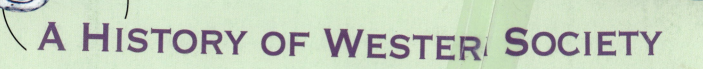

A History of Western Society

Ninth Edition

A HISTORY OF WESTERN SOCIETY

Volume I
From Antiquity to the Enlightenment

John P. McKay
University of Illinois at Urbana-Champaign

Bennett D. Hill
Late of Georgetown University

John Buckler
University of Illinois at Urbana-Champaign

Clare Haru Crowston
University of Illinois at Urbana-Champaign

Merry E. Wiesner-Hanks
University of Wisconsin–Milwaukee

HOUGHTON MIFFLIN COMPANY
Boston   New York

Publisher: Suzanne Jeans
Senior Sponsoring Editor: Nancy Blaine
Senior Marketing Manager: Katherine Bates
Development Editor: Melissa Mashburn
Senior Project Editor: Christina Horn
Art and Design Manager: Jill Haber
Cover Design Director: Tony Saizon
Senior Photo Editor: Jennifer Meyer Dare
Composition Buyer: Chuck Dutton
Editorial Associate: Adrienne Zicht
Marketing Assistant: Lauren Bussard
Editorial Assistant: Carrie Parker

Volume I cover image: *Portrait of a Man* by Antonello da Messina, ca 1475. National Gallery, London/ Bridgeman Art Library.

Printed in the U.S.A.

Library of Congress Control Number: 2007927730

Instructor's Exam Copy:
ISBN-13: 978-0-547-05263-2
ISBN-10: 0-547-05263-4

For orders, use Student Text ISBNs:
ISBN-13: 978-0-618-94633-4
ISBN-10: 0-618-94633-0

2--DJM - 08

In Memoriam

Bennett David Hill
1934 – 2005

Bennett Hill, who authored many of the chapters in earlier editions of this book, was born in Baltimore, Maryland, the son of African American Catholics. When Bennett was ten, the family moved north to Philadelphia, where his father worked for the U.S. Postal Service and his mother for the Veterans Administration. Bennett attended public schools, and his intellectual prowess was soon evident. He won a scholarship to Princeton University, where he received an excellent education that he always treasured. Majoring in history and graduating cum laude, Bennett was a trailblazer— one of the first African Americans to receive an undergraduate degree from Princeton. He subsequently earned a doctorate in European history at Princeton, joined the history department of the University of Illinois at Urbana-Champaign, and later served as department chair. Bennett was a popular but demanding teacher with a passion for medieval social history. His colleagues at Illinois remember especially his keen intellect, elegant taste, literary flair, and quick, sometimes mischievous wit. (He once persuaded some of his students that he followed medieval tradition and trimmed his front lawn with sheep rather than a lawn mower.) Establishing a scholarly reputation as a leading expert on medieval monasticism, Bennett heeded a spiritual call in midlife and became a Benedictine monk and ordained priest at St. Anselm's Abbey in Washington, D.C. He often served Mass at the parish church of his grandparents in Baltimore. Yet Bennett never lost his passion for European and world history, teaching regularly as a visiting professor at Georgetown University. An indefatigable worker with insatiable curiosity, he viewed each new edition as an exciting learning opportunity. At the time of his sudden and unexpected death in February 2005 he was working on a world history of slavery, which grew out of his research and reflected his proud heritage and intensely ethical concerns. A complex and many-sided individual, Bennett was a wonderful conversationalist, an inspiring human being, and the beloved brother and uncle of a large extended family. His sudden passing has been a wrenching loss for all who knew him.

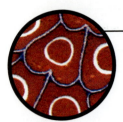

About the Authors

John P. McKay Born in St. Louis, John P. McKay received his B.A. from Wesleyan University (1961), his M.A. from the Fletcher School of Law and Diplomacy (1962), and his Ph.D. from the University of California, Berkeley (1968). He began teaching history at the University of Illinois in 1966 and became a Professor there in 1976. John won the Herbert Baxter Adams Prize for his book *Pioneers for Profit: Foreign Entrepreneurship and Russian Industrialization, 1885–1913* (1970). He has also written *Tramways and Trolleys: The Rise of Urban Mass Transport in Europe* (1976) and has translated Jules Michelet's *The People* (1973). His research has been supported by fellowships from the Ford Foundation, the Guggenheim Foundation, the National Endowment for the Humanities, and IREX. He has written well over a hundred articles, book chapters, and reviews, which have appeared in numerous publications, including *The American Historical Review, Business History Review, The Journal of Economic History,* and *Slavic Review.* He contributed extensively to C. Stewart and P. Fritzsche, eds., *Imagining the Twentieth Century* (1997).

Bennett D. Hill A native of Philadelphia, Bennett D. Hill earned an A.B. from Princeton (1956) and advanced degrees from Harvard (A.M., 1958) and Princeton (Ph.D., 1963). He taught history at the University of Illinois, where he was department chair from 1978 to 1981. He published *English Cistercian Monasteries and Their Patrons in the Twelfth Century* (1968), *Church and State in the Middle Ages* (1970), and articles in *Analecta Cisterciensia, The New Catholic Encyclopaedia, The American Benedictine Review,* and *The Dictionary of the Middle Ages.* His reviews appeared in *The American Historical Review, Speculum, The Historian,* the *Journal of World History,* and *Library Journal.* He was one of the contributing editors to *The Encyclopedia of World History* (2001). He was a Fellow of the American Council of Learned Societies and served on the editorial board of *The American Benedictine Review,* on committees of the National Endowment for the Humanities, and as vice president of the American Catholic Historical Association (1995–1996). A Benedictine monk of St. Anselm's Abbey in Washington, D.C., he was also a Visiting Professor at Georgetown University.

John Buckler Born in Louisville, Kentucky, John Buckler received his Ph.D. from Harvard University in 1973. In 1980 Harvard University Press published his *Theban Hegemony, 371–362 B.C.* He published *Philip II and the Sacred War* (Leiden, 1989) and also edited *BOIOTIKA: Vorträge vom 5. Internationalen Böotien-Kolloquium* (Munich, 1989). In 2003 he pub-

lished *Aegean Greece in the Fourth Century B.C.* In the following year appeared his editions of W. M. Leake, *Travels in the Morea* (three volumes), and Leake's *Peloponnesiaca.* Cambridge University Press published his *Central Greece and the Politics of Power in the Fourth Century*, edited by Hans Beck, in 2007.

Clare Haru Crowston Born in Cambridge, Massachusetts, and raised in Toronto, Clare Haru Crowston received her B.A. in 1985 from McGill University and her Ph.D. in 1996 from Cornell University. Since 1996, she has taught at the University of Illinois, where she has served as associate chair and Director of Graduate Studies, and is currently Associate Professor of history. She is the author of *Fabricating Women: The Seamstresses of Old Regime France, 1675–1791* (Duke University Press, 2001), which won two awards, the Berkshire Prize and the Hagley Prize. She edited two special issues of the *Journal of Women's History* (vol. 18, nos. 3 and 4) and has published numerous articles and reviews in journals such as *Annales: Histoire, Sciences Sociales, French Historical Studies, Gender and History*, and the *Journal of Economic History.* Her research has been supported with grants from the National Endowment for the Humanities, the Mellon Foundation, and the Bourse Châteaubriand of the French government. She is a past president of the Society for French Historical Studies and a former chair of the Pinkney Prize Committee.

Merry E. Wiesner-Hanks Having grown up in Minneapolis, Merry E. Wiesner-Hanks received her B.A. from Grinnell College in 1973 (as well as an honorary doctorate some years later), and her Ph.D. from the University of Wisconsin–Madison in 1979. She taught first at Augustana College in Illinois, and since 1985 at the University of Wisconsin–Milwaukee, where she is currently UWM Distinguished Professor in the department of history. She is the co-editor of the *Sixteenth Century Journal* and the author or editor of nineteen books and many articles that have appeared in English, German, Italian, Spanish, and Chinese. These include *Early Modern Europe, 1450–1789* (Cambridge, 2006), *Women and Gender in Early Modern Europe* (Cambridge, 3d ed., 2008), and *Gender in History* (Blackwell, 2001). She currently serves as the Chief Reader for Advanced Placement World History and has also written a number of source books for use in the college classroom, including *Discovering the Western Past* (Houghton Mifflin, 6th ed., 2007) and *Discovering the Global Past* (Houghton Mifflin, 3d ed., 2006), and a book for young adults, *An Age of Voyages, 1350–1600* (Oxford, 2005).

Brief Contents

Contents

Chapter 15

European Exploration and Conquest, 1450–1650 483

Chapter 16

Absolutism and Constitutionalism in Western Europe, ca 1589–1715 523

Maps

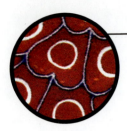

Listening to the Past

Preface

A History of Western Society grew out of the authors' desire to infuse new life into the study of Western Civilization. We knew that historians were using imaginative questions and innovative research to open up vast new areas of historical interest and knowledge. We also recognized that these advances had dramatically affected the subject of European economic, intellectual, and, especially, social history, while new research and fresh interpretations were also revitalizing the study of the traditional mainstream of political, diplomatic, and religious developments. Despite history's vitality as a discipline, however, it seemed to us at the time that both the broad public and the intelligentsia were generally losing interest in the past. That, fortunately for us all, has not proven the case.

It was our conviction, based on considerable experience introducing large numbers of students to the broad sweep of Western Civilization, that a book in which social history was the core element could excite readers and inspire a renewed interest in history. Our strategy was thus twofold. First, we incorporated recent research by social historians as we sought to re-create the life of ordinary people in appealing human terms. At the same time, we were determined to give great economic, political, cultural, and intellectual developments the attention they unquestionably deserve. We wanted to give individual readers and instructors a balanced, integrated perspective so that they could pursue—on their own or in the classroom—those themes and questions that they found particularly exciting and significant. In an effort to realize fully the potential of our fresh yet balanced approach, we made many changes, large and small, in the editions that followed.

Changes in the Ninth Edition

In preparing the Ninth Edition we have worked hard to keep our book up-to-date by including as much valuable and relevant new scholarship as possible. We have also strengthened our distinctive yet balanced approach to a wide range of topics. In addition, we have revised the layout of the chapters somewhat to foreground the histori-cal questions posed and answered in each chapter, and added a new map feature. This edition includes the best of previous editions, while blending in the most important recent findings.

Conceptual and Content Revisions

Several main lines of revision have guided our many changes. In particular, we have approached the history of the West as part of the history of the world and have devoted more space to Europe's interactions with the rest of the world. This has meant that some parts of the book have been completely reconceptualized and reorganized, as have many of the sections within chapters. Chapter 15 is now entirely devoted to European exploration, discovery, and conquest and also includes coverage of world contacts before Columbus. Chapter 7 includes fuller discussion of Central Asian steppe peoples; Chapter 19 includes discussion of European trade with Asia; and Chapter 20 incorporates extended coverage of the impact of colonial products, including sugar, tea, coffee, and tobacco. Chapter 21 has considerable new material on the Haitian revolution; Chapter 29 includes more on World War II outside of Europe; and Chapter 30 has more on decolonization in the Middle East and Africa.

A second major change is updated discussion of gender throughout the text. The development of women's and gender history has been a central part of the expansion of historical knowledge over the last several decades, and this edition includes even fuller discussion of the role of gender in shaping human experience than did previous editions. Some of this new material focuses on women, including expanded discussion of women in medieval monasticism (Chapter 10), women's role in the court culture of early modern Europe (Chapter 16), and women's work in the Industrial Revolution (Chapter 22). Some new text focuses explicitly on norms and patterns of masculinity, including those of classical Athens and Sparta (Chapter 3) and medieval knightly culture (Chapter 10). Other sections ask readers to consider the ways in which gender is related to other social hierarchies, such as social status and race (Chapters 1, 13, and 30), or ways in which religious or intellectual concepts are gendered (Chapters 2 and 16). New scholarship on gender has meant revisions in other sections as well, including discussion of the Roman family, the Reformation, the witch-hunts, the scientific revolution, nineteenth-century cities, and cold war Europe. The discussion of gender is accompanied by updates to the material on sexuality in many chapters, as this is a field of scholarship growing very rapidly.

These two major lines of revision are accompanied by continued enhancement of content that began in earlier editions. The social history focus that has been the core element of this book since its first edition continues, with more material on Roman family life (Chapter 5), popular religious practices (Chapters 10, 11, and 20), and the consumer revolution (Chapter 20), to cite just a few examples. In addition to more material on Europe in a global perspective, we have continued to incorporate more discussion of groups and regions that are frequently shortchanged in the general histories of Europe and Western Civilization. This expanded scope reflects the renewed awareness within the profession of Europe's enormous historical diversity, as well as the efforts of contemporary Europeans to understand the ambivalent and contested meanings of their national, regional, ethnic, and pan-European identities. Examples of this enlarged scope include more discussion of the Celts and Huns (Chapter 7), more on the Vikings and Magyars in eastern Europe (Chapter 8), and more material on Scandinavia in several chapters. Chapter 10 has been reconceptualized from a unit that focuses solely on Christians to one that explores Muslim and Jewish as well as Christian popular religion, and it includes discussions of similarities and differences among these three groups. The history of Jews in Europe is incorporated into a number of chapters as well. Several chapters examine notions of race during times of significant cultural change, including the Renaissance (Chapter 13), the first wave of colonization (Chapter 15), the Enlightenment (Chapter 18), and nineteenth-century urban society (Chapter 24).

An important part of this continued broader focus is material on Islam. Chapter 8 now begins with the development of Islam and includes comprehensive discussion of Muslim Spain. Chapter 9 maintains the discussion of the Arab influence in medieval Sicily highlighted in previous editions. Chapters 17, 25, and 27 all include significant new material on the Ottoman Empire. Several of the new features focus on Muslims living in Europe, as well as issues involving Christian-Muslim relations.

We believe that including examples of problems of historical interpretations in our text helps our readers de-velop the critical-thinking skills that are among the most precious benefits of studying history. Examples of this more open-ended, interpretative approach include a discussion of the importance of the Lost Gospels (Chapter 6), disagreements about the pathology of the Black Death (Chapter 12), debates about the impact of Enlightenment thought (Chapter 18), and renewed debate on personal and collective responsibility for the Holocaust (Chapter 29).

Concern with terminology is key to new ways in which history is being studied, researched, and presented, and among the historiographical issues we present are some that ask readers to consider the implications of words they (and historians) use regularly without thinking much about them. This includes a consideration of what we mean by "the West" (Chapter 1), discussion of the terms "Middle Ages" (Chapter 8), "Renaissance," and "modern" (Chapter 13), and disputes about who was and was not part of "the nation" (Chapter 25) or included in understandings of "Europe" (Chapter 31).

This edition includes several major changes in the organization of chapters. Chapter 7 now focuses explicitly on late antiquity, taking into account the exciting new scholarship on this period of transition. Chapter 9 brings together material on political developments in the High Middle Ages previously in several chapters, and Chapter 11 focuses on medieval urban life and culture. Chapter 14 now includes material on the Reformations, religious wars, and witch-hunts, while, as noted above, Chapter 15 now focuses on exploration and overseas expansion.

New Pedagogical Features

To help focus and guide the reader, we pose specific historical questions keyed to the main chapter headings at the beginning of each chapter. These questions are then answered in the course of each chapter and repeated in an end-of-chapter summary that concisely reiterates the chapter's findings. For this edition, many of the questions have been reframed, and the chapter summaries rewritten, to maximize the usefulness of this popular pedagogical device. Dates have been added to most chapter titles.

This edition also adds a new feature, "Mapping the Past." Historians have long relied on maps to help explain the stories that they tell, but we have found that students often do not pay as much attention to the maps as they should. Thus in the new "Mapping the Past" feature, one map in each chapter includes questions for discussion. Some of these questions refer only to a single map, while others encourage students to compare different maps in order to trace processes over time.

Distinctive Features

In addition to the new "Mapping the Past" feature, this edition continues to include distinctive features from earlier editions that guide the reader in the process of historical understanding.

Individuals in Society

Included in each chapter is the feature "Individuals in Society," which offers a brief study of a woman, man, or group, informing us about the societies in which they lived. Each study or biographical sketch has been carefully integrated into the body of the text. The "Individuals in Society" feature grew out of our long-standing focus on people's lives and the varieties of historical experience, and we believe that readers will empathize with these human beings as they themselves seek to define their own identities. The spotlighting of individuals, both famous and obscure, perpetuates the greater attention to cultural and intellectual developments that we used to invigorate our social history in earlier editions, and it reflects changing interests within the historical profession as well as the development of "micro-history."

The range of men and women we consider is broad. For this edition, and sometimes at readers' suggestion, we have dropped some individuals and replaced them with others who add their own contributions to history. Chapter 4 now focuses on the Greek mathematician Archimedes and the practical application of science. Chapter 10 looks at the German abbess and mystic Hildegard of Bingen and Chapter 11 at the Italian merchant Francesco Datini. In keeping with this edition's increasing attention to individuals from outside western Europe who had an impact on European developments, Chapter 17 looks at Hürrem, first the concubine and then the wife of Suleiman the Magnificent, and Chapter 21 at Toussaint L'Ouverture, leader of the revolution in the French colony of Saint-Domingue. Chapter 23 focuses on the French historian Jules Michelet, who viewed nationalism as a means of lessening social tensions, and Chapter 30 on Margaret Thatcher, the first woman to become prime minister in Britain. Chapter 31 focuses on Tariq Ramadan, the controversial European-Muslim intellectual. In addition to these new individuals, in some cases, such as Nefertiti (Chapter 1), Theodora (Chapter 7), and Leonardo da Vinci (Chapter 13), we have kept the same individuals, but completely rewritten the feature to bring it in line with current scholarship.

Listening to the Past

A two-page feature called "Listening to the Past" extends and illuminates a major historical issue considered in each of the text's chapters through the presentation of a source or small group of sources. In the new edition we have reviewed our selections and made judicious substitutions. Chapter 5 now focuses on a complex magic charm used during the Roman Empire and perhaps earlier to attract a lover. Chapter 11 again takes up the theme of love, exploring the courtly love tradition in medieval literature. Chapter 20 focuses on Louis Sebastien Mercier's comments on everyday life in eighteenth-century Paris, and Chapter 23 on the reflections of a Czech historian writing during the revolution of 1848. Chapter 27 features Arab protests regarding the establishment of the League of Nations mandates in the former Ottoman Empire and the establishment of a Jewish homeland in Palestine. Chapter 31 examines riots in the suburbs of Paris by French people of Arab descent in late 2005. As in the "Individuals in Society" feature, in addition to these brand-new sources, sources that appeared in previous editions have often been contextualized in new ways reflective of current scholarship.

Each primary source opens with a problem-setting introduction and closes with "Questions for Analysis" that invite students to evaluate the evidence as historians would. Drawn from a range of writings addressing a variety of social, cultural, political, and intellectual issues, these sources promote active involvement and critical interpretation. Selected for their interest and importance and carefully fitted into their historical context, these sources do indeed allow the student to "listen to the past" and to observe how history has been shaped by individual men and women, some of them great aristocrats, others ordinary folk.

Images in Society

This edition continues to include the photo essay "Images in Society." The complete text now contains eight essays, each consisting of a short narrative with questions, accompanied by several pictures. The goal of the feature is to encourage students to think critically: to view and compare visual illustrations and draw conclusions about the societies and cultures that produced those objects. Thus, in Chapter 1 appears the discovery of the "Iceman," the frozen remains of an unknown herdsman. "The Roman Villa at Chedworth" in Britain mirrors Roman provincial culture (Chapter 6). The essay "From Romanesque to Gothic" treats the architectural shift in medieval church building and aims to show how the Gothic cathedral reflected the ideals and values of medieval society (Chapter 11). "Art in the Reformation" (Chapter 14) examines both the Protestant and Catholic views of religious art. Chapter 17 presents the way monarchs displayed their authority visually in "Absolutist Palace Building." Moving to modern times, the focus in Chapter 19 changes to "London: The Remaking of a Great City," which depicts how Londoners rebuilt their city after a great catastrophe. "Class and Gender Boundaries in Women's Fashion, 1850–1914" studies women's clothing in relationship to women's evolving position in society and gender relations (Chapter 24). "Pablo Picasso and Modern Art" looks at some of Picasso's greatest paintings to gain insight into his principles and the modernist revolution in art (Chapter 28).

Additional Features

The illustrative component of our work has been carefully revised. We have added many new illustrations to our extensive art program, which includes more than four hundred color reproductions, letting great art and important events come alive. As in earlier editions, all illustrations have been carefully selected to complement the text, and all carry informative captions, based on thorough research, that enhance their value and have been revised for the current edition. Artwork remains an integral part of our book; the past can speak in pictures as well as in words. The use of full color serves to clarify the maps and graphs and to enrich the textual material. The maps and map captions have been updated to correlate directly to the text, and new maps, as well as the "Mapping the Past" feature, have been added.

Each chapter includes a chronology feature that lists major developments in the period discussed in the chapter. In addition, topic-specific timelines appear at key points throughout the book. Once again we provide a unified timeline at the end of the text. Comprehensive and easy to locate, this useful timeline allows students to compare developments over the centuries.

A list of Key Terms concludes each chapter. These terms are highlighted in boldface in the text. The student may use these terms to test his or her understanding of the chapter's material.

In addition to posing chapter-opening questions and presenting more problems in historical interpretation, we have quoted extensively from a wide variety of primary sources in the narrative, demonstrating in our use of these quotations how historians evaluate evidence. Thus primary sources are examined as an integral part of the narrative as well as presented in extended form in the "Listening to the Past" chapter feature. We believe that such an extensive program of both integrated and separate primary source excerpts will help readers learn to interpret and think critically.

Each chapter concludes with a carefully selected list of suggestions for further reading, revised and updated to keep them current with the vast amount of new work being done in many fields. These bibliographies are shorter than those in previous editions, as readers may now find more extensive suggestions for further reading on the website **college.hmco.com/history/west/mckay/western_society/9e/student_home.html**.

Throughout the text, icons direct students to online interactive maps and primary sources corresponding to discussions in the text and to the student and instructor websites.

Flexible Format

Western Civilization courses differ widely in chronological structure from one campus to another. To accommodate the various divisions of historical time into intervals for a two-quarter, three-quarter, or two-semester period, *A History of Western Society* is published in four versions, three of which embrace the complete work:

- One-volume hardcover edition
- Two-volume paperback: *Volume I: From Antiquity to the Enlightenment* (Chapters 1–17); *Volume II: From Absolutism to the Present* (Chapters 16–31)
- Three-volume paperback: *Volume A: From Antiquity to 1500* (Chapters 1–13); *Volume B: From the Renaissance to 1815* (Chapters 12–21); *Volume C: From the Revolutionary Era to the Present* (Chapters 21–31)
- *Since 1300* (Chapters 12–31), paperback for courses on Europe since the Renaissance

Note that overlapping chapters in both the two- and the three-volume sets permit still wider flexibility in matching the appropriate volume with the opening and closing dates of a course term.

Ancillaries

A wide array of supplements accompany this text to help students better master the material and to help instructors in teaching from the book:

- Student Website
- Instructor Website
- Online Instructor's Resource Manual
- HM Testing CD-ROM (powered by Diploma)
- Online Study Guide (powered by eCommerce)
- PowerPoint maps, images, and lecture outlines
- PowerPoint questions for personal response systems
- Blackboard™ and WebCT™ course cartridges
- Eduspace™ (powered by Blackboard™)
- Interactive ebook
- HistoryFinder

The *Student Website,* prepared by Leslie Kauffman, is a companion website for students that includes a wide range of material correlated to each book chapter such as learning objectives, chapter outlines, pre-class quizzes, interactive flashcards, chronological ordering exercises, primary sources, interactive map exercises, and ACE self-tests. Students can also find general text resources such as an online glossary, audio mp3 files of chapter summaries, and material on how to study more effectively. Throughout the text, icons direct students to relevant exercises and self-testing material located on the student website. Access the student website for this text by visiting **college.hmco.com/history/west/mckay/western_society/9e/student_home.html**.

The *Instructor Website* is a companion website for instructors. It features all of the material on the student website plus additional password-protected resources that help instructors teach the course, such as an electronic version of the *Instructor's Resource Manual* and *PowerPoint* slides. Access the instructor website for this text by visiting **college.hmco.com/history/west/mckay/western_society/9e/instructor_home.html**.

The *Instructor's Resource Manual,* prepared by John Reisbord, contains instructional objectives, chapter outlines, lecture suggestions, guidelines for using primary sources, classroom activities, map activities, audiovisual bibliographies, Internet resources, and suggested readings.

HM Testing (powered by *Diploma*) offers instructors a flexible and powerful tool for test generation and test management. Now supported by the Brownstone Research Group's market-leading *Diploma* software, this new version of *HM Testing* significantly improves on functionality and ease of use by offering all the tools needed to create, author, deliver, and customize multiple types of tests. *Diploma* is currently in use at thousands of college and university campuses throughout the United States and Canada. The *HM Testing* content for this text was developed by John Reisbord and offers key term identification, essay questions (with guidelines for how to effectively write the essay), multiple-choice questions (with page references to the correct responses), and map questions that refer to maps in the text, as well as a final exam.

The *Online Study Guide* (powered by *eCommerce*) offers students additional materials to aid their study and mastery of the text. The *Study Guide* content was developed by Carla Falkner of Northeast Mississippi Community College and offers learning objectives, chapter key points, review questions, major political ideas exercises, issues for essay and discussion, geography questions, map feature questions, and primary source analysis.

We are pleased to offer a collection of Western Civilization *PowerPoint* lecture outlines, maps, and images for use in classroom presentations. Detailed lecture outlines correspond to the book's chapters and make it easier for instructors to cover the major topics in class. The art collection includes all of the photos and maps in the text, as well as numerous other images from our Western Civilization titles. *PowerPoint* questions and answers for use with personal response system software are also offered to adopters free of charge.

A variety of assignable homework and testing material has been developed to work with the *Blackboard*™ and *WebCT*™ course management systems, as well as with *Eduspace*™: Houghton Mifflin's Online Learning Tool (powered by *Blackboard*™). *Eduspace*™ is a web-based online learning environment that provides instructors with a gradebook and communication capabilities, such as synchronous and asynchronous chats and announcement postings. It offers access to assignments such as over 650 gradable homework exercises, writing assignments, interactive maps with questions, primary sources, discussion questions for online discussion boards, and tests, which all come ready to use. Instructors can choose to use the content as is, modify it, or even add their own. *Eduspace*™ also contains an interactive ebook, which contains in-text links to interactive maps, primary sources, and audio pronunciation files, as well as review and self-testing material for students.

HistoryFinder, a new Houghton Mifflin technology initiative, helps instructors create rich and exciting classroom presentations. This online tool offers thousands of online resources, including art, photographs, maps, primary sources, multimedia content, Associated Press interactive modules, and ready-made *PowerPoint* slides. *HistoryFinder's* assets can easily be searched by keyword, or browsed from pull-down menus of topic, media type, or by textbook. Instructors can then browse, preview, and download resources straight from the website.

Acknowledgments

It is a pleasure to thank the many instructors who read and critiqued the manuscript through its development:

Hugh Agnew
George Washington University

Melanie Bailey
Centenary College of Louisiana

Rachael Ball
Ohio State University

Eugene Boia
Cleveland State University

Robert Brown
State University of New York, Finger Lakes Community College

Richard Eichman
Sauk Valley Community College

David Fisher
Texas Technical University

Wayne Hanley
West Chester University of Pennsylvania

Michael Leggiere
Louisiana State University, Shreveport

John Mauer
Tri-County Technical College

Nick Miller
Boise State University

Wyatt Moulds
Jones County Junior College

Elsa Rapp
Montgomery County Community College

Anne Rodrick
Wofford College

Sonia Sorrell
Pepperdine University

Lee Shai Weissbach
University of Louisville

Special thanks also go to Dr. Todd A. Beach, Advanced Placement History teacher at Eastview High School in Apple Valley, Minnesota, for his work on the DBQ appendix of the Advanced Placement Edition of this text.

It is also a pleasure to thank our many editors at Houghton Mifflin for their efforts over many years. To Christina Horn, who guided production, and to Tonya Lobato and Melissa Mashburn, our development editors, we express our special appreciation. And we thank Carole Frohlich for her contributions in photo research and selection.

Many of our colleagues at the University of Illinois and the University of Wisconsin–Milwaukee continue to provide information and stimulation, often without even knowing it. We thank them for it. John Buckler thanks Professor Jack Cargill for his advice on topics in Chapter 2. He also wishes to thank Professor Nicholas Yalouris, former General Inspector of Antiquities, for his kind permission to publish the mosaic from Elis, Greece, in Chapter 3. He is likewise grateful to Dr. Amy C. Smith, Curator of the Ure Museum of Archaeology of the University of Reading, for her permission to publish the vase on page 64. Sincerest thanks go also to Professor Paul Cartledge of Clare College, Cambridge University, for his kind permission to publish his photograph of the statue of Leonidas in Chapter 3. John McKay expresses his deep appreciation to Jo Ann McKay for her sharp-eyed editorial support and unfailing encouragement. For their invaluable comments and suggestions, Clare Crowston thanks the following individuals: Martin Bruegel, Antoinette Burton, Don Crummey, Max Edelson, Tara Fallon, Masumi Iriye, Craig Koslofsky, Janine Lanza, John Lynn, M. J. Maynes, Kathryn Oberdeck, Dana Rabin, and John Randolph. Merry Wiesner-Hanks would like to thank the many students over the years with whom she has used earlier editions of this book. Their reactions and opinions helped shape her revisions to this edition, and she hopes it remains worthy of the ultimate praise that they bestowed on it, that it's "not boring like most textbooks." She would, as always, also like to thank her husband, Neil, without whom work on this project would not be possible.

Each of us has benefited from the criticism of his or her coauthors, although each of us assumes responsibility for what he or she has written. John Buckler has written the first six chapters; Bennett Hill continued the narrative through Chapter 16; and John McKay has written Chapters 17 through 31. Beginning with this edition, Merry Wiesner-Hanks assumed primary responsibility for Chapters 7 through 14 and Clare Crowston assumed primary responsibility for Chapters 15 through 21. Finally, we continue to welcome the many comments and suggestions that have come from our readers, for they have helped us greatly in this ongoing endeavor.

J. P. M.   B. D. H.   J. B.   C. H. C.   M. E. W.

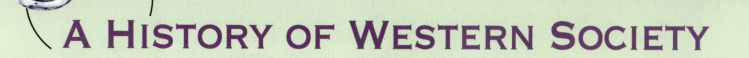

A HISTORY OF WESTERN SOCIETY

Osiris. Egyptian lord of life and death, powerful and serene, here depicted in his full regalia.
(G. Dagli-Orti/The Art Archive)

ORIGINS,
CA 400,000–1100 B.C.

The civilization and cultures of the modern Western world, like great rivers, have many sources. These sources have flowed from many places and directions. Peoples in western Europe developed numerous communities uniquely their own but also sharing some common features. They mastered such diverse subjects as astronomy, mathematics, geometry, trigonometry, engineering, religious practices, and social organization. Yet the earliest of these peoples did not record their learning and lore in systems of writing. Their lives and customs are consequently largely lost to us.

Other early peoples confronted many of the same basic challenges as those in Europe. They also made progress, but they took the important step of recording their experiences in writing. The most enduring innovations occurred in the ancient Near East, a region that includes the lands bordering the Mediterranean's eastern shore, the Arabian peninsula, parts of northeastern Africa, and perhaps above all Mesopotamia, the area of modern Iraq. Fundamental to the development of Western civilization and culture was the invention of writing by the Sumerians, which allowed knowledge of the past to be preserved. It also facilitated the spread and accumulation of learning, science, and literature. Ancient Near Eastern civilizations also produced the first written law codes, as well as religious concepts that still permeate daily life.

But how do we know and understand these things? Before embarking on the study of history, it is necessary to ask, "What is it?" Only then can the peoples and events of tens of thousands of years be placed into a coherent whole.

Understanding Western History

Most human groups have left some record of themselves. Sometimes they left artifacts, at other times pictures or signs, and at still other times written documents. In many of these records, groups set out distinctions between themselves and others. Sometimes these distinctions are between

Online Study Center
This icon will direct you to interactive activities and study materials on the website **college.hmco.com/pic/mckaywest9e**

small groups such as neighboring tribes, sometimes between countries, and sometimes between vast parts of the world. One of the most enduring of the latter is the idea of "the West" and "the East."

● *What factors are key to understanding the meaning of "the West" and its history?*

Describing the West

What do we mean by "the West"? Everyone has an answer, but these answers vary widely. Some may point to geography, others to culture and traditions, and still others to economic or political systems. Many of these answers look to the present rather than to the past, but the West as a concept has a very long history.

Ideas about the West and the distinction between West and East derived originally from the ancient Greeks. Greek civilization grew up in the shadow of earlier civilizations to the south and east of Greece, especially Egypt and Mesopotamia. Greeks defined themselves in relation to these more advanced cultures, which they saw as "Eastern." Later Europeans divided certain regions of the world into the "Near East" and the "Far East." Greeks were also the first to use the word *Europe* for a geographic area, taking the word from the name of a minor goddess. They set Europe in opposition to "Asia" (who was also a minor goddess), by which they meant both what we now call Asia and what we call Africa.

The Greeks passed this conceptualization on to the Romans, who saw themselves clearly as the West. For some Romans, Greece remained part of the West, while other Romans came to view Greek traditions as vaguely "eastern." To Romans, the East was more sophisticated and more advanced, but also decadent and somewhat immoral. Roman value judgments shape preconceptions, stereotypes, and views of differences between the West and the East—what were also called the "Occident" and the "Orient"—to this day. We can see them reflected in comments about the "mysterious East" and "oriental ways of thinking."

Greco-Roman ideas about the West—as about so much else—were passed on to people who lived in western and northern Europe, who saw themselves as the inheritors of this classical tradition and thus as the West. When these Europeans established colonies outside of Europe beginning in the late fifteenth century, they regarded what they were doing as taking Western culture with them, even though many aspects of Western culture, such as Christianity, had actually originated in what Europeans by that point regarded as the East. With colonization,

Western came to mean those cultures that included significant numbers of people of European ancestry, no matter where on the globe they were located.

In the early twentieth century educators and other leaders in the United States became worried that many people, especially young people, were becoming cut off from European intellectual and cultural traditions. They encouraged the establishment of college and university courses focusing on "Western civilization," the first of which was taught at Columbia University in 1919. The course was intended to broaden students' knowledge about the Western world as the United States emerged from its isolation to become a world leader after World War I. In designing the course, faculty included cultures that as far back as the ancient Greeks had been considered Eastern, such as Egypt and Mesopotamia, describing them as the "cradles of Western civilization." This conceptualization and the course spread to other colleges and universities, evolving into what became known as the introductory Western civilization course, the staple of historical instruction for generations of college students in North America.

After World War II divisions between the West and the East changed again. Now there was a new division between East and West within Europe, with Western coming to imply a capitalist economy and Eastern part of the Communist Eastern bloc. Japan became Western, and some Greek-speaking areas Eastern. The collapse of communism in the Soviet Union and eastern Europe in the 1980s brought yet another refiguring, with much of eastern Europe joining the European Union, originally a Western organization.

At the beginning of the twenty-first century, Western still suggests a capitalist economy, but it also has certain cultural connotations, such as individualism and competition, which some see as negative and others as positive. Islamic radicals often describe their aims as an end to Western cultural, economic, and political influence, though Islam itself is generally described, along with Judaism and Christianity, as a Western monotheistic religion. Thus, throughout its long history, the meaning of "the West" has shifted, but in every era it has meant more than a geographical location.

What Is History, and Why?

The term *history* comes from the Greek word *historie*, coined by Herodotus in the fifth century B.C. For him it meant the record of his investigations and inquiries into the past, which he published for future generations. Since his initial venture, history has remained the effort to reconstruct the past to discover what people thought, what they did, and how their beliefs and actions continue to influence human life. To appreciate the past fully, we must put it into perspective so that we can understand the factors that have helped shape us as individuals, the society in which we live, and the nature of other people's societies. Why else should we study civilizations as separated from ours through time, distance, and culture as classical Greece, medieval Germany, and modern Russia? Although most of the people involved in these epochs are long dead, what they did has touched everyone alive today.

To answer the questions mentioned above, historians examine a variety of evidence. They usually begin with primary sources, firsthand accounts by people who lived through the events, people in the best position to know what happened, who was responsible for it, why it happened, and what it meant. Individuals left numerous narratives and many other types of literary documents recording their experiences; the human tendency to keep the past alive produces a huge collection of writings. In addition to detailed narratives, there are chronicles, in which people noted events in chronological order (therefore the name) and sometimes offered brief explanations of what occurred. A unique literary source for the record of antiquity is papyrology, the study of documents written on manuscripts made from papyrus, a plant that grows abundantly in Egypt. Ancient peoples ranging from inhabitants of the Old Kingdom of Egypt to those living during the Roman period recorded not only literature but also deeds, contracts, and descriptions of local customs. In the medieval period scribes produced thousands of documents giving detailed accounts of agricultural life on manors—how they were run, what the local customs were, and how society actually functioned. These scribes, generally Christian monks, also left records of religious thinking and political affairs. Whether written thousands of years ago or reported in the morning newspapers, these records constitute the primary sources upon which history is built.

Inscriptions are another literary source of information about the past. An inscription is anything written on imperishable material such as stone. Societies have often carved their messages in stone for several important reasons. First, any literate person could understand them. They also served as public records erected in open places for all to see. Documents ranging from ancient treaties that have survived the ravages of time, to religious proclamations of faith and honorific decrees issued during the medieval period, to the Vietnam memorial in Washington can all be considered inscriptions. Even the

Chronology

3200 B.C.   Development of wheeled transport and invention of cuneiform writing

ca 3200–2200 B.C.   Sumerian and Akkadian domination in Mesopotamia

ca 3100 B.C.   Invention of Egyptian hieroglyphic writing

3100–ca 1333 B.C.   Evolution of Egyptian polytheism and belief in personal immortality

3000–1000 B.C.   Origins and development of anthropomorphic religion in Mesopotamia

ca 2700–1000 B.C.   Arrival of Indo-European peoples in western Asia and Europe

ca 2660–1640 B.C.   Old and Middle Kingdoms in Egypt

ca 2600–1200 B.C.   Expansion of Mesopotamian trade with neighbors

ca 2000–1595 B.C.   Babylonian empire in Mesopotamia

ca 1790 B.C.   *Epic of Gilgamesh* and Hammurabi's law code

ca 1600–1200 B.C.   Hittite power in Anatolia

ca 1570–1075 B.C.   New Kingdom in Egypt

ca 1400 B.C.   Development of Phoenician alphabet

ca 1300–1100 B.C.   Increased use of iron in western Asia

simple dog tag worn by a member of our armed forces is a historical inscription. Coins, too, often bear inscriptions. During the Roman Empire the emperors recorded their regnal dates on their currency, thus giving a public record of their reign. In the United States today, many recent quarters proclaim when various states entered the Union, some pertinent symbol, and the date of issue. No matter what their form, these are all written records.

Further evidence of the importance of literary sources, especially in the contemporary world, comes from official statistics covering almost everything from the annual number of deaths in automobile accidents to the daily results of the stock market. Even e-mail ensures the quick and wide dispersal of information throughout the world.

All these written materials provide historians with intriguing raw resources.

Historians also receive help from nonliterary sources such as archaeology. Excavations of various sites have revealed much information from all periods that is not present in the written record. So-called museum archaeologists make sense of what field archaeologists have found. New explorations of long lost sites have in many cases literally uncovered the physical remains of earlier cultures. Archaeology has thus proven invaluable in providing a unique, visible picture of how people actually lived, and comparisons of these findings document how cultures developed. Many travelers today walk the streets of Ephesus, where Paul the Apostle preached. Current excavations at Old Sarum in England vividly reveal how its prehistoric society gave way to the new Christianity: the old pagan mound still rises above the newly excavated early but sophisticated Christian cathedral. In the United States itself archaeology has shed light on the first years of European habitation in New York City and on the lives of Native Americans in the West.

In the face of this remarkable body of literary and nonliterary evidence, historians must try to distinguish the accurate from the false or unreliable. They do so by focusing on the earliest information first. They compare various versions of particular events or large trends with one another. Some people who have left evidence of the past were more intelligent or better informed than others, and their testimony is preferred by historians and indeed strengthened by other writers who independently reported the same things. When two or more dependable sources record the same thing in the same way, historians conclude that they present an accurate account of events.

Once historians decide which sources are reliable, they use this information to establish facts or to explain the meaning of their findings. Their conclusions, when published, are considered secondary sources, scholarly interpretations of what they and others discovered. For instance, a scholar who finds an undiscovered manuscript reads it to understand its contribution to existing historical knowledge. The next question becomes how to fit it into what is already known. The problem then becomes whether the manuscript is accurate and whether it agrees with known sources. If it does, it strengthens their value. If, however, it does not, scholars must reopen the whole question of what actually happened. In short, history must be rethought on the basis of every new piece of evidence.

Understanding of the past does not necessarily come easily—that is one of the joys and frustrations of history. Unlike chemists, historians cannot reproduce experiments under controlled conditions. No two historical events are precisely alike. People cannot be put into test tubes, and they are not as predictable as atoms or hydrocarbons. History is about people, the most complex organisms on this planet. To complicate matters, for many epochs of history only the broad outlines are known, so interpretation is especially difficult. For example, historians know that the Hittite Empire collapsed at the height of its power, but interpretations of the causes of the catastrophe are still speculative. At the other end of the spectrum, some developments are so vast and complex that historians must master mountains of data before they can even begin to interpret developments properly. Events as diverse as the end of the Western Roman Empire, the origins of the Industrial Revolution, and the causes of the French Revolution are very complicated because so many people brought so many different forces to bear for so many reasons. In such cases, there is never one simple explanation that will satisfy everyone.

Still another matter complicates an accurate understanding of the past: the attempt to understand history is uniquely human. Interpretations of the past sometimes change because people's points of view change in the course of life. The values and attitudes of one generation may not be shared by another. Despite such differences in interpretation, the efforts of historians to examine and appreciate the past can give them a perspective that is valuable to the present. It is through analysis and interpretation that historians come to appreciate not only the past but also its relation to life today.

An example of this process comes from examining what the concepts "Western civilization" and "the West" mean. Interpretations of them have changed over time and space. The Greeks, for instance, defined the West as themselves; lands and peoples to the west of them were either barbarians or unknown. The Romans likewise thought of themselves as Western and considered their neighbors in modern France, Greece, and Germany as outsiders until they adopted Greco-Roman culture. During the Middle Ages Europeans spread their civilization into eastern Europe, while the Byzantines spread classical and medieval culture into Russia. This intermingling changed the concept of the West. Social practices and traditional Mediterranean ideas resulted in a civilization that could reasonably be called European.

In the early modern period, during the age of exploration, Europeans discovered the New World, the Americas, and ventured farther into the Pacific. By geographical expansion and emigration they gradually so Europeanized the peoples there that they also entered the intellectual world of the West. West met East in social, economic, intellectual, and cultural contexts. During the nineteenth and twentieth centuries, modern technology significantly reinforced earlier Western values of individualism and private enterprise. The Chinese and Japanese willingly adopted certain aspects of Western culture, such as commercial connections and Western-style armed forces, and some learned Western languages. Yet they also retained much of their own culture. Today people the world over use computers, cellular telephones, and e-mail—all Western inventions. Therefore, the West is obviously as much a cultural concept as it is a physical place on the map. Local differences remain, but the influence of the West has far outstripped geography. Although no one should say that Western civilization has conquered the world, it is safe to say that no other culture has done as much to shape global life.

From Caves to Towns

• *How did early peoples socially develop from living in caves to creating more stable and sophisticated towns?*

Virtually every day brings startling news about the path of human evolution. We now know that by about 400,000 B.C. early peoples were making primitive stone tools, which has led historians to refer to this time as the Paleolithic period. During this period, which lasted until about 7000 B.C., people survived as nomadic gatherers and hunters, usually living in caves or temporary shelters. (See the feature "Images in Society: The Iceman.") Although they accomplished striking achievements, they contributed little to our understanding of history. They properly belong to the realm of anthropology, which studies prehistoric peoples. A reasonable dividing line between anthropology and history is the **Neolithic period,** usually dated between 7000 and 3000 B.C. The term *Neolithic* stems from the new stone tools that came into use at that time. The ways in which peoples used these tools led to fundamental changes in civilization. With them Neolithic men and women built a life primarily and permanently based on agriculture and animal husbandry. They thereby broke with previous nomadic practices.

Sustained agriculture made possible a stable and secure life. Neolithic farmers developed the primary economic activity of the ancient world and one still vital today. With this settled routine came the evolution of towns and eventually of cities. Neolithic farmers usually raised more food than they could consume, so their surpluses permitted larger, healthier populations. Population growth in turn created an even greater reliance on settled farming, as only systematic agriculture could sustain the in-

creased numbers of people. Since surpluses of food could also be bartered for other commodities, the Neolithic era witnessed the beginnings of the large-scale exchange of goods. Neolithic farmers also improved their tools and agricultural techniques. They domesticated bigger, stronger animals to work for them, invented the plow, and developed new mutations of seeds. By 3000 B.C. they had invented the wheel. Agricultural surpluses also made possible the division of labor. It freed some people to become artisans who made tools, pottery vessels, woven baskets, clothing, and jewelry. In short, these advances resulted in a wealthier, more comfortable, and more complex life.

These developments generally led to the further evolution of towns and a whole new way of life. People not necessarily related to one another created rudimentary governments that transcended the family. These governments, led by a recognized central authority, made decisions that channeled the shared wisdom, physical energy, and resources of the whole population toward a common goal. These societies made their decisions according to custom, the generally accepted norms of traditional conduct. Here was the beginning of law. Towns also meant life in individual houses or groups of them, which led to greater personal independence. Growing wealth and the need for communal cooperation prompted people to erect public buildings and religious monuments. These groups also protected their possessions and themselves by raising walls.

Many scholars consider walled towns the basic feature of Neolithic society. Yet numerous examples prove that some Neolithic towns existed without stone or mud-brick walls. For instance, at Stonehenge in England the natives erected wooden palisades for safety. At Unteruhldingen in Germany the community established its unwalled town just offshore on a lake. They let nature defend them. The most concentrated collection of walled towns is found in Mesopotamia. This fact presents a historical problem. Since generations of archaeologists and historians have concentrated their attention on this region, they have considered it typical. Yet they have failed to properly appreciate circumstances elsewhere. The fundamental points about this period are that these men and women created stable communities based on agriculture. They defended their towns in various ways by common consent and effort. This organized communal effort is far more important than the types of defenses they built.

The simplest way to support these conclusions is to examine briefly Stonehenge now and Mesopotamia afterward, each in its own unique context. A mute but engaging glimpse of a particular Neolithic society can

Images in Society

The Iceman

On September 19, 1991, two German vacationers climbing in the Italian Alps came upon one of the most remarkable finds in European history: a corpse lying face-down and covered in ice (Image 1). They had stumbled on a mystery that still intrigues archaeologists and many others in the scientific world. After chiseling the body out of the ice, various specialists examined the man. Having died 5,300 years ago, he is the earliest and best-preserved corpse from the Neolithic period (Image 2).

The skin of most corpses found in glaciers appears white and waxy, but the skin of the Iceman, as he is generally known, was brown and dry. Forces of nature had so desiccated the body that it became mummified: the body, including the internal organs, was perfectly preserved. The Iceman's less perishable possessions also survived, so scientists were able to examine him almost as though he had died recently.

The Iceman was quite fit, was between twenty-five and thirty-five years of age, and stood about five feet two inches tall. The bluish tinge of his teeth showed that he had enjoyed a diet of milled grain, perhaps millet—and also showed that he came from an environment where crops were grown. He wore an unlined robe of animal skins that he had stitched together with careful needlework, using thread made of grass, which he probably had made for himself. Over his robe he wore a cape of grass, very much like capes worn by shepherds in this region as late as the early twentieth century (even as late as the Second World War German soldiers stuffed straw into their boots to withstand the fierce Russian cold). The Iceman also wore a furry cap.

The equipment discovered with the Iceman demonstrates his mastery of several technologies. He carried a hefty copper ax (a sign of stoneworking), but he seems to have relied chiefly on archery. In his quiver were numerous wooden arrow shafts and two finished arrows, all indicating a great deal of knowledge and ingenuity (Image 3). The arrows had flint heads (another sign of stoneworking), and feathers were attached with a resin-like glue to the ends of the shafts. These simple facts convey much information about the technological knowledge of this mysterious

Image 1 **The Discovery of the Iceman** *(Paul Hanny)*

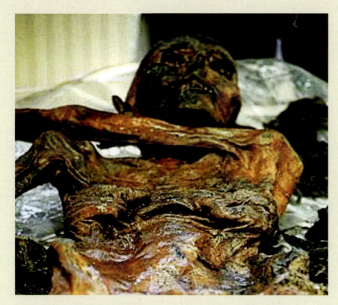

Image 2 **The Face of the Iceman** (*Keystone Press Agency Ltd./Rex Features*)

Image 3 **The Iceman's Quiver** (*S.N.S./Sipa Press*)

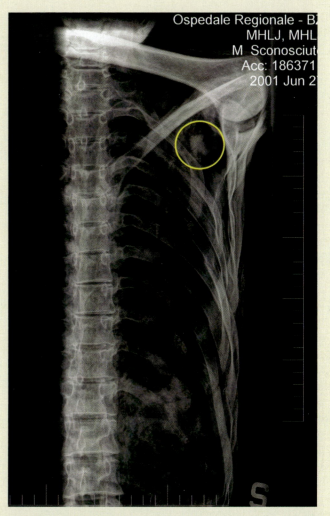

Ospedale Regionale - B
MHLJ, MHL
M Sconosciut
Acc: 186371
2001 Jun 2

S

Image 4 **X-ray of the Iceman's Shoulder** (*South Tyrol Museum of Archaeology/AP/Wide World Photos*)

man. He knew how to work stone, he knew the value of feathers to direct the arrows, and he was fully aware of the basics of ballistics. He chose for his bow the wood of the yew, some of the best wood in central Europe. Yet yew trees do not grow everywhere, so the use of yew wood proves that the Iceman had thoroughly explored his environment. He carried his necessary supplies in a primitive rucksack that he had made.

One last mystery surrounds the Iceman. When his body was first discovered, scholars assumed that he was a hapless traveler overtaken by a fierce snowstorm. But a recent autopsy found an arrowhead lodged under his left shoulder (Image 4). The Iceman was not alone on his last day. Someone accompanied him,

someone who shot him from below and behind. The Iceman is the victim in the first murder mystery of Western history.

Given this information, can you picture the circumstances of the Iceman's discovery (Image 1)? What was he doing there? From Image 2 can you imagine how nature preserved his remains? From the picture of his arrows (Image 3) can you conclude anything about the Iceman's self-reliance? From Image 4 comes the evidence for the cause of his death. Does it necessarily prove that Neolithic society was as violent as ours?

Online Study Center **Improve Your Grade**
Going Beyond Images in Society

readily be seen today in industrial England. Between 4700 and 2000 B.C. arose the Stonehenge people, named after the famous stone circle on Salisbury Plain. Though named after a single spot, this culture spread throughout Great Britain, Ireland, and Brittany in France. Circles like Stonehenge sometimes contained the houses of permanent settlers. Some were fortified enclosures in which the inhabitants established safe havens for themselves. Both were proto-urban centers. Some of these sites have yielded burial remains. Others were dedicated to religious rituals. They provided magical, not military, protection. They all served diverse social functions, another testimony to Neolithic creativity. Stonehenge and neighboring sites reveal the existence of prosperous, well-organized, and centrally led communities. They also provide evidence for cooperation among similarly constituted societies. None of them individually could have built the circle. By pooling their resources, human and material, they raised it. Thus Stonehenge itself testifies to contact and cohesion among stable groups that cooperated toward a common goal. These factors alone prove the widening horizon of these Neolithic peoples.

Stonehenge offers another insight into this Neolithic culture. It indicates an intellectual world that encompassed astronomy, the environment, and religion. The circle is oriented toward the midwinter sunset and the midsummer sunrise. Stonehenge thus marked the clocklike celestial change of the seasons. This silent evidence proves the existence of a society prosperous enough to

endure over long periods during which lore about heaven and earth could be preserved and passed along to successive generations. It also demonstrates that these communities considered themselves members of a wider world that they amiably shared with the deities of nature and the broader universe. Even the magnificent Stonehenge, however, cannot lead to history. The Stonehenge people achieved wonders, but they lacked the literacy to spread their legacy to others beyond their own culture. That breakthrough came in Mesopotamia.

Mesopotamian Civilization

The origins of Western civilization are generally traced to an area that is today not seen as part of the West: Mesopotamia, the Greek name for the land between the Euphrates and Tigris Rivers. There the arid climate confronted the peoples with the hard problem of farming with scant water supplies. Farmers learned to irrigate their land and later to drain it to prevent the buildup of salt in the soil. **Irrigation** on a large scale, like building stone circles in western Europe, demanded organized group effort. That in turn underscored the need for strong central authority to direct it. This corporate spirit led to governments in which individuals subordinated some of their particular concerns to broader interests. These factors made urban life possible in a demanding environment. By about 3000 B.C. the Sumerians, whose

Stonehenge   Seen in regal isolation, Stonehenge sits among the stars and in April 1997 was along the path of the comet Hale-Bopp. Long before Druids existed, a Neolithic society laboriously built this circle to mark the passing of the seasons. (*Jim Burgess*)

Mapping the Past

MAP 1.1 Spread of Cultures in the Ancient Near East   This map depicts the area of ancient Mesopotamia and Egypt, a region often called the "cradle of civilization." Map 1.3 on page 26 shows the balance of power that later extended far beyond the regions depicted in Map 1.1. ❶ Does this expansion indicate why Mesopotamia and Egypt earned the title of "cradle"? ❷ What geographical features of this region naturally suggest the direction in which civilization spread? ❸ Why did the first cultures of Mesopotamia spread farther than the culture of Egypt?

Online Study Center   **Improve Your Grade** Interactive Map: Spread of Cultures in the Ancient Near East

origins are mysterious, established a number of cities in the southernmost part of Mesopotamia, which became known as Sumer. The Sumerians soon turned the region into what generations have called the "cradle of civilization" (see Map 1.1). Some might argue that this phrase should be honorably retired, for civilization was advancing by various degrees from England to Mesopotamia. No one, however, can deny that the fundamental innovation of the Sumerians was the creation of writing, which helped unify this society culturally and opened it to the broader world that we still share today.

• *How did the people in Mesopotamia master their environment, invent writing to record their experiences and thoughts, and create a permanent and vibrant civilization?*

The Invention of Writing and the First Schools

The origins of writing probably go back to the ninth millennium B.C., when Near Eastern peoples used clay tokens as counters for record keeping. By the fourth millennium people had realized that drawing pictures of the tokens on clay was simpler than making tokens. This breakthrough in turn suggested that more information could be conveyed by adding pictures of still other objects. The result was a complex system of pictographs, in which each sign pictured an object. These pictographs were the forerunners of a Sumerian form of writing known as **cuneiform,** from the Latin term for "wedge-shaped," used to describe the strokes of the stylus.

MEANING	PICTOGRAPH	IDEOGRAM	PHONETIC SIGN
A Star			
B Woman			
C Mountain			
D Slave woman			
E Water In			

FIGURE 1.1 Sumerian Writing (*Source: Excerpted from S. N. Kramer,* The Sumerians: Their History, Culture and Character, *University of Chicago Press, Chicago, 1963. Copyright © 1963 by The University of Chicago Press. Reprinted by permission.*)

How did this pictographic system work, and how did it evolve into cuneiform writing? At first, if a scribe wanted to indicate a star, he simply drew a picture of it (line A of Figure 1.1) on a wet clay tablet, which became rock-hard when baked. Anyone looking at the picture would know what it meant and would think of the word for star. This complicated and laborious system had serious limitations. It could not represent abstract ideas or combinations of ideas. For instance, how could it depict a slave woman?

The solution appeared when the scribe discovered that signs could be combined to express meaning. To refer to a slave woman the scribe used the sign for woman (line B) and the sign for mountain (line C)—literally, "mountain woman" (line D). Because the Sumerians regularly obtained their slave women from the mountains, this combination of signs was easily understandable.

The next step was to simplify the system. Instead of drawing pictures, the scribe made conventionalized signs that were generally understood to represent ideas. Thus the signs became *ideograms*: they symbolized ideas. The sign for star could also be used to indicate heaven, sky, or even god.

The real breakthrough came when the scribe learned to use signs to represent sounds. For instance, the scribe

drew two parallel wavy lines to indicate the word *a* or "water" (line E). Besides water, the word *a* in Sumerian also meant "in." The word *in* expresses a relationship that is very difficult to represent pictorially. Instead of trying to invent a sign to mean "in," some clever scribe used the sign for water because the two words sounded alike. This phonetic use of signs made possible the combining of signs to convey abstract ideas.

The Sumerian system of writing was so complicated that only professional scribes mastered it, and even they had to study it for many years. By 2500 B.C. scribal schools flourished throughout Sumer. Most students came from wealthy families and were male. Each school had a master, teachers, and monitors. Discipline was strict, and students were caned for sloppy work and misbehavior. One graduate of a scribal school had few fond memories of the joy of learning:

My headmaster read my tablet, said:
"There is something missing," caned me.
. . . .
The fellow in charge of silence said:
"Why did you talk without permission," caned me.
The fellow in charge of the assembly said:
"Why did you stand at ease without permission," caned me.[1]

The Sumerian system of schooling set the educational standards for Mesopotamian culture, and the Akkadians and, later, the Babylonians adopted its practices and techniques. Mesopotamian education always had a practical side because of the economic and administrative importance of scribes. Most scribes took administrative positions in the temple or palace, where they kept records of business transactions, accounts, and inventories. But scribal schools did not limit their curriculum to business affairs. They were also centers of culture and scholarship. Topics of study included mathematics, botany, and linguistics. Advanced students copied and studied the classics of Sumerian literature. Talented students and learned scribes wrote compositions of their own. As a result, many literary, mathematical, and religious texts survive today, giving a full picture of Mesopotamian intellectual and spiritual life.

Mesopotamian Thought and Religion

The Mesopotamians made significant and sophisticated advances in mathematics using a numerical system based on units of sixty, ten, and six. They developed the concept of place value—that the value of a number depends on where it stands in relation to other numbers. The

Mesopotamians did not consider mathematics a purely theoretical science. The building of cities, palaces, temples, and canals demanded practical knowledge of geometry and trigonometry.

Mesopotamian medicine was a combination of magic, prescriptions, and surgery. Mesopotamians believed that demons and evil spirits caused sickness and that magic spells could drive them out. Or, they believed, the physician could force the demon out by giving the patient a foul-tasting prescription. As medical knowledge grew, some prescriptions were found to work and thus were true medicines. In this slow but empirical fashion medicine grew from superstition to an early form of rational treatment.

Mesopotamian thought had a profound impact in theology and religion. The Sumerians originated many beliefs, and their successors added to them. The Mesopotamians believed that many gods run the world, but they did not consider all gods and goddesses equal. Some deities had very important jobs, taking care of music, law,

sex, and victory, while others had lesser tasks, overseeing leatherworking and basketweaving. The god in charge of metalworking was hardly the equal of the god of wisdom.

Mesopotamian gods lived their lives much as human beings lived theirs. The gods were anthropomorphic, or human in form. Unlike men and women, they were powerful and immortal and could make themselves invisible. Otherwise, Mesopotamian gods and goddesses were very human: they celebrated with food and drink, and they raised families. They enjoyed their own "Garden of Eden," a green and fertile place. They could be irritable, vindictive, and irresponsible.

The Mesopotamians did not worship their deities because the gods were benevolent. Human beings were too insignificant to pass judgment on the conduct of the gods, and the gods were too superior to honor human morals. Rather, the Mesopotamians worshiped the gods because they were mighty. Likewise, it was not the place of men and women to understand the gods. The Sumerian equivalent to the biblical Job once complained to his god:

Ziggurat The ziggurat is a stepped tower that dominated the landscape of the Sumerian city. Surrounded by a walled enclosure, it stood as a monument to the gods. Monumental stairs led to the top, where sacrifices were offered for the welfare of the community. *(Charles & Josette Lemars/Corbis)*

The man of deceit has conspired against me,
And you, my god, do not thwart him,
You carry off my understanding.[2]

The motives of the gods were not always clear. In times of affliction one could only offer sacrifices to appease them.

The Mesopotamians had many myths to account for the creation of the universe. According to one Sumerian myth (echoed in Genesis, the first book of the Bible), only the primeval sea existed at first. The sea produced heaven and earth, which were united. Heaven and earth gave birth to Enlil, who separated them and made possible the creation of the other gods. Babylonian beliefs were similar. In the beginning was the primeval sea, the goddess Tiamat, who gave birth to the gods. When Tiamat tried to destroy the gods, Marduk, the chief god of the Babylonians, proceeded to kill her and divide her body and thus created the sky and earth. These myths are the earliest known attempts to answer the question, "How did it all begin?" The Mesopotamians obviously thought about these matters, as about the gods, in human terms. They never organized their beliefs into a philosophy, but their myths offered understandable explanations of natural phenomena. The myths were emotionally satisfying, and that was their greatest appeal.

Online Study Center   **Improve Your Grade**
   Primary Source: A Mesopotamian Creation Myth:
   Earth, Gods, and Humans

In addition to myths, the Sumerians produced the first epic poem, the *Epic of Gilgamesh,* which evolved as a reworking of at least five earlier myths. An epic poem is a narration of the achievements, labors, and sometimes the failures of heroes that embodies a people's or a nation's conception of its own past. Historians can use epic poems to learn about various aspects of a society, and to that extent epics can be used as historical sources. The Sumerian epic recounts the wanderings of Gilgamesh—the semihistorical king of Uruk—and his companion Enkidu, their fatal meeting with the goddess Ishtar, after which Enkidu dies, and Gilgamesh's subsequent search for eternal life. During his search Gilgamesh learns that life after death is so dreary that he returns to Uruk, where he becomes a good king and ends his life happily. The *Epic of Gilgamesh* is not only an excellent piece of literature but also an intellectual triumph. It shows the Sumerians grappling with such enduring questions as life and death, humankind and deity, and immortality. Despite its great antiquity, it addresses questions of importance to people today. (See the feature "Listening to the Past: A Quest for Immortality" on pages 32–33.)

Sumerian Social and Gender Divisions

Their harsh environment fostered a grim, even pessimistic, spirit among the Mesopotamians. The Sumerians sought to please and calm the gods, especially the patron deity of the city. Encouraged and directed by the traditional priesthood, which was dedicated to understanding the ways of the gods, the people erected shrines in the center of each city and then built their houses around them. The best way to honor the gods was to make the shrine as grand and as impressive as possible, for gods who had a splendid temple might think twice about sending floods to destroy the city.

Sumerian society was a complex arrangement of freedom and dependence, and its members were divided into four categories: nobles, free clients of the nobility, commoners, and slaves. **Nobles** consisted of the king and his family, the chief priests, and high palace officials. Generally, the king rose to power as a war leader, elected by the citizenry, who established a regular army, trained it, and led it into battle. The might of the king and the frequency of warfare quickly made him the supreme figure in the city, and kingship soon became hereditary. The symbol of royal status was the palace, which rivaled the temple in grandeur.

The king and the lesser nobility held extensive tracts of land that were, like the estates of the temple, worked by slaves and clients. **Clients** were free men and women who were dependent on the nobility. In return for their labor, the clients received small plots of land to work for themselves. Although this arrangement assured the clients of a livelihood, the land they worked remained the possession of the nobility or the temple. Thus not only did the nobility control most—and doubtless the best—land, they also commanded the obedience of a huge segment of society. They were the dominant force in Mesopotamian society.

Commoners were free. They were independent of the nobility; however, they could not rival the nobility in social status and political power. Commoners belonged to large families that owned land in their own right. Commoners could sell their land, if the family approved, but even the king could not legally take their land without their approval. Male commoners had a voice in the political affairs of the city and full protection under the law.

Until comparatively recent times, slavery has been a fact of life throughout the history of Western society. Some Sumerian slaves were foreigners and prisoners of war. Some were criminals who had lost their freedom as punishment for their crimes. Still others served as slaves to repay debts. These were more fortunate than the others, because the law required that they be freed after three years. But all slaves were subject to whatever treatment their owners might mete out. They could be beaten and even branded. Yet they were not considered dumb beasts. Slaves engaged in trade and made profits. Indeed, many slaves were able to buy their freedom. They could borrow money and received at least some legal protection.

Each of these social categories included both men and women, but their experiences were not the same, for Sumerian society made clear distinctions based on gender. Sumerian society—and all Western societies that followed, until very recently—was **patriarchal,** that is, most power was held by older adult men, especially those from the elite groups. Scholars debate the origins of patriarchy, for a hierarchy based on gender was already in place by the time the first written records appear. It may have been linked to private ownership of property and plow agriculture, which significantly increased the food supply, but also significantly increased the resources needed to produce that food. Men generally carried out the plowing and care for animals, which led to boys' being favored over girls for the work they could do for their parents while young and the support they could provide in their parents' old age. Boys became the normal inheritors of family land. Women could sometimes inherit if there were no sons in a family, but they did not gain the political rights that came with land ownership for men.

The states that developed in the ancient Middle East, beginning with Sumer, further heightened gender distinctions. They depended on taxes and tribute as well as slave labor for their support, so their rulers were very interested in maintaining population levels. All these states were dominated by hereditary aristocracies, whose members became concerned with maintaining the distinction between themselves and the majority of the population, and by male property owners who wanted to be sure the children their wives bore were theirs. These concerns led to attempts to control women's reproduction through laws governing sexual relations and, more importantly, through marriage norms and practices that set up a very unequal relationship between spouses. In most states, laws were passed mandating that women be virgins on marriage and imposing strict punishment for a married woman's adultery; sexual relations outside of marriage on the part of husbands were not considered adultery. Concern with family honor thus became linked to women's sexuality in a way that it was not for men; men's honor revolved around their work activities and, for more prominent families, around their performance of public duties, including keeping written records, in the expanding government bureaucracies. These economic and political developments were accompanied and supported by cultural norms and religious concepts that heightened gender distinctions. In some places heavenly hierarchies came to reflect those on earth, with the gods arranged in a hierarchy dominated by a single male god, who was viewed as the primary creator of life. Because other hierarchies such as those of hereditary aristocracy privileged the women connected to powerful or wealthy men, women did not see themselves as part of a coherent group and often supported the institutions and intellectual structures that subordinated them.

The Spread of Mesopotamian Culture

The Sumerians established the basic social, economic, and intellectual patterns of Mesopotamia, but the Semites played a large part in spreading Sumerian culture far beyond the boundaries of Mesopotamia. The interaction of the Sumerians and Semites, in fact, gives one of the very first glimpses of a phenomenon that can still be seen today. History provides abundant evidence of peoples of different origins coming together, usually on the borders of an established culture. The result was usually cultural change, outweighing any hostility, for each side learned from the other. The outcome in these instances was the evolution of a new culture that consisted of two or more old parts. Although the older culture almost invariably looked on the newcomers as inferior, the new just as invariably contributed something valuable to the old. So it was in 2331 B.C. The Semitic chieftain Sargon conquered Sumer and created a new empire. The symbol of his triumph was a new capital, the city of Akkad. Sargon, the first "world conqueror," led his armies to the Mediterranean Sea. Although his empire lasted only a few generations, it spread Mesopotamian culture throughout the Fertile Crescent, the belt of rich farmland that extends from Mesopotamia in the east up through Syria in the north and down to Egypt in the west (see Map 1.1).

The question is why Mesopotamian culture had such an immediate and wide appeal. In the first place it was successful and enjoyed the prestige of its success. Newcomers wanted to find a respectable place in this old and venerated culture. It also provided an easy means of communication among people on a broad scale. The Eblaites (a Semitic people) could efficiently deal with the Mesopotamians and others who embraced this culture in ways

The Triumph of Babylon

Although the empire of Sargon was extensive, it was short-lived. The Akkadians, too, failed to solve the problems posed by Mesopotamia's geography and population pattern. It was left to the Babylonians to unite Mesopotamia politically and culturally. The Babylonians were Amorites, a Semitic people who had migrated from Arabia and settled on the site of Babylon along the middle Euphrates, where that river runs close to the Tigris. Babylon enjoyed an excellent geographical position and was ideally suited to be the capital of Mesopotamia. It dominated trade on the Tigris and Euphrates Rivers: all commerce to and from Sumer and Akkad had to pass by its walls. It also looked beyond Mesopotamia. Babylonian merchants followed the Tigris north to Assyria and Anatolia. The Euphrates led merchants to Syria, Palestine, and the Mediterranean. The city grew great because of its commercial importance and soundly based power.

Babylon was also fortunate to have a farseeing and able king, Hammurabi (r. 1792–1750 B.C.). Hammurabi set out to do three things: make Babylon secure, unify Mesopotamia, and win for the Babylonians a place in Mesopotamian civilization. The first two he accomplished by conquering Assyria in the north and Sumer and Akkad in the south. Then he turned to his third goal.

Politically, Hammurabi joined in his kingship the Semitic concept of the tribal chieftain and the Sumerian idea of urban kingship. Culturally, he encouraged the spread of myths that explained how Marduk, the god of Babylon, had been elected king of the gods by the other Mesopotamian deities. Hammurabi's success in making Marduk the god of all Mesopotamians made Babylon the religious center of Mesopotamia. Through Hammurabi's genius the Babylonians made their own contribution to Mesopotamian culture—a culture vibrant enough to maintain its identity while assimilating new influences. Hammurabi's conquests and the activity of Babylonian merchants spread this enriched culture north to Anatolia and west to Syria and Palestine.

Life Under Hammurabi

One of Hammurabi's most memorable accomplishments was the proclamation of a **law code** that offers a wealth of information about daily life in Mesopotamia. Hammurabi's was not the first law code in Mesopotamia; indeed, the earliest goes back to about 2100 B.C. Like earlier lawgivers, Hammurabi proclaimed that he issued his laws on divine authority "to establish law and justice

Sargon of Akkad   This bronze head, with elaborately worked hair and beard, portrays the great conqueror Sargon of Akkad. The eyes were originally inlaid with precious jewels, which have since been gouged out. This head was found in the ruins of the Assyrian capital of Ninevah, where it had been taken as loot. *(Bildarchiv Hansmann/Interfoto)*

that all could understand. Culture ignores borders. Despite local variations, so much common ground existed that similar political and economic institutions, exchange of ideas and religious beliefs, methods of writing, and a shared etiquette served as links among all who embraced Mesopotamian culture.

• *Once they had put down roots, how did Mesopotamians spread their culture to the broader world?*

in the language of the land, thereby promoting the welfare of the people." Hammurabi's code inflicted such penalties as mutilation, whipping, and burning. Despite its severity, a spirit of justice and a sense of responsibility pervade the code. Hammurabi genuinely felt that his duty was to govern the Mesopotamians as righteously as possible. He tried to regulate the relations of his people so that they could live together in harmony.

The practical impact of Hammurabi's code is much debated. There is much disagreement about whether it recorded laws already established, promulgated new laws, or simply proclaimed what was just and proper. It is also unknown whether Hammurabi's proclamation, like others before it, was legally binding on the courts. At the very least, Hammurabi pronounced to the world the principles of justice he encouraged, while giving everyone visible evidence of his intentions as ruler of Babylonia.

The Code of Hammurabi has two striking characteristics. First, the law differed according to the social status and gender of the offender. Aristocrats were not punished as harshly as commoners, nor commoners as harshly as slaves. Certain actions that were crimes for women were not crimes for men. Second, the code demanded that the punishment fit the crime. It called for "an eye for an eye, and a tooth for a tooth," at least among equals. However, an aristocrat who destroyed the eye of a commoner or slave could pay a fine instead of losing his own eye. Otherwise, as long as criminal and victim shared the same social status, the victim could demand exact vengeance.

Hammurabi's code began with legal procedure. There were no public prosecutors or district attorneys, so individuals brought their own complaints before the court. Each side had to produce written documents or witnesses to support its case. In cases of murder, the accuser had to prove the defendant guilty; any accuser who failed to do so was put to death. This strict law was designed to prevent people from lodging groundless charges. The Mesopotamians were very worried about witchcraft and sorcery. Anyone accused of witchcraft, even if the charges were not proved, underwent an ordeal by water. The gods themselves would decide the case. The defendant was thrown into the Euphrates, which was considered the instrument of the gods. A defendant who sank was guilty; a defendant who floated was innocent. Another procedural regulation covered the conduct of judges. Once a

judge had rendered a verdict, he could not change it. Any judge who did so was fined heavily and deposed. In short, the code tried to guarantee a fair trial and a just verdict.

Consumer protection is not a modern idea; it goes back to Hammurabi's day. Merchants had to guarantee the quality of their goods and services. A boat builder who did sloppy work had to repair the boat at his own expense. A boatman who lost the owner's boat or sank someone else's boat replaced it and its cargo. House builders guaranteed their work with their lives. Careless work could result in the collapse of a house and the death of its inhabitants. If that happened, the builder was put to death. A merchant who tried to increase the interest

Law Code of Hammurabi Hammurabi ordered his code to be inscribed on a stone pillar and set up in public. At the top of the pillar Hammurabi is depicted receiving the scepter of authority from the god Shamash. *(Hirmer Verlag München)*

rate on a loan forfeited the entire amount. Hammurabi's laws tried to ensure that consumers got what they paid for and paid a just price.

Because farming was essential to Mesopotamian life, Hammurabi's code dealt extensively with agriculture. Tenant farming was widespread, and tenants rented land on a yearly basis. Instead of money they paid a portion of their crops as rent. Unless the land was carefully cultivated, it quickly reverted to wasteland. Therefore, tenants faced severe penalties for neglecting the land or not working it at all. Since irrigation was essential to grow crops, tenants had to keep the canals and ditches in good repair. Otherwise the land would be subject to floods and farmers would face crippling losses. Anyone whose neglect of the canals resulted in damaged crops had to bear all the expense of the lost crops. Those tenants who could not pay the costs were forced into slavery.

Hammurabi gave careful attention to marriage and the family. As elsewhere in the Near East, marriage had aspects of a business agreement. The prospective groom or his father and the father of the future bride arranged everything. The groom offered the father a bridal gift, usually money. If the man and his bridal gift were acceptable, the father provided his daughter with a dowry. After marriage the dowry belonged to the woman (although the husband normally administered it) and was a means of protecting her rights and status. Once the two men agreed on financial matters, they drew up a contract; no marriage was considered legal without one. Either party could break off the marriage, but not without paying a stiff penalty. Fathers often contracted marriages while their children were still young. The girl either continued to live in her father's house until she reached maturity or went to live in the house of her father-in-law. During this time she was legally considered a wife. Once she and her husband came of age, they set up their own house.

The wife was expected to be rigorously faithful. The penalty for adultery, defined as sex between a married woman and a man not her husband, was death. According to Hammurabi's code: "If the wife of a man has been caught while lying with another man, they shall bind them and throw them into the water."[3] There was no corresponding law for married men. The husband had the power to spare his wife by obtaining a pardon for her from the king. He could, however, accuse his wife of adultery even if he had not caught her in the act. In such a case she could try to clear herself before the city council that investigated the charge. If she was found innocent, she could take her dowry and leave her husband. If a woman decided to take the direct approach and kill her husband, she was impaled.

The husband had virtually absolute power over his household. He could even sell his wife and children into slavery to pay debts. Sons did not lightly oppose their fathers, and any son who struck his father could have his hand cut off. A father was free to adopt children and include them in his will. Artisans sometimes adopted children to teach them the family trade. Although the father's power was great, he could not disinherit a son without just cause. Cases of disinheritance became matters for the city to decide, and the code ordered the courts to forgive a son for his first offense. Only if a son wronged his father a second time could he be disinherited.

Prostitution, both male and female, was as common in Mesopotamia as it is today. Then as now, prostitution entailed selling sex for money. Though disreputable, it was not illegal in Mesopotamia and was instead taxed. Prostitutes, like Mesopotamians in general, differed in social status. A special type of prostitution, its meaning still disputed, was the "temple prostitute" who performed sexual acts in the temple as part of her sacred duties. Sex was a routine part of her religious life. The money went to the goddess of the temple. Other women lived as courtesans, mistresses who served clients who were their patrons on a regular basis. Courtesans were both sexual partners and social companions to wealthy and powerful men, who generally had wives and children as well. Prostitutes and courtesans differed from concubines, who were simply women who lived with men without marriage. All of them lived under the protection of the law.

Hammurabi's law code took magic as a fact of life. Magic is the invocation of the gods or the powers of the underworld to act to people's advantage. Magic was often associated with religion and medicine. Mesopotamians, like countless others, genuinely believed that supernatural forces could directly and benevolently intervene on their behalf. In devout belief they used chants and incantations to call on higher, unseen powers to bring them happiness.

Law codes, preoccupied as they are with the problems of society, provide a bleak view of things. Other Mesopotamian documents give a happier glimpse of life. Although Hammurabi's code dealt with marriage in a hard-fisted fashion, countless wills and testaments show that husbands habitually left their estates to their wives, who in turn willed the property to their children. Hammurabi's code restricted married women from commercial pursuits, but financial documents prove that many women engaged in business without hindrance. Some carried on the family business, while others became wealthy landowners in their own right.

Marriage was primarily an arrangement between families, but evidence of love has also survived. A Mesopotamian poem tells of two people meeting secretly in the city. Their parting is delightfully romantic:

Come now, set me free, I must go home,
Kuli-Enlil . . . set me free, I must go home.
What can I say to deceive my mother?[4]

Mesopotamians found their lives lightened by holidays and religious festivals. Traveling merchants brought news of the outside world and swapped marvelous tales. Despite their pessimism, the Mesopotamians enjoyed a vibrant and creative culture that left its mark on the entire Near East.

Egypt, the Land of the Pharaohs (3100–1200 B.C.)

The Greek historian and traveler Herodotus in the fifth century B.C. called Egypt the "gift of the Nile." No other single geographical factor had such a fundamental and profound impact on the shaping of Egyptian life, society, and history as the Nile (see Map 1.2). Unlike the rivers of Mesopotamia, it rarely brought death and destruction by devastating entire cities. The river was primarily a creative force. The Egyptians never feared the relatively tame Nile in the way the Mesopotamians feared the Tigris. Instead, they sang its praises:

Hail to thee, O Nile, that issues from the earth and comes to
keep Egypt alive! . . .
He that waters the meadows which Re [Ra] created,
He that makes to drink the desert . . .
He who makes barley and brings emmer [wheat] into
being . . .
He who brings grass into being for the cattle . . .
He who makes every beloved tree to grow . . .
O Nile, verdant art thou, who makest man and cattle to
live.[5]

Online Study Center Improve Your Grade
Primary Source: The Hymn to the Nile

In the mind of the Egyptians, the Nile was the supreme fertilizer and renewer of the land. Each September the Nile floods its valley, transforming it into a huge area of marsh or lagoon. By the end of November the water retreats, leaving behind a thin covering of fertile mud ready to be planted with crops.

The annual flood made the growing of abundant crops almost effortless, especially in southern Egypt. Herodotus, used to the rigors of Greek agriculture, was amazed by the ease with which the Egyptians raised crops:

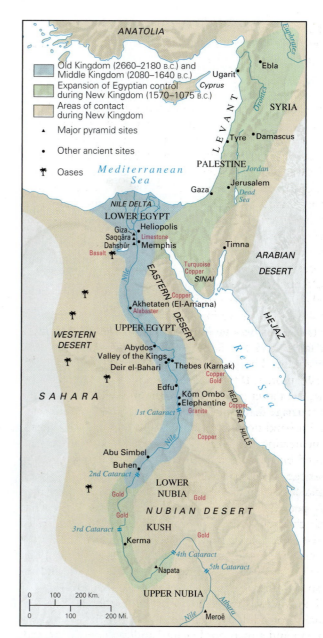

MAP 1.2 Ancient Egypt Geography and natural resources provided Egypt with centuries of peace and abundance.

Online Study Center Improve Your Grade
Interactive Map: Ancient Egypt and the Levant

For indeed without trouble they obtain crops from the land more easily than all other men. . . . They do not labor to dig furrows with the plough or hoe or do the work which other men do to raise grain. But when the river by itself inundates the fields and the water recedes, then each man, having sown his field, sends pigs into it. When the pigs trample down the seed, he waits for the harvest. Then when the pigs thresh the grain, he gets his crop.[6]

The extraordinary fertility of the Nile Valley made it easy to produce an annual agricultural surplus, which in turn sustained a growing and prosperous population. The Nile also unified Egypt. The river was the region's principal highway, promoting easy communication throughout the valley.

Egypt was fortunate in that it was nearly self-sufficient. Besides the fertility of its soil, Egypt possessed enormous quantities of stone, which served as the raw material of architecture and sculpture. Abundant clay was available for pottery, as was gold for jewelry and ornaments. The raw materials that Egypt lacked were close at hand. The Egyptians could obtain copper from Sinai and timber from Lebanon. They had little cause to look to the outside world for their essential needs, a fact that helps explain the insular quality of Egyptian life.

● *What challenges did the Egyptians face in taming their own environment, and how did they so succeed that their culture became basic to Western society?*

of kings. For modern historical purposes, however, it is more useful to divide Egyptian history into periods (see page 21). The political unification of Egypt ushered in the period known as the Old Kingdom (2660–2180 B.C.), an era remarkable for prosperity, artistic flowering, and the evolution of religious beliefs.

In religion, the Egyptians developed complex, often contradictory, ideas of their gods. They were polytheistic in that they worshiped many gods, some mightier than others. Their beliefs were all rooted in the environment and human ecology. The most powerful of these gods was Amon, a primeval sky-god, and Ra, the sun-god. Amon created the entire cosmos by his thoughts. He caused the Nile to make its annual inundations and the northern wind to blow. He brought life to the land and its people, and he sustained both. The Egyptians cherished Amon because he championed fairness and honesty, especially for the common people. The Egyptians called him the "vizier of the humble" and the "voice of the poor." He was also a magician and physician who cured ills, protected people from natural dangers,

The God-King of Egypt

Geographical unity quickly gave rise to political unification of the country under the authority of a king whom the Egyptians called "pharaoh." The precise details of this process have been lost. The Egyptians themselves told of a great king, Menes, who united Upper and Lower Egypt into a single kingdom around 3100 B.C. Thereafter the Egyptians divided their history into dynasties, or families

Ra and Horus The god Ra appears on the left in a form associated with Horus, the falcon-god. The red circle over Ra's head identifies him as the sun-god. In this scene Ra also assumes characteristics of Osiris, god of the underworld. He stands in judgment of the dead woman on the right. She meets the god with respect but without fear, as he will guide her safely to a celestial heaven. *(Egyptian Museum, Cairo)*

and protected travelers. The Egyptians considered Ra the creator of life. He commanded the sky, earth, and underworld. This giver of life could also take it without warning. Ra was associated with the falcon-god Horus, the "lord of the sky," who served as the symbol of divine kingship. Horus united Egypt and bestowed divinity on the pharaoh. The obvious similarities between Amon and Ra eventually led the Egyptians to combine them into one god, **Amon-Ra.** Yet the Egyptians never fashioned a formal theology to resolve these differences. Instead they worshiped these gods as different aspects of the same celestial phenomena.

Periods of Egyptian History

Period	Dates	Significant Events
Archaic	3100–2660 B.C.	Unification of Egypt
Old Kingdom	2660–2180 B.C.	Construction of the pyramids
First Intermediate	2180–2080 B.C.	Political chaos
Middle Kingdom	2080–1640 B.C.	Recovery and political stability
Second Intermediate	1640–1570 B.C.	Hyksos "invasion"
New Kingdom	1570–1075 B.C.	Creation of an Egyptian empire; Akhenaten's religious policy

The Egyptians likewise developed views of an afterlife that reflected the world around them. The dry air of Egypt preserves much that would decay in other climates. Thus there was a sense of permanence about Egypt: the past was never far from the present. The dependable rhythm of the seasons also shaped the fate of the dead. According to the Egyptians, Osiris, a fertility god associated with the Nile, died each year, and each year his wife, Isis, brought him back to life. Isis gave birth to Osiris's son Horus and is frequently shown in paintings and statues holding her infant son. Osiris eventually became king of the dead, and he weighed human beings' hearts to determine whether they had lived justly enough to deserve everlasting life. Osiris's care of the dead was shared by Anubis, the jackal-headed god who annually helped Isis to resuscitate Osiris. Anubis was the god of mummification, so essential to Egyptian funerary rites. The Egyptians preserved these ideas in the **Book of the Dead,** which explained that after death the soul left the body to become part of the divine. It entered gladly through the gate of heaven and remained in the presence of Aton (a sun-god) and the stars. Thus the Egyptians did not draw a firm boundary between the human and the divine, and life did not end with death.

Online Study Center **Improve Your Grade**
Primary Source: The Egyptian Book of the Dead's Declaration of Innocence

The focal point of religious and political life in the Old Kingdom was the **pharaoh,** who commanded the wealth, resources, and people of all Egypt. The pharaoh's power was such that the Egyptians considered him to be Horus in human form, a living god on earth, who became one with Osiris after death. His wife was associated with Isis, for both the queen and the goddess were viewed as protectors. The pharaoh was not simply the mediator between the gods and the Egyptian people. Above all, he was the power that achieved the integration between gods and human beings, between nature and society, that ensured peace and prosperity for the land of the Nile. The pharaoh was thus a guarantee to his people, a pledge that the gods of Egypt (strikingly unlike those of Mesopotamia) cared for their people.

The king's surroundings had to be worthy of a god. Only a magnificent palace was suitable for his home; in fact, the very word *pharaoh* means "great house." Only later, in the Eighteenth Dynasty (see page 24), did it come to mean "king." Just as the pharaoh occupied a great house in life, so he reposed in a great **pyramid** after death. The massive tomb contained all the things needed by the pharaoh in his afterlife. The walls of the burial chamber were inscribed with religious texts and spells relating to the king's journeys after death. Contrary to common belief, no curses for violation of the pyramid have been found. The pyramid also symbolized the king's power and his connection with the sun-god. After burial the entrance was blocked and concealed to ensure the pharaoh's undisturbed peace. To this day the great pyramids at Giza near Cairo bear silent but magnificent testimony to the god-kings of Egypt.

The Pharaoh's People

Because the common folk stood at the bottom of the social and economic scale, they were always at the mercy of grasping officials. The arrival of the tax collector was never a happy occasion. One Egyptian scribe described the worst that could happen:

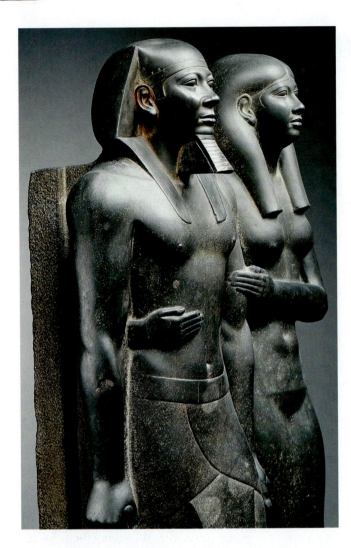

King Menkaure and Queen   The pharaoh and his wife represent all the magnificence, serenity, and grandeur of Egypt. *(Old Kingdom, Dynasty 4, reign of Mycerinus, 2532–2510 B.C.; Greywacke; H × W × D: 54¹¹/₁₆ × 22³/₈ × 21⁵/₁₆ in. (139 × 57 × 54 cm). Harvard University—Museum of Fine Arts Expedition, 11.1738. Museum of Fine Arts, Boston)*

and sowed. This was a particularly busy time, for the crops had to be planted before the land dried. The next period, from mid-March to July, saw the harvesting of crops. Rural men and women also nurtured a large variety of fruit trees, vegetables, and vines. They tended cattle and poultry, and when time permitted they hunted and fished in the marshlands of the Nile. People could routinely depend on these aspects of life. This very regularity gave a sense of calm and order to Egypt that was not found in Mesopotamia or later in Greece.

Egyptian society seems to have been a curious mixture of freedom and constraint. Slavery did not become widespread until the New Kingdom (1570–1075 B.C.). There was neither a caste system nor a color bar, and humble people could rise to the highest positions if they possessed talent. On the other hand, most ordinary folk were probably little more than serfs who could not easily leave the land of their own free will. Peasants were also subject to forced labor, including work on the pyramids and canals. Young men were drafted into the pharaoh's army, which served both as a fighting force and as a labor corps.

The vision of thousands of people straining to build the pyramids and countless artists adorning the pharaoh's tomb brings to the modern mind a distasteful picture of absolute power. Indeed, the Egyptian view of life and society is alien to those raised with modern concepts of individual freedom and human rights. To ancient Egyptians the pharaoh embodied justice and order—harmony among human beings, nature, and the divine. If the pharaoh was weak or allowed anyone to challenge his unique position, he opened the way to chaos. Twice in Egyptian history the pharaoh failed to maintain rigid centralization. During those two eras, known as the First and Second Intermediate Periods, Egypt was exposed to civil war and invasion. Yet the monarchy survived, and in each period a strong pharaoh arose to crush the rebels or expel the invaders and restore order.

And now the scribe lands on the river-bank and is about to register the harvest-tax. The janitors carry staves and the Nubians rods of palm, and they say, Hand over the corn, though there is none. The cultivator is beaten all over, he is bound and thrown into a well, soused and dipped head downwards. His wife has been bound in his presence and his children are in fetters.[7]

That was an extreme situation. Nonetheless, taxes might amount to 20 percent of the harvest, and tax collection could be brutal.

The regularity of the climate meant that the agricultural year was also routine and dependable. For the Egyptian peasants who formed the bulk of the population, the agricultural year normally began in July, when the mud of the Nile covered the land. The waters receded four months later, and then the land was plowed

The Hyksos in Egypt (1640–1570 B.C.)

While Egyptian civilization flourished behind its bulwark of sand and sea, momentous changes were taking place in

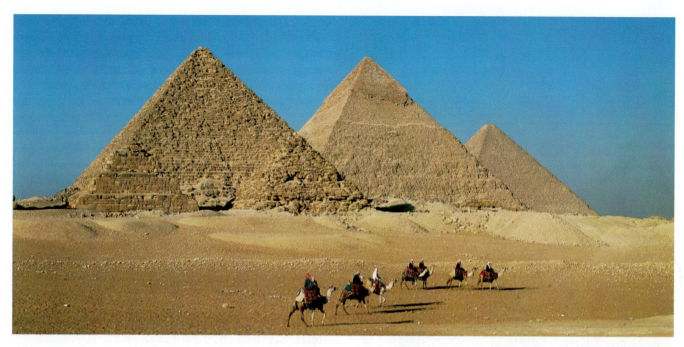

Pyramids of Giza Giza was the burial place of the pharaohs of the Old Kingdom and of their aristocracy, whose smaller rectangular tombs surround the two foremost pyramids. The small pyramid probably belonged to a pharaoh's wife. *(Jose Fuste Raga/Corbis)*

Egyptian Harvest Scene This cheerful wall painting depicts two aspects of the harvest. Workers at the top right pick bunches of ripe grapes for winemaking. Their colleagues in the center stamp the grapes, and the large pottery jars store the wine. *(Louvre/Réunion des Musées Nationaux/Art Resource, NY)*

the ancient Near East, changes that would leave their mark even on rich, insular Egypt. These changes involved enormous and remarkable movements, especially of peoples who spoke Semitic tongues.

The original home of the Semites was perhaps the Arabian peninsula. Some tribes moved into northern Mesopotamia, others into Syria and Palestine, and still others into Egypt. Shortly after 1800 B.C. people whom the Egyptians called **Hyksos,** which means "Rulers of the Uplands," began to settle in the Nile Delta. The movements of the Hyksos were part of a larger pattern of migration of peoples during this period. The history of Mesopotamia records many such wanderings of people in search of better homes for themselves. Such nomads normally settled in and accommodated themselves with the native cultures. The process was mutual, for each group had something to give to and to learn from the other.

So it was in Egypt, but Egyptian tradition, as later recorded by the priest Manetho in the third century B.C., depicted the coming of the Hyksos as a brutal invasion:

In the reign of Toutimaios—I do not know why—the wind of god blew against us. Unexpectedly from the regions of the east men of obscure race, looking forward confidently to

Shabti Figurines   The Egyptians believed in an afterlife in which earthly work must go on. They made Shabti figurines that could be called magically to life to do that work for them. The figurines fulfilled in death the tasks that ordinary human beings did in life. *(Courtesy of the Trustees of the British Museum)*

victory, invaded our land, and without a battle easily seized it all by sheer force. Having subdued those in authority in the land, they then barbarously burned our cities and razed to the ground the temples of the gods. They fell upon all the natives in an entirely hateful fashion, slaughtering them and leading both their children and wives into slavery. At last they made one of their people king, whose name was Salitis. This man resided at Memphis, leaving in Upper and Lower Egypt tax collectors and garrisons in strategic places.[8]

The Hyksos created a capital city at Avaris, located in the northeastern Nile Delta, but they probably exerted direct rule no farther south.

Although the Egyptians portrayed the Hyksos as a conquering horde, they were probably no more than no-mads looking for good land. Their entry into the delta was probably gradual and generally peaceful. The Hyksos brought with them the method of making bronze and casting it into tools and weapons that became standard in Egypt. They thereby brought Egypt fully into the **Bronze Age** culture of the Mediterranean world, a culture in which the production and use of bronze implements became basic to society. Bronze tools made farming more efficient than ever before because they were sharper and more durable than the copper tools they replaced. The Hyksos' use of bronze armor and weapons as well as horse-drawn chariots and the composite bow, made of laminated wood and horn and far more powerful than the simple wooden bow, revolutionized Egyptian warfare. However much the Egyptians learned from the Hyksos, Egyptian culture eventually absorbed the newcomers. The Hyksos came to worship Egyptian gods and modeled their monarchy on the pharaonic system.

The New Kingdom: Revival and Empire (1570–1075 B.C.)

Politically, Egypt was only in eclipse. The Egyptian sun shone again when a remarkable line of kings, the pharaohs of the Eighteenth Dynasty, arose to challenge the Hyksos. These pharaohs pushed the Hyksos out of the delta, subdued Nubia in the south, and conquered Palestine and parts of Syria in the northeast. In this way, Egyptian warrior-pharaohs inaugurated the New Kingdom—a period in Egyptian history characterized by enormous wealth and conscious imperialism. During this period, probably for the first time, widespread slavery became a feature of Egyptian life. The pharaoh's armies returned home leading hordes of slaves who constituted a new labor force for imperial building projects.

The kings of the Eighteenth Dynasty created the first Egyptian empire. They ruled Palestine and Syria through their officers and incorporated the neighboring region of Nubia into the kingdom of Egypt. Egyptian religion and customs flourished in Nubia, making a huge impact on African culture there and in neighboring areas. The warrior-kings celebrated their success with monuments on a scale unparalleled since the pharaohs of the Old Kingdom had built the pyramids. Even today the colossal granite statues of these pharaohs and the rich tomb objects of Tutankhamon ("King Tut") testify to the might and splendor of the New Kingdom.

Tutankhamon as Pharaoh   This painted casket depicts the pharaoh as the defender of the kingdom repulsing its invaders. Tutankhamon rides into battle under the signs of the sun-disk and the vulture-goddess, indicating that he and Egypt enjoy the protection of the gods. *(Egyptian Museum, Cairo)*

One of the most extraordinary of this unusual line of kings was Akhenaten (r. 1367–1350 B.C.), a pharaoh more concerned with religion than with conquest. Nefertiti, his wife and queen, encouraged his religious bent. (See the feature "Individuals in Society: Nefertiti, the 'Perfect Woman.'") The precise nature of Akhenaten's religious beliefs remains debatable. The problem began during his own lifetime. His religion was often unpopular among the people and the traditional priesthood, and its practice declined in the later years of his reign. After his death, it was condemned and denounced; consequently, not much is known about it. Most historians, however, agree that Akhenaten and Nefertiti were monotheists; that is, they believed that the sun-god Aton, whom they worshiped, was universal, the only god. They considered all other Egyptian gods and goddesses frauds and disregarded their worship. Yet their belief suffered from an obvious flaw. The pharaoh himself was considered the son of god, and monotheism obviously cannot have two gods. What Akhenaten meant by **monotheism** is that only Aton among the traditional Egyptian deities was god.

Akhenaten's monotheism, imposed from above, failed to find a place among the people. The prime reason for Akhenaten's failure is that his god had no connection with the past of the Egyptian people, who trusted the old gods and felt comfortable praying to them. Average Egyptians were no doubt distressed and disheartened when their familiar gods were outlawed, for those gods were the heavenly powers that had made Egypt powerful and unique. The fanaticism and persecution that accompanied the new monotheism were in complete defiance of the Egyptian tradition of tolerant **polytheism,** or worship of several gods. Thus, when Akhenaten died, his religion died with him.

The Hittites and the End of an Era (ca 1640–1100 B.C.)

Like the Mesopotamians and the Egyptians before them, the Hittites introduced a new element into the development of the ancient Near East. The Hittites were the first Indo-Europeans to become broadly important throughout the region. The term **Indo-European** refers to a large family of languages that includes English, most of the languages of modern Europe, including Greek and Latin, and languages as far afield as Persian and Sanskrit, spoken in ancient Turkey and India. During the eighteenth and nineteenth centuries European scholars learned that peoples who spoke related languages had

spread as far west as Ireland and as far east as Central Asia. Archaeologists were subsequently able to assign rough dates to these migrations and to put them into their historical context. As a result, historians learned that in the course of their experiences in their new world, these peoples made a singular place for themselves. They also left a lasting imprint on the Near East before the empires of the whole region suffered the shock of new peoples and widespread disruption.

• How did the Hittites rise to power, and how did they and other Near East peoples survive the collapse of the great empires?

The Coming of the Hittites (ca 1640–1200 B.C.)

The rise of the Hittites to prominence in Anatolia is reasonably clear. During the nineteenth century B.C. the

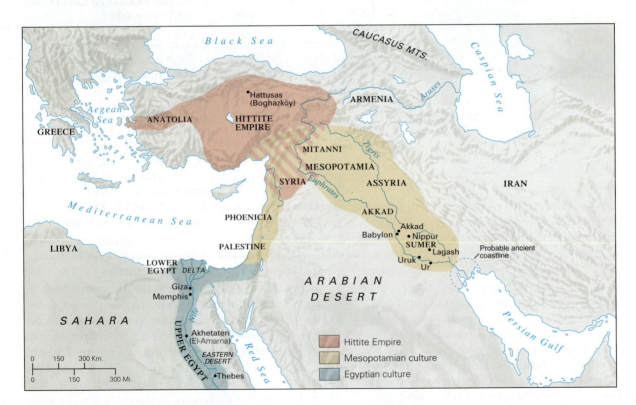

MAP 1.3 Balance of Power in the Near East   This map shows the regions controlled by the Hittites and Egyptians at the height of their power. The striped area represents the part of Mesopotamia conquered by the Hittites during their expansion eastward.

Online Study Center   **Improve Your Grade** Interactive Map: Balance of Power in the Near East

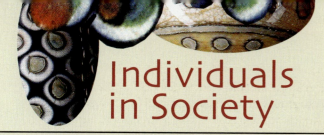

Individuals in Society

Nefertiti, the "Perfect Woman"

... be the living ... rce of law and ... ds and humans. ... ed to members of ... dren were also ... se of this, a ... ister as one of ... ood set the ... other Egyptians ... d allowed the ... Egyptian mythol- ... araoh chose one ... Vife," or principal ... gh sometimes it ... o married ... ces.

... divine allowed a ... vn right in Egypt's ... four female ... s was Hatshepsut ... er and wife of ... ed as regent for her ... vas actually the son ... trading expedi-

tions and sponsored ... hitects, ushering in a period of artistic creativity and economic prosperity. She built one of the world's great buildings, an elaborate terraced temple at Deir el Bahri, which eventually served as her tomb. Hatshepsut's status as a powerful female ruler was difficult for Egyptians to conceptualize, and she is often depicted in male dress or with a false beard, thus looking more like the male rulers who were the norm. After her death, Thutmose III tried to destroy all evidence that she had ever ruled, smashing statues and scratching her name off inscriptions, perhaps because of personal animosity and perhaps because he wanted to erase the fact that a woman had once been pharaoh. Only within the last decades have historians and archaeologists begun to (literally) piece together her story.

Though female pharaohs were very rare, many royal women had power through their position as "Great Royal Wives." The most famous of these was Nefertiti, the wife of Akhenaten. Her name means "the perfect (or beautiful) woman has come," and inscriptions also give her many other titles. Nefertiti used her position to spread the new religion of the sun-god Aton. Together

she and Akhenaten built a new palace at Akhetaten, the present Amarna, away from the old centers of power. There they developed the cult of Aton to the exclusion of the traditional deities. Nearly the only literary survival of their religious belief is the "Hymn to Aton," which declares Aton to be the only god. It describes Nefertiti as "the great royal consort whom he! Akhenaten! Loves, the mistress of the Two Lands! Upper and Lower Egypt!"

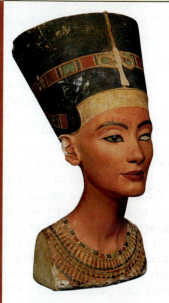

Nefertiti, queen of Egypt.
(Bildarchiv Preussischer Kulturbesitz/ Art Resource, NY)

Nefertiti is often shown the same size as her husband, and in some inscriptions she is performing religious rituals that would normally have been done only by the pharaoh. The exact details of her power are hard to determine, however. An older theory held that her husband removed her from power, though there is also speculation that she may have ruled secretly in her own right after his death. Her tomb has long since disappeared, though in 2003 an enormous controversy developed over her possible remains. There is no controversy that the bust shown above, now in a Berlin museum, represents Nefertiti, nor that it has become an icon of female beauty since it was first discovered in the early twentieth century.

Questions for Analysis

1. Why might it have been difficult for Egyptians to accept a female ruler?
2. What opportunities do hereditary monarchies such as that of ancient Egypt provide for women? How does this fit with gender hierarchies in which men are understood as superior?

Online Study Center **Improve Your Grade**
Going Beyond Individuals in Society

native kingdoms in the area engaged in suicidal warfare that left most of Anatolia's once-flourishing towns in ashes and rubble. In this climate of exhaustion the Hittite king Hattusilis I built a hill citadel at Hattusas, the modern Boghazköy, from which he led his Hittites against neighboring kingdoms (see Map 1.3). Hattusilis's grandson and successor, Mursilis I (ca 1595 B.C.), extended the Hittite conquests as far as Babylon. Upon his return home, the victorious Mursilis was assassinated by members of his own family, an act that plunged the kingdom into confusion and opened the door to foreign invasion. Mursilis's career is representative of the success and weakness of the Hittites. They were extremely vulnerable to attack by vigilant and tenacious enemies. Yet once they were united behind a strong king, the Hittites were a power to be reckoned with.

The Hittites, like the Egyptians of the New Kingdom, produced an energetic and able line of kings who built a powerful empire. Perhaps their major contribution was the introduction of iron into war and agriculture in the form of weapons and tools. Around 1300 B.C. the Hittites stopped the Egyptian army of Rameses II at the Battle of Kadesh in Syria. Having fought each other to a standstill, the Hittites and Egyptians first made peace, then an alliance. Alliance was followed by friendship, and friendship by active cooperation. The two greatest powers of the early Near East tried to make war between them impossible.

They next included the Babylonians in their diplomacy. All three empires developed an official etiquette in which they treated one another as "brothers," using this gendered familial term to indicate their connection. They made alliances for offensive and defensive protection and swore to uphold one another's authority. These contacts facilitated the exchange of ideas throughout the Near East. Furthermore, the Hittites passed much knowledge

Hittite Solar Disc   This cult standard represents Hittite concepts of fertility and prosperity. The circle surrounding the animals is the sun, beneath which stands a stag flanked by two bulls. Stylized bull's horns spread from the base of the disc. The symbol is also one of might and protection from outside harm. (*Museum of Anatolian Civilizations, Ankara*)

and lore from the Near East to the newly arrived Greeks in Europe. The details of Hittite contact with the Greeks are unknown, but enough literary themes and physical objects exist to prove the connection.

The Fall of Empires and the Survival of Cultures (ca 1200 B.C.)

As seen, the Battle of Kadesh ushered in a welcome period of peace and stability in the Near East that lasted until the thirteenth century B.C. Then, however, foreign invaders destroyed both the Hittite and the Egyptian empires. The most famous of these marauders, called the **Sea Peoples** by the Egyptians, launched a series of stunning attacks that brought down the Hittites and drove the Egyptians back to the Nile Delta. Yet the Sea Peoples and other dimly known peoples did no serious damage to the social and cultural advances made by their predecessors.

The basic social, economic, and cultural patterns of the Near East not only survived the onslaught, but also maintained their hold on the entire area. They filled an aching void in the lives of both disrupted peoples and newcomers, a pattern already seen many times before. Yet it is a mistake to think that the Egyptian and Hittite civilizations survived to face a cultural vacuum.

The Egyptians took the lead in the recovery by establishing commercial contact with their new neighbors. With the exchange of goods went ideas. Both sides shared practical concepts of shipbuilding, metal technology, and methods of trade that allowed merchants safely and efficiently to transact business over long distances. They all—old-timers and newcomers—began to establish and recognize recently created borders, which helped define them geographically and politically. One of the most striking and enduring of these developments was the cultural exchange among them.

When the worst was over, the Egyptians made contact with the Semitic peoples of Palestine and Syria whom they found living in small walled towns. Farther north in the land soon to be named Phoenicia, they also encountered a people who combined sophisticated seafaring with urban life.

The situation in northern Syria reflected life in the south. Small cities in all these places were mercantile centers rich not only in manufactured goods but also in agricultural produce, textiles, and metals. The cities flourished under royal families that shared power and dealt jointly in foreign affairs. These northerners relied heavily on their Mesopotamian heritage. While adopting Babylonian writing to communicate with their more distant neighbors to the east, they also adapted it to write their own north Semitic language. Their texts provide a wealth of information about their life. At the same time they welcomed the knowledge of Mesopotamian literature, mathematics, and culture. They worshiped both their own and Mesopotamian deities. Yet the cultural exchange remained a mixture of adoption, adaptation, contrast, and finally balance, as the two cultures came to understand and appreciate each other.

Southern Anatolia presented a similar picture. Settlements there consisted of trading colonies and small agricultural communities. Thousands of cuneiform tablets testify to commercial and cultural exchanges with Mesopotamia. Here also the Hittite heritage sturdily lived on, especially in politics and social relations. In Anatolia kingship and temple were closely allied, but the government was not a **theocracy** (rule by a priestly order). A city assembly of adult free men worked together under the king, and a prince administered the cities. Thus some men who were not members of the elite had a voice in their political and social affairs. The world of these people rested on a mixture of the Hittite past and their own native achievements. This combination enabled them to create an environment uniquely their own.

A pattern emerged in Palestine, Syria, and Anatolia. In these areas native cultures established themselves during the prehistoric period. Upon coming into contact with the Egyptian and Mesopotamian civilizations, they adopted many aspects of these cultures, adapting them to their own traditional customs. Yet they also contributed to the advance of Egyptian and Mesopotamian cultures by introducing new technologies and religious ideas. The result was the emergence of a huge group of communities stretching from Egypt in the south to Anatolia in the north and from the Levant in the west to Mesopotamia in the east. Each enjoyed its own individual character, while at the same time sharing many common features with its neighbors.

Chapter Summary

*Online Study Center*   **ACE the Test**

- *What factors are key to understanding the meaning of "the West" and its history?*
- *How did early peoples socially develop from living in caves to creating more stable and sophisticated towns?*
- *How did the people in Mesopotamia master their environment, invent writing to record their experiences and thoughts, and create a permanent and vibrant civilization?*
- *Once they had put down roots, how did Mesopotamians spread their culture to the broader world?*
- *What challenges did the Egyptians face in taming their own environment, and how did they so succeed that their culture became basic to Western society?*
- *How did the Hittites rise to power, and how did they and other Near East peoples survive the collapse of the great empires?*

Even before studying the history of Western people, historians had to decide what they meant by "the West": what made it integral while distinct from other cultures. An associated challenge was to determine what history was and how to write it. They accomplished both tasks by taking hard looks at themselves and their achievements. They decided what was important enough to record. Having done that, they created a reliable yardstick for understanding how the West differed from other cultures.

The peoples in Mesopotamia first took up this challenge by inventing writing, initially for financial records and then to record their experiences and thoughts about politics and religion. These written records indicate that their society was marked by social and gender hierarchies. The Mesopotamians advanced politically, all the while spreading their influence farther afield. Finally, the Babylonians, a new people, blended their culture with the older Mesopotamian civilization, thereby permanently furthering developments in the Near East and subsequently the broader world.

Around the same time, different peoples in Egypt confronted and triumphed over different challenges to create a new society that was distinctly their own. They developed their own government and formed a society so stable that they successfully absorbed newcomers and formed the second major cultural influence of the early West.

Finally, the Hittites, an Indo-European people, entered the Near East from the north. Distant ancestors of the modern folk of Europe and the Americas, the Hittites brought new organizational skills and methods of social and political organization. They thereby added a new and valuable ingredient to this already culturally rich area. Near East peoples received hard knocks from hostile invaders beginning around the thirteenth century B.C., but key social, economic, and cultural patterns survived to enrich future generations.

Key Terms

Neolithic period	pharaoh
irrigation	pyramid
cuneiform	Hyksos
nobles	Bronze Age
clients	monotheism
patriarchal	polytheism
law code	Indo-European
Amon-Ra	Sea Peoples
Book of the Dead	theocracy

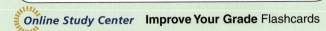*Online Study Center*   **Improve Your Grade** Flashcards

Suggested Reading

Brosius, Maria. *The Persians: An Introduction.* 2006. Covers all of Persian history from the beginnings to Alexander the Great.

Burl, Aubery. *The Stonehenge People.* 1987. An examination of the people and their monuments by the leading expert on the topic.

David, A. Rosalie. *Pyramid Builders of Ancient Egypt,* 2d ed. 1996. Studies the lives of the people who actually labored to build the pyramids for their pharaohs.

Harding, A. F. *European Societies in the Bronze Age.* 2000. A comprehensive survey of developments in Europe.

King, Helen. *Health in Antiquity.* 2005. Traces the significance of good health throughout the ancient world, rather than concentrating only on disease and its treatment.

Kuhrt, Amelie. *The Ancient Near East,* 2 vols. 1995. A broad-ranging work that covers the region from the earliest time to Alexander's conquest.

Kyle, Donald G. *Sport and Spectacle in the Ancient World.* 2006. Analyzes the history of sport and spectacle in the ancient world from the ancient Near East to the Roman Empire, using archaeological and art historical evidence to examine many aspects of sporting activities.

Leick, Gwendolyn. *The Babylonians.* 2002. Provides an introduction to all aspects of Babylonian life and culture.

McDowell, A. G. *Village Life in Ancient Egypt: Laundry Lists and Love Songs.* 1999. A readable study of the basic social and economic factors of the entire period.

Rice, Michael. *Egypt's Making: The Origins of Ancient Egypt.* 2004. Treats the prehistory and earliest history of Egypt.

Robins, Gay. *Women in Ancient Egypt.* 1993. Provides a solid overview of women's lives.

Schmandt-Besserat, Denise. *Before Writing.* 1992. A two-volume work on the origins of writing in Mesopotamia.

Silverman, David P. *Ancient Egypt.* 1997. Gives a good general account of the region.

Notes

1. Quoted in S. N. Kramer, *The Sumerians* (Chicago: University of Chicago Press, 1963), p. 238. John Buckler is the translator of all uncited quotations from a foreign language in Chapters 1–6.
2. J. B. Pritchard, ed., *Ancient Near Eastern Texts,* 3d ed. (Princeton, N.J.: Princeton University Press, 1969), p. 590. Hereafter called ANET.
3. Ibid., p. 171.
4. Kramer, p. 251.
5. ANET, p. 372.
6. Herodotus, *The Histories* 2.14.
7. Quoted in A. H. Gardiner, "Ramesside Texts Relating to the Taxation and Transport of Corn," *Journal of Egyptian Archaeology* 27 (1941): 19–20.
8. Manetho, *History of Egypt,* frag. 42.75–77.

A Quest for Immortality

The human desire to escape the grip of death, to achieve immortality, is one of the oldest wishes of all peoples. The Sumerian *Epic of Gilgamesh is the earliest recorded treatment of this topic. The oldest elements of the epic go back at least to the third millennium B.C. According to tradition, Gilgamesh was a king of Uruk whom the Sumerians, Babylonians, and Assyrians considered a hero-king and a god. In the story Gilgamesh and his friend Enkidu set out to attain immortality and join the ranks of the gods, who are determined to thwart them.*

During their quest Enkidu dies. Gilgamesh, more determined than ever to become immortal, begins seeking anyone who might tell him how to do so. His journey involves the effort not only to escape from death but also to reach an understanding of the meaning of life.

The passage begins with Enkidu speaking of a dream that foretells his own death.

Listen, my friend [Gilgamesh], this is the dream I dreamed last night. The heavens roared, and earth rumbled back an answer; between them I stood before an awful being, the sombre-faced man-bird; he had directed on me his purpose. His was a vampire eagle, his foot was a lion's foot, his hand was an eagle's talon. He fell on me and his claws were in my hair, he held me fast and I smothered; then he transformed me so that my arms became wings covered with feathers. He turned his stare towards me, and he led me away to the palace of Irkalla, the Queen of Darkness [the goddess of the underworld; in other words, an agent of death], to the house from which none who enters ever returns, down the road from which there is no coming back.

At this point Enkidu dies, whereupon Gilgamesh sets off on his quest for the secret of immortality. During his travels he meets with Siduri, the wise and good-natured goddess of wine, who gives him the following advice.

Gilgamesh, where are you hurrying to? You will never find that life for which you are looking. When the gods created man they allotted to him death, but life they retained in their own keeping. As for you, Gilgamesh, fill your belly with good things; day and night, night and day, dance and be merry, feast and rejoice. Let your clothes be fresh, bathe yourself in water, cherish the little child that holds your hand, and make your wife happy in your embrace; for this too is the lot of man.

Ignoring Siduri's advice, Gilgamesh continues his journey, until he finds Utnapishtim. Meeting Utnapishtim is especially important because, like Gilgamesh, he was once a mortal, but the gods so favored him that they put him in an eternal paradise. Gilgamesh puts to Utnapishtim the question that is the reason for his quest.

Oh, father Utnapishtim, you who have entered the assembly of the gods, I wish to question you concerning the living and the dead, how shall I find the life for which I am searching?

Utnapishtim said, "There is no permanence. Do we build a house to stand forever, do we seal a contract to hold for all time? Do brothers divide an inheritance to keep forever, does the flood-time of rivers endure? . . . What is there between the master and the servant when both have fulfilled their doom? When the Anunnaki [the gods of the underworld], the judges, come together, and Mammetun [the goddess of fate] the mother of destinies, together they decree the fates of men. Life and death they allot but the day of death they do not disclose.

Then Gilgamesh said to Utnapishtim the Faraway, "I look at you now, Utnapishtim, and your appearance is no different from mine; there is nothing strange in your features. I thought I should find you like a hero prepared for battle, but you lie here taking your ease on your back. Tell me truly, how was it that you came to enter the company of the gods and to possess everlasting life?" Utnapishtim said to Gilgamesh, "I shall reveal to you a mystery, I shall tell you a secret of the gods."

Utnapishtim then tells Gilgamesh of a time when the great god Enlil had become angered with the Sumerians and encouraged the other gods to wipe out humanity. The god Ea, however, warned Utnapishtim about the gods' decision to send a great flood to destroy the Sumerians. He commanded Utnapishtim to build a boat big enough to hold his family, various artisans, and all animals in order to survive the flood that was to come. Although Enlil was infuriated by the Sumerians' survival, Ea rebuked him. Then Enlil relented and blessed Utnapishtim with eternal paradise. After telling the story, Utnapishtim foretells Gilgamesh's fate.

Utnapishtim said, ". . . The destiny was fulfilled which the father of the gods, Enlil of the mountain, had decreed for Gilgamesh: In nether-earth the darkness will show him a light: of mankind, all that are known, none will leave a monument for generations to compare with his. The heroes, the wise men, like the new moon have their waxing and waning. Men will say, Who has ever ruled with might and power like his? As in the dark month, the month of shadows, so without him there is no light. O Gilgamesh, this was the meaning of your dream [of immortality]. You were given the kingship, such was your destiny, everlasting life was not your destiny. Because of this do not be sad at heart, do not be grieved or oppressed; he [Enlil] has given you power to bind and to loose, to be the darkness and the light of mankind. He has given unexampled supremacy over the people, victory in battle from which no fugitive returns, in forays and assaults from which there is no going back. But do not abuse this power, deal justly with your servants in the palace, deal justly before the face of the Sun."

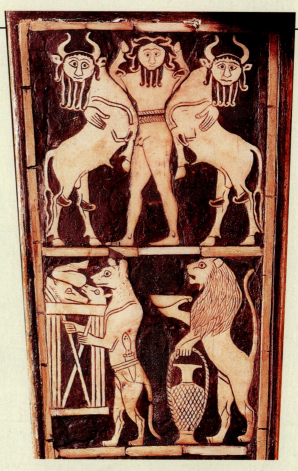

Gilgamesh, from decorative panel of a lyre unearthed at Ur. *(The University Museum, University of Pennsylvania, neg. T4-108)*

Questions for Analysis

1. What does the *Epic of Gilgamesh* reveal about Sumerian attitudes toward the gods and human beings?

2. At the end of his quest, did Gilgamesh achieve immortality? If so, what was the nature of that immortality?

3. What does the epic tell us about Sumerian views of the nature of human life? Where do human beings fit into the cosmic world?

Source: The Epic of Gilgamesh, translated by N. K. Sanders. Penguin Classics 1960, Second revised edition, 1972, pp. 91–119. Copyright © N. K. Sanders, 1960, 1964, 1972. Reproduced by permission of Penguin Books Ltd.

Reconstruction of the "Ishtar Gate," Babylon, early sixth century B.C. Located in the Berlin Museum.
(Bildarchiv Preussischer Kulturbesitz/Art Resource, NY)

chapter

2

chapter preview

Disruption and Diffusion
• *How did Egypt pass on its heritage to its African neighbors and how did new cultures develop?*

The Children of Israel
• *How did the Hebrew state evolve, and what was daily life like in Hebrew society? What forces helped shape Hebrew religious thought, still influential in today's world?*

Assyria, the Military Monarchy
• *What enabled the Assyrians to overrun their neighbors, and how did their cruelty finally cause their undoing?*

The Empire of the Persian Kings
• *How did Iranian nomads build the Persian Empire, and what sort of life did their policies create for the Near East?*

SMALL KINGDOMS AND MIGHTY EMPIRES IN THE NEAR EAST, CA 1100–513 B.C.

The migratory invasions that brought down the Hittites and stunned the Egyptians in the late thirteenth century B.C. ushered in an era of confusion and weakness. Although much was lost in the chaos, the old cultures of the ancient Near East survived to nurture new societies. In the absence of powerful empires, the Phoenicians, Hebrews, and many other peoples carved out small independent kingdoms until the Near East was a patchwork of them. During this period Hebrew culture and religion evolved under the influence of urbanism, kings, and prophets.

In the ninth century B.C. this jumble of small states gave way to an empire that for the first time embraced the entire Near East. Yet the very ferocity of the Assyrian Empire led to its downfall only two hundred years later. In 550 B.C. the Persians and Medes, who had migrated into Iran, created a "world empire" stretching from Anatolia in the west to the Indus Valley in the east. For over two hundred years the Persians gave the ancient Near East peace and stability.

Disruption and Diffusion

If the fall of empires was a time of massive political disruption, it also ushered in a period of cultural diffusion, an expansion of what had already blossomed in the broad region. Even though empires expired, many small kingdoms survived, along with a largely shared culture. These small states and local societies had learned much from the great powers, but they nonetheless retained their own lore and native traditions, which they passed on to their neighbors, thus diffusing a Near Eastern culture that was slowly becoming common in nature. The best-known examples can be found along the coast of the eastern Mediterranean, where various peoples—some of them newcomers such as the Philistines—created homes and petty kingdoms in Phoenicia and Palestine (see Map 2.1).

• *How did Egypt pass on its heritage to its African neighbors and how did new cultures develop?*

Online Study Center

This icon will direct you to interactive activities and study materials on the website **college.hmco.com/pic/mckaywest9e**

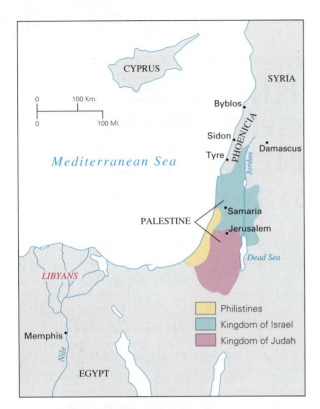

MAP 2.1 Small Kingdoms of the Near East This map illustrates the political fragmentation of the Near East after the great wave of invasions that occurred during the thirteenth century B.C.

Online Study Center **Improve Your Grade**
Interactive Map: Small Kingdoms of the Near East

The End of Egyptian Power

The invasions of the Sea Peoples brought the great days of Egyptian power to an end. The long wars against invaders weakened and impoverished Egypt, causing political upheaval and economic chaos. One scribe left behind a somber portrait of stunned and leaderless Egypt:

The land of Egypt was abandoned and every man was a law to himself. During many years there was no leader who could speak for others. Central government lapsed, small officials and headmen took over the whole land. Any man, great or small, might kill his neighbor. In the distress and vacuum that followed . . . men banded together to plunder one another. They treated the gods no better than men, and cut off the temple revenues.[1]

No longer able to dream of foreign conquests, Egypt looked to its own security from foreign invasion. Egyptians suffered four hundred years of political fragmentation, a new dark age known to Egyptian specialists as the Third Intermediate Period (eleventh–seventh centuries B.C.). (See the feature "Individuals in Society: Wen-Amon.")

In southern Egypt, meanwhile, the pharaoh's decline opened the way to the energetic Nubians, who extended their authority northward throughout the Nile Valley. Since the imperial days of the Eighteenth Dynasty (see pages 24–26), the Nubians, too, had adopted many features of Egyptian culture. Now Nubian kings and aristo-

Egyptian Plowing Despite Egyptian political defeat, ordinary life went on as usual. Here a farmer and his pair of oxen still plow the field as before. His wife follows behind sowing seeds, preparing for the new harvest. (*Deir el-Medina, Thebes/The Bridgeman Art Library*)

crats embraced Egyptian culture wholesale. Thus the Nubians and the Libyans repeated an old Near Eastern phenomenon: new peoples conquered old centers of political and military power but were assimilated into the older culture.

The reunification of Egypt occurred late and unexpectedly. With Egypt distracted and disorganized by foreign invasions, an independent African state, the kingdom of Kush, grew up in the region of modern Sudan with its capital at Nepata. Like the Libyans, the Kushites worshiped Egyptian gods and used Egyptian hieroglyphs. In the eighth century B.C. their king, Piankhy, swept through the entire Nile Valley from Nepata in the south to the delta in the north. United once again, Egypt enjoyed a brief period of peace during which Egyptians continued to assimilate their conquerors. Nonetheless, reunification of the realm did not lead to a new Egyptian empire.

Yet Egypt's legacy to its African neighbors remained vibrant and rich. By trading and exploring southward along the coast of the Red Sea, the Egyptians introduced

Chronology

ca 1100–653 B.C.	Third Intermediate Period in Egypt
ca 1100–400 B.C.	Era of the prophets in Israel
ca 1025–925 B.C.	United Hebrew kingdom
950–730 B.C.	Movement of new peoples into Egypt
ca 950–500 B.C.	Beginning of the Hebrew Bible
ca 900–612 B.C.	Assyrian Empire
ca 900–550 B.C.	Phoenician seafaring and trading in the Mediterranean
ca 710–550 B.C.	Creation of the Persian Empire
ca 600–500 B.C.	Spread of Zoroastrianism
586–538 B.C.	Babylonian Captivity of the Hebrews
ca 550–513 B.C.	Expansion of Persian trade from western Asia to India

Nubian Pyramids   The Nubians adopted many aspects of Egyptian culture and customs. The pyramids shown here are not as magnificent as their Egyptian predecessors, but they served the same purpose of honoring the dead king. Their core was constructed of bricks, which were then covered with stone blocks. At the doors of the pyramids stood monumental gates to the interiors of the tombs. *(Michael Yamashita)*

their goods and ideas as far south as the land of Punt, probably a region on the Somali coast. Egypt was the primary civilizing force in Nubia, which became another version of the pharaoh's realm, complete with royal pyramids and Egyptian deities. Egyptian religion penetrated as far south as Ethiopia.

The Rise of Phoenicia

One of the sturdy peoples who rose to prominence were the Phoenicians, Semitic-speakers who had long inhabited several cities along the coast of modern Lebanon. Although they had lived during the great days of the Hittites and Egyptians, in this period the Phoenicians came into their own. Fully independent, they put their freedom to excellent use. Unlike the Philistine newcomers, who turned from seafaring to farming, the Phoenicians took to the sea. They were master shipbuilders, their stout ships able to face the hardships of the Mediterranean. They became the seaborne merchants of their broad world. With the Greeks, one of their early customers, they traded their popular purple and blue textiles, from which originated their Greek name, Phoenicians, meaning **"Purple People."**

The growing success of the Phoenicians, combined with peace in the Near East, brought them prosperity. In addition to textiles and purple dye, they began to manufacture goods for export, such as metal tools, weapons, and cooking ware. They also expanded their trade to Egypt, where they mingled with other local traders. Egypt, however, simply opened still wider horizons. They struck out along the coast of North Africa to establish new markets in places where they encountered little competition. This route soon took them to Carthage, meaning "New City" in Phoenician, which prospered to become the leading city in the western Mediterranean. Although the Phoenicians did not found colonies, as did the later Greeks (see page 66), they planted trading posts and small farming communities along the coast. From them they shared the vital culture of the more developed Near East with less urbanized peoples. Yet they did not impose their culture, preferring instead to let the natives adopt whatever they found desirable. In this peaceful fashion the Phoenicians spread their trade and something of their customs. But they did so as merchants, not missionaries. Their trade routes eventually took them to the far western Mediterranean and beyond to the Atlantic Ocean.

Phoenician culture was urban, based on the prosperous commercial centers of Tyre, Sidon, and Byblos, all cities still thriving today. The Phoenicians' overwhelming cultural achievement was the development of an alphabet (see Figure 2.1): they, unlike other literate peoples, used one letter to designate one sound, a system that vastly simplified writing and reading. The Greeks modified this alphabet and then used it to write their own language.

Phoenician Ships   These small ships seem too frail to breast the waves. Yet Phoenician mariners routinely sailed them, loaded with their cargoes, to the far ports of the Mediterranean. (*British Museum/Michael Holford*)

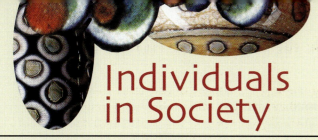

Individuals in Society

Wen-Amon

Surprising as it may sound, the life of a bureaucrat is not always easy. Wen-Amon, an official of the temple of Amon-Ra at Karnak in Egypt, learned that on an authorized mission to Phoenicia. He left his own narrative of his travels, which date to sometime in the eleventh century B.C. Egypt, the shattered kingdom, could no longer exert the authority that it had enjoyed under the pharaohs of the New Kingdom. Despite this political disruption, Egyptian officials continued to expect the traditional respect of the people whom they called "Asiatics." These Asiatics, however, had begun to doubt the power of Egypt and expressed their independence by openly opposing its authority.

Wen-Amon personally experienced this changed atmosphere when he was sent to Byblos in Phoenicia to obtain lumber for Amon-Ra's ceremonial barge. Wen-Amon's detailed account of his experiences comes in the form of an official report to the chief priest of the temple.

Entrusted with ample funds in silver to pay for the lumber, Wen-Amon set out on his voyage. He docked at Dor, in modern Israel, which was independent of the pharaoh, but the local prince received him graciously. While his ship was at anchor, one of Wen-Amon's own sailors vanished with the silver. Wen-Amon immediately reported the robbery to the prince and demanded that he investigate the theft. Wen-Amon pointed out that the silver belonged to Amon-Ra and the great men of Egypt. The prince flatly told Wen-Amon that he did not care whether Wen-Amon and the others were important men. He pointed out that an Egyptian, one of Wen-Amon's own men, had stolen the silver. It was not the prince's problem. No earlier Asian prince would have dared speak to a high Egyptian official in such terms.

Although rebuffed, Wen-Amon found a ship from Byblos and robbed it of an equivalent amount of silver. When he left Dor and entered the harbor of Byblos, the prince there, who had learned of the theft, ordered him to leave. For twenty-nine days there was an impasse. Each day that Wen-Amon remained, the prince told him to get out, but respect both for the great days of Egypt and for Amon-Ra kept the prince from laying hands on Wen-Amon. Finally, the prince sent for Wen-Amon and asked for his papers. A heated argument ensued, with the prince shouting, "I am not your servant. I am not the servant of him who sent you either." Then he asked Wen-Amon what silly voyage he was

making. By this time the Egyptian was greatly annoyed, and he reminded the prince of the greatness of Amon-Ra. He flatly stated that unless the prince honored the great god, he and his land would have neither health nor prosperity. When the two calmed down, the prince agreed to send the timber to Egypt.

After the timber was loaded aboard his ship, Wen-Amon saw eleven enemy ships entering the harbor. They anchored, and those in charge reported to the prince of Byblos that they had come for the Egyptians. He refused to hand them over, saying that he would never arrest a messenger of Amon-Ra. He agreed, however, to send Wen-Amon away first and allow the enemy ships to pursue the Egyptians. Stormy seas blew the Egyptian ship into Hittite territory. When Wen-Amon landed there, Queen Heteb granted him protection and asylum.

The papyrus breaks off at this point, but it is obvious that Wen-Amon weathered his various storms to return safely to Egypt. The document illustrates the presumption of power by Wen-Amon and his bluster at the lack of respect shown him. It also shows how Egypt's neighbors no longer feared Egyptian power. Finally, it illustrates the impact of Egyptian culture and religion on the peoples living along the coast of the Levant. Although Egyptian political power was in eclipse, its cultural legacy endured.

The essentials of Egyptian writing: a sheet of papyrus, a stylus or pen, an ink well.
(Réunion des Musées Nationaux/Art Resource, NY)

Questions for Analysis

1. What do Wen-Amon's experiences tell us about political conditions in the eastern Mediterranean?
2. Since Wen-Amon could no longer depend on the majesty of Egypt for respect, how did he fulfill his duty?

Online Study Center **Improve Your Grade**
Going Beyond Individuals in Society

HIEROGLYPHIC	REPRESENTS	UGARITIC	PHOENICIAN	GREEK	ROMAN
	Throw stick	T		Γ	G
	Man with raised arms			E	E
	Basket with handle			K	K
	Water			M	M
	Snake			N	N
	Eye		O	O	O
	Mouth			Π	P
	Head			P	R
	Pool with lotus flowers		W	Σ	S
	House			B	B
	Ox-head		K	A	A

FIGURE 2.1 Origins of the Alphabet List of Roman, hieroglyphic, Ugaritic, Phoenician, and Greek sign forms. (*Source: A. B. Knapp,* The History and Culture of Ancient Western Asia and Egypt, *Dorsey Press, Chicago, 1988, p. 191. Reprinted by permission of Wadsworth, a division of Thomson Learning, www.thomsonrights.com)*

The Children of Israel

The fall of the Hittite Empire and Egypt's collapse created a vacuum of power in the western Near East that allowed for the rise of numerous small states. South of Phoenicia arose a small kingdom, the land of the ancient Jews or Hebrews. It is difficult to say precisely who the Hebrews were and what brought them to this area, because virtually the only source for much of their history is the Bible, which is essentially a religious document. Even though it contains much historical material, it also contains many Hebrew myths and legends. Moreover, it was compiled at different times, with the earliest parts dating to between about 950 and 800 B.C.

Earlier Mesopotamian and Egyptian sources refer to people called the **Hapiru,** which seems to mean homeless, independent **nomads.** These nomads led roaming lives, always in search of pasturage for their flocks. According to Hebrew tradition, the followers of Abraham migrated from Mesopotamia, but Egyptian documents record Hapiru already in Syria and Palestine in the second millennium B.C. The Hebrews were probably a part of them. Together with other seminomadic peoples, they

probably migrated into the Nile Delta seeking good land. According to the Bible the Egyptians enslaved them. One group, however, under the leadership of Moses, perhaps a semimythical figure, left Egypt in what the Hebrews remembered as the Exodus. From Egypt they wandered in the Sinai Peninsula until they settled in Palestine in the thirteenth century B.C.

In Palestine the Hebrews encountered the Philistines; the Amorites, relatives of Hammurabi's Babylonians; and the Semitic-speaking Canaanites. Despite numerous wars, contact between the Hebrews and their new neighbors was not always hostile. The Hebrews freely mingled with the Canaanites, and some went so far as to worship **Baal,** an ancient Semitic fertility god represented as a golden calf. Archaeological research supports the biblical account of these developments. In 1990 an expedition sponsored by Harvard University discovered a statue of a golden calf in its excavations of Ashkelon in modern Israel. Despite the anger expressed in the Bible over Hebrew worship of Baal, there is nothing surprising about the phenomenon. Once again, newcomers adapted themselves to the culture of an older, well-established people.

The greatest danger to the Hebrews came from the Philistines, whose superior technology and military organization at first made them invincible. In Saul (ca 1000 B.C.), a farmer of the tribe of Benjamin, the Hebrews found a champion and a spirited leader. In the biblical account Saul carried the war to the Philistines, often without success. Yet in the meantime he established a monarchy over the twelve Hebrew tribes.

Saul's work was carried on by David of Bethlehem, who in his youth had followed Saul into battle against the Philistines. Through courage and cunning, David pushed back the Philistines and waged war against his other neighbors. To give his kingdom a capital, he captured the city of Jerusalem, which he enlarged, fortified, and made the religious and political center of his realm. David's military successes won the Hebrews unprecedented security, and his forty-year reign was a period of vitality and political consolidation. His work in consolidating the monarchy and enlarging the kingdom paved the way for his son Solomon.

Solomon (ca 965–925 B.C.) applied his energies to creating a nation out of a collection of tribes ruled by a king. He divided the kingdom into twelve territorial districts, cutting across the old tribal borders. To bring his kingdom up to the level of its more sophisticated neighbors, he set about a building program to make Israel a respectable Near Eastern state. Work was begun on a magnificent temple in Jerusalem and on cities, palaces, fortresses, and roads. Solomon dedicated the temple in grand style and made it the home of the Ark of the Covenant, the cherished chest that contained the holiest of Hebrew religious articles. The temple in Jerusalem was intended to be the religious heart of the kingdom and the symbol of Hebrew unity. Solomon turned a rude kingdom into a state with broad commercial horizons and greater knowledge of the outside world. At his death, the Hebrews broke into two political halves (see Map 2.1). The northern part of the kingdom of David and Solomon became Israel, with its capital at Samaria. The southern half was Judah, and Jerusalem remained its center. With polit-

ical division went a religious rift: Israel, the northern kingdom, established rival sanctuaries for gods other than Yahweh. The Hebrew nation was divided, but at least it was divided into two far more sophisticated political units than before the time of Solomon. Nonetheless, war soon broke out between them, as recorded in the Bible. Unexpected and independent evidence of this warfare came to light in August 1993, when an Israeli archaeologist found an inscription that refers to the "House of David," the royal line of Israel. The stone celebrates an Israelite victory from the early ninth century B.C. This discovery is the first mention of King David's royal family outside the Bible and helps confirm the biblical account of the fighting between the two kingdoms.

Eventually, the northern kingdom of Israel was wiped out by the Assyrians, but the southern kingdom of Judah survived numerous calamities until the Babylonians crushed it in 587 B.C. The survivors were sent into exile in Babylonia, a period commonly known as the **Babylonian Captivity.** In 538 B.C. the Persians, under their king Cyrus the Great, permitted some forty thousand exiles to return to Jerusalem. During and especially after the

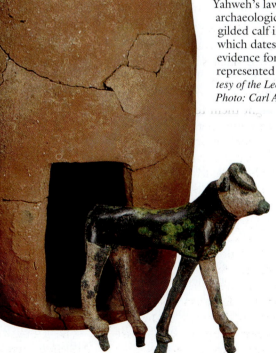

The Golden Calf According to the Hebrew Bible, Moses descended from Mount Sinai, where he had received the Ten Commandments, to find the Hebrews worshiping a golden calf, which was against Yahweh's laws. In July 1990 an American archaeological team found this model of a gilded calf inside a pot. The figurine, which dates to about 1550 B.C., is strong evidence for the existence of the cult represented by the calf in Palestine. (*Courtesy of the Leon Levy Expedition to Ashkelon. Photo: Carl Andrews*)

Babylonian Captivity, the exiles redefined their beliefs and practices and thus established what they believed was the law of Yahweh. Those who lived by these precepts can be called *Jews*.

• *How did the Hebrew state evolve, and what was daily life like in Hebrew society? What forces helped shape Hebrew religious thought, still influential in today's world?*

The Evolution of Jewish Religion

Hand in hand with their political evolution from fierce nomads to urban dwellers, the Hebrews were evolving spiritual ideas that still permeate Western society. Their chief literary product, the Hebrew Bible, has fundamentally influenced both Christianity and Islam and still exerts a compelling force on the modern world.

Online Study Center **Improve Your Grade**
Primary Source: "In the Beginning . . .": The Hebrews Explain Creation

Fundamental to an understanding of the Jewish religion is the concept of the **Covenant,** a formal agreement between Yahweh and the Hebrew people. According to the Bible, the god **Yahweh,** who in medieval Latin became "Jehovah," appeared to Moses on Mount Sinai. There Yahweh made a covenant with the Hebrews that was in fact a contract: if the Hebrews worshiped Yahweh as their only god, he would consider them his chosen people and protect them from their enemies. The Hebrews believed that Yahweh had led them out of bondage in Egypt and had helped them conquer their new land, the Promised Land. In return, the Hebrews worshiped Yahweh alone and obeyed his Ten Commandments, an ethical code of conduct revealed to them by Moses.

Online Study Center **Improve Your Grade**
Primary Source: Moses Descends Mount Sinai with the Ten Commandments

Unlike Akhenaten's monotheism, Hebrew monotheism became the religion of a whole people, deeply felt and cherished. Some might fall away from Yahweh's worship, and various holy men had to exhort the Hebrews to honor the Covenant, but on the whole the people clung to Yahweh. Yet the Hebrews did not consider it their duty to spread the belief in the one god, as later Christians did. As the chosen people, their chief duty was to maintain the worship of Yahweh as he demanded. That worship was embodied in the Ten Commandments, which forbade the Hebrews to steal, murder, lie, or commit adultery. The Covenant was a constant force in He-

brew life. (See the feature "Listening to the Past: The Covenant Between Yahweh and the Hebrews" on pages 54–55.)

From the Ten Commandments evolved Hebrew law, a code of law and custom originating with Moses and built on by priests and prophets. The earliest part of this code, the **Torah** or Mosaic law, was often as harsh as Hammurabi's code, which had a powerful impact on it. Later tradition, largely the work of prophets who lived from the eleventh to the fifth centuries B.C., put more emphasis on righteousness than on retribution.

The uniqueness of the Hebrews' religion can be seen by comparing the essence of Hebrew monotheism with the religious outlook of the Mesopotamians. Whereas the Mesopotamians considered their gods capricious, the Hebrews knew what Yahweh expected. The Hebrews believed that their god would protect them and make them prosper if they obeyed his commandments. Their devotion to Yahweh also influenced their attitude toward magic. The Jews strenuously condemned everyone and everything connected with invoking the intervention of forces from the other world. They felt that magicians, witches, astrologers, and soothsayers harmfully and wrongly usurped powers that properly belonged to Yahweh. The Mesopotamians, however, accepted magic as a natural part of their religious life. The Mesopotamians thought human beings insignificant compared to the gods, so insignificant that the gods might even be indifferent to them. The Hebrews, too, considered themselves puny in comparison with Yahweh. Yet they were Yahweh's chosen people, whom he had promised never to abandon. Finally, though the Mesopotamians believed that the gods generally preferred good to evil, their religion did not demand ethical conduct. The Hebrews could please their god only by living up to high moral standards as well as worshiping him.

Yahweh is a single god, not surrounded by lesser gods and goddesses; there is thus no female divinity in Judaism, though occasionally aspects of God are described in feminine terms, such as Sophia, the wisdom of God. Though Yahweh is conceptualized as masculine, he did not have sexual relations as Mesopotamian, Egyptian, and Greek male deities did, so that his masculinity was spiritualized, and human sexual relations were a source of ritual impurity. Despite this, sex itself was basically good because it was part of Yahweh's creation, and the bearing of children was seen in some ways as a religious function. In the codes of conduct written down in the Hebrew Bible—which Christians adopted and later termed the "Old Testament" to parallel specific Christian writings termed the "New Testament"—sex between a married woman and a man not her husband was termed an "abomination," as were incest and sex between men. Men were free to have sexual relations with concubines, servants, and slaves, along with their wives. The possibility of divorce was also gender-specific: a man could divorce his wife unilaterally (though community norms frowned on divorce for frivolous reasons), but a wife could not divorce her husband, even for desertion. In general Judaism frowned on celibacy—"chastity" is defined in Jewish law as refraining from illicit sexual activities, not from sex itself—and almost all major Jewish thinkers and rabbis were married.

Religious leaders were important in Judaism, but not as important as the written texts they interpreted; these texts came to be regarded as the word of Yahweh and thus had a status other writings did not. The most important task for observant Jews was studying religious texts, an activity limited to men until the twentieth century. Women were obliged to provide for men's physical needs so that they could study, which often meant that Jewish women were more active economically than their contemporaries of other religions. Women's religious rituals tended to center on the home, while men's centered on the temple. The reverence for a particular text or group of texts was passed down from Judaism to the other Western monotheistic religions that grew from it, Christianity and Islam, which gave (and continue to give) the statements about gender in these texts particular power.

Family Life in Israel

The nomadic Hebrews first entered modern Palestine as tribes, numerous families who thought of themselves as all related to one another. At first, good farmland, pastureland, and water spots were held in common by the tribe. Common use of land was—and still is—characteristic of nomadic peoples. Typically each family or group of families in the tribe drew lots every year to determine who worked which fields. But as formerly nomadic peoples turned increasingly to settled agriculture, communal use of land gave way to family ownership. In this respect the experience of the ancient Hebrews seems typical of that of many early peoples. Slowly the shift from nomad to farmer affected far more than just how people fed themselves. Family relationships reflected evolving circumstances. With the transition to settled agriculture, the tribe gradually became less important than the extended family. As in Mesopotamia, land was handed down within families, generally from father to son.

The development of urban life among the Jews created new economic opportunities, especially in crafts and trades. People specialized in certain occupations, such as milling flour, baking bread, making pottery, weaving, and carpentry. All these crafts were family trades. Sons worked with their father, daughters with their mother. If the business prospered, the family might be assisted by a few paid workers or slaves. The practitioners of a craft usually lived in a particular section of town, a custom still prevalent in the Middle East today. Commerce and trade developed later than crafts. Trade with neighboring countries was handled by foreigners, usually Phoenicians. Jews dealt mainly in local trade, and in most instances craftsmen and farmers sold directly to their customers.

These social and economic developments also left their mark on daily life by prompting the compilation of two significant works, the Torah and the Talmud. The Torah is basically the Mosaic law, or the first five books of the Bible. The Talmud is a later work composed during the period between the Roman destruction of the second temple in A.D. 70 and the Arab conquest of A.D. 636. The **Talmud** records civil and ceremonial law and Jewish legend. The dietary rules of the Jews provide an excellent example of both the relationship between the Torah and the Talmud and their effect on ordinary life and culture. According to the Torah, people were not to eat meat that they found in the field. This very sensible prohibition protected them from eating dangerous food. Yet if meat from the countryside could not be eaten, some rules were needed for meat in the city. The solution found in the Talmud was a set of regulations for the proper way to conduct ritual slaughter and to prepare food. Together these two works regulated and codified Jewish dietary customs.

Assyria, the Military Monarchy

Small kingdoms like those of the Phoenicians and the Hebrews could exist only in the absence of a major power. The beginning of the ninth century B.C. saw the rise of such a power: the Assyrians of northern Mesopotamia, whose chief capital was at Nineveh on the Tigris River. The Assyrians were a Semitic-speaking people heavily influenced, like so many other peoples of the Near East, by the Mesopotamian culture of Babylon to the south. They were also one of the most warlike peoples in history, largely because throughout their history they were threatened by neighboring folk. Living in an open, exposed land, the Assyrians experienced frequent and devastating attacks by the wild, war-loving tribes to their north and east and by the Babylonians to the south. The constant threat to survival experienced by the

Assyrians promoted political cohesion and military might. Yet they were also a mercantile people who had long pursued commerce with both the Babylonians in the south and other peoples in the north.

• What enabled the Assyrians to overrun their neighbors, and how did their cruelty finally cause their undoing?

The Power of Assyria

For over two hundred years the Assyrians labored to dominate the Near East. In 859 B.C. the new Assyrian king, Shalmaneser, unleashed the first of a long series of attacks on the peoples of Syria and Palestine. Year after relentless year, Assyrian armies hammered at the peoples of the West. These ominous events inaugurated two turbulent centuries marked by Assyrian military campaigns, constant efforts by Syria and the two Jewish kingdoms to maintain or recover their independence, and eventual Assyrian conquest of Babylonia and northern Egypt. In addition, periodic political instability occurred in Assyria itself, which prompted stirrings of freedom throughout the Near East.

Under the Assyrian kings Tiglath-pileser III (774–727 B.C.) and Sargon II (r. 721–705 B.C.), both mighty warriors, the Near East trembled as never before under the blows of Assyrian armies. The Assyrians stepped up their attacks on Anatolia, Syria, and Palestine. The kingdom of Israel and many other states fell; others, like the kingdom of Judah, became subservient to the warriors from the Tigris. In 717 to 716 B.C., Sargon led his army in a sweeping attack along the Philistine coast, where he defeated the pharaoh. Sargon also lashed out at Assyria's traditional enemies to the north and then turned south against a renewed threat in Babylonia. By means of almost constant warfare, Tiglath-pileser and Sargon carved out an Assyrian empire that stretched from east and north of the Tigris River to central Egypt (see Map 2.2). Revolt against the Assyrians inevitably promised the rebels bloody battles and cruel sieges.

Though atrocity and terrorism struck unspeakable fear into Assyria's subjects, Assyria's success was actually due to sophisticated, farsighted, and effective military organization. By Sargon's time the Assyrians had invented the mightiest military machine the ancient Near East had ever seen. The mainstay of the Assyrian army was the infantryman armed with spear and sword and protected by helmet and armor. The Assyrian army also featured archers, some on foot, others on horseback, still others in chariots—the latter ready to wield lances once they had expended their supply of arrows. Some infantry archers wore heavy armor. These soldiers served as a primitive

Surrender of the Jews The Jewish king Jahu finally surrendered to the Assyrians. Here his envoy kneels before the Assyrian king Shalmaneser III in total defeat. Although the Assyrian king treated Jahu well, his people were led off into slavery. *(British Museum/Michael Holford)*

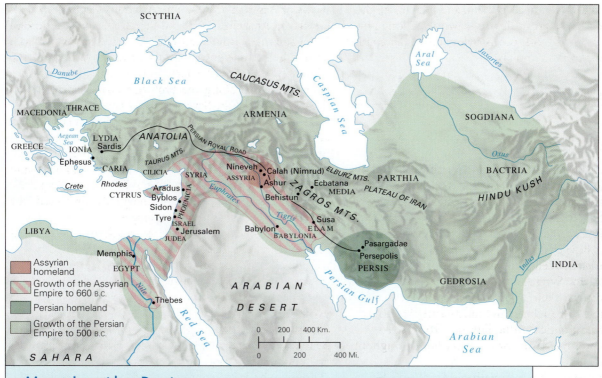

Mapping the Past

MAP 2.2 The Assyrian and Persian Empires   Compare this map showing the extent of the Assyrian and Persian Empires with Map 1.3 on page 26, which shows the earliest political extent of the Eastern states. **❶** What do these maps tell us about the growth of political power? **❷** What new areas have opened to the old cultures? **❸** What do the two maps suggest about the shift of power and the spread of civilization in the ancient Near East?

Online Study Center   **Improve Your Grade** Interactive Map: Assyrian and Persian Empires

field artillery, whose job was to sweep the enemy's walls of defenders so that others could storm the defenses. Slingers also served as artillery in pitched battles. For mobility on the battlefield, the Assyrians organized a corps of chariots.

Assyrian military genius was remarkable for the development of a wide variety of siege machinery and techniques, including excavation to undermine city walls and battering rams to knock down walls and gates. Never before in the Near East had anyone applied such technical knowledge to warfare. The Assyrians even invented the concept of a corps of engineers, who bridged rivers with pontoons or provided soldiers with inflatable skins for swimming. And the Assyrians knew how to coordinate their efforts, both in open battle and

in siege warfare. King Sennacherib's account of his siege of Jerusalem in 701 B.C. is a vivid portrait of the Assyrian war machine:

As to Hezekiah, the Jew, he did not submit to my yoke, I laid siege to 46 of his strong cities, walled forts and to the countless small villages in their vicinity, and conquered them by means of well-stamped earth-ramps, and battering rams brought thus near to the walls combined with the attack by foot soldiers, using mines, breaches as well as sapper work. . . . Himself I made prisoner in Jerusalem, his royal residence, like a bird in a cage. I surrounded him with earthwork in order to molest those who were leaving his city's gate.[2]

Royal Lion Hunt   This wall painting from the seventh century B.C. depicts an Assyrian king frightening a lion, a typical representation of the energy and artistic brilliance of Assyrian artists. The lion hunt signified the king as the protector of society, not simply as a sportsman. (*Louvre/Réunion des Musées Nationaux/Art Resource, NY*)

Online Study Center   **Improve Your Grade**
Primary Source: Jerusalem Besieged: The Assyrian King Sennacherib's Account of Events

The Jews recorded this same incident, and historians find it interesting to see how two different peoples interpreted the same event. The Jews ignored political and military events and insisted that the siege of Jerusalem resulted from Hezekiah's disbelief that Yahweh could repel the Assyrian invasion. For the Assyrians the conquest was proof of their military superiority. For the Jews it stood as a symbol of the fate of those who mistrusted their god.

Assyrian Rule and Culture

Not only did the Assyrians know how to win battles, but they also knew how to use their victories. As early as the reign of Tiglath-pileser III, the Assyrian kings began to organize their conquered territories into an empire. The lands closest to Assyria became provinces governed by Assyrian officials. Kingdoms beyond the provinces were not annexed but became dependent states that followed Assyria's lead. The Assyrian king chose their rulers either by regulating the succession of native kings or by supporting native kings who appealed to him. Against more distant states the Assyrian kings waged frequent war in order to conquer them outright or make the dependent states secure.

In the seventh century B.C. Assyrian power seemed firmly established. Yet the downfall of Assyria was swift and complete. Babylon finally won its independence in 626 B.C. and joined forces with a newly aggressive people, the Medes, an Indo-European-speaking folk from Iran. Together the Babylonians and the Medes destroyed the Assyrian Empire in 612 B.C., paving the way for the rise of the Persians. The Hebrew prophet Nahum spoke for many when he asked: "Nineveh is laid waste: who will bemoan her?"[3] Their cities destroyed and their power shattered, the Assyrians disappeared from history, remembered only as a cruel people of the Old Testament who oppressed the Hebrews. Two hundred years later, when the Greek adventurer and historian Xenophon passed by the ruins of Nineveh, he marveled at the extent of the former city but knew nothing of the Assyrians. The glory of their empire was forgotten.

Yet modern archaeology has brought the Assyrians out of obscurity. In 1839 the intrepid English archaeologist and traveler A. H. Layard began the most noteworthy excavations of Nineveh, then a mound of debris beside the Tigris. His findings electrified the world. Layard's workers unearthed masterpieces, including monumental sculpted figures—huge winged bulls, human-headed lions, and sphinxes—as well as brilliantly sculpted friezes. Equally valuable were the numerous Assyrian cuneiform documents, which ranged from royal accounts of mighty military campaigns to simple letters by common people.

Among the most renowned of Layard's finds were the Assyrian palace reliefs, whose number has been increased by the discoveries of twentieth-century archaeologists. Assyrian kings delighted in scenes of war, which their artists depicted in graphic detail. By the time of Ashurbanipal (r. 668–633 B.C.), Assyrian artists had hit on the idea of portraying a series of episodes—in fact, a visual narrative of events that had actually taken place. Scene followed scene in a continuous frieze, so that the viewer could follow the progress of a military campaign from the time the army marched out until the enemy was conquered.

Assyrian art fared better than Assyrian military power. The techniques of Assyrian artists influenced the Persians, who adapted them to gentler scenes. In fact, many Assyrian innovations, military and political as well as artistic, were taken over wholesale by the Persians. Although the memory of Assyria was hateful throughout the Near East, the fruits of Assyrian organizational genius helped enable the Persians to bring peace and stability to the same regions where Assyrian armies had spread terror.

The Empire of the Persian Kings

Like the Hittites before them, the Iranians were Indo-Europeans from central Europe and southern Russia. They migrated into the land to which they have given their name, the area between the Caspian Sea and the Persian Gulf. Like the Hittites, they then fell under the spell of the more sophisticated cultures of their Mesopotamian neighbors. Yet the Iranians went on to create one

of the greatest empires of antiquity, one that encompassed scores of peoples and cultures. The Persians, the most important of the Iranian peoples, had a farsighted conception of empire. Though as conquerors they willingly used force to accomplish their ends, they normally preferred to depend on diplomacy to rule. They usually respected their subjects and allowed them to practice their native customs and religions. Thus the Persians gave the Near East both political unity and cultural diversity. Never before had Near Eastern people viewed empire in such intelligent and humane terms.

• *How did Iranian nomads build the Persian Empire, and what sort of life did their policies create for the Near East?*

The Land of the Medes and Persians

Persia—the modern country of Iran—is a stark land of towering mountains and flaming deserts with a broad central plateau in the heart of the country (see Map 2.2). Between the Tigris-Euphrates Valley in the west and the Indus Valley in the east rises an immense plateau that cuts the interior from the sea. Iran's geographical position and topography explain its traditional role as the highway between East and West. Throughout history wild, nomadic tribes migrating from the broad steppes of Russia and Central Asia have streamed into Iran. Confronting the uncrossable salt deserts, most of them have turned either eastward or westward, moving until reaching the advanced and wealthy urban centers of Mesopotamia and India. Where cities emerged along the natural lines of east-west communications, Iran became the area in which nomads met urban dwellers, an area of unique significance for the civilizations of both East and West.

The Iranians entered this land around 1000 B.C. as part of the vast movement of Indo-European-speaking peoples whose wanderings took them from Europe to India (see page 26). These Iranians were nomads who migrated with their flocks and herds. They were also horse breeders, and the horse gave them a decisive military advantage over the prehistoric peoples of Iran. These centuries of immigration saw constant cultural interchange between conquering newcomers and conquered natives.

Two groups of Iranians gradually began coalescing into larger units. The Persians settled in Persia, the modern region of Fars in southern Iran. Their kinsmen, the Medes, occupied Media in the north, with their capital at Ecbatana, the modern Hamadan. Even though they were distracted by grave pressure from their neighbors, the

Persian Charioteers
Here are two Persians riding in a chariot pulled by four horses. The chariot is simple in construction but elegant in ornamentation. The harness of the horses is worked in elaborate and accurate detail. This chariot was used for ceremonial purposes, not for warfare. *(Courtesy of the Trustees of the British Museum)*

Medes united under one king around 710 B.C. They next extended their control over the Persians to the south. In 612 B.C. they joined the Babylonians to overthrow the Assyrian Empire. With the rise of the Medes, the balance of power in the Near East shifted for the first time east of Mesopotamia.

The Rise of the Persian Empire (550–540 B.C.)

In 550 B.C. Cyrus the Great (r. 559–530 B.C.), king of the Persians and one of the most remarkable statesmen of antiquity, conquered the Medes as the first step in the creation of one of the greatest empires of the ancient world. He also thought of Iran as a state, a concept that has survived to play its part in the contemporary world. Furthermore, Cyrus held an enlightened view of empire. He appreciated the value of the many far older, more advanced, and more sophisticated civilizations of his new realm. He nurtured and protected them so that conquered peoples continued to enjoy their institutions, religions, languages, and ways of life. His Persian Empire became a political organization sheltering many different civilizations. Consequently, the Persians gave the ancient

Near East more than two hundred years of peace, prosperity, and security.

Having united Iran, Cyrus set out to secure it from hostile neighbors. Turning west, he swept into Anatolia, easily overthrowing the young kingdom of Lydia. Its king Croesus, not only proverbial for his wealth, was also in close touch with the Greeks. Also to his west was Babylonia, enjoying a new period of power after the fall of the Assyrians. To the southwest lay Egypt, still weak and vulnerable. Turning to the east, Cyrus confronted the challenge of tough, mobile nomads capable of massive and destructive incursions deep into Iranian territory.

In a series of major campaigns, Cyrus won control of the west. His defeat of Croesus and his Lydians held lasting significance for Western civilization in that his march took him to the eastern Mediterranean. In the westernmost part of modern Turkey he encountered the Greeks, whose destiny would become deeply entwined with that of the Persians. More immediately important at the time, Cyrus the conqueror demonstrated to the world unmistakable signs of his benevolence. He spared the life of Croesus to serve him as friend and adviser. He allowed the Greeks to live according to their customs, thus making it possible for Greek culture to spread farther inland to the east. Cyrus's humanity likewise extended to the

Jews, whom he found enslaved in Babylonia. He sent them home, returned their sacred objects to them, and rebuilt the temple of Yahweh in Jerusalem. The thankful Jews considered him the shepherd of Yahweh, the lord's anointed. Cyrus's humane policy created a Persian Empire in which the culture and religions of its members were respected and honored. Seldom have conquerors been as wise, sensitive, and farsighted as Cyrus and his Persians.

Thus Spake Zarathustra

Iranian religion was originally simple. **Ahuramazda,** the chief god, was the creator and benefactor of all living creatures. Mithra, the sun-god, whose cult would later spread throughout the Roman Empire, saw to justice and redemption. As in ancient India, fire was a particularly important god. The sacred fire consumed the blood sacrifices that the early Iranians offered to all their deities. Early Iranian religion remained close to nature, unencumbered by ponderous theological beliefs. A priestly class, the **Magi,** developed among the Medes to officiate at sacrifices, chant prayers to the gods, and tend the sacred flame. In time the Iranians built fire temples for their sacrifices and rites.

Around 600 B.C. the religious thinking of Zarathustra—Zoroaster, as he is better known—breathed new meaning into Iranian religion. Zoroaster preached a novel concept of divinity and human life. Life, he taught, is a constant battleground for the two opposing forces of good and evil. Ahuramazda embodied good and truth but was opposed by Ahriman, a hateful spirit who stood for evil and lies. Ahuramazda and Ahriman were locked together in a cosmic battle for the human race, a battle that stretched over thousands of years.

Zoroaster emphasized the individual's responsibility to choose between good and evil. He taught that people possessed the free will to decide between Ahuramazda and Ahriman and that they must rely on their own conscience to guide them through life. Their decisions were crucial, Zoroaster warned, for there would be a time of reckoning. He promised that Ahuramazda would eventually triumph over evil and lies, and that at death each person would stand before the tribunal of good. Ahuramazda, like the Egyptian god Osiris, would judge whether the dead had lived righteously and on that basis would weigh their lives in the balance. In short, Zoroaster taught the concept of a last judgment at which Ahuramazda would decide each person's eternal fate.

In Zoroaster's thought, the last judgment was linked to the notion of a divine kingdom after death for those who had lived according to good and truth. Liars and the wicked, denied this blessed immortality, would be condemned to eternal pain, darkness, and punishment. Thus

Persian Saddle-Cloth   This elaborately painted piece of leather, dating from the fourth or third century B.C., served a ceremonial rather than a practical function. *(The State Hermitage Museum)*

Funeral Pyre of Croesus
This scene, an excellent example of the precision and charm of ancient Greek vase painting, depicts the Lydian king Croesus on his funeral pyre. He pours a libation to the gods, while his slave lights the fire. Herodotus has a happier ending, when he says that Cyrus the Great set fire to the pyre, but that Apollo sent rain to put it out. *(Louvre/Réunion des Musées Nationaux/Art Resource, NY)*

Zoroaster preached a last judgment that led to a heaven or a hell.

Zoroaster's teachings converted Darius (r. 521–486 B.C.), who did not, however, try to impose it on others. Under the protection of the Persian kings **Zoroastrianism** swept through Iran, winning converts and sinking roots that sustained healthy growth for centuries. Zoroastrianism survived the fall of the Persian Empire to influence liberal Judaism, Christianity, and early Islam, largely because of its belief in a just life on earth and a happy afterlife that satisfied the longings of most people. Good behavior in the world, even though unrecognized at the time, would receive ample reward in the hereafter. Evil, no matter how powerful in life, would be punished after death. In some form or another, Zoroastrian concepts still pervade the major religions of the West and every part of the world touched by Islam.

Persia's World Empire

Cyrus's successors rounded out the Persian conquest of the ancient Near East. King Darius and his son Xerxes (r. 486–464 B.C.) reached the high-water mark when they unsuccessfully tried to conquer Greece. The Persians never won a permanent foothold in Europe. Yet Darius carried Persian arms into India. Around 513 B.C.

western India became the satrapy (or province) of Hindush, which included the valley of the Indus River. Thus within thirty-seven years (550–513 B.C.) the Persians transformed themselves from a subject people to the ruler of an empire that included Anatolia, Egypt, Mesopotamia, Iran, and western India. They had created a **world empire** encompassing all the oldest and most honored kingdoms and peoples of the ancient Near East. Never before had this region been united in one such vast political organization (see Map 2.2).

The Persians knew how to preserve the peace they had won on the battlefield. Unlike the Assyrians, they did not resort to royal terrorism to maintain order. Instead, the Persians built an efficient administrative system to govern the empire. They enforced Persian laws that demanded obedience and loyalty from those governed. At the same time their system honored the customs of those governed. The Persians also protected their subjects from foreign invasion and official corruption.

Persian kings took their responsibilities seriously. They established their capital at Persepolis, "the City of the Persians," near modern Schiras, Iran. These kings received reports from their officials and entertained delegations both from their subjects and from foreign powers. From Persepolis they sent directions to the provinces. To do so they maintained a sophisticated system of roads linking the empire. The main highway, the famous **Royal Road,** spanned some 1,677 miles from the Greek city of Ephesus on the coast of Asia Minor to Susa in western Iran. Other roads branched out to link all parts of the empire from the coast of Asia Minor to the valley of the Indus River. This system of communications enabled Persian kings to keep in intimate touch with their subjects and officials. They were thereby able to make the concepts of right, justice, and good government a practical reality.

The Impact of Zoroastrianism The Persian kings embraced Zoroastrianism as the religion of the realm. This rock carving at Behistun records the bond. King Darius I is seen trampling on one rebel with others behind him. Above is the sign of Ahuramazda, the god of truth and guardian of the Persian king. *(Robert Harding World Imagery)*

The Royal Palace at Persepolis King Darius began and King Xerxes finished building a grand palace worthy of the glory of the Persian Empire. Pictured here is the monumental audience hall, where the king dealt with ministers of state and foreign envoys. *(George Holton/Photo Researchers)*

Chapter Summary

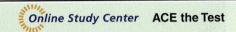
Online Study Center   **ACE the Test**

- *How did Egypt pass on its heritage to its African neighbors and how did new cultures develop?*
- *How did the Hebrew state evolve, and what was daily life like in Hebrew society? What forces helped shape Hebrew religious thought, still influential in today's world?*
- *What enabled the Assyrians to overrun their neighbors, and how did their cruelty finally cause their undoing?*
- *How did Iranian nomads build the Persian Empire, and what sort of life did their policies create for the Near East?*

Key Terms

"Purple People"	Torah
Hapiru	Talmud
nomads	Ahuramazda
Baal	Magi
Babylonian Captivity	Zoroastrianism
Covenant	world empire
Yahweh	Royal Road

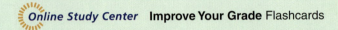
Online Study Center   **Improve Your Grade** Flashcards

Early civilizations created wealth and stability, but invasions and chaos threatened to destroy it all. Yet both well-established peoples and vigorous newcomers salvaged the best of the past, including many aspects of Egyptian culture. The Phoenicians in particular took advantage of the situation to spread commodities and ideas through trade. Through warfare with their neighbors, the Hebrews created a small kingdom centered on the temple in Jerusalem. Their kingdom was short-lived, but their religious beliefs and written codes of law and custom proved to be long-lasting. Judaism, their monotheistic religion, continues as a vibrant faith today and was an important source for Christianity and Islam.

In this world rose the Assyrians, another Semitic people who had lived on its periphery. They spread their power by brutal conquests. They disrupted life through much of the area, forging an extensive empire ruled by terror. Their enemies finally brought them down, but at least they had provided a modicum of stability to the region.

The Persians assimilated the best of the civilizations that they found around them. Through conquest that was mild compared with that of the Assyrians, they broadened the geographical horizons of the ancient world. Their empire looked west to the Greeks and east to the peoples of the Indus Valley, and they gave the Near East a long period of peace.

Suggested Reading

Alon, Gedaliah. *The Jews in Their Land.* 1989. Covers the Talmudic period.

Boyce, Mary. *Zoroastrianism.* 1979. A sound and readable treatment of the essence of Zoroastrianism.

Edwards, David N. *The Nubian Past.* 2004. Examines the history of Nubia and the Sudan, incorporating archaeological evidence to supplement historical sources.

Frye, Richard N. *History of Ancient Iran.* 1984. A comprehensive survey by one of the leading scholars in the field.

Gates, Charles. *Ancient Cities: The Archaeology of Urban Life in the Ancient Near East and Egypt, Greece, and Rome.* 2003. Provides a survey of ancient life primarily from an archaeological point of view, but one that includes cultural and social interests.

Hoffmeier, James K. *Israel in Egypt: The Evidence for the Authenticity of the Exodus Tradition.* 1997. Discusses evidence for the account in Hebrew Scripture concerning the Exodus.

Markoe, Glenn E. *The Phoenicians.* 2000. A fresh investigation of the Phoenicians at home and abroad in the western Mediterranean over their long history, with many illustrations.

Meyers, Carol. *Discovering Eve: Ancient Israelite Women in Context.* 1988. Examines the roles of Israelite women.

Morkot, Robert G. *The Black Pharaohs: Egypt's Nubian Rulers.* 2000. Examines the growth of the Kushite kingdom and its rule over pharaonic Egypt in the eighth century B.C.

Niditch, Susan. *Ancient Israelite Religion.* 1997. A brief but broad interpretation of Jewish religious developments.

Pastor, Jack. *Land and Economy in Ancient Palestine.* 1997. Discusses the basics of economic life of the period.

Redford, Donald B. *Egypt, Canaan, and Israel in Ancient Times.* 1992. Presents a study of the political, cultural, and religious relationships among the peoples of Egypt, Assyria, and the Near East during thousands of years of history.

Saggs, H. W. F. *Everyday Life in Babylonia and Assyria,* rev. ed. 1987. Offers a general and well-illustrated survey of Mesopotamian history from 3000 to 300 B.C.

Notes

1. James H. Breasted, *Ancient Records of Egypt,* vol. 4 (Chicago: University of Chicago Press, 1907), para. 398.
2. J. B. Pritchard, ed., *Ancient Near Eastern Texts,* 3d ed. (Princeton, N.J.: Princeton University Press, 1969), p. 288.
3. Nahum 3:7.

The Covenant Between Yahweh and the Hebrews

These passages from the Hebrew Bible address two themes important to Hebraic thinking. The first is the meaning of kingship; the second is the nature of the Covenant between the Hebrews and the Lord, Yahweh. The selection also raises the difficult question of how much of the Hebrew Bible can be accepted historically. As we discussed in this chapter, the Hebrew Bible is not a document that we may accept as literal truth, but it does tell us a great deal about the people who created it. From the following passages we may discern what the Hebrews thought about their own past and religion.

The background of the excerpt is a political crisis that has some archaeological support. The war with the Philistines put a huge strain on Hebrew society. The passage below describes an incident when Nahash, the king of the Ammonites, threatens to destroy the Hebrews. New and effective political and military leadership was needed to meet the situation. The elders of the tribes had previously chosen judges to lead the community only in times of crisis. The Hebrews, however, demanded that a kingship be established, even though Yahweh was their king. They turned to Samuel, the last of the judges, who anointed Saul as the first Hebrew king. In this excerpt Samuel reviews the political, military, and religious situation confronting the Hebrews, reminding them of their obligation to honor the Covenant and expressing hesitation in naming a king.

Then Nahash the Ammonite came up and encamped against Jabeshgilead: and all the men of Jabesh said unto Nahash, Make a covenant with us, and we will serve thee. And Nahash the Ammonite answered them, On this condition will I make a covenant with you, that I may thrust out all your right eyes, and lay it for a reproach upon all Israel. And the elders of Jabesh said unto him, Give us seven days' respite, that we may send messengers unto all the coasts of Israel: and then, if there be no man to save us, we will come out to thee.

Then came the messengers to Gibeah of Saul, and told the tidings in the ears of the people: and all the people lifted up their voices, and wept. And, behold, Saul came after the herd out of the field; and Saul said, What aileth the people that they weep? And they told him the tidings of the men of Jabesh. And the Spirit of God came upon Saul when he heard those tidings, and his anger was kindled greatly. And he took a yoke of oxen, and hewed them in pieces, and sent them throughout all the coasts of Israel by the hands of messengers, saying, Whosoever cometh not forth after Saul and after Samuel, so shall it be done unto his oxen. And the fear of the Lord fell on the people, and they came out with one consent. And when he numbered them in Bezek, the children of Israel were three hundred thousand, and the men of Judah thirty thousand. And they said unto the messengers that came, Thus shall ye say unto the men of Jabeshgilead, To morrow, by that time the sun be hot, ye shall have help. And the messengers came and shewed it to the men of Jabesh; and they were glad. Therefore the men of Jabesh said, To morrow we will come out unto you, and ye shall do with us all that seemeth good unto you. And it was so on the morrow, that Saul put the people in three companies; and they came into the midst of the host in the morning watch, and slew the Ammonites until the heat of the day: and it came to pass, that they which remained were scattered, so that two of them were not left together.

And the people said unto Samuel, Who is he that said, Shall Saul reign over us? bring the men, that we may put them to death. And Saul said, There shall not a man be put to death this day: for to day the Lord hath wrought salvation in Israel. Then said Samuel to the people, Come, and let us go to Gilgal, and renew the kingdom there. And all the people went to Gilgal; and there they made Saul king before the Lord in Gilgal; and there they sacrificed sacrifices of peace offerings before the Lord; and there Saul and all the men of Israel rejoiced greatly.

And Samuel said unto all Israel, Behold, I have hearkened unto your voice in all that you said to me, and have made a king over you. And now, behold, the king walks before you; and I am old and gray-headed; and behold, my sons are with you: and I have walked before you from my childhood until this day. Behold, here I am: witness against me before the Lord, and before his anointed: whose ox have I taken? or whose ass have I taken? or whom have I defrauded? whom have I oppressed? or of whose hand have I received any bribe to blind my eyes with it? and I will restore it to you.

And they said, You have not defrauded us, nor oppressed us, neither have you taken anything from any man's hand. And he said to them, the Lord is witness against you, and his anointed is witness this day, that you have not found anything in my hand. And they answered, he is witness. And Samuel said unto the people, It is the Lord that advanced Moses and Aaron, and that brought your fathers up out of the land of Egypt. Now therefore stand still, that I may reason with you before the Lord of all the righteous acts of the Lord, which he did to you and your fathers.

At this point Samuel reminds the Hebrews of their Covenant with Yahweh. He lists the times when they had broken that Covenant, the times when they had served other gods. He also reminds them of Yahweh's punishment for their backsliding. He tells them frankly that they are wrong to demand a king to rule over them, for Yahweh was their lord, god, and king. Nonetheless, Samuel gives way to their demands.

Now therefore behold the king whom you have chosen, and whom you have desired! and behold, the Lord has set a king over you. If you will fear the Lord, and serve him, and obey his voice, and not rebel against the commandment of the Lord, then shall both you and also the king who reigns over you continue following the Lord your God: But if you will not obey the voice of the Lord, but rebel against the commandment of the Lord, then shall the hand of the Lord be against you, as it was against your fathers. Now therefore stand and see this great thing, which the Lord will do before your eyes. Is it not wheat harvest today? I will call to the Lord, and he shall send thunder and rain; that you may perceive and see that your

Ark of the Covenant, depicted in a relief from Capernaum Synagogue, second century A.D. (*Ancient Art & Architecture Collection*)

wickedness is great, which you have done in the sight of the Lord, in asking you a king. So Samuel called to the Lord; and the Lord sent thunder and rain that day: and all the people greatly feared the Lord and Samuel. And all the people said to Samuel, pray for your servants to the Lord your God, so that we will not die: for we have added to all of our sins this evil, to ask us for a king. And Samuel said to the people, Fear not: you have done all this wickedness; yet turn not aside from following the Lord, but serve the Lord with all your heart; And do not turn aside; for then should you go after vain things, which cannot profit nor deliver; for they are vain. For the Lord will not forsake his people for his great name's sake: because it pleases the Lord to make you his people. Moreover, as for me, God forbid that I should sin against the Lord in ceasing to pray for you: but I will teach you the good and the right way: Only fear the Lord, and serve him in truth with all your heart: for consider how great things he has done for you. But if you shall still act wickedly, you will be consumed, both you and your king.

Questions for Analysis

1. How did Samuel explain his anointment of a king?

2. What was Samuel's attitude toward kingship?

3. What were the duties of the Hebrews toward Yahweh?

4. Might those duties conflict with those toward the secular king? If so, in what ways, and how might the Hebrews avoid the conflict?

Source: 1 Samuel 11:1–15; 12:1–7, 13–25. Abridged and adapted from *The Holy Bible,* King James Version.

Dionysos at sea. Dionysos here symbolizes the Greek sense of exploration, independence, and love of life. *(Bildarchiv Preussischer Kulturbesitz/Art Resource, NY)*

chapter preview

Hellas: The Land
• *When the Greeks arrived in Hellas, how did they adapt themselves to their new landscape?*

The Polis
• *After the Greeks had established the polis in which they lived their political and social lives, how did they shape it into its several historical forms?*

The Archaic Age (800–500 B.C.)
• *What major developments mark the Archaic Greek period in terms of spread of culture and the growth of cities?*

The Classical Period (500–338 B.C.)
• *How did the Greeks develop their literature, philosophy, religion, and art, and how did war affect this intellectual and social process?*

The Final Act (404–338 B.C.)
• *How did the Greek city-states meet political and military challenges, and how did Macedonia become dominant?*

CLASSICAL GREECE,
CA 1650–338 B.C.

The rocky peninsula of Greece was the home of the civilization that fundamentally shaped Western civilization. The Greeks were the first to explore most of the questions that continue to concern Western thinkers to this day. Going beyond mythmaking and religion, the Greeks strove to understand, in logical, rational terms, both the universe and the position of men and women in it. The result was the birth of philosophy and science—subjects that were as important to most Greek thinkers as religion. The Greeks speculated on human beings and society and created the very concept of politics.

While the scribes of the ancient Near East produced king lists, the Greeks invented history to record and understand how people and states functioned in time and space. In poetry the Greeks spoke as individuals. In drama they dealt with the grandeur and weakness of humanity and with the demands of society on the individual. The greatest monuments of the Greeks were not temples, statues, or tombs, but profound thoughts set down in terms as fresh and immediate today as they were some 2,400 years ago.

The history of the Greeks is divided into two broad periods: the Hellenic period (the subject of this chapter), roughly the time between the arrival of the Greeks (approximately 2000 B.C.) and the victory over Greece in 338 B.C. by Philip of Macedon; and the Hellenistic period (the subject of Chapter 4), the age beginning with the remarkable reign of Philip's son, Alexander the Great (336–323 B.C.) and ending with the Roman conquest of the Hellenistic East (200–146 B.C.).

Hellas: The Land

Hellas, as the Greeks still call their land, encompassed the Aegean Sea as well as the Greek peninsula (see Map 3.1). Mountains divide the land, leaving few plains and rivers that are generally no more than creeks, most of which go dry in the summer. Greece is, however, blessed with good harbors, the most important of which look to the east. The islands of the

Online Study Center
This icon will direct you to interactive activities and study materials on the website **college.hmco.com/pic/mckaywest9e**

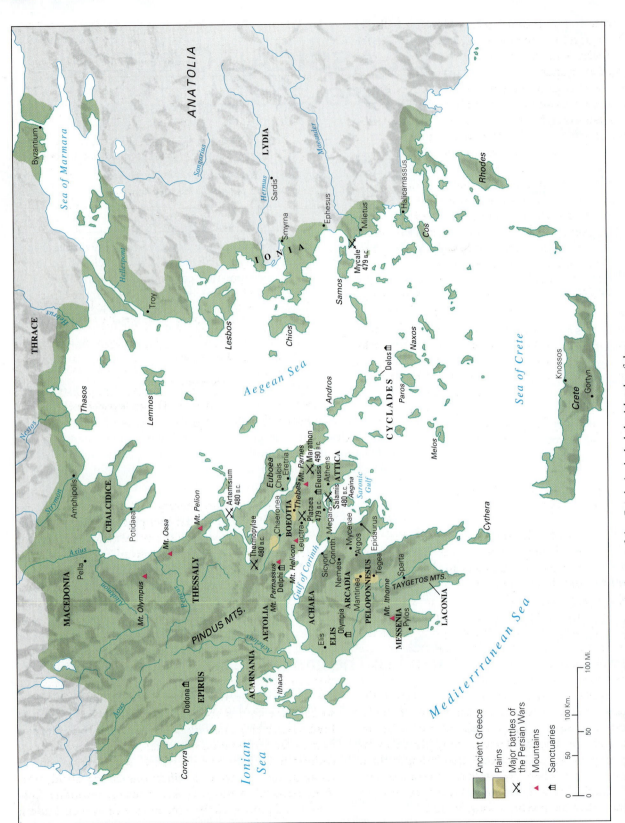

ANATOLIA

Byzantium

Sea of Marmara

Sangarius

THRACE

Hermus

LYDIA

Sardis

Smyrna

Maeander

Ephesus

Halicarnassus

Rhodes

Cos

Miletus

Mycale
479 B.C.

IONIA

Samos

Troy

Hebrus

Lesbos

Chios

Aegean Sea

Andros

Naxos

CYCLADES

Delos

Paros

Melos

Sea of Crete

Knossos

Crete

Gortyn

Thasos

Lemnos

Strymon

Amphipolis

CHALCIDICE

Potidaea

Axius

MACEDONIA

Pella

Haliacmon

Mt. Olympus

Nestos

Mt. Ossa

Peneus

THESSALY

Mt. Pelion

Artemisium
480 B.C.

Euboea

Chalcis

Eretria

Thermopylae
480 B.C.

Chaeronea

BOEOTIA

Mt. Parnes

Marathon
490 B.C.

PINDUS MTS.

Delphi

Mt. Parnassus

Mt. Helicon

Leuctra

Thebes

Plataea
479 B.C.

Eleusis
480 B.C.

Athens

Salamis

ATTICA

Megara

Aegina

Saronic Gulf

AETOLIA

ACARNANIA

Achelous

Ithaca

EPIRUS

Dodona

Aous

Corcyra

Ionian Sea

Gulf of Corinth

ACHAEA

Sicyon

Corinth

Nemea

Mycenae

Argos

Epidaurus

ELIS

Elis

Olympia

Mantinea

ARCADIA

PELOPONNESUS

Tegea

Mt. Ithome

MESSENIA

Pylos

Sparta

TAYGETOS MTS.

LACONIA

Cythera

Mediterranean Sea

Legend:
- Ancient Greece
- Plains
- ✗ Major battles of the Persian Wars
- ▲ Mountains
- 🏛 Sanctuaries

0 50 100 Mi.
0 50 100 Km.

MAP 3.1 Ancient Greece In antiquity, the home of the Greeks included the islands of the Aegean and the western shore of Turkey as well as the Greek peninsula itself.

Online Study Center **Improve Your Grade** Interactive Map: Ancient Greece

Aegean serve as steppingstones to Asia Minor, usually defined as the region from the modern Turkish coast to the Euphrates River. Thus Greece proper and the **Aegean basin** formed an intimate realm for a common Greek culture. The major regions of Greece were Thessaly and Boeotia in the north and center, lands marked by fertile plains and small rivers that flowed even in summer. Good and abundant land provided the wealth to maintain a strong population capable of fielding good cavalry and infantry. Immediately to the south of Boeotia is Attica, an area of thin soil but home to the olive and the vine. Its harbors looked to the Aegean, which invited its inhabitants, the Athenians, to concentrate on maritime commerce. Still farther south in the Peloponnesus the land is a patchwork of high mountains and small plains. These geographical features divided the area into several regions, of which the most important were Argos in the northeast, Arcadia in the center, and Laconia and Messenia in the south. The geographical fragmentation of Greece encouraged political fragmentation. Furthermore, communications were extraordinarily poor. Rocky tracks were far more common than roads, which were seldom paved. These conditions prohibited the growth of a great empire like those of the Near East.

• *When the Greeks arrived in Hellas, how did they adapt themselves to their new landscape?*

Chronology

ca 1650–1000 B.C.	Arrival of the Mycenaean Greeks in Europe
ca 1100–800 B.C.	Evolution of the polis; Greek migrations within the Aegean basin; poems of Homer and Hesiod
ca 800–500 B.C.	Rise of Sparta and Athens; flowering of lyric poetry
776 B.C.	Founding of the Olympic games
ca 750–550 B.C.	Greek colonization of the Mediterranean
ca 700–500 B.C.	Concentration of landed wealth
ca 640 B.C.	Use of coinage in western Asia
ca 525–362 B.C.	Birth and development of tragedy, historical writing, and philosophy; spread of monumental architecture
499–479 B.C.	Persian wars
431–404 B.C.	Peloponnesian War
404–338 B.C.	Spartan and Theban hegemonies; success of Philip of Macedon

The Minoans and Mycenaeans (ca 2000–ca 1100 B.C.)

The origins of Greek civilization are complicated, obscure, and diverse. Neolithic peoples had already built prosperous communities in the Aegean, but not until about 2000 B.C. did they establish firm contact with one another. By then artisans had discovered how to make bronze, which gave these Stone Age groups more efficient tools and weapons. With the adoption of metallurgy came even greater prosperity. The Aegean is a relatively small sea, and land is seldom far off. Some Cretan farmers and fishermen began to trade their surpluses with their neighbors. The central position of Crete in the eastern Mediterranean made it a crucial link in this trade. The Cretans voyaged to Egypt, Asia Minor, other islands, and mainland Greece. They thereby played a vital part in creating an Aegean economy that brought them all into close contact. These favorable circumstances produced the flourishing and vibrant **Minoan** culture on Crete, named after the mythical King Minos.

As seen earlier, only literacy can lead to history. Although the Minoans created a script now called Linear A, very little of it can be read with any certainty. Thus it cannot serve as a historical source. Instead, archaeology and art offer some glimpses of life on the island. The symbol of Minoan culture was the palace and its outlying buildings. About 1650 B.C. Crete was dotted with them, such as those at Mallia on the northern coast and Kato Zakro on the eastern tip of the island. Towering above all others in importance was the palace at Cnossus. It was the political and economic center of its society, but its relations with the other palaces are still disputed. Each palace was the political and economic center of its society. Few specifics are known about Minoan life except that at its head stood a king and his nobles, who governed the lives of their farmers, sailors, shepherds, and artisans. Minoan society, at Cnossus and elsewhere, was wealthy and, to judge by the absence of fortifications on the island, relatively peaceful. Minoan artistic remains, including frescoes and figurines, show women as well as men leading

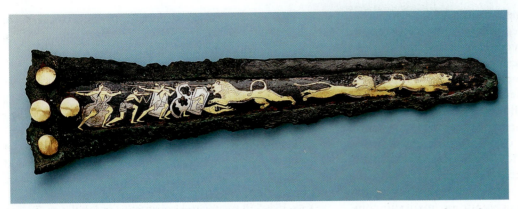

Mycenaean Lion Hunt
The Mycenaeans were a robust, warlike people who enjoyed the thrill and the danger of hunting. This scene on the blade of a dagger depicts hunters armed with spears and protected by shields defending themselves against charging lions. *(National Archaeological Museum/ Archaeological Receipts Fund)*

religious activities, watching entertainment, and engaging in athletic competitions such as leaping over a bull. We do not know if these represent daily life or mythological scenes, but many scholars see gender norms in Crete as less restrictive for women and more egalitarian than elsewhere in the ancient world.

This pleasant situation continued until the arrival of Greek-speaking peoples in the Balkans around 2000 B.C. They came gradually as individual groups who spoke various dialects of the same language. Study of these dialects, aided by archaeology, gives a reasonable idea of how the immigrants spread. The three main groups were the Aeolians, who settled in Thessaly and Boeotia. Others speaking Ionian made their homes in Attica and Euboea, but they claimed that they were indigenous. A later group whose tongue was Dorian occupied Argos, Laconia (the home of the Spartans), and Messenia. Despite these dialects, the Greeks considered themselves a distinct and related folk. By about 1650 B.C. one group had founded a powerful kingdom at Mycenae, while others spread elsewhere in Greece. They merged with native inhabitants, and from that union emerged the society that modern scholars call **Mycenaean,** after the most famous site of this new culture.

Under these conditions of foreign contact and local growth, early Mycenaean Greeks raised other palaces and established cities at Thebes, Athens, Tiryns, Pylos, and elsewhere. As in Crete, the political unit was the kingdom. The king and his warrior aristocracy stood at the top of society. The seat and symbol of the king's power and wealth was his palace, which was also the economic center of the kingdom. Within its walls royal artisans fashioned jewelry and rich ornaments, made and decorated fine pottery, forged weapons, prepared hides and wool for clothing, and manufactured the other goods needed by the king and his retainers. Palace scribes kept

records in Greek with a script known as **Linear B,** which was derived from Minoan Linear A. The scribes kept account of taxes and drew up inventories of the king's possessions. From the palace, as at Cnossus, the Mycenaean king directed the lives of his subjects. Little is known of the king's subjects except that they were the artisans, traders, and farmers of Mycenaean society. The Mycenaean economy was marked by an extensive division of labor, all tightly controlled from the palace. At the bottom of the social scale were male and female slaves, who were normally owned by the king and aristocrats but who also worked for ordinary people.

The Linear B tablets also held a surprise for those interested in Greek religion. Some of them recorded offerings to deities such as Zeus, Apollo, and Athena, the traditional Olympian gods. As late as 1995 Greek archaeologists in Thebes discovered over two hundred new Linear B tablets that are as yet unpublished. These tablets, as well as those already known, prove that the Greeks brought their traditional deities with them on their journey to Greece.

Contacts between the Minoans and Mycenaeans were originally peaceful, and Minoan culture flooded the Greek mainland. But around 1450 B.C. the Mycenaeans attacked Crete, destroying many Minoan palaces and taking possession of the grand palace at Cnossus. For about the next fifty years, the Mycenaeans ruled much of the island until a further wave of violence left Cnossus in ashes.

Whatever the explanation of these events, Mycenaean kingdoms in Greece benefited from the fall of Cnossus and the collapse of its trade. Mycenaean commerce quickly expanded throughout the Aegean, reaching as far abroad as Anatolia, Cyprus, and Egypt. Throughout central and southern Greece, Mycenaean culture flourished as never before. Palaces became grander, and citadels were often protected by mammoth stone walls. Prosperity, however, did not bring peace, and between 1300 and 1000 B.C. kingdom after kingdom suffered attack and destruction. Some modern scholars have attributed these events to the Sea Peoples, who wreaked such havoc in the eastern Mediterranean (see page 29). The best argument for absolving them from blame lies in the lack of any alien artifacts in Greece and the Aegean. If invaders, they proved remarkably tidy. Although later Greeks accused the Dorians of overthrowing the Mycenaean kingdoms, these centers undoubtedly fell because of mutual discord, just as their descendants would commit political suicide in the Peloponnesian War (see pages 73–74).

The fall of the Mycenaean kingdoms ushered in a period of such poverty, disruption, and backwardness that historians usually call it the "Dark Age" of Greece (ca 1100–800 B.C.). Even literacy, which was not widespread in any case, was a casualty of the chaos. Nonetheless, the Greeks survived the storm to preserve their culture and civilization. Greece remained Greek; nothing essential was swept away. Greek religious cults remained vital to the people, and basic elements of social organization continued to function effectively. It was a time of change and challenge, but not of utter collapse.

This period also saw a development of enormous importance for the course of Western civilization. The disruption of Mycenaean societies caused the widespread and prolonged movement of Greek peoples. They dispersed beyond mainland Greece farther south to Crete and in greater strength across the Aegean to the shores of Asia Minor. They arrived during a time when traditional states and empires had collapsed. Economic hardship was common, and various groups wandered for years. Yet by the end of the Dark Age, the Greeks had spread their culture throughout the Aegean basin.

Homer, Hesiod, Gods, and Heroes (1100–800 B.C.)

The Greeks, unlike the Hebrews, had no sacred book that chronicled their past. Instead they had Homer's *Iliad* and *Odyssey* to describe a time when gods still walked the earth. And they learned the origin and descent of the gods from the *Theogony,* an epic poem by Hesiod. Instead of authentic history, the poems of Homer and Hesiod offered the Greeks an ideal past, a largely legendary Heroic Age. These literary works deserve reading for their own sakes, but they are not reliable historical documents. Nor were they meant to be. In terms of pure history they contain scraps of information about the Bronze Age, much about the early Dark Age, and some about

the poets' own era. Chronologically, then, the Heroic Age falls mainly in the period between the collapse of the Mycenaean world and the rebirth of literacy.

The *Iliad* recounts an expedition of Mycenaeans, whom Homer called "Achaeans," to besiege the city of Troy in Asia Minor. The war was begun, as Homer tells it, by a Trojan prince's abduction of the beautiful wife of a Mycenaean king. The heart of the *Iliad,* however, concerns the quarrel between Agamemnon, the king of Mycenae, and Achilles, the tragic hero of the poem, and how their quarrel brought suffering to the Achaeans. Only when Achilles put away his anger and pride did he consent to come forward and face and kill the Trojan hero Hector. The *Odyssey,* probably composed later than the *Iliad,* narrates the adventures of Odysseus, one of the Achaean heroes who fought at Troy, during his voyage home from the fighting.

Online Study Center **Improve Your Grade**
Primary Source: Odysseus Is Rescued by the Princess Nausicaa

The splendor of these poems does not lie in their plots, although the *Odyssey* is a marvelous adventure story. Rather, both poems portray engaging but often flawed characters who are larger than life and yet typically human. Homer was also strikingly successful in depicting the great gods, who generally sit on Mount Olympus and watch the fighting at Troy like spectators at a baseball game, although they sometimes participate in the action. Homer's deities are reminiscent of Mesopotamian gods and goddesses. Hardly a decorous lot, the Olympians are raucous, petty, deceitful, and splendid. In short, they are human.

Homer at times portrayed the gods in a serious vein, but he never treated them in a systematic fashion, as did Hesiod, who lived somewhat later than Homer. Hesiod's epic poem the *Theogony* traces the descent of Zeus. Hesiod was influenced by Mesopotamian myths, which the Hittites had adopted and spread to the Aegean. Like the Hebrews, Hesiod envisaged his cosmogony—his account of the way the universe developed—in moral and gendered terms. Originally the primary deity was an earth goddess, Gaia, but through a series of incestuous relationships and generational conflicts, Zeus emerged triumphant. He established a moral order with himself at the head, ending the chaotic female-dominated system. In *Theogony* and others of his works, Hesiod attributes all human problems to the first woman, Pandora, whose curiosity led her to open the container in which pain, war, and other evils had been enclosed.

Polis of Argos   This view of modern Argos remarkably illustrates the structure of an ancient polis. Atop the hill in the background are the remains of the ancient acropolis. At its foot to the right are foundations of ancient public and private buildings, spreading beyond which are modern houses, situated where ancient houses were located. The trees and cut grain in the foreground were also major features of the *chora,* the agricultural basis of the polis. *(John Buckler)*

The Polis

After the upheavals that ended the Mycenaean period and the slow recovery of prosperity during the Dark Age, the Greeks developed their basic political and institutional unit, the **polis.** The term *polis* is generally interpreted as "city-state," one of the worst possible translations of a word that is basically untranslatable. Despite its defects, however, *city-state* is at least a term generally understood and accepted. Two problems arise in an attempt to understand the polis. The first is how it developed, and the second is what it was. Even the Greeks took the polis for granted. Although they remembered a time when kings ruled over many parts of Greece, they did not know how the polis evolved from those legendary kingdoms. In his *Politics* (1.1.9) Aristotle describes the growth of the polis in terms that are as biological as they are political. For example, he states that "man is by nature a being of the polis." He means that people developed the polis as naturally as plants and animals themselves develop. The biological analogy is wrong, but the concept of political evolution is largely correct.

• *After the Greeks had established the polis in which they lived their political and social lives, how did they shape it into its several historical forms?*

Origins of the Polis

Recent archaeological expeditions and careful study have done much to clarify the origins of the polis. Even during the late Mycenaean period, towns had grown up around palaces. These towns and even smaller villages performed basically local functions. The first was to administer the ordinary political affairs of the community. The village also served a religious purpose in that no matter how small, each had its local cult to its own deity. The exchange of daily goods made these towns and villages economically important, if only on a small scale. These settlements also developed a social system that was particularly their own. They likewise had their own views of the social worth and status of their inhabitants and the nature of their public responsibilities. In short, they relied on custom and mutual agreement to direct their ordinary affairs.

The coming of the Dorians did not significantly change this political evolution, but it had two effects. In some cases it disrupted the task of rebuilding and consolidating some of these developing communities. The Dorians at times carved out territory for themselves at the expense of the natives, but they also assimilated the culture around them. This process actually strengthened the sense of identity among the local people. The situation could have been cataclysmic, but for the most part it was not. The native inhabitants acknowledged their differences with the newcomers. They maintained their traditional religion, albeit sometimes in altered form, but they also accepted the religious validity of new cults. In addition, they looked upon the Dorians as fellow Greeks. Recent archaeological and historical studies reveal a picture of continuity and assimilation.

When fully developed, each polis normally shared a surprisingly large number of features with other poleis. Physically a polis was a society of people who lived in a city *(asty)* and cultivated the surrounding countryside *(chora)*. The city's water supply came from public fountains, springs, and cisterns. By the fifth century B.C. the city was generally surrounded by a wall. The city contained a point, usually elevated, called the **acropolis** and a public square or marketplace called the *agora*. On the acropolis, which in the early period was a place of refuge, stood the temples, altars, public monuments, and various dedications to the gods of the polis. The agora was originally the place where the warrior assembly met, but it became the political center of the polis. In the agora were porticoes, shops, and public buildings and courts.

City and Chora

Until quite recently most scholars have concentrated their attention on the city. The city provides a wealth of evidence on urban planning and daily life, and often yields public documents that illustrate the actual functioning of the polis. Nevertheless, the countryside was vital to the city and to the polis in general for a variety of reasons. Previous pictures of life there depict a scene that is dull and backward: not much happening in the country. Reality was very different. The traditional view overlooks the vitality and the basic importance of the village. The essential significance of the land is that it fed the city. Agriculture in most Greek communities indeed proved basic and far more important than local trade and urban economic dealings. Life in the polis demanded the integration of the chora and the city.

Since the Neolithic period, agriculture had provided the basis for Greek society. Farmers learned how to tame and nurture wild strains of trees and other plants. They discovered the value of irrigation to intensify their agricultural yields. The agricultural significance of the farmers on the chora and the regularity of the seasons bred a stable society. While mostly content to leave daily politics to the men of the city, male farmers made their opinions known to their fellow citizens. Although they spent most

of their days tending their fields and remained the economic basis of the polis, they never ignored the larger political issues confronting their community.

A previously unappreciated aspect of the countryside was its religious significance. Today people normally think first of the great religious festivals celebrated in the city. Although they were indeed important, most Greek religious practices were rooted in the country. The sanctuaries there were a reflection of the cults of the deities that nurtured the polis. The sanctuaries themselves and the religious rites connected with them were means of appealing to the gods to protect the crops, animals, and

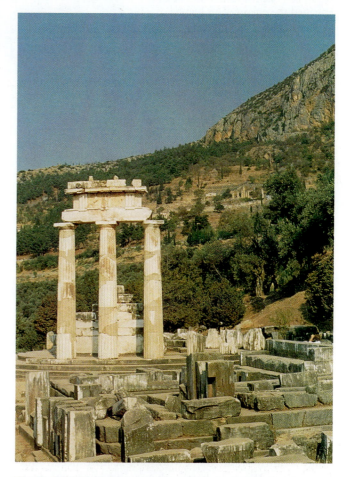

The Delphic Oracle   The Marmaria, the sanctuary of Athena, is seen here against the backdrop of the mountains that surround the sanctuary of Apollo. Around the oracle clustered many temples to various deities, shrines, and other sacred buildings, all of them in a remote mountainous area especially chosen by Apollo to be his home and the place where he answered the supplications of the faithful. *(John Buckler)*

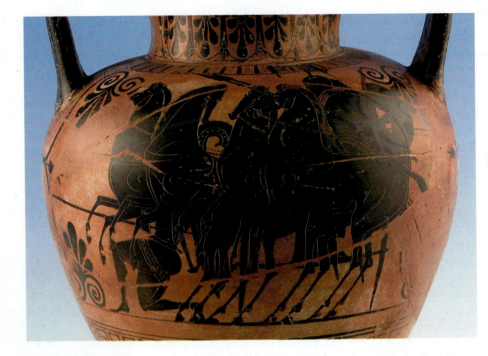

Early Greek Warfare   Before the hoplites became the backbone of the army, wealthy warriors rode into battle in a chariot, dismounted, and engaged the enemy. This scene, almost a photograph, shows on the left the warrior protecting the chariot before it returns to the rear. The painter has caught the lead horses already beginning the turn. *(Courtesy of the Ure Museum of Greek Archaeology, University of Reading)*

people who depended on the earth for survival. The sanctuaries and other religious sites on the borders of the polis linked country and city dwellers in one religious unit. They also served as sources of identification of the polis in that sacred buildings, shrines, and altars were the physical symbols of a particular people, no matter where in the polis they lived. The religious dedications in them were the possessions not only of the gods but also of the polis itself. The permanent dedications made to the gods reflected the power and prestige of the polis.

The average polis did not have a standing army. Instead it relied on its citizens for protection. Very rich citizens often served as cavalry, which was, however, never as important as the heavily armed infantry, or **hoplites.** These were the backbone of the army. They wore metal helmets and body armor, carried heavy, round shields, and armed themselves with spears and swords. They provided their own equipment and were basically amateurs. In the classical period (ca 500–338 B.C.) they were generally wealthy landowners who were accustomed to outdoor labor. When in battle, they stood in several dense lines in which cohesion and order became as valuable as courage. This effort also gave them a sense of comradeship and pride, creating a sense of masculinity that was linked to military service. Poor men made up the lightly armed infantry. Usually wielding only a javelin or two each, they used their mobility in rough areas to harass hoplites. In some instances the citizens of a polis hired

mercenaries to fight their battles. Mercenaries were expensive, untrustworthy, and willing to defect to a higher bidder. Even worse, they sometimes seized control over the polis that had hired them.

Regardless of its size or wealth, the polis was fundamental to Greek life. The polis was far more than a political institution. Above all it was a community of citizens whose customs were at the same time the laws of the polis. Even though the physical, religious, and political form of the polis varied from place to place, it was the very badge of Greekness.

Governing Structures

Greek city-states had several different types of government. **Monarchy,** rule by a king, was surprisingly not one of them. Although prevalent during the Mycenaean period, it afterwards declined. While Sparta boasted of two kings, they were only part of a more broadly based constitution. During fully developed historical times Greek states were either democracies or oligarchies. Sporadic periods of violent political and social upheaval often led to a third type of government—tyranny. **Tyranny** was rule by one man who had seized power by unconstitutional means, generally by using his wealth to win a political following that toppled the existing legal government.

Only democracy and oligarchy played lasting, broad roles in Greek political life, and these two forms flourished across Greece well into later years. **Democracy,** the power of the people, meant that all citizens, without respect to birth or wealth, administered the workings of government. Although Athens is easily the most famous of the Greek democracies, it was not alone. The people of Argos in the Peloponnesus independently governed their powerful city by a democracy quite similar to the Athenian one. So too with Corcyra, the great city that governed the island also named Corcyra, the modern Corfu. These democracies generally established friendly relations with one another, sharing many basic features while developing their own particular forms of popular rule.

Yet Greek democracy did not really live up to its name. In reality, Greek democracy meant the rule of citizens, not "the people" as a whole, and citizenship was drastically limited. In Athens and in other democracies, only free adult men who had lived in the polis a long time were citizens. Women, foreigners, slaves, and others had no rights. The 10 to 20 percent of the population who were citizens theoretically shared equally in the determination of policy and the administration of government. Moreover, they generally did so in practice. Along with military service, citizenship provided men with an opportunity to bond with one another, and it became an important component in Greek ideas of masculinity.

Most Greek states actually preferred oligarchy to democracy as their favorite form of government. **Oligarchy,** which literally means "the rule of the few," was government by a small group of wealthy citizens who were not necessarily aristocratic by birth. Oligarchy generally gave its whole population—leaders and people alike—stable government and freedom to prosper. Men could advance politically by earning enough wealth to qualify for full citizenship. Full citizenship meant the right to vote for officials and to hold office. The roll of oligarchic cities includes many of the most illustrious of the Greek states. A well-known example is Corinth, where landowners, merchants, artisans, and working people stood solidly behind a government that prospered for well over 350 years. At Corinth the wealthy governed according to the ideal called **isonomia,** meaning "equality shared under the law." Although the wealthy governed the city, they officially endorsed social mobility for capable men and application of the law equally to everyone. Corinthian oligarchs also listened to the will of the citizens, a major factor in their long success.

Several other oligarchies likewise deserve notice. Two were located in Arcadia: Mantinea in the north and Tegea in the south. These two city-states depended on agriculture for their prosperity, not on commerce as did Corinth. They too found in oligarchy the key to prosper-

ity and the means to create stable governments. They too allowed all citizens the opportunity to gain the wealth needed to join the governing class and to rise socially. Easily the most influential oligarchic state was Thebes in the region of Boeotia. It too depended on agriculture for its wealth. It was only one of the oligarchic cities in the area, but it was certainly the most powerful. Stable at home, Thebes united these other oligarchies to form the first effective federal government of city-states in Greece, the "Boeotian Confederacy." Thebes and the other oligarchies were responsible for the creation of federalism as a valid, working political principle of government. **Federalism** in Greece meant a system of government in which individual city-states joined to create one general government. This federalism is actually the same principle of the United States of America, which is a federal government of individual states joined together for the common good. The Boeotian Confederacy of oligarchic city-states proved to be so successful that elsewhere in Greece other states followed its example. It proved to be particularly popular and widespread later in the Hellenistic period (see page 98).

During the classical period, however, despite the allure of federalism, the citizens of the vast majority of city-states were determined to remain free and autonomous. The very integration of the polis proved to be one of its basic weaknesses. The political result, as earlier in Sumer, was almost constant warfare. The polis could dominate, but unlike earlier and later empires, it could not incorporate.

The Archaic Age (800–500 B.C.)

Generally known as Archaic primarily because of its art and literature, this period can be seen as a time when the Greeks recovered from the downfall of the Mycenaean kingdoms and continued the advances made during the Dark Age. These years ushered in one of the most vibrant periods of Greek history, an era of extraordinary expansion geographically, artistically, and politically. Greeks ventured as far east as the Black Sea and as far west as Spain (see Map 3.2). With the rebirth of literacy, this period also witnessed a tremendous literary flowering as poets broke away from the heroic tradition and wrote about their own lives. Politically these were the years when Sparta and Athens—the two poles of the Greek experience—rose to prominence.

● *What major developments mark the Archaic Greek period in terms of spread of culture and the growth of cities?*

Overseas Expansion

During the years 1100–800 B.C. the Greeks not only recovered from the breakdown of the Mycenaean world but also grew in wealth and numbers. This new prosperity brought new problems. The increase in population meant that many families had very little land or none at all. Land hunger and the resulting social and political tensions drove many Greek men and women to seek new homes outside of Greece. Other factors, largely intangible, played their part as well: the desire for a new start, a love of excitement and adventure, and natural curiosity about what lay beyond the horizon.

From about 750 to 550 B.C., Greeks from the mainland and Asia Minor traveled throughout the Mediterranean and even into the Atlantic Ocean in their quest for new land. They sailed in the greatest numbers to Sicily and southern Italy, where there was ample space for expansion. They also sailed farther west to Sardinia, southern France and Spain, and even the Canary Islands. In Sicily they found the Sicels, who had already adopted many Carthaginian customs, including a nascent urban culture. Fiercely independent, they greeted the coming of the Greeks just as they had the arrival of the Carthaginians. They welcomed Greek culture but not Greek demands for their land. Nonetheless, the two peoples made a somewhat uneasy accommodation, and there was some intermarriage among them. There was enough land in Sicily for Greeks and Sicels alike, so both flourished, albeit not always peacefully.

In southern Italy the Greeks encountered a number of Indo-European peoples. They were for the most part rural and enjoyed few material comforts. Some of their villages were evolving into towns, but in the mountains looser tribal units prevailed. They both welcomed Greek culture, and the Greeks found it easy to establish prosperous cities without facing significant local hostility.

Some adventurous Greeks sailed to Sardinia and the southern coast of modern France. In Sardinia they established outposts that were originally trading stations, meant primarily for bartering with the natives. Commerce was so successful that some Greeks established perma-

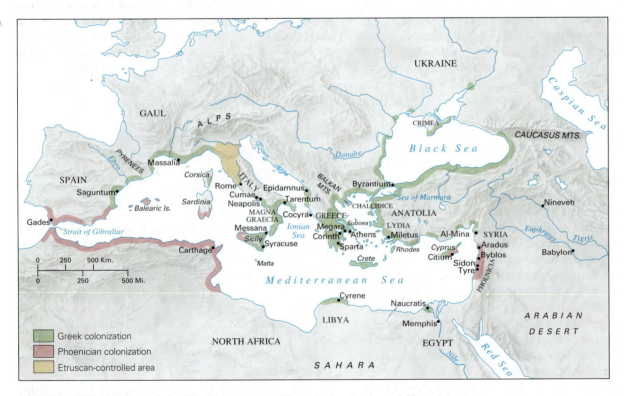

MAP 3.2 Colonization of the Mediterranean   Though the Greeks and Phoenicians colonized the Mediterranean basin at about the same time, the Greeks spread much farther.

Online Study Center   **Improve Your Grade** Interactive Map: Phoenician and Greek Colonization

nent towns there. Greek influence, in terms of physical remains and the ideas that they reflect, was far stronger on the island than was recognized even a few years ago. From these new outposts Greek influence extended to southern France. The modern city of Marseilles began as a Greek colony and later sent settlers to southern Spain.

Colonization changed the entire Greek world, both at home and abroad. In economic terms the expansion of the Greeks created a much larger market for agricultural and manufactured goods. From the east, especially from the northern coast of the Black Sea, came wheat in a volume beyond the capacity of Greek soil. In return flowed Greek wine and olive oil, which could not be produced in the harsher climate of the north. Greek-manufactured goods, notably rich jewelry and fine pottery, circulated from southern Russia to Spain. During this same period the Greeks adopted the custom of minting coins, which they apparently imported from Lydia. At first coinage was of little economic importance, and only later did it replace the common practice of barter. In the barter system one person simply exchanges one good for another without the use of money. Each person decides the value of the goods traded. Even today, especially in the backcountry of Greece, a surprisingly large number of economic transactions are done by barter. Thus Greek culture and economics, fertilized by the influences of other societies, spread throughout the Mediterranean basin.

Colonization presented the polis with a huge challenge, for it required organization and planning on an unprecedented scale. The colonizing city, called the *metropolis,* or mother city, first decided where to establish the colony, how to transport colonists to the site, and who would sail. Then the metropolis collected and stored the supplies that the colonists would need both to feed themselves and to plant their first crop. The metropolis also had to provide adequate shipping for the voyage. All preparations ready, a leader, called an **oikist,** ordered the colonists to sail. The oikist was then in full command of the band until the colony was established in its new site and capable of running its own affairs. A significant aspect of colonizing ventures was that male colonists were considered political equals and were expected to have a voice in the new colony.

Once the colonists landed, the oikist laid out the new polis, selected the sites of temples and public buildings, and established the government. Then he surrendered power to the new leaders. The colony was thereafter independent of the metropolis. For the Greeks, colonization had two important aspects. First, it demanded that the polis assume a much greater public function than

ever before, thus strengthening the city-state's institutional position. Second, colonization spread the polis and its values far beyond the shores of Greece. Even more important, colonization on this scale had a profound impact on the course of Western civilization. It meant that the prevailing culture of the Mediterranean basin would be Greek, the heritage to which Rome would later fall heir.

The Growth of Sparta

During the Archaic period the Spartans expanded the boundaries of their polis and made it the leading power in Greece. Like other Greeks, the Spartans faced the problems of overpopulation and land hunger. Unlike other Greeks, the Spartans solved these problems by conquest, not by colonization. To gain more land, the Spartans set out in about 735 B.C. to conquer Messenia, a rich, fertile region in the southwestern Peloponnesus. This conflict, the First Messenian War, lasted for twenty years and ended in a Spartan triumph. The Spartans appropriated Messenian land and turned the Messenians into *helots,* or state serfs.

In about 650 B.C. Spartan exploitation and oppression of the Messenian helots led to a helot revolt so massive and stubborn that it became known as the Second Messenian War. The Spartan poet Tyrtaeus, a contemporary of these events, vividly portrays the ferocity of the fighting:

For it is a shameful thing indeed
When with the foremost fighters
An elder falling in front of the young men
Lies outstretched,
Having white hair and grey beard,
Breathing forth his stout soul in the dust,
Holding in his hands his genitals
stained with blood.[1]

Confronted with such horrors, Spartan enthusiasm for the war waned. Finally, after some thirty years of fighting, the Spartans put down the revolt. Nevertheless, the political and social strain it caused led to a transformation of the Spartan polis.

It took the full might of the Spartan people, aristocrat and commoner alike, to win the Second Messenian War. After the victory non-noblemen, who had done much of the fighting, demanded rights equal to those of the nobility. They had taken their place in the battle line next to their aristocratic neighbors but lacked the social prestige and political rights of their noble companions. The agitation of these non-nobles disrupted society until the aristocrats agreed to remodel the state.

Periods of Greek History

Period	Significant Events	Major Writers
Bronze Age 2000–1100 B.C.	Arrival of the Greeks in Greece Rise and fall of the Mycenaean kingdoms	
Dark Age 1100–800 B.C.	Greek migrations within the Aegean basin Social and political recovery Evolution of the polis Rebirth of literacy	Homer Hesiod
Archaic Age 800–500 B.C.	Rise of Sparta and Athens Colonization of the Mediterranean basin Flowering of lyric poetry Development of philosophy and science in Ionia	Archilochus Sappho Tyrtaeus Solon Anaximander Heraclitus
Classical Period 500–338 B.C.	Persian wars Growth of the Athenian Empire Peloponnesian War Rise of drama and historical writing Flowering of Greek philosophy Spartan and Theban hegemonies Conquest of Greece by Philip of Macedon	Herodotus Thucydides Aeschylus Sophocles Euripides Aristophanes Plato Aristotle

The "Lycurgan regimen," as the reforms were called after a legendary lawgiver, was a new political, economic, and social system. Political distinctions among Spartan men were eliminated, and all citizens became legally equal. Actual governance of the polis was in the hands of two kings who were primarily military leaders. The kings and twenty-eight elders made up a council that deliberated on foreign and domestic matters and prepared legislation for the assembly, which consisted of all Spartan citizens. The real executive power of the polis was in the hands of five *ephors,* or overseers, elected from and by all the citizens. In effect, the Lycurgan regimen did nothing more than broaden the aristocracy, while at the same time setting limits on its size. Social mobility was for the most part abolished, and instead an aristocratic warrior class governed the polis.

To provide for their economic needs, the Spartans divided the land of Messenia among all citizens. Helots worked the land, raised the crops, provided the Spartans with their living, and occasionally served in the army. The Spartans kept the helots in line by means of systematic terrorism, hoping to beat them down and keep them quiet. Spartan citizens were supposed to devote their time exclusively to military training.

In the Lycurgan system every citizen owed primary allegiance to Sparta. Suppression of the individual together with emphasis on military prowess led to a barracks state. Family life itself was sacrificed to the polis. Once Spartan boys reached the age of seven, they were enrolled in separate companies with other boys their age. They lived in this **homosocial** (same-sex) setting for most of their lives. They slept outside on reed mats and underwent rugged physical and military training until age twenty-four, when they became frontline soldiers. For the rest of their lives, Spartan men kept themselves prepared for combat. Their military training never ceased, and the older men were expected to be models of endurance, frugality, and sturdiness to the younger men. In battle Spartans were supposed to stand and die rather than retreat. An anecdote frequently repeated about one Spartan mother sums up Spartan military values. As her son was setting off to battle, the mother handed him his shield and advised him to come back either victorious, carrying the shield, or dead, being carried on it. In the Lycurgan regimen, Spartan men were expected to train vigorously, disdain luxury and wealth, do with little, and like it.

In this militaristic atmosphere, citizen women were remarkably free. As in all classical cultures, there was an emphasis on childbearing, but the Spartan leadership viewed maternal health as important for the bearing of healthy, strong children and thus encouraged women to participate in athletics and to eat well. With men in military service most of their lives, citizen women owned property and ran the household; they were not physically restricted or secluded. Marriage often began with a trial marriage period to make sure the couple could have children, with divorce and remarriage the normal course if they were unsuccessful. Men saw their wives only rarely when they sneaked out of camp, and their most meaningful relations were same-sex ones. Spartan military leaders viewed such relationships as militarily advantageous, judging that men would fight more fiercely in defense of close comrades and lovers. Close links among men thus contributed to Spartan dedication to the state and understanding of civic virtue, which were admired throughout the Greek world.

The Evolution of Athens

Like Sparta, Athens faced pressing social and economic problems during the Archaic period, but the Athenian response was far different from that of the Spartans. Instead of creating an oligarchy, the Athenians extended to all citizens the right and duty of governing the polis. Indeed, the Athenian democracy was one of the most thoroughgoing in Greece.

The late seventh century B.C. was for Athens a time of turmoil, the causes of which are virtually unknown. In 621 B.C. Draco, an Athenian aristocrat, doubtless under pressure from the peasants, published the first law code of the Athenian polis. His code was thought harsh, but it nonetheless embodied the ideal that the law belonged to the citizens. Nevertheless, peasant unrest continued.

By the early sixth century B.C. social and economic conditions led to another explosive situation. The aristocracy still governed Athens oppressively. The aristocrats owned the best land, met in an assembly to govern the polis, and interpreted the law. Noble landowners were forcing small farmers into economic dependence. Many families were sold into slavery; others were exiled and their land was pledged to the rich. Poor farmers who had borrowed from their wealthy neighbors had to put up their land as collateral. If a farmer was unable to repay the loan, his creditor put a stone on the borrower's field to signify his indebtedness and thereafter took one-sixth of the annual yield until the debt was paid. If the farmer had to borrow again, he pledged himself and sometimes his family. If he was again unable to repay the loan, he became the slave of his creditor. Because the harvests of the poor farmer were generally small, he could usually raise enough crops to live on but not enough to repay his loan.

In many other city-states, conditions like those in Athens led to the rise of tyrants. One person who recognized these problems clearly was Solon, himself an aristocrat and poet, and a man opposed to tyrants. He was also the one man in Athens who enjoyed the respect of both aristocrats and peasants. Like Hesiod, Solon used his poetry to condemn the aristocrats for their greed and dishonesty. Solon recited his poems in the Athenian agora, where anyone there could hear his relentless call for justice and fairness. The aristocrats realized that Solon was no crazed revolutionary, and the common people trusted him. Around 594 B.C. the nobles elected him *archon*, chief magistrate of the Athenian polis, and gave him extraordinary power to reform the state.

Solon immediately freed all people enslaved for debt, recalled all exiles, canceled all debts on land, and made enslavement for debt illegal. He also divided society into four legal groups on the basis of wealth. In the most influential group were the wealthiest citizens, but even the poorest and least powerful men enjoyed certain rights. Solon allowed them into the old aristocratic assembly, where they could take part in the election of magistrates.

In all his work, Solon gave thought to the rights of the poor as well as the rich. He gave common men a place in government and a voice in the political affairs of Athens. Although Solon's reforms solved some immediate problems, they did not bring peace to Athens. Some aristocrats attempted to make themselves tyrants, while others banded together to oppose them. In 546 B.C. Pisistratus, an exiled aristocrat, returned to Athens, defeated his opponents, and became tyrant. Pisistratus reduced the power of the aristocracy while supporting the common people. Under his rule Athens prospered, and his building program began to transform the city into one of the splendors of Greece. His reign as tyrant promoted the growth of democratic ideas by arousing rudimentary feelings of equality in many Athenian men.

Athenian acceptance of tyranny did not long outlive Pisistratus, for his son Hippias ruled harshly, committing excesses that led to his overthrow. After a brief period of turmoil between factions of the nobility, Cleisthenes, a wealthy and prominent aristocrat, emerged triumphant in 508 B.C., largely because he won the support of lower-status men. Cleisthenes reorganized the state completely but presented every innovation to the assembly for discussion and ratification. All Athenian citizens had a voice in Cleisthenes' work.

Cleisthenes created the **deme,** a local unit, to serve as the basis of his political system. Citizenship was tightly linked to the deme, for each deme kept the roll of those men within its jurisdiction who were admitted to citizenship.

Cleisthenes also created ten new tribes as administrative units. All the demes were grouped in tribes, which thus formed the link between the demes and the central government. The central government included an assembly of all citizens and a new council of five hundred members. Cleisthenes is often credited with the institution of *ostracism,* a vote of the Athenian citizens by which the man receiving the most votes went into exile. The goal of ostracism was to rid the state peacefully of a difficult or potentially dangerous politician.

The democracy functioned on the idea that all full citizens, the *demos,* were sovereign. Yet not all citizens could take time from work to participate in government. Therefore, they delegated their power to other citizens by creating various offices meant to run the democracy. The most prestigious of them was the board of ten archons, who were charged with handling legal and military matters. Six of them oversaw the Athenian legal system. They presided over courts, fixed dates for trials, and ensured that the laws of Athens were consistent. They were all elected for one year. After leaving office they entered the *Areopagus,* a select council of ex-archons who handled cases involving homicide, wounding, and arson.

Legislation was in the hands of two bodies, the **boule,** or council, composed of five hundred members, and the **ecclesia,** the assembly of all citizens. The boule, separate from the Areopagus, was perhaps the major institution of the democracy. By supervising the various committees of government and proposing bills to the assembly, it guided Athenian political life. It received foreign envoys and forwarded treaties to the assembly for ratification. It oversaw the granting of state contracts and was responsible for receiving many revenues. It held the democracy together. Nonetheless, the assembly had the final word. Open to all male citizens over eighteen years of age, it met at a specific place to vote on matters presented to it. The assembly could either accept, amend, or reject bills put before it. Every member could express his opinion on any subject on the agenda, and a simple majority vote was needed to pass or reject a bill.

Athenian democracy was to prove an inspiring ideal in Western civilization. It demonstrated that a large group of people, not just a few, could efficiently run the affairs of state. By heeding the opinions, suggestions, and wisdom of all its citizens, the polis enjoyed the maximum amount of good counsel. Because all citizens could speak their minds, they did not have to resort to rebellion or conspiracy to express their desires. Like all democracies in ancient Greece, however, Athenian democracy was limited. Slaves, women, recent migrants, and foreigners could not be citizens; their opinions about political issues were not taken into account or recorded.

The Classical Period (500–338 B.C.)

In the years 500 to 338 B.C., Greek civilization reached its highest peak in politics, thought, and art. In this period the Greeks beat back the armies of the Persian Empire. Then, turning their spears against one another, they destroyed their own political system in a century of warfare. Some thoughtful Greeks felt prompted to record and analyze these momentous events. Herodotus (ca 485–425 B.C.), from Asia Minor, traveled the Greek world to piece together the course of the Persian wars. Although he consulted documents when he could find them, he relied largely on the memories of the participants. Not only is he the "father of history," he is also the first oral historian. Next came Thucydides (ca 460–ca 399 B.C.), whose account of the Peloponnesian War remains a classic of Western literature. Unlike Herodotus, he was often a participant in the events that he described.

This era also saw the flowering of philosophy, as thinkers in Ionia and on the Greek mainland began to ponder the nature and meaning of the universe and human experience; they used their intellects to explain the world around them and to determine humanity's place in it. The Greeks invented drama, and the Athenian tragedians Aeschylus, Sophocles, and Euripides explored themes that still inspire audiences today. Greek architects reached the zenith of their art and created buildings whose very ruins still inspire awe. Because Greek intellectual and artistic efforts attained their fullest and finest expression in these years, this age is called the "classical period." Few periods in the history of Western society can match it in sheer dynamism and achievement.

● *How did the Greeks develop their literature, philosophy, religion, and art, and how did war affect this intellectual and social process?*

The Persian Wars (499–479 B.C.)

One of the hallmarks of the classical period was warfare. In 499 B.C. the Ionian Greeks, with the feeble help of Athens, rebelled against the Persian Empire. In 490 B.C. the Persians struck back at Athens but were beaten off at the Battle of Marathon, a small plain in Attica (see Map

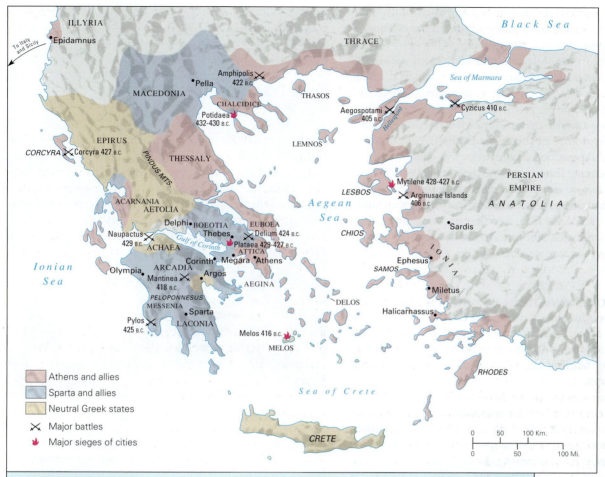

Mapping the Past

MAP 3.3 The Peloponnesian War This map shows the alignment of states during the Peloponnesian War, while Map 3.5 on page 87 shows interstate rivalry in the fourth century B.C.—two very disruptive periods in Greek history. ❶ What does Map 3.3 tell us about the balance of power during the Peloponnesian War? Which states led the others? ❷ Does Map 3.5 show the same situation? Are the leading states in Map 3.3 still the leaders in Map 3.5, or has power shifted elsewhere? What does Map 3.5 tell us about the growing political disintegration of Greece?

3.3). This victory taught the Greeks that they could defeat the Persians and successfully defend their homeland. It prompted the Persians to try again. In 480 B.C. the Persian king Xerxes led a mighty invasion force into Greece. In the face of this emergency, many of the Greeks united and pooled their resources to resist the invaders. The Spartans provided the overall leadership and commanded the Greek armies. The Athenians, led by the wily Themistocles, provided the heart of the naval forces.

The first confrontations between the Persians and the Greeks occurred at the pass of Thermopylae and in the waters off Artemisium, the northern tip of Euboea. At Thermopylae the Greek hoplites, heavily armed foot soldiers, showed their mettle. Before the fighting began, a report came in that when the Persian archers shot their bows the arrows darkened the sky. One gruff Spartan replied merely, "Fine, then we'll fight in the shade." The Greeks at Thermopylae fought heroically, but the Persians took the position. In 480 B.C. the Greek fleet, inspired by the energetic Themistocles, met the Persian armada at Salamis, an island just south of Athens. Though outnumbered by the Persians, the Greek navy won an overwhelming victory. The remnants of the Persian fleet retired, and with them went all hope of Persian victory. In the following year, a coalition of Greek forces, commanded by the Spartan Pausanias with assistance from the Athenian Aristides, smashed the last Persian army at Plataea, a small polis in Boeotia. Greece remained free.

The significance of these Greek victories is nearly incalculable. By defeating the Persians, the Greeks ensured that they would not be taken over by a monarchy, which they increasingly viewed as un-Greek. The Persian king symbolized lack of freedom and submission to one man. Monarchy had become a threat to the concept of individual Greek freedom. The decisive victories meant that Greek political forms and intellectual concepts would be handed down to later societies.

Growth of the Athenian Empire (478–431 B.C.)

For the Greeks, who had just won the Persian wars, that conflict was a beginning, not an end. Before them was a novel situation: the defeat of the Persians had created a power vacuum in the Aegean. The state with the strongest navy could turn the Aegean into its lake. In 478 B.C., to take advantage of this situation, the Athenians and their allies, again led by Aristides, formed the **Delian League,** a grand naval alliance aimed at liberating Ionia from Persian rule. The league took its name from the small island of Delos, on which stood a religious center sacred to all parties. The Delian League was intended as a free alliance under the leadership of Athens. Athenians provided most of the warships and crews and determined how many ships or how much money each member of the league should contribute to the allied effort.

The Athenians, supported by the Delian League and led by the young aristocrat Cimon, carried the war against Persia. But Athenian success had a sinister side. While the Athenians drove the Persians out of the Aegean, they also became increasingly imperialistic, even to the point of turning the Delian League into an Athenian empire. Athens began reducing its allies to the status of subjects. The Athenians sternly put down dissident or rebellious governments, replacing them with trustworthy puppets. Tribute was often collected by force, and the Athenians placed the economic resources of the Delian League under tighter and tighter control. Athenian ideas of freedom and democracy did not extend to the citizens of other cities.

Leonidas at Thermopylae This heroic statue symbolizes the sacrifice of King Leonidas at the battle. Together with his Spartans, the Thespians, and the Thebans, he heroically died to stop the Persians at the pass of Thermopylae. *(Professor Paul Cartledge)*

Athens justified its conduct by its successful leadership. In about 467 B.C. Cimon defeated a new and huge Persian force at the Battle of the Eurymedon River in Asia Minor, once again removing the shadow of Persia from the Aegean. But as the threat from Persia waned and the Athenians treated their allies more harshly, major allies such as Thasos revolted (ca 465 B.C.), requiring the Delian League to use its forces against its own members. The expansion of Athenian power and the aggressiveness of Athenian rule also alarmed Sparta and its allies. While relations between Athens and Sparta cooled, Pericles (ca 494–429 B.C.) became the leading statesman in Athens. Like the democracy he led, Pericles, an aristocrat of solid intellectual ability, was aggressive and imperialistic. At last, in 459 B.C. Sparta and Athens went to war over conflicts between Athens and some of Sparta's allies. Though the Athenians conquered Boeotia, Megara, and Aegina in the early stages of the war, they met defeat in Egypt and later in Boeotia. The war ended in 445 B.C. with no serious damage to either side and nothing settled. But this war divided the Greek world between the two great powers.

During the 440s and 430s Athens continued its severe policies toward its subject allies and came into conflict with Corinth, one of Sparta's leading supporters (see Map 3.3). In 433 B.C. Athens sided with Corcyra against Corinth in a dispute between the two. Together with the Corcyraean fleet, an Athenian squadron defeated the Corinthian navy in open combat. The next year Corinth and Athens collided again, this time over the Corinthian colony of Potidaea, in a conflict the Athenians also won. In this climate of anger and escalation, Pericles took the next step. To punish Megara for alleged sacrilege, Pericles in 432 B.C. persuaded the Athenians to pass a law, the Megarian Decree, that excluded Megarians from trading with Athens and its empire. In response the Spartans convened a meeting of their allies, whose complaints of Athenian aggression ended with a demand that Athens be stopped. Reluctantly the Spartans agreed to declare war. The real reason for war, according to the Athenian historian Thucydides, was very simple: "The truest explanation, though the one least mentioned, was the great growth of Athenian power and the fear it caused the Lacedaemonians [Spartans], which drove them to war."[2]

The Peloponnesian War (431–404 B.C.)

At the outbreak of this conflict, the Peloponnesian War, the Spartan ambassador Melesippus warned the Athenians: "This day will be the beginning of great evil for the Greeks." Few men have ever prophesied more accurately. The Peloponnesian War lasted a generation and brought in its wake fearful plagues, famine, civil wars, widespread destruction, and huge loss of life.

After a Theban attack on the nearby polis of Plataea, the Peloponnesian War began in earnest. In the next seven years, the army of Sparta and its Peloponnesian allies invaded Attica five times. The Athenians stood behind their walls, but in 430 B.C. the cramped conditions nurtured a dreadful plague, which killed huge numbers, eventually claiming Pericles himself. (See the feature "Listening to the Past: The Great Plague at Athens, 430 B.C." on pages 92–93.) The death of Pericles opened the door to a new breed of politicians, men who were rash, ambitious, and more dedicated to themselves than to Athens. One such was Cleon, a very daring and in some ways a very capable man. To divert the constant Spartan invasions of Attica, Cleon proposed a counterattack at Pylos, a rocky peninsula in Messenia immediately

opposite the Spartan-occupied island of Sphacteria. Spartan forces were defeated, yet the outcome failed to bring peace. Instead, the energetic Spartan commander Brasidas widened the war in 424 B.C. by capturing Amphipolis on the northern coast of the Aegean, one of Athens's most valuable subject states. Two years later, both Cleon and Brasidas were killed in a battle to recapture the city. Recognizing that ten years of war had resulted only in death, destruction, and stalemate, Sparta and Athens concluded the Peace of Nicias in 421 B.C.

The Peace of Nicias resulted in a cold war. But even cold war can bring horror and misery. Such was the case when in 416 B.C. the Athenians sent a fleet to the neutral island of Melos with an ultimatum: the Melians could surrender or perish. The motives of the Athenians were frankly and brutally imperialistic. The Melians resisted. The Athenians conquered them, killed the men of military age, and sold the women and children into slavery.

The cold war grew hotter, thanks to the ambitions of Alcibiades (ca 450–404 B.C.), an aristocrat, a kinsman of Pericles, and a student of the philosopher Socrates. A shameless opportunist, Alcibiades widened the war to further his own career and to increase the power of Athens. He convinced the Athenians to attack Syracuse, the leading polis in Sicily. His only valid reason lay in the argument that such an operation would cut the grain supply from Sicily to the Peloponnesus. The undertaking was vast, requiring an enormous fleet and thousands of sailors and soldiers. Trouble began at the outset. Alcibiades' political enemies indicted him, whereupon he fled to Sparta rather than stand trial. Meanwhile, in 414 B.C. the Athenians laid siege to Syracuse. The Syracusans fought back bravely, and even a huge Athenian relief force failed to conquer the city. Finally, in 413 B.C. the Syracusans counterattacked, completely crushing the Athenians. Thucydides wrote the epitaph for the Athenians: "infantry, fleet, and everything else were utterly destroyed, and out of many few returned home."[3]

The disaster in Sicily ushered in the final phase of the war, which was marked by three major developments: the renewal of war between Athens and Sparta, Persia's intervention in the war, and the revolt of many Athenian subjects. The year 413 B.C. saw Sparta's declaration of war against Athens and widespread revolt within the Athenian Empire. Yet Sparta still lacked a navy, the only instrument that could take advantage of the unrest of Athens's subjects, most of whom lived either on islands or in Ionia. The sly Alcibiades, now working for Sparta, provided a solution: he engineered an alliance between Sparta and Persia. The Persians agreed to build a fleet for Sparta. In return, the Spartans promised to give Ionia back to Persia. Now equipped with a fleet, the Spartans challenged the Athenians in the Aegean, the result being a long roll of inconclusive naval battles.

The strain of war prompted the Athenians in 407 B.C. to recall Alcibiades from exile. He cheerfully double-crossed the Spartans and Persians, but even he could not restore Athenian fortunes. In 405 B.C. Athens met its match in the Spartan commander Lysander, a man whose grasp of strategy, politics, and diplomacy easily rivaled Alcibiades'. Lysander destroyed the last Athenian fleet at the Battle of Aegospotami, after which the Spartans blockaded Athens until it was starved into submission. After twenty-seven years the Peloponnesian War was over, and the evils prophesied by the Spartan ambassador Melesippus in 431 B.C. had come true.

Athenian Arts in the Age of Pericles

In the last half of the fifth century B.C., Pericles turned Athens into the showplace of Greece. He appropriated Delian League funds to pay for a huge building program,

planning temples and other buildings to honor Athena, the patron goddess of the city, and to display to all Greeks the glory of the Athenian polis. Pericles also pointed out that his program would employ many Athenians and bring economic prosperity to the city.

Thus began the undertaking that turned the Acropolis into a monument for all time. Construction of the Parthenon began in 447 B.C., followed by the Propylaea, the temple of Athena Nike (Athena the Victorious), and the Erechtheum (see Map 3.4). Even the pollution of modern Athens, although it is destroying the ancient buildings, cannot rob them of their splendor and charm.

The planning of the architects and the skill of the workmen who erected these buildings were both very sophisticated. Visitors approaching the Acropolis first see the Propylaea, the ceremonial gateway, a building of complicated layout and grand design whose Doric columns seem to hold up the sky. On the right is the small temple of Athena Nike, whose dimensions harmonize with those of the Propylaea. The temple was built to commemorate the victory over the Persians, and the

The Acropolis of Athens These buildings embody the noblest spirit of Greek architecture. From the entrance visitors walk through the Propylaea and its pillars. Ahead opens the grand view of the Parthenon, still noble in ruins. To the left stands the Erechtheum, the whole a monument to Athens itself. *(Courtesy, Sotiris Toumbis Editions)*

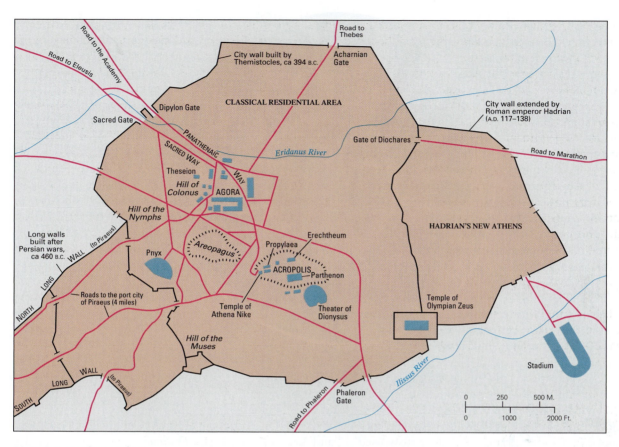

MAP 3.4 Ancient Athens   By modern standards, the city of Athens was hardly more than a town, not much larger in size than one square mile. Yet this small area reflects the concentration of ancient Greek life in the polis.

Ionic frieze above its columns depicts the struggle between the Greeks and the Persians. Here for all the world to see is a tribute to Athenian and Greek valor—and a reminder of Athens's part in the victory.

To the left of the visitors, as they pass through the Propylaea, stands the Erechtheum, an Ionic temple that housed several ancient shrines. On its southern side is the famous Portico of the Caryatids, a porch whose roof is supported by statues of Athenian maidens. The graceful Ionic columns of the Erechtheum provide a delicate relief from the prevailing Doric order of the massive Propylaea and Parthenon.

As visitors walk on, they obtain a full view of the Parthenon, thought by many to be the perfect Doric temple. The Parthenon is the chief monument to Athena and her city. The sculptures that adorn the temple portray the greatness of Athens and its goddess. The figures on the eastern pediment depict Athena's birth, those on

the west the victory of Athena over the god Poseidon in their struggle for the possession of Attica. Inside the Parthenon stood a huge statue of Athena, the masterpiece of the great sculptor Phidias.

In many ways the Athenian Acropolis is the epitome of Greek art and its spirit. Although the buildings were dedicated to the gods and most of the sculptures portray gods, these works nonetheless express the Greek fascination with the human and the rational. Greek deities were anthropomorphic, and Greek artists portrayed them as human beings. While honoring the gods, Greek artists were thus celebrating human beings. In the Parthenon sculptures it is visually impossible to distinguish the men and women from the gods and goddesses. The Acropolis also exhibits the rational side of Greek art. Greek artists portrayed action in a balanced, restrained, and sometimes even serene fashion, capturing the noblest aspects of human beings: their reason, dignity, and promise.

Other aspects of Athenian cultural life were as rooted in the life of the polis as were the architecture and sculpture of the Acropolis. The development of drama was tied to the religious festivals of the city. The polis sponsored the production of plays and required that wealthy citizens pay the expenses of their production. At the beginning of the year, dramatists submitted their plays to the archon. He chose those he considered best and assigned a theatrical troupe to each playwright. Although most Athenian drama has perished, enough has survived to prove that the archons had superb taste. Many plays were highly controversial, but the archons neither suppressed nor censored them.

Mosaic of the Muses   Not found in a great or famous urban center, this mosaic nonetheless testifies to the wide dissemination of culture and art throughout Greece. The figures of the mosaic represent the nine Muses, goddesses of the arts. The lyre of Apollo occupies the center, and Clio, the goddess of history, is represented by the scroll in the upper right of the lyre. *(Professor Nicolas Yalouris, Former General Inspector of Antiquities, Athens)*

The Athenian dramatists were the first artists in Western society to examine such basic questions as the rights of the individual, the demands of society on the individual, and the nature of good and evil. Conflict is a constant element in Athenian drama. The dramatists used their art to portray, understand, and resolve life's basic conflicts.

Aeschylus (525–456 B.C.), the first of the great Athenian dramatists, was also the first to express the agony of the individual caught in conflict. In his trilogy of plays, *The Oresteia,* Aeschylus deals with the themes of betrayal, murder, and reconciliation, urging that reason and justice be applied to reconcile fundamental conflicts. The final play concludes with a prayer that civil dissension never be allowed to destroy the city and that the life of the city be one of harmony and grace.

Sophocles (496–406 B.C.) also dealt with matters personal and political. In *Antigone* he highlights conflicts between divine and human law and comments on the gender order in Greek society. Antigone defies Creon, her uncle and king, to follow divinely established rules and bury her brother against his decree. Creon rages that she is not above the laws he has established, and that if he does not punish her she will be more man than he is. Antigone escapes her punishment by committing suicide.

Sophocles' masterpieces have inspired generations of playwrights. Perhaps his most famous plays are *Oedipus the King* and its sequel, *Oedipus at Colonus. Oedipus the King* is the ironic story of a man doomed by the gods to kill his father and marry his mother. Try as he might to avoid his fate, Oedipus's every action brings him closer to its fulfillment. When at last he realizes that he has carried out the decree of the gods, Oedipus blinds himself and flees into exile. In *Oedipus at Colonus* Sophocles dramatizes the last days of the broken king, whose patient suffering and uncomplaining piety win him an exalted position. In the end the gods honor him for his virtue. The interpretation of these two plays has been hotly debated, but Sophocles seems to be saying that human beings should obey the will of the gods, even without fully understanding it, for the gods stand for justice and order.

Euripides (ca 480–406 B.C.), the last of the three great Greek tragic dramatists, also explored the theme of personal conflict within the polis and sounded the depths of the individual. With Euripides drama entered a new, and in many ways more personal, phase. To him the gods were far less important than human beings. The essence of Euripides' tragedy is the flawed character—men and women who bring disaster on themselves and their loved ones because their passions overwhelm reason. Although Euripides' plays were less popular in his lifetime than were those of Aeschylus and Sophocles, Euripides was a dramatist of genius whose work later had a significant impact on Roman drama.

Writers of comedy treated the affairs of the polis bawdily and often coarsely. Even so, their plays also were performed at religious festivals. The comic playwrights dealt primarily with the political affairs of the polis and the conduct of its leading politicians. Best known are the comedies of Aristophanes (ca 445–386 B.C.), an ardent lover of his city and a merciless critic of cranks and quacks. He lampooned eminent generals, at times depicting them as morons. He commented snidely on Pericles, poked fun at Socrates, and hooted at Euripides. Like Aeschylus, Sophocles, and Euripides, Aristophanes used his art to dramatize his ideas on the right conduct of the citizen and the value of the polis.

Online Study Center **Improve Your Grade**
Primary Source: Socrates Has His Great Mind in the Clouds

Despite the undeniable achievements of the Athenians, many modern historians have exaggerated their importance. They have created the notion of Athenocentricism, the mistaken opinion that Athens stood solely at the center of classical Greek life. This idea fails to do justice to the other Greeks who also shaped society, culture, and history. Athenocentricism actually distorts and denies the richness of the Greek experience. Greece, like the United States, profited by incorporating many different ideas into one enduring culture.

Daily Life in Periclean Athens

In sharp contrast with the rich intellectual and cultural life of Periclean Athens stands the simplicity of its material life. The Athenians—and in this respect they were typical of Greeks in general—lived very happily with comparatively few material possessions. In the first place, there were very few material goods to own. The thousands of machines, tools, and gadgets considered essential for modern life had no counterparts in Athenian life.

The Athenian house was rather simple. Whether large or small, the typical house consisted of a series of rooms built around a central courtyard, with doors opening onto the courtyard. Many houses had bedrooms on an upper floor. Artisans often set aside a room to use as a shop or work area. Larger houses often had a room at the front where the men of the family ate and entertained guests, and a *gynaikon* (women's quarter) at the back where women worked, ate, and slept. Other rooms included the kitchen and bathroom. By modern standards there was not much furniture. In the men's dining room were couches, a sideboard, and small tables. Cups and other pottery were often hung from pegs on the wall.

In the courtyard were the well, a small altar, and a washbasin. If the family lived in the country, the stalls of the animals faced the courtyard. Country dwellers kept oxen for plowing, pigs for slaughtering, sheep for wool, goats for cheese, and mules and donkeys for transportation. Even in the city chickens and perhaps a goat or two roamed the courtyard together with dogs and cats.

Cooking, done over a hearth in the house, provided welcome warmth in the winter. Baking and roasting were done in ovens. Food consisted primarily of various grains, especially wheat and barley, as well as lentils, olives, figs, and grapes. Garlic and onion were popular garnishes, and wine was always on hand. These foods were stored at home in large jars; with them the Greek family sometimes ate fish, chicken, and vegetables. Women ground wheat into flour, baked it into bread, and on special occasions made honey or sesame cakes. The Greeks used olive oil for cooking, as families still do in modern Greece; they also used it as an unguent and as lamp fuel.

By American standards, the Greeks did not eat much meat. On special occasions, such as important religious festivals, the family ate the animal sacrificed to the god and gave the god the exquisite delicacy of the thighbone wrapped in fat. The only Greeks who consistently ate meat were the Spartan warriors. They received a small portion of meat each day, together with the infamous Spartan black broth, a ghastly concoction of pork cooked in blood, vinegar, and salt. One Greek, after tasting the broth, commented that he could easily understand why the Spartans were so willing to die.

In the city a man might support himself as a craftsman—a potter, bronzesmith, sailmaker, or tanner—or he could contract with the polis to work on public buildings, such as the Parthenon and Erechtheum. Certain crafts, including spinning and weaving, were generally done by women. Men and women without skills worked as paid laborers but competed with slaves for work. Slaves were usually foreigners and often barbarians. By "barbarians" the Greeks meant people whose native language was not Greek. Citizens, slaves, and barbarians were paid the same amount for their work.

Slavery was commonplace in Greece, as it was throughout the ancient world. In its essentials Greek slavery resembled Mesopotamian slavery. Slaves received some protection under the law and could buy their freedom. On the other hand, masters could mistreat or neglect their slaves, although killing them was illegal. Most slaves in Athens served as domestics and performed light labor around the house. Nurses for children, teachers of reading and writing, and guardians for young men were often slaves. The lives of these slaves were much like those of their owners. Other slaves were skilled workers who could be found working on public buildings or in small workshops.

Woman Grinding Grain   Here a woman takes the grain raised on the family farm and grinds it by hand in a mill. She needed few tools to turn the grain into flour. *(National Archaeological Museum, Athens/Archaeological Receipts Fund)*

Gender and Sexuality

The social condition of Athenian women has been the subject of much debate. One of the difficulties is the fragmentary nature of the evidence. Women appear frequently in literature and art, often in idealized roles, but seldom in historical contexts of a wider and more realistic nature. This is due in part to the fact that most Greek historians of the time recounted primarily the political, diplomatic, and military events of the day, events in which women seldom played a notable part. Yet that does not mean that women were totally invisible in the life of the polis. It indicates instead that ancient sources provide only a glimpse of how women affected the society in which they lived. Athenian men believed that men and women should be segregated and that women should not appear in public, but the reality was less limiting than the ideal.

The status of a free woman of the citizen class was strictly protected by law. Only her children, not those of foreigners or slaves, could be citizens. She was in charge of the household and the family's possessions, yet the law protected her primarily to protect her husband's interests. Raping a free woman was a lesser crime than seducing her, because seduction involved the winning of her affections. This law was concerned not with the husband's feelings but with ensuring that he need not doubt the legitimacy of his children.

Women in Athens and elsewhere in Greece received a certain amount of social and legal protection from their dowries. Upon marriage, the bride's father gave the couple a gift of land or money, which the husband administered. However, it was never his; and in the rare cases of divorce, it returned to the wife's domain. The same is often true in Greece today among the upper class.

A citizen woman's main functions were to bear and raise children. Childbirth could be dangerous for both mother and infant, so pregnant women often made sacrifices or visited temples to ask help from the gods. Demeter and Artemis were particularly favored. In practical terms, citizen women relied on their friends, relatives, and midwives to assist in the delivery. Greek physicians did not concern themselves with obstetrical care.

Citizen women never appeared in court or in the public political assemblies that were the heart of Athenian democracy, though they did attend public festivals, ceremonies, and funerals. They took part in annual processions to honor the goddess Athena and in harvest festivals honoring the goddess Demeter, who protected the city's crops. In a few cases, women were priestesses in

The importance of slavery in Athens must not be exaggerated. Athenians did not own huge gangs of slaves as did Roman owners of large estates. Slave labor competed with free labor and kept wages down, but it never replaced the free labor that was the mainstay of the Athenian economy.

Most Athenians supported themselves by agriculture, but unless the family was fortunate enough to possess holdings in a plain more fertile than most of the land, they found it difficult to reap a good crop from the soil. Many people must have consumed nearly everything they raised. Attic farmers were free and, though hardly prosperous, by no means destitute. They could usually expect yields of five bushels of wheat and ten of barley per acre for every bushel of grain sown. A bad harvest meant a lean year. In many places rural families grew more barley than wheat because of the nature of the soil. Wherever possible they also cultivated vines and olive trees.

the cults of various goddesses. Priestesses prayed in public on behalf of the city and, like priests, were paid for their services. The most prominent priestess was at Delphi, near Athens, where the god Apollo was understood to give messages about the future. The priestess at the oracle at Delphi interpreted these prophecies, and people came from all over Greece and beyond to hear them.

The demands of survival required some ordinary women to work in honest, if somewhat humble, jobs. Chief among them were such ordinary occupations as shopkeepers, which obviously included a public economic importance. Though the reality was more complicated than the ideal, prosperous and respectable citizen women did spend much of their time in the house. We know the names of no female poets, artists, or philosophers from classical Athens. If women wrote anything, it has not survived, as it was not considered worthy of note.

The sources surviving from ancient Athens provide a great deal of information about attitudes toward sexuality among the educated male elite. Plato and Aristotle, the two most important philosophers of ancient Athens, were both suspicious of the power of sexual passion, warning that it distracted men from reason and the search for knowledge. Both men praised a love that was intellectualized and nonsexual, the type of attachment we still term "platonic." (Neither Plato nor Aristotle was concerned about what sex does to women except as this affects men.) Plato developed a dualistic view of both humans and the world, arguing that the unseen realm of ideas was far superior to the visible material world, and that the human mind or soul was trapped in a material body. This mind-body split was a gendered concept, with men associated more with the mind and women with the body. Women's bodies were also viewed as more influenced by their sexual and reproductive organs than were men's; Plato described the womb as an

"animal" that wandered freely around the body, causing physical and mental problems. (This is why the words *hysteria* and *hysterectomy* both have the same Greek root.)

The mind-body split did not originate with Plato, but his acceptance and elaboration of it helped make this concept an important part of Western philosophy from that time on, and led some groups (though not Plato) to reject sexual activity completely. In Aristotle the mind-body split is reflected in the process of procreation (what he termed "generation"), with the male providing the "active principle" and the female simply the "material."

In classical Athens, part of an adolescent citizen's training in adulthood was supposed to entail a hierarchical sexual and tutorial relationship with an older man, who most likely was married and may have had other female sexual partners as well. These relationships between adolescents and men were often celebrated in literature and art, in part because Athenians regarded perfection as possible only in the male. The perfect body was that of the young male, and perfect love was that between an adolescent and an older man, not that between a man and an imperfect woman. This love was supposed to

Greek Courtship Here two young lovers embrace. With one arm around his girl and the other holding a wine vessel, the boy draws his girl nearer. With a smile she seems more interested in her music, for with her right thumb she turns the boy down. *(Erich Lessing/Art Resource, NY)*

Mosaic Portrait of Sappho   The Greek letters in the upper left corner identify this idealized portrait as that of Sappho. The mosaic, which was found in Sparta, dates to the Roman Empire and testifies to Sappho's popularity in antiquity. *(Museum of Sparta/Archaeological Receipts Fund)*

become intellectualized and "platonic" once the adolescent became an adult.

How often actual sexual relations between men or between men and women approached the ideal in Athens is very difficult to say, as most of our sources are prescriptive, idealized, or fictional. (This is also true for the tiny number of sources that refer to female-female sexual desire, the most famous of which are the poems of Sappho, a female poet who lived on the island of Lesbos in the sixth century B.C. Sappho and her home island were later associated with female homosexuality, but we do not know how much her poetry reflected her life.) We know that female and male prostitution was legal and common, and that female prostitutes were divided into well-educated and beautiful **hetairai** and the lower-class, ordinary prostitutes the Greeks called **pornoi.** (See the feature "Individuals in Society: Aspasia.") We also know that most Athenians married and had children, for they saw the continuation of the family line as essential. Sex-

ual desire and procreation were both important aspects of life, but they were not necessarily linked for ancient Greeks.

Greek Religion

Greek religion is extremely difficult for modern people to understand, largely because of the great differences between Greek and modern cultures. In the first place, it is not even easy to talk about "Greek religion," since the Greeks had no uniform faith or creed. Although the Greeks usually worshiped the same deities—Zeus, Hera, Apollo, Athena, and others—the cults of these gods and goddesses varied from polis to polis. The Greeks had no sacred books such as the Bible, and Greek religion was often a matter more of ritual than of belief. Nor did cults impose an ethical code of conduct. Greeks did not have to follow any particular rule of life, practice certain virtues, or even live decent lives in order to participate. Unlike the Egyptians and Hebrews, the Greeks lacked a priesthood as the modern world understands the term. In Greece priests and priestesses existed to care for temples and sacred property and to conduct the proper rituals, but not to make religious rules or doctrines, much less to enforce them. In short, there existed in Greece no central ecclesiastical authority and no organized creed.

Although temples to the gods were common, they were unlike modern churches or synagogues in that they were not normally places where a congregation met to worship as a spiritual community. Instead, the individual Greek man or woman either visited the temple occasionally on matters of private concern or walked in a procession to a particular temple to celebrate a particular festival. In Greek religion the altar, which stood outside the temple, was important; when the Greeks sought the favor of the gods, they offered them sacrifices. Greek religious observances were generally cheerful. Festivals and sacrifices were frequently times for people to meet together socially, times of high spirits and conviviality rather than of pious gloom. By offering the gods parts of the sacrifice while consuming the rest themselves, worshipers forged a bond with the gods. Some deities were particularly worshiped by men and some by women.

The most important members of the Greek pantheon were Zeus, the king of the gods, and his consort, Hera.

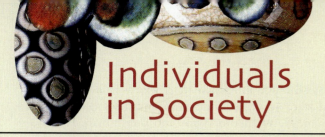

Individuals in Society

Aspasia

Idealized portrait of Aspasia.
(Alinari/Art Resource, NY)

"If it is necessary for me indeed to speak of female virtues, to those of you who have now become widows, I shall explain the entire situation briefly. It is in your hands whether you will not fall below your nature. The greatest glory to you is to be least talked about by men, either for excellence or blame" (Thucydides 2.46). These words were reportedly uttered by Pericles to the widows at a public funeral honoring those killed during the first year of the Peloponnesian War. Whether Pericles actually said the words is for the most part irrelevant. Their significance is in their expression of Athenian gender ideals. Pericles had just finished a long speech praising the dead soldiers as ideal men, then added this brief comment about women. While men's actions should be noted and recorded, he said, women's should be ignored, for their "greatest glory" was oblivion.

This ideal became the reality for most Athenian women, whose names and actions never became part of "history." It was not true, however, for the woman Pericles himself may have cared the most about—Aspasia.

Aspasia was born in the Greek city of Miletus and came to Athens in about 445 B.C. She is easily one of the most intriguing women in ancient history. Little is known about her life, but she played a role in Athenian society that was far more renowned than, and far different from, that allegedly proposed for Athenian women by Pericles.

Once in Athens, Aspasia may have become a *hetaira*, which literally means "companion." The duties of a hetaira varied. She accompanied men at dinners and drinking parties, where their wives would not have been welcome, and also served as a sexual partner. The major attractions of a successful hetaira included beauty, intelligent conversation, and proper etiquette. In return she was paid for her services. No contemporary sources specifically say that Aspasia was a hetaira, but she may have been.

Contemporary sources do make clear that Aspasia enjoyed a rare opportunity for a woman to influence the men who shaped the political life of Athens. The Roman biographer Plutarch reports that she enjoyed the company of the most famous men in Athens. Their conversation included philosophy, and in one of the philosopher Plato's dialogues Socrates claims that she taught him the art of public speaking. The story is probably not true, but it points to her public reputation.

Aspasia was introduced to Pericles, who was either already divorced from his wife or divorced her soon afterward. Because Aspasia was not an Athenian citizen, she and Pericles could not marry, but they did have a son, also named Pericles. When Pericles' sons by his wife died in an epidemic, Pericles pressured the Athenian citizenship to let his son by Aspasia become a citizen. Sons of noncitizen women were normally barred from citizenship (a law Pericles himself had introduced), but the law was waived in this case.

Pericles was powerful enough to get his way, though he could not halt criticism and ridicule. Not only had he let himself get attached to a foreign woman, but he was more devoted to her than Athenians felt was appropriate for an adult man. Even Athens's greatest statesman was expected to follow the proper gender order in his personal relationships.

Pericles died shortly after his son became a citizen, and Aspasia disappears from the historical record. We can celebrate her achievements, but we do not know what motivated her. A funeral speech attributed to her is included in one of Plato's dialogues, but whether these were her actual words we will never know.

Questions for Analysis

1. How did Aspasia's position as a foreigner in Athens shape her opportunities?
2. In what ways does her story support and in what ways does it contradict the general picture of gender roles in Athenian society?

Online Study Center **Improve Your Grade**
Going Beyond Individuals in Society

Although they were the mightiest and most honored of the deities who lived on Mount Olympus, their divine children were closer to ordinary people. Apollo was especially popular. He represented the epitome of youth, beauty, benevolence, and athletic skill. He was also the god of music and culture and in many ways symbolized the best of Greek culture. His sister Athena, who patronized women's crafts such as weaving, was also a warrior-goddess and had been born from the head of Zeus without a mother. Best known for her cult at Athens, to which she gave her name, she was highly revered throughout Greece, even in Sparta, which eventually became a fierce enemy of Athens. Artemis was Apollo's elder sister. A virgin and a huntress, she oversaw women's passage from virginity to marriage. Paradoxically, though a huntress, she also protected wildlife. There was something wild and free about her. Other divinities watched over every aspect of human life.

The Greeks also honored some heroes. A hero was born of a union of a god or goddess and a mortal and was an intermediate between the divine and the human. A hero displayed his divine origins by performing deeds beyond the ability of human beings. Herakles (or Hercules) was easily the greatest of them. He successfully fulfilled twelve labors, all of which pitted him against mythical opponents or tasks. Like other heroes, he protected mortals from supernatural dangers and provided an ideal of vigorous masculinity.

Besides the Olympian gods, each polis had its own minor deities, each with his or her own local cult. In many instances Greek religion involved the official gods and goddesses of the polis and their cults. The polis administered the cults and festivals, and all were expected to participate in this civic religion, regardless of whether they even believed in the deities being worshiped. Participating unbelievers, who seem to have been a small minority,

Temple at Bassae   The temple at Bassae stands in wild splendor in the mountains of Arcadia. It is an almost perfect Dorian temple, with its massive columns surrounding the *cella,* the inner room that contained the statue of Apollo. In such elevated, lonely places many Greeks felt that they entered a region dear to the gods. *(John Buckler)*

Sacrificial Scene Much of Greek religion was simple and festive, as this scene demonstrates. The participants include women and boys dressed in their finest clothes and crowned with garlands. Musicians add to the festivities. Only the sheep will not enjoy the ceremony. (*National Archaeological Museum, Athens/Archaeological Receipts Fund*)

were not considered hypocrites. Rather, they were seen as patriotic, loyal citizens who in honoring the gods also honored the polis. If this attitude seems contradictory, an analogy may help. Before baseball games Americans stand at the playing of the national anthem, whether they are Democrats, Republicans, or neither and whether they agree or disagree with the policies of the current administration. They honor their nation as represented by its flag in somewhat the same way an ancient Greek honored the polis and demonstrated solidarity with it by participating in the state cults.

Some Greeks turned to mystery religions like those of the Eleusinian mysteries in Attica and of Trophonios in Boeotia. These mystery religions in some ways foreshadowed aspects of early Christian practices by their rites of initiation, their acceptance of certain doctrines, and generally their promise of life after death. The basic concept of these cults was to unite individuals in an exclusive religious society with particular deities. Those who joined went through a period of preparation in which they learned the essential beliefs of the cult and its necessary rituals. Once they had successfully undergone initiation,

they were forbidden to reveal the secrets of the cult. Consequently, modern scholars know comparatively little about their tenets.

Much religion was local and indeed domestic. Each village possessed its own cults and rituals, and individual families honored various deities privately in their homes. These native rites often remained unknown far beyond their own communities. Women may have played an important part in these celebrations, which in general included all elements of society, slaves included. Many people also believed that magic rituals and spells were effective and sought the assistance of individuals reputed to have special knowledge or powers to cure disease, drive away ghosts, bring good weather, or influence the action of others.

Though Greek religion in general was individual or related to the polis, the Greeks also shared some Pan-Hellenic festivals, the chief of which were held at Olympia in honor of Zeus and at Delphi in honor of Apollo. The festivities at Olympia included the famous games, athletic contests that have inspired the modern Olympic games. Held every four years, these games were for the glory of

A Greek God Few pieces of Greek art better illustrate the conception of the gods as greatly superior forms of human beings than this magnificent statue, over six feet ten inches in height. Here the god, who may be either Poseidon or Zeus, is portrayed as powerful and perfect but human in form. *(National Archaeological Museum, Athens/Archaeological Receipts Fund)*

Zeus. They attracted visitors from all over the Greek world and lasted well into Christian times. The Pythian games at Delphi were also held every four years, but these contests differed from the Olympic games by including musical and literary contests. Both the Olympic and the Pythian games were unifying factors in Greek life, bringing Greeks together culturally as well as religiously.

The Flowering of Philosophy

The myths and epics of the Mesopotamians are ample testimony that speculation about the origin of the universe and of humans did not begin with the Greeks. The signal achievement of the Greeks was the willingness of some to treat these questions in rational rather than mythological terms. Although Greek philosophy did not fully flower until the classical period, Ionian thinkers had already begun in the Archaic period to ask what the universe was made of. These men are called the Pre-Socratics, for their work preceded the philosophical revolution begun by the Athenian Socrates. Though they were keen observers, the Pre-Socratics rarely undertook deliberate experimentation. Instead, they took individual facts and wove them into general theories. Despite appearances, they believed, the universe was actually simple and subject to natural laws. Drawing on their observations, they speculated about the basic building blocks of the universe.

Online Study Center **Improve Your Grade**
Primary Source: The Greeks Seek Answers:
The Pre-Socratic Philosophers

The first of the Pre-Socratics, Thales (ca 600 B.C.), learned mathematics and astronomy from the Babylonians and geometry from the Egyptians. Yet there was an immense and fundamental difference between Near Eastern thought and the philosophy of Thales. The Near Eastern peoples considered such events as eclipses to be evil omens. Thales viewed them as natural phenomena that could be explained in natural terms. In short, he asked why things happened. He believed the basic element of the universe to be water. Although he was wrong, the way in which he had asked the question was momentous: it was the beginning of the scientific method.

Thales' follower Anaximander (d. ca 547 B.C.) continued his work. Anaximander was the first of the Pre-Socratics to use general concepts, which are essential to abstract thought. He theorized that the basic element of the universe is the "boundless" or "endless"—something infinite and indestructible. In his view the earth floats in a void, held in balance by its distance from everything else in the universe. Heraclitus (ca 500 B.C.), however, declared the primal element to be fire. He also declared that the world had neither beginning nor end. Although the universe was eternal, it changed constantly. An outgrowth of this line of speculation was the theory of Democritus (b. ca 460 B.C.) that the universe was made up of invisible, indestructible atoms. The culmination of Pre-Socratic thought was the theory that four simple substances made up the universe: fire, air, earth, and water.

With this impressive heritage behind them, the philosophers of the classical period ventured into new areas of speculation. This development was partly due to the work of Hippocrates (second quarter of the fifth century B.C.), the father of medicine. Like Thales, Hippocrates sought natural explanations for phenomena. Basing his opinions on empirical knowledge, not on religion or magic, he taught that natural means could be employed to fight disease. The human body, he declared, contained four humors, or fluids: blood, phlegm, black bile, and yellow bile. In a healthy body the four humors were in perfect balance; too much or too little of any particular humor caused illness. But Hippocrates broke away from the mainstream of Ionian speculation by declaring that medicine was a separate craft that had its own set of principles.

The distinction between natural science and philosophy on which Hippocrates insisted was also promoted by the Sophists, who traveled the Greek world teaching young men. Despite differences of opinion on philosophical matters, the Sophists all agreed that human beings were the proper subject of study. They also believed that excellence could be taught, and they used philosophy and rhetoric to prepare young men for life in the polis. The Sophists put great emphasis on logic and the meanings of words. They criticized traditional beliefs, religion, rituals, and myths and even questioned the laws of the polis. In essence, they argued that nothing is absolute, that everything ,is relative. Hence more traditional Greeks considered them wanton and harmful, men who were interested in "making the worse seem the better cause."

One of those who was thought to be a Sophist was Socrates (ca 470–399 B.C.). He was not strictly a Sophist, because he never formally taught or collected fees from anyone. He nonetheless shared the Sophists' belief that human beings and their environment were the essential subjects of philosophical inquiry. Like the Sophists, Socrates thought that excellence could be learned and passed on to others. His approach when posing ethical questions and defining concepts was to start with a general topic or problem and to narrow the matter to its essentials. He did so by continuous questioning, a running dialogue. Never did he lecture. Socrates thought that by constantly pursuing excellence, an essential part of which

was knowledge, human beings could approach the supreme good and thus find true happiness. Yet in 399 B.C. Socrates was brought to trial, convicted, and executed on charges of corrupting the youth of the city and introducing new gods.

Socrates' student Plato (427–347 B.C.) carried on his master's search for truth. Unlike Socrates, however, Plato founded a philosophical school, the Academy. He spent his entire life trying to determine the ideal polis. This ideal state could exist only when its citizens were well educated. From education came the possibility of determining an all-comprising unity of virtues that would lead to an intelligent, moral, and ethical life. He further concluded that only divine providence could guide people to virtue. In his opinion, divine providence was one intelligible and individualistic being. In short, he equated god with the concept of good. Plato's tool was mathematics as the servant of education. Although human life is transitory, ideas are permanent. If people could master the essential ideas, guided by mathematics, their souls would become immortal. It was the highest duty of true statesmen to educate their people to reach this higher good.

Plato developed the theory that all visible, tangible things are unreal and temporary, copies of "forms" or "ideas" that are constant and indestructible. Only the mind, not the senses, can perceive eternal forms. In Plato's view the highest form is the idea of good. He discussed these ideas in *The Republic* and *The Laws*. His perfect polis was utopian and could exist only if its rulers were philosophers. Despite his efforts, Plato ultimately failed to realize his utopia, but at least he introduced the concept of trying to shape an ideal society.

Aristotle (384–322 B.C.) carried on the philosophical tradition of Socrates and Plato. Aristotle tried to understand the changes of nature—what caused them and where they led. He also attempted to bridge the gap between abstract truth and concrete perception. He argued that the universe is finite, spherical, and eternal. In the process, he discussed an immaterial being that is his conception of a god that neither created the universe nor guided it. He discussed these ideas in two masterful works, *Physics* and *Metaphysics*, in which he combined empiricism, or observation, and speculative method. He postulated the four principles of matter, form, movement, and goal. Although Aristotle considered nature impersonal, he also concluded that it had its own purpose.

For Aristotle, nature's primary purpose and aim was perfection, and Aristotle termed anything less than

Statue of Eirene   The Athenians erected this statue of Eirene (Peace) holding Ploutos (Wealth) in her left arm. Athens had seen only war for some fifty-six years, and the statue celebrated the Common Peace of 375 B.C. The bitter irony of this poignant scene is that the treaty lasted scarcely a year. *(Glyptothek, Munich/Studio Koppermann)*

perfect "monstrous." Women, in his opinion, were imperfect men, the result of something wrong with the conception that created them—their parents were too young or too old, or too diverse in age, or one of them was not healthy. Because nature always aimed at perfection, woman was thus "a deformity, but one which occurs in the ordinary course of nature."[4] Aristotle was not sure exactly why imperfect men were required in the natural scheme of things, but he decided that it must be because they performed a function necessary for men. His fundamental question about women was "What are women *for*?" whereas about men it was "What *is* man?" Aristotle did view the household and women's role within it as important, but because he regarded women as fundamentally intellectually inferior, he saw their primary function as procreation, not companionship. The philosopher Plato agreed. As we saw above, he viewed the best love and friendship as that between men, and he commented in one of his dialogues that originally all humans had been male, but some had been reborn as women when they proved to be cowardly and wicked. In his most important work, the *Republic,* Plato does include women among the group of people who governed the rest, but because he also abolishes the family for this group, these are women who have rejected or escaped the traditional female role and have become more like men.

Online Study Center **Improve Your Grade**
Primary Source: Plato on the Equality of Women
in His Republic

Athenian philosophers thus reflected their own society in their thought, but they also called for a broader examination of the universe and the place of humans in it than had earlier thinkers. Both the breadth of their vision and its limitations are important legacies to Western civilization.

The Final Act (404–338 B.C.)

The turbulent period from 404 to 338 B.C. is sometimes mistakenly seen as a period of failure and decline. It was instead a vibrant era in which Plato and Aristotle thought and wrote, one in which literature, oratory, and historical writing flourished. The architects of the fourth century B.C. designed and built some of the finest buildings of the classical period, and engineering made great strides. If the fourth century was a period of decline, this was so only in politics. The Peloponnesian War and its aftermath proved that the polis had reached the limits of its success

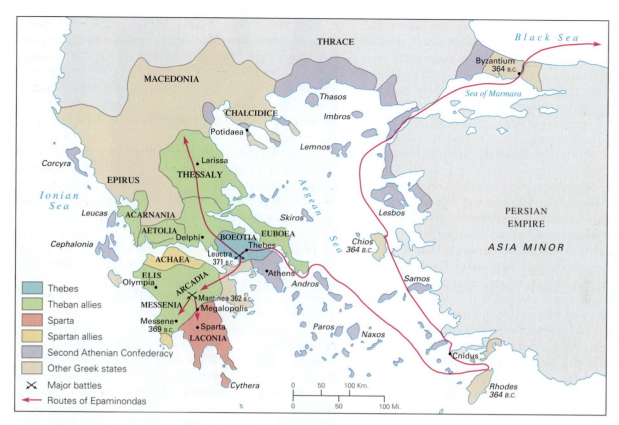

MAP 3.5 Greece in 362 B.C.   The fourth century B.C. witnessed the rapid growth of Greek federalism as states sought allies to gain security from rival powers.

as an effective political institution. The attempts of various city-states to dominate the others led only to incessant warfare. The polis system was committing suicide.

The Greeks of the fourth century B.C. experimented seriously with two political concepts in the hope of preventing war. First was the **Common Peace,** the idea that the states of Greece, whether large or small, should live together in peace and freedom, each enjoying its own laws and customs. In 386 B.C. this concept was a vital part of a peace treaty with the Persian Empire, in which the Greeks and Persians pledged themselves to live in harmony.

Federalism, the second concept to become prominent, already had a long history in some parts of Greece (see page 65). Strictly speaking, the new impetus toward federalism was intended more to gain security through numbers than to prevent war. Greek leagues had usually grown up in regions where geography shaped a well-defined area and where people shared a broad kinship. By banding together, the people of these leagues could mar-

shal their resources, both human and material, to defend themselves from outside interference. In the fourth century B.C. at least ten other federations of states either came into being or were revitalized (see Map 3.5). Federalism never led to a United States of Greece, but the concept held great importance not only for fourth-century Greeks but also for the Hellenistic period and beyond. In 1787, when the Founding Fathers met in Philadelphia to frame the Constitution of the United States, they studied Greek federalism very seriously in the hope that the Greek past could help guide the American future.

● **How did the Greek city-states meet political and military challenges, and how did Macedonia become dominant?**

The Struggle for Hegemony

If neither the Common Peace nor federalism put an end to interstate rivalry, the main reason was the stubborn desire of the principal states to dominate the others. The chief states—Sparta, Athens, and Thebes—each tried to create a **hegemony,** that is, a political ascendancy over other states, even though they sometimes paid lip service to the ideals of the Common Peace. In every instance, the ambition, jealousy, pride, and fear of the major powers doomed the effort to achieve genuine peace. In short, each major power wanted to be the leader, or *hegemon,* and refused to bow to the others that aspired to the same position.

When the Spartan commander Lysander defeated Athens in 404 B.C., the Spartans used their victory to build an empire instead of ensuring the freedom of all Greeks. Their decision quickly brought the Spartans into conflict with Persia, which now demanded the return of Ionia to its control (see page 70), and also with their own allies. The Spartan king Agesilaos, an impetuous man of mediocre ability, waged a fruitless war against the Persians in Ionia. From 400 to 386 B.C. that war eventually engulfed Greece itself. After years of stalemate the Spartans made peace with Persia and their Greek enemies. The result was the first formal Common Peace, the King's Peace of 386 B.C., which cost Sparta its empire but not its position of ascendancy in Greece.

Not content with Sparta's hegemony of Greece, Agesilaos betrayed the very concept of the Common Peace to punish cities that had opposed Sparta during the war. He treacherously ordered Thebes to be seized and even condoned an unwarranted and unsuccessful attack on Athens. Agesilaos had gone too far. Even though it appeared that his naked use of force had made Sparta supreme in Greece, his imperialism was soon to lead to Sparta's downfall at the hands of the Thebans, the very people whom he sought to tyrannize.

The first sign of Spartan failure came in 378 B.C. after an unprovoked attack on Athens. The enraged Athenians created the Second Athenian Confederacy, a federation of states to guarantee the Greeks their rights under the Common Peace (see Map 3.5). Thebes joined Athens, and the two fought Sparta until 371 B.C. Owing to its growing fear of Theban might, Athens made a separate peace with Sparta. Left alone, Thebes defended itself until later that year, when the brilliant Theban general Epaminondas routed the Spartan army on the small plain of Leuctra.

The defeat of the once-invincible Spartans stunned the Greeks, who wondered how Thebes would use its victory. Epaminondas, also a gifted statesman, immediately grappled with the problem of how to translate military success into political reality. First, in a series of invasions

The Lion of Chaeronea   This stylized lion marks the mass grave of nearly three hundred elite Theban soldiers who valiantly died fighting the Macedonians at the Battle of Chaeronea. After the battle, when Philip II viewed the bodies of these brave troops, he said: "May those who suppose that these men did or suffered anything dishonorable perish wretchedly." *(Caroline Buckler)*

he eliminated Sparta as a major power and liberated Messenia. He concluded alliances with many Peloponnesian states but made no effort to dominate them. Steadfastly refusing to create a Theban empire, he instead sponsored federalism in Greece. He also threw his support behind the Common Peace. Although he made Thebes the leader of Greece from 371 to 362 B.C., other city-states and leagues were bound to Thebes only by voluntary alliances. By his insistence on the liberty of the Greeks, Epaminondas, more than any other person in Greek history, successfully blended the three concepts of hegemony, federalism, and the Common Peace. His premature death at the Battle of Mantinea in 362 B.C. put an end to his efforts, but not to these three political ideals. The question was whether anyone or any state could realize them all.

Philip and the Macedonian Ascendancy

While the Greek states exhausted one another in endless conflicts, a new and unlikely power rose in the north. In 359 B.C. Philip II, one of the most remarkable men in history, became king of Macedonia. Macedonia was by nature potentially strong. The land, extensive and generally fertile, bordered on the east by the Aegean Sea, nurtured a numerous and hardy population. Yet Macedonia was often distracted by foreign opportunists, the Athenians among them, and divided by internal dissension. Nevertheless, under a strong king Macedonia was a power to be reckoned with. Although the Greeks considered the Macedonians backward, Philip was a brilliant, cultured, and sometimes charming man. As a youth he spent several years in Thebes, when Epaminondas was at the height of his power. In Thebes Philip learned about Greek politics and observed the military innovations of Epaminondas. He also fully understood the strengths and needs of the Macedonians, whose devotion he won virtually on the day that he ascended the throne.

The young Philip, already a master of diplomacy and warfare, quickly saw Athens as the principal threat to Macedonia. Once he had secured the borders of Macedonia against barbarian invaders, he launched a series of military operations in the northwestern Aegean. Not only did he win rich territory, but he also slowly pushed the Athenians out of the region. Yet the Greeks themselves opened to him the road to ultimate victory in Greece. The opportunity came from still another internecine Greek conflict, the Sacred War of 356 to 346 B.C. The war broke out when the Phocians seized and plundered the sanctuary of Apollo at Delphi. Their sacrilege was openly condoned by Athens and Sparta. When the

Thebans and other Greeks failed to liberate Delphi, they invited Philip to intervene. He quickly crushed the Phocians in 346 B.C. and intimidated Athens and Sparta. Athens immediately made peace with him, and he returned to his ambitions in the northern Aegean.

One man in Athens, the orator and politician Demosthenes, concluded that Philip wanted not peace but the rule of all of Greece. He accused Philip of a war of aggression, against which he warned his countrymen and the rest of Greece. Conventional wisdom holds that Demosthenes was right, but careful examination of the treaty and subsequent events prove that Athens, not Philip, broke the peace. Others also saw Philip as a threat. A comic playwright used graveyard humor to depict one of Philip's ambassadors warning the Athenians:

Do you know that your battle will be with men
Who dine on sharpened swords,
And gulp burning firebrands for wine?
Then immediately after dinner the slave
Brings us dessert—Cretan arrows
Or pieces of broken spears.
We have shields and breastplates for
Cushions and at our feet slings and arrows,
And we are crowned with catapults.[5]

These dire predictions and the progress of Philip's military operations at last had their effect. Demosthenes persuaded the Athenians to make an alliance with Thebes, which also saw the Macedonian threat. In 338 B.C. the armies of Thebes and Athens met Philip's veterans at the Boeotian city of Chaeronea. There on one summer's day Philip's army won a hard-fought victory that gave him command of Greece and put an end to classical Greek freedom. Because the Greeks could not put aside their quarrels, they fell to an invader. Yet Philip was wise enough to retain much of what the fourth-century Greeks had achieved. Not opposed to the concepts of peace and federalism, he sponsored a new Common Peace in which all of Greece, except Sparta, was united in one political body under his leadership. Philip thus used the concepts of hegemony, the Common Peace, and federalism as tools of Macedonian domination. The ironic result was the end of the age of classical Greece.

Chapter Summary

Online Study Center   ACE the Test

- When the Greeks arrived in Hellas, how did they adapt themselves to their new landscape?
- After the Greeks had established the polis in which they lived their political and social lives, how did they shape it into its several historical forms?
- What major developments mark the Archaic Greek period in terms of spread of culture and the growth of cities?
- How did the Greeks develop their literature, philosophy, religion, and art, and how did war affect this intellectual and social process?
- How did the Greek city-states meet political and military challenges, and how did Macedonia become dominant?

The Greeks entered a land of mountains and small plains, which led them to establish small communities. Sometimes these small communities were joined together in kingdoms, most prominently the Minoan kingdom on the island of Crete and the Mycenaean kingdom on the mainland. Minoans and Mycenaeans used written records, and the fall of these kingdoms led writing to disappear for centuries, a period known as the Greek Dark Age (1100–800 B.C.).

Even though kingdoms collapsed, Greek culture continued to spread, and more independent communities were formed. Such a community, called a polis, developed social and political institutions. Some were democracies, in which government was shared among all citizens, which meant adult free men. Other Greeks established smaller governing bodies of citizens, called oligarchs, who directed the political affairs of all.

During the Archaic Age (800–500 B.C.) Greeks colonized much of the Mediterranean, establishing cities in Asia Minor, southern Italy, Sicily, and southern France. This brought them into contact with many other peoples, and also spread Greek culture widely. During this period Sparta and Athens became the most important polises.

Sparta and Athens joined together to fight the Persian Empire, but later turned against one another in the Peloponnesian War (431–404 B.C.). During this time of warfare, Athenian leaders turned their city into an architectural showplace, supporting the creation of buildings and statues that are still prized. Playwrights presented tragedies and comedies that dealt with basic issues of life. Life for the men in Athens who were citizens revolved around public political assemblies, while for women it revolved around the household, for Athenian thinkers regarded women as inferior and did not think they should have a public role. Both women and men took part in ceremonies honoring gods and goddesses, though some men, most prominently the philosophers Plato and Aristotle, developed ideas about the universe and the place of humans in it that did not involve the gods.

The Greeks destroyed a good deal of their flourishing world in a series of wars. Despite their political advances, they never really learned how to routinely live peacefully with one another. Their disunity allowed for the rise of Macedonia under the leadership of King Philip II, a brilliant military leader.

Key Terms

Aegean basin	federalism
Minoan	oikist
Mycenaean	homosocial
Linear B	deme
polis	boule
acropolis	ecclesia
hoplites	Delian League
monarchy	hetairai
tyranny	pornoi
democracy	Common Peace
oligarchy	hegemony
isonomia	

Online Study Center   Improve Your Grade Flashcards

Suggested Reading

Blundell, Sue. *Women in Ancient Greece.* 1995. An accessible overview of the lives of Greek women.

Boardman, John. *The Greeks Overseas.* 2001. Provides a masterful examination of Greek expansion into the Mediterranean.

Buckler, John. *Aegean Greece in the Fourth Century B.C.* 2003. Treats in detail the history of this very influential century.

Burford, Alison. *Land and Labor in the Greek World.* 1993. Covers the entire topic of agriculture, from tools to practices of land use.

Burkert, Walter. *Greek Religion.* 1987. The authoritative study of ancient religious beliefs, with much material from the sources.

Cartledge, Paul. *The Spartans: The World of the Warrior Heroes of Ancient Greece.* 2002. Tells the story of the rise and fall of Sparta in a lively book designed for a general audience, and assesses the Spartans' legacy to Western culture.

Cohen, David. *Law, Sexuality, and Society: The Enforcement of Morals in Classical Athens.* 1992. Examines the social and legal context of adultery, same-sex relations, and other types of sexual conduct.

Fisher, N. R. E. *Slavery in Ancient Greece.* 1993. A brief analysis of the wide variety of situations faced by Greek slaves.

Gotshalk, R. R. *Homer and Hesiod, Myth and Philosophy.* 2000. Provides a good account of these authors' poetry and their purpose.

Hansen, Mogens Herman. *Polis: An Introduction to the Ancient Greek City-State.* 2006. A thorough introduction to the development and organization of Greek city-states, including famous examples such as Athens and Sparta and lesser-known ones.

Patterson, Cynthia B. *The Family in Greek History.* 2001. Treats the public and private relations of the family, which were interconnected.

Roberts, Jennifer Tolbert. *Athens on Trial: The Antidemocratic Tradition in Western Thought.* 1996. Discusses the antidemocratic tradition in Western thought from its origin in reactions to Athenian democracy to the present.

Thomas, Carol G. *Myth Becomes History.* 1993. An excellent treatment of early Greece and modern historical attitudes toward it.

Winkler, John J. *The Constraints of Desire.* 1989. Examines the anthropology of sex and gender in ancient Greece.

Notes

John Buckler is the translator of all uncited quotations from a foreign language in Chapters 1–6.

1. J. M. Edmonds, *Greek Elegy and Iambus* (Cambridge, Mass.: Harvard University Press, 1931), I.70, frag. 10.
2. Thucydides, *History of the Peloponnesian War* 1.23.
3. Ibid., 7.87.6.
4. Aristotle, *Generation of Animals,* trans. A. L. Peck. Loeb Classics (Cambridge, Mass.: Harvard University Press, 1943), IV, vi, 460.
5. J. M. Edmonds, *The Fragments of Attic Comedy* (Leiden: E. J. Brill, 1971), 2.366–369, Mnesimachos frag. 7.

The Great Plague at Athens, 430 B.C.

In 430 B.C. many of the people of Attica sought refuge in Athens to escape the Spartan invasion. The overcrowding of people, the lack of proper sanitation, and the scarcity of clean water exposed the huddled population to virulent disease. Under these conditions, a severe plague attacked the crowded masses. The great historian Thucydides lived in Athens at the time and contracted the disease himself. He was one of the fortunate people who survived the ordeal. For most people, however, the disease proved fatal. Thucydides left a vivid description of the nature of the plague and of people's reaction to it.

People in perfect health suddenly began to have burning feelings in the head; their eyes became red and inflamed; inside their mouths there was bleeding from the throat and tongue, and the breath became unnatural and unpleasant. The next symptoms were sneezing and hoarseness of voice, and before long the pain settled on the chest and was accompanied by coughing. Next the stomach was affected with stomach-aches and with vomitings of every kind of bile that has been given a name by the medical profession, all this being accompanied by great pain and difficulty. In most cases there were attacks of ineffectual retching, producing violent spasms; this sometimes ended with this stage of the disease, but sometimes continued long afterwards. Externally the body was not very hot to the touch, nor was there any pallor: the skin was rather reddish and livid, breaking out into small pustules and ulcers. But inside there was a feeling of burning, so that people could not bear the touch even of the lightest linen clothing, but wanted to be completely naked, and indeed most of all would have liked to plunge into cold water. Many of the sick who were uncared for actually did so, plunging into the water-tanks in an effort to relieve a thirst which was unquenchable; for it was just the same with them whether they drank much or little. Then all the time they were afflicted with insomnia and the desperate feeling of not being able to keep still.

In the period when the disease was at its height, the body, so far from wasting away, showed surprising powers of resistance to all the agony, so that there was still some strength left on the seventh or eighth day, which was the time when, in most cases, death came from the internal fever. But if people survived this critical period, then the disease descended to the bowels, producing violent ulceration and uncontrollable diarrhoea, so that most of them died later as a result of the weakness caused by this. For the disease, first settling in the head, went on to affect every part of the body in turn, and even when people escaped its worst effects, it still left its traces on them by fastening upon the extremities of the body. It affected the genitals, the fingers, and the toes, and many of those who recovered lost the use of these members; some, too, went blind. There were some also who, when they first began to get better, suffered from a total loss of memory, not knowing who they were themselves and being unable to recognize their friends.

Words indeed fail one when one tries to give a general picture of this disease; and as for the suffering of individuals, they seemed almost beyond the capacity of human nature to endure. Here in particular is a point where the plague showed itself to be something quite different from ordinary diseases: though there were many dead bodies lying about unburied, the birds and animals that eat human flesh either did not come near them or, if they did taste the flesh, died of it afterwards. Evidence for this may be found in the fact that there was a complete disappearance of all birds of prey: they were not to be seen either around the bodies or anywhere else. But dogs, being domestic animals, provided the best opportunity of observing this effect of the plague.

These, then, were the general features of the disease, though I have omitted all kinds of peculiarities which occurred in various individual cases. Meanwhile, during all this time there was no serious outbreak of any of the usual kinds of illness; if any such cases did occur, they ended in the plague. Some died in neglect, some in spite of every possible care being taken of them. As for a recognized method of treatment, it would be true to say that no such thing existed; what did good in some cases did harm in others. Those with naturally strong constitutions were no better able than the weak to resist the disease, which carried away all alike, even those who were treated and dieted with the greatest care. The most terrible thing of all was the despair into which people fell when they realized that they had caught the plague. Terrible, too, was the sight of people dying like sheep through having caught the disease as a result of nursing others. This indeed caused more deaths than anything else. For when people were afraid to visit the sick, then they died with no one to look after them. Indeed, there were many houses in which all the inhabitants perished through lack of attention. When, on the other hand, they did visit the sick, they lost their own lives, and this was particularly true of those who made it a point of honor to act properly. Such people felt ashamed to think of their own safety and went into their friends' houses at times when even the members of the household were so overwhelmed by the weight of their calamities that they had actually given up the usual practice of making laments for the dead. Yet still the ones who felt most pity for the sick and the dying were those who had had the plague themselves and had recovered from it. They knew what it was like and at the same time felt themselves to be safe, for no one caught the disease twice, or, if he did, the second attack was never fatal. . . .

A factor that made matters much worse than they were already was the removal of people from the country into the city, and this particularly affected the newcomers. There were no houses for them, and, living as they did during the hot season in badly ventilated huts, they died like flies. The bodies of the dying were heaped one on top of the other, and half-dead creatures could be seen staggering about in the streets or flocking around the fountains in their desire for water.

The catastrophe was so overwhelming that people, not knowing what would happen next to them, became indifferent to every rule of religion

Coin depicting the god Asclepius, represented by a snake, putting an end to urban plague. *(Bibliothèque nationale de France)*

and law. Athens owed to the plague the beginnings of a state of unprecedented lawlessness. People now began openly to venture on acts of self-indulgence which before then they used to keep in the dark. Thus they resolved to spend their money quickly and to spend it on pleasure, since money and life alike seemed equally ephemeral. As for what is called honor, no one showed himself willing to abide by its laws, so doubtful was it whether one would survive to enjoy the name for it. It was generally agreed that what was both honorable and valuable was the pleasure of the moment and everything that might conceivably contribute to that pleasure. No fear of god or law of man had a restraining influence. As for the gods, it seemed to be the same thing whether one worshiped them or not, when one saw the good and the bad dying indiscriminately. As for offenses against human law, no one expected to be punished. Instead, everyone felt that already a far heavier sentence had been passed on him and was hanging over him, and that before the time for its execution arrived, it was only natural to get some pleasure out of life.

This, then, was the calamity that fell upon Athens, and the times were hard indeed, with people dying inside the city and the land outside being laid waste.

Questions for Analysis

1. What does this account of the plague say about human nature when put in an extreme crisis?

2. Does popular religion offer any solace during such a catastrophe?

3. How did public laws and customs cope with such a disaster?

Source: R. Warner, trans., *Thucydides, History of the Peloponnesian War* (Penguin Classics, 1954), pp. 152–156. Translation copyright © Rex Warner, 1954. Introduction and Appendices copyright © M. I. Finley, 1972. Reproduced by permission of Penguin Books Ltd.

Tetrapylon of Aphrodisias. This monumental gate celebrates the beautiful and rich city of Aphrodisias in modern Turkey. *(John Buckler)*

THE HELLENISTIC WORLD, 336–146 B.C.

Two years after his conquest of Greece, Philip II of Macedon fell victim to an assassin's dagger. Philip's twenty-year-old son, historically known as Alexander the Great (r. 336–323 B.C.), assumed the Macedonian throne. This young man, one of the most remarkable personalities of Western civilization, was to have a profound impact on history. By overthrowing the Persian Empire and by spreading *Hellenism*—Greek culture, language, thought, and way of life—as far as India, Alexander was instrumental in creating a new era, traditionally called **Hellenistic** to distinguish it from the Hellenic. As a result of Alexander's exploits, the individualistic and energetic culture of the Greeks came into intimate contact with the venerable older cultures of the Near East.

Alexander and the Great Crusade

• *Why did Alexander launch his massive attack on the Persian Empire? Did he have a pressing reason to take such a huge risk?*

In 336 B.C. Alexander inherited not only Philip's crown but also his policies. After his victory at Chaeronea, Philip had organized the states of Greece into a huge league under his leadership and announced to the Greeks his plan to lead them and his Macedonians against the Persian Empire. Fully intending to carry out Philip's designs, Alexander proclaimed to the Greek world that the invasion of Persia was to be a great crusade, a mighty act of revenge for the Persian invasion of Greece in 480 B.C. It would also be the means by which Alexander would create an empire of his own in the East.

Despite his youth, Alexander was well prepared to lead the attack. Philip had groomed his son to become king and had given him the best education possible. In 334 B.C. Alexander led an army of Macedonians and Greeks into Asia Minor. With him went a staff of philosophers and poets, scientists whose job it was to map the country and study strange animals and plants, and the historian Callisthenes, who was to write an

Online Study Center

This icon will direct you to interactive activities and study materials on the website **college.hmco.com/pic/mckaywest9e**

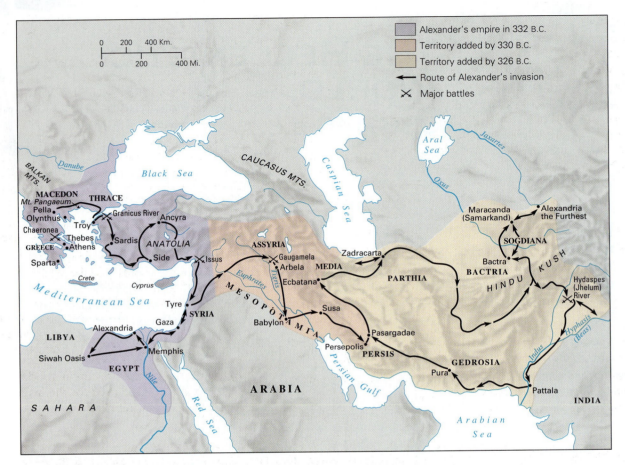

MAP 4.1 Alexander's Conquests   This map shows the course of Alexander's invasion of the Persian Empire and the speed of his progress. More important than the great success of his military campaigns was his founding of Hellenistic cities in the East.

Online Study Center   **Improve Your Grade** Interactive Map: Conquests of Alexander the Great

account of the campaign. Alexander intended not only a military campaign but also an expedition of discovery.

In the next three years Alexander won three major battles at the Granicus River, Issus, and Gaugamela. As Map 4.1 shows, these battle sites stand almost as road signs marking his march to the East. When Alexander reached Egypt, he quickly seized the land, honored the priestly class, and was proclaimed pharaoh, the legitimate ruler of the country. He next marched to the oasis of Siwah, west of the Nile Valley, to consult the famous oracle of Zeus-Amon. No one will ever know what the priest told him, but henceforth Alexander considered himself the son of Zeus. Next he marched into western Asia, where at Gaugamela he defeated the Persian army. After this victory the principal Persian capital of Persepolis easily fell

to him. There he performed a symbolic act of retribution by burning the buildings of Xerxes, the invader of Greece. In 330 B.C. he took Ecbatana, the last Persian capital, and pursued the Persian king to his death.

The Persian Empire had fallen, and the war of revenge was over, but Alexander had no intention of stopping. He dismissed his Greek troops but permitted many of them to serve on as mercenaries. Alexander then began his personal odyssey. With his Macedonian soldiers and Greek mercenaries, he set out to conquer the rest of Asia. He plunged deeper into the East, into lands completely unknown to the Greek world. It took his soldiers four additional years to conquer Bactria and the easternmost parts of the now-defunct Persian Empire, but still Alexander was determined to continue his march.

In 326 B.C. Alexander crossed the Indus River and entered India. There, too, he saw hard fighting, and finally at the Hyphasis River his troops refused to go farther. Alexander was enraged by the mutiny, for he believed he was near the end of the world. Nonetheless, the army stood firm, and Alexander relented. Still eager to explore the limits of the world, Alexander turned south to the Arabian Sea. Though the tribes in the area did not oppose him, he waged a bloody, ruthless, and unnecessary war against them. After reaching the Arabian Sea and turning west, he led his army through the grim Gedrosian Desert. The army suffered fearfully, and many soldiers died along the way; nonetheless, in 324 B.C. Alexander reached his camp at Susa. The great crusade was over, and Alexander himself died the next year in Babylon.

Alexander's Legacy

Alexander so quickly became a legend during his lifetime that he still seems superhuman. That alone makes a reasoned interpretation of him very difficult. Some historians have seen him as a high-minded philosopher, and none can deny that he possessed genuine intellectual gifts. Others, however, have portrayed him as a bloody-minded autocrat, more interested in his own ambition than in any philosophical concept of the common good. Alexander is the perfect example of the need for the historian to interpret the known facts carefully.

Chronology

340–262 B.C.	Rise of Epicurean and Stoic philosophies
336–324 B.C.	Alexander's "Great Crusade"
330–200 B.C.	Establishment of new Hellenistic cities
326–146 B.C.	Spread of Hellenistic commerce from the western Mediterranean to India
323–301 B.C.	Wars of Alexander's successors; establishment of the Hellenistic monarchies
310–212 B.C.	Scientific developments in mathematics, astronomy, and physics
305–146 B.C.	Growth of mystery religions
301–146 B.C.	Flourishing of the Hellenistic monarchies

Alexander at the Battle of Issus   At left, Alexander the Great, bareheaded and wearing a breast-plate, charges King Darius, who is standing in a chariot. The moment marks the turning point of the battle, as Darius turns to flee from the attack. (*National Museum, Naples/Alinari/Art Resource, NY*)

The historical record shows that Alexander in a drunken brawl murdered the friend who had saved his life at the Battle of the Granicus River. Alexander also used his power to have several other trusted officials, who had done nothing to offend him, assassinated. Other uglier and grimmer facts argue against the view that Alexander was a humane and tolerant man. In eastern Iran and India he savagely and unnecessarily slaughtered peoples whose only crime was their desire to be left in peace.

The only rationale to support those who see Alexander as a philosopher-king comes from a banquet held in 324 B.C. at the end of his career of carnage. This event is very important for a variety of reasons. It came immediately on the heels of a major Macedonian mutiny. The veteran and otherwise loyal Macedonians resented Alexander's new policy of giving high offices to Persians, people whom they had conquered after great suffering. Alexander realized that his Macedonians were too few to administer his new empire and that he needed the ability and experience of the Persians. As a gesture of reconciliation and to end the mutiny, Alexander named the entire Macedonian army his kinsmen and held a vast banquet to heal wounds. He reserved the place of honor for the Macedonians, giving the Persians and others positions of lesser status. At the banquet Alexander offered a public prayer for harmony and partnership between the Macedonians and the Persians, and this prayer has been interpreted as an expression of deep philosophical views. (See the feature "Listening to the Past: Alexander and the Brotherhood of Man" on pages 120–121.) But far from representing an ideal desire for the brotherhood of man, the gesture was a blatant call for Macedonians and Persians to form a superior union for the purpose of ruling his new empire. The concepts of universal harmony and the brotherhood of man became common during the Hellenistic period, but they were the creations of talented philosophers, not the battle-hardened king of Macedonia.

Alexander was instrumental in changing the face of politics in the eastern Mediterranean. His campaign swept away the Persian Empire, which had ruled the East for over two hundred years. In its place he established a Macedonian monarchy.

More important in the long run was his founding of new cities and military colonies, which scattered Greeks and Macedonians throughout the East. Thus the practical result of Alexander's campaign was to open the East to the tide of Hellenism.

● *What was Alexander's legacy to the Hellenistic world, and what did it mean to Greeks and Easterners alike? What were its effects on this new world?*

The Political Legacy

In 323 B.C. Alexander the Great died at the age of thirty-two. The main question at his death was whether his vast empire could be held together. A major part of his legacy is what he had not done. Although he fathered a successor while in Bactria, his son was an infant at Alexander's death. The child was too young to assume the duties of kingship and was cruelly murdered. That meant that Alexander's empire was a prize for the taking by the strongest of his generals. Within a week of Alexander's death a round of fighting began that was to continue for forty years. No single Macedonian general was able to replace Alexander as emperor of his entire domain. In effect, the strongest divided it among themselves. By 263 B.C. three officers had split the empire into large monarchies (see Map 4.2). Antigonus Gonatas became king of Macedonia and established the Antigonid dynasty, which ruled until the Roman conquest in 168 B.C. Ptolemy, son of Lagus, made himself king of Egypt, and his descendants, the Ptolemies, assumed the powers and position of pharaohs. Seleucus, founder of the Seleucid dynasty, carved out a kingdom that stretched from the coast of Asia Minor to India. In 263 B.C. Eumenes, the Greek ruler of Pergamum, a city in western Asia Minor, won his independence from the Seleucids and created the Pergamene monarchy. Though the Seleucid kings soon lost control of their easternmost provinces, Greek influence in this area did not wane. In modern Turkestan and Afghanistan another line of Greek kings established the kingdom of Bactria and even managed to spread their power and culture into northern India.

The political face of Greece itself changed during the Hellenistic period. The day of the polis was over; in its place rose leagues of city-states. The two most powerful and extensive were the Aetolian League in western and central Greece and the Achaean League in the Peloponnesus. Once-powerful city-states like Athens and Sparta sank to the level of third-rate powers.

The political history of the Hellenistic period was dominated by the great monarchies and the Greek leagues. The political fragmentation and incessant warfare that

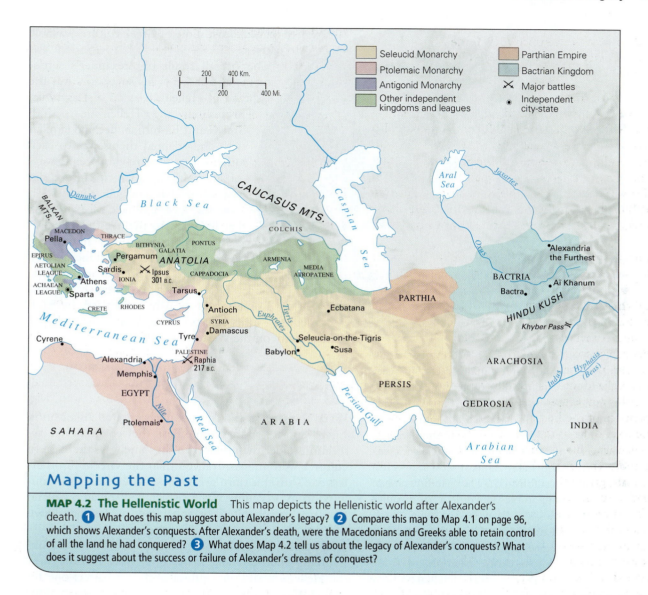

Mapping the Past

MAP 4.2 The Hellenistic World   This map depicts the Hellenistic world after Alexander's death. ❶ What does this map suggest about Alexander's legacy? ❷ Compare this map to Map 4.1 on page 96, which shows Alexander's conquests. After Alexander's death, were the Macedonians and Greeks able to retain control of all the land he had conquered? ❸ What does Map 4.2 tell us about the legacy of Alexander's conquests? What does it suggest about the success or failure of Alexander's dreams of conquest?

marked the Hellenic period continued on an even wider and larger scale during the Hellenistic period. Never did the Hellenistic world achieve political stability or lasting peace. Hellenistic kings never forgot the vision of Alexander's empire, spanning Europe and Asia, secure under the rule of one man. Try though they did, they were never able to re-create it. In this respect Alexander's legacy fell not to his generals but to the Romans of a later era.

The Cultural Legacy

As Alexander waded ever deeper into the East, distance alone presented him with a serious problem: how was he to retain contact with the Greek world behind him?

Communications were vital, for he drew supplies and reinforcements from Greece and Macedonia. Alexander had to be sure that he was never cut off and stranded far from the Mediterranean world. His solution was to plant cities and military colonies in strategic places. In these settlements Alexander left Greek mercenaries and Macedonian veterans who were no longer up to active campaigning. Besides keeping the road open to the West, these settlements served the purpose of dominating the countryside around them.

Their military significance apart, Alexander's cities and colonies became powerful instruments in the spread of Hellenism throughout the East. The Roman biographer Plutarch described Alexander's achievement in glowing

Tazza Farnese This exquisite detail of a cameo bowl from Hellenistic Egypt dates from about 125 B.C. The figure on the left represents the Nile pouring out the horn of plenty. The other figures represent the deities who gave Egypt its great riches. *(G. Dagli-Orti/ The Art Archive)*

terms: "Having founded over 70 cities among barbarian peoples and having planted Greek magistracies in Asia, Alexander overcame its wild and savage way of life."[1] Alexander had indeed opened the East to an enormous wave of immigration, and his successors continued his policy by inviting Greek colonists to settle in their realms. For seventy-five years after Alexander's death, Greek immigrants poured into the East. At least 250 new Hellenistic colonies were established. The Mediterranean world had seen no comparable movement of peoples since the days of Archilochus (see page 66), when wave after wave of Greeks had turned the Mediterranean basin into a Greek-speaking region.

One concrete and almost exotic example of these trends comes from the newly discovered Hellenistic city of Ay Khanoum. Situated on the borders of Russia and Afghanistan and not far from China, the city was predominately Greek. It had the typical Greek trappings of a gymnasium, various temples, and administration buildings. It was not, however, purely Greek. It also contained a temple and artistic remains that prove that the Greeks and the natives had already embraced aspects of each other's religions. One of the most curious discoveries was a long inscription written in Greek verse by Clearchus, a pupil of Aristotle. The inscription, carved in stone, was set up in a public place for all to see. Clearchus had simply copied the precepts of famous Greeks. The inscription was philosophy for the common people, a contribution to popular culture. It provided the Greeks with a link to their faraway homeland. It was also an easy

way to make at least some of Greek culture available to natives.

The overall result of Alexander's settlements and those of his successors was the spread of Hellenism as far east as India. Throughout the Hellenistic period, Greeks and Easterners became familiar with and adapted themselves to each other's customs, religions, and ways of life. Although Greek culture did not completely conquer the East, it gave the East a vehicle of expression that linked it to the West. Hellenism became a common bond among the East, peninsular Greece, and the western Mediterranean. This pre-existing cultural bond was later to prove supremely valuable to Rome—itself heavily influenced by Hellenism—in its efforts to impose a comparable political unity on the Western world.

The Spread of Hellenism

When the Greeks and Macedonians entered Asia Minor, Egypt, and the more remote East, they encountered civilizations older than their own. In some ways the Eastern cultures were more advanced than the Greek, in others less so. Thus this third great tide of Greek migration differed from preceding waves, which had spread over land that was uninhabited or inhabited by less-developed peoples.

What did the Hellenistic monarchies offer Greek immigrants politically and materially? More broadly, how did Hellenism and the cultures of the East affect one another? What did the meeting of East and West entail for the history of the world?

• *How far did Hellenism spread, and what effect did it have on both Greeks and those unfamiliar with Greek culture?*

Cities and Kingdoms

One of the major developments of these new kingdoms was the resurgence of monarchy, which had many repercussions. For most Greeks, monarchs were something out of the heroic past, something found in Homer's *Iliad* but not in daily life. Furthermore, most Hellenistic kingdoms embraced numerous different peoples who had little in common. Hellenistic kings thus needed a new political concept to unite them. One solution was the creation of a ruler cult that linked the king's authority with that of the gods. Thus, royal power had divine approval and was meant to create a political and religious bond between the kings and their subjects. These deified kings were not considered gods as mighty as Zeus or Apollo, and the new ruler cults probably made little religious impact on those ruled. Nonetheless, the ruler cult was an easily understandable symbol of unity within the kingdom.

Hellenistic kingship was hereditary, which gave women who were members of royal families more power than any women in democracies, in which citizenship was limited to men. Wives of kings and queen mothers had influence over their husbands and sons, and a few women ruled in their own right when there was no male heir.

Although Alexander's generals created huge kingdoms, the concept of monarchy, even when combined with the ruler cult, never replaced the ideal of the polis. Consequently, the monarchies never won the deep emotional loyalty that Greeks had once felt for the polis. Hellenistic kings needed large numbers of Greeks to run their kingdoms. Otherwise royal business would grind to a halt, and the conquerors would soon be swallowed up

by the far more numerous conquered population. Obviously, then, the kings had to encourage Greeks to immigrate and build new homes. The Hellenistic kings thus confronted the problem of making life in the new monarchies resemble the traditional Greek way of life. Since Greek civilization was urban, the kings continued Alexander's policy of establishing cities throughout their kingdoms in order to entice Greeks to immigrate. Yet the creation of these cities posed a serious political problem that the Hellenistic kings failed to solve.

To the Greeks civilized life was unthinkable without the polis, which was far more than a mere city. The Greek polis was by definition **sovereign**—an independent, autonomous state run by its citizens, free of any outside power or restraint. Hellenistic kings, however, refused to grant sovereignty to their cities. In effect, these kings willingly built cities but refused to build a polis.

Hellenistic monarchs gave their cities all the external trappings of a polis. Each had an assembly of citizens, a council to prepare legislation, and a board of magistrates to conduct the city's political business. Yet, however similar to the Greek polis they appeared, these cities could not engage in diplomatic dealings, make treaties, pursue their own foreign policy, or wage their own wars. None could govern its own affairs without interference from

The Main Street of Pergamum   No matter where in old Greece they had come from, all Greeks would immediately feel at home walking along this main street in Pergamum. They would all see familiar sights. To the left is the top of the theater where they could watch the plays of the great dramatists, climb farther to the temple, and admire the fortifications on the right. (*Faith Cimok, Turkey*)

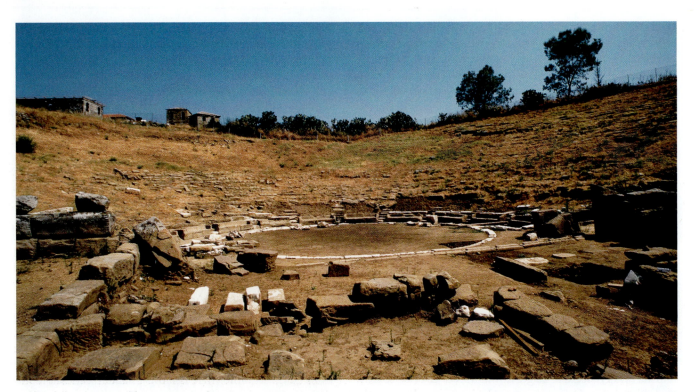

Theater of Stratos Excavation of this theater in Stratos, a major city in northwestern Greece, began only in 1994. Not a city in the mainstream of Greek affairs, Stratos nevertheless shared the love and appreciation of the arts that stamped all of Greek culture. Even in its partially excavated state, the theater boasts the remains of a stone building in the foreground, the orchestra, and behind it the seats. Beyond its many architectural refinements, the theater is of interest because most Greek plays were staged in small theaters such as this. *(John Buckler)*

the king, who, even if he stood in the background, was the real sovereign. In the eyes of the king the cities were important parts of the kingdom, but the welfare of the whole kingdom came first. The cities had to follow royal orders, and the king often placed his own officials in the cities to see that his decrees were followed.

A new Hellenistic city differed from a Greek polis in other ways as well. The Greek polis had one body of law and one set of customs. In the Hellenistic city Greeks represented an elite citizen class. Natives and non-Greek foreigners who lived in Hellenistic cities usually possessed lesser rights than Greeks and often had their own laws. In some instances this disparity spurred natives to assimilate Greek culture in order to rise politically and socially. The Hellenistic city was not homogeneous and could not spark the intensity of feeling that marked the polis.

An excellent example of this process comes from the city of Pergamum in northwestern Anatolia. Previously an important strategic site, its new Greek rulers turned it into a magnificent city complete with all the typical buildings of the polis. They built the usual government buildings, gymnasia, and baths. They founded a library second only to that in Alexandria. They erected temples to the traditional deities, but they also built an imposing temple to the Egyptian gods. Furthermore, Jews established a synagogue in the city. Especially in the agora Greeks and indigenous people met to conduct business and to learn about each other. Greeks felt as though they were at home, and the evolving culture mixed Greek and local elements.

The old Greek cities of Asia Minor actually, if unintentionally, aided this development by maintaining and spreading traditions that went back for centuries. They served as models for the new foundations by providing a rich legacy of culture and tradition. They shone with such physical beauty in buildings and arts that through their very charm they made Hellenism attractive. They also represented a gracious style of civilized life. In their very combination of refinement, sophistication, and elegance they inspired imitation of the best in Greek culture. All new cities saw in them a link between the past and the blossoming future.

In many respects the Hellenistic city resembled a modern city. It was a cultural center with theaters, temples, and libraries. It was a seat of learning, home of poets, writers, teachers, and artists. It was a place where people could find amusement. The Hellenistic city was also an economic center that provided a ready market for grain and produce raised in the surrounding countryside. The city was an emporium, scene of trade and manufacturing. In short, the Hellenistic city offered cultural and economic opportunities but did not foster a sense of united, integrated enterprise.

There were no constitutional links between city and king. The city was simply his possession. Hellenistic kings tried to make the kingdom the political focus of citizens' allegiance. If the king could secure the frontiers of his kingdom, he could give it a geographical identity. He could then hope that his subjects would direct their primary loyalty to the kingdom rather than to a particular city. However, the kings' efforts to fix their borders led only to sustained warfare. Boundaries were determined by military power, and rule by force became the chief political principle of the Hellenistic world.

Though Hellenistic kings never built a true polis, that does not mean that their urban policy failed. Rather, the Hellenistic city was to remain the basic social and political unit throughout the Hellenistic world until the sixth century A.D. Cities were the chief agents of Hellenization, and their influence spread far beyond their walls. These cities formed a broader cultural network in which Greek language, customs, and values flourished. Roman rule in the Hellenistic world would later be based on this urban culture, which facilitated the rise and spread of Christianity. In broad terms, Hellenistic cities were remarkably successful.

Men and Women in Hellenistic Monarchies

If the Hellenistic kings failed to satisfy the Greeks' political yearnings, they nonetheless succeeded in giving them unequaled economic and social opportunities. The ruling dynasties of the Hellenistic world were Macedonian, and Greeks filled all important political, military, and diplomatic positions. They constituted an upper class that sustained Hellenism in the barbarian East. Besides building Greek cities, Hellenistic kings offered Greeks land and money as lures to further immigration.

The opening of the East offered ambitious Greeks opportunities for well-paying jobs and economic success. The Hellenistic monarchy, unlike the Greek polis, did not depend solely on its citizens to fulfill its political needs. Talented Greek men could expect to rise quickly in the government bureaucracy. Appointed by the king, these administrators did not have to stand for election each year, as had many officials of a Greek polis. Since they held their jobs year after year, they had ample time to evolve new administrative techniques. Naturally, they became more efficient than the amateur officials common in Hellenic Greek city-states. The needs of the Hellenistic monarchy and the opportunities it offered thus gave rise to a professional corps of Greek administrators.

Greeks and Macedonians also found ready employment in the armies and navies of the Hellenistic monarchies. Alexander had proved the Greco-Macedonian style of warfare to be far superior to that of other peoples, and Alexander's successors, themselves

Marital Advice This small terra-cotta sculpture is generally seen as a mother advising her daughter, a new bride. Such intimate scenes of ordinary people were popular in the Hellenistic world, in contrast to the idealized statues of gods and goddesses of the classical period. (*British Museum/Michael Holford*)

experienced officers, realized the importance of trained Greek and Macedonian soldiers. Moreover, Hellenistic kings were extremely reluctant to arm the native populations or to allow them to serve in the army, fearing military rebellions among their conquered subjects. The result was the emergence of professional armies and navies consisting entirely of Greeks and Macedonians.

Greeks were able to dominate other professions as well. The kingdoms and cities recruited Greek writers and artists to create Greek literature, art, and culture on Asian soil. Architects, engineers, and skilled craftsmen found their services in great demand because of the building policies of the Hellenistic monarchs. If Hellenistic kingdoms were to have Greek cities, those cities needed Greek buildings—temples, porticoes, gymnasia, theaters, fountains, and houses. Architects and engineers were sometimes commissioned to design and build whole cities, which they laid out in checkerboard fashion and filled with typical Greek buildings. An enormous wave of construction took place during the Hellenistic period.

The Great Altar of Pergamum A new Hellenistic city needed splendid art and architecture to prove its worth in Greek eyes. The king of Pergamum ordered the construction of this monumental altar, now in Berlin. The scenes depict the mythical victory of the Greek gods over the Giants, who symbolize barbarism. The altar served the propaganda purpose of celebrating the victory of Hellenism over the East. *(Bildarchiv Preussischer Kulturbesitz/Art Resource, NY)*

Increased physical and social mobility benefited some women as well as men. More women learned to read than before, and they engaged in occupations in which literacy was beneficial, including care of the sick. During the Hellenistic period some women took part in commercial transactions. They still lived under legal handicaps; in Egypt, for example, a Greek woman needed a male guardian to buy, sell, or lease land, to borrow money, and to represent her in other transactions. Yet often such a guardian was present only to fulfill the letter of the law. The woman was the real agent and handled the business being transacted.

Online Study Center **Improve Your Grade**
Primary Source: Gender in the Hellenistic Age: A Woman of Intellectual Merit

Because real power in the Hellenistic world was held by monarchs, the political benefits of citizenship were much less than they had been in the classical period. The diminished importance of citizenship meant that it was awarded more easily. Even women sometimes received honorary citizenship from foreign cities because of aid given in times of crisis. Few women achieved these honors, however, and those who did were from the upper classes.

Despite the opportunities they offered, the Hellenistic monarchies were hampered by their artificial origins. Their failure to win the political loyalty of their Greek subjects and their policy of wooing Greeks with lucrative positions encouraged a feeling of uprootedness and self-serving individualism among Greek immigrants. Once a Greek man had left home to take service with, for instance, the army or the bureaucracy of the Ptolemies, he had no incentive beyond his pay and the comforts of life

in Egypt to keep him there. If the Seleucid king offered him more money or a promotion, he might well accept it and take his talents to Asia Minor. Why not? In the realm of the Seleucids he, a Greek, would find the same sort of life and environment that the kingdom of the Ptolemies had provided him. Thus professional Greek soldiers and administrators were very mobile and apt to look to their own interests, not their kingdom's.

One result of these developments was that the nature of warfare changed. Except in the areas of Greece and to some extent Macedonia, Hellenistic soldiers were professionals. Unlike the citizen hoplites of classical Greece, these men were regular soldiers capable of intricate maneuvers. Hellenistic kings paid them well, often giving them land as an incentive to remain loyal. Only in Macedonia among the kingdoms was there a national army that was devoted to its land, homes, and monarchy. The loyalty, skill, and bravery of Macedonian soldiers made them the most formidable in the Hellenistic world.

As long as Greeks continued to replenish their professional ranks, the kingdoms remained strong. In the process they drew an immense amount of talent from the Greek peninsula, draining the vitality of the Greek homeland. However, the Hellenistic monarchies could not keep recruiting Greeks forever, in spite of their wealth and willingness to spend lavishly. In time the huge surge of immigration slowed greatly. Even then the Hellenistic monarchs were reluctant to recruit Easterners to fill posts normally held by Greeks. The result was at first the stagnation of the Hellenistic world and finally, after 202 B.C., its collapse in the face of the young and vigorous Roman republic.

Greeks and Easterners

Because they understood themselves to be "the West," Greeks generally referred to Egypt and what we now call the Near East collectively as "the East." Many historians have continued that usage, seeing the Hellenistic period as a time when Greek and "Eastern" cultures blended to some degree. Eastern civilizations were older than Greek, and the Greeks were a minority outside of Greece. Hellenistic monarchies were remarkably successful in at least partially Hellenizing Easterners and spreading a uniform culture throughout the East, a culture to which Rome eventually fell heir. The prevailing institutions, laws, and language of the East became Greek. Indeed, the Near East had seen nothing comparable since the days when Mesopotamian culture had spread throughout the area.

Yet the spread of Greek culture was wider than it was deep. At best it was a veneer, thicker in some places than

Cultural Blending Ptolemy V, a Macedonian by birth and the Hellenistic king of Egypt, dedicated this stone to the Egyptian sacred bull of the Egyptian god Ptah. Nothing here is Greek or Macedonian, a sign that the conquered had, in some religious and ceremonial ways, won over their conquerors. *(Egyptian Museum, Cairo)*

in others. Hellenistic kingdoms were never entirely unified in language, customs, and thought. Greek culture took firmest hold along the shores of the Mediterranean, but farther east, in Persia and Bactria, it was less strong. The principal reason for this curious phenomenon is that Greek culture generally did not extend far beyond the reaches of the cities. Many urban residents adopted the aspects of Hellenism that they found useful, but others in the countryside generally did not embrace it wholly.

The Ptolemies in Egypt provide an excellent example of this situation. They made little effort to spread Greek culture, and unlike other Hellenistic kings they were not city builders. Indeed, they founded only the city of Ptolemais near Thebes. At first the native Egyptian population, the descendants of the pharaoh's people, retained their traditional language, outlook, religion, and way of life. Initially untouched by Hellenism, the natives continued to be the foundation of the state: they fed it by their labor in the fields and financed its operations with their taxes.

Under the pharaohs talented Egyptians had been able to rise to high office, but during the third century B.C. the Ptolemies cut off this avenue of advancement. Instead of converting the natives to Hellenism, the Ptolemies tied them to the land even more tightly, making it nearly impossible for them to leave their villages. The bureaucracy of the Ptolemies was ruthlessly efficient, and the native population was viciously and cruelly exploited. Even in times of hardship the king's taxes came first, although payment might mean starvation for the natives. Their desperation was summed up by one Egyptian, who scrawled the warning: "We are worn out; we will run away."[2] To many Egyptians revolt or a life of brigandage was certainly preferable to working the land under the harsh Ptolemies.

Throughout the third century B.C. the Greek upper class in Egypt had little to do with the native population. Many Greek bureaucrats established homes in Alexandria and Ptolemais, where they managed finances, served as magistrates, and administered the law. Other Greeks settled in military colonies and supplied the monarchy with fighting men. But in the second century B.C. Greeks and native Egyptians began to intermarry and mingle their cultures. The language of the native population influenced Greek, and many Greeks adopted the Egyptian religion and ways of life. Simultaneously, natives adopted Greek customs and language and began to play a role in the administration of the kingdom and even to serve in the army. While many Greeks and Egyptians remained aloof from each other, the overall result was the evolution of a widespread Greco-Egyptian culture.

Meanwhile the Seleucid kings established many cities and military colonies in western Asia Minor and along the banks of the Tigris and Euphrates Rivers in order to nurture a vigorous and large Greek population. Especially important to the Seleucids were the military colonies, for they needed Greeks to defend the kingdom. The Seleucids had no elaborate plan for Hellenizing the native population, but the arrival of so many Greeks was bound to have an impact. Seleucid military colonies were generally founded near native villages, thus exposing rural residents to all aspects of Greek life. Many Easterners found Greek political and cultural forms attractive and imitated them. In Asia Minor and Syria, for instance, numerous native villages and towns developed along Greek lines,

and some of them became Hellenized cities. Farther east, the Greek kings who replaced the Seleucids in the third century B.C. spread Greek culture to their neighbors, even into the Indian subcontinent.

For non-Greeks the prime advantage of Greek culture was its very pervasiveness. The Greek language became the common speech of Egypt and the Near East. A common dialect called **koine** even influenced the speech of peninsular Greece itself. Greek became the speech of the royal court, bureaucracy, and army. It was also the speech of commerce: anyone who wanted to compete in business had to learn it. As early as the third century B.C. some Greek cities were giving citizenship to Hellenized natives.

The vast majority of Hellenized Easterners, however, took only the externals of Greek culture while retaining the essentials of their own ways of life. Though Greeks and Easterners adapted to each other's ways, there was never a true fusion of cultures. Nonetheless, each found useful things in the civilization of the other, and the two fertilized each other. This fertilization, this mingling of Greek and Eastern elements, is what makes Hellenistic culture unique and distinctive.

Hellenism and the Jews

A prime illustration of cultural mingling is the impact of Greek culture on the Jews. At first, Jews in Hellenistic cities were treated as resident aliens. As they grew more numerous, they received permission to form a political corporation, a **politeuma,** which gave them a great deal of autonomy. The Jewish politeuma, like the Hellenistic city, obeyed the king's commands, but there was virtually no royal interference with the Jewish religion. Indeed, the Greeks were always reluctant to tamper with anyone's religion. Antiochus III (ca 242–187 B.C.), for instance, recognized that most Jews had become loyal subjects, and he treated them with great kindness and dignity. In his efforts to solidify his empire he endorsed their religious customs and ensured their political rights. He went so far as to deny any uninvited foreigner permission to enter the temple at Jerusalem. As a result, Hellenism and Judaism usually met on friendly terms. Only the Seleucid king Antiochus Epiphanes (175–ca 164 B.C.) tried to suppress the Jewish religion in Judaea. He did so not because he hated the Jews (who were a small part of his kingdom), but because he was trying to unify his realm culturally to meet the threat of Rome. To the Jews he extended the same policy that he applied to all subjects. Apart from this instance, Hellenistic Jews suffered no official religious persecution. Some Jews were given the right to become full citizens of Hellenistic cities, but few exercised that right. Citizenship would have allowed them to vote in the assembly and serve as magistrates, but it would also have obliged them to worship the gods of the city—a practice few Jews chose to follow.

Jews living in Hellenistic cities often embraced a good deal of Hellenism. So many Jews learned Greek, especially in Alexandria, that the Old Testament was translated into Greek and services in the synagogue came to be conducted in Greek. Jews often took Greek names, used Greek political forms, adopted Greek practice by forming their own trade associations, put inscriptions on graves as the Greeks did, and much else. Yet no matter how much of Greek culture or its externals Jews borrowed, they normally remained attached to their religion.

The Economic Scope of the Hellenistic World

Alexander's conquest of the Persian Empire not only changed the political face of the ancient world but also brought the East fully into the sphere of Greek economics. Yet the Hellenistic period did not see a revolution in the way people lived and worked. The material demands of Hellenistic society remained as simple as those of Athenian society in the fifth century B.C. Clothes and furniture were essentially unchanged, as were household goods, tools, and jewelry. The real achievement of Alexander and his successors was linking East and West in a broad commercial network. The spread of Greeks throughout the Near East and Egypt created new markets and stimulated trade. The economic unity of the Hellenistic world, like its cultural bonds, would later prove valuable to the Romans.

• *What economic effect did Alexander's opening of the East have on Greeks and Easterners? Did close economic contact bring them together in any significant way?*

Commerce

Alexander's conquest of the Persian Empire had immediate effects on trade. In the Persian capitals Alexander had found vast sums of gold, silver, and other treasure. This wealth financed the creation of new cities, the building of roads, and the development of harbors. Most of the great monarchies coined their money on the Attic standard, which meant that much of the money used in Hellenistic kingdoms had the same value. Traders were less in need of moneychangers than in the days when each major power coined money on a different standard. As a result of Alexander's conquests, geographical knowledge of the East increased dramatically, making the East far better known to the Greeks than previously. The Greeks spread their law and methods of transacting business. Whole new fields lay open to Greek merchants, who eagerly took advantage of the new opportunities. Commerce itself was a leading area where Greeks and non-Greeks met on grounds of common interest. In bazaars, ports, and trading centers Greeks learned of Eastern customs and traditions while spreading knowledge of their own culture.

The Seleucid and Ptolemaic dynasties traded as far afield as India, Arabia, and sub-Saharan Africa. Overland trade with India and Arabia was conducted by caravan and was largely in the hands of Easterners. The caravan trade never dealt in bulk items or essential commodities; only luxury goods could be transported in this very expensive fashion. Once the goods reached the Hellenistic monarchies, Greek merchants took a hand in the trade.

Essential to the caravan trade from the Mediterranean to Afghanistan and India were the northern route to Dura on the Euphrates River and the southern route through Arabia. The desert of Arabia may seem at first unlikely and inhospitable terrain for a line of commerce, but to the east of it lies the plateau of Iran, from which trade routes stretched to the south and still farther east to China. Commerce from the East arrived at Egypt and the excellent harbors of Palestine, Phoenicia, and Syria. From these ports goods flowed to Greece, Italy, and Spain. The backbone of this caravan trade was the camel—shaggy, ill-tempered, but durable. Only its mother could consider it beautiful, but the camel is a splendid beast of burden, and few other animals could have endured the harsh heat and aridity of the caravan routes.

Over the caravan routes traveled luxury goods that were light, rare, and expensive. In time these luxury items became more of a necessity than a luxury. In part this development was the result of an increased volume of trade. In the prosperity of the period more people could afford to buy gold, silver, ivory, precious stones, spices, and a host of other easily transportable goods. Perhaps the most prominent goods in terms of volume were tea and silk. Indeed, the trade in silk later gave the major route the name the **Great Silk Road,** for not only was this route prominent in antiquity, but it also was used in early modern times. In return the Greeks and Macedonians sent east manufactured goods, especially metal weapons, cloth, wine, and olive oil. Although these caravan routes can trace their origins to earlier times, they became far more prominent in the Hellenistic period.

Harbor and Warehouse at Delos During the Hellenistic period Delos became a thriving trading center. From Delos cargoes were shipped to virtually every part of the Mediterranean. *(Rolf Richardson/age fotostock/superstock)*

Business customs developed and became standardized, so that merchants from different nationalities communicated in a way understandable to all of them.

The durability and economic importance of the caravan routes are amply demonstrated by the fact that the death of Alexander, the ensuing wars of his successors, and the triumph of the Parthians in Iran had little effect on the trade. Numerous mercantile cities grew up along these distant tracks, places where native cultures combined with both Greco-Macedonian and Eastern cultures to create local but nonetheless cosmopolitan societies.

The commercial contacts brought people together, even if sometimes indirectly. The merchants and the caravan cities were links in a chain that reached from the Mediterranean Sea at least to Afghanistan and Iran. Ideas passed along these routes as easily as, and probably more comfortably than, gold and ivory.

The Ptolemies discovered how to use monsoon winds to establish direct contact with India. One hardy merchant has left a firsthand account of sailing this important maritime route:

Hippalos, the pilot, observing the position of the ports and the conditions of the sea, first discovered how to sail across the ocean. Concerning the winds of the ocean in this region, when with us the Etesian winds begin, in India a wind between southwest and south, named for Hippalos, sets in from the open sea. From then until now some mariners set forth from Kanes and some from the Cape of Spices. Those sailing to Dimurikes [in southern India] throw the bow of the ship farther out to sea. Those bound for Barygaza and the realm of the Sakas [in northern India] hold to the land no more than three days; and if the wind remains favorable, they hold the same course through the outer sea, and they sail along past the previously mentioned gulfs.[3]

Although this sea route never replaced overland caravan traffic, it kept direct relations between East and West alive, stimulating the exchange of ideas as well as goods.

More economically important than this exotic trade were commercial dealings in essential commodities like raw materials, grain, and industrial products. The Hellenistic monarchies usually raised enough grain for their own needs as well as a surplus for export. For the cities of Greece and the Aegean this trade in grain was essential, because many of them could not grow enough. Fortunately for them, abundant wheat supplies were available nearby in Egypt and in the Crimea in southern Russia.

Most trade in bulk commodities was seaborne, and the Hellenistic merchant ship was the workhorse of the day. The merchant ship had a broad beam and relied on sails for propulsion. It was far more seaworthy than the contemporary warship, which was long, narrow, and built for speed. A small crew of experienced sailors could handle the merchant vessel easily. Maritime trade provided opportunities for workers in other industries and trades: sailors, shipbuilders, dockworkers, accountants, teamsters, and pirates. Piracy was always a factor in the Hellenistic world and remained so until Rome extended its power throughout the East.

The Greek cities paid for their grain by exporting olive oil and wine. When agriculture and oil production developed in Syria, Greek products began to encounter competition from the Seleucid monarchy. Later in the Hellenistic period, Greek oil and wine found a lucrative market in Italy. Another significant commodity was fish, which for export was either salted, pickled, or dried. This trade was doubly important because fish provided poor people with an essential element of their diet. Salt too was often imported, and there was some very slight trade in salted meat, which was a luxury item. Far more important was the trade in honey, dried fruit, nuts, and vegetables. Of raw materials, wood was high in demand, but little trade occurred in manufactured goods.

Slaves were a staple of Hellenistic trade. The wars provided prisoners for the slave market; to a lesser extent, so did kidnapping and capture by pirates. The number of slaves involved cannot be estimated, but there is no doubt that slavery flourished. Both old Greek states and new Hellenistic kingdoms were ready slave markets, as was Rome when it emerged triumphant from the Second Punic War (see pages 141–142).

Throughout the Mediterranean world slaves were almost always in demand. Only the Ptolemies discouraged both the trade and slavery itself, and they did so only for economic reasons. Their system had no room for slaves, who would only have competed with free labor. Otherwise slave labor was to be found in the cities and temples of the Hellenistic world, in the factories and fields, and in the homes of wealthier people. In Italy and some parts of the East, slaves performed manual labor for large estates and worked the mines. They were vitally important to the Hellenistic economy.

Industry

Although demand for goods increased during the Hellenistic period, no new techniques of production appear to have developed. The discoveries of Hellenistic mathematicians and thinkers failed to produce any significant corresponding technological development. Manual labor, not machinery, continued to turn out the raw materials and few manufactured goods the Hellenistic world used. Human labor was so cheap and so abundant that kings had no incentive to encourage the invention and manufacture of laborsaving machinery.

The Ptolemies ran their gold mines along the same harsh lines. One historian gives a grim picture of the miners' lives:

The kings of Egypt condemn [to the mines] those found guilty of wrong-doing and those taken prisoner in war, those who were victims of false accusations and were put into jail because of royal anger. . . . The condemned—and they are

very many—all of them are put in chains, and they work persistently and continually, both by day and throughout the night, getting no rest, and carefully cut off from escape.[4]

The Ptolemies even condemned women and children to work in the mines. All of them—men, women, and boys—worked until they died.

Apart from gold and silver, which were used primarily for coins and jewelry, iron was the most important metal and saw the most varied use. Even so, the method of its production never became very sophisticated. The Hellenistic Greeks did manage to produce a low-grade steel by adding carbon to iron.

Pottery remained an important commodity, and most of it was made locally. The pottery used in the kitchen, the coarse ware, did not change at all. Fancier pots and bowls, decorated with a shiny black glaze, came into use during the Hellenistic period. This ware originated in Athens, but potters in other places began to imitate its style, heavily cutting into the Athenian market. In the second century B.C. a red-glazed ware, often called Samian, burst on the market and soon dominated it. Athens still held its own, however, in the production of fine pottery. Despite the change in pottery styles, the method of production of all pottery, whether plain or fine, remained essentially unchanged.

Agriculture

Hellenistic kings paid special attention to agriculture. Much of their revenue was derived from the produce of royal land, rents paid by the tenants of royal land, and taxation of agricultural land. Some Hellenistic kings even sought out and supported agricultural experts. The Ptolemies, for instance, sponsored experiments on seed grain, selecting seeds that seemed hardy and productive and trying to improve their characteristics. Indeed, the Ptolemies made the greatest strides in agriculture, and the reason for their success was largely political. Egypt had a strong tradition of central authority dating back to the pharaohs, which the Ptolemies inherited and tightened. They could decree what crops Egyptian farmers would plant and what animals would be raised, and they had the power to carry out their commands. The Ptolemies recognized the need for well-planned and constant irrigation, and much native labor went into the digging and maintenance of canals and ditches. The Ptolemies also reclaimed a great deal of land from the desert, including the Fayum, a dried lake bed near the Nile.

The centralized authority of the Ptolemies explains how agricultural advances occurred at the local level in

Egypt. But such progress was not possible in any other Hellenistic monarchy. Despite royal interest in agriculture and a more studied approach to it in the Hellenistic period, there is no evidence that agricultural productivity increased. Whether Hellenistic agricultural methods had any influence on Eastern practices is unknown.

Hellenistic Intellectual Advances

Although it was once fashionable to criticize the intellectual achievements of the Hellenistic period in contrast to those of the classical period, the critics themselves deserve the criticism. The peoples of the Hellenistic era took the ideas and ideals of the classical Greeks and advanced them to new heights. Their achievements created the intellectual and religious atmosphere that deeply influenced Roman thinking and eventually the religious thought of liberal Judaism and early Christianity. Far from being stagnant, this was a period of vigorous growth. Its achievements included new religious ideas, startling innovations in philosophy, and remarkable advances in science and medicine.

• *How did Hellenistic scientific, philosophical, medical, and religious advances affect the lives of men and women in this period?*

Religion in the Hellenistic World

In religion the most significant new ideas were developed outside of Greece. At first the Hellenistic period saw the spread of Greek religious cults throughout the Near East and Egypt. When Hellenistic kings founded cities, they also built temples and established new cults and priesthoods for the old Olympian gods. The new cults enjoyed the prestige of being the religion of the conquerors, and they were supported by public money. The most attractive aspects of the Greek cults, at least to the Greeks, were their rituals and festivities, as they were at least familiar. Greek cults sponsored literary, musical, and athletic contests, which were staged in beautiful surroundings among impressive Greek buildings. In short, the cults offered bright and lively entertainment, both intellectual and physical. They fostered Greek culture and traditional sports and thus were a splendid means of displaying Greek civilization outside of Greece.

Despite various advantages, Greek cults suffered from some severe shortcomings. They were primarily concerned with ritual. Participation in the civic cults did not even require belief (see pages 82–83). On the whole, the civic cults neither appealed to religious emotions nor embraced matters such as sin and redemption. Although the new civic cults were lavish in pomp and display, they could not satisfy deep religious feelings or spiritual yearnings.

Greeks increasingly sought solace from other sources. Educated and thoughtful people turned to philosophy as a guide to life, while others turned to superstition, magic, or astrology. Still others might shrug and speak of **Tyche,** which meant "Fate" or "Chance" or "Doom"—a capricious and sometimes malevolent force.

Hellenistic kings made no effort to spread Greek religion among their Eastern subjects. The Greeks always considered religion a matter best left to the individual. Greek cults were attractive only to those socially aspiring individuals who adopted Greek culture for personal advancement. Otherwise Easterners were little affected by Greek religion. Nor did native religions suffer from the arrival of the Greeks. Some Hellenistic kings limited the power of native priesthoods, but they also subsidized some indigenous cults with public money. Alexander the

Hellenistic Magic   This magical text, written in Greek and Egyptian, displays a snake surrounding the magical incantation. The text is intentionally obscure. *(British Library)*

Hellenistic Mystery Cult   The scene depicts part of the ritual of initiation into the cult of Dionysus. The young woman here has just completed the ritual. She now dances in joy as the official with the sacred staff looks on. *(Scala/Art Resource, NY)*

Great actually reinstated several cults that the Persians had suppressed.

Beginning in the second century B.C., some individuals were increasingly attracted to new **mystery religions,** so called because they featured a body of ritual not to be divulged to anyone not initiated into the cult. These new mystery cults incorporated aspects of both Greek and Eastern religions and had broad appeal for people who yearned for personal immortality. Since the Greeks were already familiar with old mystery cults, such as the Eleusinian mysteries in Attica, the new cults did not strike them as alien or barbarian. Familiar, too, was the concept of preparation for an initiation. Devotees of the Eleusinian mysteries and other such cults had to prepare themselves mentally and physically before entering the gods' presence. Thus the mystery cults fit well with Greek usage.

The new religions enjoyed one tremendous advantage over the old Greek mystery cults. Whereas old Greek mysteries were tied to particular places, such as Eleusis, the new religions spread throughout the Hellenistic world. People did not have to undertake long and expensive pilgrimages just to become members of the religion. In that sense the mystery religions came to the people, for temples of the new deities sprang up wherever Greeks lived.

The mystery religions all claimed to save their adherents from the worst that fate could do and promised life for the soul after death. They all had a single concept in common: the belief that by the rites of initiation devotees became united with a god, usually male, who had himself died and risen from the dead. The sacrifice of the god and his victory over death saved the devotee from eternal death. Similarly, all mystery religions demanded a period of preparation in which the convert strove to become holy, that is, to live by the religion's precepts. Once aspirants had prepared themselves, they went through an initiation in which they learned the secrets of the religion. The initiation was usually a ritual of great emotional intensity, symbolizing the entry into a new life.

The mystery religions that took the Hellenistic world by storm were the Egyptian cults of Serapis and Isis. Serapis, who was invented by King Ptolemy, combined elements of the Egyptian god Osiris with aspects of the Greek gods Zeus, Pluto (the prince of the underworld), and Asclepius. Serapis was believed to be the judge of souls, who rewarded virtuous and righteous people with eternal life. Like Asclepius, he was a god of healing. Serapis became an international god, and many Hellenistic Greeks thought of him as Zeus. Associated with Isis and Serapis was Anubis, the old Egyptian god who, like Charon in the Greek pantheon, guided the souls of initiates to the realm of eternal life.

The cult of Isis enjoyed even wider appeal than that of Serapis. Isis, wife of Osiris, claimed to have conquered Tyche and promised to save any mortal who came to her. She became the most important goddess of the Hellenistic world, and her worship was very popular among women. Her priests claimed that she had bestowed on humanity the gift of civilization and founded law and literature. She was the goddess of marriage, conception, and childbirth, and like Serapis she promised to save the souls of her believers.

Mystery religions took care of the big things in life, but many people resorted to ordinary magic for daily matters. When a cat walked across their path, they stopped until someone else had passed by them. Or they could throw three rocks across the road. A snake in the house presented a complex problem. If only an ordinary snake, people immediately invoked the god Sabazios, who was associated with the afterlife. They were on safer ground if the snake was red. They then established a shrine on the spot. People often purified their houses to protect them from Hecate, a sinister goddess associated with magic and witchcraft. People could even resurrect the dead by commanding, "I adjure you, life spirit walking in the air: enter this body, inspire it, empower it, resurrect it by the power of the eternal god, and make it walk about in this place: for I am he who acts through the power of Thayth, the holy god."[5] Many people had dreams that only seers and augurs could interpret. Today psychiatrists do the same thing for exorbitant fees. Some of these practices are familiar today because some old fears are still alive.

Philosophy and the People

Philosophy during the Hellenic period was the exclusive province of the wealthy, for only they had leisure enough to pursue philosophical studies. During the Hellenistic period, however, philosophy reached out to touch the lives of more men and women than ever before. The reasons for this development were several. Since the ideal of the polis had declined, politics no longer offered people an intellectual outlet. Moreover, much of Hellenistic life, especially in the new cities of the East, seemed unstable and without venerable traditions. Greeks were far more mobile than they had ever been before, but their very mobility left them feeling uprooted. Many people in search of something permanent, something unchanging in a changing world, turned to philosophy. Another reason for the increased influence of philosophy was the decline of traditional religion and a growing belief in Tyche. To protect against the worst that Tyche could do, many Greeks looked to philosophy.

Philosophers themselves became much more numerous, and several new schools of philosophical thought emerged. In spite of their many differences, the major branches of philosophy agreed on the necessity of making people self-sufficient. They all recognized the need to equip men and women to deal successfully with Tyche. The major schools of Hellenistic philosophy all taught that people could be truly happy only when they had turned their backs on the world and focused full attention on one enduring thing. They differed chiefly on what that enduring thing was.

Two significant philosophies caught the minds and hearts of contemporary Greeks and some Easterners, as well as some later Romans. The first was **Epicureanism,** a practical philosophy of serenity in an often tumultuous world. Epicurus (340–270 B.C.) founded this school of philosophy based on scientific theories. Accepting Democritus's idea that the universe is composed of indestructible particles, Epicurus put forward a naturalistic theory of the universe. Although he did not deny the existence of the gods, he taught that they had no effect on human life. The essence of Epicurus's belief was that the principal good of human life is pleasure, which he defined as the absence of pain. He was not advocating drunken revels or sexual dissipation, which he thought actually caused pain. Instead, Epicurus concluded that any violent emotion is undesirable and advocated mild self-discipline. Even poverty he considered good, as long as people had enough food, clothing, and shelter. Epicurus also taught that individuals can most easily attain peace and serenity by ignoring the outside world and looking into their personal feelings and reactions. Thus Epicureanism led to quietism.

Epicureanism taught its followers to ignore politics and issues, for politics led to tumult, which would disturb the soul. Although the Epicureans thought that the state originated through a social contract among individuals, they did not care about the political structure of the state. They were content to live in a democracy, oligarchy, monarchy, or any other form of government, and they never speculated about the ideal state. Their ideals stood outside all political forms.

Tyche   This statue depicts Tyche as the bringer of bounty to people. Some Hellenistic Greeks worshiped Tyche in the hope that she would be kind to them. Philosophers tried to free people from her whimsies. Others tried to placate her. *(Faith Cimok, Turkey)*

Online Study Center Improve Your Grade
Primary Source: A Materialistic Ethic: The Principal Doctrines of Epicureanism

Opposed to the passivity of the Epicureans, Zeno (335–262 B.C.), a philosopher from Citium in Cyprus, advanced a different concept of human beings and the universe. Zeno first came to Athens to form his own school, the Stoa, named after the building where he preferred to teach. **Stoicism** became the most popular Hellenistic philosophy and the one that later captured the mind of Rome. Zeno and his followers considered nature an expression of divine will; in their view, people could be happy only when living in accordance with nature. They stressed the unity of man and the universe, stating that all men were brothers and were obliged to help one another. Stoicism's science was derived from Heraclitus, but its broad and warm humanity was the work of Zeno and his followers.

Unlike the Epicureans, the Stoics taught that people should participate in politics and worldly affairs. Yet this idea never led to the belief that individuals should try to change the order of things. Time and again the Stoics used the image of an actor in a play: the Stoic plays an assigned part but never tries to change the play. To the Stoics the important question was not whether they achieved anything, but whether they lived virtuous lives. In that way they could triumph over Tyche, for Tyche could destroy achievements but not the nobility of their lives.

Though the Stoics evolved the concept of a world order, they thought of it strictly in terms of the individual. Like the Epicureans, they were indifferent to specific political forms. They believed that people should do their duty to the state in which they found themselves. The universal state they preached about was ethical, not political. The Stoics' most significant practical achievement was the creation of the concept of **natural law.** The Stoics concluded that as all men were brothers, partook of divine reason, and were in harmony with the universe, one law—a part of the natural order of life—governed them all.

The Stoic concept of a universal state governed by natural law is one of the finest heirlooms the Hellenistic world passed on to Rome. The Stoic concept of natural law, of one law for all people, became a valuable tool when the Romans began to deal with many different peoples with different laws. The ideal of the universal state gave the Romans a rationale for extending their empire to the farthest reaches of the world. The duty of individuals to their fellows served the citizens of the Roman Empire as the philosophical justification for doing their duty. In this respect, too, the real fruit of Hellenism was to ripen only under the cultivation of Rome.

Hellenistic Science

The area in which Hellenistic culture achieved its greatest triumphs was science. The most notable of the Hellenistic astronomers was Aristarchus of Samos (ca 310–230 B.C.), who was educated in Aristotle's school. Aristarchus concluded that the sun is far larger than the earth and that the stars are enormously distant from the earth. He argued against Aristotle's view that the earth was the center of the universe. Instead, Aristarchus propounded the **heliocentric theory**—that the earth and planets revolve around the sun. His work is all the more impressive because he lacked even a rudimentary telescope. Aristarchus had only the human eye and brain, but they were more than enough.

Unfortunately, Aristarchus's theories did not persuade the ancient world. In the second century A.D. Claudius Ptolemy, a mathematician and astronomer in Alexandria, accepted Aristotle's theory of the earth as the center of the universe, and this view prevailed for fourteen hundred years. Aristarchus's heliocentric theory lay dormant until resurrected in the sixteenth century by the brilliant Polish astronomer Nicolaus Copernicus.

In geometry Hellenistic thinkers discovered little that was new, but Euclid (ca 300 B.C.), a mathematician who lived in Alexandria, compiled a valuable textbook of existing knowledge. His book *The Elements of Geometry* has exerted immense influence on Western civilization, for it rapidly became the standard introduction to geometry. Generations of students, from the Hellenistic period to the present, have learned the essentials of geometry from it.

The greatest thinker of the Hellenistic period was Archimedes (ca 287–212 B.C.), a native of Syracuse. (See the feature "Individuals in Society: Archimedes and the Practical Application of Science.") As both a theoretical and a practical scientist, he was far more interested in pure mathematics than in useful inventions. His mathematical research, covering many fields, was his greatest contribution to Western thought. In his book *On Plane Equilibriums* Archimedes dealt for the first time with the basic principles of mechanics, including the principle of the lever. He once said that if he were given a lever and a suitable place to stand, he could move the world. With his treatise *On Floating Bodies* he founded the science of hydrostatics. He concluded that whenever a solid floats in a liquid, the weight of the solid is equal to the weight of the liquid displaced. He made his discovery when he stepped into a bath. He noticed that the weight of his body displaced a volume of water equal to it. He immediately ran outside shouting, "Eureka, eureka" (I have found it, I have found it).[6]

Archimedes was willing to share his work with others, among them Eratosthenes (285–ca 204 B.C.), a man of almost universal interests. From his native Cyrene in North Africa, Eratosthenes traveled to Athens, where he studied philosophy and mathematics. He refused to join any of the philosophical schools, for he was interested in too many things to follow any particular dogma. Around 245 B.C. King Ptolemy invited Eratosthenes to Alexandria. The Ptolemies had done much to make Alexandria an intellectual, cultural, and scientific center. Eratosthenes came to Alexandria to become librarian of the royal library, a position of great prestige. The library was a huge collection of Greek writings, including such classic works as the poems of Homer, the histories of Herodotus and Thucydides, and the philosophical works of Plato and Aristotle. The library became one of the foremost intellectual centers of the ancient world. Eratosthenes had the honor of becoming its head. While there he continued his mathematical work and by letter struck up a friendship with Archimedes.

Unlike Archimedes, Eratosthenes did not devote his life entirely to mathematics, although he never lost interest in it. He used mathematics to further the geographical studies for which he is most famous. He calculated the circumference of the earth geometrically, estimating it as about 24,675 miles. He was not wrong by much: the earth is actually 24,860 miles in circumference. Eratosthenes also concluded that the earth was a spherical globe, that the landmass was roughly four-sided, and that the land was surrounded by ocean. He discussed the shapes and sizes of land and ocean and the irregularities of the earth's surface. He drew a map of the earth and used his own system of explaining the divisions of the earth's landmass.

Online Study Center Improve Your Grade
Primary Source: The Genius of Hellenistic Science: Eratosthenes Computes the Earth's Circumference

Using geographical information gained by Alexander the Great's scientists, Eratosthenes tried to fit the East into Greek geographical knowledge. Although for some reason he ignored the western Mediterranean and Europe, he declared that a ship could sail from Spain either around Africa to India or directly westward to India. Not until the great days of Western exploration did sailors such as Vasco da Gama and Magellan actually prove Eratosthenes' theories. Like Eratosthenes, other Greek ge-

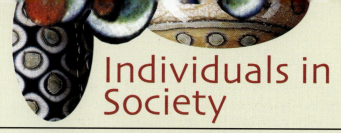

Individuals in Society

Archimedes and the Practical Application of Science

Throughout the ages generals have besieged cities to force them to surrender. Sieges were particularly hard and violent, bringing misery to soldiers and civilians alike. Between 213 and 211 B.C. the Roman general Marcellus laid close siege to the strongly walled city of Syracuse, the home of Archimedes. Not a soldier, Archimedes was the greatest scientist of his age. He towered above all others in abstract thought. The Roman siege challenged him to a practical response. Hiero, king of Syracuse and friend of Archimedes, turned to him for help.

The king persuaded Archimedes to prepare for him offensive and defensive engines to be used in every kind of warfare. These he had never used himself, because he spent the greater part of his life in freedom from war and amid the festal rites of peace. But at the present time his apparatus stood the Syracusans in good stead, and, with the apparatus, its fabricator. When, therefore, the Romans assaulted them by sea and land, the Syracusans were stricken dumb with terror. They thought that nothing could withstand so furious an onset by such forces.

Archimedes, however, began to ply his engines, and shot against the land forces of the attackers all sorts of missiles and immense masses of stones, which came down with incredible din and speed. Nothing whatever could ward off their weight, but they knocked down in heaps those who stood in their way, and threw their ranks into confusion. At the same time huge beams were suddenly projected over the ships from the walls, which sank some of them with great weights plunging down from on high. Others were seized at the prow by iron claws, or beaks like the beaks of cranes, drawn straight up into the air, and then plunged stern first into the depths, or were turned round and round by means of enginery within the city, and dashed upon the steep cliffs that jutted out beneath the wall of the city, with great destruction of the fighting men on board, who perished in the wrecks. Frequently, too, a ship would be lifted out of the water into mid-air, whirled here and there as it hung there, a dreadful spectacle, until its crew had been thrown out and hurled in all directions. Then it would fall empty upon the walls, or slip away from the clutch that had held it. As for the engine that Marcellus was bringing up on the bridge of ships, and which was called "sambuca" [large mechanically operated scaling ladders carried on ships]. While it was still some distance off in its approach to the wall, a stone of 500 pounds' weight was discharged at it, then a second and a third. Some of them, falling upon it with great noise and surge of wave, crushed the foundation of the engine, shattered its framework, and dislodged it from the platform, so that Marcellus, in perplexity, ordered his ships to sail back as fast as they could and his land forces to retire. . . .

Many of their ships, too, were dashed together, and they could not retaliate in any way upon their foes. For Archimedes had built most of his engines close behind the wall, and the Romans seemed to be fighting against the gods, now that countless mischiefs were poured out upon them from an invisible source.

At last the Romans became so fearful that whenever they saw a bit of rope or a stick of timber projecting a little over the wall, "There it is," they shouted, "Archimedes is training some engine upon us." They then turned their backs and fled. Seeing this, Marcellus desisted from all the fighting and assault, and thenceforth depended on a long siege.

Archimedes' mill. A slave turns a large cylinder fitted with blades to form a screw that draws water from a well.

(Courtesy, Soprintendenza Archeologica di Pompei. Photograph by Penelope M. Allison)

For all his genius, Archimedes did not survive the siege. His deeds of war done, he returned to his thinking and his mathematical problems, even with the siege still in the background. When Syracuse was betrayed to the Romans, soldiers streamed in, spreading slaughter and destruction throughout the city. A Roman soldier came upon Archimedes in his study and killed him outright, thus ending the life of one of the world's greatest thinkers.

Questions for Analysis

1. How did Archimedes' engines repulse the Roman attacks?
2. What effect did his weapons have on the Roman attackers?
3. What is the irony of Archimedes' death?

Source: Reprinted by permission of the publishers and the Trustees of the Loeb Classical Library™ from *Plutarch: Volume V,* Loeb Classical Library™ Volume 87, trans. Bernadotte Perrin (Cambridge, Mass.: Harvard University Press), 1917. The Loeb Classical Library™ is a registered trademark of the President and Fellows of Harvard College.

Online Study Center **Improve Your Grade**
Going Beyond Individuals in Society

Catapult This model shows a catapult as its crew would have seen it in action. The arrow was loaded on the long horizontal beam, its point fitting into the housing. There the torsion spring under great pressure released the arrow at the target, which could be some 400 yards away. *(Courtesy, Noel Kavan)*

ographers also turned their attention southward to Africa. During this period the people of the Mediterranean learned of the climate and customs of Ethiopia and gleaned some scant information about equatorial Africa.

For all of its speculation, Hellenistic science made an inestimable, if grim, contribution to practical life. The Greeks and Macedonians applied theories of mechanics to build siege machines, thus revolutionizing the art of warfare. In short, they invented the first effective artillery in Western history. Fully realizing the practical possibilities of these new machines, Philip of Macedonia introduced them to the broader world. The catapult became the first and most widely used artillery piece. The earliest catapults could shoot only large arrows and small stones. By the time Alexander the Great besieged Tyre in 332 B.C., his catapults threw stones big enough to knock down city walls. Generals soon realized that they could also hurl burning bundles over the walls to start fires in the city. To approach enemy town walls safely, engineers built siege towers, large wooden structures that served as artillery platforms, and put them on wheels so that soldiers could roll them up to the wall. Once there archers stationed on top of them swept the enemy's ramparts

with arrows, while other soldiers manning catapults added missile fire. Once the walls were cleared, soldiers from the towers swept over the enemy's ramparts and into the city. To aid the siege towers, generals added battering rams that consisted of long, stout shafts housed in reinforced shells. Inside the shell the crew pushed the ram up to the wall and then heaved the shaft against the wall. Rams proved even more effective than catapults in bringing down large portions of walls.

Right from the beginning Macedonian kings showed the way in the practical use of all these machines. There is no better example than Philip II's attack on Perinthos in 340 B.C.:

Philip launched a siege of Perinthos, advancing engines to the city and assaulting the walls in relays day after day. He built towers 120 feet tall that rose far above the towers of Perinthos. From their superior height he kept wearing down the besieged. He mined under the wall and also rocked it with battering-rams until he threw down a large section of it. The Perinthians fought stoutly and threw up a second wall. Philip rained down great destruction through his many and various arrow-shooting catapults. . . . Philip continually battered the walls with his rams and made breaches in them. With his arrow-firing catapults clearing the ramparts of defenders, he sent his soldiers in through the breaches in tight formation. He attacked with scaling-ladders the parts of the walls that had been cleared.[7]

For the Perinthians this grim story had a happy ending when their allies arrived to lift the siege. Hellenistic generals built larger, more complex, and more effective machines until no city was safe from them.

If these new engines made waging war more efficient, they also added to the misery of the people. War was no longer confined to the battlefield and fought between soldiers. Now the populations of whole cities feared for their lives. Survival of such a siege as that of Perinthos led to terror for the survivors. Many were killed in the slaughter and rape that generally came with the taking of the city. The survivors were often sold into slavery. War had come to embrace the whole population. Ironically, Hellenistic science, dedicated to improving human life, succeeded in making it more dangerous and horrible.

Despite its undeniable brilliance, Hellenistic science suffered from a remarkable weakness almost impossible for practical-minded Americans to understand. With the exception of artillery and a few other inventions, the Hellenistic people seldom turned discoveries to practical use. They generally preferred abundant slave labor to laborsaving machines. For them technology was a road not taken.

Hellenistic Medicine

The study of medicine flourished during the Hellenistic period, and Hellenistic physicians carried the work of Hippocrates into new areas. Herophilus, who lived in the first half of the third century B.C., worked at Alexandria and studied the writings of Hippocrates. He accepted Hippocrates' theory of the four humors and approached the study of medicine in a systematic, scientific fashion: he dissected dead bodies and measured what he observed. He discovered the nervous system and concluded that two types of nerves, motor and sensory, existed.

Herophilus also studied the brain, which he considered the center of intelligence, and discerned the cerebrum and cerebellum. His other work dealt with the liver, lungs, and uterus. His younger contemporary Erasistratus also conducted research on the brain and nervous system and improved on Herophilus's work. Erasistratus too followed in the tradition of Hippocrates and preferred to let the body heal itself by means of diet and air.

Both Herophilus and Erasistratus were members of the **Dogmatic school** of medicine at Alexandria. In this school speculation played an important part in research. So, too, did the study of anatomy. To learn more about human anatomy, Herophilus and Erasistratus dissected corpses and even vivisected criminals whom King Ptolemy contributed for the purpose. The practice of vivisection seems to have been short-lived, although dissection continued. Better knowledge of anatomy led to improvements in surgery. These advances enabled the Dogmatists to invent new surgical instruments and techniques.

In about 280 B.C. Philinus and Serapion, pupils of Herophilus, led a reaction against the Dogmatists. Believing that the Dogmatists had become too speculative, they founded the **Empiric school** of medicine at Alexandria. Claiming that the Dogmatists' emphasis on anatomy and physiology was misplaced, they concentrated instead on the observation and cure of illnesses. They also laid heavier stress on the use of drugs and medicine to treat illnesses. Heraclides of Tarentum (perhaps first century B.C.) carried on the Empiric tradition and dedicated himself to observation and use of medicines. He discovered the benefits of opium and worked with other drugs that relieved pain. He also steadfastly rejected the relevance of magic to drugs and medicines.

The Hellenistic world was also plagued by people who claimed to cure illnesses through incantations and magic. Their potions included such concoctions as blood from the ear of an ass mixed with water to cure fever, or the liver of a cat killed when the moon was waning and

An Unsuccessful Delivery   This funeral stele depicts a mother who has perhaps lost her own life as well as her baby's. Childbirth was the leading cause of death for adult women in antiquity, though funeral stele showing this are quite rare. Another of the few that do show death in childbirth bears the heartbreaking words attributed to the mother by her grieving family: "All my labor could not bring the child forth; he lies in my womb, among the dead." *(National Archaeological Museum, Athens/Archaeological Receipts Fund)*

preserved in salt. Broken bones could be cured by applying the ashes of a pig's jawbone to the break. The dung of a goat mixed with old wine was good for healing broken ribs. One charlatan claimed that he could cure epilepsy by making the patient drink spring water, drawn at night, from the skull of a man who had been killed but not cremated. These quacks even claimed that they could cure mental illness. The treatment for a person suffering from melancholy was calf dung boiled in wine. No doubt the patient became too sick to be depressed.

Quacks who prescribed such treatments were very popular but did untold harm to the sick and injured. They and greedy physicians also damaged the reputation of dedicated doctors who honestly and intelligently tried to heal and alleviate pain. The medical abuses that arose in the Hellenistic period were so flagrant that the Romans, who later entered the Hellenistic world, developed an intense dislike and distrust of physicians. The Romans considered the study of Hellenistic medicine beneath the dignity of a Roman, and even as late as the time of the Roman Empire, few Romans undertook the study of Greek medicine. Nonetheless, the work of men like Herophilus and Serapion made valuable contributions to the knowledge of medicine, and the fruits of their work were preserved and handed on to the West.

Chapter Summary

Online Study Center **ACE the Test**

- *Why did Alexander launch his massive attack on the Persian Empire? Did he have a pressing reason to take such a huge risk?*
- *What was Alexander's legacy to the Hellenistic world, and what did it mean to Greeks and Easterners alike? What were its effects on this new world?*
- *How far did Hellenism spread, and what effect did it have on both Greeks and those unfamiliar with Greek culture?*
- *What economic effect did Alexander's opening of the East have on Greeks and Easterners? Did close economic contact bring them together in any significant way?*
- *How did Hellenistic scientific, philosophical, medical, and religious advances affect the lives of men and women in this period?*

Although Alexander may not originally have intended to march all the way to the Indus Valley, he gained so much territory that he saw every reason to continue as far as possible. It was an almost foolhardy adventure, but it permanently changed the face of world history.

Alexander's legacy proved of essential importance to the future of the West. He brought the vital civilization of the Greeks into intimate contact with the older cultures of the East. He added enormously to Western knowledge of the culturally rich East. Neither he nor anyone else during these years brought unity to the East and West, but he at least guaranteed that they would henceforth live productive lives in the same world.

Most enduring of all, Alexander's work and that of his successors spread Hellenism far beyond its native soil. Even though it was superficial in some areas, it provided a common means of communication and shared values. The ideals and ideas of the West spread and blended with Eastern ideas and customs to create a whole new environment.

For ordinary men and women, the greatest practical boon of the Hellenistic adventure was economic. Trade connected the world on a routine basis. Economics brought people together just as surely as it brought them goods. By the end of the Hellenistic period, the ancient world had become far broader and more economically intricate than ever before.

Hellenistic achievements included intellectual advances as well as trade connections. Mystery religions, such as the worship of the goddess Isis, provided many people with answers to their questions about the meaning of life, while others turned to practical philosophies such as Stoicism for ethical guidance. Mathematicians and scientists developed theoretical knowledge and applied this to practical problems in geography, mechanics, and weaponry. Physicians also approached medicine in a systematic fashion, though many people relied on magic and folk cures for treatment of illness.

Key Terms

Hellenistic
sovereign
koine
politeuma
Great Silk Road
Tyche
mystery religions

Epicureanism
Stoicism
natural law
heliocentric theory
Dogmatic school
Empiric school

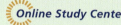 *Online Study Center*   **Improve Your Grade** Flashcards

Suggested Reading

Bosworth, A. B. *Conquest and Empire: The Reign of Alexander the Great.* 1988. Sets Alexander's career in a broad context.

Bowman, Alan K. *Egypt After the Pharaohs.* 1986. A readable account of the impact of the Greeks and Macedonians on Egyptian society.

Burkert, Walter. *Ancient Mystery Cults.* 1987. A brief comparative study of the rituals, membership, and organization of secret mystery cults of the ancient world, written by the foremost historian of Greek religion.

Cartledge, Paul. *Alexander the Great.* 2004. The story of Alexander's life and rise to power and of the impact of his conquests, by the chair of the classics department at Cambridge University.

Cohen, Getzel M. *The Hellenistic Settlements in Europe, the Islands, and Asia Minor.* 1996. A welcome contribution to the understanding of the impact of the Greeks on the world around them.

Lloyd, G. E. R. *Greek Science After Aristotle.* 1963. A good survey of Hellenistic science.

McKechnie, Paul. *Outsiders in the Greek Cities of the Fourth Century.* 1989. Provides an interesting study of the social dislocation of the Greeks in the time of Philip II and Alexander the Great.

Pomeroy, Sarah B. *Women in Hellenistic Egypt.* 1984. Studies women in the kingdom from which the most ancient evidence has survived.

Samuel, Alan E. *The Promise of the West.* 1988. Studies the connections among Greek, Roman, and Jewish culture and thought and their significance for Western history.

Sharples, R. W. *Stoics, Epicureans, Sceptics.* 1996. Provides a good synthesis of these three major branches of Hellenistic philosophy.

Shipley, Graham. *The Greek World After Alexander, 323–30 B.C.* 2000. A very thorough discussion of political, socioeconomic, intellectual, and cultural developments.

Vatai, F. L. *Intellectuals in Politics in the Greek World from Early Times to the Hellenistic Age.* 1984. A general treatment of the role of the intellectual in the classical and Hellenistic worlds.

Wallbank, F. W. *The Hellenistic World,* rev. ed. 1993. Examines political events, social systems, literature, science, and new religious movements.

Notes

1. Plutarch, *Moralia* 328E.
2. Quoted in W. W. Tarn and G. T. Griffith, *Hellenistic Civilizations,* 3d ed. (Cleveland and New York: Meridian Books, 1961), p. 199.
3. *Periplous of the Erythraian Sea* 57.
4. Diodorus 3.12.2–3.
5. G. Luck, *Arcana Mundi* (Baltimore: Johns Hopkins University Press, 2006), no. 23, p. 137.
6. Vitruvius, *On Architecture* 9 Preface, 10.
7. Diodorus 16.74.2.

Alexander and the Brotherhood of Man

One historical problem challenged historians throughout the twentieth century and has yet to be solved to everyone's satisfaction. After returning to Opis, north of Babylon in modern Iraq, Alexander found himself confronted with a huge and unexpected mutiny by his Macedonian veterans. He held a banquet to pacify them, and he included in the festivities some Persians and other Asian followers, some nine thousand in all. During the festivities he offered a public prayer for harmony and partnership in rule between the Macedonians and Persians. Many modern scholars have interpreted this prayer as an expression of his desire to establish a "brotherhood of man." The following passage provides the evidence for this view. From it all readers can determine for themselves whether Alexander attempted to introduce a new philosophical ideal or whether he harbored his own political motives for political cooperation.

8. When [Alexander] arrived at Opis, he collected the Macedonians and announced that he intended to discharge from the army those who were useless for military service either from age or from being maimed in the limbs; and he said he would send them back to their own abodes. He also promised to give those who went back as much extra reward as would make them special objects of envy to those at home and arouse in the other Macedonians the wish to share similar dangers and labours. Alexander said this, no doubt, for the purpose of pleasing the Macedonians; but on the contrary they were, not without reason, offended by the speech which he delivered, thinking that now they were despised by him and deemed to be quite useless for military service. Indeed, throughout the whole of this expedition they had been offended at many other things; for his adoption of the Persian dress, thereby exhibiting his contempt for their opinion often caused them grief, as did also his accoutring the foreign soldiers called Epigoni in the Macedonian style,

and the mixing of the alien horsemen among the ranks of the Companions. Therefore they could not remain silent and control themselves, but urged him to dismiss all of them from his army; and they advised him to prosecute the war in company with his father, deriding Ammon by this remark. When Alexander heard this . . . , he ordered the most conspicuous of the men who had tried to stir up the multitude to sedition to be arrested. He himself pointed out with his hand to the shield-bearing guards those whom they were to arrest, to the number of thirteen; and he ordered these to be led away to execution. When the rest, stricken with terror, became silent, he mounted the platform again, and spoke as follows:

9. "The speech which I am about to deliver will not be for the purpose of checking your start homeward, for, so far as I am concerned, you may depart wherever you wish; but for the purpose of making you understand when you take yourselves off, what kind of men you have been to us who have conferred such benefits upon you. . . .

10. . . . Most of you have golden crowns, the eternal memorials of your valour and of the honour you receive from me. Whoever has been killed has met with a glorious end and has been honoured with a splendid burial. Brazen statues of most of the slain have been erected at home, and their parents are held in honour, being released from all public service and from taxation. But no one of you has ever been killed in flight under my leadership. And now I was intending to send back those of you who are unfit for service, objects of envy to those at home; but since you all wish to depart, depart all of you! Go back and report at home that your king Alexander, the conqueror of the Persians, Medes, Bactrians, and Sacians; the man who has subjugated the Uxians, Arachotians, and Drangians; who has also acquired the rule of the Parthians, Chorasmians, and Hyrcanians, as far as the Caspian Sea . . . —report that when you

returned to Susa you deserted him and went away, handing him over to the protection of conquered foreigners. Perhaps this report of yours will be both glorious to you in the eyes of men and devout I ween in the eyes of the gods. Depart!"

11. Having thus spoken, he leaped down quickly from the platform, and entered the palace, where he paid no attention to the decoration of his person, nor was any of his Companions admitted to see him. Not even on the morrow was any one of them admitted to an audience; but on the third day he summoned the select Persians within, and among them he distributed the commands of the brigades, and made the rule that only those whom he proclaimed his kinsmen should have the honour of saluting him with a kiss. But the Macedonians who heard the speech were thoroughly astonished at the moment, and remained there in silence near the platform; nor when he retired did any of them accompany the king, except his personal Companions and the confidential body-guards. Though they remained most of them had nothing to do or say; and yet they were unwilling to retire. But when the news was reported to them . . . they were no longer able to restrain themselves; but running in a body to the palace, they cast their weapons there in front of the gates as signs of supplication to the king. Standing in front of the gates, they shouted, beseeching to be allowed to enter, and saying that they were willing to surrender the men who had been the instigators of the disturbance on that occasion, and those who had begun the clamour. They also declared they would not retire from the gates either day or night, unless Alexander would take some pity upon them. When he was informed of this, he came out without delay; and seeing them lying on the ground in humble guise, and hearing most of them lamenting with loud voice, tears began to flow also from his own eyes. He made an effort to say something to them, but they continued their importunate entreaties. At length one of them, Callines by name, a man conspicuous both for his age and because he was a captain of the Companion cavalry, spoke as follows, "O king, what grieves the Macedonians is that you have already made some of the Persians kinsmen to yourself, and that Persians are called Alexander's kinsmen, and have the honour of saluting you with a kiss; whereas none of the Macedonians have as yet enjoyed this honour." Then Alexander, interrupting him, said, "But all

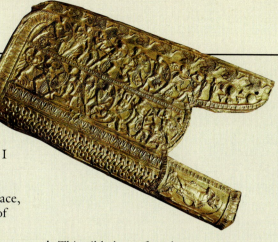

This gilded case for a bow and arrows indicates that Alexander's success came at the price of blood. These vigorous scenes portray more military conflict than philosophical compassion. *(Archaeological Museum Salonica/Dagli-Orti/The Art Archive)*

of you without exception I consider my kinsmen, and so from this time I shall call you." When he had said this, Callines advanced and saluted him with a kiss, and so did all those who wished to salute him. Then they took up their weapons and returned to the camp, shouting and singing a song of thanksgiving. After this Alexander offered sacrifice to the gods to whom it was his custom to sacrifice, and gave a public banquet, over which he himself presided, with the Macedonians sitting around him; and next to them the Persians; after whom came the men of the other nations, preferred in honour for their personal rank or for some meritorious action. The king and his guests drew wine from the same bowl and poured out the same libations, both the Grecian prophets and the Magians commencing the ceremony. He prayed for other blessings, and especially that harmony and community of rule might exist between the Macedonians and Persians.

Questions for Analysis

1. What was the purpose of the banquet at Opis?

2. Were all of the guests treated equally?

3. What did Alexander gain from bringing together the Macedonians and Persians?

Source: Arrian, *Anabasis of Alexander* 7.8.1–11.9 in F. R. B. Goldophin, ed., *The Greek Historians,* vol. 2. Copyright 1942 and renewed 1970 by Random House, Inc. Used by permission of Random House, Inc.

The Roman Forum. *(Josephine Powell)*

THE RISE OF ROME,
CA 750–44 B.C.

chapter preview

The Land and Its Early Settlers
• *How did the land help shape Roman developments?*

The Roman Republic
• *What was the nature of the Roman republic?*

Roman Expansion
• *How did the Romans expand farther into Italy?*

Old Values and Greek Culture
• *What values did the Romans embrace because of their expansion?*

The Late Republic (133–31 B.C.)
• *What were the main problems and achievements of the late republic?*

Who is so thoughtless and lazy that he does not want to know in what way and with what kind of government the Romans in less than 53 years conquered nearly the entire inhabited world and brought it under their rule—an achievement previously unheard of?"[1] This question was first asked by Polybius, a Greek historian who lived in the second century B.C. With keen awareness Polybius realized that the Romans were achieving something unique in world history.

What was that achievement? Was it simply the creation of a huge empire? Hardly. The Persians had done the same thing. For that matter, Alexander the Great had conquered vast territories in a shorter time. Was it the creation of a superior culture? Even the Romans admitted that in matters of art, literature, philosophy, and culture they learned from the Greeks. Rome's achievement lay in the ability of the Romans not only to conquer peoples but to incorporate them into the Roman system. Rome succeeded where the Greek polis had failed. Unlike the Greeks, who refused to share citizenship, the Romans extended their citizenship first to the Italians and later to the peoples of the provinces. With that citizenship went Roman government and law. Rome created a world state that embraced the entire Mediterranean area and extended northward.

Nor was Rome's achievement limited to the ancient world. Rome's law, language, and administrative practices shaped later developments in Europe and beyond. London, Paris, Vienna, and many other modern European cities began as Roman colonies or military camps. When the Founding Fathers created the American republic, they looked to Rome as a model. On the darker side, Napoleon and Mussolini paid their own tribute to Rome by aping its forms. Whether Founding Father or modern autocrat, all were acknowledging admiration for the Roman achievement.

Roman history is usually divided into two periods: the republic, the age in which Rome grew from a small city-state to ruler of an empire, and the empire, the period when the republican constitution gave way to constitutional monarchy.

⚙ *Online Study Center*

This icon will direct you to interactive activities and study materials on the website **college.hmco.com/pic/mckaywest9e**

The Land and Its Early Settlers

While the Greeks pursued their destiny in the East, other peoples in western Europe developed their own individual societies. The most historically important of them were the Etruscans and Romans who entered the peninsula of Italy and came into contact with the older cultures of the Mediterranean. The Etruscans were the first significant newcomers; their arrival can reasonably be dated to about 750 B.C. Italy gave them a genial homeland. Shaped like a boot, with the island of Sicily at its toe, Italy occupies the center of the Mediterranean basin. As Map 5.1 shows, the two geographical features of Italy and Sicily thrust southward toward the North African coast, thereby dividing the Mediterranean into two basins.

• *How did the land help shape Roman developments?*

The Etruscans and the Roman Settlement of Italy (ca 750–509 B.C.)

The Etruscans remain a mysterious people, still surrounded by numerous uncertainties. They did, however, develop the land by establishing permanent settlements that evolved into the first Italian cities. In political organization they resembled the Greek city-states, each governing itself while maintaining contact with its neighbors. The wealth of these cities, along with their political and military institutions, enabled them to form a loosely organized league of cities whose domination extended as far north as the Po Valley and as far south as Latium and Campania (see Map 5.1). Their influence spread over the surrounding countryside, which they

regularly cultivated. Having established a strong agricultural base, they mined the rich mineral resources of the land. Secure in their new home, they looked out to the wider world, especially to the East. The Mediterranean has always been a highway, and one of its major routes led to Greece. From an early period the Etruscans began to trade natural products, especially iron, in return for Greek luxury goods. They thereby built a rich cultural life that became the foundation of civilization throughout Italy. In the process they touched a small collection of villages subsequently called Rome.

The Romans, to whom the Etruscans introduced the broader world, had settled in Italy by the eighth century B.C. According to one legend of the founding of Rome, Romulus and Remus founded the city in 753 B.C. Romulus built his home on the Palatine Hill, while Remus chose the Aventine (see inset of Map 5.1). They built Rome's first walls, which were inviolable, reflecting the Etruscan concept of the **pomerium,** a sacred boundary intended to keep out anything evil or unclean. Under Etruscan influence the Romans prospered, spreading over all of Rome's seven hills.

The Etruscans soon drew the fledgling Rome into their orbit. From 753 to 509 B.C. a line of Etruscan kings ruled the city and introduced many customs. The Ro-

Sarcophagus of Lartie Seianti
The woman portrayed on this lavish sarcophagus is the noble Etruscan Lartie Seianti. Although the sarcophagus is her place of burial, she is portrayed as in life, comfortable and at rest. The influence of Greek art on Etruscan is apparent in almost every feature of the sarcophagus. (*Archaeological Museum, Florence/Nimatallah/Art Resource, NY*)

mans adopted the Etruscan alphabet, which the Etruscans themselves had adopted from the Greeks. The Romans later handed on this alphabet to medieval Europe and thence to the modern Western world. The Romans also adopted symbols of political authority from the Etruscans. The symbol of the Etruscan king's right to execute or scourge his subjects was a bundle of rods and an ax, called in Latin the **fasces,** which the king's retainer carried before him on official occasions. When the Romans expelled the Etruscan kings, they created special attendants called "lictors" to carry the fasces before their new magistrates, the consuls. Even the **toga,** the white woolen robe worn by citizens, came from the Etruscans. In engineering and architecture the Romans adopted the vault and the arch from the Etruscans. Above all, it was thanks to the Etruscans that the Romans truly became urban dwellers.

Under the Etruscans Rome enjoyed contacts with the larger Mediterranean world, while the city continued to grow. In the years 575 to 550 B.C. temples and public buildings began to grace the city. The Capitoline Hill became its religious center when the temple of Jupiter Optimus Maximus (Jupiter the Best and Greatest) was built there. The **Forum** ceased to be a cemetery and began its history as a public meeting place, a development parallel to that of the Greek agora. Trade in metalwork became common, and wealthier Romans began to import large numbers of fine Greek vases. The Etruscans had found Rome a collection of villages and made it a city.

The Roman Conquest of Italy (509–290 B.C.)

Roman expansion was hardly accidental. The Romans had to master themselves before they could rule others. Above all, that meant that they must build a political system that both governed the citizenry and directed its energy in public affairs. The Romans faced a political and social challenge in these years, the meeting of which permitted them effectively to rule themselves and eventually others.

Early Roman history is an uneven mixture of fact and legend. Roman traditions often contain an important kernel of truth, but that does not make them history. In many cases they are significant because they illustrate the ethics, morals, and ideals that Roman society considered valuable.

Several of Rome's founding legends involve sexual violence, and gender norms were deeply embedded in Roman ideals. In the story of Romulus and Remus,

Chronology

750–133 B.C.	Traditional founding of Rome; evolution of the Roman state
750–31 B.C.	Beginning of the economic growth of Rome
509–290 B.C.	Roman conquest of Italy
499–186 B.C.	Introduction of Greek deities
ca 494–287 B.C.	Struggle of the Orders
264–133 B.C.	Punic Wars and the conquest of the East
262 B.C.	Growth of large estates
239–159 B.C.	Rise of Latin literature
88–31 B.C.	Civil war
86–35 B.C.	Birth of historical and political writing

Romulus appealed to other rulers to send women to Rome to marry young Roman men. When the Sabines refused, young Roman men abducted Sabine women, raped them while their families watched, and then married them. Later the Sabine women protected their children in a war between the Sabines and the Romans, which led to a truce. There is no evidence that what became known as the "rape of the Sabine women" actually happened, but the story was frequently retold as history. Roman historians used it to highlight the centrality of marriage and legitimate birth to Roman citizenship and the way Romans integrated non-Romans into their culture; they did not emphasize the fact that this happened through rape.

Another of Rome's founding myths told the story of Tarquin, an Etruscan king, and Lucretia. During a military campaign Tarquin's men took bets on who had the most virtuous wife. Only Lucretia, the wife of Tarquin's cousin, was at home virtuously spinning wool (the other women were out with friends), and Tarquin's son decided to seduce her. She refused; he threatened to kill her, and he raped her; then she denounced him to her husband. Lucretia killed herself at the shame of the rape, which led the Roman populace to rise up against the Etruscans and found the republic, which tradition held was in 509 B.C. Like the story of the Sabine women, there is no clear evidence that these events actually happened, but the legends clearly link women's sexual honor with the Roman state. Lucretia became the symbol of virtuous Roman

Rome

QUIRINAL HILL

VIMINAL HILL

FIELD OF MARS

Tiber

ESQUILINE MT.

CAPITOLINE MT.

Senate House

Forum

Temple of
Jupiter

Regia

JANICULUM

PALATINE
MT.

Circus
Maximus

CAELIAN MT.

AVENTINE MT.

ALPS

APENNINES

Po

Arno

UMBRIA

PICENUM

ETRURIA

Tiber

SABINI

AEQUI

VESTINI

Adriatic Sea

Veii

Rome

SAMNIUM

CORSICA

LATIUM

APULIA

CAMPANIA

CALABRIA

Tarentum

SARDINIA

LUCANIA

Tyrrhenian Sea

BRUTTIUM

Mediterranean Sea

Messana

SICILY

Syracuse

Carthage

Cape
Bon

NORTH AFRICA

———	Roman boundary before the Punic Wars
———	Roman boundary before Augustus
———	Roman internal regional divisions
———	Major road

0   50   100 Km.

0   50   100 Mi.

MAP 5.1 Italy and the City of Rome The geographical configuration of the Italian peninsula shows how Rome stood astride north-south communication routes and how the state that united Italy stood poised to move into Sicily and northern Africa.

womanhood, and her suicide was portrayed in statues and paintings throughout Rome's long history, and again in the Renaissance two thousand years later.

Online Study Center Improve Your Grade
Primary Source: The Power of Myth: Livy and the Rape of Lucretia

The republic was actually founded in the years after 509 B.C., when the Romans fought numerous wars with their neighbors on the Italian peninsula. They became soldiers, and the grim fighting bred tenacity, a prominent Roman trait. At an early date the Romans also learned the value of alliances and how to provide leadership for their allies. Alliances with the Latin towns around them provided them with a large reservoir of manpower. These alliances involved the Romans in still other wars and took them farther afield in the Italian peninsula.

The growth of Roman power was slow but steady. Not until roughly a century after the founding of the republic did the Romans drive the Etruscans entirely out of Latium. Around 390 B.C. the Romans suffered a major setback when a new people, the Celts—or **Gauls,** as the Romans called them—swept aside a Roman army and sacked Rome. More intent on loot than on land, they agreed to abandon Rome in return for a thousand pounds of gold.

From 390 to 290 B.C. the Romans rebuilt their city and recouped their losses. They also reorganized their army to create the mobile legion, a flexible unit capable of fighting on either broken or open terrain. The Romans finally brought Latium and their Latin allies fully under their control and conquered Etruria (see Map 5.1). In 343 B.C. they grappled with the

Samnites in a series of bitter wars for the possession of Campania and southern Italy. The Samnites were a formidable enemy and inflicted serious losses on the Romans. But the superior organization, institutions, and manpower of the Romans won out in the end. Although Rome had yet to subdue the whole peninsula, for the first time in history the city stood unchallenged in Italy.

The Romans spread their culture by sharing their religious cults, mythology, and drama. They, like other pagans, liberally shared their religious beliefs with others, which in turn furthered the Romanization of Italy.

Roman religion opened a unique way to the appreciation of Roman law. Seen at its ideal, religion was virtually inseparable from law. Yet the spread of Roman culture was not part of a planned ideological onslaught by the Romans. Nor was it very different from the ways in which the Romans extended their political, military, and legal systems. Even so, the process eventually created a common ground for all the peoples living in Italy and made Italy Roman. In later years the Romans continued this process until all these influences spread throughout the Mediterranean basin.

Rome's success in diplomacy and politics was as important as its military victories. With many of their oldest allies, such as the Latin cities, the Romans shared full Roman citizenship. In other instances they granted citizenship without the **franchise** (*civitas sine suffragio*). Allies

Guard Dog The doorway of the house opened directly onto the street. This entrance is protected by a dog who is always on guard. The notice warns "CAVE CANEM" (beware of the dog). *(Robert Frerck/Odyssey/Chicago)*

who held this status enjoyed all the rights of Roman citizenship except that they could not vote or hold Roman offices. They were subject to Roman taxes and calls for military service but ran their own local affairs. The Latin allies were able to acquire full Roman citizenship by moving to Rome. A perhaps humble but very efficient means of keeping the Romans and their colonies together were the Roman roads, many of which were in use as late as the medieval period. These roads provided an easy route of communication between the capital and outlying areas, allowed for the quick movement of armies, and offered an efficient means of trade. They were the tangible sinews of unity.

By their willingness to extend their citizenship, the Romans took Italy into partnership. Here the political genius of Rome triumphed where Greece had failed. Rome proved itself superior to the Greek polis because it both conquered and shared the fruits of conquest with the conquered. Rome could consolidate where Greece could only dominate. The unwillingness of the Greek polis to share its citizenship condemned it to a limited horizon. Not so with Rome. The extension of Roman citizenship strengthened the state, gave it additional manpower and wealth, and laid the foundation of the Roman Empire.

The Roman Republic

The Roman republic consisted of its constitution and the people who made it. The Romans' first problem was to create the political institutions needed to govern effectively an ever-expanding and influential state. The second was the sharing of the obligations and privileges that came with that effort. The Romans did not expect these challenges, but they struggled hard to meet them. In the process they fashioned both a state and a society. If the effort was demanding, the Romans confronted it so successfully that the Roman republic became one of the preeminent institutions of the ancient world—one still admired today.

- *What was the nature of the Roman republic?*

The Roman State

The Romans summed up their political existence in a single phrase: *senatus populusque Romanum,* "the Roman senate and people." These words were a statement and a proclamation. The Romans often abbreviated this concept as "SPQR." The letters epitomized the Roman

people, their state, and their way of life. SPQR became a shorthand way of saying "Rome," just as "U.S.A." says "the United States of America." The real genius of the Romans lay in the fields of politics and law. Unlike the Greeks, they did not often speculate on the ideal state or on political forms. Instead, they realistically met actual challenges and created institutions, magistracies, and legal concepts to deal with practical problems. Change was consequently commonplace in Roman political life, and the constitution of 509 B.C. was far simpler than that of 27 B.C. Moreover, the Roman constitution, unlike the American, was not a single written document. Rather, it was a set of traditional beliefs, customs, and laws.

In the early republic social divisions determined the shape of politics. Political power was in the hands of the aristocracy—the **patricians,** who were wealthy landowners. Patrician families formed clans, as did aristocrats in early Greece. Patrician men dominated the affairs of state, provided military leadership in time of war, and monopolized knowledge of law and legal procedure. The common people of Rome, the **plebeians,** had few of the patricians' advantages. Some plebeians formed their own clans and rivaled the patricians in wealth. Many plebeian merchants increased their wealth in the course of Roman expansion, but most plebeians were poor. They were the artisans, small farmers, and landless urban dwellers. The plebeians, rich and poor alike, were free citizens with a voice in politics. Nonetheless, they were overshadowed by the patricians.

Perhaps the greatest institution of the republic was the **senate,** which had originated under the Etruscans as a council of noble elders who advised the king. During the republic the senate advised the consuls and other magistrates. Because the senate sat year after year, while magistrates changed annually, it provided stability and continuity. It also served as a reservoir of experience and knowledge. Technically, the senate could not pass legislation; it could only offer its advice. But increasingly, because of the senate's prestige, its advice came to have the force of law.

The Romans created several assemblies through which men elected magistrates and passed legislation. The earliest was the *comitia curiata,* which had religious, political, and military functions. According to Roman tradition, King Servius Tullius (578–535 B.C.), who reorganized the state into 193 *centuries* for military purposes, created the *comitia centuriata* as a political body to decide Roman policy. The comitia centuriata voted in centuries, which in this instance means political blocs. The patricians possessed the majority of centuries because they shouldered most of the burden of defense. Thus they could easily

Canopus, Hadrian's Villa   This view of Hadrian's villa embodies sublime and serene beauty. The columns and statues lend dignity, and the pond suggests rest. In the background a spacious house offers a retreat from the cares of imperial duties. *(Mark Edward Smith/TIPS Images)*

outvote the plebeians. In 471 B.C. plebeian men won the right to meet in an assembly of their own, the *concilium plebis,* and to pass ordinances. In 287 B.C. the bills passed in the concilium plebis were recognized as binding on the entire population.

The chief magistrates of the republic were the two consuls, elected for one-year terms. At first the consulship was open only to patrician men. The consuls commanded the army in battle, administered state business, convened the comitia centuriata, and supervised financial affairs. In effect, they and the senate ran the state. The consuls appointed *quaestors* to assist them in their duties, and in 421 B.C. the quaestorship became an elective office open to plebeian men. The quaestors took charge of the public treasury and prosecuted criminals in the popular courts.

In 366 B.C. the Romans created a new office, that of **praetor,** and in 227 B.C. the number of praetors was increased to four. When the consuls were away from Rome, the praetors could act in their place. The praetors dealt primarily with the administration of justice. When he took office, a praetor issued a proclamation declaring the principles by which he would interpret the law. These proclamations became very important because they usually covered areas where the law was vague and thus helped clarify the law.

Other officials included the powerful *censors,* created in 443 B.C., who had many responsibilities, the most important being supervision of public morals, the power to determine who lawfully could sit in the senate, the registration of citizens, and the leasing of public contracts. Later officials were the *aediles,* four in number, who supervised the streets and markets and presided over public festivals.

After the age of overseas conquest, the Romans divided the Mediterranean area into provinces governed by ex-consuls and ex-praetors. Because of their experience in Roman politics, they were well suited to administer the affairs of the provincials and to fit Roman law and custom into new contexts.

One of the most important achievements of the Romans was their development of law. Roman law began as a set of rules that regulated the lives and relations of citizens. This civil law, or **ius civile,** consisted of statutes, customs, and forms of procedure. Roman assemblies added to the body of law, and praetors interpreted it. The spirit of the law aimed at protecting the property, lives, and reputations of citizens, redressing wrongs, and giving satisfaction to victims of injustice.

As the Romans came into more frequent contact with foreigners, they had to devise laws to deal with disputes between Romans and foreigners and between foreigners under Roman jurisdiction. In these instances, where there was no precedent to guide the Romans, the legal decisions of the praetors proved of immense importance. The praetors adopted aspects of other legal systems and resorted to the law of equity—what they thought was right and just to all parties. Free, in effect, to determine law, the praetors enjoyed a great deal of flexibility. This situation illustrates the practicality and the genius of the Romans. By addressing specific, actual circumstances the praetors developed a body of law, the *ius gentium,* "the law of peoples," that applied to Romans and foreigners and that laid the foundation for a universal conception of law. By the time of the late republic, Roman jurists were reaching decisions on the basis of the Stoic concept of **ius naturale,** "natural law," a universal law that could be applied to all societies.

Social Conflicts in Rome

Another important aspect of early Roman history was a great social conflict, usually known as the **Struggle of the Orders,** that developed between patricians and plebeians. The plebeians wanted real political representation and safeguards against patrician domination. The plebeians' efforts to obtain recognition of their rights is the crux of the Struggle of the Orders.

Rome's early wars gave the plebeians the leverage they needed: Rome's survival depended on the army, and the army needed the plebeians. The first showdown between plebeians and patricians came, according to tradition, in 494 B.C. To force the patricians to grant concessions, the plebeians seceded from the state; they literally walked out of Rome and refused to serve in the army. The plebeians' general strike worked. Because of it the patricians made important concessions. One of these was social. In 445 B.C. the patricians passed a law, the *lex Canuleia,* which for the first time allowed patricians and plebeians to marry one another. Furthermore, the patricians recognized the right of plebeians to elect their own officials, the **tribunes.** The tribunes in turn had the right to protect the plebeians from the arbitrary conduct of patrician magistrates. The tribunes brought plebeian grievances to the senate for resolution. The plebeians were not bent on undermining the state. Rather, they used their gains only to win full equality under the law.

The law itself was the plebeians' primary target. Only the patricians knew what the law was, and only they could argue cases in court. All too often they had used the law for their own benefit. The plebeians wanted the law codified and published. The result of their agitation was the Law of the Twelve Tables, so called because the laws, which covered civil and criminal matters, were inscribed on twelve large bronze plaques. Later still, the plebeians forced the patricians to publish legal procedures as well. The plebeians had broken the patricians' legal monopoly and henceforth enjoyed full protection under the law.

The decisive plebeian victory came with the passage of the Licinian-Sextian rogations (or laws) in 367 B.C. Licinius and Sextus were plebeian tribunes who led a ten-year fight for further reform. Rich plebeians, such as Licinius and Sextus themselves, joined the poor to mount a sweeping assault on patrician privilege. Wealthy plebeians wanted the opportunity to provide political leadership for the state. They demanded that the patricians allow them access to all the magistracies of the state. If they could hold the consulship, they could also sit in the senate and advise the senate on policy. The two tribunes won approval from the senate for a law that stipulated that one of the two annual consuls must be a plebeian. Though decisive, the Licinian-Sextian rogations did not automatically end the Struggle of the Orders. That happened only in 287 B.C. with the passage of a law, the *lex Hortensia,* that gave the resolutions of the concilium plebis the force of law for patricians and plebeians alike.

The results of the compromise between the patricians and the plebeians were far-reaching. They secured economic reform and defined the access of all citizens to public land. The principal result was the definition of political leadership. Plebeians could now hold the consulship, which brought with it the consular title, places of honor in the senate, and such cosmetic privileges as wearing the purple toga, the symbol of aristocracy. Far more important, the compromise established a new nobility shared by the plebeians and the patricians. They were both groups of wealthy aristocrats who had simply agreed to share the great offices of power within the republic. This would lead not to major political reform but to an extension of aristocratic rule. Nevertheless, the patricians were wise enough to give the plebeians wider political rights than they had previously enjoyed. The compromise was typically Roman.

The Struggle of the Orders resulted in a Rome stronger and better united than before. It could have led to anarchy, but again certain Roman traits triumphed. The values fostered by their social structure predisposed the Romans to compromise, especially in the face of common danger. Resistance and confrontation in Rome never exploded into class warfare. Instead, both sides resorted to compromises to hammer out a realistic solution. Important, too, were Roman patience, tenacity, and a healthy sense of the practical. These qualities enabled both sides to keep working until they had resolved the crisis. The Struggle of the Orders ended in 287 B.C. with a new concept of Roman citizenship. All male citizens shared equally under the law. Theoretically, all men could aspire to the highest political offices.

The Struggle of the Orders made all male citizens equal before the law, but a man's independence was limited by the power that the male head of the family, termed the **paterfamilias,** had over him. This was also true for all women, who even as adults were always under the legal guardianship of some man. The paterfamilias was the oldest dominant male of the family. He held nearly absolute power over the lives of his wife and children as long as he lived. He could legally kill his wife for adultery or divorce her at will. He could kill his children or sell them into slavery. He could force the children to marry against their will. Until the paterfamilias died, his sons could not legally own property. At his death the wife and children of the paterfamilias inherited his property.

Along with his biological kin, the paterfamilias also had authority over slaves, servants, adopted children, and others who lived in his household. In poor families this group might be very small, but among the wealthy it could include hundreds of slaves and servants.

Roman Expansion

Once the Romans had settled their internal affairs, they were free to turn their attention to the larger world around them. As seen earlier, they had already come to terms with the Italic peoples in Latium. Only later did Rome achieve primacy over its Latin allies, partly because of successful diplomacy and partly because of overwhelming military power. In 282 B.C. Rome expanded even farther in Italy and extended its power across the sea to Sicily, Corsica, and Sardinia.

• *How did the Romans expand farther into Italy?*

Italy Becomes Roman

In only twenty years, from 282 to 262 B.C., the Romans dramatically built on their earlier successes. Just as they had spread their religion through cult, mythology, and drama, now they expanded politically throughout Italy. Their energy was remarkable, and the results they achieved were not always due to warfare. They established a string of colonies throughout Italy, some of them populated by Romans and others by Latins. The genius of the Romans lay in bringing these various peoples into one political system. First the Romans divided the Italians into two broad classes. Those living closest to Rome were incorporated into the Roman state. They enjoyed the full franchise and citizenship that the Romans themselves possessed. The other class comprised those Italians who lived farther afield. They were bound by treaty with the Romans and were considered allies. Although they received lesser rights of active citizenship, the allies retained their right of local self-government. The link between the allies and Rome was as much social as political, as both were ruled by aristocrats.

These contacts—social, political, and legal—with their neighbors led the Romans to a better acquaintance with the heritage, customs, and laws of their fellow Italians. Rome and the rest of Italy began to share similar views of their common welfare. By including others in the Roman political and social system, Rome was making Italy Roman.

Overseas Conquest (282–146 B.C.)

In 282 B.C., when the Romans had reached southern Italy, they embarked upon a series of wars that left them the rulers of the Mediterranean world. The nature of these wars demands attention. Unlike their attitude toward the Italians or even the Etruscans, the Romans felt that they were dealing with foreigners, people not akin to them. They were also moving into areas largely unfamiliar to them. These wars became fiercer and were fought on a larger scale than those in Italy. Yet there was nothing ideological about them. Unlike Napoleon or Hitler, the Romans did not map out grandiose strategies for world conquest. They had no idea of what lay before them. If they could have looked into the future, they would have stood amazed. In many instances the Romans did not even initiate action; they simply responded to situations as they arose. Nineteenth-century Englishmen were fond of saying, "We got our empire in a fit of absence of mind." The Romans could not go quite that far. Though they sometimes declared war reluctantly, they nonetheless felt the need to dominate, to eliminate any state that could threaten them.

The Samnite wars had drawn the Romans into the political world of southern Italy. In 282 B.C., alarmed by the powerful newcomer, the Greek city of Tarentum in southern Italy called for help from Pyrrhus, king of Epirus in western Greece. A relative of Alexander the Great and an excellent general, Pyrrhus won two furious battles but suffered heavy casualties—thus the phrase **Pyrrhic victory** for a victory involving severe losses. Roman bravery and tenacity led him to comment: "If we win one more battle with the Romans, we'll be completely washed up." Against Pyrrhus's army the Romans threw new legions, and in the end manpower proved decisive. In 275 B.C. the Romans drove Pyrrhus from Italy and extended their sway over southern Italy. Once they did, the island of Sicily became a key for them to block Carthaginian expansion northward.

The Punic Wars and Beyond (264–133 B.C.)

By 264 B.C. Carthage (see Map 5.2) was the unrivaled power of the western Mediterranean. Since the second half of the eighth century B.C., it had built its wealth on trade in tin and precious metals. It commanded one of the best harbors on the northern African coast and was supported by a fertile hinterland. The Carthaginians were for the most part merchants, not soldiers, and they made contributions to geographical knowledge by exploring as far west as the Atlantic coasts of northern Africa and Spain. They soon dominated the commerce of the western Mediterranean. By the fourth century B.C. they were fully integrated into the Hellenistic economy, which now spread from Gibraltar to the Parthian empire.

Commercial ambitions led to political conflict. Expansion led to war with the Etruscans and Greeks, but the Carthaginians won control of parts of Sardinia, Spain, and Sicily. At the end of a long string of wars, the Carthaginians held control of only the western tip of Sicily but retained considerable influence farther to the west. In fact, the Carthaginians had created and defended a mercantile empire that stretched from western Sicily to beyond Gibraltar.

This in essence is the background of the **First Punic War** between Rome and Carthage, two powers expanding into the same area. The First Punic War lasted for twenty-three years (264–241 B.C.). The Romans quickly learned that they could not conquer Sicily unless they controlled the sea. Although they lacked a fleet and hated the sea as fervently as cats hate water, with grim resolution the Romans built a navy. They fought seven major naval battles with the Carthaginians, won six, and finally wore them down. In 241 B.C. the Romans took possession of Sicily, which became their first real province. Once again Rome's resources, manpower, and determination proved decisive.

The peace treaty between the two powers brought no peace, in part because in 238 B.C. the Romans took advantage of Carthaginian weakness to seize Sardinia and Corsica. Although unable to resist, many Carthaginians concluded that genuine peace between Carthage and Rome was impossible. One such man was Hamilcar Barca, a Carthaginian commander who had come close to victory in Sicily. The only way Carthage could recoup its fortune was by success in Spain, where the Carthaginians already enjoyed a firm foothold. In 237 B.C. Hamilcar led an army to Spain in order to turn it into Carthaginian territory. With him he took his nineteen-year-old son, Hannibal, but not before he had led Hannibal to an altar and made him swear

Triumphal Column of Caius Duilius
This curious monument celebrates Rome's first naval victory in the First Punic War. In the battle Caius Duilius destroyed fifty Carthaginian ships. He then celebrated his success by erecting this column that portrays the prows of the enemy ships projecting from the column. *(Alinari/Art Resource, NY)*

ever to be an enemy to Rome. In the following years Hamilcar and his son-in-law Hasdrubal subjugated much of southern Spain and in the process rebuilt Carthaginian power. Rome responded in two ways: first, the Romans made a treaty with Hasdrubal in which the Ebro River formed the boundary between Carthaginian and Roman interests, and second, the Romans began to extend their own influence in Spain.

In 221 B.C. the young Hannibal became Carthaginian commander in Spain, and soon Roman and Carthaginian policies clashed at the city of Saguntum. When Hannibal laid siege to Saguntum, which lay within the sphere of Carthaginian interest, the Romans declared war, claiming that Carthage had attacked a friendly city. So began the Second Punic War, one of the most desperate wars ever fought by Rome. In 218 B.C. Hannibal struck first by marching more than a thousand miles over the Alps into Italy. Once there, he defeated one Roman army at the Battle of Trebia and later another at the Battle of Lake Trasimene in 217 B.C. In the following year, Hannibal won his greatest victory at the Battle of Cannae, in which he inflicted some forty thousand casualties on the Romans. He then spread devastation throughout Italy, and a number of cities in central and southern Italy rebelled against Rome. Syracuse, Rome's ally during the First Punic War, also went over to the Carthaginians. Yet Hannibal failed to crush Rome's iron circle of Latium, Etruria, and Samnium. The wisdom of Rome's political policy of extending rights and citizenship to its allies showed itself in these dark hours. And Rome fought back.

In 210 B.C. Rome found its answer to Hannibal in the young commander Scipio, later better known as Scipio Africanus. Scipio copied Hannibal's methods of mobile warfare, streamlining the legions by making their components capable of independent action and introducing new weapons. In the following years, Scipio operated in Spain, which in 207 B.C. he wrested from the Carthaginians. Also in 207 B.C. the Romans sealed Hannibal's fate in Italy. At the Battle of Metaurus, the Romans destroyed a major Carthaginian army coming to reinforce Hannibal. With Hannibal now bottled up in southern Italy, Scipio in 204 B.C. struck directly at Carthage itself. A Roman fleet landed his legions in North Africa, which prompted the Carthaginians to recall Hannibal from Italy to defend the homeland.

In 202 B.C., near the town of Zama (see Map 5.2), Scipio defeated Hannibal in one of the world's truly decisive battles. Scipio's victory meant that the world of the western Mediterranean would henceforth be Roman. Roman language, law, and culture, fertilized by Greek influences, would in time permeate this entire region. The victory at Zama meant that Rome's heritage would be passed on to the Western world.

The **Second Punic War** contained the seeds of still other wars. Unabated fear of Carthage led to the Third Punic War, a needless, unjust, and savage conflict that ended in 146 B.C. when Scipio Aemilianus, grandson of Scipio Africanus, destroyed the old hated rival. As the Roman conqueror watched the death pangs of that great city, he turned to his friend Polybius with the words: "I fear and foresee that someday someone will give the same order about my fatherland." It would, however, be centuries before an invader would stand before the gates of Rome.

During the war with Hannibal, the Romans had invaded Spain, a peninsula rich in material resources and the home of fierce warriors. When the Roman legions tried to reduce the Spanish tribes, they met with bloody and determined resistance. Not until 133 B.C., after years of brutal and ruthless warfare, did Scipio Aemilianus finally conquer Spain.

Rome Turns East (211–133 B.C.)

During the dark days of the Second Punic War, King Philip V of Macedonia made an alliance with Hannibal against Rome. Despite the mortal struggle in the West, the Romans found the strength to turn eastward to settle accounts. Their first significant victory came over the Macedonians in 197 B.C. The Roman general Titus Flamininus demanded that the Macedonians agree to give full liberty to the Greeks. Two years later he defeated the Spartans. In 189 B.C. the Seleucid kingdom fell to the Romans, but decisive victory came in 146 B.C., when the Romans conquered the Achaean League, sacked Corinth, and finally defeated Macedonia, which they made a Roman province. In 133 B.C. Attalus III, the last king of Pergamum, bequeathed his kingdom to the Romans. The Ptolemies of Egypt meekly obeyed Roman wishes.

The Romans had used the discord and disunity of the Hellenistic world to divide and conquer it. Once they had done so, they faced the formidable challenge of governing it without further warfare, which they met by establishing the first Roman provinces in the East. They ultimately succeeded in fusing the honored culture and civilization of the Hellenistic world, with its blend of Greek and Eastern cultures, with the new and vibrant Roman civilization. (See the feature "Listening to the Past: A Magic Charm" on pages 148–149.) As seen earlier, Greek cultural influence had already fertilized Roman life, but now Rome began to create the political and

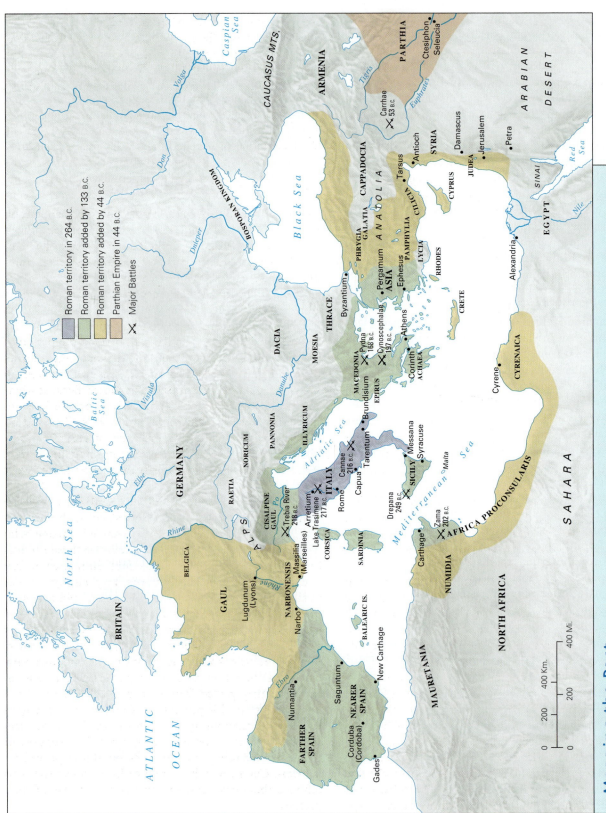

Mapping the Past

MAP 5.2 Roman Expansion During the Republic Previous maps have shown that the Greeks and Macedonians concentrated their energies on opening the East. This map indicates that Rome for the first time looked to the West. **1** What does this say about the expansion of Roman power in the Mediterranean? **2** What does this foreshadow for the subsequent development of Europe?

administrative machinery to hold the Mediterranean together under a mutually shared cultural and political system. The Romans, nonetheless, were as usual practical as well as somewhat altruistic. They declared that the Mediterranean had become *mare nostrum,* "our sea."

Old Values and Greek Culture

Rome had conquered the Mediterranean world, but some Romans considered that victory a misfortune. The historian Sallust (86–34 B.C.), writing from hindsight, complained that the acquisition of an empire was the beginning of Rome's troubles:

But when through labor and justice our Republic grew powerful, great kings defeated in war, fierce nations and mighty peoples subdued by force, when Carthage the rival of the Roman people was wiped out root and branch, all the seas and lands lay open, then fortune began to be harsh and to throw everything into confusion. The Romans had easily borne labor, danger, uncertainty, and hardship. To them leisure, riches—otherwise desirable—proved to be burdens and torments. So at first money, then desire for power grew great. These things were a sort of cause of all evils.[2]

Sallust was not alone in his feelings. At the time some senators had opposed the destruction of Carthage on the grounds that fear of their old rival would keep the Romans in check. In the second century B.C. the Romans learned that they could not return to what they fondly considered a simple life. They were world rulers. The responsibilities they faced were complex and awesome. They had to change their institutions, social patterns, and way of thinking to meet the new era. They were in fact building the foundations of a great imperial system. It was a daunting challenge, and there were failures along the way. Roman generals and politicians would destroy each other. Even the republican constitution would eventually be discarded. But in the end Rome triumphed here just as it had on the battlefield, for out of the turmoil would come the *pax Romana*—"Roman peace."

How did the Romans of the day meet these challenges? How did they lead their lives and cope with these momentous changes? Obviously there are as many answers to these questions as there were Romans. Yet two men represent the major trends of the second century B.C. Cato the Elder shared the mentality of those who longed for the good old days and idealized the traditional agrarian way of life. Scipio Aemilianus led those who embraced the new urban life, with its eager acceptance of Greek culture. Forty-nine years older than Sci-

pio, Cato was a product of an earlier generation, one that confronted a rapidly changing world. Cato and Scipio were both aristocrats, and neither of them was typical, even of the aristocracy. But they do exemplify opposing sets of attitudes that marked Roman society and politics in the age of conquest.

• *What values did the Romans embrace because of their expansion?*

Cato and the Traditional Ideal

Marcus Cato (234–149 B.C.) was born a plebeian, but his talent and energy carried him to Rome's highest offices. He created an image of himself as the bearer of "traditional" Roman virtues, perhaps to offset his rather humble origins. His description of his life is thus partly invented, but some details probably reflect the way many Romans actually lived.

Like most Romans, Cato and his family began the day early in the morning. The Romans divided the period of daylight into twelve hours and the darkness into another twelve. The day might begin as early as half past four in summer, as late as half past seven in winter. Because Mediterranean summers are invariably hot, people liked to take every advantage of the cool mornings. Cato and his family, like modern Italians, ordinarily started the morning with a light breakfast, usually nothing more than some bread and cheese. After breakfast the family went about its work.

Because of his political aspirations, Cato often used the mornings to plead law cases. He walked to the marketplace of the nearby town and defended anyone who wished his help. He received no fees for these services but did put his neighbors in his debt. In matters of law and politics Roman custom was very strong. It demanded that Cato's clients give him their political support or their votes in repayment whenever he asked for them. These clients knew and accepted their obligations to Cato for his help. The notion of clientage was a particularly Roman social and political custom: free men entrusted their lives to a more powerful man, and in exchange they gained from their patron some social entertainment and his protection. Custom, not law, governed this relationship. In return for his generosity toward his clients, the patron expected their support in public life and private matters. The bond thus proved reciprocal. Clientage helped men of lower social status to advance themselves and to advance the careers of their patrons.

Cato was married—though he never mentions the name of his wife—as were almost all Roman citizens. Grooms were generally somewhat older than their brides, who often married in their early teens. There were two types of marriage in Rome, one of which put the woman under control of her husband's family (marriage *cum manu*) and one of which kept her under her father's control (marriage *sine manu*). Each had advantages and disadvantages for women.

Women could inherit property under Roman law, though they generally received a smaller portion of any family inheritance than their brothers did. Women's inheritance usually came as a dowry on marriage. In the earliest Roman marriage laws, men could divorce their wives without any grounds while women could not divorce their husbands, but by the time of Cato these laws had changed, and both men and women could initiate divorce. Women appear to have gained greater control over their dowries, perhaps in response to the fact that Rome's military conquests meant that many husbands were away for long periods of time and women needed some say over family finances.

Both Romans and Greeks felt that children should be raised in the lap of their mother, a woman who kept her house in good order and personally saw to the welfare of her children. In wealthy homes during the period, the matron had begun to employ a slave as a wet nurse. According to Cato, his wife refused to delegate her maternal duties. Like most ordinary Roman women, she nursed her son herself and bathed and swaddled him daily.

Until the age of seven, children were under their mother's care. During this time the matron began to educate her daughters in the management of the household.

Temple of Mater Matuta   This round temple was dedicated to Mater Matuta, a very old Roman mother goddess. Its shape and architectural ornamentation indicate Hellenistic influence. *(Vanni/Art Resource, NY)*

After the age of seven, sons—and in many wealthy households daughters too—began to receive formal education. Formal education for wealthy children was generally in the hands of tutors, who were often Greek slaves, for parents wanted their children to learn Greek literature and philosophy. By the late republic, there were also a few schools. Most children learned skills from their own parents or through apprenticeships with artisans; slave boys and girls were occasionally formally apprenticed in trades such as leatherwork, weaving, or metalsmithing.

In the country Romans like Cato continued to take their main meal at midday. This meal included either coarse bread made from the entire husk of wheat or porridge made with milk or water; it also included turnips, cabbage, olives, and beans. With the midday meal the family drank ordinary wine mixed with water. Afterward any Roman who could took a nap. This was especially true in the summer, when the Mediterranean heat can be fierce. Slaves, artisans, and hired laborers, however, continued their work. In the evening Romans ate a light meal and went to bed at nightfall.

The agricultural year followed the sun and the stars—the farmer's calendar. Like Hesiod in Boeotia, the Roman farmer looked to the sky to determine when to plant, weed, shear sheep, and perform other chores. Spring was the season for plowing. Roman farmers plowed their land at least twice and preferably three times. The third plowing was to cover the sown seed in ridges and to use the furrows to drain off excess water. Farmers used oxen and donkeys to pull the plow, collecting the dung of the animals for fertilizer. Besides spreading manure, some farmers fertilized their fields by planting lupines and beans; when they began to pod, the farmers plowed them under. The main money crops, at least for rich soils, were wheat and flax. Forage crops included clover, vetch, and alfalfa. Prosperous farmers like Cato raised olive trees chiefly for the oil. They also raised grapevines for the production of wine. Cato and his neighbors harvested their cereal crops in summer and their grapes in autumn. Harvests varied depending on the soil, but farmers could usually expect yields of 5½ bushels of wheat or 10½ bushels of barley per acre.

An influx of slaves resulted from Rome's wars and conquests. The Roman attitude toward slaves and slavery had little in common with modern views. To the Romans slavery was a misfortune that befell some people, but it did not entail any racial theories. Races were not enslaved because the Romans thought them inferior. The black African slave was treated no worse—and no better—than the Spaniard. Indeed, some slaves were valued because of their physical distinctiveness: black Africans and blond Germans were particular favorites. For the talented slave the Romans always held out the hope of eventual freedom. **Manumission**—the freeing of individual slaves by their masters—became so common that it was limited by law. Not even Christians questioned the institution of slavery. It was just a fact of life.

Online Study Center Improve Your Grade
Primary Source: The Process of Freedom: Manumissions of Hellenistic Slaves

For Cato and most other Romans, religion played an important part in life. Originally the Romans thought of the gods as invisible, shapeless natural forces. Only through Etruscan and Greek influence did Roman deities take on human form. Jupiter, the sky-god, and his wife Juno became equivalent to the Greek Zeus and Hera. Mars was the god of war but also guaranteed the fertility of the farm and protected it from danger. The gods of the Romans were not loving and personal. They were stern, powerful, and aloof. But as long as the Romans honored the cults of their gods, they could expect divine favor. The shrine of the goddess Vesta, for example, was tended by six *vestal virgins* chosen from patrician families. Roman military losses were sometimes blamed on inattention by the vestal virgins, another link between female honor and the Roman state.

Along with the great gods the Romans believed in spirits who haunted fields, forests, crossroads, and even the home itself. Some of these deities were hostile; only magic could ward them off. The spirits of the dead, like ghosts in modern horror films, frequented places where they had lived. They too had to be placated but were ordinarily benign. As the poet Ovid (43 B.C.–A.D. 17) put it:

The spirits of the dead ask for little.
They are more grateful for piety than for an expensive gift—
Not greedy are the gods who haunt the Styx below.
A rooftile covered with a sacrificial crown,
Scattered kernels, a few grains of salt,
Bread dipped in wine, and loose violets—
These are enough.
Put them in a potsherd and leave them in the middle of the road.[3]

A good deal of Roman religion consisted of rituals such as those Ovid describes. These practices lived on long after the Romans had lost interest in the great gods. Even Christianity could not entirely wipe them out. Instead, Christianity was to incorporate many of these rituals into its own style of worship.

Scipio Aemilianus: Greek Culture and Urban Life

The old-fashioned ideals that Cato represented came into conflict with a new spirit of wealth and leisure. The conquest of the Mediterranean world and the spoils of war made Rome a great city. Roman life, especially in the cities, was changing and becoming less austere. The spoils of war went to build baths, theaters, and other places of amusement. Romans and Italian townspeople began to spend more of their time in leisure pursuits. Simultaneously, the new responsibilities of governing the world produced in Rome a sophisticated society. Romans developed new tastes and a liking for Greek culture and literature. They began to learn the Greek language. It became common for an educated Roman to speak both Latin and Greek. Hellenism dominated the cultural life of Rome. Even die-hards like Cato found a knowledge of Greek essential for political and diplomatic affairs. The poet Horace (64–8 B.C.) summed it up well: "Captive Greece captured her rough conqueror and introduced the arts into rustic Latium."

One of the most avid devotees of Hellenism and the new was Scipio Aemilianus, the destroyer of Carthage. Scipio realized that broad and worldly views had to replace the old Roman narrowness. The new situation called for new ways. Rome was no longer a small city on the Tiber; it was the capital of the world, and Romans had to adapt themselves to that fact. Scipio was ready to become an innovator in both politics and culture. He broke with the past in the conduct of his political career, choosing a more personal style of politics, one that reflected his own views and looked unflinchingly at the broader problems that the success of Rome brought to its people. He embraced Hellenism wholeheartedly. Perhaps more than anyone else of his day, Scipio represented the new Roman—imperial, cultured, and independent.

In his education and interests, too, Scipio broke with the past. As a boy he had received the traditional Roman training, learning to read and write Latin and becoming acquainted with the law. He mastered the fundamentals of rhetoric and learned how to throw the javelin, fight in armor, and ride a horse. But later Scipio also learned Greek and be-

came a fervent Hellenist. As a young man he formed a lasting friendship with the historian Polybius, who actively encouraged him in his study of Greek culture and in his intellectual pursuits. In later life Scipio's love of Greek learning, rhetoric, and philosophy became legendary. Scipio also promoted the spread of Hellenism in Roman society. He became the center of the Scipionic Circle, a small group of Greek and Roman artists, philosophers, historians, and poets. Conservatives like Cato tried to stem the rising tide of Hellenism, but men like Scipio carried the day and helped make the heritage of Greece an abiding factor in Roman life.

The new Hellenism profoundly stimulated the growth and development of Roman art and literature. The Roman conquest of the Hellenistic East resulted in wholesale confiscation of Greek paintings and sculpture to grace Roman temples, public buildings, and private homes. Roman artists copied many aspects of Greek art, but their emphasis on realistic portraiture carried on a native tradition.

Fabius Pictor (second half of the third century B.C.), a senator, wrote the first *History of Rome* in Greek. Other Romans translated Greek classics into Latin. Still others, such as the poet Ennius (239–169 B.C.), the father of

African Acrobat Conquest and prosperity brought exotic pleasure to Rome. Every feature of this sculpture is exotic. The young African woman and her daring gymnastic pose would catch anyone's attention. And to add to the spice of her act, she performs using a live crocodile as her platform. Americans would have loved it. *(Courtesy of the Trustees of the British Museum)*

Roman Table Manners   This mosaic is a floor that can never be swept clean. It whimsically suggests what a dining room floor looked like after a lavish dinner and also tells something about the menu: a chicken head, a wishbone, and remains of various seafood, vegetables, and fruit are easily recognizable. *(Museo Gregoriano Profano, Vatican Museums/Scala/Art Resource, NY)*

Latin poetry, studied Greek philosophy, wrote comedies in Latin, and adapted many of Euripides' tragedies for the Roman stage. Plautus (ca 254–184 B.C.) specialized in rough humor. He too decked out Greek plays in Roman dress but was no mere imitator. The Roman dramatist Terence (ca 195–159 B.C.), a member of the Scipionic Circle, wrote comedies of refinement and grace that owed their essentials to Greek models. His plays lacked the energy and the slapstick of Plautus's rowdy plays. All early Roman literature was derived from the Greeks, but it managed in time to speak in its own voice and to flourish because it had something of its own to say.

The conquest of the Mediterranean world brought the Romans leisure, and Hellenism influenced how they spent their free time. Many rich urban dwellers changed their eating habits by consuming elaborate meals of exotic dishes. A whole suckling pig stuffed with sausages was a favorite treat, and a lucky guest might even dine on peacocks, ostriches, and rare fish, all washed down with vintage wines.

During the second century B.C. the Greek custom of bathing also became a Roman passion and an important part of the day. In the early republic Romans had bathed infrequently, especially in the winter. Now large buildings containing pools and exercise rooms went up in great numbers, and the baths became an essential part of the Roman city. They became even more elaborate several centuries later. Architects built intricate systems of aqueducts to supply the bathing establishments with water. Conservatives railed at this Greek custom, calling it a waste of time and an encouragement to idleness. They were correct in that bathing establishments were more than just places to take a bath. They included gymnasia, where men exercised and played ball. Women had opportunities to bathe, generally in separate facilities or at separate times. The baths contained hot-air rooms to induce a good sweat and pools of hot and cold water to finish the actual bathing. They also contained snack bars and halls, where people chatted and read, and even libraries and lecture halls. The baths were socially important

Dressing of the Bride   Preparing for the wedding was an occasion for fun and ceremony. On the night before the event, the bride tried on her wedding dress for a favorable omen. The next morning her mother fastidiously dressed her or supervised a maid to do so. Last, the bride was crowned with a veil of flowers she had picked herself. *(Vatican Museums/Scala/Art Resource, NY)*

places where men and women went to see and be seen. Social climbers tried to talk to the right people and wangle invitations to dinner; politicians took advantage of the occasion to discuss the affairs of the day; marriages were negotiated by wealthy fathers. Prostitutes added to the attraction of many baths. These women were often slaves or members of the lower classes, who could also be found in brothels and inns. Actresses and entertainers likewise sometimes turned to prostitution as an easy way to increase their earnings, and baths provided good places to work. Despite the protests of conservatives and moralists, the baths at least furnished people—rich and poor—with places for clean and healthy relaxation.

Online Study Center **Improve Your Grade**
Primary Source: Public Space in an Urban Setting: The Sounds of a Roman Bath

Did Hellenism and new social customs corrupt the Romans? Perhaps the best answer is this: the Roman state and the empire it ruled continued to exist for six more centuries. Rome did not collapse; the state continued to prosper. The golden age of literature was still before it. The high tide of its prosperity still lay in the future. The Romans did not like change but took it in stride. That was part of their practical turn of mind and their strength.

The Late Republic (133–31 B.C.)

The wars of conquest created serious problems for the Romans, some of the most pressing of which were political. The republican constitution had suited the needs of a simple city-state but was inadequate to meet the requirements of Rome's new position in international affairs (see Map 5.2). Sweeping changes and reforms were necessary to make it serve the demands of a state holding vast territory. A system of provincial administration had to be established. Officials had to be appointed to govern the provinces and administer the law. These officials and administrative organs had to find places in the constitution. Armies had to be provided for defense, and a system of tax collection had to be created.

Other political problems were equally serious. During the wars Roman generals commanded huge numbers of troops for long periods of time. These men of great power and prestige were on the point of becoming too mighty for the state to control. Although Rome's Italian allies had borne much of the burden of the fighting, they received fewer rewards than did Roman officers and soldiers. Italians began to agitate for full Roman citizenship, including the right to vote.

● *What were the main problems and achievements of the late republic?*

Unrest in Rome and Italy

There were serious economic problems, too. Hannibal's operations and the warfare in Italy had left the countryside a shambles. The movements of numerous armies had disrupted agriculture. The prolonged fighting had also drawn untold numbers of Roman and Italian men away from their farms for long periods. The families of these soldiers could not keep the land under full cultivation. The people who defended Rome and conquered the world for Rome became impoverished for having done their duty.

These problems, complex and explosive, largely account for the turmoil of the closing years of the republic. The late republic was one of the most dramatic eras in Roman history. It produced some of Rome's most famous figures: the Gracchi, Marius, Sulla, Cicero, Pompey, and Julius Caesar, among others. In one way or another, each of these men attempted to solve Rome's problems. Yet they were also striving for the glory and honor that were the supreme goals of the senatorial aristocracy. Personal ambition often clashed with patriotism to create political tension throughout the period.

When the legionaries returned to their farms in Italy, they encountered an appalling situation. All too often their farms looked like the farms of people they had conquered. Two courses of action were open to them. They could rebuild as their forefathers had done, or they could take advantage of an alternative not open to their ancestors and sell their holdings. The wars of conquest had made some men astoundingly rich. These men wanted to invest their wealth in land. They bought up small farms to create huge estates, which the Romans called **latifundia.**

The purchase offers of the rich landowners appealed to the veterans for a variety of reasons. Many veterans had seen service in the East, where they had tasted the rich city life of the Hellenistic states. They were reluctant to return home and settle down to a dull life on the farm. Often their farms were so badly damaged that rebuilding hardly seemed worthwhile. Besides, it was hard to make big profits from small farms. Nor could the veterans supplement their income by working on the latifundia. Although the owners of the latifundia occasionally hired free men as day laborers, they preferred to use slaves. Slaves could not strike or be drafted into the army. Confronted by these conditions, veterans and their families opted to sell their land. They took what they could get for their broken farms and tried their luck elsewhere.

Most veterans migrated to the cities, especially to Rome. Although some found work, most did not. Industry and small manufacturing were generally in the hands of slaves. Even when work was available, slave labor kept the wages of free men low. Instead of a new start, veterans and their families encountered slum conditions that matched those of many modern American cities.

This trend held ominous consequences for the strength of Rome's armies. The Romans had always believed that only landowners should serve in the army, for only they had something to fight for. Landless men, even if they were Romans and lived in Rome, could not be conscripted into the army. These landless men may have been veterans of major battles and numerous campaigns; they may have won distinction on the battlefield. But once they sold their land, they became ineligible for further military service. A large pool of experienced manpower was going to waste. The landless ex-legionaries wanted a new start, and they were willing to support any leader who would provide it.

One man who recognized the plight of Rome's peasant farmers and urban poor was an aristocrat, Tiberius Gracchus (163–133 B.C.). Appalled by what he saw, Tiberius warned his countrymen that the legionaries were losing their land while fighting Rome's wars:

The wild beasts that roam over Italy have every one of them a cave or lair to lurk in. But the men who fight and die for Italy enjoy the common air and light, indeed, but nothing else. Houseless and homeless they wander about with their wives and children. And it is with lying lips that their generals exhort the soldiers in their battles to defend sepulchres and shrines from the enemy, for not a man of them has an hereditary altar, not one of all these many Romans an ancestral tomb, but they fight and die to support others in luxury, and though they are styled masters of the world, they have not a single clod of earth that is their own.[4]

Until his death Tiberius Gracchus sought a solution to the problems of the veterans and the urban poor.

After his election as tribune of the people in 133 B.C., Tiberius proposed that public land be given to the poor in small lots. Although his reform enjoyed the support of some very distinguished and popular aristocrats, he immediately ran into trouble for a number of reasons. First, his reform bill angered many wealthy aristocrats who had usurped large tracts of public land for their own use. They had no desire to give any of it back, so they bitterly resisted Tiberius's efforts. This was to be expected, yet he unquestionably made additional problems for himself. He introduced his land bill in the concilium plebis without consulting the senate. When King Attalus III left the kingdom of Pergamum to the Romans in his will, Tiberius had the money appropriated to finance his reforms—another slap at the senate. As tribune he acted

Pompeii The eruption of Mt. Vesuvius that buried this Italian city in A.D. 79 preserved a singular view of Roman life. The huge temple of Jupiter in the near foreground dominated the city. Other temples and sacred places surround it. Next to it lie the marketplace and various public buildings. *(Guido Alberto Rossi/Altitude)*

totally within his rights. Yet the way in which he proceeded was unprecedented. Many powerful Romans became suspicious of Tiberius's growing influence with the people, some even thinking that he aimed at tyranny. Others opposed him because of his unparalleled methods. After all, there were proper ways to do things in Rome, and he had not followed them. As a result, violence broke out when a large body of senators, led by the *pontifex maximus* (the chief priest), killed Tiberius in cold blood. It was a black day in Roman history. The very people who directed the affairs of state and administered the law had taken the law into their own hands. The death of Tiberius was the beginning of an era of political violence. In the end that violence would bring down the republic.

Although Tiberius was dead, his land bill became law. Furthermore, Tiberius's brother Gaius Gracchus (153–121 B.C.) took up the cause of reform. Gaius was a veteran soldier with an enviable record, but this fiery orator made his mark in the political arena. Gaius also became tribune and demanded even more extensive reform than

had his brother. To help the urban poor Gaius pushed legislation to provide them with cheap grain for bread. He defended his brother's land law and suggested other measures for helping the landless. He proposed that Rome send many of its poor and propertyless people out to form colonies in southern Italy. The poor would have a new start and lead productive lives. The city would immediately benefit because excess, nonproductive families would leave for new opportunities abroad. Rome would be less crowded, sordid, and dangerous.

Gaius went a step further and urged that all Italians be granted full rights of Roman citizenship. This measure provoked a storm of opposition, and it was not passed in Gaius's lifetime. Yet in the long run he proved wiser than his opponents. In 91 B.C. many Italians revolted against Rome over the issue of full citizenship, thus triggering the Social War, so named from the Latin word *socium,* or "ally." After a brief but hard-fought war (91–88 B.C.), the senate gave Roman citizenship to all Italians. Had the senate listened to Gaius earlier, it could have prevented a great deal of bloodshed. Yet Gaius himself was also at fault. Like his brother Tiberius, Gaius aroused a great deal of personal and factional opposition. To many he seemed too radical and too hasty to change things. Many political opponents considered him belligerent and headstrong. When Gaius failed in 121 B.C. to win the tribunate for the third time, he feared for his life. In desperation he armed his staunchest supporters, whereupon the senate ordered the consul Opimius to restore order. He did so by having Gaius killed, along with three thousand of Gaius's supporters who opposed the senate's order. Once again the cause of reform had met with violence.

The death of Gaius brought little peace, and trouble came from two sources: the outbreak of new wars in the Mediterranean basin and further political unrest in Rome. In 112 B.C. Rome declared war against the rebellious Jugurtha, king of Numidia in North Africa. Numidia had been one of Rome's **client kingdoms,** kingdoms still ruled by their own kings but subject to Rome. These kingdoms entered into a political relationship with Rome that was usually friendly but was not a relationship between equals: Rome always remained the senior partner. The kingdoms followed Rome's lead in foreign affairs but conducted their own internal business according to their own laws and customs. Client kingdoms generally lay on the outskirts of Roman control, which gave them an additional measure of local control. The benefits of these relations were mutual, for the client kingdoms enjoyed the protection of Rome while defending Rome's borders. In time many of these states became provinces of the Roman Empire.

Meanwhile, the Roman legions made little headway against Jugurtha until 107 B.C., when Gaius Marius, an Italian *new man* (a politician not from the traditional Roman aristocracy), became consul. Marius's values were those of the military camp. A man of fierce vigor and courage, Marius saw the army as the tool of his ambition. He took the unusual but not wholly unprecedented step of recruiting an army by permitting landless men to serve in the legions. Marius thus tapped Rome's vast reservoir of idle manpower. His volunteer army was a professional force, not a body of draftees. In 106 B.C. Marius and his new army handily defeated Jugurtha.

An unexpected war broke out in the following year when two German peoples, the Cimbri and Teutones, moved into Gaul and later into northern Italy. After the Germans had defeated Roman armies sent to repel them, Marius was again elected consul, even though he was legally ineligible. From 104 to 100 B.C. Marius annually held the consulship. Despite the military necessity, Marius's many consulships meant that a Roman commander repeatedly held unprecedented military power in his

hands. This would later translate into a political problem that the Roman republic never solved.

Before engaging the Cimbri and Teutones, Marius reformed the Roman army. There was, however, a disturbing side to his reforms, one that would henceforth haunt the republic. To encourage enlistments, Marius promised land to his volunteers after the war. Poor and landless veterans flocked to him, and together they conquered the Germans by 101 B.C. When Marius proposed a bill to grant land to his veterans, the senate refused to act, in effect turning its back on the soldiers of Rome. It was a disastrous mistake. Henceforth the legionaries expected the commanders—not the senate or the state—to protect their interests. Through Marius's reforms the Roman army became a professional force, but it owed little allegiance to the state. By failing to reward the loyalty of Rome's troops, the senate set the stage for military rebellion and political anarchy.

The Social War brought Marius into conflict with Sulla, who was consul in 88 B.C. First Marius and later Sulla defeated the Italian rebels. In the final stages of the war, while putting down the last of the rebels, Sulla was deposed from his consulship because of factional chaos in Rome. He immediately marched on Rome and restored order, but it was an ominous sign of the deterioration of Roman politics and political ideals. With some semblance of order restored, Sulla in 88 B.C. led an army to the East, where King Mithridates of Pontus in Asia Minor challenged Roman rule. In Sulla's absence, rioting and political violence again exploded in Rome. Marius and his supporters marched on Rome and launched a reign of terror.

Although Marius died peacefully in 86 B.C., his supporters continued to hold Rome. Once Sulla had defeated Mithridates, he once again, this time in 82 B.C., marched on Rome. After a brief but intense civil war, Sulla entered Rome and ordered a ruthless butchery of his opponents. He also proclaimed himself dictator. He launched many political and judicial reforms, including strengthening the senate while weakening the tribunate, increasing the number of magistrates in order to administer Rome's provinces better, and restoring the courts.

In 79 B.C. Sulla voluntarily abdicated his dictatorship and permitted the republican constitution to function normally once again. Yet his dictatorship cast a long shadow over the late republic. Sulla the political reformer proved far less influential than Sulla the successful general and dictator. Civil war was to be the constant lot of Rome for the next fifty years, until the republican constitution gave way to the empire of Augustus in 27 B.C. The history of the late republic is the story of the power struggles of some of Rome's most famous figures: Julius

Caesar and Pompey, Augustus and Marc Antony. One figure who stands apart is Cicero (106–43 B.C.), a practical politician whose greatest legacy to the Roman world and to Western civilization is his mass of political and oratorical writings. Yet Cicero commanded no legions, and only legions commanded respect.

Civil War

In the late republic many other Romans were grappling with the simple and inescapable fact that their old city-state constitution was unequal to the demands of overseas possessions and the governing of provinces. (See the feature "Individuals in Society: Quintus Sertorius.") Thus even Sulla's efforts to put the constitution back together proved hollow. Once the senate and other institutions of the Roman state had failed to come to grips with the needs of empire, once the authorities had lost control of their own generals and soldiers, and once the armies put their faith in commanders instead of in Rome, the republic was doomed.

Sulla's real political heirs were Pompey and Julius Caesar, with at least Caesar realizing that the days of the old republican constitution were numbered. Pompey, a man of boundless ambition, began his career as one of Sulla's lieutenants. After his army put down a rebellion in Spain, he himself threatened to rebel unless the senate allowed him to run for consul. He and another ambitious politician, Crassus, pooled political resources, and both won the consulship. They dominated Roman politics until the rise of Julius Caesar, who became consul in 59 B.C. Together the three concluded a political alliance, the **First Triumvirate,** in which they agreed to advance one another's interests.

The man who cast the longest shadow over these troubled years was Julius Caesar (100–44 B.C.). More than a mere soldier, Caesar was a cultivated man. Born of a noble family, he received an excellent education, which he furthered by studying in Greece with some of the most eminent teachers of the day. He had serious intellectual interests, and his literary ability was immense. Caesar was a superb orator, and his affable personality and wit made him popular. He was also a shrewd politician of unbridled ambition. Since military service was an effective steppingstone to politics, Caesar launched his military career in Spain, where his courage won the respect and affection of his troops. Personally brave and tireless, Caesar was a military genius who

knew how to win battles and turn victories into permanent gains.

Online Study Center **Improve Your Grade**
Primary Source: A Man of Unlimited Ambition: Julius Caesar

In 58 B.C. Caesar became governor of Cisalpine Gaul, or modern northern Italy. By 50 B.C. he had conquered all of Gaul, or modern France. Caesar's account of his operations, his *Commentaries* on the Gallic wars, became a classic in Western literature and most schoolchildren's introduction to Latin. By 49 B.C. the First Triumvirate had fallen apart. Crassus had died in battle, and Caesar and Pompey, each suspecting the other of treachery, came to blows. The result was a long and bloody civil war that raged from Spain across northern Africa to Egypt.

Online Study Center **Improve Your Grade**
Primary Source: The Tyrant Is Dead! But . . . : Cicero Offers Faint Praise for Antony

Egypt was ruled by a Greek dynasty that had been in power for centuries, and right at this point was also in the middle of a battle over who would be the supreme ruler. This fight was not between two generals, but between brother and sister, Ptolemy XIII and Cleopatra VII (69–30 B.C.). Cleopatra first allied herself with Pompey but then switched her alliance to Caesar. The two became lovers as well as allies, and she bore him a son. She returned to Rome with Caesar, but was hated by the Roman people as a symbol of the immoral East and a threat to what were viewed as traditional Roman values.

Although Pompey enjoyed the official support of the Roman government, Caesar finally defeated Pompey's forces in 45 B.C. He had overthrown the republic and made himself dictator.

Julius Caesar was not merely another victorious general. Politically brilliant, he was determined to make basic reforms, even at the expense of the old constitution. He took the first long step to break down the barriers

Julius Caesar In this bust, the sculptor portrays Caesar as a man of power and intensity. It is a study of determination and an excellent example of Roman portraiture. *(Museo Archeologico Nazionale Naples/Scala/Art Resource, NY)*

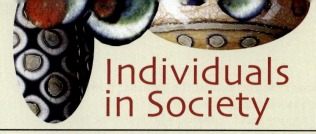

Individuals in Society

Quintus Sertorius

Quintus Sertorius, son of a prominent Italian family, stands as a prime example of the transition of the Roman republic from local power to master of the Mediterranean world. Born not in Rome itself but in nearby Nurisa (modern Norcia) in 126 B.C., he became a Roman citizen. Like many of his contemporaries, he rose to high office and took part in the political and military upheavals of the day. He became a rebel against Rome and helped shape the new Mediterranean community.

Sertorius launched his public career in Rome, where he mastered Roman law and became a gifted military officer. When two barbarian tribes invaded Gaul in 105 B.C., he fought so effectively that his ability and valor brought him to the attention of senior Roman military commanders. These events honed his martial skills and acquainted him with the new peoples gradually entering western Europe.

Sertorius's success in Gaul led him in 97 B.C. to higher command in Spain. From that time until his death, his destiny and Spain's would be intertwined. He, like Marius, Sulla, and other notable men, was swept up in this vast and chaotic episode in republican history. He chose the wrong side and upon defeat fled to Spain, where he worked to establish his own independent authority.

A surprising accident put another tool of authority into Sertorius's hands. As the story goes, one of his soldiers, while hunting, encountered a white fawn. Instead of killing the doe, he presented it to Sertorius, who made a pet of it. Sertorius declared that the animal was the gift of Diana, whose attributes included the gifts of wisdom and prophecy. The superstitious Spaniards, who had long believed in Diana's cult of the stag, believed that Diana had blessed Sertorius. This divine endorsement made him seem more Spanish and enhanced his authority among the Spaniards.

The Roman civil war soon reached Spain. Sertorius's reputation and exploits persuaded many Spaniards to invite him to lead them against the Romans. He agreed, even though he always remained a Roman at heart. He began to organize these supporters along Roman military lines. He taught them Roman principles of military command and tactics so that they could meet the greatly feared Roman army in successful, organized bodies.

These things done, Sertorius led the Spaniards against the Romans. Instead of meeting the Roman legions face-to-face, he resorted to ambushes, flanking

This statue of Quintus Sertorius still bears testimony to Rome's respect for his efforts to unite Romans and Spaniards.
(Courtesy, Luca Bonacina)

movements, and quick marches to isolate the enemy. He also struck at Roman supply lines. His success prompted many Romans to switch sides. Even some senators left Rome to join him. Welcoming them with honor, he got them involved in the civil government that he introduced. Sertorius modeled his Spanish state along Roman civil lines but under his leadership. Spain had never seen so many military, cultural, and civil developments in such a short time.

Many Greeks and Romans joined Sertorius because of his success and generosity. This flattering response seemed to bolster his plans but led to his failure and death. The Romans to whom he had bestowed a home began to insult, punish, and abuse the Spaniards while doing everything possible to thwart Sertorius's plans. Then they rebelled against him, hoping either to topple him and reign in his place or to return the province to Roman rule. Finally, with a treachery that matched that of the conspirators against Caesar, some Romans who were still considered loyal assassinated Sertorius at a banquet in 73 B.C. Roman generals from the East easily took control of Spain and ultimately reaped Sertorius's harvest.

Death and defeat did not erase Sertorius's achievements in Spain. He above any of his predecessors introduced the region to Greco-Roman culture. He gave the land and its peoples a civil government that united them. He turned their tribal hordes into an army along Roman lines. He paved the way for peaceful Spanish inclusion into the quickly evolving Roman Empire.

Questions for Analysis

1. How did Sertorius create a state in Spain?
2. What was his legacy to Spain, Rome, and Western civilization in general?

Online Study Center **Improve Your Grade**
Going Beyond Individuals in Society

between Italy and the provinces, extending citizenship to many of the provincials who had supported him. Caesar also took measures to cope with Rome's burgeoning population. By Caesar's day perhaps 750,000 people lived in Rome. Caesar drew up plans to send his veterans and some 80,000 of the poor and unemployed to colonies throughout the Mediterranean. He founded at least twenty colonies, most of which were located in Gaul, Spain, and North Africa. These colonies were important agents in spreading Roman culture in the western Mediterranean. A Roman empire composed of citizens, not subjects, was the result.

In 44 B.C. a group of conspirators assassinated Caesar and set off another round of civil war. Caesar had named his eighteen-year-old grandnephew, Octavian—or Augustus, as he is better known to history—as his heir. Augustus joined forces with two of Caesar's lieutenants, Marc Antony and Lepidus, in a pact known as the Second Triumvirate, and together they hunted down and

defeated Caesar's murderers. In the process, however, Augustus and Antony came into conflict.

In 41 B.C. Antony met Cleopatra, who had gone back to Egypt after Julius Caesar's assassination. Though Antony was already married to Augustus's sister Octavia, he became Cleopatra's lover. Augustus and other Roman leaders described Antony as a romantic and foolish captive of the seductive Cleopatra, particularly after Antony repudiated Octavia, married Cleopatra, and changed his will to favor his children by Cleopatra. Roman sources are viciously hostile to Cleopatra, and she became the model of the *femme fatale* whose sexual attraction led men to their doom. Romans turned against Antony as a traitor and a weakling, and in 31 B.C. Augustus defeated the army and navy of Cleopatra and Antony at the Battle of Actium in Greece. The two committed suicide, an incident that has been the subject of countless paintings and many movies. This victory put an end to an age of civil war that had lasted since the days of Sulla.

Chapter Summary

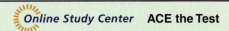
Online Study Center   **ACE the Test**

- *How did the land help shape Roman developments?*
- *What was the nature of the Roman republic?*
- *How did the Romans expand farther into Italy?*
- *What values did the Romans embrace because of their expansion?*
- *What were the main problems and achievements of the late republic?*

The land of Italy proved kinder to the Romans and their neighbors than did the peninsula of Hellas to the Greeks. The newcomers settled comfortably on the seven hills of Rome by the banks of the Tiber River. They came into contact with the Etruscans, who had settled in Italy before their arrival. Separate villages soon merged into one city, creating a single community. Under the governance of the more politically and socially advanced Etruscans, the Romans fully entered the wider world around them.

Once established, the Romans created an advanced and flexible political constitution of their own. Their society fell into two principal groups: the aristocratic patricians who led the community and the commoners who

made up the rest of the citizenry and filled the ranks of the army. Though often at odds, these two basic social groups learned how to live and work together, and thus created a powerful, unified state.

From these beginnings the Romans spread their power and influence through the rest of Italy. Beginning as conquerors, the Romans learned to use alliances and political agreements to unite their efforts with those of other Italian communities to create a common policy. They put this association on a formal political basis to create a government shared by Romans and non-Romans. Looking beyond Italy, the Romans fought three hard wars with the Carthaginians, their Punic neighbors in North Africa. In the process they included the Greeks of southern Italy in their growing empire. As these wars spread to western Europe, the Romans won control of Spain and Gaul, modern France. Further warfare next took them eastward into the Hellenistic world. Conquest followed conquest to create the nucleus of the Roman Empire.

These tumultuous events fundamentally reshaped Roman society. Though some Romans longed for what they saw as simpler times, many were dazzled by Hellenistic sophistication and ways of life. They learned to appreciate the arts and intellectual pursuits of the older Greek and Eastern cultures. They joined fully the broad cultural world of the Mediterranean, all the while making their own contribution.

Yet in some ways the Romans had moved too far and too fast from their small beginnings. Their empire had become too big for them to manage easily. Their constitution and political institutions could no longer adequately cope with the burdens and pressures that imperial life brought. After a series of bloody civil wars, the general Octavian, soon to be more generally known as Augustus, restored order and forever changed the nature of Roman life and government.

Key Terms

pomerium
fasces
toga
Forum
Gauls
franchise
patricians
plebeians
senate
praetor
ius civile (civil law)
ius naturale (natural law)

Struggle of the Orders
tribunes
paterfamilias
Pyrrhic victory
First Punic War
Second Punic War
manumission
latifundia
client kingdoms
First Triumvirate

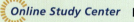 **Online Study Center** Improve Your Grade Flashcards

Suggested Reading

Bauman, Richard A. *Women and Politics in Ancient Rome.* 1992. Explores the influential role of Roman women in business, government, law, and public affairs.

Bradley, Keith R. *Slavery and Rebellion in the Roman World.* 1989. Analyzes slave revolts.

Dixon, Suzanne. *The Roman Family.* 1992. Focuses on legal and cultural changes in the Roman family and how these affected family members.

Gardner, Jane F. *Being a Roman Citizen.* 1993. A broad work that includes material on ex-slaves, the lower classes, and much else.

Gelzer, Mattias. *Caesar, Politician and Statesman*, English trans. 1968. Remains the best study of Caesar and his times, with much material from original sources.

Gruen, Erich S. *Culture and National Identity in Republican Rome.* 1992. Explores the effects of the introduction of Greek ideas, literature, and learning into central aspects of Roman life.

Gruen, Erich S. *The Last Generation of the Roman Republic.* 1974. Explores the political history of the last republic.

Haynes, Sibylle. *Etruscan Civilization: A Cultural History.* 2000. A wonderfully illustrated history of the Etruscans.

Kallet-Marx, Robert. *Hegemony to Empire.* 1995. Examines how Rome's power in the eastern Mediterranean became established between 148 and 62 B.C.

Kamm, Antony. *Julius Caesar.* 2006. An excellent brief biography designed for students that deals with his life as a politician, orator, and writer.

Lazenby, J. F. *Hannibal's War: A Military History of the Second Punic War.* 1998. An account of the conflict.

Scullard, H. H. *A History of the Roman World, 753–146 B.C.*, 4th ed. 1993. A broad account of Roman history.

Smith, Christopher J. *Early Rome and Latium: Economy and Society, c. 1000 to 500 B.C.* 1996. Examines early Roman expansion on the Italian peninsula.

Turcan, Robert. *The Gods of Ancient Rome: Religion in Everyday Life from Archaic to Imperial Times.* 2000. Examines the meaning of the gods to the Romans and the rituals associated with their worship, including family and state religions; written for students and general readers.

Williams, Craig A. *Roman Homosexuality: Ideologies of Masculinity in Classical Antiquity.* 1999. Examines ways in which Roman ideals of masculinity were linked with the sexual experiences of men in both literature and society.

Notes

1. Polybius, *The Histories* 1.1.5. John Buckler is the translator of all uncited quotations from a foreign language in Chapters 1–6.
2. Sallust, *War with Catiline* 10.1–3.
3. Ovid, *Fasti* 2.535–539.
4. Plutarch, *Life of Tiberius Gracchus* 9.5–6.

A Magic Charm

The pursuit of love is one of the oldest histories in the world. It also takes many shapes, some of them rather complicated. Not everything is as simple as boy meets girl, as this love charm demonstrates.

The following magical text comes from a papyrus found in Egypt and now housed in Paris. It dates from the period of the Roman Empire, but parts of it go back for centuries, which testifies to the popularity of these rituals. Here the lovelorn applicant is instructed to take the following steps in a rigorously prescribed order. By turning to magic he plans to win the heart of his beloved. Although the incantations sound like gibberish, the gods of the underworld understand them. The ritual not only has power over the daemons, or lesser spirits of the underworld, and over the spirits of the dead, but also can direct the actions of the living. The incantations are vital because they allow the human petitioner to contact these gods directly. In this case the applicant seeks the love of his desired whether or not she desires him in return. Similar love charms designed for women to attract men and for both men and women to attract members of the same sex have also been discovered.

Take wax [or clay] from a potter's wheel and form two figures, one male and one female. Make the male one look like Ares in arms, holding a sword in his left hand and pointing it at her right collarbone. Her arms must be (tied) behind her back, and she must kneel. Fasten the magical substance on her head or neck. On the figure of the woman you want to attract write as follows. On the head: ISEE IAO ITHI OUNE BRIDO LOTHION NEBOUTOSOUALETH. On the right ear: OUER MECHAN. On the left: LIBABA OIMATHOTHO. On the face: AMOUNABREO. On the right eye: ORORMOTHIO AETH. On the other: CHOBOUE. On the right shoulder: ADETA MEROU. On the right arm: ENE PSA ENESGAPH. On the other: MELCHIOU MELCHIEDA. On the hands: MELCHAMELCHOU AEL. On the breast write the name, on her mother's side, of the woman you want to attract. On the heart: BALAMIN THOOUTH. Under the abdomen: AOBES AOBAR. On her sexual organs: BLICHIANEOI OUOIA. On her buttocks: PISSADARA. On the sole of the right foot: ELO. On the other: ELOAIOE. Take thirteen bronze needles and stick one in the brain and say: "I am piercing your brain, NN." Stick two in the ears, two in the eyes, one in the mouth, two in the midriff, one in the hands, two in the genital organs, two in the soles, saying each time: "I am piercing such and such a member of NN, so that she may remember me, NN alone." Take a lead tablet and write on it the same formula and recite it. Tie the lead leaf [i.e., the lead tablet] to the two creatures with thread from the loom after making three hundred sixty-five knots, saying, as you have learned: "Abrasax, hold her fast." As the sun is setting, you must place it near the tomb of a person who has died an untimely or a violent death, along with the flowers of the season.

The formula to be written and recited: "I am handing over this binding spell to you, gods of the underworld, HYESEMIGADON and KORE PERSEPHONE ERESCHIGAL and ADONIS, the BARBARITHA, chthonic HERMES THOOUTH PHOKENTAZEPSEU AERCHTHATOUMI SONKTAI KALBANACHAMRE and to mighty ANUBIS PSIRINTH who has the keys to the realm of Hades, to gods and daemons of the underworld, to men and women who have died before their time, to young men and women, from year to year, from month to month, from day to day, from hour to hour. I adjure all the daemons in this place to assist this daemon. Arouse yourself for me, whoever you are, male or female, and enter every place, every neighborhood, every house, and attract and bind,

Amulet of Abrasax, the demon with the head of a cock, the body of a Roman soldier, feet of snakes, and whip in the right hand. This amulet protected against other demons. *(Kelsey Museum of Archaeology, University of Michigan, KM 26054)*

attract NN, daughter of NN, whose magical substance you have. Make NN, daughter of NN be in love with me. Let her not have sexual intercourse with another man, . . . let her not have pleasure with another man, only with me, NN, so that she, NN, is unable to drink or eat, to love, to be strong, to be healthy, to enjoy sleep, NN without me, NN, because I adjure you by the fearful, the awesome name, the name at whose sound the earth will open, the name at whose terrifying sound the daemon will panic, the name at whose sound rivers and rocks will explode. I adjure you, daemon-dead [i.e., the spirit of a dead person], male or female, in the name of BARBARITHA CHENMBRA and in the name of ABRAT ABRASAX SESENGEN BARPHARANGES and in the name of MARMAREOTH MARMARAUOTH MARMARAOTH MARECHTHANA AMARZA MARIBEOTH. Listen to my commands and to the names. Just arouse yourself from the repose that holds you, whoever you are, male or female, and enter every place, every neighborhood, every house, and bring her, NN, to me, and keep her from eating and drinking, and let her, NN, not enjoy the attempt of any other man, not even that of her own man, only my own, NN. Yes, drag her, NN, by her hair, by her heart, by her soul to me, NN, every hour of life [or: eternity], night and day, until she comes to me, NN, and let her, NN, remain inseparable from me. Do this, bind her for all the time of my life and force her, NN, to be my, NN, servant, and let her not flutter away from me for even one hour of life [or: eternity]. If you accomplish this for me, I will let you rest at once. For I am BARBAR ADONAI who hides the stars, who governs with his bright splendor the heaven; [I am] the lord of the world, ATHTHOUIN IATHOUIN SELBIOUOTH AOTH SARBA THIOUTH IATHRIERATH ADONAI LA ROURA BIA BI BIOTHE ATHOTH SABAOTH

EA NIAPHA AMARACHTHI SATAMA ZAUATHTHERE SERPHO IALADA IALE SBESI IATHTHA MARADTHA ACHIL THTHEE CHOOO OE EACHO KANSAOSA ALKMOURI THYR OSO MAI. Attract her, bind her, NN, make her love me, desire me, yearn for me, NN, (add the usual), because I adjure you, daemon-dead, in the name of the terrible, the great IAEO BAPH RENEMOUN OTHI LARIKRIPHIA EYEAI PHIRKIRALITHON YOMEN ER PHABOEA, to bring her, NN, to me.

Questions for Analysis

1. How does this magical charm invoke the help of the gods?

2. Does the woman he seeks favor him, or is she reluctant?

3. Is the charm to entice love or to force submission?

Source: G. Luck, *Magic and the Occult in the Greek and Roman Worlds: A Collection of Ancient Texts,* pp. 129–131. © 2006 The Johns Hopkins University Press. Reprinted with permission of The Johns Hopkins University Press.

Hadrian's Wall. *(D. J. Ball / Tony Stone Images / Getty Images)*

THE PAX ROMANA,
31 B.C.–A.D. 450

Had the Romans conquered the entire Mediterranean world only to turn it into their battlefield? Would they, like the Greeks before them, become their own worst enemies, destroying one another and wasting their strength until they perished? At Julius Caesar's death in 44 B.C., it must have seemed so to many. Yet finally, in 31 B.C., Augustus restored peace to a tortured world, and with peace came prosperity, new hope, and a new vision of Rome's destiny. The Roman poet Virgil expressed this vision most nobly:

You, Roman, remember—these are your arts:
To rule nations, and to impose the ways of peace,
To spare the humble and to war down the proud.[1]

In place of the republic, Augustus established what can be called a constitutional monarchy. He attempted to achieve lasting cooperation in government and balance among the people, magistrates, senate, and army. His efforts were not always successful. His settlement of Roman affairs did not permanently end civil war. Yet he carried on Caesar's work. It was Augustus who created the structure that the modern world calls the "Roman Empire." He did his work so well and his successors so capably added to it that Rome realized Virgil's hope. For the first and second centuries A.D., the lot of the Mediterranean world was the Roman peace—the **pax Romana,** a period of security, order, harmony, flourishing culture, and expanding economy. It was a period that saw the wilds of Gaul, Spain, Germany, eastern Europe, and western Africa introduced to Greco-Roman culture. By the third century A.D., Rome and its culture had left an indelible mark on the ages to come.

Augustus's Settlement (31 B.C.–A.D. 14)

When Augustus put an end to the civil wars that had raged since 88 B.C., he faced monumental problems of reconstruction. Sole ruler of the entire Mediterranean world as no Roman had ever been before, he had a rare opportunity to shape the future. But how?

Online Study Center

This icon will direct you to interactive activities and study materials on the website **college.hmco.com/pic/mckaywest9e**

Augustus could easily have declared himself dictator, as Caesar had, but the thought was repugnant to him. Augustus was neither an autocrat nor a revolutionary. His solution, as he put it, was to restore the republic. But was that possible? Some eighteen years of anarchy and civil war had shattered the republican constitution. In stark reality, by Augustus's day no one alive had even lived under the ancestral constitution. The events of the middle republic, the aftermath of the Punic Wars, and the upheavals of the civil wars had dramatically and irreversibly changed it. Nor could it be rebuilt. Augustus recognized these problems but did not let them stop him. From 29 to 23 B.C. he toiled to heal Rome's wounds. The first problem facing him was to rebuild the constitution and the organs of government. Next he had to demobilize much of the army yet maintain enough soldiers in the provinces of the empire to meet the danger of barbarians at Rome's European frontiers. Augustus was highly successful in meeting these challenges. His gift of peace to a war-torn world sowed the seeds of a literary flowering that produced some of the finest fruits of the Roman mind.

● *How did Augustus restore stability; what political and military changes did he institute; and how did he spread Roman influence to northern and western Europe?*

The Principate and the Restored Republic

Augustus claimed that in restoring constitutional government he was also restoring the republic. Typically Roman, he preferred not to create anything new; he intended instead to modify republican forms and offices to meet new circumstances. Augustus planned for the senate to take on a serious burden of duty and responsibility. He expected it to administer some of the provinces, continue to be the chief deliberative body of the state, and act as a court of law. Yet he did not give the senate enough power to become his partner in government. As a result, the senate could not live up to the responsibilities that Augustus assigned. Many of its prerogatives shifted to Augustus and his successors by default.

Augustus's own position in the restored republic was something of an anomaly. He could not simply surrender the reins of power, for someone else would only have seized them. But how was he to fit into a republican constitution? Again Augustus had his own answer. He became *princeps civitatis*, "First Citizen of the State." This prestigious title carried no power; it indicated only that

Augustus was the most distinguished of all Roman citizens. In effect, it designated Augustus as the first among equals, a little "more equal" than anyone else in the state. Clearly, much of the *principate,* as the period of First Citizen is known, was a legal fiction. Yet that need not imply that Augustus, like a modern dictator, tried to clothe himself with constitutional legitimacy. In an inscription known as *Res Gestae* (The Deeds of Augustus), Augustus described his constitutional position:

In my sixth and seventh consulships [28–27 B.C.], I had ended the civil war, having obtained through universal consent total control of affairs. I transferred the Republic from my power to the authority of the Roman people and the senate. . . . After that time I stood before all in rank, but I had power no greater than those who were my colleagues in any magistracy.[2]

Augustus as Imperator Here Augustus, dressed in breastplate and uniform, emphasizes the imperial majesty of Rome and his role as *imperator*. The figures on his breastplate represent the restoration of peace, one of Augustus's greatest accomplishments and certainly one that he frequently stressed. *(Erich Lessing/Art Resource, NY)*

What is to be made of Augustus's constitutional settlement? Despite his claims to the contrary, Augustus had not restored the republic. Augustus had created a **constitutional monarchy,** something completely new in Roman history. The title **princeps,** First Citizen, came to mean in Rome, as it does today, "prince" in the sense of a sovereign ruler.

Online Study Center **Improve Your Grade**
Primary Source: The Res Gestae of Augustus Caesar: Propaganda in the First Century A.D.

Augustus was not exactly being a hypocrite, but he carefully kept his real military power in the background. As consul he had no more constitutional and legal power than his fellow consul. Yet in addition to the consulship Augustus had many other magistracies, which his fellow consul did not. Constitutionally, his ascendancy within the state stemmed from the number of magistracies he held and the power granted him by the senate. At first he held the consulship annually; then the senate voted him proconsular power on a regular basis. The senate also voted him *tribunicia potestas*—the "full power of the tribunes." Tribunician power gave Augustus the right to call the senate into session, present legislation to the people, and defend their rights. He held either high office or the powers of chief magistrate year in and year out. No other magistrate could do the same. In 12 B.C. he became *pontifex maximus,* the chief priest of the state. By assuming this position of great honor, Augustus also became chief religious official. Without specifically saying so, he had created the office of emperor, which included many traditional powers separated from their traditional offices.

The main source of Augustus's power was his position as commander of the Roman army. His title **imperator,** with which Rome customarily honored a general after a major victory, came to mean "emperor" in the modern sense of the term. Augustus governed the provinces where troops were needed for defense. The frontiers were his special concern. There Roman legionaries held the German barbarians at arm's length. The frontiers were also areas where fighting could be expected to break out. Augustus made sure that Rome went to war only at his command. He controlled deployment of the Roman army and paid its wages. He granted it bonuses and gave veterans retirement benefits. Thus he avoided the problems with the army that the old senate had created for itself. Augustus never shared control of the army, and no Roman found it easy to defy him militarily.

Augustus made a momentous change in the army by making it a permanent, professional force. This was

Chronology

27 B.C.–A.D. 68	Julio-Claudian emperors; expansion into northern and western Europe; growth and stability of trade in the empire
17 B.C.–A.D. 17	Flowering of Latin literature
ca 3 B.C.–A.D. 29	Life of Jesus
ca A.D. 30–312	Spread of Christianity
A.D. 41–54	Creation of the imperial bureaucracy
A.D. 60–120	Composition of the New Testament
A.D. 69–96	Consolidation of the European frontiers
A.D. 70–ca 118	"Silver age" of Latin literature
A.D. 96–180	"Golden age" of prosperity and huge expansion of trade
A.D. 96–180	"Five good emperors"; increasing barbarian menace on the frontiers
A.D. 193–284	Military monarchy; extension of citizenship to all free men
A.D. 278–337	Steady spread of administration, government, and law from Britain to Syria
A.D. 284–337	Inflation and decline of trade and industry; transition to the Middle Ages in the West and the Byzantine Empire in the East
A.D. 337	Baptism of Constantine

Rome's first standing army. Soldiers received regular and standard training under career officers who advanced in rank according to experience, ability, valor, and length of service. Legions were transferred from place to place, as the need arose. They had no regular barracks. In later years of the empire soldiers could live with their families in the camps themselves. By making the army professional, Augustus forged a reliable tool for the defense of the empire. The army could also act against the central authority, much as Marius's army had earlier. Yet the mere fact that men could make a career of the army meant that it became a recognized institution of government and that its soldiers had the opportunity to achieve a military effectiveness superior to that of most of its enemies.

The very size of the army was a special problem for Augustus. Rome's legions numbered thousands of men, far more than were necessary to maintain peace. What was

Augustus to do with so many soldiers? This sort of problem had constantly plagued the late republic, whose leaders never found a solution. Augustus gave his own answer in the *Res Gestae:* "I founded colonies of soldiers in Africa, Sicily, Macedonia, Spain, Achaea, Gaul, and Pisidia. Moreover, Italy has 28 colonies under my auspices."[3] At least forty new colonies arose, most of them in the western Mediterranean. Augustus's veterans took abroad with them their Latin language and culture. His colonies, like Julius Caesar's, were a significant tool in the spread of Roman culture throughout the West.

Roman colonies were very different from earlier Greek colonies. Greek colonies were independent. Once founded, they went their own way. Roman colonies were part of a system—the Roman Empire—that linked East with West in a mighty political, social, and economic network. The glory of the Roman Empire was its great success in uniting the Mediterranean world and spreading Greco-Roman culture throughout it. Roman colonies played a crucial part in that process, and Augustus deservedly boasted of the colonies he founded.

Augustus, however, also failed to solve a momentous problem. He never found a way to institutionalize his position with the army. The ties between the princeps and the army were always personal. The army was loyal to the princeps but not necessarily to the state. The Augustan principate worked well at first, but by the third century A.D. the army would make and break emperors at will. Nonetheless, it is a measure of Augustus's success that his settlement survived as long and as well as it did.

Augustus's Administration of the Provinces

In the areas under his immediate jurisdiction, Augustus put provincial administration on an ordered basis and improved its functioning. Believing that the cities of the empire should look after their own affairs, he encouraged local self-government and urbanism. Augustus respected local customs and ordered his governors to do the same.

As a spiritual bond between the provinces and Rome, Augustus encouraged the cult of Roma, goddess and guardian of the state. In the Hellenistic East, where king-worship was an established custom, the cult of *Roma et Augustus* grew and spread rapidly. Augustus then introduced it in the West. By the time of his death in A.D. 14, nearly every province in the empire could boast an altar or a shrine to *Roma et Augustus*. In the West it was not the person of the emperor who was worshiped but his *genius*—his guardian spirit. In praying for the good health and welfare of the emperor, Romans and provincials were praying for the empire itself. The cult became a symbol of Roman unity.

Roman Expansion into Northern and Western Europe

For the history of Western civilization, one of the most momentous aspects of Augustus's reign was Roman expansion into the wilderness of northern and western Europe (see Map 6.1). In this respect Augustus was following in Julius Caesar's footsteps. Carrying on Caesar's work, Augustus pushed Rome's frontier into the region of modern Germany.

Augustus began his work in the west and north by completing the conquest of Spain. In Gaul, apart from minor campaigns, most of his work was peaceful. He founded twelve new towns, and the Roman road system linked new settlements with one another and with Italy. But the German frontier, along the Rhine River, was the scene of hard fighting. In 12 B.C. Augustus ordered a major invasion of Germany beyond the Rhine. Roman legions advanced to the Elbe River, and a Roman fleet explored the North Sea and Jutland. The area north of the Main River and west of the Elbe was on the point of becoming Roman. But in A.D. 9 Augustus's general Varus lost some twenty thousand troops at the Battle of the Teutoburger Forest. Thereafter the Rhine remained the Roman frontier.

Meanwhile more successful generals extended the Roman standards as far as the Danube. Roman legions penetrated the area of modern Austria, southern Bavaria, and western Hungary. The regions of modern Serbia, Bulgaria, and Romania fell. Within this area the legionaries built fortified camps. Roads linked these camps with one another, and settlements grew up around the camps. Traders began to frequent the frontier and to traffic with the barbarians. Thus Roman culture—the rough-and-ready kind found in military camps—gradually spread into the northern wilderness.

Although this process is most clearly seen in the provincial towns and cities, people in the countryside likewise adopted the aspects of Roman culture that appealed to them. Roman culture was adaptable and convenient, and the Romans did not force it on others. All over the empire native peoples adopted those aspects that fit in with their own ways of life. That much said, ambitious people throughout the empire knew that the surest path to political advancement lay in embracing Roman civilization and culture.

Boscoreale Cup   The central scene lavishly depicted on the side of a silver cup shows Augustus seated in majesty. In his right hand he holds an orb that represents his position as master of the world. The scroll in his left hand symbolizes his authority as lawgiver. On his right is a group of divinities who support his efforts, on his left a group of barbarians who have submitted to Rome. (© *Musée du Louvre*)

One excellent example of this process comes from the modern French city of Lyons. The site was originally the capital of a native tribe, and after his conquest of Gaul, Caesar made it a Roman military settlement. Augustus took an important step toward Romanization and conciliation in 12 B.C., when he made it a political and religious center, with responsibilities for administering the area and for honoring the gods of the Romans and Gauls. Physical symbols of this fusion of two cultures can still be seen today. For instance, the extensive remains of the amphitheater and other buildings at Lyons testify to the fact that the Gallo-Roman city was prosperous enough to afford expensive Roman buildings and the style of life that they represented. Second, the buildings show that the local population appreciated Roman culture and did not find it alien. At Lyons, as at many other of these new cities, there emerged a culture that was both Roman and native. Many such towns were soon granted Roman citizenship for their embrace of Roman culture and government and their importance to the Roman economy. (See the feature "Listening to the Past: Rome Extends Its Citizenship" on pages 186–187.)

Although Lyons is typical of the success of Romanization in new areas, the arrival of the Romans often provoked resistance from tribes of peoples who were not Greco-Roman and who simply wanted to be left alone. Romans generally referred to such people as **barbarians,** a word derived from a Greek word for those who did not speak Greek. In other cases the prosperity and wealth of the new Roman towns lured barbarians eager for plunder. The Romans maintained peaceful relations with the barbarians whenever possible, but Roman legions remained on the frontier to repel hostile barbarians. The result was the evolution of a consistent, systematic frontier policy.

Literary Flowering and Social Changes

The Augustan settlement's gift of peace inspired a literary flowering unparalleled in Roman history. With good reason this period is known as the golden age of Latin literature. Augustus and many of his friends actively encouraged poets and writers. Horace, one of Rome's finest poets, offered his own opinion of Augustus and his era:

With Caesar [Augustus] the guardian of the state
Not civil rage nor violence shall drive out peace,
Nor wrath which forges swords
And turns unhappy cities against each other.[4]

These lines are not empty flattery, despite Augustus's support of many contemporary Latin writers. To a generation that had known only vicious civil war, Augustus's settlement was an unbelievable blessing.

The tone and ideal of Roman literature, like that of the Greeks, was humanistic and worldly. Roman poets and prose writers celebrated the dignity of humanity and the range of its accomplishments. They stressed the physical and emotional joys of a comfortable, peaceful life. Their works were highly polished, elegant in style, and intellectual in conception. Roman poets referred to the gods often and treated mythological themes, but always the core of their work was human, not divine.

Virgil (70–19 B.C.), Rome's greatest poet, celebrated the new age in the *Georgics,* a poetic work on agriculture in four books. Virgil delighted in his own farm, and his poems sing of the pleasures of peaceful farm life. The poet also tells how to keep bees, grow grapes and olives,

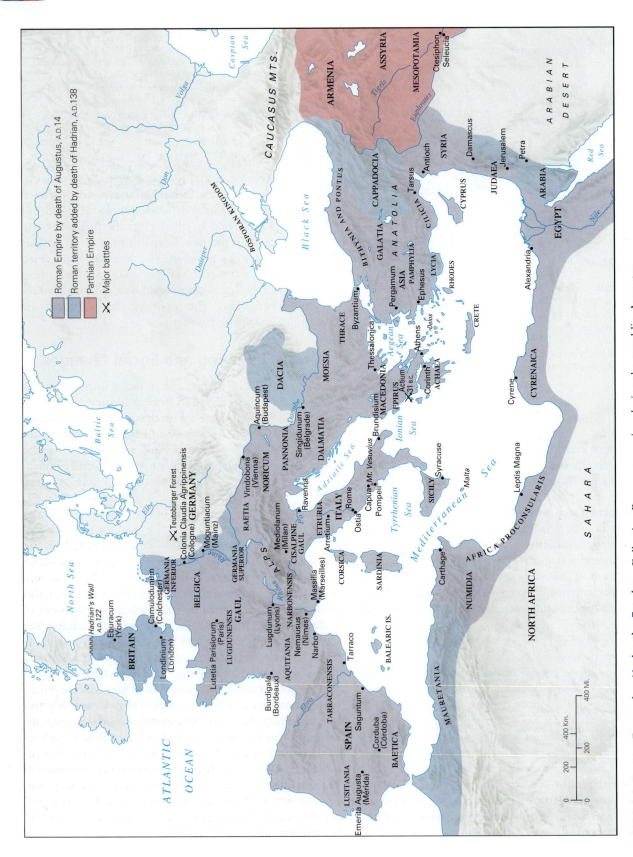

MAP 6.1 Roman Expansion Under the Empire   Following Roman expansion during the republic, Augustus added vast tracts of Europe to the Roman Empire, which the emperor Hadrian later enlarged by assuming control over parts of central Europe, the Near East, and North Africa.

Legend:

- Roman Empire by death of Augustus, A.D.14
- Roman territory added by death of Hadrian, A.D.138
- Parthian Empire
- X Major battles

Virgil and the *Aeneid* Virgil's great epic poem, the *Aeneid*, became a literary classic immediately on its appearance and has lost none of its power since. The Roman world honored Virgil for his poetic genius not only by treasuring his work but also by portraying him in art. Here two Muses flank the poet while he writes his epic poem. The Muses, nine in all, were minor Greek and Roman goddesses who were thought to inspire artists and writers. Their role as inspiration, but not authors, accurately reflects surviving Latin literature of the Augustan period, all of which is by male authors. *(C. M. Dixon/Ancient Art & Architecture Collection)*

plow, and manage a farm. Throughout the *Georgics* Virgil writes about things he himself has seen, rather than drawing from the writings of others. Virgil could be vivid and graphic as well as pastoral. Even a small event could be a drama for him. The death of a bull while plowing is hardly epic material, yet Virgil captures the sadness of the event in the image of the farmer unyoking the remaining animal:

*Look, the bull, shining under the rough plough,
falls to the ground
and vomits from his mouth blood mixed with foam,
and releases his dying groan.
Sadly moves the ploughman, unharnessing the
young steer grieving for the death of his brother
and leaves in the middle of the job
the plough stuck fast.*[5]

Virgil's poetry is robust yet graceful. A sensitive man who delighted in simple things, Virgil left in his *Georgics* a charming picture of life in the Italian countryside during a period of peace.

Virgil's masterpiece is the *Aeneid*, an epic poem that is the Latin equivalent of the Greek *Iliad* and *Odyssey*. In the *Aeneid* Virgil expressed his admiration for Augustus's work by celebrating the shining ideal of a world blessed by the pax Romana. Virgil's account of the founding of Rome and the early years of the city gave final form to the legend of Aeneas, a Trojan hero who escaped to Italy at the fall of Troy. The legend of Aeneas was a third story about the founding of Rome, along with those of Romulus and the rape of Lucretia (see page 125). This one was also gendered. As Virgil told it, Aeneas became the lover of Dido, the widowed queen of Carthage, but left her because his destiny called him to found Rome. She committed suicide, and their relationship eventually became the cause of the Punic Wars. In leaving Dido, an "Eastern" queen, Aeneas put the good of the state ahead of marriage or pleasure; the parallels between this story and the real events involving Antony and Cleopatra were not lost on Virgil's audience. Virgil believed passionately in Rome's greatness, and he portrayed Rome as the protector of the good and noble against the forces of darkness and disruption, symbolized in part by a foreign queen. This fit well with Augustus's aims; he had encouraged Virgil to write the *Aeneid* and made sure it was published immediately after Virgil died.

Ara Pacis This scene from the Ara Pacis, the Altar of Peace erected in Rome by Augustus, celebrates Augustus's restoration of peace and imperial family values. On this side, Mother Earth is depicted with twin babies on her lap, framed by nymphs representing land and sea. The sheep and the cow are both agricultural and sacrificial animals. Other sides of the altar show Romulus and Remus (another set of twins) and Augustus and his wife Livia in traditional Roman clothing. *(Scala/Art Resource, NY)*

The poet Ovid shared Virgil's views of the simple pleasures of life and also celebrated the popular culture of the day. In his *Fasti* (ca A.D. 8) he takes a personal approach to discuss and explain the ordinary festivals of the Roman year, festivals that most Romans took for granted. Without his work, the modern world would be much the poorer in its knowledge of the popular religion of imperial Rome. For instance, he tells his readers that on a journey to Rome he encountered a white-robed crowd in the middle of the road. A priest and farmers were performing an annual festival ritual. Ovid stopped to ask the priest what was happening. The priest explained that they were sacrificing to Mildew, not a farmer's favorite goddess. By burning the offerings the priest and his friends asked the goddess to be so content with them that she would not attack the crops. He further asked her not to attack the farmers' tools but to be satisfied with swords and other weapons of iron. He reminded her that "there is no need for them; the world lives in peace."[6] In his poetry Ovid, like Virgil, celebrates the pax Romana, while giving a rare glimpse of ordinary Roman life.

In its own way Livy's history of Rome, titled simply *Ab Urbe Condita* (From the Founding of the City), is the prose counterpart of the *Aeneid*. Livy (59 B.C.–A.D. 17) received training in Greek and Latin literature, rhetoric, and philosophy. He even urged the future emperor Claudius to write history. Livy loved and admired the heroes and great deeds of the republic, but he was also a friend of Augustus and a supporter of the principate. He especially approved of Augustus's efforts to restore what he saw as republican virtues. Livy's history began with the legend of Aeneas and ended with the reign of Augustus. His theme of the republic's greatness fitted admirably with Augustus's program of restoring the republic. Livy's history was colossal, consisting of 142 books, and only a quarter of it still exists. Livy was a sensitive writer and something of a moralist. Like Thucydides, he felt that history should be applied to the present. His history later became one of Rome's legacies to the modern world. During the Renaissance *Ab Urbe Condita* found a warm admirer in the poet Petrarch and left its mark on Machiavelli, who read it avidly.

The poet Horace (65–8 B.C.) rose from humble beginnings to friendship with Augustus. The son of an ex-slave and tax collector, Horace nonetheless received an excellent education. He loved Greek literature and finished his education in Athens. After Augustus's victory he returned to Rome and became Virgil's friend. Horace happily turned his pen to celebrating Rome and Augustus.

Concern with morality and with what were perceived as traditional Roman virtues was a matter not just for literature in Augustan Rome, but also for law. Augustus promoted marriage and childbearing through legal changes that released free women and freedwomen (female slaves who had been freed) from male guardianship if they had given birth to a certain number of children. Men and women who were unmarried or had no children were restricted in the inheritance of property. Adultery, defined as sex with a married woman or a woman under male guardianship, was made a crime, not simply the private family matter it had been. In imperial propaganda, Augustus had his own family depicted as a model of traditional morality, with his wife Livia at his side dressed in conservative and somewhat old-fashioned clothing rather than the more daring Greek styles that wealthy women were actually wearing in Rome at the time.

Same-sex relationships were denounced as part of the immorality of the late republic and as nonprocreative. Same-sex relationships among men in Rome had followed a pattern similar to that of Greece: often between an older man and a younger, or between men who were different in social status, such as a slave and his owner. We do not know very much about same-sex relationships among women in Rome, though court gossip and criticism of powerful women, including the wives of Augustus's successors, sometimes included charges of such relationships, along with charges of heterosexual promiscuity and other sexual slander.

The solidity of Augustus's work became obvious at his death in A.D. 14. Since the principate was not technically an office, Augustus could not legally hand it to a successor. Augustus recognized this problem and long before his death had found a way to solve it. He shared his consular and tribunician powers with his adopted son, Tiberius, thus grooming him for the principate. In his will Augustus left most of his vast fortune to Tiberius, and the senate formally requested Tiberius to assume the burdens of the principate. Formalities apart, Augustus had succeeded in creating a dynasty.

Online Study Center Improve Your Grade
  Primary Source: A Critical Assessment of the Reign
    of Augustus Caesar

The Coming of Christianity

During the reign of the emperor Tiberius (A.D. 14–37), perhaps in A.D. 29, Pontius Pilate, prefect of Judaea, the Roman province created out of the Jewish kingdom of Judah, condemned Jesus of Nazareth to death. At the time a minor event, this has become one of the best-known moments in history. How did these two men come to their historic meeting? The question is not idle, nor the answer simple. The Hellenistic world and Rome were as important as Judaism to Christianity. As seen in Chapter 4, the Hellenistic Greeks provided the entire East with a common language, widely shared literary forms, and a pervasive culture that had for years embraced Judaea. Rome contributed political administration to Hellenistic culture. The mixture was not always harmonious. Some Jews embraced aspects of Greco-Roman culture, while others shunned it. It was a situation common to other parts of the Roman Empire, where people addressed these novel developments in their own ways. In Judaea, Roman rule aroused hatred and unrest among some Jews. This climate of hostility affected the lives of all who lived there. It formed the backdrop of Jesus' life, and it had a fundamental impact on his ministry. These factors also ultimately paved the way for Christianity to spread far from its native land to the broader world of the Roman Empire. Without an understanding of this age of anxiety in Judaea, one cannot fully appreciate Jesus and his followers.

• *Why did Christianity, originally a minor local religion, sweep across the Roman world to change it fundamentally?*

Unrest in Judaea

The entry of Rome into Jewish affairs was anything but peaceful. The civil wars that destroyed the republic wasted the prosperity of Judaea and the entire eastern Mediterranean world. Jewish leaders took sides in the fighting, and Judaea suffered its share of ravages and military confiscations. The Roman senate and Augustus backed one leader, Herod (r. 37–4 B.C.) and appointed him king of Judaea. King Herod gave Judaea prosperity and security, but the Jews hated his acceptance of Greek culture. He was also a bloodthirsty prince who murdered his own wife and sons. At his death the Jews in Judaea broke out in revolt. For the next ten years Herod's successor waged almost constant war against the rebels. Added to the horrors of civil war were years of crop failure, which caused famine and plague. Men calling themselves prophets proclaimed the end of the world and the coming of the **Messiah,** the savior of Israel.

At length the Romans intervened to restore order. Augustus put Judaea under the charge of a prefect answerable directly to the emperor. Religious matters and local affairs became the responsibility of the *Sanhedrin,* the highest Jewish judicial body. Although many prefects tried to perform their duties scrupulously and conscientiously, many others were rapacious and indifferent to Jewish culture. Often acting from fear rather than cruelty, some prefects fiercely stamped out any signs of popular discontent. Pontius Pilate, prefect from A.D. 26 to 36, is typical of such incompetent officials. Especially hated were the Roman tax collectors, called "publicans," many of whom pitilessly gouged the Jews. In Christian writings, "publicans and sinners" became a common negative phrase. Clashes between Roman troops and Jewish guerrillas inflamed the anger of both sides.

Among the Jews two movements spread. First was the rise of the Zealots, extremists who worked and fought to rid Judaea of the Romans. Resolute in their worship of Yahweh, they refused to pay any but the tax levied by the Jewish temple. Their battles with the Roman legionaries were marked by savagery on both sides. As usual the innocent caught in the middle suffered grievously. As Roman policy grew tougher, even moderate Jews began to hate the conquerors. Judaea came more and more to resemble a tinderbox, ready to burst into flames at a single spark.

The second movement was the growth of militant **apocalypticism**—the belief that the coming of the Messiah was near. This belief was an old one among the Jews. But by the first century A.D. it had become more widespread and fervent than ever before. Apocalyptic predictions appeared in many texts, including the anonymous Apocalypse of Baruch, which foretold the destruction of the Roman Empire. First would come a period of great tribulation, misery, and injustice. At the worst of the suffering, the Messiah would appear. The Messiah would destroy the Roman legions and all the kingdoms that had ruled Israel. Then the Messiah would inaugurate a period of happiness and plenty for the Jews.

This was no abstract notion among the Jews. As the ravages of war became widespread and conditions worsened, more and more people prophesied the imminent coming of the Messiah. According to Christian Scripture, one such was John the Baptist, "the voice of one crying in the wilderness, Prepare ye the way of the lord."[7] Many Jews did just that. The sect described in the Dead Sea Scrolls readied itself for the end of the world. Its members were probably Essenes, an ascetic group whose social organization closely resembled that of early Christians. Members of this group shared possessions, precisely as John the Baptist urged people to do. Yet this sect, unlike the Christians, also made military preparations for the day of the Messiah.

Jewish religious aspirations were only one part of the story. What can be said of the pagan world of Rome and its empire, into which Christianity was shortly to be born? To answer that question one must first explore the spiritual environment of the pagans, many of whom would soon be caught up in the new Christian religion. The term **pagans** refers to all those who believed in the Greco-Roman gods. Paganism at the time of Jesus' birth can be broadly divided into three spheres: the official state religion of Rome, the traditional Roman cults of hearth and countryside, and the new mystery religions that flowed from the Hellenistic East. The official state religion and its cults honored the traditional deities: Jupiter, Juno, Mars, Vesta, and such newcomers as Isis (see page 111). This very formal religion was conducted on an official level by socially prominent state priests and priestesses. The state cults were a bond between the gods and the people, a religious contract to ensure the well-being of Rome. Most Romans felt that the official cults must be maintained for the welfare of the state, and Augustus was careful to link them to him. After all, observance of the traditional official religion had brought Rome victory, empire, security, and wealth.

For emotional and spiritual satisfaction, many Romans also observed cults of home and countryside. These traditional cults brought the Romans back in touch with nature and with something elemental to Roman life. Particularly popular was the rustic shrine—often a small building or a sacred tree in an enclosure—to honor the native spirit of the locality. Though familiar and simple, even this traditional religion was not enough for many. They wanted something more personal and immediate. Many common people believed in a supernatural world seen dimly through dreams, magic, miracles, and spells. They wanted some sort of revelation about this supernatural world and security in it after death. Some people turned to astrology in the belief that they could read their destiny in the stars.

Many men and women in the Roman Empire found spiritual security and an emotional outlet in the various Hellenistic mystery cults. For example, the cult of Bacchus was marked by wine drinking and often by drunken frenzy. The cult of the Great Mother, Cybele, was celebrated with emotional and even overwrought processions, and it offered its worshipers the promise of immortality. The cult of Isis also involved emotional public rituals and became so popular that Augustus banned it as an un-Roman political threat. The appeal of the mystery religions was not simply that they provided emotional release. They gave their adherents what neither the traditional cults nor philosophy could—above all, security. Yet the mystery religions were by nature exclusive, and none was truly international, open to everyone.

The Life and Teachings of Jesus

Into this climate of Roman religious yearning, political severity, fanatical Zealotry, and Messianic hope came Jesus of Nazareth (ca 3 B.C.–A.D. 29). He was raised in Galilee, stronghold of the Zealots. A typically Jewish town, Galilee had come under Roman political rule and with it Hellenism and Roman culture. Yet in Jesus' day both remained a veneer, deeper among those who had political and business dealings with the Greeks and Romans than among ordinary folk. Although most people spoke Aramaic, some Jews knew Latin and Greek, which they used for official purposes. In all, they knew the Hebrew Bible far better than Virgil's *Aeneid*. Through Galilee passed major trade routes, which means that it was hardly a backwater or isolated area. Ideas moved as easily as merchandise along these routes.

Much contemporary scholarship has attempted to understand who Jesus was and what he meant by his teachings. Views vary widely. Some see him as a visionary and a teacher, others as a magician and a prophet, and still others as a rebel and a revolutionary. The search for the historical Jesus is complicated by many factors. One is the difference between history and faith. History relies on proof for its conclusions; faith depends on belief. Thus whether Jesus is divine or not is not an issue to be decided by historians. Their role is to understand him in his religious, cultural, social, and historical context.

To sort out the various and often conflicting interpretations, historians must begin with the sources. The principal evidence for the life and deeds of Jesus are the four Gospels of the New Testament. These Gospels—the word means "good news"—are neither biographies of Jesus nor histories of his life. They are records of his teachings and religious doctrines with certain details of his life. The aim was to build a community of faith that believed that Jesus represented the culmination of the Messianic tradition. The earliest Gospels were written some seventy-five years after his death, and modern biblical scholars have used literary analysis to detect a number of discrepancies among the four. For that matter, so did ancient writers, both pagan and Christian. These discrepancies did not come from authors' having had different memories of the events of Jesus' life and mission. Instead, the writers all gave their own theological interpretations of them.

The four Gospels that are now in Christian Scripture are called "canonical," a word that means "authentic." They were the most widely circulating accounts of Jesus' teachings in the first centuries after his life, and by the fourth century officials in the Christian church decided that they, along with other types of writing such as letters and prophecies, would form Christian Scripture.

They were not the only records of Jesus' teachings, however, and in recent decades other early texts have been retrieved from the deserts of the Middle East after centuries of burial. They are also termed "Gospels," but they include teachings that differ from those in the canonical Gospels. For example, in the canonical Gospels twelve of Jesus' followers have a special status as "apostles." All are male, and one, Peter, appears as especially prominent. In one of the recently discovered Gospels, by contrast, Jesus reveals special teachings to one of his female followers, Mary Magdalene, which annoys Peter and the other men in Jesus' circle. The newest of the recently discovered Gospels is also one of the most surprising. In 2006 a small group of scholars published a papyrus document containing the Gospel of Judas Iscariot, the apostle who in the canonical Gospels betrayed Jesus. It depicts Judas not only as Jesus' most beloved disciple but also as the only one to whom he revealed his destiny. At Jesus' bidding, Judas must betray him so that Jesus can escape the prison of his mortal body. The often contradictory accounts in the various Gospels indicate that early Christians had a diversity of beliefs about Jesus' nature and purpose. Only slowly, as the Christian church became an institution, were lines drawn more clearly between what was considered correct teaching and what was considered incorrect, or **heresy.**

Despite this diversity, there were certain things about Jesus' teachings that almost all the sources agree on: he preached of a heavenly kingdom, one of eternal happiness in a life after death. His teachings were essentially Jewish. His orthodoxy enabled him to preach in the synagogue and the temple. His major deviation from orthodoxy was his insistence that he taught in his own name, not in the name of Yahweh. Was he then the Messiah? A small band of followers thought so, and Jesus claimed that he was. Yet Jesus had his own conception of the Messiah. Unlike the Messiah of the Apocalypse of

Pontius Pilate and Jesus   This Byzantine mosaic from Ravenna illustrates a dramatic moment in Jesus' trial and crucifixion. Jesus stands accused before Pilate, but Pilate symbolically washes his hands of the whole affair. *(Scala/Art Resource, NY)*

Baruch, Jesus would not destroy the Roman Empire. He told his disciples flatly that they were to "render unto Caesar the things that are Caesar's." Jesus would establish a spiritual kingdom, not an earthly one. He told his disciples that his kingdom was "not of this world."

Online Study Center **Improve Your Grade**
Primary Source: The Gospel According to Matthew: The Sermon on the Mount

Of Jesus' life and teachings the prefect Pontius Pilate knew little and cared even less. All that concerned him was the maintenance of peace and order. The crowds following Jesus at the time of the Passover, a highly emotional time in the Jewish year, alarmed Pilate, who faced a volatile situation. Some Jews believed that Jesus was the long-awaited Messiah. Others were disappointed because

he refused to preach rebellion against Rome. Still others who hated and feared Jesus wanted to be rid of him. The last thing Pilate wanted was a riot on his hands. To avert riot and bloodshed, Pilate condemned Jesus to death. According to Christian Scripture, after being scourged, he was hung from a cross until he died in the sight of family, friends, enemies, and the merely curious.

Once Pilate's soldiers had carried out the sentence, the entire matter seemed to be closed. Yet on the third day after Jesus' crucifixion, an odd rumor began to circulate in Jerusalem. Some of Jesus' followers were saying he had risen from the dead, while others accused them of having stolen his body. For the earliest Christians and for generations to come, the resurrection of Jesus became a central element of faith—and more than that, a promise: Jesus had triumphed over death, and his resurrection promised all Christians immortality. In Jerusalem, meanwhile, the tumult subsided. Jesus' followers lived quietly and peacefully, unmolested by Roman or Jew. Pilate had no quarrel with them, and Judaism already had many minor sects.

The Spread of Christianity

The memory of Jesus and his teachings sturdily survived. Believers in his divinity met in small assemblies or congregations, often in one another's homes, to discuss the meaning of Jesus' message. These meetings always took place outside the synagogue. They included such orthodox Jews as the Pharisees. These earliest Christians were clearly defining their faith to fit the life of Jesus into an orthodox Jewish context. Only later did these congregations evolve into what can be called a church with a formal organization and set of beliefs. One of the first significant events occurred in Jerusalem on the Jewish festival of Pentecost, when Jesus' followers assembled. They were joined by Jews from many parts of the world, including some from as far away as Parthia to the east, Crete to the west, Rome, and Ethiopia. These early followers were Hellenized Jews, many of them rich merchants. They were in an excellent position to spread the word throughout the known world.

The catalyst in the spread of Jesus' teachings and the formation of the Christian church was Paul of Tarsus, a Hellenized Jew who was comfortable in both the Roman and Jewish worlds. He had begun by persecuting the new sect, but on the road to Damascus he was converted to belief in Jesus. He was the single most important figure responsible for changing Christianity from a Jewish sect into a separate religion. Paul was familiar with Greek philosophy, and he had actually discussed the tenets of the new religion with Epicurean and Stoic philosophers in Athens. Indeed, one of his seminal ideas may have stemmed from the Stoic concept of the unity of mankind. He proclaimed that the mission of Christianity was "to make one of all the folk of men."[8] His vision was to include all the kindred of the earth. That concept meant that he urged the Jews to include non-Jews in the faith. He was the first to voice a universal message of Christianity.

Paul's vision proved both bold and successful. When he traveled abroad, he first met with the leaders of the local synagogue before going out among the people. He applied himself especially to the Greco-Romans, whom he did not consider common or unclean because they were not Jews. He even said that there was no difference between Jews and **Gentiles** (non-Jews), which in orthodox Jewish thought was not only revolutionary but also heresy. Paul found a ready audience among the Gentiles, who converted to the new religion with surprising enthusiasm. Paul's approach succeeded beyond expectation.

Many early Christian converts were women, who seem to have come particularly from the Greco-Roman middle classes. Paul greeted male and female converts by name in his letters, and noted that women provided financial support for his activities. Missionaries and others spreading the Christian message worked through families and friendship networks. The growing Christian communities in various cities of the Roman Empire had different ideas about many things, including the proper gender roles for believers. Some communities favored giving women a larger role, while others were more restrictive (see page 175).

Christianity might have remained just another sect had it not reached Rome, the capital of the Western world. Contrary to modern notions, the early Christians were generally tolerated. Paganism had room for many religions. Rome proved to be a dramatic step in the spread of Christianity for different reasons. First, Jesus had told his followers to spread his word throughout the world, thus making his teachings universal. The pagan Romans also considered their secular empire universal, and early Christians there combined the two concepts of **universalism.** Secular Rome provided another advantage to Christianity. If all roads led to Rome, they also led outward to the provinces of central and western Europe. The very stability and extent of the Roman Empire enabled early Christians easily to spread their faith. Paul himself said of the Christians in Rome (1 Romans 8): "First I thank my God through Jesus Christ for you all, that your faith is spoken of throughout the whole world." The **catacombs** just outside of Rome testify to the vitality of the new religion and pagan toleration of it. Although many people today think of the catacombs as secret meeting places of oppressed Christians, they were actually huge public underground cemeteries along the famous Via Appia, one of Rome's proudest lanes.

The catacombs and other archaeological sites provide a concrete idea of how Christianity spread in the West. At first pagan and Christian artistic motifs were common, and in some cases pagan influence proved stronger than Christian. Later tombs, however, were decorated more with biblical scenes. The catacombs eventually became the honored resting places of the early popes and sites of pilgrimage. Although at first the religious community in Rome was a very important one among many, in the

The Catacombs of Rome   The early Christians used underground crypts and rock chambers to bury their dead. The bodies were placed in these galleries and then sealed up. The catacombs became places of pilgrimage, and in this way the dead continued to be united with the living. *(Catacombe di Priscilla, Rome/Scala/Art Resource, NY)*

course of time it would become the center of Western Christendom. From Rome Christianity spread southward to Africa and northward into Europe and across the Channel to Britain.

The Appeal of Christianity

Christianity appealed to common people and to the poor. Its communal celebration of the Lord's Supper gave men and women a sense of belonging. Christianity also offered its adherents the promise of salvation. Christians believed that Jesus on the cross had defeated evil and that he would reward his followers with eternal life after death. Christianity also offered the possibility of forgiveness. Human nature was weak, and even the best Christians would fall into sin. But Jesus loved sinners and forgave those who repented. In its doctrine of salvation

and forgiveness alone, Christianity had a powerful ability to give solace and strength to believers.

Christianity was attractive to many because it gave the Roman world a cause. Instead of passivity, Christianity stressed the ideal of striving for a goal. Every Christian, no matter how poor or humble, supposedly worked to realize the triumph of Christianity on earth. This was God's will, a sacred duty for every Christian. By spreading the word of Christ, Christians played their part in God's plan. No matter how small, the part each Christian played was important. Since this duty was God's will, Christians believed that the goal would be achieved. The Christian was not discouraged by temporary setbacks, believing Christianity to be invincible.

Christianity gave its devotees a sense of community. No Christian was alone. All members of the Christian community strove toward the same goal of fulfilling God's plan. Each individual community was in turn a member of a greater community. And that community, according to Christian Scripture, was indestructible, for Jesus had promised, "upon this rock I will build my church; and the gates of hell shall not prevail against it."[9]

Augustus's Successors

Augustus's success in creating solid political institutions was tested by the dynasty he created, the Julio-Claudians, who schemed against one another trying to win and hold power. This situation allowed a military commander, Vespasian, to claim the throne and establish a new dynasty. Vespasian's dynasty was followed by a series of emperors who were successful militarily and politically.

• **How did Augustus's successors build on his foundation to enhance Roman power and stability?**

The Julio-Claudians and the Flavians (27 B.C.–A.D. 96)

For fifty years after Augustus's death the dynasty that he established—known as the **Julio-Claudians** because they were all members of the Julian and Claudian clans—provided the emperors of Rome. Some of the Julio-Claudians, such as Tiberius and Claudius, were sound rulers and able administrators. Others, including Caligula and Nero, were weak and frivolous men who exercised their power stupidly. Although their enemies later accused them of outrages such as murder and incest, the Julio-Claudians gave the empire a broad and welcome period of peace and prosperity.

One of the most momentous achievements of the Julio-Claudians was Claudius's creation of an imperial bureaucracy composed of professional administrators. Even the most energetic emperor could not run the empire alone. The numerous duties and immense responsibilities of the emperor prompted Claudius to delegate power. He began by giving the freedmen of his household official duties, especially in finances. It was a simple, workable system. Claudius knew his ex-slaves well and could discipline them at will. The effect of Claudius's innovations was to enable the emperor to rule the empire more easily and efficiently.

One of the worst defects of Augustus's settlement—the army's ability to interfere in politics—became obvious during the Julio-Claudian period. Augustus had created a special standing force, the Praetorian Guard, as an imperial bodyguard. In A.D. 41 one of the Praetorians murdered Caligula while others hailed Claudius as the emperor. Under the threat of violence, the senate ratified the Praetorians' choice. It was a story repeated frequently. During the first three centuries of the empire, the Praetorian Guard all too often murdered emperors they were supposed to protect and saluted emperors of their own choosing.

Claudius was murdered by his fourth wife to allow her son by a previous marriage, Nero, to become emperor. In A.D. 68 Nero's inept rule led to military rebellion and his death, thus opening the way to widespread disruption. In A.D. 69, the "Year of the Four Emperors," four men claimed the position of emperor. Roman armies in Gaul, on the Rhine, and in the East marched on Rome to make their commanders emperor. The man who emerged triumphant was Vespasian, commander of the eastern armies, who entered Rome in 70 and restored order. Nonetheless, the Year of the Four Emperors proved that the Augustan settlement had failed to end civil war.

Not a brilliant politician, Vespasian did not institute sweeping reforms, as had Augustus, or solve the problem of the army in politics. To prevent usurpers from claiming the throne, Vespasian designated his sons Titus and Domitian as his successors. By establishing the Flavian dynasty (named after his clan), Vespasian turned the principate into an open and admitted monarchy. He also expanded the emperor's power by increasing the size of the budding bureaucracy Claudius had created.

One of Vespasian's first tasks was to suppress rebellions that had erupted at the end of Nero's reign. The most famous had taken place in Judaea, which still seethed long after Jesus' crucifixion. Long-standing popular unrest and atrocities committed by Jews and Romans alike sparked a massive revolt in A.D. 66. Four years later a Roman army reconquered Judaea and reduced Jerusalem by siege. The Jewish survivors were enslaved, and their state was destroyed. The mismanagement of Judaea was one of the few—and worst—failures of the Roman imperial administration.

The Flavians carried on Augustus's work on the frontiers. Domitian, the last of the Flavians, won additional territory in Germany and consolidated it in two new provinces. He defeated barbarian tribes on the Danube frontier and strengthened that area as well. Even so, Domitian was one of the most hated of Roman emperors because of his cruelty, and he fell victim to an assassin's dagger. Nevertheless, the Flavians had given the Roman world peace and had kept the legions in line. Their work paved the way for the era of the "five good emperors," the golden age of the empire.

The Age of the "Five Good Emperors" (A.D. 96–180)

The Flavians gave way to a remarkable line of emperors, generally known as the **five good emperors,** who ruled the empire wisely, fairly, and humanely. They created an almost unparalleled period of prosperity and peace. Their generally victorious wars were confined to the frontiers, and even the serenity of Augustus's day seemed to pale in comparison. These emperors were among the noblest, most dedicated, and ablest men in Roman history. Yet fundamental political and military changes had taken place since the time of Augustus's rule.

Augustus had claimed that his influence arose from the collection of offices the senate had bestowed on him. However, there was in law no such office as emperor. Augustus was merely the First Citizen. Under the Flavians the principate became a full-blown monarchy, and by the time of the Antonines the principate was an office with definite rights, powers, and prerogatives. In the years between Augustus and the Antonines, the emperor had become an indispensable part of the imperial machinery. In short, without the emperor the empire would quickly fall to pieces. Augustus had been monarch in fact but not in theory; during their reigns, the Antonines were monarchs in both.

The five good emperors were not power-hungry autocrats. The concentration of power was the result of empire. The easiest and most efficient way to run the Roman Empire was to invest the emperor with vast powers. Furthermore, Roman emperors on the whole proved to be effective rulers and administrators. As capable and efficient emperors took on new tasks and functions, the emperor's hand was felt in more areas of life and government. Increasingly the emperors became the source of all authority and guidance in the empire. The five good emperors were benevolent and exercised their power intelligently, but they were absolute kings all the same. Lesser men would later throw off the façade of constitutionality and use this same power in a despotic fashion.

Typical of the five good emperors is the career of Hadrian, who became emperor in A.D. 117. He was born in Spain, a fact that illustrates the importance of the provinces in Roman politics. Hadrian received his education at Rome and became an ardent admirer of Greek culture. He caught the attention of his elder cousin Trajan, the future emperor, who started him on a military career. At age nineteen Hadrian served on the Danube frontier, where he learned the details of how the Roman army lived and fought and saw for himself the problems

The Emperor Marcus Aurelius   This equestrian statue, with the emperor greeting his people, represents both the majesty and the peaceful intentions of this emperor and philosopher— one of the five good emperors. Equestrian statues present an image of idealized masculinity, but most portray their subjects as fierce and warlike, not with a hand raised in peace as Marcus Aurelius's hand is here. *(Tibor Bognar/Alamy)*

of defending the frontiers. When Trajan became emperor in A.D. 98, Hadrian was given important positions in which he learned how to defend and run the empire. At Trajan's death in 117 Hadrian assumed power.

Roman government had changed since Augustus's day. One of the most significant changes was the enormous growth of the imperial bureaucracy created by Claudius. Hadrian reformed this system by putting the bureaucracy on an organized, official basis. He established imperial administrative departments to handle the

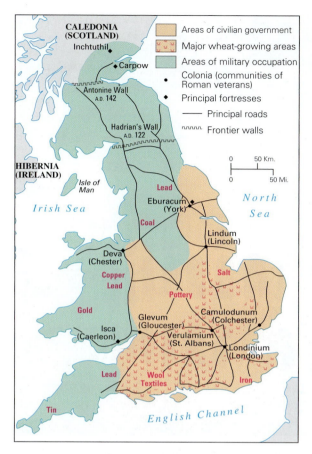

MAP 6.2 Roman Britain   Though the modern state of Great Britain plays a major role in international affairs, it was a peripheral part of the Roman Empire, a valuable area but nonetheless definitely on the frontier.

work formerly done by imperial freedmen. Hadrian also separated civil service from military service. Men with little talent or taste for the army could instead serve the state as administrators. Hadrian's bureaucracy demanded professionalism from its members. Administrators made a career of the civil service. These innovations made for more efficient running of the empire and increased the authority of the emperor—the ruling power of the bureaucracy.

The Roman army had also changed since Augustus's time. The Roman legion had once been a mobile unit, but its duties under the empire no longer called for mobility. The successors of Augustus generally called a halt to further conquests. The army was expected to defend what had already been won. Under the Flavian emperors (A.D. 69–96) the frontiers became firmly fixed, except for a brief period under Trajan, who attempted to expand the empire. Forts and watch stations guarded the borders. Behind the forts the Romans built a system of roads that allowed the forts to be quickly supplied and reinforced in times of trouble. The army had evolved into a garrison force, with legions guarding specific areas for long periods.

The personnel of the legions was changing, too. Italy could no longer supply all the recruits needed for the army. Increasingly only the officers came from Italy and from the more Romanized provinces. The legionaries were mostly drawn from the less civilized provinces, especially the ones closest to the frontiers. A major trend was already obvious in Hadrian's day: fewer and fewer Roman soldiers were really Roman. In the third century A.D. the barbarization of the army would result in an army indifferent to Rome and its traditions. In the age of the five good emperors, however, the army was still a source of economic stability and a Romanizing agent (see Map 6.2). Men from the provinces and even barbarians joined the army to learn a trade and to gain Roman citizenship. Even so, the signs were ominous. Veterans from Julius Caesar's campaigns would hardly have recognized Hadrian's troops as Roman legionaries. (See the feature "Individuals in Society: Bithus, a Typical Roman Soldier.")

Life in the "Golden Age"

Many people, both ancient and modern, have considered these years one of the happiest epochs in Western history. But popular accounts have also portrayed Rome as already decadent by the time of the five good emperors. If Rome was decadent, who kept the empire running? For that matter, can life in Rome itself be taken as representative of life in other parts of the empire? Rome was unique and must be seen as such. Surely Rome no more resembled a provincial city like Cologne than New York could possibly resemble Watseka, Illinois. Only when the uniqueness of Rome is understood in its own right can one turn to the provinces to obtain a full and reasonable picture of the empire under the Antonines.

• *What was life like in the city of Rome in the "golden age," and what was it like in the provinces?*

The Coliseum   This splendid building was the site of some of Rome's bloodiest games. In it thousands of spectators viewed gladiatorial games between men, sometimes women, and animals. Yet it stands as a monument to the Roman sense of beauty and architectural skill. *(Scala/Art Resource, NY)*

Imperial Rome

Rome was truly an extraordinary city, especially by ancient standards. It was also enormous, with a population somewhere between 500,000 and 750,000. Although it could boast of stately palaces, noble buildings, and beautiful residential areas, most people lived in jerrybuilt apartment houses. They worked at a variety of productive and service jobs. Fire and crime were perennial problems, even after Augustus created fire and urban police forces. Streets were narrow and drainage was inadequate. During the republic sanitation had been a common problem. Numerous inscriptions record prohibitions against dumping human refuse and even cadavers on the grounds of sanctuaries and cemeteries. Under the empire this situation improved. By comparison with medieval and early modern European cities, Rome was a healthy enough place to live.

Rome was such a huge city that the surrounding countryside could not feed it. Because of the danger of starvation, the emperor, following republican practice, provided the citizen population with free grain for bread and, later, oil and wine. By feeding the citizenry the emperor prevented bread riots caused by shortages and high prices. For the rest of the urban population who did not enjoy the rights of citizenship, the emperor provided grain at low prices. This measure was designed to prevent speculators from forcing up grain prices in times of crisis. By maintaining the grain supply the emperor kept the favor of the people and ensured that Rome's poor and idle did not starve.

The emperor and other wealthy citizens also entertained the Roman populace, often at vast expense. The most popular forms of public entertainment were gladiatorial contests and chariot racing. Gladiatorial fighting was originally an Etruscan funerary custom, a blood sacri-

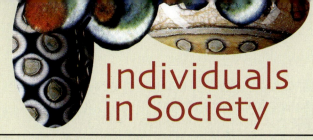

Individuals in Society

Bithus, a Typical Roman Soldier

Idealized statue of a Roman soldier.
(Deutsches Archaeologisches Institut, Rome)

Few people think of soldiers as missionaries of culture, but they often are. The culture that they spread is seldom of high intellectual or artistic merit, but they expose others to their own traditions, habits, and ways of thinking. A simple modern example may suffice. In World War II American GIs in Italy taught children there how to play baseball. From their very presence the young Americans taught their Italian friends many other things about the United States and themselves learned a great deal about Italian life and values. Even today a stranger can wander around an Italian town and see the results of this meeting of two cultures.

The same was true of the armies of the Roman Empire. The empire was so vast even by modern standards that soldiers were recruited from all parts of it to serve in distant places. A soldier from Syria might find himself keeping watch on Hadrian's Wall in Britain. He brought with him the ideas and habits of his birthplace and soon realized that others lived life differently. Yet they all lived in the same empire. Despite their ethnic differences, they were united by many commonly shared beliefs and opinions. Although the Roman Empire never became totally Romanized, soldiers, like officials and merchants, played their part in disseminating Roman ideas of government, religion, and way of life.

One such person was the infantryman Bithus, who was born in Thrace, the modern region of northeastern Greece. His career was eventful but not particularly distinguished. He is, however, typical of many others who served in the legions. Bithus's military life took him far from his native Thrace. His career started with basic training during which he learned to march and to use standard weapons.

His training over, Bithus was sent to Syria, where he spent most of his career. There he met others from as far west as Gaul and Spain, from West Africa, and from the modern Middle East. This experience gave him an idea of the size of the empire. It also taught him about life in other areas. Unlike many other cohorts that were shifted periodically, his saw service in one theater. While in the army, he raised a family, much like soldiers today. The children of soldiers like Bithus often themselves joined the army, which thereby became a fruitful source of its own recruitment. After twenty-five years of duty, Bithus received his reward on November 7, 88. Upon mustering out of the army he received the grant of Roman citizenship for himself and his family.

In his civilian life the veteran enjoyed a social status that granted him honor and privileges accorded only to Romans. From his military records there is no reason to conclude that Bithus had even seen Rome, but because of his service to it, he became as much a Roman as anyone born near the Tiber.

The example of Bithus is important because it is typical of thousands of others who voluntarily supported the empire. In the process they learned about the nature of the empire and something about how it worked. They also exchanged experiences with other soldiers and the local population that helped shape a sense that the empire was a human as well as a political unit.

Questions for Analysis

1. What did Bithus gain from his twenty-five years of service in the Roman army?
2. What effect did soldiers such as Bithus have on the various parts of the Roman Empire where they served, both in their way of seeing new cultures and in their way of sharing new experiences?

Source: Corpus Inscriptionum Latinarum, vol. 16 (Berlin: G. Reimer, 1882), no. 35.

Online Study Center **Improve Your Grade**
Going Beyond Individuals in Society

Gladiatorial Games   Though hardly games, the contests were vastly popular among the Romans. Gladiators were usually slaves, but successful ones could gain their freedom. The fighting was hard but fair, and the gladiators shown here look equally matched. *(Interphoto Press)*

fice for the dead. Even a humane man like Hadrian staged extravagant contests. In A.D. 126 he sponsored six days of such combats, during which 1,835 pairs of gladiators dueled, usually with swords and shields. Many **gladiators** were criminals, some of whom were sentenced to be slaughtered in the arena. These convicts were given no defensive weapons and stood little real chance of survival. Other criminals were sentenced to fight in the arena as fully armed gladiators. Some gladiators were the slaves of gladiatorial trainers; others were prisoners of war. Still others were free men who volunteered for the arena. Even women at times engaged in gladiatorial combat. What drove these men and women? Some obviously had no other choice. For a criminal condemned to die, the arena was preferable to the imperial mines, where convicts worked digging ore and died under wretched conditions. At least in the arena the gladiator might fight well enough to win freedom. Others no doubt fought for the love of danger or for fame. Some Romans protested gladiatorial fighting, but the emperors recognized the political value of such spectacles, and most Romans appear to have enjoyed them. Christian authors generally opposed gladiatorial and animal combat, but this did not lead to immediate bans.

The Romans were even more addicted to chariot racing than to gladiatorial shows. Under the empire four perma-nent teams competed against one another. Each had its own color—red, white, green, or blue. Some Romans claimed that people cared more about their favorite team than about the race itself. Two-horse and four-horse chariots ran a course of seven laps, about five miles. A successful driver could be the hero of the hour. One charioteer, Gaius Appuleius Diocles, raced for twenty-four years. During that time he drove 4,257 starts and won 1,462 of them. His admirers honored him with an inscription that proclaimed him champion of all charioteers.

Roman spectacles such as gladiator fights and chariot racing are fascinating subjects for movies and computer games, but they were not everyday activities for Romans. As is evident on tombstone inscriptions, ordinary Romans were proud of their work and accomplishments and affectionate toward their families and friends. They were eager to be remembered after death for these things, not for bloody entertainments.

Rome and the Provinces

The question of how much Roman civilization influenced life in the **provinces** is impossible to answer, but enough evidence survives to indicate a complex development. The problem, as usual, depends primarily on the surviving sources. The rural population throughout the empire left few records, yet the inscriptions that remain point to a melding of cultures. A growing number of inscriptions prove that indigenous peoples and newcomers alike learned at least a smattering of Latin in the West and Greek in the East. They used the official imperial languages largely for legal and state religious purposes. Moreover, knowledge of them enhanced the social and political status of their speakers. They were no longer outsiders. Language provided these people with the tool to take their place in the actual running of the empire. They became bilingual—they spoke their native language and either Latin or Greek. The provincial peoples of the Roman Empire were not linguists, but those in the West were unintentionally creating the Romance family of languages, which includes Spanish, Italian, French, Portuguese, and Romanian. This process was at first more urban than rural, but the importance of cities and towns to the life of the wider countryside ensured that its effects spread far afield. Rather than think in terms of one language and culture dominating another, it is far more accurate to observe the evolution of a new culture, with each existing culture fertilizing others.

A brief survey of the provinces proves the point. For instance, in Gaul country people retained their ancestral

Pont du Gard   Long after the Roman Empire gave way to the medieval world, this aqueduct still stands in France, where until recently it still carried water to Nîmes. The aqueduct is not only a splendid feat of Roman engineering but also a work of art. *(Yann Arthus-Bertrand/Altitude)*

gods, and there was not much difference in many parts of the province between the original Celtic villages and their Roman successors. Along the Rhine River, Romans provided the capital for commerce, agricultural development of the land, and large-scale building. Roman merchants also became early bankers, who loaned money to the natives and often brought them under financial control. The native inhabitants formed the labor force. They normally lived in villages and huts near the villas of successful merchants, whose wives brought Roman household items and clothing. Although Roman ideas spread and there was a good deal of cultural blending, native customs and religions continued to thrive. The Romans also learned about and began to respect native gods. Worship of them became popular among the Romans and the Greeks, which encouraged local peoples to preserve their religions.

Roman soldiers had originally been prohibited from marrying, though they often formed permanent relationships with local women. In the late second century the emperor permitted them to marry, and mixed-ethnicity couples became common in border areas. Because military units were moved as needed, women often ended up far from their homelands with their soldier-husbands.

The situation on the eastern bank of the Rhine was also typical of life on the borders, but it demonstrates the rawer features of frontier life. To this troubled land the Romans brought peace and stability, first by building forts and roads and then by opening the rivers to navigation. Around the forts grew native villages, and peace encouraged more intensive cultivation of the soil. The region became more prosperous than ever before, and prosperity attracted Roman settlers. Roman veterans mingled with the Celtic population and sometimes married into Celtic families. The **villa,** a country estate, not the city, was the primary unit of organized political life. This pattern of life differed from that of the Mediterranean, but it prefigured that of the early Middle Ages. The same was true in Britain, where the normal social

Images in Society

The Roman Villa at Chedworth

On the European borders of the Roman Empire, the villa was often as important as the town. Indeed, villas sometimes assumed many of the functions of towns. They were economic and social centers from which landlords directed the life of the surrounding countryside. The villa at Chedworth in Roman Britain provides an excellent example of them. The ordinary villa included a large courtyard with barns, gardens, storehouses, and buildings for processing agricultural products and manufacturing goods. The villa also included the comfortable living quarters of the owner and his family. These structures included the usual bedrooms and baths. A small temple or shrine often provided a center for religious devotions. Quarters for servants and slaves were nearby but set apart from the great houses. Equally important were the other buildings that served domestic and light industrial needs. The villa, then, was essentially a small, self-contained community. Yet it was not necessarily isolated. The villa at Chedworth was connected by roads and rivers to other similar neighboring villas. The whole picture depicts a society that, though rural, was nonetheless

cultured, comfortable, and in touch with the wider world. A good analogy is the American southern plantation before the Civil War. Like many of these villas, Chedworth survived the demise of the Roman Empire. They all remained to play a crucial role in preserving Greco-Roman civilization in northern Europe.

What did a Roman villa look like, and how can archaeological remains define and explain its functioning? Since few ancient structures remain intact, many must obviously be reconstructed from excavations. Image 1 is the archaeological ground plan of Chedworth. At first it seems to show only a series of foundations. Yet a closer look reveals its design. The large buildings marked 3, 5a, and 5 are the remains of the manorial houses. Rooms 10 through 25a are the bath structures. Number 17 is a small temple. Buildings on the northern side, numbers 26–32, were domestic quarters.

Two questions immediately arise. How do we know what these buildings looked like, and how do we know how they functioned? By analyzing the physical remains and the building techniques of the site, ar-

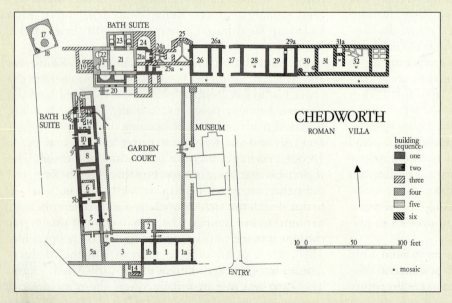

Image 1 **Ground Plan of the Roman Villa at Chedworth** *(From R. Goodburn, The Roman Villa, Chedworth. Reproduced with permission.)*

Image 2 Archaeological Reconstruction of the Villa *(Courtesy, Professor Albert Schachter)*

Image 3 Aerial View of Chedworth *(Courtesy of West Air Photography)*

Image 4 A View of the Site Today *(John Buckler)*

chaeologists and architects have made a patient reconstruction of the entire villa (see Image 2). Artifacts found in the structures reveal their functions. The most obvious example is the elaborate bath complex of numbers 19–25a. Image 3 gives an aerial view of the villa, and Image 4 provides an excellent cameo of the western wing of the villa.

From this information can you determine from the ground plan (Image 1) and the reconstruction (Image 2) what the villa actually looked like? From Image 3, an aerial view of Chedworth, together with Images 1 and 2, can you locate the landlord's houses, the temple, and the domestic buildings? Now using these three images, can you identify the buildings in Image 4? Lastly, from this material can you imagine the functions of the villa in its environmental and cultural context?

Online Study Center **Improve Your Grade**
Going Beyond Images in Society

Roman History After Augustus

Period	Important Emperors	Significant Events
Julio-Claudians 27 B.C.–A.D. 68	Augustus, 27 B.C.–A.D. 14 Tiberius, 14–37 Caligula, 37–41 Claudius, 41–54 Nero, 54–68	Augustan settlement Beginning of the principate Birth and death of Jesus Expansion into northern and western Europe Creation of the imperial bureaucracy
Year of the Four Emperors 69	Nero Galba Otho Vitellius	Civil war Major breakdown of the concept of the principate
Flavians 69–96	Vespasian, 69–79 Titus, 79–81 Domitian, 81–96	Growing trend toward the concept of monarchy Defense and further consolidation of the European frontiers
Antonines 96–180	Nerva, 96–98 Trajan, 98–117 Hadrian, 117–138 Antoninus Pius, 138–161 Marcus Aurelius, 161–180 Commodus, 180–192	The "golden age"—the era of the "five good emperors" Economic prosperity Trade and growth of cities in northern Europe Beginning of barbarian menace on the frontiers
Severi 193–235	Septimius Severus, 193–211 Caracalla, 198–217 Elagabalus, 218–222 Severus Alexander, 222–235	Military monarchy All free men within the empire given Roman citizenship
"Barracks Emperors" 235–284	Twenty-two emperors in forty-nine years	Civil war Breakdown of the empire Barbarian invasions Severe economic decline
Tetrarchy 284–337	Diocletian, 284–305 Constantine, 306–337	Political recovery Autocracy Legalization of Christianity Transition to the Middle Ages in the West Birth of the Byzantine Empire in the East

and economic structures were farms and agricultural villages. (See the feature "Images in Society: The Roman Villa at Chedworth" on pages 172–173.) Very few cities were to be found, and many native Britons were largely unacquainted with Greco-Roman culture. In Britain, as elsewhere, the Romans made local tribal leaders into their clients, though these relationships were not always amicable. In 47, for example, Boudicca, the queen of one tribe, led an army attacking Roman London.

Across eastern Europe the pattern was much the same. In the Alpine provinces north of Italy, Romans and native Celts came into contact in the cities, but native cultures flourished in the countryside. In Illyria and Dalmatia, the regions of modern Albania and the former Yugoslavia, the native population never widely embraced either Roman culture or urban life. Similarly, the Roman soldiers who increasingly settled parts of these lands made little effort to Romanize the natives, and there was less intermarriage than in Celtic areas. To a certain extent, however, Romanization occurred simply because these peoples lived in such close proximity.

The same situation existed in Asia Minor and elsewhere. In contrast with northern Europe, Asia Minor had long enjoyed the peace and stability of Roman rule. The lives of urban men and women reflected that benefit. A quiet corner of the empire, the small province of

Pamphylia in modern Turkey, gives an excellent idea of this life. The well-preserved ruins of the ancient city of Aspendos, still there today, give a full picture of a comfortable and thriving people. The city sits among fertile fields ideally suited for agriculture. The resources of the land provided raw materials for industry and trade. The Eurymedon River flowing next to the city served as an avenue to the outside world. Manufactured goods and raw materials passed along it to keep it in touch with the rest of the empire and brought in immigrants from elsewhere. For the people of Aspendos the city itself was the focus of life. There the men handled their political affairs in the council house (*bouleuterion*), and men and women frequented the ample marketplace for their ordinary needs. Temples and later a Christian basilica gave them ornate buildings in which to worship or just to think about spiritual matters. Their cultural life was surprisingly bright for an area that now seems so remote from the rest of the world. In their magnificent theater men and women enjoyed the great plays of the past and those popular in their own day. The city also offered many other places to relax. Absent was a place for gladiatorial games. That too was typical of the eastern Roman Empire, where gladiatorial contests were far less popular than horse racing.

This comfortable life also gave the Aspendians an excellent setting to pursue studies such as philosophy, literature, and history. More than just places to live, cities like Aspendos were centers of the intellectual and cultural life that spread abroad. The people here, like those elsewhere in the empire, kept fully in touch with the great thoughts and events of the day. Taken together, cities like Aspendos in the East, those along the Rhine in the West, and the many others throughout the empire united in a vibrant economic and cultural life that spanned the entire Mediterranean (see Map 6.3). They also passed it along as a rich heritage to later peoples in Europe.

Obviously the Romans went to no great lengths to spread their culture. Their chief aim was political stability, which they maintained through alliances as well as the suppression of any rebellions. As long as the empire prospered and the revenues reached the imperial coffers, the Romans were willing to live and let live. As a result, Europe fully entered into the economic and cultural life of the Mediterranean world.

The age of the five good emperors was generally one of peace, progress, and prosperity. The work of the Romans in northern and western Europe was a permanent contribution to the history of Western society. This period was also one of consolidation. Roads and secure sea-lanes linked the empire in one vast web, with men and women traveling and migrating more often than they had in earlier eras. The empire had become a commonwealth of cities, and urban life was its hallmark.

Rome in Disarray and Recovery (A.D. 177–450)

The long years of peace and prosperity abruptly gave way to a convulsed period of domestic upheaval and foreign invasion. The last of the five good emperors was followed by a long series of able but ambitious military commanders who used their legions to make themselves emperors. Law yielded to the sword. Yet even during the worst of this ordeal, many people clung to the old Roman ideals. Only the political mechanisms of the empire, its sturdy civil service and its ordinary lower officials, protected by loyal soldiers, staved off internal collapse and foreign invasion. Not until the coming of Diocletian did one man triumph over all his rivals to end the long period of strife. In 284 he reconstructed the empire and restored Roman life to peace and security.

Once Diocletian had ended the period of turmoil, succeeding emperors confronted the work of repairing the damage. Restoring the Roman Empire was the daunting challenge to the emperor Constantine (r. 306–337). While the price was high, he achieved success. Yet the Roman world, like Humpty Dumpty, could not quite be put back together again.

• *What factors led Rome into political and economic chaos, and how and to what extent did it recover?*

Civil Wars and Foreign Invasions in the Third Century

After the death of Marcus Aurelius, the last of the five good emperors, misrule by his successors led to a long and intense spasm of fighting. More than twenty different emperors ascended the throne in the forty-nine years between 235 and 284. Many rebels, loyal generals and their soldiers, and innocent civilians died in the conflagration. At various times parts of the empire were lost to mutinous generals, one of whom—Postumus—set up his own empire in Gaul for about ten years (259–269). Yet other men, like the iron-willed Aurelian (270–275), dedicated their energies to restoring order. So many military commanders ruled that the middle of the third century has become known as the age of the **barracks emperors.**

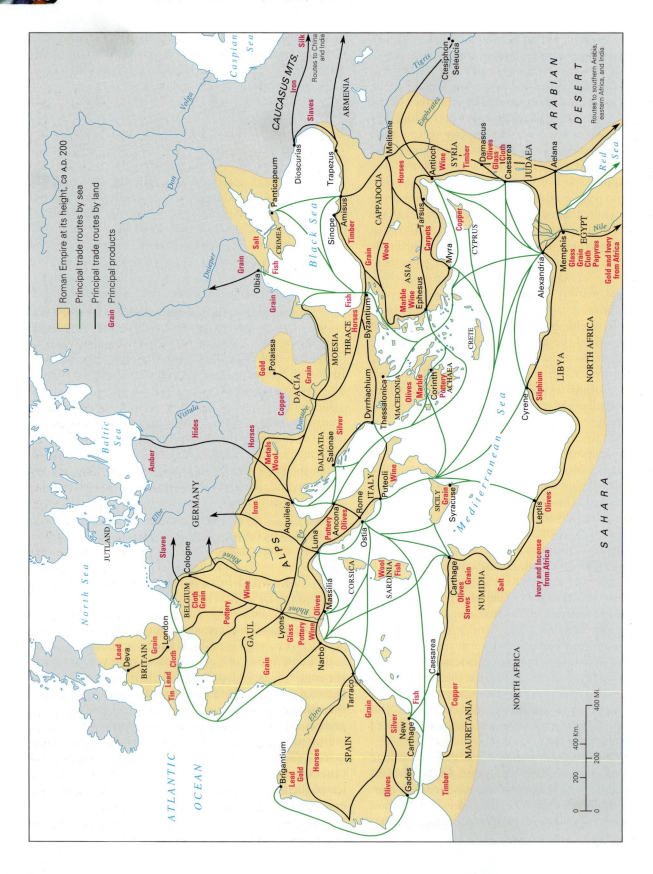

Roman Empire at its height, ca A.D. 200

Principal trade routes by sea

Principal trade routes by land

Grain Principal products

The Augustan principate had become a military monarchy, and that monarchy was nakedly autocratic.

While the empire seemed intent on committing suicide, barbarians on the frontiers took full advantage of the chaos to overrun vast areas. When they reached the Rhine and the Danube, they often found gaping holes in the Roman defenses. During much of the third century bands of Goths devastated the Balkans as far south as Greece and down into Asia Minor. The Alamanni, a Germanic people, swept across the Danube. At one point they reached Milan in Italy before being beaten back. Meanwhile, the Franks, still another Germanic folk, hit the Rhine frontier. Once loose, they invaded eastern and central Gaul and northeastern Spain. Saxons from Scandinavia sailed into the English Channel in search of loot. In the east the Sasanids overran Mesopotamia. If the army had guarded the borders instead of creating and destroying emperors, none of these onslaughts would have been successful. At the very least, the barracks emperors managed to stave off total ruin at the hands of the barbarians.

Turmoil in Farm and Village Life

This chaos also disrupted areas elsewhere in the empire, even when the local people remained distant from barbarian invaders. These convulsions gave rise to local lawlessness in which ordinary men and women suffered dreadfully. Renegade soldiers and corrupt imperial officials together with many greedy local agents preyed on local people. In many places in the countryside, farmers appealed to the government to protect them so that they could cultivate the land. Others encountered officials who requisitioned their livestock and compelled them to

do forced labor. Facing ruin, many rural families deserted the land and simply fled. Although many of those in authority were unsympathetic and even violent to villagers, many others tried justly and fairly to maintain order. They did what they could to ensure justice to all under their authority. Yet even the best of them also suffered. If they could not meet their tax quotas, they paid the deficits from their own pockets. They too were being impoverished. Because the local officials were themselves being so hard-pressed, they squeezed what they needed from rural families. By the end of the third century the entire empire tottered on the brink of ruin.

Reconstruction Under Diocletian and Constantine (A.D. 284–337)

At the close of the third century A.D. the emperor Diocletian (r. 284–305) put an end to the period of turmoil. Repairing the damage done in the third century was the major work of the emperor Constantine (r. 306–337) in the fourth. But the price was high.

Under Diocletian, Augustus's polite fiction of the emperor as first among equals gave way to the emperor as absolute autocrat. The princeps became *dominus*—"lord." The emperor claimed that he was "the elect of god"—that he ruled because of divine favor. Constantine even claimed to be the equal of Jesus' first twelve followers. To underline the emperor's exalted position, Diocletian and Constantine adopted the gaudy court ceremonies and trappings of the Persian Empire. People entering the emperor's presence prostrated themselves before him and kissed the hem of his robes. Constantine went so far as to import Persian eunuchs to run the palace. The Roman emperor had become an Eastern monarch.

No mere soldier, but rather an adroit administrator, Diocletian gave serious thought to the empire's ailments. He recognized that the empire and its difficulties had become too great for one man to handle. To solve these problems, Diocletian divided the empire into a western and an eastern half (see Map 6.4). Diocletian assumed direct control of the eastern part; he gave the rule of the western part to a colleague, along with the title **augustus,** which had become synonymous with emperor. Diocletian and his fellow augustus further delegated power by appointing two men to assist them. Each man was given the title of *caesar* to indicate his exalted rank. Although this system is known as the **Tetrarchy** because four men ruled the empire, Diocletian was clearly the senior partner and final source of authority.

Mapping the Past

MAP 6.3 The Economic Aspect of the Pax Romana
This map gives a good idea of trade routes and the economic expansion of the Roman Empire at its height. Map 11.2 on page 340 is a similar map that shows trade in roughly the same area nearly a millennium later. Examine both maps and answer the following questions: **❶** To what extent did Roman trade routes influence later European trade routes? **❷** What similarities and differences do you see in trade in the Mediterranean during these two periods?

Online Study Center **Improve Your Grade** Interactive Map: Economic Aspect of Pax Romana

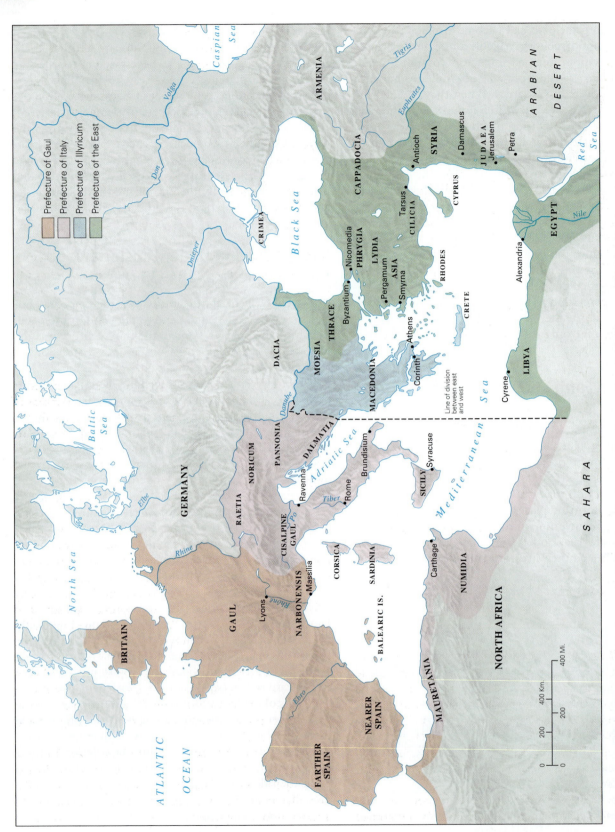

Prefecture of Gaul
Prefecture of Italy
Prefecture of Illyricum
Prefecture of the East

ATLANTIC OCEAN

North Sea

BRITAIN

Baltic Sea

GERMANY

Elbe

Rhine

GAUL

Lyons

NARBONENSIS

Massilia

Rhône

Ebro

FARTHER SPAIN

NEARER SPAIN

MAURETANIA

SAHARA

RAETIA

NORICUM

CISALPINE GAUL

Po

Ravenna

Rome

Tiber

CORSICA

SARDINIA

BALEARIC IS.

NORTH AFRICA

Carthage

NUMIDIA

PANNONIA

DALMATIA

Adriatic Sea

Brundisium

SICILY

Syracuse

Mediterranean Sea

Volga

Don

Dnieper

Caspian Sea

DACIA

MOESIA

THRACE

MACEDONIA

Danube

Corinth

Athens

Black Sea

CRIMEA

Byzantium

Nicomedia

PHRYGIA

LYDIA

Pergamum

Smyrna

ASIA

Tarsus

CILICIA

CRETE

RHODES

CYPRUS

ARMENIA

Tigris

Euphrates

CAPPADOCIA

SYRIA

Antioch

Damascus

JUDAEA

Jerusalem

Petra

ARABIAN DESERT

Red Sea

EGYPT

Nile

Alexandria

LIBYA

Cyrene

Line of division between east and west

400 Mi.

400 Km.

200

200

0

0

MAP 6.4 The Roman World Divided Under Diocletian, the Roman Empire was first divided into a western and an eastern half, a development that foreshadowed the medieval division between the Latin West and the Byzantine East.

Online Study Center **Improve Your Grade** Interactive Map: Roman World Divided

the empire into two parts became permanent. Constantine and later emperors tried hard but unsuccessfully to keep the empire together. Throughout the fourth century A.D. the eastern and the western sections drifted apart. In later centuries the western part witnessed the fall of Roman government and the rise of barbarian kingdoms, while the eastern empire evolved into the majestic Byzantine Empire.

The most serious immediate matters confronting Diocletian and Constantine were economic, social, and religious. They needed additional revenues to support the army and the imperial court. Yet the wars and the barbarian invasions had caused widespread destruction and poverty. The fighting had struck a serious blow to Roman agriculture, which the emperors tried to revive. Christianity had become too strong either to ignore or to crush. The responses to these problems by Diocletian, Constantine, and their successors helped create economic and social patterns that influenced later developments.

Inflation and Taxes

The barracks emperors had dealt with economic hardship by depreciating the currency, cutting the silver content of coins until money was virtually worthless. As a result, the entire monetary system fell into ruin. In Egypt governors had to order bankers to accept imperial money. The immediate result was crippling inflation throughout the empire.

The empire was less capable of recovery than in earlier times. Wars and invasions had disrupted normal commerce and the means of production. Mines were exhausted in the attempt to supply much-needed ores, especially gold and silver. The turmoil had hit the cities especially hard. Markets were disrupted, and travel became dangerous. Merchant and artisan families rapidly left devastated regions. The prosperous industry and commerce of Gaul and the Rhineland declined markedly. Those who owed their prosperity to commerce and the needs of urban life likewise suffered. Cities were no longer places where trade and industry thrived. The devastation of the countryside increased the difficulty of feeding and supplying the cities. The destruction was so extensive that many wondered whether the ravages could be repaired at all.

The response of Diocletian and Constantine to these problems was marked by compulsion, rigidity, and loss of individual freedom. Diocletian's attempt to curb inflation illustrates the methods of absolute monarchy. In a move unprecedented in Roman history, he issued an

Diocletian's Tetrarchy   The emperor Diocletian's attempt to reform the Roman Empire by dividing rule among four men is represented in this piece of sculpture. Here the four tetrarchs demonstrate their solidarity by clasping one another on the shoulder. Nonetheless each man has his other hand on his sword—a gesture that proved prophetic when Diocletian's reign ended and another struggle for power began. *(Alinari/Art Resource, NY)*

Each half of the empire was further split into two prefectures, each governed by a prefect responsible to an augustus. Diocletian reduced the power of the old provincial governors by dividing provinces into smaller units. He organized the prefectures into small administrative units called **dioceses,** which were in turn subdivided into small provinces. Provincial governors were also deprived of their military power, leaving them only civil and administrative duties.

Diocletian's political reforms were a momentous step. The Tetrarchy soon failed, but Diocletian's division of

Arch of Constantine Though standing in stately surroundings, Constantine's arch is decorated with art plundered from the arches of Trajan and Marcus Aurelius. He robbed them rather than decorate his own with the inferior work of his own day. *(Michael Reed, photographer/ www.mike-reed.com)*

edict that fixed maximum prices and wages throughout the empire.

The emperors dealt with the tax system just as strictly and inflexibly. As in the past, local officials bore the responsibility of collecting imperial taxes. Constantine made these officials into a hereditary class; son followed father whether he wanted to or not. In this period of severe depression many localities could not pay their taxes. In such cases these local officials had to make up the difference from their own funds. This system soon wiped out a whole class of moderately wealthy people. It was a bad policy for everyone involved.

With the monetary system in ruins, most imperial taxes became payable in kind—that is, in goods or produce instead of money. The major drawback of payment in kind is its demands on transportation. Goods have to be moved from where they are grown or manufactured to where they are needed. Accordingly, the emperors locked into their occupations all those involved in the growing, preparation, and transportation of food and essential commodities. A baker or shipper could not go into any other business, and his son took up the trade at his death. The late Roman Empire had a place for everyone, and everyone had a place.

The Decline of Small Farms

Because of worsening conditions during the third century A.D., many free tenant farmers and their families were killed, fled the land to escape the barbarians, or abandoned farms ravaged in the fighting. Consequently, large tracts of land lay deserted. Great landlords with ample resources began at once to reclaim as much of this land as they could. The huge estates that resulted, called villas, were self-sufficient. Because they often produced more than they consumed, they successfully competed with the declining cities by selling their surplus in the countryside. They became islands of stability in an unsettled world.

While the villas were growing, rural residents who remained on the land barely held their own. They were too poor and powerless to stand against the tide of chaos. They were exposed to the raids of barbarians or brigands and to the tyranny of imperial officials. For relief they turned to the great landlords. After all, the landowners were men of considerable resources, lords in their own right. They were wealthy and had many people working their land. They were independent and capable of defending themselves. If need be, they could—and at times did—field a small force of their own. Already influential, the landowning class united in protest against the demands of imperial officials.

In return for the protection and security landlords could offer, the small landholders gave over their lands. Free men and their families became clients of the landlords and lost much of their freedom. To guarantee a steady supply of labor, the landlords bound them to the soil. They could no longer decide to move elsewhere. Henceforth they and their families worked their patrons' land, not their own. Free men and women were becoming what would later be called serfs.

The Acceptance of Christianity

In religious affairs Constantine took the decisive step of recognizing Christianity as a legitimate religion. No longer would Christians suffer persecution for their beliefs as they occasionally had earlier. Constantine himself died a Christian in 337. Why had the pagans persecuted Christians in the first place? Polytheism is by nature tolerant of new gods and accommodating in religious matters. Why was Christianity singled out for violence? Such questions as these are still matters of scholarly debate to which some broad answers can be given.

A splendid approach to these problems has come from the eminent Italian scholar Marta Sordi.[10] Confronting a very complicated topic, she distinguishes among many different phases in the relationship between Christianity and official Roman acceptance of it. The Christians exaggerated the degree of pagan hostility to them, and most of the gory stories about the martyrs are fictitious. There were indeed some cases of pagan persecution of the Christians, but with few exceptions they were local and sporadic in nature. Even Nero's notorious persecution was temporary and was limited to Rome. No constant persecution of Christians occurred. Instead, pagans and Christians alike enjoyed long periods of tolerance and even friendship. Nonetheless, some pagans thought that Christians were atheists because they scorned the traditional pagan gods. Christians in fact either denied the existence of pagan gods or called them evil spirits. They went so far as to urge people not to worship pagan gods. In turn pagans, who believed in their gods as fervently as the Christians theirs, feared that the gods would withdraw their favor from the Roman Empire because of Christian blasphemy.

At first many pagans genuinely misunderstood Christian practices and rites. Even educated and cultured people like the historian Tacitus opposed Christianity because they saw it as a bizarre new sect. Tacitus believed that Christians hated the whole human race. As a rule early Christians kept to themselves. Romans distrusted and feared their exclusiveness, which seemed unsociable and even subversive. They thought that such secret rites as the Lord's Supper, at which Christians said that they ate and drank the body and blood of Jesus, were acts of cannibalism. Pagans also thought that Christians indulged in immoral and indecent rituals. They considered Christianity one of the worst of the mystery cults, for one of the hallmarks of many of those cults was rituals many Romans found unacceptable.

Another source of misunderstanding was that the pagans did not demand that Christians *believe* in pagan gods. Official Roman religion was never a matter of belief or ethics but of publicly celebrated rituals linked to the good of the state. All the pagans expected was performance of a ritual sacrifice as a demonstration of patriotism and loyalty. Those Christians who sacrificed went free, no matter what they personally believed.

As time went on, pagan hostility decreased. Pagans realized that Christians were not working to overthrow the state and that Jesus was no rival of Caesar. The emperor Trajan forbade his governors to hunt down Christians. Trajan admitted that he thought Christianity an abomination, but he preferred to leave Christians in peace.

The stress of the third century, however, seemed to some emperors the punishment of the gods. What else could account for such anarchy? With the empire threatened on every side, a few emperors thought that one way to appease the gods was by offering them the proper sacrifices. Such sacrifices would be a sign of loyalty to the empire, a show of Roman solidarity and religious piety. Consequently, a new wave of persecutions began out of desperation. Although the Christians depicted the emperor Diocletian as a fiend, he persecuted them in the hope that the gods would restore their blessings on Rome. Yet even these persecutions were never very widespread or long-lived; most pagans were not greatly sympathetic to the new round of persecutions. By the late third century, pagans had become used to Christianity. Constantine's acceptance of Christianity can be seen as the pagans' alliance with the strongest god of them all. Pagan and Christian alike must have been relieved when Constantine legalized the Christian religion.

Online Study Center **Improve Your Grade**
Primary Source: In Hoc Signo Vinces (By This Sign, Conquer): The Conversion of Constantine

In time the Christian triumph would be complete. In 380 the emperor Theodosius made Christianity the official religion of the Roman Empire. At that point

Martyrion at Aphrodisias   This trefoil building in Asia Minor is probably the remains of a *martyrion,* or martyrium, a church dedicated to a martyr. Martyrs were people killed for their belief in Jesus' divinity. There were not as many martyrs as Christians claimed, but the Christians considered them all heroes. This church probably honors a martyr now unidentified. *(M. Ali Dogenci, Turkey)*

Christians began to persecute the pagans for their beliefs. History had come full circle.

The Construction of Constantinople

The triumph of Christianity was not the only event that made Constantine's reign a turning point in Roman history. Constantine took the bold step of building a new capital for the empire. Constantinople, the New Rome, was constructed on the site of Byzantium, an old Greek city on the Bosporus. Throughout the third century emperors had found Rome and the West hard to defend. The eastern part of the empire was more easily defensible and escaped the worst of the barbarian devastation. It was wealthy and its urban life still vibrant. Moreover Christianity was more widespread in the East than in the West, and the city of Constantinople was intended to be a Christian center.

From the Classical World to Late Antiquity

Constantine had restored order, but what kind of order? Was it possible for one man to reconstruct the whole Roman Empire, indeed all of the ancient world? The answer is obviously no. Much was gone forever. Much still survived, but even more was still changing. The Roman god Janus well symbolizes this period. Janus's two faces looked both ways, in this case to the past and the future, for indeed the West was entering a vast new phase in its development. As usual in the case of major historical developments, an understanding of this whole epoch provides controversy, speculation, and new interpretations. One of the most dramatic questions is whether the Roman Empire even actually fell. Nearly all historians today agree that history, like a river, constantly flows and that all divisions of time are artificial. Historians now realize that the fourth century, which used to be seen as one of the central turning points in history, saw continuity along with change.

A great deal of the past lived on through these years of change. People still lived under the authority of the emperors and the guidance of Roman law. Essential ideas such as the value of individuals and their responsibilities to the state remained strong. In both halves of the empire, culture continued relatively unchanged. Greco-Roman architecture and art still adorned the land, not yet in the splendid and inspiring ruins that we see today, but vigorously alive. People communicated with one another as usual, in Latin throughout the West and Greek in the East, and those who could read still read the great creations of literature in these languages. The past was still the present.

Yet the gentle breeze of change also blew. Government had evolved from the SPQR of the past to the Christian monarchy of the new age. Whereas in the past the pagan gods had overseen the welfare of the state, now the Christian God with the earthly aid of the emperor and church officials protected the realm. The law of the church had increasingly mingled with that of the Caesars to govern life. The empire itself split from the unified principate of Augustus to two tenuously linked empires dividing the Western world. That in the West became the home of barbarians who absorbed much of the prevailing Roman culture while altering it with their own ideas, customs, and even languages. They were building a different world on classical foundations.

Paganism and the old gods faded into the background as Christianity came to prevail. Religion too brought its innovations. People struggled to understand Jesus' message to them. They disagreed over it, with some claiming to stand for the truth while branding those who disagreed as heretics. Christianity introduced a contest for people's souls in a way that paganism had never done. Greek philosophy, with its logic and amiable controversy, was replaced by theology, as thinkers tried earnestly to understand God and then teach others the meaning of his message. Christianity brought to religion a violence generally absent from paganism.

Through all these changes the lives of ordinary men and women did not change dramatically. They farmed, worked in cities, and hoped for the best for their families. They took new ideas, blended them with old, and created new cultural forms and ways of meeting life's challenges. The fourth century was a period of transition. The many forms that shaped it gave rise to a vibrant intellectual, spiritual, and political life that forever changed the face of Western civilization.

Chapter Summary

Online Study Center **ACE the Test**

- *How did Augustus restore stability; what political and military changes did he institute; and how did he spread Roman influence to northern and western Europe?*
- *Why did Christianity, originally a minor local religion, sweep across the Roman world to change it fundamentally?*
- *How did Augustus's successors build on his foundation to enhance Roman power and stability?*
- *What was life like in the city of Rome in the "golden age," and what was it like in the provinces?*
- *What factors led Rome into political and economic chaos, and how and to what extent did it recover?*

Once Augustus had restored order, he made it endure by remodeling the Roman government. The old constitution of the city-state gave way to the government of an empire. Although Augustus tried to save as much of the old as possible, he necessarily created a virtually new and much expanded system of rule. Furthermore, he made it endure.

As life settled down under this calming order, a small event with universal repercussions occurred in remote and insignificant Judaea. There a young Jew named Jesus taught a new religion promising salvation to all who embraced it. Some Jewish leaders opposed his teachings and persuaded Roman officials to execute him. Yet this new religion did not die with him. Instead it spread across the East, then to Rome, and by the end of the period throughout the empire.

Augustus's success in creating solid political institutions was tested by the dynasty he created, the Julio-Claudians. The fifty years during which they ruled Rome saw emperors and empresses trying to win and hold power through multiple political marriages, murder, and other tactics. In A.D. 70, Vespasian, a military commander, established a new dynasty, the Flavians, who restored some stability in Rome and expanded the empire. The Flavians were followed by a series of effective emperors, later called the "five good emperors," who created a more effective bureaucracy and larger army to govern the huge Roman Empire.

For many Romans these were rich and happy years. Much of the population enjoyed sufficient leisure time, which many spent pursuing literature and art. Others preferred watching spectacular games including gladiatorial contests and horse races. In the ever-expanding provinces, Roman and native cultures combined, and products and peoples moved easily across huge areas.

The good times fell into disarray when a series of weak, but rapacious, emperors fought all opponents for the throne. Civil war, chaos, and economic depression resulted. To worsen matters, barbarians on the frontiers took advantage of these internal troubles to invade, plunder, and destroy. These factors brought Rome near collapse. With the end apparently at hand, two stern and gifted emperors, Diocletian and Constantine, restored order and breathed fresh life into the economic and social order. By the end of this period, Christianity had made such gains that it was recognized as the official religion of the empire. By the end of Constantine's reign the Roman Empire was politically divided and religiously changing. Still, many aspects of Greco-Roman culture remained strong.

Key Terms

pax Romana	universalism
constitutional monarchy	catacombs
princeps	Julio-Claudians
imperator	five good emperors
barbarians	gladiators
Messiah	provinces
apocalypticism	villa
pagans	barracks emperors
heresy	augustus
Gentiles	Tetrarchy
	dioceses

Online Study Center **Improve Your Grade** Flashcards

Suggested Reading

Bradley, K. R. *Slaves and Masters in the Roman Empire: A Study of Social Control.* 1988. A brief book that examines how the institution of slavery was maintained over time and how the lives of slaves in the Roman world were controlled by their masters.

Burns, Thomas S. *Rome and the Barbarians, 100 B.C.–A.D. 400.* 2003. Analyzes the impact that the Romans had on the barbarians and that the barbarians had on the Romans.

Cunliffe, Barry. *Greeks, Romans and Barbarians.* 1988. Uses archaeological and literary evidence to discuss the introduction of Greco-Roman culture into western Europe.

D'Ambra, Eve. *Roman Women.* 2006. Examines women's lives in all social ranks, using material sources as well as written works.

Ehrman, Bard D. *Lost Scriptures: Books That Did Not Make It into the New Testament.* 2003. One of a series of books by this author designed for general readers that explore the diversity in early Christianity.

Esler, Philip F. *The Early Christian World.* 2004. An enormous collection by experts in the field that covers all aspects of the development of early Christianity.

Fredriksen, Paula. *From Jesus to Christ*, 2d ed. 2000. Studies the ways in which early Christians transformed the Jesus in the New Testament into the Christ of Christian tradition.

Goldsworthy, Adrian. *Roman Warfare.* 2000. Provides a concise treatment of warfare from republican to imperial times.

Goodman, Martin. *The Roman World, 44 B.C.–A.D. 180.* 1997. A good general treatment of the empire.

Greene, Kevin. *The Archaeology of the Roman Economy.* 1986. Offers an intriguing way to picture the Roman economy through physical remains.

MacMullen, Ramsay. *Christianizing the Roman Empire.* 1986. A thorough discussion by one of the leading scholars in the field.

MacMullen, Ramsay. *Roman Social Relations, 50 B.C. to A.D. 284.* 1981. Examines changes and continuities in social relations.

Noy, David. *Foreigners at Rome*. 2000. Studies the mingling of visitors and natives in the city and how tourists and locals affected each other's lives.

Shotter, David. *Augustus Caesar*. 1991. A brief study designed for students that examines the political, social, and cultural impact of the emperor's work.

Syme, Ronald. *The Augustan Aristocracy*. 1985. Studies the new order that Augustus created to help him administer the empire.

Notes

1. Virgil, *Aeneid* 6.851–853. John Buckler is the translator of all uncited quotations from a foreign language in Chapters 1–6.
2. Augustus, *Res Gestae* 6.34.
3. Ibid., 5.28.
4. Horace, *Odes* 4.15.
5. Virgil, *Georgics* 3.515–519.
6. Ovid, *Fasti* 4.925.
7. Matthew 3:3.
8. Acts 17:26.
9. Matthew 16:18.
10. See Marta Sordi, *The Christians and the Roman Empire* (London: Croom Helm, 1986).

Listening to the Past

Rome Extends Its Citizenship

One of the most dramatic achievements of the pax Romana was the extension of citizenship throughout the Roman Empire. Citizenship gave people advantages in judicial procedures, property transmission, and commercial relations. Male citizens could vote, and both female and male citizens passed citizenship on to their children. By granting citizenship to most people in the empire, the Roman government in effect took them into partnership.

Yet various emperors went even further by viewing Rome not only as a territorial but also as a political concept. In their eyes Rome was a place and an idea. Not every Roman agreed with these cosmopolitan views. The emperor Claudius (r. 41–54) took the first major step in this direction by allowing Romanized Gauls to sit in the senate. He was roundly criticized by some Romans, but in the damaged stone inscription that follows, he presents his own defense.

Surely both my great-uncle, the deified Augustus, and my uncle, Tiberius Caesar, were following a new practice when they desired that all the flower of the colonies and the municipalities everywhere—that is, the better class and the wealthy men—should sit in this senate house. You ask me: Is not an Italian senator preferable to a provincial? I shall reveal to you in detail my views on this matter when I come to obtain approval for this part of my censorship [a magistracy that determined who was eligible for citizenship and public offices]. But I think that not even provincials ought to be excluded, provided that they can add distinction to this senate house.

Look at that most distinguished and most flourishing colony of Vienna [the modern Vienne in France], how long a time already it is that it has furnished senators to this house! From that colony comes that ornament of the equestrian order—and there are few to equal him—Lucius

Vestinus, whom I cherish most intimately and whom at this very time I employ in my affairs. And it is my desire that his children may enjoy the first step in the priesthoods, so as to advance afterwards, as they grow older, to further honors in their rank. . . . I can say the same of his brother, who because of this wretched and most shameful circumstance cannot be a useful senator for you.

The time has now come, Tiberius Caesar Germanicus [Claudius himself], now that you have reached the farthest boundaries of Narbonese Gaul, for you to unveil to the members of the senate the import of your address. All these distinguished youths whom I gaze upon will no more give us cause for regret if they become senators than does my friend Persicus, a man of most noble ancestry, have cause for regret when he reads among the portraits of his ancestors the name Allobrogicus. But if you agree that these things are so, what more do you want, when I point out to you this single fact, that the territory beyond the boundaries of Narbonese Gaul already sends you senators, since we have men of our order from Lyons and have no cause for regret. It is indeed with hesitation, members of the senate, that I have gone outside the borders of the provinces with which you are accustomed and familiar, but I must now plead openly the cause of Gallia Comata [a region in modern France]. And if anyone, in this connection, has in mind that these people engaged the deified Julius in war for ten years, let him set against that the unshakable loyalty and obedience of a hundred years, tested to the full in many of our crises. When my father Drusus was subduing Germany, it was they who by their tranquility afforded him a safe and securely peaceful rear, even at a time when he had been summoned away to the war from the task of organizing the census which was still new and unaccustomed to the Gauls. How difficult such an operation is for us at this precise moment we are learning all too well from experience, even though the survey is aimed at nothing more than an official record of our resources. [The rest of the inscription is lost.]

Only later, in A.D. 212, did the emperor Caracalla (198–217) extend Roman citizenship to all freeborn men with the exception of those called dediticii, *whose identity remains a source of controversy. Caracalla claimed that he made this proclamation because the gods had saved him from a plot on his life. Some modern scholars, however, have suggested that he wanted more citizens to tax. Whatever the truth, Caracalla continued the work of Augustus (27 B.C.–A.D. 14) and Claudius. The Romans succeeded where the Greeks had failed: they built an empire of citizens. The following is a damaged copy of Caracalla's edict.*

The Emperor Caesar Marcus Aurelius Serverus Antoninus Augustus [Caracalla] declares: . . . I may show my gratitude to the immortal gods for preserving me in such [circumstances?]. Therefore I consider that in this way I can . . . rend proper service to their majesty . . . by bringing with me to the worship [?] of the gods all who enter into the number of my people. Accordingly, I grant Roman citizenship to all aliens, throughout the world, with no one remaining outside the citizen bodies except the *dediticii.* For it is proper that the multitude should not only help carry [?] all the burdens but should also now be included in my victory.

Citizenship was often granted to soldiers who had fought in the Roman army. The usual reasons were conspicuous bravery or wounds suffered in the course of duty. The emperor Trajan (98–117) made such a grant of citizenship in 106 to British soldiers who had served in the campaign in Dacia, a southern region of the former Yugoslavia. These men were also honored for their valor with an early discharge.

The Emperor Trajan . . . has granted Roman citizenship before completion of military service to the infantrymen and cavalrymen whose

Provocatio, the right of appeal, was considered a fundamental element of Roman citizenship. *(Courtesy of the Trustees of the British Museum)*

names appear below, serving in the First British Thousand-Man Ulpian Decorated Loyal Fortunate Cohort composed of Roman citizens, which is on duty in Dacia under Decimus Terentius Scaurianus, for having dutifully and faithfully discharged the Dacian campaign.

Questions for Analysis

1. What was the basic justification underlying Claudius's decision to allow Gallic nobles to sit in the senate? Did he see them as debasing the quality of the senate?

2. What do his words tell us about the changing nature of the Roman Empire?

3. What was the significance of Caracalla's extension of Roman citizenship to all freeborn men?

4. Notice that Trajan linked citizenship with military service. Can you think of modern parallels?

Source: Slightly adapted and abbreviated from N. Lewis and M. Reinhold, *Roman Civilization,* 2 vols. Copyright © 1966 by Columbia University Press, New York. Reprinted with permission of the publisher.

Hagia Sophia ("Holy Wisdom"), built by the emperor Justinian in the sixth century, was the largest Christian cathedral in the world for a thousand years. After Constantinople was conquered by the Ottoman Turks in 1453, it became a mosque, and today is a museum. *(Sadea Editore)*

LATE ANTIQUITY, 350–600

The Roman Empire, with its powerful—and sometimes bizarre—leaders, magnificent buildings, luxurious clothing, and bloody amusements, has long fascinated people. Politicians and historians have closely studied the reasons for its successes and have even more closely analyzed the weaknesses that led to its eventual collapse. From the third century onward, the Western Roman Empire slowly disintegrated. The last Roman emperor in the West, Romulus Augustus, was deposed by the Ostrogothic chieftain Odoacer in 476, but much of the empire had already come under the rule of various barbarian tribes well before this. Scholars have long seen this era as one of the great turning points in Western history, a time when the ancient world was transformed into the very different medieval world. During the last several decades, however, focus has shifted to continuities as well as changes, and what is now usually termed "late antiquity" has been recognized as a period of creativity and adaptation, not simply of decline and fall.

The two main agents of continuity were the Eastern Roman (or Byzantine) Empire and the Christian church. The Byzantine Empire lasted until 1453, a thousand years longer than the Western Roman Empire, and preserved and transmitted much of ancient law, philosophy, and institutions. Missionaries and church officials spread Christianity within and far beyond the borders of the Roman Empire, transforming a small sect into the most important and wealthiest institution in Europe. The main agents of change in late antiquity were the barbarian groups migrating into the Roman Empire. They brought different social, political, and economic structures with them, but as they encountered Roman culture and became Christian, their own ways of doing things were also transformed.

The Byzantine Empire

Constantine had tried to maintain the unity of the Roman Empire, but during the fifth and sixth centuries the Western and Eastern halves drifted apart. From Constantinople, Eastern Roman emperors worked to

Online Study Center

This icon will direct you to interactive activities and study materials on the website **college.hmco.com/pic/mckaywest9e**

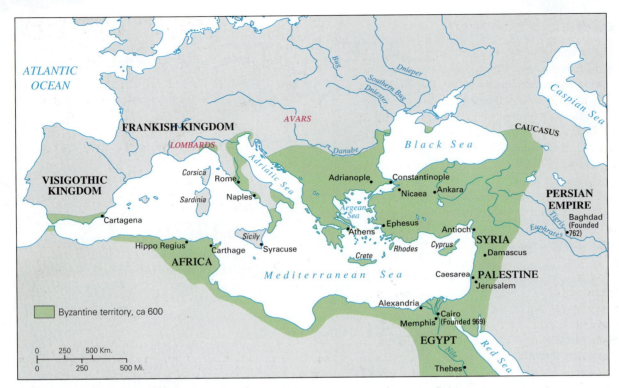

MAP 7.1 The Byzantine Empire, ca 600 The strategic position of Constantinople on the waterway between the Black Sea and the Mediterranean was clear to Constantine when he chose the city as the capital of the Eastern Roman Empire, and it was also clear to later rulers and military leaders. Byzantine territories in Italy were acquired in Emperor Justinian's sixth-century wars and were held for several centuries.

Online Study Center **Improve Your Grade** Interactive Map: Byzantine Empire, ca 600

hold the empire together and to reconquer at least some of the West from barbarian tribes. Justinian (r. 527–565) waged long and hard-fought wars against the Ostrogoths and temporarily regained Italy and North Africa, but his conquests had disastrous consequences. Justinian's wars exhausted the resources of the state, destroyed Italy's economy, and killed a large part of Italy's population. The wars also paved the way for the easy conquest of Italy by another Germanic tribe, the Lombards, shortly after Justinian's death. In the late sixth century, the territory of the Western Roman Empire came once again under Germanic sway.

However, the Roman Empire continued in the East. The Eastern Roman or Byzantine Empire (see Map 7.1) preserved the forms, institutions, and traditions of the old Roman Empire, and its people even called themselves Romans. Byzantine emperors traced their lines back past Constantine to Augustus. The senate that sat in Constantinople carried on the traditions and preserved the glory of the old Roman senate. The army that defended the empire was the direct descendant of the old Roman legions. Even the chariot factions of the Roman Empire lived on under the Byzantines, who cheered their favorites as enthusiastically as had the Romans of Hadrian's day. The Byzantine Empire maintained a high standard of living, and for centuries the Greeks were the most civilized people in the Western world. Most important, however, is the role of Byzantium as preserver of the wisdom of the ancient world. Byzantium protected the intellectual heritage of Greco-Roman civilization and then passed it on to the rest of Europe.

● *How was the Byzantine Empire able to survive for so long, and what were its most important achievements?*

Sources of Byzantine Strength

While the Western parts of the Roman Empire gradually succumbed to Germanic invaders, the Eastern Roman or Byzantine Empire survived Germanic, Persian, and Arab attacks. In 540 the Huns and Bulgars crossed the Danube and raided the Balkans as far south as the Isthmus of Corinth. In 559 a force of Huns and Slavs reached the gates of Constantinople. In 583 the Avars, a mounted Mongol people who had swept across Russia and southeastern Europe, seized Byzantine forts along the Danube and reached the walls of Constantinople. Between 572 and 630 the Sasanid Persians posed a formidable threat, and the Greeks were repeatedly at war with them. Beginning in 632 the Arabs pressured the Greek empire (see Chapter 8).

Why didn't one or a combination of these enemies capture Constantinople as the Germans had taken Rome? The answer lies in strong military leadership and even more in the city's location and its excellent fortifications. Under the skillful leadership of General Priskos (d. 612), Byzantine armies inflicted a severe defeat on the Avars in 601. Then, after a long war, the emperor Heraclius I (r. 610–641), helped by dynastic disputes among the Persians and Muslim pressures on them, crushed the Persians at Nineveh in Iraq. Massive triple walls, built by Constantine and Theodosius II (408–450) and kept in good repair, protected Constantinople from sea invasion. Within the walls huge cisterns provided water, and vast gardens and grazing areas supplied vegetables and meat. Such strong fortifications and provisions meant that, if attacked by sea, the defending people could hold out far longer than the besieging army. Attacking Constantinople by land posed greater geographical and logistical problems than a seventh- or eighth-century government could solve. The site was not absolutely impregnable—as the Venetians demonstrated in 1204 and the Ottoman Turks in 1453 (see pages 284 and 580)—but it was almost so. For centuries, the Byzantine Empire served as a bulwark for the West, protecting it against invasions from the East.

The Law Code of Justinian

One of the most splendid achievements of the Byzantine emperors was the preservation of Roman law for the medieval and modern worlds. Roman law had developed from many sources—decisions by judges, edicts of the emperors, legislation passed by the senate, and the opinions of jurists expert in the theory and practice of law. By the fourth century, it had become a huge, bewildering mass,

Chronology

312	Constantine legalizes Christianity in Roman Empire
340–419	Life of Saint Jerome; creation of the Vulgate
354–430	Life of Saint Augustine
380	Theodosius makes Christianity official religion of Roman Empire
385–461	Life of Saint Patrick
481–511	Reign of Clovis
527–565	Reign of Justinian
529	*The Rule of Saint Benedict*
542–560	"Justinian plague"

and its sheer bulk made it almost unusable. Some laws were outdated; some repeated or contradicted others.

Sweeping and systematic codification took place under the emperor Justinian. He appointed a committee of eminent jurists to sort through and organize the laws. The result was the *Code,* which distilled the legal genius of the Romans into a coherent whole, eliminated outmoded laws and contradictions, and clarified the law itself. Not content with the *Code,* Justinian set about bringing order to the equally huge body of Roman *jurisprudence,* the science or philosophy of law.

During the second and third centuries, the foremost Roman jurists had expressed varied learned opinions on complex legal problems. To harmonize this body of knowledge, Justinian directed his jurists to clear up disputed points and to issue definitive rulings. Accordingly, in 533 his lawyers published the *Digest,* which codified Roman legal thought. Finally, Justinian's lawyers compiled a handbook of civil law, the *Institutes.* These three works—the *Code,* the *Digest,* and the *Institutes*—are the backbone of the *corpus juris civilis,* the "body of civil law," which is the foundation of law for nearly every modern European nation.

Online Study Center **Improve Your Grade**
Primary Source: The Corpus Juris Civilis of Justinian Addresses the Problem of Adultery

The following excerpts on marriage and adultery from the corpus juris civilis provide valuable information on gender relations in Roman and Byzantine law:

Justinian and His Attendants   This mosaic detail is composed of thousands of tiny cubes of colored glass or stone called *tessarae*, which are set in plaster against a blazing golden background. Some attempt has been made at natura-listic portraiture. *(Scala/Art Resource, NY)*

—*Roman citizens unite in legal marriage when they are joined according to the precepts of the law, and males have attained the age of puberty and the females are capable of childbirth . . . [they must] if the latter have also the consent of the relatives under whose authority they may be, for this should be obtained and both civil and natural law require that it should be secured.*

—*The lex Julia ["Julian law," dating from 18 B.C.] declares that wives have no right to bring criminal accusations for adultery against their husbands, even though they may de-sire to complain of the violation of the marriage vow, for while the law grants this privilege to men it does not concede it to women.*[1]

Byzantine Intellectual Life

The Byzantines prized education; because of them many masterpieces of ancient Greek literature have survived to influence the intellectual life of the modern world. The literature of the Byzantine Empire was predominately Greek, although Latin was long spoken by top politi-cians, scholars, and lawyers. Indeed, Justinian's *Code* was first written in Latin. Among the large reading public, history was a favorite subject. Generations of Byzantines read the historical works of Herodotus, Thucydides, and others. Some Byzantine historians abbreviated long his-tories, such as those of Polybius, while others wrote de-tailed narratives of their own days.

The most remarkable Byzantine historian was Pro-copius (ca 500–ca 562), who left a rousing account prais-ing Justinian's reconquest of North Africa and Italy. Proof that the wit and venom of ancient writers such as Archilochus and Aristophanes lived on in the Byzantine era can be found in Procopius's *Secret History,* a vicious and uproarious attack on Justinian and his wife, the em-press Theodora. (See the feature "Individuals in Society:

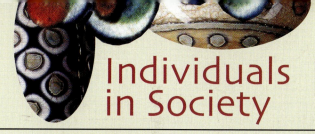

Individuals in Society

Theodora of Constantinople

The most powerful woman in Byzantine history was the daughter of a bear trainer for the circus. Theodora (ca 497–548) grew up in what her contemporaries regarded as an undignified and morally suspect atmosphere, and she worked as a dancer and burlesque actress, both dishonorable occupations in the Roman world. Despite her background, she caught the eye of Justinian, who was then a military leader and whose uncle (and adoptive father) Justin had himself risen from obscurity to become the emperor of the Byzantine Empire. Under Justinian's influence, Justin changed the law to allow an actress who had left her disreputable life to marry whom she liked, and Justinian and Theodora married in 525. When Justinian was proclaimed co-emperor with his uncle Justin on April 1, 527, Theodora received the rare title of *augusta*, empress. Thereafter her name was linked with Justinian's in the exercise of imperial power.

Most of our knowledge of Theodora's early life comes from the *Secret History*, a tell-all description of the vices of Justinian and his court, written by Procopius (ca 550), who was the official court historian and thus spent his days praising those same people. In the *Secret History*, he portrays Theodora and Justinian as demonic, greedy, and vicious, killing courtiers to steal their property. In scene after detailed scene, Procopius portrays Theodora as particularly evil, sexually insatiable, depraved, and cruel, a temptress who used sorcery to attract men, including the hapless Justinian.

In one of his official histories, *The History of the Wars of Justinian,* Procopius presents a very different Theodora. Riots between the supporters of two teams in chariot races—who formed associations somewhat like street gangs and somewhat like political parties—had turned deadly, and Justinian wavered in his handling of the perpetrators. Both sides turned against the emperor, besieging the palace while Justinian was inside it. Shouting N-I-K-A (Victory), the rioters swept through the city, burning and looting, and destroyed half of Constantinople. Justinian's counselors urged flight, but, according to Procopius, Theodora rose and declared:

For one who has reigned, it is intolerable to be an exile. . . . If you wish, O Emperor, to save yourself, there is no difficulty: we have ample funds and there are the ships. Yet reflect whether, when you have once escaped to a place of security, you will not prefer death to safety. I agree with an old saying that the purple [that is, the color worn only by emperors] is a fair winding sheet to be buried in].

Justinian rallied, had the rioters driven into the hippodrome, and ordered between thirty and thirty-five thousand men and women executed. The revolt was crushed and Justinian's authority restored, an outcome approved by Procopius.

The empress Theodora shown with the halo—symbolic of power in Eastern art. (Scala/Art Resource, NY)

Other sources describe or suggest Theodora's influence on imperial policy. Justinian passed a number of laws that improved the legal status of women, such as allowing women to own property the same way that men could and to be guardians over their own children. Justinian is reputed to have consulted her every day about all aspects of state policy, including religious policy regarding the doctrinal disputes that continued throughout his reign.

Theodora's influence over her husband and her power in the Byzantine state continued until she died, perhaps of cancer, twenty years before Justinian. Her influence may have even continued after death, for Justinian continued to pass reforms favoring women and, at the end of his life, accepted her interpretation of Christian doctrine. Institutions that she established, including hospitals, orphanages, houses for the rehabilitation of prostitutes, and churches, continued to be reminders of her charity and piety.

Theodora has been viewed as a symbol of the manipulation of beauty and cleverness to attain position and power, and also as a strong and capable co-ruler who held the empire together during riots, revolts, and deadly epidemics. Just as Procopius expressed both views, the debate has continued to today among writers of science fiction and fantasy as well as biographers and historians.

Questions for Analysis

1. How would you assess the complex legacy of Theodora?
2. Since the public and private views of Procopius are so different regarding the empress, should he be trusted at all as a historical source?

Online Study Center Improve Your Grade
Going Beyond Individuals in Society

Theodora of Constantinople.") Witness Procopius's description of Justinian's character:

For he was at once villainous and amenable; as people say colloquially, a moron. He was never truthful with anyone, but always guileful in what he said and did, yet easily hoodwinked by any who wanted to deceive him. His nature was an unnatural mixture of folly and wickedness.[2]

How much of this is true and how much the hostility of a sanctimonious hypocrite relishing the gossip he spreads, we will never know. Certainly *The Secret History* is robust reading.

Byzantine Science and Medicine

Although the Byzantines discovered little that was new in mathematics and geometry, they passed Greco-Roman learning on to the Arabs, who assimilated it and made remarkable advances with it. The Byzantines were equally uncreative in astronomy and natural science, but they faithfully learned what the ancients had to teach. Only when science could be put to military use did they make advances. For example, the best-known Byzantine scientific discovery was chemical—"Greek fire" or "liquid fire," an explosive compound of crude oil mixed with resin and sulfur that was heated and propelled by a pump through a bronze tube. As the liquid jet left the tube, it was ignited—somewhat like a modern flamethrower. Greek fire saved Constantinople from Arab assault in 678. In mechanics the Byzantines continued the work of Hellenistic and Roman inventors of artillery and siege machinery. Just as Archimedes had devised machines to stop the Romans, so Byzantine scientists improved and modified devices for defending their empire.

The Byzantines devoted a great deal of attention to medicine, and the general level of medical competence was far higher in the Byzantine Empire than in western Europe.

The Byzantines assimilated the discoveries of Hellenic and Hellenistic medicine but added very few of their own. The basis of their medical theory was Hippocrates' concept of the four humors (see page 85). Byzantine physicians emphasized the importance of diet and rest and relied heavily on herbal medicines. Perhaps their most dangerous practice was excessive use of bleeding and burning, which often further weakened already feeble patients.

Greek medical science could not cope with the terrible disease, often called the "Justinian plague," that swept through the Byzantine Empire, Italy, southern France, Iberia, and the Rhine Valley between 542 and about 560. Probably originating in northwestern India and carried to the Mediterranean region by ships, the disease was similar to modern forms of the bubonic plague. Characterized by high fever, chills, delirium, and enlarged lymph nodes (the buboes that gave bubonic plague its name), or by inflammation of the lungs that caused hemorrhages of black blood, the Justinian plague carried off tens of thousands of people. The epidemic had profound political as well as social consequences. It weakened Justinian's military resources, thus hampering his efforts to restore unity to the Mediterranean world.

Anicia Juliana (462?–528?)   The daughter of a Byzantine emperor and a great benefactor of the church and the arts, Anicia Juliana commissioned a manuscript of the works of the physician Dioscorides (fl. first century) on herbal medicines, which remained the standard reference work on the subject for centuries. She is shown here seated between two Virtues, Magnanimity and Patience. *(Austrian National Library Picture Archive)*

By the ninth or tenth century, most major Greek cities had hospitals for the care of the sick. The hospital operated by the Pantokrator monastery in Constantinople possessed fifty beds divided into five wards for different illnesses. Hospital staff included a specialist in the functions and diseases of the eye, a surgeon who performed hernia repairs, two general practitioners, two surgeons who worked an outpatient clinic, a female medical practitioner who handled diseases of women, and an attendant responsible for keeping instruments clean. The imperial Byzantine government bore the costs of this and other hospitals.

The Growth of the Christian Church

As the Western Roman Empire disintegrated in the fourth and fifth centuries, the Christian church survived and grew, becoming the most important institution in Europe. The able administrators and highly creative thinkers of the church developed permanent institutions and complex philosophical concepts.

• **What factors enabled the Christian church to expand and thrive?**

The Idea of a Church

Scriptural scholars tell us that the earliest use of the word *church* in the New Testament appears in Saint Paul's Letter to the Christians of Thessalonica in northern Greece, written about A.D. 51. *Church* means assembly or congregation (in Greek, *ekklesia*); by *ekklesia* Paul meant the local community of Christian believers. In Paul's later letters the word refers to the entire Mediterranean-wide assembly of Jesus' followers. After the legalization of Christianity by the emperor Constantine (see page 181) and the growth of institutional offices and officials, the word *church* was sometimes applied to those officials—much as we use the terms *the college* or *the university* when referring to academic administrators.

In early Christian communities the local people elected their leaders, or bishops. Bishops were men with reputations for having special spiritual charisma or with acknowledged administrative ability, learning, or preaching skills. Bishops were responsible for the community's goods and oversaw the distribution of those goods to the poor. They also were responsible for maintaining orthodox (established or correct) doctrine within the community and for preaching. Bishops alone could confirm believers in their faith and ordain men as priests.

The bishops of Rome used the text known as the Petrine Doctrine (see page 198) to support their assertions of authority over the bishops in the church. Thus the popes maintained that they represented "the church." The word *church,* therefore, has several connotations. Although modern Catholic theology frequently defines the church as "the people of God" and identifies it with local and international Christian communities, in the Middle Ages the institutional and monarchical interpretations tended to be stressed.

The Church and the Roman Emperors

The church benefited considerably from the emperors' support. In return, the emperors expected the support of the Christian church in maintaining order and unity. Constantine had legalized the practice of Christianity in the empire in 312 and encouraged it throughout his reign. He freed the clergy from imperial taxation. At churchmen's request, he helped settle theological disputes and thus preserved doctrinal unity within the church. Constantine generously endowed the building of Christian churches, and one of his gifts—the Lateran Palace in Rome—remained the official residence of the popes until the fourteenth century. Constantine also declared Sunday a public holiday, a day of rest for the service of God. Because of its favored position in the empire, Christianity slowly became the leading religion (see Map 7.2).

In 380 the emperor Theodosius made Christianity the official religion of the empire. Theodosius stripped Roman pagan temples of statues, made the practice of the old Roman state religion a treasonable offense, and persecuted Christians who dissented from orthodox doctrine. Most significant, he allowed the church to establish its own courts and to use its own body of law, called "canon law." These courts, not the Roman government, had jurisdiction over the clergy and ecclesiastical disputes. At the death of Theodosius, the Christian church was considerably independent of the Roman state. The foundation for later growth in church power had been laid.

What was to be the church's relationship to secular powers? How was the Christian to render unto Caesar the things that were Caesar's while returning to God what was due to God? This problem had troubled the earliest disciples of Christ. The toleration of Christianity and the coming to power of Christian emperors in the fourth century did not make it any easier.

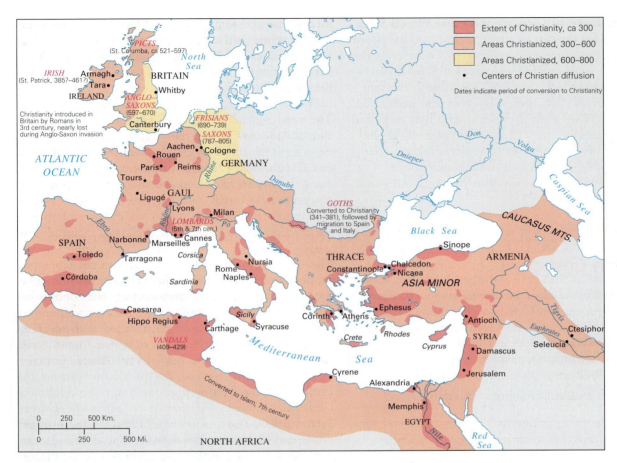

MAP 7.2 The Spread of Christianity Originating in Judaea, the southern part of modern Israel and Jordan, Christianity first spread throughout the Roman world and then beyond it in all directions.

Online Study Center **Improve Your Grade** Interactive Map: Spread of Christianity

In the fourth century, theological disputes frequently and sharply divided the Christian community. Some disagreements had to do with the nature of Christ. For example, **Arianism,** which originated with Arius (ca 250–336), a priest of Alexandria, denied that Christ was divine and co-eternal with God the Father—two propositions of orthodox Christian belief. Arius held that God the Father was by definition uncreated and unchangeable. Jesus, however, was born of Mary, grew in wisdom, and suffered punishment and death. Therefore, Arius reasoned, Jesus the Son must be less or inferior to the Unbegotten Father, who was incapable of suffering and did not die. Jesus was created by the will of the Father and thus was not co-eternal with the Father. Orthodox theologians branded Arius's position a heresy—the denial of a basic doctrine of faith.

Arianism enjoyed such popularity and provoked such controversy that Constantine, to whom religious disagreement meant civil disorder, interceded. He summoned church leaders to a council in Nicaea in Asia Minor and presided over it personally. The council produced the Nicene Creed, which defined the orthodox position that Christ is "eternally begotten of the Father" and of the same substance as the Father. Arius and those who refused to accept the creed were banished, the first case of civil punishment for heresy. This participation of the emperor in a theological dispute within the church paved the way for later emperors to do the same.

So active was the emperor Theodosius in church matters that he was eventually at loggerheads with Bishop Ambrose of Milan (339–397). Theodosius ordered Ambrose to hand over his cathedral church to the emperor.

Ambrose's response had important consequences for the future:

At length came the command, "Deliver up the Basilica"; I reply, "It is not lawful for us to deliver it up, nor for your Majesty to receive it. By no law can you violate the house of a private man, and do you think that the house of God may be taken away? . . . But do not burden your conscience with the thought that you have any right as Emperor over sacred things. . . . It is written, God's to God and Caesar's to Caesar. The palace is the Emperor's, the churches are the Bishop's. To you is committed jurisdiction over public, not over sacred buildings."[3]

Ambrose's statement was to serve as the cornerstone of the Christian theory of civil-ecclesiastical relations for centuries. Ambrose insisted that the church was independent of the state's jurisdiction and that, in matters relating to the faith or the church, the bishops were to be the judges of emperors, not the other way around. In a Christian society harmony and peace depended on agreement between the bishop and the secular ruler. But if disagreement developed, the church was ultimately the superior power because the church was responsible for the salvation of all (including the emperor). In a letter to the emperor Anastasius I, Pope Gelasius I (492–496) put this idea another way, stating that both the civil and the religious authorities were created by God and were essential to a well-ordered Christian society. Each was supreme in its own domain—the church in the spiritual, the civil in the secular—and cooperation in building a Christian society was their mutual responsibility. In later centuries, theologians, canonists, and propagandists repeatedly cited Ambrose's and Gelasius's position as the basis of relations between the two powers.

Online Study Center Improve Your Grade
Primary Source: An Emperor Brought to Heel: Saint Ambrose and Emperor Theodosius

Later Byzantine emperors continued the pattern of active involvement in church affairs. They appointed the highest officials of the church hierarchy; the emperors or their representatives presided at ecumenical councils; and the emperors controlled some of the material resources of the church—land, rents, and dependent peasantry. On the other hand, the emperors performed few liturgical functions and rarely tried to impose their views in theological disputes. Greek churchmen vigorously defended the church's independence; some even asserted the superiority of the bishop's authority over the emperor; and the church possessed such enormous economic wealth and influence over the population that it could block

government decisions. The **Orthodox church,** the name generally given to the Eastern Christian church, was less independent of secular control than the Western Christian church, but it was not simply a branch of the Byzantine state.

The steady separation of the Byzantine East and the Germanic West rests partly on the ways Christianity and classical culture were received in the two parts of the Roman Empire. In the West, Christians initially constituted a small, alien minority within the broad Roman culture; they kept apart from the rest of society. In Byzantium, by contrast, most Greeks were Christian. *Apologists,* or defenders, of Christianity insisted on harmony between Christianity and classical culture: they used Greek philosophy to buttress Christian tenets. In late antiquity the two parts of the Christian church were not completely separate, however. Most church theology in the West came from the East. Until the eighth century, the popes, who were often selected by the clergy of Rome, continued to send announcements of their elections to the emperors at Constantinople—a sign that the Roman popes long thought of themselves as bishops of the Roman Empire.

Bishops and the Pope

The early Christian church benefited from the brilliant administrative abilities of some church leaders and from identification of the authority and dignity of the bishop of Rome with the imperial traditions of the city. With the empire in decay, educated people joined and worked for the church in the belief that it was the one institution able to provide leadership. Bishop Ambrose, for example, the son of the Roman prefect of Gaul, was a trained lawyer and the governor of a province. He is typical of the Roman aristocrats who held high public office, were converted to Christianity, and subsequently became bishops. Such men later provided social continuity from Roman to Germanic rule. As bishop of Milan, Ambrose himself exercised responsibility in the temporal as well as the ecclesiastical affairs of northern Italy.

During the reign of Diocletian (284–305), the Roman Empire had been divided for administrative purposes into geographical units called dioceses. Gradually the church made use of this organizational structure. Christian bishops established their headquarters, or sees, in the urban centers of the old Roman dioceses. A bishop's jurisdiction extended throughout the diocese. The center of his authority was his cathedral (from the Latin *cathedra,* meaning "chair"). Thus, church leaders capitalized on the Roman imperial method of organization and adapted it to ecclesiastical purposes.

The bishops of Rome—known as "popes," from the Latin word *papa*, meaning "father"—claimed to speak and act as the source of unity for all Christians. They based their claim to be the successors of Saint Peter and heirs to his authority as chief of the apostles on Jesus' words:

You are Peter, and on this rock I will build my church, and the jaws of death shall not prevail against it. I will entrust to you the keys of the kingdom of heaven. Whatever you declare bound on earth shall be bound in heaven; whatever you declare loosed on earth shall be loosed in heaven.[4]

Theologians call this statement the **Petrine Doctrine.**

After the removal of the capital and the emperor to Constantinople (see page 182), the bishop of Rome exercised considerable influence in the West because he had no real competitor there. The bishops of Rome stressed that Rome had been the capital of a worldwide empire and emphasized the special importance of Rome in the framework of that empire. Successive bishops of Rome reminded Christians in other parts of the world that Rome was the burial place of Saint Peter and Saint Paul. Moreover, according to tradition, Saint Peter, the chief of Christ's first twelve followers, had lived and had been executed in Rome. No other city in the world could make such claims. Hence the bishop of Rome was called "Patriarch of the West." In the East, the bishops of Antioch, Alexandria, Jerusalem, and Constantinople, because of the special dignity of their sees, also gained the title of patriarch. Their jurisdictions extended over lands adjoining their sees; they consecrated bishops, investigated heresy, and heard judicial appeals.

In the fifth century the bishops of Rome began to stress their supremacy over other Christian communities and to urge other churches to appeal to Rome for the resolution of disputed doctrinal issues. Thus Pope Innocent I (401–417) wrote to the bishops of Africa:

We approve your action in following the principle that nothing which was done even in the most remote and distant provinces should be taken as finally settled unless it came to the notice of this See, that any just pronouncement might be confirmed by all the authority of this See.[5]

The prestige of Rome and of the church as a whole was also enhanced by the courage and leadership of the Roman bishops. As described in Chapter 6 (see page 183), church officials played important roles in addressing civil problems previously handled by Roman imperial authorities. The fact that it was Christian leaders, rather than imperial administrators, who responded to dire urban needs could not help but increase the prestige and influence of the church.

Although Popes Innocent I and Leo I (440–461) strongly asserted the primacy of the Roman papacy, local Christian communities and their leaders often exercised authority over their churches. Particular social and political situations determined the actual power of the bishop of Rome in a given circumstance. The importance of arguments for the Roman primacy rests in the fact that they served as precedents for later appeals.

The Development of Christian Monasticism

Christianity began and spread as a city religion. Since the first century, however, some especially pious Christians had felt that the only alternative to the decadence of urban life was complete separation from the world. All-consuming pursuit of material things, gross sexual promiscuity, and general political corruption disgusted them. They believed that the Christian life as set forth in the Gospel could not be lived in the midst of such immorality. They rejected the values of Roman society and were the first real nonconformists in the church.

The fourth century witnessed a significant change in the relationship of Christianity and the broader society. Until Constantine's legalization of Christianity, Christians were a persecuted minority. People were tortured and killed for their faith. Christians greatly revered these martyrs, the men and women who, like Jesus, suffered and died for their faith. When Christianity was legalized and the persecutions ended, a new problem arose. Whereas Christians had been a suffering minority, now they came to be identified with the state: non-Christians could not advance in the imperial service. And if Christianity had triumphed, so too had "the world," since secular attitudes and values pervaded the church. The church of martyrs no longer existed. Some scholars believe that the monasteries provided a way of life for those Christians who wanted to make a total response to Christ's teachings; the monks became the new martyrs. Saint Anthony of Egypt (251?–356), the earliest monk for whom there is concrete evidence and the man later considered the father of monasticism, went to Alexandria during the last persecution in the hope of gaining martyrdom. Christians believed that monks, like the martyrs before them, could speak to God and that their prayers had special influence.

Monasticism began in Egypt in the third century. At first individuals and small groups withdrew from cities and organized society to seek God through prayer in desert or mountain caves and shelters. Gradually large colonies of monks gathered in the deserts of Upper Egypt. These monks were called hermits, from the Greek word *eremos*, meaning "desert." Many devout women also were attracted to this **eremitical** life. We have no way of knowing how many hermits there were in the fourth and fifth centuries because their conscious aim was a hidden life known only to God. Although monks and nuns led isolated lives and the monastic movement represented the antithesis of the ancient ideal of an urban social existence, ordinary people soon recognized the monks and nuns as holy people and sought them as spiritual guides.

Some church leaders did not approve of eremitical life, however. Hermits sometimes claimed to have mystical experiences, direct communications with God. If hermits could communicate directly with the Lord, what need had they for the priest and the institutional church? Saint Basil (329?–379), the scholarly bishop of Caesarea in Cappadocia in Asia Minor, opposed the eremitical life on other grounds: the impossibility of material self-sufficiency; the danger of excessive concern with the self; and the fact that the eremitical life did not provide the opportunity for the exercise of charity, the first virtue of any Christian. The Egyptian ascetic Pachomius (290–346?) had organized communities of men and women at his coenobitic (communal) monastery at Tabennisi on the Upper Nile, drawing thousands of recruits. Saint Basil and the church hierarchy encouraged **coenobitic monasticism,** communal living in monasteries. Communal living, they felt, provided an environment for training the aspirant in the virtues of charity, poverty, and freedom from self-deception.

Western and Eastern Monasticism

In the fourth, fifth, and sixth centuries, information about Egyptian monasticism came to the West, and both men and women sought the monastic life. When monasticism spread to western Europe, several factors worked against the continuation of the eremitical form. The harsh weather of northern Europe that lasted for many months of the year discouraged isolated living. In the dense forests, wild animals and wandering Germanic tribes presented obvious dangers. Thus most of the monasticism that developed in Gaul, Italy, Spain, England, and Ireland was coenobitic.

In 529 Benedict of Nursia (480–543), who had experimented with both the eremitical and the communal forms of monastic life, wrote a brief set of regulations for the monks who had gathered around him at Monte Cassino between Rome and Naples. Benedict's guide for monastic life proved more adaptable than and slowly replaced all others. *The Rule of Saint Benedict* came to influence all forms of organized religious life in the Roman church. Men and women who lived in monastic houses all followed sets of rules, first those of Benedict and later those written by other individuals, and because of this came to be called **regular clergy,** from the Latin word *regulus* (rule). Priests and bishops who staffed churches in which people worshiped and who were not cut off from the world were called **secular clergy.** (According to official church doctrine, women are not members of the clergy, but this distinction was not clear to most medieval people.)

Saint Benedict conceived of his *Rule* as a simple code for ordinary men. It outlined a monastic life of regularity, discipline, and moderation in an atmosphere of silence. Each monk had ample food and adequate sleep. The monk spent part of each day in formal prayer, which Benedict called the *Opus Dei* (Work of God) and Christians later termed the divine office, the public prayer of the church. This consisted of chanting psalms and other prayers from the Bible in that part of the monastery church called the "choir." The rest of the day was passed in manual labor, study, and private prayer.

Online Study Center **Improve Your Grade**
Primary Source: The Rule of Saint Benedict: Work and Pray

Why did the Benedictine form of monasticism eventually replace other forms of Western monasticism? The answer lies partly in its spirit of flexibility and moderation and partly in the balanced life it provided. Early Benedictine monks and nuns spent part of the day in prayer, part in study or some other form of intellectual activity, and part in manual labor. The monastic life as conceived by Saint Benedict struck a balance between asceticism and activity. It thus provided opportunities for men of entirely different abilities and talents—from mechanics to gardeners to literary scholars. The Benedictine form of religious life also proved congenial to women. Five miles from Monte Cassino at Plombariola, Benedict's twin sister Scholastica (480–543) adapted the *Rule* for the use of her community of nuns. The adoption of Benedict's *Rule* by houses of women paralleled that in houses of men.

Benedictine monasticism also succeeded partly because it was so materially successful. In the seventh and eighth centuries monasteries pushed back forests and wastelands, drained swamps, and experimented with crop rotation. Benedictine houses made a significant contribution to the agricultural development of Europe. The communal nature of their organization, whereby property was held in common and profits were pooled and reinvested, made this contribution possible.

Finally, monasteries conducted schools for local young people. Some learned about prescriptions and herbal remedies and went on to provide medical treatment in their localities. A few copied manuscripts and wrote books. Local and royal governments drew on the services of the literate men and able administrators the monasteries produced. This was not what Saint Benedict had intended, but perhaps the effectiveness of the institution he designed made it inevitable.

Monasticism in the Greek Orthodox world differed in fundamental ways from the monasticism that evolved in western Europe. First, while *The Rule of Saint Benedict* gradually became the universal guide for all western European monasteries, each individual house in the Byzantine world developed its own *typikon,* or set of rules for organization and behavior. The *typika* contain regulations about novitiate, diet, clothing, liturgical functions, commemorative services for benefactors, and the election of officials, such as the *hegoumenos,* or superior of the house. Second, education never became a central feature of the Greek houses. Monks and nuns had to be literate to perform the services of the choir, but no monastery assumed responsibility for the general training of the local young.

There were also similarities between Western and Eastern monasticism. As in the West, Eastern monasteries became wealthy, with fields, pastures, livestock, and buildings. Since bishops and patriarchs of the Greek church were recruited only from the monasteries, Greek houses also exercised cultural influence.

Saint Benedict   Holding his *Rule* in his left hand, the seated and cowled patriarch of Western monasticism blesses a monk with his right hand. His monastery, Monte Cassino, is in the background. *(Biblioteca Apostolica Vaticana)*

Christian Ideas and Practices

The growth of Christianity was not simply a matter of institutions such as the papacy and monasteries, but also of ideas. Christian beliefs and practices changed as different groups of people accepted Christianity and as the political and social context changed.

● *How did Christian ideas and practices respond to changing political and social circumstances in the Roman Empire?*

Christianity and Classical Culture

Christians were initially a tiny marginal group, but Christianity eventually became the official religion of the Roman Empire. As this happened, Christian leaders and thinkers, especially those who were highly educated, gradually came to terms with classical culture. Elements of Greek and Roman philosophy and of various pre-Christian religious beliefs were incorporated into Christian teachings.

Christians in the first and second centuries believed that the end of the world was near. They expected to witness the return of Christ, and therefore they considered knowledge useless and learning a waste of time. The important duty of the Christian was to prepare for the Second Coming of the Lord. Good Christians who sought the Kingdom of Heaven through the imitation of Christ believed that they had to disassociate themselves from the "filth" that Roman culture embodied.

As Saint Paul wrote, "The wisdom of the world is foolishness, we preach Christ crucified." Tertullian (ca 160–220), an influential African church father and writer, condemned all secular literature as foolishness in the eyes of God. He called Greek philosophers such as Aristotle "hucksters of eloquence" and compared them to "animals of self-glorification." "What has Athens to do with Jerusalem," he demanded, "the Academy with the Church? We have no need for curiosity since Jesus Christ, nor for inquiry since the gospel." Tertullian insisted that Christians would find all the wisdom they needed in the Bible.

On the other hand, Christianity encouraged adjustment to the ideas and institutions of the Roman world. Some biblical texts urged Christians to accept the existing social, economic, and political establishment. Specifically addressing Christians living among non-Christians in the hostile environment of Rome, the author of the First Letter of Peter had written about the obligations of Christians:

Always behave honorably among pagans, so that they can see your good works for themselves and, when the day of reckoning comes, give thanks to God for the things which now make them denounce you as criminals. . . .

For the sake of the Lord, accept the authority of every social institution: the emperor, as the supreme authority, and the governors as commissioned by him to punish criminals and praise good citizenship. God wants you to be good citizens. . . . Have respect for everyone and love for your community; fear God and honour the emperor.[6]

Even had early Christians wanted to give up Greco-Roman ideas and patterns of thought, they would have had great difficulty doing so. Therefore, they had to adapt their Roman education to their Christian beliefs. Saint Paul himself believed that there was a good deal of truth in pagan thought, as long as it was correctly interpreted and understood.

The result was a compromise. Christians gradually came to terms with Greco-Roman culture. Saint Jerome (340–419), a distinguished theologian and linguist, remains famous for his translation of the Old and New Testaments from Hebrew and Greek into vernacular Latin. Called the "Vulgate," his edition of the Bible served as the official translation until the sixteenth century, and scholars rely on it even today. Familiar with the writings of classical authors, Saint Jerome also believed that Chris-

tians should study the best of ancient thought because it would direct their minds to God. He maintained that the best ancient literature should be interpreted in light of the Christian faith.

Christian Notions of Gender and Sexuality

Christian attitudes toward gender and sexuality illustrate the ways early Christians adopted the views of their contemporary world. In his plan of salvation, Jesus, whom Christians accept as the Messiah, considered women the equal of men. He attributed no disreputable qualities to women and did not refer to them as inferior creatures. On the contrary, women were among his earliest and most faithful converts. He discussed his mission with them (John 4:21–25), and the first persons to whom he revealed himself after his resurrection were women (Matthew 28:9–10).

Women took an active role in the spread of Christianity, preaching, acting as missionaries, being martyred alongside men, and perhaps even baptizing believers. Early Christians expected Jesus to return to earth very soon and taught that people should concentrate on this Second Coming. Because of this, marriage and normal family life should be abandoned, and Christians should depend on their new spiritual family of co-believers. Early Christians often met in people's homes and called one another brother and sister, a metaphorical use of family terms that was new to the Roman Empire in which Christianity developed. Some women embraced the ideal of virginity and either singly or in monastic communities declared themselves "virgins in the service of Christ." All this made Christianity seem dangerous to many Romans, especially when becoming Christian actually led some young people to avoid marriage, which was viewed by Romans as the foundation of society and the proper patriarchal order.

Not all Christian teachings about gender were radical, however. Many early followers of Jesus, particularly the Apostle Paul, whose letters make up a major part of the New Testament, had ambivalent ideas about women's proper role in the church, and in the first century A.D. they began to place restrictions on female believers. Paul and later writers forbade women to preach, and women were gradually excluded from holding official positions in Christianity other than in women's monasteries. Women in monasteries were to be considered not virgins who had chosen to serve Christ, but rather "brides of

The Marys at Jesus' Tomb This late-fourth-century ivory panel tells the story of Mary Magdalene and another Mary who went to Jesus' tomb to anoint the body (Matthew 28:1–7). At the top guards collapse when an angel descends from Heaven, and at the bottom the Marys listen to the angel telling them that Jesus had risen. Immediately after this, in Matthew's Gospel, Jesus appears to the women. Here the artist uses Roman artistic styles to convey Christian subject matter, an example of the assimilation of classical form and Christian teaching. *(Castello Sforzesco/Scala/Art Resource, NY)*

Christ," that is, in a dependent relationship with a man. Both Jewish and classical Mediterranean culture viewed female subordination as natural and proper, so in limiting the activities of female believers Christianity was following well-established patterns, just as it patterned its official hierarchy after that of the Roman Empire.

Christian teachings about sexuality also built on classical culture. Many early church leaders, who are often called the church fathers, renounced marriage and sought to live chaste lives not only because they expected the Second Coming imminently, but also because they accepted the hostility toward the body that derived from certain strains of Hellenistic philosophy. Just as spirit was superior to matter, the mind was superior to the body. The church fathers acknowledged that God had established marriage for the generation of children, but they believed it to be a concession to weak souls who could not bear celibacy. Though God had clearly sanctioned marriage, celibacy was the highest good. This emphasis on self-denial led to a strong streak of misogyny (hatred of women) in their writings, for they saw women and female sexuality as the chief obstacles to their preferred existence. They also saw intercourse as little more than animal lust, the triumph of the inferior body over the superior mind. Same-sex relations—which were generally acceptable in the Greco-Roman world, especially if they were between socially unequal individuals—were evil, though only slightly worse than other types of sexual relations because they could not lead to procreation. The church fathers' misogyny and hostility toward sexuality had a greater influence on the formation of later attitudes than did the relatively egalitarian actions and words of Jesus.

Saint Augustine on Human Nature, Will, and Sin

The most influential church father in the West was Saint Augustine of Hippo (354–430). Saint Augustine was born into an urban family in what is now Algeria in North Africa. His father, a minor civil servant, was a pagan; his mother, Monica, a devout Christian. Because his family was poor, the only avenue to success in a highly competitive world was a classical education.

Augustine's mother believed that a good classical education, although pagan, would make her son a better Christian, so the child received his basic education in the local school. At the age of seventeen, Augustine went to nearby Carthage to continue his education. There he experimented with several philosophies and Christian groups whose ideas differed from those of most church authorities. As was normal for young Roman men, he began relations with a concubine, who later had a son. In 383 he traveled to Rome, where he endured not only illness but also disappointment in his teaching: his students fled when their bills were due.

Augustine then took a teaching position in Milan, where he had frequent conversations with Bishop Ambrose. Through these, and through insights gained from reading Saint Paul's Letter to the Romans, Augustine became a Christian, receiving Christian baptism from Ambrose, who also baptized his son. Augustine returned to Africa, where his mother and son soon died, and later became bishop of the seacoast city of Hippo Regius. He was a renowned preacher to Christians there, a vigorous defender of orthodox Christianity, and the author of more than ninety-three books and treatises.

Augustine's autobiography, *The Confessions,* is a literary masterpiece and one of the most influential books in the history of Europe. Written in the rhetorical style and language of late Roman antiquity, it marks the synthesis of Greco-Roman forms and Christian thought. *The Confessions* describes Augustine's moral struggle, the conflict between his spiritual and intellectual aspirations and his sensual and material self. Many Greek and Roman philosophers had taught that knowledge and virtue are the same: a person who knows what is right will do what is right. Augustine rejected this idea. He believed that a person may know what is right but fail to act righteously because of the innate weakness of the human will. People do not always act on the basis of rational knowledge. For example, Augustine regarded a life of chastity as the best possible life even before he became a Christian. As he notes in *The Confessions,* as a young man he prayed to God for "chastity and continency" and added "but not yet." His education had not made his will strong enough to avoid lust or any other evil; that would come only through God's power and grace.

Augustine's ideas on sin, grace, and redemption became the foundation of all subsequent Western Christian theology, Protestant as well as Catholic. He wrote that the basic or dynamic force in any individual is the will, which he defined as "the power of the soul to hold on to or to obtain an object without constraint." The end or goal of the will determines the moral character of the individual. When Adam ate the fruit forbidden by God in the Garden of Eden (Genesis 3:6), he committed the "original sin" and corrupted the will. Adam's sin was not simply his own, but was passed on to all later humans through sexual intercourse; even infants were tainted. Original sin thus became a common social stain, in Augustine's opinion, transmitted by concupiscence, or sexual desire. Coitus

was theoretically good since it was created by God, but it had been corrupted by sin, so every act of intercourse was evil and every child was conceived through a sinful act. By viewing sexual desire as the result of disobedience to divine instructions by Adam and Eve, Augustine linked sexuality even more clearly with sin than had earlier church fathers. Because Adam disobeyed God and fell, all human beings have an innate tendency to sin: their will is weak. But according to Augustine, God restores the strength of the will through grace, which is transmitted in certain rituals that the church defined as **sacraments.** Grace results from God's decisions, not from any merit on the part of the individual.

The initial sacrament in any individual's life was baptism, and, because of his ideas about original sin, Augustine became a firm supporter of infant baptism instead of the then more commonly practiced adult baptism. Augustine held that babies who died before being baptized could not enter Heaven and that they spent eternity in Hell; this harsh view was moderated by later Catholic theologians who posited the notion of "limbo," a place where unbaptized babies remained until the Second Coming of Jesus. The fate of unbaptized babies remained a topic of debate among Catholic and later Protestant theologians for centuries. (In 2006 a papal commission recommended that Pope Benedict XVI abolish the concept of limbo and affirm that unbaptized babies go straight to Heaven. Though the pope himself had earlier noted that limbo was "only a theological hypothesis," he decided to delay making a definitive decision to abolish it.)

Augustine also argued against the Donatist heretical movement promoted by the North African bishop of Carthage, Donatus (313–347). Donatism denied the value of sacraments administered by priests or bishops who had denied their faith under persecution or had committed grave sins. For the Donatists the holiness of the minister was as important as the sacred rites he performed. Donatists viewed the true church, therefore, as a small spiritual elite that was an alternative to society. Augustine responded that, through God's action, the rites of the church have an objective and permanent validity regardless of the priest's spiritual condition. The notion of the church as a special spiritual elite recurred many times in the Middle Ages. Each time it was branded a heresy, and Augustine's arguments were marshaled against it.

When the Visigothic chieftain Alaric conquered Rome in 410, horrified pagans blamed the disaster on the Christians. In response, Augustine wrote *City of God.* This profoundly original work contrasts Christianity with the secular society in which it existed. Filled with references to ancient history and mythology, it remained for centuries

Heaven in Augustine's *City of God* Heavenly Jerusalem, from a twelfth-century Czech illuminated manuscript of Augustine's *City of God*. Augustine's writings were copied and recopied for many centuries in all parts of Europe, and they remained extremely influential. In this copy, the Czech king Wenzeslas and his grandmother are portrayed in the lower right corner; they probably paid for the manuscript. *(Erich Lessing/Art Resource, NY)*

the standard statement of the Christian philosophy of history.

According to Augustine, history is the account of God acting in time. Human history reveals that there are two kinds of people: those who live the life of the flesh in the City of Babylon and those who live the life of the spirit in the City of God. The former will endure eternal hellfire; the latter will enjoy eternal bliss.

Augustine maintained that states came into existence as the result of Adam's fall and people's inclination to sin. The state is a necessary evil, but it can work for the good by providing the peace, justice, and order that Christians need in order to pursue their pilgrimage to the City of God. The particular form of government—whether

monarchy, aristocracy, or democracy—is basically irrelevant. Any civil government that fails to provide justice is no more than a band of gangsters.

Although the state results from moral lapse—from sin—neither is the church (the Christian community) entirely free from sin. The church is certainly not equivalent to the City of God. But the church, which is concerned with salvation, is responsible for everyone, including Christian rulers. Churches later used Augustine's theory to defend their belief in the ultimate superiority of the spiritual power over the temporal. This remained the dominant political theory until the late thirteenth century.

Online Study Center **Improve Your Grade**
Primary Source: Saint Augustine Denounces Paganism and Urges Romans to Enter the City of God

Christian Missionaries and Conversion

The word *catholic* derives from a Greek word meaning "general," "universal," or "worldwide." Christ had said that his teaching was for all peoples, and Christians sought to make their faith catholic—that is, believed everywhere. This could be accomplished only through missionary activity. As Saint Paul had written to the Christian community at Colossae in Asia Minor, "there is no room for distinction between Greek and Jew, between the circumcised or the uncircumcised, or between barbarian or Scythian, slave and free man. There is only Christ; he is everything and he is in everything."[7] Paul urged Christians to bring the "good news" of Christ to all peoples. The Mediterranean served as the highway over which Christianity spread to the cities of the Roman Empire. From there missionaries took Christian teachings to the countryside, and then to areas beyond the borders of the empire.

● *What techniques did missionaries develop to convert barbarian peoples to Christianity?*

Missionaries on the Continent

During the Roman occupation, Christian communities were scattered throughout Gaul and Britain. The effective beginnings of Christianity in Gaul can be traced to Saint Martin of Tours (ca 316–397), a Roman soldier who, after giving away half his cloak to a naked beggar, had a vision of Christ and was baptized. Martin founded the monastery of Ligugé, the first in Gaul, which became a center for the evangelization of the country districts. In 372 he became bishop of Tours and introduced a rudimentary parish system. The Christianization of rural areas followed a different pattern from that of the cities.

Religion was not a private or individual matter; it was a social affair; and the religion of the chieftain or king determined the religion of the people. Thus missionaries concentrated their initial efforts not on the people, but on kings or tribal chieftains. According to custom, kings negotiated with all foreign powers, including the gods. Because Christian missionaries represented a "foreign" power (the Christian God), the king dealt with them. Germanic kings accepted Christianity because they believed that the Christian God was more powerful than pagan gods and that the Christian God would deliver victory in battle, or because Christianity taught obedience to (kingly) authority, or because Christian priests possessed knowledge and a charisma that could be associated with kingly power. Kings who converted, such as Ethelbert of Kent and the Frankish chieftain Clovis, sometimes had Christian wives. Conversion may also have indicated that barbarian kings wanted to enjoy the cultural advantages that Christianity brought, such as literate assistants and an ideological basis for their rule.

In eastern Europe, missionaries traveled far beyond the boundaries of the Byzantine Empire. In 863 the emperor Michael III sent the brothers Cyril (826–869) and Methodius (815–885) to preach Christianity in Moravia (the region of modern central Czech Republic). Other missionaries succeeded in converting the Russians in the tenth century. Cyril invented a Slavic alphabet using Greek characters, and this script (called the "Cyrillic alphabet") is still in use today. Cyrillic script made possible the birth of Russian literature. Similarly, Byzantine art and architecture became the basis and inspiration of Russian forms. The Byzantines were so successful that the Russians claimed to be the successors of the Byzantine Empire. For a time Moscow was even known as the "Third Rome" (the second Rome being Constantinople).

Christianity in the British Isles

Tradition identifies the conversion of Ireland with Saint Patrick (ca 385–461). Born in western England to a Christian family of Roman citizenship, Patrick was captured and enslaved by Irish raiders and taken to Ireland, where he worked as a herdsman for six years. He escaped and returned to England, where a vision urged him to Christianize Ireland. In preparation, Patrick stud-

ied in Gaul and was consecrated a bishop in 432. He returned to Ireland, where he converted the Irish tribe by tribe, first baptizing the king. In 445, with the approval of Pope Leo I, Patrick established his see in Armagh. The ecclesiastical organization that Patrick set up, however, differed from church structure on the continent in a fundamental way: Armagh was a monastery, and the monastery, rather than the diocese, served as the center of ecclesiastical organization. Local tribes and the monastery were interdependent, with the tribe supporting the monastery economically and the monastery providing religious and educational services for the tribe. By the time of Patrick's death, the majority of the Irish people had received Christian baptism. In his missionary work, Patrick had the strong support of Bridget of Kildare (ca 450–ca 528), daughter of a wealthy chieftain and his concubine. Bridget defied parental pressure to marry and became a nun. She and the other nuns at Kildare instructed relatives and friends in basic Christian doctrine, made religious vestments for churches, copied books, taught

Ardagh Silver Chalice This chalice, crafted about A.D. 800 and used for wine in Christian ceremonies, formed part of the treasure of Ardagh Cathedral in County Limerick, Ireland. Made of several types of metal, it is decorated with Celtic patterns in the same way that Irish manuscripts from this era are. Christianity was widespread in Ireland long before anywhere else in northern Europe, and Celtic traditions and practices differed significantly from those of Rome. *(National Museum of Ireland)*

children, and above all set a religious example by their lives of prayer. In Ireland and later in continental Europe, women shared in the process of conversion.

A strong missionary fervor characterized Irish Christianity. Perhaps the best representative of Irish-Celtic zeal was Saint Columba (ca 521–597), who established the monastery of Iona on an island in the Inner Hebrides off the west coast of Scotland (see Map 7.4 on page 214). Iona served as a base for converting the pagan Picts of Scotland. Columba's proselytizing efforts won him the title "Apostle of Scotland," and his disciples carried the Christian Gospel to the European continent.

The Christianization of the English really began in 597, when Pope Gregory I (590–604) sent a delegation of monks under the Roman Augustine to Britain. Augustine's approach, like Patrick's, was to concentrate on converting the king. When he succeeded in converting Ethelbert, king of Kent, the baptism of Ethelbert's people took place as a matter of course. Augustine established his headquarters, or see, at Canterbury, the capital of Kent.

In the course of the seventh century, two Christian forces competed for the conversion of the pagan Anglo-Saxons: Roman-oriented missionaries traveling north from Canterbury, and Celtic monks from Ireland and northwestern Britain. Monasteries were established at Iona, Lindisfarne, Jarrow, and Whitby.

The Roman and Celtic church organization, types of monastic life, and methods of arriving at the date of the central feast of the Christian calendar, Easter, differed completely. Through the influence of King Oswiu of Northumbria and the energetic abbess Hilda of Whitby, the Synod (ecclesiastical council) held at Whitby in 664 opted to follow the Roman practices. The conversion of the English and the close attachment of the English church to Rome had far-reaching consequences because Britain later served as a base for the Christianization of the continent (see Map 7.2).

Conversion and Assimilation

Between the fifth and tenth centuries, the great majority of peoples living on the European continent and the nearby islands were baptized as Christians. When a ruler marched his people to the waters of baptism, though, the work of Christianization had only begun. Baptism meant either sprinkling the head or immersing the body in water. Conversion meant awareness and acceptance of the beliefs of Christianity, including those that seemed strange or radical, such as "love your enemies" or "do good to those that hate you."

How did missionaries and priests get masses of pagan and illiterate peoples to understand and live by Christian ideals and teachings? They did so through preaching, assimilation, and the penitential system. Preaching aimed at instruction and edification. Instruction presented the basic teachings of Christianity. Edification was intended to strengthen the newly baptized in their faith through stories about the lives of Christ and the saints. But deeply ingrained pagan customs and practices could not be stamped out by words alone or even by imperial edicts. Christian missionaries often pursued a policy of assimilation, easing the conversion of pagan men and women by stressing similarities between their customs and beliefs and those of Christianity. In the same way that classically trained scholars such as Jerome and Augustine blended Greco-Roman and Christian ideas, missionaries and converts mixed pagan ideas and practices with Christian ones. Bogs and lakes sacred to Germanic gods became associated with saints, as did various aspects of ordinary life, such as traveling, planting crops, and worrying about a sick child. Aspects of existing midwinter celebrations, which often centered on the return of the sun as the days became longer, were incorporated into celebrations of Christmas. Spring rituals involving eggs and rabbits (both symbols of fertility) were added to Easter.

A letter from Pope Gregory I beautifully illustrates this policy. Sent to Augustine of Canterbury in Britain in 601, it expresses the pope's intention that pagan buildings and practices be given a Christian significance:

Therefore, when by God's help you reach our most reverent brother, Bishop Augustine, we wish you to inform him that we have been giving careful thought to the affairs of the English, and have come to the conclusion that the temples of the idols among that people should on no account be destroyed. The idols are to be destroyed, but the temples themselves are to be aspersed with holy water, altars set up in them, and relics deposited there. For if these temples are well-built, they must be purified from the worship of demons and dedicated to the service of the true God. In this way we hope that the people, seeing that their temples are not destroyed, may abandon their error and, flocking more readily to their accustomed resorts, may come to know and adore the true God.[8]

The way that assimilation works is perhaps best appreciated through the example of Saint Valentine's Day. There were two Romans named Valentine. Both were Christian priests, and both were martyred for their beliefs in the third century, around the middle of February. (Nothing in the lives of the two Christian martyrs connects them with lovers or the exchange of messages and gifts. That practice began in the later Middle Ages.) Since about

Pope Gregory I and Scribes One of the four "Doctors" (or Learned Fathers) of the Latin church, Gregory (590–604) is shown on the cover of this tenth-century ivory book writing at his desk while the Holy Spirit, in the form of a dove, whispers in his ear. Below, scribes copy Gregory's works. *(Kunsthistorisches Museum, Vienna/Art Resource, NY)*

150 B.C. the Romans had celebrated the festival of Lupercalia, at which they asked the gods for fertility for themselves, their fields, and their flocks. This celebration occurred in mid-February, shortly before the Roman New Year and the arrival of spring. Thus the early church "converted" the old festival of Lupercalia into Saint Valentine's Day. The fourteenth of February was still celebrated as a festival, but it had taken on a Christian meaning.

A process with an equally profound, if gradual, impact on the conversion of the pagan masses was the rite of reconciliation in which the sinner revealed his or her sins in order to receive God's forgiveness. In the early church, "confession" meant that the sinner publicly acknowledged charges laid against him or her and publicly carried out the penitential works prescribed by the priest or bishop. For example, the adulterer might have to stand outside the church before services wearing a sign naming his or her sin and asking the prayers of everyone who entered.

Beginning in the late sixth century, however, Irish and English missionaries brought the more private penitential system to continental Europe. **Penitentials** were manuals for the examination of conscience. The penitent knelt individually before the priest, who questioned the penitent about the sins he or she might have committed. A penance such as fasting on bread and water for a period of time or saying specific prayers was imposed as medicine for the soul. The penitential system made sin and forgiveness an individual rather than a community matter and encouraged the private examination of conscience, particularly because penitentials advised priests to ask about people's thoughts and desires as well as about their actions.

Most religious observances continued to be community matters, however, as they had been in the ancient world. People joined with family members, friends, and neighbors to attend baptisms and funerals, presided over by a priest. They prayed to saints or to the Virgin Mary to intercede with God, or they simply asked the saints for protection and blessing. The entire village participated in processions marking saints' days or points in the agricultural year, often carrying images of saints or their **relics**—bones, articles of clothing, or other objects associated with the life of a saint—around the houses and fields.

Migrating Peoples

The migration of peoples from one area to another has been a dominant and continuing feature of Western history. Mass movements of Europeans occurred in the fourth through sixth centuries, in the ninth and tenth centuries, and in the twelfth and thirteenth centuries. From the sixteenth century to the present, such movements have been almost continuous, involving not just the European continent but the entire world. The causes of early migrations varied and are not thoroughly understood by scholars. But there is no question that the migrations profoundly affected both the regions to which peoples moved and the ones they left behind.

• *How did the migration of barbarian groups such as the Celtic and Germanic tribes shape political structures and notions of ethnic identity?*

Procession to a New Church   In this sixth-century ivory carving, two men in a wagon, accompanied by a procession of people holding candles, carry a relic casket to a church under construction. Workers are putting tiles on the church roof. New churches often received holy items when they were dedicated, and processions were common ways in which people expressed community devotion. *(Amt fuer kirchliche Denmalpflege. Foto: Ann Muenchow)*

The Idea of the Barbarian

In surveying the world around them, the ancient Greeks often conceptualized things in dichotomies, or sets of opposites: light and dark, hot and cold, wet and dry, mind and body, male and female, and so on. One of their key dichotomies was Greek and non-Greek, and the Greeks coined the word *barbaros* for those whose native language was not Greek, because they seemed to the Greeks to be speaking nonsense syllables—bar, bar, bar. ("Barbar" is the Greek equivalent to "blah-blah" or "yadayada.") Barbaros originally meant someone who did not speak Greek, but gradually it also implied that the people were unruly, savage, and more primitive than people in the advanced civilization of Greece. The word brought this meaning with it when it came into Latin and other European languages, and the Romans referred to those who lived beyond the northeastern boundary of Roman territory as **barbarians.**

The modern study of ethnography (writing about the formation of ethnic groups) involves the systematic recording of the major characteristics of different human cultures. Scholars today identify three models of ethnic formation among the peoples who came in contact with the Romans and whom the Romans called barbarians.

First, there were Germanic peoples, whose identity was shaped by a militarily successful or "royal" family. For example, the Salian Franks, Lombards, and Goths attracted and controlled followers from other peoples by getting them to adhere to the cultural traditions of the leading family. Followers assimilated the "kernel family's" legendary traditions and myths, which traced their origins to a family or individual of divine ancestry. The kernel family led these followers from their original territory, won significant victories over other peoples, and settled someplace within the Roman world. In the fifth century these groups formed large political units, and their rulers began to issue law codes regulating interpersonal relations for members of the group.

A second model of ethnic formation derives from Central Asian steppe peoples such as the Huns, Avars, and Alans. These were polyethnic seminomadic and sedentary groups led by small bodies of steppe commanders. (The term *steppe* refers to the vast semiarid plain in Russian Siberia.) These peoples constituted large confederations whose success depended on constant expansion by military victory or the use of terror. Defeat in battle or the death of a leader could lead to the disintegration of the confederation, and the confederations did not develop written law codes in this era.

The Slavs of eastern Europe represent a third model of barbarian ethnic formation. They were loosely organized bands of peoples who lacked centralized leadership and intermingled with other groups as they migrated. No group records from this period survive, so the only information about the Slavs comes from outsiders. The sense of a "Slavic" identity, or of an identity that was, for example, Polish or Russian or Serbian, was the product of a later period.

One fundamental trait characterizes all barbarian peoples: the formation of the ethnic groups did not represent a single historical event. Rather, the formation was a continuous and changing process extending over long periods of time.

Migrating groups that the Romans labeled barbarians had pressed along the Rhine-Danube frontier of the Roman Empire since about A.D. 150 (see page 155). In the third and fourth centuries, increasing pressures on the frontiers from the east and north placed greater demands on military manpower, which plague and a declining birthrate had reduced. Therefore, Roman generals recruited barbarians to fill the ranks. They bribed Germanic chiefs with treaties and gold and Germanic masses with grain. By the late third century a large percentage of military recruits were Germanic.

Several types of barbarian peoples entered the empire and became affiliated with Roman government. The *laeti*, refugees or prisoners of war, and their families were settled in areas of Gaul and Italy under the supervision of Roman prefects and landowners. Generally isolated from the local Roman population, the laeti farmed regions depopulated by plague. The men had to serve in the Roman army. Free barbarian units called **foederati**, stationed near major provincial cities, represented a second type of affiliated barbarian group. Research has suggested that rather than giving them land, the Romans assigned the foederati shares of the tax revenues from the region.[9] Living in close proximity to Roman communities, the foederati quickly assimilated into Roman culture. In fact, in the fourth century, some rose to the highest ranks of the army and moved in the most cultured and aristocratic circles.

Celts, Germans, and Huns

As Julius Caesar advanced through Gaul between 58 and 50 B.C. (see page 144), the largest barbarian groups he encountered were Celts (whom the Romans called Gauls) and Germans. Modern historians have tended to use the terms *German* and *Celt* in a racial sense, but recent research stresses that *Celt* and *German* are linguistic

terms, a Celt being a person who spoke a Celtic language, an ancestor of the modern Gaelic or Breton language, and a German one who spoke a Germanic language, an ancestor of modern German, Dutch, Danish, Swedish, or Norwegian.

Celts and Germans were similar to one another in many ways. In the first century A.D., the Celts lived east of the Rhine River in an area bounded by the Main Valley and extending westward to the Somme River. Germans were more numerous along the North and Baltic Seas. Both Germans and Celts used wheeled plows and a three-field system of crop rotation. Before the introduction of Christianity, both Celtic and Germanic peoples were polytheistic, with hundreds of gods and goddesses with specialized functions whose celebrations were often linked to points in the yearly agricultural cycle. Worship was often outdoors at sacred springs, groves, or lakes.

The Celts had developed iron manufacturing, using shaft furnaces as sophisticated as those of the Romans to produce iron swords and spears. Celtic priests, called druids, had legal and educational as well as religious functions, orally passing down laws and traditions from generation to generation. Bards singing poems and ballads also passed down stories of heroes and gods, which, were written down much later. Celtic peoples conquered by the Romans often assimilated to Roman ways, adapting the Latin language and other aspects of Roman culture. By the fourth century A.D., under pressure from Germanic groups, the Celts had moved westward, settling in Brittany (modern northwestern France) and throughout the British Isles (England, Wales, Scotland, and Ireland). The Picts of Scotland as well as the Welsh, Britons, and Irish were peoples of Celtic descent (see Map 7.3).

The migrations of the Germanic peoples were important in the political and social transformations of late antiquity. Many modern scholars have tried to explain who the Germans were and why they migrated. The present consensus, based on the study of linguistic and archaeological evidence, is that there were not one but rather many Germanic peoples with very different cultural traditions. The largest Germanic tribe, the Goths, was a polyethnic group consisting of perhaps fifteen thousand to twenty thousand warriors, which with women and children amounted to one hundred thousand people. The tribe was supplemented by slaves, *coloni*, peoples who, because of their desperate situation under Roman rule, joined the Goths during their migrations.[10]

Combined with linguistic data, archaeological remains—bone fossils, cooking utensils, jewelry, weapons of war, and other artifacts—suggest three broad groupings of Germanic peoples. One group lived along the North and Baltic Seas in the regions of present-day northern Germany, southern Sweden, and Denmark. A second band inhabited the area between the Elbe and Oder Rivers. A third group lived along the Rhine and Weser Rivers, closest to the Roman frontier. Although these groupings sometimes showed cultural affiliation, they were very fluid and did not possess political, social, or ethnic solidarity.

Why did the Germans migrate? Like the Celts, in part they were pushed by groups living farther eastward, especially by the Huns from Central Asia in the fourth and fifth centuries. In part, they were searching for more regular supplies of food, better farmland, and a warmer climate. Conflicts within and among Germanic groups also led to war and disruption, which motivated groups to move. Franks fought Alemanni in Gaul; Visigoths fought Vandals in the Iberian Peninsula and across North Africa; and Angles and Saxons fought Celtic-speaking Britons in England.

All these factors can be seen in the movement of the Visigoths, one of the Germanic tribes, from an area north of the Black Sea southeastward into the Roman Empire. Pressured by defeat in battle, starvation, and the movement of the Huns, the Visigoths petitioned the emperor Valens to admit them to the empire. Seeing in the hordes of warriors the solution to his manpower problem, Valens agreed. Once the Visigoths were inside the empire, Roman authorities exploited their hunger by forcing them to sell their own people as slaves in exchange for dog flesh: "the going rate was one dog for one Goth." Still, the Visigoths sought peace. Fritigern offered himself as a friend and ally of Rome in exchange for the province of Thrace—land, crops, and livestock. With a Roman army of between thirty thousand and forty thousand men against about ten thousand Goths, Valens did not take the offer seriously, and his council voted for battle. When the two armies met on August 9, 378, near Adrianople, the Visigoths slashed down the Roman army, including thirty-five high-ranking officers and the emperor Valens himself. But the Goths had neither the equipment nor the tactical skill to take the city of Adrianople. The Battle of Adrianople created no notable change in the military or political history of the Roman Empire.

As the Visigoths migrated into Thrace and the Balkans, however, they forced the Romans to change imperial policy toward the barbarians. That policy alternated between official recognition by treaty and enmity. Alaric I's invasion of Italy and sack of Rome in 410 represents the culmination of hostility between the Visigoths and the

Vandal Landowner In this mosaic, a Vandal landowner rides out from his Roman-style house. His clothing—Roman short tunic, cloak, and sandals—reflects the way some Celtic and Germanic tribes accepted Roman lifestyles, though his beard is more typical of barbarian men's fashion. *(Courtesy of the Trustees of the British Museum)*

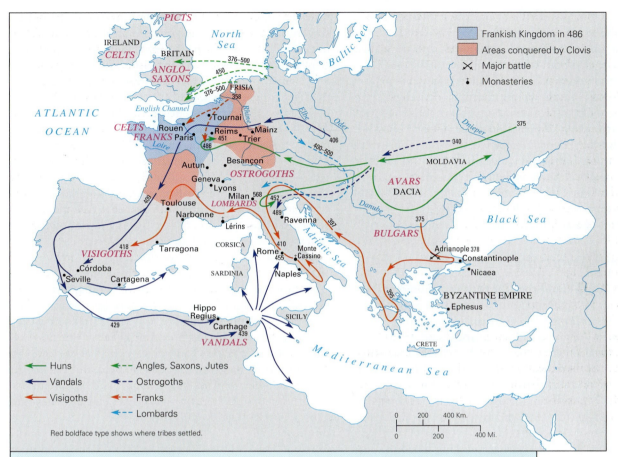

Mapping the Past

MAP 7.3 The Barbarian Migrations This map shows the migrations of various barbarian groups in late antiquity and can be used to answer the following questions: ❶ The map has no political boundaries. What does this suggest about the impact of barbarian migrations on political structures? ❷ Human migration is caused by a combination of push factors—circumstances that lead people to leave a place—and pull factors—things that attract people to a new location. Based on the information in this and earlier chapters, what push and pull factors might have shaped the migration patterns you see on the map? ❸ The movements of barbarian peoples used to be labeled "invasions" and are now usually described as "migrations." How do the dates on the map support the newer understanding of these movements?

Romans. The Goths burned and looted the city for three days, which caused many Romans to wonder whether God had deserted them. This led the imperial government to pull its troops from the British Isles and many areas north of the Alps, leaving these northern areas more vulnerable and open to migrating groups. A year later Alaric died, and his successor led his people into southwestern Gaul.[11] Establishing their headquarters at Toulouse, they exercised a weak domination over Spain until a Muslim victory at Guadalete in 711 ended Visigothic rule.

One significant factor in Germanic migration was pressure from nomadic steppe peoples from Central Asia. This included the Alans, Avars, Bulgars, Khazars, and most prominently the Huns, who attacked the Black Sea area and the Eastern Roman Empire beginning in the fourth century. Under the leadership of their warrior-king Attila, the Huns swept into central Europe in 451, attacking Roman settlements in the Balkans and Germanic settlements along the Danube and Rhine Rivers. Several Germanic groups allied with them, as did the sister of the Roman emperor, and a huge army took the city of Metz, now in eastern France. After Attila turned his army southward and crossed the Alps into Italy, a papal delegation, including Pope Leo I himself, asked him not to attack Rome. Though papal diplomacy was later credited with stopping the advance of the Huns, a plague that spread among Hunnic troops and their dwindling food supplies were probably much more important. The Huns retreated from Italy, and within a year Attila was dead. Later leaders were not as effective, and the Huns were never again an important factor in European history. Their conquests had slowed down the movements of various Germanic groups, however, allowing barbarian peoples to absorb more of Roman culture as they picked the Western Roman Empire apart.

Germanic Kingdoms

Between 450 and 565, the Germans established a number of kingdoms, but none other than the Frankish kingdom lasted very long. The Germanic kingdoms did not have definite geographical boundaries, and their locations are approximate. The Vandals, whose destructive ways are commemorated in the word *vandal,* settled in North Africa. In northern and western Europe in the sixth century, the Burgundians ruled over lands roughly circumscribed by the old Roman army camps at Lyons, Besançon, Geneva, and Autun.

In northern Italy the Ostrogothic king Theodoric (r. 471–526) established his residence at Ravenna and gradually won control of all Italy, Sicily, and the territory north and east of the upper Adriatic. Although attached to the customs of his people, Theodoric pursued a policy of assimilation between Germans and Romans. He maintained close relations with the emperor at Constantinople and attracted able scholars such as Cassiodorus to his administration. Theodoric's accomplishments were significant, but his administration fell apart after his death.

The kingdom established by the Franks in the sixth century, in spite of later civil wars, proved to be the most powerful and enduring of all the barbarian kingdoms. The Franks were a confederation of peoples who originated in the marshy lowlands north and east of the northernmost part of the Rhine frontier of the Roman Empire. They spoke a Germanic language. In the fourth and fifth centuries, they settled within the empire and allied with the Romans, some attaining high military and civil positions. In the sixth century one group, the Salian Franks, issued a law code called the **Salic Law,** the earliest description of Germanic customs. Chlodio (fifth century) is the first member of the Frankish dynasty for whom evidence survives. According to legend, Chlodio's wife went swimming, encountered a sea monster, and conceived Merowig. The Franks believed that Merowig, a man of supernatural origins, founded their ruling dynasty, which was thus called **Merovingian.**

The reign of Clovis (ca 481–511) marks the decisive period in the development of the Franks as a unified people. Through military campaigns, Clovis acquired the central provinces of Roman Gaul. The next two centuries witnessed the steady assimilation of Franks and Gallo-Romans, as many Franks adopted the Latin language and Roman ways, and Gallo-Romans copied Frankish customs and Frankish personal names. These centuries also saw Frankish acquisition of the Burgundian kingdom and of territory held by the Goths in Provence.[12]

Many writers have debated the issue of Clovis's conversion from Arian to Roman Christianity. His near-contemporary, Gregory, bishop of Tours, attributed Clovis's conversion to the influence of his Catholic wife, Chlotilde. Another contemporary writer holds that Clovis prayed to the Christian god in his war with the Alamanni (ca 496); in thanksgiving for his victory, he accepted baptism. A third contemporary witness believed that the conversion was "the personal choice of an intelligent monarch." One student of the Franks argues that Clovis was baptized in 508 (not in 496, as has been traditionally believed), at the time he was at war in southwestern Gaul with the Visigothic king Alaric II, and that there was propaganda value to be gained by appearing as the defender of Catholicism against Arianism.[13] Certainly, conversion brought Clovis the crucial support of the papacy and of the bishops of Gaul. (See the feature "Listening to the Past: The Conversion of Clovis" on pages 220–221.)

Anglo-Saxon England

The island of Britain was populated by various Celtic-speaking tribes when it was conquered by Rome during the reign of Claudius. During the first four centuries of the Christian era, it shared fully in the life of the Roman Empire. Towns were planned in the Roman fashion, with temples, public baths, theaters, and amphitheaters. In the countryside large manors controlled the surrounding lands. Roman merchants brought Eastern luxury goods and Eastern religions—including Christianity—into Britain. The Romans suppressed the Celtic chieftains, and a military aristocracy governed. In the course of the second and third centuries, many Celts assimilated to Roman culture, becoming Roman citizens and joining the Roman army.

In 407 the emperor Honorius (r. 395–423), faced with the Visigothic army attacking Rome under Alaric, withdrew imperial troops from Britain. The Picts from Scotland and the Scots from Ireland invaded British Celtic territory. According to the eighth-century historian Bede (see page 245), the Celtic king Vortigern invited the Saxons from Denmark to help him against his rivals in Britain. Saxons and other Germanic tribes from modern-day Norway, Sweden, and Denmark turned from assistance to conquest, attacking in a hit-and-run fashion. Their goal was plunder, and at first their invasions led to no permanent settlements. As more Germanic peoples arrived, however, they took over the best lands and eventually conquered most of Britain. Some Britons fled to Wales and the westernmost parts of England, north toward Scotland, and across the English Channel to Brittany. Others remained and eventually intermarried with Germanic peoples.

Historians have labeled the period 500 to 1066, the year of the Norman Conquest, "Anglo-Saxon," after the two largest Germanic tribes, the Angles and the Saxons. The Germanic tribes destroyed Roman culture in Britain. Christianity disappeared; large urban buildings were allowed to fall apart; and tribal custom superseded Roman law.

The Anglo-Saxon invasion gave rise to a rich body of Celtic mythology, particularly legends about King Arthur, who first appeared in Welsh poetry in the sixth century and later in histories, epics, and saints' lives. In the twelfth century, stories about Arthur were included in Geoffrey of Monmouth's very popular *History of the Kings of Britain,* a fictional account of British history that was regarded as fact for centuries. The legends were also spread by traveling poets and minstrels, and they gradually evolved into an elaborate story. According to these texts, when Arthur, the illegitimate son of the king of Britain, successfully drew a sword from a stone, Merlin, the court magician, revealed Arthur's royal parentage. Arthur won recognition as king, and the mysterious Lady of the Lake gave him the invincible sword Excalibur. He fought many battles and went on many quests, including a search for the Holy Grail, the cup supposedly used by Jesus at the Last Supper, which was said to have miraculous powers. Arthur held his court at Camelot, where his knights were seated at the Round Table (to avoid quarrels over precedence). Those knights—including Sir Tristan, Sir Lancelot, Sir Galahad, and Sir Percival (Parsifal)—and Arthur's wife Guinevere, whose ill-fated romance with Sir Lancelot led to the end of the Arthurian kingdom, played a large role in later medieval literature, and their stories were told again and again. In their earliest form as Welsh poems, the Arthurian legends may represent Celtic hostility to Anglo-Saxon invaders, but they later came to be more important as representations of the ideal of medieval knightly chivalry and as great stories whose retelling has continued to the present.

Whether Arthur had any basis in historical reality is hotly debated, with some scholars arguing that he was based on myths about deities, while others assert that he might have been based on one or another Romanized Celtic leader, a warrior rather than a king. Most scholars see him as a composite figure who evolved over the centuries as different stories were told about him and his associates.

The beginnings of the Germanic kingdoms in Britain are nearly as obscure as Arthur, but scholars suspect that they came into being in the seventh and eighth centuries. The scholar Bede described seven kingdoms: the Saxon kingdoms of the East Saxons (Essex), South Saxons (Sussex), and West Saxons (Wessex); the Jutish kingdom of Kent; and the kingdoms of the Angles, Mercians, and Northumbrians (see Map 7.4). The names imply that these peoples thought of themselves in tribal rather than geographical terms. Because of Bede's categorization, scholars often refer to the Heptarchy, or seven kingdoms, of Anglo-Saxon Britain. The suggestion of total Anglo-Saxon domination, however, is not entirely accurate. Germanic tribes never subdued Scotland, where the Picts remained strong, or Wales, where Celtic-speaking Welsh and Britons continued to put up stubborn resistance.

Thus Anglo-Saxon England was divided along ethnic and political lines. The Germanic kingdoms in the south, east, and center were opposed by the Britons in the west, who wanted to get rid of the invaders. The Anglo-Saxon kingdoms also fought among themselves, causing boundaries to shift constantly. Finally, in the ninth century, under pressure from the Danish, or Viking, invasions, the Celtic Britons and the Germanic Anglo-Saxons were molded together under the leadership of King Alfred of Wessex (r. 871–899).

Barbarian Society

Germanic and Celtic society had originated in the northern parts of central and western Europe and the southern regions of Scandinavia during the Iron Age (800–500 B.C.). After Germanic kingdoms replaced the Roman Empire as the primary political structure throughout much of Europe, barbarian customs and traditions formed the basis of European society for centuries.

MAP 7.4 Anglo-Saxon England   The seven kingdoms of the Heptarchy—Northumbria, Mercia, East Anglia, Essex, Kent, Sussex, and Wessex—dominated but did not subsume Britain. Scotland remained a Pict stronghold, while the Celts resisted invasion of their native Wales by Germanic tribes.

Scholars have long understood the importance of barbarian society, but they have been hampered in investigating it because most Germanic and Celtic groups did not write and thus kept no written records before their conversion to Christianity. The earliest information about them comes from *Germania,* a description of Germanic laws and customs written by the Roman politician and historian Tacitus (ca 56–ca 117). Tacitus, who had never traveled in areas with a significant Germanic population, took his information from earlier writers who had, and perhaps from soldiers or merchants who had gone beyond the borders of the Roman Empire. Thus his descriptions are secondhand at best and were also shaped

by his purpose in writing, for he thought that his fellow Romans had grown corrupt and immoral, and he saw the Germans as simpler and braver. Other Roman authors also had particular points of view when describing barbarian society, so their writings must be combined with archaeological evidence and other types of sources to gain a more accurate picture. These newer sources, from Scandinavia and the British Isles, include inscriptions carved in stone, bone, and wood and written in the **runic alphabet.** The oldest comes from shortly after the time of Tacitus. Early runic inscriptions are usually short and are limited to names, but later runes describe the actions of kings and other powerful individuals. A few with very ordinary purposes, such as letters and greetings, have been unearthed in Norway, and scholars can use them to find information about a wide range of activities.

Online Study Center **Improve Your Grade**
Primary Source: Noble Savages: Rome Encounters the Germans

● *What patterns of social, political, and economic life characterized barbarian society?*

Kinship, Custom, and Class

Barbarians generally had no notion of the state as we use the term today; they thought in social, not political, terms. The basic social unit was the tribe, a group whose members believed that they were all descended from a common ancestor. Blood united them; kinship protected them. Law was custom—unwritten, preserved in the minds of the elders of the tribe, and handed down by word of mouth from generation to generation. Every tribe had its customs, and every member of the tribe knew what they were. Members were subject to their tribe's customary laws wherever they went, and friendly tribes respected one another's laws.

Barbarian tribes were led by tribal chieftains, who are often called kings, though this implies broader power than they actually had. The chief was the member recognized as the strongest and bravest in battle and was elected from among the male members of the strongest family. He led the tribe in war, settled disputes among its members, conducted negotiations with outside powers, and offered sacrifices to the gods. The period of migrations and conquests of the Western Roman Empire witnessed the strengthening of kingship among tribes.

Closely associated with the king in some southern tribes was the **comitatus,** or "war band." Writing at the end of the first century, Tacitus described the war band as

Runic Inscriptions An eighth-century chest made of whalebone depicting warriors, other human figures, and a horse, with a border of runic letters. This chest tells a story in both pictures and words. The runes are one of the varieties from the British Isles, from a time and place in which the Latin alphabet was known as well. Runes and Latin letters were used side-by-side in some parts of northern Europe for centuries. *(Erich Lessing/Art Resource, NY)*

the bravest young men in the tribe. They swore loyalty to the chief, fought with him in battle, and were not supposed to leave the battlefield without him; to do so implied cowardice, disloyalty, and social disgrace. A social egalitarianism existed among members of the war band. The comitatus had importance for the later development of feudalism.

During the migrations of the third and fourth centuries, however, and as a result of constant warfare, the war band was transformed into a system of stratified ranks. Among the Ostrogoths, for example, a warrior nobility and several other nobilities evolved. Contact with the Romans, who produced such goods as armbands for trade with the barbarians, stimulated demand for armbands. Thus armbands, especially the gold ones reserved for the "royal families," promoted the development of hierarchical ranks within war bands. During the Ostrogothic conquest of Italy under Theodoric, warrior-nobles also sought to acquire land as both a mark of prestige and a means to power. As land and wealth came into the hands of a small elite class, social inequalities emerged and gradually grew stronger.[14] These inequalities help explain the origins of the European noble class (see pages 313–314).

Law

Early barbarian tribes had no written laws, but beginning in the late sixth century some tribal chieftains began to collect, write, and publish lists of their customs. They were encouraged to do so because the Christian missionaries who were slowly converting the barbarians to Christianity wanted to know the tribal customs. Churchmen wanted to read about barbarian ways in order to assimilate the tribes to Christianity. Augustine of Canterbury, for example, persuaded King Ethelbert of Kent to have his folk laws written down; these *Dooms of Ethelbert* date from between 601 and 604, roughly five years after Augustine's arrival in Britain. Moreover, by the sixth century many barbarian kings needed regulations for the Romans under their jurisdiction as well as for their own people.

According to the code of the Salian Franks, every person had a particular monetary value to the tribe. This value was called the **wergeld,** which literally means "man-money" or "money to buy off the spear." Men of fighting age had the highest wergeld, then women of childbearing age, children, and finally the aged. Everyone's value reflected his or her potential military worthiness. If a person accused of a crime agreed to pay the wergeld and if the victim and his or her family accepted the payment, there was peace (hence the expression "money to buy off the spear"). If the accused refused to pay the wergeld or if the victim's family refused to accept it, a blood feud ensued. Individuals depended on their kin for protection, and kinship served as a force of social control.

Historians and sociologists have difficulty interpreting the early law codes, partly because they are patchwork affairs studded with additions made in later centuries. Yet much historical information can be gleaned from these codes. For example, the Salic Law (see page 212) of the Salian Franks offers a general picture of Frankish life and problems in the early Middle Ages and is typical of the law codes of other tribes, such as the Visigoths, Burgundians, Lombards, and Anglo-Saxons.

The Salic Law lists the monetary fines to be paid to the victim or the family for such injuries as theft, rape, assault, arson, and murder:

If any person strike another on the head so that the brain appears, and the three bones which lie above the brain shall project, he shall be sentenced to 1200 denars, which make 300 shillings. . . .

If any one have killed a free woman after she has begun bearing children, he shall be sentenced to 2400 denars, which make 600 shillings. . . .

If any one shall have drawn a harrow through another's harvest after it has sprouted, or shall have gone through it with a wagon where there was no road, he shall be sentenced to 120 denars, which make 30 shillings.[15]

This is not a systematic statement of a body of law, but rather a list of fines for particular offenses. Germanic law aimed at the prevention or reduction of violence. It was not concerned with abstract justice.

Some codes had specific clauses that protected the virtue of women. For example, the Salic Law of the Franks fined a man the large amount of 15 solidi (from *solidus*, a coin originally minted by Constantine and later the basis of much European currency, such as the English shilling) if he pressed the hand of a woman, and 35 if he touched her above the elbow. The very high fine of 600 solidi for the murder of a woman of childbearing years—the same value attached to military officers of the king, to priests, and to boys preparing to become warriors—suggests the importance of women in Frankish society, at least for their childbearing capacity.

At first, Romans had been subject to Roman law and Germans to Germanic custom. As German kings accepted Christianity and as Romans and barbarians increasingly intermarried, the distinction between the two laws blurred and, in the course of the seventh and eighth centuries, disappeared. The result would be the new feudal law, to which all who lived in certain areas were subject.

Social and Economic Structures

Barbarian groups usually resided in small villages, and climate and geography determined the basic patterns of agricultural and pastoral life. Many tribes lived in small settlements on the edges of clearings where they raised barley, wheat, oats, peas, and beans. They tilled their fields with simple wooden scratch plows and harvested their grains with small iron sickles. The kernels of grain were eaten as porridge, ground up for flour, or fermented into strong, thick beer; the vast majority of people's caloric intake came from grain in some form.

Information about the gender division of labor is difficult to find, but based on later practices men probably cared for larger animals, such as cattle, while women took care of poultry. Women also had responsibility for spinning the thread that went into the manufacture of clothing and all textiles. Both sexes performed the heavy work of raising, grinding, and preserving cereals.

Within the small villages, there were great differences in wealth and status. Free men and their families constituted the largest class. The number of cattle a man possessed indicated his wealth and determined his social status. "Cattle were so much the quintessential indicator of wealth in traditional society that the modern English term 'fee' (meaning cost of goods or services), which developed from the medieval term 'fief,' had its origin in the Germanic term *fihu* . . . , meaning cattle, chattels, and hence, in general, wealth."[16] Free men also shared in tribal warfare. Slaves (prisoners of war) worked as farm laborers, herdsmen, and household servants.

Did the barbarians produce goods for trade and exchange? Ironworking represented the most advanced craft; much of northern Europe had iron deposits, and the dense forests provided wood for charcoal. Most villages had an oven and smiths who produced agricultural tools and instruments of war—one-edged swords, arrowheads, and shields. In the first two centuries A.D., the quantity and quality of Germanic goods increased dramatically, and the first steel swords were superior to the weapons of Roman troops. These goods were produced for war and for the subsistence economy, not for trade. Goods were also used for gift giving, a major social custom. Gift giving conferred status on the giver, who, in giving, showed his higher (economic) status, cemented friendship, and placed the receiver in his debt.[17] Goods that could not be produced in the village were acquired by raiding and warfare rather than by commercial exchanges. Raids between tribes brought the victors booty; the cattle and slaves captured were traded or given as gifts. Warfare determined the economy and the individual's status within barbarian society.

Barbarian tribes were understood as made up of kin groups, and those kin groups were made up of families, the basic social unit in barbarian society. Families were responsible for the debts and actions of their members and for keeping the peace in general. Barbarian law codes set strict rules of inheritance based on position in the family and often set aside a portion of land that could not be sold or given away by any family member.

Germanic society was patriarchal: within each household the father had authority over his wife, children, and slaves. Some wealthy and powerful men had more than one wife, a pattern that continued even after they became Christian, but polygamy was not widespread among ordinary people. A woman was considered to be under the legal guardianship of a man, and she had fewer rights to own property than did Roman women in the late empire. However, once they were widowed (and there must have

been many widows in such a violent, warring society), women sometimes assumed their husbands' rights over family property and held the guardianship of their children. Just as did classically trained scholars such as Augustine, Germanic religious writers and prelates doubted the spiritual equality of women. For those writers, women demonstrated their spiritual worth by converting their husbands, raising pious children, endowing churches and monasteries, and dispensing charity to the poor.

Women found outlets for their talents in monasteries and convents as writers, copyists, artists, embroiderers, teachers, and estate managers. Some houses of religious women, such as Mauberge in northern Francia under Abbess Aldegund (ca 661), produced important scholarship. The dowry required for entrance to a convent restricted admission as full sisters to upper-class women, but poorer women were taken in as lay sisters. Many women viewed the convent as a place of refuge from family pressures or tribal violence. The sixth-century queen Radegund, for example, was forced to marry Chlotar I, the murderer of several of her relatives. Radegund later escaped her polygamous union and lived out her life in a convent.

Chapter Summary

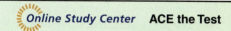
Online Study Center **ACE the Test**

- *How was the Byzantine Empire able to survive for so long, and what were its most important achievements?*
- *What factors enabled the Christian church to expand and thrive?*
- *How did Christian ideas and practices respond to changing political and social circumstances in the Roman Empire?*
- *What techniques did missionaries develop to convert barbarian peoples to Christianity?*
- *How did the migration of barbarian groups such as the Celtic and Germanic tribes shape political structures and notions of ethnic identity?*
- *What patterns of social, political, and economic life characterized barbarian society?*

Late antiquity was a period of rupture and transformation, but also of continuities and assimilation. Migrating barbarian groups broke the Western Roman Empire apart, creating much smaller states and more localized economies. As they encountered Roman culture and became Christian, their own ways of doing things were transformed, and the result was a blend of barbarian and Roman culture. In eastern Europe, the Byzantine Empire thrived throughout late antiquity, maintaining Roman traditions. Throughout Europe, leaders in the Christian church energetically developed more complex ideas and stronger institutional structures, transforming Christianity into the most powerful agent in the making of Europe.

In the east, the Byzantine Empire withstood attacks from Germanic tribes and steppe peoples and remained a state until 1453, a thousand years longer than the

Western Roman Empire. Byzantium preserved the philosophical and scientific texts of the ancient world—which later formed the basis for study in science and medicine in both Europe and the Arabic world—and produced a great synthesis of Roman law, the Justinian *Code,* which shapes legal structures in much of Europe and former European colonies to this day.

Christianity gained the support of the fourth-century emperors and gradually adopted the Roman system of hierarchical organization. The church possessed able administrators and leaders whose skills were tested in the chaotic environment of the end of the Roman Empire in the West. Bishops expanded their activities, and in the fifth century the bishops of Rome began to stress their supremacy over other Christian communities. Monasteries offered opportunities for individuals to develop deeper spiritual devotion and also provided a model of Christian living, a pattern of agricultural development, and a place for education and learning.

Christian thinkers reinterpreted the classics in a Christian sense, incorporating elements of Greek and Roman philosophy and of various pagan religious groups into Christian teachings. Prime among these were certain aspects of Greco-Roman notions of gender and sexuality. Most Christian thinkers accepted Greco-Roman ideas that men were superior to women, though they viewed sexuality and the body with greater suspicion than had ancient pagans and developed a strong sense that chastity and an ascetic life were superior to marriage and family life. Of these early thinkers, Augustine of Hippo was the most influential. His ideas about sin, free will, sexuality, and the role of government shaped western European thought from the fifth century on.

Christianity had a dynamic missionary policy, and the church slowly succeeded in assimilating—that is, adapting—barbarian peoples to Christian teaching. Christian missionaries preached the Gospel to Germanic, Celtic, and Slavic peoples, instructed them in the basic tenets of the Christian faith, and used penitentials to give them a sense of expected behavior. Christianity refashioned the Germanic and classical legacies, creating new rituals and practices that were meaningful to people.

The migration of barbarian groups into Europe from the east affected both the regions to which peoples moved and the ones they left behind. Migrations were caused by many factors, including food shortages, disputes among groups, and pressure from outside, and they sometimes involved military actions, though not always. Barbarians are often divided into large linguistic groups, such as the Celtic and Germanic tribes, with ties to other tribes based on kinship and military alliances, not on loyalty to a particular government. Most barbarian states were weak and short-lived, though that of the Salian Franks was relatively more unified and powerful. Germanic-speaking Angles and Saxons invaded Celtic-speaking England and established a group of small kingdoms that slowly became more unified.

Though barbarian states were generally feeble politically, barbarian customs and traditions formed the basis of European society for centuries. Barbarian law codes, written down for the first time in the sixth century, set out social and gender distinctions and held the family responsible for the actions of an individual. Most people lived in family groups in villages, where men, women, and children shared in the agricultural labor that sustained society. Christianity and the barbarian states absorbed many aspects of Roman culture, and the Byzantine Empire continued to thrive, but western Europe was very different in 600 from how it had been in 350.

Key Terms

Arianism	penitentials
Orthodox church	relics
Petrine Doctrine	barbarians
eremitical	foederati
coenobitic monasticism	Salic Law
regular clergy	Merovingian
secular clergy	runic alphabet
sacraments	comitatus
	wergeld

Online Study Center **Improve Your Grade** Flashcards

Suggested Reading

Brown, Peter. *Augustine of Hippo,* rev. ed. 2000. The best biography of Saint Augustine, which treats him as a symbol of change.

Brown, Peter. *The Body and Society: Men, Women, and Sexual Renunciation in Early Christianity.* 1988. Explores early Christian attitudes on sexuality and how they replaced Roman ones.

Brown, Peter. *The World of Late Antiquity,* A.D. *150–750,* rev. ed. 1989. A lavishly illustrated survey that stresses social and cultural change and has clearly written introductions to the entire period.

Burns, Thomas S. *Rome and the Barbarians, 100 B.C.–400 A.D.* 2003. Argues that Germanic and Roman culture assimilated more than they conflicted.

Cameron, Averil. *The Mediterranean World in Late Antiquity, AD 395–600.* 1993. Focuses especially on political and economic changes.

Clark, Gilian. *Women in Late Antiquity: Pagan and Christian Lifestyles.* 1994. Explores law, marriage, and religious life.

Dunn, Marilyn. *The Emergence of Monasticism: From the Desert Fathers to the Early Middle Ages.* 2003. Focuses on the beginnings of monasticism.

Evans, James Allan. *The Empress Theodora: Partner of Justinian.* 2003. Provides a brief, yet balanced and thorough treatment of the empress's life.

Fletcher, Richard. *The Barbarian Conversion: From Paganism to Christianity.* 1998. A superbly written analysis of conversion to Christianity.

Herrin, Judith. *The Formation of Christendom.* 1987. The best synthesis of the development of the Christian church from the third to the ninth centuries.

Macmullen, Ramsey. *Christianity and Paganism in the Fourth to Eighth Centuries.* 1998. Explores the influences of Christianity and paganism on each other.

Norwich, John Julius. *Byzantium: The Early Centuries.* 1989. An elegantly written brief survey.

Pelikan, Jaroslav. *The Excellent Empire: The Fall of Rome and the Triumph of the Church.* 1987. Describes how interpretations of the fall of Rome have influenced our understanding of Western culture.

Todd, Malcolm. *The Early Germans,* 2d ed. 2004. Uses archaeological and literary sources to analyze Germanic social structure, customs, and religion and to suggest implications for an understanding of migration and ethnicity.

Wells, Peter S. *The Barbarians Speak: How the Conquered Peoples Shaped Roman Europe.* 1999. Presents extensive evidence of Celtic and Germanic social and technical development.

Notes

1. Quoted in J. B. Bury, *History of the Latter Roman Empire,* vol. 1 (New York: Dover, 1958), pp. 233–234.
2. R. Atwater, trans., *Procopius: The Secret History* (Ann Arbor: University of Michigan Press, 1963), bk. 8.
3. R. C. Petry, ed., *A History of Christianity: Readings in the History of Early and Medieval Christianity* (Englewood Cliffs, N.J.: Prentice Hall, 1962), p. 70.
4. Matthew 16:18–19.
5. H. Bettenson, ed., *Documents of the Christian Church* (Oxford: Oxford University Press, 1947), p. 113.
6. Peter 2:11–20.
7. Colossians 3:9–11.
8. L. Sherley-Price, trans., *Bede: A History of the English Church and People* (Baltimore: Penguin Books, 1962), pp. 86–87.
9. See W. Goffart, *Barbarians and Romans: The Techniques of Accommodation* (Princeton, N.J.: Princeton University Press, 1980), chap. 3 and esp. Conclusion, pp. 211–230.
10. H. Wolfram, *History of the Goths* (Berkeley: University of California Press, 1988), pp. 6–10.
11. Ibid., pp. 125–131.
12. E. James, *The Franks* (New York: Basil Blackwell, 1988), pp. 3, 7–10, 58.
13. I. Wood, *The Merovingian Kingdoms, 450–751* (New York: Longman, 1994), pp. 41–45.
14. P. J. Geary, *Before France and Germany: The Creation and Transformation of the Merovingian World* (New York: Oxford University Press, 1988), pp. 108–112.
15. E. F. Henderson, ed., *Select Historical Documents of the Middle Ages* (London: G. Bell & Sons, 1912), pp. 176–189.
16. Geary, *Before France and Germany,* p. 46.
17. Ibid., p. 50.

Listening to the Past

The Conversion of Clovis

*M*odern Christian doctrine holds that *conversion is a process, the gradual turning toward Jesus and the teachings of the Christian Gospels. But in the early medieval world, conversion was perceived more as a one-time event determined by the tribal chieftain. If he accepted baptism, the mass conversion of his people followed. This selection about the Frankish king Clovis is from* The History of the Franks *by Gregory, bishop of Tours (ca 504–594), written about a century after the events it describes.*

The first child which Clotild bore for Clovis was a son. She wanted to have her baby baptized, and she kept urging her husband to agree to this. "The gods whom you worship are no good," she would say. "They haven't even been able to help themselves, let alone others. . . . Take your Saturn, for example, who ran away from his own son to avoid being exiled from his kingdom, or so they say; and Jupiter, that obscene perpetrator of all sorts of mucky deeds, who couldn't keep his hands off other men, who had his fun with all his female relatives and couldn't even refrain from intercourse with his own sister. . . .

"You ought instead to worship Him who created at a word and out of nothing heaven, and earth, the sea and all that therein is, who made the sun to shine, who lit the sky with stars, who peopled the water with fish, the earth with beasts, the sky with flying creatures, by whose hand the race of man was made, by whose gift all creation is constrained to serve in deference and devotion the man He made." However often the Queen said this, the King came no nearer to belief. . . .

The Queen, who was true to her faith, brought her son to be baptized. . . . The child was baptized; he was given the name Ingomer; but no sooner had he received baptism than he died in his white robes. Clovis was extremely angry. He

began immediately to reproach his Queen. "If he had been dedicated in the name of my gods," he said, "he would have lived without question; but now that he has been baptized in the name of your God he has not been able to live a single day!"

"I give thanks to Almighty God," replied Clotild, "the Creator of all things who has not found me completely unworthy, for He has deigned to welcome into his Kingdom a child conceived in my womb. . . ."

Some time later Clotild bore a second son. He was baptized Chlodomer. He began to ail and Clovis said, "What else do you expect? It will happen to him as it happened to his brother: no sooner is he baptized in the name of your Christ than he will die!" Clotild prayed to the Lord and at His commands the baby recovered.

Queen Clotild continued to pray that her husband might recognize the true God and give up his idol-worship. Nothing could persuade him to accept Christianity. Finally war broke out against the Alamanni and in this conflict he was forced by necessity to accept what he had refused of his own free will. It so turned out that when the two armies met on the battlefield there was a great slaughter and the troops of Clovis were rapidly being annihilated. He raised his eyes to Heaven when he saw this, felt compunction in his heart and was moved to tears. "Jesus Christ," he said, "you who Clotild maintains to be the Son of the living God, you who deign to give help to those in travail and victory to those who trust in you, in faith I beg the glory of your help. If you will give me victory over my enemies, and if I may have evidence to that miraculous power which the people dedicated to your name say that they have experienced, then I will believe in you and I will be baptized in your name. I have called upon my own gods, but, as I see only too

Ninth-century ivory carving showing Clovis being baptized by Saint Remi. *(Musée Condé, Chantilly/Laurie Platt Winfrey, Inc.)*

clearly, they have no intention of helping me. I therefore cannot believe that they possess any power for they do not come to the assistance of those who trust them. I now call upon you. I want to believe in you, but I must first be saved from my enemies." Even as he said this the Alamanni turned their backs and began to run away. As soon as they saw that their King was killed, they submitted to Clovis. "We beg you," they said, "to put an end to this slaughter. We are prepared to obey you." Clovis stopped the war. He made a speech in which he called for peace. Then he went home. He told the Queen how he had won a victory by calling on the name of Christ. This happened in the fifteenth year of his reign (496).

The Queen then ordered Saint Remigius, Bishop of the town of Rheims, to be summoned in secret. She begged him to impart the word of salvation to the King. The Bishop asked Clovis to meet him in private and began to urge him to believe in the true God, Maker of Heaven and earth, and to forsake his idols, which were powerless to help him or anyone else. The King replied: "I have listened to you willingly, holy father. There remains one obstacle. The people under my command will not agree to forsake their gods. I will go and put to them what you have just said to me." He arranged a meeting with his people, but God in his power had preceded him, and before he could say a word all those present shouted in unison: "We will give up worshipping our mortal gods, pious King, and we are prepared to follow the immortal God about whom Remigius preaches." This news was reported to the Bishop. He was greatly pleased and he ordered the baptismal pool to be made ready. . . . The baptistry was prepared, sticks of incense gave off clouds of perfume, sweet-smelling candles gleamed bright and the holy place of baptism was

filled with divine fragrance. God filled the hearts of all present with such grace that they imagined themselves to have been transported to some perfumed paradise. King Clovis asked that he might be baptized first by the Bishop. Like some new Constantine he stepped forward to the baptismal pool, ready to wash away the sores of his old leprosy and to be cleansed in flowing water from the sordid stains which he had borne so long.

King Clovis confessed his belief in God Almighty, three in one. He was baptized in the name of the Father, the Son and the Holy Ghost, and marked in holy chrism [an anointing oil] with the sign of the Cross of Christ. More than three thousand of his army were baptized at the same time.

Questions for Analysis

1. Who took the initiative in urging Clovis's conversion? What can we deduce from that?

2. According to this account, why did Clovis ultimately accept Christianity?

3. For the Salian Franks, what was the best proof of divine power?

4. On the basis of this selection, do you consider *The History of the Franks* reliable history? Why?

Sources: L. Thorpe, trans., *The History of the Franks by Gregory of Tours* (Harmondsworth, England: Penguin, 1974), p. 159; P. J. Geary, ed., *Readings in Medieval History* (Peterborough, Ontario: Broadview Press, 1991), pp. 165–166.

Garden built by Muslim rulers in Seville, Spain. Tranquil gardens such as this one represented paradise in Islamic culture, perhaps because of the religion's desert origins. *(Ric Ergenbright/Corbis)*

EUROPE IN THE EARLY MIDDLE AGES, 600–1000

In the fifteenth century writers and scholars in the growing cities of northern Italy began to think that they were living in a new era, one in which the glories of ancient Greece and Rome were being reborn. What separated their own time from classical antiquity, in their opinion, was a long period of darkness, to which a seventeenth-century professor gave the name "Middle Ages" (*Medium Aevum* in Latin). In this conceptualization, Western history was divided into three periods—ancient, medieval (a word derived from the Latin), and modern.

This three-part schema is still the primary way of organizing Western history. Exactly what marked the dividing lines between these periods was not very clear, however. For a long time the end of the Roman Empire in the West in 476 was seen as the division between the classical period and the Middle Ages, but as we saw in the last chapter, more recent historians have emphasized continuities as well as changes in the fifth and sixth centuries. The transition from ancient to medieval was a slow process, not a single event. The agents in this process included not only the Germanic tribes whose migrations broke the Roman Empire apart but also the new religion of Islam, Slavic and steppe peoples in eastern Europe, and Christian officials and missionaries. The period from the end of antiquity to about 1000, conventionally known as the "Early Middle Ages," was a time of disorder and destruction, but also of the creation of a new type of society. People at the time did not know that they were living in an era that would later be labeled "middle" or sometimes even "dark," and we can wonder whether they would have shared this somewhat negative view of their own times.

The Spread of Islam

In the seventh century A.D. two empires dominated the area today called the Middle East: the Byzantine-Greek-Christian empire and the Sasanian-Persian-Zoroastrian empire. The Arabian peninsula lay between the two. The Sasanian dynasty, which descended from Persian-speaking people of present-day southern Iran, maintained political control over very diverse

Online Study Center

This icon will direct you to interactive activities and study materials on the website **college.hmco.com/pic/mckaywest9e**

peoples through government officials and by requiring loyalty to the ancient religion of Iraq, Zoroastrianism (see pages 49–50). The Sasanian capital of Ctesiphon in what is now central Iraq had become a center of Jewish religious learning and a refuge for pagan philosophers and medical scientists from the Greek cities after Justinian forbade the teaching of pagan philosophy and law in 529. The cosmopolitan culture thus created became the source of much classical Greek philosophical and medical knowledge that later came to the European world in Arabic translations.

Around 610 in the commercial city of Mecca in what is now Saudi Arabia, a merchant called Muhammad began to have religious visions. By the time he died in 632, all Arabia had accepted his creed. A century later his followers controlled Syria, Palestine, Egypt, North Africa, Spain, and part of France. This Arabic expansion profoundly affected the development of Western civilization as well as the history of Africa and Asia.

- *How did the spread of Islam shape European history in this era?*

The Arabs

In Muhammad's time Arabia was inhabited by various tribes, most of them Bedouins. These nomadic peoples grazed goats and sheep on the sparse patches of grass that dotted the vast semiarid peninsula. Other Arabs lived in the southern valleys and coastal towns along the Red Sea in Yemen, Mecca, Medina, and the northwestern region called "Hejaz." The Hejazi led a more sophisticated life and supported themselves by agriculture and trade. Their caravan routes crisscrossed Arabia and carried goods to Byzantium, Persia, and Syria. The Hejazi had wide commercial dealings but avoided cultural contacts with their Jewish, Christian, and Persian neighbors. The wealth produced by their business transactions led to luxurious and extravagant living in the towns.

Although the nomadic Bedouins condemned the urbanized lifestyle of the Hejazi as immoral and corrupt, Arabs of both types respected one another's local tribal customs. They had no political unity beyond their tribal bonds. Custom demanded the rigid observance of family obligations and the performance of religious rituals. Custom insisted that an Arab be proud, generous, and swift to take revenge. Custom required courage in public and avoidance of behavior that could bring social disgrace.

Although the various tribes differed markedly, they had certain religious rules in common. For example, all Arabs kept three months of the year as sacred; during that time fighting stopped so that everyone could attend holy ceremonies in peace. The city of Mecca was the religious center of the Arab world, and fighting was never tolerated there. All Arabs prayed at the Kaaba, the sanctuary in Mecca. Within the Kaaba was a sacred black stone that Arabs revered because they believed it had fallen from heaven.

What eventually molded the diverse Arab tribes into a powerful political and social unity was the religion based on the teachings of Muhammad.

The Prophet Muhammad

Except for a few vague remarks in the **Qur'an,** the sacred book of Islam, Muhammad (ca 571–632) left no account of his life. Arab tradition accepts some of the sacred legends that developed about him as historically true, but those legends were not written down until about a century after his death. (Similarly, the earliest accounts of the life of Jesus, the Christian Gospels, were not written until forty to sixty years after his death.) Orphaned at the age of six, Muhammad was brought up by his grandfather. When he was a young man, he became a merchant in the caravan trade. Later he entered the service of a wealthy widow, and their subsequent marriage brought him financial independence. The Qur'an reveals him to be an extremely devout man, ascetic, self-disciplined, and literate, but not educated.

Since childhood Muhammad had been subject to seizures during which he lost consciousness and had visions. After 610 these visions apparently became more frequent. Unsure for a time about what he should do, Muhammad discovered his mission after a vision in which the angel Gabriel instructed him to preach. Muhammad described his visions in a stylized and often rhyming prose and used this literary medium as his *Qur'an,* or "prayer recitation."

Muhammad's revelations were written down by his followers during his lifetime and organized into chapters shortly after his death. In 651 Muhammad's third successor as religious leader, Othman, arranged to have an official version published. The Qur'an is regarded by Muslims as the direct words of God to his Prophet Muhammad and is therefore especially revered. (These revelations were in Arabic. When Muslims use translations in other languages, they do so alongside the original Arabic.) At the same time, other sayings and accounts of Muhammad, which gave advice on matters that went beyond the Qur'an, were collected into books termed *hadith.* Muslim tradition (*Sunna*) consists of both the Qur'an and the hadith.

Muhammad's visions ordered him to preach a message of a single God and to become God's Prophet, which he began to do in his hometown of Mecca. He gathered followers slowly but also provoked a great deal of resistance, and in 622 he migrated with his followers to Medina, an event termed the *hijra* that marks the beginning of the Muslim calendar. At Medina Muhammad was much more successful, gaining converts and working out the basic principles of the faith. In 630 Muhammad returned to Mecca at the head of a large army, and by his death in 632 he had unified most of the Arabian peninsula into a religious/political community (termed the *umma*) of *Muslims*, a word meaning those who comply with God's will. (The first umma was formed by the Charter of Medina in 622 and included the local Jewish community, which established a precedent for the later protection of Jews under Islam.) The religion itself came to be called **Islam,** which means "submission to God." The Kaaba was rededicated as a Muslim holy place, and Mecca became the most holy city in Islam. According to Muslim tradition, the Kaaba predates the creation of the world and represents the earthly counterpart of God's heavenly throne, to which "pilgrims come dishevelled and dusty on every kind of camel."[1]

The Teachings of Islam

Muhammad's religion eventually attracted great numbers of people, partly because of the straightforward nature of its doctrines. The strictly monotheistic theology outlined in the Qur'an has only a few central tenets. Allah, the Arabic word for God, is all-powerful and all-knowing. Muhammad, Allah's prophet, preached his word and carried his message. Muhammad described himself as the successor both of the Jewish patriarch Abraham and of Christ, and he claimed that his teachings replaced theirs. He invited and won converts from Judaism and Christianity.

Because Allah is all-powerful, believers must submit themselves to him. All Muslims have the obligation of the *jihad* (literally "self-exertion") to strive or struggle to lead a virtuous life and to spread God's rule and law. In some cases striving was individual against sin; in others it was social and communal and could involve armed conflict, though this was not an essential part of jihad. The Islamic belief of "striving in the path of God" is closely related to the central feature of Muslim doctrine, the coming Day of Judgment. Muslims need not be concerned about *when* judgment will occur, but they must believe with absolute and total conviction that the Day of Judgment *will* come. Consequently, all of a Muslim's

Chronology

ca 571–632	Life of the Prophet Muhammad
700	Lindisfarne Gospel produced in Northumbria
711–720	Muslim conquest of Spain
ca 720	Venerable Bede writes *Ecclesiastical History of the English People*
760s–840s	Carolingian Renaissance
768–814	Reign of Charlemagne
800–900	Free peasants in western Europe increasingly tied to the land as serfs
820	Muslim mathematician al-Khwarizmi writes first treatise on algebra
843	Treaty of Verdun divides Carolingian kingdom
850–1000	Most extensive Viking raids
ca 900	Establishment of Kievan Rus
950	Muslim Córdoba is Europe's largest and most prosperous city
1001	Establishment of kingdom of Hungary

thoughts and actions should be oriented toward the Last Judgment and the rewards of Heaven. The Muslim vision of paradise features lush green gardens surrounded by refreshing streams. There the saved, clothed in rich silks, lounge on brocade couches, nibbling ripe fruits, sipping delicious beverages, and enjoying the companionship of physically attractive people.

Online Study Center **Improve Your Grade**
Primary Source: The Qur'an: Call for Jihad

To merit the rewards of Heaven, a person must follow the strict code of moral behavior that Muhammad prescribed. The Muslim must recite a profession of faith in God and in Muhammad as God's prophet: "There is no god but God and Muhammad is his prophet." The believer must pray five times a day, fast and pray during the sacred month of Ramadan, and contribute alms to the poor and needy. If possible, the believer must make a pilgrimage to Mecca once during his or her lifetime. According to the Muslim *shari'a,* or sacred law, these five practices—the profession of faith, prayer, fasting, giving alms to the poor, and pilgrimage to Mecca—constitute the **Five Pillars of Islam.**

Muhammad and the Earlier Prophets   Muhammad, with his head surrounded by fire representing religious fervor, leads Abraham, Moses, and Jesus in prayer. Islamic tradition holds that Judaism, Christianity, and Islam all derive from the pure religion of Abraham, but humankind has strayed from that faith. Therefore, Muhammad, as "the seal (last) of the prophets," had to transmit God's revelations to humankind. *(Bibliothèque nationale de France)*

The Qur'an forbids alcoholic beverages and gambling. It condemns business *usury*—that is, lending money at interest rates or taking advantage of market demand for products by charging high prices for them. A number of foods, such as pork, are also forbidden, a dietary regulation adopted from the Mosaic law of the Hebrews.

By earlier Arab standards, the Qur'an sets forth an austere sexual morality. Muslim jurisprudence condemned licentious behavior on the part of men as well as women, which enhanced the status of women in Muslim society. So, too, did Muhammad's opposition to female infanticide. About marriage, illicit intercourse, and inheritance, the Qur'an states:

[Of] women who seem good in your eyes, marry but two, three, or four; and if ye still fear that ye shall not act equitably then only one. . . . The whore and the fornicator: whip each of them a hundred times. . . .

The fornicator shall not marry other than a whore; and the whore shall not marry other than a fornicator. . . .

Men who die and leave wives behind shall bequeath to them a year's maintenance.

And your wives shall have a fourth part of what you leave, if you have no issue [offspring]; but if you have issue, then they shall have an eighth part. . . .

With regard to your children, God commands you to give the male the portion of two females.

Polygyny, the practice of men having more than one wife, was common in Arab society before Muhammad, though for economic reasons the custom was limited to the well-to-do. Nevertheless, some commentators hold that in limiting the number of wives to four—or even one if the man could not treat all fairly—Muhammad was being revolutionary.

Westerners tend to think polygyny degrading to women, but in a military society where there were apt to be many widows, polygyny provided women with a measure of security. With respect to matters of property, Muslim women were more emancipated than Western women. For example, a Muslim woman retained complete jurisdiction over one-third of her property when she married and could dispose of it in any way she wished. Women in most European countries and the United States did not gain these rights until the nineteenth century.[2]

The Muslim who faithfully observed the laws of the Qur'an could hope for salvation. According to the Qur'an, salvation is by God's grace and choice alone. Because God is all-knowing and all-powerful, he knows from the moment of a person's conception whether that person will be saved. Although later Muslim scholars have held a number of positions on the topic of predestination, ranging from complete fatalism to a strong belief in human free will, Muhammad maintained that predestination gave believers the will and courage to try to achieve the impossible. Devout Muslims came to believe that the performance of the faith's basic rules would automatically gain them salvation. Moreover, the believer who suffered and died for his faith in battle was immediately ensured the rewards of the Muslim heaven.

What did early Muslims think of Jesus? Jesus is mentioned in ninety-three verses of the Qur'an, which affirms that he was born of Mary the Virgin. He is described as a righteous prophet who performed miracles and continued the work of Abraham and Moses, and he was a sign of the coming Day of Judgment. But Muslims held that Jesus was an apostle only, not God, and that people (that is, Christians) who called Jesus divine committed blasphemy (showing contempt for God). Muslims esteemed the Judeo-Christian Scriptures as part of God's revelation, although they believed that Christian communities had corrupted the Scriptures and that the Qur'an superseded them. The Christian doctrine of the Trinity—that there is one God in three persons (Father, Son, and Holy Spirit)—posed a powerful obstacle to Muslim-Christian understanding because of Islam's total and uncompromising monotheism.[3]

There are many similarities among Islam, Christianity, and Judaism. All three religions are monotheistic; all worship the same God. Like Jews, Muslims customarily worship together at sundown on Fridays, and no assembly or organized church is essential. Muslims call Jews and Christians *dhimmis,* or "protected people," because they were people of the book, the Hebrew Scriptures.

Expansion and Schism

Islam transcended the geographical and public aspects of the Arabic tribal religion represented by Bedouin and Hejazi societies (see page 224). Every Muslim hoped to achieve salvation by following the requirements of Islam. For the believer, the petty disputes and conflicts of tribal society paled before the simple teachings of Allah. On this basis, Muhammad united the nomads of the desert and the merchants of the cities. The doctrines of Islam, instead of the ties of local custom, bound all Arabs.

By the time Muhammad died in 632, he had welded together all the Bedouin tribes. The crescent of Islam, the Muslim symbol, prevailed throughout the Arabian peninsula. During the next century one rich province of the old Roman Empire after another came under Muslim domination—first Syria, then Egypt, and then all of North Africa (see Map 8.1). Long and bitter wars (572–591, 606–630) between the Byzantine and Persian Empires left both so weak and exhausted that they easily fell to Muslim attack. The government headquarters of this vast new empire was established at Damascus in Syria by the ruling Umayyad family. By the early tenth century a Muslim proverb spoke of the Mediterranean Sea as a Muslim lake, though the Greeks at Constantinople contested that notion. From the Arabian peninsula, Muslims carried their faith deep into Africa and across Asia all the way to India.

Despite the clarity and unifying force of Muslim doctrine, a schism soon developed within the Islamic faith. Neither the Qur'an nor the hadith gave clear guidance about how successors to Muhammad were to be chosen, but a group of Muhammad's closest followers elected Abu Bakr, who was a close friend of the Prophet's and a member of a small tribe affiliated to the Prophet's tribe, as **caliph,** a word meaning "successor." This election set a precedent for the ratification of the subsequent patriarchal caliphs, though it was unsuccessfully opposed militarily by other Arab tribes.

A more serious opposition developed later among supporters of the fourth caliph, Ali. Ali claimed the caliphate because of his blood ties with Muhammad—he was Muhammad's cousin and son-in-law—and because the Prophet had designated him as *imam,* or leader. Ali was assassinated shortly after becoming caliph, and his supporters began to assert that he should rightly have been the first caliph and that all subsequent caliphs were usurpers. These supporters of Ali—termed *Shi'ites* or *Shi'a* from Arabic terms meaning "supporters" or "partisans" of Ali—saw Ali and subsequent imams as the divinely

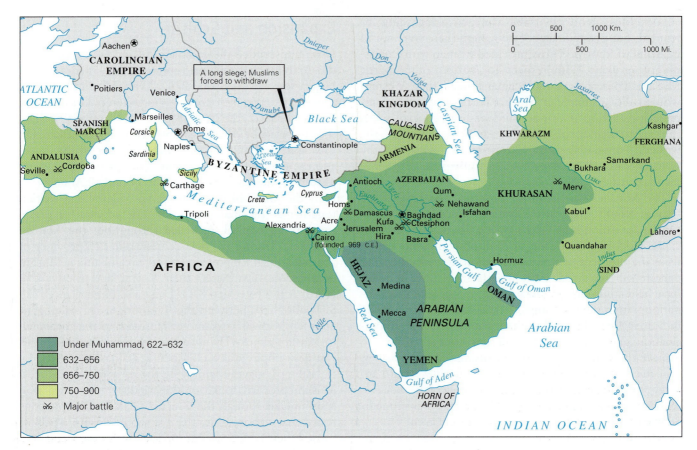

MAP 8.1 The Islamic World, ca 900   The rapid expansion of Islam in a relatively short span of time testifies to the Arabs' superior fighting skills, religious zeal, and economic organization as well as to their enemies' weakness.

Online Study Center   **Improve Your Grade** Interactive Map: The Expansion of Islam to 732

inspired leaders of the community. The larger body of Muslims who accepted the first elections—termed *Sunnis,* a word derived from *Sunna,* the traditional beliefs and practices of the community—saw the caliphs as political leaders. Since Islam did not have an organized church and priesthood, the caliphs had an additional function of safeguarding and enforcing the religious law (shari'a) with the advice of scholars (*ulama*), particularly the jurists, judges, and scholastics who were knowledgeable about the Qur'an and hadith. Over the centuries, many different kinds of Shi'ites appeared, and enmity between Sunni and Shi'a Muslims sometimes erupted into violence.

Muslim Spain

In Europe, Muslim political and cultural influence was felt most strongly in the Iberian Peninsula. In 711 a Muslim force crossed the Strait of Gibraltar and easily defeated the weak Visigothic kingdom. A few Christian princes supported by the Frankish rulers held out in northern mountain fortresses, but the Muslims took over most of Spain. A member of the Umayyad dynasty, Abd al-Rahman (r. 756–788), established a kingdom in Spain with its capital at Córdoba.

Throughout the Islamic world, Muslims used the term **al-Andalus** to describe the part of the Iberian Peninsula under Muslim control. The name al-Andalus probably derives from the Arabic for "land of the Vandals," the Germanic people who swept across Spain in the fifth century. In the eighth century al-Andalus included the entire peninsula from Gibraltar in the south to the Cantabrian Mountains in the north (see Map 8.1). Today we often use the word *Andalusia* to refer especially to southern Spain, but eighth-century Christians throughout Europe called the peninsula "Moorish Spain" because the people who invaded and conquered it were Moors—Berbers from northwest Africa. The ethnic term *Moorish* can be misleading, however, because the peninsula was home to sizable numbers of Jews and Christians as well as (Muslim) Moors. In business transactions and in much of daily life, all peoples used the Arabic language. With Muslims, Christians, and Jews trading with and learning from one another and occasionally intermarrying, Moorish Spain and Norman Sicily (see Chapter 9) were the only distinctly pluralistic societies in medieval Europe.

Between roughly the eighth and twelfth centuries, Muslims, Christians, and Jews lived close together in Andalusia, and some scholars believe that the early part of this period was an era of remarkable interfaith harmony. Jews in Muslim Spain were generally treated well, and Córdoba became a center of Jewish as well as Muslim learning. Many Christians adopted Arabic patterns of speech and dress, gave up the practice of eating pork, and developed a special appreciation for Arabic music and poetry. Some Christian women of elite status chose the Muslim practice of veiling their faces in public. Records describe Muslim and Christian youths joining in celebrations and merrymaking. These assimilated Christians, called Mozarabs, did not attach much importance to the doctrinal differences between the two religions.

Al-Andalus can be analyzed from several perspectives. From the sophisticated centers of Muslim culture in Baghdad, Damascus, and Cairo (founded 969), al-Andalus seemed a provincial backwater, a frontier outpost with little significance in the wide context of Islamic civilization. "Northern barbarians," on the other hand—the Muslim name for European peoples—acknowledged the splendor of Spanish culture. For example, the Saxon nun and writer Hroswita of Gandersheim called the city of

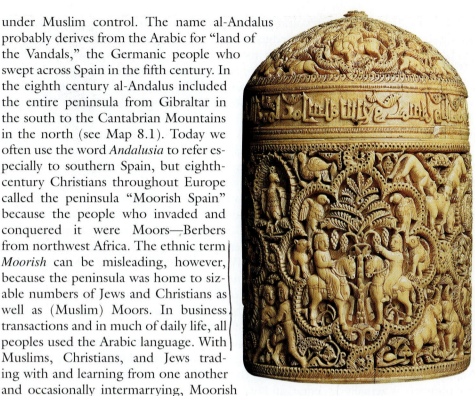

Harvesting Dates This detail from an ivory casket given to a Córdoban prince reflects the importance of fruit cultivation in the Muslim-inspired agricultural expansion in southern Europe in the ninth and tenth centuries. (*Louvre/Réunion des Musées Nationaux/Art Resource, NY*)

Córdoba "the ornament of the world." With a population of about half a million; with well-paved and well-lighted streets and an abundance of fresh water; with 1,000 mosques, 900 public baths, 213,177 houses for ordinary people, and 60,000 mansions for officials and the wealthy; with 80,455 shops and 13,000 weavers producing silks, woolens, and brocades; with 27 free schools and a library containing 400,000 volumes (the largest library in northern Europe, at the Benedictine abbey of St. Gall in Switzerland, had 600 books), Córdoba was indeed an ornament, and the Western world had no comparable urban center.

In Spain, as elsewhere in the Arab world, the Muslims had an enormous impact on agricultural development. They began the cultivation of rice, sugar cane, citrus fruits, dates, figs, eggplants, carrots, and, after the eleventh century, cotton. These crops, together with new methods of field irrigation, provided the urban population with food products unknown in the rest of Europe.

About 950 Caliph Abd al-Rahman III (912–961) of the Umayyad dynasty of Córdoba ruled most of the Iberian Peninsula from the Mediterranean in the south to the Ebro River in the north. Christian Spain consisted of the tiny kingdoms of Castile, León, Catalonia, Aragon, Navarre, and Portugal. Civil wars among al-Rahman's descendents weakened the caliphate, and the small northern Christian kingdoms expanded southward.

Science and Medicine

The Islamic world, both in Spain and elsewhere, profoundly shaped Christian European culture. Toledo, for example, became an important center of learning through which Arab intellectual achievements entered and influenced western Europe. Arabic knowledge of science and mathematics, derived from the Chinese, Greeks, and Hindus, was highly sophisticated. The Muslim mathematician al-Khwarizmi (d. 830) wrote the important treatise *Algebra,* the first work in which the word *algebra* is used mathematically. Al-Khwarizmi adopted the Hindu system of numbers (1, 2, 3, 4), used it in his *Algebra,* and applied mathematics to problems of physics and astronomy. Scholars at Baghdad translated Euclid's *Elements,* the basic text for plane and solid geometry. Muslims also instructed Westerners in the use of the zero, which permitted the execution of complicated problems of multiplication and long division. Use of the zero represented an enormous advance over clumsy Roman numerals. (Since our system of numbers is actually Hindu in origin, the term *Arabic numerals,* coined about 1847, is a misnomer.)

Middle Eastern Arabs translated and codified the scientific and philosophical learning of Greek and Persian antiquity. In the ninth and tenth centuries that knowledge was brought to Spain, where between 1150 and 1250 it was translated into Latin. Europeans' knowledge of Aristotle changed the entire direction of European philosophy and theology (see page 85). Isaac Newton's discoveries in mathematics in the seventeenth century rested on ancient Greek theories translated in Spain.

In the transmission of Greek learning, one Muslim technological accomplishment played a most significant role—paper. Second-century Chinese initially used rags to make paper, but they soon shifted to woody fibers from such plants as hemp, jute, and bamboo. The Chinese invented paper not for writing but for wrapping goods. Merchants and Buddhist missionaries carried the skills of papermaking to Samarkand in Central Asia (see Map 8.1). After Arab armies overran Central Asia in the eighth century, Muslim papermakers improved on Chinese techniques: Muslims beat the fibers of rags and then used starch to fill the pores in the surfaces of the sheets. They carried this new method to Baghdad in Iraq, Damascus in Syria, Cairo in Egypt, and the Maghrib (North Africa), from which it entered Spain. Even before the invention of printing (see page 418), papermaking had a revolutionary impact on the collection and diffusion of knowledge and thus on the transformation of society.[4]

Muslim medical knowledge far surpassed that of the West. By the ninth century Arab physicians had translated most of the treatises of Hippocrates. The Baghdad physician al-Razi (865–925) produced an encyclopedic treatise on medicine that was translated into Latin and circulated widely in the West. Al-Razi was the first physician to make the clinical distinction between measles and smallpox. The great surgeon of Córdoba, al-Zahrawi (d. 1013), produced an important work in which he discussed the cauterization of wounds (searing with a branding iron) and the crushing of stones in the bladder. Arabic science reached its peak in the physician, philologist, philosopher, poet, and scientist ibn-Sina of Bukhara (980–1037), known in the West as Avicenna. His *al-Qanun* codified all Greco-Arabic medical thought, described the contagious nature of tuberculosis and the spreading of diseases, and listed 760 pharmaceutical drugs.

Unfortunately, many of these treatises came to the West as translations from Greek to Arabic and then to Latin and inevitably lost a great deal in translation. Nevertheless, in the ninth and tenth centuries Arabic knowledge and experience in anatomy and pharmaceutical prescriptions much enriched Western knowledge.

Muslim-Christian Relations

Beyond Andalusian Spain, mutual animosity restricted contact between Muslims and Christians. The Muslim expansion into Christian Europe in the eighth and ninth centuries left a legacy of bitter hostility. Christians felt threatened by a faith that acknowledged God as creator of the universe but denied the doctrine of the Trinity and that accepted Jesus as a prophet but denied his divinity. Europeans' perception of Islam as a menace helped inspire the Crusades of the eleventh through thirteenth centuries (see pages 279–286).

By the thirteenth century Western literature sometimes displayed a sympathetic view of Islam. The Bavarian knight Wolfram von Eschenbach's *Parzival* and the Englishman William Langland's *Piers the Plowman*—two poems that survive in scores of manuscripts, suggesting that they circulated widely—reveal some broad-mindedness and tolerance toward Muslims. Some travelers in the Middle East were impressed by the kindness and generosity of Muslims and with the strictness and devotion with which Muslims observed their faith.[5]

More frequently, however, Christian literature portrayed Muslims as the most dreadful of Europe's enemies, guilty of every kind of crime. In his *Inferno* the great Florentine poet Dante placed the Muslim philosophers Avicenna and Averroes with other virtuous "heathens," among them Socrates and Aristotle, in the first circle of Hell, where they endured only moderate punishment. Muhammad, however, Dante consigned to the ninth circle, near Satan himself, where he was condemned as a spreader of discord and scandal.

Muslim views of Christians were also mixed, but here disinterest may have been more common than hostility. Muslim historical writing reflects strong knowledge of European geography but shows an almost total lack of interest in European languages, life, and culture. Muslims had a strong aversion to travel in Europe. Medieval Europe had no resident Muslim communities where a traveler could find the mosques, foods, or other things desirable for the Muslim way of life. When compelled to make diplomatic or business contacts, Muslims preferred to send Jewish or Christian intermediaries. Commercially, from the Muslim perspective, Europe had very little to offer apart from woolens from the Frisian Islands in the North Sea, which the Muslims admired, and some slaves from central and southeastern Europe.

In their understanding of the nature and purpose of the state, Muslims and Christians revealed an important similarity and a very real difference. Just as for Christians the state existed to provide the peace, order, and justice wherein the Christian could pursue his or her pilgrimage to the City of God (see page 203), so for Muslims the function of the Islamic state was "to assure that all Muslims could lead a life in keeping with the mandates of the Qur'an and discharge their obligations to Allah."[6] Thus both peoples viewed the state from a theological perspective. In the central Middle Ages European rulers reinvigorated the concept of the state, in part by defining it as an organized territory with definite geographical boundaries recognized by other states. Muslims, however, did not conceive of their states as territorial entities limited by distinct boundaries. Medieval Muslim geographers paid little attention to, or entirely ignored, territorial boundaries. Rather, what distinguished one region from another was whether most inhabitants were Muslims or nonbelievers. Territories in which the preponderance of the people were Muslims belonged to the *Dar-al-Islam,* the House of Islam; regions in which most were Christians or of some other non-Muslim faith constituted the *Dar-al-Harb,* the House of War.

Animosity between Muslims and Christians increasingly shaped relations between the two groups in Spain.

Shroud Fragment Rich and powerful people were often buried in precious fabrics. This Islamic silk cloth brocaded with gold thread was produced in Almería, a Muslim city in southern Spain, around 1100. It bears a false Arabic inscription for commercial purposes: "This was made in Baghdad, may God protect it." Made for a Christian bishop, the shroud is a fine example of cross-cultural influences. *(Silk and metallic yarns; compound weave; L × W: 16⅞ × 19¹/₁₆ in. [43 × 50 cm.]. Museum of Fine Arts, Boston, Ellen Page Hall Fund, 33.371)*

Muslim teachers feared that close contact between the two peoples would lead to Muslim contamination and become a threat to the Islamic faith. Christian bishops worried that a knowledge of Islam would lead to ignorance of essential Christian doctrines. Both Muslim scholars and Christian theologians argued that assimilation such as that of the Mozarabs was wrong.

Thus, beginning in the late tenth century, Muslim regulations increasingly defined what Christians and Muslims could do. A Christian, however much assimilated, remained an **infidel.** An infidel was an unbeliever, and the word carried a pejorative or disparaging connotation. Mozarabs had to live in special sections of cities; could not learn the Qur'an, employ Muslim workers or servants, build new churches, or ring church bells; and had to be buried in their own cemeteries. Such restrictions were enhanced in the twelfth century when al-Andalus was taken over by the Almohad dynasty, an extremist group from Morocco that outlawed Judaism and Christianity. When Christian forces conquered Muslim territory in subsequent centuries, Christian rulers regarded their Muslim and Jewish subjects as infidels and enacted similar restrictive measures.

The Frankish Kingdom

Several centuries before the Muslim conquest of Spain, the Frankish king Clovis converted to Roman Christianity and established a large kingdom in what had been Roman Gaul (see page 212). Though at the time the Frankish kingdom was established it was simply one barbarian kingdom among many, it became the most important state in Europe, expanding to become an empire. Rulers after Clovis used a variety of tactics to enhance their authority and create a stable system.

• *How did Frankish rulers govern their kingdoms?*

The Merovingians

The initial success of the Frankish king Clovis rested on three major developments: Clovis's series of military victories over other Germanic tribes; his acquisition of the wealthy provinces of Roman Gaul with their administrative machinery intact; and, after his conversion to orthodox Christianity, the ideological support of the Roman papacy and of the bishops of Gaul. By selecting Paris—the legendary scene of the martyrdom of Saint Denis, believed to be a disciple of Saint Paul—as his capital, Clovis identified himself with the cult of Saint Denis and used it to strengthen his rule. The Frankish kingdom under Clovis included much of what is now France and a large section of southwestern Germany.

Clovis established the Merovingian dynasty, named after a mythical founder Merowig. Before he died, Clovis arranged for his kingdom to be divided among his four sons, not according to strict acreage but in portions yielding roughly equal revenues. Historians have long described Merovingian Gaul in the sixth and seventh centuries as wracked by civil wars, chronic violence, and political instability as Clovis's descendants fought among themselves. So brutal and destructive were these wars and so violent the ordinary conditions of life that the term *Dark Ages* came to designate the entire Merovingian period. Recent research has presented a more complex picture. The civil wars were indeed destructive, but they "did not pose a threat to the survival of the kingdom. In a sense, they were a unifying part of the structure of the Frankish state in the sixth century and for most of the seventh."[7]

What caused the civil wars? First, the death or even reported death of a king triggered crisis and war. Lacking a clear principle of succession, any male of Merovingian blood could claim the throne, and there were often many possibilities within the Merovingian family. A prince-claimant had to prove himself worthy on the battlefield. Second, the desire for new lands provoked conflict. Royal officials and warriors had similar desires for new estates, and they sold their support to the prince who would promise them more lands. Royal armies also wanted war because war meant booty and plunder. No one disputed the Merovingian family's right to rule: it alone possessed the blood and charisma. The issue was which member. Thus the royal family and the royal court served as the focus around which conflicts arose, and in this sense the civil wars actually held the kingdom together.

Merovingian politics provided royal women with opportunities, and some queens not only influenced but occasionally also dominated events. The theoretical status of a princess or queen rested on her diplomatic importance, with her marriage sealing or divorce breaking an alliance; on her personal relationship with her husband and her ability to give him sons and heirs; on her role as the mother and guardian of princes who had not reached legal adulthood; and on her control of the royal treasury. For example, when King Chilperic I (561–584) was murdered, his wife Fredegunda controlled a large state treasury. The historian Fredegar alleges that Queen Brunhilda (d. 613), wife of King Sigebert of the East Frankish kingdom, killed twelve kings in pursuit of her political goals, including Sigebert, some of her grandchildren, and their offspring. When her sister Galswintha was found strangled to death in bed shortly after her marriage to Chilperic, ruler of the West Frankish kingdom, Brunhilda suspected that Chilperic had murdered her so that he could marry his then mistress, Fredegunda. Brunhilda instigated war between the two kingdoms. After 592 she was the real power behind her sons' and grandsons' shaky thrones, and she also ruled Burgundy, which her maneuvers had united to the East Frankish kingdom. Contemporaries may have exaggerated Brunhilda's murders, but her career reflects both the domestic violence of the Merovingian royal family and the fierce determination of some queens to exercise power.

Merovingian Army This sixth- or seventh-century ivory depicts a nobleman in civilian dress followed by seven warriors. Note that the mounted men do not have stirrups and that they seem to have fought with spears and bows and arrows. The power of the Frankish aristocracy rested on such private armies. *(Landesmuseum, Trier)*

Merovingian Government

How did Merovingian rulers govern? What were their sources of income? How did they communicate with their peoples? While local administration probably varied somewhat according to regional tradition, the **civitas**—the city and surrounding territory—served as the basis of the administrative system in the Frankish kingdom. A **comites**—senior official or royal companion, later called a count—presided over the civitas. He collected royal revenue, heard lawsuits, enforced justice, and raised troops. To receive his tax revenues, a Frankish king had to be sure of the comites's loyalty. Rebellion led to confiscation of the comites's lands.

A ruler's general sources of income were revenues from the royal estates, which were especially large in the north; the right to hospitality when he visited an area (with wives, children, servants, court officials, and several hundred warriors, plus all their horses, hospitality could be a severe drain on the resources of a region); the conquest and confiscation of new lands, which replenished lands given as monastic or religious endowments; and the "gifts" of subject peoples, such as plunder and tribute paid by peoples east of the Rhine River. Specific income derived from a land tax paid by all free landowners, which was originally collected by the Romans and continued by the Franks. In the course of the seventh century, the value of this tax declined as all Franks gradually gained immunity from it. In fact, the term **Frank** began to be associated with freedom from taxation, which may have been an incentive for Gallo-Romans to shift their ethnic allegiance to the Franks. Fines imposed for criminal offenses and tolls and customs duties on roads, bridges, and waterways (and the goods transported over them) also yielded income. As with the Romans, the minting of coins was a royal monopoly, with drastic penalties for counterfeiting. For all this the comites had responsibility.

Merovingian, Carolingian (see page 234), and later medieval rulers led peripatetic lives, traveling constantly to check up on local administrators and peoples. Merovingian kings also relied on the comites and bishops to gather and send local information to them. Gallo-Roman by descent, bishops and comites were usually native to the regions they administered and knew their areas well. Frankish royal administration involved a third official, the *dux* (duke). He was a military leader, commanding troops in the territory of several civitas, and thus responsible for all defensive and offensive strategies. Kings seem to have appointed only Franks to this position.

Clovis and his descendants in the sixth and seventh centuries also issued **capitularies,** administrative and legislative orders divided into *capitula,* chapters or articles. These laws attempted to regulate a variety of matters: for example, protecting priests, monks, nuns, and church property from violence; defining ownership and inheritance; and punishing drunkenness, robbery, arson, rape, and murder. Apart from the violent and crime-ridden realities of Merovingian society, capitularies show the strong influence of Roman law. They also reveal Merovingian kings trying to maintain law and order, holding courts, and being actively involved in exercising judicial authority.

The court or household of Merovingian kings also included scribes who kept records, legal officials who advised the king on matters of law, and treasury agents responsible for aspects of royal finance. These officials could all read and write Latin. Over them all presided the mayor of the palace, the most important secular figure after the king in the kingdom. Usually a leader of one of the great aristocratic families, the mayor governed the palace and the kingdom in the king's absence.

Kings also consulted regularly with the leaders of the aristocracy. This class represented a fusion of Franks and the old Gallo-Roman leadership. Its members possessed landed wealth—villas over which they exercised lordship, dispensing local customary, not royal, law—and they often had rich and lavish lifestyles. When they were with the king, they constituted the royal court, those around the king at a given time. If the king consulted them and they were in agreement, there was peace. Failure to consult could mean resentment and the potential for civil war.

The Rise of the Carolingians

From this aristocracy there gradually emerged in the eighth century one family that replaced the Merovingian dynasty. The emergence of the Carolingians—whose name comes from the Latin *Carolus,* or Charles—rests on several factors. First, beginning with Pippin I (d. 640), the head of the family acquired and held onto the powerful position of mayor of the palace. Pippin I served as head of the Frankish bureaucracy, governed in the king's absence, and, after the king, was the most important figure in the Frankish kingdom. Second, a series of advantageous marriage alliances brought the family estates and influence in different parts of the Frankish world. Thus Pippin II (d. 714), through his first marriage, won influence in the territory around Echternach (modern Luxembourg) and, by his second wife, estates in the Meuse Valley. The landed wealth and treasure acquired by Pippin II, his son Charles Martel (r. 714–741), and Pippin III (r. 751–768) formed the basis of Carolingian power. Although Pippin II and Charles Martel possessed more lands than any other single aristocratic family, and although they held the positions of mayor of the palace and duke, their ultimate supremacy was by no means certain. Other dukes rallied to the support of the Merovingians, and Pippin devoted much energy to fighting these magnates. Only his victory over them and King Theuderich at Tertry in 687 ensured his dominance. Such victories gave the family a reputation for military strength.

Charles Martel's successful wars against the Saxons, Frisians, Alamanni, and Bavarians further enhanced the family's prestige. In 732 Charles Martel defeated a Muslim force near Poitiers in central France. Muslims and Christians have interpreted the battle differently. To the Muslims it was a minor skirmish won by the Franks because of Muslim difficulties in maintaining supply lines over long distances and the distraction of ethnic conflicts and unrest in Islamic Spain. For Christians the Frankish victory was one of the great battles of history, halting Muslim expansion in Europe. Charles Martel and later Carolingians used it to enhance their reputation, portraying themselves as defenders of Christendom against the Muslims.

The Battle of Poitiers helped the Carolingians acquire the support of the church, perhaps their most important asset. Irish, Frankish, and Anglo-Saxon missionaries, of whom the Englishman Boniface (680–754) is the most famous, preached Christianity to pagan peoples and worked to reorganize the Frankish church. Boniface ordered the oak of Thor, a tree near the village of Fritzlar in central Germany sacred to many pagans, cut down and used the wood to build a church. When the god Thor did not respond by killing him with his lightning bolts, Boniface won many converts. With close ties to the Roman papacy, Boniface participated in establishing the abbey of Fulda and the archdiocese of Mainz, held church councils, and promoted *The Rule of Saint Benedict* in all monasteries. (Boniface was not successful in the latter. Many monasteries preferred to be guided by several monastic directives.) The Carolingian mayors of the palace, Charles Martel and Pippin III, fully supported this evangelizing activity, as missionaries also preached obedience to secular authorities as a religious duty.

Online Study Center **Improve Your Grade**
Primary Source: St. Boniface Destroys the Oak of Thor

As mayor of the palace, Charles Martel had exercised the power of king of the Franks. His son Pippin III aspired to the title as well. Against the background of collaboration between missionaries and the Frankish mayors, Pippin sent delegates to ask Pope Zacharias whether the man who held the power should also have the title of king. Pippin's ambassadors reached Rome at a diplomat-

Saint Boniface The upper panel of this piece from an early-eleventh-century Fulda Mass book shows the great missionary to Germany baptizing, apparently by full immersion. The lower panel shows his death scene, with the saint protecting himself with a Gospel book. The fluttering robes are similar to those in earlier Anglo-Saxon books, probably modeled on illustrations in books that Boniface brought to Fulda Abbey from England. (*Stadtsbibliothek Bamberg, Ms. Lit. I, fol. 126v*)

Zacharias "by virtue of his apostolic authority commanded that Pippin should be made king."[8] Chilperic, the last Merovingian ruler, was consigned to a monastery. An assembly of Frankish magnates elected Pippin king, and he was anointed by Boniface at Soissons. When, in 754, Lombard expansion again threatened the papacy, Pope Stephen II journeyed to the Frankish kingdom seeking help. On this occasion, he personally anointed Pippin and gave him the title "Patrician of the Romans." Pippin promised restitution of the papal lands.

Thus an important alliance had been struck between the papacy and the Frankish monarchs. On a successful campaign in Italy in 756, Pippin made a large donation to the papacy. The gift consisted of estates in central Italy that technically belonged to the Byzantine emperor. Because of his **anointment,** Pippin's kingship took on a special spiritual and moral character. Before Pippin only priests and bishops had received anointment. Pippin became the first to be anointed with the sacred oils and acknowledged as *rex et sacerdos* (king and priest). Anointment, rather than royal blood, set the Christian king apart. By having himself anointed, Pippin cleverly eliminated possible threats to the Frankish throne coming from other claimants, and the pope promised him support in the future. When Pippin died, his son Charles succeeded him.

The Empire of Charlemagne

Charles the Great (r. 768–814), generally known by the French version of his name, Charlemagne, built on the military and diplomatic foundations of his ancestors and on the administrative machinery of the Merovingian kings. He expanded the Frankish kingdom into what is now Germany and Italy and, late in his long reign, was crowned emperor by the pope.

• *What accounts for Charlemagne's political and diplomatic successes?*

Charlemagne's Personal Qualities and Marriage Strategies

Charlemagne's secretary and biographer Einhard wrote a lengthy idealization of this warrior-ruler. It has serious flaws, partly because it is modeled directly on the Roman author Suetonius's *Life of the Emperor Augustus*. Still, it is the earliest medieval biography of a layman, and historians consider it generally accurate:

ically opportune moment. In the eighth century the Lombards severely threatened the papacy, which, being subject to the Byzantine emperor, looked to Constantinople for support. But Byzantium, pressured from the outside by attacks from the Arabs and the Avars and wracked internally by the dispute over the veneration of icons, known as iconoclasm, was in no position to send help. Pope Zacharias therefore shifted his allegiance from the Greeks to the Franks and told Pippin that "it was better to call him king who had the royal power 'in order to prevent provoking civil war in Francia'" and that

Charles was large and strong, and of lofty stature, though not disproportionately tall . . . the upper part of his head was round, his eyes very large and animated, nose a little long, hair fair, and face laughing and merry. Thus his appearance was always stately and dignified . . . although his neck was thick and somewhat short, and his belly rather prominent; but the symmetry of the rest of his body concealed these defects. His gait was firm, his whole carriage manly and his voice clear, but not so strong as his size led one to expect. His health was excellent, except during the four years preceding his death. . . .

In accordance with the national custom, he took frequent exercise on horseback and in the chase. . . . He . . . often practiced swimming, in which he was such an adept that none could surpass him. . . . He used not only to invite his sons to his bath, but his nobles and friends.[9]

Though crude and brutal, Charlemagne was a man of enormous intelligence. He appreciated good literature, such as Saint Augustine's *City of God,* and Einhard considered him an unusually effective speaker. Recent scholarship disputes Einhard's claim that Charlemagne could not write.

Online Study Center **Improve Your Grade**
Primary Source: The Life of Charlemagne: The Emperor Himself

The security and continuation of his dynasty and the need for diplomatic alliances governed Charlemagne's complicated marriage pattern. The high rate of infant mortality required many sons. Married first to the daughter of Desiderius, king of the Lom-

Reliquary Bust of Charlemagne
This splendid twelfth-century gothic idealization portrays the emperor of legend and myth rather than the squat, potbellied ruler described by his contemporary Einhard. The jeweled helmet or crown is symbolic of Charlemagne's role as defender of church and people. *(Photo: Ann Münchow, © Domkapitel Aachen)*

bards, Charlemagne divorced her either because she failed to produce a child within a year or for diplomatic reasons. His second wife, Hildegard, produced nine children in twelve years. When she died, Charlemagne married Fastrada, daughter of an East Frankish count whose support he needed in his campaign against the Saxons. Charlemagne had a total of four legal wives and six concubines, and even after the age of sixty-five he continued to sire children. Though three sons reached adulthood, only one outlived him. Four surviving grandsons ensured perpetuation of the family.

Territorial Expansion

Continuing the expansionist policies of his ancestors, Charlemagne fought more than fifty campaigns and became the greatest warrior of the early Middle Ages. He subdued all of the north of modern France. In the south the lords of the mountainous ranges of Aquitaine fought off his efforts at total conquest. The Muslims in northeastern Spain were checked by the establishment of strongly fortified areas known as *marches.*

Charlemagne's greatest successes were in today's Germany. In the course of a thirty-year war against the Saxons, he added most of the northwestern German tribes to the Frankish kingdom. Because of their repeated rebellions, Charlemagne ordered, according to Einhard, more than four thousand Saxons slaughtered in one day.

He also achieved spectacular results in the south. In 773 to 774 the Lombards in northern Italy again threatened the papacy. Charlemagne marched south, overran fortresses at Pavia and Spoleto, and incorporated Lombardy into the Frankish kingdom. To his title king of the Franks he added king of the Lombards. Charlemagne also ended Bavarian independence and defeated the nomadic Avars, opening the Danubian plain for later settlement. He successfully fought the Byzantine Empire for Venetia (excluding the city of Venice itself), Istria, and Dalmatia and temporarily annexed those areas to his kingdom.

Charlemagne also tried to occupy Basque territory in northwestern Spain. When his long siege of Saragossa proved unsuccessful and the Saxons on his

Frankish Kingdom, 768
Areas conquered by Charlemagne
Tributary peoples
Byzantine territories

MAP 8.2 Charlemagne's Conquests Though Charlemagne's hold on much of his territory was relatively weak, the size of his empire was not equaled again until the nineteenth-century conquests of Napoleon. (*Source: Some data from Michael McCormick,* Origins of the European Economy: Communications and Commerce, A.D. 300–900 *[Cambridge: Cambridge University Press, 2001], p. 762.*)

Online Study Center **Improve Your Grade** Interactive Map: The Carolingian World

northeastern borders rebelled, Charlemagne decided to withdraw, but the Basques annihilated his rear guard, which was led by Count Roland, at Roncesvalles (778) near Pamplona in the Pyrenees. This attack represented Charlemagne's only defeat, and he forbade people to talk about it. However, the expedition inspired the great medieval epic *The Song of Roland*. Based on legend and written about 1100 at the beginning of the European crusading movement, the poem portrays Roland as the ideal chivalric knight and Charlemagne as exercising a sacred kind of kingship. Although many of the epic's details differ from the historical evidence, *The Song of Roland* is important because it reveals the popular image of Charlemagne in later centuries.

By around 805 the Frankish kingdom included all of northwestern Europe except Scandinavia (see Map 8.2). Not since the third century A.D. had any ruler controlled so much of the Western world.

The Government of the Carolingian Empire

Charlemagne ruled a vast rural world dotted with isolated estates and small villages and characterized by constant warfare. According to the chroniclers of the time, only seven years between 714 and 814 were peaceful. Charlemagne's empire was not a state as people today understand that term; it was a collection of peoples and tribes. Apart from a small class of warrior-aristocrats and clergy and a tiny minority of Jews, almost everyone engaged in agriculture. Towns served as the headquarters of bishops, as ecclesiastical centers. The Carolingians inherited the office and the administrative machinery of the Merovingian kings and the functions of the mayor of the palace. The Carolingians relied heavily on the personality and energy of the monarchs. The scholar-adviser Alcuin (see page 247) wrote that "a king should be strong against his enemies, humble to Christians, feared by pagans, loved by the poor and judicious in counsel and maintaining justice."[10] Charlemagne worked to realize that ideal. By military expeditions that brought wealth—lands, booty, slaves, and tribute—and by peaceful travel, personal appearances, and the sheer force of his personality, Charlemagne sought to awe newly conquered peoples and rebellious domestic enemies with his fierce presence and terrible justice. By confiscating the estates of great territorial magnates, he acquired lands and goods with which to gain the support of lesser lords, further expanding the territory under his control.

The political power of the Carolingians rested on the cooperation of the dominant social class, the Frankish aristocracy. By the seventh century, through mutual cooperation and frequent marriage alliances, these families exercised great power that did not derive from the Merovingian kings. The Carolingians themselves had emerged from this aristocracy, and the military and political success that Carolingians such as Pippin II achieved depended on the support of the nobility. The lands and booty with which Charles Martel and Charlemagne rewarded their followers in these families enabled the nobles to improve their economic position, but it was only with noble help that the Carolingians were able to wage wars of expansion and suppress rebellions. In short, Carolingian success was a matter of reciprocal help and reward.[11]

For administrative purposes, Charlemagne divided his entire kingdom into *counties* based closely on the old Merovingian civitas (see page 233). Each of the approximately six hundred counties was governed by a count (or in his absence by a viscount) who published royal orders, held courts and resolved legal cases, collected taxes and tolls, raised troops for the army, and supervised maintenance of roads and bridges. Counts were at first sent out from the royal court; later a person native to the region was appointed. As a link between local authorities and the central government, Charlemagne appointed officials called **missi dominici,** "agents of the lord king." The empire was divided into visitorial districts. Each year beginning in 802, two missi (singular: *missus*), usually a count and a bishop or abbot, visited assigned districts. They held courts; investigated the district's judicial, financial, and clerical activities; and organized commissions to regulate crime, moral conduct, the clergy, education, the poor, and many other matters. The missi checked up on the counts. In the marches, especially in unstable or threatened areas such as along the Spanish and Danish frontiers, officials called *margraves* had extensive powers to govern.

A modern state has institutions of government, such as a civil service, courts of law, financial agencies for collecting and apportioning taxes, and police and military powers with which to maintain order internally and defend against foreign attack. These did not exist in Charlemagne's empire. Instead, society was held together by dependent relationships cemented by oaths promising faith and loyalty.

Although the empire lacked viable institutions, some Carolingians involved in governing did have vigorous political ideas. The abbots and bishops who served as Charlemagne's advisers worked out what was for their time a sophisticated political ideology. They wrote that a ruler may hold power from God but is responsible to the law. Just as all subjects of the empire were required to obey him, he too was obliged to respect the law. They envisioned a unified Christian society presided over by a king who was responsible for maintaining peace, law, and order and doing justice, without which neither the ruler nor the kingdom had any justification. These views derived largely from Saint Augustine's theories of kingship. Inevitably, they could not be realized in an illiterate preindustrial society. But they were the seeds from which medieval and even modern ideas of government were to develop.

The Imperial Coronation of Charlemagne

In autumn of the year 800, Charlemagne paid a momentous visit to Rome. Einhard gives this account of what happened:

His last journey there [to Rome] was due to another factor, namely that the Romans, having inflicted many injuries on Pope Leo—plucking out his eyes and tearing out his tongue, he had been compelled to beg the assistance of the king. Accordingly, coming to Rome in order that he might set in order those things which had exceedingly disturbed the condition of the Church, he remained there the whole winter. It was at the time that he accepted the name of Emperor and Augustus. At first he was so much opposed to this that he insisted that although that day was a great [Christian] feast, he would not have entered the Church if he had known beforehand the pope's intention. But he bore very patiently the jealousy of the Roman Emperors [that is, the Byzantine rulers] who were indignant when he received these titles. He overcame their arrogant haughtiness with magnanimity.[12]

For centuries scholars have debated the significance of the imperial coronation of Charlemagne. Did Charlemagne plan the ceremony in Saint Peter's on Christmas Day, or did he merely accept the title of emperor? What did he have to gain from it? If, as Einhard implies, the coronation displeased Charlemagne, did that displeasure rest on Pope Leo's role in the ceremony, which, on the principle that he who gives can also take away, placed the pope in a higher position than the emperor? Did Pope Leo arrange the coronation in order to identify the Frankish monarchy with the papacy and papal policy?

Though final answers will probably never be found, several things seem certain. First, Charlemagne gained the imperial title of Holy Roman emperor and considered himself a Christian king ruling a Christian people. His motto, *Renovatio romani imperi* (Revival of the Roman Empire), suggested a revival of the Western empire in the terms of Augustinian political philosophy. Charlemagne was consciously perpetuating old Roman imperial notions while at the same time identifying with the new Rome of the Christian church. Charlemagne and his government represented a combination of Frankish practices and Christian ideals, two basic elements of medieval European society. Second, later German rulers were eager to gain the imperial title and to associate themselves with the legends of Charlemagne and ancient Rome. They wanted to use the ideology of imperial Rome to strengthen their positions. Finally, ecclesiastical authorities continually cited the event as proof that the dignity of the imperial crown could be granted only by the pope.

When Charlemagne went to Rome in 800, Pope Leo III showed him signs of respect due only to the emperor. The Carolingian family thus received official recognition from the leading spiritual power in Europe, and the papacy gained a military protector. From Baghdad, Harun al Rashid, caliph of the Abbasid Empire (786–809), congratulated the Frankish ruler with the gift of an elephant. It was named Abu'l Abbas after the founder of the Abbasid dynasty and may have served as a symbol of the diplomatic link between the Muslim world and Christian Europe. Having plodded its way to Charlemagne's court at Aachen, the elephant survived for nine years, and its death was considered important enough to be mentioned in the Frankish *Royal Annals* for the year 810.

Though the Muslim caliph recognized Charlemagne as a fellow sovereign, the Greeks regarded the papal acts as rebellious and Charlemagne as a usurper. The imperial coronation thus marks a decisive break between Rome and Constantinople. The coronation of Charlemagne, whether planned by the Carolingian court or by the papacy, was to have a profound effect on the course of German history and on the later history of Europe.

Decentralization and "Feudalism"

Charlemagne left his vast empire to his sole surviving son, Louis the Pious (r. 814–840), who attempted to keep the empire intact. This proved to be impossible. Members of the nobility engaged in plots and open warfare against the emperor, often allying themselves with one of Louis's three sons. (See the feature "Individuals in Society: Ebo of Reims.") In 843, shortly after Louis's death, those sons agreed to the **Treaty of Verdun,** which divided the empire into three parts: Charles the Bald received the western part, Lothar the middle and the title of emperor, and Louis the eastern part, from which he acquired the title "the German" (see Map 8.3). Though of course no one knew it at the time, this treaty set the pattern for political boundaries in Europe that has been maintained until today. Other than brief periods under Napoleon and Hitler, Europe would never again see as large a unified state as it had under Charlemagne, which is one reason he has become an important symbol of European unity in the twenty-first century.

The large-scale division of Charlemagne's empire was accompanied by a decentralization of power at the local level. Nobles increased their authority in their own territories and built up groups of military followers who were primarily loyal to them, not to some distant king or emperor. The nobles had different amounts of power and wealth. The most powerful were those able to gain the allegiance of others, often symbolized in an oath-swearing ceremony of homage and fealty that grew out of earlier Germanic oaths of loyalty. In this ceremony, a fighter swore his loyalty as a **vassal**—from a Celtic term meaning "servant"—to the more powerful individual, who be-

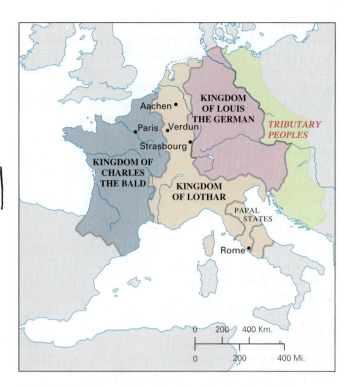

MAP 8.3 Division of the Carolingian Empire, 843 The Treaty of Verdun (843), which divided the empire among Charlemagne's grandsons, is frequently taken as the start of the separate development of Germany, France, and Italy. The "middle kingdom" of Lothar, however, lacking defensive borders and any political or linguistic unity, quickly broke up into numerous small territories.

came his lord. In return for the vassal's loyalty, aid, and military assistance, the lord promised him protection and material support, which might be a place in his household but was more likely land of his own, called a **fief** (*feudum* in Latin, from which the term **feudalism** was later coined to describe this political system). The fief theoretically still belonged to the lord, and the vassal only had the use of it. Families living on the fief produced the food and other goods necessary to maintain the warrior, and the fief might contain forests, churches, and towns.

The feudal system was thus based on personal ties of loyalty cemented by grants of land, and people had no sense of allegiance to an abstract state or governmental system. In some parts of Europe, such as Ireland and the Baltic area, warrior-aristocrats or clan chieftains who controlled relatively small regions were the ultimate political authorities; they generally did not grant fiefs to secure loyalty but relied on strictly personal ties. Thus the word *feudal* does not properly apply to these areas.

Homage and Fealty   In this manuscript illumination, a vassal kneels before the lord, places his clasped hands between those of the lord, and declares, "I become your man." Although the rite of entering a feudal relationship varied widely across Europe and sometimes was entirely verbal, we have a few illustrations of it. Sometimes the lord handed over a clump of earth, representing the fief, and the ceremony concluded with a kiss, symbolizing peace between them. *(Austrian National Library Picture Archive, Cod. VinDOB, 2262, fol. 174 [E8.037])*

Some historians argue, in fact, that the word *feudalism* should not be used at all, as it was unknown in the Middle Ages. In addition, the system that would later be called feudalism changed considerably in form and pattern between the ninth and fifteenth centuries, and differed from place to place. The feudalism of England in 1100, for example, differed greatly from that of France, scarcely fifty miles away, at the same time. The problem is that no one has come up with a better term for this loose arrangement of personal and property ties.

Whether one chooses to use the word *feudalism* or not, this system functioned as a way to organize political authority, particularly because vassals also owed obligations other than military service to the lord. They served as advisers and judges at the lord's court, provided lodging for the lord when he was traveling through their fief, gave

him gifts at important family events, such as marriages or the births of children, and might contribute ransom money if the lord was captured.

Along with granting fiefs for military service, lords rewarded officials in the Christian church with fiefs for spiritual services or promises of allegiance. In addition, the church held pieces of land on its own and granted fiefs in return for promises of assistance from knightly vassals. Abbots and abbesses of monasteries, bishops, and archbishops were either lords or vassals in many feudal arrangements.

Women other than abbesses were generally not granted fiefs, but in most parts of Europe they could inherit them if their fathers had no sons. (Because women could hold fiefs, the word *lord* does not always mean a man in the feudal context; it simply means the person or institution that holds the rights of lordship.) Occasionally, women did go through services swearing homage and fealty and swore to send fighters when the lord demanded them. More commonly, women acted as their husbands' surrogates when the men were away, defending the territory from attack and carrying out his administrative duties.

Though historians debate this, fiefs appear to have been granted extensively first by Charles Martel and then by his successors, including Charlemagne and his grandsons. These fiefs went particularly to their most powerful nobles, who often took the title of count. While countships were not hereditary in the eighth century, they tended to remain within the same family. In the ninth century regional concentrations of power depended on family connections and political influence at the king's court. The weakening of the Carolingian Empire, however, served to increase the power of regional authorities. Civil wars weakened the power and prestige of kings because there was little they could do about domestic violence. Likewise, the great invasions of the ninth century, especially the Viking invasions (see page 230), weakened royal authority. The West Frankish kings could do little to halt the invaders, and the aristocracy had to assume responsibility for defense. Common people turned for protection to the strongest local power, the counts, whom they considered their rightful rulers. Thus, in the ninth and tenth centuries great aristocratic families increased their authority in the regions of their vested

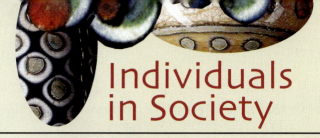

Individuals in Society

Ebo of Reims

The term *social mobility* came into broad use only in the twentieth century, but what it signifies—having the opportunity for an upward shift in status within society—is probably as old as organized society itself. "In all ages, service to the state and to men of power has raised some individuals and has enabled them to share in the social prestige that attaches to power."* In the Christian Middle Ages the Catholic Church provided the widest path for social advancement, and the archbishop symbolized political as well as religious prestige. Ebo of Reims (ca 775–851) represents one such individual.

Ebo's father was a serf freed by Charlemagne; his mother, Himiltruda, was the nurse of Louis the Pious. Ebo's mother probably launched his career, for Ebo was brought up with Louis at the "palace school" at Aachen, where nobles and others were trained for administrative and judicial service to the emperor. A bond was forged between Ebo and Louis. When Louis became king of Aquitaine, he made Ebo his librarian; when Louis succeeded as emperor in 814, he secured for Ebo the important archiepiscopal see of Reims.

Ebo proved himself a very competent administrator. He began construction of a new cathedral, gaining imperial permission to use the city walls as building blocks. Ebo organized the cathedral chapter—the local clergy who handled routine business of the diocese under the bishop. He reformed the monasteries in his see, ending the diverse forms of religious life by enforcing *The Rule of Saint Benedict* in all houses. Ebo also patronized learning and the arts. He supported the production of manuscripts and the school long associated with the cathedral, and he commissioned the production of a book that bears his name, the *Ebo Gospels.*

Ebo served the emperor as *missus* in his province, where he worked to extend royal authority. Archbishop Ebo served both church and state when, acting on behalf of Pope Pascal I and Louis the Pious, he led a mission to King Harold of Denmark, whose goal was the conversion of the Danes to Christianity and peaceful relations with the Franks. When Harold and a large Danish entourage visited Louis in 826, the Danes were baptized, and Harold became Louis's vassal.

In 830 Louis was past fifty, an old man by contemporary standards. Louis had three adult sons. Adult sons often posed a test of medieval kingship. Sons wanted power on their own, resented paternal control, and often rebelled. In 833 Archbishop Ebo served as counselor to the sons of Louis the Pious in their plot to remove Louis and replace him with Lothar. Ebo headed a commission of bishops that drew up charges against the emperor, accusing him of failing in his imperial responsibilities, promoting discord among the Frankish people, and tolerating his (second) wife Judith's adultery, thereby bringing moral scandal to the kingdom. Louis was forced to renounce the throne and to do public penance. The charges proved false, and within months Louis regained his throne. A church council deposed Ebo, consigning him to a monastery. When Louis the Pious died, Lothar restored Ebo to Reims, but the pope refused to approve the appointment. Then a dispute with Lothar led Ebo to seek the support of Louis the German, who made him bishop of Hildesheim. Ebo died at Hildesheim.

Emperor Louis the Pious confers with bishops and lay magnates. (Bibliothèque nationale de France)

Why did Ebo betray his boyhood friend and great benefactor? Was he resentful about some real or perceived slight and did he desire revenge? Was he willing to listen to dangerous advice? Did he wish to show himself the equal of any magnate who opposed the emperor? The *Annals of St.-Bertin,* the chief source of information about these events, describes Ebo as ungrateful, disobedient, disloyal, and cruel. What do you think?

Questions for Analysis

1. How does the career of Ebo of Reims illustrate social mobility?
2. What do Ebo's church appointments tell us about the Frankish state? What secular functions did bishops perform?

*K. Bosl, "On Social Mobility in Medieval Society," in *Early Medieval Society,* ed. S. L. Thrupp (New York: Appleton-Century-Crofts, 1967).

Sources: R. McKitterick, *The Frankish Kingdoms Under the Carolingians* (New York: Longman, 1983); J. L. Nelson, *Politics and Ritual in Early Medieval Europe* (London: Ronceverte, 1986).

Online Study Center **Improve Your Grade**
Going Beyond Individuals in Society

Ox Team Plowing From an eleventh-century calendar showing manorial occupations for each month, this illustration for January—the time for sowing winter wheat—shows two pairs of oxen pulling a wheeled plow, which was designed for deeper tillage. One man directs the oxen, a second prods the animals, and a third drops seeds in the ground. *(British Library Cott. Tib. B.V. 3, Min. Pt 1)*

interests. They built private castles for defense and to live in, and they governed virtually independent territories in which distant and weak kings could not interfere. Though they might officially be vassals of that king, they sometimes divided their territory into smaller parts and granted these segments to their own vassals.

Throughout western Europe, counts or earls exercised the most effective political power at the local level: they raised armies of fighting men, held courts that dispensed some form of law, coined money used in commercial transactions, and conducted relations with outside or foreign powers. Modern political scientists call these the powers of a sovereign or independent state. In the early Middle Ages local counts or earls administered these powers, and for their own personal benefit.

Feudalism actually existed at two social levels: the highest level consisted of royal officials, such as counts, who ruled great feudal principalities, while armed retainers who became knights formed a lower level, holding fiefs that may have been no larger than a small village with its surrounding land. In fact, some knights were landless and lived in the household of a king, count, or other high feudal lord. A wide and deep gap in social standing and political function separated these levels. (See the feature "Listening to the Past: Feudal Homage and Fealty" on pages 256–257.)

Manorialism, Serfdom, and the Slave Trade

Though *feudalism* is sometimes used to describe the entire social and political system of medieval Europe, the vast majority of people were not involved in the feudal system at all. They lived in family groups in villages or small towns and made their living predominantly by raising crops and animals. The village and the land surrounding it were called a *manor*, from the Latin word for "dwelling" or "homestead." Some fiefs might include only one manor, while great lords or kings might have hundreds of manors under their direct control. Residents of manors provided work for their lord in exchange for protection, a system that was later referred to as **manorialism.** Free peasants surrendered themselves and their lands to the lord's jurisdiction. The land was given back, but the peasants became tied to the land by various kinds of payments and services. Like feudalism, manorialism involved an exchange. Because the economic power of the warring class rested on landed estates worked by peasants, feudalism and manorialism were inextricably linked.

In France, England, Germany, and Italy, local custom determined precisely what services villagers would provide to their lord, but certain practices became common

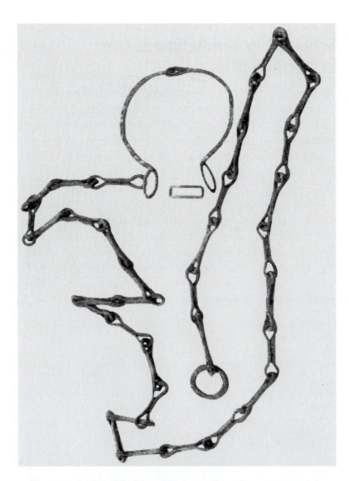

Balkan Neck Shackle (tenth century) The slave trader restrained the captive by slipping the chain through the loops in the neck collar (*top*), fastening it securely, and then attaching the chain to the captive's limbs. Similar devices for controlling slaves while allowing them to walk were later used in other parts of the world. (*Courtesy of the National Museum of History, Soa*)

everywhere. The peasant was obliged to give the lord a percentage of the annual harvest, usually in produce, sometimes in cash. The peasant paid a fee to marry someone from outside the lord's estate. To inherit property, the peasant paid a fine, often the best beast the person owned. Above all, the peasant became part of the lord's permanent labor force. With vast stretches of uncultivated virgin land and a tiny labor population, lords encouraged population growth and immigration. The most profitable form of capital was not land but laborers.

In entering into a relationship with a feudal lord, free farmers lost status. Their position became servile, and they became **serfs.** That is, they were bound to the land and could not leave it without the lord's permission. Serfdom was not the same as slavery in that lords did not own the person of the serf, but serfs were subject to the jurisdiction of the lord's court in any dispute over property and in any case of suspected criminal behavior.

The transition from freedom to serfdom was slow; its speed was closely related to the degree of political order in a given region. In the late eighth century there were still many free peasants. And within the legal category of serfdom there were many economic levels, ranging from the highly prosperous to the desperately poor. Nevertheless, a social and legal revolution was taking place. By the year 800 perhaps 60 percent of the population of western Europe—completely free a century before—had been reduced to serfdom. The ninth-century Viking assaults on Europe, discussed below, created extremely unstable conditions and individual insecurity, leading to additional loss of personal freedom.

Though serfdom was not slavery, the Carolingian trade in actual slaves was extensive, generally involving persons captured in war. Merchants in early medieval towns exchanged slaves for the luxury goods their noble and clerical customers desired, most of which came into Europe from the East. The Muslim conquest of Spain produced thousands of prisoner-slaves, as did Charlemagne's long wars against the Lombards, Avars, Saxons, and other groups. When Frankish conquests declined in the tenth century, merchants obtained people on the empire's eastern border who spoke Slavic languages, the origin of our word *slave*. Slaves sold across the Mediterranean fetched three or four times the amounts brought within the Carolingian Empire, so most slaves were sold to Muslims. For Europeans and Arabs alike, selling captives and other slaves was standard procedure. Christian moralists sometimes complained about the sale of Christians to non-Christians, but they did not object to slavery itself.

In general, the Carolingian period witnessed moderate population growth, as indicated by the steady reduction of forests and wasteland. The highest aristocrats and church officials lived well, with fine clothing and at least a few rooms heated by firewood. Male nobles hunted and managed their estates, while female nobles generally oversaw the education of their children and sometimes inherited and controlled land on their own. Craftsmen and craftswomen on manorial estates manufactured textiles, weapons, glass, and pottery, primarily for local consumption. Sometimes abbeys and manors served as markets; goods were shipped away to towns and fairs for sale; and a good deal of interregional commerce existed.

In the towns, which were generally small, artisans and merchants produced and traded luxury goods for noble and clerical patrons. The modest economic expansion benefited townspeople and nobles, but it did not alter the lives of most people very much.

Early Medieval Culture and Society

It is perhaps ironic that Charlemagne's most enduring legacy was the stimulus he gave to scholarship and learning. Barely literate himself, preoccupied with the control of vast territories, much more a warrior than an intellectual, he nevertheless set in motion a cultural revival that had widespread and long-lasting consequences.

• *What were the significant intellectual and cultural changes in Charlemagne's era?*

Scholarship and Religious Life in Northumbria

The revival of learning associated with Charlemagne and his court at Aachen drew its greatest inspiration from seventh- and eighth-century intellectual developments in the Anglo-Saxon kingdom of Northumbria, situated at the northernmost tip of the old Roman world. Despite the victory of the Roman forms of Christian liturgy at the Synod of Whitby in 664 (see page 206), Irish-Celtic culture permeated the Roman church in Britain and resulted in a flowering of artistic and scholarly activity. Northumbrian creativity owes a great deal to the intellectual curiosity and collecting zeal of Saint Benet Biscop (ca 628–689). The manuscripts and other treasures he brought back from Italy formed the library on which much later study rested.

Nuns and Learning In this tenth-century manuscript, the scholar Saint Aldhelm offers his book *In Praise of Holy Virgins* to a group of nuns, one of whom already holds a book. Early medieval nuns and monks spent much of their time copying manuscripts, preserving much of the learning of the classical world as well as Christian texts. (*His Grace the Archbishop of Canterbury and the Trustees of Lambeth Palace Library. MS 200, fol. 68v*)

Northumbrian monasteries produced scores of books: *missals* (used for the celebration of the Mass), *psalters* (which contained the 150 psalms and other prayers used by the monks in their devotions), commentaries on the Scriptures, illuminated manuscripts, law codes, and collections of letters and sermons. The finest product of Northumbrian art is probably the Gospel book produced at Lindisfarne around 700. The incredible expense involved in the publication of such a book—for vellum (calfskin or lambskin specially prepared for writing), coloring, and gold leaf—represents in part an aristocratic display of wealth. The script, *uncial,* is a Celtic version of contemporary Greek and Roman handwriting. The illustrations have a strong Eastern quality, combining the abstract, nonrepresentational style of the Christian Middle East and the narrative (storytelling) approach of classical Roman art. Likewise, the use of geometrical decorative designs shows the influence of Syrian art. Many scribes, artists, and illuminators must have participated in the book's preparation.

In Gaul and Anglo-Saxon England, women shared with men the work of evangelization and the new Christian learning. Kings and nobles, seeking suitable occupations for daughters who did not or would not marry, founded monasteries for nuns, some of which were double monasteries. A **double monastery** housed men and women in two adjoining establishments and was governed by one superior, an *abbess.* Nuns looked after the children given to the monastery as *oblates* (offerings), the elderly who retired at the monastery, and travelers who needed hospitality. Monks provided protection, since an isolated house of women invited attack in a violent age. Monks also did the heavy work on the land.

Perhaps the most famous abbess of the Anglo-Saxon period was Saint Hilda (d. 680). A noblewoman of considerable learning and administrative ability, she ruled the double monastery of Whitby on the Northumbrian coast, advised kings and princes, hosted the famous synod of 664, and encouraged scholars and poets. Five monks from Whitby later became bishops. Several generations after Hilda, Saint Boniface (see page 234) wrote many letters pleading for copies of books to Whitby and other houses of nuns; these letters attest to the nuns' intellectual reputations.[13]

The finest representative of Northumbrian, and indeed all Anglo-Saxon, scholarship is the Venerable Bede (ca 673–735). When he was seven his parents gave him as an oblate to Benet Biscop's monastery at Wearmouth. Later he was sent to the new monastery at Jarrow five miles away. Surrounded by the books Benet Biscop had brought from Italy, Bede spent the rest of his life there.

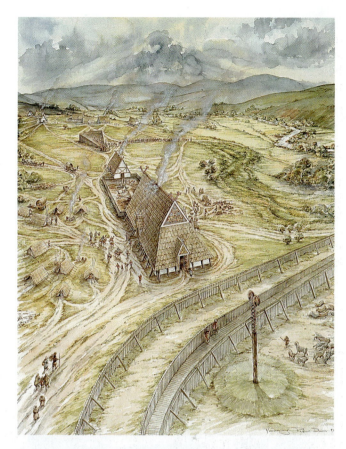

King Edwin of Northumbria's Palace Complex This modern illustration reveals a large barnlike structure protected by wooden defenses along sloped terraces. Edwin reigned from 616 to 632. (© *English Heritage, NMR*)

Modern scholars praise Bede for his *Ecclesiastical History of the English People* (ca 720), the chief source of information about early Britain. Bede searched far and wide for his information, discussed the validity of his evidence, compared various sources, and exercised rare critical judgment. For these reasons, he has been called "the first scientific intellect among the Germanic peoples of Europe."[14]

Bede popularized the system of dating events from the birth of Christ, rather than from the foundation of the city of Rome, as the Romans had done, or from the regnal years of kings, as the Germans did. He introduced the term *anno Domini,* "in the year of the Lord," abbreviated A.D. He fitted the entire history of the world into this new dating method. (The reverse dating system of B.C., "before Christ," does not seem to have been widely used before 1700.) Saint Boniface introduced this system of

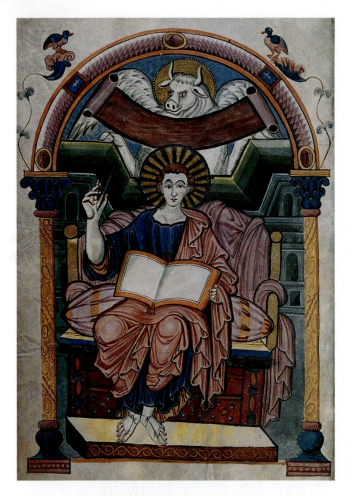

Saint Luke from the Ada Gospels (late eighth to early ninth century)   In this lavishly illuminated painting from a manuscript of the four Gospels of the New Testament, a statuesque Saint Luke sits enthroned, his clothing falling in distinct folds reminiscent of Byzantine art. He is surrounded by an elaborate architectural framework, and above him is a winged ox, the symbol of Luke in early Christian art. The Ada school of painting was attached to the court of Charlemagne and gets its name from Ada, a sister of Charlemagne who commissioned some of the school's work. *(Municipal Library, Trier, HS 22 fol. 85r)*

reckoning time throughout the Frankish empire of Charlemagne.

Is Bede representative of early medieval monasticism? Aside from brief visits to Lindisfarne and York, Bede passed his long and uneventful life in the quiet of his monastery. Using the two hundred to three hundred volumes on early Christian thought that Benet Biscop had brought back from Rome, Bede made that scholarship accessible to his barbarian present. His commentaries on sections of the biblical books of Genesis, Exodus,

Samuel, Kings, Acts, and Revelation survive in hundreds of manuscripts, indicating that they were widely studied throughout the Middle Ages. Although the monk-scholar is a fixture in the modern popular imagination, most monks spent their lives in more active work in fields and farms or in management and administration. In neither the pattern of his life nor his considerable pedagogical achievement can the "Venerable" Bede (the adjective means "marked by holiness in life") be called typical.

At about the time the monks at Lindisfarne were producing their Gospel book and Bede was writing his *History* at Jarrow, another Northumbrian monk was at work on a nonreligious epic poem that provides considerable information about the society that produced it. In contrast to the works of Bede, which were written in Latin, the poem *Beowulf* was written in the vernacular Anglo-Saxon. Although *Beowulf* is the only native English heroic epic, all the events of the tale take place in Denmark and Sweden, suggesting the close relationship between England and the continent in the eighth century. Scholars have hailed *Beowulf* as a masterpiece of Western literature.

Had they remained entirely insular, Northumbrian cultural achievements would have been of slight significance. But an Englishman from Northumbria played a decisive role in the transmission of English learning to the Carolingian Empire and continental Europe.

The Carolingian Renaissance

In Roman Gaul through the fifth century, the general culture rested on an education that stressed grammar; the works of the Greco-Roman orators, poets, dramatists, and historians; and the legal and medical treatises of the Roman world. Beginning in the seventh and eighth centuries, a new cultural tradition common to Gaul, Italy, the British Isles, and to some extent Spain emerged. This culture was based primarily on Christian sources. Scholars have called this new Christian and ecclesiastical culture, and the educational foundation on which it was based, the "Carolingian Renaissance," because Charlemagne was its major patron.

In a letter addressed to the abbot of Fulda, with copies sent to every monastery and bishopric in his kingdom, Charlemagne directed that the monasteries "should cultivate learning and educate the monks and secular clergy so that they might have a better understanding of the Christian writings." Likewise, in a "General Admonition" to all the leading clergy, he urged the establishment of cathedral and monastic schools where boys might learn to read and to pray properly. Thus the main purpose of this rebirth of learning was to promote an understanding of the Scriptures and of Christian writers and to instruct people to pray and praise God in the correct manner.

At his court at Aachen, Charlemagne assembled learned men from all over Europe. The most important scholar and the leader of the palace school was the Northumbrian Alcuin (ca 735–804). From 781 until his death, Alcuin was the emperor's chief adviser on religious and educational matters. An unusually prolific writer, he prepared some of the emperor's official documents and wrote many moral *exempla,* or "models," that set high standards for royal behavior and constitute a treatise on kingship. Alcuin's letters to Charlemagne set forth political theories on the authority, power, and responsibilities of a Christian ruler.

Aside from Alcuin's literary efforts, what did the scholars at Charlemagne's court do? They copied books and manuscripts and built up libraries. They used the beautifully clear handwriting known as "caroline minuscule," from which modern Roman type is derived. (This script is called **minuscule** because unlike the Merovingian majuscule, which had letters of equal size, minuscule had both uppercase and lowercase letters.) Caroline minuscule improved the legibility of texts and meant that a

sheet of vellum could contain more words and thus be used more efficiently. With the materials at hand, many more manuscripts could be copied. Book production on this scale represents a major manifestation of the revival of learning. Caroline minuscule illustrates the way a seemingly small technological change has broad cultural consequences.

Although scholars worked with Latin, exchanged books between monasteries, and generally collaborated in book production, the common people spoke local or vernacular languages. The Bretons, for example, retained their local dialect, and the Saxons and Bavarians could not understand each other. Some scholars believe that Latin words and phrases gradually penetrated the various vernacular languages, facilitating communication among diverse peoples.

Once basic literacy was established, monastic and other scholars went on to more difficult work. By the middle years of the ninth century, there was a great outpouring of more sophisticated books. Ecclesiastical writers imbued with the legal ideas of ancient Rome and the theocratic ideals of Saint Augustine instructed the semibarbaric rulers of the West. And it is no accident that medical study in the West began at Salerno in southern Italy in the late ninth century, *after* the Carolingian Renaissance.

Organ Music from the Utrecht Psalter The most famous of all Carolingian manuscripts, the Utrecht Psalter (ca 825–850), contains the Old Testament book of Psalms illustrated with ink drawings. Here an illustration for Psalm 150—"Praise him with blast of trumpet, praise him with strings and pipe"—shows the organ that Louis the Pious built for the palace chapel at Aachen. In the Carolingian period, books played a large role in the spread of Christianity and in the promotion of learning. *(University Library, Utrecht)*

Alcuin completed the work of his countryman Boniface—the Christianization of northern Europe. Latin Christian attitudes penetrated deeply into the consciousness of European peoples. By the tenth century the patterns of thought and the lifestyles of educated western Europeans were those of Rome and Latin Christianity.

Health and Medical Care in the Early Middle Ages

A surprising amount of information is known about medical treatment in the early Middle Ages. Medical practice consisted primarily of drug and prescription therapy. Through the monks' efforts and the recovery of Greek and Arabic manuscripts, a large body of the ancients' prescriptions was preserved and passed on. Balsam was recommended for coughs. For asthma an ointment combining chicken, wormwood, laurel berries, and oil of roses was to be rubbed on the chest. The scores of prescriptions to rid the body of lice, fleas, and other filth reflect frightful standards of personal hygiene. The large number of prescriptions for eye troubles suggests that they too must have been common.

Poor diet caused frequent stomach disorders and related ailments such as dysentery, constipation, and diarrhea. For poor circulation a potion of meadow wort, oak rind, and lustmock was recommended. Pregnancy and childbirth posed grave threats of infection for both mother and child. Infants and children were especially susceptible to a range of illnesses, and about half of the children born died before age five, though parents tried to protect them with prayers, amulets worn around the neck, and various herbal mixtures.

All wounds and open injuries invited infection, and infection invited gangrene. Several remedies were known for wounds. Physicians appreciated the antiseptic properties of honey, and prescriptions recommended that wounds be cleaned with it. When an area or a limb had become gangrenous, the physician was instructed to cut above the diseased flesh in order to hasten a cure. The juice of white poppy plants—the source of heroin—could be added to wine and drunk as an anesthetic. Egg whites, which have a soothing effect, were prescribed for burns.

The spread of Christianity in the Carolingian era had a beneficial effect on medical knowledge and treatment. Several of the church fathers expressed serious interest in medicine. The church was deeply concerned about human suffering, whether physical or mental. Christian teaching vigorously supported concern for the poor, sick, downtrodden, and miserable. Churchmen taught that, while all knowledge came from God, He had supplied it so that people could use it for their own benefit.

The foundation of a school at Salerno in southern Italy sometime in the ninth century gave a tremendous impetus to medical study by laypeople. The school's location attracted Arabic, Greek, and Jewish physicians from all over the Mediterranean region. Students flocked there from northern Europe. The Jewish physician Shabbathai Ben Abraham (931–982) left pharmacological notes that were widely studied in later centuries.

Physicians were few in the early Middle Ages, and only the rich could afford them. Local folk medicine practiced by nonprofessionals provided such help as other people could get. Apparently most illnesses simply took their course, and death came early. A forty-year-old was considered old. People's vulnerability to ailments for which there were no probable cures contributed to a fatalistic acceptance of death at an early age.

Invasions and Migrations

After the Treaty of Verdun (843), continental Europe was fractured politically. All three kingdoms controlled by the sons of Louis the Pious (see Map 8.3) were torn by domestic dissension and disorder. The frontier and coastal defenses erected by Charlemagne and maintained by Louis the Pious were neglected. No European political power was strong enough to put up effective resistance to external attacks. Three groups attacked Europe: Vikings from Scandinavia, representing the final wave of Germanic migrants; Muslims from the Mediterranean; and Magyars forced westward by other peoples (see Map 8.4).

● *What effects did the assaults and migrations of the Vikings, Magyars, and Muslims have on the rest of Europe?*

Vikings in Western Europe

From the moors of Scotland to the mountains of Sicily, there arose in the ninth century the prayer, "Save us, O God, from the violence of the Northmen." The Northmen, also known as Vikings, were Germanic peoples from Norway, Sweden, and Denmark who had remained beyond the sway of the Christianizing and civilizing influences of the Carolingian Empire. Some scholars believe that the name *Viking* derives from the old Norse

To Greenland
and North America

ICELAND

874

Faeroe Is.
800

Shetland Is.
700

Trondheim

VIKINGS

Bergen
Oslo

Uppsala

Novgorod
820

Volga

ATLANTIC

OCEAN

*North
Sea*

*Baltic
Sea*

RUSSIA

SCOTLAND
Iona

Lindisfarne

859–878

Lund

841–984

Durrow
Dublin
IRELAND
839

Jarrow

York

*Humber
Estuary*

Thames

Bremen
Hamburg
SAXONY

Kiev
882

Dnieper

Saint Wandrille
Jumièges
Rouen
Saint-
Denis
NORMANDY

Aachen
Echternach
Fulda

Elbe
Oder
Visula

895

Loire
Seine
Rhine

BAVARIA

883

843–882

BURGUNDY

Reichenau
Saint Gall

900

MAGYARS

HUNGARY

941

896–911
Bordeaux

917

Rhône

899
PROVENCE
Marseilles
Lérins

Po
LOMBARDY

895

907

866

Garonne

Santiago

Tagus

Barcelona

859–861

Balearic Is.

Danube

Black Sea

Lisbon
844

844

Corsica

Sardinia

Rome
846

Monte
Cassino

Constantinople

Ceuta

Hippo
Regius

827
Sicily

840–896

842
Carthage

MUSLIMS

Mediterranean Sea

Alexandria

•   Monasteries
→   Vikings
→   Magyars
→   Muslims

0   200   400 Km.

0   200   400 Mi.

Mapping the Past

MAP 8.4 Invasions and Migrations of the Ninth Century   This map shows the Viking, Magyar, and Arab invasions and migrations in the ninth century. Compare it with Map 7.3 (page 211) on the barbarian migrations of late antiquity to answer the following questions: ❶ What similarities do you see in the patterns of migration in these two periods? What significant differences? ❷ How is Viking expertise in shipbuilding and sailing reflected on this map? Based on the information in Map 7.3, what would you assume about the maritime skills of earlier Germanic tribes?

word *vik*, meaning "creek." A Viking, then, was a pirate who waited in a creek or bay to attack passing vessels.

The Vikings were superb seamen. Their boats, built using advanced methods, gave them great speed and maneuverability. Propelled either by oars or by sails, deckless, and about sixty-five feet long, a Viking ship could carry between forty and sixty men—enough to harass an isolated monastery or village. These ships, navigated by thoroughly experienced and utterly fearless sailors, moved through the most complicated rivers, estuaries, and waterways in Europe. The Carolingian Empire, with no navy and no notion of the importance of sea power, was helpless. The Vikings moved swiftly, attacked, and escaped to return again.

Scholars disagree about the reasons for Viking attacks and migrations. Recent research asserts that a very unstable Danish kingship and disputes over the succession led to civil war and disorder, which drove warriors abroad in search of booty and supporters. Other writers insist that the Vikings were looking for trade and new commercial contacts. In that case, there were no better targets for plunder than the mercantile centers of Francia and Frisia.

Viking attacks were savage. The Vikings burned, looted, and did extensive short-term property damage, but there is little evidence that they caused long-term destruction—perhaps because, arriving in small bands, they lacked the manpower to do so. They seized magnates and high churchmen and held them for ransom; they also demanded tribute from kings. In 844–845 Charles the Bald had to raise seven thousand pounds of silver, and across the English Channel Anglo-Saxon rulers collected a land tax, the Danegeld, to buy off the Vikings. The Vikings exploited conflicts among the Carolingians, as in 841 when they sailed up the Seine and sacked Rouen, knowing that Charles the Bald had crushed a revolt of nobles there just a few weeks earlier and that the region was vulnerable. The Carolingians also manipulated the Vikings; Lothar used his Viking ally Harald against his brothers in Frisia. In the Seine and Loire Valleys the frequent presence of Viking war bands seems to have had economic consequences, stimulating the production of food and wine and possibly the manufacture (for sale) of weapons and the breeding of horses.

In the early tenth century Danish Vikings besieged Paris with fleets of more than a hundred highly maneuverable ships, and the Frankish king Charles the Simple bought them off with a large part of northern France. The Vikings established the province of "Northmanland," or Normandy as it was later known, intermarrying with the local population and creating a distinctive Norman culture. From there they sailed around Spain and

Animal Headpost from Viking Ship Skilled woodcarvers produced ornamental headposts for ships, sledges, wagons, and bedsteads. The fearsome quality of many carvings suggests that they were intended to ward off evil spirits and to terrify. (© *University Museum of Cultural Heritage, Oslo. Photographer: Eirik Irgens Johnsen*)

into the Mediterranean, eventually conquering Sicily from the Muslim Arabs in 1060–1090, while other Normans crossed the English Channel, defeating Anglo-Saxon forces in 1066.

Between 876 and 954 Viking control extended from Dublin across the Irish Sea to Britain, across northern Britain between the Dee and the Solway Rivers, and then across the North Sea to the Vikings' Scandinavian homelands. Norwegian Vikings moved farther west than any Europeans had before, establishing permanent settlements on Iceland and short-lived settlements in Greenland and Newfoundland in what is now Canada.

In their initial attacks on isolated settlements, the Vikings put many people to the sword. From the British Isles and territories along the Baltic Sea, they took *thralls* (slaves) for the markets of Magdeburg on the Elbe River and Regensburg in Bavaria on the Danube, for the fairs of Lyons on the Rhône River, and to supply the huge demand for slaves in the Muslim world. The slave trade represented an important part of Viking commerce. The Icelander Hoskuld Dala-Kolsson of Laxardal paid three marks of silver, three times the price of a common concubine, for a pretty Irish girl; she was one of twelve offered by a Viking trader. No wonder many communities bought peace by paying tribute.

Along with destruction, the Vikings made positive contributions to the areas they settled. They carried their unrivaled knowledge of shipbuilding and seamanship everywhere. The northeastern and central parts of England where the Vikings settled became known as the *Danelaw* because Danish, not English, law and customs prevailed there. Scholars believe that some legal institutions, such as the ancestor of the modern grand jury, originated in the Danelaw. York in northern England, once a Roman army camp and then an Anglo-Saxon town, became a thriving center of Viking trade with Scandinavia. At Dublin on the east coast of Ireland, Viking ironworkers, steelworkers, and comb makers established a center for trade with the Hebrides, Iceland, and Norway. The Irish cities of Limerick, Cork, Wexford, and Waterford trace their origins to Viking trading centers.

Slavs and Vikings in Eastern Europe

In antiquity the Slavs lived in central Europe, farming with iron technology, building fortified towns, and worshiping a variety of deities. With the start of the mass migrations of the late Roman Empire, the Slavs moved in different directions and split into what later historians identified as three groups. The group labeled the West Slavs included the Poles, Czechs, Slovaks, and Wends. The South Slavs, comprising peoples who became the Serbs, Croats, Slovenes, Macedonians, and Bosnians, migrated southward into the Balkans and eventually achieved a relatively high degree of political development. In the seventh century Slavic peoples created the state of Moravia along the banks of the Danube River. Rulers of Moravia first sent for Orthodox Christian missionaries from the Byzantine Empire, but in the tenth century they decided to ally themselves with the Roman church. Most of the other West and South Slavs also slowly became Roman Christian. The pattern was similar to that of the Germanic tribes: first the ruler was baptized, and then missionaries preached, built churches, and spread Christian teachings among the common people. The ruler of Poland was able to convince the pope to establish an independent archbishopric there in 1000, the beginning of a long-lasting connection between Poland and the Roman church. In the Balkans the Serbs accepted Orthodox Christianity, while the Croats became Roman Christian, a division that has had a long impact; it was one of the factors in the civil war in this area in the late twentieth century. The Bulgars also became Orthodox Christian and in the early tenth century

built a strong state that attacked Constantinople a number of times.

Between the fifth and ninth centuries, the eastern Slavs, from whom the Ukrainians, Russians, and White Russians descend, moved into the vast and practically uninhabited area of present-day European Russia and Ukraine. This enormous area consisted of an immense virgin forest to the north, where most of the eastern Slavs settled, and an endless prairie grassland to the south. Probably organized as tribal communities, the eastern Slavs, like many North American pioneers much later, lived off the great abundance of wild game and crude "slash and burn" agriculture. After clearing a piece of the forest to build log cabins, they burned the stumps and brush. The ashes left a rich deposit of potash and lime, and the land produced several good crops before it was exhausted. The people then moved on to another untouched area and repeated the process.

In the ninth century the Vikings appeared in the lands of the eastern Slavs. Called "Varangians" in the old Russian chronicles, the Vikings were interested primarily in international trade, and the opportunities were good. Moving up and down the rivers, they soon linked Scandinavia and northern Europe to the Black Sea and to the Byzantine Empire with its capital at Constantinople. They raided and looted the cities along the Caspian Sea several times in the tenth century, taking booty and slaves. They built a few strategic forts along the rivers, from which they raided the neighboring Slavic tribes and collected tribute, especially in the form of slaves. As in the west, raids for plunder gradually turned into trading missions, and the Vikings established settlements, intermarried, and assimilated with Slavic peoples.

In order to increase and protect their international commerce, the Vikings declared themselves the rulers of the eastern Slavs. According to tradition, the semi-legendary chieftain Ruirik founded a princely dynasty about 860. In any event, the Varangian ruler Oleg (r. 878–912) established his residence at Kiev in modern-day Ukraine. He and his successors ruled over a loosely united confederation of Slavic territories known as Rus with its capital at Kiev until 1054. (The word *Russia* comes from *Rus*, though the origins of *Rus* are hotly debated, with some historians linking it with Swedish words and others with Slavic words.) The Viking prince and his clansmen quickly became assimilated into the Slavic population, taking local wives and emerging as the noble class.

Assimilation was accelerated by the conversion of the Vikings and local Slavs to Eastern Orthodox Christianity by missionaries of the Byzantine Empire. The written language of these missionaries, an early form of Slavic now known as Old Church Slavonic, was subsequently used in all religious and nonreligious documents in **Kievan Rus.** Thus the rapidly Slavified Vikings left two important legacies for the future: they created a loose unification of Slavic territories under a single ruling prince and a single ruling dynasty, and they imposed a basic religious unity by accepting Orthodox Christianity, as opposed to Roman Catholicism, for themselves and the eastern Slavs.

Online Study Center **Improve Your Grade**
Primary Source: Religious Competition in Kievan Rus

Even at its height under Great Prince Iaroslav the Wise (r. 1019–1054), the unity of Kievan Rus was extremely tenuous. Trade, not government, was the main concern of the rulers. Moreover, the Slavified Vikings failed to find a way of peacefully transferring power from one generation to the next. In medieval western Europe, this fundamental problem of government was increasingly resolved by resorting to the principle of primogeniture: the king's eldest son received the Crown as his rightful inheritance when his father died. Civil war was thus averted; order was preserved. In early Rus, however, there were apparently no fixed rules, and much strife accompanied each succession.

Possibly to avoid such chaos, Great Prince Iaroslav, before his death in 1054, divided Kievan Rus among his five sons, who in turn divided their properties when they died. Between 1054 and 1237, Kievan Rus disintegrated into more and more competing units, each ruled by a prince claiming to be a descendant of Ruirik. Even when only one prince claimed to be the great prince, the whole situation was unsettled.

The princes divided their land like private property because they thought of it as private property. A given prince owned a certain number of farms or landed estates and had them worked directly by his people, mainly slaves, called *kholops* in Russian. Outside of these estates, which constituted the princely domain, the prince exercised only limited authority in his principality. Excluding the clergy, two kinds of people lived there: the noble boyars and the commoner peasants.

The **boyars** were descendants of the original Viking warriors, and they also held their lands as free and clear private property. Although the boyars normally fought in princely armies, the customary law declared that they could serve any prince they wished. The ordinary peasants were also truly free. They could move at will wherever opportunities were greatest. In the touching phrase of the times, theirs was "a clean road, without bound-

aries."[15] In short, fragmented princely power, private property, and personal freedom all went together.

Magyars and Muslims

Along with Vikings from the north, nomadic central European steppe peoples known as Magyars moved westward in Europe in the late ninth century, crossing the Danube, attacking villages, gaining wealth, taking captives, and forcing leaders to pay tribute in an effort to prevent looting and destruction. Small groups of Magyars riding swift horses raided as far west as Spain and the Atlantic coast. They subdued northern Italy, compelled Bavaria and Saxony to pay tribute, and even penetrated into the Rhineland and Burgundy. Because of their skill with horses and their eastern origins, the Magyars were often identified with the earlier Huns by those they conquered, though they are probably unrelated ethnically. This identification may be the origin of the word *Hungarian*, though the word may also derive from a Turkish word for arrows bound together.

Magyar forces were defeated by a combined army of Frankish and other Germanic troops at the Battle of Lechfeld near Augsburg in southern Germany in 955, and the Magyars settled in the area that is now Hungary in eastern Europe. Much as Clovis had centuries earlier, their ruler Géza (r. 970–997), who had been a pagan, decided to become a Roman Christian. This gave him the support of the papacy and offered prospects for alliances with other Roman Christian rulers against the Byzantine Empire, Hungary's southern neighbor. Géza's son Stephen I (r. 997–1038) was officially crowned the king of Hungary by a papal representative on Christmas Day of 1001. He supported the building of churches and monasteries, built up royal power, and encouraged the use of Latin and the Roman alphabet. Hungary's alliance with the papacy shaped the later history of eastern Europe just as Charlemagne's alliance with the papacy shaped western European history. The Hungarians adopted settled agriculture, wrote law codes, and built towns, and Hungary became an important crossroads of trade for German and Muslim merchants.

The ninth century also saw invasions into western Europe from the south. Muslim fleets had attacked Sicily, which was part of the Byzantine Empire, beginning in the seventh century, and by the end of the ninth century they controlled most of the island. The Muslims drove northward and sacked Rome in 846. Expert seamen, they sailed around the Iberian Peninsula, braved the notoriously dangerous shoals and winds of the Atlantic coast, and captured towns along the Adriatic coast almost all the way to Venice. They attacked Mediterranean settlements along the coast of Provence and advanced on land as far as the Alps. In the tenth century Frankish, papal, and Byzantine forces were able to retake much territory, though the Muslims continued to hold Sicily. Under their rule, agricultural innovations from elsewhere in the Muslim world led to new crops such as cotton and sugar, and fortified cities became centers of Muslim learning. Disputes among the Muslim rulers on the island led one faction to ask the Normans for assistance, and between 1060 and 1090 the Normans gradually conquered the whole island.

What was the effect of these invasions on the structure of European society? From the perspective of those living in what had been Charlemagne's empire, Viking, Magyar, and Muslim attacks accelerated the fragmentation of political power. Lords capable of rallying fighting men, supporting them, and putting up resistance to the invaders did so. They also assumed political power in their territories. Weak and defenseless people sought the protection of local strongmen, and free peasants sank to the level of serfs. This period is thus often seen as one of terror and chaos.

People in other parts of Europe might have had a different opinion, however. In Muslim Spain, scholars worked in thriving cities, and new crops enhanced ordinary people's lives. In eastern Europe, states such as Moravia and Hungary became strong kingdoms. A Viking point of view might be the most positive, for by 1100 descendants of the Vikings not only ruled their homelands in Denmark, Norway, and Sweden, but also ruled Normandy, England, Sicily, Iceland, and Kievan Rus, with an outpost in Greenland and occasional voyages to North America.

Chapter Summary

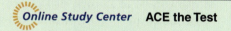
Online Study Center **ACE the Test**

- *How did the spread of Islam shape European history in this era?*
- *How did Frankish rulers govern their kingdoms?*
- *What accounts for Charlemagne's political and diplomatic successes?*
- *What were the significant intellectual and cultural changes in Charlemagne's era?*
- *What effects did the assaults and migrations of the Vikings, Magyars, and Muslims have on the rest of Europe?*

In the seventh century the diverse Arab tribes were transformed into a powerful political and social force by the teachings of the Prophet Muhammad. They conquered much of the Middle East and North Africa, and in the eighth century they crossed into Europe, eventually gaining control of most of the Iberian Peninsula. Muslim-controlled Spain, known as al-Andalus, was the most advanced society in Europe in terms of agriculture, science, and medicine. Some Christian residents assimilated to Muslim practices, but hostility between the two groups was also evident as each increasingly regarded members of the other as infidels.

In western Europe, Frankish rulers of the Merovingian dynasty built on the foundations established by Clovis in the fifth century, dividing their territories into regions and sending out royal officials, later called counts, to administer the regions. Their authority was frequently challenged by civil wars and rebellions by nobles. One of these nobles, Charles Martel, held the important position of mayor of the palace, and in the eighth century he took power and established a new dynasty, the Carolingians. The Carolingians used both military victories and strategic marriage alliances to enhance their authority.

Carolingian government reached the peak of its development under Charles Martel's grandson, Charlemagne. Building on the military and diplomatic foundations of his ancestors, Charlemagne waged constant warfare to expand his kingdom, eventually coming to control most of central and western continental Europe except Muslim

Spain. Christian missionary activity among the Germanic peoples continued, and strong ties were forged with the Roman papacy, which eventually resulted in Charlemagne's coronation as emperor. After his death his empire was divided between his grandsons in the Treaty of Verdun (843). This division of Charlemagne's empire was accompanied by a decentralization of power at the local level, and a new political form involving mutual obligations, later called "feudalism," developed. The power of the local nobles in the feudal structure rested on landed estates worked by peasants in another system of mutual obligation termed "manorialism." An overwhelmingly agricultural economy supplied food for local needs, but there was some interregional trade in glass, pottery, and woolens and a sizable long-distance trade in slaves.

Charlemagne's support of education and learning proved his most enduring legacy. The revival of learning associated with Charlemagne and his court at Aachen, sometimes styled the "Carolingian Renaissance," drew its greatest inspiration from seventh- and eighth-century intellectual developments in the Anglo-Saxon kingdom of Northumbria in northern England. Here women and men in monasteries produced beautiful illustrated texts, and the Venerable Bede popularized the Christian dating system now in use in most of the world. Monks and nuns in many parts of Europe also copied medical texts, and some Greek and Arabic medical knowledge filtered into Western Latin culture, though much was lost.

After the Treaty of Verdun, continental Europe was fractured politically, with no European political power strong enough to put up effective resistance to external attack. Vikings from Scandinavia carried out raids for plunder along the coasts and rivers of western Europe and traveled as far as Iceland, Greenland, and North America. Eventually they settled in England and France, where they established the state of Normandy. In eastern Europe Vikings traded down the rivers as far as Constantinople and formed the state of Kievan Rus, assimilating to Slavic culture and converting to the Orthodox religion. Like the Vikings, the Magyars initially invaded Europe for plunder and then established a permanent state; their ruler Stephen I was crowned as king by a papal representative two hundred years after Charlemagne's coronation. Thus, in both western and eastern Europe, civil rulers and church leaders supported each other's goals and utilized each other's prestige and power, though their alliances and disputes had little effect on the daily lives of most people in early medieval Europe.

Key Terms

Qur'an	missi dominici
Islam	Treaty of Verdun
Five Pillars of Islam	vassal
caliph	fief
al-Andalus	feudalism
infidel	manorialism
civitas	serfs
comites	double monastery
Frank	minuscule
capitularies	Kievan Rus
anointment	boyars

Online Study Center **Improve Your Grade** Flashcards

Suggested Reading

Ahmed, Leila. *Women and Gender in Islam: Historical Roots of a Modern Debate.* 1992. The starting point for all research on Islam and gender.

Barbero, Allesandro. *Charlemagne: Father of a Continent.* 2004. A wonderful biography of Charlemagne and study of the times in which he lived that argues for the complexity of his legacy.

Barford, P. M. *The Early Slavs: Culture and Society in Early Medieval Eastern Europe.* 2001. An excellent survey of developments in much of eastern Europe.

Bitel, Lisa. *Women in Early Medieval Europe, 400–1100.* 2002. Uses literary works and archaeological evidence as well as more traditional types of sources to trace all aspects of women's lives: social, intellectual, political, economic.

Duby, Georges. *The Early Growth of the European Economy: Warriors and Peasants from the Seventh to the Twelfth Century.* 1978. Relates economic behavior to other aspects of human experience in a thoroughly readable style.

Esposito, John L. *Islam: The Straight Path,* updated ed. 2004. An informed and balanced work based on the best modern scholarship and original sources.

Fletcher, Richard. *The Cross and the Crescent: Christianity and Islam from Muhammad to the Reformation.* 2003. A highly readable introduction to the intricate and controversial relationships between Christianity and Islam down to the sixteenth century.

Glick, Thomas F. *Islamic and Christian Spain in the Early Middle Ages.* 1979. A good introduction to cultural and political developments and interactions.

James, Edward. *The Origins of France: From Clovis to the Capetians, 500–1000,* 2d ed. 2006. A solid introductory survey of early French history with an emphasis on family relationships.

Lings, Martin. *Muhammad: His Life Based on the Earliest Sources.* 1987. A clearly written narrative of the life of the Prophet Muhammad and the foundation of Islam based exclusively on eighth- and ninth-century Arabic sources.

Reynolds, Susan. *Fiefs and Vassals: The Medieval Evidence Reconsidered.* 1996. A comprehensive challenge to traditional conceptions of feudalism, the fief, and vassalage that is leading to a rethinking of medieval political relationships.

Riche, Pierre. *Daily Life in the World of Charlemagne.* Trans. JoAnn McNamara. 1978. A detailed study of many facets of Carolingian society.

Sawyer, Peter, ed. *The Oxford Illustrated History of the Vikings.* 1997. A sound account of the Vikings by an international team of scholars.

Verhulst, Adriaan. *The Carolingian Economy.* 2002. A brief survey of all aspects of the economy, including agrarian production, crafts, and commerce, designed for students.

Wood, Ian. *The Merovingian Kingdoms, 450–751.* 1994. The best general treatment of the Merovingians.

Notes

1. F. E. Peters, *A Reader on Classical Islam* (Princeton, N.J.: Princeton University Press, 1994), pp. 208–209.
2. J. O'Faolain and L. Martines, eds., *Not in God's Image: Women in History from the Greeks to the Victorians* (New York: Harper & Row, 1973), pp. 108–114.
3. See Jane I. Smith, "Islam and Christendom: Historical, Cultural, and Religious Interaction from the Seventh to the Fifteenth Centuries," in *The Oxford History of Islam,* ed. John L. Esposito (New York: Oxford University Press, 1999), pp. 317–321.
4. J. M. Bloom, *Paper Before Print: The History and Impact of Paper in the Islamic World* (New Haven: Yale University Press, 2001), pp. 9–10, 17, 45, 85–89.
5. JoAnn Hoeppner Moran Cruz, "Western Views of Islam in Medieval Europe," in *Perceptions of Islam,* ed. D. Blanks and M. Frassetto (New York: St. Martin's Press, 1999), pp. 55–81.
6. See R. W. Brauer, *Boundaries and Frontiers in Medieval Muslim Geography* (Philadelphia: American Philosophical Society, 1995), p. 41.
7. I. Wood, *The Merovingian Kingdoms, 450–751* (New York: Longman, 1994), p. 101.
8. Quoted in R. McKitterick, *The Frankish Kingdoms Under the Carolingians, 751–987* (New York: Longman, 1983), p. 34.
9. Einhard, *The Life of Charlemagne,* with a foreword by S. Painter (Ann Arbor: University of Michigan Press, 1960), pp. 50–51.
10. Quoted in McKitterick, p. 77.
11. See K. F. Werner, "Important Noble Families in the Kingdom of Charlemagne," in *The Medieval Nobility: Studies on the Ruling Class of France and Germany from the Sixth to the Twelfth Century,* ed. and trans. T. Reuter (New York: North-Holland, 1978), pp. 174–184.
12. Quoted in B. D. Hill, ed., *Church and State in the Middle Ages* (New York: John Wiley & Sons, 1970), pp. 46–47.
13. J. Nicholson, "Feminae Glorisae: Women in the Age of Bede," in *Medieval Women,* ed. D. Baker (Oxford: Basil Blackwell, 1978), pp. 15–31, esp. p. 19; and C. Fell, *Women in Anglo-Saxon England and the Impact of 1066* (Bloomington: Indiana University Press, 1984), p. 109.
14. R. W. Southern, *Medieval Humanism and Other Studies* (Oxford: Basil Blackwell, 1970), p. 3.
15. Quoted in R. Pipes, *Russia Under the Old Regime* (New York: Charles Scribner's Sons, 1974), p. 48.

Feudal Homage and Fealty

Feudalism provided social and political order held together by bonds of kinship, homage, and fealty and by grants of benefices—lands or estates given by king, lay lord, or ecclesiastical officer (bishop or abbot) to another member of the nobility or to a knight. In return for the benefice, or fief, the recipient became the vassal of the lord and agreed to perform certain services, usually military ones. Feudalism developed in the ninth century during the disintegration of the Carolingian Empire because rulers needed fighting men and officials. In a society that lacked an adequate government bureaucracy, a sophisticated method of taxation, or even the beginnings of national consciousness, personal ties provided some degree of cohesiveness.

In the first document, a charter dated 876, the emperor Charles the Bald (r. 843–877), Charlemagne's grandson, grants a benefice. In the second document, dated 1127, the Flemish notary Galbert of Bruges describes homage and fealty before Count Charles the Good of Flanders (r. 1119–1127). The ceremony consists of three parts: the act of homage; the oath of fealty, intended to reinforce the act; and the investiture (apparently with property). Because all three parts are present, historians consider this evidence of a fully mature feudal system.

In the name of the holy and undivided Trinity. Charles by the mercy of Almighty God august emperor . . . let it be known to all the faithful of the holy church of God and to our now, present and to come, that one of our faithful subjects, by name of Hildebertus, has approached our throne and has beseeched our serenity that through this command of our authority we grant to him for all the days of his life and to his son after him, in right of usufruct and benefice, certain estates which are . . . called Cavaliacus, in the county of Limoges. Giving assent to his prayers for reason of his meritorious service, we have ordered this charter to be written, through which we grant to him the estates already mentioned, in all their entirety, with lands, vineyards, forests, meadows, pastures, and with the men living upon them, so that, without causing any damage through exchanges or diminishing or lessening the land, he for all the days of his life and his son after him, as we have said, may hold and possess them in right of benefice and usufruct. . . .

Done of the sixteenth kalends of August [July 15th] the thirty-seventh year of the reign of Charles most glorious emperor in France . . . at Ponthion in the palace of the emperor. In the name of God, happily. Amen.

On Thursday, the seventh of the ides of April [April 7, 1127], acts of homage were again made to the count, which were brought to a conclusion through this method of giving faith and assurance. First, they performed homage in this fashion: the count inquired if [the prospective vassal] wished completely to become his man. He replied, "I do wish it," and with his hands joined and covered by the hands of the count, the two were united by a kiss. Second, he who had done the homage gave faith to the representative of the count in these words: "I promise in my faith that I shall henceforth be faithful to Count William, and I shall fully observe the homage owed him against all men, in good faith and without deceit." Third, he took an oath on the relics of the saints. Then the count, with the rod which he had in his right hand, gave investiture to all those who by this promise had given assurance and due homage to the count, and had taken the oath.

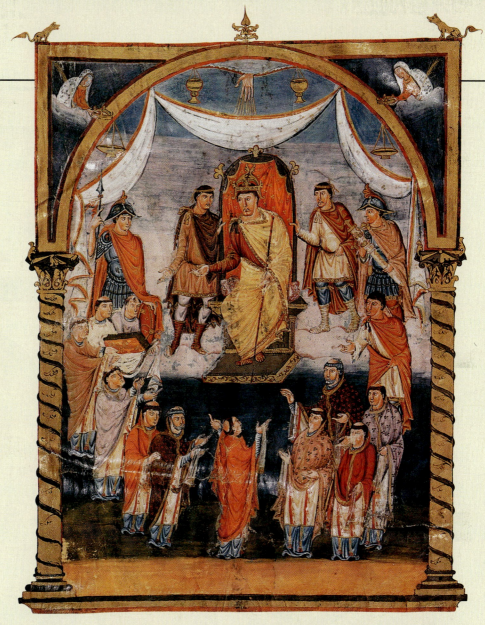

The hand of God blesses Charles the Bald as he receives the Bible, symbolic of his connection with Israelite kings David and Solomon. *(Bibliothèque nationale de France)*

Questions for Analysis

1. Why was the charter drawn up? Why did Charles grant the benefice?

2. Who were the "men living on it," and what economic functions did they perform?

3. What did the joined hands of the prospective vassal and the kiss symbolize?

4. In the oath of fealty, what was meant by the phrase "in my faith"? Why did the vassal swear on relics of the saints? What were these, and why were they used?

5. What does this ceremony tell us about the society that used it?

Source: The History of Feudalism by David Herlihy, ed. Copyright © 1970 by David Herlihy. Reprinted by permission of HarperCollins Publishers, Inc.

In this thirteenth-century manuscript, knights of King Henry II stab Archbishop Thomas Becket in 1170 in Canterbury Cathedral, a dramatic example of church-state conflict. Becket was soon made a saint, and the spot where the murder occurred became a pilgrimage site; it is still a top tourist destination. *(HIP/Art Resource, NY)*

STATE AND CHURCH IN THE HIGH MIDDLE AGES, 1000–1300

chapter preview

Political Revival
- *How did medieval rulers create larger and more stable territories?*

Finance
- *What types of institutions did medieval rulers develop to provide their realms with sufficient taxes and other income?*

Law and Justice
- *How did the administration of law contribute to the development of national states?*

The Papacy
- *How did the papacy attempt to reform the church, and what was the response from other powerful rulers?*

The Crusades
- *How did the motives, course, and consequences of the Crusades reflect and shape developments in Europe?*

The Expansion of Christianity
- *What were the effects of the expansion of Christianity into northern and eastern Europe?*

Beginning in the last half of the tenth century, the invasions that had enhanced European fragmentation gradually ended, and domestic disorder slowly subsided. Feudal rulers began to develop new institutions of government that enabled them to assert their power over lesser lords and the general population. Centralized states slowly crystallized, first in western Europe, and then in eastern and northern Europe as well. At the same time, energetic popes built their power within the Western Christian church and asserted their superiority over kings and emperors. A papal call to retake the holy city of Jerusalem led to nearly two centuries of warfare between Christians and Muslims. Christian warriors, clergy, and settlers moved out in all directions from western and central Europe, so that through conquest and colonization border regions were gradually incorporated into a more uniform European culture.

Political Revival

The eleventh century witnessed the beginnings of new political stability. Rulers in France, England, and Germany worked to reduce private warfare and civil anarchy. Domestic disorder subsided, and external invasions from the Vikings, Muslims, and Magyars (see page 248) gradually declined. In some parts of Europe, lords in control of large territories began to manipulate feudal institutions to build up their power even further, becoming kings over growing and slowly centralizing states.

- *How did medieval rulers create larger and more stable territories?*

Medieval Origins of the Modern State

Rome's great legacy to Western civilization had been the concepts of the state and the law, but for almost five hundred years after the disintegration of the Roman Empire in the West, the state as a reality did not exist. Political authority was completely decentralized. Power was spread among

Online Study Center

This icon will direct you to interactive activities and study materials on the website **college.hmco.com/pic/mckaywest9e**

many lords who gave their localities such protection and security as their strength allowed. The fiefdoms, kingdoms, and territories that covered the continent of early medieval Europe did not have the characteristics or provide the services of a modern state. They did not have jurisdiction over many people, and their laws affected a relative few. There existed many, frequently overlapping layers of authority—earls, counts, barons, knights—between a king and the ordinary people.

In these circumstances, medieval rulers had common goals. The rulers of England, France, and Germany wanted to strengthen and extend royal authority in their territories. They wanted to establish an effective means of communication with all peoples in order to increase public order. They wanted more revenue and efficient bureaucracies. The solutions they found to these problems laid the foundations for modern national states.

The modern state is an organized territory with definite geographical boundaries that are recognized by other states. It has a body of law and institutions of government. The modern national state counts on the loyalty of its citizens, or at least of a majority of them. In return it provides order so that citizens can go about their daily work and other activities. It protects its citizens and their property. The state tries to prevent violence and to apprehend and punish those who commit it. It supplies a currency or medium of exchange that permits financial and commercial transactions. It conducts relations with foreign governments. To accomplish these minimal functions, the state must have officials, bureaucracies, laws, courts of law, soldiers, information, and money. By the twelfth century medieval kingdoms and some lesser lordships possessed these attributes, at least to the extent that most modern states have them.

England

Before the Viking invasions, England had never been united under a single ruler. The victory of the remarkable Alfred, king of the West Saxons (or Wessex), over Guthrun the Dane, a Viking leader, at Edington in 878

The Bayeux Tapestry William's conquest of England was recorded in thread on a narrative embroidery panel measuring 231 feet by 19 inches. In this scene, two nobles and a bishop acclaim Harold Godwinson as king of England. The nobles hold a sword, symbol of military power, and the bishop holds a stole, symbol of clerical power. Harold himself holds a scepter and an orb, both symbols of royal power. The embroidery provides an important historical source for the clothing, armor, and lifestyles of the Norman and Anglo-Saxon warrior class. It eventually ended up in Bayeux in northern France, where it is displayed in a museum today and is incorrectly called a "tapestry," which is a different kind of needlework. *(Tapisserie de Bayeux et avec autorisation spéciale de la Ville de Bayeux)*

inaugurated a great political revival. Alfred and his immediate successors built a system of local defenses and slowly extended royal rule beyond Wessex to other Anglo-Saxon peoples until one law, royal law, took precedence over local custom. England was divided into local units called "shires," or counties, each under the jurisdiction of a shire-reeve (a word that soon evolved into "sheriff") appointed by the king. Sheriffs were unpaid officials from well-off families responsible for collecting taxes, catching and trying criminals, and raising infantry.

This unity did not prevent England from being conquered by the Vikings. In 1013 the Danish ruler Swen Forkbeard invaded England. His son Canute completed the subjugation of the island. King of England (1016–1035) and after 1030 king of Norway as well, Canute made England the center of his empire. He promoted a policy of assimilation and reconciliation between Anglo-Saxons and Vikings. King Edward the Confessor (r. 1042–1066), the son of an Anglo-Saxon father and a Norman mother who had taken Canute as her second husband, personified this assimilation. When Edward died childless, there were a number of claimants to the throne—the Anglo-Saxon noble Harold Godwinson (ca 1022–1066), who had been crowned by English nobles; the Norwegian king Harald III (r. 1045–1066), grandson of Canute; and Duke William of Normandy, who was the illegitimate son of Edward's cousin. Duke William was the descendant of Danish Vikings who had been given territory in northern France as a fief in the tenth century. He united his own vassals against external enemies and began to exert tighter control over them. He required them to personally swear homage, set up specific quotas of knights from every piece of land he distributed, and forbade them to fight with each other or build their own castles.

In 1066 William invaded England with his Norman vassals, met the exhausted forces of Harold, who had just defeated the Norwegians and had marched hundreds of miles to meet the Normans. William defeated them and later became known as William the Conqueror. He further solidified royal power on both sides of the English Channel, limiting the power of both his noble vassals and church officials and transforming the feudal system into a unified monarchy. In England William preserved the Anglo-Saxon institution of having sheriffs represent the king at the local level, but he replaced Anglo-Saxon sheriffs with Normans. He also retained another Anglo-Saxon device, the *writ*. This brief administrative order, written in the Anglo-Saxon vernacular by a government clerk, was the means by which the central government communicated with people at the local level.

Chronology

936–973	Reign of Otto I in Germany
1059	Lateran Council restricts election of the pope to the College of Cardinals
1066	Norman conquest of England
1073–1085	Pontificate of Gregory VII
1095–1291	Crusades
1154–1189	Reign of Henry II of England; revision of legal procedure; beginnings of common law
1162	Thomas Becket named archbishop of Canterbury
1180–1223	Reign of Philip II (Philip Augustus) in France
1198–1216	Innocent III; height of the medieval papacy
1215	Magna Carta
1230s	Papacy creates the Inquisition
1236	Ferdinand of Castile and León captures Córdoba
1290	Jews expelled from England
1306	Jews expelled from France
1397	Queen Margrete establishes Union of Kalmar

William retained Anglo-Saxon institutions that served his purposes and also introduced a major innovation, the Norman inquest. At his Christmas court in 1085, William discussed the state of the kingdom with his vassals and decided to conduct a systematic investigation of the entire country. The survey was to be made by means of *inquests,* or general inquiries, held throughout England. William wanted to determine how much wealth there was in his new kingdom, who held what land, and what land had been disputed among his vassals since the Conquest of 1066. Groups of royal officials were sent to every part of the country. In every village and farm, the priest and six local people were put under oath to answer the questions of the king's commissioners truthfully. In the words of a contemporary chronicler:

He sent his men over all England into every shire and had them find out how many hundred hides there were in the shire [a hide was a measure of land large enough to support

MAP 9.1 The Growth of the Kingdom of France Some scholars believe that Philip II received the title "Augustus" (from a Latin word meaning "to increase") because he vastly expanded the territories of the kingdom of France. The province of Toulouse in the south became part of France as a result of the crusade against the Albigensians (see page 284).

one family], or what land and cattle the king himself had, or what dues he ought to have in twelve months from the shire. Also . . . what or how much everybody had who was occupying land in England, in land or cattle, and how much money it was worth. So very narrowly did he have it investigated, that there was no single hide nor yard of land, nor indeed . . . one ox nor one cow nor one pig was there left out, and not put down in his record: and all these records were brought to him afterwards.[1]

The resulting record, called **Domesday Book** from the Anglo-Saxon word *doom*, meaning "judgment," still survives. It is an invaluable source of social and economic information about medieval England.

Online Study Center **Improve Your Grade**
Primary Source: William the Conqueror and Domesday Book: A Contemporary Description

The Conqueror's scribes compiled *Domesday Book* in less than a year. It provided William and his descendants with information vital for the exploitation and govern-

ment of the country. Knowing the amount of wealth every area possessed, the king could tax accordingly. Knowing the amount of land his vassals had, he could allot knight service fairly. The inclusion of material covering England helped English kings regard their country as one unit.

In 1128 William's granddaughter Matilda was married to Geoffrey of Anjou. Their son, who became Henry II of England and inaugurated the Angevin (from Anjou, his father's county) dynasty, inherited the French provinces of Normandy, Anjou, Maine, and Touraine in northwestern France. When Henry married the great heiress Eleanor of Aquitaine in 1152, he claimed lordship over Aquitaine, Poitou, and Gascony in southwestern France (see Map 9.1). Each of these provinces was separate and was only loosely linked to the others by dynastic law and personal oaths. The histories of England and France in the High Middle Ages were closely intertwined, however, leading to disputes and conflicts down to the fifteenth century.

France

France also became increasingly unified in this era. Following the death of the last Carolingian ruler in 987, an assembly of nobles selected Hugh Capet, head of a powerful clan in the West Frankish kingdom, as his successor. Soon after his own coronation, Hugh crowned his son Robert to ensure the succession and prevent disputes after his death and to weaken the feudal principle of elective kingship. The Capetian kings (so called from the *cope,* or cloak, Hugh wore as abbot of Saint-Denis) subsequently saved France from further division, but this was hardly apparent in 987. Compared with the duke of Normandy, the first rulers of the **Capetian dynasty** were weak. By hanging on to what they had, however, they laid the foundation for later political stability.

This stability came slowly. In the early twelfth century France still consisted of a number of virtually independent provinces. Each was governed by a local ruler; each had its own laws, customs, coinage, and dialect. Unlike the king of England, the king of France had jurisdiction over a very small area. Chroniclers called King Louis VI (r. 1108–1137) *roi de Saint-Denis,* king of Saint-Denis, because the territory he controlled was limited to Paris and the Saint-Denis area surrounding the city (see Map 9.1). This region, called the *Île-de-France,* or royal domain, became the nucleus of the French state. The clear goal of the medieval French king was to increase the royal domain and extend his authority.

The term *Saint-Denis* had political and religious charisma, which the Crown exploited. Following the precedent of the Frankish chieftain Clovis (see page 212), Louis VI and his Capetian successors supported and identified with the cult of Saint Denis, a deeply revered saint whom the French believed protected the country from danger. Under the saint's banner, the *oriflamme,* French kings fought their battles and claimed their victories. The oriflamme rested in the abbey of Saint-Denis, which served as the burial place of the French kings. The Capetian kings identified themselves with the cult of Saint Denis in order to tap popular devotion to him and tie that devotion and loyalty to the monarchy.

The work of unifying France began under Louis VI's grandson Philip II (r. 1180–1223). Rigord, Philip's biographer, gave him the title "Augustus" (from a Latin word meaning "to increase") because he vastly enlarged the territory of the kingdom of France. When King John of England, who was Philip's vassal for the rich province of Normandy, defaulted on his feudal obligation to come to the French court, Philip declared Normandy forfeit to the French crown. He enforced his declaration militarily, and in 1204 Normandy fell to the French. He gained other northern provinces as well, and by the end of his reign Philip was effectively master of northern France.

In the thirteenth century Philip Augustus's descendants acquired important holdings in the south. By the end of the thirteenth century most of the provinces of modern France had been added to the royal domain through diplomacy, marriage, war, and inheritance. The king of France was stronger than any group of nobles who might try to challenge his authority.

Philip Augustus devised a method of governing the provinces and providing for communication between the central government in Paris and local communities. Philip decided that each province would retain its own institutions and laws. But royal agents, called **baillis** in the north and **seneschals** in the south, were sent from Paris into the provinces as the king's official representatives with authority to act for him. Often middle-class lawyers, these men possessed full judicial, financial, and military jurisdiction in their districts. The baillis and seneschals were appointed by, paid by, and responsible to the king. Unlike the English sheriffs, they were never natives of the provinces to which they were assigned, and they could not own land there. This policy reflected the fundamental principle of French administration that royal interests superseded local interests.

Central Europe

In the middle of Europe, the German king Otto I (r. 936–973) defeated many other lords to build up his power. To do this, Otto relied on the church, getting financial support and the bulk of his army from ecclesiastical lands. Otto asserted the right to control ecclesiastical appointments. Before receiving religious consecration and being invested with the staff and ring symbolic of their offices, bishops and abbots had to perform feudal homage for the lands that accompanied the church office. This practice, later known as "lay investiture," created a grave crisis in the eleventh century, as we will see later in this chapter.

Some of our knowledge of Otto derives from *The Deeds of Otto,* a history of his reign in heroic verse written by a nun, Hroswita of Gandersheim (ca 935–ca 1003). A learned poet, she also produced six verse plays, and she is considered the first dramatist writing in Europe after the fall of the Roman Empire.

In 955 Otto I inflicted a crushing defeat on the Magyars in the Battle of Lechfeld (see page 252), which made Otto a great hero to the Germans. He used this victory to have himself crowned emperor in 962 by the pope in

**Christ Enthroned with Saints and the Emperor Otto I
(tenth century)** Between 933 and 973 Emperor Otto I
founded the church of Saint Mauritius in Magdeburg. As a
memorial to the event, Otto commissioned the production of
this ivory plaque showing Christ accepting a model of the
church from the emperor. Ivory was a favorite medium of
Ottonian artists, and squat figures in a simple geometrical
pattern characterize their work. *(The Metropolitan Museum of Art,
Bequest of George Blumenthal, 1941 [41.100.157]. Photograph ©
1986 The Metropolitan Museum of Art)*

Aachen, which had been the capital of the Carolingian
Empire. He chose this site to symbolize his intention to
continue the tradition of Charlemagne and to demonstrate papal support for his rule. It was not exactly clear
what Otto was the emperor *of*, however, though by the
eleventh century people were increasingly using the term
Holy Roman Empire to refer to a loose confederation of
principalities, duchies, cities, bishoprics, and other types
of regional governments stretching from Denmark to
Rome and from Burgundy to Poland.

In this large area of central Europe, unified nation-
states did not develop until the nineteenth century. The
Holy Roman emperors shared power with princes, dukes,
archbishops, counts, bishops, abbots, and cities. The office of emperor remained an elected one, though the

electors included only seven men—four secular rulers of
large territories within the empire and three archbishops.

Between 1000 and 1300, regionally based princely authorities emerged in the larger states in the empire as dynasties that had a strong sense of local identity and traced
their descent through the paternal line. Newly constructed stone castles bearing the family name symbolized the dynasty's power and served as the center of its
lands and rights—that is, of its *Landesherrschaft,* or territorial lordship.

Through most of the first half of the twelfth century,
civil war wracked Germany. When Conrad III died in
1152, the resulting anarchy was so terrible that the electors decided that the only alternative to continued chaos
was the selection of a strong ruler. They chose Frederick
Barbarossa of the house of Hohenstaufen.

Frederick Barbarossa (r. 1152–1190) tried valiantly to
bring peace to the empire, using his family duchy of
Swabia in southwestern Germany as a power base (see
Map 9.2). Like William the Conqueror in England and
Philip in France, Frederick required vassals to take an
oath of allegiance to him as emperor and appointed officials to exercise full imperial authority over local communities. He forbade private warfare, establishing
Landfrieden, sworn peace associations with the princes
of various regions. These peace associations had the judicial authority to punish breaches of the peace and criminals. Penalties for serious crimes, such as incendiary
conduct during a conflict, increased from maiming to execution. Barbarossa and later rulers traveled continually
and extensively, and the royal court could mete out justice anywhere. In general, however, legal jurisdiction in
the Holy Roman Empire was in the hands of local
counts, dukes, margraves, and bishops.

Frederick Barbarossa surrounded himself with men
trained in Roman law (see page 273), and he used Roman law to justify his assertion of imperial rights over the
towns of northern Italy. Between 1154 and 1188 Frederick made six expeditions into Italy. His scorched-earth
policy was successful at first, making for significant conquests in the north. The brutality of his methods, however, provoked revolts, and the Italian cities formed an
alliance with the papacy. In 1176 Frederick suffered a defeat at Legnano (see Map 9.2). This battle marked the
first time a feudal cavalry of armed knights was decisively
defeated by bourgeois infantrymen. Frederick was forced
to recognize the municipal autonomy of the northern
Italian cities. The northern and southern parts of the
Holy Roman Empire remained separate and, unlike England and France, did not become unified states until the

MAP 9.2 The Holy Roman Empire and the Kingdom of Sicily, ca 1200 Frederick Barbarossa greatly expanded the size of the Holy Roman Empire, but it remained a loose collection of various types of governments. The kingdom of Sicily included mainland areas as well as the island in 1200, with an ethnically mixed population ruled by Norman kings.

nineteenth century, when a new wave of centralization led to the formation of Germany and Italy.

The Iberian Peninsula

In the eleventh century divisions and civil war in the caliphate of Córdoba allowed Christian armies to conquer an increasingly large part of the Iberian Peninsula.

Castile, in the north-central part of the peninsula, became the strongest of the growing Christian kingdoms, and Aragon, in the northeast, the second most powerful. In 1085 King Alfonso VI of Castile and León captured Toledo on the Tagus River in central Spain, center of the old Visigothic kingdom. He immediately named Bernard, a monk of Cluny in Burgundy, as archbishop of Toledo. Alfonso, who had married a Frenchwoman, invited French knights to settle in the *meseta,* the central plateau of Spain, a region well suited for sheep farming, viticulture, and cereal agriculture.

The Almoravid dynasty, which ruled much of northwestern Africa, briefly reunified the Muslim state in the late eleventh century, but the Almoravids were themselves conquered by forces of the Almohad dynasty. Alfonso VIII (1158–1214), aided by the kings of Aragon, Navarre, and Portugal, crushed the Almohad-led Muslims at Las Navas de Tolosa in 1212, accelerating the Christian push southward. The kings of Castile, Aragon, and several smaller states established representative assemblies (the *cortes*), which were structured with separate meetings for the clergy, nobility, and urban dwellers. James the Conqueror of Aragon (r. 1213–1276) captured Valencia on the Mediterranean coast in 1233, immediately turning the chief mosque into a cathedral.

In 1236 Ferdinand of Castile and León captured the great Muslim industrial and intellectual center of Córdoba in the heart of Andalusia. The city's mosque became a Christian cathedral, and the city itself served thereafter as the main military base against Granada. When Seville fell to Ferdinand's Castilians in 1248 after a long siege, Christians controlled the entire Iberian Peninsula, save for the small state of Granada (see Map 9.3).

Once in Seville, Ferdinand's heart "was full of joy at the great reward God had given him for his labours. . . . His mother (wanted) to revive the archiepiscopal see which had of old been abandoned, despoiled (by the Muslims) . . . and a worthy foundation was established in honor of Saint Mary."[2] Ferdinand's mother thus inspired the use of the chief mosque as the diocesan cathedral. Just as the Muslims had used the sites of ancient pagan shrines for the erection of their mosques when they

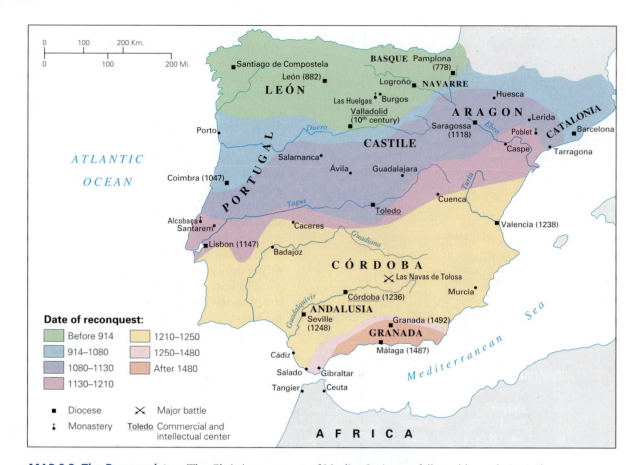

MAP 9.3 The Reconquista The Christian conquest of Muslim Spain was followed by ecclesiastical reorganization, with the establishment of dioceses, monasteries, and the Latin liturgy, which gradually tied the peninsula to the heartland of Christian Europe and to the Roman papacy. *(Source: Adapted from David Nicholas, The Evolution of the Medieval World. Copyright © 1992. Reprinted by permission of Pearson Education Limited.)*

Online Study Center **Improve Your Grade** Interactive Map: Christian Reconquista of Muslim Spain

conquered Spain in the eighth century, so Christians followed suit, and many other mosques throughout Spain were also turned into churches. Since religious buildings serve as windows into the broader culture, with valuable social, intellectual, and economic information, scholars in many fields have deplored this assimilation of mosques to Christian religious use, as it involved the destruction of Muslim art.

Muslim Spain had had more cities than any other country in Europe, and Christian Spain became highly urbanized. Victorious Christian rulers expelled the Muslims and recruited immigrants from France and elsewhere in Iberia. One example was the town of Logroño. King Alfonso VI decreed

that a town should be established there, assembling from all parts of the world burgesses of many different trades . . . Gaston, Bretons, English, Burgundians, Normans, Toulousains, Provençals and Lombards, and many other traders of various nations and foreign tongues; and thus he populated a town of no mean size.[3]

The thirteenth century thus witnessed a huge migration of peoples from the north to the depopulated cities of the central and southern parts of the peninsula.

Fourteenth-century clerical propagandists called the movement to expel the Muslims the **reconquista** (reconquest)—a sacred and patriotic crusade to wrest the country from "alien" Muslim hands. This religious myth

Almohad Banner   This finely worked embroidered banner is typical of Muslim style; it incorporates Arabic lettering on the edges and includes no representation of the human form. The Almohads were a strict Muslim dynasty from North Africa that had ruled about half of Spain in the twelfth century. In 1212 King Alfonso VIII of Castile won a decisive victory over Almohad forces at Las Navas de Tolosa, and Christian holdings in Spain increased. *(Institut Amatller d'Art Hispanic)*

became part of Spanish political culture and of the national psychology. As a consequence of the reconquista, the Spanish and Portuguese learned how to administer vast tracts of newly acquired territory. When, in the sixteenth and seventeenth centuries, they gained overseas empires in the Americas, Africa, and Asia, medieval models guided them. The precedents of medieval Spain were imposed on colonial Mexico, Brazil, Peru, Angola, and the Philippines.

 # Finance

As medieval rulers expanded their territories and extended their authority, they developed institutions to rule more effectively, including an enlarged bureaucracy of officials and larger armies. Officials and armies cost money, and rulers in various countries developed slightly different ways of acquiring more revenue and handling financial matters, some more successful than others.

• *What types of institutions did medieval rulers develop to provide their realms with sufficient taxes and other income?*

England

In England, William the Conqueror's son Henry I (r. 1100–1135) established a bureau of finance called the **Exchequer** (for the checkered cloth at which his officials collected and audited royal accounts), which became the first institution of the government bureaucracy of England. Henry's income came from a variety of sources: from taxes paid by peasants living on the king's estates; from the *Danegeld,* an old tax originally levied to pay tribute to the Danes; from the *dona,* an annual gift from the

The Pipe Rolls Twice yearly English medieval sheriffs appeared before the Barons of the Exchequer to account for the monies they had collected from the royal estates and from fines for civil and criminal offenses. Clerks recorded these revenues and royal expenditures on the pipe rolls, whose name derives from the pipelike form of the rolled parchments. A roll exists for 1129–1130, then continuously from 1156 to 1832, representing the largest series of English public records. *(Crown copyright material in the Public Record Office is reproduced by permission of the Controller of the Britannic Majesty's Stationery Office [E40 1/1565])*

church; from money paid to the Crown for settling disputes; and from fines paid by people found guilty of crimes. Henry also received income because of his position as a feudal lord. If, for example, one of his vassals died and the son wished to inherit the father's properties, the heir had to pay Henry a tax called **relief.** From the knights Henry took **scutage,** money paid in lieu of the performance of military service. With the scutage collected, Henry could hire mercenary troops. The sheriff in each county was responsible for collecting all these sums and paying them to the king's Exchequer twice a year. Henry, like other medieval kings, made no distinction between his private income and state revenues, though the officials of the Exchequer began to keep careful records of the monies paid into and out of the royal treasury.

France

The development of royal financial agencies in most continental countries lagged behind the English Exchequer. Twelfth-century French rulers derived their income from their royal estates in the Île-de-France. As Philip Augustus and his successors added provinces to the royal domain, the need for money became increasingly acute. Philip made the baillis and seneschals responsible for collecting taxes in their districts. This income came primarily from fines and confiscations imposed by the courts.

In the thirteenth century French rulers acquired some income from the church and some from people living in the towns. Townspeople paid **tallage** or the **taille**—a tax arbitrarily laid by the king. In all parts of the country, feudal vassals owed military service to the king when he called for it. Louis IX converted this military obligation into a cash payment, called "host tallage," and thus increased his revenues. Moreover, pervasive anti-Semitism allowed Philip Augustus, Louis VIII, and Louis IX to tax their Jewish subjects mercilessly.

Medieval people believed that a good king lived on the income of his own land and taxed only in time of a grave emergency—that is, a just war. Because the church, and not the state, performed what we call social services—such as education and care of the sick, the aged, and orphaned children—there was no ordinary need for the government to tax. Taxation meant war financing. The French monarchy could not continually justify taxing the people on the grounds of the needs of war. Thus the French kings were slow to develop an efficient bureau of finance. French provincial laws and institutions—in contrast to England's early unification—also retarded the growth of a central financial agency. Not until the fourteenth century, as a result of the Hundred Years' War, did a state financial bureau emerge—the Chamber of Accounts.

Sicily

The one secular government other than England that developed a financial bureaucracy was the kingdom of Sicily. Sicily is a good example of how a strong government could be built on a feudal base by determined rulers. The Sicilian administration came to have a significant Muslim component.

Like England, Sicily had come under Norman domination. Between 1061 and 1091 a bold Norman knight, Roger de Hauteville, and a small band of mercenaries defeated the Muslims and Greeks who controlled the island. Roger then governed a heterogeneous population of Sicilians, Italians, Greeks, Jews, Arabs, and Normans. Like William the Conqueror in England, he introduced Norman institutions in Sicily and made them work as a means of government. Roger distributed scattered fiefs to his followers so no vassal would have a centralized power base. He took an inquest of royal property and rights and forbade private warfare.

To these Norman practices, Roger fused Arabic and Greek governmental devices. For example, he retained the Kalbid Muslims' (previous rulers over Sicily) main financial agency, the **diwān,** a sophisticated bureau for record keeping and administration.

Under his son and heir, Count Roger II (r. 1130–1154), the process of state building continued. Roger II developed diplomatic ties with the Fatimid rulers of Egypt, exchanging letters, gifts, and embassies with the caliph al-Hafid. Because Sicilians and Muslims usually could not read each other's languages, the diwān kept official documents in Greek, Latin, and Arabic. It supervised the royal estates in Sicily, collected revenues, managed the state monopoly of the sale of salt and lumber, and registered all income to the treasury. With revenues derived from those products, Roger hired mercenaries. He encouraged appeals from local courts to his court because such appeals implied respect for the royal court.

Arabic influence in Sicily is also evident in the public presentation, or image, of the king. Following Islamic custom, Roger II became less visible, deliberately secluding himself in his palace at Palermo. On special occasions, he rode out in elegant finery surrounded by retinues of guards, household retainers, and "lords of the diwān," thereby ceremonially displaying himself. Some Christian critics considered this practice evidence of the tyranny of the Norman kings, but an Arabic courtier praised

Roger II because "he followed the way of Muslim rulers. . . . He broke with the custom of the Franks who are not acquainted with such things. . . . He treated the Muslims with respect, took them as his companions, and kept the Franks off (protected) them."[4] In the multicultural society of medieval Sicily, Muslims and Greeks, as well as Normans, staffed the army, the judiciary, and the diwān. Roger's relative seclusion did not keep him from expanding his territory, and in 1137 his forces took the city of Naples and much of the surrounding territory in southern Italy. The entire area came to be known as the kingdom of Sicily (or sometimes the kingdom of the Two Sicilies), and was often caught up in conflicts between the pope, the Holy Roman emperor, and the kings of France and Spain over control of Italy.

Frederick II

Frederick II (r. 1212–1250), grandson of Roger II of Sicily through his mother and grandson of Frederick Barbarossa of Germany through his father, was crowned king of the Germans at Aachen (1216) and Holy Roman emperor at Rome (1220). He concentrated his attention on Sicily. Frederick banned private warfare and placed all castles and towers under royal administration. He also replaced town officials with royal governors and subordinated feudal and ecclesiastical courts to the king's courts. Royal control of the nobility, of the towns, and of the judicial system added up to great centralization, which required a professional bureaucracy and sound state financing.

In 1224 Frederick founded the University of Naples to train officials for his bureaucracy. University-educated administrators and lawyers emphasized the stiff principles of Roman law, such as the maxim of the Justinian *Code* that "what pleases the prince has the force of law." Frederick's financial experts regulated agriculture, public works, and even business. Frederick secured the tacit consent of his people to regular taxation. This was a noteworthy achievement when most people believed that taxes should be levied only in time of grave emergency. Frederick defined emergency broadly. For much of his reign he was involved in a bitter dispute with the papacy, and he used this as a reason to levy taxes. Moreover, he continued the use of Muslim institutions such as the diwān, and he tried to administer justice fairly to all his subjects, declaring, "We cannot in the least permit Jews and Saracens (Muslims) to be defrauded of the power of our protection and to be deprived of all other help, just because the difference of their religious practices makes

Palatine Chapel at Palermo (1132–1140) Muslim crafts-men from Egypt painted the wooden ceiling of the royal chapel for King Roger of Sicily. This section shows the diverse peoples—Jews, Christians, Muslims—who lived in Palermo. *(Burgerbibliothek Bern Cod. 120 II, fol. 98r)*

them hateful to Christians,"[5] implying a degree of toler-ation exceedingly rare at the time.

Frederick's contemporaries called him the "Wonder of the World." He certainly transformed the kingdom of Sicily. But Sicily required constant attention, and Freder-ick's absences on crusade and on campaigns in mainland Italy took their toll. Shortly after he died, the unsuper-vised bureaucracy fell to pieces. The pope, as feudal over-lord of Sicily, called in a French prince to rule.

Frederick showed little interest in the northern part of the Holy Roman Empire. He concentrated his attention on Sicily rather than on the historic Hohenstaufen stronghold of Swabia. When he visited the German parts of the empire in the expectation of securing support for his Italian policy, he made sweeping concessions to the princes, bishops, duchies, and free cities. He exempted German churchmen and lay princes from taxation and from the jurisdiction of imperial authorities. These moves weakened imperial authority, and in the later Mid-dle Ages lay and ecclesiastical princes held sway in the Holy Roman Empire.

Law and Justice

In the early Middle Ages society perceived of major crimes as acts against an individual, and a major crime was settled when the accused made a cash payment to the victim or his or her kindred. In the High Middle Ages suspects were pursued and punished for acting against the *public* interest. Throughout Europe, however, the form and application of laws depended on local and provincial custom and practice. In the twelfth and thir-teenth centuries the law was a hodgepodge of Germanic customs, feudal rights, and provincial practices. Kings in France and England wanted to blend these elements into a uniform system of rules acceptable and applicable to all their peoples. Legal developments in continental coun-tries like France were strongly influenced by Roman law, while England slowly built up a unique unwritten com-mon law.

• *How did the administration of law contribute to the development of national states?*

France and the Holy Roman Empire

The French king Louis IX (r. 1226–1270) was famous in his time for his concern for justice. Each French province, even after being made part of the kingdom of France, retained its unique laws and procedures, but Louis IX created a royal judicial system. He established the Parlement of Paris, a kind of supreme court that wel-comed appeals from local administrators and from the courts of feudal lords throughout France. By the very act of appealing the decisions of feudal courts to the Par-lement of Paris, French people in far-flung provinces were recognizing the superiority of royal justice.

Louis sent royal judges to all parts of the country to check up on the work of the baillis and seneschals and to hear complaints of injustice. He was the first French monarch to publish laws for the entire kingdom. The Parlement of Paris registered (or announced) these laws, which forbade private warfare, judicial duels, gambling, blaspheming, and prostitution. Louis sought to identify justice with the kingship, and gradually royal justice touched all parts of the kingdom.

In the Holy Roman Empire, justice was administered at two levels. The manorial or seigneurial court, presided over by the lay or ecclesiastical lord, dealt with such matters as damage to crops and fields, trespass, boundary disputes, and debt—common conflicts at a time when princes were expanding their colonial jurisdictions over forestland and wasteland and receiving thousands of new settlers. Dukes, counts, margraves, bishops, and abbots possessed an authority called **Landgericht,** or regional magistracies. With this power, the lord's agents, or representatives, dispensed justice in serious criminal cases involving theft, arson, assault with a weapon, rape, and homicide. Regional magistrates held powers of high justice, that is, the right to execute a criminal; the imposition of the death penalty by hanging was the distinctive feature of this court.

Henry II and Thomas Becket

Under Henry II (r. 1154–1189) England developed and extended a **common law,** a law that originated in, and was applied by, the king's court and that in the next two or three centuries became common to the entire country. England was unusual in developing one system of royal courts and one secular law. Henry I had occasionally sent out **circuit judges** (royal officials who traveled a given circuit or district) to hear civil and criminal cases. Every year royal judges left London and set up court in the counties. Wherever the king's judges sat, there sat the king's court.

Henry also improved procedure in criminal justice. In 1166 he instructed the sheriffs to summon local juries to conduct inquests and draw up lists of known or suspected criminals. These lists, or indictments, sworn to by the juries, were to be presented to the royal judges when they arrived in the community. This accusing jury is the ancestor of the modern grand jury. Judges determined guilt or innocence in a number of ways. They heard testimony, sought witnesses, and read written evidence. If these were lacking and if a suspect had a bad public reputation, he or she might be submitted to trial by ordeal. An accused person could be tried by fire or water. In the latter case, the accused was tied hand and foot and dropped in a lake or river. People believed that water was

The Customs of Aragon   This illumination, imitating the style of Parisian court art, shows King James of Aragon (r. 1213–1276) presiding over a law court. King James—called "the Conqueror" because of his victories over Catalonia, Valencia, and Majorca—ordered several codifications of law. The most important of these, the Customs of Aragon (1247), drew on Roman canonical practice for legal procedures. *(Initial N: King James I of Aragon Overseeing Court of Law Vidal Mayor, 83.MQ.165, fol. 72v. © The J. Paul Getty Museum, Los Angeles)*

a pure substance and would reject anything foul or unclean. Thus a person who sank was considered innocent; a person who floated was found guilty. Trial by ordeal was a ritual that appealed to the supernatural for judgment. God determined guilt or innocence, and thus a priest had to be present to bless the water.

Henry II disliked ordeal, and it was used less during his reign than it was on the continent. Gradually, in the course of the thirteenth century, the king's judges adopted the practice of calling on twelve people (other than the accusing jury) to consider the question of innocence or guilt. This became the jury of trial, but it was very slowly accepted because medieval people had more confidence in the judgment of God than in the judgment of twelve ordinary people.

One aspect of Henry's judicial reforms encountered stiff resistance from an unexpected source: the friend and former chief adviser whom Henry had made archbishop of Canterbury—Thomas Becket. Henry selected Becket as archbishop in 1162 because he believed he could depend on Becket's support. But when Henry wanted to bring all persons in the kingdom under the jurisdiction of the royal courts, Becket's opposition led to a dramatic conflict between temporal and spiritual powers.

In the 1160s many literate people accused of crimes claimed "benefit of clergy" even though they were not clerics and often had no intention of being ordained. An accused person proved he was a cleric by his ability to read. (Later, university students and merchants—who had to keep records—could claim it.) After the courts established the practice of opening the Bible to the Fiftieth Psalm and asking the accused to read, they found that criminals had memorized the passage. Benefit of clergy gave the accused the right to be tried in church courts, which meted out mild punishments. A person found guilty in the king's court might suffer mutilation—loss of a hand or foot or castration—or even death. Ecclesiastical punishments tended to be an obligation to say certain prayers or to make a pilgrimage.

In 1164 Henry II insisted that everyone, including clerics, be subject to the royal courts. Becket vigorously protested that church law required clerics to be subject to church courts. When Becket proceeded to excommunicate one of the king's vassals, the issue became more complicated. Because no one was supposed to have any contact with an excommunicated person, it appeared that the church could arbitrarily deprive the king of necessary military forces. The disagreement between Henry II and Becket dragged on for years. The king grew increasingly bitter that his appointment of Becket had proved to be such a mistake. Late in December 1170, in a fit of rage, Henry expressed the wish that Becket be destroyed. Four knights took the king at his word. They rode to Canterbury Cathedral and, as the archbishop was leaving evening services, slashed off the crown of his head and scattered his brains on the pavement.

What Thomas Becket could not achieve in life, he gained in death. The assassination of an archbishop turned public opinion in England and throughout western Europe against the king. Miracles were recorded at Becket's tomb; Becket was made a saint; and in a short time Canterbury Cathedral became a major pilgrimage and tourist site. Henry had to back down. He did public penance for the murder and gave up his attempts to bring clerics under the authority of the royal court.

King John and Magna Carta

Henry II's sons Richard I, known as Lion-Hearted (r. 1189–1199), and John (r. 1199–1216) lacked their father's interest in the work of government. Richard looked on England as a source of revenue for his military enterprises. Soon after his accession, he departed on crusade to the Holy Land. During his reign he spent only six months in England, and the government was run by ministers trained under Henry II.

John's basic problems were financial. King John inherited a heavy debt from his father and brother. The country had paid dearly for Richard's crusading zeal. While returning from the Holy Land, Richard had been captured, and England had paid an enormous ransom—much of it in wool, England's primary export—to secure his release. Further, during the entire period of 1180–1220, England experienced severe inflation, which drove prices up. In 1204 John lost the rich province of Normandy to Philip Augustus of France and then spent the rest of his reign trying to get it back. John took scutage, and each time increased the amount due. He forced widows to pay exorbitant fines to avoid unwanted marriages. He sold young girls who were his feudal wards to the highest bidder. These actions antagonized the nobility.

John also alienated the church and the English townspeople. He rejected the pope's nominee to be archbishop of Canterbury. And he infuriated the burghers of the towns by extorting money from them and threatening to revoke their charters of self-government.

All the money John raised did not bring him success. In July 1214 John's coalition of Flemish, German, and English cavalry suffered a severe defeat at the hands of Philip Augustus of France at Bouvines in Flanders. This battle ended English hopes for the recovery of territories from France and also strengthened the barons' opposition to John. His ineptitude as a soldier in a society that idealized military glory was the final straw. Rebellion begun by northern barons eventually grew to involve many members of the English nobility, including the archbishop of Canterbury and the earl of Pembroke, the leading ecclesiastical and lay peers. After lengthy negotiations, John met the barons in 1215 at Runnymede, a meadow along the Thames River. There he was forced to approve and to attach his seal to the peace treaty called **Magna Carta,** "Magna" (great or large) because it was so long and detailed.

For contemporaries, Magna Carta was intended to redress the grievances that particular groups—the barons, the clergy, the merchants of London—had against King John. Charters were not unusual: many kings and lords at the time issued them and then sometimes revoked them, as John did almost immediately. This revocation was largely ignored, however, and every English king un-

Thieves Plunder Saint Edmund's Chapel This eleventh-century painting shows thieves searching for jewelry and rich burial fabrics and even pulling the iron nails out of the wooden structure. They are also trying to dig up the coffin of Saint Edmund, the king of East Anglia (r. 841–869), who was defeated in battle and executed by Danish invaders and whose bones could be sold as relics. Crime and violence preoccupied secular and religious authorities alike. *(Pierpont Morgan Library/ Art Resource, NY)*

til 1485 reissued Magna Carta as evidence of his promise to observe the law. Thus this charter alone acquired enduring importance. It came to signify the principle that everyone, including the king and the government, must obey the law.

Online Study Center Improve Your Grade
Primary Source: Magna Carta: The Great Charter of Liberties

Although legal scholars coined the phrase "rule of law" only in the late nineteenth century, in the later Mid-

dle Ages references to Magna Carta underlined the old Augustinian theory that a government, to be legitimate, must promote law, order, and justice. As the royal justice Henry of Bracton (d. 1268) put it, the English shall be *"Non sub homine sed sub Deo et lege"* (Not under man but under God and the law), a maxim that today appears over the entrance to Harvard Law School. Thus an English king may not disregard or arbitrarily suspend the law to suit his convenience. Drawn up initially to protect baronial interests, Magna Carta was used in later centuries to protect the interests of widows, orphans, townspeople, freemen, and the church. For example, Chapter 39 states, "No freeman shall be captured or imprisoned or disseised (dispossessed) or outlawed or exiled or in any way destroyed, nor will we go against him or send against him, except by the lawful judgment of his peers or by the law of the land." This statement contains the germ of the idea of "due process of law," meaning that a person has the right to be heard and defended in court and is entitled to the protection of the law. Because later generations referred to Magna Carta as a written statement of English liberties, it gradually came to have an almost sacred importance as a guarantee of law and justice.

In the thirteenth century the judicial precedents set under Henry II slowly evolved into permanent institutions. The king's judges asserted the royal authority and applied the same principles everywhere in the country. English people found the king's justice more rational and evenhanded than the justice meted out in the baronial courts. Respect for the king's law and courts promoted loyalty to the Crown. By the time of Henry's great-grandson Edward I (r. 1272–1307), one law, the common law, operated all over England.

Common Law and Roman Law

In the later Middle Ages the English common law developed features that differed strikingly from the system of Roman law operative in continental Europe. The common law relied on **precedent:** a decision in an important case served as an authority for deciding similar cases. By contrast, continental judges, trained in Roman law, used the fixed legal maxims of the Justinian *Code* (see page 191) to decide their cases. Thus the common-law system evolved according to the changing experience of the people, while the Roman-law tradition tended toward a more rigid or static approach. In countries influenced by the common law, such as Canada and the United States, the court is open to the public; in countries with Roman-law traditions, such as France and the Latin American nations, courts need not be public. Under the common law, people accused in criminal cases have the right to access to the evidence against them; under the other system, they do not. The common law urges judges to be impartial; in the Roman-law system, judges interfere freely in activities in their courtrooms. Finally, whereas torture is foreign to the common-law tradition, it was once widely used in the Roman legal system as a method of securing evidence or proof.

The extension of law and justice led to a phenomenal amount of legal codification all over Europe. For example, the English judge Henry of Bracton wrote *Treatise on the Laws and Customs of England*. Legal texts and encyclopedias exalted royal authority, consolidated royal power, and emphasized political and social uniformity.

The Peace of God

Along with the courts, the church also worked to promote peace. Petty crimes proved most destructive of order and stability. Attacks on churches for the ceremonial vessels and sacred objects; assaults on traveling priests, monks, and merchants for the money or goods they might be carrying; seizure of peasants' livestock and extortion through threats of burning their crops and homes; and kidnapping rustics and holding them for ransom—these kinds of violent acts were endemic across western Europe. The church had always preached peace; in the late tenth and early eleventh centuries it began to do something about it.

At a series of church councils (assemblies of bishops and abbots) in central France, where the violence was the worst, the bishops took action. Councils formed peace associations—groups of men in particular districts who assessed themselves and used the money to provide armed protection against thuggish lords. The councils also published decrees forbidding attacks on peasants, clerics, and merchants and prohibiting the destruction of crops and unfortified places under penalty of total exclusion from the Christian community. These measures had some success in reducing the violence of minor feudal lords, but not in stopping great barons from private warfare.

Another ecclesiastical effort, the Truce of God, had less impact. In this movement churchmen tried to reduce the amount of warfare by limiting the number of days on which fighting was permitted. Sundays, special feast days, and the seasons of Lent and Advent were to be free of fighting. If all the forbidden days had been observed, fighting would have been permissible only eighty days of

the year. Nobles and kings did not take the Truce of God very seriously, however, and it remained simply an ideal.

The Papacy

Kings and emperors were not the only rulers consolidating their power in the High Middle Ages. During the ninth and tenth centuries the church came under the control of kings and feudal lords, who chose priests and bishops in their territories, granting them fiefs and expecting loyalty and service in return. Popes were chosen by wealthy Roman families from among their members, and after gaining the papal office they paid more attention to their family political fortunes than to the institutional or spiritual health of the church. Church offices from village priest to pope were sources of income as well as positions of authority. They brought with them the right to collect taxes and fees and often the profits from land under the officeholder's control. They were thus sometimes sold outright—a practice called **simony,** after Simon Magus, a wealthy man mentioned in the New Testament who wanted to buy his way into Heaven. Not surprisingly, clergy at all levels who had bought their positions or had been granted them for political reasons provided little spiritual guidance, and their personal lives were rarely models of high moral standards.

Under the leadership of a series of reforming popes in the eleventh century, the church tried to correct some of these problems, though reforms were not always welcome.

● *How did the papacy attempt to reform the church, and what was the response from other powerful rulers?*

The Gregorian Reforms

The papal reform movement of the eleventh century is frequently called the Gregorian reform movement, after Pope Gregory VII (1073–1085), its most prominent advocate. Serious efforts at reform actually began somewhat earlier, under Pope Leo IX (1049–1054).

During the ninth and tenth centuries the papacy provided little leadership to the Christian peoples of western Europe. Factions in Rome sought to control the papacy for their own material gain. Popes were appointed to advance the political ambitions of their families—the great aristocratic families of the city—and not because of special spiritual qualifications. A combination of political machinations and sexual immorality damaged the pa-

Emperor Otto III Handing a Staff to Archbishop Adalbert of Prague (tenth century)   The staff, or crozier, symbolized a bishop's spiritual authority. Receiving the staff from the emperor gave the appearance that the bishop gained his spiritual rights from the secular power. Pope Gregory VII vigorously objected to this practice. *(Bildarchiv Marburg/Art Resource, NY)*

pacy's moral prestige. For example, Pope John XII (955–963) was appointed pope by his powerful father when he was only eighteen, and lacking interest in spiritual matters he concentrated on expanding papal territories.

At the local parish level, there were many married priests. Taking Christ as the model for the priestly life, the Roman church had always encouraged clerical celibacy, and celibacy had been an obligation for ordination since the fourth century. But in the tenth and eleventh centuries probably a majority of European priests were married or living with women, and in some cases they were handing down church positions and property to their children.

Leo and his successors believed that lay control was largely responsible for the church's problems, so they proclaimed the church independent from secular rulers. At a church council held in the ancient church of Saint John Lateran in 1059, representatives decided on a new method of electing the pope that would remove the influence of Roman aristocratic factions and make papal elections independent of imperial influences. Since the

eighth century the priests of the major churches in and around Rome had constituted a special group, called a "college," that advised the pope when he summoned them to meetings. These chief priests were called "cardinals," from the Latin *cardo,* meaning "hinge." The cardinals were the hinges on which the church turned. The Lateran Council of 1059 decreed that the authority and power to elect the pope rested solely in this **college of cardinals.** The college retains that power today. In the Middle Ages the college of cardinals numbered around twenty-five or thirty, most of them from Italy. In 1586 the figure was set at seventy, though today it is much larger, with cardinals from around the world. (At the death of Pope John Paul II in 2005, there were 183 cardinals, 117 of whom were under age eighty and so could vote for the next pope; this age limit on voting was set in 1975.) When the office of pope was vacant, the cardinals were responsible for governing the church.

While reform began long before Gregory's pontificate and continued after it, Gregory VII was the first pope to emphasize the *political* authority of the papacy. His belief that kings had failed to promote reform in the church prompted him to claim an active role in the politics of Western Christendom. He believed that the pope, as the successor of Saint Peter, was the vicar of God on earth and that papal orders were the orders of God. Gregory was particularly opposed to **lay investiture**—the selection and appointment of church officials by secular authority, often symbolized by laymen giving bishops and abbots their symbols of office, such as a staff and ring. In February 1075 Pope Gregory held a council at Rome that decreed that clerics who accepted investiture from laymen were to be deposed, and laymen who invested clerics were to be *excommunicated* (cut off from the sacraments and all Christian worship).

The church's penalty of **excommunication** relied for its effectiveness on public opinion. Gregory believed that the strong support he enjoyed for his *moral* reforms would carry over to his political ones; he thought that excommunication would compel rulers to abide by his changes. Immediately, however, Henry IV in the empire, William the Conqueror in England (see page 261), and Philip I in France protested.

Why did the issue of lay investiture provoke the wrath of kings? Any institution or organization needs a bureaucracy or administration to function. In the late eleventh century virtually the only people who could read and write were monks and priests. Therefore, kings appointed monks and clerics as their administrators, and they felt that it was perfectly appropriate to choose the men they wished. Because these men were also church officials, rulers used the income from church offices, bishoprics, and abbacies to provide their incomes. From the perspective of a king or emperor, this practice had the merit of financial prudence and had long stood the test of time. Gregory VII's condemnation of lay investiture, which denounced lay appointments and using church income to support royal officials, seemed revolutionary.

The struggle against lay investiture had the effect of emphasizing the distinction between priests and laypeople. For many centuries most monks had not been priests, but in the twelfth century increasing numbers of monks were ordained priests. Women could not be ordained, however. Thus the Gregorian reform movement, in building a strict hierarchical church structure and in subjecting all houses of monks and nuns to the bishop's authority, gave female monasticism a secondary status. Church councils in the eleventh and twelfth centuries forbade monks and nuns to sing church services together and ordered priests to limit their visits to convents,

heightening the sense that contact with nuns should be viewed with suspicion and avoided when possible. Church reformers put a greater emphasis on clerical celibacy and chastity. As part of these measures, in 1298 in the papal decree *Periculoso* Pope Boniface VIII ordered all female religious to be strictly **cloistered,** that is, that the nuns remain permanently inside the walls of the convent and that visits with those from outside the house, including family members, be limited. *Periculoso* was not enforced everywhere, but it did mean that convents became more cut off from medieval society. People also gave more donations to male monastic houses where monks who had been ordained as priests could say memorial masses, and fewer to women's houses, many of which became impoverished.

Emperor Versus Pope

The strongest reaction to Gregory's moves came from the Holy Roman Empire. The emperor Henry IV had supported the moral aspects of church reform within the empire, but, like most rulers, he selected and invested most high church officials. In two basic ways, however, the relationship of the emperors to the papacy differed from that of other monarchs: the pope crowned the emperor, and both the empire and the Papal States claimed northern Italy. Since the time of Charlemagne (see page 235), the emperor had controlled some territory and bishops in Italy.

An increasingly bitter exchange of letters between emperor and pope ensued. Gregory accused Henry of lack of respect for the papacy and insisted that disobedience to the pope was disobedience to God. Henry protested in a now-famous letter beginning "Henry King not by usurpation, but by the pious ordination of God, to Hildebrand, now not Pope, but false monk." Henry went on to argue that Gregory's type of reform undermined royal authority and that the pope "was determined to rob me of my soul and my kingdom or die in the attempt."[6]

Online Study Center **Improve Your Grade**
Primary Source: The Investiture Controversy Begins: Mutual Recriminations

Within the empire, those who had the most to gain from the dispute quickly took advantage of it. In January 1076 many of the German bishops who had been invested by Henry withdrew their allegiance from the pope. Gregory replied by excommunicating them and suspending Henry from the emperorship. The lay nobility delighted in the bind the emperor had been put in: with Henry IV excommunicated and cast outside the Christian fold, they did not have to obey him and could advance their own interests. Powerful nobles invited the pope to come to Germany to settle their dispute with Henry. Gregory hastened to support them. The Christmas season of 1076 witnessed an ironic situation in Germany: the clergy supported the emperor, while the great nobility favored the pope.

Henry outwitted the pope. Crossing the Alps in January 1077, he approached the castle of Countess Matilda of Tuscany, where the pope was staying. According to legend, Henry stood for three days in the snow seeking forgiveness. As a priest, Pope Gregory was obliged to grant absolution and to readmit the emperor to the Christian community. Some historians claim that this marked the peak of papal power because the most powerful ruler in Europe, the emperor, had bowed before the pope. Actually, Henry scored a temporary victory. When the sentence of excommunication was lifted, Henry regained the emperorship and authority over his rebellious subjects. But in the long run, in Germany and elsewhere, secular rulers were reluctant to pose a serious challenge to the papacy for the next two hundred years.

In Germany the controversy over lay investiture and the position of the king in Christian society continued. In 1080 Gregory VII again excommunicated and deposed the emperor. In return, Henry invaded Italy, captured Rome, and controlled the city when Gregory died in 1085. But Henry won no lasting victory. Gregory's successors encouraged Henry's sons to revolt against their father. With lay investiture the ostensible issue, the conflict between the papacy and the successors of Henry IV continued into the twelfth century.

Finally, in 1122 at a conference held at Worms, the issue was settled by compromise. Bishops were to be chosen according to canon law—that is, by the clergy—in the presence of the emperor or his delegate. The emperor surrendered the right of investing bishops with the ring and staff. But since lay rulers were permitted to be present at ecclesiastical elections and to accept or refuse feudal homage from the new prelates, they still possessed an effective veto over ecclesiastical appointments. Papal power was enhanced, but neither side won a clear victory.

The long controversy had tremendous social and political consequences in Germany. For half a century, between 1075 and 1125, civil war was chronic in the empire. The lengthy struggle between papacy and emperor allowed emerging noble dynasties to enhance their position. To control their lands, the great lords built cas-

Countess Matilda A staunch supporter of the reforming ideals of the papacy, Countess Matilda (ca 1046–1115) planned this dramatic meeting at her castle at Canossa in the Apennines. The arrangement of the figures—King Henry kneeling, Abbot Hugh of Cluny lecturing, and Matilda persuading—suggests contemporary understanding of the scene in which Henry received absolution. Matilda's vast estates in northern Italy and her political contacts in Rome made her a person of considerable influence in the late eleventh century. (*Biblioteca Apostolica Vaticana*)

tles, symbolizing their increased power and growing independence. (In no European country do more castles survive today.) The castles were both military strongholds and centers of administration for the surrounding territories. The German high aristocracy subordinated the knights, enhanced restrictions on peasants, and compelled Henry IV and Henry V to surrender certain rights and privileges. When the papal-imperial conflict ended in 1122, the nobility held the balance of power in Germany, and later German kings, such as Frederick Barbarossa (see page 264), would fail in their efforts to strengthen the monarchy against the princely families.

For these reasons, particularism, localism, and feudal independence characterized the Holy Roman Empire in the High Middle Ages. The investiture controversy had a catastrophic effect there.

The Papal Curia

In the late eleventh century and throughout the twelfth, the papacy pressed Gregory's campaign for reform of the church. The popes held a series of councils that met in the papal palace of the Lateran in Rome and that ratified the decisions made at the meeting in Worms ending lay investiture, ordered bishops to live less extravagantly, and passed other measures designed to make procedures more uniform. These Lateran councils passed a series of measures against clerical marriage and concubinage, ordering married priests to give up their wives and children or face dismissal. Most apparently obeyed, though we have little information on what happened to these families.

Pope Urban II laid the foundations for the papal monarchy by reorganizing the central government of the Roman church, the papal writing office (the chancery), and papal finances. He recognized the college of cardinals as a definite consultative body. These agencies, together with the papal chapel, constituted the papal court, or **curia Romana (Roman curia)**—the papacy's administrative bureaucracy and its court of law. The papal curia, although not fully developed until the mid-twelfth century, was the first well-organized institution of monarchical authority in medieval Europe.

The Roman curia had its greatest impact as a court of law. As the highest ecclesiastical tribunal, it formulated church law, termed **canon law,** for all of Christendom. The curia sent legates to hold councils in various parts of Europe. Councils published decrees and sought to enforce the law. When individuals in any part of Christian Europe felt they were being denied justice in their local church courts, they could appeal to Rome. In the High Middle Ages, slowly but surely, the papal curia developed into the court of final appeal for all of Christian Europe.

What kinds of appeals came to the Roman curia? The majority of cases related to disputes over church property or ecclesiastical elections and above all to questions of marriage and annulment. Since the fourth century Christian values had influenced the administration of the law, and bishops frequently sat in courts that heard marriage cases. Beginning in the tenth and eleventh centuries church officials began to claim that they had exclusive jurisdiction over marriage. Appeals to an ecclesiastical tribunal, rather than to a civil court, or appeals from a civil court to a church court implied the acceptance of the latter's jurisdiction. Moreover, most of the popes in the twelfth and thirteenth centuries were canon lawyers who pressed the authority of church courts.

Innocent III and His Successors

The most famous of the lawyer-popes was Innocent III (1198–1216), who became the most powerful pope in history. During his pontificate the church in Rome declared itself to be supreme, united and "catholic" (worldwide), responsible for the earthly well-being and eternal salvation of all citizens of Christendom. Innocent pushed the kings of France, Portugal, and England to do his will, compelling King Philip Augustus of France to take back his wife, Ingeborg of Denmark. He forced King John of England to accept as archbishop of Canterbury a man John did not want.

Innocent called the fourth Lateran Council in 1215, which affirmed the idea that ordained priests had the power to transform bread and wine during church ceremonies into the body and blood of Christ (a change termed "transubstantiation"). This power was possessed by no other group in society, not even kings. According to papal doctrine, priests now had the power to mediate for everyone with God, which set the spiritual hierarchy of the church above the secular hierarchies of kings and other rulers. The council also affirmed that Christians should confess their sins to a priest at least once a year and ordered Jews and Muslims to wear special clothing that set them apart from Christians.

By the early thirteenth century papal efforts at reform begun more than a century earlier had attained phenomenal success. Yet the seeds of future difficulties were being planted. As the volume of appeals to Rome multiplied, so did the size of the papal bureaucracy. As the number of lawyers increased, so did concern for legal niceties and technicalities, fees, and church offices. Nevertheless, the power of the curia continued to grow, as did its bureaucracy.

Thirteenth-century popes devoted their attention to the bureaucracy and to their conflicts with the German emperor Frederick II. Some, like Gregory IX (1227–1241), abused their prerogatives to such an extent that their moral impact was seriously weakened. Even worse, Innocent IV (1243–1254) used secular weapons, including military force, to maintain his leadership. These popes badly damaged papal prestige and influence. By the early fourteenth century the seeds of disorder would grow into a vast and sprawling tree, and once again cries for reform would be heard.

The Crusades

The Crusades of the eleventh and twelfth centuries were the most obvious manifestation of the papal claim to the leadership of Christian society. The **Crusades** were wars sponsored by the papacy for the recovery of the holy city of Jerusalem from the Muslims. The enormous popular response to papal calls for crusading reveals the influence of the reformed papacy. The Crusades also reflect the church's new understanding of the noble warrior class, for whom war against the church's enemies was understood as a religious duty. The word *crusade* was not actually used at the time and did not appear in English until the late sixteenth century. It means literally "taking the cross," from the cross that soldiers sewed on their garments as a Christian symbol. At the time people going off to fight simply said they were taking "the way of the cross" or "the road to Jerusalem."

Though the reconquista in Spain (see page 266) did not directly inspire the Crusades to the Middle East, the pope did sponsor groups of soldiers in this campaign as well as in the Norman campaign against the Muslims in Sicily. In both campaigns Pope Gregory VII asserted that any land conquered from the Muslims belonged to the papacy because it had been a territory held by "infidels," the word meaning unbeliever that Christians and Muslims both used to describe the other. Thus these earlier wars set a pattern for the centuries-long Crusades.

- *How did the motives, course, and consequences of the Crusades reflect and shape developments in Europe?*

Background

The Roman papacy had been involved in the bitter struggle over church reform and lay investiture with the German emperors. If the pope could muster a large army against the enemies of Christianity, his claim to be leader of Christian society in the West would be strengthened. Moreover, in 1054 a serious theological disagreement had split the Greek church of Byzantium and the Roman church of the West. The pope and the patriarch of Constantinople excommunicated each other and declared the beliefs of the other to be "anathema," that is, totally unacceptable for Christians. The pope believed that a crusade would lead to strong Roman influence in Greek territories and eventually the reunion of the two churches.

In 1071 Turkish soldiers defeated a Greek army at Manzikert in eastern Anatolia and occupied much of Asia Minor (see Map 9.4). The emperor at Constantinople appealed to the West for support. Shortly afterward the holy city of Jerusalem fell to the Turks. Pilgrimages to holy places in the Middle East became very dangerous, and the papacy claimed to be outraged that the holy city was in the hands of unbelievers. Since the Muslims had held Palestine since the eighth century, the papacy actually feared that the Seljuk Turks would be less accommodating to Christian pilgrims than the Muslim rulers had been.

In 1095 Pope Urban II journeyed to Clermont in France and on November 27 called for a great Christian holy war against the infidels. Urban's appeal at Clermont represents his policy of *rapprochement,* or reconciliation, with Byzantium, with church union his ultimate goal. (Mutual ill will, quarrels, and the plundering of Byzantine property by undisciplined Westerners were to frustrate this hope.) He urged Christian knights who had been fighting one another to direct their energies against the true enemies of God, the Muslims. Urban proclaimed an **indulgence,** or remission of the temporal penalties imposed by the church for sin, to those who would fight for and regain the holy city of Jerusalem.

Online Study Center **Improve Your Grade**
Primary Source: Call for Crusade: Urban II at the Council of Clermont

Godfrey of Bouillon, Raymond of Toulouse, and other great lords from northern France immediately had the cross of the Crusader sewn on their tunics. Encouraged by popular preachers such as Peter the Hermit and by papal legates in Germany, Italy, and England, thousands of people of all classes joined the crusade. Although most of the Crusaders were French, pilgrims from many regions streamed southward from the Rhineland, through Germany and the Balkans. Of all of the developments of the High Middle Ages, none better reveals Europeans' religious and emotional fervor and the influence of the reformed papacy than the extraordinary outpouring of support for the First Crusade. (See the feature "Listening to the Past: An Arab View of the Crusades" on pages 292–293.)

Motives and Course of the Crusades

Religious convictions inspired many Crusaders, but for the curious and the adventurous the Crusades offered foreign travel and excitement. It provided kings, who were trying to establish order and build states, with the perfect opportunity to get rid of troublemaking knights. It gave land-hungry younger sons a chance to acquire

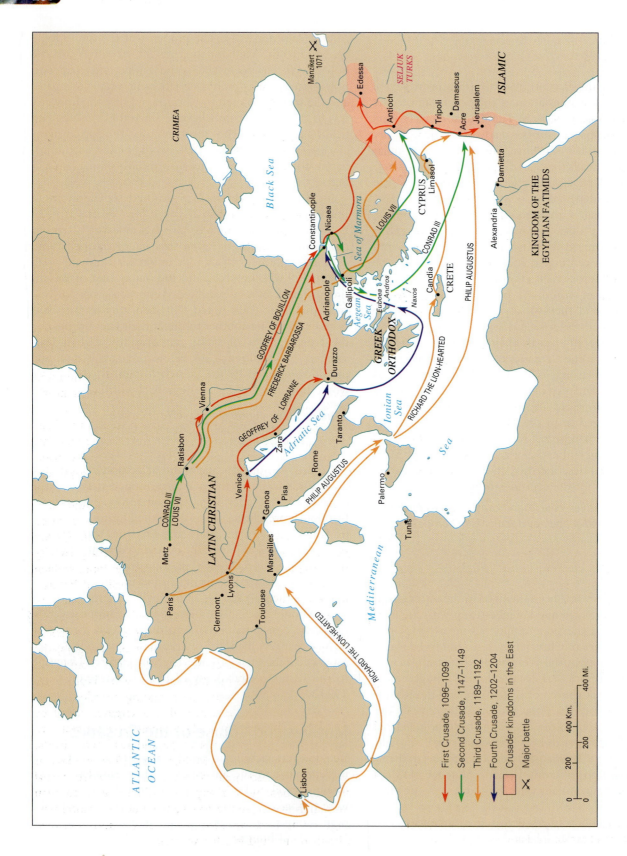

Manzikert 1071

Edessa

SELJUK TURKS

Antioch

Damascus

ISLAMIC

Tripoli

Acre

Jerusalem

Damietta

KINGDOM OF THE EGYPTIAN FATIMIDS

Alexandria

CRIMEA

Black Sea

Constantinople

Nicaea

Sea of Marmora

LOUIS VII

CYPRUS

Limasol

Adrianople

GODFREY OF BOUILLON

GREEK ORTHODOX

Gallipoli

Aegean Sea

Euboea

Andros

Naxos

Candia

CRETE

CONRAD III

PHILIP AUGUSTUS

Durazzo

FREDERICK BARBAROSSA

Vienna

RICHARD THE LION-HEARTED

Ratisbon

GEOFFREY OF LORRAINE

Ionian Sea

Zara

Adriatic Sea

Taranto

Venice

CONRAD III
LOUIS VII

Genoa

Pisa

Rome

PHILIP AUGUSTUS

Palermo

LATIN CHRISTIAN

Metz

Marseilles

Lyons

Paris

Clermont

Toulouse

Tunis

Mediterranean

RICHARD THE LION-HEARTED

ATLANTIC OCEAN

Lisbon

First Crusade, 1096–1099
Second Crusade, 1147–1149
Third Crusade, 1189–1192
Fourth Crusade, 1202–1204
Crusader kingdoms in the East
Major battle

400 Mi.
400 Km.
200
200
0
0

fiefs in the Middle East. Even some members of the middle class who stayed at home profited from the Crusades. Nobles often had to borrow money from the burghers to pay for their expeditions, and they put up part of their land as security. If a noble did not return home or could not pay the interest on the loan, the middle-class creditor took over the land.

The Crusades also brought latent Christian prejudice against the Jews to the surface. Between the sixth and tenth centuries descendants of **Sephardic** (from the modern Hebrew word *Separaddi,* meaning "Spanish" or "Portuguese") **Jews** had settled along the trade routes of western Europe; northern European Jews, those living north of the Alps, later came to be called **Ashkenazi.** In the eleventh century Jews played a major role in the international trade between the Muslim Middle East and the West. Jews also lent money to peasants, townspeople, and nobles. When the First Crusade was launched, many poor knights had to borrow from Jews to equip themselves for the expedition. Debt bred resentment. (See the feature "Individuals in Society: The Jews of Speyer: A Collective Biography.")

The First Crusade was successful, mostly because of the dynamic enthusiasm of the participants. The Crusaders had little more than religious zeal. They knew nothing about the geography or climate of the Middle East. Although there were several counts with military experience among the host, the Crusaders could never agree on a leader, and the entire expedition was marked by disputes among the great lords. Lines of supply were never set up. Starvation and disease wracked the army, and the Turks slaughtered hundreds of noncombatants. Nevertheless, convinced that "God wills it," the war cry of the Crusaders, the army pressed on, defeating the Turks in several land battles and besieging a few larger towns. Finally in 1099, after they had been on their way for three years, they reached Jerusalem, and after a month-long siege they got inside the city, where they slaugh-

tered the Muslim defenders. Fulcher of Chartres, a chaplain on the First Crusade, commented, "If you had been there your feet would have been stained to the ankles in the blood of the slain. What shall I say? None of them were left alive. Neither women nor children were spared."[7]

With Jerusalem taken, many Crusaders regarded their mission accomplished, and they set off for home again. Only the appearance of Egyptian troops convinced them that they needed to stay, and slowly institutions were set up to rule territories and the Muslim population. Four small "Crusader states"—Jerusalem, Edessa, Tripoli, and Antioch—were established; castles and fortified towns were built to defend against Muslim reconquest (see Map 9.4). Reinforcements arrived in the form of pilgrims and fighters from Europe, so that there was constant coming and going by land and more often by sea after the Crusaders conquered port cities such as Acre. Between 1096 and 1270 the crusading ideal was expressed in eight papally approved expeditions to the East, though none after the First Crusade accomplished very much. Despite this lack of success, for roughly two hundred years members of noble families in Europe went nearly every generation.

Women from all walks of life participated in the Crusades. Because of the chroniclers' belief that the *fragilitas sexus* ("weaker sex") was unfit for arms and the chroniclers' aristocratic bias, we know more about royal and noble women than about others. After her husband King Fulk died, Queen Melisande ruled the Latin kingdom of Jerusalem. When King Louis IX of France was captured on the Seventh Crusade (1248–1254), his wife Queen Marguerite negotiated the surrender of the Egyptian city of Damietta to the Muslims. In war zones some women concealed their sex by donning chain mail and helmets and fought with the knights.

Much of medieval warfare consisted of the besieging of towns and castles. Help could not enter; nor could anyone leave. The larger the number of besiegers, the greater was the chance the fortification would fall. Women swelled the numbers of besiegers. Women assisted in filling the moats surrounding fortified places with earth so that ladders and war engines could be brought close. More typically, women provided water to fighting men, a service not to be underestimated in the hot, dry climate of the Middle East. They worked as washerwomen, foraged for food, and provided sexual services. There were many more European men than women, however, so there was a fair amount of intermarriage or at least intergroup sexual relations between Christian men and Muslim women.

Mapping the Past

MAP 9.4 The Routes of the Crusades   This map shows the many different routes that Western Christians took over the centuries to reach Jerusalem. Use it and the information in the text to answer the following questions: ❶ How were the results of the various Crusades shaped by the routes that the Crusaders took? ❷ How did the routes offer opportunities for profit for Venetian and other Italian merchants? ❸ Why might the Byzantines have worried about Crusaders even before the Fourth Crusade?

Online Study Center   **Improve Your Grade** Interactive Map: Routes of the Crusades

The Capture of Jerusalem in 1099   As engines hurl stones to breach the walls, Crusaders enter on scaling ladders. Scenes from Christ's passion in the top half of the piece identify the city as Jerusalem. (*Bibliothéque nationale de France*)

The Muslim states in the Middle East were politically fragmented when the Crusaders first came, and it took about a century for them to reorganize. They did so dramatically under Saladin (Salah al-Din), who unified Egypt and Syria, and in 1187 the Muslims retook Jerusalem. Christians immediately attempted to take it back in what was later called the Third Crusade (1189–1192). Frederick Barbarossa of the Holy Roman Empire, Richard the Lion-Hearted of England, and Philip Augustus of France participated, and the Third Crusade was better financed than previous ones. But disputes among the leaders and strategic problems prevented any lasting results. The Crusaders were not successful in retaking Jerusalem, but they did keep their hold on port towns, and Saladin allowed pilgrims safe passage to Jerusalem. He also made an agreement with Christian rulers for keeping the peace. From that point on, the Crusader states were more important economically than politically or religiously, giving Italian and French merchants direct access to Eastern products such as perfumes and silk.

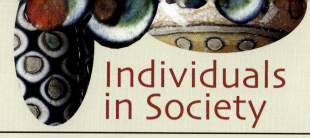

Individuals in Society

The Jews of Speyer: A Collective Biography

In the winter of 1095–1096 news of Pope Urban II's call for a crusade spread. In spring 1096 the Jews of northern France, fearing that a crusade would arouse anti-Semitic hostility, sent a circular letter to the Rhineland's Jewish community seeking its prayers. Jewish leaders in Mainz responded, "All the (Jewish) communities have decreed a fast. . . . May God save us and save you from all distress and hardship. We are deeply fearful for you. We, however, have less reason to fear (for ourselves), for we have heard not even a rumor of the crusade."* Ironically, French Jewry survived almost unscathed, while the Rhenish Jewry suffered frightfully.

Beginning in the late tenth century Jews trickled into Speyer—partly through Jewish perception of opportunity and partly because of the direct invitation of the bishop of Speyer. The bishop's charter meant that Jews could openly practice their religion, could not be assaulted, and could buy and sell goods. But they could not proselytize their faith, as Christians could. Jews also extended credit on a small scale and, in an expanding economy with many coins circulating, determined the relative value of currencies. Unlike their Christian counterparts, many Jewish women were literate and acted as moneylenders. Jews also worked as skilled masons, carpenters, and jewelers. As the bishop had promised, the Jews of Speyer lived apart from Christians in a walled enclave where they exercised autonomy: they maintained law and order, raised taxes, and provided religious, social, and educational services for their community. (This organization lasted in Germany until the nineteenth century.) Jewish immigration to Speyer accelerated; everyday relations between Jews and Christians were peaceful.

But Christians resented Jews as newcomers, outsiders, and aliens; for enjoying the special protection of the bishop; and for providing economic competition. Anti-Semitic ideology had received enormous impetus from the virulent anti-Semitic writings of Christian apologists in the first six centuries A.D. Jews, they argued, were *deicides* (Christ killers); worse, Jews could understand the truth of Christianity but deliberately rejected it; thus they were inhuman. By the late eleventh century anti-Semitism was an old and deeply rooted element in Western society.

Late in April 1096 Emich of Leisingen, a petty lord from the Rhineland who had the reputation of being a lawless thug, approached Speyer with a large band of Crusaders. Joined by a mob of burghers, they planned to surprise the Jews in their synagogue on Saturday morning, May 3, but the Jews prayed early and left before the attackers arrived. Furious, the mob randomly murdered eleven Jews. The bishop took the entire Jewish community into his castle, arrested some of the burghers, and cut off their hands. News of these events raced up the Rhine to Worms, creating confusion in the Jewish community. Some took refuge with Christian friends; others sought the bishop's protection.

A combination of Crusaders and burghers killed a large number of Jews, looted and burned synagogues, and desecrated the Torah (see page 43) and other books. Proceeding on to the old and prosperous city of Mainz, Crusaders continued attacking Jews. Facing overwhelming odds, eleven hundred Jews killed their families and themselves. Crusaders and burghers vented their hatred by inflicting barbaric tortures on the wounded and dying. The Jews were never passive; everywhere they resisted. If the Crusades had begun as opposition to Islam, after 1096 that hostility extended to all those who Christians saw as enemies of society, including heretics, Jews, and lepers. But Jews continued to move to the Rhineland and to make important economic and intellectual contributions. Crusader-burgher attacks served as harbingers of events to come in the later Middle Ages and well into modern times.

An engraving (18th century) of the mass suicide of the Jews of Worms in 1096, when they were overwhelmed by Crusaders (with shields).
(Bildarchiv Preussischer Kulturbesitz/Art Resource, NY)

Questions for Analysis

1. How do you explain Christian attacks on the Jews of Speyer? Were they defenses of faith?
2. What is meant by the phrase "dehumanization of the enemy"? Can you give other examples?

*Quoted in R. Chazan, *In the Year 1096: The First Crusade and the Jews* (Philadelphia: Jewish Publication Society, 1996), p. 28.

Online Study Center **Improve Your Grade**
Going Beyond Individuals in Society

In 1202 Innocent III sent out preachers who called on Christian knights to retake Jerusalem. Those who responded—in what would become the Fourth Crusade—decided that going by sea would be better than going by land, and they stopped in Constantinople for supplies. The supplies never materialized, and in 1204 the Crusaders decided to capture and sack Constantinople instead, destroying its magnificent library and shipping gold, silver, and relics home. The Byzantine Empire, as a political unit, never recovered from this destruction. Although the Crusader Baldwin IX of Flanders was chosen emperor, the empire splintered into three parts and soon consisted of little more than the city of Constantinople. Moreover, the assault by one Christian people on another—even though one of the goals of the Crusades was reunion of the Greek and Latin churches—made the split between the churches permanent. It also helped discredit the entire crusading movement and obviously had no effect on Muslim successes.

In 1208, in one of the most memorable episodes, two expeditions of children set out on a crusade to the Holy Land. One contingent turned back; the other was captured and sold into slavery. A seventh crusade in 1248, led by King Louis of France, tried to come in through Egypt. Louis also sent monks to the court of the Mongols in Central Asia, who were at this point led by Genghis Khan, to make a treaty that would encircle the Muslims. The monks were unsuccessful, but they brought back geographical knowledge of Asia and the peoples they had encountered.

In the late thirteenth century Turkish armies gradually conquered all other Muslim rules and then turned against the Crusader states. In 1291 their last stronghold, the port of Acre, fell in a battle that was just as bloody as the first battle for Jerusalem two centuries earlier. Knights then needed a new battlefield for military actions, which some found in Spain, where the rulers of Aragon and Castile continued fighting Muslims until 1492.

Crusades Within Europe

Crusades were also mounted against groups within Europe that were perceived as threats. In 1208 Pope Innocent III proclaimed a crusade against a group in southern France known either as the Cathars (from the Greek *katharos,* meaning "pure") or as the **Albigensians** (from the town of Albi in southern France). The Albigensians asserted that the material world was created not by the good God of the New Testament, but by a different evil God of the Old Testament. The good God had created spiritual things, and the evil God or the Devil had created material things; in this dualistic understanding, the soul was good and the body evil. Forces of good and evil battled constantly, and leading a perfect life meant being stripped of all physical and material things. To free oneself from the power of evil, a person had to lead a life of extreme asceticism. Albigensians were divided into the "perfect," who followed the principles strictly, and the "believers," who led ordinary lives until their deaths, when they repented and were saved. They used the teachings of Jesus about the evils of material goods to call for the church to give up its property, rejected the authority of the pope and the sacraments of the church, and began setting up their own bishoprics.

The Albigensians won many adherents in southern France. Faced with widespread defection, Pope Innocent III proclaimed a crusade against them. Fearing that religious division would lead to civil disorder, the French monarchy joined the crusade against the Albigensians. Under Count Simon de Montfort, a northern French noble who had been part of the disastrous Fourth Crusade in Constantinople, the French inflicted a savage defeat on the Albigensians in 1213. After more years of fighting, the leaders agreed to terms of peace, which left the French monarchy the primary beneficiary. The county of Toulouse in southern France, which had supported the Albigensians, passed to the authority of the French crown.

The end of the war did not mean an end to Albigensianism, but the papacy decided that education and investigations would be more effective ways to combat heresy than military campaigns. The pope founded the University of Toulouse, which he hoped would promote knowledge and combat ignorance, error, and incorrect belief. In the 1230s and 1240s the papacy established the papal **Inquisition,** sending out inquisitors with the power to seek out suspected heretics, question them in private without revealing who had denounced them, and sentence them to punishments ranging from penance to life imprisonment. Heretics who did not repent were handed over to the secular government to be burned, and their property was confiscated. These measures were very successful, and the last Albigensian leaders were burned in the 1320s, though their beliefs did not die out completely.

Fearful of encirclement by imperial territories, the popes also promoted crusades against Emperor Frederick II in 1227 and 1239. This use of force backfired, damaging papal credibility as the sponsor of peace.

Along with the papal Inquisition, the Crusades also inspired the establishment of new religious orders. For example, the Knights Templars, founded in 1118 with the strong backing of Saint Bernard of Clairvaux (see page 319), combined the monastic ideals of obedience and self-denial with the crusading practice of military aggression. Another order, the Teutonic Knights, waged wars against the pagan Prussians in the Baltic region. After 1230, and from a base in Poland, they established a new territory, Christian Prussia, and gradually the entire eastern shore of the Baltic came under their hegemony. Military orders served to unify Christian Europe.

Consequences of the Crusades

The Crusades provided the means for what one scholar has called "the aristocratic diaspora," the movement of knights from their homes in France to areas then on the frontiers of Christian Europe.[8] Wars of foreign conquest had occurred before the Crusades, as the Norman Conquest of England in 1066 illustrates (see page 261), but for many knights migration began with the taking of the cross. Restless, ambitious knights, many of them younger sons with no prospects, left on crusade to the Holy Land, and some of them were able to carve out lordships in Palestine, Syria, and Greece. Along the Syrian and Palestinian coasts, the Crusaders set up a string of feudal states that managed to survive for about two centuries before the Muslims reconquered them; many of the castles they built still stand today.

The Crusades introduced some Europeans to Eastern luxury goods, but their immediate cultural impact on the West remains debatable. Strong economic and intellectual ties with the East had already been developed by the late eleventh century. The Crusades did provide great commercial profits for Italian merchants, who profited from outfitting military expeditions, the opening of new trade routes, and the establishment of trading communities in the Crusader states. After those kingdoms collapsed, Muslim rulers still encouraged trade with European businessmen. Commerce with the West benefited both Muslims and Europeans, and it continued to flourish.

The Crusades proved to be a disaster for Jewish-Christian relations. The experience of the Rhenish Jews during the First Crusade (see page 283) was not unusual; later Crusades brought similar violence. Hostility between Christians and Jews increased, enhanced by Christian merchants' and financiers' resentment of Jewish business competition and by accusations that Jews engaged in the ritual murder of Christians to use their blood in religious rituals. These accusations, termed the "blood libel," were condemned by Christian rulers and higher church officials, but were often spread through sermons preached by local priests. They also charged

Jews with being "Christ killers" and of using the communion host for diabolical counter-rituals. Jews were accused of killing a Christian child and using his blood in Passover *matzot* (the unleavened bread eaten during the eight-day Passover festival) in Norwich in England in 1144, with similar accusations occurring in other cities in England, France, Germany, and Spain over the next several centuries. Such accusations led to the killing of Jewish families and sometimes entire Jewish communities, sometimes by burning people alive in the synagogue or Jewish section of town.

Legal restrictions on Jews gradually increased. The Third Lateran Council in 1179 forbade Jews to have Christian servants or employees and forbade Christians to live in Jewish parts of town, and the Fourth Lateran Council in 1215 forbade Jews to hold public office, appear in public on Christian holy days, or appear in Christian parts of town without a badge marking them as Jews. Jews were prohibited from engaging in any trade with Christians except money-lending—which only fueled popular resentment—and in 1275 King Edward I of England prohibited that as well. In 1290 he expelled the Jews from England in return for a large parliamentary grant; it would be four centuries before they would be allowed back in. King Philip the Fair of France followed Edward's example in 1306, and many Jews went to the area of southern France known as Provence, which was not yet part of the French kingdom. In July 1315 the king's need for revenue led him to readmit the Jews to France in return for a huge lump sum and for an annual financial subsidy. The returnees faced new economic pressures as well as old hostilities, however. In the thirteenth century Jews in Aragon and Castile came under increasing pressure to convert, and in the 1260s the harsh anti-Jewish measures of the Fourth Lateran Council were included in a new Castilian law code, the *Siete Partidas*.

The Crusades also left an inheritance of deep bitterness in Christian-Muslim relations. Each side dehumanized the other, viewing those who followed the other religion as unbelievers. Whereas Europeans perceived the Crusades as sacred religious movements, Muslims saw them as expansionist and imperialistic. Even today some Muslims see the conflict between Arab and Jew as just another manifestation of the medieval Crusades and view the leaders of the state of Israel as new Crusaders or as tools of Western imperialism.

The European Crusades had a profound effect in shaping the very identity of the West. They represent the first great colonizing movement beyond the geographical boundaries of the European continent. The ideal of a sacred mission to conquer or convert Muslim peoples entered Europeans' consciousness and became a continuing goal. When in 1492 Christopher Columbus sailed west, hoping to reach India, he used the language of the Crusades in his diaries, which show that he was preoccupied with the conquest of Jerusalem (see Chapter 15). Columbus wanted to establish a Christian base in India from which a new crusade against Islam could be launched.

The Crusades testify to the religious enthusiasm of the High Middle Ages, but Steven Runciman, a distinguished scholar of the Crusades, concludes in his three-volume history:

The triumphs of the Crusades were the triumphs of faith.... In the long sequence of interaction and fusion between orient and occident out of which our civilization has grown, the Crusades were a tragic and destructive episode.... High ideals were besmirched by cruelty and greed, enterprise and endurance by a blind and narrow self-righteousness; and the Holy War itself was nothing more than a long act of intolerance in the name of God, which is the sin against the Holy Ghost.[9]

The Expansion of Christianity

The Crusades had a profound impact on both Europe and the Middle East, but they were not the only example of Christian expansion in the High Middle Ages. As we saw earlier (page 266), Christian kingdoms were established in the Iberian Peninsula through the *reconquista*, and Muslim holdings were reduced to the small state of Granada in the south. The *reconquista* brought the establishment of a Roman ecclesiastical structure, and by the end of the thirteenth century Spain had fifty-one bishoprics. These bishoprics, along with new monasteries, aided the growth of Christian culture. Both also enhanced royal power, for church officials provided financial, political, and ideological support for the monarchs who had endowed their institutions.

The pattern in Spain was replicated in northern and eastern Europe in the centuries after the millennial year 1000. People and ideas moved from western France and western Germany into Ireland, Scandinavia, the Baltic lands, and eastern Europe, with significant cultural consequences for those territories. Wars of expansion, the establishment of new Christian bishoprics, and the vast migration of colonists, together with the papal emphasis on a unified Christian world, brought about the gradual Christianization of a larger area (see Map 9.5).

• *What were the effects of the expansion of Christianity into northern and eastern Europe?*

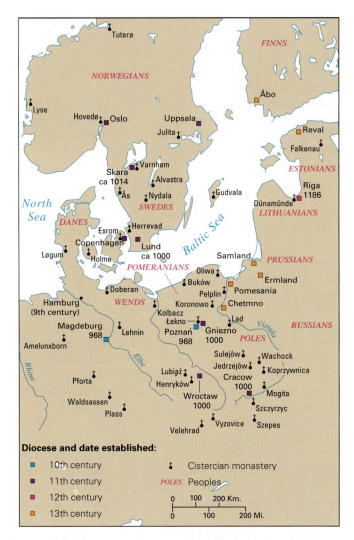

MAP 9.5 Christianization of the Baltic Region Dioceses and monasteries served as the means by which pagan Baltic peoples were Christianized and brought into the framework of Latin Christian culture. *(Source: Some data from R. Bartlett, The Making of Europe: Conquest, Colonization and Cultural Change, 950–1350 [Princeton, N.J.: Princeton University Press, 1993], pp. 16 and 259)*

Northern Europe

In 1177 John de Courcy, a Norman with small estates in Somerset (southwestern England), crossed the Irish Sea with his army and raided Ulcad in the province of Ulster. John easily defeated the local ruler, Rory MacDunlevy, seized the town of Downpatrick, and with this foothold built himself a sizable lordship. Other Anglo-Norman settlers followed. Ireland had been Christian since the days of Saint Patrick (see page 205), but John de

Courcy's intervention led to the remodeling of the Irish church from a monastic structure to an episcopal one with defined territorial dioceses. The Anglo-Norman invasion also meant the introduction of the fief, feudal cavalry, and Anglo-Norman landlords, as well as the beginnings of chartered towns on an English pattern. Similarly, Anglo-Norman, Anglo-French, and Flemish knights poured into Scotland in the twelfth century, bringing the fief and the language of feudalism. In 1286 the descendants of twelfth-century colonists held five of the thirteen Scottish earldoms. Scottish feudalism closely resembled that of western France, and immigrant knights transformed Scottish society.

Latin Christian influences entered the Scandinavian and Baltic regions primarily through the erection of dioceses. As an easily identifiable religious figure, as judge, and as the only person who could ordain priests, the bishop was the essential instrument in the spread of Christianity. Otto I (see page 263) established the first Scandinavian sees—Schleswig, Ribe, and Århus in Denmark—between 948 and 965. In 1060 a network of eight bishoprics was organized, and in 1103–1104 the Danish kingdom received its first archbishopric, Lund, in Scania (now part of Sweden). In Norway Christianity spread in coastal areas beginning in the tenth century, and King Olaf II (r. 1015–1028) brought in clergy and bishops from England and Germany to establish the church more firmly. From Norway Christianity spread to Iceland. In all of these areas, royal power advanced institutional Christianity; the traditional Norse religions practiced by the Vikings were outlawed and their adherents sometimes executed.

Christianity progressed more slowly in Sweden and Finland, in part because royal power was weaker. In the 1060s, however, six dioceses were set up in Sweden, and in 1164 Uppsala in Sweden, long a center of the pagan cults of Thor and Odin, became a Catholic archdiocese. Sweden took over much of modern-day Finland in the thirteenth century, and Swedish-speaking settlers moved into islands and coastal areas. Christian missionaries preached, baptized, and built churches, working among both the Swedish-speaking and Finnish-speaking populations, though pagan and Christian practices existed side-by-side for centuries. The Sami people of the far north in Scandinavia (formerly known as Lapps), who lived by fishing, hunting, and herding reindeer, remained pagan until the eighteenth century.

Centralized monarchy came to Scandinavia somewhat later than it did to western Europe. There was little feudalism in the classic sense of fiefs and oaths of loyalty, and during the High Middle Ages higher nobles frequently came into conflict with monarchs. In 1397 Queen Margrete I (1353–1412) united the crowns of Denmark, Sweden-Finland, and Norway in the **Union of Kalmar.** She built up royal power and worked toward creating a stronger state, checking the power of the nobility and creating a stronger financial base for the monarchy. The union gradually disintegrated in the fifteenth century, though Denmark continued to rule Norway until 1814.

Eastern Europe

In the lands between the Oder River in the east and the Elbe and Saale Rivers in the west lived the Wends, a West Slavic people, and their linguistic cousins, the Balts, the ancestors of Lithuanians, Latvians, Livonians, and Estonians. These peoples remained pagan in spite of extensive Christian missionary activity. Nevertheless, Otto I established a string of dioceses along his northern and eastern frontiers to pacify newly conquered Slavic lands and to Christianize. Among these were the archdiocese of Magdeburg, intended for "all the people of the Slavs beyond the Elbe and Saale, lately converted and to be converted to God,"[10] and the dioceses of Brandenburg, Schwerin, and Lübeck, all filled with German bishops. Repeated Slavic revolts, illustrating ethnic opposition to German lords and German bishops, indicate that the new faith did not easily penetrate the Baltic region. Only the ruthless tactics of Albert the Bear (d. 1170) pacified the region and forced the incorporation of the eastern and northern bishoprics into the structure of the Western Christian church.

A member of the Saxon nobility with experience in border warfare against the Slavs, Albert the Bear reconquered the town of Brandenburg on June 11, 1157. With this base, and to support his **Ostiedlung** (orientation to the east), Albert proclaimed a German crusade against the Slavs. He invited Dutch, Flemish, and German knights from the Rhineland to colonize conquered territories. To keep the region as far as the Oder pacified, he built castles manned by these newly recruited knights. Slav revolts were ruthlessly crushed.

Along with German knights, German (or Roman) ecclesiastical influences entered other parts of eastern Europe in the tenth and eleventh centuries. Prague in Bohemia became a bishopric in 973; from Prague missionaries set out to convert the Poles. The first diocese in Poland, Poznan, was erected in 968. Likewise, Esztergom in Hungary became a diocese in 1001, and during the eleventh century Hungarian rulers established new ecclesiastical centers along the Danube and eastward into Transylvania (modern central Romania).

Saint Hedwig of Bavaria (1174–1243) Hedwig was married to Henry, duke of Saxony, by whom she had seven children and from whom she suffered great abuse. She ruled Silesia (today partly in the Czech Republic, partly in Poland) when her husband was away at war; conducted diplomatic negotiations; and founded monasteries, including Trebnitz, the first Cistercian house for women. Hedwig and her niece, Saint Elizabeth of Hungary (1207–1231), illustrate the powerful influence of women in the spread of Christianity in central and eastern Europe. In a manuscript commissioned by her fourteenth-century descendants (shown in small-scale donor portraits), Hedwig carries a book, a rosary, and a tiny statue of the Virgin Mary, references to her devout character. *(The John Paul Getty Museum, Los Angeles, Court Atelier of Duke Ludwig I of Liegnitz and Brieg [illuminator],* Vita beatae Hedwigis, *1353. Tempera colors, colored washes and ink bound between wood boards covered with red-stained pigskin, 34.1 × 24.8 cm)*

In the twelfth and thirteenth centuries tens of thousands of German settlers poured into eastern Europe, including Silesia, Mecklenburg, Bohemia, Poland, Hungary, and Transylvania. Towns there contained the residence of the military leader of the region, the duke, and his servants and knights. The Christian baptism of Duke Mieszko (d. 992) and his court in 966 at Gniezno led to the construction of a cathedral, the arrival of churchmen, and the building of churches and monasteries for monks and nuns. All these people represented a demand for goods and services. Centers such as Gniezno, Cracow, Wroclaw, and Plock attracted craftsmen and merchant immigrants seeking business opportunities.

With urbanization came Germanization. Duke Boleslaw's charter for his new city of Cracow in Poland stated that "the city of Cracow was converted to German law and the site of the market, the houses and the courtyards was changed by the duke's officials."[11] Boleslaw specifically excluded Polish peasants from becoming burgesses because he feared the depopulation of his estates. New immigrants were German in descent, name, language, and law. Towns such as Cracow and Riga engaged in long-distance trade and gradually grew into large urban centers, and there were also hundreds of small market towns populated by German immigrants.

Christendom

Christianity began as a small group within Judaism during a time of religious questioning, and it spread to non-Jews along the trade routes of the Roman Empire during the first several centuries A.D. Christians were persecuted sporadically by Roman authorities, but most of the time they were not, and the religion spread. In the fourth century the emperor Constantine recognized Christianity as a legitimate religion and hoped that it might be useful in keeping the Roman Empire intact; he called church councils and shaped their decisions about theological and institutional matters. In 380 the emperor Theodosius made Christianity the official religion of the Roman Empire by forbidding pagan worship.

Through the actions of Constantine and Theodosius, Christianity became in some ways a state as well as a religion. Early medieval writers began to use the word **Christendom** to refer to this realm of Christianity. Sometimes notions of Christendom were linked directly to specific states, such as Charlemagne's empire or the Holy Roman Empire. More often Christendom was quite vague, a sort of loose sense of the body of all people who were Christian. When the pope called for crusades, for example, he spoke not only of the retaking of Jerusalem, but also of the defense of Christendom. When missionaries, officials, and soldiers took Christianity into the Iberian Peninsula, Scandinavia, or the Baltic region, they understood what they were doing as the expansion of Christendom.

From the point of view of popes such as Gregory VII and Innocent III, Christendom was a unified hierarchy with the papacy at the top. They pushed for uniformity of religious worship and campaigned continually for the same pattern of religious service, the Roman liturgy in Latin, in all countries and places. They forbade vernacular Christian rituals or those that differed in their pattern of worship, and in this they were successful. In 1081 Gregory wrote triumphantly to King Alfonso VI of Castile and León: "Most dearly beloved, know that one thing pleases us greatly . . . namely, that in the churches of your realm, you have caused the order of the Mother of all, the holy Roman church, to be received and celebrated in the ancient way."[12] Under Innocent (see page 278) papal directives and papal legates flowed to all parts of Europe; twelve hundred prelates obediently came to

Rome from the borderlands as well as the heartland for the Fourth Lateran Council of 1215; and the same religious service was celebrated everywhere.

As we have seen in this chapter, however, not everyone had the same view. Kings and emperors may have accepted the Roman liturgy in the areas under their control, but they had their own ideas of the way power should operate in Christendom, even if this brought them into conflict with the papacy. This did not mean that they had any less loyalty to Christendom as a concept, however, but simply a different idea about how it should be structured and who could best defend it. The battles in the High Middle Ages between popes and kings and between Christians and Muslims were signs of how deeply religion had replaced tribal, political, and ethnic structures as the essence of Western culture. Christian Europeans identified themselves first and foremost as citizens of Christendom or even described themselves as belonging to "the Christian race."[13] Whether Europeans were Christian in their observance of the Gospels remains another matter.

Chapter Summary

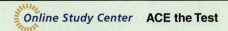

Online Study Center   **ACE the Test**

- *How did medieval rulers create larger and more stable territories?*
- *What types of institutions did medieval rulers develop to provide their realms with sufficient taxes and other income?*
- *How did the administration of law contribute to the development of national states?*
- *How did the papacy attempt to reform the church, and what was the response from other powerful rulers?*
- *How did the motives, course, and consequences of the Crusades reflect and shape developments in Europe?*
- *What were the effects of the expansion of Christianity into northern and eastern Europe?*

The end of the great invasions signaled the beginning of profound changes in European society. As domestic disorder slowly subsided, feudal rulers began to develop new institutions of government that enabled them to assert their power over lesser lords and the general population. Centralized states slowly crystallized, first in England and France, where rulers such as William the Conqueror and Philip Augustus manipulated feudal institutions to build up their power. In central Europe the German king Otto had himself declared emperor and tried to follow a similar path, but unified nation-states did not develop until the nineteenth century. Emperors instead shared power with princes, dukes, archbishops, counts, bishops, abbots, and cities. In the Iberian Peninsula Christian rulers of small states slowly expanded their territories, taking over land from Muslim rulers in the reconquista.

As medieval rulers expanded territories and extended authority, they required more officials, larger armies, and more money with which to pay for them. They developed different sorts of financial institutions to provide taxes and other income. The most effective financial bureaucracies were those developed in England, including a bureau of finance called the Exchequer, and in Sicily, where Norman rulers retained the main financial agency that had been created by their Muslim predecessors. By contrast, the rulers of France and other continental states continued to rely primarily on the income from their own lands to support their military endeavors.

In the twelfth and thirteenth centuries rulers in Europe sought to transform a hodgepodge of oral and written customs and rules into a uniform system of laws acceptable and applicable to all their peoples. In England such changes caused conflict with church officials, personified in the dispute between King Henry II and Thomas Becket, the archbishop of Canterbury. Fiscal and legal measures by Henry's son John led to opposition from the high nobles of England, who forced him to sign Magna Carta agreeing to promise to observe the law. Magna Carta had little immediate impact, but it came to signify the principle that everyone, including the king and the government, must obey the law. Legal developments in continental countries like France were strongly influenced by Roman law, while England slowly built up a unique unwritten common law.

At the same time that kings were creating more centralized realms, energetic popes built up their power within the Western Christian church and asserted their superiority over kings and emperors. The Gregorian reform movement led to a grave conflict with kings over lay investiture. The papacy achieved a technical success on the religious issue, but in Germany the greatly increased power of the nobility, at the expense of the emperor, represents the significant social consequence. Having put its own house in order, the Roman papacy built the first strong government bureaucracy in the twelfth and thirteenth centuries. In the High Middle Ages, the church exercised general leadership of European society.

A papal call to retake the holy city of Jerusalem led to the Crusades, nearly two centuries of warfare between Christians and Muslims. The enormous popular response to papal calls for crusading reveals the influence of the reformed papacy and a new sense that war against the church's enemies was a duty of nobles. The Crusades were initially successful, and small Christian states were established in the Middle East. These did not last very long, however, and other effects of the Crusades were disastrous. Jewish communities in Europe were regularly attacked; relations between the Western and Eastern Christian churches were poisoned by the Crusaders' attack on Constantinople; and Christian-Muslim relations became more uniformly hostile than they had been earlier.

These centuries also saw the penetration of Latin Christian culture into northern and eastern Europe. Christian warriors, clergy, and settlers moved out in all directions from western and central Europe, bringing the gradual Christianization of a larger area through conquest and colonization. The movement of people was particularly evident in eastern Europe, where German-speaking settlers moved into areas populated by Slavs, establishing towns and bishoprics. Both the Crusades in the Middle East and the expansion of Christianity in Iberia, Scandinavia, and the Baltic region created a stronger sense of loyalty to Christendom among many people living in Europe.

Key Terms

Domesday Book	college of cardinals
Capetian dynasty	lay investiture
baillis/seneschals	excommunication
Holy Roman Empire	cloistered
Landfrieden	curia Romana
reconquista	(Roman curia)
Exchequer	canon law
relief	Crusades
scutage	indulgence
tallage/taille	Sephardic Jews
diwān	Ashkenazi
Landgericht	Albigensians
common law	Inquisition
circuit judges	Union of Kalmar
Magna Carta	Ostiedlung
precedent	Christendom
simony	

Online Study Center **Improve Your Grade** Flashcards

Suggested Reading

Abulafia, David. *Frederick II: A Medieval Emperor.* 1992. A beautifully written biography that sets Frederick's life in a broad context.

Bartlett, Robert. *England Under the Norman and Angevin Kings, 1075–1225.* 2000. An excellent synthesis of social, cultural, and political history in highly readable prose.

Bartlett, Robert. *The Making of Europe: Conquest, Colonization and Cultural Change, 950–1350.* 1993. A broad survey of many of the developments traced in this chapter.

Chazan, Robert. *In the Year 1096: The First Crusade and the Jews.* 1996. A thorough discussion of the Rhineland Jews and many issues related to the Jews and the Crusades.

Edgington, Susan B., and Sarah Lambert, eds. *Gendering the Crusades.* 2002. Contains articles that look at the roles of men and women.

Fletcher, Richard. *The Quest for El Cid.* 1990. Provides an excellent introduction to Spanish social and political conditions through a study of Rodrigo Dias, the eleventh-century soldier of fortune who became the Spanish national hero.

Holt, J. C. *Magna Carta,* 2d ed. 1992. The authoritative study of Magna Carta.

Johns, Jeremy. *Arabic Administration in Norman Sicily.* 2002. A comprehensive account of Arabic influences on the politics of Norman Sicily.

Lowney, Chris. *A Vanished World: Medieval Spain's Golden Age of Enlightenment.* 2006. Explores the complex interactions among Jews, Muslims, and Christians in the era of practical coexistence, and traces growing intolerance.

Madden, Thomas. *The New Concise History of the Crusades.* 2005. A highly readable brief survey by the pre-eminent American scholar of the Crusades.

O'Shea, Stephen. *The Perfect Heresy: The Revolutionary Life and Death of the Medieval Cathars.* 2000. A stimulating journalistic account of this Christian heresy.

Prestwich, Michael. *Armies and Warfare in the Middle Ages: The English Experience.* 1996. An exciting and readable survey of many aspects of English warfare.

Tellenbach, Gerd. *The Church in Western Europe from the Tenth to the Twelfth Century.* 1993. A very good survey by an expert on the investiture controversy.

Tyerman, Christopher. *Fighting for Christendom: Holy War and the Crusades*. 2005. Assesses the impact of the Crusades on modern times.

Notes

1. D. C. Douglas and G. E. Greenaway, eds., *English Historical Documents,* vol. 2 (London: Eyre & Spottiswoode, 1961), p. 853.
2. Bartlett, *The Making of Europe: Conquest, Colonization and Cultural Change, 950–1350* (Princeton, N.J.: Princeton University Press, 1993), p. 13.
3. Ibid., p. 178.
4. J. Johns, *Arabic Administration in Norman Sicily: The Royal Diwān* (New York: Cambridge University Press, 2002), p. 289.
5. Ibid., p. 293.
6. I. S. Robinson, *The Papacy, 1073–1198: Continuity and Innovation* (New York: Cambridge University Press, 1990), p. 403.
7. Fulcher of Chartres, *A History of the Expedition to Jerusalem, 1095–1127,* trans. Frances Rita Ryan and ed. Harold S. Fink (Knoxville: University of Tennessee Press, 1969), p. 121.
8. Bartlett, *The Making of Europe,* p. 24.
9. S. Runciman, *A History of the Crusades,* vol. 3: *The Kingdom of Acre* (Cambridge: Cambridge University Press, 1955), p. 480.
10. Bartlett, *The Making of Europe,* p. 8.
11. Quoted in ibid., pp. 179–180.
12. Quoted in ibid., p. 249.
13. Ibid., pp. 250–255.

An Arab View of the Crusades

The Crusades helped shape the understanding that Arabs and Europeans had of each other and all subsequent relations between the Christian West and the Arab world. To medieval Christians the Crusades were papally approved military expeditions for the recovery of holy places in Palestine; to the Arabs these campaigns were "Frankish wars" or "Frankish invasions" for the acquisition of territory.

Early in the thirteenth century Ibn Al-Athir (1160–1223), a native of Mosul, an important economic and cultural center in northern Mesopotamia (modern Iraq), wrote a history of the First Crusade. He relied on Arab sources for the events he described. Here is his account of the Crusaders' capture of Antioch.

The power of the Franks first became apparent when in the year 478/1085–86* they invaded the territories of Islam and took Toledo and other parts of Andalusia. Then in 484/1091 they attacked and conquered the island of Sicily and turned their attention to the African coast. Certain of their conquests there were won back again but they had other successes, as you will see.

In 490/1097 the Franks attacked Syria. This is how it all began: Baldwin, their King, a kinsman of Roger the Frank who had conquered Sicily, assembled a great army and sent word to Roger saying: "I have assembled a great army and now I am on my way to you, to use your bases for my conquest of the African coast. Thus you and I shall become neighbors."

Roger called together his companions and consulted them about these proposals. "This will be a fine thing for them and for us!" they declared, "for by this means these lands will be converted to the Faith!" At this Roger raised one leg and farted loudly, and swore that it was of more use than their advice. "Why?" "Because if this army comes here it will need quantities of provisions and fleets of ships to transport it to Africa, as well as

reinforcements from my own troops. Then, if the Franks succeed in conquering this territory they will take it over and will need provisioning from Sicily. This will cost me my annual profit from the harvest. If they fail they will return here and be an embarrassment to me here in my own domain." . . .

He summoned Baldwin's messenger and said to him: "If you have decided to make war on the Muslims your best course will be to free Jerusalem from their rule and thereby win great honor. I am bound by certain promises and treaties of allegiance with the ruler of Africa." So the Franks made ready to set out to attack Syria.

Another story is that the Fatimids of Egypt were afraid when they saw the Seljuqids extending their empire through Syria as far as Gaza, until they reached the Egyptian border and Atsiz invaded Egypt itself. They therefore sent to invite the Franks to invade Syria and so protect Egypt from the Muslims.† But God knows best.

When the Franks decided to attack Syria they marched east to Constantinople, so that they could cross the straits and advance into Muslim territory by the easier, land route. When they reached Constantinople, the Emperor of the East refused them permission to pass through his domains. He said: "Unless you first promise me Antioch, I shall not allow you to cross into the Muslim empire." His real intention was to incite them to attack the Muslims, for he was convinced that the Turks, whose invincible control over Asia Minor he had observed, would exterminate every one of them. They accepted his conditions and in 490/1097 they crossed the Bosphorus at Constantinople. . . . They . . . reached Antioch, which they besieged.

When Yaghi Siyan, the ruler of Antioch, heard of their approach, he was not sure how the Christian people of the city would react, so he made

Miniature showing heavily armored knights fighting Muslims. *(Bibliothéque nationale de France)*

the Muslims go outside the city on their own to dig trenches, and the next day sent the Christians out alone to continue the task. When they were ready to return home at the end of the day he refused to allow them. "Antioch is yours," he said, "but you will have to leave it to me until I see what happens between us and the Franks." "Who will protect our children and our wives?" they said. "I shall look after them for you." So they resigned themselves to their fate, and lived in the Frankish camp for nine months, while the city was under siege.

Yaghi Siyan showed unparalleled courage and wisdom, strength and judgment. If all the Franks who died had survived they would have overrun all the lands of Islam. He protected the families of the Christians in Antioch and would not allow a hair of their heads to be touched.

After the siege had been going on for a long time the Franks made a deal with . . . a cuirass-maker called Ruzbih whom they bribed with a fortune in money and lands. He worked in the tower that stood over the riverbed, where the river flowed out of the city into the valley. The Franks sealed their pact with the cuirass-maker, God damn him! and made their way to the watergate. They opened it and entered the city. Another gang of them climbed the tower with their ropes. At dawn, when more than 500 of them were in the city and the defenders were worn out after the night watch, they sounded their trumpets. . . . Panic seized Yaghi Siyan and he opened the city gates and fled in terror, with an escort of thirty pages. His army commander arrived, but when he discovered on enquiry that Yaghi Siyan had fled, he made his escape by

another gate. This was of great help to the Franks, for if he had stood firm for an hour, they would have been wiped out. They entered the city by the gates and sacked it, slaughtering all the Muslims they found there. This happened in jumada I (491/April/May 1098). . . .

It was the discord between the Muslim princes . . . that enabled the Franks to overrun the country.

Questions for Analysis

1. From the Arab perspective, when did the Crusades begin?

2. How did Ibn Al-Athir explain the Crusaders' expedition to Syria?

3. Why did Antioch fall to the Crusaders?

4. The use of dialogue in historical narrative is a very old device dating from the Greek historian Thucydides (fifth century B.C.). Assess the value of Ibn Al-Athir's dialogues for the modern historian.

Sources: P. J. Geary, ed., *Readings in Medieval History* (Peterborough, Ontario: Broadview Press, 1991), pp. 443–444; E. J. Costello, trans., *Arab Historians of the Crusades* (Berkeley and Los Angeles: University of California Press, 1969).

*Muslims traditionally date events from Muhammad's *hegira,* or emigration, to Medina, which occurred in 622 according to the Christian calendar.

†Although Muslims, Fatimids were related doctrinally to the Shi'ites, and the dominant Sunni Muslims considered the Fatimids heretics.

In these scenes from a German manuscript, *Speculum Virginum*, ca 1190, the artist shows men, women, and children harvesting, raking, sowing, and digging. All residents in a village engaged in agricultural tasks. *(Rheinisches Landesmuseum, Bonn)*

chapter preview

Village Life
- *What was life like for the rural common people of medieval Europe?*

Popular Religion
- *How did religious practices and attitudes permeate everyday life?*

Nobles
- *How were the lives of nobles different from the lives of common people?*

Monasteries and Convents
- *What roles did the men and women affiliated with religious orders play in medieval society?*

THE CHANGING LIFE OF THE PEOPLE IN THE HIGH MIDDLE AGES

In one of the writings produced at the court of the late-ninth-century Anglo-Saxon king Alfred, Christian society is described as composed of those who pray, those who fight, and those who work. This image of society as divided into three **orders** gained wide circulation in the High Middle Ages. Those who used this model argued that the relationship among the three orders was beneficial rather than exploitative: peasants toiled for the other two orders, but in return they received the prayers of the monks and the physical protection of the nobles. This schema was especially popular among people who were worried about changes they saw around them, and they asserted that the three orders had been established by God. Every person had been assigned a specific social place, in their opinion, and that was the way it should remain.

Enormous social divisions certainly existed in medieval Europe, but they were not as simple or static as the tripartite model suggested or as its advocates hoped. Among the nobility and the peasantry, there were great differences in wealth and status and considerable social mobility. The model does not take townspeople and the emerging commercial classes (see pages 331–345) into consideration. It completely excludes those who were not Christian, such as Jews, Muslims, and pagans. Those who used the model, generally bishops and other church officials, ignored the fact that each of these groups was made up of both women and men; they spoke only of warriors, monks, and farmers. Despite—or perhaps because of—these limitations, the model of the three orders was a powerful mental construct. We can use it to organize our investigation of life in the High Middle Ages, though we can broaden our categories to include groups and issues that medieval authors did not.

Village Life

The evolution of localized feudal systems into more centralized states traced in the last chapter had relatively little impact on the daily lives of most people in Europe except when they involved warfare. In theory

Online Study Center
This icon will direct you to interactive activities and study materials on the website **college.hmco.com/pic/mckaywest9e**

only nobles fought, but in reality fighting often destroyed the houses, barns, and fields of ordinary people, who might also be killed either directly or as a result of the famine, disease, and devastation that often accompanied war. During times of war, people might use a local castle as a place of refuge, taking their children and animals to seek shelter within its outer walls, but most of the time they viewed castles at a distance, working and living without paying much attention to political developments concerning nobles and kings.

This lack of attention went in the other direction as well. Since villagers did not perform what were considered "noble" deeds, the aristocratic monks and clerics who wrote the records that serve as historical sources did not spend time or precious writing materials on them. When common people were mentioned, it was usually with contempt or in terms of the services and obligations they owed. Usually—but not always. In the early twelfth century Honorius, a monk and teacher at the monastery of Autun, wrote: "What do you say about the agricultural classes? Most of them will be saved because they live simply and feed God's people by means of their sweat."[1]

• *What was life like for the rural common people of medieval Europe?*

Slavery, Serfdom, and Upward Mobility

Rural common people are often lumped together and called "peasants," but it is important to remember that their conditions varied widely across Europe. Geographical and climatic features as well as human initiative and local custom determined the particular quality of rural life. The problems that faced the farmer in Yorkshire, England, where the soil was rocky and the climate rainy, were very different from those of the Italian peasant in the sun-drenched Po Valley.

Medieval theologians lumped everyone who worked the land into the category of "those who work," but in fact there were many levels of peasants, ranging from complete slaves to free and very rich farmers. The High Middle Ages was a period of considerable fluidity with significant social mobility.

Slaves were found in western Europe in the High Middle Ages, but in steadily declining numbers. The word *slave* derives from *Slav*, which attests to the widespread trade in men and women from the Slavic areas in the early Middle Ages. Around the year 1200 aristocratic and upper-middle-class households in Provence, Catalonia, Italy, and Germany had a few slaves—Slavs from the

The Three Orders of Society (fourteenth century) This book illustration shows the most common image of medieval society: those who fight, those who pray, and those who work. The group of clergy shown here includes a veiled nun; nuns were technically not members of the clergy, but most people considered them as such. (*Bibiothèque royale, Brussels*)

Baltic, Syrians, and blacks from sub-Saharan Africa. Recent research has also demonstrated the persistence of **ancillae,** female chattel slaves whose lifelong legal servitude passed to their descendants, in Scandinavia, the Balkans, Sicily, and Italian cities well into the sixteenth century.

Most rural people in western Europe in the High Middle Ages were serfs rather than slaves, though the distinction between slave and serf was not always clear. Both lacked freedom—the power to do as they wished—and both were subject to the arbitrary will of one person, the lord. Unlike a slave, however, a serf could not be bought and sold like an animal or an inanimate object.

People's legal status was based on memory and traditions, not on written documents. The serf was required to perform labor services on the lord's land, usually three days a week except during the planting or harvest seasons, when it was more. Serfs frequently had to pay arbitrary levies. When a man married, he had to pay his lord a fee. When he died, his son or heir had to pay an inheritance tax to inherit his parcels of land. The precise amounts of tax paid to the lord on these important occasions depended on local custom and tradition. A free person had to pay rent to the lord but could move and live as he or she wished.

Serfs were tied to the land, and serfdom was a hereditary condition. A person born a serf was likely to die a serf, though many serfs did secure their freedom. About 1187 Glanvill, an official of King Henry II and an expert on English law, described how **villeins** (literally, "inhabitants of small villages")—as English serfs were called—could be made free:

A person of villein status can be made free in several ways. For example, his lord, wishing him to achieve freedom from the villeinage by which he is subject to him, may quit-claim [release] him from himself and his heirs; or he may give or sell him to another with intent to free him. It should be noted, however, that no person of villein status can seek his freedom with his own money, for in such a case he could, according to the law and custom of the realm, be recalled to villeinage by his lord, because all the chattels of a villein are deemed to such an extent the property of his lord that he cannot redeem himself from villeinage with his own money, as against his lord. If, however, a third party provides the money and buys the villein in order to free him, then he can maintain himself for ever in a state of freedom as against his lord who sold him. . . . If any villein stays peaceably for a year and a day in a privileged town and is admitted as a citizen into their commune, that is to say, their gild, he is thereby freed from villeinage.[2]

909	Abbey of Cluny established
1050–1300	Steady rise in population
ca 1075–ca 1140	Life of Orderic Vitalis
1080–1180	Period of milder climate
1098–1179	Life of Hildegard of Bingen
Early 1100s	Production of iron increases greatly
1100–1200	Rapid expansion of the Cistercian Order
1200	Notion of chivalry begins to develop
1215	Fourth Lateran Council accepts seven sacraments

Thus serfs could not buy freedom with their own money, since technically all "chattels"—that is, all goods (including money)—belonged to the lord. But they could give money to a third party, who could use it to buy their freedom. Many energetic and hard-working serfs acquired their freedom through this method of **manumission** in the High Middle Ages. More than anything else, the economic revival that began in the eleventh century (see pages 331–345) advanced the cause of individual liberty. The revival saw the rise of towns, increased land productivity, the growth of long-distance trade, and the development of a money economy. With the advent of a money economy, serfs could save money and, through a third-person intermediary, use it to buy their freedom.

Another opportunity for increased personal freedom, or at least for a reduction in traditional manorial obligations and dues, was provided by the reclamation of wasteland and forestland in the eleventh and twelfth centuries. Lords organized groups of villagers to cut down forests or fill in swamps and marshes between villages to make more land available for farming. In some parts of Europe, this process of filling up empty space between existing villages was also accompanied by moving into new areas. In areas bordering the North Sea, walls and dikes were built slightly out in the water, then the water was pumped out, more soil added, and new land created behind the dikes. The thirteenth century witnessed German peasant migrations into Brandenburg, Pomerania, Prussia, and the Baltic States, with Germans establishing new villages between existing Slavic villages or pushing the Slavs eastward. In the Iberian Peninsula, Christian villagers followed after the Christian armies that were slowly reducing the area under Muslim control. In Scandinavia, farms were established in areas that had previously been used to harvest furs or lumber.

This type of agricultural advancement frequently improved the peasants' social and legal condition. A serf could clear a patch of fen or forestland, make it productive, and, through prudent saving, buy more land and eventually purchase freedom. In the thirteenth century there were many free tenants on the lands of the bishop of Ely in eastern England; these tenants had moved into the area in the twelfth century and drained the fens. Likewise, settlers on the lowlands of the abbey of Bourbourg in Flanders, who had erected dikes and extended the arable lands, possessed hereditary tenures by 1159. They secured personal liberty and owed their overlord only small payments.

In the thirteenth century the noble class frequently needed money to finance crusading, building, or other projects. For example, in 1240 when Geoffrey de Montigny became abbot of Saint-Pierre-le-Vif in the Séenonais region of France, he found the abbey church in disrepair. Geoffrey also discovered that the descendants of families who had once owed the abbey servile obligations now refused to recognize their bondage. Some of these peasants had grown wealthy. When the abbot determined to reclaim these peasants in order to get revenues to rebuild his church, a legal struggle ensued. In 1257 a compromise was worked out whereby Geoffrey manumitted 366 persons, who in turn agreed to pay him five hundred pounds a year over a twelve-year period.

Peasants who remained in the villages of their birth often benefited because landlords, threatened with the loss of serfs, relaxed ancient obligations and duties. While it would be unwise to exaggerate the social impact of the settling of new territories, frontier lands in the Middle Ages did provide opportunities for upward mobility.

The Manor

In the High Middle Ages most European peasants, free and unfree, lived in family groups in small villages. As we saw in Chapter 8 (page 242), the village and the land surrounding it were called a manor and were controlled by a noble or a church official such as a bishop, abbot, or abbess.

The manor was the basic unit of medieval rural organization and the center of rural life. All other generalizations about manors and manorial life have to be limited by variations in the quality of the soil, local climatic con-

ditions, and methods of cultivation. Manors varied from several thousand to as few as 120 acres. Recent evidence suggests that a manor might include several villages, a village whose produce was divided among several lords, or an isolated homestead.

The arable land of the manor was divided into two sections. The *demesne,* or home farm, was cultivated for the lord. The other part was held by the peasantry. Usually the peasants' portion was larger and was held on condition that they cultivate the lord's demesne. All the arable land, both the lord's and the peasants', was divided into strips that were scattered throughout the manor. If one strip yielded little, other strips (with better soil) might be more bountiful. All peasants cooperated in the cultivation of the land, working it as a group. This meant that all shared in any disaster as well as in any large harvest.

Most parts of Europe depended on grain-based agriculture, with a gender division of labor typical of that in grain-growing societies. Men were responsible for clearing new land, plowing, and the care of large animals, and women were responsible for the care of small animals, spinning, and food preparation. Both sexes harvested and planted, though often there were gender-specific tasks within each of these major undertakings. Women and men worked in the vineyards and in the harvest and preparation of crops needed by the textile industry—flax and plants used for dyeing cloth, such as madder (which produces shades of red) and woad (which yields blue dye). Along coastal areas people depended on fishing for much of their food, either eating the fish or trading them for grain and other agricultural products with those living farther inland. In fishing communities small houses and small family groups again predominated, with wives and daughters drying and salting fish for later use, while husbands and brothers went out in boats.

In western and central Europe, villages were generally made up of small houses for individual families, with one married couple, their children (including stepchildren), and perhaps one or two other relatives—a grandmother, a cousin whose parents had died, an unmarried sister or brother of one of the spouses. The household thus contained primarily a **nuclear family,** and some households contained only an unmarried person, a widow, or several unmarried people living together. Villages themselves were also *nucleated*—that is, the houses were clumped together, with the fields stretching out beyond the group of houses. In southern and eastern Europe, though nuclear families and single-person households were not unknown, extended families were more likely to live in the same household or very near to one another than in northern Europe. Father and son, or two married brothers, might share a house with the families of both, forming what demographers call a **stem** or **complex household.**

A manor usually held pasture or meadowland for the grazing of cattle, sheep, and sometimes goats. Often the manor had some forestland as well. Forests were the source of wood for building and for fuel, resin for lighting, ash for candles, ash and lime for fertilizers and all sorts of sterilizing products, and bark for the manufacture of rope. From the forests came wood for the construction of barrels, vats, and all sorts of storage containers. Last but hardly least, the forests were used for feeding pigs, cattle, and domestic animals on nuts, roots, and wild berries. If the manor was intersected by a river, it had a welcome source of fish and eels.

Lords generally appointed officials—termed **bailiffs** in England—from outside the village to oversee the legal and business operations of their manors, collect taxes and fees, and handle disputes. At regular intervals, the lords or their officials also held manorial courts, which handled legal matters such as fights, assaults or robberies, litigation between villagers, and infractions of laws or customs regarding the fields, roads, or public places. The manorial courts relied more on the collective memory of village traditions and customs than on written laws, so that groups of responsible adult men, sometimes called **jurors,** were often asked to decide issues, such as who had the rights to a certain piece of land, by simply talking among themselves or to others who might know. Because of this, jurors were chosen from among those most likely to know the facts of the case—the opposite of modern jury selection. Both plaintiff and defendant often brought in others who would swear to their view of the case or their good character. Punishments were generally fines or occasionally banishment; imprisonment and corporal punishments were rare. (Serious criminal cases were not handled by the manorial courts but rather by a royal or other higher-level court.)

The medieval village had no police as we know them, so villagers who saw a crime or infraction were expected to chase the perpetrator and yell to others to join in what was termed *raising the hue and cry*. Villages in many parts of Europe also developed institutions of self-government to handle issues such as crop rotation, and they chose additional officials such as constables and ale-tasters without the lord's interference. We do not know how these officials were chosen or elected in many cases, but we do know that they were always adult men and were generally heads of households. Women had no official voice in running the village, nor did slaves or servants (female or male), who often worked for and lived with wealthier vil-

Boarstall Manor, Buckinghamshire In 1440 Edmund Rede, lord of this estate, had a map made showing his ancestor receiving the title from King Edward I (*lower field*). Note the manor house, church, and peasants' cottages along the central road. In the common fields, divided by hedges, peasants cultivated on a three-year rotation cycle: winter wheat, spring oats, a year fallow. Peasants' pigs grazed freely in the woods, indicated by trees. We don't know whether peasants were allowed to hunt the deer. (*Buckinghamshire Record Office, Aylesbury*)

lage families. Women did buy, sell, and hold land independently and, especially as widows, headed households; when they did they were required to pay all rents and taxes. In areas of Europe where men were gone fishing or foresting for long periods of time, or where men left seasonally or more permanently in search of work elsewhere, women made decisions about the way village affairs were to be run, though they did not set up formal institutions to do this.

Manors do not represent the only form of medieval rural economy. In Frisia, in parts of Germany, and in much of southern France, free independent farmers held **allodial land**—that is, land that they owned outright, free of rents and services. These farms tended to be small and were surrounded by large estates that gradually swallowed them up. In Scandinavia the soil was so poor and the climate so harsh that people tended to live on widely scattered farms rather than in villages, but they still lived in relatively small family groups.

Agricultural Methods

The fields of the village were farmed in what historians term the **open-field system,** a pattern that differs sharply from modern farming practices. In the open-field system, the arable land of a manor was divided into two or three fields without hedges or fences to mark the individual holdings of the lord, serfs, and freemen. The village as a whole decided what would be planted in each field, rotating the crops according to tradition and need. Some fields would be planted in crops such as wheat, rye, peas, or barley for human consumption, some in oats or other crops for both animals and humans, and some would be left unworked or *fallow* to allow the soil to rejuvenate. The exact pattern of this rotation varied from location to location, but in most areas with open-field agriculture the holdings farmed by any one family did not consist of a whole field but instead of strips in many fields.

Farmers knew the value of animal fertilizers such as chicken and sheep manure. Because cattle were fed on the common pasture and were rarely stabled, gathering their manure was laborious and time-consuming. Nevertheless, whenever possible, animal manure was gathered and thinly spread. So also was house garbage—eggshells, fruit cores, onion skins—that had disintegrated in a compost heap.

Local needs, the fertility of the soil, and dietary customs determined what was planted and the method of crop rotation. Where one or several manors belonged to a great aristocratic establishment, such as the abbey of Cluny, which needed large quantities of oats for horses, more of the arable land would be planted in oats than in other cereals. The milder climate of the Mediterranean area allowed for more frequent planting and a greater range of agricultural products; families tended to farm individual square plots rather than long strips. Milder climate also meant that more work (and play) could take place outdoors, which may have somewhat alleviated crowding in households with many family members. Throughout Europe, living space—especially living space

close enough to a fire to feel some warmth in cold weather—was cramped, dark, smoky, and smelly, with animals and people both sharing tight quarters, sometimes with each other. Nobles in castles had more total space, of course, but in many parts of Europe they too huddled around fires during much of the year.

During the tenth and eleventh centuries peasants and nobles may have moved away from their fires somewhat, for Europe experienced a significant warming trend. Meteorologists believe that a slow but steady retreat of polar ice occurred between the ninth and eleventh centuries. The century between 1080 and 1180 witnessed exceptionally clement weather in England, France, and Germany, with mild winters and dry summers. Increased agricultural output had a profound impact on society: it improved Europeans' health, commerce, industry, and general lifestyle. A better diet had an enormous impact on women's lives: it meant increased body fat, which increased fertility; also, more iron in the diet meant that women were less anemic and less subject to opportunistic diseases. Some researchers believe that it was in the High Middle Ages that Western women began to outlive men. Improved opportunities also encouraged people to marry somewhat earlier, which meant larger families and further population growth. Demographers often figure that in an era before reliable artificial means of contraception, but in which women nursed their own children (which inhibits fertility), every three years earlier that people married brought on average one more child.

Agricultural Improvements

The tenth and eleventh centuries also witnessed a remarkable spurt in mechanization, especially in the use of energy. Water mills were one important part of this. In the ancient world, slaves ground the grain for bread; as slavery was replaced by serfdom, grinding became a woman's task. When water mills were introduced into an area, women turned to other tasks, such as raising animals, working in gardens or vineyards, raising and preparing flax to make linen, or spinning yarn for cloth. A water mill unearthed near Monte Cassino in Italy could grind about 1.5 tons of grain in ten hours, a quantity that would formerly have required the exertions of forty people. Both lords and villagers recognized the advantages of water-powered mills, and the increase in the number of mills along streams, under bridges, and even floating in the middle of rivers was spectacular. By the mid-ninth century, on the lands of the abbey of Saint-Germaine-des-Prés near Paris, there were 59 water mills. Succeeding generations saw a continued increase. Thus,

Windmill The mill was constructed on a pivot so that it could turn in the direction of the wind. Used primarily to grind grain, as shown here with a man carrying a sack of grain to be ground into flour, windmills were also used to process cloth, brew beer, drive saws, and provide power for iron forges. (*Bodleian Library, Oxford, MS Bodl 264, fol. 81R*)

on the Robec River near Rouen, there were 2 mills in the tenth century, 4 in the eleventh, 10 in the thirteenth, and 12 in the fourteenth. William the Conqueror ordered mills counted along with other agricultural items in the *Domesday Book,* and his assessors recorded 5,624.

Besides grinding wheat or other grains to produce flour, water mills became essential in *fulling,* the process of scouring, cleansing, and thickening cloth. No longer did men or women trample cloth in a trough; instead wooden hammers were raised and dropped on the cloth by means of a revolving drum connected to the spindle of a water wheel. Water mills revolutionized grinding and fulling by using natural, rather than human, energy. The expansion of cloth production in medieval Europe rested on a base of water power. Water-powered grain mills freed women to spin—the bottleneck in cloth production, as each weaver needed at least six spinners to supply yarn—and enabled women and men to full cloth at a much faster rate.

Successful at adapting waterpower to human needs, medieval engineers soon harnessed wind power. They replaced the wheels driven by water with sails. But while water always flows in the same direction, wind can blow from many directions. Windmill engineers solved this problem very ingeniously by mounting the framed wooden body, which contained the machinery and carried the sails, on a massive upright post free to turn in the wind. After 1180 the construction of windmills accelerated. Many were erected in the flat areas of northern Europe, including Holland, that lacked fast-flowing streams.

In the early twelfth century the production of iron increased greatly. Iron was first used in agriculture for plowshares (the part of the plow that cuts the furrow and grinds up the earth), and then for pitchforks, spades, and axes. Harrows—cultivating instruments with heavy teeth that broke up and smoothed the soil—began to have iron instead of wooden teeth.

Plows and harrows were increasingly drawn by horses. The development of the padded horse collar that rested on the horse's shoulders and was attached to the load by shafts led to dramatic improvements. The horse collar meant that the animal could put its entire weight into the task of pulling. The use of horses, rather than oxen, spread in the twelfth century because horses' greater speed brought greater efficiency to farming and reduced the amount of human labor involved. The quality of the soil and the level of rainfall in the area seem to have determined whether peasants shifted from ox teams to horses. Horses worked best on light, dry, and easily tilled soil, but they had difficulties plowing through clay soils and in places where heavy moisture caused earth to cling to the plow. Oxen, on the other hand, worked well on heavy, muddy, or clay soil, but they slipped and suffered hoof damage on dry, stony land. Thus, in England horses were employed in the light soils of Norfolk on the northeastern coast and on the stony lands of Yorkshire, while oxen remained common in the Midlands until the late sixteenth century. At the same time, horses were an enormous investment, perhaps comparable to a modern tractor. They had to be shod (another indication of increased iron production), and the oats they ate were costly.

The thirteenth century witnessed a tremendous spurt in the use of horses to haul carts to market. Consequently, goods reached market faster, and the number of markets to which the peasant had access increased. Peasants not only sold products, but also bought them as their opportunities for spending on at least a few nonagricultural goods multiplied.

Agricultural yields varied widely from place to place and from year to year. Even with good iron tools, horsepower, and careful use of seed and fertilizer, medieval peasants were at the mercy of the weather. Even today too much or too little rain can cause terrible financial loss and extreme hardship. Medieval families were far more vulnerable. Townspeople were wholly dependent on the surrounding countryside for food, which could not be shipped over long distances. A poor harvest meant that both townspeople and rural people suffered.

By twenty-first-century standards, medieval agricultural yields were very low, but there was striking improvement over time. Between the ninth and early thirteenth centuries, yields of cereals appear to have approximately doubled, and on the best-managed estates the farmer harvested 5 bushels of grain for every bushel of seed planted. (A modern Illinois farmer expects to get 40 bushels of soybeans, 150 bushels of corn, and 50 bushels of wheat for every bushel of seed planted.) Grain yields were probably greatest on large manorial estates, where there was more professional management, and may have hit 12 or 15 to 1 in good years. As low as that may seem by current standards, it marked a rise in productivity equal to that of the years just before the start of the great agricultural revolution of the eighteenth century.

Households, Work, and Food

Life for most people in medieval Europe meant country life. A person's horizons were largely restricted to the manor on which he or she was born. True, peasants who colonized such sparsely settled regions as eastern Germany must have traveled long distances. But most people rarely traveled more than twenty-five miles beyond their villages. Everyone's world was small, narrow, and provincial in the original sense of the word: limited by the boundaries of the province. This way of life did not have entirely unfortunate results. People had a strong sense of family and the certainty of its support and help in time of trouble. Men and women knew what their life's work would be—the same as their mother's or father's. They had a sense of place, and pride in that place was reflected in adornment of the village church. Religion and the village gave people a sense of identity, rootedness, and security, which some commentators argue has been lost in modern, urban, industrialized society.

Life on the manor may have been stable, but it was dull. Medieval men and women often sought escape in heavy drinking. English judicial records of the thirteenth century reveal a surprisingly large number of "accidental" deaths. Strong, robust, commonsensical people do not ordinarily fall on their knives and stab themselves, or slip out of boats and drown, or get lost in the woods on a winter's night, or fall from horses and get trampled. The victims were probably drunk. Many of these accidents occurred, as the court records say, "coming from an ale." Brawls and violent fights were frequent at taverns.

The size and quality of peasants' houses varied according to their relative prosperity, and that prosperity usually depended on the amount of land held. Poorer peasants lived in windowless cottages built of wood and clay or wattle (poles interwoven with branches or reeds) and thatched with straw. These cottages consisted of one large room that served as the kitchen and living quarters for all. The house had an earthen floor and a fireplace. The lack of windows meant that the room was very sooty. A trestle table, several stools, one or two beds, and a chest for storing clothes constituted the furniture. A shed attached to the house provided storage for tools and shelter for animals. Prosperous peasants added rooms and furniture as they could be afforded, and some wealthy peasants in the early fourteenth century had two-story houses with separate bedrooms for parents and children.

Every house had a small garden and an outbuilding. Onions, garlic, turnips, and carrots were grown and stored through the winter in the main room of the dwelling or in the shed attached to it. Cabbage was raised almost everywhere and, after being shredded, salted, and packed in vats of hot water, was turned into kraut. Peasants ate vegetables not because they appreciated their importance for good health but because there was usually little else available. Preserving and storing foods were the basic responsibility of the women and children.

Medieval households were not self-sufficient, but bought cloth, metal, leather goods, and even some food from village market stalls. They also bought ale, the universal drink of the common people in northern Europe. By modern American standards, the rate of consumption was heroic. Each monk of Abingdon Abbey in twelfth-century England was allotted three gallons a day, and a man working in the fields for ten hours probably drank much more.[3] Women dominated in the production of ale for the community market. This industry required an initial investment in large vessels and knowledge of the correct proportions of barley, water, yeast, and hops. Women found brewing hard and dangerous work: it involved carrying twelve-gallon vats of hot liquid. Records of the English coroners' courts reveal that 5 percent of women who died accidentally did so in brewing accidents, by falling into the vats of boiling liquid.[4]

The mainstay of the diet for peasants everywhere—and for all other classes—was bread. It was a hard, black substance made of barley, millet, and oats, rarely of expensive wheat flour. Bread might be baked at home, but most households did not have ovens, which were expensive to build and posed a fire danger. Thus bread was baked in communal ovens or purchased from households that specialized in bread-baking.

The diet of people living in an area with access to a river, lake, or stream would be supplemented with fish, which could be preserved by salting. People living close to the sea could gather shellfish such as oysters, mussels, and whelks. Many places had severe laws against hunting and trapping in the forests. Deer, wild boars, and other game were strictly reserved for the king and nobility. These laws were flagrantly violated, however, and stolen rabbits and wild game often found their way to peasants' tables. In places like the Bavarian Alps of southern Germany, where hundreds of sheep grazed on the mountainsides, or at Cheddar in southwestern England, cheese was a staple.

Lists of peasant obligations and services to the lord, such as the following from Battle Abbey, commonly included the payment of chickens and eggs: "John of Coyworth holds a house and thirty acres of land, and owes yearly 2 p at Easter and Michaelmas; and he owes a cock and two hens at Christmas, of the value of 4 d."[5] Chickens and eggs must have been highly valued in the prudently managed household. Animals were too valuable to be used for food on a regular basis. The weaker animals were often slaughtered in the fall so that they did not need to be fed through the winter, and their meat was

Man Stomping on Grapes   Before the invention of the winepress in 1526, grapes were crushed by human power—people treading on them in barrels. The French province of Poitou, the region of Bordeaux, and the Rhine and Moselle Valleys supplied wine to an expanding European market. The staple drinks for peasants and monks were ale, beer, and cider; wine was considered an aristocratic drink. *(Glasgow University Library, Department of Special Collections, Ms Hunter 229)*

salted and was eaten only on great feast days such as Christmas and Easter. Some scholars believe that, by the mid-thirteenth century, there was an increase in the consumption of meat generally. If so, this improvement in diet is further evidence of an improved standard of living.

Then as now, farmers ate their main meal around noon. This was often soup—a thick *potage* of boiled cabbage, onions, turnips, and peas seasoned with a bone or perhaps a sliver of meat. The evening meal, taken at sunset, consisted of leftovers from the noon meal, perhaps with bread, cheese, milk, or ale.

Once children were able to walk, they helped their parents in the hundreds of chores that had to be done. Small children were set to collecting eggs, if the family had chickens, or gathering twigs and sticks for firewood. As

Baking Bread Bread and beer or ale were the main manorial products for local consumption. While women dominated the making of ale and beer, men and women cooperated in the making and baking of bread—the staple of the diet. Most people did not have ovens in their own homes because of the danger of fire, but instead used the communal manorial oven, which, like a modern pizza oven, could bake several loaves at once. (*Bibliothèque nationale de France*)

they grew older, children had more responsible tasks, such as weeding the family's vegetable garden, milking the cows, shearing the sheep, cutting wood for fires, and helping with the planting or harvesting.

Health Care

Scholars are only beginning to explore questions of medieval health care, and there are still many aspects of public health that we know little about. The steady rise in population between the mid-eleventh and fourteenth centuries, usually attributed to warmer climate, increased food supply, and a reduction of violence with growing political stability, may also be ascribed partly to better health care. A recent study of skeletal remains in the village of Brandes in Burgundy showed that peasants enjoyed very good health: they were well built and had excellent teeth, and their bones revealed no signs of chronic disease. Obviously we cannot generalize about the health of all people on the basis of evidence from one village, but such research indicates that medieval adults were tough.

What care existed for the sick? As in the past, the sick everywhere depended above all on the private nursing care of relatives and friends. Beginning in the twelfth century in the British Isles, however, the royal family, the

clergy, noble men and women, and newly rich merchants also established institutions to care for the sick or for those who for some reason could not take care of themselves. Within city walls they built hospitals, which were not hospitals in the modern sense, but rather places where those with chronic diseases that were not contagious, poor expectant mothers, the handicapped, people recovering from injuries, foundling children, and mentally retarded or psychologically disturbed children or adults went for care. Outside city walls they built leprosariums or small hospices for people with leprosy and other contagious diseases. Such institutions might be staffed by members of religious orders, people who had less formally devoted themselves to lives of service, laymen and laywomen who were paid for their work, or a combination of the three. In the thirteenth century there were at least 113 hospitals in England with possibly as many as 3,494 beds, or one bed for every 600 to 1,000 persons. (In 1982 the ratio in England was 1 bed for every 108 persons.)

The organization of hospitals followed the structure and routine of monastic communities. Patients were segregated according to sex, wore a common uniform, and were required to keep periods of silence and to attend devotions in the hospital chapel. In the twelfth century medical personnel at hospitals were trained on the job, but by the thirteenth century some had been trained in faculties of medicine at Europe's new universities (see page 345). There were few university-trained physicians, however—one document lists ninety physicians (*medicus*) in all of England for a population of perhaps 2 million people—and day-to-day hospital care was in the hands of people whose medical training was more practical than theoretical. We have no information about rates of recovery, so we cannot judge whether those who were treated by university-trained physicians did better than other patients. University training was completely theoretical, so the food, warm bed, and nursing care provided by hospitals may have made more of a difference than the occasional doctor visit.

Outside of hospitals, university-trained physicians were a luxury only the wealthy could afford. For externally visible ailments, such as wounds, skin diseases, or broken bones, people turned to barber-surgeons who were trained in an apprenticeship system. Barber-surgeons also carried out bloodletting, using leeches or nicking a vein with a small knife to draw out blood, the most common course of treatment for many internal illnesses or as a health maintenance measure. Barber-surgeons, as their name suggests, also cut hair, for scissors were a relatively rare household item. (The barber pole, with red and blue stripes of blood running down the armlike pole, reflects this dual role; it would have been one of many markers of occupation people would have seen outside houses as they walked through the streets of a medieval town.) For other internal ailments people used apothecaries—also trained through an apprenticeship system—to suggest and mix drugs, which combined herbs, salts, metals, and more fanciful ingredients such as "dragon's blood."

People also relied on men and women who had no official training at all, but learned healing techniques from their parents or other older people. Such healers gained a reputation as "cunning men" or "wise women" through the results (or the assumed results) of their treatments, which were often mixtures of herbal remedies, sayings, specific foods, prayers, amulets, and ritual healing activities. Such combinations were also what people prescribed for themselves, for most treatment of illness was handled by home remedies handed down orally or perhaps through a cherished handwritten family herbal, cookbook, or household guide. Highly learned clergy frowned on such treatments, as they bordered on, or indeed actually included, the magical and perhaps implied doubts of God's ability to heal. Many clergy were active participants in them, however, blessing objects to be used in healing rituals or placing them under the altar cloth during the Mass.

Childbirth and Child Abandonment

The most dangerous period of life for any person, peasant or noble, was infancy and early childhood. In normal years perhaps as many as one-third of all children died before age five, and in years with plagues, droughts, or famines this share climbed to more than half. Children often died from accidents as well as from malnutrition and illness, wandering into cooking fires, drowning in potholes in the road, or getting in the way of horses or cattle. Reaching adulthood meant that people had survived the most dangerous part of their lives, and many lived well into their fifties and sixties.

Childbirth was dangerous for mothers as well as for infants. Though mortality statistics are difficult to determine, every woman would have known someone who died in childbirth, and most would have seen such a death. Women developed prayers, rituals, and special sayings to ensure safe and speedy childbirth. Village women helped their friends, relatives, sisters, and daughters through childbirth, and women who were more capable acquired specialized midwifery skills. In larger towns and cities, such women gradually developed into professional midwives who were paid for their services and who trained younger women as apprentices, just as barber-surgeons and apothecaries trained their male apprentices. For most women, however, childbirth was handled by female friends and family, not by professionals.

The abandonment of infant children seems to have been the most favored form of family limitation and was widely practiced throughout the Middle Ages. Parents or guardians left children somewhere, sold them, or legally gave authority to some other person or institution. Why did parents do this? What became of the children? What attitudes did medieval society have toward this practice?

Poverty or local natural disaster led some parents to abandon their children because they could not support them. Before the eleventh century food was so scarce that few parents could feed themselves, let alone children. Thus Saint Patrick wrote that in times of famine, fathers would sell their sons and daughters so that the children could be fed. Parents sometimes gave children away because they were illegitimate or the result of incestuous unions. An eighth-century penitential collection describes the proper treatment for a woman who exposes her unwanted child—that is, leaves it in the open to die—because she has been raped by an enemy or is unable to nourish it. She is not to be blamed, but she should do penance.[6]

Sometimes parents believed that someone of greater means or status might find the child and bring it up in

Monastic Entrance   In a world with few career opportunities for "superfluous children," monasteries served a valuable social function. Because a dowry was expected, monastic life was generally limited to the children of the affluent. Here a father—advising his son to be obedient and holding a bag of money for the monastery—hands his son over to the abbot. The boy does not look enthusiastic. *(The J. Paul Getty Museum, Los Angeles. Unknown illuminator, Initial Q: An Abbot Receiving a Child Decretum, ca 1170–1180 [83.MQ.163.fol.63])*

better circumstances than the natal parents could provide. Disappointment in the sex of the child or its physical weakness or deformity might have also led parents to abandon it. Among Christians, superfluous children could be given to monasteries as **oblates.** The word *oblate* derives from the Latin *oblatio,* meaning "offering." Boys and girls were given to monasteries or convents as permanent gifts. By the seventh century church councils and civil codes had defined the practice: "Parents of any social status could donate a child, of either sex, at least up to the age of ten." Contemporaries considered oblation a religious act, since the child was offered to God often in recompense for parental sin. But oblation also served social and economic functions. The monastery nurtured and educated the child in a familial atmosphere, and it provided career opportunities for the mature monk or nun whatever his or her origins. Oblation has justifiably been described as "in many ways the most humane form of abandonment ever devised in the West."[7]

Recent research suggests that abandonment was very common among the poor until about the year 1000. The next two hundred years, which saw great agricultural change and relative prosperity, witnessed a low point in the abandonment of poor children. On the other hand, in the twelfth and thirteenth centuries the incidence of

noble parents giving their younger sons and daughters to religious houses increased dramatically; nobles wanted to preserve their estates intact for their eldest sons. Consequently, oblates composed a high percentage of monastic populations. At Winchester in England, for example, 85 percent of the new monks between 1030 and 1070 were oblates. In the early thirteenth century the bishop of Paris observed that children were "cast into the cloister by parents and relatives just as if they were kittens or piglets whom their mothers could not nourish; so that they may die to the world not spiritually but . . . civilly, that is—so that they may be deprived of their hereditary position and that it may devolve on those who remain in the world." The abandonment of children remained socially acceptable. Ecclesiastical and civil authorities never legislated against it.[8]

Popular Religion

Apart from the land, the weather, and local legal and social conditions, religion had the greatest impact on the daily lives of ordinary people in the High Middle Ages. Religious practices varied widely from country to country and even from province to province. But nowhere was religion a one-hour-a-week affair. Most people in medieval Europe were Christian, but there were small Jewish communities scattered in many parts of Europe and Muslims in the Iberian Peninsula, Sicily, other Mediterranean islands, and southeastern Europe.

● *How did religious practices and attitudes permeate everyday life?*

Village Churches and Christian Symbols

For Christians the village church was the center of community life—social, political, and economic as well as religious—with the parish priest in charge of a host of activities. Although church law placed the priest under the bishop's authority, the manorial lord appointed him and financed such education in Latin, Scripture, and liturgy as he might receive. Parish priests were peasants and often were poor. They received a tithe of produce from their parishioners, and depending on the spiritual quality of their lives they enjoyed status and prestige. Since they often worked in the fields with the people, they understood the people's labor, needs, and frustrations. The parish priest was also responsible for the upkeep of the village church and for taking the lead in providing local poor relief.

According to official church doctrine, the center of the Christian religious life was the Mass, the re-enactment of Christ's sacrifice on the cross. Every Sunday and on holy days, the villagers stood at Mass or squatted on the floor (there were no chairs), breaking the painful routine of work. The feasts that accompanied baptisms, weddings, funerals, and other celebrations were commonly held in the churchyard. Medieval drama originated in the church. Mystery plays, based on biblical episodes, were performed first in the sanctuary, then on the church porch, which was often in front of the west door, and then at stations around the town.

From the church porch the priest read orders and messages from royal and ecclesiastical authorities to his parishioners. Royal judges traveling on circuit opened their courts on the church porch. The west front of the church, with its scenes of the Last Judgment, was the background against which the justices disposed of civil and criminal cases. In busy mercantile centers such as London, business agreements and commercial exchanges were made in the aisles of the church itself, as at Saint Paul's.

Popular religion consisted largely of rituals heavy with symbolism. Before slicing a loaf of bread, the pious woman tapped the sign of the cross on it with her knife. Before planting, the village priest customarily went out and sprinkled the fields with water, symbolizing refreshment and life. Everyone participated in village processions. The entire calendar was designed with reference to Christmas, Easter, and Pentecost, events in the life of Jesus and his disciples. The varying colors of the vestments the priests wore at Mass gave villagers a sense of the changing seasons of the church's liturgical year. The signs and symbols of Christianity were visible everywhere.

Saints and Sacraments

Along with days marking events in the life of Jesus, the Christian calendar was filled with saints' days. **Saints** were individuals who had lived particularly holy lives and were honored locally or more widely for their connection with the divine. The saints had once lived on earth and thus could well understand human problems. They could be helpful intercessors with Christ or God the Father. In the church women and men prayed to the saints; the stone in the church altar contained **relics** of the saints— bones, articles of clothing, the saint's tears, saliva, even the dust from the saint's tomb. These relics often belonged to a local saint to whom the church itself had been dedicated.

The cult of the saints had begun in the East, spread in the early Middle Ages, and gained enormous popularity in the West in the eleventh and twelfth centuries. People believed that the saints possessed supernatural powers that enabled them to perform miracles, and the saint became the special property of the locality in which his or her relics rested. Thus, to secure the saint's support and to guarantee the region's prosperity, a busy traffic in relics developed. The understanding that existed between the saint and the peasants rested on the customary medieval relationship of mutual fidelity and aid: in return for the saint's healing and support, peasants would offer the saint prayers, loyalty, and gifts at the shrine or church under his or her patronage. (See the feature "Listening to the Past: The Pilgrim's Guide to Santiago de Compostela" on pages 328–329.)

In the later Middle Ages popular hagiographies (biographies of saints based on myths, legends, and popular stories) attributed specialized functions to the saints. Saint Elmo (ca 300), who supposedly had preached unharmed during a thunder and lightning storm, became the patron of sailors. Saint Agatha (third century), whose breasts were torn with shears because she rejected the attentions of a powerful suitor, became the patron of wet nurses, women with breast difficulties, and bell ringers (because of the resemblance of breasts to bells). Saint Jude the Apostle, whom no one invoked because his name resembled that of Jesus' betrayer, Judas, became the patron of lost causes. Saint Gertrude was reputed to guard houses against the entry of mice.

How were saints chosen, and what was the official church position on them? What had been their social background when alive? Since the early days of Christianity, individuals whose exemplary virtue was proved by miracles at their tombs had been venerated by laypeople. Although, as part of the general centralization of papal power in the twelfth and thirteenth centuries, the Roman authorities insisted that they had the exclusive right to examine the lives and activities of candidates for sainthood in a formal "trial," popular opinion still continued to declare people saints. Between 1185 and 1431 only seventy official investigations were held at Rome, but hundreds of new persons across Europe were venerated as saints. Church officials and educated clergy evaluated candidates according to the "heroic virtue" of their lives, but laypeople judged solely by the saint's miracles. Some clergy preached against the veneration of relics and called it idolatry, but their appeals had little effect.

Current research suggests that a connection exists between the models of holiness and the character of the social structure in different parts of Europe. Northern and southern Europeans chose saints of different social backgrounds or classes. In Italy and Mediterranean lands saints tended to be non-aristocrats, whereas in France and Germany primarily men and women of the nobility became saints. The cult of the saints, which developed in a rural and uneducated environment, represents a central feature of popular culture in the Middle Ages.

Along with the veneration of saints, a new religious understanding developed in the High Middle Ages. Twelfth-century theologians expanded on Saint Augustine's understanding of **sacraments**—outward and visible signs regarded as instituted by Christ to give grace—and created an entire sacramental system. Only a priest could dispense a sacrament (except when someone was in danger of death), and the list of seven sacraments, originally compiled by Peter Lombard, was formally accepted by the Fourth Lateran Council in 1215.

Baptism is the rite by which a person enters the Christian community. This is signified by sprinkling the person with holy water or fully immersing him or her in water. If the person has reached the age of reason (seven), a profession of faith and repentance for previous sins are required. *Penance* (from the Latin *poena*, meaning "punishment") is the rite by which, through oral confession to a priest, sins committed after baptism are forgiven. The penitent often has to perform some act as compensation, such as paying for stolen goods or apologizing for sins against charity. **Eucharist** is the name given to the central ceremony of Christian worship (also called the Mass, the Lord's Supper, and Holy Communion) as well as to the bread and wine consecrated by the priest and consumed by believers. In *confirmation,* a person becomes a full member of the Christian community through the laying on of the bishop's hands and his anointment of the candidate's forehead with oil. *Matrimony* as a sacrament derives from Jesus' presence at the marriage feast of Cana, the first public appearance of his ministry, which medieval theologians interpreted as proof of his wish to bless marriages. In the eleventh century the church claimed exclusive jurisdiction over marriage, and civil au-

The Eucharist   The Fourth Lateran Council of 1215 encouraged all Christians to receive the Eucharist at least once a year after confession and penance. Here a priest places the consecrated bread, called a *host,* on people's tongues. *(Biblioteca Apostolica Vaticana)*

thorities acquiesced. *Orders* is the rite by which men, through the laying on of the bishop's hands and his anointment of the candidates' hands, become ordained as priests. Last, *extreme unction* or *anointment of the sick* is usually administered when a person is gravely ill and in danger of death.

Medieval Christians believed that these seven sacraments brought grace, the divine assistance or help needed to lead a good Christian life and to merit salvation. Sermons and homilies taught that at the center of the sacramental system stood the Eucharist, the small piece of bread that through the words of priestly consecration at the Mass became the living body of Christ and, when worthily consumed, became a channel of Christ's grace. The ritual of consecration, repeated at every altar of Christendom, became a unifying symbol in a complex world. The sacramental system, however, did not replace strong devotion to the saints.

Beliefs

Was popular religion largely a matter of rituals and ceremonies? What did people actually *believe?* It is difficult to say, partly because medieval peasants left few written records of their thoughts, and partly because in every age there is often great disparity between what people profess to believe and their conduct or the ways they act on their beliefs.

Peasants had a strong sense of the presence of God. They believed that God rewarded the virtuous with peace, health, and material prosperity and punished sinners with disease, poor harvests, and war. Sin was caused by the Devil, who lurked everywhere and constantly incited people to evil deeds and sin, especially sins of the flesh. Sin frequently took place in the dark. Thus evil and the Devil were connected in the peasant's mind with darkness or blackness. In some medieval literature, the Devil is portrayed as black, an identification that has had a profound and sorry impact on Western racial attitudes.

In the eleventh century theologians began to emphasize Mary's spiritual motherhood of all Christians. The huge outpouring of popular devotions to Mary concentrated on her special relationship to Christ as all-powerful intercessor with him. The most famous prayer, "Salve Regina," perfectly expresses medieval people's confidence in Mary, their advocate with Christ:

Hail, holy Queen, Mother of Mercy! Our life, our sweetness, and our hope. To thee we cry, poor banished children of Eve; to thee we send up our sighs, mourning and weeping in this valley of tears. Turn, then, most gracious advocate, thy merciful eyes upon us; and after this our exile show us the blessed fruit of thy womb, Jesus. O merciful, O loving, O sweet Virgin Mary!

The Mass was in Latin, but the priest delivered sermons on the Gospel in the vernacular. Anyway, he was supposed to. An almost universal criticism of parish priests in the twelfth and thirteenth centuries was that they were incapable of explaining basic Christian teachings to their parishioners. The growth of the universities (see page 347) did not improve the situation because few diocesan clerics attended them, and those who did and won degrees secured administrative positions with prelates or lay governments. The only parish priest to be canonized as a saint in the entire Middle Ages, the Breton lawyer and priest Saint Yves (d. 1303), had resigned a position as a diocesan judge to serve rural parishioners. At the trial for his canonization, laypeople stressed that not only had he led a simple and frugal life but he also had put his forensic skills to the service of preaching the Christian Gospels. He represents a great exception to the prevailing inability of medieval parish clergy to preach in a rural milieu. Parish priests celebrated the liturgy and administered the sacraments, but they had other short-

comings. A thirteenth-century Alsatian chronicler said that the peasants of the region did not complain that their pastors had concubines because that made them less fearful for the virtue of their daughters.[9]

Nevertheless, people grasped the meaning of biblical stories and church doctrines from the paintings on the church walls or, in wealthy parishes, the scenes in stained-glass windows. Illiterate and uneducated, they certainly could not reason out the increasingly sophisticated propositions of clever theologians. Still, Scriptural references and proverbs dotted everyone's language. The English *goodbye,* the French *adieu,* and the Spanish *adios* all derive from words meaning "God be with you." Christianity was the foundation of the common people's culture for most Europeans.

Muslims and Jews

The interpenetration of Christian ceremonies and daily life for most Europeans meant that those who did not participate or who had different religious rituals were clearly marked as outsiders. This included Muslims in the Iberian Peninsula, where Christian rulers were establishing kingdoms in territory won through the reconquista (see pages 265–267). Islam was outlawed in their territories, and some of the Muslims left Spain, leaving room for new settlers from elsewhere in Christian Europe. Other Muslims converted, becoming **conversos** or what were in Spain called "New Christians." In more isolated villages, people simply continued their Muslim rituals and practices, including abstaining from pork, reciting verses from the Qur'an, praying at specified times of the day, and observing Muslim holy days, though they might hide this from the local priest or visiting church or government officials. As in Christianity and in other Muslim areas around the world, they often venerated the tombs of individuals regarded as saints, asking them for assistance and praying for blessings.

Islam was geographically limited in medieval Europe, but by the late tenth century Jews could be found in many areas, often brought in as clients of rulers because of their skills as merchants. There were Jewish communities in Italian cities and in the cities along the Rhine such as Cologne, Worms, Speyer, and Mainz. Jews migrated from there to England and France, where they generally lived in the growing towns, often separate from the larger Christian community. Jewish dietary laws require meat to be handled in a specific way, so Jews had their own butchers; there were Jewish artisans in many other trades as well, though Jews were forbidden to join Christian guilds. Jews held weekly religious services on

Saturday, the Sabbath holy day of rest, and celebrated an annual cycle of holidays, including the High Holidays of Rosh Hashanah and Yom Kippur in the fall and Passover in the spring. Each of these holidays involved special prayers, services, and often foods, and many of them commemorated specific events from Jewish history, including various times that they had been rescued from captivity.

The Crusades brought violence against Jews in many cities (see pages 281–283), and restrictions on Jews increased in much of Europe. Christian officials meeting in the Third and Fourth Lateran Councils limited Jewish-Christian relations and required Jews to wear badges of identification. In the late thirteenth century Jews were expelled from England and in the early fourteenth century from France. Many of them went to Muslim and Christian areas of the Iberian Peninsula, where the rulers of both faiths initially welcomed them, though restrictions and violence gradually became more common there as well. Jews continued to live in the independent cities of the Holy Roman Empire and Italy, and some migrated eastward into new towns that were being established in Slavic areas.

Religion and the Cycle of Life

Increasing suspicion and hostility marked relations between religious groups throughout the Middle Ages, but there were also important similarities in the ways Christians, Jews, and Muslims in Europe understood and experienced their religions. In all three traditions, every major life transition was marked by a ceremony that included religious elements. Christian weddings might be held in the village church or at the church door, though among well-to-do families the wedding was held in the house of the bride or bridegroom. A priest's blessing was often sought, though it was not essential to the marriage, for Christian doctrine defined marriage as an agreement between a man and a woman. As long as consent was given freely, the spouses were old enough to know what they were doing, and the agreement was made in words of present tense (that is, not promising to marry some time in the future), the marriage was theologically valid. Exchanging rings and a kiss solemnized this contract between the spouses. Muslim weddings were also finalized by a contract between the bride and groom and were often overseen by a wedding official, though any man with knowledge of Islamic principles could officiate. Jewish weddings were guided by statements in Talmudic law that weddings were complete when the bride had entered the "chuppah," which medieval Jewish authorities

interpreted to mean a room in the groom's house. (By the sixteenth century the chuppah was often a cloth canopy held by four tall posts, a practice that continues in Jewish wedding ceremonies today.) Among wealthy families, this room might be decorated for the occasion with tapestries and flowers.

A wedding generally meant a party of some sort, with food, music, dancing, and lots of drinking. It often included rituals that symbolized the proper hierarchical relations between the spouses—such as placing the husband's shoe on the bedstead over the couple, symbolizing his authority—or that worked to ensure the couple's fertility—such as untying all the knots in the household, for tying knots was one way that people reputed to have magical powers bound up the reproductive power of a man. All this came together in what was often the final event of a wedding, the priest blessing the couple in their marriage bed, often with family and friends standing around or banging on pans, yelling, or otherwise making as much noise as possible. The friends and family members had generally been part of the discussions, negotiations, and activities leading up to the marriage; marriage united two families and was far too important to leave up to two young people alone. Among serfs the lord's permission was often required, with a special fee paid to obtain this. (This permission did *not* include the right to deflower the bride; the idea that lords had the "right of first night," the *jus primae noctis,* had a particularly long life, but there is no evidence of its existence in any legal sources.)

The involvement of family and friends in choosing one's spouse might lead to conflict, but more often the wishes of the young people and their parents, kin, and community were quite similar; all hoped for marriages that provided economic security, honorable standing, and a good number of healthy children. The best marriages offered companionship, emotional support, and even love, but these were understood to grow out of the marriage, not necessarily precede it. Jewish authorities described the best marriages as predestined in heaven and allowed divorce for truly bad matches that clearly did not reflect such heavenly matching. Although earlier Jewish customs had given the right to divorce only to men, by the medieval period German Jewish courts allowed women to petition for divorce as well and held that they could not be divorced without their consent. Among Christians, marriage was increasingly regarded as officially indissoluble, though wealthy people could generally obtain annulment in return for payment to a church official, while poorer folk could use abandonment or simply moving apart as a last resort. Breaking up a

Foolish Maidens on a Wedding Door of the Cathedral in Strasbourg (thirteenth century) Medieval cathedrals sometimes had a side door depicting a biblical story of ten young women who went to meet a bridegroom. Five of them were wise and took extra oil for their lamps, and five were foolish and did not (Matthew 25:1–13). In the story, which is a parable about always being prepared for the end of the world, the foolish maidens were out of oil when the bridegroom arrived and missed the wedding feast. The "maidens' door" became a popular site for weddings, which were held right in front of it. *(Erich Lessing/Art Resource, NY)*

marriage meant breaking up the basic production and consumption unit, however, which was a very serious matter, so marital dissolution by any means other than the death of one spouse was rare.

Children and Religion

Most brides hoped to be pregnant soon after their weddings, and if the rituals during the weddings had not been effective in bringing this about, there were other avenues to try. Christian women hoping for children said special prayers to the Virgin Mary or her mother Anne; wore amulets of amber, bone, or mistletoe thought to increase fertility; repeated charms and verses they had learned from other women; or, in desperate cases, went on pilgrimages to make special supplications. Muslim and Jewish women wore small cases with sacred verses or

asked for blessings from religious leaders. Women continued these prayers and rituals through pregnancy and childbirth, often combining religious traditions with folk beliefs handed down orally. Women in southern France, for example, offered prayers for easy childbirth and healthy children to Saint Guinefort, a greyhound who had been mistakenly killed by his owner after saving the owner's child from a poisonous snake. The fact that Guinefort was a dog meant he could never become an official saint, but women saw him as a powerful and martyred protector of children.

Judaism, Christianity, and Islam all required women to remain separate from the community after childbirth and often had special ceremonies welcoming them back once this period was over. Muslim women were prohibited from touching the Qur'an, entering a mosque, or engaging in religious fasts for forty days, after which their relatives brought special clothes and gifts for the child. Six weeks after giving birth, a Jewish woman underwent a ritual bath of purification, called a *mikvah,* in a special room or building in the Jewish part of town. By the Middle Ages the Virgin Mary's purification bath after the birth of Jesus had become a Christian holiday called Candlemas celebrated on February 2. A Christian woman also went through a ritual of thanksgiving and purification, called *churching,* six weeks after giving birth. During churching the mother went to church with the women who had assisted in the birth; in English these women were known as her "god-siblings," a word that became shortened to "gossip." The new mother made an offering of money or perhaps yarn she had spun and was blessed by the priest. This ritual varied from parish to parish, but it often included a prayer such as "Almighty and everlasting God, who has freed this woman from the danger of bearing a child, consider her to be strengthened from every pollution of the flesh so that with a clean heart and pure mind she may deserve to enter into the bosom of our mother, the church, and make her devoted to Your service."[10]

Religious ceremonies also welcomed children into the community. Among Christian families, infants were baptized quickly after they were born, for without baptism they could not enter Heaven. Thus midwives who delivered children who looked especially weak and sickly often baptized them in an emergency service. Mothers whose children had died before they could be baptized sometimes carried them many miles to special chapels where the priest was thought to have powers of revitalization; he blew "life" back into the children just long enough for baptism, and then the children were buried. (These chapels became surrounded by graveyards with hundreds of infant bodies; from those bodies archaeologists can tell that the children had sometimes been dead for weeks before they were buried.) In normal baptisms, the women who had assisted the mother in the birth often carried the baby to church, where carefully chosen godparents vowed their support. Godparents were often close friends or relatives, but parents might also choose prominent villagers or even the local lord in the hope that he might later look favorably on the child and provide for it in some way. When a child was baptized, a few grains of salt were dropped on its tongue. Salt had been the symbol of purity, strength, and incorruptibility for the ancient Hebrews, and the Romans had used it in their sacrifices. It was used in Christian baptism to drive away demons and to strengthen the infant in its new faith.

Within Judaism, a boy was circumcised and given his name in a ceremony when he was in his eighth day of life. This *brit milah,* or "covenant of circumcision," was viewed as a reminder of the covenant between God and Abraham described in Hebrew Scripture. There was no corresponding ceremony for girls, who were generally named during the first regular worship service after their birth. (Within the last several decades, Jews in many parts of the world have developed a naming ceremony for girls called *simhat bat.*) Muslims also circumcised boys in a special ritual, though the timing varied from a few days after birth to adolescence. Circumcision is not mentioned in the Qur'an, but Muhammad was understood to have been circumcised, so the practice was part of following his example. For both Jews and Muslims, circumcision was often accompanied by a family celebration or, in the case of wealthy families, a lavish feast; for sons of rulers, circumcision celebrations could be public occasions and go on for many days.

Death and the Afterlife

Death was similarly marked by religious ceremonies. Christians called for a priest when they thought the hour of death was near. The priest brought a number of objects and substances regarded as having power over death and the sin related to it: holy water to be sprinkled on and around the dying person; holy oil for anointing him or her; a censer with incense to be waved around; the priest's stole for the dying person to touch; a crucifix with an image of the dying Christ to remind him or her of Christ's own agony and death; lighted candles to drive back the darkness both figuratively and literally, which was often placed in the person's hand as he or she was just about to take a last breath (or "give up the ghost" as

the phrase still goes); and the communion host consecrated by the priest during the sacrament of extreme unction and then consumed by the dying person.

Once the person had died, the body was washed—usually by female family members or women who made their living this way—and was put in special clothing or a sack of plain cloth and buried within a day or two. Family and friends joined in a funeral procession, again with candles, holy water, incense, and a crucifix and marked by the ringing of church bells; sometimes extra women were hired so that the mourning and wailing were especially loud. The procession carried the body into the church, where there were psalms, prayers, and a funeral Mass, and then to a consecrated space for burial, the wealthy sometimes inside the church—in the walls, un-

Jewish Cemetery   Tomb in Worms of a thirteenth-century German Jewish rabbi who was imprisoned by the emperor and died in prison. Jewish and Christian cemeteries were separated in medieval Europe, with Christian cemeteries generally next to churches and Jewish ones often outside town walls. *(Erich Lessing/Art Resource, NY)*

three separate types of merchants: the sedentary merchant who ran the "home office," financing and organizing the firm's entire export-import trade; the carriers who transported goods by land and sea; and the company agents resident in cities abroad who, on the advice of the home office, looked after sales and procurements. Commercial correspondence, unnecessary when one businessperson oversaw everything and made direct bargains with buyers and sellers, proliferated. Regular courier service among commercial cities began. Commercial accounting became more complex when firms had to deal with shareholders, manufacturers, customers, branch offices, employees, and competing firms. Tolls on roads became high enough to finance what has been called a "road revolution," involving new surfaces, bridges, new passes through the Alps, and new inns and hospices for travelers. The growth of mutual confidence among merchants facilitated the growth of sales on credit.

In all these transformations, merchants of the Italian cities led the way. (See the feature "Individuals in Society: Francesco Datini.") They formalized their agreements with new types of contracts, including permanent partnerships termed *compagnie* (literally "bread together," that is, sharing bread, and the root of the English word *company*). Many of these compagnie began as agreements between brothers or other relatives and in-laws, but quickly grew to include people who were not family members. In addition, they began to involve individuals—including a few women—who invested only their money, leaving the actual running of the business to the active partners.

The ventures of the German Hanseatic League also illustrate these new business procedures. The **Hanseatic League** was a mercantile association of towns. Though scholars trace the league's origin to the foundation of the city of Lübeck in 1143, the mutual protection treaty later signed by Lübeck and Hamburg marks the league's actual expansion. Lübeck and Hamburg wanted mutual security, exclusive trading rights, and, where possible, a monopoly. During the next century, perhaps two hundred cities from Holland to Poland, including Cologne, Brunswick, Dortmund, Danzig, and Riga, joined the league, but Lübeck always remained the dominant member. From the thirteenth to the sixteenth centuries, the Hanseatic League controlled trade along the axis of Novgorod-Reval-Lübeck-Hamburg-Bruges-London, that is, the trade of northern Europe (see Map 11.2). In the fourteenth century the Hanseatics branched out into southern Germany and Italy by land and into French, Spanish, and Portuguese ports by sea.

Across regular, well-defined trade routes along the Baltic and North Seas, the ships of league cities carried furs, wax, copper, fish, grain, timber, and wine. These goods were exchanged for finished products, mainly cloth and salt, from western cities. At cities such as Bruges and London, Hanseatic merchants secured special trading concessions exempting them from all tolls and allowing them to trade at local fairs. Hanseatic merchants established foreign trading centers, called "factories," the most famous of which was the London Steelyard, a walled community with warehouses, offices, a church, and residential quarters for company representatives. By the late thirteenth century Hanseatic merchants had developed an important business technique, the business register. Merchants publicly recorded their debts and contracts and received a league guarantee for them.

The dramatic increase in trade ran into two serious difficulties in medieval Europe. One was the problem of money. Despite investment in mining operations to increase the production of metals, the amount of gold, silver, and copper available for coins was simply not adequate for the increased flow of commerce. Merchants developed paper letters of exchange, in which coins or goods in one location were exchanged for a sealed letter (much like a modern deposit statement), which could be used in place of metal coinage elsewhere. This made the long, slow, and very dangerous shipment of coins unnecessary. Begun in the late twelfth century, the bill of exchange was the normal method of making commercial payments by the early fourteenth century among the cities of western Europe, and it proved to be a decisive factor in the later development of credit and commerce in northern Europe.

The second problem was a moral and theological one. Church doctrine, relying on Scripture (Leviticus 25:36–37, Psalms 37:26, Luke 11:15), frowned on lending money at interest, termed **usury.** It had developed this doctrine in the early Middle Ages when loans were mainly for consumption, tiding someone over, for instance, until the next harvest. Theologians reasoned that it was wrong for a Christian to take advantage of the bad luck or need of another Christian, so loans should be made *pro amore* (out of love), not with an eye for profit. This restriction on Christians is one reason why Jews were frequently moneylenders in early medieval society; it was one of the few occupations not forbidden them by Christian authorities.

The church's prohibition of usury meant that merchants often felt the need to hide their interest and disguise their profit. Gradually the church relaxed the total

Wismar Founded in 1229 in Mecklenburg on the Baltic Sea, Wismar won full rights of self-government in 1236 from the dukes of Mecklenburg-Pomerania, who resided there. A fishing and shipbuilding center, Wismar became one of the most powerful members of the Hanseatic League. Warehouses lined the shore, while the town's many church steeples dominated the skyline. *(Biblioteca Civica "Angelo Mai," Bergamo)*

prohibition of interest, declaring that some interest was legitimate as a payment for the risk the investor was taking, and that only interest above a certain level would be considered usury. (This definition of usury has continued; modern governments generally set limits on the rate legitimate businesses may charge for loaning money.) The church itself then got into the money-lending business, opening pawnshops in cities and declaring that the shops were benefiting the poor by charging a lower rate of interest than that available from secular moneylenders. In rural areas, Cistercian monasteries loaned money at interest.

The stigma attached to lending money was in many ways attached to all the activities of a medieval merchant. Trade was not like agriculture, mining, or making a product; a merchant simply handled goods produced by someone else. Medieval people were uneasy about persons making a profit merely from the investment of money; the investment of labor, skill, and time warranted

a profit, but did the investment of merely money? Merchants themselves shared these ideas to some degree, so they gave generous donations to the church and to charities and agreed, at least in principle, that profit should be limited to what was judged to be fair and just. They also took pains not to flaunt their wealth, but instead to dress and furnish their homes in a way that would convey financial stability rather than flashy extravagance. By the end of the Middle Ages, society had come to accept the role of the merchant somewhat, with preachers in Italian cities comparing merchants to Christ, who had "redeemed" the human race from the snares of the Devil in the same way that merchants redeemed loans and merchandise.

The Commercial Revolution

Changes in business procedures, combined with the growth in trade, led to a transformation of the European

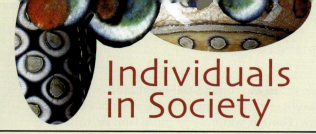

Individuals in Society

Francesco Datini

In 1348, when he was a young teenager, Francesco Datini (1335–1410) lost his father, his mother, a brother, and a sister to the Black Death epidemic that swept through Europe (see pages 374–381). Leaving his hometown of Prato in northern Italy, he apprenticed himself to merchants in nearby Florence for several years to learn accounting and other business skills. At fifteen, he moved to the city of Avignon in southern France. The popes were living in Avignon instead of Rome, and the city offered many opportunities for an energetic and enterprising young man. Datini first became involved in the weapons trade, which offered steady profits, and then handled spices, wool and silk cloth, and jewels. He was very successful, and when he was thirty-one he married the young daughter of another merchant in an elaborate wedding that was the talk of Avignon.

In 1378 the papacy returned to Italy, and Datini soon followed, setting up trading companies in Prato, Pisa, Florence, and eventually other cities as well. He focused on cloth and leather and sought to control the trade in products used for preparation as well, especially the rare dyes that created the brilliant colors favored by wealthy noblemen and townspeople. He eventually had offices all over Europe and became one of the richest men of his day, opening a mercantile bank and a company that produced cloth as well as his many branch offices.

Datini was more successful than most, but what makes him particularly stand out was his record keeping. He kept careful account books and ledgers, all of them headed by the phrase "in the name of God and profit." He wrote to the managers of each of his offices every week, providing them with careful advice and blunt criticism: "You cannot see a crow in a bowl of milk." Taking on the son of a friend as an employee, he wrote to the young man: "Do your duty well, and you will acquire honor and profit, and you can count on me as if I were your own father. But if you do not, then do not count on me; it will be as if I had never known you."

When Datini was away from home, which was often, he wrote to his wife every day, and she sometimes responded in ways that were less deferential than we might expect of a woman who was many years younger. "I think it is not necessary," she wrote at one point "to send me a message every Wednesday to say that you will be here on Sunday, for it seems to me that on every Friday you change your mind."

Datini's obsessive record-keeping lasted beyond his death, for someone put all of his records—hundreds of ledgers and contracts, eleven thousand business letters, and over a hundred thousand personal letters—in sacks in his opulent house in Prato, where they were found in the nineteenth century. They provide a detailed picture of medieval business practices and also reveal much about Datini as a person. Ambitious, calculating, luxury-loving, and a workaholic, Datini seems similar to a modern CEO. Like many of today's self-made super-rich people, at the end of his life Datini began to think a bit more about God and less about profit. In his will, he set up a foundation for the poor in Prato and a home for orphans in Florence, both of which are still in operation. In 1967 scholars established an institute for economic history in Prato, naming it in Datini's honor; the institute now manages the collection of Datini documents and gathers other relevant materials in its archives.

Statue of Francesco Datini outside the city hall in Prato.
(Peter Horree/Alamy)

Questions for Analysis

1. How would you evaluate Datini's motto: as an honest statement of his aims, a hypocritical justification of greed, a blend of both, or something else?
2. Changes in business procedures in the Middle Ages have been described as a "commercial revolution." Do Datini's activities support this assessment? Why?

Source: Iris Origo, *The Merchant of Prato: Francesco di Marco Datini, 1335–1410* (New York: Alfred A. Knopf, Inc., 1957).

Online Study Center **Improve Your Grade**
Going Beyond Individuals in Society

economy often called the **commercial revolution** by historians, who see it as the beginning of the modern capitalist economy. Though you may be most familiar with using *revolution* to describe a violent political rebellion such as the American Revolution or the French Revolution, the word is also used more broadly to describe economic and intellectual changes such as the Industrial Revolution and the scientific revolution. These do not necessarily involve violence and may last much longer than political revolutions. What makes them revolutions is the extent of their effects on society. In calling this transformation the "commercial revolution," historians point not only to an increase in the sheer volume of trade and in the complexity and sophistication of business procedures, but also to the new attitude toward business and making money. Some even detect a "capitalist spirit" in which making a profit is regarded as a good thing in itself, regardless of the uses to which that profit is put.

Part of this capitalist spirit was a new attitude toward time. Country people needed only approximate times—dawn, noon, sunset—for their work. Monasteries needed much more precise times to call monks together for the recitation of the Divine Office. In the early Middle Ages monks used a combination of hourglasses, sundials, and water-clocks to determine the time, and then rang bells by hand. About 1280 new types of mechanical mechanisms seem to have been devised in which weights replaced falling water and bells were rung automatically. Records begin to use the word *clock* (from the Latin word for bell) for these machines, which sometimes figured the movement of astronomical bodies as well as the hours. The merchants who ran city councils quickly saw clocks as both useful and a symbol of their prosperity. Beautiful and elaborate mechanical clocks, usually installed on the cathedral or town church, were in general use in Italy by the 1320s, in Germany by the 1330s, in England by the 1370s, and in France by the 1380s. Buying and selling goods had initiated city people into the practice of quantification, and clocks contributed to the development of a mentality that conceived of the universe in quantitative terms.

Capitalism in the Middle Ages primarily involved trade rather than production, so it is termed **mercantile capitalism.** In a few places, such as Florence, cloth production was organized along capitalist lines, with a cloth merchant owning the raw materials, the finished product, and sometimes the tools, and with workers paid simply for their labor. Most production in the Middle Ages was carried out by craft guilds or by people working on their own, however.

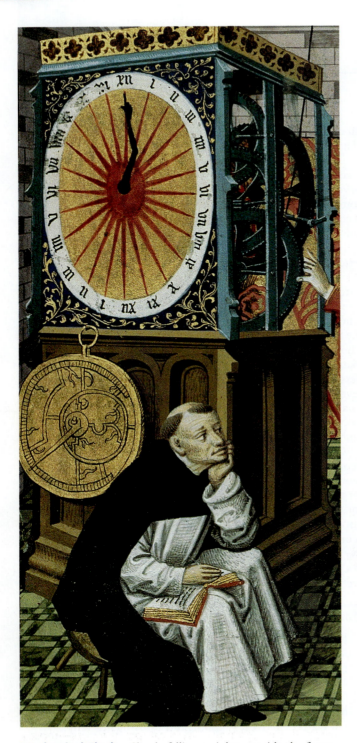

Mechanical Clock Slowly falling weights provide the force that pushes the hand on the twenty-four-hour face of this large, public sixteenth-century German clock. The gears also regulated the striking of bells, so that the sound of a machine marked time. *(Bibliothèque royale Albert 1er, Brussels)*

The commercial revolution created a great deal of new wealth, which did not escape the attention of kings and other rulers. Wealth could be taxed, and through taxation kings could create strong and centralized states. In the years to come, alliances with the middle classes enabled kings to defeat feudal powers and aristocratic interests and to build the states that came to be called "modern." The commercial revolution also provided the opportunity for thousands of serfs to improve their social position. The slow but steady transformation of European society from almost completely rural and isolated to relatively more sophisticated constituted the greatest effect of the commercial revolution that began in the eleventh century.

Even so, merchants and business people did not run medieval communities other than in central and northern Italy and in the county of Flanders. Most towns remained small, and urban residents were never more than 10 percent of the population. The castle, the manorial village, and the monastery dominated the landscape. The feudal nobility and churchmen determined the preponderant social attitudes, values, and patterns of thought and behavior. The commercial changes of the eleventh through thirteenth centuries did, however, lay the economic foundations for the development of urban life and culture.

Medieval Universities

Just as the first strong secular states emerged in the thirteenth century, so did the first universities. This was no coincidence. The new bureaucratic states and the church needed educated administrators, and universities were a response to this need. The word *university* derives from the Latin *universitas,* meaning "corporation" or "guild." Medieval universities were educational guilds that produced educated and trained individuals, and they continue to influence institutionalized learning in the Western world.

• *How did universities evolve, and what needs of medieval society did they serve?*

Origins

In the early Middle Ages, outside of the aristocratic court or the monastery, anyone who received an education got it from a priest. Priests instructed the clever boys on the manor in the Latin words of the Mass and taught them the rudiments of reading and writing. Few boys acquired elementary literacy, however, and peasant girls did not obtain even that. The peasant father who wished to send his son to school had to secure the permission of his lord because the result of formal schooling tended to be a career in the church or some trade. If a young man were to pursue either, he would have to leave the manor and gain free status. Because the lord stood to lose the services of educated peasants, he limited the number of serfs sent to school.

Since the time of the Carolingian Empire, monasteries and cathedral schools had offered most of the available formal instruction. The monasteries were geared to religious concerns, and the monastic curriculum consisted of studying the Scriptures and the writings of the church fathers. Monasteries wished to maintain an atmosphere of seclusion and silence and were unwilling to accept large numbers of noisy lay students. In contrast, schools attached to cathedrals and run by the bishop and his clergy were frequently situated in bustling cities, and in the eleventh century in Italian cities like Bologna, wealthy businessmen had established municipal schools. In the course of the twelfth century, cathedral schools in France and municipal schools in Italy developed into educational institutions that attracted students from a wide area (see Map 11.3). These schools were called *studium generale* ("general center of study") or *universitas magistrorum et scholarium* ("universal society of teachers and students"), the origin of the English word *university.* The first European universities appeared in Italy in Bologna and Salerno.

The growth of the University of Bologna coincided with a revival of interest in Roman law during the investiture controversy. The study of Roman law as embodied in the Justinian *Code* had never completely died out in the West, but in the late eleventh century a complete manuscript of the *Code* was discovered in a library in Pisa. This discovery led scholars in nearby Bologna, beginning with Irnerius (ca 1055–ca 1130), to study and teach Roman law intently again. His fame attracted students from all over Europe. Irnerius not only explained the Roman law of the Justinian *Code,* but also applied it to difficult practical situations.

At Salerno in southern Italy interest in medicine had persisted for centuries. Medical practitioners—mostly men, but apparently also a few women—received training first through apprenticeship and then in an organized medical school. Individuals associated with Salerno, such as Constantine the African (fl. 1065–1085)—who was a convert from Islam and later a Benedictine monk—

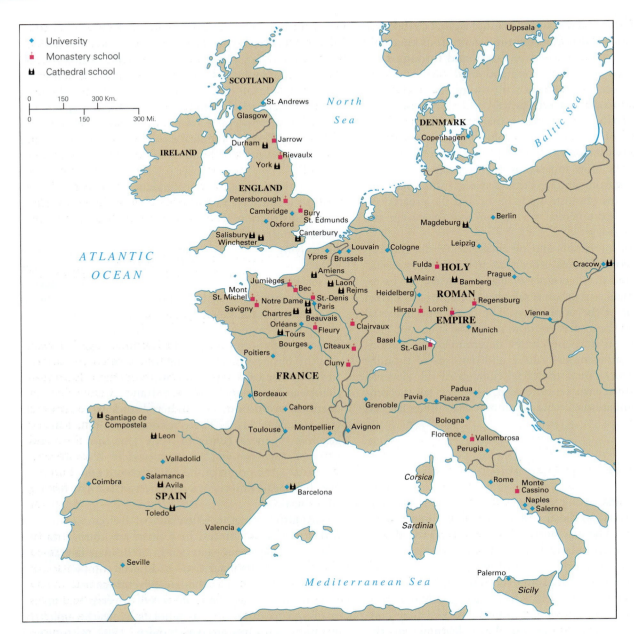

MAP 11.3 Intellectual Centers of Medieval Europe Universities obviously provided more sophisticated instruction than did monastery and cathedral schools. What other factors distinguished the three kinds of intellectual centers?

Online Study Center **Improve Your Grade** Interactive Map: Intellectual Centers of Medieval Europe

began to translate medical works out of Arabic. These translations included writings by the ancient Greek physicians and Muslim medical writers. Students of medicine poured into Salerno and soon attracted royal attention. In 1140, when King Roger II of Sicily took the practice of medicine under royal control, his ordinance stated:

Who, from now on, wishes to practice medicine, has to present himself before our officials and examiners, in order to pass their judgment. Should he be bold enough to disregard this, he will be punished by imprisonment and confiscation of his entire property. In this way we are taking care that our subjects are not endangered by the inexperience of the physicians.[5]

In the first decades of the twelfth century, students converged on Paris. They crowded into the cathedral school of Notre Dame and spilled over into the area later called the "Latin Quarter"—whose name reflects either the Italian origin of many of the students attracted to Paris by the surge of interest in the classics, logic, and theology, or the Latin language spoken in the area. The cathedral school's international reputation drew scholars from all over Europe to Paris.

Abelard and Heloise

One of the young men drawn to Paris was Peter Abelard (1079–1142), the son of a minor Breton knight. Abelard studied in Paris, quickly absorbed a large amount of material, and set himself up as a teacher. He was fascinated by logic, which he believed could be used to solve most problems. He had a brilliant mind and, though orthodox in his philosophical teaching, appeared to challenge ecclesiastical authorities. His book *Sic et Non* (Yes and No) was a list of apparently contradictory propositions drawn from the Bible and the writings of the church fathers. One such proposition, for example, stated that sin is pleasing to God and is not pleasing to God. Abelard used a method of systematic doubting in his writing and teaching. As he put it in the preface to *Sic et Non,* "By doubting we come to questioning, and by questioning we perceive the truth." While other scholars merely asserted theological principles, Abelard discussed and analyzed them. Through reasoning he even tried to describe the attributes of the three persons of the Trinity, the central mystery of the Christian faith. Abelard was severely censured by a church council, but his cleverness, boldness, and imagination made him a highly popular figure among students.

In a supposedly autobiographical statement, *A History of My Calamities,* Abelard described his academic career and his private life. His reputation for intellectual brilliance drew the attention of one of the cathedral canons, Fulbert, who hired Abelard to tutor his clever niece Heloise. The relationship between teacher and pupil passed beyond the intellectual. Abelard said that he seduced Heloise to learn about sexuality. She became pregnant, and Canon Fulbert pressured the couple to marry. Abelard insisted that the union be kept secret for the sake of his career, an arrangement Heloise much resented. Distrusting Abelard, Canon Fulbert hired men to castrate him. Wounded in spirit as well as body, Abelard persuaded Heloise to enter a convent. He became a monk of Saint-Denis; and their baby, baptized Astrolabe for a recent Muslim navigational invention, was given to her

family for adoption. Heloise secured a copy of Abelard's *History* and took great exception to his statement that their relationship had been based solely on physical desire. She considered her religious life hypocritical. Abelard spent his later years as abbot of an obscure monastery in Brittany, where he wrote Heloise letters of spiritual direction. The two unfortunate lovers were united in death and later buried together in a cemetery in Paris. Some scholars consider *A History of My Calamities* the most famous autobiography of the twelfth century, a fine example of the new self-awareness of the period's rebirth of learning. Other scholars believe the entire *History* a forgery, the source of a romantic legend with no basis in historical fact.[6]

Online Study Center **Improve Your Grade**
Primary Source: Letter to Abelard: "I beseech thee. . . ."

Instruction and Curriculum

The influx of students eager for learning, together with dedicated and imaginative teachers, created the atmosphere in which universities grew. In northern Europe—at Paris and later at Oxford and Cambridge in England—associations or guilds of professors organized universities. They established the curriculum, set the length of time for study, and determined the form and content of examinations. By the end of the fifteenth century there were at least eighty universities in Europe. Some universities also offered younger students training in the liberal arts that could serve as a foundation for more specialized study in all areas.

Students at universities were generally considered to be lower-level members of the clergy—this was termed being in "minor orders"—so that any students accused of legal infractions were tried in church, rather than in city courts. This clerical status, along with widely held ideas about women's lesser intellectual capabilities, meant that university education was restricted to men; even more than feudal armies—which were often accompanied by women who did laundry, found provisions, cooked meals, and engaged in sex for money—universities were all-male communities. The few women trained at Salerno during its early years of development were the last women in Europe to receive formal university training in any subject until the nineteenth century, although a handful of professor's daughters in one or two places were reputed to have listened to lectures from behind a curtain. (Most European universities did not admit or grant degrees to women until after World War I.) Though university classes were not especially expensive,

Law Lecture at Bologna This beautifully carved marble sculpture, with the fluid drapery characteristic of late Gothic style, suggests the students' intellectual intensity. Medieval students often varied widely in age; here some have moustaches and some look like adolescents. *(Museo Civico, Bologna/Scala/Art Resource, NY)*

the many years that university required meant that the sons of peasants or artisans could rarely attend, unless they could find wealthy patrons who would pay their expenses while they studied. Most students were the sons of urban merchants or lower-level nobles, especially the younger sons who would not inherit family lands.

University faculties grouped themselves according to academic disciplines—law, medicine, arts, theology. The professors (a term first used in the fourteenth century) were known as "schoolmen" or **Scholastics.** They developed a method of thinking, reasoning, and writing in which questions were raised and authorities cited on both sides of the question. The goal of the Scholastic method was to arrive at definitive answers and to provide a rational explanation for what was believed on faith. Schoolmen held that reason and faith constituted two harmonious realms whose truths complemented each other.

The Scholastic approach rested on the recovery of classical philosophical texts. Ancient Greek and Arabic texts had entered Europe in the early twelfth century. Knowledge of Aristotle and other Greek philosophers came to Paris and Oxford by way of Islamic intellectual centers at Baghdad, Córdoba, and Toledo. These texts, which formed the basis of Western philosophical and theological speculation, were not the only Islamic gifts. The major contribution of Arabic culture to the new currents of Western thought rested in the stimulus Arabic philosophers and commentators gave to Europeans' reflection on the Greek texts. For example, in Islam a strong tension exists between faith and reason. Western scholars' understanding of Aristotle's philosophy was closely tied to their discovery of Arabic thought. The tension between reason and faith became a fundamental theme in Christian thought.

Aristotle had stressed the importance of the direct observation of nature, as well as the principles that theory must follow fact and that knowledge of a thing requires an explanation of its causes. The schoolmen reinterpreted Aristotelian texts in a Christian sense. But in their exploration of the natural world, they did not precisely follow Aristotle's axioms. Medieval scientists argued from authority, such as the Bible, the Justinian *Code,* or an ancient scientific treatise, rather than from direct observation and experimentation as modern scientists do. Thus the conclusions of medieval scientists were often wrong. Nevertheless, natural science gradually emerged as a discipline distinct from philosophy, and Scholastics laid the foundations for later scientific work.

Many of the problems that Scholastic philosophers raised dealt with theological issues. For example, they addressed the question that interested all Christians, educated and uneducated: how is a person saved? Saint Augustine's thesis—that, as a result of Adam's fall, human beings have a propensity to sin—had become a central feature of church doctrine. The church taught that it possessed the means to forgive the sinful: grace conveyed through the sacraments. However, although grace provided a predisposition to salvation, the Scholastics held that one must also *decide* to use the grace received. In other words, a person must use his or her will and reason to advance to God.

At all universities the standard method of teaching was the *lecture*—that is, a reading. The professor read a passage from the Bible, the Justinian *Code,* or one of Aristotle's treatises. He then explained and interpreted the passage; his interpretation was called a *gloss.* Texts and glosses were sometimes collected and reproduced as textbooks. For example, the Italian Peter Lombard (d. 1160), a professor at Paris, wrote what became the standard textbook in theology, *Sententiae* (The Sentences), a compilation of basic theological principles.

Because books had to be copied by hand, they were extremely expensive, and few students could afford them. Students therefore depended for study on their own or friends' notes accumulated over a period of years. The choice of subjects was narrow. The syllabus at all universities consisted of a core of ancient texts that all students studied and, if they wanted to get ahead, mastered.

Examinations were given after three, four, or five years of study, when the student applied for a degree. The professors determined the amount of material students had to know for each degree, and students frequently insisted that the professors specify precisely what that material was. Examinations were oral and very difficult. If the candidate passed, he was awarded a license to teach, which was the earliest form of academic degree. Initially these licenses granted the title of *master* or *doctor,* still in use today and both derived from Latin words meaning "teach." Bachelor's degrees came later. Most students, however, did not become teachers. They staffed the expanding diocesan, royal, and papal administrations.

Students did not spend all their time listening to lectures or debating, however. Much information about medieval students concerns what we might call their "extracurricular" activities: university regulations forbade them to throw rocks at professors; sermons talked about students' breaking and entering, raping local women, attacking town residents, or disturbing church services; court records discussed their engaging in drunken brawls and riots or stabbing each other in fights and duels. The money sent by parents or patrons was often not sufficient for all expenses, so students augmented this by begging, thieving, or doing odd jobs. They also delayed finishing their studies because life as a student could be very pleasant, without the responsibilities that came with becoming fully adult. Student life was also described by those who knew it best—students themselves—in poems, usually anonymous, that celebrated the joys of Venus (the goddess of love), Bacchus (the god of wine), and Decius (the god of dice).

Thomas Aquinas and the Teaching of Theology

Thirteenth-century Scholastics devoted an enormous amount of time to collecting and organizing knowledge on all topics. These collections were published as **summa,** or reference books. There were summa on law, philosophy, vegetation, animal life, and theology. Saint Thomas Aquinas (1225–1274), a professor at Paris, produced the most famous collection, the *Summa Theologica,* which deals with a vast number of theological questions.

Online Study Center **Improve Your Grade**
Primary Source: Summa Theologica: On Dispensing the Eucharist

Aquinas drew an important distinction between faith and reason. He maintained that, although reason can demonstrate many basic Christian principles such as the existence of God, other fundamental teachings such as the Trinity and original sin cannot be proved by logic. That reason cannot establish them does not, however, mean they are contrary to reason. Rather, people understand such doctrines through revelation embodied in

Scripture. Scripture cannot contradict reason, nor reason Scripture:

The light of faith that is freely infused into us does not destroy the light of natural knowledge [reason] implanted in us naturally. For although the natural light of the human mind is insufficient to show us these things made manifest by faith, it is nevertheless impossible that these things which the divine principle gives us by faith are contrary to these implanted in us by nature [reason]. Indeed, were that the case, one or the other would have to be false, and, since both are given to us by God, God would have to be the author of untruth, which is impossible. . . . [I]t is impossible that those things which are of philosophy can be contrary to those things which are of faith.[7]

Aquinas also investigated the branch of philosophy called *epistemology,* which is concerned with how a person knows something. Aquinas stated that one knows, first, through sensory perception of the physical world—seeing, hearing, touching, and so on. He maintained that there can be nothing in the mind that is not first in the senses. Second, knowledge comes through reason, the mind exercising its natural abilities. Aquinas stressed the power of human reason to know, even to know God. Proofs of the existence of God exemplify the Scholastic method of knowing.

Aquinas began with the things of the natural world—earth, air, trees, water, birds. Then he inquired about their original source or cause: the mover, creator, planner who started it all. Everything, Aquinas maintained, has an ultimate and essential explanation, a reason for existing. Here he was following Aristotle. Aquinas went further and identified this reason for existing, or first mover, with God. Aquinas and all medieval intellectuals held that the end of faith and reason was the knowledge of and union with God. His work later became the fundamental text of Roman Catholic doctrine.

Teaching the Law

Legal scholars as well as theologians attempted to create an all-inclusive system based on logical principles. Irnerius and other teachers at Bologna taught law not as a group of discrete bits of legislation, but as an organic whole related to the society it regulated. Thus, as social and economic structures changed, law would change with them. Like theology, law was something that was created and developed by the human mind, not an unchanging body of immutable customs, which is how law had generally been viewed in the early Middle Ages.

Jurists educated at Bologna and later at other universities—such as Montpellier in France, where Roman law formed an increasingly large part of the legal curriculum—were hired by rulers to systematize their law codes and write legal treatises. In the 1260s the English jurist Henry Bracton wrote a comprehensive treatise bringing together the laws and customs of England, and King Alfonso X of Castile issued the *Siete Partidas* (Book in Seven Parts) that set out a detailed plan for administering his whole kingdom according to Roman legal principles.

When cities gained their freedom from feudal lords, they had to write city charters and law codes for both civil and criminal matters, which grew longer and longer as new issues arose. These law codes were a combination of earlier Germanic law codes and Roman law, blended together in ways that addressed local needs and fit with local customs. Lawyers served as advisers and consultants for city councils, though they themselves were generally not members of the city government.

Canon law (see page 278) was also shaped by the reinvigoration of Roman law, and canon lawyers in ever greater numbers were hired by church officials or became prominent church officials themselves. In about 1140 the Benedictine monk Gratian put together a collection of nearly 3,800 texts covering all areas of canon law. His collection, known as the *Decretum,* became the standard text on which teachers of canon law lectured and commented. The *Decretum* presented material in dialectical form as a series of questions and answers about practical problems judges and lawyers in church courts might confront, such as issues surrounding marriage or cases involving members of the clergy or university students. Canon lawyers worked with the popes—indeed, some popes were canon lawyers—to make sure that the scope of jurisdiction for those courts continued to expand.

Jewish scholars as well as Christian ones produced elaborate commentaries on law and religious tradition. Medieval universities were closed to Jews, but in some cities in the eleventh century special rabbinic academies opened that concentrated particularly on the study of the Talmud, a compilation of legal arguments, proverbs, sayings, and folklore that had been produced in the fifth century in Babylon (present-day Iraq). The Talmud was written in Aramaic, so that simply learning to read it required years of study, and medieval scholars began to produce commentaries on the Talmud to help facilitate this. The most famous of these was that of Rabbi Solomon bar Isaac, known as Rashi (1040–1105), who lived in Troyes, a city in France. Men seeking to become rabbis—highly respected figures within the Jewish community with authority over economic and social as well as religious matters—spent long periods of time studying the Talmud, which served as the basis for their legal decisions in all areas of life.

Medical Training

Like philosophy and law, medical studies at medieval universities were based on classical ideas, particularly those of Hippocrates and Aristotle (see page 85). For the ancient Greeks, ideas about the human body were very closely linked to philosophy and to ideas about the natural world in general. Prime among these was the notion of the four bodily humors, four fluids—blood, phlegm, black bile, and yellow bile—contained in the body that influenced bodily health. Each individual was thought to have a characteristic temperament or *complexion* determined by the balance of the four humors, in the same way that we might describe a person today as having a "positive outlook" or a "Type-A" personality. These four humors corresponded to four qualities—hot, cold, wet, and dry—and to the four basic elements in the Aristotelian universe—earth, air, fire, and water. The organs were primarily viewed as channels for the humors, rather than as having specific functions. Disease was primarily regarded as an imbalance of bodily humors, which could be diagnosed by taking a patient's pulse or examining his or her urine. Treatment was thus an attempt to bring the humors back into balance, which might be accomplished through diet or drugs—usually mixtures of herbal or mineral substances regarded as therapeutic—or as a direct attempt to rebalance the humors through emetics, purgatives, or bloodletting. The bodily humors were somewhat gender-related—women were regarded as tending toward the cold and wet and men toward the hot and dry—so that therapies were also gender-distinctive. The exact balance of humors was different for each individual, however, and heat could cause one fluid to transform into another.

Heat was also viewed as important in reproduction. The sex of an infant, for example, was believed to be determined largely by the amount of heat present during intercourse and gestation; males resulted when there was the proper amount of heat, which caused their sexual organs to be pushed outside the body, and females when there was too little heat, which caused their sexual organs to remain internal. Men's greater heat continued throughout their lives, causing them to burn up their hair and go bald and to develop broader shoulders and

bigger brains (because heat rises and causes things to expand).

Although disagreements existed, the ideas of this medical literature spread throughout Europe from Salerno and became the basis of university medical training. University training gave physicians high social status and

Physician's Diagnosis University-trained physicians rarely touched patients, but instead diagnosed illness by looking at patients' urine. This illustration appeared in a French translation of *De Proprietatibus Rerum* (The Properties of Things), the first encyclopedia of the Middle Ages, by Bartholomaeus Anglicus (Bartholomew the Englishman). Bartholomaeus was an English Franciscan who taught at the universities of Paris and Magdeburg in Germany. This encyclopedia, which was widely copied and translated into several languages, includes material from Greek, Arabic, and Jewish medical writers. (*Snark/Art Resource, NY*)

allowed them to charge high fees. They were generally hired directly by their patients as they were needed, though some had more permanent positions as members of the household staffs of especially wealthy nobles or rulers or in hospitals such rulers had founded (see pages 304–305). In the fifteenth century city governments sometimes hired official city physicians to advise them on medical matters and give opinions in legal cases on such issues as how long a person had been dead or whether a child had taken a breath before it had died. (The latter emerged in cases of suspected infanticide.)

The influence of learned medical literature did not stop with those who could read Greek and Latin, however, for beginning in the fourteenth century in Europe translations and compilations were made in the vernacular languages. Once the printing press was developed in the mid-fifteenth century, these vernacular medical works, along with Latin and Greek medical works, were frequently printed. It is difficult to gauge how often the treatments they recommend were actually applied, but the ideas they contain were shared by most of the population, from the highly learned to the illiterate, until well into the sixteenth century.

Vernacular Culture

University education was conducted completely in Latin, and all learned philosophical, theological, and medical works were written in Latin as well. So were many works of literature, including poetry, plays, stories, and chronicles, particularly those written by monks and nuns. In contrast to Roman times, however, by the High Middle Ages no one spoke Latin as his or her original mother tongue. The barbarian invasions, the mixture of peoples, and evolution over time had resulted in a variety of local **dialects** that blended words and linguistic forms in various ways. These dialects were specific to one region, and as kings increased the size of their holdings they often ruled people who spoke many different dialects. In the early Middle Ages almost all written works continued to be in Latin, but in the High Middle Ages some authors began to write in their local dialect, that is, in the everyday language of their region, which linguistic historians call the vernacular. This new **vernacular literature** gradually transformed some local dialects into literary languages, such as French, German, Italian, and English, while other dialects remained (and remain to this day) simply means of oral communication. Most people in the High Middle Ages could no more read vernacular literature than they could read Latin, however, so oral trans-

mission continued to be the most important way information was conveyed and traditions passed down.

- *What do oral traditions and vernacular literature reveal about medieval culture?*

Oral Traditions and Entertainment

The treatment of illness was only one of many aspects of life in which traditions were handed down orally. Children heard stories about saints, heroes, and magical creatures from their parents; apprentices and journeymen learned the tasks associated with their craft by watching and listening to their masters; people of all types gathered when wandering preachers gave sermons urging them to live better lives or go on pilgrimages. Much of this oral culture is difficult to recover because it was never written down; writing was for important legal or intellectual matters, done by highly trained scribes on expensive parchment or vellum (stretched goatskin or sheepskin).

By the thirteenth century, however, techniques of making paper from old linen cloth and rags began to spread from Spain, where they had been developed by the Arabs, providing a much cheaper material on which to write. People started to write down things that were more mundane and less serious—personal letters, lists, poems, songs, recipes, rules, instructions—in various vernacular dialects, using spellings that were often personal and idiosyncratic. The writings included fables, legends, stories, and myths that had circulated orally for generations, and slowly a body of written vernacular literature developed. From written vernacular records and from discussions in more learned literature, we can gain some access to medieval popular culture, though its full range cannot be completely reconstructed.

The recreation of all classes reflected the fact that medieval society was organized for war and that violence was common. The aristocracy engaged in tournaments or jousts; archery and wrestling had great popularity among ordinary people. The hangings and mutilations of criminals were exciting and well-attended events, with all the festivity of a university town before a Saturday football game. Chroniclers exulted in describing executions, murders, and massacres. Here a monk gleefully describes the gory execution of William Wallace (ca 1270–1305), the Scottish hero who led a revolt against Edward I of England and retains importance as a symbol of resistance to English rule and of Scottish nationalism:

Wilielmus Waleis, a robber given to sacrilege, arson and homicide . . . was condemned to most cruel but justly de-

Spanish Bullfight In this fourteenth-century painting, spectators goad a bull with whips. The Romans may have introduced bullfighting in Spain, but the Muslims popularized it, and Christians continued the tradition. In its medieval version, bullfighters fought from horseback; bullfighters on foot were added in the eighteenth century. *(From the* Cantigas *of Alfonso X, ca 1283. El Escorial/Laurie Platt Winfrey, Inc.)*

served death. He was drawn through the streets of London at the tails of horses, until he reached a gallows of unusual height, there he was suspended by a halter; but taken down while yet alive, he was mutilated, his bowels torn out and burned in a fire, his head then cut off, his body divided into four, and his quarters transmitted to four principal parts of Scotland.[8]

Games and sports were common forms of entertainment and relaxation. There were games akin to modern football, rugby, and soccer in which balls were kicked and thrown, and other games in which balls were hit by sticks, paddles, and rackets much like modern tennis and field hockey. There were wrestling matches ranging from informal bouts between two individuals to organized team matches between two cities. People played card and board games of all types, with paper providing the material for the cards themselves and for writing down rules. They played with dice carved from stone or bone, or with the knucklebones of animals or wood carved in knucklebone shape, somewhat like modern jacks. They trained dogs to fight each other or put them in an enclosure to fight a captured bear. In Spain, Muslim knights confronted and killed bulls from horseback as part of religious feast days, developing a highly ritualized ceremony that would later be further adapted by Spain's Christian conquerors. All these sports and games were occasions for wagering and gambling, which preachers sometimes condemned (especially when the games were attached to holiday or saints' day celebrations) but had little power to control.

Religious and family celebrations also meant dancing, which the church also attempted to ban or at least regulate, again with little success. Men and women danced in lines toward a specific object, such as a tree or a maypole, or in circles, groups, or pairs with specific step patterns. They were accompanied by a variety of instruments: reed pipes such as the chalumeau (an ancestor of the clarinet) and shawm; woodwinds such as flutes, panpipes, and recorders; stringed instruments including dulcimers, harps, lyres, lutes, zithers, and mandolins; brass instruments such as horns and trumpets; and percussion instruments like drums and tambourines. Many of these instruments were simple and were made by their players.

If nothing else was available, someone often had a Jew's harp, a tiny iron frame with a vibrating strip of metal, which was held between the teeth and plucked, with the notes changing depending on the shape of the mouth. (The origins of the name "Jew's harp" are very obscure and hotly debated, but it appears to have nothing to do with Jews and may have been invented in many different places.) Musicians playing string or percussion instruments often sang as well, and people sang without instrumental accompaniment on festive occasions or while working.

Drama, derived from the church's liturgy, emerged as a distinct art form during the High Middle Ages. For centuries skits based on Christ's Nativity and Resurrection had been performed in monasteries and cathedrals. Beginning in the thirteenth century plays based on these and other biblical themes and on the lives of the saints were performed in the towns. Students of theater history distinguish three kinds of medieval plays: *mystery* plays financed and performed by "misteries," members of the craft guilds; *miracle* plays acted by amateurs or professional actors, not guild members; and *morality* plays in which the characters personified virtues and vices and the actors represented the struggle between good and evil. Performed first at the cathedral altar, then in the church square, later at stations around the town, and finally in the town marketplace, mystery plays enjoyed great popularity. By combining comical farce based on ordinary life with serious religious scenes, they gave ordinary people an opportunity to identify with religious figures and think about the mysteries of their faith.

Troubadour Poetry

In addition to amateur musicians who played and sang for village dances and peasant weddings, professional musicians and poets performed and composed at the courts of nobles and rulers. In Germany and most of northern Europe, they favored stories and songs recounting the great deeds of warrior heroes, such as the knight Roland who fought against the Muslims and Hildebrand who fought the Huns. These epics, known as *chansons de geste* ("songs of great deeds"), celebrate violence, slaughter, revenge, and physical power. In southern Europe, especially in the area of southern France known as Provence, poets who called themselves **troubadours** wrote and sang lyric verses celebrating love, desire, beauty, and gallantry. (See the feature "Listening to the Past: Courtly Love" on pages 366–367.) The word *troubadour* comes from the Provençal word *trobar*, which in

turn derives from the Arabic *taraba*, meaning "to sing" or "to sing poetry." A troubadour was a poet who wrote lyric verse in Provençal, the regional spoken language of southern France, and sang it at one of the noble courts. Troubadours included a few women, called *trobairitz*, most of whose exact identities are not known.

Troubadour lyric poetry enjoyed the patronage of many of the great lords of southern France, including William IX, duke of Aquitaine, himself a famed author. William's granddaughter, Eleanor of Aquitaine, may have taken troubadour poetry to England when she married Henry II. Since the songs of the troubadours were widely imitated in Italy, England, and Germany, they spurred the development of vernacular literature there. In the thirteenth century, for example, German Minnesängers (love singers) such as Walther von der Wogelweide (1170–1220) wrote stylized verses on a variety of topics in an early version of German.

The romantic motifs of the troubadours also influenced the northern French *trouvères*, who wrote adventure-romances in the form of epic poems in a language we call Old French, the ancestor of modern French. At the court of his patron, Marie of Champagne, Chrétien de Troyes (ca 1135–ca 1190) used the legends of the fifth-century British king Arthur (see page 213) to relate stories of lovers who occasionally lapsed in their purity. Chrétien told the story of the noble Lancelot, whose love for Guinevere, the wife of King Arthur, his lord, became physical as well as spiritual. Their sexual relationship led to everyone's ruin, but it also became the best-known part of the "Arthurian cycle" of stories about the legendary king Arthur and his knights at Camelot. Combining chivalric romance and battle-strewn epic, Chrétien wrote down many of these stories, which remained popular for centuries and were later written down in slightly different forms by other authors. Such poems as *Lancelot, Percival and the Holy Grail*, and *Tristan and Isolde* reveal Chrétien as the most innovative figure in the twelfth-century vernacular literature.

Online Study Center **Improve Your Grade**
Primary Source: The Temptation of Sir Lancelot

Most of the troubadours and trouvères came from and wrote for the aristocratic classes, and their poetry suggests the interests and values of noble culture. Their influence eventually extended to all social groups, however, for people who could not read heard the poems and stories from people who could, so that what had originally come from oral culture was recycled back into it every generation.

Architecture and Art

The development of secular vernacular literature focusing on human concerns did not mean any lessening of the importance of religion in medieval people's lives. As we have seen, religious devotion was expressed through daily rituals, holiday ceremonies, and the creation of new institutions such as universities and religious orders. People also wanted permanent visible representations of their piety, and both church and city leaders wanted physical symbols of their wealth and power. These aims found their outlet in the building of tens of thousands of churches, chapels, abbeys, and, most spectacularly, **cathedrals** in the twelfth and thirteenth centuries. (A cathedral is the church of a bishop and the administrative headquarters of a diocese, a church district headed by a bishop. The word comes from the Greek word *kathedra,* meaning "seat," because the bishop's throne, a symbol of the office, is located in the cathedral.)

It is difficult for people today to appreciate the extraordinary amounts of energy, imagination, and money involved in building cathedrals. Between 1180 and 1270 in France alone, eighty cathedrals, about five hundred abbey churches, and tens of thousands of parish churches were constructed. This construction represents a remarkable investment for a country of scarcely 18 million people. More stone was quarried for churches in medieval France than had been mined in ancient Egypt, where the Great Pyramid alone consumed 40.5 million cubic feet of stone.

- *How did cathedrals express the ideals, attitudes, and interests of medieval people?*

Romanesque Churches and Cathedrals

Most of the churches in the early Middle Ages had been built primarily of wood, which meant they were very susceptible to fire. They were often small, with a flat roof, in a rectangular or slightly cross-shaped form called a *basilica,* based on earlier Roman public buildings. The long part of the cross, called the *nave,* was arranged on an east-west axis, so that as people entered the main central door at the foot of the nave they looked eastward, toward Jerusalem. The altar was at the head of the nave, at the point where the arms of the cross, called the *transept,* intersected it. A small rounded *apse* formed the head of the cross.

With the end of the Viking and Magyar invasions and the increasing political stability of the eleventh century,

bishops and abbots supported the construction of larger and more fire-resistant churches made almost completely out of stone. These were based on the basilican style, but their cross shape was made more pronounced by increasing the size of the transept and apse and adding a rectangular section called a *choir* between the apse and the altar. As the size of the church grew horizontally, it also grew vertically, as builders adapted Roman-style rounded barrel vaults made of stone for the ceiling; this use of Roman forms led this style to be labeled **Romanesque.** The nave, apse, and each arm of the transept had its own barrel-vault ceiling, which met in the middle over the altar in what was called a *cross vault.* All of these ceilings were extremely heavy and generated a great deal of downward and outward thrust, so that the walls of the church needed to be very thick and sturdy to support them. Thus windows were small, and Romanesque churches could be dark and gloomy. This was alleviated by painting the ceilings and walls in light, bright colors and by filling the church with sculptures, tapestries, paintings, and gold and silver ornaments, all of which would catch the light. Along with the central altar, the side aisles of the nave often contained altars erected by prominent families, wealthy individuals, or craft guilds, often dedicated to specific saints. Lighted candles or priests and monks saying mass could often be found at these side altars, so that larger churches were rarely completely empty.

The exteriors of Romanesque churches became more elaborate as well, with sculptured figures over each door representing biblical figures, saints, rulers, or scenes from the Bible, and with towers over the church with bells that tolled the hours of services. The scenes over each door were specialized in some churches; scenes representing Heaven and Hell were carved over doors designated for pilgrims to enter, while the story of the wise and foolish maidens was carved over a side door in front of which weddings were held or through which wedding parties entered. In northern Europe, twin bell towers often crowned Romanesque churches, giving them a powerful, fortresslike appearance. Built primarily by monasteries, Romanesque churches reflect the quasi-military, aristocratic, and pre-urban society that built them.

Gothic Cathedrals

The inspiration for a new style of architecture originated in the brain of one monk, Suger, abbot of Saint-Denis (1122–1151). When Suger became abbot, he decided to reconstruct the old Carolingian abbey church at Saint-

From Romanesque to Gothic

The word *church* has several meanings: assembly, congregation, sect. The Greek term from which it is derived means "a thing belonging to the Lord," and this concept was applied to the building where a congregation assembled. In the Middle Ages people understood the church building to be "the house of God and the gate to Heaven"; it served as an image or representation of supernatural reality (Heaven). A church symbolized faith. Christians revealed and exercised faith; they communicated with God through prayer—that is, by raising their minds and hearts to God. The church building seemed the ideal place for prayer: communal prayer built faith, and faith encouraged prayer.

Architecture became the dominant art form of the Middle Ages. Nineteenth-century architectural historians coined the term *Romanesque,* meaning "in the Roman manner," to describe church architecture in most of Europe between the tenth and twelfth centuries. The main features of the Romanesque style—solid walls, rounded arches, and masonry vaults—had been the characteristics of large Roman buildings. With the massive barrel vaulting of the roof, heavy walls were required to carry the weight (see Image 1). Romanesque churches had a massive quality, reflecting the increasing political and economic stability of the period and suggesting that they were places of refuge and security in times of attack. A Romanesque church was a "fortress of God."

Gothic churches, by contrast, were walls of light. Visitors and worshipers approached the west end of the building, noticing the carved statues in the *tympanum* (space above the portal, or door), perhaps awestruck by the lancets and rose window over the portal. Inside, a long row of columns directed their gaze down the *nave* (center aisle), and they proceeded to the *transept* (cross aisle), which separated the sanctuary and the choir (reserved for the clergy) from the body of the church (the laypeople's area). See Image 2. So that the flow of pilgrims would not disturb the clergy in their chants, *ambulatories* (walkways) were constructed around the sanctuary. Off the ambulatories, radiating

Image 1 **Saint-Savin-sur-Gartempe (Romanesque), Early Twelfth Century.** *(Editions Gaud)*

chapels surrounded the *apse,* the semicircular domed projection at the east end of the building. Apsidal chapels, each dedicated to and containing the relics of a particular saint, were visible from the exterior, as were the *flying buttresses* that supported the outward thrusts of the interior vaults. Above the apse and the west, south, and north portals, circular windows emerged from the radiating stone tracery in the form of roses.

Study the model of Chartres Cathedral (Image 3). Cover it with a piece of paper. In the photo of Notre Dame Cathedral on page 359, identify the following parts of a Gothic church: west portal, nave, transept, ambulatory, apse, pointed arch, flying buttress, spire,

Image 2 Amiens Cathedral, Mid-Thirteenth Century.
(Editions Gaud)

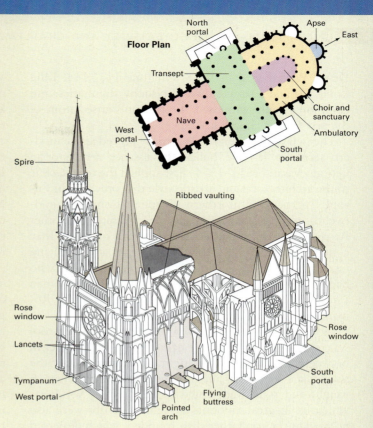

Image 3 Elements of a Gothic Church (Chartres Cathedral).

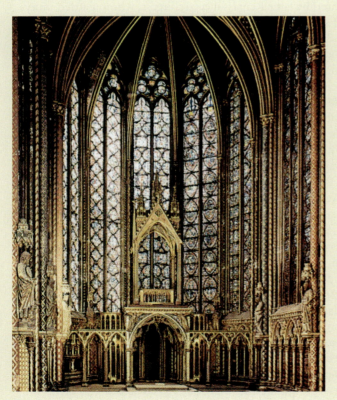

Image 4 Sainte-Chapelle, Paris, Mid-Thirteenth Century. *(Scala/Art Resource, NY)*

lancet, rose window. Explain the function of each feature you identify. How do you account for the fact that some churches were never finished?

Compare the interior of the abbey church of Saint-Savin-sur-Gartempe (Image 1), a Romanesque church built in about 1100 in Poitou, France, and the interior of Amiens Cathedral (Image 2), a Gothic church built from 1220 to 1288. What are the most striking differences? What developments made the changes from Romanesque to Gothic structurally possible?

Architecture reveals the interests and values of a society, its goals and aspirations. What does Sainte-Chapelle (Image 4), built by King Louis IX of France to house relics—the crown of thorns placed on Jesus' head before the Crucifixion, a nail from the Crucifixion, a fragment of Jesus' cross—tell us about the values and aspirations of thirteenth-century French society?

A Gothic church represents more than a house of prayer or worship. Medieval people did not compartmentalize the various aspects of their lives as modern people tend to do. What civic, social, economic, and political functions did a church building serve?

Online Study Center **Improve Your Grade**
Going Beyond Images in Society

Denis. Work began in 1137. On June 11, 1144, King Louis VII and a large crowd of bishops, dignitaries, and common people witnessed the solemn consecration of the first **Gothic** church in France.

The new architectural style actually preceded the modern term for it. The Italian Renaissance art historian Giorgio Vasari (1511–1574) first applied the term *Gothic* to the architectural and artistic style that prevailed in Europe (particularly northern Europe) from the mid-twelfth to the sixteenth centuries. Vasari and other Renaissance artists used *Gothic* as a word of abuse: they condemned medieval architecture as barbaric, implying incorrectly that it was the style of the Gothic tribes who had destroyed the classical architecture of the Roman Empire. (See the feature "Images in Society: From Romanesque to Gothic" on pages 356–357.)

In Gothic churches the solid stone barrel-vaulted roof was replaced by a roof made of stone ribs with plaster in between. This made the ceiling much lighter, so that the side pillars and walls did not need to carry so much weight and solid walls could be replaced by windows, which let in great amounts of light. The ribs were also pointed at the top rather than rounded, which dispersed the thrust of the archway in a new way. In addition to ribs that ran down the walls of the church, additional arched stone supports outside the walls, called *flying buttresses*, carried some of the weight and thrust of the roof, allowing builders to go higher and more open still. Thus, in contrast to solid Romanesque structures, Gothic churches became walls of light in which the eye is led upward by the pointed arches and ribbed vaulting; plain glass windows were replaced by colored stained-glass in elaborate designs, often painted or arranged to show biblical scenes.

Begun in the Île-de-France, Gothic architecture spread throughout France with the expansion of royal power. From France the new style spread to England, Germany, Italy, Spain, and eastern Europe. In those countries, the Gothic style competed with strong indigenous architectural traditions and thus underwent transformations that changed it to fit local usage. French master masons were soon invited to design and supervise the construction of churches in other parts of Europe. For example, William of Sens was commissioned to rebuild Canterbury Cathedral after a disastrous fire in 1174.

Organizing and Building

The bishop and the clergy of the cathedral made the decision to build, but they depended on the support of all social classes. Bishops raised revenue from contributions of people in their dioceses, and the clergy appealed to the king and the nobility. Since Suger deliberately utilized the Gothic style to glorify the French monarchy, it was called "French royal style" from its inception. Thus the French kings were generous patrons of many cathedrals. Louis IX endowed churches in the Île-de-France—most notably, Sainte-Chapelle, a small chapel to house relics. Noble families often gave contributions to have their crests in the stained-glass windows. Above all, the church relied on the help of those with the greatest amount of ready cash, the commercial classes.

Money was not the only need. A great number of artisans had to be assembled: quarrymen, sculptors, stone-cutters, masons, mortar makers, carpenters, blacksmiths, glassmakers, roofers. Each master craftsman had apprentices, and unskilled laborers had to be recruited for the heavy work. The construction of a large cathedral was rarely completed in a lifetime; many were never finished at all. Because generation after generation added to the building, many Gothic churches show the architectural influences of two or even three centuries. (These variations in style were one of the aspects of Gothic buildings hated by later Renaissance architects, who regarded unity of style as essential in an attractive building.)

Bishops and abbots sketched out what they wanted and set general guidelines, but they left practical needs and aesthetic considerations to the master mason. He held overall responsibility for supervision of the project. (Medieval chroniclers applied the term *architect* to the abbots and bishops who commissioned the projects or the lay patrons who financed them, not to the draftsmen who designed them.) **Master masons** were paid higher wages than other masons; their contracts usually ran for several years, and great care was taken in their selection. Being neither gentlemen, clerics, nor laborers, master masons fit uneasily into the social hierarchy.

Since cathedrals were symbols of civic pride, towns competed to build the largest and most splendid church. In northern France in the late twelfth and early thirteenth centuries, cathedrals grew progressively taller. In 1163 the citizens of Paris began Notre Dame Cathedral, planning it to reach the height of 114 feet. When reconstruction on Chartres Cathedral was begun in 1194, it was to be 119 feet. The people of Beauvais exceeded everyone: their church, started in 1247, reached 157 feet. Unfortunately, the weight imposed on the vaults was too great, and the building collapsed in 1284. Another part collapsed in 1573, and Beauvais Cathedral was never finished, leaving a transept, choir, and apse with no

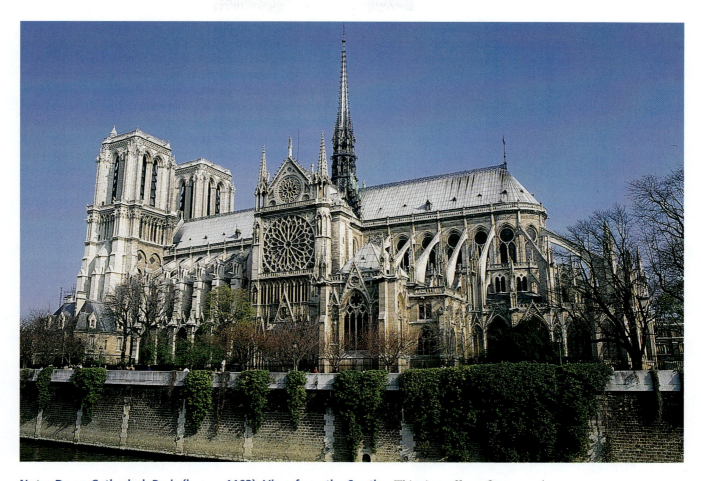

Notre Dame Cathedral, Paris (begun 1163), View from the South   This view offers a fine example of the twin towers (*left*), the spire, the great rose window over the south portal, and the flying buttresses that support the walls and the vaults. Like hundreds of other churches in medieval Europe, it was dedicated to the Virgin. With a nave rising 226 feet, Notre Dame was the tallest building in Europe. *(David R. Frazier/Photo Researchers)*

nave; these parts contain the highest ceiling of any Gothic cathedral, tall enough to hold a fifteen-story office building. Such a collapse was very rare, however, and many cathedrals well over 100 feet tall were built as each bishop and town sought to outdo the neighbors. Medieval people built cathedrals to glorify God—and if mortals were impressed, all the better.

Cathedrals served secular as well as religious purposes. The sanctuary containing the altar and the bishop's chair belonged to the clergy, but the rest of the church belonged to the people. In addition to marriages, baptisms, and funerals, there were scores of feast days on which the entire town gathered in the cathedral for festivities.

Amiens Cathedral could hold the entire town population. Local guilds met in the cathedrals to arrange business deals and plan recreational events and the support of disabled members. Magistrates and municipal officials held political meetings there. Some towns never built town halls because all civic functions took place in the cathedral. Pilgrims slept there; lovers courted there; traveling actors staged plays there. The cathedral belonged to all.

First and foremost, however, the cathedral was intended to teach the people the doctrines of Christian faith through visual images. Architecture became the servant of theology. The main altar was at the east end, pointing toward Jerusalem. The west front of the cathedral faced

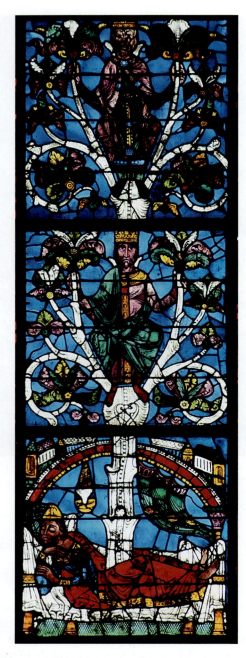

Tree of Jesse In Christian symbolism, a tree stands for either life or death. Glassmakers depicted the ancestors of Christ as a tree's branches, based on the prophecy of Isaiah (11:1–2)—"a shoot shall sprout from the stump of Jesse, and from his roots a bud shall blossom, the spirit of the Lord shall rest upon him"—and the genealogy of Jesus in Matthew (1:1–16). In this stained glass from the west façade of Chartres Cathedral (ca 1150–1170), Jesse, David, and Solomon are shown from bottom to top, with Mary holding the Christ child (unseen) at the top. The glass is set within a rectilinear framework. (© Clive Hicks)

the setting sun, and its wall was usually devoted to the scenes of the Last Judgment. The north side, which received the least sunlight, displayed events from the Old Testament. The south side, washed in warm sunshine for much of the day, depicted scenes from the New Testament. This symbolism implied that the Jewish people of the Old Testament lived in darkness and that the Gospel brought by Christ illuminated the world. Every piece of sculpture, furniture, and stained glass had religious or social significance.

Stained glass beautifully reflects the creative energy of the High Middle Ages. It is both an integral part of Gothic architecture and a distinct form of painting. The ancient Egyptians had invented the process. The designer first sketched a picture on a wooden panel the size of the window opening, noting the colors of each form or shape in the planned composition. Then glass blowers made sheets of colored glass, adding metallic oxides—cobalt for blue, manganese for red or purple, silver for yellow—to a basic mixture of sand and ash or lime, which was fused at a high temperature. From the large sheets of stained glass, artisans cut small pieces and laid them out on the wooden panel. Details were added with an enamel emulsion, and the glass was reheated to fuse the enamel. Last, the designer assembled the pieces and linked them together with narrow strips of lead, called *cames*. The assembled window was then set into an iron frame prepared to fit the window opening.[9] As Gothic churches became more skeletal and had more windows, stained glass replaced manuscript illumination as the leading form of painting.

Contributors to the cathedral and workers left their imprints on it. Stonecutters cut their individual marks in each block of stone, partly so that they would be paid. At Chartres the craft and merchant guilds—drapers, furriers, haberdashers, tanners, butchers, bakers, fishmongers, and wine merchants—donated money and are memorialized in stained-glass windows. Thousands of scenes in the cathedral celebrate nature, country life, and the activities of ordinary people.

Tapestry making also came into its own in the fourteenth century. Heavy woolen tapestries were first made in the monasteries and convents as wall hangings for churches. Because they could be moved and lent an atmosphere of warmth, they replaced mural paintings. Early tapestries depicted religious scenes, but later hangings produced for the knightly class bore secular designs, especially romantic forests and hunting spectacles.

Romanesque and Gothic churches housed relics of Jesus, Mary, or the saints. Abbey and cathedral churches at-

Fifteenth-Century Flemish Tapestry   The weavers of Tournai (in present-day Belgium) spent twenty-five years (1450–1475) producing this magnificent tapestry, which is based on the Old Testament story of Jehu, Jezebel, and the sons of Ahab (2 Kings, 9–10). *(Isabella Stewart Gardner Museum, Boston)*

tracted pilgrims from far and near to pray near the relics, which provided economic opportunities for merchants and innkeepers.

Once at least part of a Gothic cathedral had been built, the building began to be used for religious services. The Mass and other services became increasingly complex to fit with their new surroundings. Originally, services were chanted in unison, termed *plainsong* or *Gregorian chant,* but by the eleventh century additional voices singing on different pitches were added to create *polyphony.* Certain parts of the service were broken off into standalone polyphonic pieces called *motets,* a style that composers soon adapted to secular music as well as ecclesiastical. Church leaders sometimes fumed that motets and polyphony made the text impossible to understand—Pope John XXII called this style an "avalanche of notes" in 1324—but, along with incense, candles, stained-glass windows, and the building itself, music made any service in a Gothic cathedral a rich experience.

Cities and the Church

The soaring towers of Gothic cathedrals were visible symbols of the Christian faith and civic pride of medieval urban residents, but many city people also felt that the church did not meet their spiritual needs. The bishops, usually drawn from the feudal nobility, did not understand urban culture and were suspicious of it. Christian theology, formulated for an earlier rural age, did not address the problems of the more sophisticated mercantile society. The new monastic orders of the twelfth century, such as the Cistercians, situated in remote, isolated areas had little relevance to the towns. Townspeople wanted a pious clergy capable of preaching the Gospel, and they disapproved of clerical ignorance and luxurious living. Critical of the clergy, neglected, and spiritually unfulfilled, townspeople turned to heretical sects.

• *Why did towns become the center of religious heresy, and what was the church's response?*

Heretical Groups

The term *heresy,* which derives from the Greek *hairesis,* meaning "individual choosing," is older than Christianity. At the end of the fourth century, when Christianity became the official religion of the Roman Empire, religious issues took on a legal dimension. Theologians and kings defined the Roman Empire as a Christian society. Since religion was thought to bind society in a fundamental way, religious unity was essential for social cohesion. A heretic, therefore, threatened not only the religious part of the community, but the community itself. Beginning with Emperor Theodosius in the fourth century (page 195), civil authority could (and did) punish heresy. In the early Middle Ages the term *heresy* came to be applied to the position of a Christian who held to doctrines that the church defined as incorrect.

Ironically, the eleventh-century Gregorian reform movement, which had worked to purify the church of disorder, led to some twelfth- and thirteenth-century heretical movements. Papal efforts to improve the sexual morality of the clergy, for example, had largely succeeded. When Gregory VII forbade married priests to celebrate church ceremonies, he expected public opinion to force priests to put aside their wives and concubines. But Gregory did not foresee the consequences of this order. Laypersons assumed they could, and indeed should, remove priests for any type of immorality or for not living according to standards that the parishioners judged appropriate.

In northern Italian towns, Arnold of Brescia, a vigorous advocate of strict clerical poverty, denounced clerical wealth. In France, Peter Waldo, a rich merchant of Lyons, gave his money to the poor and preached that only prayers, not sacraments, were needed for salvation. The **Waldensians**—as Peter's followers were called—bitterly attacked the sacraments and church hierarchy, and they carried these ideas across Europe. As we saw in Chapter 9, the Albigensians asserted that the material world was evil and that religious leaders should be those who rejected worldly things, not the wealthy bishops or the papacy (see pages 284–285).

The Friars

In its continuing struggle against heresy, the church gained the support of two remarkable men, Saint Dominic and Saint Francis, and of the orders they founded. Born in Castile, the province of Spain famous for its zealous Christianity and militant opposition to Islam, Domingo de Gúzman (1170?–1221) received a sound education and was ordained a priest. In 1206 he accompanied his bishop on a mission to preach to the Albigensian heretics in Languedoc. Although the austere simplicity in which they traveled contrasted favorably with the pomp and display of the papal legate in the area, Dominic's efforts had little practical success. Determined to win the heretics back with ardent preaching, Dominic subsequently returned to France with a few followers. In 1216 the group—officially known as the "Preaching Friars" though often called **Dominicans**—won papal recognition as a new religious order. Their name indicates their goal; they were to preach, and in order to preach effectively, they had to study. Dominic sent his recruits to the universities for training in theology.

Francesco di Bernardone (1181–1226), son of a wealthy cloth merchant from the northern Italian town of Assisi, was an extravagant wastrel until he had a sudden conversion. Directed by a vision to rebuild the dilapidated chapel of Saint Damiano in Assisi, Francis sold some of his father's cloth to finance the reconstruction. His enraged father insisted that he return the money and enlisted the support of the bishop. When the bishop told Francis to obey his father, Francis took off all his clothes and returned them to his father. Thereafter he promised to obey only his Father in Heaven. Francis was particularly inspired by two biblical texts: "If you seek perfection, go, sell your possessions, and give to the poor. You will have treasure in heaven. Afterward, come back and follow me" (Matthew 19:21); and Jesus' advice to his disciples as they went out to preach, "Take nothing for the journey, neither walking staff nor travelling bag, nor bread, nor money" (Luke 9:3). Over the centuries, these words have inspired countless young people. With Francis, however, there was a radical difference: he intended to observe them literally and without compromise. He set out to live and preach the Gospel in absolute poverty.

Francis went to live in a cave near Assisi. His father cut him off from any more family money, but Francis took delight in this situation, saying that he was now married to "Lady Poverty." His asceticism did not emphasize withdrawal from the world, but joyful devotion; in contrast to the Albigensians, who saw the material world as evil, Francis saw all creation as God-given and good. He wrote hymns to natural objects such as "brother moon" and was widely reported to perform miracles involving animals, which is how he has become the patron saint of birdbaths in the contemporary world.

The simplicity, humility, and joyful devotion with which Francis carried out his mission soon attracted companions. Although he resisted pressure to establish an order, his followers became so numerous that he was obliged to develop some formal structure. In 1221 the papacy approved the "Rule of the Little Brothers of Saint Francis," as the **Franciscans** were known.

The new Dominican and Franciscan orders differed significantly from older monastic orders such as the Benedictines and the Cistercians. First, the Dominicans and Franciscans were **friars,** not monks. Their lives and work focused on the cities and university towns, the busy centers of commercial and intellectual life, not the secluded and cloistered world of monks. They did not chant the Divine Office (see page 321), and they thought that *more* contact with ordinary Christians, not less, was a better spiritual path.

Second, the friars stressed apostolic poverty, a life based on the Gospel's teachings, in which they would own no property and depend on Christian people for their material needs. Hence they were called **mendicants** or mendicant orders, that is, begging friars. Benedictine and Cistercian abbeys, on the other hand, held land—not infrequently great tracts of land. The Franciscans originally vowed absolute poverty—Francis wanted them never to have more at one time than they would need in a day—but the order grew so fast that this became impossible to maintain, and Francis's original standards were relaxed.

Finally, the friars usually drew their members largely from the burgher class, from small property owners and shopkeepers. The monastic orders, by contrast, gathered their members (at least until the thirteenth century) overwhelmingly from the nobility.

The friars represented a response to the spiritual and intellectual needs of the thirteenth century. While the Franciscans initially accepted uneducated men, the Dominicans showed a marked preference for university graduates. A more urban and sophisticated society required a highly educated clergy. The Dominicans soon held professorial chairs at leading universities, and they count Thomas Aquinas, probably the greatest medieval philosopher in Europe, as their most famous member. But the Franciscans followed suit at the universities and also produced intellectual leaders. The friars interpreted

Christian doctrine for the new urban classes. By living Christianity as well as by preaching it, they won the respect of the medieval bourgeoisie.

As the orders of friars were being established, women sought to develop similar women's orders devoted to active service out in the world. Clare of Assisi (1193–1253), like Francis the child of a wealthy Italian urban family, refused to marry, sought to live in poverty, and became a follower of Francis, who established a place for her to live in a nearby church. She was joined by other women, and they attempted to establish a rule for life in their community that would follow Francis's ideals of absolute poverty and allow them to serve the poor. Her rule was accepted by the papacy only after many decades, and then only because she agreed that the order, called the **Poor Clares,** would be enclosed.

In the growing cities of Europe, especially in the Netherlands, groups of women seeking to live religious lives came together as what later came to be known as **Beguines.** (The origins of the word are debated.) They lived communally in small houses called beguinages, combining a life of prayer with service to the needy, but took no formal vows. In a few cities these beguinages grew quite large, eventually incorporating churches and other buildings as well as housing for several hundred women. Beguine spirituality emphasized direct personal communication with God, sometimes through mystical experiences, rather than through the intercession of a saint or official church rituals. Many Beguines were also devoted to the church's sacraments, however, especially the Eucharist, and initially some church officials gave guarded approval of the movement. By the fourteenth century, however, they were declared heretical and much of their property was confiscated, for church officials were clearly uncomfortable with women who were neither married nor cloistered nuns.

The Friars and Papal Power

Beginning in 1233 the papacy used the friars to staff its new ecclesiastical court, the Inquisition (see pages 284–285). Popes selected the friars to direct the Inquisition because bishops proved unreliable and because special theological training was needed. *Inquisition* means "investigation," and the Franciscans and Dominicans developed expert methods of rooting out unorthodox thought. Ironically, within a hundred years of Francis's death one of the Inquisition's targets was the Spiritual Franciscans, a breakaway group that wanted to follow

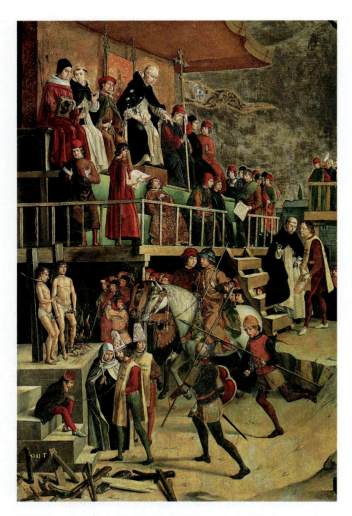

Saint Dominic and the Inquisition   The fifteenth-century court painter to the Spanish rulers Ferdinand and Isabella, Pedro Berruguete here portrays an event from the life of Saint Dominic: Dominic presides at the trial of Count Raymond of Toulouse, who had supported the Albigensian heretics. Raymond, helmeted and on horseback, repented and was pardoned; his companions, who would not repent, were burned. Smoke from the fire has put one of the judges to sleep, and other officials, impervious to the human tragedy, chat among themselves. *(Museo del Prado, Madrid/Institut Amatller d'Art Hispanic)*

Francis's original ideals of poverty and denied the pope's right to countermand that ideal.

Modern Americans consider the procedures of the Inquisition exceedingly unjust, and there was substantial criticism of it in the Middle Ages. The accused did not learn the evidence against them or see their accusers; they were subjected to lengthy interrogations often designed to trap them; and torture could be used to extract confessions. Medieval people, however, believed that heretics destroyed the souls of their neighbors. By attacking religion, it was also thought, heretics destroyed the very bonds of society. By the mid-thirteenth century secular governments steadily pressed for social conformity, and they had the resources to search out and punish heretics. So successful was the Inquisition as a tool of royal power that within a century heresy had been virtually extinguished.

Popes and kings jointly supported the Inquisition, but in the late thirteenth century the papacy came into a violent dispute with several of Europe's leading rulers. In 1294 King Edward I of England and Philip the Fair of France declared war on each other. To finance this war, both kings laid taxes on the clergy. Kings had been taxing the church for decades. Pope Boniface VIII (1294–1303), arguing from precedent, insisted that kings gain papal consent for taxation of the clergy and forbade churchmen to pay the taxes. But Edward and Philip refused to accept this decree, partly because it hurt royal finances and partly because the papal order threatened royal authority within their countries. Edward immediately denied the clergy the protection of the law, an action that meant its members could be attacked with impunity. Philip halted the shipment of all ecclesiastical revenue to Rome. Boniface had to back down.

Philip the Fair and his ministers continued their attack on all powers in France outside royal authority. Philip arrested a French bishop who was also the papal legate. When Boniface defended the ecclesiastical status and diplomatic immunity of the bishop, Philip declared that the pope was a heretic. The papacy and the French monarchy waged a bitter war of propaganda. Finally, in 1302, in a letter titled **Unam Sanctam** (because its opening sentence spoke of one holy Catholic Church), Boniface insisted that all Christians were subject to the pope. Although the letter made no specific reference to Philip, it held that kings should submit to papal authority. Philip's university-trained advisers responded with an argument drawn from Roman law. They maintained that the king of France was completely sovereign in his kingdom and responsible to God alone. French mercenary troops went to Italy and assaulted and arrested the aged pope at Anagni. Although Boniface was soon freed, he died shortly afterward. The confrontation at Anagni foreshadowed serious difficulties in the Christian church, but religious struggle was only one of the crises that would face Western society in the fourteenth century.

Chapter Summary

- *How did medieval cities originate, and what impact did they have on the economy and on culture?*
- *How did universities evolve, and what needs of medieval society did they serve?*
- *What do oral traditions and vernacular literature reveal about medieval culture?*
- *How did cathedrals express the ideals, attitudes, and interests of medieval people?*
- *Why did towns become the center of religious heresy, and what was the church's response?*

Medieval cities—whether beginning around the sites of cathedrals, fortifications, or market towns—recruited people from the countryside with the promise of greater freedom and new possibilities. Cities provided economic opportunity, which, together with the revival of long-distance trade and a new capitalistic spirit, led to greater wealth, a higher standard of living, and upward social mobility for many people. Merchants and artisans formed guilds to protect their means of livelihood. Not everyone in medieval cities shared in the prosperity, however; many residents lived hand-to-mouth on low wages.

The towns that became centers of trade and production in the High Middle Ages developed into cultural and intellectual centers. Trade brought in new ideas as well as merchandise, and in many cities a new type of educational institution—the university—emerged from cathedral and municipal schools. Universities developed theological, legal, and medical courses of study based on classical models and provided trained officials for the new government bureaucracies. University-trained professionals joined merchants and guild masters as well-off members of the urban elite, heading large households staffed with servants and charging high prices for their services.

University education was in Latin and was limited to men, but the High Middle Ages also saw the creation of new types of vernacular literature. Poems, songs, and stories, written down in local dialects, celebrated things of concern to ordinary people. In this, the troubadours of southern France led the way, using Arabic models to create romantic stories of heterosexual love. The ability to read the vernacular was still limited, however, so oral transmission continued as the most important way that information was conveyed and traditions passed down. The oral culture of medieval cities included plays with re-ligious themes, but also violent entertainments, bawdy songs, and dancing.

Economic growth meant that merchants, nobles, and guild masters had disposable income they could spend on artistic products and more elaborate consumer goods. They supported the building of churches and cathedrals as visible symbols of their Christian faith and their civic pride; cathedrals in particular grew larger and more sumptuous, with high towers, stained-glass windows, and multiple altars. The sturdy Romanesque style was replaced by the soaring Gothic, in which sophisticated building techniques allowed windows to grow ever taller and wider. Cathedrals were places for socializing as well as worship, and increasingly complex music added to the experience.

Town residents demonstrated their deep religious faith in the construction of Gothic cathedrals, but many urban people thought that the church did not fulfill their spiritual needs. They turned instead to heresies, many of which, somewhat ironically, denied the value of material wealth. Combating heresy became a principal task of new types of religious orders, most prominently the Dominicans and Franciscans, who preached, ministered to city dwellers, and also staffed the papal Inquisition, a special court designed to root out heresy. These efforts were largely successful, and the church continued to exercise leadership of Christian society in the High Middle Ages, though the clash between the papacy and the kings of France and England at the end of the thirteenth century seriously challenged papal power.

Key Terms

town liberties	troubadours
merchant guild	cathedrals
craft guilds	Romanesque
livery	Gothic
sumptuary laws	master masons
Hanseatic League	Waldensians
usury	Dominicans
commercial revolution	Franciscans
mercantile capitalism	friars
Scholastics	mendicants
summa	Poor Clares
dialects	Beguines
vernacular literature	*Unam Sanctam*

 *Online Study Center*   **Improve Your Grade** Flashcards

(continued on page 368)

Courtly Love

Whether female or male, the troubadour poets celebrated fin'amor, a Provençal word for the pure or perfect love a knight was supposed to feel for his lady, which has in English come to be called chivalry or "courtly love." In courtly love lyrics, the writer praises his or her love object, idealizing the beloved and promising loyalty and great deeds. Most of these songs are written by, or from the perspective of, a male lover who is socially beneath his female beloved; her higher status makes her unattainable, so the lover's devotion can remain chaste and pure, rewarded by her handkerchief, or perhaps a kiss, but nothing more. The noblemen and noblewomen who listened to these songs viewed such love as ennobling, and some authors even wrote courtly love lyrics directed to the Virgin Mary, the ultimate unattainable woman.

Scholars generally agree that poetry praising perfect love originated in the Muslim culture of the Iberian Peninsula, where heterosexual romantic love had long been the subject of poems and songs. Southern France was a border area where Christian and Muslim cultures mixed; Spanish Muslim poets sang at the courts of Christian nobles, and Provençal poets picked up their romantic themes.

Other aspects of courtly love are hotly debated. Was it simply a literary convention, or did it shape actual behavior? Did it celebrate adultery, or was true courtly love pure (and unrequited)? How should we interpret medieval physicians' reports of people (mostly young men) becoming gravely ill from "lovesickness"; did the doctors really believe in the physical power of love? Were there actually "courts of love" in which women judged lovers based on a system of rules? Did courtly love lead to greater respect for women or toward greater misogyny, as desire for a beloved so often ended in frustration?

It is very difficult to know whether courtly love literature influenced the treatment of real women to any great extent—peasant women were certainly no less in danger of rape from knightly armies in the thirteenth century than they had been in the tenth—but it did introduce an ideal of heterosexual romance into Western literature that had not been there in the classical or early medieval period. People who study contemporary popular culture note how much courtly love ideals still shape romantic conventions. Countless movies, songs, and novels explore love between people of different social groups, though now the love generally remains pure by having either the lover or the beloved tragically die young.

The following poem was written by Arnaut Daniel, a thirteenth-century troubadour praised by writers from Dante in the thirteenth century to Ezra Pound in the twentieth. Not much is known about him, but the songs that have survived capture courtly love conventions perfectly.

I only know the grief that comes to me,
to my love-ridden heart, out of over-loving,
since my will is so firm and whole
that it never parted or grew distant from her
whom I craved at first sight, and afterwards:
and now, in her absence, I tell her burning
 words;
then, when I see her, I don't know, so much I
 have to, what to say.

To the sight of other women I am blind, deaf
 to hearing them
since her only I see, and hear and heed,
and in that I am surely not a false slanderer,
since heart desires her more than mouth may
 say;
wherever I may roam through fields and valleys,
 plains and mountains
I shan't find in a single person all those qualities
which God wanted to select and place in her.

I have been in many a good court,
but here by her I find much more to praise:
measure and wit and other good virtues,
beauty and youth, worthy deeds and fair
 disport;
so well kindness taught and instructed her
that it has rooted every ill manner out of her:
I don't think she lacks anything good.

No joy would be brief or short
coming from her whom I endear to guess [my
    intentions],
otherwise she won't know them from me,
if my heart cannot reveal itself without words,
since even the Rhone [River], when rain swells
    it,
has no such rush that my heart doesn't stir
a stronger one, weary of love, when I behold
    her.

Joy and merriment from another woman seems
    false and ill to me,
since no worthy one can compare with her,
and her company is above the others'.
Ah me, if I don't have her, alas, so badly she has
    taken me!
But this grief is amusement, laughter and joy,
since in thinking of her, of her am I gluttonous
    and greedy:
ah me, God, could I ever enjoy her otherwise!

And never, I swear, I have liked game or ball so
    much,
or anything has given my heart so much joy
as did the one thing that no false slanderer
made public, which is a treasure for me only.
Do I tell too much? Not I, unless she is
    displeased:
beautiful one, by God, speech and voice
I'd lose ere I say something to annoy you.

And I pray my song does not displease you
since, if you like the music and lyrics,
little cares Arnaut whether the unpleasant ones
    like them as well.

*Far fewer poems by female troubadours
(trobairitz) have survived than by male, but those
that have express strong physical and emotional
feelings. The twelfth-century Countess of Dia may
have been the wife of a Provençal nobleman, but
biographies of both troubadours and trobairitz were
often made up later to fit the conventions of courtly
love, so we don't know for sure. We do know that the
words to at least four of her songs have survived, one
of them with the melody, which is very rare.*

I've suffered great distress
From a knight whom I once owned.
Now, for all time, be it known:
I loved him—yes, to excess.
    His jilting I've regretted,
Yet his love I never really returned.
Now for my sin I can only burn:
    Dressed, or in my bed.

O if I had that knight to caress
Naked all night in my arms,
He'd be ravished by the charm

In this fourteenth-century
painting, a lady puts the helmet on
her beloved knight. *(akg-images)*

Of using, for cushion, my breast.
    His love I more deeply prize
Than Floris did Blancheor's
Take that love, my core,
    My sense, my life, my eyes!

Lovely lover, gracious, kind,
When will I overcome your fight?
O if I could lie with you one night!
Feel those loving lips on mine!
    Listen, one thing sets me afire:
Here in my husband's place I want you,
If you'll just keep your promise true:
    Give me everything I desire.

Questions for Analysis

1. Both of these songs focus on a beloved who
   does not return the lover's affection. What
   similarities and differences do you see in them?

2. How does courtly love reinforce other aspects
   of medieval society? Are there aspects of
   medieval society it contradicts?

3. Can you find examples from current popular
   music that parallel the sentiments expressed in
   these two songs?

Source: First poem: Leonardo Malcovati, *Prosody in Eng-
land and Elsewhere: A Comparative Approach* (London:
Gival Press, 2006), and online at http://www.trobar.org/
troubadours/; second poem: quoted in J. J. Wilhelm, ed.,
Lyrics of the Middle Ages: An Anthology (New York: Garland
Publishers, 1993), pp. 83–84.

Suggested Reading

Bruckner, Matilda. *Songs of the Women Troubadours*. 2000. Provides analysis and excerpts of songs.

De Ridder-Symoens, Hilde, ed. *A History of the University in Europe,* vol. 1: *Universities in the Middle Ages.* 1991. Up-to-date interpretations by leading scholars.

Gaunt, Simon, and Sarah Kay, eds. *The Troubadours: An Introduction.* 1999. A collection of essays that trace the development of troubadour song and the reception of troubadour poetry.

Gimpel, Jean. *The Medieval Machine: The Industrial Revolution of the Middle Ages.* 1977. Discusses the mechanical and scientific problems involved in constructing cathedrals and other buildings and the invention of new types of tools.

Lambert, Malcolm. *Medieval Heresy: Popular Movements from the Gregorian Reform to the Reformation,* 3d ed. 2000. Analyzes the development and suppression of heresy over several centuries.

LeGoff, Jacques. *Time, Work, and Culture in the Middle Ages.* 1980. Looks at the broad cultural impact of economic change.

Moore, R. I. *The First European Revolution: 970–1215.* 2000. A bold assessment of the long-term significance of the changes discussed in this chapter.

Moore, R. I. *The Formation of a Persecuting Society.* 1990. Sets the Inquisition and medieval heresy within a broad cultural, social, and political context.

Pirenne, Henri. *Economic and Social History of Medieval Europe.* 1956. Remains a valuable study of the economic revival of Europe by a leading French medievalist.

Radding, Charles M. *The Origins of Medieval Jurisprudence.* 1988. Analyzes legal training and the development of law.

Radding, Charles M., and William W. Clark. *Medieval Architecture, Medieval Learning: Builders and Masters in the Age of Romanesque and Gothic.* 1992. A valuable survey of the evolution of architectural styles and their relation to broader intellectual and cultural developments.

Reynolds, Susan. *An Introduction to the History of English Medieval Towns.* 1982. A good survey of the growth of English towns.

Robertson, D. W., Jr. *Abélard and Héloise.* 1972. A highly readable and commonsensical look at the famous relationship.

Siraisi, Nancy. *Medieval and Early Renaissance Medicine: An Introduction to Knowledge and Practice.* 1990. The best place to start for information about both theory and practice.

Spufford, Peter. *Money and Its Use in Medieval Europe.* 1988. Explores coinage, credit, and other aspects of the monetary economy.

Notes

1. Quoted in R. S. Lopez, "Of Towns and Trade," in *Life and Thought in the Early Middle Ages,* ed. R. S. Hoyt (Minneapolis: University of Minnesota Press, 1967), p. 33.
2. Douglas and Greenaway, *English Historical Documents,* vol. 2, pp. 969–970.
3. H. Rothwell, ed., *English Historical Documents,* vol. 3 (London: Eyre & Spottiswoode, 1975), p. 854.
4. M. M. Postan, *The Medieval Economy and Society: An Economic History of Britain in the Middle Ages* (Baltimore: Penguin Books, 1975), pp. 213–214.
5. Quoted in H. E. Sigerist, *Civilization and Disease* (Chicago: University of Chicago Press, 1943), p. 102.
6. See John F. Benton, "Fraud, Fiction and Borrowing in the Correspondence of Abelard and Heloise," in *Culture, Power and Personality in Medieval France,* ed. T. N. Bisson (London and Rio Grande: The Hambledon Press, 1991), pp. 417–449, esp. pp. 430–443, which convincingly demonstrates that "the most personal parts of the correspondence are not genuine" and that the letters were probably written in the later thirteenth century; and the same scholar's "The Correspondence of Abelard and Heloise," in the same volume, pp. 487–512.
7. Quoted in J. H. Mundy, *Europe in the High Middle Ages, 1150–1309* (New York: Basic Books, 1973), pp. 474–475.
8. A. F. Scott, ed., *Everyone a Witness: The Plantagenet Age* (New York: Thomas Y. Crowell, 1976), p. 263.
9. See "The Technique of Stained Glass Windows," in M. Stokstad, *Art History* (New York: Harry N. Abrams, 1995), p. 559, on which I have leaned.

In this lavishly illustrated French chronicle, Wat Tyler, the leader of the English Peasant's Revolt, is stabbed during a meeting with the king. Tyler died soon afterward, and the revolt was ruthlessly crushed. *(Bibliothèque nationale de France)*

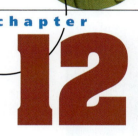

THE CRISIS OF THE LATER MIDDLE AGES, 1300–1450

During the later Middle Ages, the last book of the New Testament, the Book of Revelation, inspired thousands of sermons and hundreds of religious tracts. The Book of Revelation deals with visions of the end of the world, with disease, war, famine, and death. It is no wonder this part of the Bible was so popular. Between 1300 and 1450 Europeans experienced a frightful series of shocks: climate change, economic dislocation, plague, war, social upheaval, and increased crime and violence. Death and preoccupation with death make the fourteenth century one of the most wrenching periods of Western civilization. Yet, in spite of the pessimism and crises, important institutions and cultural forms, including representative assemblies and national literatures, emerged. Even institutions that experienced severe crisis, such as the Christian church, saw new types of vitality.

Prelude to Disaster

In the first half of the fourteenth century, Europe experienced a series of climate changes that led to lower levels of food production, which had dramatic and disastrous ripple effects. Political leaders attempted to find solutions, but were unable to deal with the economic and social problems that resulted.

● *What were the demographic and economic consequences of climate change?*

Climate Change and Famine

The period from about 1000 to about 1300 saw warmer than usual climate in Europe, which underlay all the changes and vitality of the High Middle Ages. About 1300 the climate changed, becoming colder and wetter. Historical geographers refer to the period from 1300 to 1450 as a "little ice age," which they can trace through both natural and human records.

Online Study Center
This icon will direct you to interactive activities and study materials on the website **college.hmco.com/pic/mckaywest9e**

Death from Famine   In this fifteenth-century painting, dead bodies lie in the middle of a path, while a funeral procession at the right includes a man with an adult's coffin and a woman with the coffin of an infant under her arm. People did not simply allow the dead to lie in the street in medieval Europe, though during famines and epidemics it was sometimes difficult to maintain normal burial procedures. *(Erich Lessing/Art Resource, NY)*

Evidence from nature emerges through the study of Alpine and polar glaciers, tree rings, and pollen left in bogs. Human-produced sources include written reports of rivers freezing and crops never ripening, as well as archaeological evidence such as the abandoned villages of Greenland, where ice floes cut off contact with the rest of the world and the harshening climate meant that the few hardy crops grown earlier could no longer survive. The Viking colony on Greenland died out completely, though Inuit people who relied on hunting sea mammals continued to live in the far north, as they had before the arrival of Viking colonists.

An unusual number of storms brought torrential rains, ruining the wheat, oat, and hay crops on which people and animals almost everywhere depended. Since long-distance transportation of food was expensive and difficult, most urban areas depended for bread and meat on areas no more than a day's journey away. Poor harvests—and one in four was likely to be poor—led to scarcity and starvation. Almost all of northern Europe suffered a

"Great Famine" in the years 1315–1322, which contemporaries interpreted as a recurrence of the biblical "seven lean years" (Genesis 42). Even in non-famine years, the cost of grain, livestock, and dairy products rose sharply.

Reduced caloric intake meant increased susceptibility to disease, especially for infants, children, and the elderly. Workers on reduced diets had less energy, which in turn meant lower productivity, lower output, and higher grain prices. The Great Famine proved to be a demographic disaster in France; in Burgundy perhaps one-third of the population died. The many religious houses of Flanders experienced a high loss of monks, nuns, and priests. In Scandinavia and the Baltic countries, low cereal harvests, declines in meat and dairy production, economic recessions, and the lack of salt, used for preserving herring, resulted in terrible food shortages.

Hardly had western Europe begun to recover from this disaster when another struck: an epidemic of typhoid fever carried away thousands. In 1316, 10 percent of the population of the city of Ypres may have died between

May and October alone. Then in 1318 disease hit cattle and sheep, drastically reducing the herds and flocks. Another bad harvest in 1321 brought famine and death.

The province of Languedoc in France presents a classic example of agrarian crisis. For more than 150 years Languedoc had enjoyed continual land reclamation, steady agricultural expansion, and enormous population growth. Then the fourteenth century opened with four years of bad harvests. Torrential rains in 1310 ruined the harvest and brought on terrible famine. Harvests failed again in 1322 and 1329. In 1332 desperate peasants survived the winter on raw herbs. In the half century from 1302 to 1348, poor harvests occurred twenty times. These catastrophes had grave social consequences. Poor harvests and famine led to the abandonment of homesteads. In parts of the Low Countries and in the Scottish-English borderlands, entire villages were abandoned. This meant a great increase in the number of vagabonds, what we call "homeless people." In Flanders and East Anglia (eastern England), where aspects of the famine have been carefully analyzed, some peasants were forced to mortgage, sublease, or sell their holdings to get money to buy food. Rich farmers bought out their poorer neighbors. When conditions improved, debtors tried to get their lands back, leading to a very volatile land market. To reduce the labor supply and the mouths to feed in the countryside, young men and women sought work in the towns. Poor harvests probably meant that marriage had to be postponed. Later marriages and the deaths caused by famine and disease meant a reduction in population. Meanwhile, the international character of trade and commerce meant that a disaster in one country had serious implications elsewhere. For example, the infection that attacked English sheep in 1318 caused a sharp decline in wool exports in the following years. Without wool, Flemish weavers could not work, and thousands were laid off. Without woolen cloth, the businesses of Flemish, Hanseatic, and Italian merchants suffered. Unemployment encouraged people to turn to crime.

Government Ineptitude

To none of these problems did governments have effective solutions. The three sons of Philip the Fair who sat on the French throne between 1314 and 1328 condemned speculators, who held stocks of grain back until conditions were desperate and prices high; forbade the sale of grain abroad; and published legislation prohibiting fishing with traps that took large catches. These measures had few positive results. As the subsistence crisis deepened, popular discontent and paranoia increased.

Chronology

1309–1376	Babylonian Captivity; papacy in Avignon
1310–1320	Dante, *Divine Comedy*
1315–1322	Famine in northern Europe
1324	Marsiglio of Padua, *Defensor Pacis*
1337–1453	Hundred Years' War
1348	Black Death arrives in mainland Europe
1358	Jacquerie peasant uprising in France
1378	Ciompi revolt in Florence
1378–1417	Great Schism
1381	Peasants' Revolt in England
1387–1400	Chaucer, *Canterbury Tales*
1415	English smash the French at Agincourt
1429	French victory at Orléans; Charles VII crowned king
1431	Joan of Arc declared a heretic and burned at the stake

Starving people focused their anger on the rich, speculators, and the Jews, who were targeted as creditors fleecing the poor through pawnbroking. (Expelled from France in 1306, Jews were readmitted in 1315 and were granted the privilege of lending at high interest rates.) Rumors spread of a plot by Jews and their agents, the lepers, to kill Christians by poisoning the wells. Based on "evidence" collected by torture, many lepers and Jews were killed, beaten, or hit with heavy fines.

In England Edward I's incompetent son, Edward II (r. 1307–1327), used Parliament to set price controls, first on the sale of livestock after disease and poor lambing had driven prices up, and then on ale, which was made from barley (the severe rains of 1315 had contributed to molds and mildews, sharply reducing the crop). Baronial conflicts and wars with the Scots dominated Edward II's reign. Fearing food riots and violence, Edward condemned speculators, which proved easier than enforcing price controls. He did try to buy grain abroad, but yields in the Baltic were low; the French crown, as we have seen, forbade exports; and the grain shipped from Castile in northern Spain was grabbed by Scottish, English, and rogue Hanseatic pirates on the high seas. Such grain as reached southern English ports was stolen by looters and sold on the black market. The Crown's efforts at famine relief failed.

The Black Death

Royal attempts to provide food from abroad were unsuccessful, but they indicate the extent of long-distance shipping by the beginning of the fourteenth century. In 1291 Genoese sailors had opened the Strait of Gibraltar to Italian shipping by defeating the Moroccans. Then, shortly after 1300, important advances were made in the design of Italian merchant ships. A square rig was added to the mainmast, and ships began to carry three masts instead of just one. Additional sails better utilized wind power to propel the ship. The improved design permitted year-round shipping for the first time, and Venetian and Genoese merchant ships could sail the dangerous Atlantic coast even in the winter months.

Ships continually at sea carried all types of cargo, and they also carried vermin of all types, especially insects and rats, which often harbored disease pathogens. Rats, fleas, and cockroaches could live for months on the cargo carried along the coasts, disembarking at ports with the grain, cloth, or other merchandise. Just as modern air travel has allowed diseases such as AIDS and SARS to spread quickly over very long distances, medieval shipping did the same. The most frightful of these diseases first emerged in western Europe in 1347, carried on Genoese ships, a disease that was later called the **Black Death.**

• How did the spread of the plague shape European society?

Pathology

Most historians and almost all microbiologists identify the disease that spread in the fourteenth century as the bubonic plague, caused by the bacillus *Yersinia pestis.* The disease normally afflicts rats. Fleas living on the infected rats drink their blood; the bacteria that cause the plague multiply in the flea's gut; and the flea passes them on to the next rat it bites by throwing up into the bite. Usually the disease is limited to rats and other rodents, but at certain points in history—perhaps when most rats have been killed off—the fleas have jumped from their rodent hosts to humans and other animals. One of these times appears to have been in the Eastern Roman Empire in the sixth century, when a plague killed millions of people. Another was in China and India in the 1890s,

when millions died. Doctors and epidemiologists closely studied this outbreak, identified the bacillus as bubonic plague, and learned about the exact cycle of infection for the first time.

The fourteenth-century outbreak showed many similarities to the nineteenth-century outbreak, but also some differences. There are no reports of massive rat dieoffs in fourteenth-century records. The plague was often transmitted directly from one person to another through coughing and sneezing (what epidemiologists term *pneumonic* transmission) as well as through flea bites. The fourteenth-century outbreak spread much faster than the nineteenth-century outbreak and was much more deadly, killing as much as one-third of the population when it first spread to an area. These differences have led some historians to question whether the fourteenth-century disease was actually bubonic plague or whether it was some other disease, perhaps something like the Ebola virus. In the late 1990s French paleomicrobiologists studying the tooth pulp from bodies in two plague cemeteries found DNA from *Y. pestis,* a finding that has been viewed as convincing by most medical historians, though similar studies of English plague cemeteries have not yielded the same results.

These debates fuel continued study of medical aspects of the plague. Some scholars suggest that the type of fleas that normally live on humans might have also been agents in plague transmission in the fourteenth century (which would account for the lack of a rat die-off), or that the fourteenth-century strain of the disease might have been particularly deadly, or that improvements in sanitation and public health by the nineteenth century— even in poor countries such as India—might have limited the mortality rate significantly.

Though there is some disagreement about exactly what kind of disease the plague was, there is no dispute about its dreadful effects on the body. The classic symptom of the bubonic plague was a growth the size of a nut or an apple in the armpit, in the groin, or on the neck. This was the boil, or **bubo,** that gave the disease its name and caused agonizing pain. If the bubo was lanced and the pus thoroughly drained, the victim had a chance of recovery. The next stage was the appearance of black spots or blotches caused by bleeding under the skin. (This syndrome did not give the disease its common name; contemporaries did not call the plague the Black Death. Sometime in the fifteenth century, the Latin phrase *atra mors,* meaning "dreadful death," was translated as "black death," and the phrase stuck.) Finally, the victim began to cough violently and spit blood. This stage, indicating the presence of millions of bacilli in the

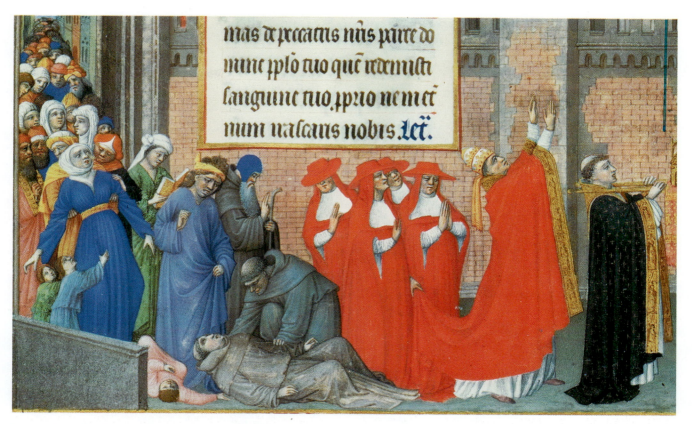

Procession of Saint Gregory According to the *Golden Legend,* a thirteenth-century collection of saints' lives, the bubonic plague ravaged Rome when Gregory I was elected pope (590–604). This fourteenth-century painting, produced at a time when plague was again striking Europe, shows Gregory leading a procession around the city as new victims fall (*center*). The artist shows everyone in fourteenth-century clothing and may have seen similar plague processions in his own city. (*Musée Condé, Chantilly/Art Resource, NY*)

bloodstream, signaled the end, and death followed in two or three days.

Spread of the Disease

Plague symptoms were first described in 1331 in southwestern China, part of the Mongol Empire. Plague-infested rats accompanied Mongol armies and merchant caravans carrying silk, spices, and gold across Central Asia in the 1330s. Then they stowed away on ships, carrying the disease to the ports of the Black Sea by the 1340s. Later stories told of more dramatic means of spreading the disease as well, reporting that Mongol armies besieging the city of Kaffa on the shores of the Black Sea catapulted plague-infected corpses over the walls to infect those inside. The city's residents dumped the corpses into the sea as fast as they could, but they were already infected.

In October 1347 Genoese ships brought the plague from Kaffa to Messina, from which it spread across Sicily. Venice and Genoa were hit in January 1348, and from the port of Pisa the disease spread south to Rome and east to Florence and all of Tuscany. By late spring southern Germany was attacked. Frightened French authorities chased a galley bearing the disease away from the port of Marseilles, but not before plague had infected the city, from which it spread to Languedoc and Spain. In June 1348 two ships entered the Bristol Channel and introduced it into England. All Europe felt the scourge of this horrible disease (see Map 12.1).

Although urban authorities from London to Paris to Rome had begun to try to achieve a primitive level of sanitation by the fourteenth century, urban conditions remained ideal for the spread of disease. Narrow streets filled with refuse and human excrement were as much cesspools as thoroughfares. Dead animals and sore-covered

Mapping the Past

MAP 12.1 The Course of the Black Death in Fourteenth-Century Europe   Use the map and the information in the text to answer the following questions: ❶ How did the expansion of trade that resulted from the commercial revolution contribute to the spread of the Black Death? ❷ When did the plague reach Paris? Why do you think it got to Paris before it spread to the rest of northern France or to southern Germany? ❸ Which cities were spared? What might account for this? ❹ Which regions were spared? Would the reasons for this be the same as those for cities, or might other causes have been operating in rural areas?

Online Study Center **Improve Your Grade** Interactive Map: Bubonic Plague and Social Upheaval in Fourteenth-Century Europe

beggars greeted the traveler. Houses whose upper stories projected over the lower ones blocked light and air. And extreme overcrowding was commonplace. When all members of an aristocratic family lived and slept in one room, it should not be surprising that six or eight persons in a middle-class or poor household slept in one bed—if they had one. Closeness, after all, provided warmth. Houses were beginning to be constructed of

brick, but many wood, clay, and mud houses remained. A determined rat had little trouble entering such a house.

Standards of personal hygiene remained frightfully low. True, most large cities had public bathhouses, but we have no way of knowing how frequently ordinary people used them. Lack of personal cleanliness, combined with any number of temporary ailments such as diarrhea and the common cold, weakened the body's resistance to serious disease. Fleas and body lice were universal afflictions: everyone from peasants to archbishops had them. One more bite did not cause much alarm. But if that nibble came from a bacillus-bearing flea, an entire household or area was doomed.

Mortality rates cannot be specified because population figures for the period before the arrival of the plague do not exist for most countries and cities. The largest amount of material survives for England, but it is difficult to use; after enormous scholarly controversy, only educated guesses can be made. Of a total English population of perhaps 4.2 million, probably 1.4 million died of the Black Death in its several visits. Densely populated Italian cities endured incredible losses. Florence lost between one-half and two-thirds of its 1347 population of 85,000 when the plague visited in 1348. The most widely accepted estimate for western Europe is that the plague killed about one-third of the population in the first wave of infection.

Nor did central and eastern Europe escape the ravages of the disease. Moving northward from the Balkans, eastward from France, and southward from the Baltic, the plague swept through the German Empire. In the Rhineland in 1349, Cologne and Mainz endured heavy losses. In 1348 it swept through Bavaria, entered the Moselle Valley, and pushed into northern Germany. One chronicler records that, in the summer and autumn of 1349, between five hundred and six hundred died every day in Vienna. Styria, in what today is central Austria, was very hard hit, with cattle straying unattended in the fields.

As the Black Death took its toll on the German Empire, waves of emigrants fled to Poland, Bohemia, and Hungary. The situation there was better, though disease was not completely absent. The plague seems to have entered Poland through the Baltic seaports and spread from there. Still, population losses were lower than elsewhere in Europe. The plague spread from Poland to Russia, reaching Pskov, Novgorod, and Moscow. No estimates have been made of population losses there or in the Balkans. In Serbia, though, the plague left vast tracts of land unattended, which prompted an increase in Albanian immigration to meet the labor shortage.

Across Europe the Black Death recurred intermittently from the 1360s to 1400. It reappeared with reduced virulence from time to time over the following centuries, making its last appearance in the French port city of Marseilles in 1721. Survivors became more prudent. Because periods of famine had caused malnutrition, making people vulnerable to disease, Europeans controlled population growth so that population did not outstrip food supply. Western Europeans improved navigation techniques and increased long-distance trade, which permitted the importation of grain from sparsely populated Baltic regions. They strictly enforced quarantine measures. They worked on the development of vaccines. But it was only in 1947, six centuries after the arrival of the plague in the West, that the American microbiologist Selman Waksman discovered an effective vaccine, streptomycin. Plague continues to infect rodent and human populations sporadically today.

Care

Fourteenth-century medical literature indicates that physicians could sometimes ease the pain, but they had no cure. Medical doctors observed that crowded cities had high death rates, especially when the weather was warm and moist. We understand that warm, moist conditions make it easier for germs, viruses, and bacteria to grow and spread, but fourteenth-century people—lay, scholarly, and medical—thought in terms of "poisons" in the air or "corrupted air" rather than germs. This "corrupted air" came from swamps, unburied animal or human corpses, too much rain, the position of planets or stars, or perhaps other causes. The poisons caused illness, which doctors thought of as an imbalance in the fluids in the body, especially blood. Certain symptoms of the plague, especially bleeding and vomiting, were believed to be the body's natural reaction to too much fluid. These were often symptoms of other illnesses as well, and doctors frequently prescribed bloodletting, that is, taking blood from the body by applying leeches or making small cuts in veins, as standard treatment.

If the plague came from poisoned air, people reasoned, then strong-smelling herbs or other substances, like rosemary, juniper, or sulfur, held in front of the nose or burned as incense might stop it. Perhaps loud sounds like ringing church bells or firing the newly invented cannon might help. Medicines made from plants that were bumpy or that oozed liquid might work, keeping the more dangerous swelling and oozing of the plague away. Because the plague seemed to strike randomly, perhaps wearing jewelry with random number and letter combinations, or drinking water in which ink used to write these magical combinations had been dissolved, would help. Such letter and number combinations, called *cryptograms*, were especially popular in Muslim areas. They were often the first letters of words in prayers or religious sayings, and they gave people a sense of order when faced with the randomness with which the plague seemed to strike.

The Italian writer Giovanni Boccaccio (1313–1375), describing the course of the disease in Florence in the preface to his book of tales, *The Decameron*, identified what many knew—that the disease passed from person to person:

Moreover, the virulence of the pest was the greater by reason that intercourse was apt to convey it from the sick to the whole, just as fire devours things dry or greasy when they are brought close to it. Nay, the evil went yet further, for not merely by speech or association with the sick was the malady communicated to the healthy with consequent peril of common death, but any that touched the clothes of the sick or aught else that had been touched or used by them, seemed thereby to contract the disease.[1]

Online Study Center **Improve Your Grade**
Primary Source: The Plague Hits Florence

Wealthier people often fled cities for the countryside, though sometimes this simply spread the plague faster. Some cities tried shutting their gates to prevent infected people and animals from coming in, which worked in a few cities. They also walled up houses in which there was plague, trying to isolate those who were still healthy from the sick. When the disease struck the town of Salé in Morocco, Ibu Abu Madyan shut in the members of his household with sufficient food and water and allowed no one to enter or leave until the plague had passed. Abu Madyan was entirely successful.

Along with looking for medical causes and cures, people also searched for scapegoats, and savage cruelty sometimes resulted. Many people believed that the Jews had poisoned the wells of Christian communities and thereby infected the drinking water. This charge led to the murder of thousands of Jews across Europe. According to one chronicler, sixteen thousand were killed at the imperial city of Strasbourg alone in 1349. Though sixteen thousand is probably a typical medieval numerical exaggeration, the horror of the massacre is not lessened. Scholars have yet to explain the economic impact that the loss of so many productive people had on Strasbourg and other cities.

If medical science had no effective treatment, could victims' suffering be eased? Perhaps it could, in hospitals. What was the geographical distribution of hospitals, and, although our estimates of medieval populations remain rough, what was the hospital-to-population ratio? How many patients could a hospital serve? Whereas earlier the feudal lord had made philanthropic foundations, beginning in the thirteenth century individual merchants—out of compassion, generosity, and the custom of giving to

parish collections, and in the belief that the sick would be prayerful intercessors with God for the donors' sins—endowed hospitals. Business people established hospitals in the towns of northern France and Flanders; Milan, Genoa, and Venice were well served, and the thirty hospitals in Florence provided a thousand beds in 1339. Sixty hospitals served Paris in 1328—but probably not enough for its population of two hundred thousand. The many hospitals in the Iberian Peninsula continued the Muslim tradition of care for the poor and ill. Merchants in the larger towns of the German Empire, in Poland, and in Hungary also founded hospitals in the fourteenth century, generally later than those in western Europe. Sailors, long viewed as potential carriers of disease, benefited from hospitals reserved for them; in 1300 the Venetian government paid a surgeon to care for sick sailors. At the time the plague erupted, therefore, most towns and cities had hospital facilities.

When trying to determine the number of people a hospital could accommodate, the modern researcher considers the number of beds, the size of the staff, and the building's physical layout. Since each medieval hospital bed might serve two or more patients, we cannot calculate the number of patients on the basis of the beds alone. We do know that rural hospices usually had twelve to fifteen beds, and city hospitals, as at Lisbon, Narbonne, and Genoa, had on average twenty-five to thirty beds, but these figures do not tell us how many patients were accommodated. Only the very rare document listing the number of wrapping sheets and coffins for the dead purchased in a given period provides the modern scholar with information on the number of patients a hospital had. Hospitals could offer only shelter, compassion, and care for the dying.

Many people did not see the plague as a medical issue, but instead interpreted it as the result of something within themselves. God must be punishing them for terrible sins, they thought, so the best remedies were religious ones: asking for forgiveness, praying, trusting in God, making donations to churches, and trying to live better lives. In Muslim areas, religious leaders urged virtuous living in the face of death: give to the poor, reconcile with your enemies, free your slaves, and say a proper goodbye to your friends and family.

Social, Economic, and Cultural Consequences

It is noteworthy that, in an age of mounting criticism of clerical wealth, the behavior of the clergy during the

Patients in a Hospital Ward, Fifteenth Century   In many cities hospitals could not cope with the large numbers of plague victims. The practice of putting two or more adults in the same bed, as shown here, contributed to the spread of the disease. At the Hôtel-Dieu in Paris, nurses complained of being forced to put eight to ten children in a single bed in which a patient had recently died. *(Giraudon/The Bridgeman Art Library)*

plague was often exemplary. Priests, monks, and nuns cared for the sick and buried the dead. In places like Venice, from which even physicians fled, priests remained to give what ministrations they could. Consequently, their mortality rate was phenomenally high. The German clergy especially suffered a severe decline in personnel in the years after 1350.

In taking their pastoral responsibilities seriously, some clergy did things that the church in a later age would vigorously condemn. The institutional church has traditionally opposed letting laymen and, especially, laywomen administer the sacraments. But the shortage of priests was so great that in 1349 Ralph, bishop of Bath and Wells in England (1329–1363), advised his people that "if they are on the point of death and cannot secure the services of a priest, then they should make confession to each other, as is permitted in the teaching of the Apostles, whether to a layman or, if no man is present, even to a woman."[2]

Economic historians and demographers sharply dispute the impact of the plague on the economy in the late fourteenth century. The traditional view that the plague had a disastrous effect has been greatly modified. The clearest evidence comes from England, where the agrarian economy showed remarkable resilience. While the severity of the disease varied from region to region, it appears that by about 1375 most landlords enjoyed revenues near those of the pre-plague years. By the early fifteenth century seigneurial prosperity reached a medieval peak. Why? The answer appears to lie in the fact that England and many parts of Europe suffered from overpopulation in the early fourteenth century. Population losses caused by the Black Death led to increased productivity by restoring a more efficient balance between labor, land, and capital.

What impact did visits of the plague have on urban populations? The rich evidence from a census of the city of Florence and its surrounding territory taken between

1427 and 1430 is fascinating. The region had suffered repeated epidemics since 1347. In a total population of 260,000 persons, 15 percent were age sixty or over (a very high proportion), suggesting that the plague took the young rather than the mature. Children and youths up to age nineteen constituted 44 percent of the people. Adults between the ages of twenty and fifty-nine, the most economically productive group, represented 41 percent of Florentine society.

The high mortality rate of craftsmen led Florentine guilds to recruit many new members. For example, between 1328 and 1347 the silk merchants guild accepted 730 members, and between 1408 and 1427 it admitted 784. It appears that economic organizations tried to keep their numbers constant, even though the size of the population and its pool of potential guild members was shrinking. Moreover, in contrast to the pre-1348 period, many new members of the guilds were not related to existing members. Thus the post-plague years represent an age of "new men."

The Black Death brought on a general European inflation. High mortality produced a fall in production, shortages of goods, and a general rise in prices. The shortage of labor and workers' demands for higher wages put guild masters on the defensive. They retaliated with measures such as the Statute of Laborers (1351), an attempt by the English Parliament to freeze the wages of English workers at pre-1347 levels. Such statutes could not be enforced and thus were unsuccessful. The price of wheat in most of Europe increased, as did the costs of meat, sausage, and cheese. This inflation continued to the end of the fourteenth century. But wages in the towns rose faster, and the broad mass of people enjoyed a higher standard of living. Population decline meant a sharp increase in per capita wealth. The greater demand for labor meant greater mobility for peasants in rural areas and for industrial workers in the towns and cities. Labor shortages caused by the Black Death throughout the Mediterranean region, from Constantinople to Spain, presented aggressive businessmen with a golden opportunity, and the price of slaves rose sharply.

Even more significant than the social effects were the psychological consequences. The knowledge that the disease meant almost certain death provoked the most profound pessimism. Imagine an entire society in the grip of the belief that it was at the mercy of a frightful affliction

Flagellants   In this manuscript illumination from 1349, shirtless flagellants scourge themselves with whips as they walk through the streets of the Flemish city of Tournai. The text notes that they are asking for God's grace to return to the city after it had been struck with the "most grave" illness. *(HIP/Art Resource, NY)*

about which nothing could be done, a disgusting disease from which family and friends would flee, leaving one to die alone and in agony. It is not surprising that some sought release in wild living, while others turned to the severest forms of asceticism and frenzied religious fervor. Some extremists joined groups of **flagellants,** who whipped and scourged themselves as penance for their and society's sins in the belief that the Black Death was God's punishment for humanity's wickedness. Groups of flagellants traveled from town to town, often provoking hysteria against Jews and growing into unruly mobs. Officials worried that they would provoke violence and riots, and ordered groups of them to disband or forbade them to enter cities.

Plague ripped apart the social fabric. In the thirteenth century, funerals, traditionally occasions for the mutual consolation of the living as much as memorial services for the dead, grew increasingly elaborate, with large corteges and many mourners. In the fourteenth century, public horror at the suffering of the afflicted and at the dead reduced the size of mourning processions and eventually resulted in failure even to perform the customary death rites. Fear of infection led to the dead being buried hastily, sometimes in mass graves.

People often used pilgrimages to holy places as justification for their flight from cities. Suspected of being carriers of plague, travelers, pilgrims, and the homeless aroused deep hostility. All European port cities followed the example of Ragusa (modern Dubrovnik in southwestern Croatia on the Dalmatian coast) and quarantined arriving ships, crews, passengers, and cargoes to determine whether they brought the plague. Deriving from a Venetian word, the English term *quarantine* originally meant forty days' isolation.

Popular endowments of educational institutions multiplied. The years of the Black Death witnessed the foundation of new colleges at old universities, such as Corpus Christi and Clare Colleges at Cambridge and New College at Oxford, and of entirely new universities. The beginnings of Charles University in Prague (1348) and the Universities of Florence (1350), Vienna (1364), Cracow (1364), and Heidelberg (1385) were all associated with the plague: their foundation charters specifically mention the shortage of priests and the decay of learning. Whereas universities such as those at Bologna and Paris had international student bodies, new institutions established in the wake of the Black Death had more national or local constituencies. Thus the international character of medieval culture weakened. The decline of cultural cohesion paved the way for schism in the Catholic Church even before the Reformation.

The literature and art of the fourteenth century reveal a terribly morbid concern with death. One highly popular artistic motif, the Dance of Death, depicted a dancing skeleton leading away a living person.

The Hundred Years' War

The plague ravaged populations in Asia, North Africa, and Europe; in western Europe a long international war added further misery to the frightful disasters of the plague. England and France had engaged in sporadic military hostilities from the time of the Norman Conquest in 1066, and in the middle of the fourteenth century these became more intense. From 1337 to 1453, the two countries intermittently fought one another in what was the longest war in European history, ultimately dubbed the Hundred Years' War though it actually lasted 116 years.

● *What were the causes of the Hundred Years' War, and how did the war affect European politics, economics, and cultural life?*

Causes

The Hundred Years' War had both distant and immediate causes. In 1259 France and England signed the Treaty of Paris, in which the English king agreed to become—for himself and his successors—vassal of the French crown for the duchy of Aquitaine. The English claimed Aquitaine as an ancient inheritance. French policy, however, was strongly expansionist, and the French kings resolved to absorb the duchy into the kingdom of France.

In January 1327 Queen Isabella of England, her lover Mortimer, and a group of barons, having deposed and murdered Isabella's incompetent husband, King Edward II, proclaimed his fifteen-year-old son king as Edward III. Isabella and Mortimer, however, held real power until 1330, when Edward seized the reins of government. In 1328 Charles IV of France, the last surviving son of Philip the Fair, died childless. With him ended the Capetian dynasty. An assembly of French barons, meaning to exclude Isabella—who was Charles's sister and the daughter of Philip the Fair—and her son Edward III from the French throne, proclaimed that "no woman nor her son could succeed to the [French] monarchy." French lawyers defended the position with the claim that the exclusion of women from ruling or passing down the right to rule was part of Salic Law, a sixth-century Germanic law code (see page 216), and that Salic Law itself

English Merchants in Flanders   In this 1387 illustration, an English merchant requests concessions from the count of Flanders to trade English wool at a favorable price. Flanders was officially on the French side during the Hundred Years' War, but Flemish cities depended heavily on English wool for their textile manufacturing. Hence the count of Flanders agreed to the establishment of the Merchant Staple, an English trading company with a monopoly on trade in wool. *(British Library)*

Economic factors involving the wool trade and the control of Flemish towns had served as justifications for war between France and England for centuries. The wool trade between England and Flanders served as the cornerstone of both countries' economies; they were closely interdependent. Flanders was a fief of the French crown, and the Flemish aristocracy was highly sympathetic to the monarchy in Paris. But the wealth of Flemish merchants and cloth manufacturers depended on English wool, and Flemish burghers strongly supported the claims of Edward III. The disruption of commerce with England threatened their prosperity.

The Popular Response

The governments of both England and France manipulated public opinion to support the war. Whatever significance modern scholars ascribe to the economic factor, public opinion in fourteenth-century England held that the war was waged for one reason: to secure for King Edward the French crown he had been unjustly denied. Edward III issued letters to the sheriffs describing the evil deeds of the French in graphic terms and listing royal needs. Kings in both countries instructed the clergy to deliver sermons filled with patriotic sentiment. The royal courts sensationalized the wickedness of the other side and stressed the great fortunes to be made from the war. Philip VI sent agents to warn communities about the dangers of invasion and to stress the French crown's revenue needs to meet the attack.

The royal campaign to rally public opinion was highly successful, at least in the early stage of the war. Edward III gained widespread support in the 1340s and 1350s. The English developed a deep hatred of the French and feared that King Philip intended "to have seized and slaughtered the entire realm of England." When England was successful in the field, pride in the country's military proficiency increased.

Most important of all, the Hundred Years' War was popular because it presented unusual opportunities for wealth and advancement. Poor knights and knights who were unemployed were promised regular wages. Criminals who enlisted were granted pardons. The great nobles expected to be rewarded with estates. Royal exhortations to the troops before battles repeatedly stressed that, if

was part of the fundamental law of France. They used this invented tradition to argue that Edward should be barred from the French throne. (This notion became part of French legal tradition until the end of the monarchy in 1789.) The barons passed the crown to Philip VI of Valois (r. 1328–1350), a nephew of Philip the Fair.

In 1329 Edward III paid homage to Philip VI for Aquitaine. In 1337 Philip, eager to exercise full French jurisdiction in Aquitaine, confiscated the duchy. Edward III interpreted this action as a gross violation of the treaty of 1259 and as a cause for war. Moreover, Edward argued, as the eldest directly surviving male descendant of Philip the Fair, he must assume the title of king of France in order to wield his rightful authority in Aquitaine. In short, Edward rejected the decision of the French barons excluding him from the throne. Edward III's dynastic argument upset the feudal order in France: to increase their independent power, French vassals of Philip VI used the excuse that they had to transfer their loyalty to a more legitimate overlord, Edward III. One reason the war lasted so long was that it became a French civil war, with some French barons supporting English monarchs in order to thwart the centralizing goals of the French crown.

victorious, the men might keep whatever they seized. The French chronicler Jean Froissart wrote that, at the time of Edward III's expedition of 1359, men of all ranks flocked to the English king's banner. Some came to acquire honor, but many came "to loot and pillage the fair and plenteous land of France."[3]

Online Study Center **Improve Your Grade**
Primary Source: Warfare Without Chivalry:
The Sack of Limoges

The Course of the War to 1419

The war was fought almost entirely in France and the Low Countries (see Map 12.2). It consisted mainly of a series of random sieges and cavalry raids. In 1335 the French began supporting Scottish incursions into northern England, ravaging the countryside in Aquitaine, and

sacking and burning English coastal towns, such as Southampton. Such tactics lent weight to Edward III's propaganda campaign. In fact, royal propaganda on both sides fostered a kind of early nationalism.

During the war's early stages, England was highly successful. At Crécy in northern France in 1346, English longbowmen scored a great victory over French knights and crossbowmen. Although the aim of the longbow was not very accurate, it allowed for rapid reloading, and an English archer could send off three arrows to the French crossbowman's one. The result was a blinding shower of arrows that unhorsed the French knights and caused mass confusion. The ring of cannon—probably the first use of artillery in the West—created further panic. Thereupon the English horsemen charged and butchered the French.

This was not war according to the chivalric rules that Edward III would have preferred. Nevertheless, his son, Edward the Black Prince, used the same tactics ten years

Siege of the Castle of Mortagne Near Bordeaux (1377) Medieval warfare usually consisted of small skirmishes and attacks on castles. This miniature shows the French besieging an English-held castle, which held out for six months. Most of the soldiers use longbows, although at the left two men shoot primitive muskets above a pair of cannon. Painted in the late fifteenth century, the scene reflects military technology available at the time it was painted, not the time of the actual siege. (*British Library*)

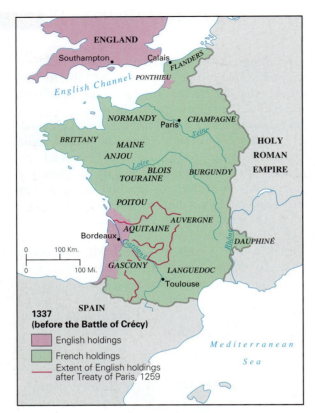

1337
(before the Battle of Crécy)

ENGLAND
Southampton
Calais
FLANDERS
PONTHIEU
English Channel
NORMANDY
Paris
CHAMPAGNE
Seine
BRITTANY
MAINE
ANJOU
HOLY
ROMAN
EMPIRE
BLOIS
TOURAINE
BURGUNDY
Loire
POITOU
AUVERGNE
AQUITAINE
Bordeaux
Garonne
DAUPHINÉ
Rhône
GASCONY
LANGUEDOC
Toulouse
0   100 Km.
0   100 Mi.
SPAIN
Mediterranean Sea

- English holdings
- French holdings
- Extent of English holdings after Treaty of Paris, 1259

1360
(after the Battle of Poitiers)

ENGLAND
Calais
FLANDERS
English Channel
Crécy 1346
Rouen
NORMANDY
Paris
CHAMPAGNE
Seine
BRITTANY
MAINE
ANJOU
HOLY
ROMAN
EMPIRE
BLOIS
TOURAINE
BURGUNDY
Loire
Poitiers 1356
POITOU
AUVERGNE
AQUITAINE
Bordeaux
Garonne
DAUPHINÉ
Rhône
GASCONY
LANGUEDOC
Toulouse
0   100 Km.
0   100 Mi.
SPAIN
Mediterranean Sea

- English holdings
- French holdings
- ✕ Major battles

ca 1429
(after the siege of Orléans)

ENGLAND
Calais
FLANDERS
Agincourt 1415
English Channel
Rouen
Reims
NORMANDY
Paris
CHAMPAGNE
Domrémy
Seine
BRITTANY
MAINE
ANJOU
Orléans
HOLY
ROMAN
EMPIRE
BLOIS
TOURAINE
Bourges
DUCHY OF BURGUNDY
COUNTY OF BURGUNDY
Loire
POITOU
AUVERGNE
AQUITAINE
Bordeaux
Garonne
DAUPHINÉ
Rhône
GASCONY
LANGUEDOC
Toulouse
0   100 Km.
0   100 Mi.
SPAIN
Mediterranean Sea

- English holdings
- French holdings
- Burgundian lands allied with England to 1435
- ✕ Major battle

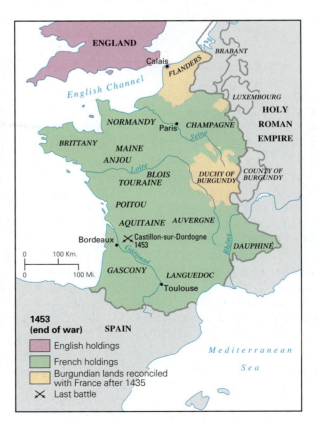

1453
(end of war)

ENGLAND
Calais
FLANDERS
BRABANT
English Channel
LUXEMBOURG
HOLY
ROMAN
EMPIRE
NORMANDY
Paris
CHAMPAGNE
Seine
BRITTANY
MAINE
ANJOU
DUCHY OF BURGUNDY
COUNTY OF BURGUNDY
Loire
BLOIS
TOURAINE
POITOU
AQUITAINE
AUVERGNE
Bordeaux
✕ Castillon-sur-Dordogne 1453
Garonne
DAUPHINÉ
Rhône
GASCONY
LANGUEDOC
Toulouse
0   100 Km.
0   100 Mi.
SPAIN
Mediterranean Sea

- English holdings
- French holdings
- Burgundian lands reconciled with France after 1435
- ✕ Last battle

MAP 12.2 English Holdings in France During the Hundred Years' War The year 1429 marked the greatest extent of English holdings in France.

later to smash the French at Poitiers, where he captured the French king and held him for ransom. Again, at **Agincourt** near Arras in 1415, the chivalric English soldier-king Henry V (r. 1413–1422) gained the field over vastly superior numbers. Henry followed up his triumph at Agincourt with the reconquest of Normandy. By 1419 the English had advanced to the walls of Paris (see Map 12.2). But the French cause was not lost. Though England had scored the initial victories, France won the war.

Joan of Arc and France's Victory

The ultimate French success rests heavily on the actions of an obscure French peasant girl, **Joan of Arc,** whose vision and work revived French fortunes and led to victory. A great deal of pious and popular legend surrounds Joan the Maid because of her peculiar appearance on the scene, her astonishing success, her martyrdom, and her canonization by the Catholic Church. The historical fact is that she saved the French monarchy, which was the embodiment of France.

Born in 1412 to well-to-do peasants in the village of Domrémy in Champagne, Joan of Arc grew up in a religious household. During adolescence she began to hear voices, which she later said belonged to Saint Michael, Saint Catherine, and Saint Margaret. In 1428 these voices spoke to her with great urgency, telling her that the dauphin (the uncrowned King Charles VII) had to be crowned and the English expelled from France. Joan went to the French court, persuaded the king to reject the rumor that he was illegitimate, and secured his support for her relief of the besieged city of Orléans.

The astonishing thing is not that Joan the Maid overcame serious obstacles to see the dauphin, and not even that Charles and his advisers listened to her. What is amazing is the swiftness with which they were convinced. French fortunes had been so low for so long that the court believed that only a miracle could save the country. Because Joan cut her hair short and dressed like a man, she scandalized the court. But hoping she would provide the miracle, Charles allowed her to accompany the army that was preparing to raise the English siege of Orléans.

In the meantime Joan, herself illiterate, dictated this letter calling on the English to withdraw:

King of England . . . , do right in the King of Heaven's sight. Surrender to The Maid sent hither by God the King of Heaven, the keys of all the good towns you have taken and laid waste in France. She comes in God's name to establish the Blood Royal, ready to make peace if you agree to abandon France and repay what you have taken. And you,

archers, comrades in arms, gentles and others, who are before the town of Orléans, retire in God's name to your own country.[4]

Joan arrived before Orléans on April 28, 1429. Seventeen years old, she knew little of warfare and believed that if she could keep the French troops from swearing and frequenting brothels, victory would be theirs. On May 8 the English, weakened by disease and lack of supplies, withdrew from Orléans. Ten days later Charles VII was crowned king at Reims. These two events marked the turning point in the war.

Online Study Center **Improve Your Grade**
Primary Source: The Trial of Joan of Arc

Joan's presence at Orléans, her strong belief in her mission, and the fact that she was wounded enhanced her reputation and strengthened the morale of the army. In 1430 England's allies, the Burgundians, captured Joan and sold her to the English. When the English handed her over to the ecclesiastical authorities for trial, the French court did not intervene. While the English wanted Joan eliminated for obvious political reasons, sorcery (witchcraft) was the ostensible charge at her trial. Witch persecution was increasing in the fifteenth century, and Joan's wearing of men's clothes appeared not only aberrant but indicative of contact with the Devil. In 1431 the court condemned her as a heretic—her claim of direct inspiration from God, thereby denying the authority of church officials, constituted heresy—and burned her at the stake in the marketplace at Rouen. A new trial in 1456 rehabilitated her name. In 1920 she was canonized and declared a holy maiden, and today she is revered as the second patron saint of France, along with King Louis IX. The nineteenth-century French historian Jules Michelet extolled Joan of Arc as a symbol of the vitality and strength of the French peasant classes.

The relief of Orléans stimulated French pride and rallied French resources. As the war dragged on, loss of life mounted, and money appeared to be flowing into a bottomless pit, demands for an end increased in England. The clergy and intellectuals pressed for peace. Parliamentary opposition to additional war grants stiffened. Slowly the French reconquered Normandy and, finally, ejected the English from Aquitaine. At the war's end in 1453, only the town of Calais remained in English hands.

Costs and Consequences

In France the English had slaughtered thousands of soldiers and civilians. In the years after the sweep of the

Black Death, this additional killing meant a grave loss of population. The English had laid waste to hundreds of thousands of acres of rich farmland, leaving the rural economy of many parts of France a shambles. The war had disrupted trade and the great fairs, resulting in the drastic reduction of French participation in international commerce. Defeat in battle and heavy taxation contributed to widespread dissatisfaction and aggravated peasant grievances.

In England only the southern coastal ports experienced much destruction, and the demographic effects of the Black Death actually worked to restore the land-labor balance (see page 379). The costs of the war, however, were tremendous. England spent over £5 million on the war effort, a huge sum at the time. Manpower losses had greater social consequences. The knights who ordinarily handled the work of local government as sheriffs, coroners, jurymen, and justices of the peace were abroad, and their absence contributed to the breakdown of order at the local level. The English government attempted to finance the war effort by raising taxes on the wool crop. Because of steadily increasing costs, Flemish and Italian buyers could not afford English wool. Consequently, raw wool exports slumped drastically between 1350 and 1450.

Many men of all social classes had volunteered for service in France in the hope of acquiring booty and becoming rich. The chronicler Walsingham, describing the period of Crécy, wrote: "For the woman was of no account who did not possess something from the spoils of . . . cities overseas in clothing, furs, quilts, and utensils . . . tablecloths and jewels, bowls of murra [semiprecious stone] and silver, linen and linen cloths."[5] Walsingham is referring to 1348, in the first generation of war. As time went on, most fortunes seem to have been squandered as fast as they were made.

If English troops returned with cash, they did not invest it in land. In the fifteenth century returning soldiers were commonly described as beggars and vagabonds, roaming about making mischief. Even the large sums of money received from the ransom of the great—such as the £250,000 paid to Edward III for the freedom of King John of France—and the money paid as indemnities by captured towns and castles did not begin to equal the more than £5 million spent. England suffered a serious net loss.

The war stimulated technological experimentation, especially with artillery. Cannon revolutionized warfare, making the stone castle no longer impregnable. Because only central governments, not private nobles, could afford cannon, they strengthened the military power of national states.

The long war also had a profound impact on the political and cultural lives of the two countries. Most notably, it stimulated the development of the English Parliament. Between 1250 and 1450, **representative assemblies** flourished in many European countries. In the English Parliament, German diets, and Spanish cortes, deliberative practices developed that laid the foundations for the representative institutions of modern liberal-democratic nations. While representative assemblies declined in most countries after the fifteenth century, the English Parliament endured. Edward III's constant need for money to pay for the war compelled him to summon not only the great barons and bishops, but knights of the shires and burgesses from the towns as well. Parliament met in thirty-seven of the fifty years of Edward's reign.[6]

The frequency of the meetings is significant. Representative assemblies were becoming a habit. Knights and wealthy urban residents—or the "Commons," as they came to be called—recognized their mutual interests and began to meet apart from the great lords. The Commons gradually realized that they held the country's purse strings, and a parliamentary statute of 1341 required that all nonfeudal levies have parliamentary approval. By signing the law, Edward III acknowledged that the king of England could not tax without Parliament's consent. During the course of the war, money grants were increasingly tied to royal redress of grievances: to raise money, the government had to correct the wrongs its subjects protested.

In England, theoretical consent to taxation and legislation was given in one assembly for the entire country. France had no such single assembly; instead, there were many regional or provincial assemblies. Why did a national representative assembly fail to develop in France? The initiative for convening assemblies rested with the king, who needed revenue almost as much as the English ruler. But the French monarchy found the idea of representative assemblies thoroughly distasteful. Large gatherings of the nobility potentially or actually threatened the king's power. The advice of a counselor to King Charles VI (r. 1380–1422), "above all things be sure that no great assemblies of nobles or of *communes* take place in your kingdom," was accepted.[7] Charles VII (r. 1422–1461) even threatened to punish those proposing a national assembly.

No one in France wanted a national assembly. Linguistic, geographical, economic, legal, and political differences were very strong. People tended to think of themselves as Breton, Norman, Burgundian, or whatever, rather than French. Through much of the fourteenth and early fifteenth centuries, weak monarchs lacked the power to call a national assembly. Provincial assemblies, highly jealous of their independence, did not want a national assembly. The costs of sending delegates to it would be high, and the result was likely to be increased taxation.

In both countries, however, the war did promote the growth of **nationalism**—the feeling of unity and identity that binds together a people. After victories, each country experienced a surge of pride in its military strength. Just as English patriotism ran strong after Crécy and Poitiers, so French national confidence rose after Orléans. French national feeling demanded the expulsion of the enemy not merely from Normandy and Aquitaine but from all French soil. Perhaps no one expressed this national consciousness better than Joan of Arc when she exulted that the enemy had been "driven out of *France*."

Challenges to the Church

In times of crisis or disaster, people of all faiths have sought the consolation of religion. In the fourteenth century, however, the official Christian church offered little solace. In fact, the leaders of the church added to the sorrow and misery of the times. In response to this lack of leadership, members of the clergy challenged the power of the pope, and laypeople challenged the authority of the church itself. Women and men increasingly relied on direct approaches to God, often through mystical encounters, rather than on the institutional church.

• *What challenges faced the Christian church in the fourteenth century, and how did church leaders, intellectuals, and ordinary people respond?*

The Babylonian Captivity and Great Schism

In order to control the church and its policies, Philip the Fair of France pressured Pope Clement V to settle permanently in Avignon in southeastern France, where the popes already had their summer residence (see Map 11.3 on page 346). Clement, critically ill with cancer, lacked the will to resist Philip. The popes lived in Avignon from 1309 to 1376, a period in church history often called the **Babylonian Captivity** (referring to the seventy years the ancient Hebrews were held captive in Mesopotamian Babylon).

The Babylonian Captivity badly damaged papal prestige. The Avignon papacy reformed its financial administration and centralized its government. But the seven popes at Avignon concentrated on bureaucratic matters to the exclusion of spiritual objectives. Though some of the popes led austere lives, the general atmosphere was one of luxury and extravagance. (See the feature "Individuals in Society: Francesco Datini" in Chapter 11 on page 343.) The leadership of the church was cut off from its historic roots and the source of its ancient authority, the city of Rome. In the absence of the papacy, the Papal States in Italy lacked stability and good government. The economy of Rome had been based on the presence of the papal court and the rich tourist trade the papacy attracted. The Babylonian Captivity left Rome poverty-stricken.

In 1377 Pope Gregory XI brought the papal court back to Rome. Unfortunately, he died shortly after the return. At Gregory's death, Roman citizens demanded an Italian pope who would remain in Rome. Between the time of Gregory's death and the opening of the conclave, great pressure was put on the cardinals to elect an Italian. At the time, none of them protested this pressure, and they chose a distinguished administrator, the archbishop of Bari, Bartolomeo Prignano, who took the name Urban VI.

Urban VI (1378–1389) had excellent intentions for church reform, but he went about this in a tactless and bullheaded manner. He attacked clerical luxury, denouncing individual cardinals by name, and even threatened to excommunicate certain cardinals.

The cardinals slipped away from Rome and met at Anagni. They declared Urban's election invalid because it had come about under threats from the Roman mob, and they asserted that Urban himself was excommunicated. The cardinals then elected Cardinal Robert of Geneva, the cousin of King Charles V of France, as pope. Cardinal Robert took the name Clement VII. There were thus two popes—Urban at Rome and Clement VII (1378–1394), who set himself up at Avignon in opposition to Urban. So began the **Great Schism,** which divided Western Christendom until 1417.

The powers of Europe aligned themselves with Urban or Clement along strictly political lines. France naturally recognized the French pope, Clement. England, France's historic enemy, recognized the Italian pope, Urban. Scotland, whose attacks on England were subsidized by France, followed the French and supported Clement. Aragon, Castile, and Portugal hesitated before deciding for Clement at Avignon. The emperor, who bore ancient hostility to France, recognized Urban. At first the Italian city-states recognized Urban; when he alienated them, they opted for Clement.

John of Spoleto, a professor at the law school at Bologna, eloquently summed up intellectual opinion of the schism, or division: "The longer this schism lasts, the more it appears to be costing, and the more harm it does; scandal, massacres, ruination, agitations, troubles and disturbances."[8] The common people, wracked by inflation, wars, and plague, were thoroughly confused about which pope was legitimate. The schism weakened the religious faith of many Christians and brought church leadership into serious disrepute. The schism also brought to the fore conciliar ideas about church government.

The Conciliar Movement

Theories about the nature of the Christian church and its government originated in the very early church, but the years of the Great Schism witnessed their maturity. **Conciliarists** believed that reform of the church could best be achieved through periodic assemblies, or general councils, representing all the Christian people. While acknowledging that the pope was head of the church, conciliarists held that the pope derived his authority from the entire Christian community, whose well-being he existed to promote. Conciliarists favored a balanced or constitutional form of church government, with papal authority shared with a general council, in contrast to the monarchical one that prevailed.

A half century before the Great Schism, in 1324, Marsiglio of Padua, then rector of the University of Paris, had published *Defensor Pacis* (The Defender of the Peace). Marsiglio argued that the state was the great unifying power in society and that the church was subordinate to the state. He put forth the revolutionary ideas that the church had no inherent jurisdiction and should own no property. Authority in the Christian church, according to Marsiglio, should rest in a general council made up of laymen as well as priests, and the council should be superior to the pope. These ideas directly contradicted the medieval notion of a society governed by the church and the state, with the church supreme. *Defensor Pacis* was condemned by the pope, and Marsiglio was excommunicated.

Even more earthshaking than the theories of Marsiglio of Padua were the ideas of the English scholar and theologian John Wyclif (ca 1330–1384). Wyclif wrote that papal claims of temporal power had no foundation in the Scriptures and that the Scriptures alone should be the standard of Christian belief and practice. He urged the abolition of such practices as the veneration of saints, pilgrimages, pluralism, and absenteeism. Sincere Christians, according to Wyclif, should read the Bible for themselves. In response to that idea, the first English translation of the Bible was produced and circulated. Wyclif's views had broad social and economic significance. He urged that the church be stripped of its property. His idea that every Christian free of mortal sin possessed lordship was seized on by peasants in England during a revolt in 1381 and used to justify their goals.

In advancing these views, Wyclif struck at the roots of medieval church structure. Consequently, he has been hailed as the precursor of the Protestant Reformation of the sixteenth century. Although Wyclif's ideas were vigorously condemned by ecclesiastical authorities, they were widely disseminated by humble clerics and enjoyed great popularity in the early fifteenth century. Wyclif's followers were called "Lollards." The term, which means "mumblers of prayers and psalms," refers to what they criticized. Lollard teaching allowed women to preach. Women, some well educated, played a significant role in the movement. After Anne, sister of Wenceslaus, king of Germany and Bohemia, married Richard II of England, members of her household carried Lollard books back to Bohemia.

In response to continued calls throughout Europe for a council, the two colleges of cardinals—one at Rome, the other at Avignon—summoned a council at Pisa in 1409. That gathering of prelates and theologians deposed both popes and selected another. Neither the Avignon pope nor the Roman pope would resign, however, and the appalling result was the creation of a threefold schism.

Finally, because of the pressure of the German emperor Sigismund, a great council met at the imperial city of Constance (1414–1418). It had three objectives: to end the schism, to reform the church "in head and members" (from top to bottom), and to wipe out heresy. The council condemned the Czech reformer Jan Hus (see the feature "Individuals in Society: Jan Hus"), and he was burned at the stake. The council eventually deposed both the Roman pope and the successor of the pope chosen at Pisa, and it isolated the Avignon antipope. A conclave elected a new leader, the Roman cardinal Colonna, who took the name Martin V (1417–1431).

Martin proceeded to dissolve the council. Nothing was done about reform. The schism was over, and though councils subsequently met at Basel and at Ferrara-Florence, in 1450 the papacy held a jubilee celebrating its triumph over the conciliar movement. In the later fifteenth century the papacy concentrated on Italian problems to the exclusion of universal Christian interests. But the schism and the conciliar movement had exposed the crying need for ecclesiastical reform, thus laying the foundation for the great reform efforts of the sixteenth century.

Spoon with Fox Preaching to Geese (southern Nether-lands, ca 1430) Taking as his text a contemporary proverb, "When the fox preaches, beware your geese," the artist shows, in the bowl of a spoon, a fox dressed as a monk or friar, preaching with three dead geese in his hood, while another fox grabs one of the congregation. The preaching fox reads from a scroll bearing the word *pax* (peace), implying the perceived hypocrisy of the clergy. The object suggests the widespread criticism of churchmen in the later Middle Ages. *(Painted enamel and gilding on silver; 17.6 cm [6 ⅞ in]. Museum of Fine Arts, Boston, Helen and Alice Coburn Fund, 51.2472)*

Lay Piety and Mysticism

During the fourteenth and fifteenth centuries the laity began to exercise increasing control over parish affairs. The constant quarrels of the mendicant orders (the Franciscans and Dominicans), the mercenary and grasping attitude of the parish clergy, the scandal of the Great Schism, and a divided Christendom all did much to weaken the spiritual mystique of the clergy in the popular mind. The laity steadily took responsibility for the management of parish lands and secured jurisdiction over the structure of the church building and its vestments, books, and furnishings. Lay Christian men and women often formed **confraternities,** voluntary lay groups organized by occupation, devotional preference, neighborhood, or charitable activity. Confraternities expanded rapidly in larger cities and many villages with the growth of the mendicant orders in the thirteenth century. Some confraternities specialized in praying for souls in purga-

tory, either for specific individuals or for the anonymous mass of all souls. In England they were generally associated with a parish, so are called parish guilds, parish fraternities, or lights; by the late Middle Ages they held dances, church ales, and collections to raise money to clean and repair church buildings and to supply the church with candles and other liturgical objects. Like craft guilds, most confraternities were groups of men, but separate women's confraternities were formed in some towns, often to oversee the production of vestments, altar cloths, and other items made of fabric.

In Holland, beginning in the late fourteenth century, a group of pious laypeople called the Brethren and Sisters of the Common Life lived in stark simplicity while daily carrying out the Gospel teaching of feeding the hungry, clothing the naked, and visiting the sick. The Brethren also taught in local schools with the goal of preparing devout candidates for the priesthood. They sought to make religion a personal inner experience. The spirituality of the Brethren and Sisters of the Common Life found its finest expression in the classic ***The Imitation of Christ*** by Thomas à Kempis, which gained wide appeal among laypeople. It urges Christians to take Christ as their model, seek perfection in a simple way of life, and look to the Scriptures for guidance in living a spiritual life. In the mid-fifteenth century the movement had founded houses in the Netherlands, in central Germany, and in the Rhineland.

Online Study Center Improve Your Grade
Primary Source: *The Imitation of Christ: On True Charity*

Most of this lay piety centered on prayer, pious actions, and charitable giving, but for some individuals, religious devotion included mystical experiences. Bridget of Sweden (1303–1373) was a noblewoman who journeyed to Rome after her husband's death. She began to see visions and gave advice based on these visions to both laypeople and church officials. Because she could not speak Latin, she dictated her visions in Swedish; these were later translated and eventually published in Latin. At the end of her life, Bridget made a pilgrimage to Jerusalem, where she saw visions of the Virgin Mary, who described to her exactly how she was standing "with my knees bent" when she gave birth to Jesus, and how she "showed to the shepherds the nature and male sex of the child."[9] Bridget's visions convey her deep familiarity with biblical texts taught to her through sermons or stories, as there was no Bible available in Swedish. They also provide evidence of the ways in which laypeople used their own experiences to enhance their religious understanding;

Bridget's own experiences of childbirth shaped the way she viewed the birth of Jesus, and she related to the Virgin Mary in part as one mother to another.

Economic and Social Change

In the fourteenth century economic and political difficulties, disease, and war profoundly affected the lives of European peoples. Decades of slaughter and destruction, punctuated by the decimating visits of the Black Death, made a grave economic situation virtually disastrous. In many parts of France and the Low Countries, fields lay in ruin or untilled for lack of labor power. In England, as taxes increased, criticisms of government policy and mismanagement multiplied. Crime and new forms of business organization aggravated economic troubles, and throughout Europe the frustrations of the common people erupted into widespread revolts.

• *How did economic and social tensions contribute to revolts, crime, violence, and a growing sense of ethnic and national distinctions?*

Peasant Revolts

Nobles, clergy, and city dwellers lived on the produce of peasant labor. Early in the thirteenth century the French preacher Jacques de Vitry asked rhetorically, "How many serfs have killed their lords or burnt their castles?"[10] And in the fourteenth and fifteenth centuries social and economic conditions caused a great increase in peasant uprisings (see Map 12.3). They were very common and provide most of the evidence of peasants' long suffering and exploitation.

We will never be able fully to answer Jacques de Vitry's questions, for peasants were not literate and, apart from their explosive uprisings, left no record of their aspirations. The clerical writers who mentioned the rebellions viewed the peasants with aristocratic disdain and hostility. Recent research provides some insight into **peasant revolts** in Flanders in the 1320s. Long-existing conflicts along the Flemish-French border came to a head at Courtrai in July 1302 when Flemish infantry smashed a French army, killing many knights and nobles (their golden spurs retrieved from the battlefield gave the battle its name, the Battle of the Spurs). The Flemish victory failed to resolve disputes over the French crown's claim to fiscal rights over the county of Flanders. Moreover, the peace agreements imposed heavy indemnities on Flemish peasants, who in 1323 began to revolt in protest of officials' demands for taxes and of the misappropriation of the money collected. Also, monasteries pressed peasants for fees higher than the customary tithes. In retaliation, peasants subjected castles and aristocratic country houses to arson and pillage. A French army intervened and on August 23, 1328, near the town of Cassel in southwestern Flanders, crushed peasant forces. Savage repression and the confiscation of peasant property followed in the 1330s.

In 1358, when French taxation for the Hundred Years' War fell heavily on the poor, the frustrations of the French peasantry exploded in a massive uprising called the **Jacquerie,** after a mythical agricultural laborer, Jacques Bonhomme (Good Fellow). Two years earlier the English had captured the French king John and many nobles and held them for ransom. The peasants resented paying for their lords' release. Recently hit by plague, experiencing famine in some areas, and harassed by nobles, peasants in Picardy, Champagne, and the Île-de-France erupted in anger and frustration. Crowds swept through the countryside, slashing the throats of nobles, burning their castles, raping their wives and daughters, and killing or maiming their horses and cattle. Peasants blamed the nobility for oppressive taxes, for the criminal brigandage of the countryside, for defeat in war, and for the general misery. Artisans, small merchants, and parish priests joined the peasants. Urban and rural groups committed terrible destruction, and for several weeks the nobles were on the defensive. Then the upper class united to repress the revolt with merciless ferocity. Thousands of the "Jacques," innocent as well as guilty, were cut down. That forcible suppression of social rebellion, without any effort to alleviate its underlying causes, served to drive protest underground.

The Peasants' Revolt in England in 1381 involved thousands of people (see Map 12.3). Its causes were complex and varied from place to place. In general, though, the thirteenth century had witnessed the steady commutation of labor services for cash rents, and the Black Death had drastically cut the labor supply. As a result, peasants demanded higher wages and fewer manorial obligations. The parliamentary Statute of Laborers of 1351 (see page 380) had declared:

Whereas to curb the malice of servants who after the pestilence were idle and unwilling to serve without securing excessive wages, it was recently ordained . . . that such servants, both men and women, shall be bound to serve in return for salaries and wages that were customary . . . five or six years earlier.[11]

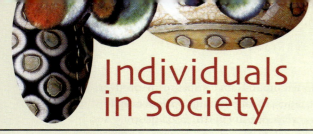

Individuals in Society

Jan Hus

In May 1990 the Czech Republic's parliament declared July 6, the date of Jan Hus's execution in 1415, a Czech national holiday. The son of free farmers, Hus (ca 1369–1415) was born in Husinec in southern Bohemia, an area of heavy German settlement, and grew up conscious of the ethnic differences between Czechs and Germans. Most of his professors at Charles University in Prague were Germans. In 1396 he received a master's degree, and just before his ordination as a priest in 1400 he wrote that he would not be a "clerical careerist," implying that ambition for church offices motivated many of his peers.

The young priest lectured at the university and preached at the private Bethlehem Chapel. During his twelve years there Hus preached only in Czech. He denounced superstition, the sale of indulgences, and other abuses, but his remarks were thoroughly orthodox. He attracted attention among artisans and the small Czech middle class, but not Germans. His austere life and lack of ambition enhanced his reputation.

Around 1400, Czech students returning from study at Oxford introduced into Bohemia the reforming ideas of the English theologian John Wyclif. When German professors condemned Wyclif's ideas as heretical, Hus and the Czechs argued "academic freedom," the right to read and teach Wyclif's works regardless of their particular merits. When popular demonstrations against ecclesiastical abuses and German influence at the university erupted, King Vaclav IV (1378–1419) placed control of the university in Czech hands. Hus was elected rector, the top administrative official.

The people of Prague, with perhaps the largest urban population in central Europe, 40 percent of it living below the poverty line and entirely dependent on casual labor, found Hus's denunciations of an overendowed church appealing. Hus considered the issues theological; his listeners saw them as socioeconomic.

Church officials in Prague were split about Hus's ideas, and popular unrest grew. The king forced Hus to leave the city, but he continued to preach and write. He disputed papal authority, denounced abuses, and argued that everyone should receive both bread and wine in the Eucharist. (By this time, in standard Western Christian practice, the laity received only the bread; the priest received the wine *for* the laity, a mark of his distinctiveness.) Hus also defended transubstantiation (see page 449); insisted that church authority rested on Scripture, conscience, and tradition (in contrast to sixteenth-century Protestant reformers, who placed

authority in Scripture alone); and made it clear that he had no intention of leaving the church or inciting a popular movement.

The execution of Jan Hus.
(University of Prague/The Art Archive)

In 1413 the emperor Sigismund urged the calling of a general council to end the schism. Hus was invited, and, given the emperor's safe conduct (protection from attack or arrest), agreed to go. What he found was an atmosphere of inquisition. The safe conduct was disregarded, and Hus was arrested. Under questioning about his acceptance of Wyclif's ideas, Hus repeatedly replied, "I have not held; I do not hold." Council members were more interested in proving Hus a Wyclite than in his responses. They took away his priesthood, banned his teachings, burned his books, and burned Hus himself at the stake. He then belonged to the ages.

The ages have made good use of him. His death aggravated the divisions between the bishops at Constance and the Czech clerics and people. In September 1415, 452 nobles from all parts of Bohemia signed a letter saying that Hus had been unjustly executed and rejecting council rulings. This event marks the first time that an ecclesiastical decision was publicly defied. Revolution swept through Bohemia, with Hussites—Czech nobles and people—insisting on clerical poverty and both the bread and wine at the Eucharist, and with German citizens remaining loyal to the Roman church. In the sixteenth century reformers hailed Hus as the forerunner of Protestantism. In the eighteenth century Enlightenment philosophes evoked Hus as a defender of freedom of expression. In the nineteenth century central European nationalists used Hus's name to defend national sentiment against Habsburg rule. And in the twentieth century Hus's name was used against German fascist and Russian communist tyranny.

Questions for Analysis

1. Since Jan Hus lived and died insisting that his religious teaching was thoroughly orthodox, why has he been hailed as a reformer?
2. What political and cultural interests did the martyred Hus serve?

Online Study Center **Improve Your Grade**
Going Beyond Individuals in Society

MAP 12.3 Fourteenth-Century Peasant Revolts   In the later Middle Ages, peasant and urban uprisings were endemic, as common as factory strikes in the industrial world. The threat of insurrection served to check unlimited exploitation.

Online Study Center   **Improve Your Grade**
Interactive Map: Fourteenth-Century Peasant Revolts

frightened and insecure. Moreover, decades of aristocratic violence against the weak peasantry had bred hostility and bitterness. Social and religious agitation by the popular preacher John Ball fanned the embers of discontent. Ball's famous couplet "When Adam delved and Eve span; Who was then the gentleman?" reflected real revolutionary sentiment.

The straw that broke the camel's back in England was the reimposition of a head tax on all adult males. Despite widespread opposition to the tax in 1380, the royal council ordered the sheriffs to collect it again in 1381 on penalty of a huge fine. Beginning with assaults on the tax collectors, the uprising in England followed a course similar to that of the Jacquerie in France. Castles and manors were sacked. Manorial records were destroyed. Many nobles, including the archbishop of Canterbury, who had ordered the collection of the tax, were murdered.

The center of the revolt lay in the highly populated and economically advanced south and east, but sections of the north and the Midlands also witnessed rebellions. Violence took different forms in different places. Urban discontent merged with rural violence. In English towns where skilled Flemish craftsmen were employed, fear of competition led to their being attacked and murdered. Apprentices and journeymen, frustrated because the highest positions in the guilds were closed to them, rioted.

The boy-king Richard II (r. 1377–1399) met Wat Tyler and other leaders of the revolt, agreed to charters ensuring peasants' freedom, tricked them with false promises, and then crushed the uprising with terrible ferocity. The nobility tried to restore ancient duties of serfdom, but nearly a century of freedom had elapsed, and the commutation of manorial services continued. Rural serfdom disappeared in England by 1550.

Urban Conflicts

In Flanders, France, and England, peasant revolts often blended with conflicts involving workers in cities. Unrest also occurred in other cities. In Florence in 1378 the *ciompi*, the poor propertyless workers, revolted. Serious

But this attempt to freeze wages and social mobility could not be enforced. Some scholars believe that in most places the peasantry was better off in the period 1350 to 1450 than it had been for centuries before or was to be for four centuries after.

Why then was the outburst in England in 1381 so serious? It was provoked by a crisis of rising expectations. The relative prosperity of the laboring classes led to demands that the upper classes were unwilling to grant. Unable to climb higher, the peasants sought release for their economic frustrations in revolt. Economic grievances combined with other factors. The south of England, where the revolt broke out, had been subjected to destructive French raids. The English government did little to protect the south, and villagers grew increasingly

social trouble occurred in Lübeck, Brunswick, and other German cities. In Spain in 1391 aristocratic attempts to impose new forms of serfdom, combined with demands for tax relief, led to massive working-class and peasant uprisings in Seville and Barcelona.

These revolts often occurred in cities where the conditions of work were changing for many people. In the thirteenth century craft guilds had organized production of most goods, with masters, journeymen, and apprentices working side by side. Beginning in the fourteenth century in a few areas of Europe such as Florence and Flanders, individuals who had made money in trade and banking invested in production. They wanted to make products on a larger scale than guilds would allow, so they hired many households, with each household performing only one step of the process. Craft guilds sometimes protested these changes, but in other cities more enterprising or wealthier masters recognized the benefits of this new system and began to hire other households to work for them. This promoted a greater division within guilds between wealthier masters and the poorer masters and journeymen they hired. Some masters became so wealthy that they no longer had to work in a shop themselves, nor did their wives and family members. Instead of being artisans, they became capitalist investors, though they still generally belonged to the craft guild.

While capitalism provided opportunities for some artisans to become investors and entrepreneurs, especially in cloth production, for many it led to a decrease in income and status. Guilds often responded to competition by limiting membership to existing guild families, which meant that journeymen who were not master's sons or who could not find a master's widow or daughter to marry could never become masters themselves. They remained journeymen their entire lives, losing their sense of solidarity with the masters of their craft and in some cities forming separate journeymen's guilds. These journeymen's guilds tried to prevent anyone who was not a member of the guild from working in any craft shop, enforcing their aims with boycotts, strikes, and riots. Such actions often led cities to prohibit journeymen's guilds, but they were still set up illegally, and their secrecy made them stronger. Journeymen developed elaborate initiation rituals and secret ceremonies to enhance group solidarity, and they carried their organizations with them when they traveled in search of work.

Urban uprisings were most often touched off by economic issues, as low- and middle-class workers deeply resented the widening economic and social gap separating them from mercantile elites, but they were also sparked by issues involving honor, such as employers' requiring

workers to do tasks they regarded as beneath them. As their actual status and economic prospects declined and their work became basically wage labor, journeymen and poorer masters emphasized skill and honor as qualities that set them apart from less-skilled workers.

The sense of honor developed by craft and journeymen's guilds was a gendered one. When urban economies were expanding in the High Middle Ages, the master's wife and daughters worked alongside him, and the journeymen and apprentices and female domestic servants also carried out productive tasks. (See the feature "Listening to the Past: Christine de Pizan" on pages 404–405.) Women and girls served as a labor reservoir to be utilized when guild needs required. Masters' widows ran shops after the death of their husbands and were expected to pay all guild fees, though they could not participate in running the guild. This informal participation began to change in the fourteenth century, as guilds increasingly came to view the honor of their work as tied to an all-male workplace. First, masters' widows were limited in the amount of time they could keep operating a shop or were prohibited from hiring journeymen; then female domestic servants were excluded from any productive tasks; then the number of his daughters a master craftsman could employ was limited. The timing of these restrictions varied from craft to craft, town to town, and country to country, but because women's participation in guild shops was generally not guaranteed by guild regulations and because widows had no political voice in running the guilds, women as a group were not able to protect their right to work. A few might be allowed to work, but this was on an individual basis and was viewed as a substitute for charity. The separate journeymen's guilds were even more hostile to women's work and never allowed female members. Their secret rituals offered opportunities for men to bond with one another and to express their resentment of economic change through hostility toward women's work as well as toward merchants' privileges.

Sex in the City

Peasant and urban revolts and riots had clear economic bases, but some historians have suggested that late medieval marital patterns may have also played a role in unrest. At what age did people usually marry? The largest amount of evidence on age at first marriage survives from Italy. For girls, population surveys at Prato place the age at 16.3 years in 1372 and at 21.1 years in 1470. Noble and wealthy urban women in cities elsewhere in Europe also generally married while in their late teens, but peasant and poorer urban women, especially in northwestern Europe—including the British Isles, Scandinavia, France, and Germany—waited until their mid- or late twenties to marry. The northwestern European marriage pattern resulted largely from the idea that couples should be economically independent before they married, so both spouses spent long periods as servants or workers in other households saving money and learning skills, or they waited until their own parents had died and the family property was distributed.

The most unusual feature of this pattern was the late age of marriage for women. Women entered marriage as adults and took charge of running a household immediately. They were thus not as dependent on their husbands or their mothers-in-law as were women who married at younger ages. They had fewer pregnancies than women who married earlier, though not necessarily fewer surviving children.

Men of all social groups were older when they married. An Italian chronicler writing about 1354 says that men did not marry before the age of thirty. At Prato in 1371 the average age of men at first marriage was twenty-four years, very young for Italian men, but these data may signal an attempt to regain population losses due to the recent attack of the plague. In general, men were in their middle or late twenties at first marriage, with wealthier urban merchants often much older. Journeymen and apprentices were often explicitly prohibited from marrying, as were the students at universities, as they were understood to be in "minor orders" and thus like clergy, even if they were not intending on careers in the church.

The prohibitions on marriage for certain groups of men and the late age of marriage for most men meant that cities and villages were filled with large numbers of young adult men with no family responsibilities who often formed the core of riots and unrest. Not surprisingly, this situation also contributed to a steady market for sexual services outside of marriage, what in later centuries was termed *prostitution*. Research on the southern French province of Languedoc in the fourteenth and fifteenth centuries has revealed the establishment of legal houses of prostitution in many cities. Municipal authorities in Toulouse, Montpellier, Albi, and other towns set up houses or red-light districts either outside the city walls or away from respectable neighborhoods. For example, authorities in Montpellier set aside Hot Street for prostitution, required public women to live there, and forbade anyone to molest them. Prostitution thus passed from being a private concern to a social matter requiring public supervision. The towns of Languedoc were not unique. Public authorities in Amiens, Dijon, Paris,

Venice, Genoa, London, Florence, Rome, most of the larger German towns, and the English port of Sandwich set up brothels.

Many cities set down rules for the women and their customers, and they justified the existence of municipal brothels with the comment that such women protected honorable girls and women from the uncontrollable lust of young men, an argument at least as old as Saint Augustine. In a few cities such as Florence, authorities also noted that brothels might keep young men from homosexual relations, another, far worse alternative in their eyes. Visiting brothels was associated with achieving manhood in the eyes of young men, though for the women themselves their activities were work. Indeed, in some cases the women had no choice, for they had been traded to the brothel manager by their parents or other people in payment for debt, or had quickly become indebted to him (or, more rarely, her) for the clothes and other finery regarded as essential to their occupation. Poor women—and men—also sold sex illegally outside of city brothels, combining this with other sorts of part-time work such as laundering or sewing. Prostitution was an urban phenomenon because only populous towns had large numbers of unmarried young men, communities of transient merchants, and a culture accustomed to a cash exchange.

Though selling sex for money was legal in the Middle Ages, the position of women who did so was always marginal. In the late fifteenth century cities began to limit brothel residents' freedom of movement and choice of clothing, requiring them to wear distinctive head coverings or bands on their clothing so that they would not be mistaken for "honorable" women. The cities also began to impose harsher penalties on women who did not live in the designated house or section of town. A few prostitutes did earn enough to donate money to charity or buy property, but most were very poor.

Along with buying sex, young men also took it by force. Unmarried women often found it difficult to avoid sexual contacts. Many of them worked as domestic servants, where their employers or employers' sons or male relatives could easily coerce them, or they worked in proximity to men. Female servants were sent on errands alone or with men or worked by themselves in fields far from other people. Notions of female honor kept upper-class women secluded in their homes, particularly in southern and eastern Europe, but there was little attempt anywhere to keep female servants or day laborers from the risk of seduction or rape. Rape was a capital crime in many parts of Europe, but the actual sentences handed out were more likely to be fines and brief imprisonment,

Prostitute Invites a Traveling Merchant Poverty drove women into prostitution, which, though denounced by moralists, was accepted as a normal part of the medieval social fabric. In the cities and larger towns where prostitution flourished, public officials passed laws requiring prostitutes to wear a special mark on their clothing, regulated hours of business, forbade women to drag men into their houses, and denied business to women with the "burning sickness," gonorrhea. *(Bodleian Library, MS. Bodl. 264, fol. 245V)*

with the severity of the sentence dependent on the social status of the victim and the perpetrator. According to a study of the legal evidence from Venice in the years 1338 to 1358, rape was not considered a particularly serious crime against either the victim or society. Noble youths committed a higher percentage of rapes than their small numbers in Venetian society would imply. The rape of a young girl of marriageable age or a child under twelve was considered a graver crime than the rape of a married woman. Nevertheless, the punishment for rape of a noble marriageable girl was only a fine or about six months' imprisonment. In an age when theft and robbery could be punished by mutilation and forgery and sodomy by burning, this penalty was mild indeed. When an upper-class youth was convicted of the rape of a non-noble girl, his punishment was even lighter. By contrast, the sexual assault of a noblewoman by a working-class man, which was extraordinarily rare, resulted in severe penalization because the crime had social and political overtones.

According to laws regarding rape in most parts of Europe, the victim had to prove that she had cried out and had attempted to repel the attacker, and she had to bring the charge within a short period of time after the attack had happened. Women bringing rape charges were often more interested in getting their own honorable reputations back than in punishing the perpetrators, and for this reason they sometimes asked the judge to force their rapists to marry them.

Same-sex relations—what in the late nineteenth century would be termed *homosexuality*—were another feature of medieval urban life (and of village life, though there are very few sources relating to sexual relations of any type in the rural context). Same-sex relations were of relatively little concern to church or state authorities in the early Middle Ages, but this attitude changed beginning in the late twelfth century. By 1300 most areas had defined such actions as "crimes against nature," with authorities seeing them as particularly reprehensible because they thought they did not occur anywhere else in creation. Same-sex relations, usually termed *sodomy*, became a capital crime in most of Europe, with adult offenders threatened with execution by fire. The Italian cities of Venice, Florence, and Lucca created special courts to deal with sodomy, which saw thousands of investigations.

How prevalent was homosexuality? This is difficult to answer, even in modern society, but Florence provides a provocative case study. The city of Florence passed legislation against sodomy in 1415 and 1418, and in 1432 it set up a special magistracy, the Office of the Night, to "root out . . . the abominable vice of sodomy." This board of professional men at least forty-five years of age and married was elected annually and charged with pursuing and punishing sodomitical activity between males.[12] The name of the magistracy derived from the nocturnal activities of most male encounters, especially in the spring and summer months and on feast days and

Sundays. Between 1432 and the abolition of the magistracy in 1502, about seventeen thousand men came to its attention, which, even over a seventy-year period, represents a great number in a population of about forty thousand. Moreover, careful statistical analysis of judicial records shows that all classes of society engaged in it— men in the textile trade, in commerce, in education, and in the food industry, especially butchers, as well as construction workers, tavern keepers, artists, and innkeepers. Sodomy was not a marginal practice, which may account for the fact that, despite harsh laws and special courts, actual executions for sodomy were rare in Italy. They were also uncommon in England, where despite harsh laws there were only six trials for sodomy during the entire long reign of Queen Elizabeth I (1564–1603). Trials were more common in the Iberian Peninsula, where those charged with sodomy were sometimes tortured to reveal other names, so that sodomy accusations often occurred in waves.

Almost all cases heard by the Florentine court and courts in other cities involved an adult man and an adolescent boy and ranged from sex exchanged for money or gifts to long-term affectionate relationships. Florentines believed in a generational model in which different roles were appropriate to different stages in life. In a socially and sexually hierarchical world, the boy in the passive role was identified as subordinate, dependent, and mercenary, words usually applied to women. Florentines, however, never described the dominant partner in feminine terms, for he had not compromised his masculine identity or violated a gender ideal; in fact, the adult partner might be married or have female sexual partners as well as male. Only if an adult male assumed the passive role was his masculinity jeopardized. Such cases were extremely rare. Same-sex relations often developed within the context of all-male environments, such as the army, the craft shop, and the artistic workshop, and were part of the collective male experience. Homoerotic relationships played important roles in defining stages of life, expressing distinctions of status, and shaping masculine gender identity.

Same-sex relations involving women almost never came to the attention of legal authorities, so it is difficult to find out much about them. Most commentators about sexual relations were male clergy who viewed sex between women as categorically different than sex between men, if they regarded it as sex at all. Female-female desire is expressed in songs, plays, and stories, as is male-male desire. Such literary sources can be used as evidence of the way people understood same-sex relations, though not how common such relations were.

Same-Sex Relations   This illustration, from a thirteenth-century French book of morals, interprets female and male same-sex relations as the work of devils, who hover over the couples. This illustration was painted at the time that religious and political authorities were increasingly criminalizing same-sex relations. *(Austrian National Library, Vienna, Cod. 2554, fol. 2r)*

Fur-Collar Crime

The Hundred Years' War had provided employment and opportunity for thousands of idle and fortune-seeking knights. But during periods of truce and after the war finally ended, many nobles once again had little to do. Inflation hurt them. Although many were living on fixed incomes, their chivalric code demanded lavish generosity and an aristocratic lifestyle. Many nobles turned to crime as a way of raising money. The fourteenth and fifteenth centuries witnessed a great deal of "fur-collar crime," so called for the miniver fur nobles alone were allowed to wear on their collars.

Fur-collar crime rarely involved such felonies as homicide, robbery, rape, and arson. Instead, nobles used their superior social status to rob and extort from the weak and then to corrupt the judicial process. Groups of noble brigands roamed the English countryside stealing from both rich and poor. Sir John de Colseby and Sir William Bussy led a gang of thirty-eight knights who stole goods worth £3,000 in various robberies. Operating like modern urban racketeers, knightly gangs demanded that peasants pay "protection money" or else have their hovels burned and their fields destroyed.

Attacks on the rich often took the form of kidnapping and extortion. Wealthy travelers were seized on the highways and held for ransom. In northern England a gang of gentry led by Sir Gilbert de Middleton abducted Sir Henry Beaumont; his brother, the bishop-elect of Durham; and two Roman cardinals in England on a peacemaking visit. Only after ransom was paid were the victims released.

Fur-collar criminals were terrorists, but like some modern-day white-collar criminals who commit nonviolent crimes, medieval aristocratic criminals got away with their outrages. When accused of wrongdoing, fur-collar criminals intimidated witnesses. They threatened jurors. They used "pull" or cash to bribe judges. As a fourteenth-century English judge wrote to a young nobleman, "For the love of your father I have hindered charges being brought against you and have prevented execution of indictment actually made."[13] Criminal activity by nobles continued decade after decade because governments were too weak to stop it.

The ballads of Robin Hood, a collection of folk legends from late medieval England, describe the adventures of the outlaw hero and his band of followers who lived in Sherwood Forest and attacked and punished those who violated the social system and the law. Most of the villains in these simple tales are fur-collar criminals—grasping landlords, wicked sheriffs such as the famous sheriff of Nottingham, and mercenary churchmen. Robin and his merry men performed a sort of retributive justice. Robin Hood was a popular figure because he symbolized the deep resentment of aristocratic corruption and abuse; he represented the struggle against tyranny and oppression.

Ethnic Tensions and Restrictions

Large numbers of people in the twelfth and thirteenth centuries migrated from one part of Europe to another: the English into Scotland and Ireland; Germans, French, and Flemings into Poland, Bohemia, and Hungary; the French into Spain. The colonization of frontier regions meant that peoples of different ethnic backgrounds lived side by side. Everywhere in Europe, towns recruited people from the countryside (see pages 333). In frontier regions, townspeople were usually long-distance immigrants and, in eastern Europe, Ireland, and Scotland, ethnically different from the surrounding rural population. In eastern Europe, German was the language of the towns; in Irish towns, French, the tongue of Norman or English settlers, predominated.

In the early periods of conquest and colonization, and in all regions with extensive migrations, a legal dualism existed: native peoples remained subject to their traditional laws; newcomers brought and were subject to the laws of the countries from which they came. On the Prussian and Polish frontier, for example, the law was that "men who come there . . . should be judged on account of any crime or contract engaged in there according to Polish custom if they are Poles and according to German custom if they are Germans."[14] Likewise, in Spain Mudéjars, Muslim subjects of Christian kings, received guarantees of separate but equal judicial rights. King Alfonso I of Aragon's charter to the Muslims of Toledo states, "They shall be in lawsuits and pleas under their (Muslim) qadi (judges) . . . as it was in the times of the Moors."[15] Thus conquered peoples, whether Muslims in Spain or minority immigrant groups such as Germans in eastern Europe, had legal protection and lived in their own juridical enclaves. Subject peoples experienced some disabilities, but the broad trend was toward legal pluralism.

The great exception to this broad pattern was Ireland. From the start, the English practiced an extreme form of discrimination toward the native Irish. The English distinguished between the free and the unfree, and the entire Irish population, simply by the fact of Irish birth, was unfree. In 1210 King John declared that "English law and custom be established there (in Ireland)." Accordingly, a legal structure modeled on that of England, with county courts, itinerant justices, and the common law (see pages 271–274), was set up. But the Irish had no access to the common-law courts. In civil (property) disputes, an English defendant need not respond to his Irish plaintiff; no Irish person could make a will. In criminal procedures, the murder of an Irishman was not considered a felony. In 1317–1318 Irish princes sent a Remonstrance to the pope complaining that "any non-Irishman is allowed to bring legal action against an Irishman, but an Irishman . . . except any prelate (bishop or abbot) is barred from every action by that fact alone." An English defendant in the criminal matter would claim "that he is not held to answer . . . since he [the plaintiff] is Irish and not of free blood."[16] Naturally, this emphasis on blood descent provoked bitterness.

Other than in Ireland, although native peoples commonly held humbler positions, both immigrant and native townspeople prospered during the expanding economy of the thirteenth century. When economic recession hit during the fourteenth century, ethnic tensions multiplied.

The later Middle Ages witnessed a movement away from legal pluralism or dualism and toward legal homogeneity and an emphasis on blood descent. Competition for ecclesiastical offices and the cultural divisions between town and country people became arenas for ethnic tension. Since bishoprics and abbacies carried religious authority, spiritual charisma, and often rights of appointment to subordinate positions, they were natural objects of ambition. When prelates of a language or "nationality" different from those of the local people gained church positions, the latter felt a loss of influence. Bishops were supposed to be pastors. Their pastoral work involved preaching, teaching, and comforting, duties that could be performed effectively only when the bishop (or priest) could communicate with the people. Ideally, in a pluralistic society, he should be bilingual; often he was not.

In the late thirteenth century, as waves of Germans migrated into Danzig on the Baltic, into Silesia, and into the Polish countryside and towns, they encountered Jakub Swinka, archbishop of Gniezno (1283–1314), whose jurisdiction included these areas of settlement. The bishop hated Germans and referred to them as "dog heads." His German contemporary, Bishop John of Cracow, detested the Poles, wanted to expel all Polish people, and refused to appoint Poles to any church office. In Ireland, English colonists and the native Irish competed for ecclesiastical offices until 1217, when the English government in London decreed:

Since the election of Irishmen in our land of Ireland has often disturbed the peace of that land, we command you . . . that henceforth you allow no Irishman to be elected . . . or preferred in any cathedral . . . (and) you should seek by all means to procure election and promotion to vacant bishoprics of . . . honest Englishmen.[17]

Although criticized by the pope and not totally enforceable, this law remained in effect in many dioceses for centuries.

Likewise, the arrival of Cistercians and mendicants (Franciscans and Dominicans) from France and Germany in Baltic and Slavic lands provoked ethnic hostilities. Slavic prelates and princes saw the German mendicants as "instruments of cultural colonization," and Slavs were strongly discouraged from becoming friars. In 1333, when John of Drazic, bishop of Prague, founded a friary at Roudnice (Raudnitz), he specified that "we shall admit no one to this convent or monastery of any nation except a Bohemian [Czech], born of two Czech-speaking parents."[18] In the fourteenth-century *Dalimil Chronicle*, a survey of Bohemian history written in Czech and pervaded with Czech hostility toward Germans, one anti-German prince offered 100 marks of silver "to anyone who brought him one hundred noses cut off from the Germans."[19] Urban residents, who were German, countered with their own restrictions. Cobblers in fourteenth-century Beeskow, a town close to the large Slavic population of Lausitz in Silesia, required that "an apprentice who comes to learn his craft should be brought before the master and guild members. . . . We forbid the sons of barbers, linen workers, shepherds, Slavs." The bakers of the same town decreed: "Whoever wishes to be a member must bring proof to the councillors and guildsmen that he is born of legitimate, upright, German folk. . . . No one of Wendish (Slavic) race may be in the guild."[20]

Ethnic purity can be maintained across generations only by prohibiting marriage among groups, and laws did just this. Intermarriage was forbidden in many places, such as Riga on the Baltic (now the capital of Latvia), where legislation for the bakers guild stipulated that "whoever wishes to have the privilege of membership in our company shall not take as a wife any woman who is ill-famed . . . or non-German; if he does marry such a woman, he must leave the company and office." Not only the guilds but also eligibility for public office depended on ethnic purity, as at the German burgher settlement of Pest in Hungary, where a town judge had to have four German grandparents.

The most extensive attempt to prevent intermarriage and protect ethnic purity is embodied in Ireland's **Statute of Kilkenny** (1366), which states that "there were to be no marriages between those of immigrant and native stock; that the English inhabitants of Ireland must employ the English language and bear English names; that they must ride in the English way (that is, with saddles) and have English apparel; that no Irishmen were to be granted ecclesiastical benefices or admitted to monasteries in the English parts of Ireland."[21] Rulers of the Christian kingdoms of Spain drew up comparable legislation discriminating against the Mudéjars.

Late medieval chroniclers used words such as *gens* (race or clan) and *natio* (species, stock, or kind) to refer to different groups. They held that peoples differed according to language, traditions, customs, and laws. None of these were unchangeable, however, and commentators increasingly also described ethnic differences in terms of "blood"—"German blood," "English blood," and so on—which made ethnicity heritable. Religious beliefs also came to be conceptualized as blood, with people re-

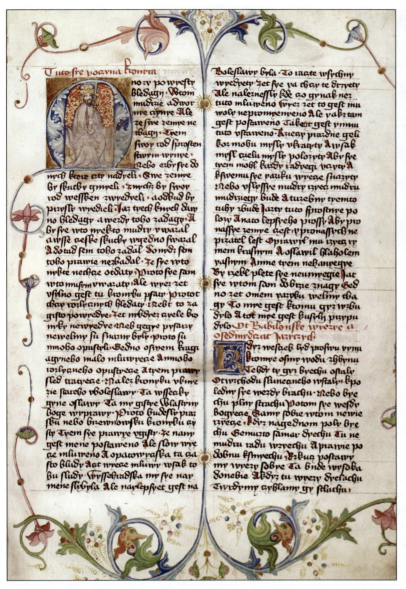

Opening Page from the *Dalimil Chronicle* This history of Bohemia (now part of the Czech Republic) was the first book to be written in the Czech language, and was an important tool in the creation of a Czech national identity. The section reproduced here includes references to "our people" and "our land." The book remains an important part of Czech identity; in 2005 the National Library of the Czech Republic purchased a fragment of an illustrated fourteenth-century Latin translation for nearly half a million dollars. Similar historical chronicles were written in the vernacular languages of many parts of Europe in the fifteenth century and contributed to a growing sense of ethnic and national distinctions. *(Austrian National Library, Vienna)*

garded as having Jewish blood, Muslim blood, or Christian blood. The most dramatic expression of this was in Spain, where "purity of the blood"—having no Muslim or Jewish ancestors—became an obsession. Blood was also used as a way to talk about social differences, especially for nobles. Just as Irish and English were prohibited from marrying each other, those of "noble blood" were prohibited from marrying commoners in many parts of Europe. As Europeans increasingly came into contact with people from Africa and Asia, and particularly as they developed colonial empires, these notions of blood also became a way of conceptualizing racial categories (see page 429).

Literacy and Vernacular Literature

The development of ethnic identities had many negative consequences, but a more positive effect was the increasing use of national languages. In the High Middle Ages most official documents and works of literature were written in Latin. Beginning in the fourteenth century, however, national languages—the **vernacular**—came into widespread use not only in verbal communication but in literature as well. Two masterpieces of European culture, Dante's *Divine Comedy* (1310–1320) and Chaucer's *Canterbury Tales* (1387–1400), brilliantly manifest this new national pride.

Dante Alighieri (1265–1321) descended from a landowning family in Florence, where he held several positions in the city government. Dante called his work a "comedy" because he wrote it in Italian and in a different style from the "tragic" Latin; a later generation added the adjective *divine,* referring both to its sacred subject and to Dante's artistry. The *Divine Comedy* is an allegorical trilogy of one hundred cantos (verses), each of whose three equal parts (1 + 33 + 33 + 33) describes one of the realms of the next world: Hell, Purgatory, and Paradise. The Roman poet Virgil, representing reason, leads Dante through Hell, where he observes the torments of the damned and denounces the disorders of his own time, especially ecclesiastical ambition and corruption. Passing up into Purgatory, Virgil shows the poet how souls are purified of their disordered inclinations. From Purgatory, Beatrice, a woman

Schoolmaster and Schoolmistress Teaching Ambrosius Holbein, elder brother of the more famous Hans Holbein, produced this signboard for the Swiss educator Myconius; it is an excellent example of what we would call commercial art—art used to advertise, in this case Myconius's profession. The German script above promised that all who enrolled, girls and boys, would learn to read and write. Most schools were for boys only, but a few offered instruction for girls as well. By modern standards the classroom seems bleak: the windows have glass panes but they don't admit much light, and the schoolmaster is prepared to use the sticks if the boy makes a mistake. *(Kunstmuseum Basel/Martin Buhler, photographer)*

Dante once loved and the symbol of divine revelation in the poem, leads him to Paradise. In Paradise, home of the angels and saints, Saint Bernard—representing mystic contemplation—leads Dante to the Virgin Mary. Through her intercession, he at last attains a vision of God.

The *Divine Comedy* portrays contemporary and historical figures, comments on secular and ecclesiastical affairs, and draws on Scholastic philosophy. Within the framework of a symbolic pilgrimage to the City of God, the *Divine Comedy* embodies the psychological tensions of the age. A profoundly Christian poem, it also contains bitter criticism of some church authorities. In its symmetrical structure and use of figures from the ancient world, such as Virgil, the poem perpetuates the classical tradition, but as the first major work of literature in the Italian vernacular, it is distinctly modern.

Geoffrey Chaucer (1342–1400), the son of a London wine merchant, was an official in the administrations of the English kings Edward III and Richard II and wrote poetry as an avocation. Chaucer's *Canterbury Tales* is a collection of stories in lengthy rhymed narrative. On a pilgrimage to the shrine of Saint Thomas Becket at Canterbury (see page 271), thirty people of various social backgrounds tell tales. The Prologue sets the scene and describes the pilgrims, whose characters are further re-

vealed in the story each one tells. For example, the gross Miller tells a vulgar story about a deceived husband; the earthy Wife of Bath, who has buried five husbands, sketches a fable about the selection of a spouse; and the elegant Prioress, who violates her vows by wearing jewelry, delivers a homily on the Virgin. In depicting the interests and behavior of all types of people, Chaucer presents a rich panorama of English social life in the fourteenth century. Like the *Divine Comedy, Canterbury Tales* reflects the cultural tensions of the times. Ostensibly Christian, many of the pilgrims are also materialistic, sensual, and worldly, suggesting the ambivalence of the broader society's concern for the next world and frank enjoyment of this one.

Beginning in the fourteenth century, a variety of evidence attests to the increasing literacy of laypeople. Wills and inventories reveal that many people, not just nobles, possessed books—mainly devotional, but also romances, manuals on manners and etiquette, histories, and sometimes legal and philosophical texts. In England the number of schools in the diocese of York quadrupled between 1350 and 1500. Information from Flemish and German towns is similar: children were sent to schools and were taught the fundamentals of reading, writing, and arithmetic. Laymen increasingly served as managers or stewards of estates and as clerks to guilds and town governments; such positions obviously required that they be able to keep administrative and financial records.

The penetration of laymen into the higher positions of governmental administration, long the preserve of clerics, also illustrates rising lay literacy. For example, in 1400 beneficed clerics held most of the posts in the English Exchequer; by 1430 clerics were the exception. With growing frequency, the upper classes sent their daughters to convent schools, where, in addition to instruction in singing, religion, needlework, deportment, and household management, girls gained the rudiments of reading and sometimes writing. Reading and writing were taught separately, and many young people, especially girls, were taught to read but not to write.

The spread of literacy represents a response to the needs of an increasingly complex society. Trade, commerce, and expanding government bureaucracies required more and more literate people. Late medieval culture remained an oral culture in which most people received information by word of mouth. But by the mid-fifteenth century, even before the printing press was turning out large quantities of reading materials, the evolution toward a literary culture was already perceptible.

Chapter Summary

Online Study Center   ACE the Test

- *What were the demographic and economic consequences of climate change?*
- *How did the spread of the plague shape European society?*
- *What were the causes of the Hundred Years' War, and how did the war affect European politics, economics, and cultural life?*
- *What challenges faced the Christian church in the fourteenth century, and how did church leaders, intellectuals, and ordinary people respond?*
- *How did economic and social tensions contribute to revolts, crime, violence, and a growing sense of ethnic and national distinctions?*

The crises of the fourteenth and fifteenth centuries were acids that burned deeply into the fabric of traditional medieval society. Bad weather brought poor harvests, which contributed to widespread famine and disease and an international economic depression. Political leaders attempted to find solutions, but were unable to deal with the economic and social problems that resulted.

In 1348 a new disease, most likely the bubonic plague, came to mainland Europe, carried from the Black Sea by ships. It spread quickly by land and sea and within two years may have killed as much as one-third of the European population. Contemporary medical explanations for the plague linked it to poisoned air or water, and treatments were ineffective. Many people regarded the plague as a divine punishment and sought remedies in religious practices such as prayer, pilgrimages, or donations to churches. Population losses caused by the Black Death led to inflation but in the long run may have contributed to more opportunities for the peasants and urban workers who survived the disease.

The miseries of the plague were enhanced in England and France by the Hundred Years' War, which was fought intermittently in France from 1337 to 1453. The war began as a dispute over the succession to the French crown, and royal propaganda on both sides fostered a kind of early nationalism. The English won most of the battles and in 1419 advanced to the walls of Paris. The appearance of Joan of Arc rallied the French cause, and French troops eventually pushed English forces out of all of France except the port of Calais. The war served as a catalyst for the development of representative government in England. In France, on the other hand, the war stiffened opposition to national assemblies.

Religious beliefs offered people solace through these difficult times, but the Western Christian church was going through a particularly difficult period in the fourteenth and early fifteenth centuries. The Avignon papacy and the Great Schism weakened the prestige of the church and people's faith in papal authority. The conciliar movement, by denying the church's universal sovereignty, strengthened the claims of secular governments to jurisdiction over all their peoples. As members of the clergy challenged the power of the pope, laypeople challenged the authority of the church itself. Women and men increasingly relied on direct approaches to God, often through mystical encounters, rather than on the institutional church. Some, including John Wyclif and Jan Hus, questioned basic church doctrines.

The plague and the war both led to higher taxes and economic dislocations, which sparked peasant revolts in Flanders, France, and England. Peasant revolts often blended with conflicts involving workers in cities, where working conditions were changing to create a greater gap between wealthy merchant-producers and poor propertyless workers. Unrest in the countryside and cities may have been further exacerbated by marriage patterns that left large numbers of young men unmarried and rootless. The pattern of late marriage for men contributed to a growth in prostitution, which was an accepted feature of medieval urban society. Along with peasant revolts and urban crime and unrest, violence perpetrated by nobles was a common part of late medieval life. The economic and demographic crises of the fourteenth century also contributed to increasing ethnic tensions in the many parts of Europe where migration had brought different population groups together. A growing sense of ethnic and national identity led to restrictions and occasionally to violence, but also to the increasing use of national languages for works of literature. The increasing number of schools that led to the growth of lay literacy represents another positive achievement of the later Middle Ages.

Key Terms

Great Famine
Black Death
bubo
flagellants
Agincourt
Joan of Arc
representative
  assemblies
nationalism
Babylonian Captivity

Great Schism
conciliarists
confraternities
*The Imitation of
  Christ*
peasant revolts
Jacquerie
Statute of Kilkenny
vernacular

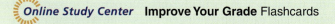 *Online Study Center* **Improve Your Grade** Flashcards

Suggested Reading

Allmand, Christopher. *The Hundred Years War: England and France at War, ca 1300–1450,* rev. ed. 2005. Designed for students; examines the war from political, military, social, and economic perspectives and compares the way England and France reacted to the conflict.

Boswell, John. *Christianity, Social Tolerance, and Homosexuality: Gay People in Western Europe from the Beginning of the Christian Era to the Fourteenth Century.* 1981. Remains an important broad analysis of attitudes toward same-sex relations throughout the Middle Ages.

Dunn, Alastair. *The Peasants' Revolt: England's Failed Revolution of 1381.* 2004. Offers new interpretations of the causes and consequence of the English Peasants' Revolt.

Dyer, Christopher. *Standards of Living in the Later Middle Ages.* 1989. Examines economic realities and social conditions more generally.

Herlihy, David. *The Black Death and the Transformation of the West,* 2d ed. 1997. A fine treatment of the causes and cultural consequences of the disease that remains the best starting point for study of the great epidemic.

Holt, James Clarke. *Robin Hood.* 1982. A soundly researched and highly readable study of the famous outlaw.

Jordan, William Chester. *The Great Famine: Northern Europe in the Early Fourteenth Century.* 1996. Discusses catastrophic weather, soil exhaustion, and other factors that led to the Great Famine and the impact of the famine on community life.

Karras, Ruth M. *Sexuality in Medieval Europe: Doing onto Others.* 2005. A brief overview designed for undergraduates that incorporates the newest scholarship.

Kieckhefer, Richard. *Unquiet Souls: Fourteenth-Century Saints and Their Religious Milieu.* 1984. Sets the ideas of the mystics in their social and intellectual contexts.

Koch, H. W. *Medieval Warfare.* 1978. A beautifully illustrated book covering strategy, tactics, armaments, and costumes of war.

Lehfeldt, Elizabeth, ed. *The Black Death.* 2005. Includes excerpts from debates about many aspects of the Black Death.

Oakley, Frances. *The Western Church in the Later Middle Ages.* 1979. An excellent broad survey.

Robertson, D. W., Jr. *Chaucer's London.* 1968. Evokes the social setting of *Canterbury Tales* brilliantly.

Swanson, R. N. *Religion and Devotion in Europe, c. 1215– c. 1515.* 2004. Explores many aspects of spirituality.

Tuchman, Barbara. *A Distant Mirror: The Calamitous Fourteenth Century.* 1978. Written for a general audience, this remains a vivid description of this tumultuous time.

Notes

1. J. M. Rigg, trans., *The Decameron of Giovanni Boccaccio* (London: J. M. Dent & Sons, 1903), p. 6.
2. Quoted in D. Herlihy, *The Black Death and the Transformation of the West* (Cambridge, Mass.: Harvard University Press, 1997), p. 42.
3. Quoted in J. Barnie, *War in Medieval English Society: Social Values and the Hundred Years' War* (Ithaca, N.Y.: Cornell University Press, 1974), p. 34.
4. W. P. Barrett, trans., *The Trial of Jeanne d'Arc* (London: George Routledge, 1931), pp. 165–166.
5. Quoted in Barnie, *War in Medieval English Society,* pp. 36–37.
6. See G. O. Sayles, *The King's Parliament of England* (New York: W. W. Norton, 1974), app., pp. 137–141.
7. Quoted in P. S. Lewis, "The Failure of the Medieval French Estates," *Past and Present* 23 (November 1962): 6.
8. Quoted in J. H. Smith, *The Great Schism, 1378: The Disintegration of the Medieval Papacy* (New York: Weybright & Talley, 1970), p. 15.
9. Quoted in Katharina M. Wilson, ed., *Medieval Women Writers* (Athens: University of Georgia Press, 1984), p. 245.
10. Quoted in M. Bloch, *French Rural History,* trans. J. Sondeimer (Berkeley: University of California Press, 1966), p. 169.
11. C. Stephenson and G. Marcham, eds., *Sources of English Constitutional History,* rev. ed. (New York: Harper & Row, 1972), p. 225.
12. M. Rocke, *Forbidden Friendships: Homosexuality and Male Culture in Renaissance Florence* (New York: Oxford University Press, 1996), p. 45.
13. Quoted in B. A. Hanawalt, "Fur Collar Crime: The Pattern of Crime Among the Fourteenth-Century English Nobility," *Journal of Social History* 8 (Spring 1975): 7.
14. Quoted in R. Bartlett, *The Making of Europe: Conquest, Colonization and Cultural Change, 950–1350* (Princeton, N.J.: Princeton University Press, 1993), p. 205.
15. Quoted ibid., p. 208.
16. Quoted ibid., p. 215.
17. Quoted ibid., p. 224.
18. Quoted ibid., p. 228.
19. Quoted ibid., p. 236.
20. Quoted ibid., p. 238.
21. Quoted ibid., p. 239.

Christine de Pizan

Christine de Pizan (1364?–1430; earlier spelled "Pisan") was the daughter and wife of highly educated men who held positions at the court of the king of France. She was widowed at twenty-five with young children and an elderly mother to support. Christine, who herself had received an excellent education, decided to support her family through writing, an unusual choice for anyone in this era before the printing press and unheard of for a woman. She began to write prose works and poetry, sending them to wealthy individuals in the hope of receiving their support. Her works were well received, and Christine gained commissions to write specific works, including a biography of the French king Charles V, several histories, a long poem celebrating Joan of Arc's victory, and a book of military tactics. She became the first woman in Europe to make her living as a writer.

Among Christine's many works were several in which she considered women's nature and proper role in society, which had been a topic of debate since ancient times. The best known of these was The City of Ladies *(1404), in which she ponders why so many men have a negative view of women and provides examples of virtuous women to counter this view. Immediately afterward she wrote* The Treasure of the City of Ladies *(1405, also called* The Book of Three Virtues*), which provides moral suggestions and practical advice on behavior and household management for women of all social classes. Most of the book is directed toward princesses and court ladies (who would have been able to read it), but she also includes shorter sections for the wives of merchants and artisans, serving-women, female peasants, and even prostitutes. This is her advice to the wives of artisans, whose husbands were generally members of urban craft guilds, such as blacksmiths, bakers, or shoemakers.*

All wives of artisans should be very painstaking and diligent if they wish to have the necessities of life. They should encourage their husbands or their workmen to get to work early in the morning and work until late, for mark our words, there is no trade so good that if you neglect your work you will not have difficulty putting bread on the table. And besides encouraging the others, the wife herself should be involved in the work to the extent that she knows all about it, so that she may know how to oversee his workers if her husband is absent, and to reprove them if they do not do well. She ought to oversee them to keep them from idleness, for through careless workers the master is sometimes ruined. And when customers come to her husband and try to drive a hard bargain, she ought to warn him solicitously to take care that he does not make a bad deal. She should advise him to be chary of giving too much credit if he does not know precisely where and to whom it is going, for in this way many come to poverty, although sometimes the greed to earn more or to accept a tempting proposition makes them do it.

In addition, she ought to keep her husband's love as much as she can, to this end: that he will stay at home more willingly and that he may not have any reason to join the foolish crowds of other young men in taverns and indulge in unnecessary and extravagant expense, as many tradesmen do, especially in Paris. By treating him kindly she should protect him as well as she can from this. It is said that three things drive a man from his home: a quarrelsome wife, a smoking fireplace and a leaking roof. She too ought to stay at home gladly and not go every day traipsing hither and yon gossiping with the neighbours and visiting her chums to find out what everyone is doing. That is done by slovenly housewives roaming about the town in groups. Nor should

Several manuscripts of Christine's works included illustrations showing her writing, which would have increased their appeal to the wealthy individuals who purchased them. *(British Library)*

she go off on these pilgrimages got up for no good reason and involving a lot of needless expense. Furthermore, she ought to remind her husband that they should live so frugally that their expenditure does not exceed their income, so that at the end of the year they do not find themselves in debt.

If she has children, she should have them instructed and taught first at school by educated people so that they may know how better to serve God. Afterwards they may be put to some trade by which they may earn a living, for whoever gives a trade or business training to her child gives a great possession. The children should be kept from wantonness and from voluptuousness above all else, for truly it is something that most shames the children of good towns and is a great sin of mothers and fathers, who ought to be the cause of the virtue and good behavior of their children, but they are sometimes the reason (because of bringing them up to be finicky and indulging them too much) for their wickedness and ruin.

Questions for Analysis

1. How would you describe Christine's view of the ideal artisan's wife?

2. The regulations of craft guilds often required that masters who ran workshops be married. What evidence does Christine's advice provide for why guilds would have stipulated this?

3. How are economic and moral virtues linked for Christine?

Source: Christine de Pisan, *The Treasure of the City of Ladies,* translated with an introduction by Sarah Lawson (Peguin Classics, 1985). This translation copyright © 1985 by Sarah Lawson. Reprinted by permission of Penguin Books Ltd. For more on Christine, see C. C. Willard, *Christine de Pisan: Her Life and Works* (1984), and S. Bell, *The Lost Tapestries of the City of Ladies: Christine de Pizan's Renaissance Legacy* (2004).

Michelangelo's frescoes in the Sistine Chapel in the Vatican, commissioned by the pope. The huge ceiling includes biblical scenes, and the far wall, painted much later, shows a dramatic and violent Last Judgment. *(Vatican Museum)*

chapter

13

chapter preview

Economic and Political Developments
• *What economic and political developments in Italy provided the setting for the Renaissance?*

Intellectual Change
• *What were the key ideas of the Renaissance, and how were they different for men and women and for southern and northern Europeans?*

Art and the Artist
• *How did changes in art both reflect and shape new ideas?*

Social Hierarchies
• *What were the key social hierarchies in Renaissance Europe, and how did ideas about hierarchy shape people's lives?*

Politics and the State in the Renaissance (ca 1450–1521)
• *How did the nation-states of western Europe evolve in this period?*

EUROPEAN SOCIETY IN THE AGE OF THE RENAISSANCE, 1350–1550

While the Four Horsemen of the Apocalypse seemed to be carrying war, plague, famine, and death across northern Europe, a new culture was emerging in southern Europe. The fourteenth century witnessed the beginnings of remarkable changes in many aspects of Italian intellectual, artistic, and cultural life. Artists and writers thought that they were living in a new golden age, but not until the sixteenth century was this change given the label we use today—the **Renaissance,** from the French version of a word meaning "rebirth." That word was first used by the artist and art historian Giorgio Vasari (1511–1574) to describe the art of "rare men of genius" such as his contemporary Michelangelo. Through their works, Vasari judged, the glory of the classical past had been reborn—or perhaps even surpassed—after centuries of darkness. Vasari used *Renaissance* to describe painting, sculpture, and architecture, what he termed the "Major Arts." Gradually, however, the word was used to refer to many aspects of life at this time, first in Italy and then in the rest of Europe. This new attitude had a slow diffusion out of Italy, with the result that the Renaissance "happened" at different times in different parts of Europe: Italian art of the fourteenth through the early sixteenth century is described as "Renaissance," and so is English literature of the late sixteenth century, including Shakespeare's plays and poetry.

About a century after Vasari coined the word *Renaissance*, scholars began to use the words *Middle Ages* to refer to the millennium between the ancient world and the Renaissance. They increasingly saw the cultural and political changes of the Renaissance, along with the religious changes of the Reformation (see Chapter 14) and the European voyages of exploration (see Chapter 15), as ushering in the "modern" world. Since then, some historians have chosen to view the Renaissance as a bridge between the medieval and modern eras because it corresponded chronologically with the late medieval period and because there were many continuities along with the changes. Others have questioned whether the word *Renaissance* should be used at all to describe an era in which many social groups saw decline rather than advance. These debates remind us that these labels—medieval, Renaissance, modern—are

Online Study Center
This icon will direct you to interactive activities and study materials on the website **college.hmco.com/pic/mckaywest9e**

407

intellectual constructs, devised after the fact. They all contain value judgments, just as do other chronological designations, such as the "golden age" of Athens and the "Roaring Twenties."

Economic and Political Developments

The cultural achievements of the Renaissance rest on the economic and political developments of earlier centuries. Economic growth laid the material basis for the Italian Renaissance, and ambitious merchants gained political power to match their economic power. They then used their money and power to buy luxuries and hire talent.

• **What economic and political developments in Italy provided the setting for the Renaissance?**

Commercial Developments

In the great commercial revival of the eleventh century, northern Italian cities led the way. By the middle of the twelfth century Venice, supported by a huge merchant marine, had grown enormously rich through overseas trade. Genoa and Milan also enjoyed the benefits of a large volume of trade with the Middle East and northern Europe. These cities fully exploited their geographical positions as natural crossroads for mercantile exchange between the East and the West. Furthermore, in the early fourteenth century Genoa and Venice made important strides in shipbuilding that for the first time allowed their ships to sail all year long. Advances in ship construction greatly increased the volume of goods that could be transported; improvements in the mechanics of sailing accelerated speed.

Scholars tend to agree that the first artistic and literary manifestations of the Italian Renaissance appeared in Florence, which possessed enormous wealth despite geographical constraints: it was an inland city without easy access to sea transportation. But toward the end of the thirteenth century, Florentine merchants and bankers acquired control of papal banking. From their position as tax collectors for the papacy, Florentine mercantile families began to dominate European banking on both sides of the Alps. These families had offices in Paris, London, Bruges, Barcelona, Marseilles, Tunis and other North African ports, and, of course, Naples and Rome. The profits from loans, investments, and money exchanges that poured back to Florence were pumped into urban industries. Such profits contributed to the city's economic vitality. Banking families, such as the Medici in Florence, controlled the politics and culture of their cities.

By the first quarter of the fourteenth century, the economic foundations of Florence were so strong that even severe crises could not destroy the city. In 1344 King Edward III of England repudiated his huge debts to Florentine bankers and forced some of them into bankruptcy. Florence suffered frightfully from the Black Death, losing at least half its population. Serious labor unrest, such as the *ciompi* revolts of 1378 (see page 392), shook the political establishment. Nevertheless, the basic Florentine economic structure remained stable. Driving enterprise, technical know-how, and competitive spirit saw Florence through the difficult economic period of the late fourteenth century.

A Bank Scene, Florence   Originally a "bank" was just a counter; moneychangers who sat behind the counter became "bankers," exchanging different currencies and holding deposits for merchants and business people. In this scene from fifteenth-century Florence, the bank is covered with an imported Ottoman geometric rug, one of many imported luxury items handled by Florentine merchants. (*Prato, San Francesco/Scala/Art Resource, NY*)

Communes and Republics

The northern Italian cities were **communes,** sworn associations of free men seeking complete political and economic independence from local nobles. The merchant guilds that formed the communes built and maintained the city walls, regulated trade, raised taxes, and kept civil order. In the course of the twelfth century, communes at Milan, Florence, Genoa, Siena, and Pisa fought for and won their independence from surrounding feudal nobles. The nobles, attracted by the opportunities of long-distance and maritime trade, the rising value of urban real estate, the new public offices available in the expanding communes, and the chances for advantageous marriages into rich commercial families, frequently settled in the cities. Marriage vows often sealed business contracts between the rural nobility and wealthy merchants, with the large dowries of brides providing cash for their new husbands' businesses. This merger of the northern Italian feudal nobility and the commercial elite created a powerful **oligarchy,** or small group that ruled a city and its surrounding countryside. The ruling oligarchy in any city was tied together by blood, economic interests, and social connections, but was also often divided by hostilities of kinship groups toward one another. Such hostilities sometimes erupted in violence, and Italian communes were often politically unstable.

Conflict between families within the ruling oligarchy was exacerbated by unrest coming from below. Merchant elites made citizenship in the communes dependent on a property qualification, years of residence within the city, and social connections. Only a tiny percentage of the male population possessed these qualifications and thus could hold office in the commune's political councils. The common people, called the **popolo,** were disenfranchised and heavily taxed, and they bitterly resented their exclusion from power. The popolo wanted places in the communal government and equality of taxation. Throughout most of the thirteenth century, in city after city, the popolo used armed force and violence to take over the city governments. Republican governments—in which political power theoretically resides in the people and is exercised by their chosen representatives—were established in Bologna, Siena, Parma, Florence, Genoa, and other cities. The victory of the popolo proved temporary, however, because they could not establish civil order within their cities. Merchant oligarchies reasserted their power and sometimes brought in powerful military leaders to establish order. These military leaders, called **condottieri** (singular, condottiero), had their own mercenary armies, and in many cities they took over political

power as well. The military leader often invented a long noble lineage to justify his takeover of power, pretending he descended from a Germanic king or Roman leader. There was not much that merchant oligarchies could do to retain their power, and many cities in Italy became **signori,** in which one man ruled and handed down the right to rule to his son. Some signori (the word is plural in Italian and is used for both persons and forms of government) kept the institutions of communal government in place, but these had no actual power.

For the next two centuries the Italian city-states were ruled by signori or by merchant oligarchies. Oligarchic regimes possessed constitutions and often boasted about how much more democratic their form of government was than the government in neighboring signori. In actuality, there wasn't much difference. In oligarchies, a small, restricted class of wealthy merchants exercised the judicial, executive, and legislative functions of government. Thus, in 1422 Venice had a population of eighty-four thousand, but two hundred men held all the power; Florence had about forty thousand people, but only six hundred men were part of the government. Even this number is an illusion, for real power in Florence for most of the fifteenth century was actually held by the Medici family. Oligarchic regimes maintained only a façade of republican government. The Renaissance nostalgia for the Roman form of government, combined with calculating shrewdness, prompted the leaders of Venice, Milan, and Florence to use the old forms.

Chronology

1350–1353	Boccaccio, *The Decameron*
1434–1494	Medici family in power in Florence
1440s	Invention of movable metal type
1469	Marriage of Isabella of Castile and Ferdinand of Aragon
1486	Pico della Mirandola, *On the Dignity of Man*
1494	Invasion of Italy by Charles VIII of France
1508–1512	Michelangelo paints ceiling of Sistine Chapel
1513	Machiavelli, *The Prince*
1516	More, *Utopia*
1528	Castiglione, *The Courtier*

In the fifteenth century the signori in many cities and the most powerful merchant oligarchs in others transformed their households into **courts.** They built magnificent palaces in the centers of cities and required all political business be done there. They hired architects to design and build these palaces, artists to fill them with paintings and sculptures, and musicians and composers to fill them with music. They supported writers and philosophers, flaunting their patronage of learning and the arts. They used ceremonies connected with family births, baptisms, marriages, funerals, or triumphant entrances into the city as occasions for magnificent pageantry and elaborate ritual. Courtly culture afforded signori and oligarchs the opportunity to display and assert their wealth and power. The courts of the rulers of Milan, Florence, and other cities were models for those developed later by rulers of nation-states.

The Balance of Power Among the Italian City-States

Renaissance Italians had a passionate attachment to their individual city-states: political loyalty and feeling centered on the local city. This intensity of local feeling perpetuated the dozens of small states and hindered the development of one unified state.

In the fifteenth century five powers dominated the Italian peninsula: Venice, Milan, Florence, the Papal States, and the kingdom of Naples (see Map 13.1). The rulers of the city-states—whether signori in Milan, patrician elitists in Florence, or oligarchs in Venice—governed as monarchs. They crushed urban revolts, levied taxes, killed their enemies, and used massive building programs to employ, and the arts to overawe, the masses.

Venice, with its enormous trade and vast colonial empire, ranked as an international power. Though Venice had a sophisticated constitution and was a **republic** in name, an oligarchy of merchant aristocrats actually ran the city. Milan was also called a republic, but the condottieri-turned-signori of the Sforza family ruled harshly and dominated the smaller cities of the north. Likewise, in Florence the form of government was republican, with authority vested in several councils of state. In reality, between 1434 and 1494, power in Florence was held by the great Medici banking family. Though not public officers, Cosimo (1434–1464) and Lorenzo (1469–1492) ruled from behind the scenes.

Central Italy consisted mainly of the Papal States, which during the Babylonian Captivity had come under the sway of important Roman families. Pope Alexander VI (1492–1503), aided militarily and politically by his son Cesare Borgia, reasserted papal authority in the papal lands. Cesare Borgia became the hero of Machiavelli's *The Prince* (see page 415) because he began the work of uniting the peninsula by ruthlessly conquering and exacting total obedience from the principalities making up the Papal States.

South of the Papal States was the kingdom of Naples, consisting of virtually all of southern Italy and, at times, Sicily. The kingdom of Naples had long been disputed by the Aragonese and by the French. In 1435 it passed to Aragon.

The major Italian city-states controlled the smaller ones, such as Siena, Mantua, Ferrara, and Modena, and competed furiously among themselves for territory. The large cities used diplomacy, spies, paid informers, and any other available means to get information that could be used to advance their ambitions. While the states of northern Europe were moving toward centralization and consolidation, the world of Italian politics resembled a jungle where the powerful dominated the weak.

In one significant respect, however, the Italian city-states anticipated future relations among competing European states after 1500. Whenever one Italian state appeared to gain a predominant position within the peninsula, other states combined to establish a *balance of power* against the major threat. In the formation of these alliances, Renaissance Italians invented the machinery of modern diplomacy: permanent embassies with resident ambassadors in capitals where political relations and commercial ties needed continual monitoring. The resident ambassador was one of the great achievements of the Italian Renaissance.

At the end of the fifteenth century Venice, Florence, Milan, and the papacy possessed great wealth and represented high cultural achievement. However, their imperialistic ambitions at one another's expense and their resulting inability to form a common alliance against potential foreign enemies made Italy an inviting target for invasion. When Florence and Naples entered into an agreement to acquire Milanese territories, Milan called on France for support.

At Florence the French invasion had been predicted by Dominican friar Girolamo Savonarola (1452–1498). In a number of fiery sermons between 1491 and 1494, Savonarola attacked what he called the paganism and moral vice of the city, the undemocratic government of Lorenzo de' Medici, and the corruption of Pope Alexander VI. For a time Savonarola enjoyed popular support among the ordinary people; he became the religious

•MAP 13.1 The Italian City-States, ca 1494   In the fifteenth century the Italian city-states represented great wealth and cultural sophistication. The political divisions of the peninsula invited foreign intervention.

leader of Florence and as such contributed to the fall of the Medici dynasty. Eventually, however, people tired of his moral denunciations, and he was excommunicated by the pope and executed. Savonarola stands as proof that the common people did not share the worldly outlook of the commercial and intellectual elite. His career also illustrates the internal instability of Italian cities such as Florence, an instability that invited foreign invasion.

The invasion of Italy in 1494 by the French king Charles VIII (r. 1483–1498) inaugurated a new period in Italian and European power politics. Italy became the focus of international ambitions and the battleground of foreign armies, particularly those of France and the Holy Roman Empire in a series of conflicts called the Habsburg-Valois Wars (named for the German and French dynasties). The Italian cities suffered severely from

Uccello: Battle of San Romano   Fascinated by perspective—the representation of spatial depth or distance on a flat surface—the Florentine artist Paolo Uccello (1397–1475) celebrated the Florentine victory over Siena (1432) in a painting with three scenes. Though a minor battle, it started Florence on the road to domination over smaller nearby states. The painting hung in Lorenzo de' Medici's bedroom. *(National Gallery, London/Erich Lessing/Art Resource, NY)*

continual warfare, especially in the frightful sack of Rome in 1527 by imperial forces under the emperor Charles V. Thus the failure of the city-states to form some federal system, to consolidate, or at least to establish a common foreign policy led to centuries of subjection by outside invaders. Italy was not to achieve unification until 1870.

Intellectual Change

The Renaissance was characterized by self-conscious awareness among fourteenth- and fifteenth-century Italians that they were living in a new era. The realization that something new and unique was happening first came to men of letters in the fourteenth century, especially to the poet and humanist Francesco Petrarch (1304–1374). Petrarch thought that he was living at the start of a new age, a period of light following a long night of Gothic gloom.

Medieval people had believed that they were continuing the glories that had been ancient Rome and had recognized no cultural division between the world of the emperors and their own times. But for Petrarch, the Germanic migrations had caused a sharp cultural break with the glories of Rome and inaugurated what he called the "Dark Ages." Along with many of his contemporaries, Petrarch believed that he was witnessing a new golden age of intellectual achievement.

● *What were the key ideas of the Renaissance, and how were they different for men and women and for southern and northern Europeans?*

Humanism

Petrarch and other poets, writers, and artists showed a deep interest in the ancient past, in both the physical remains of the Roman Empire and classical Latin texts. The study of Latin classics became known as the *studia humanitates,* usually translated as "liberal studies" or the "liberal arts." Like all programs of study, they contained an implicit philosophy, generally known as **humanism,** a term devised by the Florentine rhetorician and historian Leonardo Bruni (1370–1444). The words *humanism* and *humanist* derive ultimately from the Latin *humanitas,* which the ancient Roman writer Cicero had used to mean the literary culture needed by anyone who would be considered educated and civilized. Humanists studied the Latin classics to learn what they reveal about human nature. Humanism emphasized human beings and their achievements, interests, and capabilities.

Appreciation for the literary culture of the Romans had never died in the West, but medieval writers had studied the ancients in order to come to know God. Medieval scholars had interpreted the classics in a Christian sense and had invested the ancients' poems and histories with Christian meaning.

Renaissance humanists approached the classics differently. Whereas medieval writers looked to the classics to reveal God, Renaissance humanists studied the classics to understand human nature. They viewed humanity from a strongly Christian perspective, however: men (and women, though to a lesser degree) were made in the image and likeness of God. For example, in a remarkable essay, *On the Dignity of Man* (1486), the Florentine writer Giovanni Pico della Mirandola (1463–1494) stressed that man possesses great dignity because he was made as Adam in the image of God before the Fall and as Christ after the Resurrection. According to Pico, man's place in the universe is somewhere between the beasts and the angels, but because of the divine image planted in him, there are no limits to what he can accomplish. Humanists generally rejected classical ideas that were opposed to Christianity, or they sought through reinterpretation an underlying harmony between the pagan and secular and the Christian faith.

Interest in human achievement led humanists to emphasize the importance of the individual. Groups such as families, guilds, and religious organizations continued to provide strong support for the individual and to exercise great social influence. Yet in the Renaissance, intellectuals, unlike their counterparts in the Middle Ages, prized their own uniqueness.

The Renaissance witnessed the emergence of many distinctive personalities who gloried in their individuality; they had enormous confidence in their ability to achieve great things. Leon Battista Alberti (1404–1472), a writer, architect, and mathematician, remarked, "Men can do all things if they will."[1] Florentine goldsmith and

Benvenuto Cellini: Saltcellar of Francis I (ca 1540)   In gold and enamel, Cellini depicts the Roman sea god, Neptune (with trident, or three-pronged spear), sitting beside a small boat-shaped container holding salt from the sea. Opposite him, a female figure personifying Earth guards pepper, which derives from a plant. Portrayed on the base are the four seasons and the times of day, symbolizing seasonal festivities and daily meal schedules. Classical figures portrayed with grace, poise, and elegance were common subjects in Renaissance art. *(Kunsthistorisches Museum, Vienna/The Bridgeman Art Library)*

sculptor Benvenuto Cellini (1500–1574) prefaced his *Autobiography* with a declaration:

My cruel fate hath warr'd with me in vain:
Life, glory, worth, and all unmeasur'd skill,
Beauty and grace, themselves in me fulfil
That many I surpass, and to the best attain.[2]

Cellini, certain of his genius, wrote so that the whole world might appreciate it.

This attitude of **individualism** stressed personality, uniqueness, genius, and full development of one's capabilities and talents. Thirst for fame, the quest for glory, a driving ambition, and a burning desire for success drove people such as Alberti and Cellini.

The fourteenth- and fifteenth-century humanists loved the language of the classics and considered it superior to the corrupt Latin of the medieval schoolmen. The leading humanists of the early Renaissance were rhetoricians, seeking effective and eloquent oral and written communication. Literary humanists of the fourteenth century wrote each other highly stylized letters imitating ancient authors, and they held witty philosophical dialogues in conscious imitation of the Platonic Academy of the fourth century B.C. They eventually became concerned about form more than about content, however, and more about the way an idea was expressed than about the significance and validity of the idea.

Education

One of the central preoccupations of the humanists was education and moral behavior. Humanists poured out treatises, often in the form of letters, on the structure and goals of education and the training of rulers. They taught that a life active in the world should be the aim of all educated individuals and that education was not simply for private or religious purposes, but benefited the public good. In one of the earliest systematic programs for the young, Peter Paul Vergerio (1370–1444) wrote Ubertinus, the ruler of Carrara:

For the education of children is a matter of more than private interest; it concerns the State, which indeed regards the right training of the young as, in certain aspects, within its proper sphere. . . .

We call those studies liberal which are worthy of a free man; those studies by which we attain and practice virtue and wisdom; that education which calls forth, trains, and develops those highest gifts of body and mind which ennoble men, and which are rightly judged to rank next in dignity to virtue only.[3]

Part of Vergerio's treatise specifies subjects for the instruction of young men in public life: history teaches virtue by examples from the past, ethics focuses on virtue itself, and rhetoric or public speaking trains for eloquence.

Humanists did not simply talk about education, but also put their ideas into practice. They opened schools and academies in Italian cities and courts in which pupils began with Latin grammar and rhetoric, went on to study Roman history and political philosophy, and then learned Greek in order to study Greek literature and philosophy. These classics, humanists taught, would provide models of how to write clearly, argue effectively, and speak persuasively, important skills for future diplomats, lawyers, military leaders, businessmen, and politicians. Merchants and bankers sent their sons to humanist schools, and ambitious young men from outside Italy flocked to these schools or to schools that opened later in their own cities. Humanist teachers and their ideas spread out from Florence across the Alps and eventually to northern European cities like London and Paris. Gradually humanist education became the basis for intermediate and advanced education for a large share of middle- and upper-class males.

Their emphasis on the public role and reputation of the educated individual made humanists ambivalent in their attitudes about education for women. If the best models of moral behavior and clear thought were to be found in classical authors, why should women be denied access to these? Should the new virtues of self-confidence and individualism be extended to include women? Most humanists thought that a program of study that emphasized eloquence and action was not proper for women, for women were not to engage in public activities. They agreed with Leonard Bruni that "rhetoric in all its forms lies absolutely outside the province of women" and that the "field of religion and morals" should be the primary focus of women's education.[4] The Italian humanist and polymath Leon Battista Alberti (1404–1472), discussing morality in his *On the Family,* stressed that a wife's role should be restricted to the orderliness of the household, food and the serving of meals, the education of children, and the supervision of servants. (Alberti never married, so he never put his ideas into practice in his own household.) Humanists never established schools for girls, though a few women of very high social status did gain a humanist education from private tutors. The ideal Renaissance woman looked a great deal more like her medieval counterpart than did the Renaissance man, leading the historian Joan Kelly to ask, in a now-famous essay, "Did women have a Renaissance?" (Her answer was no.)

No book on education had broader influence than Baldassare Castiglione's *The Courtier* (1528). This treatise sought to train, discipline, and fashion the young man into the courtly ideal, the gentleman. According to Castiglione, who himself was a courtier serving several different rulers, the educated man of the upper class should have a broad background in many academic subjects, and his spiritual and physical as well as intellectual capabilities should be trained. The courtier should have easy familiarity with dance, music, and the arts. Castiglione envisioned a man who could compose a sonnet, wrestle, sing a song and accompany himself on an instrument, ride expertly, solve difficult mathematical problems, and, above all, speak and write eloquently. Castiglione also included discussion of the perfect court lady, who, like the courtier, was to be well-educated and able to play a musical instrument, to paint, and to dance. Physical beauty, delicacy, affability, and modesty were also important qualities for court ladies, however, though these were not expected of gentlemen.

maintain, and increase it. Machiavelli implicitly addresses the question of the citizen's relationship to the state. As a good humanist, he explores the problems of human nature and concludes that human beings are selfish and out to advance their own interests. This pessimistic view of humanity led him to maintain that the prince might have to manipulate the people in any way he finds necessary:

For a man who, in all respects, will carry out only his professions of good, will be apt to be ruined amongst so many who are evil. A prince therefore who desires to maintain himself must learn to be not always good, but to be so or not as necessity may require.[5]

The prince should combine the cunning of a fox with the ferocity of a lion to achieve his goals. Asking rhetorically whether it is better for a ruler to be loved or feared, Machiavelli writes, "It will naturally be answered that it would be desirable to be both the one and the other; but as it is difficult to be both at the same time, it is much more safe to be feared than to be loved, when you have to choose between the two."[6]

Online Study Center **Improve Your Grade**
Primary Source: *The Prince:* Power Politics During the Italian Renaissance

Medieval political theory had derived ultimately from Saint Augustine's view that the state arose as a consequence of Adam's fall and people's propensity to sin. The test of good government was whether it provided justice, law, and order. Political theorists and theologians from Alcuin to Marsiglio of Padua had stressed the way government *ought* to be; they had set high moral and Christian standards for the ruler's conduct.

Machiavelli maintained that the ruler should be concerned not with the way things ought to be but with the way things actually are. The sole test of a "good" government is whether it is effective, whether the ruler increases his power. Machiavelli did not advocate amoral behavior, but he believed that political action cannot be restricted by moral considerations. While amoral action might be the most effective approach in a given situation, he did not argue for generally amoral, rather than moral, behavior. Nevertheless, on the basis of a crude interpretation of *The Prince,* the word *Machiavellian* entered the language as a synonym for the politically devious, corrupt, and crafty, indicating actions in which the end justifies the means. The ultimate significance of Machiavelli rests on two ideas: first, that one permanent social order reflecting God's will cannot be established, and second, that politics has its own laws, based on expediency, not morality.

Raphael: Portrait of Castiglione In this portrait by Raphael, the most sought-after portrait painter of the Renaissance, Castiglione is shown dressed exactly as he advised courtiers to dress, in elegant, but subdued, clothing that would enhance the splendor of the court, but never outshine the ruler. *(Scala/Art Resource, NY)*

In the sixteenth and seventeenth centuries, *The Courtier* was translated into every European language and widely read. It influenced the social mores and patterns of conduct of elite groups in Renaissance and early modern Europe. Echoes of its ideal for women have perhaps had an even longer life.

Political Thought

No Renaissance book on any topic has been more widely read and studied in all the centuries since its publication (1513) than the short political treatise **The Prince** by Niccolò Machiavelli (1469–1527). The subject of *The Prince* is political power: how the ruler should gain,

Secular Spirit

Machiavelli's *The Prince* is often seen as a prime example of another aspect of the Renaissance, secularism. **Secularism** involves a basic concern with the material world instead of with the eternal world of spirit. A secular way of thinking tends to find the ultimate explanation of everything and the final end of human beings within the limits of what the senses can discover. Even though medieval business people ruthlessly pursued profits and medieval monks fought fiercely over property, the dominant ideals focused on the otherworldly, on life after death. Renaissance people often had strong and deep spiritual interests, but in their increasingly secular society, attention was concentrated on the here and now. Wealth allowed greater material pleasures, a more comfortable life, and the leisure time to appreciate and patronize the arts. The rich, social-climbing residents of Venice, Florence, Genoa, and Rome came to see life more as an opportunity to be enjoyed than as a painful pilgrimage to the City of God.

In *On Pleasure,* humanist Lorenzo Valla (1406–1457) defends the pleasures of the senses as the highest good. Scholars praise Valla as a father of modern historical criticism. His study *On the False Donation of Constantine* (1444) demonstrates by careful textual examination that an anonymous eighth-century document supposedly giving the papacy jurisdiction over vast territories in western Europe was a forgery. Medieval people had accepted the Donation of Constantine as a reality, and the proof that it was an invention weakened the foundations of papal claims to temporal authority. Lorenzo Valla's work exemplifies the application of critical scholarship to old and almost sacred writings as well as the new secular spirit of the Renaissance.

The tales in *The Decameron* (1350–1353) by the Florentine Giovanni Boccaccio (1313–1375), which describe ambitious merchants, lecherous friars, and cuckolded husbands, portray a frankly acquisitive, sensual, and worldly society. Although Boccaccio's figures were stock literary characters, *The Decameron* contains none of the "contempt of the world" theme so pervasive in medieval literature. Renaissance writers justified the accumulation and enjoyment of wealth with references to ancient authors.

Nor did church leaders do much to combat the new secular spirit. In the fifteenth and early sixteenth centuries, the papal court and the households of the cardinals were just as worldly as those of great urban patricians. Of course, most of the popes and higher church officials had come from the bourgeois aristocracy. Renaissance popes beautified the city of Rome, patronized artists and men of letters, and expended enormous enthusiasm and

huge sums of money. Pope Julius II (1503–1513) tore down the old Saint Peter's Basilica and began work on the present structure in 1506. Michelangelo's dome for Saint Peter's is still considered his greatest work. Papal interests, which were far removed from spiritual concerns, fostered, rather than discouraged, the new worldly attitude.

Despite their interest in secular matters, however, few people (including Machiavelli) questioned the basic tenets of the Christian religion. Italian humanists and their aristocratic patrons were anti-ascetic, but they were not agnostics or skeptics. The thousands of pious paintings, sculptures, processions, and pilgrimages of the Renaissance period prove that strong religious feeling persisted.

Christian Humanism

The blend of religious and secular concerns of the Italian humanists is even more pronounced among humanists from northern Europe. In the last quarter of the fifteenth century, students from the Low Countries, France, Germany, and England flocked to Italy, imbibed the "new learning," and carried it back to their countries. Northern humanists, often called **Christian humanists,** interpreted Italian ideas about and attitudes toward classical antiquity, individualism, and humanism in terms of their own traditions. They developed a program for broad social reform based on Christian ideals.

Christian humanists were interested in an ethical way of life. To achieve it, they believed that the best elements of classical and Christian cultures should be combined. For example, the classical ideals of calmness, stoical patience, and broad-mindedness should be joined in human conduct with the Christian virtues of love, faith, and hope. Northern humanists also stressed the use of reason, rather than acceptance of dogma, as the foundation for an ethical way of life. Like the Italians, they were impatient with Scholastic philosophy. Christian humanists had profound faith in the power of human intellect to bring about moral and institutional reform. They believed that, although human nature had been corrupted by sin, it was fundamentally good and capable of improvement through education.

The Englishman Thomas More (1478–1535) towered above other figures in sixteenth-century English social and intellectual history. Trained as a lawyer, More lived as a student in the London Charterhouse, a Carthusian monastery. He subsequently married and practiced law but became deeply interested in the classics. His household served as a model of warm Christian family life and as a mecca for foreign and English humanists, who were

Bennozzo Gozzoli: Procession of the Magi, 1461 This segment of a huge fresco covering three walls of a chapel in the Medici Palace in Florence shows members of the Medici family and other contemporary individuals in a procession accompanying the biblical three wise men (*magi* in Italian) as they brought gifts to the infant Jesus. The painting was ordered by Cosimo and Piero de' Medici, who had just finished building the family palace in the center of the city. Reflecting the self-confidence of his patrons, Gozzoli places the elderly Cosimo and Piero at the head of the procession, accompanied by their grooms. The group behind them includes Pope Pius II (in the last row in a red hat that ties under the chin) and the artist (in the second to the last row in a red hat with gold lettering). *(Scala/Art Resource, NY)*

particularly impressed with the linguistic skills of More's daughters, whom he had trained in Latin and Greek. In the career pattern of such Italian humanists as Petrarch, More entered government service under Henry VIII and was sent as ambassador to Flanders. There More found the time to write *Utopia* (1516), which presents a revolutionary view of society.

Utopia, which means "nowhere," describes an ideal socialistic community on an island somewhere off the mainland of the New World. All children receive a good education, primarily in the Greco-Roman classics, and learning does not cease with maturity, for the goal of all education is to develop rational faculties. Adults divide their days between manual labor or business pursuits and intellectual activities.

Because profits from business and property are held in common, there is absolute social equality. The Utopians use gold and silver to make chamber pots and to prevent wars by buying off their enemies. By this casual use of precious metals, More meant to suggest that the basic problems in society are caused by greed. Citizens of Utopia lead an ideal, nearly perfect existence because they live by reason; their institutions are perfect. More punned on the word *utopia,* which he termed "a good place. A good place which is no place."

More's ideas were profoundly original in the sixteenth century. Contrary to the long-prevailing view that vice and violence existed because people were basically corrupt, More maintained that acquisitiveness and private property promoted all sorts of vices and civil disorders. Since society protected private property, society's flawed institutions were responsible for corruption and war. According to More, the key to improvement and reform of the individual was reform of the social institutions that molded the individual. Today this view is so much taken for granted that it is difficult to appreciate how radical More's approach was in the sixteenth century.

Online Study Center **Improve Your Grade**
Primary Source: *Utopia:* A Question over Diplomatic Advice

Better known by contemporaries than Thomas More was the Dutch humanist Desiderius Erasmus (1466?–1536) of Rotterdam. Orphaned as a small boy, Erasmus was forced to enter a monastery. Although he hated the monastic life, he developed an excellent knowledge of the Latin language and a deep appreciation for the Latin classics. During a visit to England in 1499, Erasmus met the scholar John Colet, who decisively influenced his life's work: the application of the best humanistic learning to the study and explanation of the Bible. As a mature scholar with an international reputation stretching from Cracow to London, a fame that rested largely on his exceptional knowledge of Greek, Erasmus could boast with truth, "I brought it about that humanism, which among the Italians . . . savored of nothing but pure paganism, began nobly to celebrate Christ."[7]

Erasmus's long list of publications includes *The Education of a Christian Prince* (1504), a book combining idealistic and practical suggestions for the formation of a ruler's character through the careful study of Plutarch, Aristotle, Cicero, and Plato; *The Praise of Folly* (1509), a satire of worldly wisdom and a plea for the simple and spontaneous Christian faith of children; and, most important, a critical edition of the Greek New Testament (1516). In the preface to the New Testament, Erasmus explained the purpose of his great work:

For I utterly dissent from those who are unwilling that the sacred Scriptures should be read by the unlearned translated into their vulgar tongue, as though Christ had taught such subtleties that they can scarcely be understood even by a few theologians. . . . Christ wished his mysteries to be published as openly as possible. I wish that even the weakest woman should read the Gospel—should read the epistles of Paul. And I wish these were translated into all languages, so that they might be read and understood, not only by Scots and Irishmen, but also by Turks and Saracens.[8]

Two fundamental themes run through all of Erasmus's work. First, education is the means to reform, the key to moral and intellectual improvement. The core of education ought to be study of the Bible and the classics. (See the feature "Listening to the Past: An Age of Gold" on pages 442–443.) Second, the essence of Erasmus's thought is, in his own phrase, "the philosophy of Christ." By this Erasmus meant that Christianity is an inner attitude of the heart or spirit. Christianity is not formalism, special ceremonies, or law; Christianity is Christ—his life and what he said and did, not what theologians have written. The Sermon on the Mount, for Erasmus, expresses the heart of the Christian message.

The Printed Word

The fourteenth-century humanist Petrarch and the sixteenth-century humanist Erasmus had similar ideas about many things, but the immediate impact of their ideas was very different because of one thing: the printing press with movable metal type. The ideas of Petrarch were spread the same way that ideas had been for centuries, from person to person by hand copying. The ideas

of Erasmus were spread through print, in which hundreds or thousands of identical copies could be made in a short time. Erasmus actually spent his later years living with printer friends, checking his own and others' work for errors as well as translating and writing. Print shops were gathering places for those interested in new ideas. Though printers were trained through apprenticeships just like blacksmiths or butchers, they had connections to the world of politics, art, and scholarship that other craftsmen did not.

Printing with movable metal type developed in Germany in the middle of the fifteenth century as a combination of existing technologies. Several metal-smiths, most prominently Johan Gutenberg, recognized that the metal stamps used to mark signs on jewelry could be covered with ink and used to mark symbols onto a surface, in the same way that other craftsmen were using carved wood stamps. These craftsmen carved a whole page in wood, inked it, and pressed it on paper, and then assembled the paper into a book called a *block-book*. Block printing had been used in China and Korea since at least the eighth century and had spread to Europe by the thirteenth. The carvings could be used only a few dozen times before they became ink-soaked and unreadable, however; and since each word, phrase, or picture was on a separate block, this method of reproduction was extraordinarily expensive and time-consuming.

Using molds as smiths did for tableware or other metal items, Gutenberg and his assistants made stamps—later called *type*—for every letter of the alphabet and built racks that held the type in rows. This type could be rearranged for every page and so used over and over; it could also be melted down and remade once it became flattened through repeated use. They experimented with different types of ink, settling on a type of artists' ink, and with different types of presses, adapting the presses used to press grapes for wine, stamp patterns on fabric, or make block-books.

Books were printed on paper, and by the middle of the fifteenth century, acquiring paper was no problem. The knowledge of paper manufacture had originated in China, and the Arabs introduced it to the West in the twelfth century. Europeans quickly learned that durable paper was far less expensive than the vellum (calfskin) and parchment (sheepskin) on which medieval scribes had relied for centuries. By the fifteenth century the increase in urban literacy, the development of primary schools, and the opening of more universities had created an expanding market for reading materials of all types (see pages 400–401). When Gutenberg developed what he saw at first as a faster way to copy, professional copyists writing by hand

The Print Shop This sixteenth-century engraving captures the busy world of a print shop: On the left, men set pieces of type, and an individual wearing glasses checks a copy. At the rear, another applies ink to the type, while a man carries in fresh paper on his head. At the right, the master printer operates the press, while a boy removes the printed pages and sets them to dry. The well-dressed figure in the right foreground may be the patron checking to see whether his job is done. *(Giraudon/Art Resource, NY)*

and block-book makers, along with monks and nuns in monasteries, were already churning out reading materials on paper as fast as they could for the growing number of people who could read.

Gutenberg's invention involved no special secret technology or materials, and he was not the only one to recognize the huge market for books. Other craftsmen made their own type, built their own presses, and bought their own paper, setting themselves up in business in the cities of Germany, Switzerland, and the Netherlands, and then in Italy, England, and France. By 1480 about 110 cities in Europe had presses, with Venice employing the most and producing about one-eighth of all printed books in Europe. Printing continued to spread to Spain and Scandinavia, and by 1500, roughly fifty years after the first printed books, more than 200 cities and towns in Europe had presses (see Map 13.2). Historians estimate that somewhere between 8 million and 20 million books were printed in Europe before 1500, many more than the number of books produced in all of Western history up to that point.

The effects of the invention of movable-type printing were not felt overnight. Nevertheless, within a half century of the publication of Gutenberg's Bible of 1456, movable type had brought about radical changes. Printing transformed both the private and the public lives of Europeans. It gave hundreds or even thousands of people identical books, so that they could more easily discuss the ideas that the books contained with one another in person or through letters. Printed materials reached an invisible public, allowing silent individuals to join causes and groups of individuals widely separated by geography to form a common identity; this new group consciousness could compete with older, localized loyalties.

Government and church leaders both used and worried about printing. They printed laws, declarations of war, battle accounts, and propaganda, and they also attempted to censor books and authors whose ideas they thought were wrong. Officials developed lists of prohibited books and authors, enforcing their prohibitions by confiscating books, arresting printers and booksellers, or destroying the presses of printers who disobeyed. None of this was very effective, and books were printed secretly, with fake title pages, authors, and places of publication, and smuggled all over Europe.

Printing also stimulated the literacy of laypeople and eventually came to have a deep effect on their private lives. Although most of the earliest books and pamphlets dealt with religious subjects, students, merchants, and upper- and middle-class people sought books on all subjects, and printers produced anything that would sell. They produced law codes bound in fancy leather bindings

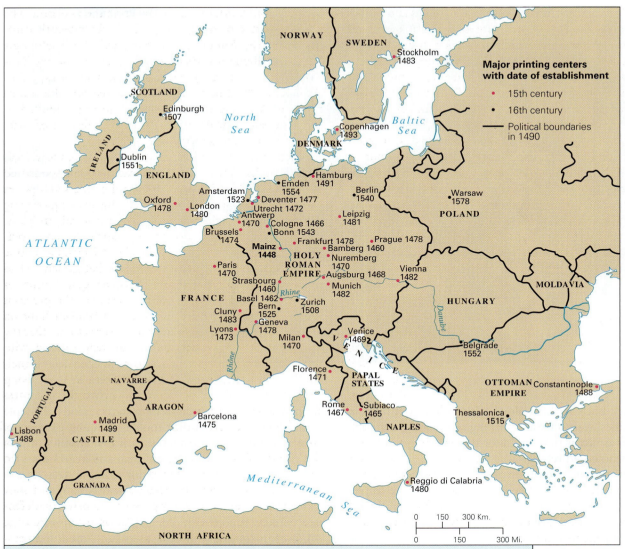

Mapping the Past

MAP 13.2 The Growth of Printing in Europe The speed with which artisans spread printing technology across Europe provides strong evidence for the existing market in reading material. Presses in the Ottoman Empire were first established by Jewish immigrants who printed works in Hebrew, Greek, and Spanish. Use this map and those in other chapters to answer the following questions: **1** What part of Europe had the greatest number of printing presses by 1550? Why might this be? **2** Printing was developed in response to a market for reading materials. Use Maps 11.2 and 11.3 (pages 340 and 346) to help explain why printing spread the way it did. **3** Many historians also see printing as an important factor in the spread of the Protestant Reformation. Use Map 14.2 (page 468) to test this assertion.

Online Study Center **Improve Your Grade** Interactive Map: The Growth of Printing

in matching sets for lawyers; medical manuals and guides to healing herbs for doctors, surgeons, pharmacists, and midwives; grammars and dictionaries for students, often in small sizes with paper covers so that they were cheap and could be carried to class; and books of prayers and sermons for members of the clergy. They printed historical romances, biographies, and how-to manuals, such as cookbooks and books of home remedies. They discovered that illustrations increased a book's sales, so published both history and pornography full of woodcuts and engravings. Single-page broadsides and flysheets allowed great public festivals, religious ceremonies, political events, and "wonders" such as comets or two-headed calves to be experienced vicariously by the stay-at-home. Since books and other printed materials were read aloud to illiterate listeners, print bridged the gap between the written and oral cultures.

Art and the Artist

No feature of the Renaissance evokes greater admiration than its artistic masterpieces. The 1400s (*quattrocento*) and 1500s (*cinquecento*) bore witness to dazzling creativity in painting, architecture, and sculpture. In all the arts, the city of Florence led the way. According to Vasari, the painter Perugino once asked why it was in Florence and not elsewhere that men achieved perfection in the arts. The first answer he received was, "There were so many good critics there, for the air of the city makes men quick and perceptive and impatient of mediocrity."[9] But Florence was not the only artistic center, for Rome and Venice also became important, and northern Europeans perfected their own styles.

• *How did changes in art both reflect and shape new ideas?*

Art and Power

In early Renaissance Italy, art manifested corporate power. Powerful urban groups such as guilds or religious confraternities commissioned works of art. The Florentine cloth merchants, for example, delegated Filippo Brunelleschi to build the magnificent dome on the cathedral of Florence and selected Lorenzo Ghiberti to design the bronze doors of the Baptistery. These works represented the merchants' dominant influence in the community. Corporate patronage was also reflected in the Florentine government's decision to hire Michelangelo to create the

sculpture of David, the great Hebrew hero and king. The subject matter of art through the early fifteenth century, as in the Middle Ages, remained overwhelmingly religious. Religious themes appeared in all media—woodcarvings, painted frescoes, stone sculptures, paintings. As in the Middle Ages, art served an educational purpose. A religious picture or statue was intended to spread a particular doctrine, act as a profession of faith, or recall sinners to a moral way of living.

Increasingly in the later fifteenth century, individuals and oligarchs, rather than corporate groups, sponsored works of art. Patrician merchants and bankers and popes and princes supported the arts as a means of glorifying themselves and their families, becoming artistic **patrons.** Vast sums were spent on family chapels, frescoes, religious panels, and tombs. Writing about 1470, Florentine oligarch Lorenzo de' Medici declared that his family had spent the astronomical sum of 663,755 gold florins for artistic and architectural commissions over the previous thirty-five years. Yet "I think it casts a brilliant light on our estate [public reputation] and it seems to me that the monies were well spent and I am very pleased with this."[10] Powerful men wanted to exalt themselves, their families, and their offices. A magnificent style of living enriched by works of art served to prove the greatness and the power of the despot or oligarch.

In addition to power, art reveals changing patterns of consumption in Renaissance Italy. In the rural world of the Middle Ages, society had been organized for war. Men of wealth spent their money on military gear—swords, armor, horses, crenelated castles, towers, family compounds—all of which represent offensive or defensive warfare. As Italian nobles settled in towns (see page 333), they adjusted to an urban culture. Rather than employing knights for warfare, cities hired mercenaries. Expenditure on military hardware declined. For the rich merchant or the noble recently arrived from the countryside, the urban palace represented the greatest outlay of cash. It was his chief luxury, and although a private dwelling, the palace implied grandeur. Within the palace, the merchant-prince's chamber, or bedroom, where he slept and received his intimate guests, was the most important room. In the fourteenth and fifteenth centuries a large, intricately carved wooden bed, a chest, and perhaps a bench served as its sole decorations. The chest held the master's most precious goods—silver, tapestries, jewelry, clothing. Other rooms, even in palaces of fifteen to twenty rooms, were sparsely furnished. As the fifteenth century advanced and wealth increased, the other rooms were gradually furnished with carved chests, tables,

Botticelli: Primavera, or Spring (ca 1482)   Framed by a grove of orange trees, Venus, goddess of love, is flanked on her left by Flora, goddess of flowers and fertility, and on her right by the Three Graces, goddesses of banquets, dance, and social occasions. Above, Venus's son Cupid, the god of love, shoots darts of desire, while at the far right the wind god Zephyrus chases the nymph Chloris. The entire scene rests on classical mythology, though some art historians claim that Venus is an allegory for the Virgin Mary. Botticelli captured the ideal for female beauty in the Renaissance: slender, with pale skin, a high forehead, red-blond hair, and sloping shoulders. *(Digital image © The Museum of Modern Art/Licensed by Scala/Art Resource, NY)*

benches, chairs, tapestries for the walls, paintings (an innovation), and sculptural decorations, and a private chapel was added. Wealthy individuals and families ordered gold dishes, embroidered tablecloths, and paintings of all sizes as art became a means of displaying wealth. By the late sixteenth century the Strozzi banking family of Florence spent more on household goods than on anything else except food; the value of those furnishings was three times that of their silver and jewelry.

After the palace itself, the private chapel within the palace symbolized the largest expenditure. Equipped with the ecclesiastical furniture—tabernacles, chalices, thuribles, and other liturgical utensils—and decorated with religious scenes, the chapel served as the center of the household's religious life and its cult of remembrance of the dead. In fifteenth-century Florence, only the Medici had a private chapel, but by the late sixteenth century most wealthy Florentine families had private chapels.

Subjects and Style

The content and style of Renaissance art were often different from those of the Middle Ages. The individual portrait emerged as a distinct artistic genre. In the fifteenth century members of the newly rich middle class often had themselves painted in scenes of romantic chivalry or courtly society. Rather than reflecting a spiritual ideal, as medieval painting and sculpture tended to do, Renaissance portraits showed human ideals, often portrayed in a more realistic style. The Florentine painter Giotto (1276–1337) led the way in the use of realism; his treatment of the human body and face replaced the formal stiffness and artificiality that had long characterized representation of the human body. Piero della Francesca (1420–1492) and Andrea Mantegna (1430/31–1506) seem to have pioneered *perspective* in painting, the linear representation of distance and space on a flat surface.

As the fifteenth century advanced, the subject matter of art in Italy became steadily more secular. The study of classical texts brought deeper understanding of ancient ideas. Classical themes and motifs, such as the lives and loves of pagan gods and goddesses, figured increasingly in painting and sculpture. Religious topics, such as the Annunciation of the Virgin and the Nativity, remained popular among both patrons and artists, but frequently the patron had himself and his family portrayed. People were conscious of their physical uniqueness and wanted their individuality immortalized.

The sculptor Donatello (1386–1466) probably exerted the greatest influence of any Florentine artist before Michelangelo. His many statues express an appreciation of the incredible variety of human nature. Whereas medieval artists had depicted the nude human body in a spiritualized and moralizing context only, Donatello revived the classical figure, with its balance and self-awareness. The short-lived Florentine Masaccio (1401–1428), sometimes called the father of modern painting, inspired a new style characterized by great realism, narrative power, and remarkably effective use of light and dark. *The Last Supper* by Leonardo da Vinci (1452–1519), with its stress on the tension between Christ and the disciples, is an incredibly subtle psychological interpretation.

Andrea Mantegna: Adoration of the Magi (ca 1495–1505) Applying his study of ancient Roman relief sculpture, Mantegna painted for the private devotion of the Gonzaga family of Mantua this scene of the three wise men coming to visit the infant Christ. The three wise men, depicted as kings, represent the entire world—that is, the three continents known to medieval Europeans: Europe, Asia, and Africa. They also symbolize the three stages of life: youth, maturity, and old age. Here Melchior, the oldest, his large cranium symbolizing wisdom, personifies Europe. He offers gold in a Chinese porcelain cup from the Ming Dynasty. Balthazar, with an olive complexion and dark beard, stands for Asia and maturity. He presents frankincense in a stunning vessel of Turkish tombac ware. Caspar, representing Africa and youth, gives myrrh in an urn of striped marble. The three wise men were a common subject in Renaissance art (compare the illustration on page 417), as they allowed artists to show exotic figures and sumptuous clothing. (© *The J. Paul Getty Museum, Los Angeles. Mantegna, Andrea.* Adoration of the Magi, *ca 1495–1505, distemper on linen, 54.6 × 70.7 cm [85.PA.417]*)

As humanists looked to the classical past for inspiration in their writing, so did architects in constructing buildings. The Florentine architect Filippo Brunelleschi (1377–1446) designed a new hospital for orphans and foundlings set up by the silk-workers' guild in Florence, in which all proportions—of the windows, height, floor plan, and covered walkway with a series of rounded arches—were carefully thought out to achieve a sense of balance and harmony. Brunelleschi later turned his talents to designing and constructing a dome for the Florence Cathedral, based to some degree on Roman domes, but higher and more graceful.

Art produced in northern Europe in the fourteenth and fifteenth centuries tended to be more religious in orientation than that produced in Italy. Some Flemish painters, notably Rogier van der Weyden (1399/1400–1464) and Jan van Eyck (1366–1441), were considered the artistic equals of Italian painters and were much admired in Italy. Van Eyck, one of the earliest artists to use oil-based paints successfully, shows the Flemish love for detail in paintings such as *Ghent Altarpiece* and the portrait *Giovanni Arnolfini and His Bride;* the effect is great realism and remarkable attention to human personality. Northern architecture was little influenced by the classical revival so obvious in Renaissance Italy.

In the fifteenth century Florence was the center of the new art in Italy, but in the early sixteenth century this shifted to Rome, where wealthy cardinals and popes wanted visual expression of the church's and their own families' power and piety. Michelangelo, a Florentine who had spent his young adulthood at the court of Lorenzo de' Medici, went to Rome about 1500 and began the series of statues, paintings, and architectural projects from which he gained an international reputation: the Pieta, Moses, the redesigning of the Capitoline Hill in central Rome, and, most famously, the ceiling and altar wall of the Sistine Chapel. Pope Julius II, who commissioned the Sistine Chapel, demanded that Michelangelo work as fast as he could and frequently visited the artist at his work with suggestions and criticisms. Michelangelo complained in person and by letter about the pope's meddling, but his reputation did not match the

Rogier van der Weyden: Deposition Taking as his subject the suffering and death of Jesus, a popular theme of Netherlandish piety, van der Weyden describes (in an inverted T) Christ's descent from the cross, surrounded by nine sorrowing figures. An appreciation of human anatomy, the rich fabrics of the clothes, and the pierced and bloody hands of Jesus were all intended to touch the viewers' emotions. *(Museo del Prado/Scala/Art Resource, NY)*

power of the pope, and he kept working. Raphael Sanzio (1483–1520), another Florentine, got the commission for frescoes in the papal apartments, and in his relatively short life he painted hundreds of portraits and devotional images, becoming the most sought-after artist in Europe. Raphael also oversaw a large workshop with many collaborators and apprentices—who assisted on the less difficult sections of some paintings—and wrote treatises on his philosophy of art in which he emphasized the importance of imitating nature and developing an orderly sequence of design and proportion.

Venice became another artistic center in the sixteenth century. Titian (1490–1576) produced portraits, religious subjects, and mythological scenes, developing techniques of painting in oil without doing elaborate drawings first, which speeded up the process and pleased patrons eager to display their acquisition. Titian and other sixteenth-century painters developed an artistic style known in English as "mannerism" (from *maniera* or "style" in Italian) in which artists sometimes distorted figures, exaggerated musculature, and heightened color to express emotion and drama more intently. (This is the style in which Michelangelo painted the Last Judgment in the Sistine Chapel, shown in the frontispiece to this chapter.) Until the twentieth century, "mannerism" was a negative term; critics and art historians preferred the more naturalistic and elegant style of Botticelli and Raphael, but modern critics and artists have appreciated its sense of movement, vivid colors, and passionate expressions.

Patronage and Creativity

Artists in the Renaissance did not produce unsolicited pictures or statues for the general public, but usually worked on commission from patrons. A patron could be an individual, a group such as a guild, a convent, a ruler, or a city council. Patrons varied in their level of involvement as a work progressed; some simply ordered a specific subject or scene, while others oversaw the work of the artist or architect very closely, suggesting themes and styles and demanding changes while the work was in progress.

The right patrons rewarded certain artists very well. Lorenzo Ghiberti's salary of 200 florins a year compared favorably with that of the head of the city government, who earned 500 florins. Moreover, at a time when a person could live in a princely fashion on 300 ducats a year, Leonardo da Vinci was making 2,000 ducats annually.

Renaissance society respected the distinguished artist. In 1537 the prolific letter writer, humanist, and satirizer of princes Pietro Aretino (1492–1556) wrote to Michelangelo while he was painting *The Last Judgment* behind the altar in the Sistine Chapel:

To the Divine Michelangelo: Sir, just as it is disgraceful and sinful to be unmindful of God so it is reprehensible and dishonourable for any man of discerning judgment not to honour you as a brilliant and venerable artist whom the very stars use as a target at which to shoot the rival arrows of their favour. . . . It is surely my duty to honour you with this salutation, since the world has many kings but only one Michelangelo.[11]

Aretino was not alone in addressing Michelangelo as "divine," for the word was widely applied to him, and to a few other artists as well. (See the feature "Individuals in Society: Leonardo da Vinci.") Vasari described a number of painters, sculptors, and architects, in fact, as "rare men of genius." This adulation of the artist has led many historians to view the Renaissance as the beginning of the concept of the artist as genius. In the Middle Ages people believed that only God created, albeit through individuals; the medieval conception recognized no particular value in artistic originality. Renaissance artists and humanists came to think that a work of art was the deliberate creation of a unique personality who transcended traditions, rules, and theories. A genius had a peculiar gift, which ordinary laws should not inhibit.

Renaissance artists were not only aware of their creative power, but they also boasted about it. Describing his victory over five others, including Brunelleschi, in the competition to design the bronze doors of Florence's Baptistery, Ghiberti exulted, "The palm of victory was conceded to me by all the experts and by all my fellow-competitors. By universal consent and without a single exception the glory was conceded to me."[12] Some medieval painters and sculptors had signed their works; Renaissance artists almost universally did so, and many of them incorporated self-portraits, usually as bystanders, in their paintings.

It is important not to overemphasize the Renaissance notion of genius. As certain artists became popular and well-known, they could assert their own artistic styles and pay less attention to the wishes of patrons, but even major artists like Raphael generally worked according to the patron's specific guidelines. Whether in Italy or northern Europe, most Renaissance artists trained in the workshops of older artists; Botticelli, Raphael, Titian, and at times even Michelangelo were known for their large, well-run, and prolific workshops. Though they might be "men of genius," artists were still expected to

Gentile and Giovanni Bellini: Saint Mark Preaching in Alexandria (1504–1507)   The Venetian artists Gentile and Giovanni Bellini combine figures and architecture in this painting of Saint Mark, the patron saint of Venice. Saint Mark (on the platform) is wearing ancient Roman dress. Behind him are male citizens of Venice in sixteenth-century Italian garb. In front of him are Ottoman Muslim men in turbans, Muslim women in veils, and various other figures. The buildings in the background are not those of first-century Alexandria (where Saint Mark is reported to have preached) but of Venice and Constantinople in the sixteenth century. The setting is made even more fanciful with a camel and a giraffe in the background. The painting glorifies cosmopolitan Venice's patron saint, a more important feature for the Venetian patron who ordered it than was historical accuracy. Its clear colors and effective perspective and the individuality of the many faces make this a fine example of Renaissance art. *(Scala/Art Resource, NY)*

be well-trained in proper artistic techniques and stylistic conventions, for the notion that artistic genius could show up in the work of an untrained artist did not emerge until the twentieth century. Beginning artists spent years copying drawings and paintings, learning how to prepare paint and other artistic materials, and, by the sixteenth century, reading books about design and composition. Younger artists gathered together in the evenings for further drawing practice; by the later sixteenth century some of these informal groups had turned into more formal artistic "academies," the first of which was begun in 1563 in Florence by Vasari under the patronage of the Medicis.

As Vasari's phrase indicates, the notion of artistic genius that developed in the Renaissance was gendered. All the most famous and most prolific Renaissance artists were male; there are no female architects whose names are known and only one female sculptor. The types of art in which more women were active, such as textiles, needlework, and painting on porcelain, were not re-

garded as "major arts," but only as "minor" or "decorative" arts. (The division between "major" and "minor" arts begun in the Renaissance continues to influence the way museums and collections are organized today.) Like painting, embroidery changed in the Renaissance to become more classical in its subject matter, naturalistic, and visually complex. Embroiderers were not trained to view their work as products of individual genius, however, so they rarely included their names on their works, and there is no way to discover who they were.

Several women did become well-known as painters in their day. Stylistically, their works are different from one another, but their careers show many similarities. The majority of female painters were the daughters of painters or of minor noblemen with ties to artistic circles. Many were eldest daughters or came from families in which there were no sons, so their fathers took unusual interest in their careers. Many women began their careers before they were twenty and produced far fewer paintings after they married, or stopped painting entirely. Women were

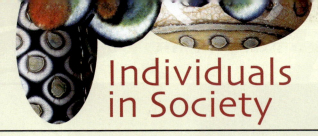

Individuals in Society

Leonardo da Vinci

What makes a genius? An infinite capacity for taking pains? A deep curiosity about an extensive variety of subjects? A divine spark as manifested by talents that far exceed the norm? Or is it just "one percent inspiration and ninety-nine percent perspiration," as Thomas Edison said? To most observers, Leonardo da Vinci was one of the greatest geniuses in the history of the Western world. In fact, Leonardo was one of the individuals that the Renaissance label "genius" was designed to describe: a special kind of human being with exceptional creative powers.

Leonardo (who, despite the title of a recent bestseller, is always called by his first name) was born in Vinci, near Florence, the illegitimate son of Caterina, a local peasant girl, and Ser Piero da Vinci, a notary public. Caterina later married another native of Vinci. When Ser Piero's marriage to Donna Albrussia produced no children, he and his wife took in Leonardo. Ser Piero secured Leonardo's apprenticeship with the painter and sculptor Andrea del Verrocchio in Florence. In 1472, when Leonardo was just twenty years old, he was listed as a master in Florence's "Company of Artists."

Leonardo's most famous portrait, *Mona Lisa,* shows a woman with an enigmatic smile that Giorgio Vasari described as "so pleasing that it seemed divine rather than human." The portrait, probably of the young wife of a rich Florentine merchant (her exact identity is hotly debated), may actually be the best-known painting in the history of art. One of its competitors in that designation would be another work of Leonardo's, *The Last Supper,* which has been called "the most revered painting in the world."

Leonardo's reputation as a genius does not rest simply on his paintings, however, which are actually few in number, but rather on the breadth of his abilities and interests. In these, he is often understood to be the first "Renaissance man," a phrase we still use for a multi-talented individual. He wanted to reproduce what the eye can see, and he drew everything he saw around him, including executed criminals hanging on gallows as well as the beauties of nature. Trying to understand how the human body worked, Leonardo studied live and dead bodies, doing autopsies and dissections to investigate muscles and circulation. He carefully analyzed the effects of light, and he experimented with perspective.

Leonardo used his drawings as the basis for his paintings and also as a tool of scientific investigation.

He drew plans for hundreds of inventions, many of which would become reality centuries later, such as the helicopter, tank, machine gun, and parachute. He was hired by one of the powerful new rulers in Italy, Duke Ludovico Sforza of Milan, to design weapons, fortresses, and water systems, as well as to produce works of art. Leonardo left Milan when Sforza was overthrown in war and spent the last years of his life painting, drawing, and designing for the pope and the French king.

Leonardo da Vinci, Lady with an Ermine. *The enigmatic smile and smoky quality of this portrait can be found in many of Leonardo's works.*
(Czartoryski Museum, Krakow/The Bridgeman Art Library)

Leonardo experimented with new materials for painting and sculpture, some of which worked and some of which did not. The experimental method he used to paint *The Last Supper* caused the picture to deteriorate rapidly, and it began to flake off the wall as soon as it was finished. Leonardo actually regarded it as never quite completed, for he could not find a model for the face of Christ that would evoke the spiritual depth he felt it deserved. His gigantic equestrian statue in honor of Ludovico's father, Duke Francesco Sforza, was never made and the clay model collapsed. He planned to write books on many subjects but never finished any of them, leaving only notebooks. Leonardo once said that "a painter is not admirable unless he is universal." The patrons who supported him—and he was supported very well—perhaps wished that his inspirations would have been a bit less universal in scope, or at least accompanied by more perspiration.

Questions for Analysis

1. In what ways do the notion of a "genius" and of a "Renaissance man" both support and contradict one another? Which better fits Leonardo?
2. Has the idea of artistic genius changed since the Renaissance? How?

Sources: Giorgio Vasari, *Lives of the Artists,* vol. 1, trans. G. Bull (London: Penguin Books, 1965); S. B. Nuland, *Leonardo da Vinci* (New York: Lipper/Viking, 2000).

Online Study Center **Improve Your Grade**
Going Beyond Individuals in Society

Artemisia Gentileschi: Esther Before Ahasuerus (ca 1630)   In this oil painting, Gentileschi shows an Old Testament scene of the Jewish woman Esther who saved her people from being killed by her husband, King Ahasuerus. This deliverance is celebrated in the Jewish holiday of Purim. Both figures are in the elaborate dress worn in Renaissance courts. Typical of a female painter, Artemisia Gentileschi was trained by her father. She mastered the dramatic style favored in the early seventeenth century and became known especially for her portraits of strong biblical and mythological heroines. *(Image copyright © The Metropolitan Museum of Art/Art Resource, NY)*

not allowed to study the male nude, which was viewed as essential if one wanted to paint large history paintings with many figures. Women could also not learn the technique of fresco, in which colors are applied directly to wet plaster walls, because such works had to be done out in public, which was judged inappropriate for women. Joining a group of male artists for informal practice was also seen as improper, and the artistic academies that were established were for men only. Like universities, humanist academies, and most craft guild shops, artistic workshops were male-only settings in which men of different ages came together for training and created bonds of friendship, influence, patronage, and sometimes intimacy.

Women were not alone in being excluded from the institutions of Renaissance culture. Though a few "rare men of genius" such as Leonardo or Michelangelo emerged from artisanal backgrounds, most scholars and artists came from families with at least some money. Renaissance culture did not influence the lives of most people in cities and did not affect life in the villages at all. A small, highly educated minority of literary humanists and artists created the culture of and for an exclusive elite. The Renaissance maintained, or indeed enhanced, a gulf between the learned minority and the uneducated multitude that has survived for many centuries.

Social Hierarchies

The division between educated and uneducated people was only one of many social hierarchies evident in the Renaissance. Every society has social hierarchies; in ancient Rome, for example, there were patricians and plebeians (see page 128). Such hierarchies are to some degree descriptions of social reality, but they are also idealizations—that is, they describe how people *imagined* their society to be, without all the messy reality of social-climbing plebeians or groups that did not fit the standard categories. Social hierarchies in the Renaissance built on those of the Middle Ages but also developed new features that contributed to modern social hierarchies.

• *What were the key social hierarchies in Renaissance Europe, and how did ideas about hierarchy shape people's lives?*

Race

Renaissance ideas about what we would term "race" were closely linked with those about ethnicity and "blood" discussed in Chapter 12 (see page 399). In law codes, histories, and other writings, ethnic and religious groups were referred to as *gens* or *natio*, words generally translated as "people" or "nation": the German nation, the Irish people, the Jewish people, and so on. What exactly *made* them German or Irish or Jewish was viewed as a mixture of language, traditions, and customs, but these were also conceptualized as "blood," and people were described as having French blood or Jewish blood. The word *race* was also used in several European languages in the Renaissance to describe such groupings—the French race, the Spanish race—or other social groups, such as "the race of learned gentlemen" or "the race of mankind." It was also used to refer to family line, kindred, or lineage. With all these words—nation, people, blood, race—people did not clearly distinguish between things that we would regard as biologically heritable, such as hair color, and as socially constructed, such as being well-dressed. (The boundaries between these two are not always clear today, of course, as arguments about certain groups being "naturally" gifted musicians or mathematicians demonstrate.)

The contemporary meaning of *race* as a system dividing people into very large groups by skin color and other physical characteristics originated in the eighteenth century, when European natural scientists sought to develop one single system that would explain human differences. They first differentiated "races" by continent of origin—Americanus, Europaeus, Asiaticus, and Africanus—and then by somewhat different geographical areas. The word *Caucasian* was first used by the German anatomist and naturalist Johann Friedrich Blumenbach (1752–1840) to describe light-skinned people of Europe and western Asia because he thought that the Caucasus Mountains on the border between Russia and Georgia

were most likely their original home. He thought that they were the first humans, and the most attractive. (His judgment about Caucasian attractiveness came through studying a large collection of skulls and measuring all other skulls against one from Georgia that he judged to be "the most beautiful form of the skull.") This meaning of *race* has had a long life, though biologists and anthropologists today do not use it, as it has no scientific meaning or explanatory value. Renaissance people thus did not use *race* the way we do, but they did make distinctions based on skin color. These distinctions were interwoven with ethnic, national, and religious distinctions, and they provide some of the background for later conceptualizations of race.

Ever since the time of the Roman republic, a few black Africans had lived in western Europe. They had come, along with white slaves, as the spoils of war. Even after the collapse of the Roman Empire, Muslim and Christian merchants continued to import them. Unstable political conditions in many parts of Africa enabled enterprising merchants to seize people and sell them into slavery. Local authorities afforded them no protection. Long tradition, moreover, sanctioned the practice of slavery. The evidence of medieval art attests to the continued presence of Africans in Europe throughout the Middle Ages and to Europeans' awareness of them.

Beginning in the fifteenth century sizable numbers of black slaves entered Europe. Portuguese explorers imported perhaps a thousand a year and sold them at the markets of Seville, Barcelona, Marseilles, and Genoa. In the late fifteenth century this flow increased, with thousands of people leaving the West African coast. By 1530 between four thousand and five thousand were being sold to the Portuguese each year. By the mid-sixteenth century blacks, slave and free, constituted about 10 percent of the population of the Portuguese cities of Lisbon and Évora; other cities had smaller percentages. In all, blacks made up roughly 3 percent of the Portuguese population. In the Iberian Peninsula, African slaves intermingled with the people they lived among and sometimes intermarried. Cities such as Lisbon had significant numbers of people of mixed African and European descent.

Although blacks were concentrated in the Iberian Peninsula, there must have been some Africans in northern Europe as well. In the 1580s, for example, Queen Elizabeth I of England complained that there were too many "blackamoores" competing with needy English people for places as domestic servants.[13] Black servants were much sought after; the medieval interest in curiosities, the exotic, and the marvelous continued in the

Carpaccio: Black Laborers on the Venetian Docks (detail)   Enslaved and free blacks, besides working as gondoliers on the Venetian canals, served on the docks: here, seven black men careen—clean, caulk, and repair—a ship. Carpaccio's reputation as one of Venice's outstanding painters rests on his eye for details of everyday life. *(Gallerie dell'Accademia, Venice/Scala/Art Resource, NY)*

Renaissance. Italian aristocrats had their portraits painted with their black pageboys to indicate their wealth (see the illustration on page 417, in which Gozzoli's depiction of Cosimo de' Medici shows him with a black groom). Blacks were so greatly in demand at the Renaissance courts of northern Italy, in fact, that the Venetians defied papal threats of excommunication to secure them. In the late fifteenth century Isabella, the wife of Gian Galazzo Sforza, took pride in the fact that she owned ten blacks, seven of them females. A black lady's maid was both a curiosity and a symbol of wealth. In 1491 Isabella of Este, duchess of Mantua, instructed her agent to secure a black girl between four and eight years old, "shapely and as black as possible." The duchess saw the child as a source of entertainment: "We shall make her very happy and shall have great fun with her." She hoped the girl would become "the best buffoon in the world,"[14] as the cruel ancient practice of a noble household's retaining a professional "fool" for the family's amusement persisted through the Renaissance—and down to the twentieth century. Tradition, stretching back at least as far as the thirteenth century, connected blacks with music and dance. In Renaissance Spain and Italy, blacks performed as dancers, as actors and actresses in courtly

dramas, and as musicians, sometimes making up full orchestras.

Africans were not simply amusements at court. Adult black slaves served as maids, valets, and domestic servants in Spanish and Italian cities. The Venetians employed blacks—slave and free—as gondoliers and stevedores on the docks. In Portugal, kings, nobles, laborers, monasteries and convents, and prostitutes owned slaves. Slaves supplemented the labor force in virtually all occupations—as agricultural laborers, as craftsmen, and as seamen on ships going to Lisbon and Africa. Agriculture in Europe did not involve large plantations, so large-scale agricultural slavery did not develop there; African slaves formed the primary workforce on the sugar plantations set up by Europeans on the Atlantic islands in the late fifteenth century, however (see page 505).

Until the voyages down the African coast in the late fifteenth century, Europeans had little concrete knowledge of Africans and their cultures. What Europeans did know was based on biblical accounts. The European attitude toward Africans was ambivalent. On the one hand, Europeans perceived Africa as a remote place, the home of strange people isolated by heresy and Islam from superior European civilization. Africans' contact, even as slaves, with Christian Europeans could only "improve" the blacks. Theologians taught that God was light and linked black skin color with the hostile forces of the underworld: evil, sin, and the Devil. Thus the Devil was commonly represented as a black man in medieval and early Renaissance art (see the illustration on page 396). On the other hand, blackness possessed certain positive qualities. It symbolized the emptiness of worldly goods and the humility of the monastic way of life. Black clothes permitted a conservative and discreet display of wealth. Black vestments and funeral trappings indicated grief, and Christ had said that those who mourn are blessed. Negative preconceptions about blackness largely outweighed positive ones, however, and the expanding slave trade only reinforced these.

Class

Just as *race* did not develop its current meaning until after the Renaissance, neither did *class*. The notion of class—working class, middle class, upper class—was developed by nineteenth-century social theorists, most prominently Karl Marx. Looking at their own industrial societies, they decided that the most basic social division was between men who owned the "means of production," that is, factories and equipment, and those who did not and worked for wages. The former were the "bourgeoisie" (the middle class) and the latter the "proletariat" (the working class). (How women fit into this division was not clear. Married women in the nineteenth century could not own property and had no right to their wages, which belonged to their husbands.) This was a system of social differentiation based primarily on wealth.

By contrast, the medieval system of social differentiation was based on function—or least theoretical function—in society. Medieval Europeans conceptualized society in three basic groups: those who pray, or the clergy; those who fight, or the nobility; and those who work, or everyone else (see page 295). These groups were termed **"orders"** or "estates," and many medieval representative assemblies, including those of France and the Low Countries, were organized into three houses by estate. The society of orders worked fairly well in setting out sociolegal categories for membership in representative bodies. It also highlighted the most important social distinction in both medieval and Renaissance Europe, that between noble and commoner. Status as a noble generally brought freedom from direct taxation and rights of jurisdiction over a piece of property and the people who lived on it.

By the thirteenth century, however, and even more so by the fifteenth, the more fixed and inherited hierarchy of orders was interwoven with a more changeable hierarchy based on wealth, what would later come to be termed "social class." This was particularly true in towns. Most residents of towns were technically members of the "third estate," that is, not nobles or clergy, but they included wealthy merchants who oversaw vast trading empires and lived in splendor that rivaled the richest nobles. As we saw above, in many cities these merchants had gained political power to match their economic might, becoming merchant oligarchs who ruled through city councils.

The development of a hierarchy of wealth did not mean an end to the hierarchy of orders, however. Those in the first estate were far more likely to be wealthy than those in the third, but even if they were poorer, they had higher status. If this had not been the case, wealthy Italian merchants would not have bothered to buy noble titles and country villas as they began doing in the fifteenth century, nor would wealthy English or Spanish merchants have been eager to marry their daughters and sons into often impoverished noble families. The nobility maintained its status in most parts of Europe not by maintaining rigid boundaries, but by taking in and integrating the new social elite of wealth. Wealth allowed some male commoners to buy or gain noble titles and female commoners to marry into noble families.

Along with being tied to the hierarchy of orders, social status was also linked with considerations of honor. Among the nobility, for example, certain weapons and battle tactics were favored because they were viewed as more honorable. Among urban dwellers, certain occupations, such as city executioner or manager of the municipal brothel, might be well paid but were understood to be "dishonorable" and so of low status.

Cities were where the hierarchy of orders met the hierarchy of wealth most dramatically. In many cities, a number of urban merchants and bankers were wealthier than all but the highest level of the nobility. Some of these men climbed into the nobility through marriage, service to a monarch, or purchase of a title. More of them heightened social and political distinctions within cities, trying to set themselves off as a privileged social group. Wealthy merchants often dominated city councils, and they made it increasingly difficult for new residents to become citizens. They passed sumptuary laws, essentially urban dress codes that created easily visible distinctions between social groups (see page 338). Nobles and wealthy urban residents could wear fine silk clothing, jewelry, and bright colors and guild masters and artisans

Italian City Scene In this detail from a fresco of the life of Saint Barbara by the Italian painter Lorenzo Lotto, the artist captures the mixing of social groups in a Renaissance Italian city. The crowd of men in the right foreground surrounding the biblical figures includes wealthy merchants in elaborate hats and colorful coats. Two mercenary soldiers (carrying a sword and a pike), probably in hire to a condottiero, wear short doublets and tight hose stylishly slit to reveal colored undergarments, while boys play with toy weapons at their feet. Clothing like that of the soldiers, which emphasized the masculine form, was frequently the target of sumptuary laws for both its expense and its "indecency." At the left, women sell vegetables and bread, which would have been a common sight at any city marketplace. At the very rear, men judge the female saint, who was thought to have been martyred for her faith in the third century. *(Scala/Art Resource, NY)*

linen garments, while servants were restricted to rough, dark clothes and aprons. Individuals tried to evade these laws by wearing the clothing restricted to the group above them, though there were fines for doing so. Sumptuary laws also regulated spending on celebrations such as weddings or baptisms according to social class, and they were justified as a way to limit frivolous spending on luxuries and promote local production, for many laws restricted the purchase of imported clothing or foodstuffs. Along with setting out a hierarchy of wealth, sumptuary laws marked certain groups as outside the social order: Jews were obliged to wear specific symbols on their clothes or hats of a specific color (often yellow) so that they would be easily recognizable, and prostitutes might also be ordered to sew stripes of yellow or red on their clothing, wear a specific type or color of cloak, or keep their hair uncovered so people would not mistake them for "honorable" women.

Gender

While "race" is an eighteenth-century concept and "class" a nineteenth-century concept, "gender" is a concept that grew out of the women's movement that began in the 1970s. Advocates of women's rights increasingly distinguished between "sex," by which they meant physical and anatomical differences (what are often called "biological differences") and "gender," by which they meant a culturally constructed and historically changing system of differences. The boundaries between "sex" and "gender" are debated (are men "biologically" better at math,

and women "biologically" more peaceful, or do such differences simply come from their upbringing?), and the recently emerged transgender movement has questioned whether a model with two sexes or two genders is adequate. The word *gender* is becoming increasingly common, however, even on government forms.

Renaissance people would have understood the word *gender* to refer to categories of nouns in many European languages, not categories of people, but they would have easily grasped the concept. Toward the end of the fourteenth century, learned men (and a few women) began what was termed the **"debate about women"** (*querelle des femmes*), a debate about women's character and nature that would last for centuries. Misogynist critiques of women from both clerical and secular authors denounced females as devious, domineering, and demanding. In answer, several authors, including Giovanni Boccaccio and Christine de Pizan, compiled long lists of famous and praiseworthy women exemplary for their loyalty, bravery, and morality. (See the feature "Listening to the Past: Christine de Pizan" in Chapter 12 on pages

404–405.) Boccaccio's tribute is somewhat ambiguous, for the highest praise he can bestow on a woman is that she is like a man: "What can we think except that it was an error of nature to give female sex to a body which had been endowed by God with a magnificent virile spirit?"[15] Christine de Pizan and several other writers were interested not only in defending women, but also in exploring the reasons behind women's secondary status—that is, why the great philosophers, statesmen, and poets had generally been men. In this they were anticipating recent discussions about the "social construction of gender" by six hundred years.

Online Study Center Improve Your Grade
Primary Source: *The Book of the City of Ladies: Advice for a "Wise Princess"*

Some authors who wrote defenses of women also wrote attacks, or, like Baldassare Castiglione in *The Courtier*, included both sides of the argument in a single work, so that it is difficult to gauge their actual opinions. The debate was clearly more than a literary game among intellectuals, however. With the development of the printing press, popular interest in the debate about women grew, and works were translated, reprinted, and shared around Europe. The debate about women also found visual expression, particularly in single-sheet prints that were hung in taverns or people's homes. Prints that juxtaposed female virtues and vices were very popular, with the virtuous women depicted as those of the classical or biblical past and the vice-ridden dressed in contemporary clothes. The favorite metaphor for the virtuous

wife was either the snail or the tortoise, both animals that never leave their "houses" and are totally silent, although such images were never as widespread as those depicting wives beating their husbands or hiding their lovers from them.

Beginning in the sixteenth century, the debate about women also became one about female rulers, sparked primarily by dynastic accidents in many countries, including Spain, England, France, and Scotland, which led to women serving as advisers to child kings or ruling in their own right (see pages 436 and 463). The questions vigorously and at times viciously disputed directly concerned the social construction of gender: could a woman's being born into a royal family and educated to rule allow her to overcome the limitations of her sex? Should it? Or stated another way: which was (or should be) the stronger determinant of character and social role, gender or rank? There were no successful rebellions against female rulers simply because they were women, but in part this was because female rulers, especially Queen Elizabeth I of England, emphasized qualities regarded as masculine—physical bravery, stamina, wisdom, duty—whenever they appeared in public. Machiavelli also linked rule and masculinity, using "effeminate" to describe the worst kind of ruler. (*Effeminate* in the Renaissance carried different connotations than it does today, however; strong heterosexual passion was not a sign of manliness, but could make one "effeminate," that is, dominated by as well as similar to a woman.) Male rulers also made sure that they appeared and were portrayed on horseback with armor, weapons, and other symbols of masculinity. The ideal Renaissance king or courtier may have been able to sing and dance, but he was also careful to have people see him as a warrior.

Renaissance Wedding Chest (Tuscany, late fifteenth century) Well-to-do brides provided huge dowries to their husbands in Renaissance Italy, and grooms often gave smaller gifts in return, such as this wedding chest. Appreciated more for their decorative value than for practical storage purposes, such chests were prominently displayed in people's homes. This 37-inch by 47-inch by 28-inch chest is carved with a scene from classical mythology in which Ceres, the goddess of agriculture, is searching for her daughter Proserpina (also known as Persephone), who has been abducted by Pluto, the god of the underworld. The subject may have been a commentary on Renaissance marriage, in which young women often married much older men and went to live in their houses. (*Philadelphia Museum of Art. Purchased with the Bloomfield Moore Fund and with Museum Funds, 1944 [1944-15-7]*)

Ideas about women's and men's proper roles shaped the actions of the most powerful Renaissance monarchs and determined those of ordinary men and women even more forcefully. The dominant notion of the "true" man was that of the married head of household, so men whose class and age would have normally conferred political power but who remained unmarried did not participate on the same level as their married brothers. Unmarried men in Venice, for example, could not be part of the ruling council. Women were also understood as "married or to be married," even if the actual marriage patterns in Europe left many women (and men) unmarried until quite late in life (see page 394). This meant that women's work was not viewed as supporting a family—even if it did—and was valued less than men's. If they worked for wages, and many women did, women earned about half to two-thirds of what men did even for the same work, and they received less food (and much less ale or wine) if wages included food.

The maintenance of appropriate power relationships between men and women, with men dominant and women subordinate, served as a symbol of the proper functioning of society as a whole. Disorder in the proper gender hierarchy was linked with other types of social upheaval and was viewed as the most threatening way in which the world could be turned upside down. Carnival plays, woodcuts, and stories frequently portrayed domineering wives in pants and henpecked husbands washing diapers alongside professors in dunce caps and peasants riding princes. Men and women involved in relationships in which the women were thought to have power—an older woman who married a younger man, or a woman who scolded her husband—were often subjected to public ridicule, with bands of neighbors shouting insults and banging sticks and pans in disapproval. Of all the ways in which Renaissance society was hierarchically arranged—class, age, level of education, rank, race, occupation—gender was regarded as the most "natural" and therefore the most important to defend.

Politics and the State in the Renaissance (ca 1450–1521)

The High Middle Ages had witnessed the origins of many of the basic institutions of the modern state. Sheriffs, inquests, juries, circuit judges, professional bureaucracies, and representative assemblies all trace their origins to the twelfth and thirteenth centuries (see pages 259–273). The linchpin for the development of states, however, was

strong monarchy, and during the period of the Hundred Years' War, no ruler in western Europe was able to provide effective leadership. The resurgent power of feudal nobilities weakened the centralizing work begun earlier.

Beginning in the fifteenth century, rulers utilized the aggressive methods implied by Renaissance political ideas to rebuild their governments. First in Italy, then in France, England, and Spain, rulers began the work of reducing violence, curbing unruly nobles, and establishing domestic order. They emphasized royal majesty and royal sovereignty and insisted on the respect and loyalty of all subjects. These monarchs ruthlessly suppressed opposition and rebellion, especially from the nobility. They loved the business of kingship and worked hard at it.

- *How did the nation-states of western Europe evolve in this period?*

France

The Hundred Years' War left France drastically depopulated, commercially ruined, and agriculturally weak. Nonetheless, the ruler whom Joan of Arc had seen crowned at Reims, Charles VII (r. 1422–1461), revived the monarchy and France. He seemed an unlikely person to do so. Frail, indecisive, and burdened with questions about his paternity (his father had been deranged; his mother, notoriously promiscuous), Charles VII nevertheless began France's long recovery.

Charles reconciled the Burgundians and Armagnacs, who had been waging civil war for thirty years. By 1453 French armies had expelled the English from French soil except in Calais. Charles reorganized the royal council, giving increased influence to middle-class men, and strengthened royal finances through such taxes as the **gabelle** (on salt) and the *taille* (land tax). These taxes remained the Crown's chief sources of income until the Revolution of 1789.

By establishing regular companies of cavalry and archers—recruited, paid, and inspected by the state—Charles created the first permanent royal army. In 1438 Charles published the **Pragmatic Sanction of Bourges,** asserting the superiority of a general council over the papacy, giving the French crown major control over the appointment of bishops, and depriving the pope of French ecclesiastical revenues. The Pragmatic Sanction established Gallican (or French) liberties because it affirmed the special rights of the French crown over the French church. Greater control over the church and the army helped consolidate the authority of the French crown.

Charles's son Louis XI (r. 1461–1483), called the "Spider King" because of his treacherous character, was very much a Renaissance prince. Facing the perpetual French problem of reduction of feudal disorder, he saw money as the answer. Louis promoted new industries, such as silk weaving at Lyons and Tours. He welcomed foreign craftsmen and entered into commercial treaties with England, Portugal, and the towns of the Hanseatic League (see page 341). He used the revenues raised through these economic activities and severe taxation to improve the army. With the army, Louis stopped aristocratic brigandage and slowly cut into urban independence.

Luck favored his goal of expanding royal authority and unifying the kingdom. On the timely death of Charles the Bold, duke of Burgundy, in 1477, Louis invaded Burgundy and gained some territories. Three years later, the extinction of the house of Anjou brought Louis the counties of Anjou, Bar, Maine, and Provence.

Two further developments strengthened the French monarchy. The marriage of Louis XII (r. 1498–1515) and Anne of Brittany added the large western duchy of Brittany to the state. Then the French king Francis I and Pope Leo X reached a mutually satisfactory agreement in 1516. The new treaty, the Concordat of Bologna, rescinded the Pragmatic Sanction's assertion of the superiority of a general council over the papacy and approved the pope's right to receive the first year's income of new bishops and abbots. In return, Leo X recognized the French ruler's right to select French bishops and abbots. French kings thereafter effectively controlled the appointment and thus the policies of church officials in the kingdom.

England

English society suffered severely from the disorders of the fifteenth century. The aristocracy dominated the government of Henry IV (r. 1399–1413) and indulged in mischievous violence at the local level. Population, decimated by the Black Death, continued to decline. Between 1455 and 1471 adherents of the ducal houses of York and Lancaster waged civil war, commonly called the **Wars of the Roses** because the symbol of the Yorkists was a white rose and that of the Lancastrians a red one. The chronic disorder hurt trade, agriculture, and domestic industry. Under the pious but mentally disturbed Henry VI (r. 1422–1461), the authority of the monarchy sank lower than it had been in centuries.

The Yorkist Edward IV (r. 1461–1483) began establishing domestic tranquillity. He succeeded in defeating the Lancastrian forces and after 1471 began to recon-struct the monarchy. Edward, his brother Richard III (r. 1483–1485), and Henry VII (r. 1485–1509) of the Welsh house of Tudor worked to restore royal prestige, to crush the power of the nobility, and to establish order and law at the local level. All three rulers used methods that Machiavelli himself would have praised—ruthlessness, efficiency, and secrecy.

The Hundred Years' War had been financed by Parliament. Dominated by baronial factions, Parliament had been the arena in which the nobility exerted its power. As long as the monarchy was dependent on the Lords and the Commons for revenue, the king had to call Parliament. Edward IV and subsequently the Tudors, excepting Henry VIII, conducted foreign policy on the basis of diplomacy, avoiding expensive wars. Thus the English monarchy did not depend on Parliament for money, and the Crown undercut that source of aristocratic influence.

Henry VII did summon several meetings of Parliament in the early years of his reign, primarily to confirm laws, but the center of royal authority was the **royal council,** which governed at the national level. There Henry VII revealed his distrust of the nobility: though not completely excluded, very few great lords were among the king's closest advisers. Regular representatives on the council numbered between twelve and fifteen men, and while many gained high ecclesiastical rank (the means, as it happened, by which the Crown paid them), their origins were in the lesser landowning class, and their education was in law. They were, in a sense, middle class.

The royal council handled any business the king put before it—executive, legislative, and judicial. For example, the council conducted negotiations with foreign governments and secured international recognition of the Tudor dynasty through the marriage in 1501 of Henry VII's eldest son Arthur to Catherine of Aragon, the daughter of Ferdinand and Isabella of Spain. The council dealt with real or potential aristocratic threats through a judicial offshoot, the **court of Star Chamber,** so called because of the stars painted on the ceiling of the room. The court applied principles of Roman law, and its methods were sometimes terrifying: accused persons were not entitled to see evidence against them; sessions were secret; torture could be applied to extract confessions; and juries were not called. These procedures ran directly counter to English common-law precedents, but they effectively reduced aristocratic troublemaking.

Unlike the continental countries of Spain and France, England had no standing army or professional civil service bureaucracy. The Tudors relied on the support of unpaid local officials, the **justices of the peace.** These influential landowners in the shires handled all the work of local government. They apprehended and punished criminals, enforced parliamentary statutes, fixed wages and prices, maintained proper standards of weights and measures, and even checked up on moral behavior.

The Tudors won the support of the influential upper middle class because the Crown linked government policy with the interests of that class. A commercial or agricultural upper class fears and dislikes few things more than disorder and violence. The Tudors promoted peace and social order, and the gentry did not object to arbitrary methods, like those of the court of Star Chamber, because the government had halted the long period of anarchy.

Secretive, cautious, and thrifty, Henry VII rebuilt the monarchy. He encouraged the cloth industry and built up the English merchant marine. English exports of wool and the royal export tax on that wool steadily increased. Henry crushed an invasion from Ireland and secured peace with Scotland through the marriage of his daughter Margaret to the Scottish king. When Henry VII died in 1509, he left a country at peace both domestically and internationally, a substantially augmented treasury, and the dignity and role of the royal majesty much enhanced.

Spain

While England and France laid the foundations of unified nation-states during the Renaissance, Spain remained a conglomerate of independent kingdoms. Castile and León formed a single political organization, but Aragon consisted of the principalities of Aragon, Valencia, Majorca, Sicily, Cardeña, and Naples, each tied to the crown of Aragon in a different way. On the one hand, the legacy of Hispanic, Roman, Visigothic, Jewish, and Muslim peoples made for rich cultural diversity; on the other hand, the Iberian Peninsula lacked a common cultural tradition.

The centuries-long reconquista—the wars of the northern Christian kingdoms to control the entire peninsula (see pages 265–267)—had military and religious objectives: conversion or expulsion of the Muslims and Jews and political control of the south. By the middle of the fifteenth century, the kingdoms of Castile and Aragon dominated the weaker Navarre, Portugal, and Granada, and the Iberian Peninsula, with the exception of Granada, had been won for Christianity. But even the wedding in 1469 of the dynamic and aggressive Isabella of Castile and the crafty and persistent Ferdinand of Aragon did not bring about administrative unity. Rather, their marriage constituted a dynastic union of two royal houses, not the political union of two peoples. Although Ferdinand and Isabella (r. 1474–1516) pursued a common foreign policy, until about 1700 Spain existed as a loose confederation of separate kingdoms (see Map 13.3), each maintaining its own *cortes* (parliament), laws, courts, and systems of coinage and taxation.

To curb the rebellious and warring aristocracy, Ferdinand and Isabella revived an old medieval institution: the **hermandades,** or "brotherhoods," which were popular groups in the towns given authority to act as local police forces and judicial tribunals. The hermandades repressed violence with such savage punishments that by 1498 they could be disbanded.

The decisive step Ferdinand and Isabella took to curb aristocratic power was the restructuring of the royal council. Aristocrats and great territorial magnates were rigorously excluded; thus the influence of the nobility on state policy was greatly reduced. Ferdinand and Isabella intended the council to be the cornerstone of their government system, with full executive, judicial, and legislative powers under the monarchy. The council was also to be responsible for the supervision of local authorities. The king and queen therefore appointed only people of middle-class background to the council. The council and various government boards recruited men trained in Roman law, which exalted the power of the Crown as the embodiment of the state.

In the extension of royal authority and the consolidation of the territories of Spain, the church was the linchpin. If the Spanish crown could select the higher clergy, the monarchy could influence ecclesiastical policy, wealth, and military resources. Through a diplomatic alliance with the Spanish pope Alexander VI, the Spanish monarchs secured the right to appoint bishops in Spain and in the Hispanic territories in America. This power enabled the "Catholic Kings of Spain," a title granted Ferdinand and Isabella by the papacy, to establish, in effect, a national church.

Revenues from ecclesiastical estates provided the means to raise an army to continue the reconquista. The victorious entry of Ferdinand and Isabella into Granada on January 6, 1492, signaled the culmination of eight centuries of Spanish struggle against the Arabs in southern Spain and the conclusion of the reconquista (see Map 9.3 on page 266). Granada in the south was incorporated into the Spanish kingdom, and in 1512 Ferdinand conquered Navarre in the north.

There still remained a sizable and, in the view of the majority of the Spanish people, potentially dangerous minority, the Jews. During the long centuries of the reconquista, Christian kings had renewed Jewish rights and privileges; in fact, Jewish industry, intelligence, and money had supported royal power. While Christians of

MAP 13.3 Spain in 1492 The marriage of Ferdinand of Aragon and Isabella of Castile in 1469 represented a dynastic union of two houses, not a political union of two peoples. Some principalities, such as León (part of Castile) and Catalonia (part of Aragon), had their own cultures, languages, and legal systems. Barcelona, the port city of Catalonia, controlled a commercial empire throughout the Mediterranean. Most of the people in Granada were Muslims, and Muslims and Jews lived in other areas as well.

all classes borrowed from Jewish moneylenders and while all who could afford them sought Jewish physicians, a strong undercurrent of resentment of Jewish influence and wealth festered. When the kings of France and England had expelled the Jews from their kingdoms (see page 310), many had sought refuge in Spain. In the fourteenth century Jews formed an integral and indispensable part of Spanish life. With vast numbers of Muslims, Jews, and Moorish Christians, medieval Spain represented the most diverse and cosmopolitan country in Europe. Diversity and cosmopolitanism, however, were not medieval social ideals.

Since ancient times, governments had seldom tolerated religious pluralism; religious faiths that differed from the official state religion were considered politically dangerous. But in the fourteenth century anti-Semitism in Spain rose more from popular sentiment than from royal poli-

cies. Rising anti-Semitic feeling was aggravated by fiery anti-Jewish preaching, by economic dislocation, and by the search for a scapegoat during the Black Death. In 1331 a mob attacked the Jewish community of Gerona in Catalonia. In 1355 royal troops massacred Jews in Toledo. On June 4, 1391, inflamed by "religious" preaching, mobs sacked and burned the Jewish community in Seville and compelled the Jews who survived to accept baptism. From Seville anti-Semitic pogroms swept the towns of Valencia, Barcelona, Burgos, Madrid, and Segovia. One scholar estimates that 40 percent of the Jewish population of Spain was killed or forced to convert.[16] Those converted were called *conversos* or **New Christians.**

Conversos were often well-educated and successful. In the administration of Castile, New Christians held the royal secretaryship, controlled the royal treasury, and composed a third of the royal council. In the church,

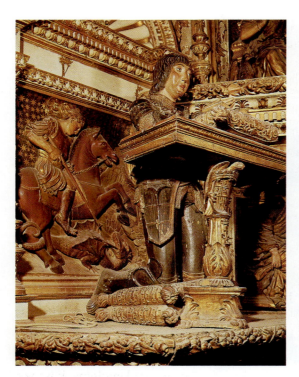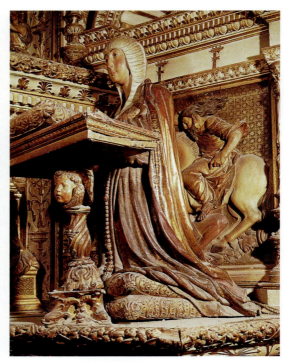

Felipe Bigarny: Ferdinand and Isabella In these wooden sculptures, the Burgundian artist Felipe Bigarny portrays Ferdinand and Isabella as paragons of Christian piety, kneeling at prayer. Ferdinand is shown in armor, a symbol of his military accomplishments and masculinity. Isabella wears a simple white head-covering rather than something more elaborate to indicate her modesty, a key virtue for women, though her actions and writings indicate that she was more determined and forceful than Ferdinand. *(Capilla Real, Granada/Laurie Platt Winfrey, Inc.)*

they held high positions as archbishops, bishops, and abbots. In the administration of the towns, conversos often held the highest public offices; in Toledo they controlled the collection of royal revenues. They included some of the leading merchants and business people. They also served great magnates, and by intermarrying with the nobility they gained political leverage. In the professions of medicine and law, New Christians held the most prominent positions. Numbering perhaps two hundred thousand in a total Spanish population of about 7.5 million, New Christians and Jews exercised influence disproportionate to their numbers.

Such successes bred resentment. Aristocratic grandees resented their financial dependence; the poor hated the converso tax collectors; and churchmen doubted the sincerity of their conversions. Queen Isabella shared these suspicions, and she and Ferdinand sought permission to set up an Inquisition in Spain. Pope Sixtus IV's bull authorizing the Inquisition reached Spain in November 1478, and on September 28, 1480, Ferdinand and Isabella ordered the establishment of tribunals to "search out and punish converts from Judaism who had transgressed against Christianity by secretly adhering to Jewish beliefs and performing rites of the Jews."[17] Investigations and trials began immediately, as officials of the Inquisition looked for conversos who showed any sign of incomplete conversion, such as not eating pork.

Recent scholarship has carefully analyzed documents of the Inquisition. Most conversos identified themselves as Christians. They insisted that they were happy to be Christians and failed to see why they should be labeled New Christians: many came from families that had received baptism generations before.

In response, officials of the Inquisition developed a new type of anti-Semitism. A person's status as a Jew, they argued, could not be changed by religious conversion, but was in the person's nature as a human being. Judaism was in their blood and was heritable, so Jews could never be true Christians. In what were known as "purity of the blood" laws, having pure Christian blood became a requirement for noble status. Intermarriage between Old and New Christians had been common for centuries, but now many families sought to hide their ancestors. Ideas about Jews developed in Spain were important components in European concepts of race, and discussions of "Jewish blood" later expanded into notions of the "Jewish race."

This new racially based anti-Semitism emerged at the very time a Spanish national feeling was emerging, a national sentiment that looked to the building of a single nation. Whereas earlier anti-Semitism, such as that during the time of the Black Death, alleged Jewish schemes to kill off entire Christian populations—by poisoning the wells, for example, from which Jews derived no profit—fifteenth-century theories held that Jews or New Christians planned to take over all public offices in Spain. Jews, therefore, represented a grave threat to national unity.

Although the Inquisition was a religious institution established to ensure the Catholic faith, it was controlled by the Crown and served primarily as a politically unifying tool. Because the Spanish Inquisition commonly applied torture to extract confessions, first from conversos, then from Muslims, and later from Protestants, it gained a notorious reputation. Thus the word *inquisition*, meaning "any judicial inquiry conducted with ruthless severity," came into the English language. The methods of the Spanish Inquisition were cruel, though not as cruel as the investigative methods of some twentieth-century governments.

Shortly after the conquest of the Moorish stronghold at Granada in 1492, Isabella and Ferdinand issued an edict expelling all practicing Jews from Spain. Of the community of perhaps 200,000 Jews, 150,000 fled. (Efforts were made, through last-minute conversions, to retain good Jewish physicians.) Many Muslims in Granada were forcibly baptized and became another type of New Christian investigated by the Inquisition. Absolute religious orthodoxy and purity of blood ("untainted" by Jews or Muslims) served as the theoretical foundation of the Spanish national state.

The diplomacy of the Catholic rulers of Spain achieved a success they never anticipated. Partly out of hatred for the French and partly out of a desire to gain international recognition for their new dynasty, in 1496 Ferdinand and Isabella married their second daughter Joanna, heiress to Castile, to the archduke Philip, heir through his mother to the Burgundian Netherlands and through his father to the Holy Roman Empire. Philip and Joanna's son, Charles V (r. 1519–1556), thus succeeded to a vast patrimony. When Charles's son Philip II joined Portugal to the Spanish crown in 1580, the Iberian Peninsula was at last politically united. The various kingdoms, however, were administered separately.

Chapter Summary

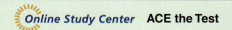 Online Study Center   ACE the Test

- *What economic and political developments in Italy provided the setting for the Renaissance?*
- *What were the key ideas of the Renaissance, and how were they different for men and women and for southern and northern Europeans?*
- *How did changes in art both reflect and shape new ideas?*
- *What were the key social hierarchies in Renaissance Europe, and how did ideas about hierarchy shape people's lives?*
- *How did the nation-states of western Europe evolve in this period?*

The Italian Renaissance rested on the phenomenal economic growth of the High Middle Ages. In the period from about 1050 to 1300, a new economy emerged based on Venetian and Genoese shipping and long-distance trade and on Florentine banking and cloth manufacture. These commercial activities, combined with the struggle of urban communes for political independence from surrounding feudal lords, led to the appearance of a new ruling group in Italian cities—merchant oligarchs. Unrest in some cities led to their being taken over by single rulers, but however Italian cities were governed, they jockeyed for power with one another and prevented the establishment of a single Italian nation-state.

The Renaissance was characterized by self-conscious awareness among fourteenth- and fifteenth-century Italians, particularly scholars and writers known as humanists, that they were living in a new era. Key to this attitude was a serious interest in the Latin classics, a belief in individual potential, and a more secular attitude toward life. All these are evident in political theory developed in the Renaissance, particularly that of Machiavelli. Humanists opened schools for boys and young men to train them for an active life of public service, but they had doubts about whether humanist education was appropriate for women. As humanism spread to northern Europe, religious concerns became more pronounced, and Christian humanists set out plans for the reform of church and society. Their ideas were spread to a much wider audience than those of early humanists because of the development of the printing press with movable metal type, which revolutionized communication.

Interest in the classical past and in the individual also shaped Renaissance art in terms of style and subject matter. Painting became more naturalistic, and the individual portrait emerged as a distinct artistic genre. Wealthy merchants, cultured rulers, and powerful popes all hired painters, sculptors, and architects to design and ornament public and private buildings. Art in Italy became more secular and classical, while that in northern Europe retained a more religious tone. Artists began to understand themselves as having a special creative genius, though they continued to produce works on order for patrons, who often determined the content and form.

Social hierarchies in the Renaissance built on those of the Middle Ages, but also developed new features that contributed to the modern social hierarchies of race, class, and gender. Black Africans entered Europe in sizable numbers for the first time since the collapse of the Roman Empire, and Europeans fit them into changing understandings of ethnicity and race. The medieval hierarchy of orders based on function in society intermingled with a new hierarchy based on wealth, with new types of elites becoming more powerful. The Renaissance debate about women led many to discuss women's nature and proper role in society, a discussion sharpened by the presence of a number of ruling queens in this era.

With taxes provided by business people, kings in western Europe established greater peace and order, both essential for trade. Feudal monarchies gradually evolved in the direction of nation-states. In Spain, France, and England, rulers also emphasized royal dignity and authority, and they utilized Machiavellian ideas to ensure the preservation and continuation of their governments.

Like the merchant oligarchs and signori of Italian city-states, Renaissance monarchs manipulated culture to enhance their power.

Key Terms

Renaissance	orders
communes	debate about
oligarchy	women
popolo	gabelle
condottieri	Pragmatic Sanction
signori	of Bourges
courts	Wars of the Roses
republic	royal council
humanism	court of Star
individualism	Chamber
The Prince	justices of the
secularism	peace
Christian humanists	hermandades
patrons	New Christians

Online Study Center **Improve Your Grade** Flashcards

Suggested Reading

Clark, Samuel. *State and Status: The Rise of the State and Aristocratic Power.* 1995. Discusses the relationship between centralizing states and the nobility.

Earle, T. F., and K. J. P. Lowe, eds. *Black Africans in Renaissance Europe.* 2005. Includes essays discussing many aspects of ideas about race and the experience of Africans in Europe.

Eisenstein, Elizabeth. *The Printing Press as an Agent of Change: Communications and Cultural Transformations in Early Modern Europe.* 1979. The definitive study of the impact of printing.

Ertman, Thomas. *The Birth of Leviathan: Building States and Regimes in Medieval and Early Modern Europe.* 1997. A good introduction to the creation of nation-states.

Grafton, Anthony, and Lisa Jardine. *From Humanism to the Humanities: Education and the Liberal Arts in Fifteenth and Sixteenth Century Europe.* 1986. Discusses humanist education and other developments in Renaissance learning.

Hale, J. R. *The Civilization of Europe in the Renaissance.* 1994. A comprehensive treatment of the period, arranged thematically.

Hale, J. R. *Machiavelli and Renaissance Italy.* 1966. A sound short biography.

Harbison, Craig. *The Mirror of the Artist: Northern Renaissance Art in Its Historical Context.* 1995. The best introduction to the art of northern Europe.

Holmes, George, ed. *Art and Politics in Renaissance Italy.* 1993. Treats the art of Florence and Rome against a political background.

Jardine, Lisa. *Worldly Goods: A New History of the Renaissance.* 1998. Discusses changing notions of social status, artistic patronage, and consumer goods.

Lubkin, Gregory. *A Renaissance Court: Milan Under Galeazzo Maria Sforza.* 1994. A wonderful study of one of the most important Renaissance courts.

Man, John. *Gutenberg Revolution: The Story of a Genius and an Invention That Changed the World.* 2002. Presents a rather idealized view of Gutenberg, but has good discussions of his milieu and excellent illustrations.

McConica, James. *Erasmus.* 1991. A sensitive treatment of the leading northern humanist.

Nauert, Charles. *Humanism and the Culture of Renaissance Europe.* 1995. A thorough introduction to humanism throughout Europe.

Netanyahu, Benjamin. *The Origins of the Inquisition in Fifteenth Century Spain.* 1995. An analysis of issues relating to the expulsion of the Jews by the former prime minister of Israel.

Wiesner, Merry E. *Women and Gender in Early Modern Europe,* 2d ed. 2000. Discusses all aspects of women's lives and ideas about gender.

Notes

1. Quoted in J. Burckhardt, *The Civilization of the Renaissance in Italy* (London: Phaidon Books, 1951), p. 89.
2. *Memoirs of Benvenuto Cellini; A Florentine Artist; Written by Himself* (London: J. M. Dent & Sons, 1927), p. 2.
3. Quoted in W. H. Woodward, *Vittorino da Feltre and Other Humanist Educators* (Cambridge: Cambridge University Press, 1897), p. 102.
4. Ibid., p. 127.
5. C. E. Detmold, trans., *The Historical, Political and Diplomatic Writings of Niccolò Machiavelli* (Boston: J. R. Osgood, 1882), pp. 51–52.
6. Ibid., pp. 54–55.
7. Quoted in E. H. Harbison, *The Christian Scholar and His Calling in the Age of the Reformation* (New York: Charles Scribner's Sons, 1956), p. 109.
8. Quoted in F. Seebohm, *The Oxford Reformers* (London: J. M. Dent & Sons, 1867), p. 256.
9. B. Burroughs, ed., *Vasari's Lives of the Artists* (New York: Simon & Schuster, 1946), pp. 164–165.
10. L. Martines, *Power and Imagination: City-States in Renaissance Italy* (New York: Vintage Books, 1980), p. 253.
11. G. Bull, trans., *Aretino: Selected Letters* (Baltimore: Penguin Books, 1976), p. 109.
12. Quoted in P. Murray and L. Murray, *A Dictionary of Art and Artists* (Baltimore: Penguin Books, 1963), p. 125.
13. J. Hale, *The Civilization of Europe in the Renaissance* (New York: Atheneum, 1994), p. 44.
14. Quoted in J. Devisse and M. Mollat, *The Image of the Black in Western Art,* vol. 2, trans. W. G. Ryan (New York: William Morrow, 1979), pt. 2, pp. 187–188.
15. Boccaccio, *Concerning Famous Women,* trans. Guido Guarino (New Brunswick, N.J., Rutgers University Press, 1963), p. 87.
16. See B. F. Reilly, *The Medieval Spains* (New York: Cambridge University Press, 1993), pp. 198–203.
17. B. Netanyahu, *The Origins of the Inquisition in Fifteenth Century Spain* (New York: Random House, 1995), p. 921.

An Age of Gold

As the foremost scholar of the early sixteenth century and a writer with international contacts, Desiderius Erasmus (1466?–1536) maintained a vast correspondence. In the letters here, he explains his belief that Europe was entering a golden age. The letters also reflect the spiritual ideals of northern European humanists. Wolfgang Capito (1478?–1541), a German scholar, was professor of theology at the University of Basel. Pope Leo X (1513–1521), second son of Lorenzo de' Medici, extended the hospitality of the papal court to men of letters, sought to rebuild Rome as a Renaissance capital, and pushed the building of the new Saint Peter's Basilica by licensing the sale of indulgences (see page 448).

To Capito

It is no part of my nature, most learned Wolfgang, to be excessively fond of life; whether it is that I have, to my own mind, lived nearly long enough, having entered my fifty-first year, or that I see nothing in this life so splendid or delightful that it should be desired by one who is convinced by the Christian faith that a happier life awaits those who in this world earnestly attach themselves to piety. But at the present moment I could almost wish to be young again, for no other reason but this, that I anticipate the near approach of a golden age, so clearly do we see the minds of princes, as if changed by inspiration, devoting all their energies to the pursuit of peace. The chief movers in this matter are Pope Leo and Francis, King of France.

There is nothing this king does not do or does not suffer in his desire to avert war and consolidate peace . . . and exhibiting in this, as in everything else, a magnanimous and truly royal character. Therefore, when I see that the highest sovereigns of Europe—Francis of France, Charles the King Catholic, Henry of England, and the Emperor Maximilian—have set all their warlike

preparations aside and established peace upon solid and, as I trust, adamantine foundations, I am led to a confident hope that not only morality and Christian piety, but also a genuine and purer literature, may come to renewed life or greater splendour; especially as this object is pursued with equal zeal in various regions of the world—at Rome by Pope Leo, in Spain by the Cardinal of Toledo,* in England by Henry, eighth of the name, himself not unskilled in letters, and among ourselves by our young King Charles.† In France, King Francis, who seems as it were born for this object, invites and entices from all countries men that excel in merit or in learning. Among the Germans the same object is pursued by many of their excellent princes and bishops, and especially by Maximilian Caesar,‡ whose old age, weary of so many wars, has determined to seek rest in the employments of peace, a resolution more becoming to his own years, while it is fortunate for the Christian world. To the piety of these princes it is due, that we see everywhere, as if upon a given signal, men of genius are arising and conspiring together to restore the best literature.

Polite letters, which were almost extinct, are now cultivated and embraced by Scots, by Danes, and by Irishmen. Medicine has a host of champions. . . . The Imperial Law is restored at Paris by William Budé, in Germany by Udalric Zasy; and mathematics at Basel by Henry of Glaris. In the theological sphere there was no little to be done, because this science has been hitherto mainly professed by those who are most pertinacious in their abhorrence of the better

---

*Francisco Jiménez de Cisneros (1436–1517), Spanish statesman and adviser to Queen Isabella, who gained renown for his reform of the monasteries and the Spanish church.
† After 1516 king of Spain and much of the Netherlands; after 1519 Holy Roman emperor.
‡Holy Roman emperor (1493–1519); he was succeeded by his grandson Charles (above).

Hans Holbein the Younger, *Erasmus* (ca 1521). Holbein persuaded his close friend Erasmus to sit for this portrait and portrayed him at his characteristic work, writing. *(Louvre/Scala/Art Resource, NY)*

literature,§ and are the more successful in defending their own ignorance as they do it under pretext of piety, the unlearned vulgar being induced to believe that violence is offered to religion if anyone begins an assault upon their barbarism. . . . But even here I am confident of success if the knowledge of the three languages continues to be received in schools, as it has now begun. . . .

The humblest part of the work has naturally fallen to my lot. Whether my contribution has been worth anything I cannot say; . . . although the work was not undertaken by me with any confidence that I could myself teach anything magnificent, but I wanted to construct a road for other persons of higher aims, so that they might be less impeded by pools and stumbling blocks in carrying home those fair and glorious treasures.

Why should I say more? Everything promises me the happiest success. But one doubt still possesses my mind. I am afraid that, under cover of a revival of ancient literature, paganism may attempt to rear its head—as there are some among Christians that acknowledge Christ in name but breathe inwardly a heathen spirit—or, on the other hand, that the restoration of Hebrew learning may give occasion to a revival of Judaism. This would be a plague as much opposed to the doctrine of Christ as anything that could happen. . . . Some books have lately come out with a strong flavour of Judaism. I see how Paul exerted himself to defend Christ against Judaism, and I am aware that some persons are secretly sliding in that direction. . . . So much the more do I wish you to undertake this province; I know that your sincere piety will have regard to nothing but Christ, to whom all your studies are devoted. . . .

To Pope Leo X

While on the one hand, as a private matter, I acknowledge my own felicity in obtaining the approbation not only of the Supreme Pontiff but of Leo, by his own endowments supreme among the supreme, so on the other hand, as a matter of public concern, I congratulate this our age— which bids fair to be an age of gold, if ever such there was—wherein I see, under your happy auspices and by your holy counsels, three of the

§Latin, Greek, and Hebrew.

chief blessings of humanity are about to be restored to her. I mean, first, that truly Christian piety, which has in many ways fallen into decay; secondly, learning of the best sort, hitherto partly neglected and partly corrupted; and thirdly, the public and lasting concord of Christendom, the source and parent of piety and erudition. These will be the undying trophies of the tenth Leo, which, consecrated to eternal memory by the writings of learned men, will forever render your pontificate and your family‖ illustrious. I pray God that he may be pleased to confirm this purpose in you, and so protract your life, that after the affairs of mankind have been ordered according to your designs, Leo may make a long-delayed return to the skies.

Questions for Analysis

1. What does Erasmus mean by a "golden age"?

2. Do education and learning ensure improvement in the human condition, in his opinion? Do you agree?

3. What would you say are the essential differences between Erasmus's educational goals and those of modern society?

‖The Florentine House of Medici, whose interests Leo X, himself a Medici, was known always to support.

Source: Epistles 522 and 530, from *The Epistles of Erasmus,* trans. F. M. Nichols (London: Longmans, Green & Co., 1901).

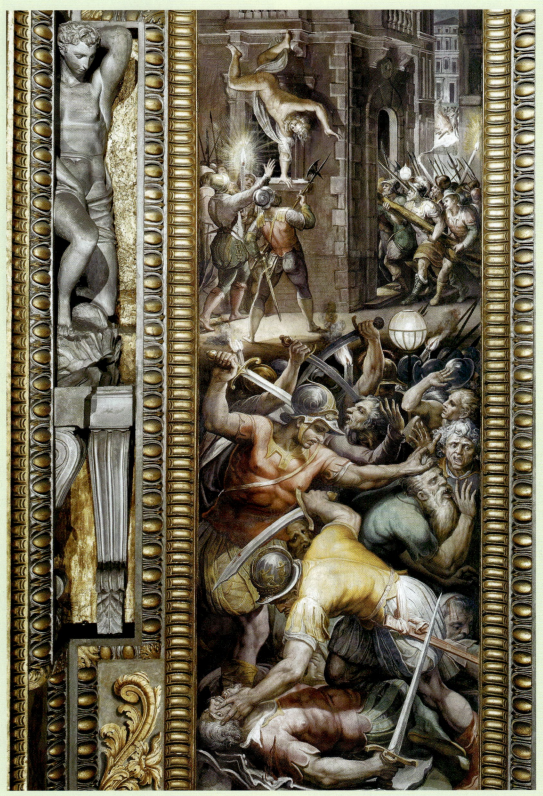

Giorgio Vasari: *Massacre of Coligny and the Huguenots* (1573). This fresco shows the Saint Bartholomew's Day massacre in Paris, one of many bloody events in the religious wars that accompanied the Reformation. *(Vatican Palace/Scala/Art Resource, NY)*

REFORMATIONS AND RELIGIOUS WARS, 1500–1600

Calls for reform of the Christian church began very early in its history. When Christianity became the official religion of the Roman Empire in the fourth century, many believers thought that the church had abandoned its original mission, and they called for a return to a church that was not linked to the state. Throughout the Middle Ages individuals and groups argued that the church had become too wealthy and powerful and urged monasteries, convents, bishoprics, and the papacy to give up their property and focus on service to the poor. Some asserted that basic teachings of the church were not truly Christian and that changes were needed in theology as well as in institutional structures and practices. The Christian humanists of the late fifteenth and early sixteenth centuries urged reform, primarily through educational and social change.

Sixteenth-century cries for reformation were hardly new. Throughout the centuries, men and women believed that the early Christian church represented a golden age, akin to the golden age of the classical past celebrated by Renaissance humanists. What was new was the breadth of acceptance and the ultimate impact of the calls for reform. In 1500 there was one Christian church in western Europe to which all Christians at least nominally belonged. Fifty years later there were many, a situation that continues today.

Along with the Renaissance, the Reformation is often seen as a key element in the creation of the "modern" world. This radical change contained many elements of continuity, however. Sixteenth-century reformers looked back to the early Christian church for their inspiration, and many of their reforming ideas had been advocated for centuries.

The Early Reformation

Calls for reform in the church came from many quarters in early-sixteenth-century Europe—from educated laypeople such as Christian humanists and urban residents, from villagers and artisans, and from church officials themselves. This dissatisfaction helps explain why the

Online Study Center

This icon will direct you to interactive activities and study materials on the website **college.hmco.com/pic/mckaywest9e**

ideas of an obscure professor from a new and not very prestigious German university found a ready audience. Within a decade of his first publishing his ideas (using the new technology of the printing press), much of central Europe and Scandinavia had broken with the Catholic Church and even more radical concepts of the Christian message were being developed and linked to calls for social change.

● *What were the central ideas of the reformers, and why were they appealing to different social groups?*

The Christian Church in the Early Sixteenth Century

If external religious observances are a measure of depth of heartfelt conviction, Europeans in the early sixteenth century were deeply pious and remained loyal to the Roman Catholic Church. Villagers participated in processions honoring the local saints. Middle-class people made pilgrimages to the great shrines, such as Saint Peter's in Rome. The upper classes continued to remember the church in their wills. People of all social classes devoted an enormous amount of their time and income to religious causes and foundations.

Despite—or perhaps because of—the depth of their piety, many people were also highly critical of the Roman Catholic Church and its clergy. The papal conflict with the German emperor Frederick II in the thirteenth century, followed by the Babylonian Captivity and then the Great Schism, badly damaged the prestige of church leaders. Humanists denounced corruption in the church. In *The Praise of Folly,* Erasmus condemned the superstitions of the parish clergy and the excessive rituals of the monks (see page 325). Many ordinary people agreed. Court records, bishop's visitations of parishes, and even popular songs and printed images show widespread **anticlericalism,** or opposition to the clergy.

Online Study Center Improve Your Grade
Primary Source: *The Praise of Folly:* Erasmus on Popular Religious Practice

In the early sixteenth century critics of the church concentrated their attacks on three disorders—clerical immorality, clerical ignorance, and clerical pluralism, with the related problem of absenteeism. Many priests, particularly those ministering to country people, had concubines, and reports of neglect of the rule of celibacy were common. Clerical drunkenness, gambling, and indulgence in fancy dress were also frequent charges. Because such conduct was completely at odds with the church's rules and moral standards, it scandalized the educated faithful.

The bishops only casually enforced regulations regarding the education of priests. As a result, standards for ordination were shockingly low. Many priests could barely read and write, and critics laughed at illiterate priests mumbling Latin words of the Mass that they could not understand. In northern Europe—in England, for example—recent research shows an improvement in clerical educational standards in the early sixteenth century. Nevertheless, parish priests throughout Europe were not as educated as the educated laity, who condemned the irregularity and poor quality of sermons.

In regard to absenteeism and **pluralism,** many clerics, especially higher ecclesiastics, held several *benefices* (or offices) simultaneously but seldom visited the benefices, let alone performed the spiritual responsibilities those offices entailed. Instead, they collected revenues from all of them and hired a poor priest, paying him just a fraction of the income to fulfill the spiritual duties of a particular local church. Many Italian officials in the papal curia held benefices in England, Spain, and Germany. Revenues from those countries paid the Italian priests' salaries, provoking not only charges of absenteeism but also nationalistic resentment.

There was also local resentment of clerical privileges and immunities. Priests, monks, and nuns were exempt from civic responsibilities, such as defending the city and paying taxes. Yet religious orders frequently held large amounts of urban property, in some cities as much as one-third. City governments were increasingly determined to integrate the clergy into civic life by reducing their privileges and giving them public responsibilities. This brought city leaders into opposition with bishops and the papacy, which for centuries had stressed the independence of the church from lay control and the distinction between members of the clergy and laypeople.

Martin Luther

By itself, widespread criticism of the church did not lead to the dramatic changes of the sixteenth century. Those resulted from the personal religious struggle of a German university professor, Martin Luther (1483–1546), who was also an Augustinian friar. The Augustinian friars were a mendicant order, like the Dominicans and Franciscans, whose members often preached, taught, and assisted the poor. Martin Luther was born at Eisleben in Saxony and was the second son of a copper miner and, later, mine owner. At considerable sacrifice, his father sent him to school and then to the University of Erfurt, where he earned a master's degree with distinction at the young age of twenty-one. Hans Luther intended his son to proceed to the study of law and a legal career, which for centuries had been the steppingstone to public office and material success. Badly frightened during a thunderstorm, however, Martin Luther vowed to become a friar. Much to his father's dismay, he entered the monastery of the Augustinian friars at Erfurt in 1505. Luther was ordained a priest in 1507 and after additional study earned a doctorate of theology. From 1512 until his death in 1546, he served as professor of the Scriptures at the new University of Wittenberg. Luther was deadly serious when he said, years later, "I would not take all the world's goods for my doctorate." His doctorate led to his professorship, and his professorship conferred on him the authority to teach: throughout his life, he frequently cited his professorship as justification for his reforming work.

Martin Luther was a very conscientious friar. His scrupulous observance of the religious routine, frequent confessions, and fasting, however, gave him only temporary relief from anxieties about sin and his ability to meet God's demands. These apprehensions in turn led him to doubt the value of the monastic life itself. Since the medieval church had long held that the monastic life was a sure and certain road to salvation, Luther's confusion and anxieties increased.

Luther's wise and kindly confessor, John Staupitz, directed him to study Saint Paul's letters in the New Testament. Gradually Luther arrived at a new understanding of the Pauline letters and of all Christian doctrine. His understanding is often summarized as "faith alone, grace alone, Scripture alone" (*sola fide, sola gratia, sola Scriptura*). For Christians, salvation and justification come through faith, not good works, though true faith leads to love and to the active expression of faith in helping others. Faith is a free gift of God, not the result of human effort. God's word is revealed only in Scripture, not in the traditions of the church.

At the same time Luther was engaged in scholarly reflections and professorial lecturing, Archbishop Albert of Mainz, who controlled the area in which Wittenberg was located, sought to become the bishop of several other territories as well. He borrowed money from the Fuggers, a wealthy banking family of Augsburg, to pay for the papal dispensation of the rules regarding pluralism. Meanwhile, Pope Leo X, a member of the Medici family, was constructing family chapels and tombs (for which he hired Michelangelo) and continuing the building of St. Peter's Basilica in Rome. He authorized a special St. Pe-

Chronology

1477	Union of Burgundian and Habsburg dynasties
1517	Martin Luther, "Ninety-five Theses on the Power of Indulgences"
1521	Diet of Worms
1521–1559	Habsburg-Valois Wars
1525	Peasants' War in Germany
1526	Turkish victory at Mohács, which allows spread of Protestantism in Hungary
1536	John Calvin, *The Institutes of the Christian Religion*
1540	Papal approval of Society of Jesus (Jesuits)
1542	Sacred Congregation of the Holy Office and Roman Inquisition
1545–1563	Council of Trent
1553–1558	Reign of Mary Tudor and temporary restoration of Catholicism in England
1555	Peace of Augsburg, official recognition of Lutheranism
1558–1603	Reign of Elizabeth and the "Elizabethan Settlement" in England
1559	Treaty of Cateau-Cambrésis
1560–1660	Height of the European witch-hunt
1568–1578	Civil war in the Netherlands
1572	Saint Bartholomew's Day massacre
1598	Edict of Nantes

ter's indulgence and allowed Albert to keep a portion of the revenue collected in the territories over which he was bishop to pay back the Fuggers.

Albert hired a friar from the Dominican order, Johann Tetzel, to run the indulgence sale. Tetzel mounted an advertising blitz. He was a very effective salesman, hawking indulgences—printed on the newly developed printing press—in a way that promised full forgiveness for sins or the end of time in purgatory for one's friends and relatives. One of his slogans—"As soon as coin in coffer rings, the soul from purgatory springs"—brought phenomenal success. Tetzel even drew up a chart with prices for the forgiveness of particular sins.

The Folly of Indulgences In this woodcut from the early Reformation, the church's sale of indulgences is viciously satirized. With one claw in holy water, another resting on the coins paid for indulgences, and a third stretched out for offerings, the church, in the form of a rapacious bird, writes out an indulgence with excrement. The creature's head and gaping mouth represent Hell, with foolish Christians inside, others being cooked in a pot above, and a demon delivering the pope in a three-tiered crown and holding the keys to Heaven, a symbol of papal authority. Illustrations such as this, often printed as single-sheet broadsides and sold very cheaply, clearly conveyed criticism of the church to people who could not read. (*Kunstsammlungen der Veste Coburg*)

What exactly was an **indulgence?** According to Catholic theology, individuals who sin alienate themselves from God. To be reconciled to God, the sinner must confess his or her sins to a priest and do an assigned **penance,** a religious act such as praying or fasting. Sometimes earthly penance is not enough, and beginning in the twelfth century learned theologians increasingly emphasized the idea of **purgatory,** a place where souls on their way to Heaven after death went to make amends for their earthly sins. (Those on their way to Hell went

straight there.) When it was first discussed, purgatory was a rather neutral place, unpleasant largely because one was separated from God, but by the fifteenth century it had acquired the fire and brimstone of Hell. Time in purgatory could be shortened by actions of the living, however, such as arranging for memorial masses or saying prayers for the dead.

According to Catholic theology, the church has the authority to grant sinners the remission of the penalties for sin by drawing on what was termed the "treasury of merits." This was a collection of all the virtuous acts that Christ, the apostles, and the saints had done during their lives; their virtue was infinite, and so was the treasury of merit. People thought of it as a sort of strongbox, like those in which merchants carried coins. An indulgence was a piece of parchment (and later paper), signed by the pope or another church official, that substituted a virtuous act from the treasury of merit for penance. The papacy and bishops had given Crusaders such indulgences, and by the later Middle Ages they were offered for making pilgrimages or other pious activities and also sold outright. People widely believed that indulgences secured total remission of penalties for sin and could substitute for both penance and time in purgatory. They ensured swift entry into Heaven and, like prayers for the dead, were effective on behalf of relatives or friends already dead.

Luther was severely troubled that ignorant people believed that they had no further need for repentance once they had purchased indulgences. He wrote a letter to Archbishop Albert on the subject and enclosed in Latin "Ninety-five Theses on the Power of Indulgences." His argument was that indulgences undermined the seriousness of the sacrament of penance, competed with the preaching of the Gospel, and downplayed the importance of charity in Christian life. After Luther's death, biographies reported that the theses were also posted on the door of the church at Wittenberg Castle on October 31, 1517. Such an act would have been very strange—they were in Latin and written for those learned in theology, not for normal churchgoers—but it has become a standard part of Luther lore. In any case, Luther intended the theses for academic debate, but by December 1517 they had been translated into German and were read throughout the Roman Empire.

Online Study Center **Improve Your Grade**
Primary Source: "Ninety-five Theses on the Power and Efficacy of Indulgences"

Luther was ordered to come to Rome, which he was able to avoid because of the political situation in the empire, but he did engage in formal scholarly debate with a representative of the church, Johann Eck, at Leipzig in 1519. He denied both the authority of the pope and the infallibility of a general council. The Council of Constance, he said, had erred when it had condemned Jan Hus (see page 391).

The papacy responded with a letter condemning some of Luther's propositions, ordering that his books be burned, and giving him two months to recant or be excommunicated. Luther retaliated by publicly burning the letter. By January 3, 1521, when the excommunication was supposed to become final, the controversy involved more than theological issues. The papal legate wrote, "All Germany is in revolution. Nine-tenths shout 'Luther' as their war cry; and the other tenth cares nothing about Luther, and cries 'Death to the court of Rome.'"[1]

In this highly charged atmosphere, the twenty-one-year-old emperor Charles V held his first diet (assembly of the Estates of the empire) in the German city of Worms. Charles summoned Luther to appear before the **Diet of Worms.** When ordered to recant, Luther replied in language that rang all over Europe:

Unless I am convinced by the evidence of Scripture or by plain reason—for I do not accept the authority of the Pope or the councils alone, since it is established that they have often erred and contradicted themselves—I am bound by the Scriptures I have cited and my conscience is captive to the Word of God. I cannot and will not recant anything, for it is neither safe nor right to go against conscience. God help me. Amen.[2]

Protestant Thought

As he developed his ideas, Luther gathered followers, who came to be called Protestants. The word **Protestant** derives from the protest drawn up by a small group of reforming German princes at the Diet of Speyer in 1529. The princes "protested" the decisions of the Catholic majority. At first Protestant meant "Lutheran," but with the appearance of many protesting sects, it became a general term applied to all non-Catholic western European Christians.

The most important early reformer other than Luther was the Swiss humanist, priest, and admirer of Erasmus, Ulrich Zwingli (1484–1531). In Zurich, Zwingli announced in 1519 that he would preach not from the church's prescribed readings but, relying on Erasmus's New Testament, go right through the New Testament "from A to Z," that is, from Matthew to Revelation.

Zwingli was convinced that Christian life rested on the Scriptures, which were the pure words of God and the sole basis of religious truth. He went on to attack indulgences, the Mass, the institution of monasticism, and clerical celibacy. In his gradual reform of the church in Zurich, where he remained the rest of his life, he had the strong support of the city authorities, who had long resented the privileges of the clergy.

Luther, Zwingli, and other Protestants agreed on many things. First, how is a person to be saved? Traditional Catholic teaching held that salvation is achieved by both faith and good works. Protestants held that salvation comes by faith alone. Women and men are saved by the arbitrary decision of God, irrespective of good works or the sacraments. God, not people, initiates salvation. (See the feature "Listening to the Past: Martin Luther, *On Christian Liberty*" on pages 480–481.) Second, where does religious authority reside? Christian doctrine had long maintained that authority rests both in the Bible and in the traditional teaching of the church. For Protestants, authority rests in the Word of God as revealed in the Bible alone and as interpreted by an individual's conscience. For a doctrine or issue to be valid, it had to have a scriptural basis. Because of this, most Protestants rejected Catholic teachings about the sacraments (see page 308), holding that only baptism and the Eucharist have scriptural support.

Third, what is the church? Protestants held that the church is a spiritual *priesthood of all believers,* an invisible fellowship not fixed in any place or person, which differed markedly from the Roman Catholic practice of a clerical, hierarchical institution headed by the pope in Rome. Luther re-emphasized the Catholic teaching that the church consists of the entire community of Christian believers. Medieval churchmen, in contrast, had tended to identify the church with the clergy. Fourth, what is the highest form of Christian life? The medieval church had stressed the superiority of the monastic and religious life over the secular. Luther argued that all vocations, whether ecclesiastical or secular, have equal merit and that every person should serve God in his or her individual calling. Celibacy was not superior to marriage, and vows of celibacy went against both human nature and God's commandment.

Protestants did not agree on everything. One important area of dispute was the ritual of the Eucharist (also called communion, or the Lord's Supper). Catholics hold the dogma of **transubstantiation:** by the consecrating words of the priest during the Mass, the bread and wine become the actual body and blood of Christ, who is then fully present in the bread and wine. In opposition,

Lucas Cranach the Elder: The Ten Commandments, 1516 Cranach, who was the court painter for the elector of Saxony from 1505 to 1553, painted this giant illustration of the Ten Commandments (more than 5 feet by 11 feet) for the city hall in Wittenberg just at the point that Luther was beginning to question Catholic doctrine. Cranach became an early supporter of Luther, and many of his later works depict the reformer and his ideas. This close association, and the fact that the painting captures the Protestant emphasis on biblical texts very well, led it to be moved to the Luther House in Wittenberg, the largest museum of the Protestant Reformation in the world. Paintings were used by both Protestants and Catholics to teach religious ideas. (*Lutherhalle, Wittenberg/The Bridgeman Art Library*)

Luther believed that Christ is really present in the consecrated bread and wine, but this is the result of God's mystery, not the actions of a priest. Zwingli understood the Lord's Supper as a *memorial,* in which Christ was present in spirit among the faithful, but not in the bread and wine. The Colloquy of Marburg, summoned in 1529 to unite Protestants, failed to resolve these differences, though Protestants reached agreement on almost everything else.

The Appeal of Protestant Ideas

Every encounter Luther had with ecclesiastical or political authorities attracted attention. Pulpits and printing presses spread his message all over Germany. By the time of his death, people of all social classes had become Lutheran. What was the immense appeal of Luther's religious ideas and those of other Protestants?

Educated people and humanists were much attracted by Luther's words. He advocated a simpler personal religion based on faith, a return to the spirit of the early church, the centrality of the Scriptures in the liturgy and in Christian life, and the abolition of elaborate ceremonies—precisely the reforms the Christian humanists had been calling for. His insistence that everyone should read and reflect on the Scriptures attracted the literate and thoughtful middle classes partly because Luther appealed to their intelligence. This included many priests and monks, who became clergy in the new Protestant churches. There was no official position for women in Protestant churches, but Protestant literature was smuggled into convents. Some nuns (most famously Katharina von Bora, who became Luther's wife) accepted Luther's idea that celibacy was not especially worthy and left their convents, while others remained in their convents but otherwise accepted Protestant teachings.

As we saw above, many townspeople envied the church's wealth, disapproved of the luxurious lifestyle of some churchmen, and resented tithes and ecclesiastical taxation. Protestant doctrines of the priesthood of all believers not only raised the religious status of laypeople, but also provided greater income for city treasuries. After

Zurich became Protestant, the city council taxed the clergy and placed them under the jurisdiction of civil courts.

Hymns, psalms, and Luther's two catechisms (1529), compendiums of basic religious knowledge, show the power of language in spreading the ideals of the Reformation. Such hymns as the famous "A Mighty Fortress Is Our God" (which Luther wrote) expressed deep human feelings, were easily remembered, and imprinted central points of doctrine on the mind. Luther's *Larger Catechism* contained brief sermons on the main articles of faith, whereas the *Shorter Catechism* gave concise explanations of doctrine in question-and-answer form. Both catechisms stressed the importance of the Ten Commandments, the Lord's Prayer, the Apostle's Creed, and the sacraments for the believing Christian. Although originally intended for the instruction of pastors, these catechisms became powerful techniques for the indoctrination of men and women of all ages, especially the young.

Scholars in many disciplines have attributed Luther's fame and success to the invention of the printing press, which rapidly reproduced and made known his ideas. Many printed works included woodcuts and other illustrations, so that even those who could not read could grasp the main ideas. (See the feature "Images in Society: Art in the Reformation" on pages 452–453.) Equally important was Luther's incredible skill with language. Luther's linguistic skill, together with his translation of the New Testament into German in 1523, led to the acceptance of his dialect of German as the standard version of German.

Both Luther and Zwingli recognized that if reforms were going to be permanent, political authorities as well as concerned individuals and religious leaders would have to accept them. Zwingli worked closely with the city council of Zurich, and in other cities and towns of Switzerland and south Germany city councils similarly took the lead. They appointed pastors that they knew had accepted Protestant ideas, required them to swear an oath of loyalty to the council, and oversaw their preaching and teaching.

Luther lived in a territory ruled by a noble—the elector of Saxony—and he also worked closely with political authorities, viewing them as fully justified in asserting control over the church in their territories. Indeed, in his 1520 *Address to the Christian Nobility of the German Nation* he demanded that German rulers reform the papacy and ecclesiastical institutions, and in *On Secular Government* he instructed all Christians to obey their secular rulers, whom he saw as divinely ordained to maintain order. In terms of the process of the Reformation, Luther's hopes were largely fulfilled. Individuals may have been convinced of the truth of Protestant teachings by hearing sermons, listening to hymns, or reading pamphlets, but a territory became Protestant when its ruler, whether a noble or a city council, brought in a reformer or to re-educate the territory's clergy, sponsored public sermons, and confiscated church property. This happened in many of the states of the empire during the 1520s. In every area that became Protestant, there was aslightly differ-ent balance between popular religious ideas and the aims of the political authorities. In some areas certain groups, such as clergy or journeymen, pushed for reforms, while in others the ruler or city council forced religious change on a population that was disinterested or hostile.

The first area outside the empire to officially accept the Reformation was the kingdom of Denmark-Norway under King Christian III (r. 1536–1559). Danish scholars studied at the University of Wittenberg, and Lutheran ideas spread into Denmark very quickly. In the 1530s the king officially broke with the Catholic Church, and most clergy followed. The process went smoothly in Denmark, but in northern Norway and Iceland (which Christian also ruled) there were violent reactions, and Lutheranism was only gradually imposed on a largely unwilling populace. In Sweden, Gustavus Vasa (r. 1523–1560), who came to the throne during a civil war with Denmark, also took over control of church personnel and income, and Protestant ideas spread, though the Swedish church did not officially accept Lutheran theology until later in the century.

The Radical Reformation

Some individuals and groups rejected the idea that church and state needed to be united, and sought to create a voluntary community of believers as they understood it to have existed in New Testament times. In terms of theology and spiritual practices, these individuals and groups varied widely, though they are generally termed "radicals" for their insistence on a more extensive break with the past. Many of them repudiated infant baptism, for they wanted only members who had intentionally chosen to belong. Some adopted the baptism of believers—for which they were given the title of "Anabaptists" or rebaptizers by their enemies—while others saw all outward sacraments or rituals as misguided and concentrated on inner spiritual transformation. Some groups attempted to follow Christ's commandments in the Gospels literally, while others reinterpreted the nature

Images in Society

Art in the Reformation

In the Reformation era, controversy raged over the purpose and function of art. Protestants and Catholics disagreed, and Protestant groups disagreed with one another. The Bible specifically prohibits making images of anything "in the heavens above or the earth below or the waters beneath the earth" (Exodus 20:4–6 and Deuteronomy 5:8–10). Based on this, some Protestant leaders, including Ulrich Zwingli, stressed that "the Word of God" should be the only instrument used in the work of evangelization. Martin Luther disagreed, saying he was not "of the opinion that the Gospel should blight and destroy all the arts." Luther believed that painting and sculpture had value in spreading the Gospel message because "children and simple folk are more apt to retain the divine stories when taught by pictures and parables than merely by words or instruction." Similar debates involved music, with Luther supporting and even writing hymns, and Swiss Protestants removing organs from their churches.

Lucas Cranach the Elder (1472–1553), a close friend of Luther's, is the finest representative of Protestant Reformation artists. He and Luther collaborated on the production of woodcuts and paintings, such as *The Ten Commandments* (see page 450), that spread the new evangelical theology. Each square in Cranach's painting represents one of the Ten Commandments.

Lucas Cranach the Younger (1515–1586) continued his father's work of spreading Luther's message. His woodcut *The True and False Churches* (Image 1) contains blatant and more subtle messages. At the center Luther stands in a pulpit, preaching the word of God from an open Bible. At the right, a flaming open mouth symbolizing the jaws of Hell engulfs the pope, cardinals, and friars, one kind of "false church." The scene at the left actually suggests another kind of "false church," however. Cranach shows a crucified Christ emerging out of the

"lamb of God" on the altar as people are receiving communion. This image represents the Lutheran understanding of the Lord's Supper, in which Christ is really present in the bread and wine, in contrast to other Protestants who saw the ceremony as a memorial (see page 450). The woodcut thus could be understood on different levels by different viewers, which is true of much effective religious art.

For John Calvin, the utter transcendence of God made impossible any attempt to bring God down to human level through visual portraiture; to domesticate or to humanize God would deprive him of his glory. In houses of worship Calvin emphasized the centrality of the divine word, allowing wall inscriptions from the Bible. In later life, Calvin tolerated narrative biblical scenes as long as they did not include pictures of God or Jesus Christ. In the Netherlands, which adopted a Calvinist version of Protestantism, many formerly Catholic churches were stripped of all statues, images, and decoration and were redesigned with a stark, bare simplicity that mirrored the Calvinist ideal. Notice the interior of the church of Saint Bavo in Haarlem (Image 2).

The Catholic Church officially addressed the subject of art at the Council of Trent in December 1563. The church declared that honor and veneration should be given to likenesses of Christ, the Virgin Mary, and the

Image 1 Lucas Cranach the Younger: The True and False Churches
(Staatliche Kunstsammlungen Dresden)

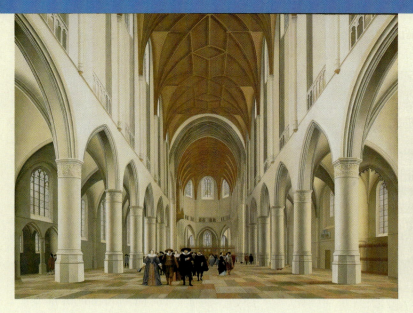

Image 2 Church of Saint Bavo, Haarlem (*Pieter Jansz, Saenredam, S. Bavo in Haarlem. John G. Johnson Collection, Philadelphia Museum of Art [J 599]*)

Image 3 Jesuit Priest Distributing Holy Pictures (*From Pierre Chenu,* The Reformation *[New York: St. Martin's Press, 1986]*)

Image 4 Ceiling of the Gesù (*Scala/Art Resource, NY*)

saints; that images would remind people of the saints' virtues, which should be imitated; and that pictorial art would promote piety and the love of God. Examine the painting *Jesuit Priest Distributing Holy Pictures* (Image 3). Such pictures and images of saints were often given to children to help educate them on matters of doctrine. How do these pictures serve the same function as the Protestant *Ten Commandments*?

Both Protestants and Catholics used religious art for propaganda purposes, to oppose religious heterodoxy, and to arouse piety in laypeople. Catholic Reformation art came into full flowering with the style later known as baroque (see page 539). Baroque art originated in Rome and reflected the dynamic and proselytizing spirit of the Counter-Reformation. The church encouraged artists to appeal to the senses, to touch the souls and kindle the faith of ordinary people while proclaiming the power and confidence of the reformed Catholic Church.

In addition to this underlying religious emotionalism, the baroque drew from the Catholic Reformation a sense of drama, motion, and ceaseless striving. The interior of the Jesuit Church of Jesus—the Gesù—combined all these characteristics in its lavish, shimmering, wildly active decorations and frescoes (Image 4). This triumphant, elaborate, and flamboyant church celebrates both the Catholic baroque and Rome as the artistic capital of Europe. How would you compare the Gesù with the Saint Bavo Church (Image 2)?

Domestic Scene   The Protestant notion that the best form of Christian life was marriage and a family helps explain its appeal to middle-class urban men and women, such as those shown in this domestic scene. The engraving, titled "Concordia" (harmony), includes the biblical inscription of what Jesus called the greatest commandment—"You shall love the Lord your God with all your heart and all your soul and your neighbor as yourself " (Deuteronomy 6; Matthew 22)—on tablets at the back. The father presides as his son says grace; the mother passes bread; the older daughters seem to have begun eating; and small children and animals complete the scene. The large covered bed at the back was both a standard piece of furniture in urban homes and a symbol of proper marital sexual relations. *(Mary Evans Picture Library)*

of Christ. Radicals were often pacifists and refused to hold office or swear oaths, which were required of nearly everyone with any position of authority, including city midwives and toll collectors, as well as anyone involved in court proceedings. Some groups attempted communal ownership of property, living very simply and rejecting anything they thought unbiblical. Different groups blended these practices in different ways and often reacted harshly to a member who deviated, banning the person from the group and requiring other group members—sometimes including the spouse—to shun, or have no contact with, the offending member until he or she changed behavior and asked for forgiveness. Others, however, argued for complete religious toleration and individualism.

Ideas such as absolute pacifism and the distinction between the Christian community and the state brought down on these unfortunate people fanatical hatred and bitter persecution. Protestants and Catholics all saw—quite correctly—the separation of church and state as leading ultimately to the secularization of society. The powerful rulers of Swiss and German society immediately saw the connection between religious heresy and economic dislocation. Civil authorities feared that the combination of religious differences and economic grievances would lead to civil disturbances. In Saxony, in Strasbourg, and in the Swiss cities, radicals were either banished or cruelly executed by burning, beating, or drowning. Their community spirit and the edifying example of their lives, however, contributed to the survival of radical ideas. Later, the Quakers, with their gentle pacifism; the Baptists, with their emphasis on inner spiritual light; the Congregationalists, with their democratic church organization; and in 1787 the authors of the U.S. Constitution, with their opposition to the "establishment of religion" (state churches), would all trace their origins, in part, to the radicals of the sixteenth century.

The German Peasants' War

The radicals represent one way that the ideas of early reformers were pushed farther; as we have seen, many of their ideas had social, economic, and political implications, which is in part why they were seen as so dangerous. Groups that linked Protestant ideas directly to various political and social programs were also threatening. The most far-reaching of these was the German Peasants' War of 1525.

Peasant revolts had erupted in many parts of Europe in the fourteenth and fifteenth centuries (see page 390). In the early sixteenth century the economic condition of the peasantry varied from place to place but was generally worse than it had been in the fifteenth century and was deteriorating. Crop failures in 1523 and 1524 aggravated an explosive situation. In 1525 representatives of the Swabian peasants met at the city of Memmingen and drew up the Twelve Articles expressing their grievances. The Twelve Articles condemned lay and ecclesiastical lords and summarized the agrarian crisis of the early sixteenth century. They complained that nobles had seized village common lands, which traditionally had been used by all; that they had imposed new rents on manorial properties and new services on the peasants working those properties; and that they had forced the poor to pay unjust death duties in the form of the peasants' best horses or cows. Wealthy, socially mobile peasants especially resented these burdens, which they emphasized as new. The peasants believed that their demands conformed to the Scriptures and cited Luther as a theologian who could prove that they did.

Luther wanted to prevent rebellion. Initially he sided with the peasants, and he blasted the lords in his tract *An Admonition to Peace* (1525):

We have no one on earth to thank for this mischievous rebellion, except you lords and princes, especially you blind bishops and mad priests and monks. . . . In your government you do nothing but flay and rob your subjects in order that you may lead a life of splendor and pride, until the poor common folk can bear it no longer.[3]

But, he warned, nothing justified the use of armed force: "The fact that rulers are unjust and wicked does not excuse tumult and rebellion; to punish wickedness does not belong to everybody, but to the worldly rulers who bear the sword." As for biblical support for the peasants' demands, he maintained that Scripture had nothing to do with earthly justice or material gain, a position that Zwingli supported.[4]

Massive revolts first broke out near the Swiss frontier and then swept through Swabia, Thuringia, the Rhineland, and Saxony. The crowds' slogans came directly from Protestant writings. "God's righteousness" and the "Word of God" were invoked in an effort to secure social and economic justice. The peasants who expected Luther's support were soon disillusioned. Freedom for Luther meant independence from the authority of the Roman church; it did *not* mean opposition to legally established secular powers. Firmly convinced that rebellion would hasten the end of civilized society, he wrote the tract *Against the Murderous, Thieving Hordes of the Peasants:* "Let everyone who can smite, slay, and stab [the peasants], secretly and openly, remembering that nothing can be more poisonous, hurtful or devilish than a rebel."[5] The nobility ferociously crushed the revolt. Historians estimate that more than seventy-five thousand peasants were killed in 1525.

The German Peasants' War of 1525 greatly strengthened the authority of lay rulers. Not surprisingly, the Reformation lost much of its popular appeal after 1525, though peasants and urban rebels sometimes found a place for their social and religious ideas in radical groups. Peasants' economic conditions did moderately improve, however. For example, in many parts of Germany, enclosed fields, meadows, and forests were returned to common use.

The Reformation and Marriage

At the same time they were reacting so harshly to radicals and peasants, Luther and Zwingli decided to marry, Luther to a former nun, Katharina von Bora (1499–1532), and Zwingli to a Zurich widow, Anna Reinhart (1491–1538). Both women quickly had several children. Most other Protestant reformers also married, and their wives had to create a new and respectable role for themselves—pastor's wife—to overcome being viewed as simply a new type of priest's concubine. They were living demonstrations of their husband's convictions about the superiority of marriage to celibacy, and they were expected to be models of wifely obedience and Christian charity.

Though they denied that marriage was a sacrament, many Protestant reformers praised marriage in formal treatises, commentaries on the Book of Genesis, household guides, and—most importantly—wedding sermons. They stressed that it had been ordained by God when he presented Eve to Adam, served as a "remedy" for the unavoidable sin of lust, provided a site for the pious rearing of the next generation of God-fearing Christians, and offered husbands and wives companionship and consolation. A proper marriage was one that reflected both the spiritual equality of men and women and the proper social hierarchy of husbandly authority and wifely obedience.

Protestants did not break with medieval scholastic theologians in their idea that women were to be subject to men, a subjection rooted in their original nature and made more pronounced by Eve's primary responsibility for the Fall. Women were advised to be cheerful rather than grudging in their obedience, for in doing so they

Martin Luther and Katharina von Bora, by Lucas Cranach the Elder   Cranach painted this double marriage portrait to celebrate Luther's wedding in 1525 to Katharina von Bora, a former nun. The artist was one of the witnesses at the wedding and, in fact, had presented Luther's marriage proposal to Katharina. Using a go-between for proposals was very common, as was having a double wedding portrait painted. This particular couple quickly became a model of the ideal marriage, and many churches wanted their portraits. More than sixty similar paintings, with slight variations, were produced by Cranach's workshop and hung in churches and wealthy homes. (*Uffizi, Florence/Scala/Art Resource, NY*)

demonstrated their willingness to follow God's plan. Men were urged to treat their wives kindly and considerately, but also to enforce their authority, through physical coercion if necessary. Both continental and English marriage manuals use the metaphor of breaking a horse for teaching a wife obedience, though laws did set limits on the husband's power to do so. A few women took Luther's idea about the priesthood of all believers to heart and wrote religious pamphlets and hymns, but no sixteenth-century Protestants officially allowed women to hold positions of religious authority, though monarchs such as Elizabeth I of England and female territorial rulers of the states of the Holy Roman Empire did determine religious policies.

Catholics viewed marriage as a sacramental union that, if validly entered into, could not be dissolved. Protestants saw marriage as a contract in which each partner promised the other support, companionship, and the sharing of mutual goods. Because, in Protestant eyes, marriage was created by God as a remedy for human weakness, marriages in which spouses did not comfort or support one another physically, materially, or emotionally endangered their own souls and the surrounding community. The only solution might be divorce and remarriage, which most Protestants came to allow. Protestant marital courts in Germany, Switzerland, Scandinavia, and later

Scotland and France allowed divorce for adultery and impotence, and sometimes for contracting a contagious disease, "malicious" desertion (meaning intentional desertion, as opposed to unintentional desertion such as extended army service), conviction for a capital crime, or deadly assault. Some of them allowed both parties to marry again, and some only the innocent.

This was a dramatic change in marital law, as Catholic canon law had allowed only separation from bed and board with no remarriage, but it had a less than dramatic impact. Because marriage was the cornerstone of society socially and economically, divorce was a desperate last resort. In many Protestant jurisdictions the annual divorce rate hovered around 0.02 to 0.06 per thousand people. (By contrast, in 2000 the U.S. divorce rate was 4.1 per thousand people.)

Marriage was the proper remedy for lust, and Protestants uniformly condemned prostitution. The licensed brothels that were a common feature of late medieval urban life (see page 394) were closed in Protestant cities, and harsh punishments were set for prostitution. Selling sex was couched in moral rather than economic terms, as simply one type of "whoredom," a term that also included premarital sex, adultery, and other unacceptable sexual activities. Religious reformers such as Luther described women who sold sex in very negative terms and also regarded "whore" as the worst epithet they could hurl at their theological opponents.

Closing the official brothels did not end the exchange of sex for money, of course, but simply reshaped it. Smaller illegal brothels were established, or women moved to areas right outside city walls. Police and other authorities were influenced or bribed to overlook such activities. For Italian city authorities, this fluid situation was more worrisome, and they tended to favor regulation over suppression. They also viewed selling sex as a significant source of municipal income. From 1559 until the mid-eighteenth century in Florence, for example, all women registered as prostitutes were required to contribute an annual tax based on their income, which went to support a convent for women who wished to give up prostitution. Payment of extra taxes would allow a woman to live where she wished in the city and wear any type of clothes she chose, rather than having to follow the sumptuary laws requiring prostitutes to dress a certain way (see page 394).

The Protestant Reformation clearly had a positive impact on marriage, but its impact on women was more mixed. Many nuns had lacked a religious vocation, but convents nevertheless provided women of the upper classes with scope for their literary, artistic, medical, or administrative talents if they could not or would not marry. The Reformation generally brought the closing of monasteries and convents, and marriage became virtually the only occupation for upper-class Protestant women. Women in some convents recognized this and fought the Reformation, or argued that they could still be pious Protestants within convent walls. Most nuns left, however, and we do not know what happened to them. The Protestant emphasis on marriage made unmarried women (and men) suspect, for they did not belong to the type of household regarded as the cornerstone of a proper, godly society.

The Reformation and German Politics

Criticism of the church was widespread in Europe in the early sixteenth century, and calls for reform came from many areas. It was no accident, however, that the reformer whose ideas had the most impact lived in the politically divided Holy Roman Empire. Unlike Spain, France, and England, the Holy Roman Empire lacked a strong central power. The emperor was elected in a process established by the Golden Bull of 1356, a decree issued by the Holy Roman emperor Charles IV (and

named after the golden seal attached to it). There were only seven electors—the archbishops of Mainz, Trier, and Cologne, the margrave of Brandenburg, the duke of Saxony, the count palatine of the Rhine, and the king of Bohemia. All these individuals were powerful, but so were many other nobles and church officials who ruled the hundreds of largely independent states in the empire.

Against this background of decentralization and strong local power, Martin Luther had launched a movement to reform the church. Two years after Luther published the Ninety-five Theses, the electors chose as emperor a nineteen-year-old Habsburg prince who ruled as Charles V. The course of the Reformation was shaped by this election and by the political relationships surrounding it.

- **How did the political situation in Germany shape the course of the Reformation?**

The Rise of the Habsburg Dynasty

War and diplomacy were important ways that states increased their power in sixteenth-century Europe, but so was marriage. Because almost all of Europe was ruled by hereditary dynasties—the Papal States and a few cities being the exceptions—claiming and holding resources involved shrewd marital strategies, for it was far cheaper to gain land by inheritance than by war. Royal and noble sons and daughters were important tools of state policy. Even popes and city leaders were often part of such marital strategies; papal nieces, nephews, and sometimes children were coveted marriage partners, as were the wealthy daughters of urban elites. Wealthy urban families, especially in Italy, also transformed themselves into hereditary dynasties through coups and alliances during this period, and they cemented their position through marriages with more established ruling houses.

The benefits of an advantageous marriage, particularly if the wife had no brothers and thus inherited territory, stretched across generations, a process that can be seen most dramatically with the Habsburgs. The Holy Roman emperor Frederick III, a Habsburg who was the ruler of most of Austria, acquired only a small amount of territory—but a great deal of money—with his marriage to Princess Eleonore of Portugal in 1452. He arranged for his son Maximilian to marry Europe's most prominent heiress, Mary of Burgundy, in 1477; she inherited the Netherlands, Luxembourg, and the County of Burgundy in what is now eastern France. Through this union with the rich and powerful duchy of Burgundy, the Austrian house of Habsburg, already the strongest ruling family in the empire, became an international power. The marriage of Maximilian and Mary angered the French, however, who considered Burgundy French territory, and inaugurated centuries of conflict between the Austrian house of Habsburg and the kings of France.

"Other nations wage war; you, happy Austria, marry." Historians dispute the origins of this adage, but no one questions its accuracy, at least in terms of marriage. (The frequency with which the Habsburgs went to war make the saying somewhat ironic.) Maximilian learned the lesson of marital politics well, marrying his son and daughter to the children of Ferdinand and Isabella, the rulers of Spain, much of southern Italy, and eventually the Spanish New World empire. His grandson Charles V (1500–1558) fell heir to a vast conglomeration of territories. Through a series of accidents and unexpected deaths, Charles inherited Spain from his mother, her New World possessions, and the Spanish dominions in Italy, Sicily, and Sardinia. From his father he inherited the Habsburg lands in Austria, southern Germany, the Low Countries, and Franche-Comté in east-central France. Charles would eventually rule about half of Europe.

Charles's inheritance was an incredibly diverse collection of states and peoples, each governed in a different manner and held together only by the person of the emperor (see Map 14.1 on page 460). Charles's Italian adviser, the grand chancellor Gattinara, told the young ruler, "God has set you on the path toward world monarchy." Charles not only believed this but also was convinced that it was his duty to maintain the political and religious unity of Western Christendom.

The Political Impact of the Protestant Reformation

In the sixteenth century the practice of religion remained a public matter. Everyone participated in the religious life of the community, just as almost everyone shared in the local agricultural work. Whatever spiritual convictions individuals held in the privacy of their consciences, the emperor, king, prince, magistrate, or other civil authority determined the official form of religious practice in his (or occasionally her) jurisdiction. Almost everyone believed that the presence of a faith different from that of the majority represented a political threat to the security of the state. Only a tiny minority, and certainly none of the rulers, believed in religious liberty.

Against this background, the religious storm launched by Martin Luther swept across Germany. Anticlericalism blended with hostility to the papacy, which was increasingly seen as Italian rather than international. Papal tax

collectors had long been more active in the empire than they were in the more unified nation-states such as France, where royal power restricted them. Luther and other reformers highlighted papal financial exploitation of Germany in their sermons and pamphlets. Though Germany was not a nation, people did have an understanding of being German because of their language and traditions. Luther frequently used the phrase "we Germans" in his attacks on the papacy. Luther's appeal to German patriotism gained him strong support, and national feeling influenced many rulers otherwise confused by or indifferent to the complexities of the religious issues. Some German rulers were sincerely attracted to Lutheran ideas, but material considerations swayed many others to embrace the new faith. The rejection of Roman Catholicism and adoption of Protestantism would mean the legal confiscation of lush farmlands, rich monasteries, and wealthy shrines. A steady stream of duchies, margraviates, free cities, and bishoprics secularized church property, accepted Lutheran theological doctrines, and adopted simpler services conducted in German. Thus many political authorities in the empire used the religious issue to extend their financial and political power and to enhance their independence from the emperor.

Charles V was a vigorous defender of Catholicism, however, so it is not surprising that the Reformation led to religious wars. The first battleground was Switzerland, which was officially part of the Holy Roman Empire, though it was really a loose confederation of thirteen largely autonomous territories called "cantons." Some cantons remained Catholic, and some became Protestant, and in the late 1520s the two sides went to war. Zwingli was killed on the battlefield in 1531, and both sides quickly decided that a treaty was preferable to further fighting. The treaty basically allowed each canton to determine its own religion and ordered each side to give up its foreign alliances, a policy of neutrality that has been characteristic of modern Switzerland.

Trying to halt the spread of religious division, Charles V called an Imperial Diet in 1530, to meet at Augsburg. The Lutherans developed a statement of faith, later called the Augsburg Confession, and the Protestant princes presented this to the emperor. (The Augsburg Confession remained an authoritative statement of belief for many Lutheran churches for centuries.) Charles refused to accept it and ordered all Protestants to return to the Catholic Church and give up any confiscated church property. This threat backfired, and Protestant territories in the empire—mostly north German princes and south German cities—formed a military alliance. The emperor could not respond militarily, as he was in the midst of a

Giorgio Vasari: Fresco of Pope Clement VII and the Emperor Charles V In this double portrait, Vasari uses matching hand gestures to indicate agreement between the pope and the emperor, though the pope's red hat and cape make him the dominant figure. Charles V remained loyal to Catholicism, though the political situation and religious wars in Germany eventually required him to compromise with Protestants. *(Palazzo Vecchio, Florence/Scala/Art Resource, NY)*

series of wars with the French: the Habsburg-Valois Wars, fought in Italy along the eastern and southern borders of France and eventually in Germany. The Turks had also taken much of Hungary and in 1529 were besieging Vienna.

The 1530s and early 1540s saw complicated political maneuvering among many of the powers of Europe. The emperor, the pope, France, England, Protestant and Catholic princes and cities in Germany, Scotland, Sweden, Denmark, and even the Turks made and broke alliances, and the Habsburg-Valois rivalry continued to be played out militarily. Various attempts were made to heal the religious split with a church council, but intransigence on both sides made it increasingly clear that this would not be possible and that war was inevitable. Charles V realized that he was fighting not only for religious unity, but also for a more unified state against territorial rulers who wanted to maintain their independence. He was thus defending both church and empire.

Fighting began in 1546, and initially the emperor was very successful. This success alarmed both France and the pope, however, who did not want Charles to become even more powerful. The pope withdrew papal troops, and the Catholic king of France sent money and troops to the Lutheran princes. Finally, in 1555 Charles agreed to the Peace of Augsburg, which, in accepting the status quo, officially recognized Lutheranism. The political authority in each territory was permitted to decide whether the territory would be Catholic or Lutheran. Most of northern and central Germany became Lutheran, while the south remained Roman Catholic. There was no freedom of religion, however. Princes or town councils established state churches to which all subjects of the area had to belong. Dissidents had to convert or leave.

Online Study Center **Improve Your Grade**
Primary Source: The Religious Peace of Augsburg

There were limitations and problems in the Peace of Augsburg that would become clear by the late sixteenth century, but it accomplished what its makers hoped it would. It ended religious war in Germany for many decades, and it put political, religious, and economic life clearly in the hands of the territorial rulers. It was immediately evident that this agreement ended Charles V's hope of creating a united empire with a single church. He abdicated in 1556 and moved to a monastery, transferring power over his Spanish and Netherlandish holdings to his son Philip and his imperial power to his brother Ferdinand.

The Spread of the Protestant Reformation

States within the empire and the kingdom of Denmark-Norway were the earliest territories to accept the Protestant Reformation, but by the later 1520s Protestant ideas and dynastic considerations combined to bring religious

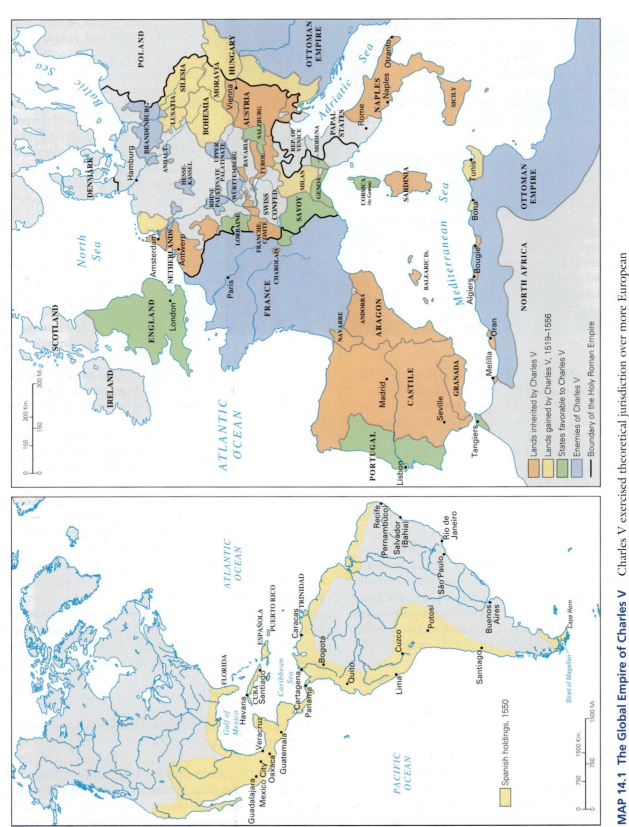

MAP 14.1 The Global Empire of Charles V Charles V exercised theoretical jurisdiction over more European territory than anyone since Charlemagne. He also claimed authority over large parts of North and South America, though actual Spanish control was weak in much of this area.

Online Study Center **Improve Your Grade** Interactive Map: Global Empire of Charles V

change to England. Protestant ideas also spread into France and eastern Europe. In all these areas, a second generation of reformers built on Lutheran and Zwinglian ideas to develop their own theology and plans for institutional change. The most important of the second-generation reformers was John Calvin, whose ideas would come to shape Christianity over a much wider area than did Luther's.

• *How did Protestant ideas and institutions spread beyond German-speaking lands?*

The Reformation in England and Ireland

As on the continent, the Reformation in England had economic as well as religious causes. When the personal matter of the divorce of King Henry VIII (r. 1509–1547) became enmeshed with political issues, a complete break with Rome resulted.

Henry was married to Catherine of Aragon, the daughter of Ferdinand and Isabella. Catherine had originally been married to his older brother Arthur, who had died as a youth. Marriage to a brother's widow went against canon law, and Henry had been required to obtain a special papal dispensation to marry Catherine. The marriage was about average for royal marriages—they neither especially hated nor loved one another—but it had produced only one living heir, a daughter, Mary. By 1527 Henry decided that God was showing his displeasure with the marriage by denying him a son, and he appealed to the pope to have the marriage annulled. He was also in love with a court lady-in-waiting, Anne Boleyn, and assumed that she would give him the son he wanted. Normally an annulment would not have been a problem, but the troops of Emperor Charles V were in Rome at that point, and Pope Clement VII was essentially their prisoner. Charles V was the nephew of Catherine of Aragon and thus was vigorously opposed to an annulment, which would have declared his aunt a fornicator and his cousin Mary a bastard. (An annulment declares that there never was a marriage, making children of such a union illegitimate.) The military situation in Rome, added to the fact that an annulment would have called into question the pope's right to grant a dispensation from something proscribed by the Bible, led the pope to stall.

Since Rome appeared to be thwarting Henry's matrimonial plans, he decided to remove the English church from papal jurisdiction. Henry used Parliament to legalize the Reformation in England. The Act in Restraint of Appeals (1533) declared the king to be the supreme sovereign in England and forbade judicial appeals to the papacy, thus establishing the Crown as the highest legal authority in the land. The Supremacy Act (1534) declared the king the supreme head of the Church of England. Both the Act in Restraint of Appeals and the Supremacy Act led to heated debate in the House of Commons. Some opposed the king. John Fisher, the bishop of Rochester, a distinguished scholar and a humanist, lashed the clergy with scorn for its cowardice in abjectly bending to the king's will. Another humanist, Thomas More, resigned the chancellorship: he could not take the oath required by the Supremacy Act because it rejected papal authority and made the king head of the English church. Fisher, More, and other dissenters were beheaded.

When Anne Boleyn failed twice to produce a male child, Henry VIII charged her with adulterous incest and in 1536 had her beheaded. Parliament promptly proclaimed Anne's daughter, the princess Elizabeth, illegitimate and, with the royal succession thoroughly confused, left the throne to whomever Henry chose. His third wife, Jane Seymour, gave Henry the desired son, Edward, but died in childbirth. Henry went on to three more wives. Before he died in 1547, he got Parliament to reverse the decision of 1536, relegitimating Mary and Elizabeth and fixing the succession first in his son and then in his daughters.

Between 1535 and 1539, under the influence of his chief minister, Thomas Cromwell, Henry decided to dissolve the English monasteries because he wanted their wealth. The king ended nine hundred years of English monastic life, dispersing the monks and nuns and confiscating their lands. Hundreds of properties were sold to the middle and upper classes and the proceeds spent on war. The dissolution of the monasteries did not achieve a more equitable distribution of land and wealth. Rather, the redistribution of land strengthened the upper classes and tied them to the Tudor dynasty.

Henry's motives combined personal, political, social, and economic elements. Theologically he retained such traditional Catholic practices and doctrines as confession, clerical celibacy, and transubstantiation. Meanwhile, Protestant literature circulated, and Henry approved the selection of men of Protestant sympathies as tutors for his son.

Did the religious changes accompanying this political upheaval have broad popular support? Some people were certainly dissatisfied with the church in England, but traditional Catholicism exerted an enormously strong and vigorous hold over the imagination and loyalty of the people. The surviving evidence does not allow us to gauge the degree of opposition to (or support for) Henry's

Allegory of the Tudor Dynasty   The unknown creator of this work intended to glorify the virtues of the Protestant succession; the painting has no historical reality. Enthroned Henry VIII (r. 1509–1547) hands the sword of justice to his Protestant son Edward VI (r. 1547–1553). The Catholic Queen Mary (r. 1553–1558) and her husband Philip of Spain are followed by Mars, god of war, signifying violence and civil disorder. At right the figures of Peace and Plenty accompany the Protestant Elizabeth I (r. 1558–1603), symbolizing England's happy fate under her rule. *(Yale Center for British Art, Paul Mellon Collection/The Bridgeman Art Library)*

break with Rome. Most clergy and officials accepted Henry's moves, but all did not quietly acquiesce. In 1536 popular opposition in the north to the religious changes led to the Pilgrimage of Grace, a massive multiclass rebellion that proved the largest in English history. The "pilgrims" accepted a truce, but their leaders were arrested, tried, and executed. Recent scholarship points out that people rarely "converted" from Catholicism to Protestantism overnight, particularly where changes were piecemeal and the religious policies of the Crown itself varied, as in England. People responded to an action of the Crown that was played out in their own neighborhood—the closing of a monastery, the ending of Masses for the dead—with a combination of resistance, acceptance, cooperation, and collaboration.

Loyalty to the Catholic Church was particularly strong in Ireland. Ireland had been claimed by English kings since the twelfth century, but in reality the English had

firm control of only the area around Dublin, known as the Pale. In 1536, on orders from London, the Irish parliament, which represented only the English landlords and the people of the Pale, approved the English laws severing the church from Rome. The Church of Ireland was established on the English pattern, and the (English) ruling class adopted the new reformed faith. Most of the Irish people remained Roman Catholic, thus adding religious antagonism to the ethnic hostility that had been a feature of English policy toward Ireland for centuries (see page 397). Irish armed opposition to the Reformation led to harsh repression by the English. Catholic property was confiscated and sold, and the profits were shipped to England. With the Roman church driven underground, Catholic clergy acted as national as well as religious leaders.

The nationalization of the church and the dissolution of the monasteries led to important changes in government administration in both England and Ireland. Vast tracts of formerly monastic land came temporarily under the Crown's jurisdiction, and new bureaucratic machinery had to be developed to manage those properties. Cromwell reformed and centralized the king's household, the council, the secretariats, and the Exchequer. New departments of state were set up. Surplus funds from all departments went into a liquid fund to be applied to areas where there were deficits. This balancing resulted in greater efficiency and economy. Henry VIII's reign saw the growth of the modern centralized bureaucratic state.

In the short reign of Henry's sickly son, Edward VI (r. 1547–1553), strongly Protestant ideas exerted a significant influence on the religious life of the country. Archbishop Thomas Cranmer simplified the liturgy, invited Protestant theologians to England, and prepared the first **Book of Common Prayer** (1549). In stately and dignified English, the *Book of Common Prayer* included, together with the Psalter, the order for all services of the Church of England.

The equally brief reign of Mary Tudor (r. 1553–1558) witnessed a sharp move back to Catholicism. The devoutly Catholic daughter of Catherine of Aragon, Mary rescinded the Reformation legislation of her father's reign and restored Roman Catholicism. Mary's marriage to her cousin Philip of Spain, son of the emperor Charles V, proved highly unpopular in England, and her execution of several hundred Protestants further alienated her subjects. During her reign, many Protestants fled to the continent. Mary's death raised to the throne her sister Elizabeth (r. 1558–1603) and inaugurated the beginnings of religious stability.

Elizabeth had been raised a Protestant, but at the start of her reign sharp differences existed in England. On the one hand, Catholics wanted a Roman Catholic ruler. On the other hand, a vocal number of returning exiles wanted all Catholic elements in the Church of England eliminated. The latter, because they wanted to "purify" the church, were called "Puritans." Probably one of the shrewdest politicians in English history, Elizabeth chose a middle course between Catholic and Puritan extremes. She insisted on dignity in church services and political order in the land. She required her subjects to attend church or risk a fine, but did not care what they actually believed as long as they kept quiet about it. She required officials, clergy, and nobles to swear allegiance to her as the "supreme governor of the Church of England." She initially chose the word *governor* rather than *head* to provide a loophole for English Catholics to remain loyal to her without denying the primacy of the pope. She also realized that *head* might be viewed as inappropriate for a woman, for treatises about the family and proper gender relations always referred to men as the "head."

The parliamentary legislation of the early years of Elizabeth's reign—laws sometimes labeled the **Elizabethan Settlement**—required outward conformity to the Church of England and uniformity in all ceremonies. In 1563 a convocation of bishops approved the Thirty-nine Articles, a summary in thirty-nine short statements of the basic tenets of the Church of England. During Elizabeth's reign, the Anglican church (from the Latin *Ecclesia Anglicana*), as the Church of England was called, moved in a moderately Protestant direction. Services were conducted in English, monasteries were not reestablished, and clergymen were (grudgingly) allowed to marry. But the episcopate was not abolished, and the bishops remained as church officials; apart from language, the services were quite traditional.

Calvinism

In 1509, while Luther was studying for a doctorate at Wittenberg, John Calvin (1509–1564) was born in Noyon in northwestern France. Luther inadvertently launched the Protestant Reformation. Calvin, however, had the greater impact on future generations. His theological writings profoundly influenced the social thought and attitudes of Europeans and English-speaking peoples all over the world, especially in Canada and the United States. Although he had originally intended to have an ecclesiastical career, Calvin studied law, which had a decisive impact on his mind and later thought. In 1533 he experienced a religious crisis, as a result of which he converted to Protestantism.

Convinced that God selects certain people to do his work, Calvin believed that God had specifically called him to reform the church. Accordingly, he accepted an invitation to assist in the reformation of the city of Geneva. There, beginning in 1541, Calvin worked assiduously to establish a Christian society ruled by God through civil magistrates and reformed ministers. Geneva, "a city that was a church," became the model of a Christian community for sixteenth-century Protestant reformers.

To understand Calvin's Geneva, it is necessary to understand Calvin's ideas. These he embodied in **The Institutes of the Christian Religion,** first published in 1536 and definitively issued in 1559. The cornerstone of Calvin's theology was his belief in the absolute sovereignty and omnipotence of God and the total weakness of humanity. Before the infinite power of God, he asserted, men and women are as insignificant as grains of sand.

Calvin did not ascribe free will to human beings because that would detract from the sovereignty of God. Men and women cannot actively work to achieve salvation; rather, God in his infinite wisdom decided at the beginning of time who would be saved and who damned. This viewpoint constitutes the theological principle called **predestination:**

Predestination we call the eternal decree of God, by which he has determined in himself, what he would have become of every individual. . . . For they are not all created with a similar destiny; but eternal life is foreordained for some, and eternal damnation for others. . . . In conformity, therefore, to the clear doctrine of the Scripture, we assert, that by an eternal and immutable counsel, God has once for all determined, both whom he would admit to salvation, and whom he would condemn to destruction. . . . To those whom he devotes to condemnation, the gate of life is closed by a just and irreprehensible, but incomprehensible, judgment. How exceedingly presumptuous it is only to inquire into the causes of the Divine will; which is in fact, and is justly entitled to be, the cause of everything that exists. . . . For the will of God is the highest justice; so that what he wills must be considered just, for this very reason, because he wills it.[6]

Many people consider the doctrine of predestination, which dates back to Saint Augustine and Saint Paul, to be a pessimistic view of the nature of God, who, they feel, revealed himself in the Old and New Testaments as merciful as well as just. But "this terrible decree," as even Calvin called it, did not lead to pessimism or fatalism. Rather, the Calvinist believed in the redemptive work of Christ and was confident that God had elected (saved) him or her. Predestination served as an energizing dynamic, forcing a person to undergo hardships in the constant struggle against evil.

Calvin aroused Genevans to a high standard of morality. He had two remarkable assets: complete mastery of the Scriptures and exceptional eloquence. Through his sermons and a program of religious education, God's laws and man's were enforced in Geneva. Calvin's powerful sermons delivered the Word of God and thereby monopolized the strongest contemporary means of communication: preaching. Through his *Genevan Catechism,* published in 1541, children and adults memorized set questions and answers and acquired a summary of their faith and a guide for daily living. Calvin's sermons and his *Catechism* gave a whole generation of Genevans thorough instruction in the reformed religion.[7]

Young John Calvin Even in youth, Calvin's face showed the strength and determination that were later to characterize his religious zeal. *(Bibliothèque de Genève, Département iconographique)*

In the reformation of the city, the Genevan Consistory also exercised a powerful role. This body consisted of twelve laymen plus the Company of Pastors, of which Calvin was the permanent moderator (presider). The duties of the Consistory were "to keep watch over every man's life [and] to admonish amiably those whom they see leading a disorderly life." Even though Calvin emphasized that the Consistory's activities should be thorough and "its eyes may be everywhere," corrections were considered only "medicine to turn sinners to the Lord."[8]

Although all municipal governments in early modern Europe regulated citizens' conduct, none did so with the severity of Geneva's Consistory under Calvin's leadership. Nor did it make any distinction between what we would consider crimes against society and simple unChristian conduct. Absence from sermons, criticism of ministers, dancing, card playing, family quarrels, and heavy drinking were all investigated and punished by the

Consistory. Serious crimes and heresy were handled by the civil authorities, which, with the Consistory's approval, sometimes used torture to extract confessions. Between 1542 and 1546 alone seventy-six persons were banished from Geneva and fifty-eight executed for heresy, adultery, blasphemy, and witchcraft.

Calvin reserved his harshest condemnation for religious dissenters, declaring them "dogs and swine":

God makes plain that the false prophet is to be stoned without mercy. We are to crush beneath our heel all affections of nature when His honor is concerned. The father should not spare his child, . . . nor husband his own wife or the friend who is dearer to him than life. No human relationship is more than animal unless it be grounded in God.[9]

In the 1550s Spanish humanist Michael Servetus had gained international notoriety for his publications denying the Christian dogma of the Trinity. Servetus had been arrested by the Inquisition but escaped to Geneva, where he was promptly rearrested. At his trial, he not only held to his belief that there is no scriptural basis for the Trinity but also rejected child baptism and insisted that a person under twenty cannot commit a mortal sin. The city fathers considered this last idea dangerous to public morality, "especially in these days when the young are so corrupted." Though Servetus begged that he be punished by banishment, Calvin and the town council maintained that the denial of child baptism and the Trinity amounted to a threat to all society. Servetus was burned at the stake.

Online Study Center Improve Your Grade
Primary Source: The Trial of Michael Servetus in Calvin's Geneva

To many sixteenth-century Europeans Calvin's Geneva seemed "the most perfect school of Christ since the days of the Apostles." Religious refugees from France, England, Spain, Scotland, and Italy visited the city. Subsequently, the Reformed church of Calvin served as the model for the Presbyterian church in Scotland, the Huguenot church in France, and the Puritan churches in England and New England.

Calvinism became the compelling force in international Protestantism. The Calvinist ethic of the "calling" dignified all work with a religious aspect. Hard work, well done, was pleasing to God. This doctrine encouraged an aggressive, vigorous activism. These factors, together with the social and economic applications of Calvin's theology, made Calvinism the most dynamic force in sixteenth- and seventeenth-century Protestantism.

The Establishment of the Church of Scotland

Calvinism found a ready audience in Scotland. There as elsewhere, political authority was the decisive influence in reform. The monarchy was weak, and factions of virtually independent nobles competed for power. King James V and his daughter Mary, Queen of Scots (r. 1560–1567), staunch Catholics and close allies of Catholic France, opposed reform. The Scottish nobles supported it. One man, John Knox (1505?–1572), dominated the movement for reform in Scotland.

In 1559 Knox, a dour, single-minded, and fearless man with a reputation as a passionate preacher, set to work reforming the church. He was determined to structure the Scottish church after the model of Geneva, where he had studied and worked with Calvin. In 1560 Knox persuaded the Scottish parliament, which was dominated by reform-minded barons, to enact legislation ending papal authority. The Mass was abolished. Knox then established the Presbyterian Church of Scotland, so named because *presbyters,* or ministers, not bishops, governed it. The Church of Scotland was strictly Calvinist in doctrine, adopted a simple and dignified service of worship, and laid great emphasis on preaching. Knox's *Book of Common Order* (1564) became the liturgical directory for the church. The Presbyterian Church of Scotland was a national, or state, church, and many of its members maintained close relations with English Puritans.

The Reformation in Eastern Europe

While political and economic issues determined the course of the Reformation in western and northern Europe, ethnic factors often proved decisive in eastern Europe. In the later Middle Ages, the migration of diverse peoples into Bohemia, Poland, and Hungary meant that those countries had heterogeneous populations in the sixteenth century. Ethnic background tended to resolve religious matters.

In Bohemia in the fifteenth century, the ethnic grievances of the Czech majority against German economic and ecclesiastical domination (see page 391) fused with Czech resentment at the corruption of the Roman church. By 1500 most Czechs had adopted the ideas of Jan Hus, and the emperor had been forced to recognize a separate Hussite church. Lutheranism spread rapidly among Germans in Bohemia in the 1520s and 1530s; many Germans lived near the border of Luther's Saxony. Moreover, the nobility's identification of Lutheranism with opposition to the Habsburgs contributed, as in Germany, to the growth of Protestantism. The forces of the Catholic Reformation promoted a Catholic spiritual revival in Bohemia, and some areas reconverted. This complicated situation would be one of the causes of the Thirty Years' War (see pages 562–565).

By 1500 Poland and the Grand Duchy of Lithuania were united in a dynastic union. A king, senate, and diet (parliament) governed, but the two territories retained separate officials, judicial systems, armies, and forms of citizenship. In the fifteenth century rulers had granted the Polish *szlachta* (nobility) extensive rights; though hereditary, the monarchy was weak and had to cooperate with the szlachta. The combined realms covered about 440,150 square miles, making Poland-Lithuania the largest European polity. A population of only about 7.5 million people was very thinly scattered over that land.

In comparison with western Europe, Poland-Lithuania was overwhelmingly rural; its largest cities—Gdansk (30,000) and Cracow (15,000)—were very small in population by Italian or French standards. Yet with Germans, Italians, Tartars, and Jews, Poland-Lithuania represented great diversity. Such peoples had come as merchants, invited by medieval rulers because of their wealth or to make agricultural improvements. Each group spoke its native language, though all educated people spoke Latin. In the late fifteenth century Italian Renaissance humanism influenced Polish art, architecture, literature, and historical writing.

Luther's ideas spread first to the German-speaking Baltic towns, then to the University of Cracow, where his works were translated. His ideas met two major obstacles: King Sigismund I (r. 1506–1548) banned Luther's teachings in Poland, and strong anti-German feeling among Poles meant that Lutheranism would have limited success outside Germanized towns.

The Reformed tradition of John Calvin, with its stress on the power of church elders, appealed to the Polish szlachta, however. The fact that Calvinism originated in France, not in Germany, also made it more attractive than Lutheranism. Several Polish magnates, including Jan Laski (1499–1560), converted to Calvinism, and Calvinist nobles dominated the important diet of 1555. But doctrinal differences among Calvinists, Lutherans, and other groups prevented united opposition to Catholicism.

Under Stanislaus Hosius (1505–1579), who attended the Council of Trent, a systematic Counter-Reformation gained momentum. Hosius pressed for reform within the Catholic Church, held provincial synods, and published a comprehensive and clear statement of Roman Catholic

faith and morals. The Jesuits (see page 469) complemented his work by establishing schools for the sons of the szlachta. By 1650 the identification of Poland and Roman Catholicism was well established.

Merchants from Poland carried the first news about Martin Luther to Hungary in 1521. Hungarian students flocked to Wittenberg; they became the major agents for the spread of Lutheranism in Hungary, and sympathy for it developed at the royal court at Buda. But concern about "the German heresy" by the Catholic hierarchy and among the magnates found expression in a decree of the Hungarian diet in 1523 that "all Lutherans and those favoring them . . . should have their property confiscated and themselves punished with death as heretics."[10]

A military event on August 26, 1526, had profound consequences for both the Hungarian state and the Protestant Reformation there. On the plain of Mohács in southern Hungary, the Ottoman sultan Suleiman the Magnificent (see page 566) inflicted a crushing defeat on the Hungarians, killing King Louis II, many of the magnates, and more than sixteen thousand ordinary soldiers. Rival factions elected different kings, and the Hungarian kingdom was divided into three parts: the Ottoman Turks absorbed the great plains, including the capital, Buda; the Habsburgs ruled the north and west; and Ottoman-supported Janos Zapolya held eastern Hungary and Transylvania. The Turks were indifferent to the religious conflicts of the infidels.

Mohács led to a great advance of Protestantism. Many Magyar (Hungarian) magnates accepted Lutheranism; Lutheran schools and parishes headed by men educated at Wittenberg multiplied; and peasants welcomed the new faith. In spite of the foundation of Jesuit colleges, in 1585 the papal nuncio noted that 85 percent of the population was Protestant, 10 percent remained Greek Orthodox, and just 5 percent (concentrated in Croatia) stayed Catholic. Hungary seemed lost to Catholicism. Then, in the late seventeenth century, Hungarian nobles' recognition of Habsburg (Catholic) rule and Ottoman Turkish withdrawal in 1699 led to Catholic restoration.

The Catholic Reformation

Between 1517 and 1547 Protestantism made remarkable advances. Nevertheless, the Roman Catholic Church made a significant comeback. After about 1540 no new large areas of Europe, other than the Netherlands, accepted Protestant beliefs (see Map 14.2). Many historians see the developments within the Catholic Church after the Protestant Reformation as two interrelated movements: one a drive for internal reform linked to earlier reform efforts, and the other a Counter-Reformation that opposed Protestants intellectually, politically, militarily, and institutionally. In both movements, the papacy, new religious orders, and the Council of Trent that met from 1545 to 1563 were important agents.

• *How did the Catholic Church respond to the new religious situation?*

The Reformed Papacy

The Renaissance princes who sat on the throne of Saint Peter were not blind to the evils that existed. Modest reform efforts were undertaken, but the idea of reform was closely linked to the idea of a general council representing the entire church. Remembering fifteenth-century conciliar attempts to limit papal authority, early sixteenth-century popes resisted calls for a council. The papal bureaucrats who were the popes' intimates warned the popes against a council, fearing loss of power, revenue, and prestige.

This changed beginning with Pope Paul III (1534–1549), and the papal court became the center of the reform movement rather than its chief opponent. Paul appointed reform-minded cardinals, abbots, and bishops who improved education for the clergy, tried to enforce moral standards among them, and worked on correcting the most glaring abuses. Reform measures that had been suggested since the late Middle Ages, such as prohibiting pluralism and absenteeism, were gradually adopted during the sixteenth century. Paul III and his successors supported the establishment of new religious orders that preached to the common people, the opening of seminaries for training priests, the end of the selling of church offices, and stricter control of clerical life. Their own lives were models of decorum and piety, in contrast to Renaissance popes who had concentrated on building and decorating churches and palaces and on enhancing the power of their own families.

In 1542 Pope Paul III established the Sacred Congregation of the **Holy Office,** with jurisdiction over the Roman Inquisition, a powerful instrument of the Catholic Reformation. The Inquisition was a committee of six cardinals with judicial authority over all Catholics and the power to arrest, imprison, and execute. Under the fervent Cardinal Caraffa, it vigorously attacked heresy.

The Roman Inquisition operated under the principles of Roman law. It accepted hearsay evidence, was not obliged to inform the accused of charges against them, and sometimes applied torture. Echoing one of Calvin's remarks about heresy, Cardinal Caraffa wrote, "No man is to lower himself by showing toleration towards any sort of heretic, least of all a Calvinist."[11] The Holy Office published the *Index of Prohibited Books,* a catalogue of forbidden reading.

Within the Papal States, the Inquisition effectively destroyed heresy (and some heretics). Outside the papal territories, however, its influence was slight. In Venice, a major publishing center, the *Index* had no influence on scholarly research in nonreligious areas such as law, classical literature, and mathematics.

The Council of Trent

Pope Paul III also called an ecumenical council, which met intermittently from 1545 to 1563 at Trent, an imperial city close to Italy. It was called not only to reform the church but also to secure reconciliation with the Protestants. Lutherans and Calvinists were invited to participate, but their insistence that the Scriptures be the sole basis for discussion made reconciliation impossible. International politics repeatedly cast a shadow over the theological debates. Charles V opposed discussions on any matter that might further alienate his Lutheran subjects, fearing the loss of additional imperial territory to Lutheran princes. Meanwhile, the French kings worked against the reconciliation of Roman Catholicism and Lutheranism. As long as religious issues divided the German states, the empire would be weakened, and a weak and divided empire meant a stronger France. Portugal, Poland, Hungary, and Ireland sent representatives, but very few German bishops attended.

In spite of the obstacles, the achievements of the Council of Trent were impressive. The council dealt with both doctrinal and disciplinary matters. It gave equal validity to the Scriptures and to tradition as sources of religious truth and authority. It reaffirmed the seven sacraments and the traditional Catholic teaching on transubstantiation. Thus it rejected Lutheran and Calvinist positions.

The council tackled the problems arising from ancient abuses by strengthening ecclesiastical discipline. Tridentine (from *Tridentum,* the Latin word for Trent) decrees required bishops to reside in their own dioceses, suppressed pluralism and simony, and forbade the sale of indulgences. Clerics who kept concubines were to give them up. The jurisdiction of bishops over all the clergy of their dioceses was made almost absolute, and bishops were ordered to visit every religious house within the diocese at least once every two years. In a highly original decree, the council required every diocese to establish a

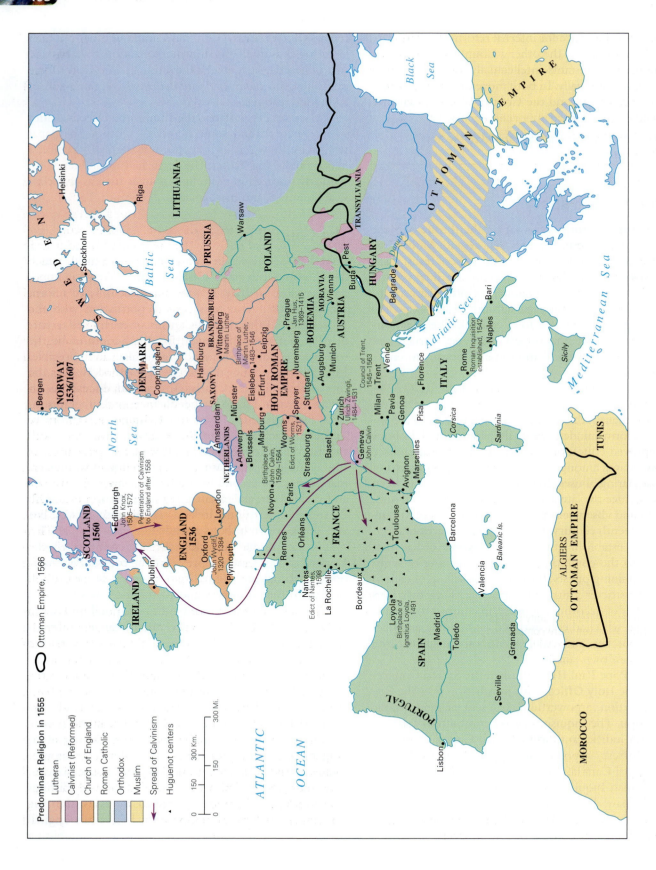

Predominant Religion in 1555

Lutheran
Calvinist (Reformed)
Church of England
Roman Catholic
Orthodox
Muslim
Spread of Calvinism
▲ Huguenot centers

◯ Ottoman Empire, 1566

NORWAY 1536/1607
SWEDEN
Bergen
Stockholm
Helsinki
Riga
LITHUANIA
Warsaw
PRUSSIA
POLAND
DENMARK
Copenhagen
Hamburg
BRANDENBURG
Wittenberg
Birthplace of Martin Luther
SAXONY
Münster
Eisleben
1483–1546
Erfurt
Leipzig
Prague
Jan Hus, 1369–1415
BOHEMIA
MORAVIA
Nuremberg
HOLY ROMAN EMPIRE
Speyer
Stuttgart
Augsburg
Munich
AUSTRIA
Vienna
TRANSYLVANIA
HUNGARY
Buda
Pest
Belgrade
Danube
Council of Trent, 1545–1563
Trent
Venice
Milan
Pavia
Genoa
ITALY
Florence
Rome
Roman Inquisition established, 1542
Naples
Bari
Sicily
Corsica
Sardinia
Adriatic Sea
Mediterranean Sea
Black Sea
OTTOMAN EMPIRE

Baltic Sea
North Sea

NETHERLANDS
Amsterdam
Antwerp
Brussels
Marburg
Birthplace of Marburg
John Calvin, 1509–1564
Worms
1521
Edict of Worms
Strasbourg
Basel
Zurich
Ulrich Zwingli, 1484–1531
Geneva
John Calvin
Noyon
Paris
Avignon
Marseilles
Toulouse
Barcelona
Balearic Is.
Valencia
Granada
Seville
Toledo
Madrid
Loyola
Birthplace of Ignatius Loyola, 1491
SPAIN
PORTUGAL
Lisbon
FRANCE
Orléans
Rennes
Nantes
Edict of Nantes, 1598
La Rochelle
Bordeaux
Pisa

SCOTLAND 1560
Edinburgh
John Knox, 1505–1572
Penetration of Calvinism to England after 1558
ENGLAND 1536
London
Oxford
John Wyclif, 1320–1384
Plymouth
IRELAND
Dublin

ATLANTIC OCEAN

MOROCCO
ALGIERS
OTTOMAN EMPIRE
TUNIS

300 Mi.
300 Km.
150
150
0
0

seminary for the education and training of the clergy; the council even prescribed the curriculum and insisted that preference for admission be given to sons of the poor. Seminary professors were to determine whether candidates for ordination had *vocations,* genuine callings as determined by purity of life, detachment from the broader secular culture, and a steady inclination toward the priesthood. This was a novel idea, since from the time of the early church, parents had determined their sons' (and daughters') religious careers. Finally, great emphasis was laid on preaching and instructing the laity, especially the uneducated.

One decision had especially important social consequences for laypeople. Since the time of the Roman Empire, many couples had treated marriage as a completely personal matter, had exchanged vows privately without witnesses, and had thus formed what were called clandestine (secret) unions. This widespread practice frequently led later to denials by one party, conflicts over property, and disputes in the ecclesiastical courts that had jurisdiction over marriage once it became a sacrament (which occurred in the twelfth century). The Tridentine decree Tametsi (November 1563) stipulated that for a marriage to be valid, consent (the essence of marriage) as given in the vows had to be made publicly before witnesses, one of whom had to be the parish priest. Trent thereby ended secret marriages in Catholic countries. (They remained a problem for civil and church courts in England until the Hardwicke Act of 1753 abolished them.)

The Council of Trent did not meet everyone's expectations. Reconciliation with Protestantism was not achieved, nor was reform brought about immediately. Nevertheless, the Tridentine decrees laid a solid basis for the spiritual renewal of the church and for the enforcement of correction. For four centuries the doctrinal and disciplinary legislation of Trent served as the basis for Roman Catholic faith, organization, and practice.

New Religious Orders

The establishment of new religious orders within the church reveals a central feature of the Catholic Reformation. Most of these new orders developed in response to one crying need: to raise the moral and intellectual level of the clergy and people. (See the feature "Individuals in Society: Teresa of Ávila.") Education was a major goal of the two most famous orders.

The Ursuline order of nuns, founded by Angela Merici (1474–1540), attained enormous prestige for the education of women. The daughter of a country gentleman, Angela Merici worked for many years among the poor, sick, and uneducated around her native Brescia in northern Italy. In 1535 she established the Ursuline order to combat heresy through Christian education. The first women's religious order concentrating exclusively on teaching young girls, the Ursulines sought to re-Christianize society by training future wives and mothers. Because the Council of Trent placed great stress on the *claustration* (strict enclosure) of religious women and called for the end of all active ministries for women, Angela had great difficulty gaining papal approval. Official recognition finally came in 1565, and the Ursulines rapidly spread to France and the New World. Their schools in North America, stretching from Quebec to New Orleans, provided superior education for young women and inculcated the spiritual ideals of the Catholic Reformation.

The Society of Jesus, or **Jesuits,** founded by Ignatius Loyola (1491–1556), a former Spanish soldier, played a powerful international role in resisting the spread of Protestantism, converting Asians and Latin American Indians to Catholicism, and spreading Christian education all over Europe. While recuperating from a severe battle wound in his legs, Loyola studied a life of Christ and other religious books and decided to give up his military career and become a soldier of Christ. During a year spent in seclusion, prayer, and personal mortification, he gained insights that went into his great classic, *Spiritual Exercises* (1548). This work, intended for study during a four-week period of retreat, directed the individual imagination and will to the reform of life and a new spiritual piety.

Mapping the Past

MAP 14.2 Religious Divisions in Europe The Reformations shattered the religious unity of Western Christendom. The situation was even more complicated than a map of this scale can show. Many cities within the Holy Roman Empire, for example, accepted a different faith than the surrounding countryside; Augsburg, Basel, and Strasbourg were all Protestant, though surrounded by territory ruled by Catholic nobles. Use the map and the information in the book to answer the following questions: **1** Why was the Holy Roman Empire the first arena of religious conflict in sixteenth-century Europe? **2** Are there similarities in regions where a particular branch of the Christian faith was maintained or took root? **3** To what degree can nonreligious factors be used as an explanation for the religious divisions in sixteenth-century Europe?

Online Study Center **Improve Your Grade** Interactive Map: Protestant and Catholic Reformations

School of Titian: The Council of Trent Since the early sessions were sparsely attended, this well-attended meeting seems to be a later session or an idealization. The seated figures in the tall white hats are bishops, while the dark-clothed figures around the edges are church lawyers and officials. The guards in the foreground are members of the Swiss guards, founded by Pope Julius II in 1505 to defend the papacy and still serving in that role (and in similar uniforms) today. In the sixteenth century Switzerland was a poor country, as its mountainous terrain was not good for agriculture, and mercenary soldiers were one of its chief "exports." *(Louvre/ Réunion des Musées Nationaux/Art Resource, NY)*

Loyola was a man of considerable personal magnetism. After study at universities in Salamanca and Paris, he gathered a group of six companions and in 1540 secured papal approval of the new Society of Jesus. The first Jesuits, recruited primarily from the wealthy merchant and professional classes, saw the Reformation as a pastoral problem, its causes and cures related not to doctrinal issues but to people's spiritual condition. Reform of the church, as Luther and Calvin understood that term, played no role in the future the Jesuits planned for themselves. Their goal was "to help souls." Loyola also possessed a gift for leadership that consisted in spotting talent and in seeing "how at a given juncture change is more consistent with one's scope than staying the course."[12]

The Society of Jesus developed into a highly centralized, tightly knit organization. Candidates underwent a two-year novitiate, in contrast to the usual one-year probation. In addition to the traditional vows of poverty, chastity, and obedience, professed members vowed "special obedience to the sovereign pontiff regarding missions."[13] Thus as stability—the promise to live his life in the monastery—was what made a monk, so mobility—the commitment to go anywhere for the help of souls—was the defining characteristic of a Jesuit. Flexibility and the willingness to respond to the needs of time and circumstance formed the Jesuit tradition. In this respect, Jesuits were very modern, and they attracted many recruits. They achieved phenomenal success for the papacy and the reformed Catholic Church. Jesuit schools adopted

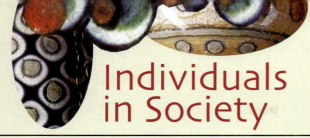

Individuals in Society

Teresa of Ávila

Her family derived from Toledo, center of the Moorish, Jewish, and Christian cultures in medieval Spain. Her grandfather, Juan Sanchez, made a fortune in the cloth trade. A "New Christian" (see pages 437–439), he was accused of secretly practicing Judaism. Although he endured the humiliation of a public repentance, he moved his family south to Ávila. Beginning again, he recouped his wealth and, aspiring to the prestige of an "Old Christian," bought noble status. Juan's son Alzonzo Sanchez de Cepeda married a woman of thoroughly Christian background, giving his family an aura of impeccable orthodoxy. The third of their nine children, Teresa, became a saint and in 1970 was the first woman declared a Doctor of the Church, a title given to a theologian of outstanding merit.

At age twenty, inspired more by the fear of Hell than the love of God, Teresa (1515–1582) entered the Carmelite Convent of the Incarnation in Ávila. Most of the nuns were daughters of Ávila's leading citizens; they had entered the convent because of a family decision about which daughters would marry and which would become nuns. Their lives were much like those of female family members outside the convent walls, with good food, comfortable surroundings, and frequent visits from family and friends. Teresa was frequently ill, but she lived quietly in the convent for many years. In her late thirties, she began to read devotional literature intensely and had profound mystical experiences—visions and voices in which Christ chastised her for her frivolous life and friends. She described one such experience in 1560:

It pleased the Lord that I should see an angel. . . . Short, and very beautiful, his face was so aflame that he appeared to be one of the highest types of angels. . . . In his hands I saw a long golden spear and at the end of an iron tip I seemed to see a point of fire. With this he seemed to pierce my heart several times so that it penetrated to my entrails. When he drew it out . . . he left me completely afire with the great love of God.*

Teresa responded with a new sense of purpose: although she encountered stiff opposition, she resolved to found a reformed house. Four basic principles were to guide the new convent. First, poverty was to be fully observed, symbolized by the nuns' being barefoot, hence *discalced*. Charity and the nuns' own work must support the community. Second, the convent must keep strict enclosure; the visits of powerful benefactors with

material demands were forbidden. Third, Teresa intended an egalitarian atmosphere in which class distinctions were forbidden. She had always rejected the emphasis on "purity of blood," a distinctive and racist feature of Spanish society that was especially out of place in the cloister. All sisters, including those of aristocratic background, must share the manual chores.

Seventeenth-century cloisonné enamelwork illustrating Teresa of Ávila's famous vision of an angel piercing her heart.
(By gracious permission of Catherine Hamilton Kappauf)

Finally, like Ignatius Loyola and the Jesuits, Teresa placed great emphasis on obedience, especially to one's confessor.

Between 1562 and Teresa's death in 1582, she founded or reformed fourteen other houses of nuns, traveling widely to do so. Though Teresa did not advocate institutionalized roles for women outside the convent, she did chafe at the restrictions placed on her because of her sex, and she thought of the new religious houses she founded as answers to the Protestant takeover of Catholic churches elsewhere in Europe. From her brother, who had obtained wealth in the Spanish colonies, Teresa learned about conditions in Peru and instructed her nuns "to pray unceasingly for the missionaries working among the heathens." Through prayer, Teresa wrote, her nuns could share in the exciting tasks of evangelization and missionary work otherwise closed to women. Her books, along with her five hundred extant letters, show her as a practical and down-to-earth woman as well as a mystic and a creative theologian.

Questions for Analysis

1. How did sixteenth-century convent life reflect the values of Spanish society?
2. How is the life of Teresa of Ávila typical of developments in the Catholic Reformation? How is her life unusual?

**The Autobiography of St. Teresa of Ávila*, trans. and ed. E. A. Peers (New York: Doubleday, 1960), pp. 273–274.

Online Study Center **Improve Your Grade**
Going Beyond Individuals in Society

Juan de Valdes Leal: Pope Paul III Approves the Jesuit Constitutions   This painting by a Spanish artist celebrates the founding of the Jesuits by his fellow countryman Ignatius Loyola. When the Jesuit constitutions were read to him, Paul III supposedly murmured, "There is the finger of God." Judging by other portraits, the depiction of Loyola here is a reasonable likeness, that of the pope an idealization: in 1540 he was a very old man. *(Institut Amatller d'Art Hispanic)*

the modern humanist curricula and methods, and though they first concentrated on the children of the poor, they were soon educating the sons of the nobility. As confessors and spiritual directors to kings, Jesuits exerted great political influence. Operating on the principle that the end sometimes justifies the means, they were not above spying. Indifferent to physical comfort and personal safety, they carried Christianity to India and Japan before 1550 and to Brazil, North America, and the Congo in

the seventeenth century. Within Europe the Jesuits brought southern Germany and much of eastern Europe back to Catholicism.

Religious Violence

In 1559 France and Spain signed the Treaty of Cateau-Cambrésis, which ended the long conflict known as the Habsburg-Valois Wars. Spain was the victor. France, exhausted by the struggle, had to acknowledge Spanish dominance in Italy, where much of the fighting had taken place. The Treaty of Cateau-Cambrésis did not bring peace, however. Instead, over the next century religious differences led to riots, civil wars, and international conflicts. Especially in France and the Netherlands, Protestants and Catholics used violent actions as well as preaching and teaching against each other, for each side regarded the other as a poison in the community that would provoke the wrath of God. Catholics continued to believe that Calvinists and Lutherans could be reconverted; Protestants persisted in thinking that the Roman church should be destroyed. Catholics and Protestants alike feared people of other faiths, who they often saw as agents of Satan. Even more, they feared those who were explicitly identified with Satan: witches living in their midst. The era of religious wars was also the time of the most virulent witch persecutions in European history, as both Protestants and Catholics tried to make their cities and states more godly.

• *What were the causes and consequences of religious violence, including riots, wars, and witch-hunts?*

French Religious Wars

The Habsburg-Valois Wars, waged intermittently through the first half of the sixteenth century, cost more than the French government could afford. In addition to the time-honored practices of increasing taxes and engaging in heavy borrowing, King Francis I (r. 1515–1547) tried two new devices to raise revenue: the sale of public offices and a treaty with the papacy. The former proved to be only a temporary source of money. The offices sold tended to become hereditary within a family, and once a man bought an office he and his heirs were exempt from taxation.

The treaty with the papacy was the Concordat of Bologna (see page 435), in which Francis agreed to recognize the supremacy of the papacy over a universal council. In return, the French crown gained the right to appoint all French bishops and abbots. This understanding gave the monarchy a rich supplement of money and offices and a power over the church that lasted until the Revolution of 1789. The Concordat of Bologna helps explain why France did not later become Protestant: in effect, it established Catholicism as the state religion. Because French rulers possessed control over appointments and had a vested financial interest in Catholicism, they had no need to revolt against Rome.

Luther's tracts first appeared in France in 1518, and his ideas attracted some attention. After the publication of Calvin's *Institutes* in 1536, sizable numbers of French people were attracted to the "reformed religion," as Calvinism was called. Because Calvin wrote in French rather than Latin, his ideas gained wide circulation. Initially, Calvinism drew converts from among reform-minded members of the Catholic clergy, the industrious middle classes, and artisan groups. Most French Calvinists (called **Huguenots**) lived in major cities, such as Paris, Lyons, and Rouen. When Henry II died in 1559, perhaps one-tenth of the population had become Calvinist.

The feebleness of the French monarchy was the seed from which the weeds of civil violence sprang. The three weak sons of Henry II who occupied the throne could not provide the necessary leadership, and they were often dominated by their mother, Catherine de' Medici. The French nobility took advantage of this monarchical weakness. In the second half of the sixteenth century between two-fifths and one-half of the nobility at one time or another became Calvinist. Just as German princes in the Holy Roman Empire had adopted Lutheranism as a means of opposition to Emperor Charles V, so French nobles frequently adopted the reformed religion as a religious cloak for their independence. Armed clashes between Catholic royalist lords and Calvinist antimonarchical lords occurred in many parts of France. Both Calvinists and Catholics believed that the others' books, services, and ministers polluted the community. Preachers incited violence, and ceremonies such as baptisms, marriages, and funerals triggered it.

Protestant teachings called the power of sacred images into question, and mobs in many cities took down and smashed statues, stained-glass windows, and paintings. They ridiculed and tested religious images, throwing them into latrines, using them as cooking fuel or building material, or giving them as toys or masks for children. Though it was often inspired by fiery Protestant sermons, this **iconoclasm** is an example of men and women carrying out the Reformation themselves, rethinking the church's system of meaning and the relationship between the unseen and the seen. Catholic mobs responded by defending images, and crowds on both sides killed their opponents, often in gruesome ways.

A savage Catholic attack on Calvinists in Paris on August 24, 1572 (Saint Bartholomew's Day), followed the usual pattern. The occasion was a religious ceremony, the marriage of the king's sister Margaret of Valois to the Protestant Henry of Navarre, which was intended to help reconcile Catholics and Huguenots. Instead Huguenot wedding guests in Paris were massacred, and other Protestants were slaughtered by mobs. Religious violence spread to the provinces, where thousands were killed. This **Saint Bartholomew's Day massacre** led to a civil war that dragged on for fifteen years. Agriculture in many areas was destroyed; commercial life declined severely; and starvation and death haunted the land.

What ultimately saved France was a small group of moderates of both faiths called **politiques** who believed that only the restoration of strong monarchy could reverse the trend toward collapse. No religious creed was worth the incessant disorder and destruction. Therefore, the politiques favored accepting the Huguenots as an officially recognized and organized pressure group. (But religious toleration, the full acceptance of peoples of different religious persuasions within a pluralistic society, with minorities having the same civil liberties as the majority, developed only in the eighteenth century.) The death of Catherine de' Medici, followed by the assassination of King Henry III, paved the way for the accession of Henry of Navarre (the unfortunate bridegroom of the Saint Bartholomew's Day massacre), a politique who became Henry IV (r. 1589–1610).

Henry knew that the majority of the French were Roman Catholics. Allegedly saying "Paris is worth a Mass," Henry knelt before the archbishop of Bourges and was received into the Roman Catholic Church. Henry's willingness to sacrifice religious principles to political necessity saved France. The **Edict of Nantes,** which Henry published in 1598, granted liberty of conscience and liberty of public worship to Huguenots in 150 fortified towns, such as La Rochelle. The reign of Henry IV and the Edict of Nantes prepared the way for French absolutism in the seventeenth century by helping restore internal peace in France.

The Netherlands Under Charles V

Hostility to a monarch was also part of religious wars in the Netherlands. What began as a movement for the reformation of the church developed into a struggle for Dutch independence.

Emperor Charles V (r. 1519–1556) had inherited the seventeen provinces that compose present-day Belgium and the Netherlands (see page 458). Each of the seventeen provinces of the Netherlands possessed historical liberties: each was self-governing and enjoyed the right to make its own laws and collect its own taxes. In addition to important economic connections, only the recognition of a common ruler in the person of Emperor Charles V united the provinces. The cities of the Netherlands made their living by trade and industry.

In the Low Countries as elsewhere, corruption in the Roman church and the critical spirit of the Renaissance provoked pressure for reform, and Lutheran ideas spread. Charles V had grown up in the Netherlands, however, and he was able to limit their impact. In 1556 Charles V abdicated, dividing his territories between his brother Ferdinand, who received Austria and the Holy Roman Empire, and his son Philip, who inherited Spain, the Low Countries, Milan and the kingdom of Sicily, and the Spanish possessions in the Americas. Philip had grown up in Spain and did not understand the Netherlands.

By the 1560s Protestants in the Netherlands were primarily Calvinists, not Lutherans, and were more militant in their beliefs. Calvinism appealed to the middle classes because of its intellectual seriousness, moral gravity, and emphasis on any form of labor well done. It took deep root among the merchants and financiers in Amsterdam and the northern provinces. Working-class people were also converted. Whereas Lutherans taught respect for the powers that be, Calvinism tended to encourage opposition to "illegal" civil authorities.

In the 1560s Spanish authorities attempted to suppress Calvinist worship and raised taxes, which sparked riots. Thirty churches in Antwerp were sacked and the religious images in them destroyed in a wave of iconoclasm. From Antwerp the destruction spread to Brussels and Ghent and north to the provinces of Holland and Zeeland. From Madrid Philip II sent twenty thousand Spanish troops under the duke of Alva to pacify the Low Countries. Alva interpreted "pacification" to mean the ruthless extermination of religious and political dissidents. On top of the Inquisition, he opened his own tribunal, soon called the "Council of Blood." On March 3, 1568, fifteen hundred men were executed.

For ten years, between 1568 and 1578, civil war raged in the Netherlands between Catholics and Protestants and between the seventeen provinces and Spain. Eventually the ten southern provinces, the Spanish Netherlands (the future Belgium), came under the control of the Spanish Habsburg forces. The seven northern provinces, led by Holland, formed the **Union of Utrecht** and in

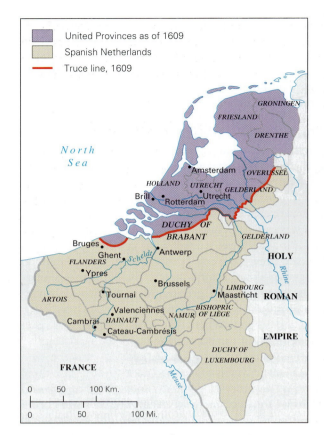

MAP 14.3 The Netherlands, 1559–1609 This map shows the division of the seventeen provinces as a result of the religious wars. Some provinces were overwhelmingly agricultural; some were involved in manufacturing; and others were heavily commercial.

1581 declared their independence from Spain. The north was Protestant; the south remained Catholic (see Map 14.3). Philip did not accept this, and war continued, with the Dutch troops gaining victories under the leadership of a local nobleman, William of Nassau, prince of Orange (1533–1584), known as William the Silent. William was shot by a French assassin loyal to Philip (the first known assassination of a political leader by a handgun), and the leaders of the United Provinces looked beyond their borders to other Protestant areas for assistance against the Spanish.

They particularly appealed to the Protestant queen of England, Elizabeth, for assistance. Fearing that the next step would be a Spanish invasion of England, Elizabeth reluctantly sent money and troops. Philip responded by planning and launching an invasion of England, but the Spanish fleet scattered in the English Channel and only half the ships made it back to Spain (see pages 512–513).

Fighting continued off and on in the Netherlands, but the borders set by the Union of Utrecht gradually became permanent, and in 1609 Spain agreed to a truce that recognized the independence of the United Provinces.

The Great European Witch-Hunt

The relationship between the Reformation and the up-surge in trials for witchcraft that occurred at roughly the same time is complex. Increasing persecution for witch-craft actually began before the Reformation in the 1480s, but it became especially common about 1560. Religious reformers' extreme notions of the Devil's powers and the insecurity created by the religious wars contributed to this increase. Both Protestants and Catholics tried and executed witches, with church officials and secular authorities acting together. They regarded both their religious opponents and witches as deluded by the Devil but made a clear distinction between them; heretics might merit burning, but they were only rarely accused of witchcraft. Witches were a special kind of heretic, but their primary crime was a pact with the Devil, not incorrect doctrine.

The heightened sense of God's power and divine wrath in the Reformation era was an important factor in the witch-hunts, but other factors were also significant. One of these was a change in the idea of what a witch was. Nearly all premodern societies believe in witchcraft and make some attempts to control witches, who are understood to be people who use magical forces to do evil deeds. Witches themselves often believe in their own powers, which they can use to earn a living or gain influence over their neighbors. In the later Middle Ages, however, many educated Christian theologians, canon lawyers, and officials added a demonological component to this notion of what a witch was. For them, the essence of witchcraft was making a pact with the Devil that required the witch to do the Devil's bidding. Witches were no longer simply people who used magical power to get what they wanted, but rather people used by the Devil to do what *he* wanted. This demonological or Satanic idea of witchcraft was fleshed out, and witches were thought to engage in wild sexual orgies with the Devil, fly through the night to meetings called sabbats, which parodied the Mass, and steal communion wafers and unbaptized babies to use in their rituals. Some demonological theorists also claimed that witches were organized in an international conspiracy to overthrow Christianity, with a hierarchy similar to the hierarchy of angels and archangels that Christian philosophers had invented. Witchcraft was

Iconoclasm in the Netherlands Calvinist men and women break stained-glass windows, remove statues, and carry off devotional altarpieces. Iconoclasm, or the destruction of religious images, is often described as a "riot," but here the participants seem very purposeful. Calvinist Protestants regarded pictures and statues as sacrilegious and saw removing them as a way to purify the church. *(The Fotomas Index/The Bridgeman Art Library)*

thus spiritualized, and witches became the ultimate heretics, enemies of God.

Trials involving this new notion of witchcraft as diabolical heresy began in Switzerland and southern Germany in the late fifteenth century, became less numerous in the early decades of the Reformation when Protestants and Catholics were busy fighting each other, and then picked up again about 1560. Because so many records have been lost or destroyed, it is difficult to make an estimate for all of Europe, but most scholars agree that during the sixteenth and seventeenth centuries somewhere between 100,000 and 200,000 people were officially tried for witchcraft and between 40,000 and 60,000 were executed.

Though the gender balance varied widely in different parts of Europe, between 75 and 85 percent of those tried and executed were women. Ideas about women, and the roles women actually played in society, were thus important factors shaping the witch-hunts. Some demonologists expressed virulent **misogyny,** or hatred of women, and particularly emphasized women's powerful sexual desire, which could be satisfied only by a demonic lover. Most people viewed women as weaker and so more likely to give in to any kind of offer by the Devil, including better food or nicer clothing. Women were associated with nature, disorder, and the body, all of which were linked with the demonic. Women's actual lack of power in society and gender norms about the use of violence meant that they were more likely to use scolding and cursing to get what they wanted instead of taking people to court or beating them up. Curses were generally expressed (as they often are today) in religious terms; "go to Hell" was calling on the powers of Satan. Women also had more contact with areas of life in which bad things happened unexpectedly, such as preparing food or caring for new mothers, children, and animals.

Learned ideas about the diabolical nature of witchcraft gradually filtered down to common people. Illustrated pamphlets and broadsides portrayed witches riding on pitchforks to sabbats where they engaged in anti-Christian acts such as spitting on the communion host and having sexual relations with demons. Though witch trials were secret, executions were not; they were public spectacles witnessed by huge crowds, with the list of charges read out for all to hear. By the late sixteenth century popular accusations of witchcraft in many parts of Europe involved at least some parts of the demonic conception of witchcraft.

Legal changes also played a role in causing, or at least allowing for, massive witch trials. One of these was a change from an accusatorial legal procedure to an inquisitorial procedure. In the former, a suspect knew the accusers and the charges they had brought, and an accuser could in turn be liable for trial if the charges were not proven; in the latter, legal authorities themselves brought the case. This change made people much more willing to accuse others, for they never had to take personal responsibility for the accusation or face the accused's relatives. Inquisitorial procedure involved intense questioning of the suspect, often with torture; areas in Europe that did not make this change saw very few trials. Torture was also used to get the names of additional sus-

pects, as most lawyers firmly believed that no witch could act alone.

The use of inquisitorial procedure did not always lead to witch-hunts, however. The most famous inquisitions in early modern Europe, those in Spain, Portugal, and Italy, were in fact very lenient in their treatment of people accused of witchcraft: the Inquisition in Spain executed only a handful of witches, the Portuguese Inquisition only one, and the Roman Inquisition none, though in each of these areas there were hundreds of cases. Inquisitors certainly believed in the power of the Devil and were no less misogynist than other judges, but they doubted very much whether the people accused of witchcraft had actually made pacts with the Devil that gave them special powers. They viewed such people not as diabolical Devil-worshipers but as superstitious and ignorant peasants who should be educated rather than executed. Thus most people brought up before the Inquisition for witchcraft were sent home with a warning and a penance.

Most witch trials began with a single accusation in a village or town. Individuals accused someone they knew of using magic to spoil food, make children ill, kill animals, raise a hailstorm, or do other types of harm. Tensions within families, households, and neighborhoods often played a role in these accusations. Women number very prominently among accusers and witnesses as well as among those accused of witchcraft because the actions witches were initially charged with, such as harming children or curdling milk, were generally part of women's sphere. A woman also gained economic and social security by conforming to the standard of the good wife and mother and by confronting women who deviated from it.

Once a charge was made, judges began to question other neighbors and acquaintances, building up a list of suspicious incidents that might have taken place over decades. Historians have pointed out that one of the reasons those accused of witchcraft were often older was that it took years to build up a reputation as a witch. At this point, the suspect was brought in for questioning by legal authorities. Judges and inquisitors sought the exact details of a witch's demonic contacts, including sexual ones. Suspects were generally stripped and shaved in a search for a "witch's mark," or "pricked" to find a spot insensitive to pain, and then tortured.

Detailed records of witch trials survive for many parts of Europe. They have been used by historians to study many aspects of witchcraft, but they cannot directly answer what seems to us an important question: did people really practice witchcraft and think they were witches? They certainly

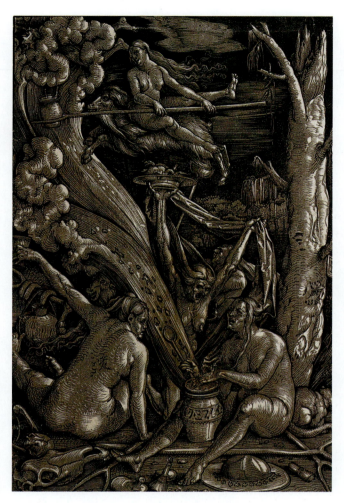

Hans Baldung Grien: Witches' Sabbat (1510) In this woodcut, Grien combines learned and popular beliefs about witches: they traveled at night, met at sabbats (or assemblies), feasted on infants (in dish held high), concocted strange potions, and had animal "familiars" that were really demons (here a cat). Grien also highlights the sexual nature of witchcraft by portraying the women naked and showing them with goats, which were common symbols of sexuality. *(Germanisches Nationalmuseum Nürnberg)*

confessed to evil deeds and demonic practices, sometimes without torture, but where would we draw the line between reality and fantasy? Clearly people were not riding through the air on pitchforks, but did they think they did? Did they actually invoke the Devil when they were angry at a neighbor, or was this simply in the mind of their accusers? Trial records cannot tell us, and historians have answered these questions very differently, often using insights from psychoanalysis or the study of more recent victims of torture in their explanations.

Once the initial suspect had been questioned, and particularly if he or she had been tortured, the people who had been implicated were brought in for questioning. This might lead to a small hunt, involving from five to ten victims, and it sometimes grew into a much larger hunt, what historians have called a "witch panic." Panics were most common in the part of Europe that saw the most witch accusations in general—the Holy Roman Empire, Switzerland, and parts of France. Most of this area consisted of very small governmental units, which were jealous of each other and after the Reformation were divided by religion. The rulers of these small territories often felt more threatened than did the monarchs of western Europe, and they saw persecuting witches as a way to demonstrate their piety and concern for order.

Sometimes witch panics were the result of legal authorities' rounding up a group of suspects together. Such panics often occurred after some type of climatic disaster, such as an unusually cold and wet summer, and they came in waves. In large-scale panics a wider variety of suspects were taken in—wealthier people, children, a greater proportion of men. Mass panics tended to end when it became clear to legal authorities, or to the community itself, that the people being questioned or executed were not what they understood witches to be, or that the scope of accusations was beyond belief. Some from their community might be in league with Satan, they thought, but not this type of person and not as many as this.

Similar skepticism led to the gradual end of witch-hunts in Europe. Even in the sixteenth century a few individuals questioned whether witches could ever do harm, make a pact with the Devil, or engage in the wild activities attributed to them. Doubts about whether secret denunciations were valid or torture would ever yield a truthful confession gradually spread among the same type of religious and legal authorities who had so vigorously persecuted witches. Prosecutions for witchcraft became less common and were gradually outlawed. Sporadic trials continued into the eighteenth century, but by then people who thought themselves witches were more likely to be regarded as deluded or mentally defective, meriting pity rather than persecution, even by people who still firmly believed in the Devil. Belief in the power of witches continued among uneducated people, but educated people now sneered at this as superstition. People ceased to bring formal accusations when they knew they would simply be dismissed, and witch trials ended. The last official execution for witchcraft in England was in 1682, though the last one in the Holy Roman Empire was not until 1775.

Chapter Summary

- *What were the central ideas of the reformers, and why were they appealing to different social groups?*
- *How did the political situation in Germany shape the course of the Reformation?*
- *How did Protestant ideas and institutions spread beyond German-speaking lands?*
- *How did the Catholic Church respond to the new religious situation?*
- *What were the causes and consequences of religious violence, including riots, wars, and witch-hunts?*

The Catholic Church in the early sixteenth century had serious problems, and many individuals and groups had long called for reform. This background of discontent helps explain why Martin Luther's ideas found such a ready audience. Luther and other Protestants developed a new understanding of Christian doctrine that emphasized faith, the power of God's grace, and the centrality of the Bible. Protestant ideas were attractive to educated people and urban residents, and they spread rapidly through preaching, hymns, and the printing press. By 1530 many parts of the Holy Roman Empire and Scandinavia had broken with the Catholic Church. Some reformers developed more radical ideas about infant baptism, the ownership of property, and separation between church and state. Both Protestants and Catholics regarded these as dangerous, and radicals were banished or executed. The German Peasants' War, in which Luther's ideas were linked to calls for social and economic reform, was similarly put down harshly. The Protestant reformers did not break with medieval ideas about the proper gender hierarchy, though they did elevate the status of marriage and viewed orderly households as the key building blocks of society.

The progress of the Reformation was shaped by the political situation in the Holy Roman Empire. The Habsburg emperor, Charles V, ruled almost half of Europe along with Spain's overseas colonies. Within the empire his authority was limited, however, and local princes, nobles, and cities actually held most power. This decentral-

ization allowed the Reformation to spread. Charles remained firmly Catholic, and in the 1530s religious wars began in Germany. These were brought to an end with the Peace of Augsburg in 1555, which allowed rulers to choose whether their territory would be Catholic or Lutheran.

In England the political issue of the royal succession triggered the break with Rome, and a Protestant church was established. Protestant ideas also spread into France and eastern Europe. In all these areas, a second generation of reformers built on Lutheran and Zwinglian ideas to develop their own theology and plans for institutional change. The most important of the second-generation reformers was John Calvin, whose ideas would come to shape Christianity over a much wider area than did Luther's.

The Roman Catholic Church responded slowly to the Protestant challenge, but by the 1530s the papacy was leading a movement for reform within the church instead of blocking it. Catholic doctrine was reaffirmed at the Council of Trent, and reform measures such as the opening of seminaries for priests and a ban on holding multiple church offices were introduced. New religious orders such as the Jesuits and the Ursulines spread Catholic ideas through teaching, and in the case of the Jesuits through missionary work.

Religious differences led to riots, civil wars, and international conflicts in the later sixteenth century. In France and the Netherlands, Calvinist Protestants and Catholics used violent actions against one another, and religious differences mixed with political and economic grievances. Long civil wars resulted, which in the case of the Netherlands became an international conflict. War ended in France with the Edict of Nantes in which Protestants were given some civil rights, and in the Netherlands with a division of the country into a Protestant north and Catholic south. The era of religious wars was also the time of the most extensive witch persecutions in European history, as both Protestants and Catholics tried to rid their cities and states of people they regarded as linked to the Devil.

Key Terms

anticlericalism
pluralism
indulgence
penance
purgatory
Diet of Worms
Protestant
transubstantiation
Book of Common Prayer
Elizabethan Settlement
The Institutes of the Christian Religion

predestination
Holy Office
Jesuits
Huguenots
iconoclasm
Saint Bartholomew's Day massacre
politiques
Edict of Nantes
Union of Utrecht
misogyny

 Online Study Center **Improve Your Grade** Flashcards

Suggested Reading

Bossy, John. *Christianity in the West, 1500–1700.* 1985. A lively brief overview.

Bouwsma, William J. *John Calvin: A Sixteenth-Century Portrait.* 1988. An authoritative study that situates Calvin within Renaissance culture.

Elton, Geoffrey R. *Reform and Reformation: England, 1509–1558.* 1977. Combines religious, political, and social history.

Holt, Mack P. *The French Wars of Religion, 1562–1629.* 1995. A thorough survey designed for students.

Hsia, R. Po-Chia. *The World of Catholic Renewal, 1540–1770.* 1998. Situates the Catholic Reformation in a global context and provides coverage of colonial Catholicism.

Levack, Brian. *The Witchhunt in Early Modern Europe*, 3d ed. 2007. A good introduction to and helpful bibliographies of the vast literature on witchcraft.

Levi, Anthony. *Renaissance and Reformation: The Intellectual Genesis.* 2002. Surveys the ideas of major Reformation figures against the background of important political issues.

Lindbergh, Carter. *The European Reformations.* 1996. A thorough discussion of the Protestant Reformation and some discussion of Catholic issues.

Monter, William E. *Calvin's Geneva.* 1967. Shows the effect of Calvin's reforms on the social life of the Swiss city.

Oberman, Heiko. *Luther: Man Between God and the Devil.* 1989. Provides a thorough grounding in his thought.

O'Malley, John W. *Trent and All That: Renaming Catholicism in the Early Modern Era.* 2000. Provides an excellent historiographical review of the literature and explains why and how early modern Catholicism influenced early modern European history.

Roper, Lyndal. *The Holy Household: Women and Morals in Reformation Augsburg.* 1991. An important study in local religious history as well as the history of gender and the family.

Shagan, Ethan. *Popular Politics and the English Reformation.* 2003. Analyzes the process of the Reformation in local areas.

Wheatcroft, Andrew. *The Habsburgs: Embodying Empire.* 1995. A solid study of political developments surrounding the Reformation.

Notes

1. Quoted in O. Chadwick, *The Reformation* (Baltimore: Penguin Books, 1976), p. 55.
2. Quoted in E. H. Harbison, *The Age of Reformation* (Ithaca, N.Y.: Cornell University Press, 1963), p. 52.
3. Quoted in S. E. Ozment, *The Age of Reform, 1250–1550: An Intellectual and Religious History of Late Medieval and Reformation Europe* (New Haven, Conn.: Yale University Press, 1980), p. 280.
4. Quoted ibid., p. 281.
5. Quoted ibid., p. 284.
6. J. Allen, trans., *John Calvin: The Institutes of the Christian Religion* (Philadelphia: Westminster Press, 1930), bk. 3, chap. 21, paras. 5, 7.
7. E. W. Monter, *Calvin's Geneva* (New York: John Wiley & Sons, 1967), pp. 98–108.
8. Ibid., p. 137.
9. Quoted in R. H. Bainton, *Women of the Reformation in Germany and Italy* (Minneapolis: Augsburg, 1971), pp. 69–70.
10. Quoted in D. P. Daniel, "Hungary," in *The Oxford Encyclopedia of the Reformation,* vol. 2, ed. H. J. Hillerbrand (New York: Oxford University Press, 1996), p. 273.
11. Quoted in Chadwick, *The Reformation,* p. 270.
12. See J. W. O'Malley, *The First Jesuits* (Cambridge, Mass.: Harvard University Press, 1993), p. 376.
13. Ibid., p. 298.

Martin Luther, *On Christian Liberty*

T he idea of liberty or freedom has played a *powerful role in the history of Western society and culture, but the meaning and understanding of liberty has undergone continual change and interpretation. In the Roman world, where slavery was a basic institution, liberty meant the condition of being a free man, independent of obligations to a master. In the Middle Ages possessing liberty meant having special privileges or rights that other persons or institutions did not have. A lord or a monastery, for example, might speak of his or its liberties, and citizens in London were said to possess the "freedom of the city," which allowed them to practice trades and own property without interference. Likewise, the first chapter of Magna Carta (1215), often called the "Charter of Liberties," states: "Holy Church shall be free and have its rights entire and its liberties inviolate," meaning that the English church was independent of the authority of the king.*

The idea of liberty also has a religious dimension, and the reformer Martin Luther formulated a classic interpretation of liberty in his treatise On Christian Liberty (*sometimes translated* On the Freedom of a Christian), *arguably his finest piece. Written in Latin for the pope but translated immediately into German and published widely, it contains the main themes of Luther's theology: the importance of faith, the relationship of Christian faith and good works, the dual nature of human beings, and the fundamental importance of Scripture. Luther writes that Christians were freed from sin and death through Christ, not through their own actions.*

Christian faith has appeared to many an easy thing; nay, not a few even reckon it among the social virtues, as it were; and this they do because they have not made proof of it experimentally, and have never tasted of what efficacy it is. For it is not possible for any man to write well about it, or to understand well what is rightly written, who has not at some time tasted of its spirit, under the pressure of tribulation; while he who has tasted

of it, even to a very small extent, can never write, speak, think, or hear about it sufficiently. . . .

I hope that . . . I have attained some little drop of faith, and that I can speak of this matter, if not with more elegance, certainly with more solidity. . . .

A Christian man is the most free lord of all, and subject to none; a Christian man is the most dutiful servant of all, and subject to everyone.

Although these statements appear contradictory, yet, when they are found to agree together, they will do excellently for my purpose. They are both the statements of Paul himself, who says, "Though I be free from all men, yet have I made myself a servant unto all" (I Cor. 9:19), and "Owe no man anything but to love one another" (Rom. 13:8). Now love is by its own nature dutiful and obedient to the beloved object. Thus even Christ, though Lord of all things, was yet made of a woman; made under the law; at once free and a servant; at once in the form of God and in the form of a servant.

Let us examine the subject on a deeper and less simple principle. Man is composed of a twofold nature, a spiritual and a bodily. As regards the spiritual nature, which they name the soul, he is called the spiritual, inward, new man; as regards the bodily nature, which they name the flesh, he is called the fleshly, outward, old man. The Apostle speaks of this: "Though our outward man perish, yet the inward man is renewed day by day" (II Cor. 4:16). The result of this diversity is that in the Scriptures opposing statements are made concerning the same man, the fact being that in the same man these two men are opposed to one another; the flesh lusting against the spirit, and the spirit against the flesh (Gal. 5:17).

We first approach the subject of the inward man, that we may see by what means a man becomes justified, free, and a true Christian; that is, a spiritual, new, and inward man. It is certain that absolutely none among outward things, under whatever name they may be reckoned, has any influence in producing Christian righteousness or liberty, nor, on the other hand, unrighteousness or slavery. This can be shown by an easy argument.

What can it profit to the soul that the body should be in good condition, free, and full of life, that it should eat, drink, and act according to its pleasure, when even the most impious slaves of every kind of vice are prosperous in these matters? Again, what harm can ill health, bondage, hunger, thirst, or any other outward evil, do to the soul, when even the most pious of men, and the freest in the purity of their conscience, are harassed by these things? Neither of these states of things has to do with the liberty or the slavery of the soul.

And so it will profit nothing that the body should be adorned with sacred vestment, or dwell in holy places, or be occupied in sacred offices, or pray, fast, and abstain from certain meats, or do whatever works can be done through the body and in the body. Something widely different will be necessary for the justification and liberty of the soul, since the things I have spoken of can be done by an impious person, and only hypocrites are produced by devotion to these things. On the other hand, it will not at all injure the soul that the body should be clothed in profane raiment, should dwell in profane places, should eat and drink in the ordinary fashion, should not pray aloud, and should leave undone all the things above mentioned, which may be done by hypocrites.

. . . One thing, and one alone, is necessary for life, justification, and Christian liberty; and that is the most Holy Word of God, the Gospel of Christ, as He says, "I am the resurrection and the life; he that believeth in me shall not die eternally" (John 9:25), and also, "If the Son shall make you free, ye shall be free indeed" (John 8:36), and "Man shall not live by bread alone, but by every word that proceedeth out of the mouth of God" (Matt. 4:4).

Let us therefore hold it for certain and firmly established that the soul can do without everything except the Word of God, without which none at all of its wants is provided for. But, having the Word, it is rich and wants for nothing, since that is the Word of life, of truth, of light, of peace, of justification, of salvation, of joy, of liberty, of wisdom, of virtue, of grace, of glory, and of every good thing. . . .

But you will ask, "What is this Word, and by what means is it to be used, since there are so many words of God?" I answer, "The Apostle Paul (Rom. 1) explains what it is, namely the Gospel of God, concerning His Son, incarnate, suffering, risen, and glorified through the Spirit, the Sanctifier." To preach Christ is to feed the soul, to justify it, to set it free, and to save it, if it believes the preaching. For faith alone, and the efficacious use of the Word of

On effective preaching, especially to the uneducated, Luther urged the minister "to keep it simple for the simple." *(Church of St. Marien, Wittenberg/The Bridgeman Art Library)*

God, bring salvation. "If thou shalt confess with thy mouth the Lord Jesus, and shalt believe in thine heart that God hath raised Him from the dead, thou shalt be saved" (Rom. 9:9); . . . and "The just shall live by faith" (Rom. 1:17). . . .

But this faith cannot consist of all with works; that is, if you imagine that you can be justified by those works, whatever they are, along with it. . . . Therefore, when you begin to believe, you learn at the same time that all that is in you is utterly guilty, sinful, and damnable, according to that saying, "All have sinned, and come short of the glory of God" (Rom. 3:23). . . . When you have learned this, you will know that Christ is necessary for you, since He has suffered and risen again for you, that, believing on Him, you might by this faith become another man, all your sins being remitted, and you being justified by the merits of another, namely Christ alone.

. . . [A]nd since it [faith] alone justifies, it is evident that by no outward work or labour can the inward man be at all justified, made free, and saved; and that no works whatever have any relation to him. . . . Therefore the first care of every Christian ought to be to lay aside all reliance on works, and strengthen his faith alone more and more, and by it grow in knowledge, not of works, but of Christ Jesus, who has suffered and risen again for him, as Peter teaches (I Peter 5).

Questions for Analysis

1. What did Luther mean by liberty?
2. Why, for Luther, was Scripture basic to Christian life?

Source: Luther's Primary Works, ed. H. Wace and C. A. Buchheim (London: Holder and Stoughton, 1896). Reprinted in *The Portable Renaissance Reader,* ed. James Bruce Ross and Mary Martin McLaughlin (New York: Penguin Books, 1981), pp. 721–726.

A detail from an early-seventeenth-century Flemish painting depicting maps, illustrated travel books, a globe, a compass, and an astrolabe. *(Reproduced by courtesy of the Trustees, The National Gallery, London)*

EUROPEAN EXPLORATION AND CONQUEST, 1450–1650

Prior to 1400 Europeans were relatively marginal players in a centuries-old trading system that linked Africa, Asia, and Europe. Elite classes everywhere prized Chinese porcelains and silks, while wealthy members of the Celestial Kingdom, as China called itself, wanted ivory and black slaves from East Africa, and exotic goods and peacocks from India. African people wanted textiles from India and cowrie shells from the Maldive Islands. Europeans craved spices and silks, but they had few desirable goods to offer their trading partners.

Within little more than a century, European nations had embarked on a remarkably ambitious project to dominate this trading system. The European search for Southeast Asian spices led to a new overseas empire in the Indian Ocean and the accidental discovery of the Western Hemisphere. Within a short time, South and North America had joined a worldwide economic and imperial web. The results were trading networks and political empires of truly global proportions. The era of "globalization" had begun.

European states' intrusions into Indian Ocean trade and into new economies in the New World gave them wealth and power. Over time the old Asian-dominated trading world gave way to a new European-dominated one that encompassed the vast territories of the Americas and the Pacific Ocean. Global contacts created new forms of cultural exchange, assimilation, conversion, and resistance. Europeans sought to impose their cultural values on the people they encountered and struggled to comprehend the peoples and societies they found. New forms of racial prejudice emerged in this period, but so did new openness and curiosity about different ways of life. Together with the developments of the Renaissance and the Reformation, the Age of Discovery laid the foundations for the modern world as we know it today.

World Contacts Before Columbus

Columbus did not sail west on a whim. To understand his voyages—and the European explorations that preceded and succeeded them—we must

Online Study Center

This icon will direct you to interactive activities and study materials on the website **college.hmco.com/pic/mckaywest9e**

first understand late medieval trade networks. Historians now recognize important ties between Europe and other parts of the world prior to Columbus's voyages, arguing that a type of "world economy" linked the products and people of Europe, Asia, and Africa in the fifteenth century. The West was not the dominant player in 1492, and the European voyages derived from the possibilities and constraints of this system. The global impact of the discoveries in the New World must be viewed in the context of this world trading system, which it would in turn revolutionize.

- *What was the Afro-Eurasian trading world before Columbus?*

The Trading World of the Indian Ocean

The center of the pre-Columbian world trade network was the Indian Ocean, the globe's third-largest waterway (after the Atlantic and Pacific). To the west its arms reach into the Red and Arabian Seas, through the former to the Mediterranean Sea, and through the latter into the Persian Gulf and southwestern Asia. To the north the Indian Ocean joins the Bay of Bengal; to the east the Pacific; and to the south the west coast of Australia (see Map 15.1). The monsoon winds blow from the west or south between April and August, and from the northwest or northeast between December and March. These seasonal climate patterns determined the rhythms of trade.

The location of the Indian Ocean made it a crossroads for commercial and cultural exchange. Since Han and Roman times, seaborne trade between China (always the biggest market for Southeast Asian goods), India, the Middle East, Africa, and Europe had flowed across the Indian Ocean. From the seventh through the thirteenth centuries, the volume of this trade steadily increased. After a period of decline resulting from the Black Death, demand for Southeast Asian goods accelerated once more in the late fourteenth century.

Merchants congregated in a series of port cities strung around the ocean that harbored a bewildering array of peoples and cultures. The most developed area of this commercial web lay to the east on the South China Sea. In the fifteenth century the port of **Malacca** became a great commercial **entrepôt,** to which goods were shipped for temporary storage while awaiting redistribution to other places. To Malacca came Chinese porcelains, silks, and camphor (used in the manufacture of many medications, including those to reduce fevers); pepper, cloves, nutmeg, and raw materials such as sappanwood and san-

dalwood from the Moluccas; sugar from the Philippines; and Indian printed cotton and woven tapestries, copper weapons, incense, dyes, and opium. Merchants at Malacca stockpiled goods in fortified warehouses while waiting for the next monsoon. With its many mosques and elegant homes, Malacca enjoyed the reputation of being a sophisticated city, full of "music, ballads, and poetry."[1]

Women in Southeast Asia enjoyed relatively high autonomy. Their important role in planting and harvesting rice, the traditional agricultural crop, gave them authority and economic power. In contrast to Europe, the more daughters a Southeast Asian man had, the richer he was. At marriage the groom paid the bride (or sometimes her family) a sum of money, called bride wealth, which remained under her control. This practice was in sharp contrast to the European dowry, which was provided by the wife's family and came under the husband's control. Married couples usually resided in the wife's village and administered property jointly. All children, regardless of gender, inherited equally, and even after Islam took root in parts of the region, the rule that sons receive double the inheritance of daughters was never implemented.

This respect for women's capacity to handle financial affairs carried over to the commercial sphere. Women participated in business as independent entrepreneurs or partners in family businesses, even undertaking long sea voyages to accompany their wares. When Portuguese and Dutch men settled in the region and married local women, their wives continued to play an important role in trade and commerce.

China played a key role in the fifteenth-century revival of Indian Ocean trade. Given its size and its sophisticated artisanal production, China was an economic powerhouse. Historians agree that medieval China had the most advanced economy in the world; one scholar's controversial theory is that its economic superiority to the West continued to 1800.[2]

The Mongol emperors opened the doors of China to the West, encouraging European traders like Marco Polo to do business there. Marco Polo's tales of his travels from 1271 to 1295 and his encounter with the Great Khan fueled Western fantasies about the exotic "Orient." Unbeknownst to the West, the Mongols fell to the new Ming Dynasty in 1368. During the Ming Dynasty (1368–1644), China entered a period of agricultural and commercial expansion, population growth, and urbanization. By the end of the dynasty, the Chinese population had doubled to perhaps 100 million people. The city of Nanjing had one million inhabitants, making it the largest city in the world, while the new capital, Beijing, had more than six hundred thousand inhabitants.

Population growth was one reason for the Chinese desire for more goods. Another was the celebrated naval expeditions led by **Admiral Zheng He.** Between 1405 and 1433 Zheng He led seven voyages to achieve the emperor Yongle's diplomatic, political, geographical, and commercial goals. Yongle wanted to secure China's hegemony over tributary states and form new tribute-paying relations with profitable trade centers. Zheng He's first fleet was composed of 317 ships—including junks, supply ships, water tankers, warships, transports for horses, and patrol boats—carrying twenty-eight thousand sailors and soldiers. Because it bore tons of beautiful porcelains, elegant silks, lacquer ware, and exquisite artifacts to be exchanged for goods abroad, the Chinese called it the "treasure fleet." Sailing as far west as Egypt, the expeditions brought back spices, books, hardwood, and a giraffe from the kingdom of Mali for the imperial zoo. Zheng He may have been appointed commander because as a Muslim he could more easily negotiate with Muslim merchants on the Indian Ocean.

Court conflicts and the need to defend against renewed Mongol encroachment led to the abandonment of the expeditions and shipbuilding after the deaths of Zheng He and the emperor. Despite the Chinese decision not to pursue overseas voyages, trade continued in the South China Sea. A vast immigration of Chinese people to Southeast Asia, sometimes called the Chinese diaspora, followed the expeditions. Immigrants carried with them Chinese culture, including social customs, diet, and practical objects of Chinese technology—calendars, books, scales for weights and measures, and musical instruments.

Another center of trade in the Indian Ocean was India, the crucial link between the Persian Gulf and the Southeast Asian and East Asian trade networks. The subcontinent had ancient links with its neighbors to the northwest: trade between South Asia and Mesopotamia dates back to the origins of civilization. Fashionable women of the Roman Empire were addicted to Indian cotton; and until the decline of Rome exotic animals, ivory, and Chinese silk also made their way to Europe through India. Trade with the Indian Ocean was revived by Arab merchants who circumnavigated India on their way to trade in the South China Sea. The need for stopovers led to the establishment of trading posts at Gujarat and on the Malabar coast, where the cities of Calicut and Quilon became thriving commercial centers.

The inhabitants of India's southeast, Coromandel Coast, traditionally looked east to Southeast Asia, where they had ancient trading and cultural ties. Hinduism and Buddhism arrived in Southeast Asia from India during the Middle Ages, and a brisk trade between Southeast

Chronology

1443	Portuguese establish first African trading post at Arguim
1450–1650	Age of Discovery
1492	Columbus lands on San Salvador
1511	Portuguese capture Malacca from Muslims
1518	Atlantic slave trade begins
1519–1522	Magellan's expedition circumnavigates the world
1520	Spaniards defeat Aztec army
1532	Pizarro arrives in Peru and defeats Inca Empire
1547	Oviedo, *General History of the Indies*
1570–1630	Worldwide commercial boom
1602	Dutch East India Company established

Asian and Coromandel port cities persisted through the early modern period. India itself was an important contributor of goods to the world trading system. Most of the world's pepper was grown in India, and Indian cotton and silk textiles, mainly from the Gujarat region, were also highly prized.

The Indian Ocean trading system was characterized by ancient and active trade conducted from multicultural, cosmopolitan port cities, most of which had some form of autonomous self-government. When the Portuguese arrived, they found a rich commercial world in which mutual self-interest had largely limited violence and attempts to monopolize trade. As one historian stated, "before the arrival of the Portuguese . . . in 1498 there had been no organised attempt by any political power to control the sea-lanes and the long-distance trade of Asia. . . . The Indian Ocean as a whole and its different seas were not dominated by any particular nations or empires."[3]

Africa

Often neglected by historians, Africa played an important role in the world trade system before Columbus. Around 1450 Africa had a few large and developed empires along with hundreds of smaller polities. From 1250 until its defeat by the Ottomans in the sixteenth century, the Mameluke Egyptian empire was one of the most

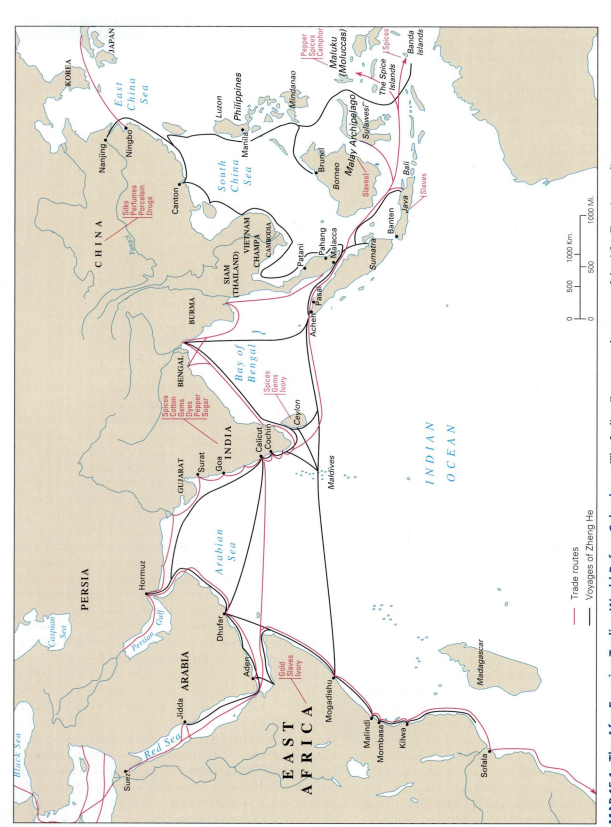

MAP 15.1 The Afro-Eurasian Trading World Before Columbus The Indian Ocean was the center of the Afro-Eurasian trading world. After a period of decline following the Black Death and the Mongol invasions, trade revived in the fifteenth century. Muslim merchants dominated trade, linking ports in East Africa and the Red Sea with those in India and the Malay Archipelago. The Chinese Admiral Zheng He's voyages (1405–1433) followed the most important Indian Ocean trade routes, hoping to impose Ming dominance of trade and tribute. (*Source: Some data from The Times Atlas of World History, 3d ed., page 146.*)

The Port of Banten in Western Java   Influenced by Muslim traders and emerging in the early sixteenth century as a Muslim kingdom, Banten evolved into a thriving entrepôt. The city stood on the trade route to China and, as this Dutch engraving suggests, in the seventeenth century the Dutch East India Company used Banten as an important collection point for spices purchased for sale in Europe. *(Archives Charmet/The Bridgeman Art Library)*

powerful on the continent. Its capital, Cairo, was a center of Islamic learning and religious authority as well as a hub for Indian Ocean trade goods, which the Mamelukes helped to re-orient through the Red Sea. Sharing in the newfound Red Sea prosperity was the African highland state of Ethiopia, which in 1270, saw the rise of a new dynasty claiming descent from the biblical King Solomon and the Queen of Sheba. On the east coast of Africa Swahili-speaking city-states engaged in the Indian Ocean trade, exchanging ivory, rhinoceros horn, tortoise shells, copra, and slaves for textiles, spices, cowrie shells, porcelain, and other goods. The most important cities were Mogadishu, Mombasa, and Kilwa, which had converted to Islam by the eleventh century. Peopled by confident and urbane merchants, they were known for their prosperity and culture.

Another important African contribution to world trade was gold. In the fifteenth century most of the gold that reached Europe came from Sudan in West Africa and from the Akan peoples living near present-day Ghana. After the introduction of camels around A.D. 300, trade routes crisscrossed the Sahara. In exchange for Saharan salt, Arab and African traders brought gold from the cities of Niani and Timbuktu to be sold in the Mediterranean ports of Fez, Marrakesh, Tunis, and Tripoli. Other trading routes led to the Egyptian cities of Alexandria and Cairo, where the Venetians held commercial privileges.

Nations in the inland savannah that sat astride the north-south caravan routes grew wealthy from this trade. In the mid-thirteenth century Sundiata Keita founded the powerful kingdom of Mali. African merchants carried not only goods, but also ideas, helping spread Islam to West Africa. The celebrated pilgrimage of Keita's successor, **Mansa Musa,** to Mecca in 1324 underscores the links between West Africa and the Muslim world in this period. On his way to Mecca, Musa arrived in Cairo with a caravan that included sixty thousand people and eighty camels, with more than two tons of gold for gifts. Word of this spectacular caravan spread across Europe. The famous Spanish world map of 1375, known as the Catalan atlas, depicts Musa as the king of Africa with scepter in one hand and gold nugget in another. He reportedly even discussed sending vessels to explore the Atlantic Ocean, suggesting that not only Europeans envisaged westward naval exploration.

Mansa Musa used his wealth to invest in new mosques and religious schools, making Timbuktu a renowned center of culture and learning. The Muslim traveler Ibn Battuta visited the city and remarked on the rigorous discipline in its religious schools and also on the "extraordinary" state of affairs between men and women. Not only did families trace descent through the mother's line, but the "women show no bashfulness before men and do not veil themselves, though they are assiduous in attending the prayers."[4] Both husbands and wives, he reported, could have "friends" and "companions" of the opposite sex without provoking dishonor or jealousy. By the time the Portuguese arrived, however, the Malian empire was fading, to be replaced by the Songhay, who themselves fell to Moroccan invasion at the end of the sixteenth century. The Portuguese diversion of gold away from the trans-Sahara routes weakened this area politically and economically, and led to its decline as a center of Islamic scholarship.

Gold was one important object of trade; slaves were another. Slavery was practiced in Africa, as virtually everywhere else in the world, before the arrival of Europeans. Arabic and African merchants crossed the Sahara in both directions with slaves. They took West African slaves to the Mediterranean to be sold in European, Egyptian, or Mideastern markets and also brought eastern Europeans—a major element of European slavery—to West Africa as slaves. In addition, Indian and Arabic merchants traded slaves in the coastal regions of East Africa. European contact would revolutionize the magnitude and character of African slavery (see page 508).

Africa—or legends about Africa—played an important role in Europeans' imagination of the outside world. They long cherished the belief in a Christian nation in Africa ruled by a mythical king, Prester John, thought to be a descendant of one of the three kings who visited Jesus after his birth. In 1165 a letter purportedly written by Prester John to the Byzantine emperor describing the king's vast wealth and the fantastic subjects over whom he ruled appeared in Europe. The letter also promised friendship and solidarity with Christian Europe against Islam. Portuguese explorers carried letters of introduc-tion to Prester John on their voyages along the African coast and were convinced they had found him when, in 1520, a Portuguese embassy reached the Christian Ethiopian court.

The Ottoman and Persian Empires

The Middle East was crucial to the late medieval world trade system, serving as an intermediary for trade from all points of the compass. It was situated at the crossroads between the Baltic States, Central Asia, and Russia to the north; Arabia, Egypt, and East Africa to the south; the Mediterranean, Europe, and West and North Africa to the west; and Southeast and East Asia to the east. In addition to serving as a conduit to trade, the Middle East was an important supplier of goods for foreign exchange, especially silk and cotton.

The most famous trade route leading through the Middle East was the ancient Silk Road that linked the West to the Far East. After its collapse in the aftermath of Mongol rule in the fourteenth century, merchants turned to a northern overland route, which led from the Baltic Sea to Russia, Central Asia, and China. Along this route traveled slaves, fur and timber to the east, and Asian luxury goods to the west. Even more important were the two southern sea routes that brought products from the Indian Ocean trading system. The first came across the Arabian Sea and then up the Red Sea past Aden to Cairo. The second led past Hormuz up the Persian Gulf and on to Baghdad. Standing at the mouths of two seas, Aden and Hormuz had vital economic and strategic importance. From the magnificent capitals of Cairo and Baghdad, goods were sent to bustling trading posts on the eastern Mediterranean coast, such as Alexandria, Damascus, Beirut, and Aleppo.

Two great rival Islamic empires, the Turkish Ottomans and the Persian Safavids, dominated this region. The Ottomans combined excellent military strategy with efficient administration of their conquered territories. Under Sultan Mohammed II (r. 1451–1481), the Ottomans captured **Constantinople** in May 1453, sending shock waves through Europe. Renamed Istanbul, the city became the capital of the Ottoman Empire. With a population of 600,000 to 750,000, it was by far the largest city in Europe and the Middle East and rivaled the great Chinese cities in size.

Online Study Center **Improve Your Grade**
Primary Source: The Fall of Constantinople to the Ottomans: A Lamentation

Having completed the conquest of Anatolia in 1461, the emperor Suleiman I (1494–1566) pressed northwest into the Balkans and by the early sixteenth century controlled the sea trade on the eastern Mediterranean. In 1516 the sultan's forces took Syria and Palestine, followed by Egypt in 1517 and the rest of northern Africa. After defeating the Hungarian king in 1526 and bringing portions of his kingdom into the empire, Suleiman turned to the Habsburg state ruled by Ferdinand I, brother to Habsburg emperor Charles V. In 1529 the Turks besieged the Habsburg capital of Vienna. After a siege of several weeks and high casualties on both sides, the Turks retreated, leaving Vienna as the westward limit of Ottoman expansion into Europe.

Ottoman expansion had political, economic, and religious goals. The Ottomans wished to control the Balkans and the Mediterranean so as to monopolize trade routes with the West and spread Islamic rule. The Balkans themselves were a precious source of timber, dye, and silver. With the defeat of the Mameluke empire, expansion into Egypt gave the Ottomans new access to sources of African gold and control over Red Sea shipping. Similarly, conquest of Baghdad brought control of shipping west out of the Persian Gulf.

Turkish expansion badly frightened Europeans. Ottoman armies seemed nearly invincible and the empire's desire for expansion limitless. In France in the sixteenth century, twice as many books were printed about the Turkish threat as about the American discoveries. The strength of the Ottomans helps explain some of the missionary fervor Christians brought to new territories. It also raised economic concerns. With trade routes to the east in the hands of the Ottomans, Europeans were convinced that they needed new trade routes.

Europeans were not alone in opposing Ottoman ambitions. In the early sixteenth century the Persian Safavid Empire became a powerful Muslim state, reaching its height under Shah Abbas I (r. 1587–1629). Like the Ottomans, the Persians were important intermediary figures in the Afro-Eurasian trading system. Persian merchants could be found throughout this trading world in diaspora communities they formed as far away as the Indian Ocean. Persia was also a major producer and exporter of silk.

The Safavids had complex, often hostile relations with their Ottoman neighbors. Although both were Muslim states, the Ottomans' Sunni faith clashed with the Persians' adherence to Shi'ism. Economically, the two competed for control over trade routes to the east. These conflicts led to the Ottoman-Safavid war of 1615–1618 and to periodic confrontations in the following years.

The Taking of Constantinople by the Turks, April 22, 1453 The Ottoman conquest of the capital of the Byzantine Empire in 1453 sent waves of shock and despair through Europe. Capitalizing on the city's strategic and commercial importance, the Ottomans made it the center of their empire. *(Bibliothèque nationale de France)*

However, the two empires also relied on each other economically; for example, the Ottoman silk industry depended on raw silk imported from Iran.[5]

Despite the fear generated by the Ottomans and the military clashes between Ottoman and European forces, it is important to emphasize that no "iron curtain" separated Christian Europe from the Muslim Middle East. Despite explicit religious laws dividing the world into Muslims and infidels, in practice the Ottoman state tolerated religious differences, protecting Christian and Jewish lives and property. Foreign merchants, travelers, and pilgrims were permitted to enter, and the cities of the empire had established settlements of Christian merchants (see Chapter 17).

It is also important to emphasize the disunities within each world. "Muslims" could be Mameluke Egyptians, Ottomans, Persians, Indians, Africans, or Southeast Asians. In many ways Islam helped foster commerce by offering a common Islamic commercial law and culture; however, there were also many divisions among Muslims. Rivalries among European powers as well as among Muslim states like the Sunni Ottomans and the Shi'ite Persians encouraged a shifting pattern of pragmatic and self-interested alliances that breached the borders supposedly dividing East and West. Eventually the Turks formed a loose alliance with the Portuguese against the Persians, which helped both sides ameliorate their trading positions. For his part, Shah Abbas I sent emissaries to Europe seeking alliances against the Ottomans. He offered trade concessions to the English for their help in eliminating the Portuguese from Hormuz. Before then the Safavids had purchased arms from the Portuguese (acquired from India) to use in combat with the Ottomans.

Genoese and Venetian Middlemen

Europe was the western terminus of the world trading system. Before the Portuguese and Spanish voyages, the Italian city-states of Venice and Genoa controlled the European luxury trade with the East. Centuries-old rivals for this trade, Venice and Genoa both lost importance with the rise of Ottoman power in the eastern Mediterranean and with Portuguese, then Dutch, intrusion into the **spice trade** at its source. After a brilliant period during the late Middle Ages, they entered a long period of decline. However, Italian experience in colonial administration, slaving, and international trade and finance served as crucial models for the Iberian states as they pushed European expansion to new heights. Mariners, merchants, and financiers from Venice and Genoa—most notably Christopher Columbus—played a crucial role in bringing the fruits of this experience to the Iberian Peninsula.

Venice grew in importance with the creation of the Crusader kingdoms, gaining territory and special trading concessions in return for aiding the Crusader armies. The Venetian fleet sacked Constantinople in 1204, placing a new emperor on the throne and gaining exclusive trading rights. When the political situation reversed and they lost those privileges, the Venetians turned their attention south. In 1304 the city established formal relations with the sultan of Mameluke Egypt, opening permanent offices in Cairo, the gateway to trade from India, Southeast Asia, and China.

Venice specialized in expensive luxury goods like spices, silks, and carpets. Venetian traders did not, as later Europeans did, explore new routes to get to the sources of supply of these goods. Instead, they obtained them from middlemen in the eastern Mediterranean and Asia Minor. A little went a long way. Venetians purchased no more than five hundred tons of spices a year around 1400, but with a profit of around 40 percent. The most important by far was pepper, grown in India and Indonesia, which composed 60 percent of the spices they purchased in 1400. In all, one historian has estimated that 70 percent of the Western trade in spices belonged to the Venetians.[6] Other imported goods included grain and sugar from Egypt and silk and cotton from Syria. Venetian merchants redistributed these goods throughout Europe.

Another major element of Venetian trade was slavery. Venetian merchants purchased slaves, many of whom were fellow Christians, in the Balkans. The men went to Egypt for the sultan's army or to work as agricultural laborers on Venetian possessions in the Mediterranean. Young girls, who made up the majority of the trade, were sold in western Mediterranean ports as servants or concubines.

The Venetians exchanged Eastern luxury goods for European products they could trade abroad, including Spanish and English wool, German metal goods, Flemish textiles, and silk cloth made in their own manufactures with imported raw materials. The demand for such goods in the East, however, was low. To make up the difference, the Venetians earned currency in the shipping industry and through trade in firearms and slaves. At least half of what they traded with the East took the form of precious metal, much of it acquired in Egypt and North Africa. When the Portuguese arrived in Asia, they found Venetian coins everywhere.

The spice trade brought riches and power to Venice. After the catastrophe of the Black Death, Venice reached the height of its glory in the 1400s. By 1500 the city's population was 120,000, making it one of the largest in Europe. From its origins as a small fishing village in the sixth century A.D., Venice had created a sizable empire. It controlled an expansive region on the Italian peninsula and had trading posts in North Africa, the Levant, and northern Europe in addition to outright colonies on the west coast of the Adriatic. The islands of Crete and later Cyprus were also controlled by Venice.

Merchant wealth endowed the city with beautiful buildings, art, and a rich and vibrant culture, whose legacy can

Bellini: Procession in the Piazza San Marco The Piazza San Marco was, and remains, the principal square of Venice. Located on the Grand Canal, it is home to Saint Mark's Basilica and the palace of the doge, the officer elected for life by the city's aristocracy to rule the city. Many Venetian festivals, like this procession recorded in 1496 by the great artist Gentile Bellini, took place in the square. *(Erich Lessing/Art Resource, NY)*

still be appreciated today. The Venetian city-state organized international trade meticulously; its impressive fleet of state-sponsored ships was one of the finest naval forces in Europe.

French invasions in the 1490s distracted and weakened the city, as did the new claims on the spice trade made by the Portuguese in the early 1500s, which the Venetians' Egyptian allies were unable to counter. The Ottoman conquest of Egypt in 1516 raised Venice's hopes briefly. Eager to improve Red Sea trade and to oppose Portuguese attempts to monopolize the spice trade, the Ottomans encouraged traders to bypass Portuguese ports. Spices began to flow again through the Red Sea to Venetian merchants in Cairo. By the 1600s, however, the Dutch had succeeded in monopolizing this trade, ending Venice's centuries-old role as the main European entrepôt for Asian spices. Venice also lost its eastern Mediterranean colonies to Ottoman conquest, leading to a loss of supplies of slaves and other trade goods.

Venice's ancient rival was Genoa. As was the case with Venice, Genoa's fortunes rose with its participation in the Crusades. Having undone Venetian control of Constan-

tinople, Genoa dominated the northern route to Asia through the Black Sea. Expansion in the thirteenth and fourteenth centuries took the Genoese as far as Persia and the Far East. In 1291 they sponsored an expedition into the Atlantic in search of "parts of India" by the Vivaldi brothers. The ships were lost, and their exact destination and motivations remain unknown. However, the voyage underlines the long history of Genoese aspirations for Atlantic exploration.

In the fifteenth century Genoa made a bold change of direction. With Venice claiming victory over the spice trade, the Genoese shifted focus from trade to finance and from the Black Sea to the western Mediterranean. Given its location on the northwestern coast of Italy, Genoa had always been active in the western Mediterranean, trading with North African ports, southern France, Spain, and even England and Flanders through the Strait of Gibraltar. When new voyages took place in the western Atlantic, Genoese merchants, navigators, and financiers provided their skills to the Iberian monarchs, whose own subjects had much less commercial experience. The Genoese, for example, ran many of the sugar plantations established on the Atlantic islands colonized by the Portuguese. From their settlement in Seville, Genoese merchants financed Spanish colonization of the New World and conducted profitable trade with its colonies.

The Genoese were also enthusiastic slavers. Like the Venetians, they supplied slaves for agricultural labor on their colonial possessions and as slave soldiers to Mameluke Egypt. Once more, the majority of the slaves were young women sent to serve in southern Europe or Genoa. It was a brutal trade:

In a ship sailing from the Crimea to Chios in 1455 30 per cent of the slaves on board died. Genoese law accepted that a master could beat his slave to death, whilst for the rape of a female the punishment was merely a modest fine combined with the obligation to compensate her owner for the damage to his property.[7]

After the loss of the Black Sea—and thus the source of slaves—to the Ottomans, the Genoese sought new supplies in the West, taking the Guanches (indigenous peoples from the Canary Islands), Muslim prisoners and Jewish refugees from Spain, and by the early 1500s both black and Berber Africans. With the growth of Spanish colonies in the New World, Genoese merchants became important players in the Atlantic slave trade.

The European Voyages of Discovery

As we have seen, Europe was by no means isolated before the voyages of exploration and the "discovery" of the New World; the Europeans were aware of and in contact with the riches of the Indian Ocean trading world. From the time of the Crusades, Italian merchants brought the products of the East to luxury markets in Europe eager for silks, spices, porcelain, and other fine goods. But because they did not produce many products desired by Eastern elites, Europeans were relatively modest players in the Afro-Eurasian trading world. Their limited role was reduced even further in the mid-fourteenth century, when the Black Death, combined with the ravages of the Mongol warlord Tamerlane, led to a collapse in trade routes and commercial markets.

From these lows, however, Europeans would soon undertake new and unprecedented expansion. As population and trade recovered, new European players entered the scene, eager to spread Christianity and to undo Italian dominance of trade with the East. A century after the plague, Iberian explorers began the overseas voyages that helped create the modern world, with staggering conse-

quences for their own continent and the rest of the planet.

• *How and why did Europeans undertake ambitious voyages of expansion that would usher in a new era of global contact?*

Causes of European Expansion

European expansion had multiple causes. By the middle of the fifteenth century, Europe was experiencing a revival of population and economic activity after the lows of the Black Death. While this revival was not sufficient to create population pressure in Europe, it did create new demands for luxury goods from the East and for spices in particular. The fall of Constantinople in 1453 and subsequent Ottoman control of trade routes created obstacles to fulfilling these desires. Europeans needed to find new sources of precious metal to trade with the Ottomans or sources of supply for themselves and thereby eliminate Ottoman interference.

Why were spices so desirable? Introduced into western Europe by the Crusaders in the twelfth century, pepper, nutmeg, ginger, mace, cinnamon, and cloves added flavor and variety to the monotonous diet of Europeans. Spices evoked the scent of the Garden of Eden; they seemed a marvel and a mystery. It is also important to remember that the term *spices* referred not only to flavorings added to food but also to perfumes, medicines, drugs, and dyes. Take, for example, cloves, for which Europeans found many uses. If picked green and sugared, the buds could be transformed into conserve (a kind of jam); if salted and pickled, cloves became a flavoring for vinegar. Cloves sweetened the breath. When added to food or drink, cloves were thought to stimulate the appetite and clear the intestines and bladder. When crushed and powdered, they were a medicine rubbed on the forehead to relieve head colds and applied to the eyes to strengthen vision. Taken with milk, cloves were believed to enhance the pleasures of sexual intercourse.

Apart from a desire for trade goods, religious fervor was another important catalyst for expansion. The passion and energy ignited by the Iberian reconquista encouraged the Portuguese and Spanish to continue the Christian crusade. Just seven months separated Isabella and Ferdinand's entry into Granada on January 2 and Columbus's departure westward on August 3, 1492. Overseas exploration was in some ways a transfer of their religious zeal, enthusiasm for conquest and expansion, and certainty of God's blessing on their ventures from the European continent to new non-Christian territories.

Since organized Muslim polities such as the Ottoman Empire were too strong to defeat, Iberians turned their attention to non-Christian peoples elsewhere.

Combined with eagerness for profits and to spread Christianity was the desire for glory and the urge to chart new waters. Scholars have frequently described the European discoveries as a manifestation of Renaissance curiosity about the physical universe—the desire to know more about the geography and peoples of the world. The detailed journals kept by such voyagers as Christopher Columbus and Antonio Pigafetta (a survivor of Magellan's world circumnavigation) attest to their wonder and fascination with the new peoples and places they visited.

Individual explorers combined these motivations in unique ways. Christopher Columbus was a devout Christian who was increasingly haunted by messianic obsessions in the last years of his life. As Bartholomew Diaz put it, his own motives were "to serve God and His Majesty, to give light to those who were in darkness and to grow rich as all men desire to do." When Vasco da Gama reached the port of Calicut, India, in 1498 and a native asked what the Portuguese wanted, he replied, "Christians and spices."[8] The bluntest of the Spanish conquistadors, Hernando Cortés, announced as he prepared to conquer Mexico, "I have come to win gold, not to plow the fields like a peasant."[9]

Eagerness for exploration could be heightened by a lack of opportunity at home. After the reconquista, enterprising young men of the Spanish upper classes found their economic and political opportunities greatly limited. As a study of the Castilian city of Ciudad Real shows, the ancient aristocracy controlled the best agricultural land and monopolized urban administrative posts. Great merchants and a few nobles (surprisingly, since Spanish law forbade participation by nobles in commercial ventures) dominated the textile and leather-glove manufacturing industries. Consequently, many ambitious men turned to the Americas to seek their fortunes.[10]

Whatever the motivations, the voyages were made possible by the growth of government power. Mariners and explorers did not possess the massive sums needed to explore mysterious oceans and control remote continents. Reassertion of monarchical authority and state centralization in the fifteenth century provided rulers with such resources. In the fifteenth century Isabella and Ferdinand had consolidated their several kingdoms to achieve a more united Spain and had revamped the Spanish bureaucracy. The Spanish monarchy was stronger than before and in a position to support foreign ventures. In Portugal the steadfast financial and moral support of **Prince Henry the Navigator** led to Portugal's phenome-

nal success in the spice trade. Like voyagers, monarchs shared a mix of motivations, from desire to please God to desire to win glory and profit from trade.

For ordinary sailors, life at sea was dangerous, overcrowded, unbearably stench-ridden, filled with hunger, and ill-paid. For months at a time, 100 to 120 people lived and worked in a space of between 150 and 180 square meters, with no available water except a small amount for drinking. Each person had an average of 1.5 meters of space, with more going to officers and wealthy passengers.[11] A lucky sailor would find enough space on deck to unroll his sleeping mat. This is not to mention the horses, cows, pigs, chickens, rats, and lice that accompanied the voyages. As one scholar concluded, "traveling on a ship must have been one of the most uncomfortable and oppressive experiences in the world."[12]

Why did men choose to go to sea? They did so to escape poverty at home, to continue a family trade, to win a few crumbs of the great riches of empire, or to find a better life as illegal immigrants in the colonies. Moreover, many orphans and poor boys were placed on board as young pages and had little say in the decision. Women also paid a price for the voyages of exploration. Left alone for months or years at a time, and frequently widowed, sailors' wives struggled to feed their families. The widow of a sailor lost on Magellan's 1519 voyage had to wait until 1547 to collect her husband's salary from the Crown.[13]

The people who stayed at home had a powerful impact on the process. Court coteries and factions influenced a monarch's decisions and could lavishly reward individuals or cut them out of the spoils of empire. Then there was the public: the small number of people who could read were a rapt audience for tales of fantastic places and unknown peoples. Cosmography, natural history, and geography aroused enormous interest among educated people in the fifteenth and sixteenth centuries. Just as science fiction and speculation about life on other planets excite readers today, quasi-scientific literature about Africa, Asia, and the Americas captured the imaginations of literate Europeans. Gonzalo Fernández de Oviedo's *General History of the Indies* (1547), a detailed eyewitness account of plants, animals, and peoples, was widely read. Indeed, the elite's desire for the exotic goods brought by overseas trade helped propel the whole process of expansion.

Technological Stimuli to Exploration

Technological developments in shipbuilding, weaponry, and navigation provided another impetus for European expansion. Since ancient times, most seagoing vessels had been narrow, open boats called *galleys,* propelled largely by manpower. Slaves or convicts who had been sentenced to the galleys manned the oars of the ships that sailed the Mediterranean, and both cargo ships and warships carried soldiers for defense. Though well suited to the placid and thoroughly explored waters of the Mediterranean, galleys could not withstand the rough winds and uncharted shoals of the Atlantic. The need for sturdier craft, as well as population losses caused by the Black Death, forced the development of a new style of ship that would not require soldiers for defense or much manpower to sail.

In the course of the fifteenth century, the Portuguese developed the **caravel,** a small, light, three-masted sailing ship. Though somewhat slower than the galley, the caravel held more cargo. Its triangular lateen sails and sternpost rudder also made the caravel a much more maneuverable vessel. When fitted with cannon, it could dominate larger vessels, such as the round ships commonly used as merchantmen.

By 1350 *cannon*—iron or bronze guns that fired iron or stone balls—had been fully developed. These pieces of artillery emitted frightening noises and great flashes of fire and could batter down fortresses and even city walls.

Early cannon posed serious technical difficulties. Iron cannon were cheaper than bronze to construct, but they were difficult to cast effectively and were liable to crack and injure artillerymen. Bronze guns, made of copper and tin, were less subject than iron to corrosion, but they were very expensive. All cannon were extraordinarily difficult to move, required considerable time for reloading, and were highly inaccurate. They thus proved inefficient for land warfare. However, they could be used at sea.

Great strides in cartography and navigational aids were also made in this period. Around 1410 Arab scholars reintroduced Europeans to **Ptolemy's *Geography.*** Written in the second century A.D. by a Hellenized Egyptian, the work was a formidable synthesis of the geographical knowledge of the classical world. Its republication provided significant improvements over medieval cartography, showing the world as round and introducing the idea of latitude and longitude to plot position accurately. Ptolemy's work also contained crucial errors. Ignorant of the existence of the Americas, he showed the world as much smaller than it is, so that Asia appeared not very distant from Europe to the west. Based on this work, cartographers fashioned new maps that combined classical knowledge with the latest information from mariners.

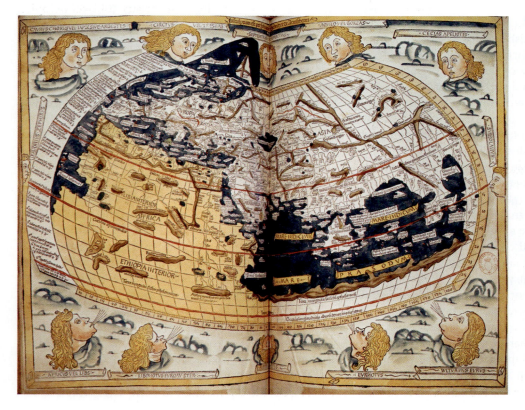

Ptolemy's *Geography* The recovery of Ptolemy's *Geography* in the early fifteenth century gave Europeans new access to ancient geographical knowledge. This 1486 world map, based on Ptolemy, is a great advance over medieval maps but contains errors with significant consequences for future exploration. It shows the world watered by a single ocean, with land covering three-quarters of the world's surface and with Europe, Africa, and Asia as the only continents. Africa and Asia are joined, making the Indian Ocean a landlocked sea and rendering the circumnavigation of Africa impossible. The continent of Asia is stretched far to the east, greatly shortening the distance from Europe to Asia. *(Giraudon/Art Resource, NY)*

First the Genoese and Venetians, and then the Portuguese and Spanish, took the lead in these advances.[14]

The magnetic compass enabled sailors to determine their direction and position at sea. The astrolabe, an instrument invented by the ancient Greeks and perfected by Muslim navigators, was used to determine the altitude of the sun and other celestial bodies. It permitted mariners to plot their latitude, or position north or south of the equator.

Many scholars have argued that it was superior European weaponry, shipbuilding, and navigational skill that allowed them to undertake such astonishing voyages and to overcome the resistance of numerically far superior forces. As in the Industrial Revolution, they have argued, the key to European success over others was its openness to new technology and its interest in developing and adopting the most advanced technologies.

These arguments have encountered criticism in recent years. Some scholars have emphasized the extent to which European technology was borrowed from the East. For example, gunpowder, the compass, and the sternpost rudder were all Chinese inventions. The lateen sail, which allowed European ships to tack against the wind, was a product of the Indian Ocean trading world and was brought to the Mediterranean on Arab ships. Navigational aids, such as the astrolabe, were also acquired from others, and advances in cartography drew on the rich tradition of Judeo-Arabic mathematical and astronomical learning in Iberia. This assistance sometimes assumed human form. It was not his own seafaring abilities but assistance from a local guide that helped Vasco da Gama find a sea route from the East African coast to India. In exploring new territories, European sailors thus called on techniques and knowledge developed over centuries in China and the trading world of the Indian Ocean.

Other historians have argued that technological advances were in themselves not that important. Not only were cannon inaccurate and unreliable, but in the tropical conditions of Africa, India, and South America gunpowder got wet and cannon did not fire. Native populations quickly acquired firepower from Europeans who were eager to profit from the weapons trade. These historians have concluded that technological developments arose to meet the needs of exploration, rather than being a necessary precursor to them. To support this case, one scholar points out that the first Portuguese voyages took place in whatever boats were available and with crews unable to make use of a compass or a sea chart. Columbus himself relied on dead reckoning—at which he proved extremely adept—rather than on new navigational devices. As this

Nocturnal   An instrument for determining the hour of night at sea by finding the progress of certain stars around the polestar (center aperture). *(National Maritime Museum, London)*

historian concludes, "Neither in Asia nor anywhere else was empire the inevitable corollary of technological superiority."[15]

The Portuguese Overseas Empire

At the end of the fourteenth century Portugal was a small and poor nation on the margins of European life whose principal activities were fishing and subsistence farming. It would have been hard for a European to predict Portugal's phenomenal success overseas in the next two centuries. Yet Portugal had a long history of seafaring and navigation. Blocked from access to western Europe by Spain, the Portuguese turned to the Atlantic and North Africa, whose waters they knew better than almost any other Europeans. Nature favored the Portuguese: winds blowing along their coast offered passage to Africa, its Atlantic islands, and, ultimately, Brazil.

In the early phases of Portuguese exploration, Prince Henry (1394–1460), a younger son of the king, played a leading role. A nineteenth-century scholar dubbed Henry "the Navigator" because of his support for the study of geography and navigation and for the annual expeditions he sponsored down the western coast of Africa. Although he never personally participated in voyages of exploration, Henry's enthusiasm for discovery and his financial support

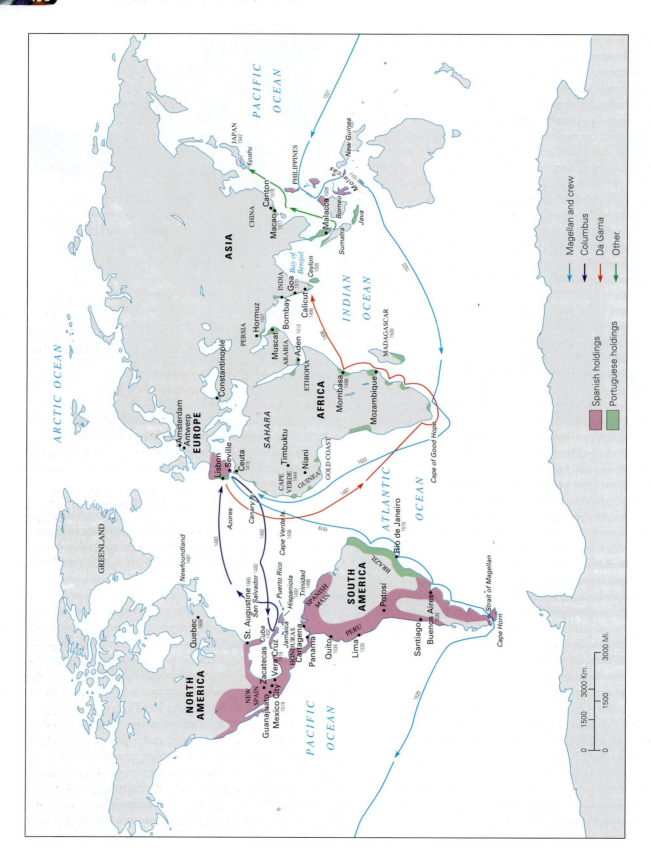

PACIFIC OCEAN

1521

JAPAN
1542

Kyushu

PHILIPPINES

New Guinea

CHINA

Canton
1513

MOLUCCAS
1521

Macao
1577

Malacca
1511

Borneo
1509

Java

Sumatra

ASIA

Bay of Bengal

INDIA

Goa
1510

Bombay

Calicut
1498

Ceylon
1505

INDIAN OCEAN

1498

Hormuz
1507

Muscat

Aden
1513

PERSIA

ARABIA

ETHIOPIA

MADAGASCAR
1500

Constantinople

EUROPE

Amsterdam
Antwerp

AFRICA

Mombasa
1498

Mozambique

SAHARA

Lisbon
Seville
Ceuta
1415

Timbuktu

Niani
1444

GUINEA

CAPE VERDE

GOLD COAST

1522

ATLANTIC OCEAN

Cape of Good Hope

1522

ARCTIC OCEAN

GREENLAND

Azores

Canary Is.
1492

Cape Verde Is.
1456

1497

1493

1519

Newfoundland
1497

Quebec
1608

St. Augustine
1565

San Salvador 1492

Cuba
1492

Puerto Rico
1493

Hispaniola
1492

Trinidad
1498

Jamaica

HONDURAS

NORTH AMERICA

NEW SPAIN

Guanajuato
Zacatecas
Mexico City
1519

Vera Cruz

Cartagena

Panama

SPANISH MAIN

SOUTH AMERICA

BRAZIL

Rio de Janeiro
1516

Potosi

Quito
1534

Lima
1535

Santiago

Buenos Aires
1535

PERU

1516

1519

1520

Strait of Magellan

Cape Horn

PACIFIC OCEAN

3000 Mi.

3000 Km.

1500

1500

0

0

Spanish holdings

Portuguese holdings

Magellan and crew

Columbus

Da Gama

Other

ensured that Portugal did not abandon the effort despite early disappointments.

The objectives of Portuguese policy included aristocratic desires for martial glory, the historic Iberian crusade to Christianize Muslims, and the quest to find gold, slaves, an overseas route to the spice markets of India, and the mythical king Prester John. Portugal's conquest of Ceuta, an Arab city in northern Morocco, in 1415 marked the beginning of European exploration and control of overseas territory. In the late 1420s, under Henry's direction, the Portuguese began to settle the Atlantic islands of Madeira (ca 1420) and the Azores (1427). In 1443 the Portuguese founded their first African commercial settlement at Arguim in present-day Mauritania. By the time of Henry's death in 1460, his support for exploration was vindicated by thriving plantations on the Atlantic islands and new access to gold.

Under King John II (r. 1481–1495) the Portuguese established trading posts and forts on the gold-rich Guinea coast and penetrated into the African continent all the way to Timbuktu (see Map 15.2). Portuguese ships transported gold to Lisbon, and by 1500 Portugal controlled the flow of African gold to Europe. The golden century of Portuguese prosperity had begun.

Still the Portuguese pushed farther south down the west coast of Africa. In 1487 Bartholomew Diaz rounded the Cape of Good Hope at the southern tip, but storms and a threatened mutiny forced him to turn back. On a later expedition in 1497 **Vasco da Gama** commanded a fleet of four ships in search of a sea route to the Indian Ocean trade. Da Gama's ships rounded the Cape and sailed up the east coast of Africa. With the help of an Indian guide, da Gama sailed across the Arabian Sea to the port of Calicut in India. Overcoming local hostility, he returned to Lisbon loaded with spices and samples of In-

The Portuguese Fleet Embarked for the Indies This image shows a Portuguese trading fleet in the late fifteenth century, bound for the riches of the Indies. Between 1500 and 1635, over nine hundred ships sailed from Portugal to ports on the Indian Ocean, in annual fleets composed of five to ten ships. *(British Museum/HarperCollins Publishers/The Art Archive)*

Mapping the Past

MAP 15.2 Overseas Exploration and Conquest, Fifteenth and Sixteenth Centuries The voyages of discovery marked a dramatic new phase in the centuries-old migrations of European peoples. This map depicts the voyages of Ferdinand Magellan, Christopher Columbus, and Vasco da Gama. ❶ What was the contemporary significance of each of these voyages? ❷ Was the importance of the voyages primarily economic, political, or cultural? ❸ Which voyage had the most impact, and why?

Online Study Center **Improve Your Grade** Interactive Map: World Exploration, 1492–1535

dian cloth. He had failed to forge any trading alliances with local powers, and Portuguese arrogance ensured the future hostility of Muslim merchants who dominated the trading system. Nonetheless, he had proved the possibility of lucrative trade with the East via the Cape route.

King Manuel (r. 1495–1521) promptly dispatched thirteen ships under the command of Pedro Alvares Cabral, assisted by Diaz, to set up trading posts in India. On April 22, 1500, Cabral's fleet sighted the coast of Brazil in South America and claimed it for the Crown of Portugal. Cabral then proceeded south and east around the Cape of Good Hope and reached India. Half the fleet was lost on the return voyage, but the six spice-laden vessels that dropped anchor in Lisbon harbor in July 1501 more than paid for the entire expedition. Thereafter, a Portuguese convoy set out for passage around the Cape every March. Lisbon became the entrance port for Asian goods into Europe—but this was not accomplished without a fight.

For centuries, port city-states had controlled the rich spice trade of the Indian Ocean, and they did not surrender it willingly. Portuguese commercial activities were accompanied by the destruction or seizure of strategic coastal forts, which later served Portugal as both trading posts and military bases. Alfonso de Albuquerque, whom the Portuguese crown appointed as governor of India (1509–1515), decided that these bases, not inland territories, should control the Indian Ocean. Accordingly, his cannon blasted open the ports of Malacca, Calicut, Ormuz, and Goa, the vital centers of Muslim domination of South Asian trade. This bombardment laid the foundation for Portuguese imperialism in the sixteenth and seventeenth centuries—a strange way to bring Christianity to "those who were in darkness." As one scholar wrote about the opening of China to the West, "while Buddha came to China on white elephants, Christ was borne on cannon balls."[16]

In March 1493, between the voyages of Diaz and da Gama, Spanish ships under a triumphant Genoese mariner named **Christopher Columbus** (1451–1506), in the service of the Spanish crown, entered Lisbon harbor. Spain also had begun the quest for an empire.

The Problem of Christopher Columbus

The year 1992, which marked the quincentenary of Columbus's first voyages to the Americas, spawned an enormous amount of discussion about the significance of his voyages. Journalists, scholars, amateurs, and polemicists debated Columbus's accomplishments and failures. Until the 1980s most writers would have generally agreed with Harvard historian Samuel Eliot Morison in his 1942 biography of the explorer:

The whole history of the Americas stems from the Four Voyages of Columbus; today a score of independent nations and dominions unite in homage to Columbus, the stout-hearted son of Genoa, who carried Christian civilization across the Ocean Sea.[17]

In 1942, the Western Powers believed they were engaged in a life-and-death struggle to defend "Christian civilization" against the evil of fascism.

In contrast to this lavish praise, Columbus has recently been severely criticized. He enslaved and sometimes killed the Indians he encountered. He was a cruel and ineffective governor of Spain's Caribbean colony. Moreover, he did not discover the Americas: Native Americans had occupied the New World for millennia before Columbus, and other Europeans, including the Vikings, had been there before him. Not only did he not discover the continents, but he also misunderstood what he found. Other writers have faulted Columbus as an opportunistic adventurer who originated European exploitation of the non-European world.

Rather than judging Columbus by debates and standards of our time, it is more important to put him into the context of his own time. First, what kind of man was Columbus, and what forces or influences shaped him? Second, in sailing westward from Europe, what were his goals? Third, did he achieve his goals, and what did he make of his discoveries?

Columbus grew up in Genoa and thus drew on the centuries-old tradition of Genoese participation in international trade. In his dream of a westward passage to the Indies, he embodied a long-standing Genoese ambition to circumvent Venetian domination of eastward trade, which was now being claimed by the Portuguese. Columbus was also very knowledgeable about the sea. He had worked as a mapmaker, and he was familiar with such fifteenth-century Portuguese navigational developments as *portolans*—written descriptions of the courses along which ships sailed, showing bays, coves, capes, ports, and the distances between these places—and the use of the magnetic needle as a nautical instrument. As he implied in his *Journal,* he had acquired not only theoretical but also practical experience: "I have spent twenty-three years at sea and have not left it for any length of time worth mentioning, and I have seen everything from east to west [meaning he had been to England] and I have been to Guinea [north and west Africa]."[18] Although some of Columbus's geographical information, such as his measurement of the distance from Portugal to Japan as 2,760 miles when it is actually 12,000, proved inaccurate, his successful thirty-three-day voyage to the Caribbean owed a great deal to his seamanship.

Columbus was also a deeply religious man. He began the *Journal* of his voyage to the Americas in the form of a letter to Ferdinand and Isabella of Spain:

On 2 January in the year 1492, when your Highnesses had concluded their war with the Moors who reigned in Europe, I saw your Highnesses' banners victoriously raised on the towers of the Alhambra, the citadel of the city, and the Moor-

ish king come out of the city gates and kiss the hands of your Highnesses and the prince, My Lord. And later in that same month, on the grounds of information I had given your Highnesses concerning the lands of India . . . your Highnesses decided to send me, Christopher Columbus, to see these parts of India and the princes and peoples of those lands and consider the best means for their conversion.[19]

Columbus had witnessed the Spanish reconquest of Granada and shared fully in the religious and nationalistic fervor surrounding that event. Like the Spanish rulers and most Europeans of his age, Columbus understood Christianity as a missionary religion that should be carried to places and peoples where it did not exist. Although Columbus certainly had material and secular goals, first and foremost, as he wrote in 1498, he believed he was a divine agent: "God made me the messenger of the new heaven and the new earth of which he spoke in the Apocalypse of St. John . . . and he showed me the post where to find it."[20]

What was the object of this first voyage? Columbus gave the answer in the very title of the expedition, "The Enterprise of the Indies." He wanted to find a direct ocean trading route to Asia. Rejected by the Portuguese in 1483 and by Ferdinand and Isabella in 1486, the project finally won the backing of the Spanish monarchy in 1492. The **Santa Fe capitulations** named Columbus viceroy over any territory he might discover and gave him one-tenth of the material rewards of the journey. Inspired by the stories of Marco Polo, Columbus dreamed of reaching the court of the Great Khan (not realizing that the Ming Dynasty had overthrown the Mongols in 1368). Based on Ptolemy's *Geography* and other texts, he expected to pass the islands of Japan and then land on the east coast of China. He carried letters from Ferdinand and Isabella to the khan and an Arabic interpreter, for he assumed that the Great Khan must be in dialogue with Arabic-speaking powers.

How did Columbus interpret what he had found, and in his mind did he achieve what he had set out to do? Columbus's small fleet left the seaport of Palos on August 3 bound for a first stop at the Canary Islands, the westernmost outpost of European civilization. He landed in the Bahamas on October 12, which he christened San Salvador. Columbus believed he had found some small islands off the east coast of Cipangu (Japan). On encountering natives of the islands, he gave them some beads and "many other trifles of small value," pronouncing them delighted with these gifts and eager to trade. In a letter he wrote to Ferdinand and Isabella on his return

to Spain, Columbus described the natives as handsome, peaceful, and primitive people whose body painting reminded him of the Canary Islands natives. He concluded that they would make good slaves and could quickly be converted to Christianity. (See the feature "Listening to the Past: Columbus Describes His First Voyage" on pages 518–519.)

Columbus received reassuring reports—via hand gestures and mime—of the presence of gold and of a great king in the vicinity. From San Salvador, Columbus sailed southwest, believing that this course would take him to Japan or the coast of China. He landed on Cuba on October 28. Deciding that he must be on the mainland near the coastal city of Quinsay (Hangzhou), he sent a small embassy inland with letters from Ferdinand and Isabella and instructions to locate the grand city.

The landing party, however, found only sparsely populated villages. In response to this disappointment, Columbus set a course that is still controversial among historians. Instead of continuing north, he turned southwest, apparently giving up on his aim to meet the Great Khan in preference to trying to find gold among the peoples he had discovered. In January, having failed to find the source of gold but having made contact with natives seemingly apt for Christianization and confident of the existence of gold somewhere in the vicinity, he headed back to Spain.

Over the next decades, Columbus's change of course was reconfirmed as the Spanish adopted the model of conquest and colonization they had already introduced in the Canary Islands rather than one of exchange with equals (as envisaged for the Mongol khan). On his second voyage, Columbus forcibly subjugated the island of Hispaniola, enslaved its indigenous peoples, and laid the basis for a system of land grants tied to their labor service. Columbus himself, however, had little interest in or capacity for governing. Revolt soon broke out against him and his brother on Hispaniola. A royal expedition sent to investigate returned the brothers to Spain in chains. Columbus was quickly cleared of wrongdoing, but he did not recover his authority over the territories. Instead, they came under royal control.

Columbus was very much a man of his times. To the end of his life in 1506, he believed that he had found small islands off the coast of Asia. He never realized the scope of his achievement: to have found a vast continent unknown to Europeans, except for a fleeting Viking presence centuries earlier. He could not know that the scale of his discoveries would revolutionize world power, raising issues of trade, settlement, government bureaucracy, and the rights of native and African peoples.

Later Explorers

News of Columbus's first voyage rapidly spread across Europe. On April 1, 1493, a printer in Barcelona published Columbus's letter to Ferdinand and Isabella describing what he had found. By the end of that month the letter had been translated into Latin and published in Rome. Within a year printers in Paris, Basel, Antwerp, and Venice had brought out six more Latin editions, which were soon followed by translations into other European languages. In a 1503 letter Florentine navigator Amerigo Vespucci (1454–1512) wrote about his discoveries on the coast of modern-day Venezuela, stating: "Those new regions which we found and explored with the fleet . . . we may rightly call a New World." This letter, titled *Mundus Novus* (The New World), was the first document to describe America as a continent separate from Asia. In recognition of Amerigo's bold claim, the continent was named for him. (When later cartographers realized that Columbus had made the discovery first, it was too late to change the maps.)

To settle competing claims to the Atlantic discoveries, Spain and Portugal turned to Pope Alexander VI. The **Treaty of Tordesillas** (1494) gave Spain everything to the west of an imaginary line drawn down the Atlantic and Portugal everything to the east. This arbitrary division worked in Portugal's favor when in 1500 an expedition led by Pedro Alvares Cabral landed on the coast of Brazil, which Cabral claimed as Portuguese territory. The country's name derives from the brazilwood trees found there, an important source of red dye (from the word *brasa,* or the reddish color of burning coals).

The search for profits determined the direction of Spanish exploration and expansion into South America. When it became apparent that placer mining (in which ore is separated from soil by panning) in the Caribbean islands was unrewarding and that the Portuguese were reaping enormous riches in Asian trade, new routes to the East and new sources of gold and silver were sought. In 1519 the Spanish ruler Charles V commissioned the Portuguese mariner **Ferdinand Magellan** (1480–1521) to find a direct route to the spices of the Moluccas off the southeast coast of Asia. Magellan sailed southwest across the Atlantic to Brazil, and after a long search along the coast he located the treacherous straits that now bear his name (see Map 15.2). The new ocean he sailed into after a rough passage through the straits seemed so peaceful that Magellan dubbed it the Pacific. He was soon to realize his mistake. His fleet sailed north up the west coast of South America and then headed west into the immense expanse of the Pacific toward the Malay Archipelago. (Some of these islands were conquered in the 1560s and named the "Philippines" for Philip II of Spain.)

Terrible storms, disease, starvation, and violence haunted the expedition. Magellan had set out with a fleet of five ships and around 270 men. Sailors on two of the

World Map of Diogo Ribeiro, 1529   This map integrates the wealth of new information provided by European explorers in the decades after Columbus's 1492 voyage. Working on commission for the Spanish king Charles V, the mapmaker incorporated new details on Africa, South America, India, the Malay Archipelago, and China. Note the inaccuracy in his placement of the Moluccas, or Spice Islands, which are much too far east. This "mistake" was intended to serve Spain's interests in trade negotiations with the Portuguese. *(Biblioteca Apostolica Vaticana)*

ships attempted mutiny on the South American coast; one ship was lost, and another ship deserted and returned to Spain before even traversing the straits. The trip across the Pacific took ninety-eight days, and the men survived on rats and sawdust. Magellan himself was killed in a skirmish in the Philippines. The expedition had enough survivors to man only two ships, and one of them was captured by the Portuguese. One ship with eighteen men returned to Spain from the east by way of the Indian Ocean, the Cape of Good Hope, and the Atlantic in 1522. The voyage had taken almost exactly three years.

Despite the losses, this voyage revolutionized Europeans' understanding of the world by demonstrating the vastness of the Pacific. The earth was clearly much larger than Columbus had believed. The voyage actually made a small profit in spices, but Magellan had proved the westward passage to the Indies to be too long and dangerous for commercial purposes. Turning to its New World colonies, Spain abandoned the attempt to oust Portugal from the Eastern spice trade.

Resounding success in this arena belonged to the Dutch. By the end of the sixteenth century Amsterdam had overtaken Antwerp as the financial capital of Europe. The Dutch had also embarked on foreign exploration and conquest. The Dutch East India Company, founded in 1602, became the major organ of Dutch imperialism and within a few decades expelled the Portuguese from Ceylon and other East Indian islands. By 1650 the Dutch West India Company had successfully intruded on the Spanish possessions in the Americas, in the process gaining control of much of the African and American trade.

English and French explorations lacked the immediate, sensational results of those of the Spanish and Portuguese. In 1497 John Cabot, a Genoese merchant living in London, sailed for Brazil but discovered Newfoundland. The next year he returned and explored the New England coast, perhaps going as far south as Delaware. Since these expeditions found no spices or gold, Henry VII lost interest in exploration. Between 1534 and 1541 Frenchman Jacques Cartier made several voyages and explored the St. Lawrence region of Canada. The first permanent French settlement, at Quebec, was founded in 1608.

New World Conquest

In the West Indies the slow recovery of gold, the shortage of a healthy labor force, and sheer restlessness sped up Spain's search for wealth. In 1519, the year Magellan departed on his worldwide expedition, a brash and determined Spanish adventurer named **Hernando Cortés** (1485–1547) crossed from Hispaniola to mainland Mexico with six hundred men, seventeen horses, and ten cannon. The conquest of Aztec Mexico had begun.

Cortés landed at Vera Cruz in February 1519. In November he entered **Tenochtitlán** (now Mexico City), capital of the sophisticated Aztec Empire ruled by Montezuma II (r. 1502–1520). Larger than any European city of the time, the capital was the heart of a civilization with advanced mathematics, astronomy, and engineering, with a complex social system, and with oral poetry and historical traditions. In less than two years Cortés had destroyed the monarchy, gained complete control of the capital city, and extended his jurisdiction over much of the Aztec Empire. Why did a strong people defending its own territory succumb to a handful of Spaniards fighting in dangerous and unfamiliar circumstances? Scholars continue to debate this question. The best answer is that, at the time of the Spanish arrival, the Aztec Empire faced internal weaknesses brought on by the resentment of recently subjugated tribes and by the Aztecs' own psychology and attitudes toward war.

Online Study Center **Improve Your Grade**
Primary Source: Cortés on the Aztecs: Two Letters to Charles V

The Spaniards arrived in late summer, when the Aztecs were preoccupied with harvesting their crops and not thinking of war. From the Spaniards' perspective, the timing was ideal. A series of natural phenomena, signs, and portents seemed to augur disaster for the Aztecs. A comet was seen in daytime, and two temples were suddenly destroyed, one by lightning unaccompanied by thunder. These and other apparently inexplicable events had an unnerving and demoralizing effect on the Aztecs.

Even more important was the alienation of newly conquered tribes and the Aztecs' failure to provide an effective military resistance. The Aztec state religion, the sacred cult of Huitzilopochtli, necessitated constant warfare against neighboring peoples to secure captives for religious sacrifice and laborers for agricultural and infrastructural work. When Cortés landed, recently defeated tribes were not yet fully integrated into the empire. Increases in tribute provoked revolt, which led to reconquest, retribution, and demands for higher tribute, which in turn sparked greater resentment and fresh revolt. When the Spaniards appeared, the Totonacs greeted them as liberators, and other subject peoples joined them against the Aztecs.[21]

Montezuma himself refrained from attacking the Spaniards as they advanced toward his capital and welcomed Cortés and his men into Tenochtitlán. Historians have

The Aztec Capital of Tenochtitlán Occupying a large island, Tenochtitlán was laid out in concentric circles. The administrative and religious buildings were at the heart of the city, which was surrounded by residential quarters. Cortés himself marveled at the city in his letters: "It has four approaches by means of artificial causeways. . . . The city is as large as Seville or Cordoba. . . . There are bridges, very large, strong, and well constructed, so that, over many, ten horsemen can ride abreast. . . . The city has many squares where markets are held. . . . There is one square, twice as large as that of Salamanca, all surrounded by arcades, where there are daily more than sixty thousand souls, buying and selling. In the service and manners of its people, their fashion of living was almost the same as in Spain, with just as much harmony and order." *(The Newberry Library)*

often condemned the Aztec ruler for vacillation and weakness. But he relied on the advice of his state council, itself divided, and on the dubious loyalty of tributary communities. When Cortés—with incredible boldness—took Montezuma hostage, the emperor's influence over his people crumbled.

Forced to leave Tenochtitlán to settle a conflict elsewhere, Cortés placed his lieutenant, Alvarado, in charge. Alvarado's harsh rule drove the Aztecs to revolt, and they almost succeeded in destroying the Spanish garrison. When Cortés returned just in time, the Aztecs allowed his reinforcements to join Alvarado's besieged force. No threatened European or Asian state would have conceived of doing such a thing: dividing an enemy's army and destroying the separate parts was basic to their mili-

tary tactics. But for the Aztecs warfare was a ceremonial act in which "divide and conquer" had no place.

Having allowed the Spanish forces to reunite, the entire population of Tenochtitlán attacked the invaders and killed many Spaniards. In retaliation, the Spaniards executed Montezuma. The Spaniards escaped from the city and inflicted a crushing defeat on the Aztec army at Otumba near Lake Texcoco on July 7, 1520. Aztec weapons proved no match for the terrifyingly noisy and lethal Spanish cannon, muskets, crossbows, and steel swords. After this victory Cortés began the systematic conquest of Mexico.

More amazing than the defeat of the Aztecs was the Spanish victory over the remote Inca Empire perched at 9,800 to 13,000 feet above sea level. Like the Aztecs, the

Incas had created a civilization that rivaled the Europeans in population and complexity. The borders of this vast empire were well fortified and were threatened by no foreign invaders. Like the Romans, the Incas had built an extensive network of roads linking all parts of the empire, which permitted the operation of a highly efficient postal service. The imperial government taxed, fed, and protected its subjects. Grain was plentiful. Apart from an outbreak of smallpox in a distant province—introduced by the Spaniards—no natural disaster upset the general peace. An army of fifty thousand loyal troops stood at the ruler's disposal.

The Incas were totally isolated. They had no contact with other Amerindian cultures and knew nothing of Aztec civilization or its collapse in 1520. Since about 1500 Inca scouts had reported "floating houses" on the seas manned by white men with beards, and tradesmen told of strange large animals with feet of silver (the appearance of horseshoes in the brilliant sunshine). The Spanish told the Incas that they were sent by God—whom Incans may have associated with their creator-god **Virocha**—and the Incas initially believed these claims of good faith.

From 1493 to 1525 the Inca Huayna Capac ruled as a benevolent despot (the word *Inca* refers both to the ruler of the Andeans who lived in the valleys of the Andes in present-day Peru and to the people themselves). His millions of subjects considered him a link between the earth and the sun-god. In 1525 Huascar succeeded his father as Inca and was crowned at Cuzco, the Incas' capital city, with the fringed headband symbolizing his imperial office. However, his rule was threatened by the claims of his half-brother Atauhualpa. Civil war ensued, and Atauhualpa emerged victorious.[22] The five-year struggle may have exhausted him and damaged his judgment.

Francisco Pizarro (ca 1475–1541), a conquistador of modest Spanish origins, landed on the northern coast of Peru on May 13, 1532, the very day Atauhualpa won the decisive battle. The Spaniard soon learned about the war and its outcome. As Pizarro advanced across the steep Andes toward Cuzco, Atauhualpa was proceeding to the capital for his coronation. Like Montezuma in Mexico, Atauhualpa was kept fully informed of the Spaniards' movements, and he stopped at the provincial town of Cajamarca. His plan was to lure the Spaniards into a trap, seize their horses and ablest men for his army, and execute

Doña Marina Translating for Hernando Cortés During His Meeting with Montezuma In April 1519 Doña Marina (or La Malinche as she is known in Mexico) was among twenty women given to the Spanish as slaves. Fluent in Nahuatl and Yucatec Mayan (spoken by a Spanish priest accompanying Cortés), she acted as an interpreter and diplomatic guide for the Spanish. She had a close personal relationship with Cortés and bore his son Don Martín Cortés in 1522. Doña Marina has been seen as a traitor to her people, as a victim of Spanish conquest, and as the founder of the Mexican people. She highlights the complex interaction between native peoples and the Spanish and the particular role women often played as cultural mediators between the two sides. *(American Museum of Natural History. Image VC #31)*

the rest. What had the Inca, surrounded by his thousands of troops, to fear? Atauhualpa thus accepted Pizarro's invitation to meet in the central plaza of Cajamarca with his bodyguards "unarmed so as not to give offense." The Spaniards captured him and collected an enormous ransom in gold. Instead of freeing the new emperor, however, they killed him.

Decades of violence ensued, marked by Incan resistance and internal struggles among Spanish forces for the spoils of empire. By the 1570s the Spanish crown had succeeded in imposing control. With Spanish conquest, a new chapter opened in European relations with the New World.

Europe and the World After Columbus

Europeans had maintained commercial relations with Asia and sub-Saharan Africa since Roman times. In the Carolingian era the slave trade had linked northern Europe and the Islamic Middle East. The High Middle Ages had witnessed a great expansion of trade with Africa and Asia. But with the American discoveries, for the first time commercial and other relations became worldwide, involving all the continents except Australia. European involvement in the Americas led to the acceleration of global contacts. In time, these contacts had a profound influence on European society and culture.

- **What effect did overseas expansion have on the conquered societies, on enslaved Africans, and on world trade?**

Spanish Settlement and Indigenous Population Decline

In the sixteenth century perhaps two hundred thousand Spaniards immigrated to the New World. Mostly soldiers demobilized from the Spanish and Italian campaigns and adventurers and drifters unable to find employment in Spain, they did not come to work. After assisting in the conquest of the Aztecs and the subjugation of the Incas, these drifters wanted to settle down and become a ruling class. They carved out vast estates in temperate grazing areas and imported Spanish sheep, cattle, and horses for the kinds of ranching with which they were familiar. In coastal tropic areas unsuited for grazing the Spanish erected huge sugar plantations. Columbus had introduced sugar into the West Indies; Cortés had introduced

it into Mexico. Sugar was a great luxury in Europe, and demand was high. Around 1550 the discovery of silver at Zacatecas and Guanajuato in Mexico and Potosí in present-day Bolivia stimulated silver rushes. How were the cattle ranches, sugar plantations, and silver mines to be worked? Obviously, by the Amerindians.

The Spanish quickly established the **encomienda system.** The Crown granted the conquerors the right to employ groups of Amerindians as agricultural or mining laborers or as tribute payers. Theoretically, the Spanish were forbidden to enslave the natives; in actuality, the encomiendas were a legalized form of slavery. The European demand for sugar, tobacco, and silver prompted the colonists to exploit the Amerindians mercilessly. Unaccustomed to forced labor, especially in the blistering heat of tropical cane fields or in the dark, dank, and dangerous mines, they died in staggering numbers.

Students of the history of medicine have suggested another crucial explanation for indigenous population losses: disease. Contact with disease builds up bodily resistance; peoples isolated from other societies are not exposed to some diseases and thus do not build resistance. At the beginning of the sixteenth century Amerindians probably had the unfortunate distinction of longer isolation from the rest of humankind than any other people on earth. Crowded concentrations of laborers in the mining camps bred infection, which the miners carried to their home villages. Having little or no resistance to diseases brought from the Old World, the inhabitants of the highlands of Mexico and Peru, especially, fell victim to smallpox, typhus, influenza, and other diseases. According to one expert, smallpox caused "in all likelihood the most severe single loss of aboriginal population that ever occurred."[23] (The old belief that syphilis was a New World disease imported to Europe by Columbus's sailors has been discredited by the discovery of pre-Columbian skeletons in Europe bearing signs of the disease.)

Although disease was the most important cause of indigenous population decline, there were many others. With the native population diverted from traditional agricultural work, cultivation of crops suffered, leading to malnutrition, reduced fertility rates, and starvation. Women forced to work were separated from their infants, leading to high infant mortality rates in a population with no livestock to supply alternatives to breast milk. Malnutrition and hunger in turn reduced resistance to disease.

Many indigenous peoples died through outright violence.[24] According to the Franciscan missionary Bartolomé de Las Casas (1474–1566), the Spanish maliciously murdered thousands:

This infinite multitude of people [the Indians] was . . . without fraud, without subtilty or malice . . . toward the Spaniards whom they serve, patient, meek and peaceful. . . .

To these quiet Lambs . . . came the Spaniards like most c(r)uel Tygres, Wolves and Lions, enrag'd with a sharp and tedious hunger; for these forty years past, minding nothing else but the slaughter of these unfortunate wretches, whom with divers kinds of torments neither seen nor heard of before, they have so cruelly and inhumanely butchered, that of three millions of people which Hispaniola itself did contain, there are left remaining alive scarce three hundred persons.[25]

Las Casas's remarks concentrate on the tropical lowlands, but the death rate in the highlands was also overwhelming.

The Franciscan, Dominican, and Jesuit missionaries who accompanied the conquistadors and settlers played an important role in converting the Amerindians to Christianity, teaching them European methods of agriculture, and inculcating loyalty to the Spanish crown. In terms of numbers of people baptized, missionaries enjoyed phenomenal success, though the depth of the Amerindians' understanding of Christianity remains debatable. Missionaries, especially Las Casas, asserted that the Amerindians had human rights, and through Las Casas's persistent pressure the emperor Charles V abolished the worst abuses of the encomienda system in 1531.

For colonial administrators the main problem posed by the astronomically high death rate was the loss of a subjugated labor force. As early as 1511 King Ferdinand of Spain observed that the Amerindians seemed to be "very frail" and that "one black could do the work of four Indians."[26] Thus was born an absurd myth and the new tragedy of the Atlantic slave trade.

Sugar and Slavery

Throughout the Middle Ages slavery was deeply entrenched in the Mediterranean. The bubonic plague, famines, and other epidemics created a severe shortage of agricultural and domestic workers throughout Europe, encouraging Italian merchants to buy slaves from the Balkans, Thrace, southern Russia, and central Anatolia. During the Renaissance the slave trade represented an important aspect of Italian business enterprise: where profits were high, papal threats of excommunication failed to stop slave traders. The Genoese set up colonial stations in the Crimea and along the Black Sea, and according to an international authority on slavery, these outposts were "virtual laboratories" for the development of slave plantation agriculture in the New World.[27] This form of slavery had nothing to do with race; almost all slaves were white. How, then, did black African slavery enter the European picture and take root in South and then North America?

In 1453 the Ottoman capture of Constantinople halted the flow of white slaves from the Black Sea region and the Balkans. Mediterranean Europe, cut off from its traditional source of slaves, then turned to sub-Saharan Africa, which had a long history of slave trading. The centuries-old trans-Saharan trade was greatly stimulated by the existence of a ready market for slaves in the vineyards and sugar plantations of Sicily and Majorca. (See the feature "Individuals in Society: Juan de Pareja.")

Native to the South Pacific, **sugar** was taken in ancient times to India, where farmers learned to preserve cane juice as granules that could be stored and shipped. From there, sugar traveled to China and the Mediterranean, where islands like Crete, Sicily, and Cyprus had the necessary warm and wet climate. When Genoese and other Italians colonized the Canary Islands and the Portuguese settled on the Madeira Islands, sugar plantations came to the Atlantic. In this stage of European expansion, "the history of slavery became inextricably tied up with the history of sugar."[28] Originally sugar was an expensive luxury that only the very affluent could afford, but population increases and monetary expansion in the fifteenth century led to an increasing demand for it.

Resourceful Italians provided the capital, cane, and technology for sugar cultivation on plantations in southern Portugal, Madeira, and the Canary Islands. Meanwhile, in the period 1490 to 1530, Portuguese traders brought between three hundred and two thousand black slaves to Lisbon each year (see Map 15.3), where they performed most of the manual labor and constituted 10 percent of the city's population. From there slaves were transported to the sugar plantations of Madeira, the Azores, and the Cape Verde Islands. Sugar and the small Atlantic islands gave New World slavery its distinctive shape. Columbus himself, who spent a decade in Madeira, brought sugar plants on his voyages to "the Indies."

Online Study Center **Improve Your Grade**
Primary Source: Fifteenth-Century Slave Trade: The Portuguese in West Africa

As already discussed, European expansion across the Atlantic led to the economic exploitation of the Americas. In the New World, the major problem settlers faced was a shortage of labor. As early as 1495 the Spanish solved the problem by enslaving the native Indians. In

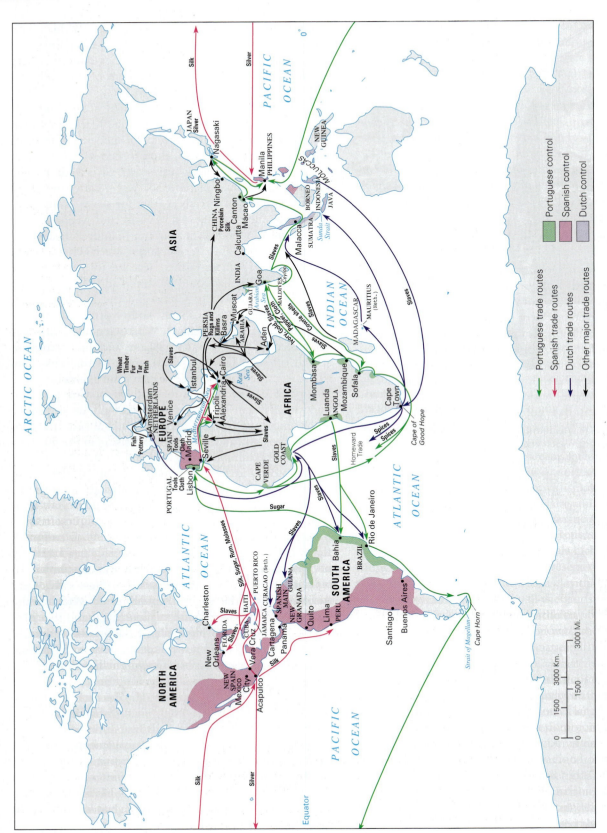

MAP 15.3 Seaborne Trading Empires in the Sixteenth and Seventeenth Centuries By the mid-seventeenth century, trade linked all parts of the world, except for Australia. Notice that trade in slaves was not confined to the Atlantic but involved almost all parts of the world.

*Online **Study Center*** **Improve Your Grade** Interactive Map: Worldwide Slave Trade

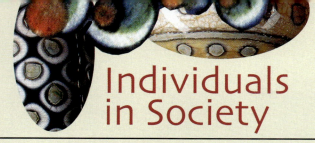

Individuals in Society

Juan de Pareja

A marginal person is one who lives outside the mainstream of the dominant society, who is not fully assimilated into or accepted by that society. Apart from revealing little known aspects of past cultures, marginalized people teach us much about the values and ideals of the dominant society. Such a person was the Spanish religious and portrait painter Juan de Pareja.

Pareja was born in Antequera, an agricultural region and the old center of Muslim culture near Seville in southern Spain. Of his parents we know nothing. Because a rare surviving document calls him a "mulatto," one of his parents must have been white and the other must have had some African blood. The Spanish word *mulatto* derives from the Arabic *muwallad,* a person of mixed race, and some scholars, using religion to describe ethnic category, speak of Pareja's "Muslim descent." The region from which he came makes that possible, but we do not know whether he actually believed in or practiced Islam.

In 1630 Pareja applied to the mayor of Seville for permission to travel to Madrid to visit his brother and "to perfect his art." The document lists his occupation as "a painter in Seville." Since it mentions no other name, it is reasonable to assume that Pareja arrived in Madrid a free man. Sometime between 1630 and 1648, however, he came into the possession of the artist Diego Velázquez (1599–1660); Pareja became a slave.

In the twelfth century Muslim slaves helped build the cathedral of Saint James at Santiago de Compostela, one of the great shrines of medieval Christendom. During the long wars of the reconquista, Muslims and Christians captured each other in battle and used the defeated as slaves. The fifteenth and sixteenth centuries had seen a steady flow of sub-Saharan Africans into the Iberian Peninsula. Thus early modern Spain was a slaveholding society.

How did Velázquez acquire Pareja? By purchase? As a gift? Had Pareja fallen into debt or committed some crime and thereby lost his freedom? We do not know. Velázquez, the greatest Spanish painter of the seventeenth century, had a large studio with many assistants. Pareja was set to grinding powders to make colors and to preparing canvases. He must have demonstrated ability because, when Velázquez went to Rome in 1648, he chose Pareja to accompany him.

In 1650, as practice for a portrait of Pope Innocent X, Velázquez painted Pareja. That same year, Velázquez signed the document that gave Pareja his freedom, to become effective in 1654. From 1654 until his death Pareja worked in Madrid as an independent painter. Although he received recognition for his work, only one painting survives: *The Calling of Saint Matthew,* signed and dated 1661 (see page 540). Modern art historians dispute its merit. Some believe it shows a forceful baroque energy and considerable originality; others consider it derivative of Velázquez.

Velázquez, Juan de Pareja *(1650).* (The Metropolitan Museum of Art, Fletcher Fund, Rogers Fund, and Bequest of Miss Adelaide Milton de Groot (1876–1967), by exchange, supplemented by gifts from friends of the Museum, 1971. [1971.86]. Photograph © 1986 The Metropolitan Museum of Art)

What does the public career of this seventeenth-century marginal person tell us about the man and his world? After living in Seville and Madrid, he traveled widely, visiting Genoa, Venice, Rome, and Naples. Travel may have broadened him, producing a cosmopolitan man. Pareja's career suggests that a person of talent and ability could rise in Spanish society despite the social and religious barriers that existed at the time. Jonathan Brown, the leading authority on Velázquez, describes Pareja's appearance in Velázquez's portrait as "self-confident." A more enthusiastic student writes, "The Metropolitan is probably the greatest museum in the world . . . and this [Velázquez's portrait of Pareja] is its greatest painting. . . . The man was technically a slave. . . . However, we can see from Velázquez's painting that the two were undeniably equals. That steady look of self-controlled power can even make us wonder which of the two had a higher opinion of himself."

Questions for Analysis

1. Since slavery was an established institution in Spain, speculate on Velázquez's possible reasons for giving Pareja his freedom.
2. What issues of cultural diversity might Pareja have faced in seventeenth-century Spain?

Sources: Jonathan Brown, *Velázquez: Painter and Courtier* (New Haven, Conn.: Yale University Press, 1986); *Grove Dictionary of Art* (New York: Macmillan, 2000); *Sister Wendy Beckett's 1000 Masterpieces* (New York: Dorling Kindersley Inc., 1999).

A New World Sugar Refinery, Brazil   Sugar was the most important and most profitable plantation crop in the New World. This image shows the processing and refinement of sugar on a Brazilian plantation. Sugar cane was grown, harvested, and processed by African slaves who labored under brutal and ruthless conditions to generate enormous profits for plantation owners. *(The Bridgeman Art Library/Getty Images)*

the next two centuries the Portuguese, Dutch, and English followed suit. The horrifyingly rapid decline of the Amerindian population, however, led to the search for new forms of labor.

In Africa, where slavery was entrenched (as it was in the Islamic world, southern Europe, and China), African kings and dealers sold black slaves to European merchants who participated in the transatlantic trade. The Portuguese brought the first slaves to Brazil; by 1600 four thousand were being imported annually. After its founding in 1621, the Dutch West India Company, with the full support of the government of the United Provinces, transported thousands of Africans to Brazil and the Caribbean. In the late seventeenth century, with the chartering of the Royal African Company, the English got involved. Altogether, traders from all these countries brought an estimated ten million African slaves to the Americas from 1650 to 1870.

European sailors found the Atlantic passage cramped and uncomfortable, but conditions for African slaves were lethal. Before 1700, when slavers decided it was better business to improve conditions, some 20 percent of slaves died on the voyage.[29] The most common cause of death was from dysentery induced by poor-quality food and water, intense crowding, and lack of sanitation. Men were often kept in irons during the passage, while women and girls were fair game for sailors. To increase profits, slave traders packed several hundred captives on each ship. One slaver explained that he removed his boots before entering the slave hold because he had to crawl over their packed bodies.[30]

The eighteenth century witnessed the peak of the Atlantic slave trade. In 1790 there were 757,181 blacks in a total U.S. population of 3,929,625. When the first census was taken in Brazil in 1798, blacks numbered about 2 million in a total population of 3.25 million.

The Columbian Exchange

An important historical study asserts that the most significant changes brought about by the Columbian voyages were biosocial. The Age of Discovery led to the migration of peoples, which in turn led to an exchange of fauna and flora—of animals, plants, and disease, a complex process known as the **Columbian Exchange.** Spanish and Portuguese immigrants to the Americas wanted the lifestyle and diet with which they were familiar. Foods that Iberian settlers considered essential—wheat for bread, grapes for wine, olive oil for both culinary and sacramental purposes—were not grown in America. So the migrants sought to turn the New World into the Old: they searched for climatic zones favorable to those crops. Everywhere they settled they raised wheat—in the highlands of Mexico, the Rio de la Plata, New Granada (in northern South America), and Chile. By 1535 Mexico was exporting wheat. Grapes did well in parts of Peru and Chile. It took the Spanish longer to discover areas where suitable soil and adequate rainfall would nourish olive trees, but by the 1560s the coastal valleys of Peru and Chile were dotted with olive groves. Columbus had brought sugar plants on his second voyage; Spaniards also introduced rice and bananas from the Canary Islands, and the Portuguese carried these items to Brazil. All nonindigenous plants and trees had to be brought from Europe, but not all plants arrived intentionally. In clumps of mud on shoes and in the folds of textiles came immigrant grasses such as Kentucky bluegrass, daisies, and the common dandelion.

Apart from wild turkeys and game, Native Americans had no animals for food; apart from alpacas and llamas, they had no animals for travel or to use as beasts of burden. (Human power had moved the huge stones needed to build the monumental Aztec temples.) On his second voyage in 1493 Columbus introduced horses, cattle, sheep, dogs, pigs, chickens, and goats. The multiplication of these animals proved spectacular. By the 1550s, when the Spaniards explored, they brought along herds of swine. The horse enabled the Spanish conquerors and the Amerindians to travel faster and farther and to transport heavy loads.

In return, the Spanish and Portuguese took back to Europe the main American cereal, maize (corn), from Mexico; white potatoes from Peru; and many varieties of beans, squash, pumpkins, avocados, and tomatoes (which Europeans distrusted, fearing that they were sexually stimulating). Maize was the great gift of the Amerindians to all the peoples of the world as food for humans and livestock. Because maize grows in climates too dry for rice and too wet for wheat, gives a high yield per unit of land, and has a short growing season, it proved an especially important crop for Europeans. Initially they looked on the white potato with contempt, but they gradually recognized its nutritional value. Its cultivation slowly spread from west to east—to Ireland, England, and France in the seventeenth century; and to Germany, Poland, Hungary, and Russia in the eighteenth. Ironi-

cally, the white potato reached New England from old England in 1718.

Silver and the Economic Effects of Spain's Discoveries

The sixteenth century has often been called Spain's golden century, but silver was far more important than gold. The influence of Spanish armies, Spanish Catholicism, and Spanish wealth was felt all over Europe. This greatness rested largely on the influx of silver from the Americas.

In 1545, at an altitude of fifteen thousand feet where nothing grew because of the cold, and after a two-and-a-half-month journey by pack animal from Lima, Peru, the Spanish discovered an incredible source of silver at Potosí (in present-day Bolivia) in territory conquered from the Inca Empire. The place had no population. By 1600, 160,000 people lived there, making it about the size of the city of London. In the second half of the sixteenth century Potosí yielded perhaps 60 percent of all the silver mined in the world. From Potosí and the mines at Zacatecas and Guanajuato in Mexico, huge quantities of precious metals poured forth. To protect this treasure from French and English pirates, armed convoys transported it to Spain each year. Between 1503 and 1650, 16 million kilograms of silver and 185,000 kilograms of gold entered Seville's port. Spanish predominance, however, proved temporary.

In the sixteenth century Spain experienced a steady population increase, creating a sharp rise in the demand for food and goods. Spanish colonies in the Americas also represented a demand for products. Since Spain had expelled some of its best farmers and businessmen—the Muslims and Jews—in the fifteenth century, the Spanish economy was suffering and could not meet the new demands, and prices rose. Because the cost of manufacturing cloth and other goods increased, Spanish products could not compete with cheaper products made elsewhere in the international market. The textile industry was badly hurt. Prices spiraled upward faster than the government could levy taxes to dampen the economy. (Higher taxes would have cut the public's buying power; with fewer goods sold, prices would have come down.)

Did the flood of silver bullion from America cause the inflation? Prices rose most steeply before 1565, but bullion imports reached their peak between 1580 and 1620. Thus there is no direct correlation between silver imports and the inflation rate. Did the substantial population growth accelerate the inflation rate? It may have done so. After 1600, when population pressure declined, prices gradually stabilized. One fact is certain: the **price revolution** severely strained government budgets. Several times between 1557 and 1647, Spain's King Philip II and his successors repudiated the state debt, thereby undermining confidence in the government and leaving the economy in shambles.

As Philip II paid his armies and foreign debts with silver bullion, Spanish inflation was transmitted to the rest of Europe. Between 1560 and 1600 much of Europe experienced large price increases. Prices doubled and in some cases quadrupled. Spain suffered most severely, but all European countries were affected. Because money bought less, people who lived on fixed incomes, such as the continental nobles, were badly hurt. Those who owed fixed sums of money, such as the middle class, prospered: in a time of rising prices, debts had less value each year. Food costs rose most sharply, and the poor fared worst of all.

In many ways, it was not Spain but China that controlled the world trade in silver. The Chinese demanded silver for its products and for the payment of imperial taxes. China was thus the main buyer of world silver, serving as a "sink" for half the world's production of silver. Just as China was the heart of world trade, so was it, not Europe, the center of the early modern bullion trade. The silver market drove world trade, with the Americas and Japan being mainstays on the supply side and China dominating the demand side.

The Birth of the Global Economy

With the Europeans' discovery of the Americas and their exploration of the Pacific, the entire world was linked for the first time in history by seaborne trade. That trade brought into being three successive commercial empires: the Portuguese, the Spanish, and the Dutch.

In the sixteenth century naval power and shipborne artillery gave Portugal hegemony over the sea route to India. To Lisbon the Portuguese fleet brought spices, which the Portuguese paid for with textiles produced at Gujarat and Coromandel in India and with gold and ivory from East Africa (see Map 15.3). From their fortified bases at Goa on the Arabian Sea and at Malacca on the Malay Peninsula, ships of Malabar teak carried goods to the Portuguese settlement at Macao in the South China Sea. From Macao Portuguese ships loaded with Chinese silks and porcelains sailed to the Japanese port of Nagasaki and to the Philippine port of Manila, where Chinese goods were exchanged for Spanish (that is, Latin

American) silver. Throughout Asia the Portuguese traded in slaves—black Africans, Chinese, and Japanese. The Portuguese exported to India horses from Mesopotamia and copper from Arabia; from India they exported hawks and peacocks for the Chinese and Japanese markets.

Across the Atlantic Portuguese Brazil provided most of the sugar consumed in Europe in the sixteenth and early seventeenth centuries. African slave labor produced the sugar on the plantations of Brazil, and Portuguese merchants controlled both the slave trade between West Africa and Brazil and the commerce in sugar between Brazil and Portugal. The Portuguese were the first worldwide traders, and Portuguese was the language of the Asian maritime trade.

Spanish possessions in the New World constituted basically a land empire, and in the sixteenth century the Spaniards devised a method of governing that empire (see page 538). But across the Pacific the Spaniards also built a seaborne empire centered at Manila in the Philippines, which had been "discovered" by Ferdinand Magellan in 1521. Between 1564 and 1571 the Spanish navigator Miguel Lopez de Legazpi sailed from Mexico and through a swift and almost bloodless conquest took over the Philippine Islands. The city of Manila henceforth served as the transpacific bridge between Spanish America and the extreme Eastern trade.

Chinese silk, sold by the Portuguese in Manila for American silver, was transported to Acapulco in Mexico, and from there it was carried overland to Vera Cruz for re-export to Spain. Because hostile Pacific winds prohibited direct passage from the Philippines to Peru, large shipments of silk also went south from Acapulco to Peru (see Map 15.3). Spanish merchants could never satisfy the European demand for silk, so huge amounts of bullion went from Acapulco to Manila. In 1597, for example, 12 million pesos of silver, almost the total value of the transatlantic trade, crossed the Pacific. After about 1640 the Spanish silk trade declined because it could not compete with Dutch imports.

Stimulated by a large demand for goods in Europe, India, China, and Japan, a worldwide commercial boom occurred from about 1570 to 1630. Many people throughout the world profited: capitalists who advanced money for voyages, captains and crews of ships, and port officials. As spices moved westward or northward, as silks and porcelains moved southward and westward, and as cloth moved eastward and westward, these various goods grew more valuable in the boom of long-distance trade.[31]

In the latter half of the seventeenth century the worldwide Dutch seaborne trade predominated. The Dutch Empire was built on spices. In 1599 a Dutch fleet re-

Chinese Porcelain This porcelain from a seventeenth-century Chinese ship's cargo, recovered from the sea, was intended for European luxury markets. (*Christie's Images*)

crative spice trade. The seaborne empires of Portugal, Spain, and Holland paved the way for the eighteenth-century mercantilist empires of France and Great Britain.

Spain's Global Empire

Spanish expansion into the New World and Asia are even more amazing when considered in light of Spanish expansion within Europe itself. As discussed in Chapter 14, Charles V combined vast and scattered territories across Europe under his rule. From his father's side, he inherited in 1506 the Burgundian lands, which included the Low Countries and Flanders, and in 1519 the Habsburg domains in Austria. As the grandson of Ferdinand and Isabella, in 1516 he became the first monarch to rule a united Spain. In 1530 he capped off this list by being named Holy Roman emperor. Under his reign, Spanish conquistadors brought new territories to Spain's colonial empire. Charles ruled over a vast and multiethnic array of territories (see Map 14.1 on page 460) and thus ruled the first global empire in history.

By 1556 Charles was exhausted by decades of administering this great empire. He had warred with France and the Ottoman Empire throughout his reign. He had also devoted enormous energy to a futile attempt to stamp out the burgeoning Protestant Reformation. (It was he who summoned Martin Luther to the Diet of Worms.) Charles abdicated the Spanish crown and the Netherlands to his son Philip II of Spain and Austria, and other territories in central Europe and the title of Holy Roman emperor to his brother Ferdinand.

Philip inherited his father's overseas Spanish Empire as well as the cascade of silver now flowing from the Americas. In today's world we might view the birth of globalization as a monumental turning point; Philip, however, was more concerned with religious rivalries in Europe. Traditional scholarship has depicted Philip as morose and melancholic, a religious bigot determined to re-impose Roman Catholicism on northern Europe. Recent research portrays him as a more complicated figure. In his youth, "he had visited northern Italy, the Alps, southern Germany, the Rhineland, the Netherlands, parts of France, and southern England."[32] He had walked the streets of Antwerp, Augsburg, Brussels, Cologne, London, and Trent. With the exception of his father, no other European ruler of the time had traveled or seen so much or had accumulated so much political experience in international relations.

turned to Amsterdam carrying 600,000 pounds of pepper and 250,000 pounds of cloves and nutmeg. Those who had invested in the expedition received a 100 percent profit. The voyage led to the establishment in 1602 of the Dutch East India Company, founded with the stated intention of capturing the spice trade from the Portuguese.

The Dutch fleet, sailing from the Cape of Good Hope and avoiding the Portuguese forts in India, steered directly for the Sunda Strait in Indonesia (see Map 15.3). The Dutch wanted direct access to and control of the Indonesian sources of spices. In return for assisting Indonesian princes in local squabbles and disputes with the Portuguese, the Dutch won broad commercial concessions. Through agreements, seizures, and outright war, they gained control of the western access to the Indonesian archipelago. Gradually, they acquired political domination over the archipelago itself. Exchanging European manufactured goods—armor, firearms, linens, and toys—the Dutch soon had a monopoly on the very lu-

Philip II, ca 1533   This portrait of Philip II as a young man and crown prince of Spain is by the celebrated artist Titian, who was court painter to Philip's father, Charles V. After taking the throne, Philip became another great patron of the artist. *(Scala/Art Resource, NY)*

After Philip buried his fourth wife, Anna of Austria, to whom he had been deeply devoted, contemporaries noticed a more marked devotion to religion. He relied more and more on God for political help. On the issues of the Inquisition and religious toleration, Philip was completely inflexible. He identified toleration with the growth of heresy, civil disorder, violence, and bloodshed: "Had there been no inquisition (in Spain) there would

have been more heretics, and the country would be in a lamentable state like others (the Netherlands) where there is no inquisition as we have in Spain."[33] In this respect, Philip II differed little from the Protestant reformers Luther and Calvin, who initially called for individual liberty of conscience and then insisted on the right of church and civil powers to extirpate heresy within their jurisdictions. Philip was a man of his times, and the times did not favor religious toleration.

With his determination to crush heresy in the Low Countries and with the enormous wealth of American silver enabling him to hire the mercenary armies he needed, why did Philip II have such trouble achieving his goal? Philip was preoccupied with other parts of his vast empire, especially the advance of the Ottoman Turks into the western Mediterranean. This issue—combined with the death of his son and heir Don Carlos and then a revolt of the Moriscos (Muslims) in Granada—made it impossible to concentrate on the Netherlands. At one point in 1566 he complained, "I have so much on my mind that I rarely know what I am doing or saying." Only after Philip learned of the death of Suleiman the Magnificent did he feel able to focus on the Netherlands.[34]

But the Netherlands could not be separated in Philip's mind from what he perceived as the "British problem." In 1586 Mary, Queen of Scots, cousin and heir of Elizabeth of England, became implicated in a plot to assassinate Elizabeth. Hoping to reunite England with Catholic Europe through Mary, Philip gave the conspiracy his full backing. Mary was discovered and beheaded on February 18, 1587. News of her execution reached Philip in mid-April. When Pope Sixtus V (1585–1590) learned of Mary's death on March 24 (the dates suggest the slowness of communication in the late sixteenth century), he promised to pay Philip one million gold ducats the moment Spanish troops landed in England. Conquering England promised the additional benefit of cutting off financial support to the Dutch rebels.

As plans for a naval expedition to attack England proceeded in 1587, two serious difficulties burdened the king. First, he was so badly crippled by gout that he could not sign documents and needed a cane to walk, painfully. Second, official reports indicated that the Ottoman Turks might seize the moment of preoccupation with the Netherlands and England to attack Spain from the Mediterranean. Philip prepared a vast fleet to sail from Lisbon to Flanders, fight off Elizabeth's navy if it attacked, rendezvous with the duke of Parma, commander of Spanish forces in the Netherlands, and escort barges carrying Parma's troops across the English Channel. On May 9, 1588, *la felicissima armada*—"the most fortunate fleet," as it was ironically called in official documents—sailed from Lisbon harbor composed of more than 130 vessels. The **Spanish Armada** met an English fleet in the Channel. The English ships were smaller, faster, and more maneuverable, and many of them had greater firing power than their Spanish counterparts. A combination of storms and squalls, spoiled food and rank water, inadequate Spanish ammunition, and, to a lesser extent, English fire ships that caused the Spanish to scatter gave England the victory. The Armada was defeated before it even reached the Netherlands. On the journey home many Spanish ships went down around Ireland; perhaps 65 managed to reach home ports.

The battle in the Channel has frequently been described as one of the decisive battles in world history. In fact, it had mixed consequences. Spain soon rebuilt its navy, and after 1588 the quality of the Spanish fleet improved. The destruction of the Spanish Armada did not halt the flow of silver from the New World. More silver reached Spain between 1588 and 1603 than in any other fifteen-year period. The war between England and Spain dragged on for years.

The defeat of the Spanish Armada was decisive, however, in the sense that it prevented Philip II from reimposing religious unity on western Europe by force. He did not conquer England, and Elizabeth continued her financial and military support of the Dutch. In the Netherlands neither side gained significant territory. The borders of 1581 tended to become permanent. In 1609 Philip III of Spain (r. 1598–1621) agreed to a truce, in effect recognizing the independence of the United Provinces. In seventeenth-century Spain memory of the loss of the Spanish Armada contributed to a spirit of defeatism. In England the victory contributed to a David and Goliath legend that enhanced English national sentiment.

Changing Attitudes and Beliefs

The age of religious wars and overseas expansion was characterized by an extraordinary degree of intellectual and artistic ferment. This effervescence can be seen in the development of the essay as a distinct literary genre, in other prose, in poetry, in drama, in art, and in music. In many ways, literature, the visual arts, music, and the drama of the period mirrored the social and cultural conditions that gave rise to them. An important theme running through the culture of this time was the encounter with radically new places and peoples.

• *How did culture and art in this period respond to social and cultural transformation?*

New Ideas About Race

Ancient Greeks and Romans were in close contact with Africa and they also practiced slavery, but they did not associate one with the other. Slavery, which was endemic in the ancient world, stemmed from either capture in war or debt. Although generations could be born in captivity, no particular ethnic or racial associations were involved (see page 137). How did slavery come to be so closely associated with race in the Age of Discovery?

Settlers brought to the Americas the racial attitudes they had absorbed in Europe. Their beliefs and attitudes toward Africans derived from Christian theological speculation and Arab ideas. In the sixteenth and seventeenth centuries the English, for example, were extremely curious about Africans' lives and customs, and slavers' accounts were extraordinarily popular. Travel literature depicted Africans as savages because of their eating habits, morals, clothing, and social customs; as barbarians because of their language and methods of war; and as heathens because they were not Christian (nearly the identical language with which the English described the Irish—see page 398). Africans were believed to possess a potent sexuality; African women were considered sexually aggressive, with a "temper hot and lascivious."[35]

"At the time when Columbus sailed to the New World, Islam was the largest world religion, and the only world religion that showed itself capable of expanding rapidly in areas as far apart and as different from each other as Senegal [in northwest Africa], Bosnia [in the Balkans], Java, and the Philippines."[36] Medieval Arabic literature spoke of blacks' physical repulsiveness, mental inferiority, and primitivism. In contrast to civilized peoples from the Mediterranean to China, some Arab writers absurdly claimed, sub-Saharan blacks were the only peoples who had produced no sciences or stable states. Though black kings, the Muslim historian Ibn Khaldun alleged, sold their subjects without even a pretext of crime or war, the victims bore no resentment because they gave no thought to the future and had "by nature few cares and worries; dancing and rhythm are for them inborn."[37]

Medieval Christians and Arabs therefore had similar notions of blacks as primitive people ideally suited to enslavement. The racial biases that the Portuguese, Spanish, Dutch, and English brought to the New World, however, derived primarily from Christian theological speculation. As Europeans turned to Africa for new sources of slaves, they used ideas about Africans' primitiveness and barbarity to defend slavery and even argue that enslavement benefited Africans by bringing the light of Christianity to heathen peoples. Thus, the institution of slavery contributed to the dissemination of more rigid notions of racial inferiority. From rather vague assumptions and prejudices, Europeans developed more elaborate ideological notions of racial superiority and inferiority to safeguard the ever-increasing profits gained from plantation slavery.

Michel de Montaigne and Cultural Curiosity

Racism was not the only possible reaction to the new worlds emerging in the sixteenth century. Decades of religious fanaticism, bringing civil anarchy and war, led both Catholics and Protestants to doubt that any one faith contained absolute truth. Added to these doubts was the discovery of peoples in the New World who had radically different ways of life. These shocks helped produce ideas of **skepticism** and cultural relativism in the sixteenth and seventeenth centuries. Skepticism is a school of thought founded on doubt that total certainty or definitive knowledge is ever attainable. The skeptic is cautious and critical and suspends judgment. Cultural relativism suggests that one culture is not necessarily superior to another, just different. Both notions found expression in the work of Frenchman Michel de Montaigne (1533–1592).

Montaigne descended from a bourgeois family that had made a fortune selling salted herring and wine and in 1477 had purchased the title and property of Montaigne in Gascony. His mother came from a Jewish family that had been forced to flee Spain. Montaigne received a classical education, studied law, and secured a judicial appointment in 1554. He condemned the ancient nobility for being more concerned with war and sports than with the cultivation of the mind.

At the age of thirty-eight Montaigne resigned his judicial post, retired to his estate, and devoted the rest of his life to study, contemplation, and an effort to understand himself. His wealth provided him with the leisure time to do so. A humanist, he believed that the object of life was to "know thyself," for self-knowledge teaches men and women how to live in accordance with nature and God. Montaigne developed a new literary genre, the essay—from the French *essayer,* meaning "to test or try"—to express his thoughts and ideas.

Montaigne's *Essays* provides insight into the mind of a remarkably civilized man. From the ancient authors, especially the Roman Stoic Seneca, Montaigne acquired a sense of calm, patience, tolerance, and broad-mindedness. Mon-

taigne had grown up during the French civil wars, perhaps the worst kind of war. Religious ideology had set family against family, even brother against brother. He wrote:

In this controversy . . . France is at present agitated by civil wars, the best and soundest side is undoubtedly that which maintains both the old religion and the old government of the country. However, among the good men who follow that side . . . we see many whom passion drives outside the bounds of reason, and makes them sometimes adopt unjust, violent, and even reckless courses.[38]

Though he remained a Catholic, Montaigne possessed detachment, independence, openness of mind, and the willingness to look at all sides of a question. As he wrote, "other people's reasons can serve to support me, but seldom to change my course. I listen to them all favorably and decently; but so far as I can remember, I have never up to this moment followed any but my own. I set little value on my own opinion, but I set just as little on those of others."[39]

Montaigne's essay "On Cannibals" reveals the impact of overseas discoveries on one European's consciousness. His tolerant mind rejected the notion that one culture is superior to another:

I long had a man in my house that lived ten or twelve years in the New World, discovered in these latter days, and in that part of it where Villegaignon landed [Brazil]. . . .

I find that there is nothing barbarous and savage in [that] nation, . . . excepting, that every one gives the title of barbarism to everything that is not in use in his own country. As, indeed, we have no other level of truth and reason, than the example and idea of the opinions and customs of the place wherein we live.[40]

Montaigne's rejection of dogmatism, his secularism, and his skepticism thus represented a basic change. In his own time and throughout the seventeenth century, few would have agreed with him. The publication of his ideas, however, anticipated a basic shift in attitudes. Montaigne inaugurated an era of doubt. "Wonder," he said, "is the foundation of all philosophy, research is the means of all learning, and ignorance is the end."[41]

Online Study Center **Improve Your Grade**
Primary Source: Michel de Montaigne on the Fallibility of Human Understanding

Elizabethan and Jacobean Literature

In addition to the essay as a literary genre, the period fostered remarkable creativity in other branches of literature. England, especially in the latter part of Elizabeth's reign and in the first years of her successor, James I (r. 1603–1625), witnessed remarkable literary expression. The terms *Elizabethan* and *Jacobean* (referring to the reign of James) are used to designate the English music, poetry, prose, and drama of this period. The poetry of Sir Philip Sidney (1554–1586), such as *Astrophel and Stella*, strongly influenced later poetic writing. *The Faerie Queene* of Edmund Spenser (1552–1599) endures as one of the greatest moral epics in any language. The rare poetic beauty of the plays of Christopher Marlowe (1564–1593), such as *Tamburlaine* and *The Jew of Malta*, paved the way for the work of Shakespeare. Above all, the immortal dramas of William Shakespeare (1564–1616) and the stately prose of the Authorized, or King James, Bible marked the Elizabethan and Jacobean periods as the golden age of English literature.

William Shakespeare, the son of a successful glove manufacturer in Stratford-on-Avon, chose a career on the London stage. By 1592 he had gained recognition as an actor and playwright. He performed in the Lord Chamberlain's Company and became co-owner of the Globe Theatre, which after 1603 presented his plays. Shakespeare's genius lay in the originality of his characterizations, the diversity of his plots, his understanding of human psychology, and his unexcelled gift for language. Shakespeare was a Renaissance man in his deep appreciation of classical culture, individualism, and humanism. Such plays as *Julius Caesar, Pericles,* and *Antony and Cleopatra* deal with classical subjects and figures. Several of his comedies have Italian Renaissance settings. The nine history plays, including *Richard II, Richard III,* and *Henry IV,* enjoyed the greatest popularity among Shakespeare's contemporaries. Written during the decade after the defeat of the Spanish Armada, the history plays express English national consciousness.

Shakespeare's later tragedies, including *Hamlet, Othello,* and *Macbeth,* explore an enormous range of human problems and are open to an almost infinite variety of interpretations. *Othello* portrays an honorable man destroyed by a flaw in his own character and the satanic evil of his supposed friend Iago. *Macbeth*'s central theme is

Titus Andronicus   With classical allusions, fifteen murders and executions, a Gothic queen who takes a black lover, and incredible violence, this early Shakespearean tragedy (1594) was a melodramatic thriller that enjoyed enormous popularity with the London audience. Modern critics believe that it foreshadowed *King Lear* with its emphasis on suffering and madness. *(Reproduced by permission of the Marquess of Bath, Longleat House, Warminster, Wilts)*

exorbitant ambition. Shakespeare analyzes the psychology of sin in the figures of Macbeth and Lady Macbeth, whose mutual love under the pressure of ambition leads to their destruction. The central figure in *Hamlet,* a play suffused with individuality, wrestles with moral problems connected with revenge and with the human being's relationship to life and death.

Shakespeare's last play, *The Tempest*, is now viewed by critics as one of his best. The sorcerer-prince Prospero and his daughter Miranda are stranded on an island by Prospero's treacherous brother. There Prospero finds and raises Caliban, whom he instructs in his own language and religion. After Caliban's attempted rape of Miranda, Prospero enslaves him, earning the rage and resentment of his erstwhile pupil. Modern scholars often note the echoes between this play and the realities of imperial conquest and settlement in Shakespeare's day. It is no accident, they argue, that the poet portrayed Caliban as a monstrous, dark-skinned island native whose natural condition is servitude. The author himself borrows words from Montaigne's essay "On Cannibals," suggesting that his portrayal may have implied criticism of superior colonial attitudes rather than an unqualified endorsement.

Another great masterpiece of the Jacobean period was the Authorized Bible. At a theological conference in 1604, a group of Puritans urged James I to support a new translation of the Bible. The king assigned the task to a committee of scholars, and their version was published in 1611. Divided into chapters and verses, the Authorized Version is actually more a revision of earlier Bibles than an original work. Yet it provides a superb expression of the mature English vernacular of the early seventeenth century. Consider Psalm 37:

Fret not thy selfe because of evill doers, neither bee thou envious against the workers of iniquitie.
For they shall soone be cut downe like the grasse; and wither as the greene herbe.
Trust in the Lord, and do good, so shalt thou dwell in the land, and verely thou shalt be fed.

The Authorized Version, so called because it was produced under royal sponsorship (it had no official ecclesiastical endorsement), represented the Anglican and Puritan desire to encourage laypeople to read the Scriptures. It quickly achieved great popularity and displaced all earlier versions. British settlers carried this Bible to the North American colonies, where it became known as the King James Bible. For centuries the King James Bible has had a profound influence on the language and lives of English-speaking peoples.

Chapter Summary

Online Study Center **ACE the Test**

- **What was the Afro-Eurasian trading world before Columbus?**
- **How and why did Europeans undertake ambitious voyages of expansion that would usher in a new era of global contact?**
- **What effect did overseas expansion have on the conquered societies, on enslaved Africans, and on world trade?**
- **How did culture and art in this period respond to social and cultural transformation?**

Prior to Columbus's voyages, well-developed trade routes linked the peoples and products of Africa, Asia, and Europe. The Indian Ocean was the center of the Afro-Eurasian trade world, ringed by cosmopolitan commercial cities such as Mombasa, Malacca, and Macao. Venetian and Genoese merchants brought sophisticated luxury goods, like silks and spices, into western Europe from the East. Overall, though, Europeans played a minor role in the Afro-Eurasian trading world, since they did not produce many products desired by Eastern elites.

In the sixteenth and seventeenth centuries Europeans gained access to large parts of the globe for the first time. European peoples had the intellectual curiosity, driving ambition, and material incentive to challenge their marginal role in the pre-existing trade world. The revived monarchies of the sixteenth century now possessed sufficient resources to back ambitious seafarers like Christopher Columbus and Vasco da Gama. Exploration and exploitation contributed to a more sophisticated standard of living, in the form of spices and Asian luxury goods, and to a terrible international inflation resulting from the influx of South American silver and gold. Governments, the upper classes, and the peasantry were badly hurt by the resulting inflation. Meanwhile, the middle class of bankers, shippers, financiers, and manufacturers prospered for much of the seventeenth century.

Other consequences of European expansion had global proportions. Indian Ocean trade, long dominated by Muslim merchants operating from autonomous city-ports, increasingly fell under the control of Portuguese merchants sponsored by their Crown. In the New World Europeans discovered territories wholly unknown to them and forcibly established new colonies. The resulting Columbian exchange decimated native populations and fostered exchange of a myriad of plant, animal, and viral species. The slave trade took on new proportions of scale and intensity, as many millions of Africans were transported to labor in horrific conditions in the mines and plantations of the New World.

Cultural attitudes were challenged as well. While most Europeans did not question the superiority of Western traditions and beliefs, new currents of religious skepticism and new ideas about race were harbingers of developments to come. The essays of Montaigne, the plays of Shakespeare, and the King James Bible remain classic achievements of the Western cultural heritage. They both reflected dominant cultural values and projected new ideas into the future.

Key Terms

Malacca
entrepôt
Admiral Zheng He
Mansa Musa
Constantinople
spice trade
Prince Henry
  the Navigator
General History of
  the Indies
caravel
Ptolemy's *Geography*
Vasco da Gama
Christopher
  Columbus

Santa Fe
  capitulations
Treaty of Tordesillas
Ferdinand Magellan
Hernando Cortés
Tenochtitlán
Virocha
Francisco Pizarro
encomienda system
sugar
Columbian
  exchange
price revolution
Spanish Armada
skepticism

Online Study Center **Improve Your Grade** Flashcards

Suggested Reading

Crosby, Alfred W. *The Columbian Exchange: Biological and Cultural Consequences of 1492,* 30th anniversary ed. 2003. An innovative and highly influential account of the environmental impact of Columbus's voyages.

Davis, David B. *Slavery and Human Progress.* 1984. A moving and authoritative account of New World slavery.

Fernández-Armesto, Felip. *Columbus.* 1992. An excellent biography of Christopher Columbus.

Frederickson, George M. *The Arrogance of Race: Historical Perspectives on Slavery, Racism, and Social Inequality.* 1988. Analyzes the social and economic circumstances associated with the rise of plantation slavery.

Greenblatt, Stephen. *Marvelous Possessions: The Wonder of the New World.* 1991. Describes the cultural impact of New World discoveries on Europeans.

Northrup, David, ed. *The Atlantic Slave Trade.* 1994. Collected essays by leading scholars on many different aspects of the slave trade.

Pérez-Mallaína, Pablo E. *Spain's Men of the Sea*: *Daily Life on the Indies Fleet in the Sixteenth Century.* 1998. A description of recruitment, daily life, and career paths for ordinary sailors and officers in the Spanish fleet.

Pomeranz, Kenneth, and Steven Topik. *The World That Trade Created: Society, Culture and the World Economy, 1400 to the Present.* 1999. The creation of a world market presented through rich and vivid stories of merchants, miners, slaves, and farmers.

Restall, Matthew. *Seven Myths of Spanish Conquest.* 2003. A re-examination of common ideas about why and how the Spanish conquered native civilizations in the New World.

Scammell, Geoffrey V. *The World Encompassed: The First European Maritime Empires, c. 800–1650.* 1981. A detailed overview of the first European empires, including the Italian city-states, Portugal, and Spain.

Schwarz, Stuart B., ed. *Implicit Understandings: Observing, Reporting and Reflecting on the Encounters Between Europeans and Other Peoples in the Early Modern Era.* 1994. A collection of articles examining the cultural and intellectual impact of encounters between Europeans and non-Europeans during the Age of Discovery.

Subrahamanyam, Sanjay. *The Career and Legend of Vasco da Gama.* 1998. A probing biography that places Vasco da Gama in the context of Portuguese politics and society.

(continued on page 520)

Columbus Describes His First Voyage

On his return voyage to Spain in January 1493, Christopher Columbus composed a letter intended for wide circulation and had copies of it sent ahead to Isabella and Ferdinand and others when the ship docked at Lisbon. Because the letter sums up Columbus's understanding of his achievements, it is considered the most important document of his first voyage. Remember that his knowledge of Asia rested heavily on Marco Polo's Travels, published around 1298.

Since I know that you will be pleased at the great success with which the Lord has crowned my voyage, I write to inform you how in thirty-three days I crossed from the Canary Islands to the Indies, with the fleet which our most illustrious sovereigns gave me. I found very many islands with large populations and took possession of them all for their Highnesses; this I did by proclamation and unfurled the royal standard. No opposition was offered.

I named the first island that I found "San Salvador," in honour of our Lord and Saviour who has granted me this miracle. . . . When I reached Cuba, I followed its north coast westwards, and found it so extensive that I thought this must be the mainland, the province of Cathay.* . . . From there I saw another island eighteen leagues eastwards which I then named "Hispaniola."†

Hispaniola is a wonder. The mountains and hills, the plains and meadow lands are both fertile and beautiful. They are most suitable for planting crops and for raising cattle of all kinds, and there are good sites for building towns and villages. The harbours are incredibly fine and there are many great rivers with broad channels and the majority contain gold.‡ The trees, fruits and plants are very different from those of Cuba. In Hispaniola there are many spices and large mines of gold and other metals. . . .§

The inhabitants of this island, and all the rest that I discovered or heard of, go naked, as their mothers bore them, men and women alike. A few of the women, however, cover a single place with a leaf of a plant or piece of cotton which they weave for the purpose. They have no iron or steel or arms and are not capable of using them, not because they are not strong and well built but because they are amazingly timid. All the weapons they have are canes cut at seeding time, at the end of which they fix a sharpened stick, but they have not the courage to make use of these, for very often when I have sent two or three men to a village to have conversation with them a great number of them have come out. But as soon as they saw my men all fled immediately, a father not even waiting for his son. And this is not because we have harmed any of them; on the contrary, wherever I have gone and been able to have conversation with them, I have given them some of the various things I had, a cloth and other articles, and received nothing in exchange. But they have still remained incurably timid. True, when they have been reassured and lost their fear, they are so ingenuous and so liberal with all their possessions that no one who has not seen them would believe it. If one asks for anything they have they never say no. On the

---

*Cathay is the old name for China. In the log-book and later in this letter Columbus accepts the native story that Cuba is an island that they can circumnavigate in something more than twenty-one days, yet he insists here and later, during the second voyage, that it is in fact part of the Asiatic mainland.

†Hispaniola is the second largest island of the West Indies; Haiti occupies the western third of the island, the Dominican Republic the rest.

‡This did not prove to be true.

§These statements are also inaccurate.

contrary, they offer a share to anyone with demonstrations of heartfelt affection, and they are immediately content with any small thing, valuable or valueless, that is given them. I forbade the men to give them bits of broken crockery, fragments of glass or tags of laces, though if they could get them they fancied them the finest jewels in the world.

I hoped to win them to the love and service of their Highnesses and of the whole Spanish nation and to persuade them to collect and give us of the things which they possessed in abundance and which we needed. They have no religion and are not idolaters; but all believe that power and goodness dwell in the sky and they are firmly convinced that I have come from the sky with these ships and people. In this belief they gave me a good reception everywhere, once they had overcome their fear; and this is not because they are stupid—far from it, they are men of great intelligence, for they navigate all those seas, and give a marvellously good account of everything— but because they have never before seen men clothed or ships like these. . . .

In all these islands the men are seemingly content with one woman, but their chief or king is allowed more than twenty. The women appear to work more than the men and I have not been able to find out if they have private property. As far as I could see whatever a man had was shared among all the rest and this particularly applies to food. . . . In another island, which I am told is larger than Hispaniola, the people have no hair. Here there is a vast quantity of gold, and from here and the other islands I bring Indians as evidence.

In conclusion, to speak only of the results of this very hasty voyage, their Highnesses can see that I will give them as much gold as they require, if they will render me some very slight assistance; also I will give them all the spices and cotton they want. . . . I will also bring them as much aloes as they ask and as many slaves, who will be taken from the idolaters. I believe also that I have found rhubarb and cinnamon and there will be countless other things in addition. . . .

So all Christendom will be delighted that our Redeemer has given victory to our most illustrious King and Queen and their renowned kingdoms, in this great matter. They should hold great celebrations and render solemn thanks to the Holy Trinity with many solemn prayers, for the great triumph which they will have, by the

Christopher Columbus, by Ridolpho Ghirlandio. Friend of Raphael and teacher of Michelangelo, Ghirlandio (1483–1561) enjoyed distinction as a portrait painter, and so we can assume that this is a good likeness of the older Columbus. *(Scala/Art Resource, NY)*

conversion of so many peoples to our holy faith and for the temporal benefits which will follow, for not only Spain, but all Christendom will receive encouragement and profit.

This is a brief account of the facts. Written in the caravel off the Canary Islands.‖
15 February 1493

At your orders
THE ADMIRAL

Questions for Analysis

1. How did Columbus explain the success of his voyage?

2. What was Columbus's view of the Native Americans he met?

3. Evaluate his statements that the Caribbean islands possessed gold, cotton, and spices.

4. Why did Columbus cling to the idea that he had reached Asia?

‖Actually, Columbus was off Santa Maria in the Azores.

Source: The Four Voyages of Christopher Columbus (Penguin Classics, 1958), pp. 115–123. Copyright © J. M. Cohen, 1958. Reproduced by permission of Penguin Books Ltd.

Notes

1. A. Reid, *Southeast Asia in the Age of Commerce, 1450–1680,*. vol. 2: *Expansion and Crisis* (New Haven, Conn.: Yale University Press, 1993), Chaps. 1 and 2, pp. 1–131.

2. Andre Gunder Frank, *Re-Orient: Global Economy in the Asian Age* (Berkeley: University of California Press, 1998).

3. K. N. Chaudhuri, *Trade and Civilisation in the Indian Ocean: An Economic History from the Rise of Islam to 1750* (Cambridge: Cambridge University Press, 1985), p. 14.

4. Quoted in Erik Gilbert and Jonathan T. Reynolds, *Africa in World History: From Prehistory to the Present* (Upper Saddle River, N.J.: Pearson, 2004), p. 93.

5. Halil Inalcik and Donald Quataert, eds., *An Economic and Social History of the Ottoman Empire, 1300–1914* (Cambridge: Cambridge University Press, 1994), p. 219.

6. G. V. Scammell, *The World Encompassed: The First European Maritime Empires, c. 800–1650* (Berkeley: University of California Press, 1981), pp. 101, 104.

7. Ibid., p. 174.

8. Quoted in C. M. Cipolla, *Guns, Sails, and Empires: Technological Innovation and the Early Phases of European Expansion, 1400–1700* (New York: Minerva Press, 1965), p. 132.

9. Quoted in F. H. Littell, *The Macmillan Atlas: History of Christianity* (New York: Macmillan, 1976), p. 75.

10. See C. R. Phillips, *Ciudad Real, 1500–1750: Growth, Crisis, and Readjustment in the Spanish Economy* (Cambridge, Mass.: Harvard University Press, 1979), pp. 103–104, 115.

11. Pablo E. Pérez-Mallaína, *Spain's Men of the Sea: Daily Life on the Indies Fleet in the Sixteenth Century* (Baltimore: Johns Hopkins University Press, 1998), p. 130.

12. Ibid., p. 133.

13. Ibid., p. 19.

14. Scammell, *The World Encompassed,* p. 207.

15. Ibid., p. 265.

16. Quoted in Cipolla, *Guns, Sails, and Empires,* pp. 115–116.

17. S. E. Morison, *Admiral of the Ocean Sea: A Life of Christopher Columbus* (Boston: Little, Brown, 1942), p. 339.

18. Quoted in F. Maddison, "Tradition and Innovation: Columbus' First Voyage and Portuguese Navigation in the Fifteenth Century," in *Circa 1492: Art in the Age of Exploration,* ed. J. A. Levenson (Washington, D.C.: National Gallery of Art, 1991), p. 69.

19. J. M. Cohen, ed. and trans., *The Four Voyages of Christopher Columbus* (New York: Penguin Books, 1969), p. 37.

20. Quoted in R. L. Kagan, "The Spain of Ferdinand and Isabella," in *Circa 1492: Art in the Age of Exploration,* ed. J. A. Levenson (Washington, D.C.: National Gallery of Art, 1991), p. 60.

21. G. W. Conrad and A. A. Demarest, *Religion and Empire: The Dynamics of Aztec and Inca Expansionism* (New York: Cambridge University Press, 1993), pp. 67–69.

22. Ibid., pp. 135–139.

23. Quoted in Crosby, *The Columbian Exchange: Biological and Cultural Consequences of 1492* (Westport, Conn.: Greenwood, 1972), p. 39.

24. Ibid., pp. 35–59.

25. Quoted in C. Gibson, ed., *The Black Legend: Anti-Spanish Attitudes in the Old World and the New* (New York: Knopf, 1971), pp. 74–75.

26. Quoted in L. B. Rout, Jr., *The African Experience in Spanish America* (New York: Cambridge University Press, 1976), p. 23.

27. C. Verlinden, *The Beginnings of Modern Colonization,* trans. Y. Freccero (Ithaca, N.Y.: Cornell University Press, 1970), pp. 5–6, 80–97.

28. This section leans heavily on D. B. Davis, *Slavery and Human Progress* (New York: Oxford University Press, 1984), pp. 54–62; the quotation is on p. 58.

29. Herbert S. Klein, "Profits and the Causes of Mortality," in David Northrup, ed., *The Atlantic Slave Trade* (Lexington, Mass.: D. C. Heath and Co., 1994), p. 116.

30. Malcolm Cowley and Daniel P. Mannix, "The Middle Passage," in David Northrup, ed., *The Atlantic Slave Trade* (Lexington, Mass.: D. C. Heath and Co., 1994), p. 101.

31. Reid, *Southeast Asia,* vol. 2, pp. 10–26.

32. H. Kamen, *Philip of Spain* (New Haven: Yale University Press, 1997), p. 77.

33. Quoted in ibid., p. 235.

34. Parker, *Grand Strategy of Philip II* (New Haven, Conn.: Yale University Press, 2000), pp. 115–122; the quotation is on p. 119.

35. Quoted in D. P. Mannix, with M. Cowley, *Black Cargoes: A History of the Atlantic Slave Trade* (New York: Viking Press, 1968), p. 19.

36. See P. Brown, "Understanding Islam," *New York Review of Books,* February 22, 1979, pp. 30–33.

37. Quoted in Davis, *Slavery and Human Progress,* pp. 43–44.

38. D. M. Frame, trans., *The Complete Works of Montaigne* (Stanford, Calif.: Stanford University Press, 1958), pp. 175–176.

39. Ibid., p. 618.

40. C. Cotton, trans., *The Essays of Michel de Montaigne* (New York: A. L. Burt, 1893), pp. 207, 210.

41. Ibid., p. 523.

Hyacinthe Rigaud, *Louis XIV, King of France and Navarre* (1701). Louis XIV is surrounded by the symbols of his power: the sword of justice, the scepter of power, and the crown. The vigor and strength of the king's stocking-covered legs contrast with the age and wisdom of his lined face. *(Scala/Art Resource, NY)*

chapter

16

chapter preview

Seventeenth-Century Crisis and Rebuilding
- *What were the common crises and achievements of seventeenth-century states?*

Absolutism in France and Spain
- *To what extent did French and Spanish monarchs succeed in creating absolute monarchies?*

The Culture of Absolutism
- *What cultural forms flourished under absolutist governments?*

Constitutionalism
- *What is constitutionalism, and how did this form of government emerge in England and the Dutch Republic?*

ABSOLUTISM AND CONSTITUTIONALISM IN WESTERN EUROPE, CA 1589–1715

The seventeenth century was a period of crisis and transformation. Agricultural and manufacturing slumps meant that many people struggled to feed themselves and their families. After a long period of growth, population rates stagnated or even fell. Religious and dynastic conflicts led to almost constant war, visiting violence and destruction on ordinary people.

The demands of war reshaped European states. Armies grew larger than they had been since the time of the Roman Empire. To pay for these armies, governments greatly increased taxes. They also created new bureaucracies to collect the taxes and to foster economic activity that might increase state revenue. Despite numerous obstacles, European states succeeded in gathering more power during this period. What one historian described as the long European "struggle for stability" that originated with the Reformation in the early sixteenth century was largely resolved by 1680.[1]

Important differences existed, however, in terms of *which* authority within the state possessed sovereignty—the Crown or privileged groups. Between roughly 1589 and 1715 two basic patterns of government emerged in Europe: absolute monarchy and the constitutional state. Almost all subsequent European governments have been modeled on one of these patterns.

Seventeenth-Century Crisis and Rebuilding

Historians often refer to the seventeenth century as an "age of crisis." After the economic and demographic growth of the sixteenth century, Europe faltered into stagnation and retrenchment. This was partially due to climate changes beyond anyone's control, but it also resulted from the bitterness of religious divides, the increased pressures exerted by governments, and the violence and dislocation of war. Overburdened peasants and city-dwellers took action to defend themselves, sometimes profiting

Online Study Center

This icon will direct you to interactive activities and study materials on the website **college.hmco.com/pic/mckaywest9e**

523

from elite conflicts to obtain redress of their grievances. In the long run, however, governments proved increasingly able to impose their will on the populace. This period witnessed a spectacular growth in army size as well as new forms of taxation, government bureaucracies, and increased state sovereignty.

• *What were the common crises and achievements of seventeenth-century states?*

Economic and Demographic Crisis

In the seventeenth century the vast majority of western Europeans lived in the countryside. The hub of the rural world was the small peasant village centered on a church and a manor. Life was in many ways circumscribed by the village, although we should not underestimate the mobility induced by war, food shortage, fortune-seeking, and religious pilgrimage.

A small number of peasants in each village owned enough land to feed themselves and the livestock and ploughs necessary to work their land. These independent farmers were leaders of the peasant village. They employed the landless poor, rented out livestock and tools, and served as agents for the noble lord. Below them were small landowners and tenant farmers who did not have enough land to be self-sufficient. These families sold their best produce on the market to earn cash for taxes, rent, and food. At the bottom were the rural proletariat who worked as dependent laborers and servants.

Rich or poor, bread was the primary element of the diet. Ignoring our modern health concerns, the richest ate a white loaf, leaving brown bread to those who could not afford better. Peasants paid stiff fees to the local miller for grinding grain into flour and sometimes to the lord for the right to bake bread in his oven. Bread was most often accompanied with a soup made of roots, herbs, beans, and perhaps a small piece of salt pork. One of the biggest

An English Food Riot Nothing infuriated ordinary women and men more than the idea that merchants and landowners were withholding grain from the market in order to push high prices even higher. In this cartoon an angry crowd hands out rough justice to a rich farmer accused of hoarding. *(Courtesy of the Trustees of the British Museum)*

annual festivals in the rural village was the killing of the family pig. The whole family gathered to help, sharing a rare abundance of meat with neighbors and carefully salting the extra and putting down the lard. In some areas, menstruating women were careful to stay away from the kitchen for fear they might cause the lard to spoil.

Rural society lived on the edge of subsistence. A bad harvest, an illness, or a drop in prices could lead to debt and the loss of one's land. Because of the crude technology and low crop yield, peasants were constantly threatened by scarcity and famine. The fear of hunger marked popular culture, and death was a familiar presence.

The seventeenth century put new stresses on this fragile balance. A colder and wetter climate meant a shorter farming season. Conditions were so bad that scholars refer to this period as a "little ice age." A bad harvest created dearth; a series of bad harvests could lead to famine. Recurrent famines had a significant effect on the population levels of early modern Europe. Using parish registers, historians have traced the correspondence between high prices on the one hand and burials and low birth and marriage rates on the other. Most people did not die of outright starvation, but rather of diseases brought on by malnutrition and exhaustion. Facilitated by the weakened population, outbreaks of bubonic plague continued in Europe until the 1720s.

Industry also suffered. While the evidence does not permit broad generalizations, it appears that the output of woolen textiles, one of the most important European manufactures, declined sharply in the first half of the century. Food prices were high, wages stagnated, and unemployment soared. This economic crisis was not universal: it struck various regions at different times and to different degrees. In the middle decades of the century, Spain, France, Germany, and England all experienced great economic difficulties; but these years were the golden age of the Netherlands.

Peasants and the urban poor were the first to suffer from bad harvests and economic depression. When the price of bread rose beyond their capacity to pay, they frequently took action. In towns they invaded the bakers' shop to seize bread and resell it at a "just price." In rural areas groups of peasants attacked convoys taking grain away to the cities and also redistributed it for what they considered a fair price. Women often took the lead in these actions, since their role as mothers with children to feed gave them some impunity in authorities' eyes. Historians have labeled this vision of a world in which community needs predominate over competition and profit a **moral economy.**

Chronology

1589–1610	Henry IV in France
1598	Edict of Nantes
1602	Dutch East India Company founded
1605–1715	Food riots common across Europe
1635	Birth of French Academy
1640–1680	Golden age of Dutch art (Vermeer, Van Steen, Rembrandt)
1642–1649	English civil war ends with execution of Charles I
1643–1715	Louis XIV in France
1648–1653	The Fronde
1653–1658	Military rule in England under Oliver Cromwell
1659	Treaty of the Pyrenees marks end of Spanish imperial dominance
1660	Restoration of English monarchy under Charles II
1665–1683	Jean-Baptiste Colbert applies mercantilism to France
1685	Edict of Nantes revoked
1688–1689	Glorious Revolution in England
1701–1713	War of the Spanish Succession
1713	Peace of Utrecht

Seventeenth-Century State-Building: Common Obstacles and Achievements

In this context of economic and demographic depression, monarchs began to make new demands on their people. Traditionally, historians have distinguished sharply between the "absolutist" governments of France, Spain, central Europe, and Russia and the constitutionally limited governments of England and the Dutch Republic. Whereas absolutist monarchs gathered all power under their personal control, Dutch and English rulers were obliged to respect laws passed by representative institutions. More recently, historians have emphasized commonalities among these powers. Despite their political differences, absolutist and constitutional monarchs shared common projects of protecting and expanding their frontiers, raising new taxes, and consolidating state control.

Rulers who wished to increase their authority encountered formidable obstacles. Some were purely material. Without paved roads, telephones, or other modern technology, it took weeks to convey orders from the central government to the provinces. States like France and Spain were vast, especially if we take their overseas empires into account. Rulers also suffered from a lack of information about their realms, due to the limited size of their bureaucracies. Without accurate knowledge of the number of inhabitants and the wealth they possessed, it was impossible to police and tax the population effectively. Cultural and linguistic differences presented their own obstacles. Seventeenth-century Basques, Bretons, Languedocians, and Alsatians spoke not French but their own languages. These differences decreased even further their willingness to obey a distant monarch's commands.

A more concrete obstacle was the array of privileged groups who shared in authority and its spoils. The traditional enemy of monarchical power was the nobility. Across Europe, nobles retained great legal, military, political, and financial powers, not to mention the traditional social prestige they commanded. Nobles were not alone in opposing monarchs' new claims. Other competitors included the church, the legislative corps, town councils, guilds, and other bodies that had acquired autonomy over the course of the Middle Ages. In some countries whole provinces held separate privileges and exemptions granted when they entered the kingdom. This special status reinforced local power structures and identities.

A long historical consensus held that absolutist monarchs succeeded in breaking the power of these institutions, with Louis XIV of France serving as the model for absolutist power across Europe. By contrast, mighty kings were humbled in England and the Dutch Republic and were forced to concede political power to elected representatives. Today, historians paint a more nuanced picture of this divide. On the one hand, they emphasize the extent to which absolutist monarchs had to compromise with existing power structures. Louis XIV succeeded because he co-opted and convinced nobles, rather than by crushing their power. On the other hand, historians also recognize that traditional elites retained power in England and the Netherlands. Constitutional limits did not mean democracy, the rule of the people.

If we take a step back from the political differences, we see that these states all succeeded—albeit to varying degrees—in overcoming the obstacles and achieving new levels of central control. Four achievements stand out in particular: greater taxation, growth in armed forces, larger and more efficient bureaucracies, and the increased ability to compel obedience from their subjects.

Increasing the size and power of the state required new sources of revenue. Medieval kings frequently found temporary financial support through bargains with the nobility: the nobility agreed to an ad hoc grant of money in return for freedom from future taxation. Over the course of the seventeenth century, rulers succeeded in generating new levels of income by either forcing direct taxes ever higher or devising alternative methods of raising money.

Taxation both permitted and required a larger government apparatus. This period witnessed the expansion of government bureaucracies and the creation of administrative techniques to improve communication and efficiency. Bureaucracies were now composed of career officials appointed by and solely accountable to the king. The backgrounds of these civil servants varied. They sometimes came from the middle classes, as in France, the Netherlands, and England. In Spain and eastern Europe, monarchs utilized members of the nobility instead (see Chapter 17).

Over time, government power added up to something close to **sovereignty.** A state may be termed sovereign when it possesses a monopoly over the instruments of justice and the use of force within clearly defined boundaries. In a sovereign state, no system of courts, such as ecclesiastical tribunals, competes with state courts in the dispensation of justice; and private armies, such as those of feudal lords, present no threat to central authority because the state's army is stronger. State law touches all persons in the country. While seventeenth-century states did not acquire total sovereignty, they made important strides toward that goal.

Warfare and the Growth of Army Size

The driving force of seventeenth-century state-building was warfare, characterized by dramatic changes in the size and style of armies. Medieval armies had been raised by feudal lords for particular wars or campaigns, after which the troops were disbanded. In the seventeenth century monarchs took command of recruiting and maintaining armies—in peacetime as well as wartime. Kings deployed their troops both inside and outside the country in the interests of the monarchy. Instead of serving their own interests, army officers were required to be loyal and obedient to the monarchs who commanded them. New techniques for training and deploying soldiers meant a rise in the professional standards of the army.

Along with professionalization came an explosive growth in army size. The French took the lead, with the army growing from roughly 125,000 men in the Thirty Years' War (1630–1648) to 250,000 during the Dutch War (1672–1678) and 340,000 during the War of the League of Augsburg (1688–1697).[2] This growth was caused in part by changes in the style of armies. Mustering a royal army took longer than simply hiring a mercenary band, giving enemies time to form coalitions. The large coalitions Louis XIV confronted required him to fight on multiple fronts with huge armies. In turn, the relative size and wealth of France among European nations allowed Louis to field enormous armies and thereby to pursue the ambitious foreign policies that caused his alarmed neighbors to form coalitions against him.

The death toll was startlingly high for noble officers, who personally led their men in battle. The paramount value of honor for noblemen outshone concerns for safety or material benefit. Nobles had to purchase their positions in the army and supply horses, food, uniforms, and weapons for themselves and their troops. Royal stipends did not begin to cover these expenses, and an officer's position could not be sold if he died in battle. The only legacy an officer's widow received was the debt incurred to fund her husbands' military career. It was not until the 1760s that the French government assumed the costs of equipping troops.

Other European powers were quick to follow the French example. The rise of absolutism in central and eastern Europe was similarly marked by a vast expansion in the size of armies (see Chapter 17). Great Britain followed a similar, albeit distinctive pattern. Instead of building a land army, the British focused on naval forces and eventually built the largest navy in the world.

Many historians believe that the new loyalty, professionalism, and size of the French army is the best case for the success of absolutism under Louis XIV. Whatever his compromises elsewhere, the French monarch had firm control of his armed forces. As in so many other matters, Louis's model was followed across Europe.

Popular Political Action

In the seventeenth century increased pressures of taxation and warfare turned bread riots into armed uprisings. **Popular revolts** were extremely common in England, France, Spain, Portugal, and Italy in the mid-seventeenth century.[3] In 1640 Philip IV of Spain faced revolt in Catalonia, the economic center of his realm. This was the same time he was struggling to put down an uprising in Portugal and the revolt of the northern provinces of the Netherlands. In 1647 the city of Palermo, in Spanish-occupied Sicily, exploded in protest over food shortages caused by a series of bad harvests. Fearing public unrest, the city government subsidized the price of bread, attracting even more starving peasants from the countryside. When Madrid ordered an end to

The Spider and the Fly In reference to the insect symbolism (*upper left*), the caption on the lower left side of this illustration states, "The noble is the spider, the peasant the fly." The other caption (*upper right*) notes, "The more people have, the more they want. The poor man brings everything—wheat, fruit, money, vegetables. The greedy lord sitting there ready to take everything will not even give him the favor of a glance." This satirical print summarizes peasant grievances. (*The New York Public Library/Art Resource, NY*)

subsidies, municipal leaders decided to lighten the loaf rather than raise prices. Not fooled by this change, local women led a bread riot, shouting "Long live the king and down with the taxes and the bad government!" The uprising spread to the rest of the island and eventually to Naples on the mainland. Apart from affordable food, rebels demanded the suppression of extraordinary taxes and participation in municipal government. Some dreamed of a republic in which noble tax exemptions would be abolished. Despite initial successes, the revolt lacked unity and strong leadership and could not withstand the forces of aristocratic reaction.[4]

In France urban disorders became so frequent an aspect of the social and political landscape as to be "a distinctive feature of life."[5] Major insurrections occurred at Dijon in 1630 and 1668, at Bordeaux in 1635 and 1675, at Montpellier in 1645, at Lyons in 1667–1668 and 1692, and at Amiens in 1685, 1695, 1704, and 1711. All were characterized by deep popular anger, a vocabulary of violence, and what a recent historian calls "the culture of retribution"—that is, the punishment of royal "outsiders," officials who attempted to announce or collect taxes.[6] These officials were sometimes seized, beaten, and hacked to death. For example, in 1673 Louis XIV's imposition of new taxes on legal transactions, tobacco, and pewter ware provoked an uprising in Bordeaux.

Municipal and royal authorities often struggled to overcome popular revolt. They feared that stern repressive measures, such as sending in troops to fire on crowds, would create martyrs and further inflame the situation, while forcible full-scale military occupation of a city would be very expensive. The limitations of royal authority gave some leverage to rebels. Royal edicts were sometimes suspended, prisoners released, and discussions initiated.

By the end of the seventeenth century, this leverage had largely disappeared. Municipal governments were better integrated into the national structure, and local authorities had prompt military support from the central government. People who publicly opposed royal policies and taxes received swift and severe punishment.[7]

Absolutism in France and Spain

In the Middle Ages jurists held that as a consequence of monarchs' coronation and anointment with sacred oil, they ruled "by the grace of God." Law was given by God; kings discovered or "found" the law and acknowledged that they must respect and obey it. In the absolutist state, kings amplified these claims, asserting that, as they were chosen by God, they were responsible to God alone. They claimed exclusive power to make and enforce laws, denying any other institution or group the authority to check their power.

In 1651 in *Leviathan,* the English philosopher Thomas Hobbes provided a theoretical justification for absolute monarchical authority, arguing that any limits on or divisions of government power would lead only to paralysis or civil war. At the court of Louis XIV the theologian Bossuet proclaimed that the king was the "image" of God on earth and that it was a sacred duty to obey him: "The prince need render account of his acts to no one. . . . Without this absolute authority the king could neither do good nor repress evil. It is necessary that his power be such that no one can hope to escape him, and, finally, the only protection of individuals against the public authority should be their innocence." Historians have been debating since his reign how successfully Louis XIV and other absolutist monarchs realized these claims.

● ***To what extent did French and Spanish monarchs succeed in creating absolute monarchies?***

The Foundations of Absolutism: Henry IV, Sully, and Richelieu

Louis XIV's absolutism had long roots. In 1589 his grandfather Henry IV (r. 1589–1610), the founder of the Bourbon dynasty, acquired a devastated country. Civil wars had wracked France since 1561. Catastrophically poor harvests meant that peasants across France lived on the verge of starvation. Commercial activity had fallen to one-third its 1580 level. Nobles, officials, merchants, and peasants wanted peace, order, and stability. "Henri le Grand" (Henry the Great), as the king was called, promised "a chicken in every pot" and inaugurated a remarkable recovery. He was beloved because of the belief that he cared about the people; he was the only king whose statue the Paris crowd did not tear down in the Revolution of 1789.

Aside from a short war in 1601, Henry kept France at peace. Maintaining that "if we are without compassion for the people, they must succumb and we all perish with them," Henry sharply lowered taxes on the overburdened peasants. In compensation for lost revenues, in 1602–1604 he introduced the *paulette,* an annual fee paid by royal officials to guarantee heredity in their offices. (Although effective at the time, the long-term effect of this tax was to reduce royal control over officeholders.)

Along with his able chief minister, the Protestant Maximilien de Béthune, duke of Sully, Henry IV laid the foundations for the growth of state power. He combined the indirect taxes on salt, sales, and transit and leased their collection to financiers. Although the number of taxes declined, revenues increased because of the revival of trade.[8] Henry improved the infrastructure of the country, building new roads and canals and repairing the ravages of years of civil war. In only twelve years he restored public order in France.

As a divinely appointed leader of his people, Henry sought to heal the religious divisions that had torn France apart. In 1598 he issued the **Edict of Nantes** as a compromise between Catholics and Huguenots. The edict allowed Protestants the right to worship in 150 traditionally Protestant towns throughout France; the king gave the towns 180,000 écus to support the maintenance of their military garrisons. This was too much for some devout Catholics. Henry was murdered in 1610 by François Ravaillac, a Catholic zealot, setting off national crisis.

Online Study Center **Improve Your Grade**
Primary Source: Henry IV's Edict of Nantes Grants Limited Toleration to the Huguenots

After the death of Henry IV his wife, the queen-regent Marie de' Medici, headed the government for the child-king Louis XIII (r. 1610–1643). In 1624 Marie de' Medici secured the appointment of Armand Jean du Plessis—Cardinal Richelieu (1585–1642)—to the council of ministers. It was a remarkable appointment. The next year Richelieu became president of the council, and after 1628 he was first minister of the French crown. Richelieu used his strong influence over King Louis XIII to exalt the French monarchy as the embodiment of the French state. One of the greatest servants of that state, Richelieu struggled through the turmoil of the Thirty Years' War to maintain the monarchy's position within Europe and within its own borders.

Richelieu's goal was to subordinate competing groups and institutions to the French monarchy. The nobility constituted the foremost threat. Nobles ran the army, controlled large provinces of France, sat in royal councils, and were immune from direct taxation. Richelieu sought to curb their power. In 1624 he succeeded in reshuffling the royal council, eliminating potential power brokers. Thereafter Richelieu dominated the council in an unprecedented way.

The constructive genius of Cardinal Richelieu is best reflected in the administrative system he established to strengthen royal control. He extended the use of the royal commissioners called **intendants.** France was divided into thirty-two *généralités* (districts), in each of which after 1634 a royal intendant held a commission to perform specific tasks, often financial but also judicial and policing. Intendants painstakingly collected information from local communities for Paris and delivered royal orders from the capital to their districts. Almost always recruited from the newer judicial nobility, the *noblesse de robe* or robe nobility, intendants were appointed directly by the monarch, to whom they were solely responsible. They could not be natives of the districts where they held authority; thus they had no vested interest in their localities. The intendants recruited men for the army, supervised the collection of taxes, presided over the administration of local law, checked up on the local nobility, and regulated economic activities—commerce, trade, the guilds, marketplaces—in their districts. They were to use their power for three related purposes: to inform the central government about their généralités, to enforce royal orders, and to undermine the influence of the regional nobility. As the intendants' power increased under Richelieu, so did the power of the centralized French state.

Under Richelieu the French monarchy also reasserted the principle of one people united by one faith. In 1627 Louis XIII decided to end Protestant military and political independence because, he said, it constituted "a state within a state." According to Louis, Huguenots demanded freedom of conscience but did not allow Catholics to worship in their cities. He interpreted this inequity as *political* disobedience.[9] Attention focused on La Rochelle, fourth largest of the French Atlantic ports and a major commercial center with strong ties to the northern Protestant states of Holland and England. Louis personally supervised the siege of La Rochelle. After the city fell in October 1628, its municipal government was suppressed and its walled fortifications were destroyed. Although Protestants retained the right of public worship, the king reinstated the Catholic liturgy, and Cardinal Richelieu himself celebrated the first Mass. The fall of La Rochelle weakened the influence of aristocratic Huguenots and was one step in the removal of Protestantism as a strong force in French life.

The elimination of potential dissidents at home did not mean hostility to Protestants abroad. Foreign policy under Richelieu aimed primarily at the destruction of the fence of Habsburg territories that surrounded France. Consequently, Richelieu supported the Habsburgs' enemies, including Protestants. In 1631 he signed a treaty with the Lutheran king Gustavus Adolphus promising French support against the Catholic Habsburgs in what has been called the Swedish phase of the Thirty Years' War (see page 562). French influence became an important factor in the political future of the German Empire. Richelieu acquired for France extensive rights in Alsace in the east and Arras in the north.

In building the French state, Richelieu knew that his approach sometimes seemed to contradict traditional Christian teaching. As a priest and bishop, how did he justify his policies? He developed his own *raison d'état* (reason of state): "Where the interests of the state are concerned, God absolves actions which, if privately committed, would be a crime."[10]

Richelieu's successor as chief minister for the boy-king Louis XIV was Cardinal Jules Mazarin (1602–1661). Along with the regent, Queen Mother Anne of Austria, Mazarin continued Richelieu's centralizing policies. His struggle to increase royal revenues to meet the costs of war with Spain led to the uprisings of 1648–1653 known as the **Fronde.** The word *fronde* means "slingshot" or "catapult," and a *frondeur* was originally a street urchin who threw mud at the passing carriages of the rich. The word came to be applied to the many individuals and groups who opposed the policies of the government. The Fronde began among the robe nobility when the judges of the Parisian high law court (the *Parlement*) rejected Anne and Mazarin's proposal to raise new revenues by rescinding judicial salaries. The arrest of several magistrates sparked a popular riot in the capital, whose inhabitants had suffered to meet the costs of war. With the boy-king, Anne of Austria fled the capital for safety. Essentially traditional and conservative, the magistrates agreed to a compromise with the government that largely favored their demands.

The second stage of the Fronde saw the conflict extend to the **noblesse d'épée** or sword nobility, who were also angered by the increasing powers of the central government. The Prince de Condé, one of the highest nobles in France, entered open warfare against the Crown, followed by other nobles and their followers. Popular rebellions led by aristocratic factions broke out in the provinces and spread to Paris.[11] As rebellion continued, civil order broke down completely. In 1651 Anne's regency ended with the declaration of Louis as king in his own right. Much of the rebellion died away, and its leaders came to terms with the government.

The conflicts of the Fronde had significant results for the future. First, it became apparent that compromise between the king and the sword and robe nobility was nec-

essary. Neither side was strong enough to subjugate the other; only violence and disorder could come from a refusal to negotiate. This meant, in some ways, a victory for the forces opposing the king, who were guaranteed the preservation of their traditional privileges. However, the Fronde also quelled—and in some cases killed—the most vociferous opponents of the Crown. The twin evils of noble factionalism and popular riots left the French wishing for peace and for a strong monarch to re-impose order. This was the legacy that Louis XIV inherited when he assumed personal rule in 1661. Humiliated by his flight from Paris, he was determined to avoid any recurrence of rebellion.

Louis XIV and Absolutism

In the reign of Louis XIV (r. 1643–1715), the longest in European history, the French monarchy reached the peak of absolutist development. In the magnificence of his court, in the brilliance of the culture that he presided over and that permeated all of Europe, and in his remarkably long life, the "Sun King" dominated his age.

The boy-king received an education appropriate for his position. He learned to speak Italian and Spanish fluently, spoke and wrote elegant French, and knew some French history and a great deal of European geography. Louis also imbibed the devout Catholicism of his mother, Anne of Austria, and throughout his long life scrupulously performed his religious duties. Religion, Anne, and Mazarin all taught Louis the doctrine of the **divine right of kings:** God had established kings as his rulers on earth, and they were answerable ultimately to God alone. Though kings were divinely anointed and shared in the sacred nature of divinity, they could not simply do as they pleased. They had to obey God's laws and rule for the good of the people.

Louis worked very hard at the business of governing. He ruled his realm through several councils of state, which he personally attended, and through the intendants who acted for the councils in the provinces. A stream of questions and instructions flowed between local districts and Versailles, helping centralize and standardize a hopelessly complex administration. Louis insisted on taking a personal role in many of the decisions issued by the councils.

Councilors of state came from the recently ennobled or the upper middle class. Royal service provided a means of social mobility. These professional bureaucrats served the state in the person of the king, but they did not share power with him. Louis stated that he chose bourgeois officials because he wanted "people to know by the rank of the men who served him that he had no intention of

Rubens: The Death of Henry IV and the Proclamation of the Regency (1622–1625) In 1622 the regent Marie de' Medici commissioned Peter Paul Rubens to paint a cycle of paintings depicting her life. This one portrays two distinct moments: the assassination of Henry IV (shown on the left ascending to Heaven), and Marie's subsequent proclamation as regent. The queen is seated on a throne in mourning clothes, with the goddess Athena on her right (representing Prudence), a woman in the air holding a rudder (symbolizing regency), and the personification of France kneeling before her offering an orb (symbolizing government). The other twenty-three canvasses in the cycle similarly glorify Marie, a tricky undertaking given her unhappy marriage to Henry IV and her tumultuous relationship with her son Louis XIII, who removed her from the regency in 1617. As in this image, Rubens frequently resorted to allegory and classical imagery to elevate the events of Marie's life. *(Réunion des Musées Nationaux/Art Resource, NY)*

sharing power with them."[12] If great ones were the king's advisers, they would seem to share the royal authority; professional administrators from the middle class would not.

Despite increasing financial problems, Louis never called a meeting of the Estates General. The nobility therefore had no means of united expression or action. Nor did Louis have a first minister; he kept himself free from worry about the inordinate power of a Richelieu. Louis also used spying and terror—a secret police force, a system of informers, and the practice of opening private letters—to eliminate potential threats.

Religion was also a tool of national unity under Louis, who continued Richelieu's persecution of Protestants. In 1685 Louis revoked the Edict of Nantes, by which his grandfather Henry IV had granted liberty of conscience to French Huguenots. The new law ordered the destruction of Huguenot churches, the closing of schools, the

Catholic baptism of Huguenots, and the exile of Huguenot pastors who refused to renounce their faith. The result was the departure of some of his most loyal and industrially skilled subjects.

There had been so many mass conversions of Protestants in France that the king's second wife, Madame de Maintenon, could say that "nearly all the Huguenots were converted." Moreover, Richelieu had already deprived French Calvinists of political rights. Why, then, did Louis XIV undertake such an apparently unnecessary, cruel, and self-destructive measure? First, Louis considered religion primarily a political question. Although he was personally tolerant, he hated division within the realm and insisted that religious unity was essential to his royal dignity and to the security of the state. As he put it, his goal was "one king, one law, one faith." Second, while France in the early years of Louis's reign permitted religious liberty, it was not a popular policy. Aristocrats had long petitioned Louis to crack down on Protestants. His decision to do so won him enormous praise: "If the flood of congratulation means anything, it . . . was probably the one act of his reign that, at the time, was popular with the majority of his subjects."[13]

Louis's personal hold on power, his exclusion of great nobles from his councils, and his ruthless pursuit of religious unity persuaded many earlier historians that his reign witnessed the creation of an **absolute monarchy.** Louis supposedly crushed the political pretensions of the nobility, leaving them with social grandeur and court posing but no real power. A later generation of historians has revised that view, showing the multiple constraints on Louis's power and his need to cooperate with the nobles. Louis may have declared his absolute power, but in practice he governed through collaboration with nobles, who maintained tremendous prestige and authority in their ancestral lands. Scholars also underline the traditional nature of Louis's motivations. Like his predecessors, Louis XIV sought to enhance the glory of his dynasty and his country, mostly through war. The creation of a new state apparatus was a means to that goal, not an end in itself.

Financial and Economic Management Under Louis XIV: Colbert

France's ability to build armies and fight wars depended on a strong economy. The king named Jean-Baptiste Colbert (1619–1683), the son of a wealthy merchant-financier of Reims, as controller general of finances. Colbert came to manage the entire royal administration and proved himself a financial genius. His central principle was that the wealth and the economy of France should serve the state. He did not invent the system called "mercantilism," but he rigorously applied it to France.

Mercantilism is a collection of governmental policies for the regulation of economic activities, especially commercial activities, by and for the state. In seventeenth- and eighteenth-century economic theory, a nation's international power was thought to be based on its wealth, specifically its gold supply. Because resources were limited, mercantilist theory held, state intervention was needed to secure the largest part of a limited resource. To accumulate gold, a country always had to sell more goods abroad than it bought. Colbert thus insisted that France should be self-sufficient, able to produce within its borders everything French subjects needed. Consequently, the outflow of gold would be halted; debtor states would pay in bullion; unemployment and poverty would greatly

diminish; and with the wealth of the nation increased, its power and prestige would be enhanced.

Colbert attempted to accomplish self-sufficiency by supporting old industries and creating new ones, especially in textiles, the most important sector of the economy. To ensure high-quality finished products, Colbert reinforced the system of state inspection and regulation and formed guilds in many industries. Colbert encouraged foreign craftsmen to immigrate to France, and he gave them special privileges. He also took measures to bring more female workers into the labor force. To protect French goods, he abolished many domestic tariffs and enacted high foreign tariffs, which prevented foreign products from competing with French ones.

One of Colbert's most ambitious projects was the creation of a merchant marine to transport French goods. He gave bonuses to French shipowners and shipbuilders and established a method of maritime conscription, arsenals, and academies for training sailors. In 1661 France possessed 18 unseaworthy vessels; by 1681 it had 276 frigates, galleys, and ships of the line. In 1664 Colbert founded the Company of the East Indies with (unfulfilled) hopes of competing with the Dutch for Asian trade.

Online Study Center **Improve Your Grade**
Primary Source: Colbert Promotes "The Advantages of Overseas Trade"

Colbert also hoped to make Canada—rich in untapped minerals and some of the best agricultural land in the world—part of a vast French empire. He gathered four thousand peasants from western France and shipped them to Canada, where they peopled the province of Quebec. (In 1608, one year after the English arrived at Jamestown, Virginia, Sully had established the city of Quebec, which became the capital of French Canada.) Subsequently, the Jesuit Jacques Marquette and the merchant Louis Joliet sailed down the Mississippi River and took possession of the land on both sides as far south as present-day Arkansas. In 1684 the French explorer Robert La Salle continued down the Mississippi to its mouth and claimed vast territories and the rich delta for Louis XIV. The area was called, naturally, "Louisiana."

Colbert's most pressing concern was tax collection. Extensive military reform, war, an expanding professional bureaucracy, and the court at Versailles cost a great deal of money. Yet there were many difficulties in raising taxes. English kings relied on one national assembly, Parliament, for consent to taxation for the entire country. The French system was both more complicated and more inequitable. In some provinces, provincial **estates** (representative bodies of clergy, nobles, and commoners) held the authority to negotiate with the Crown over taxes. In provinces without estates, the king held direct control over taxation through his intendants. Throughout France the nobility and clergy enjoyed exemption from the direct property tax, or *taille*; even bourgeois city-dwellers often gained exemption from it. This meant that the tax burden fell most heavily on those with the least wealth. Finally, the practice of subcontracting tax collection to financiers, known as tax-farmers, meant that a good portion of state money fell into private hands.

Despite these difficulties, Colbert managed to raise revenues significantly by cracking down on inefficiencies and corruption. During Colbert's tenure as controller general, Louis was able to pursue his goals without massive tax increases and without creating a stream of new offices. The constant pressure of warfare after Colbert's death, however, undid many of his economic achievements.

Louis XIV's Wars

Louis XIV wrote that "the character of a conqueror is regarded as the noblest and highest of titles." In pursuit of the title of conqueror, he kept France at war for thirty-three of the fifty-four years of his personal rule. In 1666 Louis appointed François le Tellier (later, marquis de Louvois) as secretary of state for war. Under the king's watchful eye, Louvois created a professional army that was modern in the sense that the French state, rather than private nobles, employed the soldiers. Louvois utilized several methods in recruiting troops: dragooning, in which press gangs seized men off the streets; conscription; and, after 1688, lottery. With these techniques, the French army grew to some 340,000 men at its height, enormous by the standards of the day. Louvois also imposed new levels of professionalization. Uniforms and weapons were standardized and a rational system of training and promotion devised. This new military machine gave one state the potential to dominate the affairs of the continent for the first time in European history.

Louis's supreme goal was to expand France to what he considered its "natural" borders and to secure those lands from any threat of outside invasion. A defensive

MAP 16.1 The Acquisitions of Louis XIV, 1668–1713
The desire for dynastic glory and the weakness of his German neighbors encouraged Louis's wars, but his country paid a high price for his acquisitions.

policy in his eyes, it appeared frighteningly aggressive to onlookers. In 1667, using a dynastic excuse, he invaded Flanders, part of the Spanish Netherlands, and Franche-Comté in the east. In consequence, he acquired twelve towns, including the important commercial centers of Lille and Tournai (see Map 16.1). Five years later Louis personally led an army of over one hundred thousand men into Holland, and the Dutch ultimately saved themselves only by opening the dikes and flooding the countryside. The Dutch war lasted six years and eventually involved the Holy Roman Empire and Spain. At the Treaty of Nijmegen (1678), Louis gained additional Flemish towns and all of Franche-Comté. In 1681 Louis seized the city of Strasbourg, and three years later he sent his armies into the province of Lorraine. At that moment the king seemed invincible. In fact, Louis had reached the limit of his expansion. The wars of the 1680s and 1690s brought no additional territories.

Louis understood his wars largely as defensive undertakings, but his enemies naturally viewed French expansion with great alarm. Louis's wars inspired the formation of Europe-wide coalitions against him. As a result, he was obliged to support a huge army in several different theaters of war. This task placed unbearable strains on French resources, especially given the inequitable system of taxation.

Claude Le Peletier, Colbert's successor as minister of finance, resorted to the devaluation of the currency and the old device of selling offices and tax exemptions. Colbert's successors also created new income taxes in 1695 and 1710, which nobles and clergymen had to pay for the first time. In exchange for this money, the king reaffirmed the traditional social hierarchies by granting honors, pensions, and titles to the nobility. Moreover, he did not lessen the burden on commoners, who had to pay the new taxes as well as the old ones.

A series of bad harvests between 1688 and 1694 added social to fiscal catastrophe. The price of wheat skyrocketed. The result was widespread starvation, and in many provinces the death rate rose to several times the normal figure. Parish registers reveal that France buried at least one-tenth of its population in those years, perhaps 2 million in 1693 and 1694 alone. Rising grain prices, new taxes for war, a slump in manufacturing, and the constant nuisance of pillaging troops all meant great suffering for the French people. France wanted peace at any price and won a respite for five years, which was shattered by the War of the Spanish Succession (1701–1713).

In 1700 the childless Spanish king Charles II (r. 1665–1700) died, opening a struggle for control of Spain and its colonies. His will bequeathed the Spanish crown and its empire to Philip of Anjou, Louis XIV's grandson (Louis's wife, Maria-Theresa, had been Charles's sister). This testament violated a prior treaty by which the European powers had agreed to divide the Spanish possessions between the king of France and the Holy Roman emperor, both brothers-in-law of Charles II. Claiming that he was following both Spanish national interests and French dynastic and national interests, Louis broke with the treaty and accepted the will.

In 1701 the English, Dutch, Austrians, and Prussians formed the Grand Alliance against Louis XIV. The allied powers united to prevent France from becoming too strong in Europe and to check France's expanding commercial power in North America, Asia, and Africa. The war dragged on until 1713. The **Peace of Utrecht,** which ended the war, applied the principle of partition. Louis's grandson Philip remained the first Bourbon king of Spain on the understanding that the French and Spanish crowns would never be united. France surrendered Newfoundland, Nova Scotia, and the Hudson Bay territory to England, which also acquired Gibraltar, Minorca, and control of the African slave trade from Spain. The Dutch gained little because Austria received the former Spanish Netherlands (see Map 16.2).

The Peace of Utrecht had important international consequences. It represented the balance-of-power principle in operation, setting limits on the extent to which any one power—in this case, France—could expand. The treaty completed the decline of Spain as a great power. It vastly expanded the British Empire, and it gave European powers experience in international cooperation. The Peace of Utrecht also marked the end of French expansion. Thirty-five years of war had brought rights to all of Alsace and the gain of important cities in the north such as Lille, as well as Strasbourg. But at what price? In 1714 an exhausted France hovered on the brink of bankruptcy. It is no wonder that when Louis XIV died on September 1, 1715, many subjects felt as much relief as they did sorrow.

The Decline of Absolutist Spain in the Seventeenth Century

Spanish absolutism and greatness had preceded those of the French. In the sixteenth century Spain (or, more precisely, the kingdom of Castile) had developed the standard features of absolutist monarchy: a permanent bureaucracy staffed by professionals employed in the various councils of state, a standing army, and national taxes, the *servicios,* which fell most heavily on the poor. France depended on financial and administrative unification within its borders; Spain had developed an international absolutism on the basis of silver bullion from Peru. Spanish gold and silver, armies, and glory had dominated the continent for most of the sixteenth century. In 1580 the Spanish crown annexed Portugal, putting an end to earlier conflicts over the boundaries of their overseas empires.

The Inquisition continued to ensure a dogmatic Catholic orthodoxy in Spain. Converted Jews and Muslims were always under suspicion and subject to imprisonment and even execution. In 1609 Philip III expelled all converted Muslims, known as Moriscos, from Spain. Some three hundred thousand individuals left the country, many going to the Ottoman Empire and North Africa. This measure satisfied the king's Catholic conscience and his fears of potential insurrection, but it was destructive for Spanish society, which lost precious skilled workers and merchants.

Tiepolo: The Triumph of Spain   This painting is from the ceiling of the Royal Palace in Madrid. Arguably the greatest Italian painter of the eighteenth century, Giovanni Tiepolo depicted the Spanish Empire as the self-assured champion of Christian cultural values in Europe and America. *(Palacio Real de Madrid/The Bridgeman Art Library)*

By the early seventeenth century the seeds of disaster were sprouting. By 1715 agricultural crisis and population decline, the loss of artisans and merchants, failure to invest in productive enterprises, and intellectual isolation and psychological malaise all combined to reduce Spain to a second-rate power. The fabulous and seemingly inexhaustible flow of silver from Mexico and Peru, together with the sale of cloth, grain, oil, and wine to the colonies, had greatly enriched Spain. In the early seventeenth century, however, the Dutch and English began to trade with the Spanish colonies, cutting into the revenues that had gone to Spain. Mexico and Peru themselves developed local industries, further lessening their need to buy from Spain. Between 1610 and 1650 Spanish trade with the colonies fell 60 percent. At the same

time, the native Indians and African slaves who toiled in the South American silver mines suffered frightful epidemics of disease. Ultimately, the lodes started to run dry, and the quantity of metal produced steadily declined.

In Madrid, however, royal expenditures constantly exceeded income. To meet mountainous state debt and declining revenues, the Crown repeatedly devalued the coinage and declared bankruptcy. In 1596, 1607, 1627, 1647, and 1680, Spanish kings found no solution to the problem of an empty treasury other than to cancel the national debt. Given the frequency of cancellation, national credit plummeted.

In contrast to the other countries of western Europe, Spain had only a tiny middle class. Public opinion, taking its cue from the aristocracy, condemned moneymaking

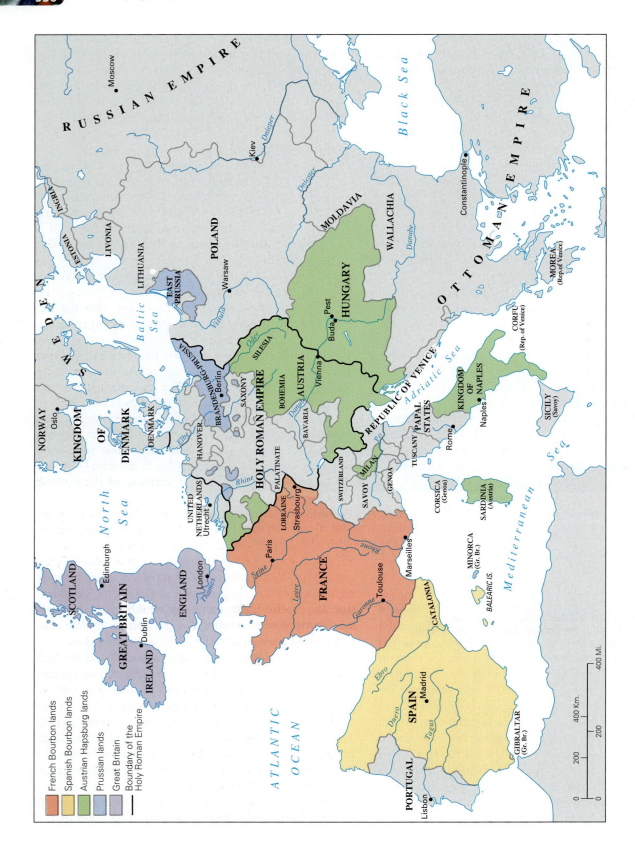

RUSSIAN EMPIRE

Moscow

OTTOMAN EMPIRE

Black Sea

Kiev

Dnieper

Dniester

NORWAY

Oslo

SWEDEN

FINLAND

ESTONIA

LIVONIA

Baltic Sea

LITHUANIA

POLAND

Warsaw

EAST PRUSSIA

Vistula

MOLDAVIA

WALLACHIA

Danube

HUNGARY

Pest

Buda

Vienna

AUSTRIA

SILESIA

Oder

BRANDENBURG-PRUSSIA

Berlin

SAXONY

BOHEMIA

BAVARIA

HOLY ROMAN EMPIRE

Danube

REPUBLIC OF VENICE

Adriatic Sea

CORFU
(Rep. of Venice)

MOREA
(Rep. of Venice)

Constantinople

KINGDOM OF DENMARK

DENMARK

HANOVER

Elbe

Rhine

UNITED NETHERLANDS

Utrecht

PALATINATE

LORRAINE

Strasbourg

SWITZERLAND

SAVOY

MILAN

GENOA

TUSCANY

PAPAL STATES

Rome

KINGDOM OF NAPLES

Naples

SICILY
(Savoy)

Po

North Sea

SCOTLAND

Edinburgh

GREAT BRITAIN

ENGLAND

London

Thames

IRELAND

Dublin

Paris

Seine

Loire

FRANCE

Rhône

Marseilles

Toulouse

Garonne

CORSICA
(Genoa)

SARDINIA
(Austria)

MINORCA
(Gr. Br.)

BALEARIC IS.

Mediterranean Sea

ATLANTIC OCEAN

CATALONIA

Ebro

SPAIN

Madrid

Duero

Tagus

GIBRALTAR
(Gr. Br.)

PORTUGAL

Lisbon

French Bourbon lands
Spanish Bourbon lands
Austrian Hapsburg lands
Prussian lands
Great Britain
Boundary of the
Holy Roman Empire

400 Mi.

400 Km.

200

200

0

0

as vulgar and undignified. Those with influence or connections sought titles of nobility and social prestige. Thousands entered economically unproductive professions: there were said to be nine thousand monasteries in the province of Castile alone. The flood of gold and silver had produced severe inflation, pushing the costs of production in the textile industry to the point that Castilian cloth could not compete in colonial and international markets. Many businessmen found so many obstacles in the way of profitable enterprise that they simply gave up.[14]

Spanish aristocrats, attempting to maintain an extravagant lifestyle they could no longer afford, increased the rents on their estates. High rents and heavy taxes in turn drove the peasants from the land. Agricultural production suffered, and peasants departed for the large cities, where they swelled the ranks of unemployed beggars.

Their most Catholic majesties, the kings of Spain, had no solutions to these dire problems. If one can discern personality from pictures, the portraits of Philip III (r. 1598–1622), Philip IV (r. 1622–1665), and Charles II (r. 1665–1700) hanging in the Prado, the Spanish national museum in Madrid, reflect the increasing weakness of the dynasty. Philip III, a pallid, melancholy, and deeply pious man handed the government over to the duke of Lerma, who used it to advance his personal and familial wealth. Philip IV left the management of his several kingdoms to Gaspar de Guzmán, count-duke of Olivares.

Olivares was an able administrator who has often been compared to Richelieu. He did not lack energy and ideas, and he succeeded in devising new sources of revenue.

Mapping the Past

MAP 16.2 Europe in 1715 The series of treaties commonly called the Peace of Utrecht (April 1713–November 1715) ended the War of the Spanish Succession and redrew the map of Europe. A French Bourbon king succeeded to the Spanish throne. France surrendered to Austria the Spanish Netherlands (later Belgium), then in French hands, and France recognized the Hohenzollern rulers of Prussia. Spain ceded Gibraltar to Great Britain, for which it has been a strategic naval station ever since. Spain also granted to Britain the *asiento,* the contract for supplying African slaves to America. ❶ Identify the areas on the map that changed hands as a result of the Peace of Utrecht. How did these changes affect the balance of power in Europe? ❷ How and why did so many European countries possess scattered or discontiguous territories? What does this suggest about European politics in this period? ❸ Does this map suggest potential for future conflict?

But he clung to the grandiose belief that the solution to Spain's difficulties rested in a return to the imperial tradition. Unfortunately, the imperial tradition demanded the revival of war with the Dutch at the expiration of a twelve-year truce in 1622 and a long war with France over Mantua (1628–1659). Spain thus became embroiled in the Thirty Years' War. These conflicts, on top of an empty treasury, brought disaster.

In 1640 Spain faced serious revolts in Catalonia and Portugal. The Portuguese succeeded in regaining independence from Habsburg rule under their new king, John IV (r. 1640–1656). In 1643 the French inflicted a crushing defeat on a Spanish army at Rocroi in what is now Belgium. By the Treaty of the Pyrenees of 1659, which ended the French-Spanish conflict, Spain was compelled to surrender extensive territories to France. This treaty marked the decline of Spain as a great power. Spain's long conflict with France ended with the bequeathing of the Spanish crown to a French prince, igniting the War of the Spanish Succession.

Seventeenth-century Spain was the victim of its past. It could not forget the grandeur of the sixteenth century and look to the future. The bureaucratic councils of state continued to function as symbols of the absolute Spanish monarchy. But because those councils were staffed by aristocrats, it was the aristocracy that held real power. Spanish absolutism had been built largely on slave-produced gold and silver. When the supply of bullion decreased, the power and standing of the Spanish state declined.

The most cherished Spanish ideals were military glory and strong Roman Catholic faith. In the seventeenth century Spain lacked the finances and the manpower to fight the expensive wars in which it got involved. Spain also ignored the new mercantile ideas and scientific methods because they came from heretical nations, Holland and England. The incredible wealth of South America destroyed what remained of the Spanish middle class and created contempt for business and manual labor.

The decadence of the Habsburg dynasty and the lack of effective royal councilors also contributed to Spanish failure. Spanish leaders seemed to lack the will to reform. Pessimism and fatalism permeated national life. In the reign of Philip IV, a royal council was appointed to plan the construction of a canal linking the Tagus and Manzanares Rivers in Spain. After interminable debate, the committee decided that "if God had intended the rivers to be navigable, He would have made them so."

In the brilliant novel **Don Quixote,** Spanish writer Miguel de Cervantes (1547–1616) produced one of the

Peeter Snayers: Spanish Troops (detail) The long wars that Spain fought over Dutch independence, in support of Habsburg interests in Germany, and against France left the country militarily exhausted and financially drained by the mid-1600s. Here Spanish troops—thin, emaciated, and probably unpaid—straggle away from battle. *(Museo Nacional del Prado, Madrid. Photo: José Baztan y Alberto Otero)*

great masterpieces of world literature. *Don Quixote* delineates the whole fabric of sixteenth-century Spanish society. The main character, Don Quixote, lives in a world of dreams, traveling about the countryside seeking military glory. From the title of the book, the English language has borrowed the word *quixotic*. Meaning "idealistic but impractical," the term characterizes seventeenth-century Spain. As a leading scholar has written, "The Spaniard convinced himself that reality was what he felt, believed, imagined. He filled the world with heroic reverberations. Don Quixote was born and grew."[15]

Colonial Administration

Whatever its problems within Europe, Spain continued to rule a vast empire in the Americas. Columbus, Cortés, and Pizarro had claimed the lands they had "discovered" for the Crown of Spain. How were these lands governed? According to the Spanish theory of absolutism, the Crown was entitled to exercise full authority over all im-

perial lands. In the sixteenth century the Crown divided its New World territories into four **viceroyalties,** or administrative divisions: New Spain, which consisted of Mexico, Central America, and present-day California, Arizona, New Mexico, and Texas, with the capital at Mexico City; Peru, originally all the lands in continental South America, later reduced to the territory of modern Peru, Chile, Bolivia, and Ecuador, with the viceregal seat at Lima; New Granada, including present-day Venezuela, Colombia, Panama, and, after 1739, Ecuador, with Bogotá as its administrative center; and La Plata, consisting of Argentina, Uruguay, and Paraguay, with Buenos Aires as the capital.

Within each territory, the viceroy, or imperial governor, exercised broad military and civil authority as the direct representative of the sovereign in Madrid. The viceroy presided over the *audiencia,* a board of twelve to fifteen judges that served as his advisory council and the highest judicial body. The reform-minded Spanish king Charles III (r. 1759–1788) introduced the system of *in-*

tendants, pioneered by the Bourbon kings of France, to the New World territories. These royal officials possessed broad military, administrative, and financial authority within their intendancies and were responsible not to the viceroy but to the monarchy in Madrid.

From the early sixteenth century to the beginning of the nineteenth century, the Spanish monarchy acted on the mercantilist principle that the colonies existed for the financial benefit of the home country. The mining of gold and silver was always the most important industry in the colonies. The Crown claimed the **quinto,** one-fifth of all precious metals mined in South America. Gold and silver yielded the Spanish monarchy 25 percent of its total income. In return, it shipped manufactured goods to the Americas and discouraged the development of native industries.

The Portuguese governed their colony of Brazil in a similar manner. After the union of the Crowns of Portugal and Spain in 1580, Spanish administrative forms were introduced. Local officials called *corregidores* held judicial and military powers. Mercantilist policies placed severe restrictions on Brazilian industries that might compete with those of Portugal. In the seventeenth century the use of black slave labor made possible the cultivation of coffee and cotton, and in the eighteenth century Brazil led the world in the production of sugar. The unique feature of colonial Brazil's culture and society was its thoroughgoing intermixture of Indians, whites, and blacks.

The Culture of Absolutism

Under absolutist monarchs, culture became an instrument of state power. The baroque style in art and music flourished in the context of the Catholic Reformation. Baroque masters like Rubens painted portraits celebrating the glory of European monarchs. The baroque was particularly popular in Spain, Italy, and central Europe. Along with art, architecture became an important tool for absolutist monarchs. Louis XIV made the magnificent palace of Versailles the center of his kingdom, inspiring imitators across Europe (see Chapter 17). Even language reflected the growing power of the Crown. Within France Richelieu established an academy to oversee French literature and language. Outside its borders French became the common language of the European elite.

• *What cultural forms flourished under absolutist governments?*

Baroque Art and Music

Throughout European history, the cultural tastes of one age have often seemed unsatisfactory to the next. So it was with the baroque. The term **baroque** itself may have come from the Portuguese word for an "odd-shaped, imperfect pearl" and was commonly used by late-eighteenth-century art critics as an expression of scorn for what they considered an overblown, unbalanced style. These critics also scorned the Gothic style of medieval cathedrals in favor of a classicism inspired by antiquity and the Renaissance. Specialists now agree that the baroque style marked one of the high points in the history of Western culture.

Rome and the revitalized Catholic Church of the later sixteenth century played an important role in the early development of the baroque. The papacy and the Jesuits encouraged the growth of an intensely emotional, exuberant art. These patrons wanted artists to go beyond the Renaissance focus on pleasing a small, wealthy cultural elite. They wanted artists to appeal to the senses and thereby touch the souls and kindle the faith of ordinary churchgoers while proclaiming the power and confidence of the reformed Catholic Church. In addition to this underlying religious emotionalism, the baroque drew its sense of drama, motion, and ceaseless striving from the Catholic Reformation. The interior of the famous Jesuit Church of Jesus in Rome—the Gesù—combined all these characteristics in its lavish, shimmering, wildly active decorations and frescoes.

Taking definite shape in Italy after 1600, the baroque style in the visual arts developed with exceptional vigor in Catholic countries—in Spain and Latin America, Austria, southern Germany, and Poland. Yet baroque art was more than just "Catholic art" in the seventeenth century and the first half of the eighteenth. True, neither Protestant England nor the Netherlands ever came fully under the spell of the baroque, but neither did Catholic France. And Protestants accounted for some of the finest examples of baroque style, especially in music. The baroque style spread partly because its tension and bombast spoke to an agitated age that was experiencing great violence and controversy in politics and religion.

In painting, the baroque reached maturity early with Peter Paul Rubens (1577–1640), the most outstanding and most representative of baroque painters. Studying in his native Flanders and in Italy, where he was influenced by masters of the High Renaissance such as Michelangelo, Rubens developed his own rich, sensuous, colorful style, which was characterized by animated figures, melodramatic contrasts, and monumental size. Rubens excelled

Juan de Pareja: The Calling of Saint Matthew   Using rich but subdued colors, Pareja depicts the biblical text (Mark 2:13–17), with Jesus in traditional first-century dress and the other figures, arranged around a table covered with an Oriental carpet, in seventeenth-century apparel. Matthew, at Jesus' right hand, seems surprised by the "call." Pareja, following a long tradition, includes himself (*standing, rear center*). (*Museo Nacional del Prado, Madrid/The Bridgeman Art Library*)

in glorifying monarchs such as Queen Mother Marie de' Medici of France (see the painting on page 531). He was also a devout Catholic; nearly half of his pictures treat Christian subjects. Yet one of Rubens's trademarks was fleshy, sensual nudes who populate his canvases as Roman goddesses, water nymphs, and remarkably voluptuous saints and angels.

Rubens was enormously successful. To meet the demand for his work, he established a large studio and hired many assistants to execute his rough sketches and gigantic murals. Sometimes the master artist added only the finishing touches. Rubens's wealth and position—on occasion he was given special diplomatic assignments by the Habsburgs—affirmed that distinguished artists continued to enjoy the high social status they had won in the Renaissance.

In music, the baroque style reached its culmination almost a century later in the dynamic, soaring lines of the endlessly inventive Johann Sebastian Bach (1685–1750).

Organist and choirmaster of several Lutheran churches across Germany, Bach was equally at home writing secular concertos and sublime religious cantatas. Bach's organ music combined the baroque spirit of invention, tension, and emotion in an unforgettable striving toward the infinite. Unlike Rubens, Bach was not fully appreciated in his lifetime, but since the early nineteenth century his reputation has grown steadily.

Court Culture

For much of the seventeenth century, the courts of Europe looked to France, and to the palace of Versailles, for cultural as well as political inspiration. (See the feature "Listening to the Past: The Court at Versailles" on pages 556–557.) Versailles began as a modest hunting lodge. Under Louis XIV's orders, his architects, Le Nôtre and Le Vau, turned what the duke of Saint-Simon called "the most dismal and thankless of sights" into a magnificent palace. Everywhere, the viewer had a sense of grandeur, vastness, and elegance. Enormous staterooms became display galleries for inlaid tables, Italian marble statuary, tapestries woven at the royal factory in Paris, and beautiful furniture. In the gigantic Hall of Mirrors, hundreds of candles illuminated the domed ceiling, where allegorical paintings celebrated the king's victories. The formal gardens celebrated the rationality and order imposed by the Sun King; its classical sculptures depicted Louis as Apollo, king of the gods.

In 1682 Louis formally established his court at Versailles, which became the center of the kingdom: a model of rational order and the perfect symbol of the king's power. The art and architecture of Versailles were tools of Louis's policy, used to overawe his subjects and foreign visitors. The Russian tsar Peter the Great imitated Versailles in the construction of his palace, Peterhof, as did the Prussian emperor Frederick the Great in his palace at Potsdam outside Berlin and the Habsburgs at Schonbrunn outside Vienna. (See the feature "Images in Society: Absolutist Palace Building" on pages 568–569.)

The palace was the summit of political, social, and cultural life. The king required all great nobles to spend at least part of the year in attendance on him at Versailles. Between three thousand and ten thousand people occupied the palace each day. Given the demand for space, even high nobles had to make do with cramped and uncomfortable living quarters. The palace gardens, and the palace itself on some occasions, were open to the public, allowing even local peasants a glimpse of their sovereign. More than a royal residence or administrative center, Versailles was a mirror of French greatness to the world.

Much has been made of the "domestication" of the nobility at Versailles. Elaborate rituals attended every moment of Louis's day, from waking up and dressing in the morning to removing his clothing and retiring at night. Nobles had to follow a tortuous system of court etiquette, and they vied for the honor of serving the monarch, with the highest in rank claiming the privilege to hand the king his shirt. Endless squabbles broke out over what type of chair one could sit on at court and the order in which great nobles entered and were seated in the chapel for Mass.

These rituals were far from meaningless or trivial. The king controlled immense resources and privileges; access to him meant favored treatment for pensions, military and religious posts, honorary titles, and a host of other benefits. Courtiers sought these rewards for themselves and for their family members and followers. As in ancient Rome, patron-client relations—in which a higher-ranked individual protected a lower-ranked one in return for loyalty and services—dominated political life. **Patronage** flowed from the court to the provinces; it was the mechanism through which Louis gained cooperation from social elites.

One family demonstrates the interplay between the state's rationalizing impulses and its reliance on very traditional patterns of nepotism and patronage. Long credited as the "modernizer" of the French army, the minister Louvois acquired his position through family ties, not merit. His father, Michel LeTellier was secretary of war from 1643 to 1677; Louvois succeeded his father in this position from 1677 to his death in 1691 and was succeeded in turn by his own son Barbézieux from 1691 to 1701. The Louvois family not only had powerful connections within the French bureaucracy, but also bought court offices for younger family members to ensure their influence at Versailles.

Although they were denied public offices and posts, women played a central role in the patronage system. At court, the king's wife, mistresses, and other female relatives used their high rank to establish their own patronage relations. They recommended individuals for honors, advocated policy decisions, and brokered alliances between noble factions. Noblewomen played a similar role, bringing their family connections to marriage to form powerful social networks. Onlookers sometimes resented the influence of powerful women at court. The Duke of Saint-Simon said of Madame de Maintenon, Louis XIV's mistress and secret second wife:

The power of Madame de Maintenon was, as may be imagined, immense. She had everybody in her hands, from the highest and most favored ministers to the meanest subject of the realm. Many people have been ruined by her, without having been able to discover the author of the ruin, search as they might.

French Classicism

To this day, culture is a central element of French national pride and identity. French emphasis on culture dates back to Cardinal Richelieu, whose efforts at state centralization embraced cultural activities. In 1635 he gave official recognition to a group of scholars interested in grammar and rhetoric. Thus was born the French Academy. With Richelieu's encouragement, the French Academy began the preparation of a dictionary to standardize the French language; the dictionary was completed in 1694 and has been updated in many successive editions. The Academy survives today as a prestigious society, and retains authority over correct usage in the French language.

Scholars characterize the art and literature of the age of Louis XIV as **French classicism.** By this they mean that the artists and writers of the late seventeenth century imitated the subject matter and style of classical antiquity, that their work resembled that of Renaissance Italy, and that French art possessed the classical qualities of discipline, balance, and restraint. This was a movement away from the perceived excesses of baroque style.

Louis XIV danced gracefully at court ballets in his youth and was an enthusiastic patron of the arts. Music and theater frequently served as backdrops for court ceremonials. Louis favored Jean-Baptiste Lully (1632–1687), whose orchestral works combined lively animation with the restrained austerity typical of French classicism. Lully also composed court ballets, and his operatic productions were a powerful influence throughout Europe. Louis supported François Couperin (1668–1733), whose harpsichord and organ works possessed the regal grandeur the king loved, and Marc-Antoine Charpentier (1634–1704), whose solemn religious music entertained him at meals. Charpentier received a pension for the *Te Deums,* hymns of thanksgiving, he composed to celebrate French military victories.

Louis XIV loved the stage, and in the plays of Molière and Racine his court witnessed the finest achievements in the history of the French theater. When Jean-Baptiste Poquelin (1622–1673), the son of a prosperous tapestry maker, refused to join his father's business and entered the theater, he took the stage name "Molière." As playwright, stage manager, director, and actor, Molière produced comedies that exposed the hypocrisies and follies of society through brilliant caricature. *Tartuffe* satirized the religious hypocrite; *Le Bourgeois Gentilhomme* (The Bourgeois Gentleman) attacked the social parvenu; and *Les Précieuses ridicules* (The Pretentious Young Ladies) mocked the pretensions of the *précieuses,* elite women who ran intellectual salons and wrote and spoke in an elegant and pretentious manner. In structure Molière's plays followed classical models, but they were based on careful social observation. Molière made the bourgeoisie the butt of his ridicule; he stopped short of criticizing the high nobility, reflecting the policy of his royal patron.

Online Study Center **Improve Your Grade**
Primary Source: Molière's Bourgeois Gentlewoman, Mme. Jourdain, Rejects a Noble Son-in-Law

While Molière dissected social mores, his contemporary Jean Racine (1639–1699) based his tragic dramas on Greek and Roman legends. His persistent theme was the conflict of good and evil. Several plays—*Andromaque, Bérénice, Iphigénie,* and *Phèdre*—bear the names of

women and deal with the power of female passion. Louis preferred *Mithridate* and *Britannicus* because of the "grandeur" of their themes. For simplicity of language, symmetrical structure, and calm restraint, the plays of Racine represent the finest examples of French classicism. His tragedies and Molière's comedies are still produced today.

With Versailles as the center of European politics, French culture grew in international prestige. Beginning in the reign of Louis XIV, French became the language of polite society and international diplomacy. French also gradually replaced Latin as the language of scholarship and learning. The royal courts of Sweden, Russia, Poland, and Germany all spoke French. In the eighteenth century the great Russian aristocrats were more fluent in French than in Russian. In England the first Hanoverian king, George I, spoke fluent French and only halting English. France inspired a cosmopolitan European culture in the late seventeenth century, which looked to Versailles as its center.

Constitutionalism

While France and later Prussia, Russia, and Austria solved the question of sovereignty with the absolutist state, England and Holland evolved toward the constitutional state. **Constitutionalism** is the limitation of government by law. Constitutionalism also implies a balance between the authority and power of the government, on the one hand, and the rights and liberties of the subjects, on the other.

A nation's constitution may be written or unwritten. It may be embodied in one basic document, occasionally revised by amendment, like the Constitution of the United States. Or it may be only partly formalized and include parliamentary statutes, judicial decisions, and a body of traditional procedures and practices, like the English and Dutch constitutions. Whether written or unwritten, a constitution gets its binding force from the government's acknowledgment that it must respect that constitution—that is, that the state must govern according to the laws. In a constitutional monarchy, a king or queen serves as the head of state and possesses some residual political authority, but the ultimate, or sovereign, power rests in the electorate.

A constitutional government is not the same as a democratic government. In a complete democracy, *all* the people have the right to participate either directly or indirectly (through their elected representatives) in the government of the state. Most men could not vote in Europe until the late nineteenth century, and women gained the franchise only in the twentieth century.

• *What is constitutionalism, and how did this form of government emerge in England and the Dutch Republic?*

Absolutist Claims in England (1603–1649)

In 1588 Queen Elizabeth I of England exercised very great personal power; by 1689 the English monarchy was severely circumscribed. Change in England was anything but orderly. Seventeenth-century England executed one king and experienced a bloody civil war; experimented with military dictatorship, then restored the son of the murdered king; and finally, after a bloodless revolution, established constitutional monarchy. Political stability came only in the 1690s. After such a violent and tumultuous century, how did England produce a constitutional monarchy? What combination of political, socioeconomic, and religious factors brought on a civil war in 1642–1649 and then the constitutional settlement of 1688–1689?

The extraordinary success of Elizabeth I rested on her political shrewdness and flexibility, her careful management of finances, her wise selection of ministers, her clever manipulation of Parliament, and her sense of royal dignity and devotion to hard work. A rare female monarch, Elizabeth imposed her authority in part by refusing to marry. If she had married, proper wifely submission to her husband would have made it difficult to assert royal authority over her subjects. The problem with this strategy was that it left the queen with no immediate heir to continue her legacy.

In 1603 Elizabeth's Scottish cousin James Stuart succeeded her as James I (r. 1603–1625). King James was well educated, learned, and, with thirty-five years' experience as king of Scotland, politically shrewd. But he was not as interested in displaying the majesty of monarchy as Elizabeth had been. Urged to wave at the crowds who waited to greet their new ruler, James complained that he was tired and threatened to drop his breeches "so they can cheer at my arse." The new king failed to live up to the role expected of him in England. Moreover, in contrast to Elizabeth, James was a poor judge of character, and in a society already hostile to the Scots, James's Scottish accent was a disadvantage.[16]

James's greatest problems, however, arose in resistance to his claims for monarchical authority. Like his French counterpart, James was devoted to the theory of the divine right of kings. He expressed his ideas in his essay "The Trew Law of Free Monarchy." According to James

I, a monarch has a divine (or God-given) right to his authority and is responsible only to God. Rebellion is the worst of political crimes. If a king orders something evil, the subject should respond with passive disobedience but should be prepared to accept any penalty for noncompliance. James went so far as to lecture the House of Commons: "There are no privileges and immunities which can stand against a divinely appointed King." This notion, implying total royal jurisdiction over the liberties, persons, and properties of English men and women, formed the basis of the Stuart concept of absolutism. Such a view ran directly counter to the long-standing English idea that a person's property could not be taken away without due process of law. James's expression of such views before the English House of Commons was a grave political mistake.

The House of Commons guarded the state's pocketbook, and James and later Stuart kings badly needed to open that pocketbook. Elizabeth had left James a sizable royal debt. Elizabeth had managed to escape public disapprobation for the debt, but James was left to face the consequences. Elizabeth had also left her Stuart successors a House of Commons that appreciated its own financial strength and intended to use that strength to acquire a greater say in the government of the state. The knights and burgesses who sat at Westminster in the late sixteenth and early seventeenth centuries wanted a voice in royal expenditures, religious reform, and foreign affairs. Essentially, the Commons wanted a measure of sovereignty.

Profound social changes had occurred since the sixteenth century. The English House of Commons during the reigns of James I and his son Charles I (r. 1625–1649) was very different from the assembly Henry VIII had manipulated into passing his Reformation legislation. The dissolution of the monasteries and the sale of monastic land had enriched many people. Enclosure of the common lands and new agricultural techniques had also enriched landowners, while many people invested successfully in commercial ventures, such as the expanding cloth industry. These developments led to a great deal of social mobility. Both in commerce and in agriculture, the English in the late sixteenth and early seventeenth centuries were capitalists, investing their profits to make more money.

The typical pattern was for the commercially successful to set themselves up as country gentry, thus creating an elite group that possessed a far greater proportion of land and of the national wealth in 1640 than had been the case in 1540. Small wonder that in 1640 someone could declare in the House of Commons that "We could buy

Van Dyck: Charles I (ca 1635) Anthony Van Dyck was the greatest of Rubens's many students. In 1633 he became court painter to Charles I. His portrait of Charles just dismounted from a horse emphasizes the aristocratic bearing, elegance, and innate authority of the king. This monarch seemingly needs no pomp or magnificence to display his sovereignty. Van Dyck's success led to innumerable commissions by members of the court and aristocratic society. He had a profound influence on English portraiture and was revered, for example, by Gainsborough. Some scholars believe that this portrait influenced Rigaud's 1701 portrait of Louis XIV (see page 522). *(Scala/Art Resource, NY)*

the House of Lords three times over." Increased wealth had also produced a better-educated and more articulate House of Commons. Many members had acquired at least a smattering of legal knowledge, which they used to search for medieval precedents from which to argue against the king.

In England, unlike France, there was no social stigma attached to paying taxes. Members of the House of Commons were willing to assess and pay taxes provided they had some say in the expenditure of those taxes and

in the formulation of state policies. The Stuart kings, however, considered such ambitions intolerable and a threat to their divine-right prerogative. Consequently, at every Parliament between 1603 and 1640, bitter squabbles erupted between the Crown and the articulate and legally minded Commons. Charles I's attempt to govern without Parliament (1629–1640) and to finance his government by arbitrary nonparliamentary levies, brought the country to a crisis.

Religious Divides

Religious issues also embittered relations between the king and the House of Commons. In the early seventeenth century increasing numbers of English people felt dissatisfied with the Church of England established by Henry VIII and reformed by Elizabeth. Many **Puritans** (see page 463) believed that the Reformation had not gone far enough. They wanted to "purify" the Anglican church of Roman Catholic elements—elaborate vestments and ceremonials, bishops, and even the giving and wearing of wedding rings.

It is difficult to establish what proportion of the English population was Puritan. According to present scholarly consensus, the dominant religious groups in the early seventeenth century were Calvinist; their more zealous members were Puritans. It also seems clear that many English people were attracted by the socioeconomic implications of John Calvin's theology. Calvinism emphasized hard work, sobriety, thrift, competition, and postponement of pleasure, and it tended to link poverty with weakness and moral corruption. These values, which have frequently been called the "Protestant ethic" or "capitalist ethic," fit in precisely with the economic approaches and practices of many successful business people and farmers. While it is hazardous to identify capitalism with Protestantism—there were many successful Catholic capitalists, for example—the "Protestant virtues" represented the prevailing values of members of the House of Commons.

Puritans wanted to abolish bishops in the Church of England, and when James I said, "No bishop, no king," he meant that the bishops were among the chief supporters of the throne. His son Charles I gave the impression of being sympathetic to Roman Catholicism. First, Charles married the French Catholic princess Henrietta Maria, a daughter of Henry IV. Charles also supported the policies of William Laud (1573–1645), archbishop of Canterbury, who tried to impose elaborate ritual on all churches. Laud insisted on complete uniformity of church services and enforced that uniformity through an ecclesiastical court called the "Court of High Commission." People believed that the country was being led back to Roman Catholicism.

In 1637 Laud attempted to impose two new elements on church organization in Scotland: a new prayer book, modeled on the Anglican *Book of Common Prayer,* and bishoprics, which the Presbyterian Scots firmly rejected. The Scots therefore revolted. To finance an army to put down the Scots, King Charles was compelled to summon Parliament in November 1640.

Charles I was an intelligent man, but contemporaries found him deceitful, dishonest, and treacherous. After quarreling with Parliament over his right to collect customs duties on wine and wool and over what the Commons perceived as religious innovations, Charles had dissolved Parliament in 1629. From 1629 to 1640, he ruled without Parliament, financing his government through extraordinary stopgap levies considered illegal by most English people. For example, the king revived a medieval law requiring coastal districts to help pay the cost of ships for defense, but he levied the tax, called "ship money," on inland as well as coastal counties. Most members of Parliament believed that such taxation without consent amounted to despotism. Consequently, they were not willing to trust the king with an army. Moreover, many supported the Scots' resistance to Charles's religious innovations and had little wish for military action against them. Accordingly, this Parliament, called the "Long Parliament" because it sat from 1640 to 1660, enacted legislation that limited the power of the monarch and made arbitrary government impossible.

In 1641 the Commons passed the Triennial Act, which compelled the king to summon Parliament every three years. The Commons impeached Archbishop Laud and abolished the Court of High Commission, then went further and threatened to abolish bishops. King Charles, fearful of a Scottish invasion—the original reason for summoning Parliament—accepted these measures. Understanding and peace were not achieved, however, partly because radical members of the Commons pushed increasingly revolutionary propositions, and partly because Charles maneuvered to rescind those he had already approved.

The next act in the conflict was precipitated by the outbreak of rebellion in Ireland. Ever since Henry II had conquered Ireland in 1171, English governors had mercilessly ruled the land, and English landlords had ruthlessly exploited the Irish people. The English Reformation had made a bad situation worse: because the Irish remained Catholic, religious differences united with economic and political oppression. In 1641 the Catholic gentry led an uprising in response to a feared invasion by anti-Catholic forces of the Long Parliament.

Puritan Occupations   These twelve engravings depict typical Puritan occupations and show that the Puritans came primarily from the artisan and lower middle classes. The governing classes and peasants adhered to the traditions of the Church of England. *(Visual Connection Archive)*

Without an army, Charles I could neither come to terms with the Scots nor respond to the Irish rebellion, and the Long Parliament remained unwilling to place an army under a king it did not trust. After a failed attempt to arrest parliamentary leaders, Charles left London for the north of England. There, he recruited an army drawn from the nobility and its cavalry staff, the rural gentry, and mercenaries. The parliamentary army was composed of the militia of the city of London, country squires with business connections, and men with a firm belief in the spiritual duty of serving.

The English civil war (1642–1649) tested whether sovereignty in England was to reside in the king or in Parliament. In 1645 Parliament reorganized its forces into the **New Model Army** under the leadership of Sir Thomas Fairfax and Oliver Cromwell, a member of the House of Commons who had emerged as a military leader during the war. After three years of inconclusive fighting, parliamentary forces finally defeated the king's armies at the Battles of Naseby and Langport in the summer of 1645. To all appearances, the war was over and the parliamentary side had prevailed. The only remaining issue was to obtain formal recognition from Charles on restrictions on royal authority and church reform. Charles, though, refused to concede defeat. Both sides jockeyed for position, waiting for a decisive event. This arrived in the form of the army. In 1647 Cromwell's forces captured the king and dismissed members of the Parliament who opposed his actions. In 1649 the remaining representatives, known as the "Rump Parliament," put Charles on trial for high treason, a severe blow to the theory of divine-right monarchy. Charles was found guilty and beheaded on January 30, 1649, an act that sent shockwaves around Europe.

Puritanical Absolutism in England: Cromwell and the Protectorate

With the execution of Charles, kingship was abolished. A *commonwealth,* or republican government, was proclaimed. Theoretically, legislative power rested in the surviving members of Parliament, and executive power was lodged in a council of state. In fact, the army that had defeated the king controlled the government, and Oliver Cromwell controlled the army. Though called the **Protectorate,** the rule of Cromwell (1653–1658) constituted military dictatorship.

The army prepared a constitution, the Instrument of Government (1653), that invested executive power in a lord protector (Cromwell) and a council of state. The instrument provided for triennial parliaments and gave Par-

Cartoon of 1649: "The Royall Oake of Brittayne" Chopping down this tree signifies the end of royal authority, stability, Magna Carta (see page 272), and the rule of law. As pigs graze (representing the unconcerned common people), being fattened for slaughter, Oliver Cromwell, with his feet in Hell, quotes Scripture. This is a royalist view of the collapse of Charles I's government and the rule of Cromwell. *(Courtesy of the Trustees of the British Museum)*

liament the sole power to raise taxes. But after repeated disputes, Cromwell tore the document up. He continued the standing army and proclaimed quasi-martial law. He divided England into twelve military districts, each governed by a major general. The state rigorously censored the press, forbade sports, and kept the theaters closed in England. On the issue of religion, Cromwell favored some degree of toleration, and the Instrument of Government gave all Christians except Roman Catholics the right to practice their faith. As for Irish Catholicism, Cromwell identified it with sedition and heresy. In September 1649 his army crushed a rebellion at Drogheda and massacred the garrison. Another massacre followed in October. These brutal acts left a legacy of Irish hatred for England that has not yet subsided. Cromwell defended his actions by claiming to have acted only against soldiers in arms and said that a strong deterrent would prevent future bloodshed. After Cromwell's departure for England, the atrocities worsened. Sir William Petty, who served the English government in Ireland, estimated that over six hundred thousand people, or one-third of Ireland's population, died or were exiled as a result of the civil wars. The English banned Catholicism in Ireland, executed priests, and confiscated land from Catholics for English and Scottish settlers.

In England, Cromwell's regulation of the nation's economy had features typical of seventeenth-century absolutism. The lord protector's policies were mercantilist, similar to those Colbert established in France. Cromwell enforced a Navigation Act (1651), requiring that English goods be transported on English ships. The Navigation Act was a great boost to the development of an English merchant marine and brought about a short but successful war with the commercially threatened Dutch. Cromwell also welcomed the immigration of Jews because of their skills, and they began to return to England after four centuries of absence.

Military government collapsed when Cromwell died in 1658 and his ineffectual son succeeded him. Fed up with military rule, the English longed for a return to civilian government, restoration of the common law, and social stability. Government by military dictatorship was an experiment that the English never forgot or repeated. By 1660 they were ready to restore the monarchy.

The Restoration of the English Monarchy

The Restoration of 1660 re-established the monarchy in the person of Charles II (r. 1660–1685), eldest son of

Charles I, who returned from exile on the continent to take the throne. At the same time, both houses of Parliament were restored, together with the established Anglican church, the courts of law, and the system of local government through justices of the peace. The Restoration failed to resolve two serious problems, however. What was to be the attitude of the state toward Puritans, Catholics, and dissenters from the established church? And what was to be the relationship between the king and Parliament?

About the first of these issues, Charles II, an easygoing and sensual man, was basically indifferent. He was not interested in doctrinal issues. Members of Parliament were, and they enacted a body of laws that sought to compel religious uniformity. Those who refused to receive the Eucharist of the Church of England could not vote, hold public office, preach, teach, attend the universities, or even assemble for meetings, according to the **Test Act** of 1673. But these restrictions could not be enforced. When the Quaker William Penn held a meeting of his Friends and was arrested, the jury refused to convict him.

In politics Charles II was determined "not to set out in his travels again," which meant that he intended to get along with Parliament. Generally good rapport existed between the king and the strongly royalist Parliament that had restored him. This rapport was due largely to the king's appointment of a council of five men who served both as his major advisers and as members of Parliament, thus acting as liaison agents between the executive and the legislature. This body—known as the "Cabal" from the names of its five members (Clifford, Arlington, Buckingham, Ashley-Cooper, and Lauderdale)—was an ancestor of the later cabinet system. Although its members sometimes disagreed and intrigued among themselves, it gradually came to be accepted that the Cabal was answerable in Parliament for the decisions of the king. This development gave rise to the concept of ministerial responsibility: royal ministers must answer to the Commons.

Harmony between the Crown and Parliament rested on the understanding that Charles would summon frequent Parliaments and that Parliament would vote him sufficient revenues. But Parliament did not grant him an adequate income. Accordingly, in 1670 Charles entered into a secret agreement with his cousin Louis XIV (Charles's mother Henrietta-Maria was the daughter of Henry IV, Louis' grandfather). The French king would give Charles two hundred thousand pounds annually, and in return Charles would relax the laws against Catholics, gradually re-Catholicize England, support French policy against the Dutch, and convert to Catholicism himself. When the details of this treaty leaked out, a great wave of anti-Catholic fear swept England. This fear was compounded by a crucial fact: with no legitimate heir, Charles would be succeeded by his Catholic brother, James, duke of York. A combination of hatred for French absolutism and hostility to Catholicism produced virtual hysteria. The Commons passed an exclusion bill denying the succession to a Roman Catholic, but Charles quickly dissolved Parliament, and the bill never became law.

When James II (r. 1685–1688) succeeded his brother, the worst English anti-Catholic fears, already aroused by Louis XIV's revocation of the Edict of Nantes, were realized. In violation of the Test Act, James appointed Roman Catholics to positions in the army, the universities, and local government. When these actions were challenged in the courts, the judges, whom James had appointed, decided for the king. The king was suspending the law at will and appeared to be reviving the absolutism of his father and grandfather. He went further. Attempting to broaden his base of support with Protestant dissenters and nonconformists, James issued a declaration of indulgence granting religious freedom to all.

Two events gave the signals for revolution. First, seven bishops of the Church of England petitioned the king that they not be forced to read the declaration of indulgence because of their belief that it was an illegal act. They were imprisoned in the Tower of London but subsequently acquitted amid great public enthusiasm. Second, in June 1688 James's second wife produced a male heir. A Catholic dynasty seemed ensured. The fear of a Roman Catholic monarchy supported by France and ruling outside the law prompted a group of eminent persons to offer the English throne to James's Protestant daughter Mary and her Dutch husband, Prince William of Orange. In December 1688 James II, his queen, and their infant son fled to France and became pensioners of Louis XIV. Early in 1689 William and Mary were crowned king and queen of England.

The Triumph of England's Parliament: Constitutional Monarchy and Cabinet Government

The English call the events of 1688 and 1689 the "Glorious Revolution" because it replaced one king with another with a minimum of bloodshed. It also represented the destruction, once and for all, of the idea of divine-right monarchy. William and Mary accepted the English throne from Parliament and in so doing explicitly recog-

nized the supremacy of Parliament. The revolution of 1688 established the principle that sovereignty, the ultimate power in the state, was divided between king and Parliament and that the king ruled with the consent of the governed.

The men who brought about the revolution quickly framed their intentions in the Bill of Rights, the cornerstone of the modern British constitution. The principles of the Bill of Rights were formulated in direct response to Stuart absolutism. Law was to be made in Parliament; once made, it could not be suspended by the Crown. Parliament had to be called at least once every three years. Both elections to and debate in Parliament were to be free in the sense that the Crown was not to interfere in them (this aspect of the bill was widely disregarded in the eighteenth century). The independence of the judiciary was established. No longer could the Crown get the judicial decisions it wanted by threats of removal. There was to be no standing army in peacetime—a limitation designed to prevent the repetition of Cromwellian military government. The Bill of Rights granted "that the subjects which are Protestants may have arms for their defense suitable to their conditions and as allowed by law,"[17] meaning that Catholics could not possess arms because the Protestant majority feared them. Additional legislation granted freedom of worship to Protestant dissenters and nonconformists and required that the English monarch always be Protestant.

The Glorious Revolution found its best defense in political philosopher John Locke's *Second Treatise of Civil Government* (1690). Locke (1632–1704) maintained that people set up civil governments to protect life, liberty, and property. A government that oversteps its proper function—protecting the natural rights of life, liberty, and property—becomes a tyranny. (By "natural" rights Locke meant rights basic to all men because all have the ability to reason.) Under a tyrannical government, the people have the natural right to rebellion. Such rebellion can be avoided if the government carefully respects the rights of citizens and if people zealously defend their liberty. Arguing for a close relationship between economic and political freedom, Locke linked economic liberty and private property with political freedom. On the basis of this link, he justified limiting the vote to property owners. Locke served as the great spokesman for the liberal English revolution of 1688 and 1689 and for representative government. His idea that there are natural or universal rights equally valid for all peoples and societies was especially popular in colonial America. (Colonists also appreciated his arguments that Native Americans had no property rights since they did not cultivate the land and, by extension, no political rights because they possessed no property.)

Online Study Center   Improve Your Grade
Primary Source: John Locke's Vindication for the
Glorious Revolution: The Social Contract

The events of 1688 and 1689 did not constitute a *democratic* revolution. The revolution placed sovereignty in Parliament, and Parliament represented the upper classes. The great majority of English people acquired no say in their government. The English revolution established a constitutional monarchy; it also inaugurated an age of aristocratic government that lasted at least until 1832 and in many ways until 1928, when women received full voting rights.

The Dutch Republic in the Seventeenth Century

In the late sixteenth century the seven northern provinces of the Netherlands fought for and won their independence from Spain as the Republic of United Provinces of the Netherlands—an independence that was confirmed by the Peace of Westphalia ending the Thirty Years' War in 1648 (see page 563). The seventeenth century witnessed an unparalleled flowering of Dutch scientific, artistic, and literary achievement. In this period, often called the "golden age of the Netherlands," Dutch ideas and attitudes played a profound role in shaping a new and modern worldview. At the same time, the United Provinces was another model of the development of the modern constitutional state.

Within each province, an oligarchy of wealthy merchants called "regents" handled domestic affairs in the local Estates. The provincial Estates held virtually all the power. A federal assembly, or **States General,** handled matters of foreign affairs, such as war. But the States General did not possess sovereign authority; all issues had to be referred back to the local Estates for approval. The States General appointed a representative, the **stadholder,** in each province. As the highest executive there, the stadholder carried out ceremonial functions and was responsible for defense and good order. Maurice and

Jan Steen: The Christening Feast   As the mother, surrounded by midwives, rests in bed (*rear left*) and the father proudly displays the swaddled child, thirteen other people, united by gestures and gazes, prepare the celebratory meal. Very prolific, Steen was a master of warm-hearted domestic scenes. In contrast to the order and cleanliness of many seventeenth-century Dutch genre paintings, Steen's more disorderly portrayals gave rise to the epithet "a Jan Steen household," meaning an untidy house. (*Wallace Collection, London/The Bridgeman Art Library*)

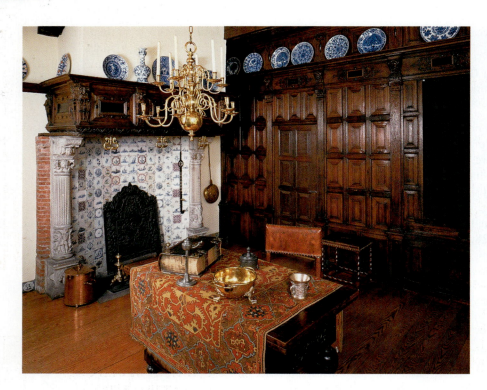

Room from Het Scheepje (The Little Ship) A retired sea captain who became a successful brewer in Haarlem owned the house (adjacent to his brewery) that included this room. The brass chandelier, plates, tiles, Turkish rug on the table (probably from Transylvania in the Ottoman Empire), oak mantelpiece, and paneling make this a superb example of a Dutch domestic interior during the golden age. A bed built into the wall paneling was warmed at night by coals in the pan hanging by the fireplace. *(Room from Het Scheepje, Haarlem, The Netherlands, early 17th century. Philadelphia Museum of Art, Gift of Edward W. Bok. 1928-66-1)*

William Louis, the sons of William the Silent, held the office of stadholder in all seven provinces. As members of the House of Orange, they were closely identified with Dutch patriotism. The regents in each province jealously guarded local independence and resisted efforts at centralization. Nevertheless, Holland, which had the largest navy and the most wealth, dominated the republic and the States General. Significantly, the Estates assembled at Holland's capital, The Hague.

The government of the United Provinces had none of the standard categories of seventeenth-century political organization. The Dutch were not monarchical but rather fiercely republican. The government was controlled by wealthy merchants and financiers. Though they were rich, their values were strongly middle class, not aristocratic. The Dutch republic was not a strong federation but a confederation—that is, a weak union of strong provinces. The provinces were a temptation to powerful neighbors, yet the Dutch resisted the long Spanish effort at reconquest and withstood both French and English attacks in the second half of the century.

The political success of the Dutch rested on the phenomenal commercial prosperity of the Netherlands. The moral and ethical bases of that commercial wealth were thrift, frugality, and religious toleration. John Calvin had written, "From where do the merchant's profits come except from his own diligence and industry?" This attitude

encouraged a sturdy people who had waged a centuries-old struggle against the sea.

Alone of all European peoples in the seventeenth century, the Dutch practiced religious toleration. Peoples of all faiths were welcome within their borders. Although there is scattered evidence of anti-Semitism, Jews enjoyed a level of acceptance and assimilation in Dutch business and general culture unique in early modern Europe. (See the feature "Individuals in Society: Glückel of Hameln.") For example, Benedict Spinoza (1632–1677), a descendant of Spanish Jews who fled the Inquisition, passed his entire life in Amsterdam, supporting himself as a lens grinder while producing important philosophical treatises. The urbanity of Dutch society allowed a rare degree of religious freedom. As long as business people conducted their religion in private, the government did not interfere with them.

In the Dutch Republic, toleration paid off: it attracted a great deal of foreign capital and investment. Deposits at the Bank of Amsterdam were guaranteed by the city council, and in the middle years of the century the bank became Europe's best source of cheap credit and commercial intelligence and the main clearing-house for bills of exchange. People of all races and creeds traded in Amsterdam, at whose docks on the Amstel River five thousand ships were berthed. Joost van den Vondel, the poet of Dutch imperialism, exulted:

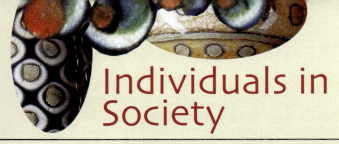

Individuals in Society

Glückel of Hameln

In 1690 a Jewish widow in the small German town of Hameln* in Lower Saxony sat down to write her autobiography. She wanted to distract her mind from the terrible grief she felt over the death of her husband and to provide her twelve children with a record "so you will know from what sort of people you have sprung, lest today or tomorrow your beloved children or grandchildren came and know naught of their family." Out of her pain and heightened consciousness, Glückel (1646–1724) produced an invaluable source for scholars.

She was born in Hamburg two years before the end of the Thirty Years' War. In 1649 the merchants of Hamburg expelled the Jews, who moved to nearby Altona, then under Danish rule. When the Swedes overran Altona in 1657–1658, the Jews returned to Hamburg "purely at the mercy of the Town Council." Glückel's narrative proceeds against a background of the constant harassment to which Jews were subjected—special papers, permits, bribes—and in Hameln she wrote, "And so it has been to this day and, I fear, will continue in like fashion."

When Glückel was "barely twelve," her father betrothed her to Chayim Hameln. She married at age fourteen. She describes him as "the perfect pattern of the pious Jew," a man who stopped his work every day for study and prayer, fasted, and was scrupulously honest in his business dealings. Only a few years older than Glückel, Chayim earned his living dealing in precious metals and in making small loans on pledges (articles held on security). This work required his constant travel to larger cities, markets, and fairs, often in bad weather, always over dangerous roads. Chayim consulted his wife about all his business dealings. As he lay dying, a friend asked if he had any last wishes. "None," he replied. "My wife knows everything. She shall do as she has always done." For thirty years Glückel had been his friend, full business partner, and wife. They had thirteen children, twelve of whom survived their father, eight then unmarried. As Chayim had foretold, Glückel succeeded in launching the boys in careers and in providing dowries for the girls.

Glückel's world was her family, the Jewish community of Hameln, and the Jewish communities into which her children married. Social and business activities took her to Amsterdam, Baiersdorf, Bamberg, Berlin, Cleves, Danzig, Metz, and Vienna, so her world was not narrow or provincial. She took great pride that Prince Frederick of Cleves, later king of Prussia, danced at the wedding of her eldest daughter. The rising prosperity of Chayim's businesses allowed the couple to maintain up to six servants.

Glückel was deeply religious, and her culture was steeped in Jewish literature, legends, and mystical and secular works. Above all, she relied on the Bible. Her language, heavily sprinkled with scriptural references, testifies to a rare familiarity with the basic book of Western civilization. The Scriptures were her consolation, the source of her great strength in a hostile world.

Gentleness and deep mutual devotion seem to pervade Rembrandt's The Jewish Bride. (Rijksmuseum-Stichting Amsterdam)

Students who would learn about business practices, the importance of the dowry in marriage, childbirth, the ceremony of bris, birthrates, family celebrations, and even the meaning of life can gain a good deal from the memoirs of this extraordinary woman who was, in the words of one of her descendants, the poet Heinrich Heine, "the gift of a world to me."

Questions for Analysis

1. Consider the ways in which Glückel of Hameln was both an ordinary and an extraordinary woman of her times. Would you call her a marginal or a central person in her society?
2. How was Glückel's life affected by the broad events and issues of the seventeenth century?

* A town immortalized by the Brothers Grimm. In 1284 the town contracted with the Pied Piper to rid it of rats and mice; he lured them away by playing his flute. When the citizens refused to pay, he charmed away their children in revenge.

Source: The Memoirs of Glückel of Hameln, (New York: Schocken Books, 1977).

Online Study Center Improve Your Grade
Going Beyond Individuals in Society

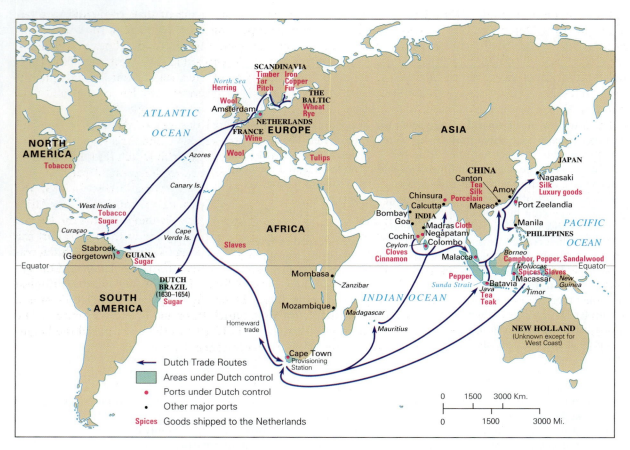

MAP 16.3 Seventeenth-Century Dutch Commerce Dutch wealth rested on commerce, and commerce depended on the huge Dutch merchant marine, manned by perhaps forty-eight thousand sailors. The fleet carried goods from all parts of the globe to the port of Amsterdam.

God, God, the Lord of Amstel cried, hold every conscience
   free;
And Liberty ride, on Holland's tide, with billowing sails
   to sea,
And run our Amstel out and in; let freedom gird the bold,
And merchant in his counting house stand elbow deep
   in gold.[18]

The fishing industry was the original cornerstone of the Dutch economy. For half the year, from June to December, fishing fleets combed the dangerous English coast and the North Sea and raked in tiny herring. Profits from herring stimulated shipbuilding, and even before 1600 the Dutch were offering the lowest shipping rates in Europe. The Dutch merchant marine was the largest in Europe. In 1650 contemporaries estimated that the Dutch had sixteen thousand merchant ships, half the Eu-

ropean total. All the wood for these ships had to be imported: the Dutch bought whole forests from Norway. They also bought entire vineyards from French growers before the grapes were harvested. They controlled the Baltic grain trade, buying entire wheat and rye crops in Poland, east Prussia, and Swedish Pomerania. Because the Dutch dealt in bulk, nobody could undersell them. Foreign merchants coming to Amsterdam could buy anything from precision lenses for the microscope (recently invented by Dutchman Anton van Leeuwenhoek) to muskets for an army of five thousand. Although Dutch cities became famous for their exports—diamonds and linens from Haarlem, pottery from Delft—Dutch wealth depended less on exports than on transport.

In 1602 a group of the regents of Holland formed the **Dutch East India Company,** a joint stock company. The investors each received a percentage of the profits proportional to the amount of money they had put in. Within half a century the Dutch East India Company had cut heavily into Portuguese trading in East Asia. The Dutch seized the Cape of Good Hope, Ceylon, and Malacca and established trading posts in each place. In the 1630s the Dutch East India Company was paying its investors about a 35 percent annual return on their investments. The Dutch West India Company, founded in 1621, traded extensively with Latin America and Africa (see Map 16.3).

Trade and commerce brought the Dutch prodigious wealth. In the seventeenth century the Dutch enjoyed the highest standard of living in Europe, perhaps in the world. Amsterdam and Rotterdam built massive granaries where the surplus of one year could be stored against possible shortages the next. Thus, except in the 1650s, when bad harvests reduced supplies, food prices fluctuated very little. By the standards of Cologne, Paris, or London, salaries were high for all workers—except women, but even women's wages were high when compared with those of women in other parts of Europe. All classes of society, including unskilled laborers, ate well.

The low price of bread meant that, compared to other places in Europe, a higher percentage of the worker's income could be spent on fish, cheese, butter, vegetables, and even meat. A scholar has described the Netherlands as "an island of plenty in a sea of want." Consequently, the Netherlands experienced very few of the food riots that characterized the rest of Europe.[19]

Although the initial purpose of the Dutch East and West India Companies was commercial—the import of spices and silks to Europe—the Dutch found themselves involved in the imperialist exploitation of parts of East Asia and Latin America, with great success. In 1652 the Dutch founded Cape Town on the southern tip of Africa as a fueling station for ships planning to cross the Pacific. But war with France and England in the 1670s hurt the United Provinces. The long War of the Spanish Succession—in which the Dutch prince William of Orange, who was King William III of England, utilized English wealth in the Dutch fight against Louis XIV—was a costly drain on Dutch labor and financial resources. The peace signed in 1713 to end the war marked the beginning of Dutch economic decline.

Chapter Summary

Online Study Center   **ACE the Test**

- *What were the common crises and achievements of seventeenth-century states?*
- *To what extent did French and Spanish monarchs succeed in creating absolute monarchies?*
- *What cultural forms flourished under absolutist governments?*
- *What is constitutionalism, and how did this form of government emerge in England and the Dutch Republic?*

Most parts of Europe experienced the seventeenth century as a period of severe economic, social, and military crisis. Across the continent, rulers faced popular rebellions from their desperate subjects, who were pushed to the brink by poor harvests, high taxes, and decades of war. Many forces, including powerful noblemen, the church, and regional and local loyalties, constrained the state's

authority. Despite these obstacles, most European states emerged from the seventeenth century with increased powers and more centralized control. Whether they ruled through monarchical fiat or parliamentary negotiation, European governments strengthened their bureaucracies, raised more taxes, and significantly expanded their armies.

According to Thomas Hobbes, the central drive in every human is "a perpetual and restless desire of Power, after Power, that ceaseth only in Death." The seventeenth century solved the problem of sovereign power in two fundamental ways: absolutism and constitutionalism. Under Louis XIV France witnessed the high point of absolutist ambition in western Europe. The king saw himself as the representative of God on earth, and it has been said that "to the seventeenth century imagination God was a sort of image of Louis XIV."[20] Under Louis's rule, France developed a centralized bureaucracy, a professional army, and a state-directed economy, all of which he personally supervised.

Despite his claims to absolute power, historians now agree that Louis XIV ruled, in practice, by securing the collaboration of high nobles. In exchange for confirmation of their ancient privileges, the nobles were willing to cooperate with the expansion of state power. This was a common pattern in attempts at absolutism across Europe. In Spain, where monarchs made similar claims to absolute power, the seventeenth century witnessed economic catastrophe and a decline in royal capacities. Spanish rule continued in the colonies and foreshadowed a revival of Spanish fortunes in the eighteenth century.

France's dominant political role in Europe elevated its cultural influence as well. French became the common language of the European elite, as all heads turned to Versailles and the radiant aristocratic culture emanating from it. Within France, the Bourbon monarchy pursued culture as one more aspect of absolutist policy, creating cultural academies, sponsoring playwrights and musicians, and repressing Protestantism with a bloody hand.

As Louis XIV personified absolutist ambitions, so Stuart England exemplified the evolution of the constitutional state. The conflicts between Parliament and the first two Stuart rulers, James I and Charles I, tested where sovereign power would reside. The resulting civil war did not solve the problem. The Instrument of Government provided for a balance of government authority and recognition of popular rights; as such, the Instrument has been called the first modern constitution. Unfortunately, it lacked public support. James II's absolutist tendencies brought on the Glorious Revolution of 1688 and 1689, and the people who made that revolution settled three basic issues: sovereign power was divided between king and Parliament, with Parliament enjoying the greater share; government was to be based on the rule of law; and the liberties of English people were made explicit in written form in the Bill of Rights.

Having won independence from Spain, the United Provinces of the Netherlands provided another model of constitutional government, one dominated by wealthy urban merchants rather than the landed gentry who controlled the English system. The federal constitution of the Netherlands invested power in the Estates General, but diluted their authority by giving veto power to provincial assemblies. Dominated by Holland, the Netherlands provided a shining example of industriousness, prosperity, and relative tolerance for the rest of Europe.

Key Terms

moral economy
sovereignty
popular revolts
Edict of Nantes
intendants
noblesse de robe
  (robe nobility)
Fronde
noblesse d'épée
  (sword nobility)
divine right of kings
absolute monarchy
mercantilism
estates
Peace of Utrecht
Don Quixote

viceroyalties
quinto
baroque
patronage
French classicism
constitutionalism
Puritans
New Model Army
Protectorate
Test Act
*Second Treatise of
  Civil Government*
States General
stadholder
Dutch East India
  Company

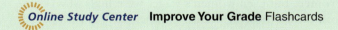

Online Study Center **Improve Your Grade** Flashcards

Suggested Reading

Beik, William. *Urban Protest in Seventeenth-Century France*. 1997. Explores urban violence in France during harsh years of economic and social crisis.

Benedict, Philip, and Myron P. Gutmann, eds. *Early Modern Europe: From Crisis to Stability*. 2005. A helpful introduction to the many facets of the seventeenth-century crisis.

Burke, Peter. *The Fabrication of Louis XIV*. 1992. Explains the use of architecture, art, medals, and other symbols to promote the king's image.

Collins, James B. *The State in Early Modern France*. 1995. A detailed and well-argued survey of French administration from Louis XIII to Louis XVI.

Elliott, John H. *Richelieu and Olivares*. 1984. A comparison of the chief ministers of France and Spain that also reveals differences and similarities in the countries they led.

Gaunt, Peter, ed. *The English Civil War: The Essential Readings*. 2000. A collection showcasing leading historians' interpretations of the civil war.

Hutton, Ronald. *Charles II: King of England, Scotland and Ireland*. 1989. A reliable and highly readable biography of King Charles II.

Israel, Jonathan. *The Dutch Republic: Its Rise, Greatness and Fall, 1477–1806*. 1995. A thorough study of the political history of the republic.

Kettering, Sharon. *Patronage in Sixteenth- and Seventeenth-Century France*. 2002. A collection of essays exploring the role of patronage in politics and noble life, including women's role in patronage networks.

Lynn, John A. *Giant of the Grand Siècle: The French Army, 1610–1715*. 1997. Examines the tremendous growth and professionalization of the French army under Louis XIV.

Pagden, Anthony. *Spanish Imperialism and the Political Imagination*. 1990. Explores Spanish ideas of empire, primarily in Italy and the Americas.

Schama, Simon. *The Embarrassment of Riches: An Interpretation of Dutch Culture in the Golden Age*. 1987. A lengthy but vivid and highly readable account of Dutch culture in the seventeenth century, including a chapter on the mania for speculation on the tulip market.

Te Brake, Wayne. *Shaping History: Ordinary People in European Politics, 1500–1700*. 1998. Examines the political activities of the non-elite in early modern Europe.

Underdown, David. *Revel, Riot, and Rebellion*. 1985. Discusses ordinary people's roles in the English civil war.

Wrightson, Keith. *English Society, 1580–1680*. 1982. Good coverage of English political and social issues of the seventeenth century.

Young, John, ed. *Celtic Dimensions of the British Civil Wars*. 1997. Explores Scotland and Ireland and their involvement in the civil wars in Great Britain.

Notes

1. The classic study Theodore K. Rabb, *The Struggle for Stability in Early Modern Europe* (Oxford: Oxford University Press, 1975).
2. John A. Lynn, "Recalculating French Army Growth," in *The Military Revolution Debate: Readings on the Military Transformation of Early Modern Europe*, ed. Clifford J. Rogers (Boulder, Colo.: Westview Press, 1995), p. 125.
3. G. Parker and L. M. Smith, "Introduction," and N. Steensgaard, "The Seventeenth Century Crisis," in *The General Crisis of the Seventeenth Century*, ed. G. Parker and L. M. Smith (London: Routledge & Kegan Paul, 1985), pp. 1–53, esp. p. 12.
4. H. G. Koenigsberger, "The Revolt of Palermo in 1647," *Cambridge Historical Journal* 8 (1944–1946): 129–144.
5. See W. Beik, *Urban Protest in Seventeenth-Century France: The Culture of Retribution* (New York: Cambridge University Press, 1997), p. 1.
6. Ibid.
7. See ibid., chaps. 1, 2, 3, and 11.
8. Ibid., pp. 22–26.
9. See M. Turchetti, "The Edict of Nantes," in *The Oxford Encyclopedia of the Reformation*, ed. H. J. Hillerbrand, vol. 3 (New York: Oxford University Press, 1996), pp. 126–128.
10. Quoted in J. H. Elliott, *Richelieu and Olivares* (Cambridge: Cambridge University Press, 1984), p. 135; and in W. F. Church, *Richelieu and Reason of State* (Princeton, N.J.: Princeton University Press, 1972), p. 507.
11. James B. Collins, *The State in Early Modern France* (Cambridge: Cambridge University Press, 1995), pp. 65–78.
12. Quoted in J. Wolf, *Louis XIV* (New York: W. W. Norton, 1968), p. 146.
13. Ibid.
14. J. H. Elliott, *Imperial Spain, 1469–1716* (New York: Mentor Books, 1963), pp. 306–308.
15. B. Bennassar, *The Spanish Character: Attitudes and Mentalities from the Sixteenth to the Nineteenth Century*, trans. B. Keen (Berkeley: University of California Press, 1979), p. 125.
16. For a revisionist interpretation, see J. Wormald, "James VI and I: Two Kings or One?" *History* 62 (June 1983): 187–209.
17. C. Stephenson and G. F. Marcham, *Sources of English Constitutional History* (New York: Harper & Row, 1937), p. 601.
18. Quoted in D. Maland, *Europe in the Seventeenth Century* (New York: Macmillan, 1967), pp. 198–199. Copyright © 1967 by A & C Black Ltd.
19. S. Schama, *The Embarrassment of Riches: An Interpretation of Dutch Culture in the Golden Age* (New York: Alfred A. Knopf, 1987), pp. 165–170; quotation is on p. 167.
20. C. J. Friedrich and C. Blitzer, *The Age of Power* (Ithaca, N.Y.: Cornell University Press, 1957), p. 112.

The Court at Versailles

Although the duke of Saint-Simon (1675–1755) was a soldier, courtier, and diplomat, his enduring reputation rests on The Memoirs *(1788), his eyewitness account of the personality and court of Louis XIV. A nobleman of extremely high status, Saint-Simon resented Louis's high-handed treatment of the ancient nobility and his promotion of newer nobles and the bourgeoisie.* The Memoirs, *excerpted here, remains a monument of French literature and an indispensable historical source, partly for its portrait of the court at Versailles.*

Very early in the reign of Louis XIV the Court was removed from Paris, never to return. The troubles of the minority had given him a dislike to that city; his enforced and surreptitious flight from it still rankled in his memory; he did not consider himself safe there, and thought cabals would be more easily detected if the Court was in the country, where the movements and temporary absences of any of its members would be more easily noticed. . . . No doubt that he was also influenced by the feeling that he would be regarded with greater awe and veneration when no longer exposed every day to the gaze of the multitude.

His love-affair with Mademoiselle de la Vallière, which at first was covered as far as possible with a veil of mystery, was the cause of frequent excursions to Versailles. . . . The visits of Louis XIV becoming more frequent, he enlarged the *château* by degrees till its immense buildings afforded better accommodation for the Court than was to be found at St. Germain, where most of the courtiers had to put up with uncomfortable lodgings in the town. The Court was therefore removed to Versailles in 1682, not long before the Queen's death. The new building contained an infinite number of rooms for courtiers, and the King liked the grant of these rooms to be regarded as a coveted privilege.

He availed himself of the frequent festivities at Versailles, and his excursions to other places, as a means of making the courtiers assiduous in their attendance and anxious to please him; for he nominated beforehand those who were to take part in them, and could thus gratify some and inflict a snub on others. He was conscious that the substantial favours he had to bestow were not nearly sufficient to produce a continual effect; he had therefore to invent imaginary ones, and no one was so clever in devising petty distinctions and preferences which aroused jealousy and emulation. The visits to Marly later on were very useful to him in this way; also those to Trianon [Marly and Trianon were small country houses], where certain ladies, chosen beforehand, were admitted to his table. It was another distinction to hold his candlestick at his *coucher;* as soon as he had finished his prayers he used to name the courtier to whom it was to be handed, always choosing one of the highest rank among those present. . . .

Not only did he expect all persons of distinction to be in continual attendance at Court, but he was quick to notice the absence of those of inferior degree; at his *lever* [formal rising from bed in the morning], his *coucher* [preparations for going to bed], his meals, in the gardens of Versailles (the only place where the courtiers in general were allowed to follow him), he used to cast his eyes to right and left; nothing escaped him, he saw everybody. If any one habitually living at Court absented himself he insisted on knowing the reason; those who came there only for flying visits had also to give a satisfactory explanation; any one who seldom or never appeared there was certain to incur his displeasure. If asked to bestow a favour on such persons he would reply haughtily: "I do not know him"; of such as rarely presented themselves he would say, "He is a man I never see"; and from these judgements there was no appeal.

He always took great pains to find out what was going on in public places, in society, in private houses, even family secrets, and maintained an immense number of spies and tale-bearers. These were of all sorts; some did not know that their reports were carried to him; others did know it; there were others, again, who used to write to him directly, through channels which he prescribed; others who were admitted by the backstairs and saw him in his private room. Many a man in all ranks of life was ruined by these methods, often very unjustly, without ever being able to discover the reason; and when the King had once taken a prejudice against a man, he hardly ever got over it. . . .

No one understood better than Louis XIV the art of enhancing the value of a favour by his manner of bestowing it; he knew how to make the most of a word, a smile, even of a glance. If he addressed any one, were it but to ask a trifling question or make some commonplace remark, all eyes were turned on the person so honored; it was a mark of favour which always gave rise to comment. . . .

He loved splendour, magnificence, and profusion in all things, and encouraged similar tastes in his Court; to spend money freely on equipages [the king's horse carriages] and buildings, on feasting and at cards, was a sure way to gain his favour, perhaps to obtain the honour of a word from him. Motives of policy had something to do with this; by making expensive habits the fashion, and, for people in a certain position, a necessity, he compelled his courtiers to live beyond their income, and gradually reduced them to depend on his bounty for the means of subsistence. This was a plague which, once introduced, became a scourge to the whole country, for it did not take long to spread to Paris, and thence to the armies and the provinces; so that a man of any position is now estimated entirely according to his expenditure on his table and other luxuries. This folly, sustained by pride and ostentation, has already produced widespread confusion; it threatens to end in nothing short of ruin and a general overthrow.

Louis XIV was extremely proud of the gardens at Versailles and personally led ambassadors and other highly ranked visitors on tours of the extensive palace grounds. *(Erich Lessing/Art Resource, NY)*

Questions for Analysis

1. What was the role of etiquette and ceremony at the court of Versailles? How could Louis XIV use them in everyday life at court to influence and control nobles?

2. How important do you think Louis's individual character and personality were to his style of governing? What challenges might this present to his successors?

3. Consider the role of ceremony in some modern governments, such as the U.S. government. How does it compare to Louis XIV's use of ceremony as portrayed by Saint-Simon?

4. Do you think Saint-Simon is an objective and trustworthy recorder of life at court? Why?

Source: F. Arkwright, ed., *The Memoirs of the Duke de Saint-Simon,* vol. 5 (New York: Brentano's, n.d.), pp. 271–274, 276–278.

Peter the Great's magnificent new crown, created for his joint coronation in 1682 with his half-brother Ivan. *(State Museum of the Kremlin, Moscow)*

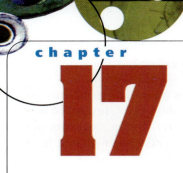

chapter preview

Warfare and Social Change in Central and Eastern Europe

• *What social and economic changes affected central and eastern Europe from 1400 to 1650?*

The Rise of Austria and Prussia

• *How and why did the rulers of Austria and Prussia, each in different political and social environments, manage to build powerful absolute monarchies that proved more durable than that of Louis XIV?*

The Development of Russia and the Ottoman Empire

• *What were the distinctive features of Russian and Ottoman absolutism in this period?*

ABSOLUTISM IN CENTRAL AND EASTERN EUROPE
TO 1740

The crises of the seventeenth century—religious division, economic depression, and war—were not limited to the West. Central and eastern Europe experienced even more catastrophic dislocation, with German lands serving as the battleground of the Thirty Years' War and borders constantly vulnerable to attack from the east. In Prussia and Habsburg Austria absolutist states emerged in the aftermath of this conflict.

Russia and the Ottoman Turks also developed absolutist governments. These empires seemed foreign and exotic to western Europeans, who saw them as the antithesis of their political, religious, and cultural values. To Western eyes, their monarchs respected law—either divine or constitutional—while Eastern despots ruled with an iron fist. The Ottoman Muslim state was home to fanaticism and heresy, and even Russian Orthodoxy had rituals and traditions, if not core beliefs, that differed sharply from either Catholicism or Protestantism. Beneath the surface, however, these Eastern governments shared many similarities with Western ones.

The most successful Eastern empires lasted until 1918, far longer than monarchical rule endured in France, the model of absolutism under Louis XIV. Eastern monarchs had a powerful impact on architecture and the arts, encouraging new monumental construction to reflect their glory. Questions about the relationship between East and West remain potent today, when Turkey's bid for membership in the European Union is controversial both at home and abroad.

Warfare and Social Change in Central and Eastern Europe

When absolute monarchy emerged in the seventeenth century, it built on social and economic foundations laid between roughly 1400 and 1650. In those years the elites of eastern Europe—with the major exception of the Ottoman rulers in the Balkans—rolled back the gains made by the peasantry during the High Middle Ages and re-imposed a harsh serfdom on the rural masses. The nobility also reduced the importance of the

Online Study Center

This icon will direct you to interactive activities and study materials on the website **college.hmco.com/pic/mckaywest9e**

towns and the middle classes. This process differed from developments in western Europe, where peasants won greater freedom and the urban middle class continued its rise. The Thirty Years' War represented the culmination of these changes. Decades of war in central Europe led to depopulation and economic depression, which allowed lords to impose ever-harsher controls on the peasantry.

• *What social and economic changes affected central and eastern Europe from 1400 to 1650?*

Origins of Serfdom

The period from 1050 to 1300 was a time of general economic expansion in eastern Europe characterized by the growth of trade, towns, and population. This meant clearing the forests and colonizing the frontier beyond the Elbe River. Eager to attract settlers to sparsely populated lands, the rulers of eastern Europe offered newcomers economic and legal incentives, providing land on excellent terms and granting greater personal freedom. These benefits were also gradually extended to the local Slavic populations, even those of central Russia. Thus, by 1300 **serfdom** had all but disappeared in eastern Europe. Peasants bargained freely with their landlords and moved about as they pleased. Opportunities and improvements in the East had a positive impact on the West, where the weight of serfdom was also reduced between 1100 and 1300. Thus fundamental social and economic developments moved in tandem across Europe in the High Middle Ages.

After about 1300, however, as Europe's population and economy declined grievously, mostly as a result of the Black Death, East and West parted paths. Across Europe, lords sought to solve their economic problems by more heavily exploiting the peasantry. This reaction generally failed in the West, where by 1500 almost all peasants were free or had their serf obligations greatly reduced. East of the Elbe, however, the landlords won.

Eastern landlords successfully used their political and police power against the peasantry in two ways. First, they restricted or eliminated the peasants' time-honored right of freedom of movement. Thus a peasant could no longer leave the land without his lord's permission, and the lord had no reason to make such concessions. In Prussian territories by 1500 the law required that runaway peasants be hunted down and returned to their lords. Until the mid-fifteenth century, medieval Russian peasants were free to move wherever they wished. Thereafter this freedom was gradually curtailed, so that by 1497 a Russian peasant had the right to move only during a two-week period after the fall harvest. Eastern peasants were losing their status as free and independent men and women.

Second, lords steadily took more of their peasants' land and imposed heavier labor obligations. Instead of being independent farmers paying freely negotiated rents, peasants became forced laborers on the lords' estates. By the early 1500s, lords in many territories could command their peasants to work without pay as many as six days a week.

The gradual erosion of the peasantry's economic position was bound up with manipulation of the legal system. The local lord was also the local prosecutor, judge, and jailer. There were no independent royal officials to provide justice or uphold the common law, allowing lords to rule in their own favor in disputes with peasants.

The Consolidation of Serfdom

Between 1500 and 1650 the social, legal, and economic conditions of peasants in eastern Europe continued to decline, and free peasants became serfs. In Poland nobles gained complete control over their peasants in 1574, after which they could legally inflict the death penalty whenever they wished. In Prussia in 1653 peasants were assumed to be tied to their lords in **hereditary subjugation**—bound to their lords and the land from one generation to the next. In Russia peasants' right to move from an estate was permanently abolished in 1603. In 1649 the tsar lifted the nine-year time limit on the recovery of runaways and eliminated all limits on lords' authority over their peasants. Although political development in the various Eastern states differed, the legal re-establishment of permanent hereditary serfdom was the common fate of Eastern peasants by the mid-seventeenth century.

The consolidation of serfdom accompanied the growth of estate agriculture, particularly in Poland and eastern Germany. In the sixteenth century European economic expansion and population growth resumed after the great declines of the late Middle Ages. Prices for agricultural commodities also rose sharply as gold and silver flowed in from the New World. Thus Polish and German lords had powerful economic incentives to increase the production of their estates. And they did. Lords seized more peasant land for their own estates and then demanded more unpaid labor on those enlarged estates. Though the estates were generally inefficient and technically backward, the great Polish nobles and middle-rank German lords squeezed sizable profits from their impoverished peasants. Surpluses in wheat and timber were sold to foreign merchants, who exported them to the growing cities of the West. Thus the poor East helped feed the wealthier West.

The re-emergence of serfdom in eastern Europe cannot be explained by economic factors alone. Western Europe experienced similar agricultural and population decline in the fourteenth and fifteenth centuries, but its peasants won better rather than harsher conditions. It seems likely that political, rather than economic, factors were crucial. Eastern lords enjoyed much greater political power than did their Western counterparts. In the late Middle Ages central and eastern Europe experienced innumerable wars and general political chaos, which allowed noble landlords to increase their political power. There were, for example, many disputed royal successions, so that weak kings were forced to grant political

Estonia in the 1660s The Estonians were conquered by German military nobility in the Middle Ages and reduced to serfdom. The German-speaking nobles ruled the Estonian peasants with an iron hand, and Peter the Great reaffirmed their domination when Russia annexed Estonia (see Map 17.3 on page 573). *(Mansell Collection/Time Life Pictures/Getty Images)*

Chronology

ca 1400–1650	Re-emergence of serfdom in eastern Europe
1462–1505	Reign of Ivan III in Russia
1533–1584	Reign of Ivan the Terrible in Russia
1620	Habsburgs crush Protestantism in Bohemia
1620–1740	Growth of absolutism in Austria and Prussia
1640–1688	Reign of Frederick William in Prussia
1652	Nikon reforms Russian Orthodox Church
1670–1671	Cossack revolt led by Razin
ca 1680–1750	Construction of palaces by absolutist rulers
1683–1718	Habsburgs defend Vienna, win war with Ottoman Turks
1702	Peter the Great founds St. Petersburg
1713–1740	Growth of Prussian military

favors to win the nobility's support. Thus while strong monarchs and effective central government were rising in Spain, France, and England, kings were generally losing power in the East and could not resist the demands of lords regarding peasants.

Moreover, most Eastern monarchs did not oppose the growth of serfdom. The typical king was only first among noble equals. He, too, wanted to squeeze his peasants. The Western concept of sovereignty, as embodied in a king who protected the interests of all his people, was not well developed in eastern Europe before 1650.

It was not only the peasants who suffered. Also with the approval of kings, landlords systematically undermined the medieval privileges of the towns and the power of the urban classes. Instead of selling products to local merchants, landlords sold directly to foreigners. For example, Dutch ships sailed up the rivers of Poland and eastern Germany to the loading docks of the great estates, completely bypassing the local towns. Moreover, "town air" no longer "made people free," for the Eastern towns had lost their medieval right of refuge and were now compelled to return runaways to their lords. The population of the towns and the importance of the urban middle classes declined greatly.

The Thirty Years' War

The Holy Roman Empire was a confederation of hundreds of principalities, independent cities, duchies, and other polities loosely united under an elected emperor. An uneasy truce had prevailed in the Holy Roman Empire since the Peace of Augsburg of 1555 (see page 459). According to the settlement, the faith of the prince determined the religion of his subjects. Later in the century, however, Catholics grew alarmed because Lutherans, in violation of the Peace of Augsburg, were steadily acquiring German bishoprics. The spread of Calvinism further confused the issue: the Augsburg settlement had pertained only to Lutheranism and Catholicism, so Calvinists ignored it and converted several princes. Also, the militantly active Jesuits had reconverted several Lutheran princes to Catholicism. Lutherans feared that the Augsburg principles would be undermined by Catholic and Calvinist gains. Lutheran princes felt compelled to form the **Protestant Union** (1608), and Catholics retaliated with the Catholic League (1609). Each alliance was determined that the other should make no religious or territorial advance. Dynastic interests were also involved; the Spanish Habsburgs strongly supported the goals of their Austrian relatives—the unity of the empire and the preservation of Catholicism within it.

Violence erupted in 1617 when Ferdinand of Styria, the new Catholic king in Bohemia, closed some Protestant churches. On May 23, 1618, Protestants hurled two of Ferdinand's officials from a castle window in Prague. They fell seventy feet but survived: Catholics claimed that angels had caught them; Protestants said that the officials had fallen on a heap of soft horse manure. Called the "defenestration of Prague," this event marked the beginning of the Thirty Years' War (1618–1648).

The war is traditionally divided into four phases. The first, or Bohemian, phase (1618–1625) was characterized by civil war in Bohemia between the Catholic League, led by Ferdinand, and the Protestant Union, headed by Frederick, the elector of the Palatinate. The Bohemians fought for religious liberty and independence from Habsburg rule. In 1620 Catholic forces defeated Frederick at the Battle of the White Mountain. Ferdinand, who had recently been elected Holy Roman emperor as Ferdinand II, followed up his victories by wiping out Protestantism in Bohemia through forcible conversions and Jesuit missionary work. Within ten years Bohemia was completely Catholic.

The second, or Danish, phase of the war (1625–1629)—so called because of the leadership of the Protestant king Christian IV of Denmark (r. 1588–1648)—

witnessed additional Catholic victories. The Catholic imperial army led by Albert of Wallenstein swept through Silesia, north to the Baltic, and east into Pomerania, scoring smashing victories. Wallenstein, an unscrupulous opportunist who used his vast riches to build an army loyal only to himself, seemed interested more in carving out his own empire than in aiding the Catholic cause. He quarreled with the Catholic League, and soon the Catholic forces were divided. Religion was eclipsed as a basic issue of the war.

Habsburg power peaked in 1629. The emperor issued the Edict of Restitution, whereby all Catholic properties lost to Protestantism since 1552 were restored, and only Catholics and Lutherans were allowed to practice their faiths. When Wallenstein began ruthless enforcement, Protestants throughout Europe feared the collapse of the balance of power in north-central Europe.

The third, or Swedish, phase of the war (1630–1635) began with the arrival in Germany of the Swedish king Gustavus Adolphus (r. 1594–1632). The ablest administrator of his day and a devout Lutheran, he intervened to support the empire's oppressed Protestants. Cardinal Richelieu, chief minister of King Louis XIII of France (r. 1610–1643), subsidized the Swedes, hoping to weaken Habsburg power in Europe. In 1631, with a small but well-disciplined army equipped with superior muskets, Gustavus Adolphus won a brilliant victory at Breitenfeld. Again in 1632 he was victorious at Lützen, though he was fatally wounded in the battle.

The participation of the Swedes in the Thirty Years' War proved decisive for the future of Protestantism and German history. When Gustavus Adolphus landed on German soil, he headed a Baltic empire under Swedish influence. The Swedish victories ended the Habsburg ambition to unite the German states under imperial authority.

Gustavus Adolphus's death in 1632, followed by the Swedes' defeat at the Battle of Nördlingen in 1634, prompted the French to enter the war on the Protestant side, beginning the French, or international, phase of the Thirty Years' War (1635–1648). For almost a century French foreign policy was based on opposition to the Habsburgs because a weak empire enhanced France's international stature. In 1635 Cardinal Richelieu declared war on Spain and again sent financial and military assistance to the Swedes and the German Protestant princes. The war dragged on. The French, Dutch, and Swedes, supported by Scots, Finns, and German mercenaries, burned, looted, and destroyed German agriculture and commerce. The Thirty Years' War lasted so long because neither side had the resources to win a quick, decisive victory. Finally, in October 1648 peace was achieved.

Soldiers Pillage a Farmhouse Billeting troops among civilian populations caused untold hardships. In this late-seventeenth-century Dutch illustration, brawling soldiers take over a peasant's home, eat his food, steal his possessions, and insult his family. Peasant retaliation sometimes proved swift and bloody. (*Rijksmuseum-Stichting Amsterdam*)

Consequences of the Thirty Years' War

The 1648 **Peace of Westphalia** that ended the Thirty Years' War marked a turning point in European history. Conflicts fought over religious faith ended. The treaties recognized the sovereign, independent authority of more than three hundred German princes (see Map 17.1). Since the time of Holy Roman Emperor Frederick II (1194–1250) , Germany had followed a pattern of state-building different from that of France and England: the emperor shared authority with the princes. After the Peace of Westphalia, the emperors' power continued to be severely limited, and the Holy Roman Empire remained a loosely knit federation.

The peace agreement acknowledged the independence of the United Provinces of the Netherlands. France acquired the province of Alsace along with the advantages of the weakened status of the empire. Sweden received a large cash indemnity and jurisdiction over German territories along the Baltic Sea, leaving it as a major threat to

the future kingdom of Brandenburg-Prussia. The agreement also denied the papacy the right to participate in central European religious affairs—a restriction symbolizing the reduced political role of the church. In religion, the Peace of Westphalia made the Augsburg agreement of 1555 permanent, with the sole modification that Calvinism, along with Catholicism and Lutheranism, would be a legally permissible creed. The north German states remained Protestant, the south German states Catholic.

The Thirty Years' War was probably the most destructive event for the central European economy and society prior to the twentieth century. Perhaps one-third of urban residents and two-fifths of the rural population died. Entire areas were depopulated by warfare, by the flight of refugees, and by disease. Typhus, dysentery, bubonic plague, and syphilis accompanied the movements of armies.

Because the Thirty Years' War was fought on German soil, the empire experienced untold losses in agricultural land, livestock, trade, and commerce. The trade of south-

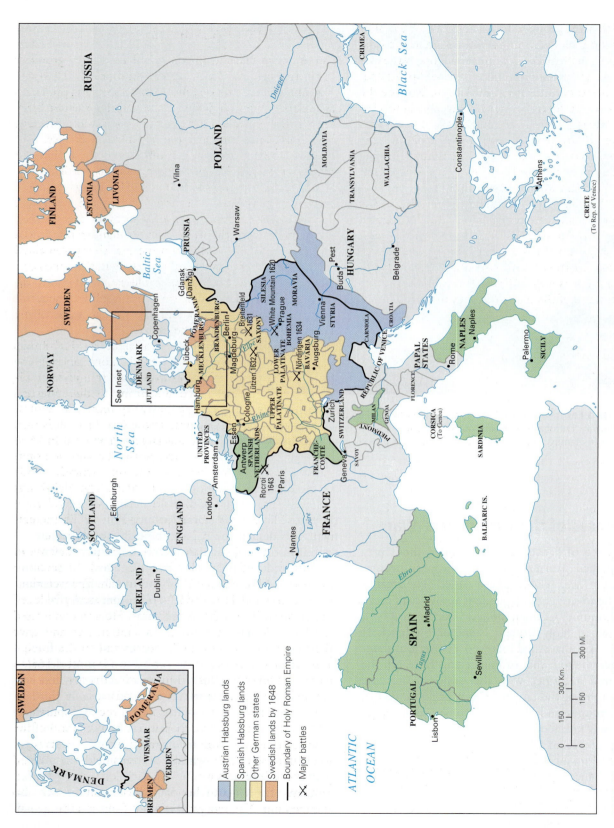

MAP 17.1 Europe After the Thirty Years' War Which country emerged from the Thirty Years' War as the strongest European power? What dynastic house was that country's major rival in the early modern period?

Online Study Center **Improve Your Grade** Interactive Map: Europe During Thirty Years' War

ern cities such as Augsburg, already hard hit by the shift in transportation routes from the Mediterranean to the Atlantic, was virtually destroyed. All of Europe was experiencing severe inflation due to the influx of Spanish silver, but the destruction of land and foodstuffs made the price rise worse in central Europe than anywhere else. Agricultural areas suffered catastrophically. Many small farmers lacked the revenue to rework their holdings and had to become day laborers. In parts of central Europe, especially in areas east of the Elbe River, loss of land contributed to the consolidation of serfdom.[1]

Although the Thirty Years' War contributed to the legal and economic decline of the majority of the population, some people prospered. Nobles and landlords bought the land of failed small farmers, thereby acquiring even greater estates. Northern towns such as Lübeck, Hamburg, and Bremen as well as Essen in the Ruhr area also prospered because of the many refugees they attracted.

The Rise of Austria and Prussia

Serfdom and the Thirty Years' War aided Eastern rulers greatly in their attempts to build absolute monarchies. These rulers not only fought one another but also battled with armies of invaders from Asia. In this atmosphere of continual wartime emergency, monarchs were able to increase the powers of the central state. In exchange for leaving nobles the unchallenged masters of their peasants, the would-be absolutist monarchs of central and eastern Europe gradually gained political power in three key areas. First, they imposed permanent taxes without consent. Second, they maintained permanent standing armies to police the country and fight abroad. Third, they conducted relations with other states as they pleased.

As with all general historical developments, there were important variations on the absolutist theme in eastern Europe. Royal **absolutism** in Prussia was stronger and more effective than in Austria. This would give Prussia a thin edge in the struggle for power in east-central Europe in the eighteenth century. Prussian-style absolutism had great long-term political significance, for it was a rising Prussia that unified the German people in the nineteenth century and imposed on them a militaristic stamp.

• *How and why did the rulers of Austria and Prussia, each in different political and social environments, manage to build powerful absolute monarchies that proved more durable than that of Louis XIV?*

The Austrian Habsburgs

The Austrian Habsburgs controlled a scattered group of territories in central and eastern Europe. By 1618 the Habsburg realm included the German-speaking provinces of Austria, Tyrol, and Styria; the Czech-speaking kingdom of Bohemia; and parts of the kingdom of Hungary. Habsburg lands encompassed different languages, ethnicities, and religious affiliations; some lay within the Holy Roman Empire and some beyond its borders.

Like all of central Europe, the Habsburgs emerged from the Thirty Years' War impoverished and exhausted. Their efforts to destroy Protestantism in the German lands and to turn the weak Holy Roman Empire into a real state had failed. Although the Habsburgs remained the hereditary emperors, real power lay in the hands of a bewildering variety of separate political jurisdictions, including independent cities, small principalities, medium-size states such as Bavaria and Saxony, and some of the territories of Prussia and the Habsburgs.

Defeat in central Europe encouraged the Habsburgs to turn away from a quest for imperial dominance and to focus inward and eastward in an attempt to unify their diverse holdings. An important step in this direction had occurred in Bohemia during the Thirty Years' War. Protestantism had been strong among the Czechs in Bohemia. The lesser Czech nobility was largely Protestant in 1600 and had considerable political power because it dominated the **Bohemian Estates**—the representative body of the different estates, or legal orders. The Habsburgs believed that religious diversity fatally weakened royal power. If they could not impose Catholicism in the empire, at least they could do so in their own domains.

In 1618 the Bohemian Estates rose up in defense of Protestant rights. The Habsburgs crushed the revolt in 1620 at the Battle of the White Mountain. The victorious king, Ferdinand II (r. 1619–1637), drastically reduced the power of the Bohemian Estates. He also confiscated the landholdings of many Protestant nobles and gave them to a few loyal Catholic nobles and to the foreign aristocratic mercenaries who led his armies. After 1650 a large portion of the Bohemian nobility was of recent origin and owed everything to the Habsburgs.

With the help of this new nobility, the Habsburgs established direct rule over Bohemia. The condition of the enserfed peasantry worsened substantially: three days per week of unpaid labor—the *robot*—became the norm, and a quarter of the serfs worked for their lords every day but Sundays and religious holidays. Protestantism was also stamped out. The reorganization of Bohemia was a giant

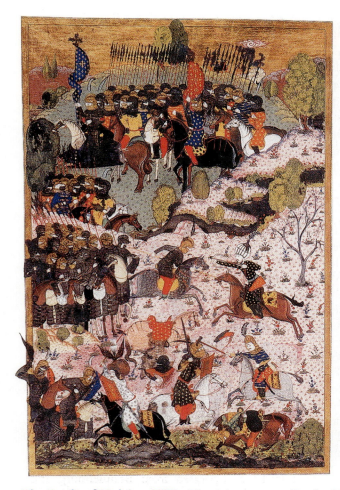

The Battle of Mohács, 1526   The *Süleymanname* (Book of Suleiman), a biography, contains these fascinating illustrations of the great Ottoman victory at Mohács, which enabled the Turks to add Hungary to their expanding empire. In the right panel, Suleiman in a white turban sits on a black horse surrounded by his personal guard, while his janissary soldiers fire their muskets and cannon at the enemy. In the left panel, the Europeans are in disarray, in contrast to the Turks' discipline and order. *(Topkapi Saray Museum)*

step toward creating absolutist rule. As in France in the same years, the pursuit of religious unity was an essential element of absolutism.

After the Thirty Years' War, Ferdinand III (r. 1637–1657) continued to build state power. He centralized the government in the hereditary German-speaking provinces, which formed the core Habsburg holdings. For the first time, a permanent standing army was ready to put down any internal opposition.

Austrian Rule in Hungary

The Habsburg monarchy then turned toward the plains of Hungary. After the **Battle of Mohács** in 1526, the kingdom of Hungary was divided between the Ottomans and the Habsburgs. Transylvania in the east became an Ottoman dependent, while the Habsburgs ruled the west and north. In the 1540s the Ottomans organized their Hungarian territories into provinces of the empire. Warfare between the Ottomans and the Habsburgs devastated Hungary during the sixteenth century. Between 1683 and 1699 the Habsburgs pushed the Ottomans from most of Hungary and Transylvania. The recovery of all of the former kingdom of Hungary was completed in 1718.

The Hungarian nobility, despite its reduced strength, effectively thwarted the full development of Habsburg absolutism. Throughout the seventeenth century Hungarian nobles—the most numerous in Europe—rose in revolt against attempts to impose absolute rule. They never triumphed decisively, but neither were they crushed the way the Czech nobility had been in 1620.

The Hungarians resisted because many of them remained Protestants, especially in areas formerly ruled by the Turks. Ottoman rule had been relatively light-handed compared to the harsh reconversion efforts of the Habsburgs. Until the end of the seventeenth century the Ottomans still ruled parts of Hungary, providing a powerful military ally to nobles in areas recovered by the Habsburgs. Finally, the Hungarian nobility, and even part of the peasantry, became attached to a national ideal long before most of the other peoples of eastern Europe. Hungarian nobles were determined to maintain as much independence and local control as possible. In 1703, with the Habsburgs bogged down in the War of the Spanish Succession (see page 534), the Hungarians rose in one last patriotic rebellion under Prince Francis Rákóczy.

Rákóczy and his forces were eventually defeated, but the Habsburgs had to accept a compromise. Charles VI restored many of the traditional privileges of the aristocracy in return for Hungarian acceptance of hereditary Habsburg rule. Thus Hungary, unlike Austria and Bohemia, was never fully integrated into a centralized, absolute Habsburg state.

Despite checks on their ambitions in Hungary, the Habsburgs made significant achievements in state-building by forging consensus with the church and the nobility. A sense of common identity and loyalty to the monarchy grew among elites in Habsburg lands, even to a certain extent in Hungary. The best evidence for this consensus is the spectacular sums approved by the estates for the growth of the army. By the end of the seventeenth century Emperor Leopold commanded a standing army of a hundred thousand men funded by contributions from the provincial estates. German became the language of the common culture and, with ongoing Protestant conversion and emigration, zealous Catholicism also helped fuse a collective identity. Vienna became the political and cultural center of the empire. By 1700 it was a thriving city with a population of one hundred thousand, with its own version of Versailles, the royal palace of Schönbrunn. (See the feature "Images in Society: Absolutist Palace Building" on pages 568–569.)

Empowered by the imperial government, the landed nobility took charge of economic recovery. The nobles increased the burdens of serfdom and profited from the war's population losses to take over vast tracts of land. With technical and commercial innovations, they created a new form of capitalist, market-oriented agriculture, which allowed them to increase their holdings even more at the expense of smaller landowners.

In 1713 Charles VI (r. 1711–1740) proclaimed the so-called **Pragmatic Sanction,** which stated that Habsburg possessions were never to be divided, even if it meant allowing a woman to take the throne. Lacking a male heir, Charles spent much of his reign trying to get this principle accepted within and beyond his realm. His success resulted in the crowning of his daughter Maria Theresa upon Charles's death in 1740.

Prussia in the Seventeenth Century

After 1400 a revitalized landed nobility became the undisputed ruling class in eastern Germany. The Hohenzollern family, which ruled through its senior and junior branches as the imperial electors of Brandenburg and the dukes of Prussia, had little real power. Nothing suggested that this family and its territories would ever play an important role in European or even regional affairs. The **elector of Brandenburg** had the right to help choose the Holy Roman emperor, which bestowed prestige, but the elector had no military strength of his own. Moreover, Brandenburg, the area around Berlin and the elector's power base, was a land-locked combination of sand and swamp (see Map 17.2) that lacked defensible natural frontiers. Contemporaries contemptuously called it the "sand-box of the Holy Roman Empire."[2]

The territory of the elector's cousin, the duke of Prussia, was completely separated from Brandenburg and was part of the kingdom of Poland. By 1600 Prussia's German-speaking peasants had much in common with Polish peasants, for both ethnic groups had seen most of their freedoms reduced or revoked by their noble landlords. (Poland's numerous lesser nobles dominated the Polish state, which was actually a constitutional republic headed by an elected king who had little real power.) In 1618 the junior branch of the Hohenzollern family died out, and Prussia reverted to the elector of Brandenburg.

The elector of Brandenburg was a helpless spectator in the Thirty Years' War, his territories alternately ravaged by Swedish and Habsburg armies. Population fell drastically, and many villages disappeared. Yet this devastation paved the way for Hohenzollern absolutism because foreign armies dramatically weakened the political power of the estates, which helped the very young elector Frederick William (r. 1640–1688), later known as the "Great Elector," to ride roughshod over traditional representative rights and to take a giant step toward royal absolutism. This constitutional struggle was the most crucial in Prussian history until that of the 1860s.

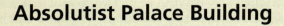

Absolutist Palace Building

By 1700 palace building had become a veritable obsession for the rulers of central and eastern Europe. Their dramatic palaces symbolized the age of absolutist power, just as soaring Gothic cathedrals had expressed the idealized spirit of the High Middle Ages. With its classically harmonious, symmetrical, and geometric design, Versailles, shown in Image 1, served as the model for the wave of palace building that began in the last decade of the seventeenth century.

Located ten miles southwest of Paris, Versailles began as a modest hunting lodge built by Louis XIII in 1623. His son, Louis XIV, loved the site so much that he spent decades enlarging and decorating the original chateau. Between 1668 and 1670, his architect Louis Le Vau enveloped the old building within a much larger second structure that still exists today. In 1682 the new palace became the official residence of the Sun King and his court, although construction continued until 1710, when the royal chapel was completed. At any one time, several thousand people lived in the bustling and crowded palace. The awesome splendor of the eighty-yard Hall of Mirrors, replete with floor-to-ceiling mirrors and ceiling murals illustrating the king's triumphs, contrasted with the strong odors from the courtiers who commonly relieved themselves in discreet corners. Royal palaces like Versailles were intended to overawe the people and proclaim their owners' authority and power.

In 1693 Charles XI of Sweden, having reduced the power of the aristocracy, ordered the construction of his Royal Palace, which dominates the center of Stockholm to this day. Another such palace was Schönbrunn, an enormous Viennese Versailles begun in 1695 by Emperor Leopold to celebrate Austrian military victories and Habsburg might. Image 2 shows architect Joseph Bernhard Fischer von Erlach's ambitious plan for Schönbrunn palace. Erlach's plan emphasizes the palace's vast size and its role as a site for military demonstrations. Ultimately financial constraints resulted in a more modest building.

Petty German princes contributed mightily to the palace-building mania. Frederick the Great of Prussia noted that every descendant of a princely family "imagines himself to be something like Louis XIV. He builds his Versailles, has his mistresses, and maintains his army."* The elector-archbishop of Mainz, the ruling prince of that city, confessed apologetically that "building is a craze which costs much, but every fool likes his own hat."†

In central and eastern Europe, the favorite noble servants of royalty became extremely rich and powerful, and they too built grandiose palaces in the capital cities. These palaces were in part an extension of the monarch, for they surpassed the buildings of less-favored nobles and showed all the high road to fame and fortune. Take, for example, the palaces of Prince Eugene of Savoy, a French nobleman who became Austria's most famous military hero. It was Eugene who led the Austrian army, smashed the Turks, fought Louis XIV to a standstill, and generally guided the triumph of absolutism in Austria. Rewarded with great wealth by his grateful king, Eugene called on the leading architects of the day, J. B. Fischer von Erlach and

Image 1 Pierre-Denis Martin: View of the Chateau de Versailles, 1722 *(Châteaux de Versailles et de Trianon, Versailles/ Réunion des Musées Nationaux/Art Resource, NY)*

Image 2 Project for the Palace at Schönbrunn (ca 1700) (*Austrian National Library, Vienna*)

Image 4 View of the Petit Parc at Versailles from the Canal (*Bibliothèque nationale de France*)

Image 3 Prince Eugene's Summer Palace, Vienna (*Erich Lessing/Art Resource, NY*)

Johann Lukas von Hildebrandt, to consecrate his glory in stone and fresco. Fischer built Eugene's Winter (or Town) Palace in Vienna, and he and Hildebrandt collaborated on the prince's Summer Palace on the city's outskirts, shown in Image 3. The prince's summer residence featured two baroque gems, the Lower Belvedere and the lovely Upper Belvedere, completed in 1722 and shown here. The building's interior is equally stunning, with crouching giants serving as pillars and a magnificent great staircase.

Palace gardens were an extension of the architecture. The rational orderliness and symmetry of a garden showed that the ruler's force extended even to nature, which offered its subjugated pleasures to the delight of sovereign and courtiers. The terraces and waterworks of these gardens served as showcases for the latest techniques in military and civil engineering. Exotic plants and elaborate designs testified to the sovereign's global trading networks and elevated taste.

The gardens at Versailles, shown in Image 4, exemplify absolutist palace gardens. In the foreground of this image we see a mock naval campaign being enacted on the canal for the edification of courtiers. For diplomatic occasions, Louis XIV himself wrote lengthy guides for viewing the gardens of Versailles. Modern visitors can still follow his itineraries. The themes of the sculptures in the Versailles gardens also hailed Louis's power, with images of Apollo, the sun-god, and Neptune, the sea-god, making frequent appearances.

Compare the image of Prince Eugene's summer palace with the plans for Schönbrunn and the palace of Versailles. What did concrete objects and the manipulation of space accomplish for these rulers that mere words could not? What disadvantages might stem from using architecture in this way? Is the use of space and monumental construction still a political tool in today's world?

---

*Quoted in R. Ergang, *The Potsdam Fuhrer: Frederick William I, Father of Prussian Militarism* (New York: Octagon Books, 1972), p. 13.
†Quoted in J. Summerson, in *The Eighteenth Century: Europe in the Age of Enlightenment,* ed. A. Cobban (New York: McGraw-Hill, 1969), p. 80.

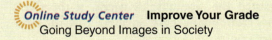

Online Study Center **Improve Your Grade**
Going Beyond Images in Society

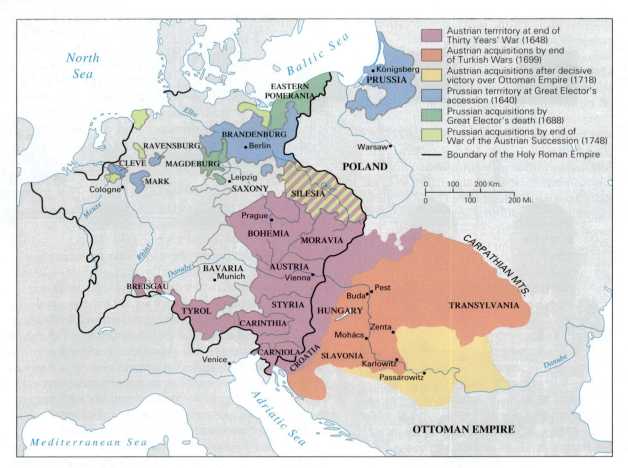

MAP 17.2 The Growth of Austria and Brandenburg-Prussia to 1748 Austria expanded to the southwest into Hungary and Transylvania at the expense of the Ottoman Empire. It was unable to hold the rich German province of Silesia, however, which was conquered by Brandenburg-Prussia.

When he came to power in 1640, the twenty-year-old Great Elector was determined to unify his three provinces and enlarge them by diplomacy and war. These provinces were Brandenburg; Prussia, inherited in 1618; and scattered holdings along the Rhine, inherited in 1614 (see Map 17.2). Each was inhabited by German-speakers, but each had its own estates. Although the estates had not met regularly during the chaotic Thirty Years' War, taxes could not be levied without their consent. The estates of Brandenburg and Prussia were dominated by the nobility and the landowning classes, known as the **Junkers.** But this was also the case in most European countries that had representative bodies, including the English Parliament before and after the civil war. Had the estates successfully resisted the absolutist demands of the Great Elector, they too might have evolved toward more broadly based constitutionalism.

The struggle between the Great Elector and the provincial estates was long and intense. After the Thirty Years' War, noble representatives zealously reasserted the estates' control over taxes. Yet first in Brandenburg in 1653 and then in Prussia between 1661 and 1663, the Great Elector eventually had his way.

To pay for the permanent standing army he first established in 1660, Frederick William forced the estates to accept the introduction of permanent taxation without consent. The estates' power declined rapidly thereafter, for the Great Elector had both financial independence and superior force. The state's total revenue tripled during his reign, and the size of the army leaped by ten. In 1688 a population of one million was supporting a peacetime standing army of thirty thousand.

Two factors were central to the Great Elector's triumph. First, as in the formation of every absolutist state, war was a decisive factor. The ongoing struggle between Sweden and Poland for control of the Baltic after 1648 and the wars of Louis XIV in western Europe created an atmosphere of permanent crisis. The nomadic Tatars of the Crimea in southern Russia swept through Prussia in the winter of 1656–1657, killing and carrying off thousands as slaves. This invasion softened up the estates and strengthened the urgency of the Great Elector's demands for more military funding.

Second, the nobility proved willing to accept Frederick William's new claims in exchange for reconfirmation of their own privileges. The Junkers had long dominated the government through the estates, but they refused to join representatives of the towns in a common front. Instead, they accepted a compromise with the state whereby the bulk of the new taxes fell on towns and the Junkers received legal confirmation of their authority over the serfs. The elector used naked force to break the liberties of the towns; the main leader of urban opposition in the key city of Königsberg, for example, was arrested and imprisoned for life without trial.

Like Louis XIV, the Great Elector built his absolutist state on collaboration with traditional elites, reaffirming their privileges in return for loyal service and revenue. He also created a larger centralized government bureaucracy to oversee his realm and to collect the new taxes. Preexisting representative institutions were bypassed. The Diet of Brandenburg did not meet again after 1652. In 1701 the elector's son, Frederick I, received the elevated title of king of Prussia (instead of elector) as a reward for aiding the Holy Roman emperor in the War of the Spanish Succession.

The Consolidation of Prussian Absolutism

Frederick William I, "the Soldiers' King" (r. 1713–1740), completed his grandfather's work. Though crude and ruthless, Frederick William I was the most talented reformer produced by the Hohenzollern family. Under his rule, Prussia built the best army in Europe for its size and transformed into a model military state. It was he who truly established Prussian absolutism and gave it its unique character. In the words of a famous historian of Prussia:

For a whole generation, the Hohenzollern subjects were victimized by a royal bully, imbued with an obsessive bent for military organization and military scales of value. This left a deep mark upon the institutions of Prussiandom and upon the molding of the "Prussian spirit."[3]

Frederick William was intensely attached to military life. He had, for example, an extreme fondness for tall soldiers, whom he credited with superior strength and endurance. Profoundly militaristic in temperament, Frederick William always wore an army uniform, and he lived the highly disciplined life of the professional soldier. He began his work by five or six in the morning; at ten he almost always went to the parade ground to drill or inspect his troops. His love of the army was based on a hardheaded conception of the struggle for power. Years later he summed up his life's philosophy in his instructions to his son: "A formidable army and a war chest large enough to make this army mobile in times of need can create great respect for you in the world, so that you can speak a word like the other powers."[4] This unshakable belief that the welfare of king and state depended on the army above all else reinforced Frederick William's passion for the soldier's life.

The cult of military power provided the rationale for a great expansion of absolutism in Prussia. As the king put it: "I must be served with life and limb, with house and wealth, with honour and conscience, everything must be committed except eternal salvation—that belongs to God, but all else is mine."[5] To achieve these extraordinary demands, Frederick William created a strong centralized bureaucracy and eliminated the last traces of the parliamentary estates and local self-government.

The king's power grab brought him into considerable conflict with the Junkers. In his early years he even threatened to destroy them; yet, in the end, the Prussian nobility was not destroyed but enlisted—into the army. Responding to a combination of threats and opportunities, the Junkers became the officer caste. A new compromise was worked out whereby the proud nobility imperiously commanded the peasantry in the army as well as on the estates.

Penny-pinching and hard-working, Frederick William achieved results. Above all, he built a first-rate army with third-rate resources. The standing army increased from thirty-eight thousand to eighty-three thousand during his reign. Prussia, twelfth in Europe in population, had the fourth largest army by 1740. Moreover, soldier for soldier, the Prussian army was the best in Europe, astonishing foreign observers with its precision, skill, and discipline. For the next two hundred years Prussia and then Prussianized Germany would win many crucial military battles.

Frederick William and his ministers also built an exceptionally honest and conscientious bureaucracy to administer the country and foster economic development. Like the miser he was known to be, the king loved his

A Prussian Giant Grenadier Frederick William I wanted tall, handsome soldiers. He dressed them in tight bright uniforms to distinguish them from the peasant population from which most soldiers came. He also ordered several portraits of his favorites from his court painter, J. C. Merk. Grenadiers wore the miter cap instead of an ordinary hat so that they could hurl their heavy grenades unimpeded by a broad brim. *(The Royal Collection © 2007, Her Majesty Queen Elizabeth II)*

"blue boys" so much that he hated to "spend" them. This most militaristic of kings was, paradoxically, almost always at peace.

Nevertheless, Prussians paid a heavy and lasting price for the obsessions of their royal drillmaster. Civil society became rigid and highly disciplined, and Prussia became the "Sparta of the North"; unquestioning obedience was the highest virtue. As a Prussian minister later summed up, "To keep quiet is the first civic duty."[6] Thus the policies of Frederick William I combined with harsh peasant bondage and Junker tyranny to lay the foundations for a highly militaristic country.

The Development of Russia and the Ottoman Empire

A favorite parlor game of nineteenth-century intellectuals was debating whether Russia was a Western (European) or non-Western (Asian) society. This question was particularly fascinating because it was unanswerable. To this day Russia differs fundamentally from the West in some basic ways, though its history has paralleled that of the West in other aspects.

There was no question in the mind of Europeans, however, that the Ottomans were outsiders. Even absolutist rulers disdained Ottoman sultans as cruel and tyrannical despots. Despite stereotypes, the Ottomans were in many ways more tolerant than the West, providing protection and security to other religions while steadfastly maintaining their Muslim faith. The Ottoman state combined the Byzantine heritage of the territory they conquered with Persian and Arab traditions. Flexibility and openness to other ideas and practices were sources of strength for the empire.

• *What were the distinctive features of Russian and Ottoman absolutism in this period?*

The Mongol Yoke and the Rise of Moscow

The eastern Slavs might have emerged from the Middle Ages weak and politically divided had it not been for the Mongol conquest of the Kievan principality. The Mongols were nomadic tribes from present-day Mongolia who had been temporarily unified in the thirteenth century by Chinggis Khan (1162–1227). In five years his armies subdued all of China. His successors then turned westward, smashing everything in their path and reaching the plains of Hungary before pulling back in 1242. The Mongol army—the Golden Horde—used terror to reduce con-

Mapping the Past

MAP 17.3 The Expansion of Russia to 1725 After the disintegration of the Kievan state and the Mongol conquest, the princes of Moscow and their descendants gradually extended their rule over an enormous territory. ❶ Compare this map with Map 17.4, which shows Ottoman expansion from 1300. What explains the fantastic success of both the Russians and the Ottomans in expanding their territories? Why was the sixteenth century such an important period for expansion? ❷ How do you explain the geographical direction that expansion followed in each case? ❸ What happened after the periods shown on these maps? Did the territorial development of the two states diverge from each other or follow the same trajectory?

Online Study Center **Improve Your Grade** Interactive Map: Expansion of Russia to 1725

---

quered peoples to submission. As a show of force, the army would destroy an entire city, slaughtering the whole population before burning the city to the ground.

The Mongols ruled the eastern Slavs for more than two hundred years, the period of the so-called **Mongol Yoke.** They built their capital of Saray on the lower Volga (see Map 17.3) and forced the rival Slavic princes to submit to their rule and to give them tribute and slaves. If conquered peoples rebelled, the Mongols used ruthless violence to re-impose control. The Mongol khan was acknowledged by all the eastern Slavs as the supreme ruler.

Online Study Center **Improve Your Grade**
Primary Source: Russia's Conquest by the Mongols: A Song to Lost Lands

Unification transformed the internal political situation. Although the Mongols conquered, they were quite willing to use local princes as obedient servants and tax collectors. Thus, they did not abolish the title of "great prince," bestowing it instead on the prince who served them best and paid them most handsomely. Beginning with Alexander Nevsky in 1252, the princes of Moscow became particularly adept at serving the Mongols. They loyally put down popular uprisings and collected the khan's taxes. As reward, the princes of Moscow emerged as hereditary great princes. Eventually the Muscovite princes were able to destroy their princely rivals. Ivan III (r. 1462–1505) consolidated power around Moscow and won Novgorod, almost reaching the Baltic Sea (see Map 17.3).

By about 1480 Ivan III felt strong enough to stop acknowledging the khan as his supreme ruler. To legitimize their new authority, the princes of Moscow drew on two sources of authority. First, they declared themselves *autocrats*, meaning that, like the khans, they were the sole source of power. In addition to political authority, Moscow also took over Mongol tribute relations and borrowed institutions like the tax system, postal routes, and the census.

The second source of legitimacy lay in Moscow's claim to the political and religious inheritance of the Byzantine Empire. The title **tsar** is a contraction of *caesar*. After the fall of Constantinople to the Turks in 1453, the princes of Moscow saw themselves as the heirs of both the caesars and Orthodox Christianity, the one true faith. All the other kings of Europe were heretics; only the tsars were rightful and holy rulers. The idea was promoted by Orthodox churchmen, who spoke of "holy Russia" as the "Third Rome." Ivan's marriage to the daughter of the last Byzantine emperor further enhanced the aura of Moscow's imperial inheritance.

Historians long took at face value the tsars' claims to unlimited autocratic power over their people, from the peasants to the highest-ranking nobles or **boyars.** More recently they have begun to emphasize the considerable consensus that existed between the nobility and the self-styled *autocrat*. Along with Mongol tribute relations, Moscow inherited a tradition of ruling in cooperation with local elites. The tsars' success in combining grandiose claims to power with an extremely limited government apparatus is explained through their collaboration with boyars in Moscow and with the provincial gentry. The Russian Orthodox Church helped cement this consensus. Since the national borders of Russia corresponded to the borders of the church, religion was a source of patriotic nationalism and loyalty to the Crown.

The tsars ensured the loyalty of the elite in part by creating new nobles personally loyal to them. These new nobles made up the **service nobility,** whose members held the tsar's land on the explicit condition that they serve in his army.

Tsar and People to 1689

Developments in Russia took a chaotic turn with the reign of Ivan IV (r. 1533–1584), the famous "Ivan the Terrible," who ascended the throne at age three. His mother died, possibly poisoned, when he was eight, leaving Ivan to suffer insults and neglect from the boyars at court. At age sixteen he suddenly pushed aside his hated advisers, and in an awe-inspiring ceremony, complete

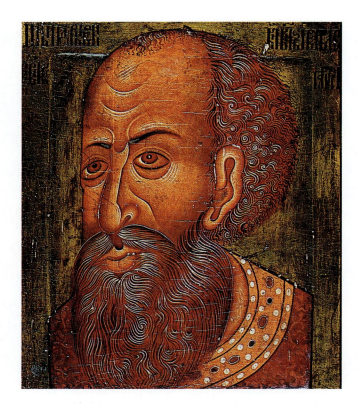

Ivan the Terrible   Ivan IV, the first to take the title tsar of Russia, executed many Muscovite boyars and their peasants and servants. His ownership of all the land, trade, and industry restricted economic development. *(National Museum, Copenhagen, Denmark)*

with gold coins pouring down on his head, Ivan majestically crowned himself, taking the august title of tsar for the first time.

Selecting the beautiful and kind Anastasia of the Romanov family as his queen, the young tsar soon declared war on the remnants of Mongol power. He defeated the khanates of Kazan and Astrakhan between 1552 and 1556, adding vast new territories to the realm and laying the foundations for the huge, multiethnic Russian empire. In the course of these wars, Ivan virtually abolished the old distinction between hereditary boyar private property and land temporarily granted for service. All nobles, old and new, had to serve the tsar in order to hold land.

In 1557 Ivan turned westward, and for the next twenty-five years he waged an exhausting, unsuccessful war primarily against the large Polish-Lithuanian state. Quarreling with the boyars over the war and suspecting them of a role in the sudden death of his beloved Anastasia in 1560, the increasingly demented Ivan struck down all who stood in his way. A reign of terror ensued in which Ivan jailed and executed anyone he suspected of opposing him. He created a special corps of black-clad soldiers to execute his alleged enemies, along with their families, friends, servants, and peasants. Many victims were intimates of the court from the leading boyar families of Moscow. Their large estates were broken up and reapportioned. Ivan gave about half of the land acquired through such purges to the lower service nobility; the rest he maintained as a personal domain.

Ivan also took strides toward making all commoners servants of the tsar. His endless wars and violent purges depopulated much of central Russia. As the service nobles demanded more from the remaining peasants, growing numbers fled toward wild, recently conquered territories to the east and south. There they formed free groups and outlaw armies known as **Cossacks** and maintained a precarious independence. The solution to the problem of peasant flight was to tie peasants ever more firmly to the land and to the noble landholders, who in turn served the tsar.

Simultaneously, urban traders and artisans were also bound to their towns and jobs so that the tsar could tax them more heavily. Ivan assumed that the tsar owned Russia's trade and industry, just as he owned all the land. The urban classes had no security in their work or property, and even the wealthiest merchants were dependent agents of the tsar. Royal monopolization and service obligations checked the growth of the Russian middle classes and stood in sharp contrast to developments in western Europe, where the middle classes were gaining security in their private property.

As so often in Russia, the death of an iron-fisted tyrant—in this case, Ivan the Terrible in 1584—opened an era of violent struggles for power. Ivan's son, Theodore, died in 1598 without an heir, ushering in the "Time of Troubles" (1598–1613). The close relatives of the deceased tsar intrigued against and murdered one another, alternately fighting and welcoming the invading Swedes

Saint Basil's Cathedral, Moscow With its sloping roofs and colorful onion-shaped domes, Saint Basil's is a striking example of powerful Byzantine influences on Russian culture. According to tradition, an enchanted Ivan the Terrible blinded the cathedral's architects to ensure that they would never duplicate their fantastic achievement, which still dazzles the beholder in today's Red Square. *(George Holton/Photo Researchers)*

and Poles. Cossack bands, led by a former slave named Ivan Bolotnikov, marched northward, rallying peasants and slaughtering nobles and officials. Cossacks and peasants called for the "true tsar," who would restore their freedom of movement, reduce their heavy taxes, and lighten the yoke imposed by the landlords.

This social explosion from below brought the nobles, big and small, to their senses. They put aside their quarrels and finally crushed the Cossack rebellion at the gates of Moscow. In 1613 the nobles elected Ivan the Terrible's sixteen-year-old grandnephew, Michael Romanov, the new hereditary tsar (r. 1613–1645). Michael's election was represented as a restoration of tsarist autocracy. (See the feature "Listening to the Past: A Foreign Traveler in Russia" on pages 586–587.)

Although the new tsar successfully reconsolidated central authority, social and religious uprisings continued through the seventeenth century. In 1652 the patriarch Nikon determined to bring "corrupted" Russian practices of worship into line with the Greek Orthodox model. The self-serving church hierarchy quickly went along, but the intensely religious common people resisted. They saw Nikon as the Antichrist who was stripping them of the only thing they had—the true religion of "holy Russia." Great numbers left the church and formed communities of "Old Believers," who were hunted down and persecuted. As many as twenty thousand people burned themselves alive, singing the "hallelujah" in their chants three times rather than twice, as Nikon had demanded. After the Great Schism, the Russian masses were alienated from the established church, which became dependent on the state for its authority.

The Cossacks revolted once more against a state that was doggedly trying to reduce them to serfdom. Under Stenka Razin they moved up the Volga River in 1670 and 1671, attracting a great army of urban poor and peasants, killing landlords and government officials, and proclaiming freedom from oppression. Eventually this rebellion was defeated.

The normal obstacles to state-building were exacerbated in Russia's case by the huge size of its territory, its thinly spread population, and the economic devastation wrought by the Time of Troubles. Nevertheless, Romanov tsars made several important achievements during the second half of the seventeenth century. After a long war, Russia gained a large mass of Ukraine from weak and decentralized Poland in 1667 (see Map 17.3) and completed the conquest of Siberia by the end of the century. Territorial expansion was accompanied by growth of the bureaucracy and the army. Russian tsars turned to imported foreign experts to help build and reform the Russian army. The great profits from Siberia's natural resources, especially furs, funded the Romanov's bid for great power status.

The Reforms of Peter the Great

Heir to the first efforts at state-building, Peter the Great (r. 1682–1725) embarked on a tremendous campaign to accelerate and complete these processes. A giant for his time, at six feet seven inches, and possessing enormous energy and willpower, Peter was determined to build and improve the army. He was equally determined to continue the tsarist tradition of territorial expansion. After 1689 Peter ruled independently for thirty-six years, only one of which was peaceful.

Fascinated by weapons and foreign technology, the tsar led a group of 250 Russian officials and young nobles on an eighteen-month tour of western European capitals. Traveling unofficially to avoid lengthy diplomatic ceremonies, Peter worked with his hands at various crafts and met with foreign kings and experts. He was particularly impressed with the growing power of the Dutch and the English, and he considered how Russia could profit from their example.

Returning to Russia, Peter entered into a secret alliance with Denmark and Poland to wage a sudden war of aggression against Sweden. Despite the country's small population and limited agricultural resources, Swedish rulers in the seventeenth century had developed a strong absolutist state and had built an excellent standing army. Like other absolutist rulers, Charles XI of Sweden built a beautiful palace in his capital, modeled after Louis XIV's Versailles. Expanding beyond its borders, Sweden held substantial territory in northern Germany, Finland, and Estonia. Yet these possessions were scattered and appeared vulnerable. Above all, Peter and his allies believed that their combined forces could win easy victories because Sweden was in the hands of a new and inexperienced king.

Eighteen-year-old Charles XII (1697–1718) surprised Peter. He defeated Denmark quickly in 1700, then turned on Russia. In a blinding snowstorm, his well-trained professional army attacked and routed unsuspecting Russians besieging the Swedish fortress of Narva on the Baltic coast. Peter and the survivors fled in panic to Moscow. It was, for the Russians, a grim beginning to the long and brutal Great Northern War, which lasted from 1700 to 1721.

Suffering defeat and faced with a military crisis, the energetic Peter responded with a long series of practical but far-reaching measures designed to increase state power,

Gustaf Cederstrom: The Swedish Victory at Narva (1701) This poignant re-creation focuses on the contrast between the Swedish officers in handsome dress uniforms and the battered Russian soldiers laying down their standards in surrender. Charles XII of Sweden scored brilliant, rapid-fire victories over Denmark, Saxony, and Russia, but he failed to make peace with Peter while he was ahead and eventually lost Sweden's holdings on the Baltic coast. *(The National Museum of Fine Arts, Stockholm)*

strengthen his armies, and gain victory. Tightening up Muscovy's old service system, he required every noble-man, great or small, to serve in the army or in the civil administration—for life. Since a more modern army and government required skilled technicians and experts, Peter created schools and universities to produce them. One of his most hated reforms was requiring a five-year education away from home for every young nobleman. Peter established an interlocking military-civilian bureaucracy with fourteen ranks, and he decreed that all had to start at the bottom and work toward the top. Some people of non-noble origins rose to high positions in this embryonic meritocracy. Drawing on his experience abroad, Peter searched out talented foreigners and

placed them in his service. These measures gradually combined to make the army and government more powerful and efficient.

Peter also greatly increased the service requirements of commoners. In the wake of the Narva disaster, he established a regular standing army of more than two hundred thousand peasant-soldiers commanded by officers from the nobility. In addition, special forces of Cossacks and foreigners numbered more than one hundred thousand. The departure of a drafted peasant boy was celebrated by his family and village almost like a funeral, since the recruit was drafted for life. The peasantry also served with its taxes, which increased threefold during Peter's reign. Serfs were arbitrarily assigned to work in the growing

Peter the Great in 1723 This compelling portrait by Grigory Musikiysky captures the strength and determination of the warrior-tsar after more than three decades of personal rule. In his hand Peter holds the scepter, symbol of royal sovereignty, and across his breastplate is draped an ermine fur, a mark of honor. In the background are the battleships of Russia's new Baltic fleet and the famous St. Peter and St. Paul Fortress that Peter built in St. Petersburg. *(Kremlin Museums, Moscow/The Bridgeman Art Library)*

number of factories and mines. Most of these industrial enterprises were directly or indirectly owned by the state, and they were worked almost exclusively for the military.

The constant warfare of Peter's reign consumed 80 to 85 percent of all revenues and brought only modest territorial expansion. Yet the Great Northern War with Sweden was crowned in the end by Russian victory. Peter's new war machine crushed the smaller army of Sweden in Ukraine at Poltava in 1709, one of the most significant battles in Russian history. The war dragged on until 1721, but Sweden never regained the offensive. Estonia and present-day Latvia (see Map 17.3) came under Russian rule for the first time. Russia became the dominant power on the Baltic Sea and very much a European Great Power. If victory or defeat is the ultimate historical criterion, Peter's reforms were a success.

There were other important consequences of Peter's reign. Because of his feverish desire to use modern technology to strengthen the army, many Westerners and Western ideas flowed into Russia for the first time. For Peter, modernization meant westernization. He thus required nobles to shave their heavy beards and wear Western clothing, previously banned in Russia. He required them to attend parties where young men and women would mix together and freely choose their own spouses. He forced a warrior elite to accept administrative service as an honorable occupation. From these efforts a new class of Western-oriented Russians began to emerge.

Online Study Center **Improve Your Grade**
Primary Source: Peter the Great Imposes Western Styles on the Russians

At the same time, vast numbers of Russians hated Peter's massive changes. For nobles, one of Peter's most detested reforms was the imposition of unigeniture—inheritance of land by one son alone—cutting daughters and other sons from family property. For peasants, the reign of the reforming tsar saw a significant increase in the bonds of serfdom. The gulf between the enserfed peasantry and the educated nobility widened more, even though all were caught up in the demands of the sovereign.

Thus Peter built on the service obligations of old Muscovy. His monarchical absolutism was truly the culmination of the long development of a unique Russian civilization. Yet the creation of a more modern army and state introduced much that was new and Western to Russia. This development paved the way for Russia to move somewhat closer to the European mainstream in its thought and institutions during the Enlightenment, especially under Catherine the Great.

The Growth of St. Petersburg

Nothing exemplifies the scope of Peter's reforms like his creation of St. Petersburg. In 1700, when the Great Northern War began, the city did not exist; there was only a small Swedish fortress on one of the waterlogged islands at the mouth of the Neva River, where it flows into the Baltic Sea. In 1702 Peter the Great's armies seized this desolate outpost. Within a year the reforming tsar decided to build a new city there and to make it, rather than ancient Moscow, his capital.

To secure the Baltic coast, military construction was the main concern for the next eight years. A mighty fortress was built on the newly named Peter Island, and a port and shipyards were built across the river on the mainland as a Russian navy came into being. From the inhospitable northern marshland Peter would create a future metropolis gloriously bearing his name.

After the decisive Russian victory at Poltava in 1709 greatly reduced the threat of Swedish armies, Peter moved into high gear. In one imperious decree after another, he ordered his people to build a city equal to any in the world. Such a city had to be Western and modern, just as Peter's

army had to be Western and permanent. From such a "window on Europe," Peter believed, it would be easier to reform the country militarily and administratively.

These general political goals matched Peter's architectural ideas, which had been influenced by his travels in western Europe. First, Peter wanted a comfortable, "modern" city. Modernity meant broad, straight, stone-paved avenues; houses built in a uniform line and not haphazardly set back from the street; large parks; canals for drainage; stone bridges; and street lighting. Second, all buildings had to conform to detailed architectural regulations set down by the government. Finally, each social group—the nobility, the merchants, the artisans, and so on—was to live in a certain section of town. In short, the city and its population were to conform to a carefully defined urban plan.

Peter used the traditional methods of Russian autocracy to build his modern capital. Its creation was just one

St. Petersburg, ca 1760 Rastrelli's remodeled Winter Palace, which housed the royal family until the Russian Revolution of 1917, stands on the left along the Neva River. The Navy Office with its famous golden spire and other government office buildings are nearby and across the river. Russia became a naval power and St. Petersburg a great port. *(Michael Holford)*

of the heavy obligations he dictatorially imposed on all of Russian society. The peasants bore the heaviest burdens. Just as the government drafted peasants for the army, it also drafted twenty-five thousand to forty thousand men each summer to labor in St. Petersburg for three months without pay. Every ten to fifteen peasant households had to furnish one worker each summer and then pay a special tax in order to feed him in St. Petersburg.

Peasants hated this forced labor, and each year one-fourth to one-third of those sent risked brutal punishment to run away. Many peasant construction workers died from hunger, sickness, and accidents. Thus beautiful St. Petersburg was built by the shoveling, carting, and paving of a mass of conscripted serfs.

Peter also drafted more privileged groups to his city. Nobles were summarily ordered to build costly stone houses and palaces in St. Petersburg and to live in them most of the year. The more serfs a noble possessed, the bigger his dwelling had to be. Merchants and artisans were also commanded to settle and build in St. Petersburg. These nobles and merchants were then required to pay for the city's avenues, parks, canals, embankments, and bridges, all of which were costly in money and lives because they were built on a swamp. The building of St. Petersburg was, in truth, an enormous direct tax levied on the wealthy, which in turn forced the peasantry to do most of the work.

By the time of Peter's death in 1725, there were at least six thousand houses and numerous impressive government buildings in St. Petersburg. The city blossomed in the eighteenth century, at least in its wealthy showpiece sections. Peter's youngest daughter, Elizabeth (r. 1741–1762), named as her chief architect Bartolomeo Rastrelli, who came to Russia from Italy as a boy of fifteen in 1715. Combining Italian and Russian traditions into a unique, wildly colorful St. Petersburg style, Rastrelli built many palaces for the nobility and all the larger government buildings erected during Elizabeth's reign. He also rebuilt the Winter Palace as an enormous, aqua-colored royal residence, now the Hermitage Museum. All the while St. Petersburg grew rapidly, and its almost three hundred thousand inhabitants in 1782 made it one of the world's largest cities. Peter and his successors created a magnificent royal city from nothing, which unmistakably proclaimed the power of Russia's rulers and the creative potential of the absolutist state.

The Growth of the Ottoman Empire

Most Christian Europeans perceived the Ottomans as the antithesis of their own values and traditions and viewed the empire as driven by an insatiable lust for warfare and conquest. In their view the fall of Constantinople was a catastrophe and the taking of the Balkans a despotic imprisonment of those territories. The Ottoman Empire seemed the epitome of Eastern exoticism, religious fanaticism, and tyranny. From the perspective of the Ottomans, the world looked very different. The siege of Constantinople liberated a glorious city from its long decline under the Byzantines. Rather than being a despoiled captive, the Balkans became a haven for refugees fleeing the growing intolerance of Western Christian powers. The Ottoman Empire provided Jews, Muslims, and even some Christians safety from the Inquisition and religious war: the Iberian powers tried to impose Christianity through conversion or exile, but Islam and Judaism remained part of the conversation of post-Reformation Europe because of the presence of the Ottoman Empire at Europe's gate.

The Ottomans came out of Central Asia as conquering warriors, settled in Anatolia (present-day Turkey), and created one of history's greatest empires (see pages 466 and 566). At their peak in the mid-sixteenth century under Sultan Suleiman the Magnificent (r. 1520–1566), they ruled the most powerful empire in the world. Their possessions stretched from western Persia across North Africa and into the heart of central Europe (see Map 17.4). In 1690 a Turkish visitor to Versailles wrote in his travel diary: "The King of France is the Sultan Suleiman of our time."

Ottoman expansion borrowed from the peoples they conquered. They were heirs to the Byzantine Empire and, through it, of Rome and its vision of universal empire. From the Byzantines, they adopted the tax structure and the use of religion to bind together a diverse empire. From the Persians, the Ottomans borrowed political and financial practices, and from the Arabs, religion and spirituality. This openness and adaptability—missing from most Western accounts of the Ottomans—was largely responsible for the empire's longevity.

When the Ottomans captured Constantinople in 1453, they fulfilled a long-held Islamic dream. They also shattered a bulwark of Christian identity. Founded by the emperor who introduced the Christian church to mighty Rome, for a millennium Constantinople had stood as a symbol of Christianity and its links to imperial power. Though the Byzantine Empire gradually shrank, the city itself had withstood numerous sieges. The loss of Constantinople was not just symbolic but strategic as well. The city stands at the natural gateway between the Black and Mediterranean Seas, between Europe and the Balkans. With the capture of Constantinople—renamed

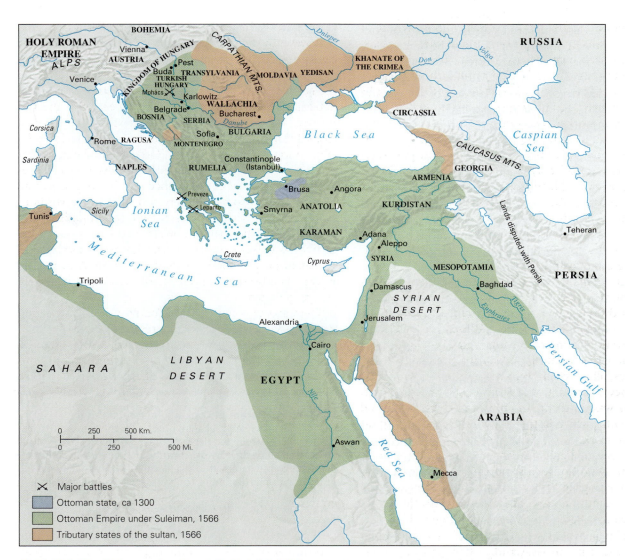

MAP 17.4 The Ottoman Empire at Its Height, 1566 The Ottomans, like their great rivals the Habsburgs, rose to rule a vast dynastic empire encompassing many different peoples and ethnic groups. The army and the bureaucracy served to unite the disparate territories into a single state under an absolutist ruler.

Istanbul—the Ottomans and Islam occupied a permanent place in the European landscape. By 1600 Istanbul was one of the largest cities in the world, with a population of seven hundred thousand.

Ottoman expansion continued to the south as well. The Ottomans first conquered Syria and Iraq, and in 1517 Sultan Selim I (r. 1512–1520) invaded the Egyptian Mameluke empire and quickly captured Egypt, North Africa, and the Arabian peninsula. His successor, Suleiman the Magnificent, turned north, capturing Bosnia, Croatia, Romania, Ukraine, and part of Hungary at the Battle of Mohács in 1526. For the next hundred and fifty years, the Ottomans ruled the many different

ethnic groups living in southeastern Europe and the eastern Mediterranean. In 1529 their European expansion was halted with a failed siege of the Habsburg capital, Vienna. The Ottoman loss at the Battle of Lepanto in 1571, against the Christian Holy League, confirmed the limits of their ambitions in Europe.

The Ottoman Empire was originally built on a unique model of state and society. There was an almost complete absence of private landed property. Agricultural land was the personal hereditary property of the **sultan,** and peasants paid taxes to use the land. There was therefore no security of landholding and no hereditary nobility, two key features of western European society.

The Ottomans also employed a distinctive form of government administration. The top ranks of the bureaucracy were staffed by the sultan's slave corps. Because Muslim law prohibited enslaving other Muslims, the sultan's agents purchased slaves along the borders of the empire. Within the realm, the sultan levied a "tax" of one thousand to three thousand male children on the conquered Christian populations in the Balkans every year. Young slaves were raised in Turkey as Muslims and were trained to fight and to administer. The most talented rose to the top of the bureaucracy, where they might acquire wealth and power; the less fortunate formed the brave and skillful core of the sultan's army, the janissary corps. Lurid accounts of weeping Christian boys being carried off into Ottoman slavery did much to foster the idea of the brutal, fanatical Turk in the European mind.

After 1453 Istanbul became the capital of the empire and, with the transfer of the caliphate from Cairo, the religious center of Sunni Islam. The "old palace" was for the sultan's female family members, who lived in isolation under the care of eunuchs. The newly constructed Topkapi Palace was where officials worked and young slaves trained for future administrative or military careers. To prevent wives from bringing foreign influence into government—a constant concern in the West—sultans procreated only with their concubines and not with official wives. They also adopted a policy of allowing each concubine to produce only one male heir. At a young age, each son went to govern a province of the empire under his mother's supervision. These practices were intended to stabilize power and prevent a recurrence of the civil wars of the late fourteenth and early fifteenth centuries.

Sultan Suleiman undid these policies when he boldly married his concubine and had several children with her. He established a wing in the Topkapi Palace for his own female family members and his brothers' families. Starting with Suleiman, imperial wives began to take on more power. Marriages were arranged between sultans' daughters and high-ranking servants, creating powerful new members of the imperial household. Over time, the sultan's exclusive authority waned in favor of a more bureaucratic administration. These changes brought the Ottoman court closer to the European model of factionalism, intrigue, and informal female power. (See the feature "Individuals in Society: Hürrem.")

In this period the Ottoman Empire experienced the same economic and social crises that affected the rest of Europe. In the 1580s and 1590s rebellions broke out among many different groups in the vast empire: frustrated students, underpaid janissaries, and ambitious provincial governors. Revolts continued during the sev-

The Sultan's Harem at Topkapi Palace, Istanbul   Sultan Suleiman I created separate quarters at the Topkapi Palace for his wife Hürrem and her ladies-in-waiting. His successors transferred all of their wives, concubines, and female family members to the harem at Topkapi, carefully situated out of sight of the staterooms and courtyards where public affairs took place. The harem was the object of intense curiosity and fascination in the West. *(Vanni/Art Resource, NY)*

enteenth century as the janissaries formed alliances with court factions that resulted in the overthrow or execution of several Ottoman sultans.

In the late seventeenth century the Ottomans succeeded in marshaling their forces for one last attack on the Habsburgs, and a huge Turkish army laid siege to Vienna in 1683. After holding out against great odds for two months, the city was relieved at the last minute by reinforcements, and the Ottomans were forced to retreat. Soon the retreat became a rout. As Russian and Venetian allies attacked on other fronts, the Habsburgs conquered almost all of Hungary and Transylvania by 1699 (see Map 17.4). The Habsburgs completed their victory in 1718, with the Treaty of Passarowitz. These defeats might have led to reform of Ottoman political, military, and economic structures. They did not, and the empire's strength slowly eroded and with it Western fears of the Ottoman threat.

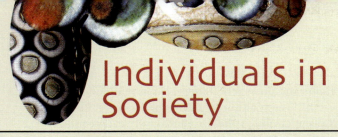

Individuals in Society

Hürrem

In Muslim culture *harem* means a sacred place or a sanctuary, which is forbidden to profane outsiders. The term was applied to the part of the household occupied by women and children and forbidden to men outside the family. The most famous member of the Ottoman sultan's harem was Hürrem, wife of Suleiman the Magnificent.

Hürrem (1505?–1558) came to the harem as a slave-concubine. Like many of the sultan's concubines, Hürrem was of foreign birth. Tradition holds that she was born Aleksandra Lisowska in what was the kingdom of Poland and today is Ukraine. She was captured during a Tatar raid and enslaved. Between 1517 and 1520, when she was about fifteen years old, she entered the imperial harem. Venetian reports insist that she was not outstandingly beautiful but was possessed of wonderful grace, charm, and good humor. These qualities gained her the Turkish nickname Hürrem, or "joyful one." After her arrival in the harem, Hürrem quickly became the imperial favorite.

Suleiman's love for Hürrem led him to break all precedents for the role of a concubine, including the rule that concubines must cease having children once they give birth to a male heir. By 1531 Hürrem had given birth to one daughter and five sons. In 1533 or 1534 Suleiman entered formal marriage with his consort—an unprecedented honor for a concubine. He reportedly gave his exclusive attention to his wife and also defied convention by allowing Hürrem to remain in the palace throughout her life instead of accompanying her son to a provincial governorship as other concubines had done.

Contemporaries were shocked by Hürrem's influence over the sultan and resentful of the apparent role she played in politics and diplomacy. The Venetian ambassador Bassano wrote that "the Janissaries and the entire court hate her and her children likewise, but because the Sultan loves her, no one dares to speak."[*] She was suspected of using witchcraft to control the sultan and accused of ordering the death of the sultan's first-born son (with another mother) in 1553. These stories were based on court gossip and rumor. The correspondence between Suleiman and Hürrem, unavailable until the nineteenth century, along with Suleiman's own diaries, confirms her status as the sultan's most trusted confidant and adviser. During his frequent absences, the pair exchanged passionate love letters. Hürrem included information about the political situation and warnings about any potential uprisings. She also intervened in affairs between the empire and her former home. She wrote to Polish king Sigismund Augustus and seems to have helped Poland attain its

privileged diplomatic status. She brought a particularly feminine touch to diplomatic relations, sending the Persian shah and the Polish king personally embroidered articles.

Hürrem used her enormous pension to contribute a mosque, two schools, a hospital, a fountain, and two public baths to Istanbul. In Jerusalem, Mecca, and Istanbul, she provided soup kitchens and hospices for pilgrims and the poor. She died in 1558, eight years before her husband. Her son Selim II (r. 1566–1574) inherited the throne.

Hürrem and her ladies in the harem.
(Bibliothèque nationale de France)

Drawing from reports of contemporary Western observers, historians depicted Hürrem as a manipulative and power-hungry social climber. They saw her career as the beginning of a "sultanate of women" in which strong imperial leadership gave way to court intrigue and dissipation. More recent historians have emphasized the intelligence and courage Hürrem demonstrated in navigating the ruthlessly competitive world of the harem.

Hürrem's journey from Ukrainian maiden to harem slave girl to sultan's wife captured enormous public attention. She is the subject of numerous paintings, plays, and novels as well as of an opera, a ballet, and a symphony by the composer Haydn. Interest in and suspicion of Hürrem continues. In 2003 a Turkish miniseries once more depicted her as a scheming intriguer.

Questions for Analysis

1. Compare Hürrem to other powerful early modern women such as Isabella of Castile, Elizabeth I of England, and Catherine de' Medici of France.
2. What can an exceptional woman like Hürrem reveal about the broader political and social world in which she lived?

[*]Cited in Galina Yermolenko, "Roxolana: The Greatest Empresse of the East," in *The Muslim World* 95 (2005): 2.

Source: Leslie P. Pierce, *The Imperial Harem: Women and Sovereignty in the Ottoman Empire* (New York: Oxford University Press, 1993).

Online Study Center **Improve Your Grade**
Going Beyond Individuals in Society

Religious Diversity in the Ottoman Empire

Despite Western perceptions, the Ottomans were more tolerant of religious differences than were the Europeans. They recognized Christians and Jews as "peoples of the Book" who followed the same biblical tradition as Islam. Building on the practices of the great Middle Eastern empires, the Ottomans divided their subjects into religious communities, and each *millet,* or "nation," enjoyed autonomous self-government under its religious leaders. (The Ottoman Empire recognized Orthodox Christians, Jews, Armenian Christians, and Muslims as distinct millets.) The **millet system** created a powerful bond between the Ottoman ruling class and the different religious leaders, who supported the sultan's rule in return for extensive authority over their own communities. Each millet collected taxes for the state, regulated group behavior, and maintained law courts, schools, synagogues, and hospitals for its people. Individuals outside the ruling elite had status only through their millet membership.

Supported and reassured by religious toleration and cultural autonomy, non-Muslim minorities coexisted and commingled with the Muslim majority. Greek, Jewish, and Armenian merchants moved easily to and from Europe, drawing Ottomans and Europeans closer together despite recurring war and conflict. Armenian merchants excelled as international silk merchants, Jews as textile manufacturers and financiers, and Greeks as mariners and shipowners, although all three groups participated in all Ottoman occupations in the sixteenth and seventeenth centuries.[7] Religious diversity was mostly a source of strength for the Ottomans, allowing them to integrate many different ethnicities into the empire and to profit from the skills and networks of each group.

Despite its tolerance, the Ottoman Empire was an explicitly Islamic state. Members of the Muslim religious elite were educated at religious schools (*medreses*) attached to mosques. *Muftis* supervised mosques and religious schools and wrote interpretations of Islamic law, and state-appointed *kadis* administered the law. Whereas non-Muslims had their own courts for dealings among themselves, any conflict involving a Muslim was regulated by a kadi in an Islamic court. Wariness of the Islamic courts encouraged non-Muslims to deal with their own as much as possible. However, the Ottomans showed the same openness in law as in empire building. They adopted the most flexible of Muslim law traditions, and they accepted provincial law codes that respected pre-existing local laws. Under Suleiman the Magnificent and his successors, a process of legal centralization began; provincial laws were codified and standardized. The sultan's claim to be caliph—the guide for the community of all Muslims—helped legitimize this process of legal centralization. The legal reforms won Suleiman the title "the Lawgiver" from his subjects.

Chapter Summary

Online Study Center   **ACE the Test**

- *What social and economic changes affected central and eastern Europe from 1400 to 1650?*
- *How and why did the rulers of Austria and Prussia, each in different political and social environments, manage to build powerful absolute monarchies that proved more durable than that of Louis XIV?*
- *What were the distinctive features of Russian and Ottoman absolutism in this period?*

From about 1400 to 1650 social and economic developments in eastern Europe diverged from those in western Europe. In the East, after enjoying relative freedom in the Middle Ages, peasants and townspeople lost freedom and fell under the economic, social, and legal authority of the nobles, who increased their power and prestige.

Within this framework of resurgent serfdom and entrenched nobility, Austrian and Prussian monarchs fashioned absolutist states in the seventeenth and early eighteenth centuries. These monarchs won absolutist control over standing armies, taxation, and representative bodies, but they did not question underlying social and economic relationships. Indeed, they enhanced the privileges of the nobles, who filled enlarged armies and growing state bureaucracies. In exchange for entrenched privileges over their peasants, nobles thus cooperated with the growth of state power.

In Russia the social and economic trends were similar, but the timing of political absolutism was different. Mongol conquest and rule were a crucial experience, and a harsh indigenous tsarist autocracy was firmly in place by the reign of Ivan the Terrible in the sixteenth century. More than a century later Peter the Great succeeded in modernizing Russia's traditional absolutism by reforming the army and the bureaucracy. Farther to the east, the Ottoman sultans developed a distinctive political and economic system in which all land theoretically belonged to the sultan, who was served by a slave corps of administrators and soldiers. The Ottoman Empire was relatively tolerant on religious matters and served as a haven for Jews and other marginalized religious groups.

Triumphant absolutism interacted spectacularly with the arts. Central and eastern European rulers built grandiose palaces, and even whole cities, like St. Petersburg, to glorify their power and majesty.

Key Terms

serfdom
hereditary subjugation
Protestant Union
Peace of Westphalia
absolutism
Bohemian Estates
Battle of Mohács
Pragmatic Sanction
elector of Brandenburg
Junkers
Mongol Yoke
tsar
boyars
service nobility
Cossacks
sultan
millet system

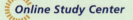 *Online Study Center* **Improve Your Grade** Flashcards

Suggested Reading

Bushkovitch, Paul. *Peter the Great: The Struggle for Power, 1671–1725*. 2001. An outstanding biography of the Russian tsar.

Engel, Barbara A. *Women in Russia, 1700–2000*. 2004. An excellent account of the role of women in Russian society over three centuries.

Goffman, Daniel. *The Ottoman Empire and Early Modern Europe*. 2002. An original and valuable study of Ottoman relations with the European world.

Hagen, William W. *Ordinary Prussians: Brandenburg Junkers and Villagers, 1500–1840*. 2002. Provides a fascinating encounter with the people of a Prussian estate.

Hughes, Lindsey, ed. *Peter the Great and the West: New Perspectives*. 2001. Essays by leading scholars on the reign of Peter the Great and his opening of Russia to the West.

Ingrao, Charles W. *The Habsburg Monarchy, 1618–1815*, 2d ed. 2000. An excellent synthesis of the political and social development of the Habsburg empire in the early modern period.

Kappeler, Adreas. *The Russian Empire: Ethnicity and Nationalism*. 2001. Explains the rise of a multiethnic empire in Russia from the seventeenth century on.

Kollmann, N. Shields. *By Honor Bound: State and Society in Early Modern Russia*. 1999. An excellent study of politics and values among the Russian elite.

Lincoln, W. Bruce. *Sunlight at Midnight: St. Petersburg and the Rise of Modern Russia*. 2001. Captures the spirit of Peter the Great's new northern capital.

McKay, Derek. *The Great Elector: Frederick William of Brandenburg-Prussia*. 2001. Examines the formative years of Prussian power.

Murphey, Rhoads. *Ottoman Warfare, 1500–1700*. 1999. A good introduction to Ottoman military history, including warfare between the Ottomans and European states.

Ogilvie, Sheilagh, and Bob Scribner, eds. *Germany: A New Economic and Social History, 1450–1800*, 2 vols. 1996. A broad overview of life in central Europe in the early modern period.

Parker, Geoffrey. *The Thirty Years War*, 2d ed. 1997. The standard account of the Thirty Years' War.

Quataert, Donald. *The Ottoman Empire, 1700–1922*. 2000. A recent synthesis of Ottoman history by a leading historian.

Riasanovsky, Nicholas V., and Mark Steinberg. *A History of Russia to 1855*. 2004. An excellent starting place for students interested in Russian history.

Notes

1. H. Kamen, "The Economic and Social Consequences of the Thirty Years' War," *Past and Present* 39 (April 1968): 44–61.
2. Quoted in F. L. Carsten, *The Origins of Prussia* (Oxford: Clarendon Press, 1954), p. 175.
3. H. Rosenberg, *Bureaucracy, Aristocracy, and Autocracy: The Prussian Experience, 1660–1815* (Boston: Beacon Press, 1966), p. 38.
4. Ibid., p. 43.
5. Quoted in R. A. Dorwart, *The Administrative Reforms of Frederick William I of Prussia* (Cambridge, Mass.: Harvard University Press, 1953), p. 226.
6. Quoted in Rosenberg, *Bureaucracy, Aristocracy, and Autocracy*, p. 40.
7. D. Goffman, *The Ottoman Empire and Early Modern Europe* (Cambridge: Cambridge University Press, 2002), pp. 9–18, 83–91.

Listening to the Past

A Foreign Traveler in Russia

Seventeenth-century Russia remained a remote and mysterious land for western and even central Europeans, who had few direct contacts with the tsar's dominion. Developing their ideas of refined society and gradual progress (see Chapter 18), Westerners portrayed eastern Europe as more "barbaric" and less "civilized" than their homelands. Thus they expanded eastern Europe's undeniably harsher social and economic conditions to encompass a very debatable cultural and moral inferiority.

Knowledge of Russia came mainly from occasional travelers who had visited Muscovy and sometimes wrote accounts of what they saw. The most famous of these accounts was by the German Adam Olearius (ca 1599–1671), who was sent to Moscow by the duke of Holstein on three diplomatic missions in the 1630s. These missions ultimately proved unsuccessful, but they provided Olearius with a rich store of information for his Travels in Muscovy, from which the following excerpts are taken. Published in German in 1647 and soon translated into several languages (but not Russian), Olearius's unflattering but well-informed study played a major role in shaping European ideas about Russia.

The government of the Russians is what political theorists call a "dominating and despotic monarchy," where the sovereign, that is, the tsar or the grand prince who has obtained the crown by right of succession, rules the entire land alone, and all the people are his subjects, and where the nobles and princes no less than the common folk—townspeople and peasants—are his serfs and slaves, whom he rules and treats as a master treats his servants. . . .

If the Russians be considered in respect to their character, customs, and way of life, they are justly to be counted among the barbarians. . . . The vice of drunkenness is so common in this nation,

among people of every station, clergy and laity, high and low, men and women, old and young, that when they are seen now and then lying about in the streets, wallowing in the mud, no attention is paid to it, as something habitual. If a cart driver comes upon such a drunken pig whom he happens to know, he shoves him onto his cart and drives him home, where he is paid his fare. No one ever refuses an opportunity to drink and to get drunk, at any time and in any place, and usually it is done with vodka. . . .

The Russians being naturally tough and born, as it were, for slavery, they must be kept under a harsh and strict yoke and must be driven to do their work with clubs and whips, which they suffer without impatience, because such is their station, and they are accustomed to it. Young and half-grown fellows sometimes come together on certain days and train themselves in fisticuffs, to accustom themselves to receiving blows, and, since habit is second nature, this makes blows given as punishment easier to bear. Each and all, they are slaves and serfs. . . .

Because of slavery and their rough and hard life, the Russians accept war readily and are well suited to it. On certain occasions, if need be, they reveal themselves as courageous and daring soldiers. . . .

Although the Russians, especially the common populace, living as slaves under a harsh yoke, can bear and endure a great deal out of love for their masters, yet if the pressure is beyond measure, then it can be said of them: "Patience, often wounded, finally turned into fury." A dangerous indignation results, turned not so much against their sovereign as against the lower authorities, especially if the people have been much oppressed by them and by their supporters and have not been protected by the higher authorities. And once they are aroused and enraged, it is not easy to appease them. Then, disregarding all dangers that may ensue, they resort to every kind of

The brutality of serfdom is shown in this illustration from Olearius's *Travels in Muscovy*. (University of Illinois Library, Champaign)

violence and behave like madmen. . . . They own little; most of them have no feather beds; they lie on cushions, straw, mats, or their clothes; they sleep on benches and, in winter, like the non-Germans [natives] in Livonia, upon the oven, which serves them for cooking and is flat on the top; here husband, wife, children, servants, and maids huddle together. In some houses in the countryside we saw chickens and pigs under the benches and the ovens. . . . Russians are not used to delicate food and dainties; their daily food consists of porridge, turnips, cabbage, and cucumbers, fresh and pickled, and in Moscow mostly of big salt fish which stink badly, because of the thrifty use of salt, yet are eaten with relish. . . .

The Russians can endure extreme heat. In the bathhouse they stretch out on benches and let themselves be beaten and rubbed with bunches of birch twigs and wisps of bast (which I could not stand); and when they are hot and red all over and so exhausted that they can bear it no longer in the bathhouse, men and women rush outdoors naked and pour cold water over their bodies; in winter they even wallow in the snow and rub their skin with it as if it were soap; then they go back into the hot bathhouse. And since bathhouses are usually near rivers and brooks, they can throw themselves straight from the hot into the cold bath. . . .

Generally noble families, even the small nobility, rear their daughters in secluded chambers, keeping them hidden from outsiders; and a bridegroom is not allowed to have a look at his bride until he receives her in the bridal chamber. Therefore some happen to be deceived, being given a misshapen and sickly one instead of a fair one, and sometimes a kinswoman or even a maidservant instead of a daughter; of which there have been examples even among the highborn. No wonder therefore that often they live together like cats and dogs and that wife-beating is so common among Russians. . . .

In the Kremlin and in the city there are a great many churches, chapels, and monasteries, both within and without the city walls, over two thousand in all. This is so because every nobleman who has some fortune has a chapel built for himself, and most of them are of stone. The stone churches are round and vaulted inside. . . . They allow neither organs nor any other musical instruments in their churches, saying: Instruments that have neither souls nor life cannot praise God. . . .

In their churches there hang many bells, sometimes five or six, the largest not over two hundredweights. They ring these bells to summon people to church, and also when the priest during mass raises the chalice. In Moscow, because of the multitude of churches and chapels, there are several thousand bells, which during the divine service create such a clang and din that one unaccustomed to it listens in amazement.

Questions for Analysis

1. In what ways were all social groups in Russia similar, according to Olearius?

2. How did Olearius characterize the Russians in general? What supporting evidence did he offer for his judgment?

3. Does Olearius's account help explain Stenka Razin's rebellion? In what ways?

4. On the basis of these representative passages, why do you think Olearius's book was so popular and influential in central and western Europe?

Source: G. Vernadsky and R. T. Fisher, Jr., eds., *A Source Book for Russian History from Early Times to 1917*, vol. 1 (New Haven: Yale University Press, 1972), pp. 249–251. Copyright © 1972 by Yale University Press. Reprinted by permission of Yale University Press.

Index

Timeline A History of Western Society: A Brief Overview

	Government	Society and Economy
3200 B.C.	Dominance of Sumerian cities in Mesopotamia, ca 3200–2340 Unification of Egypt; Archaic Period, ca 3100–2660 Old Kingdom of Egypt, ca 2660–2180 Dominance of Akkadian empire in Mesopotamia, ca 2331–2200 Middle Kingdom in Egypt, ca 2080–1640	Neolithic peoples rely on settled agriculture, while others pursue nomadic life, ca 7000–ca 3000 Development of wheeled transport in Mesopotamia, by ca 3200 Expansion of Mesopotamian trade and culture into modern Turkey, the Middle East, and Iran, ca 2600
2000 B.C.	Babylonian empire, ca 2000–1595 Hyksos invade Egypt, ca 1640–1570 Hittite Empire, ca 1600–1200 New Kingdom in Egypt, ca 1570–1075	First wave of Indo-European migrants, by 2000 Extended commerce in Egypt, by ca 2000 Horses introduced into western Asia, by ca 2000
1500 B.C.	Third Intermediate Period in Egypt, ca 1100–700 Unified Hebrew Kingdom under Saul, David, and Solomon, ca 1025–925	Use of iron increases in western Asia, by ca 1300–1100 Second wave of Indo-European migrants, by ca 1200
1000 B.C.	Hebrew Kingdom divided into Israel and Judah, 925 Assyrian Empire, ca 900–612 Phoenicians found Carthage, 813 Kingdom of Kush conquers and reunifies Egypt, 8th c. Medes conquers Persia, 710 Babylon wins independence from Assyria, 626 Dracon issues law code at Athens, 621 Cyrus the Great conquers Medes, founds Persian Empire, 550 Solon's reforms at Athens, ca 549 Persians complete conquest of ancient Near East, 521–464 Reforms of Cleisthenes in Athens, 508	Concentration of landed wealth in Greece, ca 750–600 Greek overseas expansion, ca 750–550 Beginning of coinage in western Asia, ca 640
500 B.C.	Battle of Marathon, 490 Xerxes' invasion of Greece, 480–479 Delian Confederacy, 478/7 Twelve Tables in Rome, 451/0 Valerio-Horatian laws in Rome, 449 Peloponnesian War, 431–404 Rome captures Veii, 396 Gauls sack Rome, 390 Roman expansion in Italy, 390–290 Conquests of Alexander the Great, 334–323 Punic Wars, 264–146 Reforms of the Gracchi, 133–121	Building of the Via Appia begins, 312 Growth of Hellenistic trade and cities, ca 300–100 Beginning of Roman silver coinage, 269 Growth of slavery, decline of small farmers in Rome, ca 250–100 Agrarian reforms of the Gracchi, 133–121

Religion and Philosophy	Science and Technology	Arts and Letters
Growth of anthropomorphic religion in Mesopotamia, ca 3000–2000 Emergence of Egyptian polytheism and belief in personal immortality, ca 2660 Spread of Mesopotamian and Egyptian religious ideas as far north as modern Anatolia and as far south as central Africa, ca 2600	Development of wheeled transport in Mesopotamia, by ca 3200 Use of widespread irrigation in Mesopotamia and Egypt, ca 3000 Construction of the first pyramid in Egypt, ca 2600	Sumerian cuneiform writing, ca 3200 Egyptian hieroglyphic writing, ca 3100
Emergence of Hebrew monotheism, ca 1700 Mixture of Hittite and Near Eastern religious beliefs, ca 1595	Construction of the first ziggurats in Mesopotamia, ca 2000 Widespread use of bronze in the ancient Near East, ca 1900 Babylonian mathematical advances, ca 1800	*Epic of Gilgamesh,* ca 1900 Code of Hammurabi, ca 1790
Exodus of the Hebrews from Egypt into Palestine, 13th c. Religious beliefs of Akhenaten, ca 1367	Hittites introduce iron technology, ca 1400	Phoenicians develop alphabet, ca 1400 Naturalistic art in Egypt under Akhenaten, ca 1367 Egyptian Book of the Dead, ca 1300
Era of the prophets in Israel, ca 1100–500 Intermixture of Etruscan and Roman religious cults, ca 753–509 Growing popularity of local Greek religious cults, ca 700 B.C.–A.D. 337 Babylonian Captivity of the Hebrews, 586–539	Babylonian astronomical advances, ca 750–400	Beginning of the Hebrew Bible, ca 9th c. First Olympic Games, 776 Babylonian astronomical advances, ca 750–400 Homer, traditional author of the *Iliad* and *Odyssey,* ca 700 Hesiod, author of the *Theogony* and *Works and Days,* ca 700 Archilochos, lyric poet, 648 Aeschylus, first significant Athenian tragedian, 525/4–456
Pre-Socratic philosophers, 5th c. Socrates, 469–399 Plato, 429–347 Diogenes, leading proponent of cynicism, ca 412–323 Aristotle, 384–322 Epicurus, 340–270 Zeno, founder of Stoic philosophy, 335–262 Emergence of Mithraism, ca 300 Spread of Hellenistic mystery religions, 2nd c. Greek cults brought to Rome, ca 200	Hippocrates, formal founder of medicine ca 430 Theophrastus, founder of botany, ca 372–288 Aristarchos of Samos, advances in astronomy, ca 310–230 Euclid codifies geometry, ca 300 Herophilus, discoveries in medicine, ca 300–250 Archimedes, works on physics and hydrologics, ca 287–212	Sophocles, tragedian who used his plays to explore moral and political problems, ca 496–406 Euripides, the most personal of the Athenian tragedians, ca 480–406 Thucydides, historian of the Peloponnesian War, ca 460–400 Aristophanes, the greatest writer of Old Comedy, ca 457–ca 385 Herodotus, the father of history, ca 450

	Government	Society and Economy
100 B.C.	Dictatorship of Sulla, 88–79 Civil war in Rome, 78–27 Dictatorship of Caesar, 45–44 Principate of Augustus, 31 B.C.–A.D. 14	Reform of the Roman calendar, 46
A.D. 300	Constantine removes capital of Roman Empire to Constantinople, ca 315 Visigoths defeat Roman army at Adrianople (378), signaling massive German invasions into the empire Bishop Ambrose asserts church's independence from the state, 380 Death of emperor Romulus Augustus marks end of Roman Empire in the West, 476 Clovis issues Salic law of the Franks, ca 490	Growth of serfdom in Roman Empire, ca 200–500 Economic contraction in Roman Empire, 3rd c.
500	Law Code of Justinian, 529 Dooms of Ethelbert, king of Kent, ca 604 Spread of Islam across Arabia, the Mediterranean region, Spain, North Africa, and Asia as far as India, ca 630–733	Gallo-Roman aristocracy intermarries with Germanic chieftains Decline of towns and trade, ca 500–700 Agrarian economy predominates in the West, ca 500–1800
700	Charles Martel defeats Muslims at Tours, 732 Pippin III anointed king of the Franks, 754 Charlemagne secures Frankish crown, r. 768–814	Height of Muslim commercial activity, ca 700–1300, with western Europe
800	Imperial coronation of Charlemagne, Christmas 800 Treaty of Verdun, 843 Viking, Magyar, and Muslim invasions, ca 845–900	Byzantine commerce and industry, ca 800–1000 Invasions and unstable conditions lead to increase of serfdom
1000	Seljuk Turks conquer Muslim Baghdad, 1055 Norman conquest of England, 1066 Penance of Henry IV at Canossa, 1077	Decline of Byzantine free peasantry, ca 1025–1100 Growth of towns and trade in the West, ca 1050–1300 Domesday Book, 1086
1100	Henry I of England, r. 1100–1135 Louis VI of France, r. 1108–1137 Frederick I of Germany, r. 1152–1190 Henry II of England, r. 1154–1189 Thomas Becket murdered, 1170 Philip Augustus of France, r. 1180–1223	Henry I of England establishes the Exchequer, 1130 Beginnings of the Hanseatic League, 1159

Religion and Philosophy	Science and Technology	Arts and Letters
Mithraism spreads to Rome, 27 B.C.–A.D. 270 Dedication of the Ara Pacis Augustae, 9 Traditional birth of Jesus, ca 3	Pliny the Elder, student of natural history, 23 B.C.–A.D. 79 Frontinus, engineering advances in Rome, 30 B.C.–A.D. 104	Virgil, 70–19 B.C. Livy, ca 59 B.C.–A.D. 17 Ovid, 43 B.C.–A.D. 17
Constantine legalizes Christianity, 312 Theodosius declares Christianity the official state religion, 380 Donatist heretical movement at its height, ca 400 St. Augustine, *The City of God,* ca 425 Clovis adopts Roman Christianity, 496		St. Jerome publishes the Latin *Vulgate,* late 4th c. St. Augustine, *Confessions,* ca 390 Byzantines preserve Greco-Roman culture, ca 400–1000
Rule of St. Benedict, 529 Monasteries established in Anglo-Saxon England, 7th c. Muhammad preaches reform, ca 610 Publication of the Qu'ran, 651 Synod of Whitby, 664	Using watermills, Benedictine monks exploit energy of fast-flowing rivers and streams Heavy plow and improved harness facilitate use of multiple-ox teams; harrow widely used in northern Europe	Boethius, *The Consolation of Philosophy,* ca 520 Justinian constructs church of Santa Sophia, 532–537 Pope Gregory the Great publishes *Dialogues, Pastoral Care, Moralia,* 590–604
Missionary work of St. Boniface in Germany, ca 710–750 Iconoclastic controversy in Byzantine Empire, 726–843 Pippin III donates Papal States to the papacy, 756	Byzantines successfully use "Greek fire" in naval combat against Arab fleets attacking Constantinople, 673, 717	Lindisfarne Gospel Book, ca 700 Bede, *Ecclesiastical History of the English Nation,* ca 700 *Beowulf,* ca 700 Carolingian Renaissance, ca 780–850
Foundation of abbey of Cluny, 909 Byzantine conversion of Russia, late 10th c.	Stirrup and nailed horseshoes become widespread in shock combat Paper, invented in China ca 2d c., enters Europe through Muslim Spain in 10th c.	Byzantines develop the Cyrillic script, late 10th c.
Beginning of reformed papacy, 1046 Schism between Roman and Greek Orthodox churches, 1054 Pope Gregory VII, 1073–1085 Peter Abelard, 1079–1142 St. Bernard of Clairvaux, 1090–1153 First Crusade, 1095–1099	Arab conquests bring new irrigation methods, cotton cultivation, and manufacture to Spain, Sicily, southern Italy Avicenna, Arab scientist, d. 1037	Romanesque style in architecture and art, ca 1000–1200 *Song of Roland,* ca 1095 Muslim musicians introduce lute, rebec—stringed instruments and ancestors of violin
Universities begin, ca 1100–1300 Concordat of Worms ends investiture controversy, 1122 Height of Cistercian monasticism, 1125–1175 Aristotle's works translated into Latin, ca 1140–1260 Third Crusade, 1189–1192 Pope Innocent III, 1198–1216	In castle construction Europeans, copying Muslim and Byzantine models, erect rounded towers and crenelated walls Windmill invented, ca 1180 Some monasteries, such as Clairvaux and Canterbury Cathedral Priory, supplied by underground pipes with running water and indoor latrines, elsewhere rare until 19th c.	*Rubaiyat of Umar Khayyam,* ca 1120 Dedication of abbey church of Saint-Denis launches Gothic style, 1144 Hildegard of Bingen, 1098–1179 Court of troubador poetry, especially that of Chrétien de Troyes, circulates widely

	Government	Society and Economy
1200	Spanish victory over Muslims at Las Navas de Tolosa, 1212 Frederick II of Germany and Sicily, r. 1212–1250 Magna Carta, 1215 Louis IX of France, r. 1226–1270 Mongols end Abbasid caliphate, 1258 Edward I of England, r. 1272–1307 Philip IV (the Fair) of France, r. 1285–1314 England and France at war, 1296	Economic revival, growth of towns, clearing of wasteland contribute to growth of personal freedom, 13th c. Crusaders capture Constantinople (Fourth Crusade) and spur Venetian economy, 1204 Agricultural expansion leads to population growth, ca 1225–1300
1300	Philip IV orders arrest of Pope Boniface at Anagni, 1303 Hundred Years' War, 1337–1453 Political disorder in Germany, ca 1350–1450 Merchant oligarchies or despots rule Italian city-states	European economic depression, ca 1300–1450 Black Death appears ca 1347; returns intermittently until 18th c. Height of the Hanseatic League, 1350–1450 Peasant and working-class revolts: Flanders, 1302; France, 1358; Florence, 1378; England, 1381
1400	Joan of Arc rallies French monarchy, 1429–1431 Medici domination of Florence begins, 1434 Princes in Germany consolidate power, ca 1450–1500 Ottoman Turks under Mahomet II capture Constantinople, May 1453 Wars of the Roses in England, 1453–1471 Ferdinand and Isabella complete reconquista in Spain, 1492 French invasion of Italy, 1494	Population decline, peasants' revolts, high labor costs contribute to decline of serfdom in western Europe Christopher Columbus reaches the Americas, October 1492 Portuguese gain control of East Indian spice trade, 1498–1511 Flow of Balkan slaves into eastern Mediterranean; of African slaves into Iberia and Italy, ca 1400–1500
1500	Charles V, Holy Roman emperor, 1519–1556 Imperial sack of Rome, 1527 Philip II of Spain, r. 1556–1598 Revolt of the Netherlands, 1566–1609 St. Bartholomew's Day massacre, August 24, 1572 Defeat of the Spanish Armada, 1588 Henry IV of France issues Edict of Nantes, 1598	Balboa discovers the Pacific, 1513 Magellan's crew circumnavigates the earth, 1519–1522 Spain and Portugal gain control of regions of Central and South America, ca 1520–1550 Peasants' Revolt in Germany, 1524–1525 "Time of Troubles" in Russia, 1598–1613
1600	Thirty Years' War, 1618–1648 Richelieu dominates French government, 1624–1643 Frederick William, Elector of Brandenburg, r. 1640–1688 English Civil War, 1642–1649	Chartering of British East India Company, 1600 Famine and taxation lead to widespread revolts, decline of serfdom in western Europe, ca 1600–1650 English Poor Law, 1601

Religion and Philosophy	Science and Technology	Arts and Letters
Maimonides, d. 1204 Founding of Franciscan order, 1210 Fourth Lateran Council, 1215 Founding of Dominican order, 1216 Thomas Aquinas (1225–1274) marks height of Scholasticism Pope Boniface VIII, 1294–1303	*Notebooks* of Villard de Honnecourt, a master mason (architect), a major source for Gothic engineering, ca 1250 Development of double-entry bookkeeping in Florence and Genoa, ca 1250–1340 Venetians purchase secrets of glass manufacture from Syria, 1277 Mechanical clock invented, ca 1290	*Parzifal, Roman de la Rose, King Arthur and the Round Table* celebrate virtues of knighthood Height of Gothic style, ca 1225–1300
Babylonian Captivity of the papacy, 1307–1377 John Wyclif, ca 1330–1384 Great Schism in the papacy, 1377–1418	Edward III of England uses cannon in siege of Calais, 1346	Petrarch, 1304–1374 Paintings of Giotto, ca 1305–1337 Dante, *Divine Comedy,* ca 1310 Boccaccio, *The Decameron,* ca 1350 Jan van Eyck, 1366–1441 Brunelleschi, 1377–1446 Chaucer, *Canterbury Tales,* ca 1385–1400
Council of Constance, 1414–1418 Pragmatic Sanction of Bourges, 1438 Expulsion of Jews from Spain, 1492	Water-powered blast furnaces operative in Sweden, Austria, the Rhine Valley, Liège, ca 1400 Leonardo Fibonacci's *Liber Abaci* (1202) popularizes use of Hindu-Arabic numerals, "a major factor in the rise of science in the Western world" Paris and largest Italian cities pave streets, making street cleaning possible Printing and movable type, ca 1450	Masaccio, 1401–1428 Botticelli, 1444–1510 Leonardo da Vinci, 1452–1519 Albrecht Dürer, 1471–1528 Michelangelo, 1475–1564 Raphael, 1483–1520 Rabelais, ca 1490–1553
Lateran Council attempts reforms of church abuses, 1512–1517 Machiavelli, *The Prince,* 1513 Concordat of Bologna, 1516 More, *Utopia,* 1516 Luther, *Ninety-five Theses,* 1517 Henry VIII of England breaks with Rome, 1532–1534 Loyola establishes Society of Jesus, 1540 Calvin establishes theocracy in Geneva, 1541 Merici establishes Ursuline order for education of women, 1544 Council of Trent, 1545–1563 Peace of Augsburg, 1555 Hobbes, 1588–1679 Descartes, 1596–1650	Copernicus, *On the Revolutions of the Heavenly Bodies,* 1543 Galileo, 1564–1642 Kepler, 1571–1630 Harvey, 1578–1657	Erasmus, *The Praise of Folly,* 1509 Castiglione, *The Courtier,* 1528 Cervantes, 1547–1616 Baroque movement in the arts, ca 1550–1725 Shakespeare, 1564–1616 Rubens, 1577–1640 Montaigne, *Essays,* 1598 Velazquez, 1599–1660
Huguenot revolt in France, 1625	Bacon, *The Advancement of Learning,* 1605 Boyle, 1627–1691 Leeuwenhoek, 1632–1723	Rembrandt van Rijn, 1606–1669 Golden Age of Dutch culture, 1625–1675 Vermeer, 1632–1675 Racine, 1639–1699

	Government	Society and Economy
1600 (cont.)	Louis XIV, r. 1643–1715 Peace of Westphalia, 1648 The Fronde in France, 1648–1660	Chartering of Dutch East India Company, 1602 Height of Dutch commercial activity, ca 1630–1665
1650	Protectorate in England, 1653–1658 Leopold I, Habsburg emperor, r. 1658–1705 Treaty of the Pyrenees, 1659 English monarchy restored, 1660 Ottoman Siege of Vienna, 1683 Glorious Revolution in England, 1688–1689 Peter the Great of Russia, r. 1689–1725	Height of mercantilism in Europe, ca 1650–1750 Principle of peasants' "hereditary subjugation" to their lords affirmed in Prussia, 1653 Colbert's economic reforms in France, ca 1663–1683 Cossack revolt in Russia, 1670–1671
1700	War of the Spanish Succession, 1701–1713 Peace of Utrecht, 1713 Frederick William I of Prussia, r. 1713–1740 Louis XV of France, r. 1715–1774 Maria Theresa of Austria, r. 1740–1780 Frederick the Great of Prussia, r. 1740–1786	Foundation of St. Petersburg, 1701 Last appearance of bubonic plague in western Europe, ca 1720 Enclosure movement in England, ca 1730–1830 Jeremy Bentham, 1748–1823
1750	Seven Years' War, 1756–1763 Catherine the Great of Russia, r. 1762–1796 Partition of Poland, 1772–1795 Louis XVI of France, r. 1774–1792 American Revolution, 1776–1783 Beginning of the French Revolution, 1789	Start of general European population increase, ca 1750 Growth of illegitimate births, ca 1750–1850 Adam Smith, *The Wealth of Nations,* 1776 Thomas Malthus, *Essay of the Principle of Population,* 1798
1800	Napoleonic era, 1799–1815 Congress of Vienna, 1814–1815 "Battle of Peterloo," Great Britain, 1819	European economic imperialism, ca 1816–1880
1825	Greece wins independence, 1830 French conquest of Algeria, 1830 Revolution in France, 1830 Great Britain: Reform Bill of 1832; Poor Law reform, 1834; Chartists, repeal of Corn Laws, 1838–1848 British complete occupation of India, 1848 Revolutions in Europe, 1848	Height of French utopian socialism, 1830s–1840s German Zollverein founded, 1834 European capitalists begin large-scale foreign investment, 1840s Great Famine in Ireland, 1845–1851 Marx, *Communist Manifesto,* 1848
1850	Second Empire in France, 1852–1870 Crimean War, 1853–1856 Unification of Italy, 1859–1870 Civil War, United States, 1861–1865 Bismarck leads Germany, 1862–1890 Unification of Germany, 1864–1871 Britain's Second Reform Bill, 1867 Third Republic in France, 1870–1940	Crédit Mobilier founded in France, 1852 Japan opened to European influence, 1853 Mill, *On Liberty,* 1859 Russian serfs emancipated, 1861 First Socialist International, 1864–1871 Marx, *Das Capital,* 1867

Religion and Philosophy	Science and Technology	Arts and Letters
Patriarch Nikon's reforms split Russian Orthodox church, 1652 Test Act in England excludes Roman Catholics from public office, 1673 Revocation of Edict of Nantes, 1685 James II tries to restore Catholicism as state religion, 1685–1688 Montesquieu, 1689–1755 Locke, *Second Treatise on Civil Government,* 1690 Pierre Bayle, *Historical and Critical Dictionary,* 1697	Tull (1674–1741) encourages innovation in English agriculture Newton, *Principia Mathematica,* 1687 Newcomen develops steam engine, 1705	Construction of baroque palaces and remodeling of capital cities throughout central and eastern Europe, ca 1650–1725 J. S. Bach, 1685–1750 Fontenelle, *Conversations on the Plurality of Worlds,* 1686 The Enlightenment, ca 1690–1790 Voltaire, 1694–1778
Wesley, 1703–1791 Hume, 1711–1776 Diderot, 1713–1784 Condorcet, 1743–1794	Charles Townsend introduces four-year crop rotation, 1730	Montesquieu, *The Spirit of Laws,* 1748
Ricardo, 1772–1823 Fourier, 1772–1837 Papacy dissolves the Jesuits, 1773 Church reforms of Joseph II in Austria, 1780s Reorganization of the church in France, 1790s	Hargreaves's spinning jenny, ca 1765 Arkwright's water frame, ca 1765 Watt's steam engine promotes industrial breakthroughs, 1780s War widens the gap in technology between Britain and the continent, 1792–1815 Jenner's smallpox vaccine, 1796	*Encyclopedia,* edited by Diderot and d'Alembert, published, 1751–1765 Mozart, 1756–1791 Rousseau, *The Social Contract,* 1762 Beethoven, 1770–1827 Wordsworth, 1770–1850 Romanticism, ca 1790–1850 Wollstonecraft, *A Vindication of the Rights of Women,* 1792
Napoleon signs Concordat with Pope Pius VII regulating Catholic church in France, 1801 Spencer, 1820–1903		Staël, *On Germany,* 1810 Liszt, 1811–1886
Comte, *System of Positive Philosophy,* 1830–1842 List, *National System of Political Economy,* 1841 Nietzsche, 1844–1900 Sorel, 1847–1922	First railroad, Great Britain, 1825 Faraday studies electromagnetism, 1830–1840s	Balzac, *The Human Comedy,* 1829–1841 Delacroix, *Liberty Leading the People,* 1830 Hugo, *Hunchback of Notre Dame,* 1831
Decline in church attendance among working classes, ca 1850–1914 Pope Pius IX, *Syllabus of Errors,* denounces modern thoughts, 1864 Doctrine of papal infallibility, 1870	Modernization of Paris, ca 1850–1870 Great Exhibition, London, 1851 Darwin, *Origin of Species,* 1859 Pasteur develops germ theory of disease, 1860s Suez Canal opened, 1869 Mendeleev develops the periodic table, 1869	Realism, ca 1850–1870 Freud, 1856–1939 Flaubert, *Madame Bovary,* 1857 Tolstoy, *War and Peace,* 1869 Impressionism in art, ca 1870–1900 Eliot (Mary Ann Evans), *Middlemarch,* 1872

	Government	Society and Economy
1875	Congress of Berlin, 1878 European "scramble for Africa," 1880–1900 Britain's Third Reform Bill, 1884 Dreyfus affair in France, 1894–1899 Spanish-American War, 1898 Boer War, 1899–1902	Full property rights for women, Great Britain, 1882 Social welfare legislation, Germany, 1883–1889 Second Socialist International, 1889–1914 Witte directs modernization of Russian economy, 1892–1899
1900	Russo-Japanese War, 1904–1905 Revolution in Russia, 1905 Balkan wars, 1912–1913	Women's suffrage movement, England, ca 1900–1914 Social welfare legislation, France, 1904, 1910; England, 1906–1914 Agrarian reforms in Russia, 1907–1912
1914	World War I, 1914–1918 Armenian genocide, 1915 Easter Rebellion, 1916 U.S. declares war on Germany, 1917 Bolshevik Revolution, 1917–1918 Treaty of Versailles, 1919	Planned economics in Europe, 1914 Auxiliary Service Law in Germany, 1916 Bread riots in Russia, March 1917
1920	Mussolini seizes power, 1922 Stalin uses forced collectivization, police terror, ca 1929–1939 Hitler gains power, 1933 Rome-Berlin Axis, 1936 Nazi-Soviet Non-Aggression Pact, 1939 World War II, 1939–1945	New Economic Policy in the Soviet Union, 1921 Dawes Plan for reparations and recovery, 1924 The Great Depression, 1929–1939 Rapid industrialization in Soviet Union, 1930s Roosevelt's "New Deal," 1933
1940	United Nations, 1945 Cold war begins, 1947 Fall of colonial empires, 1947–1962 Communist government in China, 1949 Korean War, 1950–1953 "De-Stalinization," 1955–1962	The Holocaust, 1941–1945 Marshall Plan, 1947 European economic progress, ca 1950–1969 European Coal and Steel Community, 1952 European Economic Community, 1957
1960	The Berlin Wall goes up, 1961 United States in Vietnam, ca 1961–1973 Student rebellion in France, 1968 Soviet tanks end Prague Spring, 1968 Détente, 1970s Soviets in Afghanistan, 1979	Civil rights movement in United States, 1960s Collapse of postwar monetary system, 1971 OPEC oil price increases, 1973 and 1979 Stagflation, 1970s Women's movement, 1970s
1980	U.S. military buildup, 1980s Solidarity in Poland, 1980 Unification of Germany, 1989 Revolutions in eastern Europe, 1989–1990 End of Soviet Union, 1991 War in former Yugoslavia, 1991–1995 War in Chechnya, 1991–present	Growth of debt, 1980s Economic crisis in Poland, 1988 Maastricht Treaty proposes monetary union, 1990 European Community becomes European Union, 1993 Migration to western Europe grows, 1990s
2000	Terrorist attack on U.S., Sept. 11, 2001 War in Afghanistan, 2001 War in Iraq, 2003–present	Euro note enters circulation, 2002 Voters reject new constitution for the European Union, 2005 Immigrant riots in France, 2005

Religion and Philosophy	Science and Technology	Arts and Letters
Growth of public education in France, ca 1880–1900 Growth of mission schools in Africa, 1890–1914	Emergence of modern immunology, ca 1875–1900 Trans-Siberian Railroad, 1890s Marie Curie, discovery of radium, 1898 Electrical industry: lighting and streetcars, 1880–1900	Zola, *Germinal,* 1885 Kipling, "The White Man's Burden," 1899
Separation of church and state, France, 1901–1905 Jean-Paul Sartre, 1905–1980	Planck develops quantum theory, ca 1900 First airplane flight, 1903 Einstein develops relativity theory, 1905–1910	"Modernism," ca 1900–1929 Conrad, *Heart of Darkness,* 1902 Cubism in art, ca 1905–1930 Proust, *Remembrance of Things Past,* 1913–1927
Schweitzer, *Quest of the Historical Jesus,* 1906	Submarine warfare, 1915 Ernest Rutherford splits the atom, 1919	Spengler, *The Decline of the West,* 1918
Emergence of modern existentialism, 1920s Wittgenstein, *Essay on Logical Philosophy,* 1922 Revival of Christianity, 1920s and 1930s	"Heroic age of physics," 1920s First major public radio broadcasts in Great Britain and the United States, 1920 Heisenberg, "principle of uncertainty," 1927 Talking movies, 1930 Radar system in England, 1939	Gropius, the Bauhaus, 1920s Dadaism and surrealism, 1920s Woolf, *Jacob's Room,* 1922 Joyce, *Ulysses,* 1922 Eliot, *The Waste Land,* 1922 Remarque, *All Quiet on the Western Front,* 1929 Picasso, *Guernica,* 1937
De Beauvoir, *The Second Sex,* 1949 Communists fail to break Catholic church in Poland, 1950s	Oppenheimer, 1904–1967 "Big Science" in United States, ca 1940–1970 U.S. drops atomic bombs on Japan, 1945 Watson and Crick discover structure of DNA molecule, 1953 Russian satellite in orbit, 1957	Cultural purge in Soviet Union, 1946–1952 Van der Rohe, Lake Shore Apartments, 1948–1951 Orwell, *1984,* 1949 Pasternak, *Doctor Zhivago,* 1956 The "beat" movement in the U.S., late 1950s
Catholic church opposes the legalization of divorce and abortion, 1970 to present Pope John Paul II electrifies Poland, 1979	European Council for Nuclear Research (CERN), 1960 Space race, 1960s Russian cosmonaut first to orbit globe, 1961 American astronaut first person on the moon, 1969	The Beatles, 1960s Solzhenitsyn, *One Day in the Life of Ivan Denisovitch,* 1962 Friedan, *The Feminine Mystique,* 1963 Servan-Schreiber, *The American Challenge,* 1967
Revival of religion in Soviet Union, 1985 to present Fukuyama proclaims "end of history," 1991 Growth of Islam in Europe, 1990s	Reduced spending on Big Science, 1980s Computer revolution continues, 1980s and 1990s U.S. Genome Project begins, 1990 First WWW server/browser, 1991 Pentium processor invented, 1993 "Dolly," first genetically cloned sheep, 1996	Solzhenitsyn returns to Russia, 1994 Author Salman Rushdie is exiled from Iran, 1989 Gehry, Guggenheim Museum, Bilbao, 1997
Ramadan, *Western Muslims and the Future of Islam,* 2004 Conservative elected as Pope Benedict XVI, 2005	Growing concern about global warming, 2000s First hybrid car, 2003	Calatrava, Tenerife Concert Hall, 2003